DATE DUE

BS
1171.2
S46
1992

"Sha'arei Talmon"

"Sha'arei Talmon"

*Studies in the Bible, Qumran,
and the Ancient Near East
Presented to Shemaryahu Talmon*

Edited by
Michael Fishbane and Emanuel Tov
with the assistance of Weston W. Fields

Eisenbrauns
Winona Lake, Indiana
1992

*Published with the support
of the Leo Polak Fund and the Philip Sang Fund.*

© 1992 by Eisenbrauns.
All rights reserved.
Printed in the United States of America.

Library of Congress Cataloging-in-Publication Data

Shaʿarei Talmon : studies in the Bible, Qumran, and the Ancient Near East
   presented to Shemaryahu Talmon / edited by Michael Fishbane and
   Emanuel Tov with the assistance of Weston W. Fields.
      p. cm.
   English and Hebrew.
   Title on added t.p.: Shaʿare Ṭalmon.
   Includes bibliographical references and index.
   ISBN 0-931464-61-7
   1. Bible. O.T.—Criticism, interpretation, etc. 2. Dead Sea scrolls—
Criticism, interpretation, etc. 3. Middle East—Religion. I. Talmon,
Shemaryahu, 1920-. II. Fishbane, Michael A. III. Tov, Emanuel.
IV. Fields, Weston W. V. Title: Shaʿare Ṭalmon.
BS1171.2.S46   1992
221.6—dc20   91-3286

CONTENTS

ix *Editors' Preface*
xiii *Abbreviations*
xv *Abstracts of Hebrew Articles*
xxv *The Published Writings of Shemaryahu Talmon*

Biblical Literature and Exegesis

3 MICHAEL FISHBANE • University of Chicago
   The Well of Living Water: A Biblical Motif and Its Ancient Transformations
17 WESTON W. FIELDS • Hebrew University
   The Motif "Night as Danger" Associated with Three Biblical Destruction Narratives
33 JAN P. FOKKELMAN • University of Leiden
   Structural Remarks on Judges 9 and 19
47 CYRUS H. GORDON • New York University
   "This Time" (Genesis 2:23)
53 BARUCH HALPERN • York University
   Sociological Comparativism and the Theological Imagination: The Case of the Conquest
69 PAUL D. HANSON • Harvard University
   1 Chronicles 15–16 and the Chronicler's Views on the Levites
79 SARA JAPHET • Hebrew University
   The Israelite Legal and Social Reality as Reflected in Chronicles: A Case Study
93 OTTO KAISER • Philipps University, Marburg
   The Law as Center of the Hebrew Bible
105 KLAUS KOCH • University of Hamburg
   Ezra and Meremoth: Remarks on the History of the High Priesthood
111 NORBERT LOHFINK • Philologisch-Theologische Hochschule Sankt Georgen
   Deuteronomy 6:24: לְחַיֹּתֵנוּ 'To Maintain Us'

121 CAROL L. MEYERS and ERIC M. MEYERS • Duke University
Jerusalem and Zion after the Exile: The Evidence of First Zechariah
137 JACOB MILGROM • University of California, Berkeley
The Priestly Laws of Sancta Contamination
147 SHALOM M. PAUL • Hebrew University
Polysensuous Polyvalency in Poetic Parallelism
165 ROLF RENDTORFF • University of Heidelberg
The Image of Postexilic Israel in German Bible Scholarship from Wellhausen to von Rad
175 NAHUM M. SARNA • Brandeis University, Emeritus
Legal Terminology in Psalm 3:8
183 JACK M. SASSON • University of North Carolina
Time . . . to Begin
195 J. ALBERTO SOGGIN • University of Rome
Jacob in Shechem and in Bethel (Genesis 35:1–7)
199 MATITIAHU TSEVAT • Hebrew Union College, Cincinnati
Was Samuel a Nazirite?

Textual Criticism

207 MICHAEL V. FOX • University of Wisconsin, Madison
The Redaction of the Greek Alpha-Text of Esther
221 MOSHE GOSHEN-GOTTSTEIN • Hebrew University
Editions of the Hebrew Bible—Past and Future
243 SARAH KAMIN ז״ל
The Theological Significance of the *Hebraica Veritas* in Jerome's Thought
255 EMANUEL TOV • Hebrew University
Interchanges of Consonants between the Masoretic Text and the *Vorlage* of the Septuagint
267 EUGENE ULRICH • University of Notre Dame
The Canonical Process, Textual Criticism, and Latter Stages in the Composition of the Bible

Qumran

295 JAMES H. CHARLESWORTH • Princeton Theological Seminary
An Allegorical and Autobiographical Poem by the *Moreh haṣ-Ṣedeq* (1QH 8:4–11)
309 JONAS C. GREENFIELD • Hebrew University
Two Notes on the Apocryphal Psalms
315 ALEXANDER ROFÉ • Hebrew University
A Neglected Meaning of the Verb כול and the Text of 1QS vi:11–13
323 JAMES A. SANDERS • Claremont School of Theology
The Dead Sea Scrolls and Biblical Studies

Judaism

339 W. D. DAVIES • Duke University, Emeritus
     Reflections on Territory in Judaism
345 JACOB NEUSNER • University of Southern Florida
     Biblical Exegesis and the Formation of Judaism: Sifra and the Problem of the Mishnah

Ancient Near East

367 TZVI ABUSCH • Brandeis University
     Ritual and Incantation: Interpretation and Textual History of *Maqlû* vii:58–105 and ix:152–59
381 WILLIAM W. HALLO • Yale University
     Royal Ancestor Worship in the Biblical World
403 THORKILD JACOBSEN • Harvard University, Emeritus
     The Spell of Nudimmud

417 *Index of References*
    417 Hebrew Bible
    427 Apocrypha and Pseudepigrapha
    427 New Testament
    428 Qumran / Dead Sea Scrolls
    429 Mishnaic and Other Rabbinic Writings
    429 Other Ancient Near Eastern Texts

EDITORS' PREFACE

It is a pleasure to offer this *Festschrift* to our dear friend and colleague, Prof. Shemaryahu Talmon, who now celebrates a half-century of life and study in Israel. Immigrating to (then) Palestine from Germany in 1939, Talmon began his Bible studies at the Hebrew University of Jerusalem. He subsequently taught at British and Israeli universities before returning to Jerusalem, where he served as the J. L. Magnes Professor of Bible. Combining the skill of a master teacher with a passion for his subject matter, Talmon has contributed to many areas of biblical studies during a full and distinguished academic career.

One of Shemaryahu Talmon's oldest interests has been the text and versions of the Hebrew Bible, an area within which he wrote his doctoral dissertation. That work, focusing on "double readings" in the biblical text, set a standard of excellence for his research, and introduced an innovative focus to the field. Over the years he refined and supplemented these studies—through challenging investigations and theories on the history of the text and the growth of the canon; through years of devoted work as one of the editors of the Hebrew University Bible Project and as the editor of its annual *Textus*; and through the application of text-critical procedures to the cultural and literary history of ancient Israel. This remarkable ability to synthesize diverse interests and produce fruitful and integrative inquiries is the hallmark of Talmon the scholar, and one of the indelible marks he has left on us and others as a teacher.

Shemaryahu Talmon's sociological approach to text history and his penetrating study of the ancient text witnesses have yielded many important contributions to our understanding of various aspects of the biblical text, especially in light of the finds in the Judean Desert. One continues to read his studies on the exegetical aspects of the large Isaiah scroll with profit after many years. His summary articles on the textual history of the Bible are frequently quoted in the scholarly literature. Talmon's interests in the texts found at Qumran and in sociological research were fruitfully combined in his study of the nature and history of the Qumran covenanters. Among his significant contributions is his essay on the meaning and social background of the term *yaḥad*. Talmon's parallel work in other areas of ancient sociology or social institutions—one thinks of his studies of kingship or ʿam hā-ʾāretz in ancient Israel and his ongoing research on the books of Ezra and Nehemiah—has opened new perspectives and challenged his colleagues to read more widely in the social sciences. Talmon's programmatic essay on the comparative method drew on this interest and is a valuable contribution to an important area of ancient studies.

Prof. Talmon's research has also pointed the way to an innovative combination of textual criticism with literary analysis and redaction criticism. His quick eye for textual repetitions, honed on "simultaneous" or "double" readings in the versions, produced studies on the "simultaneity" of episodes in the biblical narrative as well as on the role of "resumptive repetition" in the editorial process that created the biblical books. His abiding interest in the recurrence of motifs has led to other valuable essays. Among these, his study of the "Desert Motif" is a model analysis in this genre—combining literary insight with keen evaluations of ancient social attitudes.

Ever creative, each piece of research from the pen of Shemaryahu Talmon shows a synthetic and developing scholarly mind at work. It was certainly this feature of his life and work that has inspired numerous students. Talmon has not only taught at the major Israeli universities, but has also served as a visiting professor at many distinguished institutions, including University of Leeds, Brandeis University, Harvard University, University of Hiedelberg, University of California at Berkeley, Johns Hopkins University, and Vanderbilt University. In this capacity, and through an active lecture schedule, Prof. Talmon has served very much as an ambassador of Bible Studies. But he has seen his cultural task in even larger terms, as can be attested in the roles he played in the building of educational institutions in the illegal immigrant camps in Cyprus and in forging cultural and intellectual links with the World Council of Churches and the Vatican. For example, many students at universities, seminaries, and theological institutes in Europe, Africa, and America, having participated in workshops led by Shemaryahu Talmon, subsequently returned to Jerusalem for further studies at the Hebrew University. These ecumenical efforts have been acknowledged at the highest levels of the Vatican and elsewhere. His efforts on behalf of the Institute for Judaic Studies in Heidelberg show a further dimension of his diplomatic, educational, and administrative work. All these skills were nurtured and focused in Israel as well—where he served as the academic head of Haifa University College, as dean of the Faculty of Humanities at the Hebrew University, and as a leader in the ongoing Jewish-Christian dialogue.

The large number of colleagues, who have so quickly and warmly responded to our invitation to join this celebration of his work, will equally remember their own talks with Shemaryahu, and gladly acknowledge his many contributions to our field of study. The scope and quality of the studies included here—in Hebrew and English—appropriately reflect the wide range of Shemaryahu's interests.

Our editorial work has been made considerably easier and more pleasant through the interest and support of Shemaryahu's wife, Peninah, and their children, Efrat Livny, Tamar Elad, Noga Levine, and Tammy Morag. We owe a special debt of gratitude to Dr. Weston Fields. He was involved in all stages of the project, and he enthusiastically and skillfully offered his help and expertise. We are also indebted to Ms. Dalia Amarah and Ms. Dorit Yosef, who graciously helped with the copyediting of the Hebrew articles, and to Ms. Ronit Shamgar-Handelman, who designed and typeset the Hebrew pages in Jerusalem. We also wish to thank Mr. James Eisenbraun, Mr. David Aiken, and the staff of Eisenbrauns, who carried through the project with their usual diligence and efficiency. Special thanks are due to Mr. David Aiken for his thorough and professional copyediting.

Finally, a word of explanation about the title of this work, שערי טלמון, šaʿărê ṭalmôn. In the Bible "Talmon" is the name of a family of שוערים, gatekeepers, among the returning exiles from Babylon (Ezra 2:42; Neh 7:45, 11:19, 12:25; 1 Chr 9:17), and this fact is alluded to by the title of the Festschrift, שערי טלמון. Moreover, since שער not only means "gate" but "section" as well (in post-biblical Hebrew), we have subdivided שערי טלמון, the "Gateways of Talmon," into several sections (שערים) to convey the range of Shemaryahu Talmon's scholarly interests and influence. The fact that gatekeepers *guard* (in Hebrew, the root שמ"ר) the gates of the temple also reminds us of שמריהו.

Shemaryahu, we know we speak on behalf of everyone involved and of many others not represented in this volume, when we thank you for your work and example, which has not only influenced us so profoundly, but left us with a deep sense of gratitude for having been your students and friends.

ABBREVIATIONS

AB	Anchor Bible
AfO	*Archiv für Orientforschung*
AHW	W. von Soden, *Akkadisches Handwörterbuch*
ANET	J. B. Pritchard (ed.), *Ancient Near Eastern Texts Relating to the Old Testament*
AOS	American Oriental Series
BA	*Biblical Archaeologist*
BASOR	*Bulletin of the American Schools of Oriental Research*
BDB	F. Brown, S. R. Driver, and C. A. Briggs, *Hebrew and English Lexicon of the Old Testament*
Bib	*Biblica*
BJS	Brown Judaic Studies
BZAW	Beihefte zur Zeitschrift für die Alttestamentliche Wissenschaft
CAD	*The Assyrian Dictionary of the Oriental Institute of the University of Chicago*
CBQ	*Catholic Biblical Quarterly*
DJD	Discoveries in the Judaean Desert
EI	*Eretz-Israel*
EncJud	*Encyclopaedia Judaica*
GKC	*Gesenius' Hebrew Grammar*, edited by E. Kautzsch, translated by A. E. Cowley
HAT	Handbuch zum Alten Testament
HSS	Harvard Semitic Studies
HTR	*Harvard Theological Review*
ICC	International Critical Commentary
IDBSup	K. Crim (ed.), *Interpreter's Dictionary of the Bible, Supplementary Volume*
JANES	*Journal of the Ancient Near Eastern Society*
JAOS	*Journal of the American Oriental Society*
JB	Jerusalem Bible
JBL	*Journal of Biblical Literature*
JCS	*Journal of Cuneiform Studies*

JJS	*Journal of Jewish Studies*
JNES	*Journal of Near Eastern Studies*
JPSV	Jewish Publication Society Version
JSOT	*Journal for the Study of the Old Testament*
JSOTSup	Journal for the Study of the Old Testament, Supplement Series
KAI	H. Donner and W. Röllig, *Kanaanäische und aramäische Inschriften*
KAT	Kommentar zum Alten Testament
KB	L. Koehler and W. Baumgartner, *Lexicon in Veteris Testamenti Libros*
LXX	Septuagint
MSL	Materials for the Sumerian Lexicon
MT	Masoretic Text
NAB	New American Bible
NEB	New English Bible
NJPSV	New Jewish Publication Society Version
OBO	Orbis Biblicus et Orientalis
OED	*Oxford English Dictionary*
Or	*Orientalia*
OTL	Old Testament Library
RA	*Revue d'Assyriologie et d'Archeologie Orientale*
RB	*Revue Biblique*
RevQ	*Revue de Qumran*
RLA	*Reallexikon der Assyriologie*
RSV	Revised Standard Version
SBLDS	Society of Biblical Literature, Dissertation Series
ScrHier	Scripta Hierosolymitana
STDJ	Studies on the Texts of the Desert of Judah
TDNT	G. Kittel and G. Friedrich (eds.), *Theological Dictionary of the New Testament*
TEV	Today's English Version
TWAT	G. J. Botterweck and H. Ringgren (eds.), *Theologisches Wörterbuch zum Alten Testament*
UF	*Ugarit-Forschungen*
UT	C. H. Gordon, *Ugaritic Textbook*
VT	*Vetus Testamentum*
VTSup	Vetus Testamentum Supplements
ZA	*Zeitschrift für Assyriologie*
ZAW	*Zeitschrift für die Alttestamentliche Wissenschaft*

ABSTRACTS OF HEBREW ARTICLES

DID JOB REALLY EXIST?
AN ISSUE OF MEDIEVAL EXEGESIS
Moshe Greenberg
(pp. 3*–11*)

Whether the Book of Job is factual or fictive has exercised Jewish Bible interpreters from early times. While the preponderant talmudic view is that it is factual, a tradition of its fictiveness persisted into medieval times. It was so read by Maimonides (allegorically), who argued for fictiveness from the absence of a fixed tradition of the book's origin and the scandalous bargain struck between God and Satan at the opening scene. A later disciple of his, Zerahiah of Barcelona (end of the thirteenth century), carried the argument to great lengths, adding criteria remarkable for their boldness. Zerahiah's arguments are:

1. theological: the aforesaid bargain is too scandalous to be true
2. literary-historical: one cannot imagine how the book was composed on the assumption that it is a true record
3. literary-stylistic: fablelike features (e.g., absence of identifying particulars), plot improbabilities (especially Job's double reward at the end), and the uniform style of all the speeches indicate a single author

Zerahiah offers three grounds for rejecting the reference to Job in Ezekiel 14 as evidence of the hero's factualness.

Zerahiah's criteria could cast doubt on the factualness of other biblical narratives; it is no wonder, then, that his work fell into oblivion.

For an English version of Zerahiah's arguments, see pp. 9*–11*.

PSALM 104: A LITERARY EXAMINATION
Yair Hoffman
(pp. 13*–24*)

Psalm 104 is a hymn and, as such, it has the characteristics of the hymn genre. Yet, since hymns are not as limited in their motifs as other *Gattungen* in the psalter, the main poetical problem of their authors is not how to maneuver between the conventions of the genre and their own artistic individuality. An examination of the poetic nature of this psalm suggests that the author was trying, whether consciously or not, to overcome three major problems while composing his poem: (1) the existence in Israel of numerous short sayings praising God, (2) his acquaintance with the Egyptian hymn to Aton, and (3) the existence of many creation traditions in Israel. The two main literary devices applied to overcome these difficulties were (1) a sophisticated use of the genre of the catalog and (2) employment of the literary device of "the unexpected turn of events." Our awareness of these literary devices contributes to a better understanding of the psalm.

THE BIBLE AS LITERATURE

Moshe Weinfeld

(pp. 25*-30*)

The literary-esthetic approach to the Bible cannot be fully realized without the literary-critical approach. In order to analyze a pericope from a literary-esthetic standpoint one should take into consideration both philological analysis and redactional criticism. Conversely, in order to better understand the layout of a pericope, one must be cognizant of its literary-esthetic nature. At the same time one cannot use the same standard for the whole biblical corpus. Chronicles and legal material cannot be measured solely by esthetic tools, just as narratives and poetic material cannot be analyzed only by means of historical-critical criteria. The literary approach is vital for biblical study on the condition that it is accompanied by the philological and historical-critical method.

PSALM 23: THE PSALMIST ON GOD'S CARE

Meir Weiss

(pp. 31*-41*)

The meaning of Psalm 23 is embodied in the psalm's form and language. In contrast to the widespread view, the sole image employed by the psalmist is that of the shepherd (vv. 2-4a); in the concretization which follows, the image is left behind. The transition is achieved by means of the multivalent word נפש, which in v. 3a serves both in its primary meaning ('throat'), thus functioning as part of the image of the hungry, thirsty sheep, and in its extended sense ('vitality'): "He [i.e., the LORD] renews my [i.e., the psalmist's] life." The subject of v. 5 is God, and not, as generally held, a metaphoric "host." The image and its elaboration are connected not by means of a coherent literary transition but rather by contiguous association. The word יְנַחֲמֻנִי 'comfort me' in v. 4, which in its immediate context refers to the encouragement the psalmist receives from God's sustenance as well as from his chastisement, draws in its wake the transformed image of a set table, aroused by association with the practice of preparing a table to comfort a mourner.

Psalm 23 is not a prayer of petition or hope but rather an affirmation of the psalmist's sense of God's all-encompassing care. This feeling intensifies as the psalm progresses. While the psalmist initially feels that God is with him as he walks "through a valley of deepest darkness" (v. 4), he goes on to speak of God's mindfulness in the presence of his enemies (v. 5) and finally comes to the realization that throughout "all the days of his life" his only pursuers are "the goodness and steadfast love" of the LORD.

ETHNOLOGY, ETIOLOGY, GENEALOGY, AND HISTORIOGRAPHY IN THE TALE OF LOT AND HIS DAUGHTERS (GENESIS 19:30–38)

Zeev Weisman
(pp. 43*–52*)

Attempts to answer the question of the meaning of the tale of Lot and his daughters in its present context by a separation between an original Moabite-Ammonite saga and a later Israelite etiological-derogatory layer are inconclusive. Whatever might be the original intention of the tale, by its incorporation within the context of the Abrahamic narrative, it functions to explain why Abraham had to send as far as Mesopotamia for a wife for his son Isaac, rather than finding one among the descendants of Lot, his close neighbor and nephew. The exclusion of Lot's descendants from intermarriage with Abraham's descendants reflects the tendency of a late historiographer to discard—right from the outset—any close kinship ties between Israelites and Moabites or Ammonites on the ground of the incestuous genealogy of the latter two nations. The historical locus of this tendency has to be the endeavor of Ezra and Nehemiah to consolidate the "holy seed" as the only legitimate heir of the covenant with Abraham.

"ELISHA DIED ... HE CAME TO LIFE AND STOOD UP" (2 KINGS 13:20–21): A SHORT "SHORT STORY" IN EXEGETICAL CIRCLES

Yair Zakovitch
(pp. 53*–62*)

Almost every analysis of a biblical story shows that the meaning of an isolated tale differs from the sense it acquires when read within its wider narrative context—the tales which precede and follow it, the entire cycle dealing with this story's central hero, the biblical book in which it appears, and even the entire historiographical complex beginning with Genesis to the end of the Book of Kings. Each contextual circle adds a measure of depth to the tale and also offers different answers to the questions facing the reader. This dynamic process of understanding and interpreting is exemplified by an analysis of a very short and ambiguous tale—the death of Elisha (2 Kgs 13:20–21).

THE ORIGINAL LANGUAGE OF THE STORY OF THE THREE YOUTHS (1 ESDRAS 3–4)
Zipora Talshir and David Talshir
(pp. 63*–75*)

The language of the story of the three youths is translation Greek and its *Vorlage* is Aramaic rather than Hebrew.

The Greek of the story owes its fairly good standard to the character of the translator, as proven from the other, undoubtedly translated, parts of 1 Esdras. Nevertheless, the Greek of 1 Esdras, including this story, cannot be confused with that of works originally written in Greek. When checked against various linguistic criteria (e.g., the frequency of καί, the position of πᾶς, the relation between main verbs and subordinate verbs), its language betrays the gap between independent Greek and Greek bound to a Semitic *Vorlage*. In addition, there are many expressions, phrases, loan-translations, and some mistaken renderings that, when taken together, prove that the work is actually a translation.

In spite of the difficulty in separating Hebrew and Aramaic, two closely related languages, it is possible to adduce enough material in favor of an Aramaic *Vorlage*. Besides the well-known and frequent use of τότε, reflecting אדין, there are other phrases attested in Aramaic rather than in Hebrew, as well as some problems in content, which seem to be best explained as originating in an Aramaic *Vorlage*.

Since the link between the story and its context (1 Esdr 5:1–6) is particularly Semitic, it seems that the story was first set in its present context in a stage previous to its translation into Greek.

"IF YOU RACE WITH THE FOOT-RUNNERS AND THEY EXHAUST YOU" (JEREMIAH 12:5)
Abraham Malamat
(pp. 77*–79*)

Jeremiah 12:5 continues: "How then can you compete with horses? / If you בוטח in a tranquil land, / How will you fare in the jungle of the Jordan?"

(NJPSV). This curious verse is listed in the midrashic literature as one of the biblical instances of the *a minori ad majus* or *qal wa-ḥomer* argument. The imagery here is of two races—between foot-runners and foot-runners against horses, the latter referring most likely to chariots, perhaps in a military context. The Bible mentions several long-distance runners; and there is also comparative material from Egypt, dating only a few decades prior to Jeremiah.

The crux in the second half of the verse is the meaning of the verb בוטח, generally understood here (as elsewhere) as "you are safe, secure." Yet, in order to obtain a coherent understanding of the entire verse we have to accept a meaning suggested by the medieval lexicographer Al-Fasi on the basis of Arabic and adapted by various commentators, namely "(if in a safe territory) *you fall down (flat on your face)*." Thus, the final part of the verse also deals with the image of the race and the failing of the runner.

וישתחו: GROUP FORMULAS IN BIBLICAL PROSE AND POETRY

Frank H. Polak
(pp. 81*–91*)

The verb השתחוה occurs around ninety times in Old Testament prose narrative and some forty times in poetry. In Ugaritic epic poetry this verb occurs in a fixed phrase: *lpʿn ʾil thbr wtql, tštḥwy wtkbdh* (*CTA* 4 iv:25–26). Although this formula has no obvious parallels in biblical poetry, it is matched by various frequent prose formulas and cognate expressions, as specified in the following table:

	Abraham, Jacob, Balaam	Joseph	David	Other tales	Ruth, Job, Ezra	Chronicles	Total
ויפל וישתחו	0	0	6	2	2	(1)	10
ויקד וישתחו	3	1	4	3	1	2	14
ויקם וישתחו	2	0	2	1	0	0	5
וישתחו אפים ארצה	0	2	4	0	0	(1)	6
וישתחו ארצה	3	2	0	1	0	0	6
ויבא וישתחו	0	2	5	3	0	1	11
Total	8	7	21	10	3	3	52

Only the last phrase, ויבא וישתחו, has parallels in biblical poetry (nine examples). The other formulas are only matched by some rare expressions in exilic prophecy (Isa 49:7, 23; 60:14); the form of these phrases shows them to be later replicas of the prose formulas. Hebrew prose narrative has inherited these formulas from ancient Northwest Semitic epic poetry. This result corroborates the Cross–Cassuto thesis: pre-Israelitic epic poetry is the ultimate ancestor of biblical prose narrative.

MILITARY ELITE AND POLITICS: DISMAL EPISODES IN THE HISTORY OF THE NORTHERN KINGDOM

Hanoch Reviv ז"ל

(pp. 93*–97*)

During the period following the division of the Solomonic Empire there was a consolidation of a military elite. These high-ranking officers took an active part in the politics of the Kingdom of Israel. This period was characterized by successive efforts of officers, supported by army units and fractions within the civil population, to influence or control the government. The efforts (which had no link to the alleged tribal heterogeneity) point to the weakness of the royalty and to struggles between army commanders differing in matters concerning warfare against Judah and Philistia or domestic policy.

BIBLICAL PROPHECY IN THE QUMRAN SCROLLS

Gershon Brin

(pp. 101*–112*)

The complex status of prophecy in the Qumran scrolls is exemplified by the sect's belief that prophecy did not exist in its time. On the one hand they awaited the renewal of prophecy, yet on the other hand they appointed themselves as the living substitute for the defunct office of the prophet. This substitution took the form of the kind of interpretations of Scripture exemplified in the pesharim, which applied biblical prophetic texts to their own era. At the same time the eschatological concepts of future salvation and the coming of a Messiah are found within the sect. A prophet was even included among the elements of salvation (1QS 9:10–11). Their system of quoting the biblical text revealed their attitude toward the institution of prophecy.

THE HEBREW BIBLE IN THE DEAD SEA SCROLLS: TORAH QUOTATIONS IN THE *DAMASCUS COVENANT*

Devorah Dimant

(pp. 113*–122*)

The work known as the *Damascus Covenant* (=CD) belongs to the writings produced by the Qumran community or a related group. Written in a peculiar style, it employs biblical materials extensively. As an early post-biblical Qumranic writing, extant in the original form and language, it offers a unique opportunity for the study of the function and purpose of biblical materials in a Second Temple document of this kind. The use made of such biblical materials can be divided into two categories: explicit and nonexplicit usages, each category including a number of subtypes.

The analysis of explicit quotations in the *Damascus Covenant* is of special interest due to the peculiar character of this document—a unique combination of historical and parenetic materials, side by side with halakic sections, all of which are interspersed with explicit quotations. The explicit quotations in the *Damascus Covenant* fall into two well-defined groups: (1) Quotations interpreted according to the pesher method, applied to historical circumstances; significantly, this group includes not only quotations from the prophets (e.g., CD 7:8–13, 19:10–13) but also quotations from a few Torah songs (e.g, CD 8:9–12, quoting Deut 32:33; CD 7:19–21, quoting Num 24:17; CD 6:3–11, quoting Num 21:18), which must have been considered prophecies. (2) Quotations from the Torah for the purpose of legal exegesis, in two subtypes: (*a*) quotations of Torah laws in contexts of polemics against opponents, found only in the first, historical section of the *Damascus Covenant* (e.g., CD 5:1–4, 8–12); and (*b*) quotations of Torah laws for the purpose of legal interpretation and clarification. Not surprisingly, instances belonging to this second subgroup are found only in the halakic section of the *Damascus Covenant*. They present special interest because most of the halakic materials in this section are formulated as abstract rules, very much like the Mishnah. Only occasionally is a Torah quotation introduced.

Quotations are adduced in the *Damascus Covenant* in cases where the authors of the Halakah in question differed from the practice of the opponent school. In a few cases the rule formulated in a specific case applies to the members of the community, rather than to Israel at large (CD 9:2–8).

11QPs[a] AND THE COMPOSITION OF THE BOOK OF PSALMS

Menahem Haran
(pp. 123*–128*)

11QPs[a] comprises about forty psalms from Psalms 93–150 of the canonical book and eight extracanonical works. The literary units in this scroll display an apparent confusion, as their order differs entirely from that of the canonical book. The editor of 11QPs[a], J. A. Sanders, labels it *The Psalms Scroll* (not, e.g., *A Scroll of Psalms*), thus taking for granted that it represents a certain stage in a long and complicated process by which the canonical book reached its final form. Moreover, since the scope of the scroll is obviously smaller than that of the canonical book, he assumes that it has to do with the consolidation of only the two final "books" of Psalms which are taken to be separated by the fourth doxology (Ps 106:47–48). In addition, presupposing that the Qumran community regarded this scroll as the official, *bona fide*, psalter, Sanders is forced to claim that it saw no difference between the eight extracanonical works and the biblical psalms included therein. Sanders also argues that all the works in that scroll, both canonical and extracanonical, were ascribed to King David.

צַדִּיק = 'WISE' IN BIBLICAL HEBREW AND THE WISDOM CONNECTIONS OF PSALM 37

Avi Hurvitz
(pp. 131*–135*)

The word צדיק, meaning 'just, righteous', is very common in Biblical Hebrew and appears throughout the Old Testament. However, with the specific connotation 'wise', צדיק is attested in the Bible almost exclusively in the wisdom writings of Proverbs and Qoheleth, and once in the Book of Psalms—in Psalm 37. Furthermore, the antonym of צדיק, רשע with the meaning 'stupid', is also peculiar to wisdom literature (Qoheleth, Ben-Sira; the standard connotation of רשע has nothing to do with 'foolishness', but, rather, with 'wickedness').

The distribution pattern of צדיק = 'wise' and רשע = 'stupid' thus clearly shows that these forms belong to the wisdom vocabulary of Biblical Hebrew. The distribution also confirms the widely held view that Psalm 37, the only work in the entire Psalter which uses צדיק = 'wise', reflects a sapiential milieu and should be classified as a wisdom composition.

THE STRUCTURE OF SEMANTIC AND ASSOCIATIVE FIELDS IN BIBLICAL HEBREW AND CLASSICAL ARABIC

Shelomo Morag
(pp. 137*–143*)

The notion *associative field* refers to a group of semantic fields which are associatively connected. The connection is created as the result of the appearance of certain semantemes (semantic units) in a number of fields within the group. Thus, for example, in Biblical Hebrew the fields of "growing," "movement," "anger," and "pride" ("vanity") are associatively connected: semantemes derived from the root עבר appear in all of them.

The distribution of semantemes in various semantic fields may be observed in the following roots: (1) רדד (in Biblical Hebrew and Classical Arabic), (2) נטי (in Biblical Hebrew) and its semantic parallel גני (in Post-Biblical Hebrew, Aramaic, and Classical Arabic), (3) אסר (in Biblical Hebrew), and (4) חלל (in Biblical Hebrew and Classical Arabic).

The associative aspects inherent in the development of the meanings of some semantemes is emphasized by tracing the full extent of this development in each of the languages treated. The following Biblical Hebrew words illustrate the principle of associative fields: וַיֵּרֶד (1 Kgs 6:32), רְדִיד (Isa 3:23, Cant 5:7), צָעִיף (Gen 24:65; 38:14, 19), נְטָיו (Num 24:6), יַטּוּ (Amos 2:8, לֶאֱסֹר (Ps 105:22), יְחַבֵּם (Ps 105:22), and וַיָּחֵלוּ (Hos 8:10).

THE INTERPRETATION OF RHETORICAL QUESTIONS IN THE BIBLE

Benjamin Kedar
(pp. 145*–152*)

A question need not be formulated in an interrogative sentence; it may be expressed in an imperative or a declarative sentence. On the other hand, not every interrogative sentence asks for information: it may express a rhetorical question. Since this term is rather vague, there arises the need to analyze more accurately what the intention of such noninformational questions may be in any specific case. These general considerations apply to the corpus of biblical texts. Some verses are ambiguous in this respect, and the various, often contradictory, interpretations need to be analyzed as offered by the classical versions and traditional Jewish commentators.

THE AUTHORITY OF MASORETIC ACCENTS IN TRADITIONAL BIBLICAL EXEGESIS

Simcha Kogut
(pp. 153*–165*)

The system of Masoretic accents (te‘amim) came to be considered authoritative in traditional biblical exegesis, influencing traditional exegesis in several ways. Because they mark syntactical features, such as pauses, they influenced these exegetes' understanding of certain biblical texts. Sometimes a difference in meaning was even predicated upon the phonetic role of the accents—marking the tone-syllable.

Many traditional interpreters (from the sages to the medieval period) felt obligated to interpret within the boundaries of the range of meanings permitted by the accents. This adherence to the accentuation system is evident in traditional commentators. Only rarely did traditional commentators dare explicitly to disagree with the authority of the Masoretic accentuation system.

THE PUBLISHED WRITINGS OF SHEMARYAHU TALMON

A. Books

1. מלאכת הסיפור במקרא. Jerusalem: Hebrew University, 1956.

2. כפלי גירסה: תופעת יסוד בתולדות המסירה של נוסח המקרא. Ph.D. thesis. Academon, Hebrew University of Jerusalem, 1957.

3. דרכי הסיפור במקרא. Jerusalem: Hebrew University, 1965.
   [English excerpts in no. D206]

4. *Eschatology and History in Biblical Judaism.* The Ecumenical Institute for Advanced Theological Study, Tantur, Occasional Papers 2. Jerusalem: Ecumenical Institute, 1986.
   [Translation (from German) of no. D165]

5. *King, Cult and Calendar in Ancient Israel: Collected Studies.* Jerusalem: Magnes, 1986.
   [Includes nos. D13, D21, D45, D55, D79, D92, D118, D157, D178, and D210]

6. *Gesellschaft und Literatur in der hebräischen Bibel: Gesammelte Aufsätze.* Volume 1. Information Judentum 8. Neukirchen-Vluyn: Neukirchener Verlag, 1988.
   [Includes nos. D20, D21, D79, D92, D98, D108, D150, D157, and D199]

7. *The World of Qumran from Within: Collected Studies.* Jerusalem: Magnes/Leiden: Brill, 1989.
   [Includes nos. D3, D7, D8, D11, D14, D20, D26, D36, D44, D54, D75, D150, D209, and D224]

8. *Juden und Christen im Gespräch: Gesammelte Aufsätze.* Volume 2. Information Judentum 11. Neukirchen-Vluyn: Neukirchener Verlag, 1991.
   [Includes nos. D87, D119, D132, D151, D152, D153, D158, D159, D160, D171, D178, D179, D200, D203, and D223]

9. *The Hebrew Bible in the Making: Form and Content. Collected Studies.* Jerusalem: Magnes, forthcoming (1991).
[Includes nos. D43, D138, D147, D149, D168, D169, D197, D202, and D228]

B. Books Edited

1. לקט פרקים מן התורה על פי נוסחת השומרונים. Jerusalem: Hebrew University, 1958.

2. פני עולם המקרא. Volume 2: *Former Prophets*. Edited by Shemaryahu Talmon, Michael Avi-Yonah, and Avraham Malamat. Ramat Gan: International Publishing, 1960.

3. י' בן צבי, ספר השומרונים. Edited by Shemaryahu Talmon with the assistance of Yeshayahu Gafni. New edition. Jerusalem: Yad Yitzak Ben Zvi, 1970.

4. תולדות נוסח המקרא במחקר החדיש. Jerusalem: Academon, Hebrew University, 1973.

5. *Qumran and the History of the Biblical Text*. Edited by Frank M. Cross and Shemaryahu Talmon. Cambridge: Harvard University Press, 1975.
[Includes nos. D36, D54, D86, and D115]

6. *Religion und Politik in der Gesellschaft des 20. Jahrhunderts: Ein Symposion mit israelischen und deutschen Wissenschaftlern.* Edited by Shemaryahu Talmon and Gregor Siefer. Bonn: Keil, 1978.
[Includes no. D152]

7. כאן ועכשיו: עיונים בהגות החברתית והדתית של מ"מ בובר. Edited by Shemaryahu Talmon, Kalman Yaron, and Yosef Emanuel. Jerusalem: Martin Buber Center, University of Jerusalem, 1982.
[Revised edition in no. B12; includes nos. D184 and D185]

8. *Lutherans and Jews: First Official International Consultation, Copenhagen, 6-8 July 1981.* Edited by Shemaryahu Talmon and Magnus Saebø. London: Institute of Jewish Affairs, 1982. Issued as *Christian Jewish Relations* 15/2 (June 1982), with the theme "The Concept of the Human Being in the Lutheran and Jewish Traditions."

9. *Zukunftshoffnung und Heilserwartung in den monotheistischen Religionen.* Edited by Abdoldjavad Falaturi, Walter Strolz, and Shemaryahu Talmon. Veröffentlichungen der Stiftung Oratio Dominica: Weltgespräch der Religionen 9. Freiburg: Herder, 1982.
[Includes no. D188]

10. מחקרים בספרות קומראן. Jerusalem: Academon, Hebrew University, 1984.

11. *Mitte der Schrift? Ein jüdisch-christliches Gespräch: Texte des Berner Symposions vom 6.-12. Januar 1985.* Edited by Martin Klopfenstein, Ulrich Luz, Shemaryahu Talmon, and Emanuel Tov. Judaica et Christiana 11. Bern/New York: Lang, 1987.
[Includes no. D207]

12. כאן ועכשיו: עיונים בהגותו החברתית והדתית של מ"מ בובר. Edited by Shemaryahu Talmon, Kalman Yaron, and Yosef Emanuel. Enlarged edition. Jerusalem: Martin Buber Center, University of Jerusalem, 1989.
[Revised edition of no. B7]

13. *Jewish Civilization in the Hellenistic-Roman Period.* Sheffield: Sheffield Academic Press, forthcoming (1991).

14. מגילות קומראן: בין מקרא למשנה: כנס ירושלים לציון ארבעים שנות מחקר של מגילות מדבר יהודה. Edited by Magen Broshi, Shemaryahu Talmon, Sara Japhet, and Daniel Schwartz. Jerusalem: Israel Exploration Society/Bialik, forthcoming.
[Includes no. D240]

C. Series and Projects Edited

1. *The Hebrew University Bible Project.* Edited by Moshe H. Goshen-Gottstein, Chaim Rabin, Shemaryahu Talmon, and Emanuel Tov.

2. *Textus: Annual of the Hebrew University Bible Project.* Volumes 4–10. 1964–1982.

3. *Encyclopedia of the Biblical World.* Jerusalem: Revivim [Hebrew illustrated commentaries; "Exodus" and "Judges" planned for release in 1991].

4. Member of editorial committee for the following publications:
Explorations
Hebrew Studies
Jewish Quarterly Review
Judaism
Kirche und Israel
Theological Dictionary of the Old Testament
Theologisches Wörterbuch zum Alten Testament
Vetus Testamentum

D. Articles

1950

1. The History of Modern Hebrew Education in Israel. *Chayenu* 14:8–9.

2. The Case for Unified Education (in Israel). *Zionist Review* (London) Nov. 18.

1951

3. Notes on the Habakkuk Scroll. *Vetus Testamentum* 1:33–37.
   [Reprinted in no. A7, pp. 142b1-46]

4. קווים לחקירת הנוסח השומרוני של התורה. *Tarbiz* 22:124–28.

5. The Samaritan Pentateuch Version. *Journal of Jewish Studies* 2:144–50.

6. Samaritan Decalogue Inscriptions. *Bulletin of the John Rylands Library* 33:211–36.
   [With John Bowman]

7. Yom Hakippurim in the Habakkuk Scroll. *Biblica* 32:549–63.
   [Reprinted in no. A7, pp. 186–99]

1953

8. The Sectarian יחד—A Biblical Noun. *Vetus Testamentum* 3:133–40.
   [Reprinted in no. A7, pp. 53–60]

1954

9. חתן דמים. Pp. 93-96 in *Eretz-Israel 3: Dedicated to the Memory of M. D. U. Cassuto, 1883–1951*. Edited by Hayyim Z. Hirschberg, Benjamin Mazar (Maisler), Naftali H. Tur-Sina (Torczyner). Jerusalem: Israel Exploration Society/Bialik.

10. A Case of Abbreviation Resulting in Double Readings. *Vetus Testamentum* 4:206–8.

1955

11. לשאלת חילופי הגירסה במגילת ישעיה א׳. Pp. 147–56 in *Elias Auerbach Jubilee Volume*. Edited by Arthur Biram. Publications of the Israel Society for Biblical Research 1. Jerusalem: Kiryat Sepher for the Israel Society for Biblical Research.
    [English translation in no. A7, pp. 117–30]

12. A Case of Faulty Harmonization. *Vetus Testamentum* 5:206–8.

1956

13. משפט המלך. Pp. 45–56 in *Arthur Biram Jubilee Volume*. Edited by Haim Gevaryahu, Ben-Zion Lurie, and Israel Melman. Publications of the Israel Society for Biblical Research 2. Jerusalem: Kiryat Sepher for the Israel Society for Biblical Research.
[English translation in no. A5, pp. 53–67]

1957

14. A Note on DJD vi, 11–13. *Journal of Jewish Studies* 8:113–15.
[Reprinted in no. A7, pp. 68–70]

15. עיונים במגילות מדבר יהודה: חשבון הלוח של כת מדבר יהודה. Pp. 24–39 in עיונים במגילות מדבר יהודה: *Papers Read at the Third Eliezer Lippa Sukenik Memorial Meeting*. Edited by Jacob Liver. Publications of the Israel Society for Biblical Research 4. Jerusalem: Kiryat Sepher for the Israel Society for Biblical Research.
[Revised and enlarged version in no. D30; English translation in no. D20]

16. הקונגרס העולמי השני למדעי היהדות. Pp. 45–53 in *Second World Congress of Jewish Studies*, section 12. Jerusalem: World Union of Jewish Studies.

17. כת ים המלח גרסה: מולד יום בבוקר. *Ha-Aretz* (Tel Aviv) July 4.

18. לוחות השנה של כת מדבר יהודה. *Molad* 103:53–58.

19. Review of המגילות הגנוזות ממדבר יהודה, by Yigael Yadin. *Ha-Aretz* (Tel Aviv) Feb. 15.

1958

20. The Calendar Reckoning of the Sect from the Judaean Desert. Pp. 162–99 in *Aspects of the Dead Sea Scrolls*. Edited by Chaim Rabin and Yigael Yadin. Scripta Hierosolymitana 4. Jerusalem: Magnes.
[Translation (from Hebrew) of no. D15; reprinted in no. A7, pp. 147–85; German translation in no. A6, pp. 152–89]

21. Divergences in Calendar-Reckoning in Ephraim and Judah. *Vetus Testamentum* 8:48–74.
[Reprinted in no. A5, pp. 113–39; German translation in no. A6, pp. 56–79]

22. "המה הקינים הבאים מחמת אבי בית רכב" (דה״א ב, נה). Pp. 111–13 in *Eretz-Israel 5: Dedicated to Professor Benjamin Mazar on His Fiftieth*

Birthday. Edited by Michael Avi-Yonah, Hayyim Z. Hirschberg, Yigael Yadin, and Hayim Tadmor. Jerusalem: Israel Exploration Society/ Hebrew University.
[English translation in no. D25]

1959

23. לשאלת הלוח של כת מדבר יהודה. *Molad* 109–110: 383–84.

1960

24. Double Readings in the Massoretic Text. *Textus* 1:144–84.

25. "המה הקינים הבאים מחמת אבי בית־רכב": 1 Chron. ii, 55. *Israel Exploration Journal* 10:174–80.
[Translation (from Hebrew) of no. D22]

26. The "Manual of Benedictions" of the Sect of the Judaean Desert. *Revue de Qumran* 2:475–500.
[Translation (from Hebrew) of no. D27; combined with no. D150 and reprinted in no. A7, pp. 200–243]

27. מחזור הברכות של כת מדבר יהודה. *Tarbiz* 29:1–20.
[English translation in no. D26]

28. הערה להערה. *Tarbiz* 29:394–95.

1961

29. Synonymous Readings in the Textual Traditions of the Old Testament. Pp. 335–83 in *Studies in the Bible*. Edited by Chaim Rabin. Scripta Hierosolymitana 8. Jerusalem: Magnes.

30. חשבון הלוח של כת מדבר יהודה. Pp. 77–105 in *Essays on the Dead Sea Scrolls in Memory of E. L. Sukenik*. Edited by Yigael Yadin and Chaim Rabin. Jerusalem: Shrine of the Book.
[Revised and enlarged version of no. D15]

31. 1 Sam. XV 32b—A Case of Conflated Readings? *Vetus Testamentum* 11:456–57.

32. The Masoretic Text of the Old Testament. *Christian Friends* 18:3–6.

33. Review of *Sefér Abišaᶜ*, by F. F. Perez Castro. *Erasmus* 14:24–28.
[Hebrew translation in no. D34]

34. Review of *Sefér Abišaᶜ*, by F. F. Perez Castro. *Molad* 148:580–81
[Translation (from English) of no. D33]

35. Search for the Text of the Original Hebrew Scriptures. *Jewish Digest* (Houston) August: 24–26.

1962

36. DSIa as a Witness to Ancient Exegesis of the Book of Isaiah. *Annual of the Swedish Theological Institute* 1:62–72.
[Reprinted in in no. A7, pp. 131–41, and no. B5, pp. 116–26]

37. The Three Scrolls of the Law That Were Found in the Temple Court. *Textus* 2:14–27.
[Hebrew translation in no. D56]

38. מלחמות ה', ספר מלחמות ה'. *Encyclopaedia Miqra'it* 2:1064–65. Jerusalem: Bialik.

39. Review of *Ancient Israel—Its Life and Institutions*, by Roland de Vaux. *Christian News from Israel* 13/3–4: 40–44.

40. Review of *Old Testament Translation Problems*, by S. R. Hulst. *Noticias Cristianas de Israel* 13/1:27–30.
[Translation (from English) of no. D58]

41. Review of *Old Testament Translation Problems*, by S. R. Hulst. *Nouvelles Chretiennes d'Israel* 13/1:25–28.
[Translation (from English) of no. D58]

42. Techniques of Augmenting the Hebrew Vocabulary. *Iggeret: Newsletter of the National Association of Professors of Hebrew* 22:2–4.

1963

43. "Wisdom" in the Book of Esther. *Vetus Testamentum* 13:419–55.
[Reprinted in no. A9; excerpts in no. D206]

44. A Further Link between the Judean Covenanters and the Essenes. *Harvard Theological Review* 56:313–19.
[Reprinted in no. A7, pp. 61–67]

45. The Gezer Calendar and the Seasonal Cycle of Ancient Canaan. *Journal of the American Oriental Society* 83:177–87.
[Reprinted in no. A5, pp. 89–112; Hebrew translation in no. D74]

46. Some Unrecorded Fragments of the Hebrew Pentateuch in the Samaritan Version. *Textus* 3:60–73.

47. Review of *The Interpreter's Dictionary of the Bible*, edited by George A. Buttrick. *Journal of Bible and Religion* 31:332–34.

48. Review of *Memory and Tradition in Israel*, by Brevard S. Childs. *Journal of Biblical Literature* 82:330, 332–33.

49. Arcaismo. Pp. 695–96 in *Enciclopedia de la Biblia*, volume 1. Madrid/Barcelona: Garriga.

50. Balthasar. Pp. 1032–33 in *Enciclopedia de la Biblia*, volume 1. Madrid/Barcelona: Garriga.

51. Ben Hadad. Pp. 1108–9 in *Enciclopedia de la Biblia*, volume 1. Madrid/Barcelona: Garriga.

52. Darda^c. P. 784 in *Enciclopedia de la Biblia*, volume 2. Madrid/Barcelona: Garriga.

53. Rhetórica. Pp. 180–88 in *Enciclopedia de la Biblia*, volume 6. Madrid/Barcelona: Garriga.

1964

54. Aspects of the Textual Transmission of the Bible in the Light of Qumran Manuscripts. *Textus* 4:95–132.
[Reprinted in no. A7, pp. 71–116, and in no. B5, pp. 226–63]

55. The New Hebrew Letter from the Seventh Century B.C. in Historical Perspective. *Bulletin of the American Schools of Oriental Research* 176:29–38.
[Reprinted in no. A5, pp. 79–88; Hebrew translation in no. D61]

56. שלשה ספרים מצאו בעזרה. Pp. 252–64 in *Studies in the Bible Presented to Professor M. H. Segal*. Edited by Jehoshua M. Grintz and Jacob Liver. Publications of the Israel Society for Biblical Research 17. Jerusalem: Kiryat Sepher for the Israel Society for Biblical Research.
[Translation (from English) of no. D37]

57. למשנתו של יחזקאל קויפמן, דברים לזכרו. *University College Haifa*: 19–26.
[Spanish translation in no. D96; English translation in no. D97]

58. Review of *Old Testament Translation Problems*, by S. R. Hulst. *Journal of Semitic Studies* 9:370–72.
[Spanish translation in no. D40; French translation in no. D41]

59. תולדות החינוך בתקופת המקרא. Cols. 52–72 in *Encyclopedia of Education*. Edited by Martin Buber and Chaim Ormian. Volume on *History of Education*. Jerusalem: Ministry of Education and Culture/Bialik.
[With Moshe Weinfeld]

1965

60. The Town Lists of Simeon. *Israel Exploration Journal* 15:235–41.
[Hebrew translation in no. D81]

61. הכתובת העברית החדשה מימי יאשיהו. *Beth Mikra* 11:3–14.
[Translation (from English) of no. D55]

62. למשנתו של קויפמן בחקר המקרא. *Ha-Boqer* (Tel Aviv) April 22: 7.

63. Review of מלכות שמים, by Martin Buber. *Ha-Boqer* (Tel Aviv) Oct. 22: 5.
64. איוב. Pp. 38–39 in *Bible Lexicon*, volume 1. Tel Aviv: Dvir.
65. חמש שמרוני. Pp. 292–94 in *Bible Lexicon*, volume 1. Tel Aviv: Dvir.
66. מלוכה. Pp. 522–25 in *Bible Lexicon*, volume 2. Tel Aviv: Dvir.
67. משלי. Pp. 574–76 in *Bible Lexicon*, volume 2. Tel Aviv: Dvir.
68. משפחה. Pp. 576–81 in *Bible Lexicon*, volume 2. Tel Aviv: Dvir.
69. קהלת. Pp. 783–84 in *Bible Lexicon*, volume 2. Tel Aviv: Dvir.
70. שופטים; ספר שופטים; מעשי השופטים. Pp. 825–26 in *Bible Lexicon*, volume 2. Tel Aviv: Dvir.
71. שמרונים. Pp. 858–60 in *Bible Lexicon*, volume 2. Tel Aviv: Dvir.

1966

72. The "Desert Motif" in the Bible and in Qumran Literature. Pp. 31–63 in *Biblical Motifs: Origins and Transformations*. Edited by Alexander Altmann. Philip W. Lown Institute of Advanced Judaic Studies: Studies and Texts 3. Cambridge: Harvard University Press.
[Excerpts in no. D206; Hebrew translation in no. D104]

73. Pisqah Beʾemṣaʿ Pasuq and 11QPsᵃ. *Textus* 5:11–21.

74. לוח גזר ומחזור העונות בכנען הקדומה. *Beth Mikra* 12:3–17.
[Translation (from English) of no. D45]

75. מזמרים חיצוניים בלשון העברית מקומראן — מזמור קנא. *Tarbiz* 35:214–34.
[English translation in no. A7, pp. 244–72]

76. יסוד אוגריתי בעמוס ז,ד. *Tarbiz* 35:301–3.

77. שופטים פרק א׳. Pp. 14–29 in עיונים בספר שופטים. Publications of the Israel Society for Biblical Research. Jerusalem: Kiryat Sepher for the Israel Society for Biblical Research.

78. Review of *Bibliographie zu den Handschriften vom Toten Meer*, by Christoph Burchard. *Tarbiz* 35:195–97.

1967

79. The Judaean ʿam Haʾareṣ in Historical Perspective. Pp. 71–76 in *Fourth World Congress of Jewish Studies: Papers*, volume 1. Jerusalem: World Union of Jewish Studies.
[Reprinted in no. A5, pp. 68–78; Hebrew translation in no. D80; German translation in no. A6, pp. 80–91]

80. תולדות עם הארץ בממלכת יהודה. *Beth Mikra* 12:27–55.
[Translation (from English) of no. D79]

81. רשימת ערי שמעון. Pp. 265–68 in *Eretz-Israel 8: E. L. Sukenik Memorial Volume (1889–1953)*. Edited by Nachman Avigad, Michael Avi-Yonah, Hayyim Z. Hirschberg, and Benjamin Mazar (Maisler). Jerusalem: Israel Exploration Society.
[Translation (from English) of no. D60]

1969

82. *Amen* as an Introductory Oath Formula. *Textus* 7:124–29.

83. Prolegomenon. Pp. i–xxvii in the reprint of *The Ten Nequdoth of the Torah; or, The Meaning and Purpose of the Extraordinary Points of the Pentateuch (Massoretic Text): A Contribution to the History of Textual Criticism among the Ancient Jews*, by Romain Butin. New York: Ktav.

84. המקרא בהומניסמוס של דורנו. *The University* (Jerusalem) 14:6–9.
[English translation in nos. D91 and D99; Spanish translation in no. D106]

85. Review of *The Psalms Scroll of Qumran Cave 11*, by James A. Sanders. *Tarbiz* 37:99–104.

1970

86. The Old Testament Text. Pp. 159–99 in *The Cambridge History of the Bible*, volume 1: *From the Beginnings to Jerome*. Edited by Peter R. Ackroyd and Christopher F. Evans. Cambridge: Cambridge University Press.
[Reprinted in no. B5, pp. 1–41]

87. Die Bedeutung Jerusalems in der Bibel. Pp. 135–52 in *Jüdisches Volk, gelobtes Land: Die biblischen Landverheissungen als Problem des jüdischen Selbstverständnisses und der christlichen Theologie*. Edited by Willehad P. Eckert, Nathan P. Levinson, and Martin Stöhr. Abhandlungen zum christlich-jüdischen Dialog 3. Munich: Kaiser.
[Reprinted in no. A8, pp. 83–97; English translation in no. D93; Spanish translations in nos. D88 and D100; French translation in no. D142; Italian translation in no. D143; Dutch translation in no. D177]

88. Jerusalem en el Antiguo Testamento. *Tierra Santa* Jan./Feb.: 25–31.
[Translation (from German) of no. D87]

89. Martin Bubers Wege in der Bibel. *Emunah-Horizonte zur Diskussion über Israel und das Judentum* 5:93–95.

90. Review of ההיסטוריה של עם ישראל: סידרה ראשונה: הזמן העתיק, vol. 1, edited by Ephraim A. Speiser; and vol. 2/2, edited by Benjamin Mazar. *Qadmoniot* 3:34–35.

91. The Bible in Contemporary Israeli Humanism. *Ha-Shalom* (Durban) 47:12–15.
[Translation (from Hebrew) of no. D84; reprinted in no. D99]

1971

92. Typen der Messiaserwartung um die Zeitwende. Pp. 571–88 in *Probleme biblischer Theologie: Gerhard von Rad zum 70. Geburtstag*. Edited by Hans W. Wolff. Munich: Kaiser.
[Reprinted in no. A6, pp. 209–24; English translation in no. A5, pp. 202–24, and nos. D130 and D196]

93. The Biblical Concept of Jerusalem. *Journal of Ecumenical Studies* 8:300–316.
[Translation (from German) of no. D87; reprinted in no. D109]

94. The New Covenanters of Qumran. *Scientific American* 225/5 (November): 72–81.

95. עַם הָאָרֶץ. *Encyclopaedia Miqra'it* 6:239–42. Jerusalem: Bialik.

96. El Enfoque de la Investigacion Biblica de Yehezkel Kaufmann. *Maj'shavot—Pensamientos* (Buenos Aires) 10:63–70.
[Translation (from Hebrew) of no. D57]

97. Yehezkel Kaufmann's Approach to Biblical Research. *Conservative Judaism* 25:20–28.
[Translation (from Hebrew) of no. D57]

1972

98. בימים ההם אין מלך בישראל. Pp. 135–44 in *Proceedings of the Fifth World Congress of Jewish Studies*, volume 1. Edited by Pinchas Peli. Jerusalem: World Union of Jewish Studies.
[English translation in no. D118; German translation in no. A6, pp. 44–55]

99. The Bible in Contemporary Israeli Humanism. *Judaism* 21:79–83.
[Reprinted from no. D91]

100. El Concepto Biblico de Jerusalem. Pp. 22–40 in *Jerusalem en la Historia Judía*. Biblioteca Popular Judía 60. Buenos Aires: Congreso Judío Latinoamericano.
[Translation (from English) of no. D93]

101. Die Samaritaner in Vergangenheit und Gegenwart. *Frankfurter Universitätsreden* 42:71–83 (Woche der Hebräischen Universität Jerusalem an der Johann Wolfgang Goethe-Universität, Frankfurt am Main, 15.–19. Januar 1968).
[Reprinted in no. D234; Spanish translation in no. D161]

102. Qumran und das Alte Testament. *Frankfurter Universitätsreden* 42:84–100 (Woche der Hebräischen Universität Jerusalem an der Johann Wolfgang Goethe-Universität, Frankfurt am Main, 15.–19. Januar 1968).

103. Review of *The Book of Amos: A Commentary*, by Erling Hammershaimb. *Journal of Biblical Literature* 91:253–54.

1973

104. והנה אין יוסף: מוטיב המדבר במקרא ובספרות קומראן. Pp. 73–107 in *Joseph Amorai Memorial Volume*. Tel Aviv: Privately printed.
[Translation (from English) of no. D72]

105. An Apparently Redundant MT Reading—Jeremiah 1:18. *Textus* 8:160–63.

106. La Biblia en el Humanismo Israeli Contemporaneo. *Maj'shavot—Pensamientos* (Buenos Aires) 12:92–96.
[Translation (from Hebrew) of no. D84]

107. Interfaith Dialogue in Israel: Retrospect and Prospect. *Immanuel*, Special Supplement (Autumn): 9–20.
[Reprinted in nos. D112 and D144; German translation in no. D110]

1974

108. מסורות במקרא על ראשית תולדות השומרונים. Pp. 19–33 in *The Land of Samaria: The Thirtieth Israeli Conference on the Study of the Land of Israel*. Jerusalem: Israel Exploration Society.
[German translation in no. A6, pp. 132–51]

109. The Biblical Concept of Jerusalem. Pp. 189–203 in *Jerusalem*. Edited by John M. Oesterreicher and Anne Sinai. New York: John Day.
[Reprinted from no. D93]

110. Der interkonfessionelle Dialog in Israel—Rükblick und Ausblick. *Freiburger Rundbriefe* 26:140–46.
[Translation (from English) of no. D107]

111. The Hebrew University Bible Project. *Immanuel* 3:22–27.

112. Interfaith Dialogue in Israel: Retrospect and Prospect. *Encounter Today—Judaism and Christianity in the Contemporary World* 9:18-29.
[German translation in no. D107]

113. Towards World Community: Resources and Responsibilities for Living Together—A Jewish View. *Ecumenical Review* 26:604-18.

114. Majority and Minority Cultures. Pp. 6-7 in *Congress Bi-Weekly*. Special Issue: Jewishness and the Creative Process (New York: American Jewish Congress).

1975

115. The Textual Study of the Bible—A New Outlook. Pp. 321-400 in *Qumran and the History of the Biblical Text* [no. B5]. Edited by Frank M. Cross and Shemaryahu Talmon. Cambridge: Harvard University Press.

116. סוגיות בסידור ספר יחזקאל. *Beth Mikra* 20:315-27.
[Reprinted in no. D182]

117. הַר *har*; גִּבְעָה *gibʿāh*. Cols. 459-83 in *Theologisches Wörterbuch zum Alten Testament*, volume 2. Edited by G. Johannes Botterweck and Helmer Ringgren. Stuttgart: Kohlhammer.
[English translation in no. D154]

118. "In Those Days There Was No King in Israel." *Immanuel* 5:27-36.
[Translation (from Hebrew) of no. D98; reprinted in no. A5, pp. 39-52]

119. Martin Buber als Bibelinterpret. *Freiburger Rundbrief* 27:6-11.
[Reprinted in no. A8, pp. 130-44, and nos. D155 and D187; English translation in no. D131; Spanish translation in no. D163; Hebrew translation in no. B7, pp. 124-39, and no. D185]

120. Particularity and Universality—A Jewish View. Pp. 36-42 in *Jewish-Christian Dialogue: Six Years of Christian-Jewish Consultations*. Geneva: World Council of Churches.
[Reprinted in no. D121; German translation in no. D132]

121. Particularity and Universality—A Jewish View. *CCAR Journal* (Spring): 13-19.
[Reprinted from no. D120]

122. Review of *The Gospel and the Land: Early Christianity and Jewish Territorial Doctrine*, by W. D. Davies. *Christian News from Israel* 25:132-36.

123. Die Kommune von Qumran. *Frankfurter Allgemeine Zeitung* (Frankfurt am Main) Aug. 2.

1976

124. סוגיות בסידורם של פרקי ספר יחזקאל. *Tarbiz* 42:27–41.

125. The Structuring of Biblical Books: Studies in the Book of Ezekiel. *Annual of the Swedish Theological Institute* 10:129–53.
[With Michael Fishbane]

126. Some Aspects of the Text of the Hebrew Bible. Pp. 50–69 in *Armenian and Biblical Studies*. Edited by Michael E. Stone. Jerusalem: St. James Press.

127. Conflate Readings (OT). Pp. 170–73 in *The Interpreter's Dictionary of the Bible, Supplementary Volume*. Edited by Keith Crim. Nashville: Abingdon.

128. Ezra and Nehemiah (Books and Men). Pp. 317–28 in *The Interpreter's Dictionary of the Bible, Supplementary Volume*. Edited by Keith Crim. Nashville: Abingdon.

129. Wilderness. Pp. 946–49 in *The Interpreter's Dictionary of the Bible, Supplementary Volume*. Edited by Keith Crim. Nashville: Abingdon.

130. Types of Messianic Expectation at the Turn of the Era. *CCAR Journal* (Spring): 1–11.
[Translation (from German) of no. D92; reprinted in no. A5, pp. 202–24, and no. D196]

131. Martin Buber's Ways of Interpreting the Bible. *Journal of Jewish Studies* 27:195–209.
[Translation (from German) of no. D119]

132. Partikularismus und Universalismus aus jüdischer Sicht. *Freiburger Rundbrief* 28:33–36.
[Translation (from English) of no. D120; reprinted in no. A8, pp. 159–65]

133. Jerusalem—Glaube und Geschichte. *Süddeutsche Zeitung am Wochenende* (Munich) March 20–21: 83–84.
[Reprinted in no. D134]

134. Jerusalem—Glaube und Geschichte. *Zur Debatte: Themen der Katholischen Adademie in Bayern* 6/3:1–3.
[Reprinted from no. D133]

135. Die Samaritaner. *Süddeutsche Zeitung am Wochenende* (Munich) May 22–23: 129–30.

136. Dialogue: How Useful? *Jewish Chronicle* (London) May 21: 21.

1977

137. טבור הארץ והמחקר ההשוואתי. *Tarbiz* 45:1–15.
[Reprinted in no. D183; English translation in no. D138]

138. The "Navel of the Earth" and the Comparative Method. Pp. 243–68 in *Scripture in History and Theology: Essays in Honor of J. Coert Rylaarsdam*. Edited by Arthur L. Merrill and Thomas W. Overholt. Pittsburgh Theological Monograph Series 17. Pittsburgh: Pickwick.
[Translation (from Hebrew) of no. D137; reprinted in no. A9]

139. The Book of Judges Examined by Statistical Linguistics. *Biblica* 58:469–99.
[With Yehuda T. Radday, Giora Leb, and Dieter Wickmann]

140. The Samaritans. *Scientific American* 236/1 (January): 100–108.

141. Jerusalem in Ancient Times. *CCAR Journal* (Winter): 11–18.

142. La Notion Biblique de Jérusalem. *Rencontre* 11:251–65.
[Translation (from German) of no. D87]

143. Il Concetto di Gerusalemme nella Bibbia. *Documenti e Fatti* (Milan) 20–21: 10–13.
[Translation (from German) of no. D87]

144. Interfaith Dialogue in Israel: Retrospect and Prospect. *Face to Face: An Interreligious Bulletin* 2:3–5.
[Reprinted from no. D107]

145. Israel: Significance and Realities. *Immanuel* 7:92–98.

146. Review of *Arad Inscriptions*, by Yohanan Aharoni; and *Bullae and Seals from a Post-Exilic Judean Archive*, by Nahman Avigad. *Christian News from Israel* 26:113–16.

1978

147. The "Comparative Method" in Biblical Interpretation—Principles and Problems. Pp. 320–56 in *Congress Volume: Göttingen 1977*. Vetus Testamentum Supplement 29. Leiden: Brill.
[Reprinted in no. A9]

148. "יגיד עליו רעו" (איוב לו, 33): ביאורי כתובים ותיקוני נוסח במקרא על סמך מקבילות מספרות אוגרית. Pp. 117–24 in *Eretz-Israel 14: H. L. Ginsberg*

Volume. Edited by Menahem Haran. Jerusalem: Israel Exploration Society/Jewish Theological Seminary.
[English translation in no. D204]

149. The Presentation of Synchroneity and Simultaneity in Biblical Narrative. Pp. 9–26 in *Studies in Hebrew Narrative Art throughout the Ages.* Edited by Joseph Heinemann and Shmuel Werses. Scripta Hierosolymitana 27. Jerusalem: Magnes.
[Reprinted in no. A9]

150. The Emergence of Institutionalized Prayer in Israel in the Light of the Qumrân Literature. Pp. 265–84 in *Qumrân: Sa Piété, sa Théologie et son Milieu.* Edited by Mathias Delcor. Bibliotheca Ephemeridum Theologicarum Lovaniensium 46. Paris/Gembloux: Duculot/Louvain: Louvain University Press.
[Combined with no. D26 and reprinted in no. A7, pp. 200–243; German translation in no. A6, pp. 190–208]

151. Exil und Rückkehr in der Ideenwelt des Alten Testaments. Pp. 31–55 in *Exil, Diaspora, Rückkehr: Zum theologischen Gespräch zwischen Juden und Christen.* Edited by Rudolf Mosis. Schriften der Katholischen Akademie in Bayern 81. Düsseldorf: Patmos.
[Reprinted in no. A8, pp. 61–82; Spanish translation in no. D162]

152. Sakralisierung der Geschichte und Säkularisierung des Glaubens im jüdischen Denken. Pp. 134–47 in *Religion und Politik in der Gesellschaft des 20. Jahrhunderts: Ein Symposion mit israelischen und deutschen Wissenschaftlern* [no. B6]. Edited by Shemaryahu Talmon and Gregor Siefer. Bonn: Keil.
[Reprinted in no. A8, pp. 178–87]

153. Kritische Anfrage der jüdischen Theologie an das europäische Christentum. Pp. 139–57 in *Israel hat dennoch Gott zum Trost: Festschrift für Schalom Ben-Chorin.* Edited by Gotthold Müller. Trier: Paulinus.
[Reprinted in no. A8, pp. 209–25, and no. D175]

154. הַר *har*; גִּבְעָה *gibhʿāh*. Pp. 427–47 in *Theological Dictionary of the Old Testament*, volume 3. Edited by G. Johannes Botterweck and Helmer Ringgren. Translated by John T. Willis, Geoffrey W. Bromiley, and David E. Green. Grand Rapids: Eerdmans.
[Translation (from German) of no. D117]

155. Martin Buber als Bibelinterpret. Pp. 42–54 in *Leben als Begegnung: Ein Jahrhundert Martin Buber, 1878–1978: Vorträge und Aufsätze.* Veröffentlichungen aus dem Institut Kirche und Judentum 7. Berlin: Institut Kirche und Judentum.
[Reprinted from no. D119]

156. Martin Buber und die Bibel. Pp. 11–21 in *Martin Buber: Festakt der hessischen Landesregierung und der Johann Wolfgang Goethe-Universität, Frankfurt am Main am 8. Februar 1978 in der Frankfurter Paulskirche*. Frankfurt am Main: Pressestelle der Universität.

1979

157. Kingship and the Ideology of the State. Pp. 3–26 in *The World History of the Jewish People*, volume 4/2: *The Age of the Monarchies: Culture and Society*. Edited by Abraham Malamat. Jerusalem: Massada.
    [Reprinted in no. A5, pp. 9–38; German translation in no. A6, pp. 11–43]

158. Torah as a Concept and Vital Principle in the Hebrew Bible. *Greek Orthodox Theological Review* 24:271–89.
    [German translation in no. A8, pp. 31–47]

159. Utopie und Wirklichkeit im Denken Martin Bubers. Pp. 127–36 in *Toleranz heute: 250 Jahre nach Mendelssohn und Lessing*. Edited by Peter von der Osten-Sacken. Veröffentlichungen aus dem Institut Kirche und Judentum bei der Kirchlichen Hochschule Berlin 9. Berlin: Institut Kirche und Judentum.
    [Reprinted in no. A8, pp. 166–77; English translation in no. D174; Hebrew translation in no. B7, pp. 16–27, no. B12, pp. 45–56, and no. D184; German translation in no. 186]

160. Das Verhältnis von Judentum und Christentum im Verständnis Franz Rosenzweigs. Pp. 119–42 in *Offenbarung im Denken Franz Rosenzweigs*. Essen: Wolfsburg.
    [Reprinted in no. A8, pp. 188–200; English translation in no. D173]

161. Los Samaritanos: Pasado y Presente. *Helmantica* 30:317–30.
    [Translation (from German) of no. D101]

162. "Exilio" y "Retorno" en el Pensamiento del Antiguo Testamento. Pp. 165–92 in *Identidad y Testimonio: Actas del IV Simposio Hispano-Israelí, Abril 1978*. Madrid: Centro de Estudios Judeo-Christianos.
    [Translation (from German) of no. D151; abridged reprint in no. D232]

163. Los Caminos de Buber en la Interpretacion de la Biblia. Pp. 193–212 in *Identidad y Testimonio: Actas del IV Simposio Hispano-Israelí, Abril 1978*. Madrid: Centro de Estudios Judeo-Christianos.
    [Translation (from German) of no. D119]

1980

164. The Biblical Idea of Statehood. Pp. 239–48 in *The Bible World: Essays in Honor of Cyrus H. Gordon*. Edited by Gary Rendsburg, Ruth Adler, Milton Arfa, and Nathan H. Winter. New York: Ktav/ Institute of Hebrew Culture and Education of New York University.

165. Eschatologie und Geschichte im biblischen Judentum. Pp. 13–50 in *Zukunft: Zur Eschatologie bei Juden und Christen*. Edited by Rudolf Schnackenburg. Düsseldorf: Patmos.
[English translation in no. A4]

166. Eschatologie im biblischen Judentum. *Zur Debatte: Themen der Katholischen Adademie in Bayern* 10/2:10–11.

1981

167. The Ancient Hebrew Alphabet and Biblical Text Criticism. Pp. 497–530 in *Mélanges Dominique Barthélemy: Études Bibliques Offertes à l'Occasion de son 60ᵉ Anniversaire*. Edited by Pierre Casetti, Othmar Keel, and Adrian Schenker. Orbis Biblicus et Orientalis 38. Göttingen: Vandenhoeck & Ruprecht/ Freiburg: Éditions Universitaires.

168. Did There Exist a Biblical National Epic? Pp. 41–61 in *Proceedings of the Seventh World Congress of Jewish Studies*, volume 2: *Studies in the Bible and the Ancient Near East*. Jerusalem: Perry Foundation for Biblical Research/ World Union of Jewish Studies.
[Reprinted in no. A9]

169. Polemics and Apology in Biblical Historiography—2 Kings 17:24–41. Pp. 57–68 in *The Creation of Sacred Literature: Composition and Redaction of the Biblical Text*. Edited by Richard E. Friedman. University of California Publications: Near Eastern Studies 22. Berkeley/ Los Angeles: University of California Press.
[Reprinted in no. A9]

170. A Commentary on the Text of Jeremiah, 1: The LXX of Jer. 1:1–7. *Textus* 9:1–15.
[With Emanuel Tov]

171. Grundzüge des Offenbarungsverständnisses in biblischer Zeit. Pp. 12–36 in *Offenbarung im jüdischen und christlichen Glaubensverständnis*. Edited by Jakob J. Petuchowski und Walter Strolz. Freiburg: Herder.
[Reprinted in no. A8, pp. 11–30; English translation in no. D202]

172. Israel und Diaspora. Pp. 179–201 in *Unter dem Bogen des Bundes: Beiträge aus jüdischer und christlicher Existenz*. Edited by Hans H. Henrix. Aachener Beiträge zu Pastoral- und Bildungsfragen 11. Aachen: Einhard.

173. Judaism and Christianity in Franz Rosenzweig's Perspective. Pp. 587–98 in *De la Tôrah au Messie: Études d'Exégèse et d'Herméneutique Bibliques Offertes à Henri Cazelles.* Edited by Maurice Carrez, Joseph Doré, and Pierre Grelot, Paris: Desclée.
[Translation (from German) of no. D160]

174. Utopia and Reality in Martin Buber's Thought. Pp. 375–86 in *Standing before God: Studies on Prayer in Scriptures and in Tradition with Essays in Honor of John M. Oesterreicher.* Edited by Asher Finkel and Lawrence Frizzell. New York: Ktav.
[Translation (from German) of no. D159]

175. Kritische Anfrage der jüdischen Theologie an das europäische Christentum. Pp. 58–80 in *Einladung ins Lehrhaus: Beiträge zum jüdischen Selbstverständnis.* Edited by Werner Licharz and Martin Stöhr. Arnoldshainer Texte 4. Frankfurt am Main: Haag & Herchen.
[Reprinted from no. D153]

176. Der Gesalbte Jahwes. *Zur Debatte: Themen der Katholischen Akademie in Bayern* 11/2:10–11.

177. Jeruzalem als Bijbles Begrip. *Gesprekken in Israel–Nes Ammim Lezingen* 6/4:2–22.
[Translation (from German) of no. D87]

1982

178. Der Gesalbte Jahwes: Biblische und früh–nachbiblische Messias- und Heilserwartungen. Pp. 27–68 in *Jesus-Messias? Heilserwartungen bei Juden und Christen.* Regensburg: Pustet.
[Reworked and reprinted in no. A8, pp. 98–129; English revision and translation in no. A5, pp. 140–64]

179. Wissenschaft vom Judentum und christliche Theologie: Prinzipien und Probleme einer Zusammenarbeit. *Freiburger Rundbrief* 34:12–15.
[Reprinted in no. A8, pp. 226–33]

180. נוסח — תנ״ך. *Encyclopaedia Miqraʾit* 8:621–41. Jerusalem: Bialik.

181. "הערות לשוניות" רבין ח׳ של מאמרו בעקבי. *Shnaton* 5–6: 227–30.

182. עיונים בספר יחזקאל in Pp. 131–50. סוגיות בסידור ס׳ יחזקאל. Edited by Yitzchak Avishur. Jerusalem: Kiryat-Sefer.
[Reprinted from no. D116]

183. עיונים בספר יחזקאל in Pp. 151–76. "טבור הארץ" והשיטה ההשוואתית. Edited by Yitzchak Avishur. Jerusalem: Kiryat-Sefer.
[Reprinted from no. D137]

184. כאן ועכשיו: עיונים במחשבתו של בובר. אוטופיה ומציאות במחשבתו של בובר. Pp. 16–27 in בהגותו החברתית והדתית של מ״מ בובר [nos. B7 and B12]. Edited by Shemaryahu Talmon, Kalman Yaron, and Yosef Emanuel. Jerusalem: Martin Buber Center, Hebrew University of Jerusalem.
[Translation (from German) of no. D159]

185. כאן ועכשיו: עיונים בהגותו של בובר כפרשן המקרא. דרכו של בובר כפרשן המקרא. Pp. 124–39 in החברתית והדתית של מ״מ בובר [nos. B7 and B12]. Edited by Shemaryahu Talmon, Kalman Yaron, and Yosef Emanuel. Jerusalem: Martin Buber Center, Hebrew University of Jerusalem.
[Translation (from German) of no. D119]

186. Utopie und Wirklichkeit im Denken Martin Bubers. Pp. 108–24 in *Dialog mit Martin Buber*. Edited by Werner Licharz. Arnoldshainer Texte 7. Frankfurt am Main: Haag & Herchen.
[Reprinted from no. D159]

187. Martin Buber als Bibelinterpret. Pp. 269–89 in *Dialog mit Martin Buber*. Edited by Werner Licharz. Arnoldshainer Texte 7. Frankfurt am Main: Haag & Herchen.
[Reprinted from no. D119]

188. Partikularität und Universalismus in der biblischen Zukunftserwartung. Pp. 21–48 in *Zukunftshoffnung und Heilserwartung in den monotheistischen Religionen* [no. B9]. Edited by Abdoldjavad Falaturi, Walter Strolz, and Shemaryahu Talmon. Veröffentlichungen der Stiftung Oratio Dominica: Weltgespräch der Religionen 9. Freiburg: Herder.

1983

189. ההיסטוריה של עם ישראל: שיבת ציון- ראשיתה של שיבת ציון. Pp. 28–39 in שיבת ציון- ימי שלטון פרס. Edited by Hayim Tadmor, Israel Ephal, and Jonas C. Greenfield. Jerusalem: Pelli.

190. Exil und Rückkehr. Pp. 27–53 in *Geschichte der Juden von der biblischen Zeit bis zur Gegenwart*. Edited by Franz J. Bautz. Beck'sche Schwarze Reihe 268. Munich: Beck.

191. Biblical *repā'îm* and Ugaritic *rpu/i(m)*. *Hebrew Annual Review* 7 (Biblical and Other Studies in Honor of Robert Gordis; edited by Reuben Ahroni): 235–49.
[Hebrew translation in no. D192]

192. רפאים שבמקרא ו-rpu-i(m) בספרות אוגרית. *Beth Mikra* 30:16–27.
[Translation (from English) of no. D191]

193. Ägypten und Israel aus biblischer Sicht. Pp. 129–39 in *5000 Jahre Ägypten: Genese und Permanenz pharaonischer Kunst*. Edited by Jan Assmann and Günter Burkard. Nussloch: IS-Edition.

194. Cardinal Bea and the Christian-Jewish Dialogue. *Communio* (Rome) N.S. 14 (Card. Agostino Bea Fest.): 103–10.

195. מִדְבָּר *miḏbār*; עֲרָבָה *ᶜᵃrāḇāh*. Cols. 660–95 in *Theologisches Wörterbuch zum Alten Testament*, volume 4. Edited by G. Johannes Botterweck, Helmer Ringgren, and Heinz-Josef Fabry. Stuttgart: Kohlhammer.

196. Messianic Expectations at the Turn of the Era. *Face to Face: An Interreligious Bulletin* 10:4–12.
[Reprinted from no. D130]

1984

197. Yād Wāšēm: An Idiomatic Phrase in Biblical Literature and Its Variations. *Hebrew Studies* 25:8–17.
[Reprinted in no. A9; Hebrew translation in no. D217]

1985

198. The Ancient Hebrew Alphabet and Biblical Text Criticism. Pp. 387–402 in *Mélanges Bibliques et Orientaux en l'Honneur de M. Mathias Delcor*. Edited by André Caquot, Simon Légasse, and Michel Tardieu. Alter Orient und Altes Testament 215. Neukirchen-Vluyn: Neukirchener Verlag/Kevelaer: Butzon & Bercker.

199. Jüdische Sektenbildung in der Frühzeit des zweiten Tempels: Ein Nachtrag zu Max Webers Studie über das antike Judentum. Pp. 233–80 in *Max Webers Sicht des antiken Christentums: Interpretation und Kritik*. Edited by Wolfgang Schluchter. Suhrkamp Taschenbuch Wissenschaft 548. Frankfurt am Main: Suhrkamp.
[Reprinted in no. A6, pp. 95–131; English translation in no. A5, pp. 165–201, and no. D210]

200. Die Wertung von "Leben" in der hebräischen Bibel. Pp. 15–30 in *Der Herr des Lebens: Jüdische und christliche Interpretationen in der Ökumene*. Edited by Hans-Georg Link and Martin Stöhr. Arnoldshainer Texte 39. Frankfurt am Main: Haag & Herchen.
[Reprinted in no. A8, pp. 48–60]

201. A Bible Scholar's Evaluation. Pp. 225–35 in *Genesis: An Authorship Study in Computer-Assisted Statistical Linguistics*, by Yehuda T. Radday and Haim Shore. Analecta Biblica 103. Rome: Pontifical Biblical Institute.

202. Revelation in Biblical Times. *Hebrew Studies* 26 (In Honor of Abraham I. Katsh): 53–70.
[Translation (from German) of no. D171; reprinted in no. A9]

1986

203. Gott und Mensch—eine zeitgenössische jüdische Ansicht. Pp. 185–90 in *"Wie gut sind deine Zelte Jaakow": Festschrift zum 60. Geburtstag von Reinhold Mayer.* Edited by Ernst L. Ehrlich, Bertold Klappert, and Ursula Ast. Gerlingen: Bleicher.
[Reprinted in no. A8, pp. 201–8]

204. Emendation of Biblical Texts on the Basis of Ugaritic Parallels. Pp. 279–300 in *Studies in Bible.* Edited by Sara Japhet. Scripta Hierosolymitana 31. Jerusalem: Magnes.
[Translation (from Hebrew) of no. D148]

205. Ezra and Nehemiah, Books of. Pp. 349–52 in *Illustrated Dictionary and Concordance of the Bible.* Edited by Geoffrey Wigoder. New York: Macmillan.

206. [Untitled.] Pp. 28–30, 48–50, 137–38, 246–47, and 366–68 in *The Hebrew Bible in Literary Criticism.* Edited by Alex Preminger and Edward L. Greenstein. New York: Ungar.
[Excerpts from nos. A3, D43, and D72]

1987

207. Heiliges Schrifttum und kanonische Bücher aus jüdischer Sicht: Überlegungen zur Ausbildung der Grösse "Die Schrift" im Judentum. Pp. 45–79 in *Mitte der Schrift? Ein jüdisch-christliches Gespräch: Texte des Berner Symposions vom 6.-12. January 1985* [no. B11]. Edited by Martin Klopfenstein, Ulrich Luz, Shemaryahu Talmon, and Emanuel Tov. Judaica et Christiana 11. Bern/New York: Lang.

208. Har and Midbār: An Antithetical Pair of Biblical Motifs. Pp. 117–42 in *Figurative Language in the Ancient Near East.* Edited by Murray Mindlin, Mark J. Geller, and John E. Wansbrough. London: School of Oriental and African Studies, University of London.

209. Waiting for the Messiah: The Spiritual Universe of the Qumran Covenanters. Pp. 111–37 in *Judaisms and Their Messiahs at the Turn of the Christian Era.* Edited by Jacob Neusner, William S. Green, and Ernest S. Frerichs. Cambridge: Cambridge University Press.
[Reprinted in no. A7, pp. 273–300]

210. The Emergence of Jewish Sectarianism in the Early Second Temple Period. Pp. 587–616 in *Ancient Israelite Religion: Essays in Honor of Frank Moore Cross.* Edited by Patrick D. Miller Jr., Paul D. Hanson, and S. Dean McBride. Philadelphia: Fortress.
[Translation (from German) and revision of no. D199; preprinted in no. A5, pp. 165–201]

211. The Biblical Understanding of Creation and the Human Commitment. *Christian-Jewish Relations* (London) 20:69–89.
   [Revised in no. D213; German translation in no. D212]

212. Das biblische Verständnis der Schöpfung und der Verpflichtung des Menschen. Pp. 19–32 in *Ursprung: Vortragszyklus 1986/87 über die Entstehung des Menschen und der Welt in den Mythen der Völker*. Edited by Mark Münzel. Interim 6. Frankfurt am Main: Museum für Völkerkunde.
   [Translation (from English) of no. D211]

213. The Biblical Understanding of Creation and the Human Commitment. *Ex Auditu* 3:98–119.
   [Revised and enlarged version of no. D211]

214. Daniel. Pp. 343–56 in *The Literary Guide to the Bible*. Edited by Robert Alter and Frank Kermode. Cambridge: Harvard University Press.

215. Ezra and Nehemiah. Pp. 357–64 in *The Literary Guide to the Bible*. Edited by Robert Alter and Frank Kermode. Cambridge: Harvard University Press.

216. 1 and 2 Chronicles. Pp. 365–72 in *The Literary Guide to the Bible*. Edited by Robert Alter and Frank Kermode. Cambridge: Harvard University Press.

217. "יד ושם"—גלגולי מטבע לשון בספרות המקרא. Pp. 137–48 in *Studies in Bible: Dedicated to the Memory of U. Cassuto on the 100th Anniversary of His Birth*. Edited by Hayim Beinart and Samuel E. Loewenstamm. Jerusalem: Magnes.
   [Translation (from English) of no. D197]

218. Mose und Aaron—zentrale Gestalten in der Bibel: Erwägungen zu A. Schönbergs Oper "Mose und Aaron." Pp. 151–62 in *Festschrift für Walter Strolz (1927–1987)*. Freiburg: Privately printed.

219. Jerusalem. Pp. 495–503 in *Contemporary Jewish Religious Thought: Original Essays on Critical Concepts, Movements, and Beliefs*. Edited by Arthur A. Cohen and Paul Mendes-Flohr. New York: Scribner.

220. Review of *Critique Textuelle de l'Ancien Testament*, volume 1: *Isaié, Jérémie, Lamentations*, by Dominique Barthélemy. *Theologie und Philosophie* 62:588–89.

221. Faith to Faith: A Conversation. *Immanuel* 21:118–21.
   [With Thomas Idinopulos]

1988

222. Literary Motifs and Speculative Thought. *Hebrew University Studies in Literature and the Arts* 16:150-68.

223. Zur Bibelinterpretation von Franz Rosenzweig und Martin Buber. Pp. 273-85 in *Der Philosoph Franz Rosenzweig (1886-1929): Internationaler Kongress, Kassel 1986*, volume 1: *Die Herausforderung jüdischen Lernens*. Edited by Wolfdietrich Schmied-Kowarzik. Freiburg: Alber.
[Reprinted in no. A8, pp. 145-56]

1989

224. Between the Bible and the Mishna. Pp. 11-52 in *The World of Qumran from Within: Collected Studies* [no. A9]. Jerusalem: Magnes/ Leiden: Brill.
[Hebrew translation in no. B14]

225. The Collocation משתין בקיר ועצור ועזוב and Its Meaning. *Zeitschrift für die Alttestamentliche Wissenschaft* 101:85-112.
[With Weston W. Fields]

226. קטעי כתבים כתובים עברית ממצדה. Pp. 278-86 in *Eretz-Israel 20: Yigael Yadin Memorial Volume*. Edited by Amnon Ben-Tor, Jonas C. Greenfield, and Abraham Malamat. Jerusalem: Israel Exploration Society.

227. צַח *ṣaḥ*; צָחִיחַ *ṣāḥîaḥ*; צְחִיחָה *ṣeḥîḥāh*. Cols. 983-86 in *Theologisches Wörterbuch zum Alten Testament*, volume 6. Edited by G. Johannes Botterweck, Helmer Ringgren, and Heinz-Josef Fabry. Stuttgart: Kohlhammer.

1990

228. "400 Jahre" oder "vier Generationen": Geschichtliche Zeitangaben oder literarische Motive? Pp. 13-25 in *Die hebräische Bibel und ihre zweifache Nachgeschichte: Festschrift für Rolf Rendtorff zum 65. Geburtstag*. Edited by Erhard Blum, Christian Macholz, and Ekkehard W. Stegemann. Neukirchen-Vluyn: Neukirchener Verlag.
[English translation in no. A9]

229. קֵץ *qēṣ*. Cols. 84-92 in *Theologisches Wörterbuch zum Alten Testament*, vol. 7. Edited by G. Johannes Botterweck, Helmer Ringgren, and Heinz-Josef Fabry. Stuttgart: Kohlhammer.

230. והמשכיל בעת ההיא ידם (עמוס ה, 13). *Shnaton* 10:115-22.
[With Esti Eshel]

231. שי לחיים רבין in 147–57 .Pp .קטע ממגילה חיצונית לספר יהושע ממצדה. Edited by Moshe H. Goshen-Gottstein, Shelomoh Morag, and Simchah Kogut. Jerusalem: Academon.

232. "Exilio" y "Retorno": En el Pensamiento del Antiguo Testamento. *La Biblia: Suplemento Cultural de Ultimas Noticias* (Caracas) June 24: 36–37.
[Abbreviated translation of no. D162]

1991

233. Prophetic Rhetoric and Agricultural Metaphora. Pp. 267–79 in *Storia e Tradizioni d'Israeli: Studi in Onore di J. A. Soggin*. Edited by Daniele Garrone and Felice Israel. Rome: Paideia.

234. Die Samaritaner in Vergangenheit und Gegenwart. Pp. 240–48 in *Die Samaritaner*. Edited by Ferdinand Dexinger and Reinhard Pummer. Wege der Forschung 604. Darmstadt: Wissenschaftliche Buchgesellschaft.
[Reprinted from no. D101]

Forthcoming

235. Esra–Nehemia: Historiographie oder Theologie? In *Klaus Koch Festschrift*. Edited by Dwight R. Daniels, Uwe Glessmer, and Martin Rösel. Neukirchen-Vluyn: Neukirchener Verlag.

236. The Concepts of Mašiaḥ and Messianism in Early Judaism. In *The Messiah*. Edited by James H. Charlesworth. Minneapolis: Augsburg Fortress.

237. "Oral Tradition" and "Written Transmission," or the "Heard" and the "Seen" Word in Judaism of the Second Temple Period. In *Jesus and the Oral Gospel Tradition: Oral Tradition in, before, and outside the Gospels*. Edited by Henry Wansbrough. Sheffield: Sheffield Academic Press.

238. The "Topped Triad" in the Hebrew Bible and the "Ascending Numerical Pattern." In *Maarav* 7–8 ("Let Your Colleagues Praise You": Stanley Gevirtz Memorial Volume; edited by Robert J. Ratner).

239. Tora-Nomos-Gesetz: Die Bedeutung des Judentums für die christliche Theologie.

240. מגילות קומראן: בין מקרא למשנה; כנס ירושלים לציון בין מקרא למשנה. In ארבעים שנות מחקר של מגילות מדבר יהודה [no. B14]. Edited by Magen Broshi, Shemaryahu Talmon, Sara Japhet, and Daniel Schwartz. Jerusalem: Israel Exploration Society/Bialik.

Biblical Literature and Exegesis

THE WELL OF LIVING WATER: A BIBLICAL MOTIF AND ITS ANCIENT TRANSFORMATIONS

Michael Fishbane

Motif analysis is one of the methods whereby the recurrent concerns of a literary corpus may be traced and their variations delineated. Moreover, since these topics frequently derive from the concrete life of a society, the literary motifs provide a valuable index to its patterns of culture as well. The careful investigator must therefore shuttle between the literary images themselves and the concrete realia which nourished them. At the same time, these same images frequently serve as the basis for their renewed reinterpretation. The result is a rich texture of transformations, bound by threads of creativity and continuity. In his own classical study of "The 'Desert Motif' in the Bible and in Qumran Literature," Shemaryahu Talmon formulated this matter with methodological precision:

> A literary motif is a representative complex theme which recurs within the framework of the Old Testament in variable forms and connections. It is rooted in an actual situation of anthropological or historical nature. In its secondary literary setting, the motif gives expression to ideas and experiences inherent in the original situation, and is employed to reactualize in the audience the reactions of the participants in the original situation. The motif... is not a mere reiteration of the sensations involved, but rather a heightened and intensified representation of them.[1]

In the study which follows, I hope to exemplify these observations with respect to the well motif in biblical and early post-biblical literature. In particular, I shall show that the concrete phenomenological power of the

---

Author's note: It is a pleasure to dedicate this essay to Shemaryahu Talmon in esteem and friendship.

  1. S. Talmon, "The 'Desert Motif' in the Bible and in Qumran Literature," in *Biblical Motifs* (ed. A. Altmann; Cambridge, MA, 1966) 39.

well as a source of sustenance is retained long after the motif is reinterpreted as a fount of heavenly wisdom. This bold refiguration has notable consequences for ancient Jewish religious thought—at once demonstrating the early hypostasization of the sources of divine wisdom, and adding to the growing evidence that many motifs of medieval Jewish mysticism are nourished by channels flowing from ancient Israel and its formative exegetical energies.[2] Aspects of this chapter in literary and cultural history will be reviewed below.

The Biblical Motif: Concrete Fact and Religious Metaphor

The concrete nature of the well is repeatedly marked in all strata and genres of the Hebrew Bible. Particularly striking is the common reference to a "well [באר] of living water" (Gen 26:16, Cant 4:15). This image apparently refers to the upsurge of springs of flowing rivers—as against stagnant pools or cisterns—and focuses attention on the well as a source of life and nourishment. This primordial character of natural springs (variously called מעין, מקור, or עין), from which water bursts forth from the depths of the earth, should not be forgotten. It is only surprising that so few theophanies are recorded at these sites (Gen 16:14; cf. Gen 25:11), or that traces of ancient cults are not recorded in connection with them. More regularly, these texts depict the social character of these loci and their function as places of meeting outside the areas of settlement. Particularly vivid portrayals of the well as a matrix for social intercourse recur in the old epic narratives of Genesis and Exodus. The centrality of the well in the episode describing the journey of Abraham's steward to Padan Aram is well known (Genesis 24). Indeed, the events around this well provide diagnostic conditions whereby he divines whether God will fulfill his mission to find a wife for Isaac (vv. 12–27, 42–48). The heroic encounter between Moses and the shepherds at a well, which results in his marriage to Zipporah, is another case in point (Exod 2:15–21). Beyond such literary *topoi*, the importance of cisterns and water supplies within the fortified cities of the period of settlement has been abundantly confirmed by archeological excavations. Accordingly, the prospect of blocked wells and cisterns was a curse to be avoided at all costs (cf. Hos 13:15, 2 Chr 32:4). The concise account of the contention over wells in the days of Isaac is exemplary in this regard (Gen 26:15–25), and, through the naming of the wells, also attests to the vital link between "living waters" and fertile growth (cf. vv. 19, 23). Thus, if open wells repeatedly serve in biblical texts as a metonymy for sustenance and life, their stoppage signals mortal danger and death.

---

2. M. Idel, *Kabbalah: New Perspectives* (New Haven, 1988), chaps. 5–8, has drawn attention to numerous phenomenological and literary links between ancient rabbinic sources and medieval Jewish mysticism. The present essay supports this effort.

In other texts, we may observe how millennia of social life oriented around springs and wells stimulated the production of concrete metaphors of different sorts. Among these images is the notable association of wells with wisdom—presumably because the teachings of the wise were considered living sources of help and guidance. Thus in one proverb we read that "the instruction of the wise man is a fountain [מקור] of life, enabling one to avoid deadly snares" (Prov 13:14; cf. 10:11, 18:4). At the same time, the well was also an image of eschatological promise. For example, the prophet Isaiah predicts that waters of renewal will be drawn from the fountains (מעיני) of salvation (Isa 12:3); while Joel later portrays the restoration of the temple and natural bounty in terms of a flowing fountain (Joel 4:18). This tradition recalls other postexilic traditions of "living water" flowing from Jerusalem (Zech 14:8), and thus gives mythic depth to historical hope.

In the biblical world view, however, natural springs are ultimately the bounty of the Lord—the supernatural source of sustenance and salvation. It is therefore not surprising that this theologoumenon is also epitomized by the imagery of a well. The psalmist prays:

> How precious is your abiding care, O God!
> Mankind is protected by the shadow of your wings.
>   They feast on the bounty of your house;
>   You let them drink at your refreshing stream.
> With you is the fountain of life [מקור חיים];
>   And by your light do we see light.   (Ps 36:8–10)

In this encomium, the natural springs of earthly life are metaphorically transposed on two planes: the first is the concrete temple, which is portrayed here in terms of a stream of spiritual renewal; while the second is God himself, who is presented as the fountain of all life and light. The religious depths of this imagery take us to the heart of biblical spirituality and the religious experience of the temple. Both the primordial awareness of light and the concrete dependence on water vitalize the prayer with images of the bounty of divine transcendence: "Bestow your abiding care on those devoted to you, and your kindness to the upright of heart" (Ps 36:11).

The creative dynamic that links the concrete fact of wells with their new metaphorical applications may be more precisely perceived through an instance of inner-biblical interpretation.[3] The starting point is the sermon of Moses found in Deut 6:10–13. Here the people are warned not to forget the Lord when they enter the promised land; for it was he, Moses exhorts, who delivered them from Egyptian bondage to give them "great and goodly

---

3. For this phenomenon in the Hebrew Bible, see my discussion in *Biblical Interpretation in Ancient Israel* (Oxford, 1985), part III.

cities that you did not build, houses full of good things that you did not fill (and) hewn cisterns [ברת חצובים] which you did not hew." Each of the images is concrete and physical: emblems of God's grace at the settlement. By contrast, in an apparent reuse of this deuteronomic paranesis, Jeremiah chides the people for having "abandoned" God, "the Fount [מקור] of living water," and for having "hewed . . . out cisterns [לחצב להם בארות], broken cisterns which cannot even hold water" (Jer 2:13). Two changes are immediately apparent. The first is the spiritualization of the overall imagery: God is called "the Fount of living water." The second transformation is the reuse of the cistern imagery to express apostasy. To dig new wells becomes a metaphor for misdirected spiritual labors, even as water serves as a metaphor for religious instruction. Only God is the source of truth, the prophet says, and only he is the fount of salvation. A similar point is made when Jeremiah later says that the people have "abandoned" the Lord—"the hope [מקוה] of Israel" and "Fount [מקור] of living water" (17:13). The use of the epithet מקוה ('hope') adds a rich theological resonance to this rebuke, since the word can also mean 'pool of water'. The same theological pun recurs in another oracle of Jeremiah (14:1–8). In this case, the physical drought of the land is directly related to the people's rejection of their spiritual source (מקור). The theologoumenon מקוה ישראל thus captures the complex belief in God as both a fount of physical sustenance and the unique source of spiritual hope. The metaphors arise from concrete reality, and this continues to vitalize their ongoing applications.

Transformations in the Scrolls of the Judean Desert

The exegetical dynamic between concrete and metaphorical aspects of the well motif are mostly fully exemplified by the so-called Song of the Well (Num 21:17–18) and its post-biblical *Nachleben*:

> Then Israel sang [אז ישיר] this song [השירה הזאת];
> Spring up, O well [באר]—sing to it—
> The well which the chieftains dug,
> Which the nobles of the people started
> with mace [במחוקק], with their staves.

The continuation of this song states: "And from Midbar to Mattanah" (v. 19). This notice ostensibly constitutes the continuation of the desert itinerary plotted repeatedly in the chapter (21:4, 10, 11, 14, 15, 16). But since the stop immediately prior to the recitation of this song was Beᵓer ('well', v. 16), and also because the account routinely repeats the preceding toponym along with the intended destination, it is possible that the place name Midbar is an error for Beᵓer. This is, in fact, the very toponym recorded in the Septuagint. Accordingly, it may be supposed that an old incantationary song to the well (be'er) was associatively inserted into an itinerary list just after the mention of Be'er. The inclusion was subsequently bracketed off by a *Wiederaufnahme*, so that the itinerary resumes (with Be'er) where it left off.[4] A similar inclusion of a song into an historical narrative occurs in the Book of Exodus: Moses' hymn of praise to God (Exod 15:1-18) occurs after a narrative report of the Israelite crossing of the sea (Exod 14:28-29) and prior to its repetition (v. 19). The repetitive phraseology which frames the song suggests that, here too, the song is a secondary component, and that the means of inclusion was by the technique of *Wiederaufnahme*. Also similar to the "Song of the Well" is the editorial superscription to Moses' hymn, which states, "Then Moses sang [אז ישיר] this song [השירה הזאת]" (Exod 15:1). An old stylistic pattern is clearly in use.

The concrete significance of this well in the desert is heightened by the request for water in the preceding narrative (Num 20:5-11). By contrast with that complaint and the fiasco of Moses' response, the water given here is portrayed as a free gift of God (21:6)—natural sustenance provided by supernatural grace. No further mention is made of this *topos* in the Hebrew Bible, nor is there any metaphorical reinterpretation of the divine gift involved. But just this is the burden of the exegesis of Num 21:18 in the *Damascus Document* (6:3-10). After citing the lemma, the words are interpreted thus:

> The "well" [באר] is the Torah and "its diggers" are the penitent (or returnees) of Israel who left Judea to dwell in the land of Damascus, where God called them all "chieftains," for they sought him and their fame was not rejected. "The lawgiver" [מחוקק] is the seeker to dig the well [באר] with maces [מחוקקות] which the lawgiver established [חקק המחוקק]. . . .[5]

The particulars of this extended exegesis thus transform the biblical passage into a religious history of the sect. Following the atomizing style of the *pesharim*, though without this technical term, the באר in the desert has become a symbol for the Torah which the community and its leadership interprets according to their esoteric mode.[6] The issue is therefore not the revelation of a new Torah, but the reinterpretation of the teachings of Moses—now applied to the community as the true Israel in the period of

---

4. For other examples, cf. M. Fishbane and S. Talmon, "The Structuring of Biblical Books: Studies in the Book of Ezekiel," *Annual of the Swedish Theological Institute* 15 (1976) 129-53; and Talmon, "The Presentation of Synchroneity and Simultaneity in Biblical Narrative," in *Studies in Hebrew Narrative Art* (ed. J. Heinemann and S. Werses; ScrHier 27; Jerusalem, 1978) 9-26.

5. See the edition and commentary of C. Rabin, *The Zadokite Documents* (Oxford, 1958), ad loc.

6. For an overview of exegesis at Qumran, see now my discussion, "Use, Authority and Interpretation of Mikra at Qumran," in *Mikra* (ed. M. J. Mulder; Compendia Rerum Iudaicarum ad Novum Testamentum 2.1; Philadelphia, 1989) 339-77.

the "end." The point as well as the metaphor occur earlier in the document, though without the benefit of exegesis:

> (God) established his covenant with Israel forever, to reveal to them hidden things concerning which all Israel erred.... He opened for them (the true practice of) his holy sabbaths, (the time of) his glorious festivals ... and the ways of his truth ..., and they dug a well [באר] for much water—and all who despise them (viz., these waters; the new interpretations) will not live." (CD 3:13–17)

The symbolic identification of the Torah and its interpretation with a desert well presumably derive from the experience of the Torah as a source of living instructions, and desert springs as the sources of natural life. Both provide sustenance from mysterious depths. Indeed, as a metaphorical vehicle for transcendent sources of divine blessing, the well was also hypostasized and projected as a heavenly fount in the cosmological account of the Two Ways found in the *Rule of the Community*. Alongside a "reservoir [מקוה] of darkness" which is the source of all "evil," there is a "spring [מעין] of light" from which derives all manner of "truth" (1QS 3:17–19).[7] This cosmic source of wisdom is also the source of other divine qualities which are depicted as founts of transcendent mystery given by God to his chosen ones:

> For the truth of God is the rock of my steps, and his power the stay of my right hand. From the source [מקור] of his righteousness is my justification. The light in my heart stems from his glorious mysteries. My eye has seen what is everlasting. Deep wisdom which was hidden from mortal man, knowledge and clever plan hidden from the sons of man, fount [מקור] of righteousness, reservoir [מקוה] of power, with the spring [מעין] of glory from the community of flesh. But to those whom God has chosen he has given these things as an eternal possession.... (1QS 11:5–7)

A profound religious, perhaps even mystical, experience underlies this text. The speaker testifies that he has perceived the hidden mysteries of divine wisdom, and has had revealed to him the founts of God's attributes of power and glory. Therefore his heart is enlightened with divine truth. Such an inner transformation through contact with transcendent wisdom is

---

7. In light of the parallelism here and elsewhere (e.g., 1QS 11:4–8, cited below), the reading must be *maʿăyān ʾôr* ('spring of light') and not *meʿôn ʾôr* ('abode of light'), as some have suggested. A similar scribal variation occurs in the later medieval text called *Beraitha de-Maʿaśeh Berešit*; see versions A and B, published by N. Séd, "Une Cosmologie Juive du Haut Moyen Age," *Revue des études juives* 124 (1965) 48. For the cosmological background in the midrash, cf. *Gen. Rab.* 1:8 and the *Tanḥuma* fragments published by E. Urbach in *Qobetz al-Yad* (Jerusalem, 1966), 6:1:19.

also expressed in several hymns found in the *Thanksgiving Scroll*. In these prayers, the speaker (possibly the founder himself) describes himself as a God-given source of life and instruction for the fellowship: "You have set in my heart to open a source of knowledge [מקור דעת] for all those who understand" (1QH 2:18); and elsewhere he avers that "You have strengthened a foundation of truth in my heart, and well-waters for those who seek it" (1QH 5:10–11).[8] This profound sense of being a channel of divine wisdom also expresses itself in a striking personalization of edenic imagery. In 1QH 8:4–8 the speaker thanks God for having made him a "fount [מקור] of flowing waters in the dry land," "an overflowing fountain [מבוע] of waters in a parched soil," and an "eternal fountain" for the community of salvation. The waters he releases to the fellowship are called מים חיים. In this context, this idiom cannot merely mean 'flowing' or 'living water', but rather the esoteric waters of wisdom and salvation.[9] These streams flow from hypostatic sources to God's chosen adepts on earth. A dynamic relationship is thus effected between the physical fact of the Qumran community, set near a desert oasis and nourished by living springs and mountain torrents, and the teacher's own identification with the group, which he enlivens by the stream of spiritual water that flows through him.

In sum, the well motif occurs on three distinct (though interrelated) levels in the Dead Sea Scrolls: the cosmic, the earthly, and the personal. The Torah is the dynamic link between these realms. As an earthly expression of divine truth, the Torah functions as a well of instruction through the exegesis of teachers who have attained divine enlightenment. The sources of divine truth are themselves portrayed as hypostatic founts from which heavenly wisdom flows. This wisdom is concretized in the Torah and absorbed by teachers and students. These individuals are, in turn, mystically transformed by contact with God's heavenly fountain. Further reflections of this ancient mystical theology—focused both on hypostatic sources of wisdom and pneumatic instruction—occur in a variety of other nonbiblical sources of the Second Temple period and its aftermath.

In the Pseudepigrapha and in Ancient Christian and Gnostic Sources

In pseudepigraphical sources a recurrent stream of tradition uses the well motif to refer to the cosmic sources of divine wisdom. Thus in 1 Enoch (Ethiopic) 48:1 we read how that worthy was transported to the heavenly dwellings of the blessed where, he says,

---

8. Following the understanding of M. Wallenstein, "A Hymn from the Scrolls," *VT* 5 (1955) 278, 280 (and notes); cf. J. Licht, *Megillat ha-Hodayot* (Jerusalem, 1957) 100.

9. See J. Charlesworth, "Les Odes de Salomon et Les Manuscrits de la Mer Morte," *RB* 72 (1970) 534–38.

I saw the well of righteousness which was inexhaustible; and around it were many fountains of wisdom: and all the thirsty drank of them, and were filled with wisdom, and their dwellings were with the righteous and holy and elect.[10]

This reference to a "well of righteousness" alongside "fountains of wisdom" recalls the association of מקור צדקה ('fount of righteousness') with divine "wisdom" in 1QS 11:6–8, cited earlier. In a further reuse of traditional language, 1 Enoch 48:1–2a applies the epithets of the Davidic messiah in Isa 11:2 to the Heavenly Man. Fountain imagery adds to the picture:

For wisdom is poured out like water, and the glory fails not before him evermore. And on him awaits the spirit of wisdom, and the spirit of understanding and of might, and the spirit of those who have fallen asleep in righteousness.[11]

In other sources, this wisdom is identified with the esoteric content of seventy books: "For in them is the spring of understanding, the fountain of wisdom, and the streams of knowledge" (4 Ezra 14:47). According to 2 Bar (Syriac) 59:7, Moses received at Sinai both the Torah and "the root of wisdom, the riches of understanding, and the fount of knowledge." This latter is the esoteric wisdom of supernal mysteries.

Like the situation in the Qumran hymns, 4 Ezra (2 Esdr) 14:38–41 also emphasizes the internalization of divine knowledge and the mystical transformation which this induces:

... a voice called me, saying: "Ezra, open thy mouth and drink what I give thee to think." Then I opened my mouth, and lo! there was reached unto me a full cup, which was full as it were with water, but the color of it was like fire. And I took it and drank and when I had drank my heart poured forth understanding, wisdom grew in my breast, and my spirit retained its memory. . . .[12]

The central image of this passage is the widespread motif of drinking from the founts of wisdom.[13] A typical expression of this is found in the somewhat mystical teaching of Jesus reported in John 7:37–38: "If anyone is thirsty let him come to me; whoever believes in me let him drink. As Scripture says: 'Streams of living water [ὕδατος ζῶντος] shall flow out from

---

10. Following R. H. Charles, *The Apocrypha and Pseudepigrapha of the Old Testament* (Oxford, 1913), 2:216.
11. Ibid., 217. Cf. also the messianic use of Num 24:17 in the *Testament of Judah* 24:1–4, where fountain imagery is used. According to Charles, *Apocrypha and Pseudepigrapha of the Old Testament*, 2:324, this is a gloss.
12. Charles, *Apocrypha and Pseudepigrapha of the Old Testament*, 2:623.
13. See H. Levy, *Sobria Ebrietas* (Giesen, 1929), passim.

within him.'"[14] While it is somewhat debatable whether this reference is a true or pseudo-citation from the Bible, it is nevertheless clear that spiritual instruction is imparted here through belief in an incarnate being. Drinking the "living water [מיא חיה]" of eternal life from the "fountain [מבוגא] of the Lord" is also mentioned in the Odes of Solomon (11:6–7)—and "this (draught) was not without knowledge [ידעתא]."[15] One suspects a Johannine impact on the terminology used here and in Odes Sol. 30:1–7, where the instruction found in John 7:37–38 is developed in mystical and rhapsodic terms.

> Fill ye water for yourselves from the living fountain [מבוגא חיא] of the Lord for it is opened to you: And come all ye thirsty and take a draught, and rest by the fountain of the Lord. For it is fair and pure; and it gives rest to the soul . . . it flows from the lips of the Lord, and from the heart of the Lord it runs. . . .[16]

The transformation of the adept into a fountain of divine truth is also reflected in John 4:14. Here Jesus says that "the water which I give" will transform the receiver into "a fountain of springing water [πηγὴ ὕδατος ἁλλομένου] for eternal life [εἰς ζωὴν αἰώνιον]." This theme assumes a more polemical tone in other early Christian texts. For example, in his *Dialogue with Trypho* Justin avers that "as a fountain of living water [πηγὴ ὕδατος ζῶντος] from God, in the land destitute of knowledge of God . . . has our Christ gushed forth" (69:26; *Patrologia Graeca* 6:637). He also says that Jews cannot understand this teaching since they "cannot drink from the living fountain of God." Reverting to the older argument of Jeremiah (2:13), Justin goes on to say that the same Jews rather drink "of the broken cisterns of God, as Scripture says, 'They have abandoned the living fountain [πηγὴν ὕδατος ζῶσαν], to hew them out broken cisterns which cannot even hold water'" (*Dialogue with Trypho* 114:82; *Patrologia Graeca* 6:740).

The theme of a fountain of spiritual instruction for the faithful is repeatedly mentioned in Mandaic sources. For example, we read that "the Life placed itself in the midst of the fountains of water [בגו מאמוגיא דמיא] that was formed for it . . . and into its splendor dwelled (lit., sat] the name of the living teaching in which it clad itself."[17] In other passages the

---

14. For a discussion of this citation, see R. E. Brown, *The Gospel According to John (I–XII)* (AB 29; New York, 1966) 319–29.

15. See R. Harris, *The Odes and Psalms of Solomon* (Manchester, 1916–20), 1:12–13, 2:266.

16. Ibid., 1:73, 2:366.

17. *Ginzā Yamina* (GR) 10:240:9–12, in M. Lidzbarski, *Der Ginza oder der Grosse Schatz der Mandäer* (Göttingen, 1925). Cf. also *Qolasta* 45, in M. Lidzbarski, *Mandäische*

messenger is himself identified with the fountain,[18] or the teaching is called the "fountain of life [אמבוגא דמיא]" which is poured out from heavenly founts to the people.[19] A related complex of ideas occurs in Gnostic doctrines reported by the Church Fathers. Thus, in his refutation of Justin the Gnostic, Hippolytus reports that the initiates of this sect drank from "the well of living, springing water [πηγὴ ζῶντος ὕδατος ἁλλομένου]" (*Refutation* 5:27).[20] He also states that the Sethian initiates drink of "the cup of the living, springing water [τὸ ποτήριον ζῶντος ὕδατος ἁλλομένου]" (*Refutation* 5:19).[21] The exegetical link with the Gospel of John (πηγὴ ὕδατος ἁλλομένου) is evident. The main difference is that in these Gnostic sects the mystical transformation of the believer is ritualized through a ceremony in which the initiate drinks waters symbolizing knowledge and life. The accuracy of Hippolytus's report is now confirmed by the original Gnostic sources. Thus, in the *First Thought in Three Forms* the Logos says: "I alone am the ineffable . . . the hidden light that brings forth living water from the invisible, incorruptible, immeasurable wellspring" (46:16–18).[22] Similarly, in the *Secret Book according to John* the First Principle is called the "immeasurable, incorruptible light" (4:9) and "the wellspring of living water" (4:21).[23]

The same confluence of imagery and terminology is also reflected in a hymn of thanksgiving at Qumran, where the psalmist says that "the fountain [מעין] of light shall become an everlasting well [למקור עולם], inexhaustible" (1QH 6:18–19). One cannot, therefore, avoid the impression that these Qumran scrolls not only influenced the Pauline stratum of early Christianity but had an appreciable impact upon a varied stream of later tradition as well.[24] In all cases, the motif of a well or fountain symbolizes the heavenly source of wisdom that is transmitted to the lower world by inspired teachers who are, moreover, spiritually transformed thereby. As we have seen, this point is made prescriptively in John 4:14 ("the water . . . *will become in him* [αὐτῷ γενήσεται]"); it occurs as a matter of pneumatic testimony in 4 Ezra 14:38–41. In Qumran the experience of divine wisdom is called the "light" and "fountain of truth in my heart" (1QS 11, 1QH

Liturgien (Abhandlungen der königlichen Gesellschaft der Wissenschaften zu Göttingen, Philologisch-historische Klasse, n.s. 17/1; Berlin, 1920), 77:1–2.

18. Cf. *Qolasta* 45 (*Mandäische Liturgien*, 76:9–10, 77:1).
19. Cf. *Qolasta* 24 (ibid., 38:2–4).
20. P. Wendland, *Hippolytus Werke* (Leipzig, 1916), vol. 3.
21. Ibid.
22. B. Layton, *The Gnostic Scriptures* (New York, 1989) 98.
23. Ibid., 30.
24. This point continues the important line of argument begun by D. Flusser, "The Dead Sea Sect and Pre-Pauline Christianity," in *Aspects of the Dead Sea Scrolls* (ed. C. Rabin and Y. Yadin; ScrHier 4; Jerusalem, 1958) 215–66.

11:18); while Ben Sira testifies that through contact with divine wisdom, "I . . . became a stream from a river" and "will pour out instruction like prophecy" (Sir 24:31, 35).

In Ancient and Early Medieval Rabbinic Sources

Early rabbinic sources reflect typology for the well motif, which is remarkably similar to the traditions so far considered. Thus, as in the *Damascus Document* (6:3–10), Num 21:18 serves as a frequent point of departure. The exegetical elaboration found in *Targum Jonathan* 2 gives typical expression to the issues at play: "The well which the patriarchs of the world, Abraham, Isaac, and Jacob, dug from olden times; (and) the wise of the world, the Sanhedrin of seventy wise men who separate themselves, perfected; Moses and Aaron, the scribes of Israel, drew (it) forth with their staves. . . ."[25] The history of this well is thus a genealogy of leadership and instruction. According to a parallel tradition, this well is a remanifestation of Miriam's well which faithfully followed Israel in its desert wanderings—but had disappeared at her death.[26] In a number of sources, the genealogy of this well is given the mythic status of one of the special things created by God prior to the first sabbath.[27]

Speaking more metaphorically, the rabbis also refer to the "living" words of the Torah as "living water" (cf. *b. Taʿan.* 7a), and sometimes compare the Torah or its components to a well (*b. B. Bat.* 72b, *Gen. Rab.* 64:8). In other cases, the link between wells and instruction serves to neutralize a messianic impulse of Scripture. For example, in the Targum to Isa 12:3, the ancient biblical prophecy, "You shall joyfully draw water from the fountains of salvation," is translated, "You shall joyfully receive new teaching from the choicest of righteous men."[28] The correlation between wells and wise men as expressed here comes to paradigmatic expression with regard to R. Eleazar ben Arak who was compared to a surging well, so great was his capacity to nourish the nation with interpretations of

---

25. Cf. the similar versions in *Targum Jonathan* 1 and *Targum Neofiti* 1; see A. Diéz Macho, *Neofiti*, vol. 4: *Números* (Madrid, 1974) 199. A briefer version of this paraphasis occurs in *Targum Onqelos*. Typical is the midrashic exposition in *Tanḥuma, Ḥuqqat* 48 (ed. S. Buber; Vilna, 1885) 64*a*.

26. See *Tg. Jon.* Num 21:17, and especially *Tg. Jon.* Num 20:2. Healing properties are associated with Miriam's well in *Gen. Rab.* 18:22 and *Lev. Rab.* 20:4. For medieval customs connected with this well, see I. Ta-Shma's essay "Miriam's Well: Transformation of an Ashkenazi Custom Connected with the Third Sabbath Meal," in *Jerusalem Studies in Jewish Thought* 4 (1986) 251–70 [Hebrew].

27. E.g., *ʾAbot R. Nat.* B/37 (ed. S. Schechter; New York, 1945) 95.

28. This shift parallels the recurrent shift from prophets to sages in early Jewish sources. In general, see the remarks of N. N. Glatzer, "A Study of the Talmudic Interpretation of Prophecy," *Review of Religion* 10 (1945/46) 115–37.

Torah (m. ʾAbot 2:11, ʾAbot R. Nat. A/1:14). It may be added that even Joshua bin Nun, who is described in Scripture as "filled with the spirit of wisdom" (Deut 34:9), is compared in the midrash to a "well" which waters the entire nation (*Exod. Rab.* 30:3).[29]

On a more pneumatic level, the well also serves as a metaphor for the source from which the Holy Spirit is drawn (*Gen. Rab.* 70:8; cf. *Tg.* Isa 44:3). In fact, the very study of Torah may spiritually transform the sage into a fountain overflowing with the esoteric mysteries of Scripture. According to R. Meir,

> Whoever devotedly studies the Torah for its own sake merits many things; and not only this but (one may even say) that the entire world is found deserving for his sake. He is called Beloved Companion, who loves the divine Presence and love all creatures, (and) makes the divine Presence glad and makes glad all creatures. And it (Torah study) robes him with humility and fear; enables him to be righteous, pious, upright, and faithful; and keeps him far from sin and near to merit. And people shall benefit from his counsel, discernment, understanding, and fortitude ... and the mysteries of the Torah are revealed to him, and he becomes like never-failing fountain [מעין] and surging torrent ... ; and it makes him great and lifts him above the entire creation. (*m. ʾAbot* 6:1)[30]

This teaching reveals something of the spiritual world of the Tannaite sages, and their belief in the transformative effects of study. For them, God's grace flows to those who are occupied with Torah without precondition or presumption; they are then granted such divine gifts as humility and piety, as well as revelations of the hidden mysteries of the Law. Graced by the splendor of mystical illumination, the sage becomes a living fount of divine wisdom to the people.

An even more striking characterization of the pneumatic power of Torah study is expressed in a midrashic fragment, whose value for the Jewish mystical tradition has been recognized. Speaking of two great mystics, R. Aqiba and Ben Azzai, the *Midrash Hallel* preserves the following interpretation of Ps 114:8:

---

29. The term used here is *gipyôn*; the parallel version in *Tanḥuma, Mišpaṭim* 8, has *namsînan*. The medieval *Arukh Completum* understood the latter as derived from *nampîn*, meaning 'pit' or 'well'. This reading would seem to underlie the reconstruction of S. Krauss, who traced *gipyôn* to *nampyôn*, and the hypothetical Greek word νυμφαῖον ('Springbrunnen'); see *Griechische und lateinische Lehnwörter im Talmud, Midrasch und Targum* (Berlin, 1898) 364. Significantly, the late medieval commentator *Matnot Kehunah* suggested *napyôn* here.

30. Following the edition of M. Higger, "*Pereq Qinyan Torah*," *Horeb* 2 (1935–36) 285–96; the saying also appears in *Pseudo-Seder Eliahu Zuta* (ed. M. Friedmann; Vienna, 1904) 15–16. This text is the point of departure for the study of D. Flusser and S. Safrai, "The Essence Doctrine of Hypostasis and Rabbi Meir," *Immanuel* 14 (1982) 47–57. The link between Meir's *logion* and the well motif is explored in ways similar to the present, independent study.

Who turned the rock into a pool of water. This indicates that R. Aqiba and Ben Azzai were at the beginning as crude rock; but because of the privations they suffered in the study of Torah, God opened the threshold of Torah for them. Thus (concerning) those matters which the schools of Hillel and Shammai could not determine whether they were forbidden or permitted, Ben Azzai arose and explained, as is written, *he put forth his hand upon the flinty rock, he overturns the mountains by the roads* [Job 28:9]. And (concerning) matters which were mysteries, R. Aqiba arose and explained (them), as is written, *he binds up the streams so that they do not trickle and the thing that is hidden he brings to light* [Job 28:11]. This indicates that R. Aqiba viewed the Heavenly Chariot in the same way as the prophet Ezekiel; therefore it is written, *who turns the rock into a pool of water, the flint into a fountain of water.*[31]

In this text, two ancient worthies are described as being transformed through study from "flinty rocks" into "fountains of water." "God opened the threshold of Torah" to Ben Azzai and R. Aqiba—so that the former easily explained the exoteric difficulties of the law, while the latter "explained ... matters which were mysteries."[32] He even perceived the very glory of the divine Chariot (*Merkavah*) like Ezekiel of old. In other mystical sources, the fountains of wisdom are not merely portrayed as within the sage but appear as heavenly hypostases. Just this thematic occurs in the *Book of Bahir*, a classic of medieval Jewish mysticism.[33] Of particular interest is the following passage, which bears a striking thematic link to the interpretation just cited from *Midrash Hillel*.

The king slivers stones and hews rocks and the fountain [מעין] flows out; this being the superfluity of wisdom, which is blessing [ברכה]—which is revealed from the Upper Pool [בריכה] which flows from the rock hewn from the Ancient Quarry....[34]

This discussion goes on to describe the emanation of divine wisdom from founts of heavenly truth. More so than earlier reflexes of the well motif, in fact, this medieval text is a bold mythological account of the hypostatic sources of wisdom—which are revealed in and through the process of mystical hermeneutics. It may be granted that the mythological topography and even the exegetical daring in this text are striking and innovative. But

---

31. Following the text of J. Eisenstein, *Otzar ha-Midrashim* (New York, 1915) 1:131; see also A. Jellinek, *Bet ha-Midrasch* (Jerusalem, 1938), 5:97. For a discussion of some links to Jewish mysticism, see S. Lachs, "Midrash Hallel and Merkabah Mysticism," *Gratz College Anniversary Volume* (Philadelphia, 1971) 193–203; and in connection with the praxis of weeping, see Idel, *Kabbalah*, 77–78.

32. For an earlier use of the rock motif in connection with Aqiba's scholarly beginnings, see ʾAbot R. Nat. A/6 (ed. Schechter) 28–29.

33. Cf. *Sefer ha-Bahir* (ed. R. Margulies; Jerusalem, 1978) §5, where the *topos* is again linked to hewn rocks.

34. See G. Scholem, *Reʾšit ha-Qabbalah ve-Sefer ha-Bahir* (Jerusalem, 1962) 290ff.

one should not thereby conclude that we have here a *novum* in the history of Jewish religious thought. As we have repeatedly seen, the transcendent nature of divine wisdom and the transformative power of its proper understanding is a dominant feature of the well motif in the Qumran scrolls—a full millennium earlier. Accordingly, to appreciate this continuity is also to take cognizance of both the great antiquity of such imagery and the spiritual experiences which they reflect. With this in mind, let us return to the profound biblical theologoumenon which states: "With you is the fount of life; and by your light do we see light" (Ps 36:10). Commenting on Jer 2:13, Philo adds (*De Fuga* 198): "God is more than life; he is the everflowing fountain of life [πηγὴ τοῦ ζῆν], as he himself has said." His words clearly allude to the psalmist's encomium (LXX 35:10, πηγὴ ζωῆς), and testify to a mystical awareness only slightly masked by the language of philosophical exegesis. One may wonder, in turn, at the sensibility which nurtured the biblical figure itself—and which continued to sustain it as an active metaphor of the religious imagination.

THE MOTIF "NIGHT AS DANGER" ASSOCIATED WITH THREE BIBLICAL DESTRUCTION NARRATIVES

Weston W. Fields

Recurring Motifs

Time-space relationships are a salient feature of many biblical narratives. Where and especially when something happens, whether in the day or night, and during what part of the day or night, are all very carefully recorded—at times more prominently than the order in which the events themselves transpired. Some time-space notices, in fact, recurrently become motifs, that is, repeated themes used in similar stories. In the present context I propose to focus attention upon one such motif, the "night-as-danger" motif, contained in the accounts of subsidiary events leading up to (Sodom and Gomorrah, Genesis 19; Jericho, Joshua 2) or following (Gibeah, Judges 19-21) three related destruction narratives. These three stories, representative of the type plot "destruction of a city or people" are closely interrelated in more than one way: on the level of ideas, in phraseology, and, what is to be the focus of the present study, on the level of shared motifs.

The terms "type plot" and "type scene"[1] have been used to designate a type or category of plot or scene in narrative. In the unfolding of biblical history certain experiences are reported more than once, with the settings

---

Author's note: It is a great honor to dedicate this essay to Shemaryahu Talmon: mentor, master teacher, friend. I am indebted to Prof. Talmon for the suggestion of the term "type plot," as well as many of the ideas in this article; see his "Daniel," in *The Literary Guide to the Bible* (ed. R. Alter and F. Kermode; Cambridge, MA, 1987) 350-52; and idem, "Literary Motifs and Speculative Thought in the Hebrew Bible," *Hebrew University Studies in Literature and the Arts* 16 (1988) 150-68. I would also like to thank professors D. Segal and Y. Zakovitch for their valuable criticisms and suggestions.

1. R. Alter, *The Art of Biblical Narrative* (New York, 1981).

and details only slightly changed.² Much of this can be attributed to the sameness of human experience, for in the course of life many events recur: courtship and marriage, the birth of children (or lack of such), the confrontation with and overcoming of or succumbing to difficulties or disappointments or dangers, protection of family, vanquishing of enemies, encounters with evil/good actions of people, and death. These and many other types of life experiences will be reported in conventional ways as the literary norm. Looked at from this perspective, variations in the reporting of parallel episodes in life are not necessarily random, and repetitions are not always, or even necessarily, duplications of an *Ur*-story. Thus, literary convention associated with a particular type plot has caused a good deal of the similarity, as has the human commonality of the experience itself.

How an incident is reported is crucial to the feeling evoked in the reader. If an event is reported within the somewhat fluid limits of a type plot, then the reader feels that all is well with the world, because events continue to happen as one would expect, even if the events themselves are disquieting. For this reason, similar or even nearly identical reports about similar or nearly identical events may say more about commonality of experiences and rather less about the literary interdependence of the reports. More than this, similarities in stories demonstrate implicit mutual agreements within the given society between author and audience as to the information the audience expects to receive and the form in which it expects to receive it. To put it another way, similar accounts draw upon a cultural *fundus*, a store of conventions, in the reporting of similar events in fixed ways, however loosely or tightly prescribed those might be.

All this does not preclude one author's borrowing or copying from another, but it may call for the exercise of caution and restraint in the predication of crude plagiarism or sloppy, haphazard editing in apparent cases of borrowing or copying. Borrowing, copying, or repetition often occur precisely because a writer at a particular time and in a particular place wants to be certain that he is reporting something in the traditional manner. He may borrow in order to connect between one story and another, or he may borrow in order to highlight the differences between stories.³ At all events, the author wants his report to be acceptable to the readers and thus capable of conveying whatever message he wants to convey. After all, if nonadherence to expected conventions offends or disappoints the expectations of the reader, the message may never be

---

2. Some of the more prominent type plots in Hebrew narrative are the barren woman who ultimately bears a famous son, a wife met at a well, a wife passed off as a sister, and the discouraged prophet. On the first of these, see Talmon, "Literary Motifs and Speculative Thought," 157–65; on the second, see M. Fishbane, "The Well of Living Water: A Biblical Motif and Its Ancient Transformations," pp. 3–16 in this volume.

3. See Y. Zakovitch, "סיפור בבואה—מימד נוסף להערכת הדמויות בסיפור המקראי," *Tarbiz* 54 (1985) 165–76.

communicated. So it is the better part of wisdom for an author to work more or less within the conventions of the type plot he is employing, and use conventions which are anticipated by his readers, the better to convey his message (i.e., the wider field of "reader's reception").

Definition of Terminology

Among the several elements comprising a type plot are word motif, motif, theme, and action sequence.[4] It is perhaps helpful to make a distinction at the outset between word motif and motif. Word motifs, also known as *Leitwörter*, are individual words or roots that are repeated within a story, within a series of stories of the same type plot, or in various stories between which one author or another wants to make a connection.[5] Such shared and repeated lexemes or roots are the *modus operandi* of allusions in biblical narrative.[6]

The term motif, whose history in English is ably surveyed by Ben-Amos,[7] is used in literary study with a variety of similar, but not identical, meanings. Encompassing the main ways in which the term is used in modern literature (for it is a rather modern term) is this definition: "a recurrent character, event, situation, or theme" (*OED* Supplement). This definition alludes to the confusion in terminology, for motif is used both to describe a rather more restricted phenomenon like a recurring character or theme, as well as a broader one like a recurring event or situation. There is doubtless place for both employments of the term.

A broader definition, which as proven both useful and enduring, was proposed by Talmon some years ago:

> A literary motif is a representative complex theme which recurs within the framework of the Old Testament in variable forms and connections. It is rooted in a presumed actual situation of anthropological or historical nature. In its secondary literary setting, the motif gives expression to ideas and experiences inherent in the original situation, and is employed to reactualize in the audience the reactions of the participants in that original situation. The motif represents the essential meaning of the situation, not the situation itself. It is not a mere reiteration of the sensations involved, but rather a heightened and intensified representation of them.[8]

---

4. Alter, *Art of Biblical Narrative*, 95.
5. See M. Buber, דרכו של מקרא (Jerusalem, 1955) 284–307.
6. The following are examples of some of the many shared words which serve to link these three accounts through allusion: סבב, שכב, לילה, שחת, ערב, בשדה, סגר, רחוב, נוח, הר, חתן, שער, שכם, מנער ועד זקן, מלאך, לון, דלת.
7. D. Ben-Amos, "The Concept of Motif in Folklore," *Folklore Studies in the Twentieth Century* (ed. V. Newell; London, 1980) 17–36.
8. S. Talmon, "The 'Desert Motif' in the Bible and in Qumran Literature," *Biblical Motifs* (ed. A. Altmann; Cambridge, MA, 1966) 39.

For the sake of convenience and simplicity, I will use the term motif in this discussion in a more restricted sense, to refer to repeated themes. By way of contrast, the "representative complex theme," as Talmon puts it, or complex of themes of which each of the three stories to be analyzed consists, and constitute a group when taken together, I will call a type plot.

Interconnections between different instances of the same type plot are established by means of allusions (sometimes explicit, sometimes not so obvious), as well as by means of their shared motifs. Thus, the stories of Sodom, Gibeah, and Jericho are related because they share the same kind of plot or scene—destruction of a city/people—but also because they share motifs and because there are allusions in one to the other. In what follows I will use the term motif to refer to a recurrent individual theme, specifically, the "danger-at-night" theme shared by the three destruction narratives investigated.

Although I am focusing on a single motif, it should be remarked that a motif in isolation is not important by itself. Its importance transpires in the recurrence in combination with other motifs. Its recurrence may be explicit (i.e., there is literary confirmation of instances of recurrence) or implicit (i.e., there is no surviving instance of recurrence, but its usage leads one to predicate recurrence based on the way it is employed). In the case of the night motif, its recurrence is confirmed in many instances, so its repetition is actualized.

More important, a motif communicates a message beyond the action, object, character, or situation it portrays. That is, the very presence of a motif in a narrative communicates something to the reader beyond the surface level of the story. Biblical motifs reveal ancient underlying concepts of society and history, of behavioral norms and concepts. The surface level of a narrative tells a story; the subsurface level serves, among other things, as a vehicle for the expression of concepts. Motifs are condensations of the biblical authors' and editors' ideas and thoughts. The communication of such messages naturally relies on the reader's ability and willingness to receive it, and the reader's reception is conditioned at least in part by his cultural literary expectations. He is much more likely to receive the message of a narrative for which his literary expectation has prepared him than he is to receive a story couched in strange and unfamiliar conventions. Thus, recurrent motifs are used by the narrator to orient his readers,[9] to assure them that the tale is being told in the prescribed manner. But beyond that, motifs convey deeper information, the real heart of the tale. It is this culturally bound information that must be the ultimate focus of this inves-

---

9. As U. Simon points out, "Warren and Wellek are undoubtedly correct in their general assertion that 'Man's pleasure in a literary work is compounded of the sense of novelty and the sense of recognition.... The totally familiar and repetitive pattern is boring; the totally novel form will be unintelligible—is indeed unthinkable'"; "Samuel's Call to Prophecy: Form Criticism with Close Reading," *Prooftexts* 1 (1981) 121, citing R. Wellek and A. Warren, *Theory of Literature* (New York, 1956) 225.

The Motif "Night as Danger"

tigation. In other words, a motif is a literary device which functions on two levels: on the surface it connects similar type plots, on a deeper level it conveys the essential cultural meaning of the narrative.

The Night-as-Danger Motif

I turn now to the analysis of the night-spelling-danger motif shared by the above-mentioned three destruction narratives.[10] It is not by accident that the authors of all three narratives set the events leading up to the destructions at night. The very first sentence of the Sodom story finds Lot sitting at the gate in the evening (ויבאו . . . סדמה בערב), and over one third of the story will have been told by the time the morning dawns. From the point at which it is reported in Judges 19 that the Levite leaves Bethlehem late in the day, it is clear that night will play an important part in the story. The two spies and Rahab in Jericho could never have been presented in Joshua as they are had the author of that story not set the scene in the night, for both her hiding of them and their escape depend, narratively speaking, on the nocturnal setting. Such close-ups of the time-space relationship, are an important and widely used device in biblical literature, reflecting a culture substantially more attuned than our own to the light-dark rhythm of the solar day. The setting of these biblical stories at night is all the more remarkable because, apart from battle scenes in which armies make use of darkness for tactical purposes,[11] the rule for normal life seems to have been, start a task early in the morning, continue during the day, and finish it in time to be home before darkness.[12]

---

10. The connection between Genesis 19 and Judges 19 is well known and has been frequently noted: see M. Güdemann, "Tendenz und Abfassungszeit der letzten Kapitel des Buches der Richter," *Monatsschrift für Geschichte und Wissenschaft des Judentums* 18 (1869) 357–68; C. F. Burney, *The Book of Judges* (London, 1918) 444–45; G. F. Moore, *A Critical and Exegetical Commentary on Judges* (ICC; Edinburgh, 1895) 407; and T. Rudin-O'Brasky, מאלוני ממרא עד סדום (Jerusalem, 1982) 103–6.

11. Examples of the utilization of darkness as a stratagem in battle are Abram against King Chedorlaomer and his allies (Gen 14:15), Joshua against Ai (Josh 8:3), Gideon attacking the Midianites (Judg 7:9), Abimelech against Gaal son of Ebed at Shechem (Judg 9:32, 34), Saul sending out messengers before the battle with the Ammonites (1 Sam 11:5–10), Saul against the Philistines (1 Sam 14:36), David against Saul (1 Sam 26:7), the King of Aram planning to capture Elisha in Dothan (2 Kgs 6:14), Joram (Jehoram) against Edom (2 Kgs 8:21, 2 Chr 21:9), the מלאך יהוה striking down the Assyrians (2 Kgs 19:35). Examples of the use of darkness for escape or stealth are David escaping during the night with Michal's help (1 Sam 19:11–12); the men of Jabesh-Gilead removing the bodies of Saul and his sons from the wall of Beth-shan (1 Sam 31:12), Abner escaping from Joab (2 Sam 2:29), Rechab and Baanah escaping after the murder of Ish-bosheth (2 Sam 4:7), David escaping from Absalom (2 Sam 17:16), and King Zedekiah and his soldiers escaping from the Babylonians besieging Jerusalem (2 Kgs 25:4, Jer 39:4).

12. Some examples of this are Moses as magistrate among the people (Exod 18:13), Joshua and the elders of Israel prostrating themselves before the Ark after the defeat at Ai (Josh 7:6), Israelites lamenting before the Lord after their defeat at Gibeah (Judg 20:23, 26),

The importance of the employment of this motif for setting the tone of these three narratives can hardly be overstated. By setting the events leading up to the destruction at night (and in the case of Sodom, also the incestuous aftermath of the destruction), the authors evoke an ominous and sinister feeling in their readers. This ancient dread of malevolent darkness can be most fully appreciated only by those who have spent time in places without artificial lighting. Deep darkness—צלמות—is a metaphor for things evil and feared, not for things good and loved. For the ancient reader the evening/night setting would almost certainly have imbued each narrative from the outset with an aura of foreboding and sinister premonition, of trepidation and anxiety, for night and violence, danger and darkness were inseparably joined.[13] Evening was the time to make for the safety of the private home, where at least some light from a fire or oil lamp or candle was available. Night was the time to remain within the bounds of this safe haven.[14]

I begin my examination of the three narratives under consideration by listing their references to time, and discover in them an overriding concern with the connection of events to a specific time of day. This reporting of when something happened is not only important for the general flow of the narration, but adds importance to the event itself. An event set in the early morning or at noon portends something to the reader quite different from the same event set at dusk or in the deep darkness of night. The ambience imparted to the story by the messengers who come to Abraham at noon (Genesis 18) is entirely different from the ambience imparted by the visitors who show up at night in Sodom, Jericho, and Gibeah.

The list below demonstrates the degree to which the Sodom story evinces such a keen interest in fixing chronological relationships. Not only does the narrative begin with בערב, but it is continually punctuated by chronological notices, which can be brought under four headings: daylight, darkness, and both transitions from one to the other (dawn=sunrise, dusk=sunset).

Israelites lamenting before the Lord after the Benjaminites were nearly wiped out (Judg 21:2), David fighting against the Amalakites (מהנשף ועד הערב 'from dawn to dusk', 1 Sam 30:17), and David and his men lamenting Saul and Jonathan (2 Sam 1:12).

13. Some examples of the association between violent acts and night are Gideon and the destruction of the altar of Baal (Judg 6:27), and the plot against Samson and his destruction of the gates of Gaza (Judg 16:2–3). One who kills a thief working at night is not held guilty (Exod 22:1) in contrast to one who kills him after "sunup" (Exod 22:2; cf. Gen 19:15, 23).

14. Except in times of warfare, as indicated in n. 11. A convenient listing and categorization of the various uses of night, but with very little accompanying analysis, may be found in G. B. Bruzzone, "*Lajla* nell'Antico Testamento," *Bibbia e Oriente* 25 (1983) 155–61. Cf. also idem, "*ʿereb* nell'Antico Testamento," *Bibbia e Oriente* 23 (1981) 65–70; idem, "*Bōqer* nell'Antico Testamento," *Bibbia e Oriente* 23 (1981) 175–83; H. Stiglmair, "לַיְלָה/לֵיל," *TWAT* 4:551–62. Compare with לילה the words עלטה, נשף, חשך, אפלה, אמש.

Gen 19:1	בערב	evening=dusk
Gen 19:2	ולינו	spend the night=darkness
Gen 19:2	נלין	spend the night=darkness
Gen 19:4	טרם ישכבו	before lying down=darkness
Gen 19:5	הלילה	night=darkness
Gen 19:33	בלילה	night=darkness
Gen 19:2	והשכמתם	rise up early=daylight
Gen 19:27	וישכם . . . בבקר	rise up early=daylight
Gen 19:15	וכמו השחר עלה	at dawn=daylight
Gen 19:23	השמש יצא	the sun rose=light

Thus, it is quite clear that the temporal emphasis of the account of the events leading up to the destruction at Sodom is night and darkness. Dawn is highlighted only as it contrasts with darkness or, simply, as a period of transition from darkness to light (Gen 19:15–22), and in the case of dusk in the Gibeah story, from light to darkness.

The author of the Sodom story puts Lot and his guests inside at night as would be the custom at the time. After bringing them together at the city gate בערב, he transfers them immediately to Lot's home, where they were to spend the night. But out of the darkness comes an evil crowd bent on unspeakable deeds. The narrative's threatening tone is immensely heightened by constant reminders that it is night—it is dark—and the omens are unpropitious.

The Gibeah narrative is similarly constructed around a framework of chronological references.[15] The plethora of expressions for the latter part of the day creates again a sense of ominous foreboding:[16]

Judg 19:8	עד נטות היום	dusk=darkness
Judg 19:9	רפה היום לערב	twilight at dusk=darkness
Judg 19:11	והיום רד מאד	dusk=darkness

---

15. It should be noted that וישכם . . . בבקר (Gen 19:27) and בבקר (Judg 20:19) are indications of a shift of scene: the next day . . . in another location. . . . On the other hand בלילה (Gen 19:33) is probably a synchronous indicator.

16. The expressions denoting the progression from full light to full dark in Judg 19:8–14 have their counterparts in the expressions denoting the progression from full dark to full light in Judg 19:25–26:

Judg 19:8–14	Judg 19:25–26
1. עד נטות היום	4. כל הלילה עד הבקר
2. רפה היום לערב	3. בעלות השחר
3. והיום רד מאד	2. לפנות הבקר
4. ותבא להם השמש	1. עד האור

Although not stated specifically in the Judges narrative, the counterpart of ותבא . . . השמש (sunset) is found in the Sodom narrative, השמש יצא (sunrise, Gen 19:23).

Judg 19:14	ותבא להם השמש	sundown=darkness
Judg 19:15	ללון . . . ברחוב	spend night=darkness
Judg 19:16	בערב	evening=darkness
Judg 19:25	כל הלילה	all night=darkness
Judg 19:25	עד הבקר	till (before) morning=darkness
Judg 19:27	ויקם . . . בבקר	got up (after night)
Judg 20:23	עד הערב	evening=darkness
Judg 20:26	עד הערב	evening=darkness
Judg 21:2	עד הערב	evening=darkness
Judg 19:25	בעלות השחר	at dawn=daylight
Judg 19:26	לפנות הבקר	twilight at dawn=daylight
Judg 19:26	עד האור	sunrise=daylight
Judg 20:19	בבקר	in the morning=daylight

Of the three narratives discussed here, Judges 19–21 utilizes the atmosphere-charging potential of the danger-at-night motif to the greatest extent. The extraordinary effect of this motif on the emotion-filled account of the rape of the concubine in Gibeah does not find its power in the mere number of references to approaching darkness and the night itself. It is the way in which the motif is combined with the other details of the story that gives it its signal prominence in the creation of an atmosphere of tension and gloom. The narrative exudes anxiety, disquietude, and danger from the report that after several unsuccessful previous attempts the Levite finally extricates himself from his father-in-law's household only late in the day (עד נטות היום, 19:8), through the recounting of his hurried journey from Bethlehem past Jerusalem to Gibeah during the waning hours of that day (רפה היום לערוב, והיום רד מאד, 19:9, 11), to the disclosure that by the time he and his concubine arrived at Gibeah the sun has set (ותבא להם השמש, 19:14), it is evening (איש זקן בא . . . בערב, 19:16),[17] and consequently they will have to spend the night in the street. The apprehension, the suspense, the worry and concern formed in the emotions of the audience are all enhanced by the narrator's masterful employment of the danger-at-night motif. One imagines the characters of the story repeating to each other as they pass each village, "Where will we spend the night? Where will we spend the night?" The gravity of their plight—caught in unfamiliar territory at night without protection—is especially evident in their deliberations whether to turn in at Jerusalem. As Josephus says, "The servant counseled

---

17. The use of the *yqtl* ויבא(ו) in reference to the traveler (19:15) and the *qtl* בא in reference to the "old man" who sojourned in Gibeah reveals the simultaneity of these apparently unrelated events. See S. Talmon, "The Presentation of Synchroneity and Simultaneity in Biblical Narrative," *Studies in Hebrew Narrative Art throughout the Ages* (ed. J. Heinemann and S. Werses; ScrHier 27; Jerusalem, 1978) 11–12.

them to lodge somewhere, lest, journeying by night, some misadventure should befall them, above all when they were not far from foes, *that hour oft rendering perilous and suspect even the offices of friends*" (*Antiquities* 5:139 [2:8], emphasis added).

A journey from Bethlehem to Gibeah need be little more than a short trip, and would certainly merit but passing notice. But a journey undertaken at a time of day inappropriate by any standard of that era, a journey transformed into a virtual race against the sun, was not only worthy of rehearsal, but served as an eminently appropriate introduction to the tale of Gibeah's inhospitality, which culminated in the rape, murder, and grisly dismemberment of the concubine from Bethlehem.

In the account of the ensuing intertribal war precipitated by the vile actions of the men of Gibeah, the expression עד הערב turns up three times (20:23, 26; 21:2). In view of the unprecedented slaughter of one faction of Israel by another,[18] the Israelites come weeping, fasting, sacrificing, and inquiring before the Lord until evening (עד הערב). The seriousness of the situation might have demanded that they stay on through the night; but the unacceptability of being outside protective surroundings at night overruled whatever urgency the exigencies of the situation may have imposed on them.[19]

No less ominous is the mood set in the Jericho story. Quite early in the sequence of events it is reported to the king of Jericho that spies had entered the city that night (אנשים באו הנה הלילה, Josh 2:2). Thereupon the important function of evening/night in the narrative begins to emerge, as the cumulative impact of the variegated expressions for the dark half of the solar cycle make themselves felt. The terms employed to describe the spies' instructions, their arrival, Rahab's arrangements for them, and the disposition of the city gate in relation to their movements, all add to the rising apprehension.

Josh 2:1	וישכבו	they lay down=darkness
Josh 2:2	הלילה	tonight=darkness
Josh 2:5	השער לסגור בחשך	gate shut=darkness
Josh 2:7	והשער סגרו	gate shut=darkness
Josh 2:8	טרם ישכבון	before lying down=darkness

---

18. Except, perhaps, for the slaughter of forty-two thousand Ephraimites at the hands of the Gileadites (Judges 12).

19. עד הערב in this instance does not refer to the motif of danger at night, but is an idiom used to describe the length of their inquiries into the divine pleasure. Nevertheless, any such usage on the level of tradition illuminates the level of literary motif and this occasion is no exception. The divine pleasure was forthcoming only in the morning, following the traditional dictum of prayer in the evening, divine deliberation during the night, and response the next morning.

The spies are portrayed as expecting from the outset to spend at least one night in Jericho. Having entered the city that night late in the evening (אנשים באו הנה הלילה, Josh 2:2), but before the city gates were closed at dark for the night (ויהי השער לסגור בחשך, Josh 2:5), they come to Rahab's house and settle down there for the night (וישכבו . . . הלילה, Josh 2:1, 2). Rahab is portrayed as having hidden the men by the time the royal emissaries came to find them,[20] and after sending away the search party, she returns to the men on the roof, who are still waiting in the darkness for her, though they had not yet gone to sleep (טרם ישכבון, Josh 2:8). For this reason וישכבו may be considered proleptic. לילה is missing from the LXX of Josh 2:2, possibly because it was thought to be premature in the chronological development of the story.[21] In any event, after she and the men have discussed the coming invasion and struck a bargain by which both Rahab and her family will be spared, she effects their escape by lowering them from her house. The author can include such a means of escape because under the cover of darkness the men successfully escape the danger they face, undetected.

Thus, all the events of the entire episode of the spies in Jericho, including their arrival, reception, hiding, warning to Rahab, and planning with her, and their escape, are represented as having been accomplished in the short space of one dark evening and night.[22]

Subsidiary Motifs

I turn now to two subsidiary or "allo-motifs" (a term suggested by M. Fishbane) which relate to the night motif in the stories under consideration here. The first of these submotifs involves reproachable sexuality of one sort or another. Or, to put it another way, sexuality is usually associated with night,[23] not just in the narratives within our limited purview here, but

---

20. Y. Zakovitch suggests that Rahab is actually portrayed as setting up the two spies by betraying them to the authorities so that they will be grateful when she protects them and thus will save her and her family when the Israelites conquer the city. Thus the story becomes a parody of which Joshua and his spies are the butt of the joke; see "Humor and Theology or the Successful Failure of Israelite Intelligence: A Literary-Folkloristic Approach to Jos. 2," *Semeia* (forthcoming).

21. The possibly sexual implications of the expression employed to depict Rahab's return to the men on the room (עלתה עליהם) are not made explicit.

22. Upon the spies' return, Joshua mobilizes the people to travel to the east bank of the Jordan. There they spend the night. The account of the commencement of the daily encirclement of Jericho also reports that at the end of each circuit the people returned to spend the night in the camp (וילינו במחנה, Josh 6:11). I emphasize again, because the story itself stresses this, that in this society it was of paramount importance to have a safe place to spend the night, and this accounts for the continual notices about where and how the principals of a narrative do just that.

23. Stiglmair maintains that since night is the "Zeit der Ruhe und des Schlafes steht *lajlāh* in einem besonderen Zusammenhang mit dem Sexualleben des Menschen"; "לַיְלָה/לֵיל, לַיִל," 556.

also in biblical narrative literature as a whole.[24] One is reminded, for example, of the account of Samson's foray into Gaza described in Judg 16:1–3. In this narrative, the writer employs the night motif for similar purposes in a context of sexual relations, surrounding or besieging with evil intent, and the prelude to destruction, albeit in this case a rather mild case of destruction. In this condensed, laconic version of one of the adventures of Samson, it is recorded that he journeyed to Gaza, where he met the אשה זונה, with whom he consorted (ויבא אליה). The townspeople surrounded him (ויסבו) to ambush him (ויארבו), and during the entire night (עד אור הבקר, כל הלילה) they made plans to kill him. Samson stayed in bed (וישכב) with the prostitute until midnight (חצי הלילה), when he got up, pulled down the gates of the city, and carried them off to Hebron. The shared use of the danger-at-night motif as well as key words recalls to the reader's mind the stories of Sodom, Jericho, and Gibeah.

In each of the three destruction stories being considered in this essay sexuality turns up in one form or another, each occurrence containing something unusual or abnormal. That is, the sexual relations described are outside the purview of normal family relationships.

Gen 19:5	איה האנשים . . . הוציאם אלינו ונדעה אתם
Gen 19:33	ותבא הבכירה ותשכב את אביה
Gen 19:35	ותקם הצעירה ותשכב עמו
Judg 19:22	הוצא את האיש אשר בא אל ביתך ונדענו
Judg 19:25	וידעו אותה ויתעללו בה כל הלילה

Not as explicit, but perhaps implied, is something of sexuality in the Rahab story:

| Josh 2:1 | ויבאו בית אשה זונה |
| Josh 2:8 | והיא עלתה עליהם על הגג |

---

24. Besides Judg 16:2–3, other examples of a connection between לילה and שכב with a sexual connotation are Jacob and Leah (Gen 29:23, 30:15–16), David and Bathsheba (he saw her late in the day, לעת הערב, so they lay together that night, 2 Sam 11:2–4), and Ruth and Boaz (Ruth 3:1–14). On the relationship between Gen 19:30–38 and Ruth 3 see Y. Zakovitch, "בין תמונת הגורן במגילת רות למעשה בנות לוט," *Shnaton* 3 (1976) 29–33. Conception and night are linked in Job 3:3, 6. The narrator of the incident of the attempted seduction of Joseph at the hands of Potiphar's wife uses this culturally anticipated conjunction of night and sexual relations to great advantage by setting the scene of the seduction in chronologically unanticipated circumstances. It is ביום, in the day (Gen 39:11–12), that she makes her play, by which the author communicates to his readers her desperation; she could not even wait for nightfall. The ceremonial impurity associated with seminal emission and sexual intercourse lasts "until evening." This period extends from the morning after such sexual events (for it is assumed that they happened at night) until evening, that is, one entire period of daylight (Lev 15:16–18; cf. Deut 23:11–12).

Two kinds of irregular sexual relations appear in the Sodom narrative: Preceding the destruction there is homosexuality (the sort of relations the Sodomites wanted to have with the messengers),[25] and following the destruction there is the incest of Lot and his daughters.[26] The pre-destruction scene is centered around the violent confrontation between the entire sex-crazed, homosexually inclined male population of Sodom, from the youngest to the oldest, and the innocent guests and their protector Lot. Although Lot is willing to sacrifice his virgin daughters in order to fulfill his responsibility to protect the visitors, in the end they are saved by the suddenly and divinely imposed (temporary?) blindness (סנורים, Gen 19:11).[27] Nevertheless Lot is punished measure for measure by the very daughters whom he so cavalierly proffered to his assailants. It is they who trick him into incestuous copulation at the end of the story.

The incest of Lot and his daughters also forms a not too subtle anti-Moabite, anti-Ammonite polemic.[28] The author of the story uses the incest, committed as expected at night, to blacken the reputation of the peoples descended from Lot.[29]

At Gibeah the sexuality takes a somewhat different twist. There it is both the unsuccessful attempt to engage in homosexual relations, as at

---

25. Given the explicit legal prohibition of homosexuality in biblical law, one might have expected the prophets and post-biblical writers to have ascribed the destruction of Sodom to their attempted homosexual relations—the aberration to which Sodom has given the name sodomy (מעשה סדום). In his comparison of Israel with Sodom, Ezekiel actually uses the word זמה (16:58), a word carrying overtones of sexual depravity. But when he specifies the sin of Sodom he focuses not on her aberrant sexuality but on her parsimonious callousness toward the poor and needy (16:49): הנה זה היה עון סדם אחותך גאון שבעת לחם ושלות השקט היה לה ולבנותיה ויד עני ואביון לא החזיקה.

26. The law prohibits almost every conceivable incestuous relationship (Lev 18:6–18, 20:10–21), but sexual relations between a father and his own daughter are not explicitly mentioned. Nevertheless, father-daughter incest is understood to be excluded by the law on the basis of the general rule: איש איש אל כל שאר בשרו לא תקרבו לגלות ערוה (Lev 18:6). The incestuous origins of Lot's sons Moab and Ammon are undoubtedly related to the stories regarding the animosity between the Moabites and Ammonites and the Israelite congregation traveling from Egypt to Canaan, and their subsequent long-standing enmity. The negative presentation of the origins of the enemies of Israel is itself a prominent recurring motif, of which this is one instance. See n. 28 below.

27. The only other occurrence of this word is 2 Kgs 6:18. There Elisha is besieged at Dothan at night by an Aramean force, whom the Lord strikes blind at his request. Not only this word is shared by Genesis 19 and 2 Kings 6, but there are others as well: אש, הר, נקף (often parallel to סבב; see Josh 6:3), שכם, סבב, נערו.

28. This thesis will be defended elsewhere.

29. In the present Hebrew text of Deuteronomy 23 the reason given for the exclusion of Ammonites and Moabites from the congregation of Israel is their refusal of help during the Exodus and their hiring of Balaam (Deut 23:4–7). But it is clear from the preceding context (vv. 1–3), which deals with sexual sins and sexual incapacitation, that the exclusion of Moab and Ammon is mentioned in this particular passage precisely because in the Sodom story their origins are reported to have been incestuous.

Sodom, and, as a substitute for that frustrated urge, rape. The portrayal of the men of Gibeah, so bent on homosexual relations that they would forcibly take a stranger and abuse him, is an extremely anti-Benjaminite statement. By introducing these sexual crimes into his narrative the writer puts the men of Gibeah into the same category as the Sodomites, who, by the time he is writing are probably already a byword for this particular sexual aberration.[30] Such brazen, public, shameless behavior seizes the attention of the reader because the sociological, religious, and legal climate should have precluded this kind of behavior. Could this be the reason that either the text followed by Josephus or Josephus himself recasts the entire story so that the men ask not for the Levite, but for his concubine?[31]

The gang rape and murder of the Levite's concubine stand among the most horrifying acts of all recorded ancient biblical tradition. The story also epitomizes a general attitude toward women in the society. Just as in the Genesis 19 account, where Lot is represented as willing to sacrifice his daughters for his own safety and the safety of his guests, so the old man in Gibeah was willing to sacrifice his own daughter and the guests' concubine for the same purpose. In short, women were considered expendable if the alternative was harm to a man. The kidnapping of the women to provide wives for the Benjaminites further exemplifies the tenuous social status of women.

At Jericho, Rahab the זונה was the host for the two מלאכים who came to her. Whether זונה means prostitute and what it may have meant besides prostitute has been widely debated, but some kind of sexual overtones were undoubtedly evoked in the minds of ancient receptors of the story, even though it is unclear whether the writer meant to imply sexual relations between the spies and Rahab.[32]

30. This assumes the priority of the Sodom story, which I will defend elsewhere.

31. "But some of the young men of Gaba, who had seen the woman in the marketplace and admired her comeliness, when they learned that she lodged with the old man, scorning the feebleness of these few, came to the doors; and when the old man bade them begone and not to resort to violence and outrage, they required him to hand over his woman guest if he wished to avoid trouble. The old man replying that he was a kinsman and a Levite and that they would be guilty of a dreadful crime in violating the laws at the beck of pleasure, they recked little of righteousness, mocked at it, and threatened to kill him if he thwarted their lusts. Driven to such a pass and unwilling to suffer his guests to be abused, he offered the men his own daughter, declaring that it would be more legitimate for them thus to gratify their lust than by doing violence to his guests, and for his part thinking by this means to avoid wronging those whom he had received. But they in no wise abated their passion for the stranger, being insistent in their demands to have her, and while he was yet imploring them to perpetrate no iniquity, they seized the woman and, yielding still more to the force of their lust, carried her off to their homes and then, after sating their lewdness all night long, let her go toward the break of day" (*Antiquities* 5:143–46 [2:8]).

32. According to Josephus (*Antiquities* 5:7–8 [1:2]), Rahab was an innkeeper. Josephus follows the Palestinian interpretation found in the Targum on Josh 2:1, where זונה is translated פונדקיתא, derived from the Greek verb πανδοκεύειν 'to keep an inn' (see the note of

Thus, in all three of these destruction stories the accounts of the events leading up to the destruction conjoin danger at night and reproachable sexuality. This juxtaposition in the events preliminary to and following the destructions functions in the stories as an agent of defamation, a means of vilifying the inhabitants of a place and of scandalizing the readers of the narrative. It is the more subtle, the more effective way to convey the message of censure and condemnation. Rather than make some baldfaced and unadorned statement such as "they were evil and deserved punishment," the introduction of abnormal sexuality into the narrative allows the authors to win the sympathies of their audiences unawares, and having so won it, to count on their approbation for their causes and their understanding of their recriminatory messages.

The second submotif common to accounts of the events leading up to the destructions at Sodom and Gibeah, and subsidiary to the motif of danger at night, is the surrounding of the host's house in the darkness. This combination of siege and lurking darkness imparts to the stories a heightened sense of foreboding. The Genesis and Judges stories may be compared as follows:

Gen 19:4	ואנשי העיר אנשי סדם נסבו על הבית
Judg 19:22	אנשי העיר אנשי בני בליעל נסבו את הבית
Judg 20:5	ויסבו עלי את הבית

There is no more natural stratagem in any kind of conflict between one group and another than "surrounding." An individual or a smaller group surrounded by a larger group or even just a superior group in any kind of a fight or battle is automatically at a serious disadvantage.[33] It is to be anticipated, therefore, that the narrators of these three stories would record that the Sodomites surrounded the house of Lot, that the men of Gibeah surrounded the residence of the hospitable old man, and that a group of the king's men gathered outside Rahab's house. What is natural to real life

---

Antiquities 3:276 [12:2] in Loeb Classical Library no. 242). L. M. Epstein suggests that the connection between the term זונה and innkeeping may have had its roots in the ancient practice of metronymic marriage; see *Sex Laws and Customs in Judaism* (New York, 1967) 159–63. The reputation of innkeepers probably placed Rahab in the general category of prostitute. Abarbanel suggests that prostitutes became innkeepers after retirement; נבאים ראשונים (Jerusalem, 1956) 21.

33. "Surrounding" as a stratagem (at night) is also found elsewhere in biblical literature: the men of Gaza and their ambush of Samson (Judg 16:1–3), the Israelites against the Moabites in Kirhareseth (2 Kgs 3:25), the king of Aram besieging Dothan to capture Elisha (2 Kgs 6:15), and the Edomites who surround Joram (but Joram was defeated by trying to escape the siege at night; 2 Kgs 8:21, 2 Chr 21:9). In 1 Sam 22:22 לסבב seems to be used metonymically for destroying (אנכי סבתי בכל נפש בית אביך), and it is used in parallel structure with להלחם in Ps 109:3.

becomes a motif, an expected component of a narrative, to the extent that one could hardly relate a tale of conflict without including the surrounding motif.[34] Besieging is employed to create a sense of reality and tension in the stories. Because the surrounding falls into two categories, it is used in two different applications. First there is the surrounding of the house by the mobs in Sodom, Gibeah, and perhaps, Jericho.[35] Then there is the surrounding in battle at Jericho and Gibeah. In all cases surrounding conveys a message of strength of opponents, imminent attack, and danger, especially when used in conjunction with the night motif.

Conclusion

What message, then, is communicated by this night motif? What does it mean that the authors set their stories in the dark? I have pointed out the sexual aberrations at Sodom, in the cave outside Zoar, and at Gibeah, and the sexual overtones of the lodging of the spies with the זונה Rahab. I have also pointed out that night was the time for crime, and thus a time of danger. Wicked men committed great sins at night (and the punishment of the righteous God was carried out in the day).[36] But most important is the general tone given to these stories by their chronological setting. It is quite similar to the apprehension that would be evoked by a modern story which began with the condensed time-space notice: New York–midnight–the subway. The ancient preoccupation with fear of the night and darkness,

---

34. Of particular interest in the present instance is the fact that there are only three places in the Hebrew Bible in which the *Niphal* of סבב is used in the sense of 'surround, close round upon': Gen 19:4, Josh 7:9 (preceding the destruction of העי), and Judg 19:22. In the former two instances the construction is נסבו על, and in the latter the construction is נסבו את. Thus, on the most basic level, the level of grammar, there is already a link established between two of the three stories being compared. It is true that Josh 7:9 may be read as "to turn upon" (KB 647) as well as "to surround" (BDB 686), but the latter fits the context best. Of further interest is the single use of a synonym for סבב, the verb כתר (Judg 20:43). כתר is used elsewhere in the Hebrew Bible with the meaning 'surround' only in Ps 22:13 and Hab 1:4. Psalm 22 is of interest because there the word appears in parallel with סבב and a number of other words also employed in the Sodom story (e.g., נבט, מלט, זרע, זכר, דבק, גור, שחר, שחה, נפש, and others). As I have indicated above, some of these words may be vehicles for allusions.

35. The group of messengers from the king in the Rahab story may be compared to the mob who surrounds the house in Sodom and Gibeah. All three groups were seeking to harm the two messengers in one way or another. Although not specifically told that the messengers of the king of Jericho surround the house in so many words, we are left to infer that inasmuch as it was physically possible they blocked off escape from the house, and thus in that sense they surrounded or besieged it when they came to question Rahab.

36. Two examples are the destruction in Genesis 19, which took place after the sun rose (השמש יצא על הארץ... ויהוה המטיר על סדם ועל עמרה גפרית ואש...), vv. 23–24) and Nathan's description of God's coming punishment upon David (כי אתה עשית בסתר ואני אעשה את הדבר הזה נגד כל ישראל ונגד השמש, 2 Sam 12:12).

combined with the practical fact that it was dangerous or even impossible to carry on with normal activities at night in the scarcity of widespread artificial lighting, led to a real-life situation in which public life came to a virtual standstill with the setting of the sun. Such historical-sociological reality is the basis for the powerful impact of this vivid motif. This is true to such an extent that the mere mention of evening or night in an ancient Hebrew narrative imparted to the narrative a mood of menacing and ill-omened portent. It is just so in the accounts of the events leading up to the destructions at Sodom, Gibeah, and Jericho.

STRUCTURAL REMARKS ON JUDGES 9 AND 19

Jan P. Fokkelman

The Strength and Weakness of Abimelech (Judges 9)

The story of Abimelech in Judges 9 takes place after the act about judge Gideon and before that about Jephthah. The strength and the weakness of this tyrant of Shechem can be interpreted correctly only if we properly understand the internal structure of this very long chapter and its relations forward and backward. I would like to discuss them here by following some proper names and numbers, by sketching the actantial model and its reversal, and by considering the male/female polarity and the framework through speeches and violence.

The name Abimelech is active on at least three levels. On the first and traditional level, the name is a confession of faith from the parents, who say at birth: "My father [i.e., God] is king." In this case we are to see it as a statement by Gideon. As an element of narrative art, however, it is already a literary game on the first level. The father has given that name, not to one of his official sons growing up in his house, but to the child born to him by a concubine in the city of Shechem. It is as if he does not want to be reminded each day of the contents of the statement of faith אבימלך. Are his own ambitions perhaps at stake? After his successes as a liberator, Gideon firmly refused the offer to become ruler over his people (8:23), but it is doubtful whether he did so with all his heart; in 8:25–30 his behavior still gives the impression of a prince.[1] If the idea that he might have been king was strong in his subconscious, that wish has now found an outlet on the

---

Author's note: I dedicate this article with gratitude and warmth to Shemaryahu Talmon, an ambassador of scholarship and tolerance, who in the season of 1982–1983 was my neighbor in the Institute for Advanced Studies of the Hebrew University, Givat Ram, Jerusalem.

For the sake of precise references, I divide each verse into clauses and mark them with letters, e.g., 9:18c indicates the third clause of v. 18.

1. David Gunn, "Joshua and Judges," in *The Literary Guide to the Bible* (ed. R. Alter and F. Kermode; Cambridge, MA, 1987) 114.

margin of his official life. Now there is a boy roaming about in the distance, whose name on a second level can be read as "my father [i.e., Gideon] is king."

In this reading the name next affects its bearer. Abimelech knows from the start that he is no more than "the son of a handmaid" or at least will be considered as such by all who do not like him. One of the acknowledged sons, his half-brother Jotham, is to call him so later on (9:18c) in a great speech. Putting it mildly, Abimelech is not very happy with such a position as an outsider, and he is dominated by a ruthless craving to change his marginal existence. He seeks compensation by aspiring to power and he succeeds in becoming the king of Shechem. What the father had suppressed within himself now bursts forth in brutal and cruel overtness with the son. He acts out his hatred for Gideon's official family by murdering the seventy accepted sons on his way to the throne. His kingship provides the proper name Abimelech with a third level and creates a quite ironical link between the message "my father [i.e., Gideon] is king" and the original reading, "my father [i.e., God] is king." The new king of Shechem does not take into account that the original אבימלך might generate a scenario against him.

The irony and the son's hatred of the father are to be found in the text, where Abimelech takes over a key word from his father. In 8:23 Gideon had used the combination משל + בכם as many times in three clauses when turning down a position as ruler.[2] In the electoral speech which we hear as early as 9:2 and which consists of four lines,[3] the very same combination is central as an ironical copy (twice in v. 2cd). Around it the syllable כם occurs twice; however, the first time it is not the suffix but, surprisingly, part of the city name Shechem. In this way the ending of v. 2a rhymes with that of v. 2b, as well as with the words "your bones and your flesh" of v. 2e, as a literary expression of the idea that Shechem and you are identical.[4] However, the contrast with 8:23 is sharp. This time the verb and the suffix are used, not to express theocratic respect toward the people, but to influence a faction (the next-of-kin in Shechem) and to perpetrate dirty politics. In this way Abimelech pays his father back for being a

---

2. His speech is a tricolon with 4 + 4 + 3 beats. The three members end on בכם as a perfect rhyme; opposite the negations of v. 23b and v. 23c (with an inner rhyme of the explicit subject, בני and אני, "neither me nor my son") stands the positive thesis of v. 23d, "the Lord alone shall rule over you." This clue is a variant of the statement of faith "my father is king." Notice how Judges 9 does and does not fulfill the statement of v. 23c.

3. With its imperative to the next of kin in Shechem, v. 2a is a first-degree speech and introduction. Then follow the four lines mentioned, which are a second-degree speech. They have a kind of ABBA structure: a short question as heading in v. 2b, fleshed out by two central lines (v. 2cd) offering a twofold question (indicated by the particles ha and ʾim), and next in v. 2e an exhortation and appeal to kinship. The זכר of v. 2e stands opposite—and is identical with—forgetting (לא זכר) the true God in 8:34.

4. Notice the contrast between the words at the end of v. 2a and the three words at the end of v. 2c: כל בעלי שכם versus כל בני ירבעל.

quantité négligeable in the family. The reverse of v. 2e, the line that is to win over the Shechemites with the phoney[5] argument of kinship, is the polemical message that Abimelech has cut the bonds with the family in Ophra. So he splits his next-of-kin into two irreconcilable factions: the relatives on his mother's side may raise him to the throne, the brothers on his father's side will all have to be put to death.

Abimelech is called "son of Jerubbaal" in 9:1a and his seventy half-brothers on his father's side are called "the sons of Jerubbaal" in v. 2c—which is a hint from the narrator that Abimelech and the seventy do not differ as much as the solitary one thinks they do. Jerubbaal is another name of Gideon[6] and the narrator has Jotham use this theophoric variant as well (in vv. 16b and 19a). Both names occur side by side in the ending of chap. 8, which prepares for chap. 9, in 8:35a. That is, however, part of a passage (8:33–35) about the little influence Gideon has and about his decease—a sequence in which the Canaanite Baals again gain the upper hand in Israel. The narrator brings a "Baal" motif into his story by regularly calling Abimelech's supporters now "all the masters [or citizens, i.e., בעלי] of Shechem."[7] To make matters worse, the seventy silver pieces to finance the slaughter of Gideon's sons come from "the temple of Baal-berith."[8] All these details illustrate that Abimelech is making a program out of the theophoric name in a heathen (Canaanite) manner: Jerubbaal means "the master is powerful." With this policy, too, Abimelech is undermining his father through irony.

How long can he sustain this program? Taking power over the ancient and respectable city of Shechem, Abimelech announces his nomination as hero of the story. But an actantial analysis of the plot and the stakes in Judges 9 easily shows that Abimelech will soon be pushed aside. Let me first give the division of the text, which consists of four parts:

I   = vv. 1–6:   exposition, Abimelech takes control through a massacre
II = vv. 7–24: great speech by Jotham (fable + application)

---

5. Further on in the Deuteronomistic History, in 2 Samuel among other places, the factor of kinship is severely criticized as a principle to act on politically. See my *Narrative Art and Poetry in the Books of Samuel*, vol. 1: King David (Studia Semitica Neerlandica 20; Assen, 1981) 208, 290, 294–97.

6. The name Gideon is avoided in the whole of Judges 9, which is a significant choice and omission. The name Jerubbaal occurs in 9:1a, 2c, 5bc, 16b, 19a, 24a, 57b (where it is the last word, in an ironical conjunction with the yahwistic name Jotham, as in v. 5c!).

7. All the places in chap. 9 are vv. 2a, 3a, 6a, 7a, 23ab, 24c, 25a, 26c, 39a, 46a, 47b; compare v. 51b. Notice that in the final v. 57 the naming is eventually changed in "the men of Shechem," as if to honor God who is the agent there and has let nemesis take its course in order to fulfill Jotham's curse.

8. Thus says v. 4a. The temple returns in v. 27 as a location of wantonness (the הלל of the Shechemites becomes quite oral there—eating and drinking—and culminates in the קלל of Abimelech). Finally, see v. 46b with "the temple of El-berith" and the preparatory line 8:33d.

III = vv. 25-41: subplot, fight between Gaal and Zebul
IV = vv. 42-57: sieges by Abimelech, a woman kills him

These four parts can also be read as two halves, because the narrator asserts himself strongly at the ends of parts II and IV. There he discloses his dominating point of view and his ideology by giving a look behind the curtain and explaining that Providence had decided to organize Abimelech's downfall. The terms that signify the balance between Abimelech's hubris and the nemesis launched by God are especially repeated from v. 24 in vv. 56-57. Moreover, the narrator assigns a genre name to Jotham's speech afterward, in the line that points out the downfall of Shechem and Abimelech as the fulfillment of "Jotham's curse" (v. 57b). At the end we understand that the narrator's point of view does not differ perceptibly from the points of view Jotham and God have. The double mention of the evil that Abimelech and the Shechemites, conspiring together, have brought about (v. 24bc and vv. 56-57a) is covered and prepared by Jotham's double curse in v. 15 (still in disguise, under the terms of the fable) and v. 20. The mutuality of the destruction which will fall upon both evil parties and which manifests itself in vv. 15 and 20 is reflected in v. 23a, in the subplot of part III, and in the syntactic chiasmus that controls vv. 56-57a.[9] The narrator has drawn the reader into his camp by sharing his foreknowledge and omniscient position with him in vv. 23-24.

At the start it seems clear how the actantial positions are occupied. Abimelech is the subject and the object of his quest is power. He has two groups of helpers: the relatives from Shechem and a band of hired murderers. Their wage, seventy pieces of silver, of course corresponds to the number of victims, so that the story has enabled us to compute the value of one human life to Abimelech and his faction: exactly one piece of silver. Then there is the axis of destination. On it, Abimelech is the sender (*destinateur*) who via the massacre sends a message to a receiver, the *destinataire*. That is the milieu or the survivors of Gideon's family. Then, however, a unique character comes to the fore, "the youngest son of Jerubbaal" having succeeded in escaping from the bloodbath. He is called

---

9. Accounting more for the boundaries of the parts I-IV: part I ends with the solemn coronation in v. 6b (where a threefold מלך fills out, substitutes, undermines, etc., the threefold משל turned down by the father). Then an unexpected antagonist appears on a spot that is just as unexpected, the Gerizim mountain (one of the two peaks which overlook Shechem). So Jotham holds his speech, which takes up almost the entire part II, in the lion's den. The information of vv. 22-24 (i.e., including the data about Abimelech's government in v. 22) marks the ending of part II and/or the transition to part III. Part III is the only one to be characterized by dialogue and it has its own subplot of two lesser bosses, Gaal versus Zebul. The competitor Gaal's coming and going in vv. 26 and 41 rounds off part III. Part IV is introduced by a time designation and contains a series of sieges by Abimelech which results in his head being crushed. Notice that its third clause (v. 42a) is identical to the third clause of part III (i.e., v. 25c).

Jotham and in part II he gets all the space he needs from the narrator to execute a special function of being (part of) the receiver: he assesses the shocking event precisely and on two levels (fable and application). The message from sender Abimelech is: Look at me! See what I can do and dare to; nobody can get around me anymore; you will be my slaves!

The position of Jotham the receiver on the mountain symbolizes having the overall picture and moral superiority. His extraordinarily big speech is so special because its point lies in the explicit introduction of a value, a moral criterion as touchstone. It is the measure of what is *integer*, honest: תמים. How important this word is appears from the fact that it is supported directly by and alliterates with אמת, and at the same time it is part of the proper name Jotham, "the Lord is honest." Moreover, the word for honesty is *the* connecting element of the two halves; it occurs at the end of the fable in v. 15, immediately after that at the start of the application in v. 16a, and after the parenthesis of vv. 17–18 it is resumed in v. 19a.

Now we understand that the name is programmatic, too, and that the actantial substance of part II is that here a counter-quest is being announced and introduced during the public testing. After v. 6 Abimelech has lost all initiative! He may win some additional military victories, but those campaigns are no more than reactions on his part; the action comes from the treacherous Shechemites, as is announced by v. 23b and proven by the opening of part III (v. 25: ambushes on the mountain peaks). Standing up against Abimelech is given an extra dimension in part III with the appearance of a supposedly Hivite element, Gaal, who tries to outwit Abimelech with his claim (v. 28) to be still more Shechemite. For a short while, some two or three campaigns, Abimelech may be under the illusion that he can maintain his power (vv. 39–49), but it all ends badly for him under the citadel wall of the city Thebez. There, the sturdy agent of old becomes totally *patiens* and his desperate effort not to be the victim of a woman's action (his speech to the arms bearer in v. 54) can do no more than underline how much he has become the actantial object of the nemesis launched by Providence. The special contribution from the narrator in vv. 23–24 (who plays a trump card in this aside by revealing that God has decided to bring evil upon Abimelech; compare 2 Sam 17:14 about Absalom's chances) confirms in an early stage that Jotham has initiated the counter-quest with his speech. The whoring after the Baals (as 8:33 has it) is highlighted clearly and punished through the pure norm of YHWH and his party.

The usurper's demise can also be traced by following the isotopy of the family terms, especially the man/woman polarity that appears with Abimelech. This outsider really wants to have his cake and eat it, and this form of dualism cannot stand. He is inspired by his father in the desire to be king, but at the same time he rejects and hates his parent. He divides the family into one-half on his father's side, which is killed by him, and for that he uses the half on his mother's side, which is pampered by him. The first and subtle signs of divisiveness that characterizes Abimelech as regards his roots appear immediately in v. 1. The line v. 1a is stretched between father and mother by drawing Abimelech's trajectory: this runs from אבי (part of the personal name!) to אמו. In v. 1b the term for family, בית אב, which in the case of Abimelech already has an ironic effect, expands to both sides, into the remarkable phrase משפחת בית אבי אמו. This combination discloses how the actual principle "on mother's side" that the outsider wants so much to respect is already undermined. The paternal values cannot be deleted, not even with the deepest pathological determination. Accordingly, almost everything that is observed in this article can be used as an argument for the position that Judges 9 is not an independent narrative, but a part of, and the crown of, the Gideon act.

"His mother's brothers" enter on Abimelech's behalf and canvas Shechem in v. 3. The two short words in direct speech with which the city consents[10] repeat nothing but the turbid argument of kinship: "he is our relative [lit., brother]" (v. 3d). In order to kill "his brothers" Abimelech returns "to his father's house" in Ophra with a band (v. 5); this phrase counts doubly, as a designation of space and family. And so on: in this way one can and should trace all references to mother and father, to men and women in his chapter in the light of Abimelech's pathological polarizing.[11] Also, there is the return of the term "brother(s)," with an increasing charge that is incriminating for the tyrant.[12] In vv. 49–51 we meet two groups of citizens who are being besieged by Abimelech. One group is burnt, the other will survive. Both are entrenched in a "tower" and explicitly consist of men as well as women who appear in a chiasmus:

v. 49e	איש ואשה	כל אנשי מגדל שכם
v. 51b	כל בעלי העיר	כל האנשים והנשים

The fire with which Abimelech destroys the Tower of Shechem in vv. 47–49 is of course the fulfillment of Jotham's curse about fire in v. 20abc. But how about the fire in v. 20de that is to consume Abimelech? The answer given by the narrator is a pun. After v. 49, which in lines a, d,

---

10. With an echo clearly in Jotham's speech, in v. 18d.

11. The male/female polarity is eminently important for the whole of Judges. Barak is eclipsed by Deborah as well as by Jael, the great victory song in Judges 5 comes from a woman, Jephthah is determined by the whore-virgin tension (=mother-daughter respectively!), the whoremonger Samson is fascinated by one Philistine woman after another (which among other things is a sign of an authority conflict with his parents), not to speak of the horrors and chaos brought upon women in chaps. 19–21.

12. See esp. v. 24 with the reciprocity of "their brother" and "his brothers," which is important because of the omniscient narrator's point of view. "Brother(s)" occurs in vv. 1a, 3a, 5b, 18d, 21c, 56b, 31b, and 41b (the last two connected with Gaal); "father" in vv. 1b, 5a, 17a, 18a, 28f, 56b; "mother" in vv. 1ab, 3a; and "woman/women" in vv. 49e, 51b, 53a, 54e.

and e uses the words איש, אש, and איש ואשה, and after the mention of the men and women in v. 51b, Abimelech plans to destroy the citadel of Thebez also by fire (אש). Then a woman comes to the fore who hits him unexpectedly and fatally. With the word אשה, the story not only realizes the second half of the curse, but also makes the man/woman polarity acute at the *moment suprême*, to the tyrant's detriment.[13] With the most graphical effect, the happenings in Judges 9—the two acts of violence which form beginning and end—are attuned to one another and in this way frame the whole.

The woman offering Abimelech such an ignominious ending is not only אשה, but אשה אחת. Strictly speaking, the numeral is redundant, but it is present as the end point of a series of numbers which take part in a literary game several times. The millstone from the single woman is of course the counterpart of the single stone on which Abimelech performed his bloodbath, so that hubris has found its nemesis.[14] The contrast between seventy and one—with which Abimelech suggested that oligarchy is a confused and inefficient form of government and that monarchy is preferable—returns in the single stone and the seventy pieces of silver. The millstone that crushes the tyrant's head (ראש) itself marks the end of a decreasing series of numbers. When Abimelech quells Gaal's rebellion, he still has "four columns" (ראשים) at his disposal (v. 34b; the ambush, incidentally, being a striking counterpart of v. 25a). The next day he sends three ראשים against the Shechemites (vv. 43b, 44a) in such a way that two columns (ראשים in v. 44c) slaughter the citizens in the field. For a short while Abimelech may think he is powerful, but then the single woman rolls her millstone to the fore and smashes his own ראש (v. 53).

Abimelech has tried to compensate for his inner divisiveness by a great display of power. His weakness comes from his position as an outsider and it is in this very aspect that he deserves to be compared with the next group of stories dedicated to judge Jephthah. Jephthah is not only an outsider, but also an outcast, literally so, on the grounds that he is the son of a whore (11:1–3). He, too, is seeking compensation by gathering power and he becomes the commander of a band abroad. Called back in times of distress as the strong man who is to save the nation, he fails at the decisive moment: he dares not trust his charisma (he is chosen by God's spirit), but makes a doubtful vow that will cost him his only child, a daughter. She is a virgin, a condition forcefully underlined by the passage 11:37–40. The state

---

13. Opposite the connection and the pun between fire and woman stands the combination shadow and men (warriors) in part III (in v. 36), about which Gaal and Zebul have their argument.

14. For Judges 9 as a story of retribution see T. A. Boogaart, "Stone for Stone: Retribution in the Story of Abimelech and Shechem," *JSOT* 32 (1985) 45–56; and J. Gerald Janzen, "A Certain Woman in the Rhetoric of Judges 9," *JSOT* 38 (1987) 33–37.

of being intact and the innocence that were a source of hope and inspiration for Jephthah's tormented psyche are lost and cruelly sacrificed. In this way judge Jephthah's life is determined and ruined by the connection of the two poles whore and virgin. As "the son of a handmaid," Abimelech is a station halfway along this tragic development. He, too, is stamped, though differently, by the polarity man/woman and marginal origin.

I conclude this section with the remarkable distribution shown by the spoken word in Judges 9. Part III, with its subplot Gaal versus Zebul, alone offers dialogue in a statistically normal quantity.[15] Part II is excessive by being complete speech on two levels, from a character who is absent further on. The hero/villain Abimelech is allowed to speak only at the boundaries of the chapter, in vv. 2, 48fg, and 54cde—and nowhere else! The speeches in parts I and IV—especially Abimelech's first and last speeches—have the common feature that Abimelech commands others to take pains on his behalf and that they themselves contain embedded (i.e., second-degree) speech, which shows how much Abimelech is preoccupied with his image. In v. 2 he tells his relatives what they should say in their election campaign for him. In v. 54 his shield bearer is asked to commit an exceptional act, with the impossible purpose of keeping the tyrant free from the stigma that "a woman has killed him." Whether this plan succeeded we see in 1 Sam 11:21, where the general Joab quotes military history and recalls nothing of Abimelech other than that he was killed by a woman indeed, with the lucky drop of a millstone. Together with the peaks of violence and the game of numbers, these speeches by Abimelech give the whole its closure.

The Outrage in Gibeah (Judges 19)

My contribution on Judges 19 is mainly a short note on the correct structure of the story. Some recent publications have mentioned the importance of the elementary system of coordinates consisting of time and space designations, but have not yet fully exploited those data.[16] However, the

---

15. In the Books of Samuel the proportions of report and speech are roughly fifty-fifty. For figures of report versus speech in two large sections of Samuel see *Narrative Art and Poetry in the Books of Samuel*, vol. 2: *The Crossing Fates* (Studia Semitica Neerlandica 23; Assen, 1986), chap. 16.

16. Hans-Winfried Jüngling, *Richter 19: Ein Plädoyer für das Königtum: Stilistische Analyse der Tendenzerzählung Ri 19,1–30a; 21,25* (Analecta Biblica 84; Rome, 1981); and Phyllis Trible, *Texts of Terror: Literary-Feminist Readings of Biblical Narratives* (Philadelphia, 1984), whose chap. 3 (pp. 65–91) discusses Judges 19 and is a curious combination of good stylistic analysis and wrong value judgments. Feminist zeal leads Trible into some fundamental errors: (*a*) she takes for granted that the narrator is a man(!), and she puts him among all the wicked males of the story because she confuses his reticent art of storytelling with his point of view (pp. 76, 80, 86), but this overlooks the fact that the narrator reveals his moral stance unequivocally by disqualifying the men from Gibeah at the very moment that he

interpretation of the text cannot be given a solid foundation, nor can all the details fall into place until the correct proportions of the sequences are delineated:

A	B	C		D	E	F		G	H	I
1–2	3–4	5–7	+	8–10	11–14	15–21	+	22–26	27–28	29–30
introduction	journey	stay	+	stay	journey	stay	+	stay	journey	appeal

A short stylistic account of the boundaries of these nine elements is as follows. Segment A poses the problem the plot is going to elaborate. It is framed by a double ימים and the mentioning of four months. Segment B contains the journey out plus the welcome in Bethlehem and it finishes on the detail "three days," a round figure which makes the reader think, "This should be enough." Segment C begins "on the fourth day" and contains two rounds of carousing, given form in a double action of persuading the guest to stay a little longer, and in his spending the night there. Segment D begins explicitly with a double time indication that links up chiastically with the phrases of v. 5ab. With the addition of ללכת, this device gives the impression that the Levite will depart now, "on the fifth day." However, the point of D is that this does not work out for the time being and that the fifth day is also given two halves around noon. The Levite tarries[17] until after the siesta. The longest speech by the host (a verb + היום three times) then has no further effect and finally the Levite is on his way, at a peculiar moment in the afternoon, so that he will not be able to reach his home in a one-day march.

The ending of segment D is marked by the place-name Jebus; as a conspicuous station on the way back, less than two hours by foot from Bethlehem, this indication of space is also a designation of time and prepares for the discussion between master and servant in vv. 11–12. The central segment E is marked by an inclusio; in v. 11a the day is almost over

---

introduces them; (*b*) she does not understand that quasi-objective narration and the precise description of horrors is a much more effective critique of violence than snorting out moral indignation, nor that the narrator is morally in order by the very creation and handing down of this story; (*c*) she overlooks that the transition from the accidental or personal to the national level arises out of the event; and (*d*) she ignores that the two men in 19:22 are themselves driven into an appalling predicament, in the face of which the reader should refrain from passing a quick and premature judgment.

17. The word התמהמהו in the MT, v. 8d, should be kept! It is an imperative, it is still part of the direct speech (and so it is not said by the narrator), and it puts the hedonistic Levite beside Lot (Gen 19:16), whose התמהמה reveals a similar mentality (hanging on from love of ease).

and in v. 14b the sun is setting. These data form a chiasmus with the place-names Jebus and Gibeah. The paragraph is all dialogue. Around the rejection of v. 12bc there are two speeches which are a parallelism: both begin with לכה + cohortative of a verb of movement + place-name, and they close on a form of לין + preposition ב + spatial term. This structure points to the middlemost clause of the speech in v. 12 as the center. There we have the opinion that "foreign cities" like Jebus "do not belong to the Israelites," an attractive prejudice that will be put to shame.

Segment F has its own mini-quest: the Levite looks for shelter in the beginning, and at the end has found it. Two clusters of report by means of narrative forms and information (especially vv. 15–16) frame three speeches by the new, aged host and his guests. Segment G begins just like v. 11a with a typical circumstantial clause and by introducing a new character, a horrifying collective. This paragraph, too, is rounded off by its own quest: the rabble's menacing desire in v. 22 and the satisfaction in v. 25, a multiple crime. There is a symmetry of deliverance (demanded in v. 22) and return of the victim (v. 26). Around the boundary between segments G and H, five successive clauses end on a time designation (the night is all horror, the dawn does not bring liberation but simply throws light on the crime), while three clauses show the stagnation of a horrible death at the threshold, ending as they do in space designations: vv. 25e–27a and 27bcd. Segment H mainly follows the heartless Levite's point of view: his discovery of the lifeless woman and his departure. His callous command (קומי ונלכה) and his return home (ויקם וילך) close a series of movements with הלך + קום (see vv. 3ab and 10b). Segment I stands as homecoming opposite v. 3. There are two disjunctions: one of them makes I the counterpart of segment A, because the Levite is again separated from his concubine; the other is new and shocking: the cutting of her body limb by limb. But by sending the body parts throughout the land, the Levite makes a national issue out of an incident or a personal loss. In this way he lifts the stakes to the higher plane where they belong, that is, a moral-religious assessment of the outrage by the tribes of Israel.

At this point, historical-critical scholars like Jüngling and many of his predecessors have seriously slipped. Due to a lack of narratological knowledge and training, they have wrongly separated the text of 19:1–30a from v. 30b plus chaps. 20 and 21, and have practiced diachronical hypercriticism. What they have overlooked is this: as is usual elsewhere, the plot of Judges 19 also begins with a lack (in this case the runaway woman) and the quest consists of the effort (by the Levite here) to remedy the lack. The success of a quest easily completes plot and story. But when the quest fails, the hero is back to square one, and then what? In the case of Judges 19, v. 30 cannot possibly function as an ending, because the very act of cutting the woman into pieces implies a new and much more serious lack: it is the enormous black hole which was brought about by the rapists from Gibeah and which affects the moral stature of an entire nation. What the Levite is concerned with is the sexual crime, not a case of mere loss of property.[18] He does so in a manner that is just as abhorrent as it is effective. The great outrage that breaks out answers his intentions exactly and the words with which the people respond in v. 30bcde go far beyond the dimension of property or such laws.

This plot analysis offers a better understanding of the relationship between chap. 19 and chaps. 20–21. After all, and without any underestimation of the woman's experience, the crime of chap. 19 is merely an incident. But it becomes the spark in a powder keg: it serves as the exposition to, and an opportunity for, the emotional chaos and civil war of chaps. 20–21. The national level of violence and confusion there and the resulting problem of the right form of government are really the level on which the narrator wants to work, as the coda to his book.[19] The inclusio with which he delineates Judges 17–21—the striking formula "in those days there was no king in Israel, everyone did as he pleased"—is a helping hand and a hermeneutical hint to the readers: the narrator himself indicates the framework within which we are supposed to interpret his material.

It is not for nothing that he offers the formula in a shortened version in 18:1a and 19:1a. In this way he provides a bridge from 17:6 to 21:25, which, as the very last verse, takes up a strategical position and is of extra importance to understanding section and book. I note that 18:1a and 19:1a are attuned to each other by a modest chiasmus, מלך אין versus אין מלך "in Israel," and that both verses omit the line that "everyone did what was right in his eyes." In the case of chap. 19, the relevance of the ellipse is that it is the reverse side of the fact that the story proper is itself an exploration of some modalities carried by the root יטב/טוב and its antipole רעע.

The diagram of the structure shows how much space is given to enjoying hospitality—segments C, D, and F—and at first the reader wonders what all this triviality has to do with the crime and its horrors. The answer is that the story signifies how much the Levite is attached to "carousing" (יטב לב and synonyms) and that such hedonism and materialism lead to a situation in which throwing women out as a sexual prey for the rabble will be called right. It is the impossible position in which the host (being aged and a resident alien only, i.e., neither physically nor

---

18. Contra Trible, *Texts of Terror*, 82, who makes a serious misjudgment in this case, too: "Outrage erupts at the harm done to a man through his property but ignores the violence done against the woman herself." That is untenable. She does not see that from 19:30 on the nation is just as shocked as she is. How else could we explain that "a conflict of incredible proportions" (p. 83) is imminent?

19. I borrow the term coda from the interpretation given by Barry G. Webb, *The Book of the Judges: An Integrated Reading* (JSOTSup 46; Sheffield, 1987), chap. 5. Note that the materialist of Judges 19 traveling to the south has been preceded by another money-loving Levite traveling to the north.

juridically able to wield any power against the intruding band) and the Levite land in segment G. The picture of male carousing, which was given so much space in the counterparts C and D, returns on the boundary of segments F and G, in vv. 21d and 22a; then, however, all hell breaks loose. The host makes a desperate attempt at rescue in a long speech (vv. 23-24). He begins well in v. 23c‖v. 23e with a double prohibitive form: "Do not commit such a wrong" (here we have רעע!) and, "Do not perpetrate this outrage!" But when the second half of the speech comes to טוב, he is already confused morally and says something unbelievable in the face of the imminent crime: "Have your pleasure of them, do to them what is right in your eyes."[20] Here is the culminating point (and at the same time the nadir) of the exploration of good and evil, with which the story itself fills out the ellipse in 19:1a.

The importance of weighing good and evil is not yet sufficiently established as regards Judges 19. I look into the diagram and find the symmetries to be evident. Due to the correspondences of the journeys to and fro, and due to the motif of staying and enjoyment as elaborated in vv. 3-9 as well as in vv. 15-21, the series ABCDEFGHI can easily be rewritten as ABCD-X-DCBA.[21] This structure shows that the journey of vv. 11-14, so halfheartedly begun after the siesta and proceeding only halfway, is of crucial importance. What is so peculiar about this sequence is that it reports a non-event, in the sense of a rejection option, an unrealized stay in Jerusalem. Without any difficulty, the narrator could have continued his story after v. 10 with v. 14b, but instead he has the master and his servant talk to each other. The concentric structure of the speeches in vv. 11-13 points at v. 12c as the axis of element X. The non-event prepares for the *Umwertung aller Werte* that becomes event and action in Gibeah! For the narrator puts both the Levite and the reader on the wrong footing via the pleasant idea that spending the night in a town of Benjamin is better than staying with the foreign Jebusites. However, what seems right proves to be wrong, and what seems bad might very well have had a fortunate

---

20. Many commentators write high-toned words in connection with Gen 19:8 (Lot's daughters as a sexual sell-off) and Judg 19:24, in the sense that hospitality was such a valued asset in Israel, that people would even give up their women if necessary. To me, this seems to be not only a terrible cliché, but worse: it might well be incorrect. On the one hand the two chapters are exceptional (no lawgiver can foresee such situations) and on the other hand they show something that happens all over the world: under the pressures of terror and crime, good manners and morals crumble like a house of cards. We find a variant of the cliché in Trible, *Texts of Terror*, 75: Genesis 19 and Judges 19 "show that rules of hospitality in Israel protect only males." I do not believe this.

21. The symmetry A-A′ consists of a small lack versus a big one. Segments B and B′ are the journey to and fro, and have a reversal of disjunctions and conjunctions between the Levite and his concubine: v. 3 wife run away + v. 4 reunion, v. 26 reunion of man and wife, but also separation by death. The great amount of space given to "male carousing" by segments C, D, and F gives it effective criticism (contra Trible).

ending. The master is wrong in his prejudice, the servant is perhaps right in his matter-of-fact and open attitude—that, too, is a reversal of values in this world of decay. At this very moment the sun sets; a night begins that is obscure in so many respects and will know no ending for the anonymous woman.[22]

22. The symbolics of time designations in this chapter is a subject apart, especially those of sunset and daybreak. Here, too, the reversal of values is operational: the appearance of the light, so often a sign of liberation, is only the manifestation of abomination and death in vv. 25-26.

"THIS TIME" (GENESIS 2:23)

Cyrus H. Gordon

Before the creation of Eve by Yahweh-Elohim (Gen 2:21–22), a woman had already been fashioned by Elohim (Gen 1:27). The commandment to the first man and woman was, "Be fruitful and multiply, fill the earth, master it, and rule over all of the fish of the sea, fowl of the heavens, and over every living creature that moves on the earth" (Gen 1:28). But their inability to reproduce or rule over the earth and animal kingdom required another creation. To make sure that Adam and Eve would be attracted to each other and mate, Eve was fashioned from a part of Adam so that "therefore [עַל כֵּן] man shall forsake his father and mother and cleave unto his wife and they shall become one flesh" (Gen 2:24). There follow genealogies that indicate the couple "this time" was fertile, for they would mate to regain their pristine unity. Thus we see that, imbedded in the account of the second creation of man and woman, there is the assumption of a first unsuccessful fashioning of a man and a woman. This combination of two (or more) parallel narratives is a widespread phenomenon in the Bible (and indeed throughout the ancient Near East) which I will call "Buildup and Climax" (hereafter abbreviated BUC).

There is also in the *textus receptus* a reference in the first creation to the second creation. The initial words of Genesis (בְּרֵאשִׁית בָּרָא) imply that the account thus introduced will subsequently be followed by another account in accordance with the pervasive principle of BUC. The best parallel is provided by Hos 1:2: תְּחִלַּת דִּבֶּר ('the first time [God] spoke [to Hosea]'), which implies a second time. On the first occasion God commanded Hosea to marry a bad woman (1:2); on the second occasion he ordered him to repeat the performance and again (עוֹד) marry a bad woman (3:1). The key word in the latter passage is עוֹד.

It will be noted that both בְּרֵאשִׁית בָּרָא and תְּחִלַּת דִּבֶּר are the same formation: a noun (indicating temporal primacy) in the construct before a

47

verb in the perfect. This identity of formation was noted by Rashi, who, however, did not sense that either (let alone both) reflected anything like BUC.

To state things differently: the opening words of Genesis anticipate a second creation, even as the same formation in Hos 1:2 tells the reader that he will eventually encounter a second divine command to Hosea (3:1) to wed a lewd tramp.

There are literally hundreds of BUCs in the Bible and other literatures of the ancient Near East. The principle of parallelism is not limited to words,[1] phrases, or verses: it also applies to longer units. An instructive illustration comes from Ugaritic literature. Anath goes on a rampage killing people left and right but "she was not satisfied," so she embarks on another blood bath "until she was satisfied."[2] Judges 21 narrates that the decimated tribe of Benjamin needed an adequate supply of wives if the tribe was to survive. So four hundred virgins captured from Jabesh-Gilead were given to the Benjaminites וְלֹא מָצְאוּ לָהֶם כֵּן (21:14), 'but they did not [thereby] get for themselves [the] right [number]'. So a climactic parallel account is necessary for the BUC. Accordingly the Benjaminites took advantage of a festival at Shiloh to snatch maidens who were dancing and kept them as their brides (21:19ff.). This time they carried off the number required (וישאו נשים למספרם, v. 23). Otto Eissfeldt misunderstood me regarding the two accounts as consciously forming a BUC unit and insisted that we are instead dealing with two entirely different sources about the same event: (1) a Jabesh-Gilead tradition and (2) a Shiloh tradition. That the two accounts are different is obvious, but my point is simply that Hebrew style required the parallelism of BUC. By the same token, the two creation accounts in Genesis 1–2 are full of differences but the text has combined them into one BUC unit and each account refers to the other. Indeed the combination, far from being due to careless or illogical editing, is implied in the first two words of the Bible.

---

1. Thus, in the ubiquitous examples of hendiadys; for example, אגידה ואדברה (Ps 40:6), 'let me declare and say'. There can be more than two synonyms to express a single idea: for instance, צדק ומשפט ומישרים (Prov 1:3), which we can translate 'piety, and justice, and rightness' but actually the triad simply designates the idea of "the decent thing." In the Prophets and the Wisdom Literature these words refer to the right kind of behavior (often miscalled "social justice"). It includes always defending the weaker against the stronger in any conflict of interest. For example, widows and orphans are always right vis-à-vis their creditors, even though the letter of the law be on the side of the creditor. Thus the widow who is unable to pay her rent or mortgage is "right" and the landlord who would evict her or force her to pay it by working it off (= enslavement) is always "wrong." Since such "social justice" is not really "justice" in the legal sense, it is not a good rendering. I therefore use the admittedly colloquial "decent thing" which at least conveys a truer meaning.

2. ᶜAnat, ii:19–20; see C. H. Gordon, *Ugaritic Textbook* (Analecta Orientalia 38; Rome, 1965) 253.

No modern reader with an Occidental education likes the needless slaughter in the Scroll of Esther. Ahasuerus authorizes (8:10–13) the Jews to defend themselves and slay their enemies on the day when an earlier decree had allowed the non-Jewish population to massacre all the Jews (3:13). So the Jews, instead of being slain, slew a large number of the inimical populace (9:6–12). For our taste, that was enough carnage. But no—a second request by Queen Esther (9:12) to embark on another (עוד) round of mass killing is granted and this time a far larger number of anti-Semites are massacred (9:16). For whatever consolation it may give the modern lover of Scripture, we are not dealing with historical bloodshed but with ancient literary style. Just as Anath required two "pogroms" so does the Scroll of Esther in accordance with BUC.

The Book of Jonah comes in two distinct parts: chaps. 1–2 deal with Jonah and the fish, while chaps. 3–4 narrate the tale of Jonah at Nineveh. No one denies that the narrative content of the two stories is quite different. But the fact is that they are consciously combined as a BUC unit. Both tales deal with God dispatching Jonah to Nineveh. In the first account the prophet tries to evade his duty and flees westward instead of going to Nineveh. The second account has him going east to Nineveh and prophesying there as he was told. Thus the tale in chaps. 1–2 is non-fulfillment while chaps. 3–4 are the climactic fulfillment. Obviously there are other factors. The book as a whole indicates that God's will will be done and if we try to evade we will learn to our sorrow that by not obeying promptly we bring grief upon ourselves[3] and eventually we have to fit in with God's plan. There are other significant features of the Book of Jonah; for example, God's concern not only for his "chosen people" but for all mankind[4] and even cattle (4:11). The point I am making is that the book as a whole is a composition consciously unified in accordance with the stylistic principle of BUC. The introduction to the first half is God's command to Jonah: ויהי דבר יהוה אל יונה . . . קום לך אל נינוה (1:1–2): 'Yahweh's word was [addressed] to Jonah . . . : "Arise, go to Nineveh!"'; while the second half begins: ויהי דבר יהוה אל יונה שנית לאמר קום לך אל נינוה (3:1–2): 'Yahweh's word was [addressed] to Jonah a second time, saying: "Arise, go to Nineveh!"' The key word here is שנית 'a second time' (for which I shall cite another example below). Stylistically, the BUC here is just as necessary as the parallel hemistichs that make up a verse.

---

3. Compare the wrath of Meleager in the *Iliad*. By allowing his anger to keep him from defending his fellow citizens promptly, Meleager caused mischief and finally when he performed his duty, he lost out on the greater honor that would have been his had he acted properly on time.

4. In Jonah 1, the pagan sailors are portrayed as very decent people, while the Hebrew prophet is the one who has behaved irresponsibly. The theme of innocent Gentiles *vis-à-vis* a foolish Hebrew prophet therefore emerges as an *inclusio*, opening the Book of Jonah in chap. one, and closing it at the end of the book.

The prophecy of Haggai aims at inspiring the Jews of the Second Commonwealth to build the temple under the leadership of Zerubbabel as heir to the Davidic line. He was to be aided by Joshua as the legitimate heir to the high priesthood. The first statement is, "In the second year of King Darius, on the first day of the sixth month Yahweh's words were [addressed] through the prophet Haggai to Zerubbabel, son of Sheʾaltiʾel, governor of Judea, and to Joshua, son of Yehoṣedeq, the high priest." There follows the command to build the temple (1:7ff.). The book ends (2:20–23) thus: . . . ויהי דבר יהוה שנית אל הגי . . . לאמר: אמר אל זרובבל פחת יהודה: 'Yahweh's word was [addressed] to Haggai . . . a second time as follows: "Say to Zerubbabel, governor of Judea, . . ." This time God's choice of Zerubbabel as leader is reaffirmed succinctly and emphatically. שנית is again the key word of the BUC structure. Here the divine election of Zerubbabel for the task can also be regarded as an *inclusio*, beginning and ending the book with slight variations of the same formula.

I now return to the two creations combined in Genesis 1–2 in accordance with the BUC principle. The consistent use of אלהים as the first creator and of יהוה אלהים as the second creator has taken on a new look since the discovery of the Baal and Anath Cycle at Ugarit. There the head of the pantheon, who is sometimes called El and sometimes called by his epithet Lṭpn 'the Kindly One', states: *šm.bny.yw.il* ['the name of my son is Yw-ʾIl' (cf. the PN יואל 'Joel').[5] The longer form of *Yw* is Yahweh, even as the longer form of El is Elohim. Accordingly the name of El(ohim)'s son is יו אל whose longer form is יהוה אלהים. Such compound names occur in Israel (no one questions that יהוה אלהים is one god, not two) and even beyond in the ancient Near East; for example, at Ugarit (Qdš-Amrr) and in Egypt (Amon-Re). The concept of dual creations is widespread but I need point only to one other example in the Old Testament. In Prov 30:1–4, Agur of Maśśaʾ challenges his audience (or readers) to come up with the names of the creator and his son. I need only cite the finale of that creation account (v. 4): מי הקים כל אפסי ארץ מה שמו ומה שם בנו כי תדע, 'Who established all the ends of the earth? What is his name and what is the name of his son? if you know'. That this polytheistic tradition from the northern region of משא (see Prov 30:1, 31:1) was not palatable to the monotheistic mainstream of the Hebrew and Jewish community requires no explanation, but it does enable us to understand the configuration of evidence in the Ugaritic ʿAnat tablet, Genesis 1–2, and Proverbs 30. All three illuminate each other.

Another factor enters the picture. There are pivot words in the Bible that can be described as supplying asymmetric Janus parallelism. The best example is Cant 2:12: הנצנים נראו בארץ עת הזמיר הגיע וקול התור נשמע בארצנו, 'The blossoms have appeared in the land / The time of the *zāmîr* has

---

5. ʿAnat, pl. x: iv:14; see Gordon, *Ugaritic Textbook*, 256.

arrived / And the voice of the turtledove has been heard in our land.' The verse is a tristich with the middle stich simultaneously paralleling the first and third. The pivot word is *zāmîr* which has two entirely different meanings: one is agricultural (often translated 'pruning'), the other has to do with 'song'. *Zāmîr* provides asymmetric Janus parallelism; retrospectively it parallels the first stich botanically, prospectively it parallels the third stich musically. The notion that a word must have only one meaning in *all* contexts is incorrect. All the commentaries I have consulted insist either that *zāmîr* in Cant 2:12 can mean (1) only 'pruning' or (2) only 'singing'—and all are mistaken. It means *both* here; one retrospectively and the other prospectively; and this ambiguity is intentional.

In Gen 2:1 there is another asymmetric Janus word that can (unlike *zāmîr*) be adequately translated into English by a single word with both the meanings of the ambiguous Hebrew word. After the six days of creation in Genesis 1, we read in Gen 2:1: וַיְכֻלּוּ הַשָּׁמַיִם וְהָאָרֶץ, 'and the heavens and the earth were finished'. Now the Hebrew לְכַלּוֹת, like the English "to finish" has the same two quite different meanings: 'to complete' or 'to destroy'. Retrospectively, וַיְכֻלּוּ means that the heavens and earth 'were completed'; prospectively, it means they 'were destroyed'. My translation 'they were finished' conveys the ambiguity precisely. Gen 2:5 tells us that before Yahweh-Elohim began the second creation there was no vegetation in existence nor any human being to till the soil, although the first account includes Elohim's creation of vegetation and of mankind, male and female. While most exegetes opt for the translation of וַיְכֻלּוּ 'they were completed', Rabbi Efes of Antioch (in *Berešit Rabba*) states "ויכלו can only mean a catastrophic and total annihilation." Both extremes are erroneous. Retrospectively, ויכלו refers to the first creation by Elohim; but prospectively, to the later work of Yahweh-Elohim.

The Bible abounds in subtleties. It is an accomplishment of the wise להבין משל ומליצה דברי חכמים וחידתם, 'to understand proverbs and clever sayings, the words of the sages and their riddles' (Prov 1:6).

An achievement of the current generation of Old Testament scholars is their refinement in analyzing countless stylistic devices in biblical literature. Much of this comes in the wake of discoveries at Ugarit in the last sixty years.

SOCIOLOGICAL COMPARATIVISM AND THE THEOLOGICAL IMAGINATION: THE CASE OF THE CONQUEST

Baruch Halpern

Theology and the Historical Imagination

One gauge of how far scholarship has recaptured an antique culture lies in the realm of imagination. If artists can bring historical figures or a historical era to life, without offending the sensibilities of a tolerant professional, then scholars have developed an articulated conceptual framework, a matrix of cultural categories and political fraction, that transcends a disconnected chronicle of events and constitutes an organic—if nevertheless hypothetical—recreation of the past.

For some periods, successful artistic treatments abound. Historical romances, for example, range from the American gangster and the American West to traditional China (one thinks of Judge Dee). Elizabethan England and revolutionary and Napoleonic Europe have evoked prolific work. And there have been several realistic and, in E. M. Forster's terminology, three-dimensional treatments of Rome, dwarfed in common by Robert Graves's Claudius dilogy. Yet, for all that Akhenaten is celebrated as the "first individual in history," for all that David is the first individual in historiography, no historically persuasive biblical romance has left the presses in modern times.

Israelite history, in a word, is dehumanized. The vilification of Jezebel, the canonization of Elijah, and the self-canonization of Amos are translated from the text into art. Full of saints and demons, the past shrivels into a

---

Author's note: Shemaryahu Talmon has long stood in the forefront of those scholars demanding a balanced approach toward comparativism. It is joyous work indeed to dedicate this study to him.

cartoon: a Michelangelo fresco, cluttered with immaculately robed, carefully coiffed, granite-chinned Abrahams and Moseses: David and Bathsheba as Gregory Peck and Susan Hayward. Israelite history is reduced to a tapestry, a cardboard monument to a god's or a nation's literary prowess.

Why is Israel a less-fit subject for romance than revolutionary France or Imperial Rome? A shortage of deists. Classical history is not plagued, after all, by catechists from the Capitoline and ecstatics from Eleusis, to whom it is a life-and-death matter whether Aeneas came from Troy to sow the empire. The Punic Wars are, unlike the Exodus, inessential to scholars' identities. Biblical romance is impoverished by the emotional and ontological centrality of its subject in Western culture. Whom the gods wish to destroy, at least artistically, they first make sacred.

Scholarship expresses the cultural centrality of Israel's history in a preoccupation with ideas. De Wette wrote, "The most important object for the scholar of Israelite history must be the history of religion and worship."[1] And this has been the rule: with rare exceptions, theology, not geopolitics, has been the cynosure of research. The study of Israel has bleached, not obliterated, its theological spots.

Yet it is naïve to tilt with the theological windmill. Social and political history are legitimate objects of investigation. But ideas and convictions condition them. The two intertwine in a lush, patterned fabric of dialectical causation.

Thus, nothing is wrong with the windmill. The problem is with the wind. The very scholars who make doctrine an object of primary scrutiny marginalize it historically in one of two ways: they treat it as a divine or moral absolute; or, they affirm that it follows mechanically as a sort of appendix, a cut-flower aftergrowth, idly mirroring current economic relations. The history of Israelite ideas is linked always with short-term political developments. Monotheism was a repudiation of Egypt, or of Canaan, or a product of the desert. Or exilic theologians produced it to avoid the painful inference of YHWH's and Judah's powerlessness.

Though an event can trigger an idea, the state of culture best explains the dissemination of that idea. The Voting Rights Act did not come down with the Thirteenth Amendment or Plessy *vs.* Ferguson. Nor did gun control begin when John Wilkes Booth broke a leg at the Ford Theater. Yet our reconstructions are often just that flat, that one-dimensional. Amos's rantings show Israel was irremediably corrupt—as though Amos were not appealing to norms shared by the community of his auditors. The Deuteronomic program? Samarian refugees brought it "south" in 722—had Jerusalem jammed the samizdats of Israelite dissidents before that time? Did the fugitives rise straight to power? Job explains unmerited pain(!) and can only have come from the Exile: the question "Why me?" first arose in the sixth century.

---

1. W. M. L. de Wette, *Beiträge zur Einleitung in das Alte Testament* (Halle, 1806), 1:4.

The peripheral periods, of which least is known, are those of which most is surmised: the premonarchic period and the Exile together spawned about nine-tenths of Israel's theology. The Exile is a particular favorite. Among the notions that have been traced to this single event are covenant, monotheism, ritual, history, and law. No wonder Zechariah, that famous pollyanna, predicted that the fast of the 9th of Ab would be transformed to festal joy. Were it not for the Exile, the Bible would be no more than a pamphlet!

Biblical scholars generally take one of two views. Either ideas arose in some pristine Mosaic revelation, such that the personal religion of Moses has its first competent exposition in the preaching of Deutero-Isaiah, or they mirrored events perfectly, immediately, indivisibly. This latter view is most common: it is the one that Marx promoted in polemics, but quietly abandoned when writing historical narrative, as in his *Eighteenth Brumaire*.

The one hope for an exception to this rule lies with recent attempts to recast history in sociological terms. If one can separate the generation of ideas from their dissemination, from the complex mechanics of their socialization and their ratification in policy, then a nuanced, faction- and function-sensitive history of ideas is possible. As yet, the sociological approach to the history of Israelite theology has only outfitted the tattered old approaches in a nattier raiment: sociology and "models" are used chiefly to sustain epistemic claims against those of historical-critical method. Like the old methods, the sociological approach ciphers theological agendas. It exaggerates the authority of theory and comparative evidence, applying them speculatively to a culture in the study of which the disciplined historical imagination has historically been impoverished.

Unpleasant Peasants: Poverty in Evidence

No theory more exemplifies these points than the "Peasants' Revolt" model, the flagship hypothesis of the sociological method. Its original formulation by G. E. Mendenhall in 1962 may justly be said to have inspired, directly or indirectly, much of the present interest among biblicists in social scientific research.

Mendenhall proposed that Canaanite peasants, disgruntled with monarchy and "bureaucratic socialism," withdrew from the urban system. They defected to some escaped Egyptian slaves, adopting a god who by dictating that they could have no other sovereign precluded their reintegration into the city-state political framework. Their league dichotomized Canaan along city : village lines.[2]

Mendenhall's hypothesis, regarded at a remove of a quarter century, had an astounding appeal. Some of this should be credited to Norman

---

2. G. Mendenhall, "The Hebrew Conquest of Palestine," *BA* 25 (1962) 66–87, cited here from *Biblical Archaeologist Reader* (ed. E. F. Campbell Jr. and D. N. Freedman; Garden City, NY, 1970), 3:100–120.

Gottwald's masterful consolidation.³ Still, one suspects that the idea was generated by a junction of events and attitudes different from those that have perpetuated it. Before turning to this point, one should ask from the outset what first actuated the thesis intellectually, and what its chief defects are.

The pilasters of Mendenhall's argument were two. The first was based upon his work on the covenant. Dating the covenant (and the Decalogue) to the start of Israelite history, he reasoned that YHWH's regulation of society and demand for exclusive loyalty preempted human sovereignty: Yahwism denied that any human agency, foreign or domestic, could be vested with a monopoly on the legitimate use of force. So the rise of the state under Saul, David, and Solomon was a betrayal of Moses' revelation; this, in turn, was kept alive only by "the prophets," at least until the rise of Christianity.⁴

Mendenhall quarried his other pier from the Amarna archive: Amarna-era peasants overthrew kings in order to throw in with invaders.⁵ Identifying the appellation "Hebrew" with the Amarna "Habiru," he took the latter to denote peasants who renounced state authority. So Israel's ethnic designation and the evidence of its covenant converged.

Mendenhall also appealed to biblical narratives to sustain his "ideal model." So Balak resorted to cursing Israel in Numbers 22–24 to dissuade Moabites from defecting, as Sihon's subjects must have done for the Song of Heshbon to have been preserved. Reubenite place-names and clan-names in Cisjordan and a reference to Gileadites as "fugitives of Ephraim" (Judg 12:4) were the residue of defections eastward from Cisjordan and revolts (without narrative reflex) against kings of the central hills (as Josh 12:17–18a, 24a). Israel's formation was recorded in Joshua 24, which Mendenhall dated early: the abjuration of "other gods" from Mesopotamia and Egypt contradicted the notion of Exod 3:6 that YHWH was originally the "god of the fathers." And, the Aramaisms of the Song of Deborah and the expression "fugitive Aramean" in Deuteronomy 26 meant that Israel came from Aram, with the Amorites in EB IV.⁶

These references are of no avail. The "Aramaisms" reflect a recombinant continuum in Canaanite dialects that persisted throughout the Iron Age.⁷ Like the reference in Deuteronomy 26, they imply that the ties to

---

3. N. Gottwald, *The Tribes of Yahweh* (New York, 1979).

4. Mendenhall, "Hebrew Conquest of Palestine," 108–9, 119. Cf. idem, "Ancient Oriental and Biblical Law," *BA* 17 (1954) 26–46; "Covenant Forms in Israelite Tradition," *BA* 17 (1954) 50–76. Both of these items are reprinted in *The Biblical Archaeologist Reader* (ed. E. F. Campbell Jr. and D. N. Freedman; Garden City, NY, 1970), 3:3–24, 25–53.

5. Mendenhall, "Hebrew Conquest of Palestine," 111–12.

6. Ibid. 114–18. The phrase "ideal model" is from p. 100.

7. See my "Dialect Distribution in Canaan and the Deir Alla Inscriptions," in *"Working with No Data": Semitic and Egyptian Studies Presented to Thomas O. Lambdin* (ed. D. Golomb; Winona Lake, IN, 1987) 119–39; G. Rendsburg, "The Ammonite Phoneme /ṭ/," *BASOR* 269 (1988) 73–79.

Aram were recent: otherwise, the languages should have diverged more widely. Joshua 24 does not contradict Exodus; it claims that Israel divested herself of "other gods" *than* Y*HWH* from before (24:3) and after the time that Y*HWH* became the "god of the fathers." The Transjordanian links to Cisjordan all relate to parts of the hill country that were uninhabited to Canaanites in the Late Bronze Age. And Mendenhall's psychologizing of Balak, as though he were the subject of a documentary film interview, neglects a vast literature of imprecations against enemies.

The Peasants' Revolt suffers from all the defects of any randomly applied "model." Iron Age and Amarna-era peasants exhibit restiveness only under siege; they never flee to uninhabited regions, or constitute a separate socioethnic group.[8] Also, traditions (Abraham, the births of Jacob's sons, Joshua) of allochthonous origins contradict the thesis that Israel was autochthonous and the antedating of its entry into the third millennium (the latter demands an analogical reading of anagogic folklore in Genesis). The model covers up an absence of data.

In the hills, the process of settlement contradicts the model. The population of urban LB Canaan was already depleted, as shrinkage in fortresses and settlement surveys reveal. In Iron I, the hills population burgeons at a rate far exceeding that of natural increase. The demography is diagnostic: the earliest homesteaders chose regions best suited to a pastoral economy; even ᶜIzbet Ṣarṭah III, on a watershed between pastureland and dry-farming land, took the form of a pastoral enclosure supplying meat to Canaanite Apheq.

The settlers, then, were not vagrants. They had converted their assets into livestock and migrated either from the Canaanite lowlands or, as refugees from Assyrian taxation, from Syria by way of Transjordan.[9] Probably of a recent agrarian background, they entered the hills with established herds.

This is why the Merneptah stela pictures the "people, Israel" as the "Shasu," the transhumants of Transjordan, of Ramesses II.[10] These are the peoples for whom Israel felt a special affinity. Their material culture most resembles that of the Israelites. And they are peoples Israel identified, like

---

8. See my *Emergence of Israel in Canaan* (Society of Biblical Literature Monograph Series 29; Chico, CA, 1983) 55–63, 88; N. Naʾaman, "Habiru and Hebrews: The Transfer of a Social Term to the Literary Sphere," *JNES* 45 (1986) 271–88, esp. 276–88.

9. See I. Finkelstein, *The Archaeology of the Israelite Settlement* (Jerusalem, 1988); M. Weippert, "The Israelite 'Conquest' and the Evidence from Transjordan," in *Symposia Celebrating the Seventy-Fifth Anniversary of the Founding of the American Schools of Oriental Research (1900–1975)* (ed. F. M. Cross; Cambridge, MA, 1979) 15–34; Halpern, *Emergency of Israel in Canaan*, 100–104.

10. D. Redford, "The Ashkelon Relief at Karnak and the Israel Stela," *Israel Exploration Journal* 36 (1986) 188–200; cf. L. Stager, "Merenptah, Israel and Sea Peoples," *EI* 18 (1985) 59–60; I. Singer, "Merneptah's Campaign to Canaan," *BASOR* 269 (1988) 1–10. For the Shasu in the south and Transjordan, see M. Weippert, "Semitische Nomaden des zweiten Jahrtausends," *Bib* 55 (1974) 265–80.

themselves, as alien agents of vengeance upon autochthonous populations (Deut 2:2–23; Gen 12:1–3, 15:16). Israelite traditions about the migrations of "Hebrews," like those about Philistines (as Amos 9:7, Gen 10:14) and Arameans (as Amos 9:7, Gen 11:31), are specific. And, they answer to archaeological and epigraphic data.

Mendenhall stressed the non-ethnic, apolitical construction of early Israel—peasants from diverse regions banded together to resist royalism. Gottwald concurs, adding somewhat naïvely, as Mendenhall observed, a commitment not just to ecumenism, but to "egalitarianism."

Israel's xenophobia contraindicates ecumenism. Joshua 12, a late compilation, lists kings that Israel killed. But the preceding narrative is replete with warfare against populations. Early texts (as Exod 15:13–14, Judges 5) share the same xenophobia. The kings, thus, are trophies because they are Canaanite, not because they are kings; one rejoices at Sisera's demise (Judges 5) not because he is a general, but because he is an *enemy* general. Similarly, Hivite ethnicity persisted in the face of Israelite homesteading (Joshua 9, 2 Samuel 21); nativism prevented assimilation (note Judg 1:27–36). Egalitarianism in Israel was inwardly directed: ecumenism is a chimera.

Second, evidence is emerging for avoidance of pigs by Israel even in border zones. This, like circumcision, distinguished Israel from the Philistines and from the autochthonous inhabitants of the plains. Canaanites were less fond of pork than the Philistines, of whose meat consumption it represented up to 40 percent. But despite exiguous representation at some sites, pig was a staple of Canaanite cuisine (8 percent of the sample at Tel Miqneh). Boar was hunted at Laish (seven of eighty LB specimens), thus, until Israel's arrival.[11] All this indicates that the Israelites did not eschew pig for environmental reasons (though pigs require large quantities of water). Rather, this peculiar pattern of consumption suggests cultural, and by extension ethnic, homogeneity. Here, xenophobia, or a contributing factor, leaves an archeological reflex.

Mendenhall's defenders do cite archeological data: proto-Israelite material culture appears in Late Bronze–Iron I Transjordan. But this material is typical of a spectrum of peoples in Syro-Palestine at the Late Bronze II–Iron I transition. Its components are homogeneous in the hills and Transjordanian sites of Iron I Israel and Ammon, at least. Probably, it was the shared material culture of the so-called Hebrew peoples (Gen 10:25–30,

---

11. On pig-bone distribution, see P. Wapnish and B. Hesse, "Philistine/Israelite Animal Use in Iron Age Canaan" and "Faunal Remains from Tell Dan," both forthcoming; S. Hellwing and Y. Adjeman, "Animal Bones," in ʿIzbet Ṣarṭah: An Early Iron Age Site near Rosh Haʿayin, Israel (ed. I. Finkelstein; Oxford, 1986) 141–52; Hesse, "Animal Use at Tel Miqne-Eqron in the Bronze Age and Iron Age," *BASOR* 264 (1986) 17–28; Hesse, M. Metzger, and S. Henson, "Rural-Urban Exchange in Animal Products in Eastern Mediterranean Societies," forthcoming. On the implications of mutilation, note J. Goody, *Comparative Studies in Kinship* (London, 1969).

11:14ff.), whose nations crystallized into the states of the Iron Age along the King's Highway and in Cisjordan as the Egyptian empire receded: Israel, Ammon, Edom, Moab, possibly Geshur, and so on.[12]

Further, despite continuity in the pottery traditions, the predilection for collared-rim store jars in the hills has no parallel in the valleys, where few have been found; the only one in a LB II context crops up in shouting distance of a contemporary Israelite settlement. Nor is the mix of ware the same in the hills and the valleys: at Giloh, for example, 60 percent of the pottery consisted of collared-rim jars and cooking pots. This distribution is unexampled in Canaanite sites.[13] The same holds for the "four-room house," a typical "Hebrew" dwelling. So far, the only possible local antecedent to it is a single similar house at LB IIA Tel Batashi. At no time do Canaanite sites exhibit the concentrated construction of such buildings that characterizes most Israelite settlements. Early Israelite material culture is distinctive.

Mendenhall assumed, too, that Canaan's city-states were seething with sedition in the Amarna era (ca. 1370–1345). The "peasantry" of Amarna Canaan do defect, but usually under external military pressure, and also within the context of professions of loyalty either to an Egyptian or to a Hittite (one presumes) overlord; further, the peasants flee their towns only under famine conditions, and take refuge in the next town over, never in the hills. Mendenhall's characterization of the situation either twists the evidence, or ignores the polemical character of references to enemy factions.

Worse yet, archeological surveys afford no sign of a LB II community of ḫabiru in the hills, nor even in the land of Shechem, said to have been given to the ḫabiru.[14] Indeed, few texts refer to genuine ḫabiru at Amarna (EA 195; Kumidi 1, 2; possibly EA 71:20–22, 28–31; 76:17–20).[15] Nearly all passages cited to support a thesis of a large-scale ḫabiru presence consist of accusations that the kings of Amurru, Shechem, or Jerusalem are in revolt. To "join the ḫabiru" is to ally with the correspondent's enemies, to

---

12. See J. Sauer, "Transjordan in the Bronze and Iron Ages," *BASOR* 263 (1986) 1–26, esp. 10–14; M. M. Ibrahim, "The Collared-Rim Jar of the Early Iron Age," in *Archaeology in the Levant: Essays for Kathleen Kenyon* (ed. R. Moorey and P. Parr; Warminster, 1978) 117–26; note J. M. Miller, "Recent Archaeological Developments Relevant to Ancient Moab," in *Studies in the History and Archaeology of Jordan* (ed. A. Hadidi; Amman, 1982), 1:169–73.

13. See I. Finkelstein, "Pottery and Stone Artifacts," in *ʿIzbet Ṣarṭah: An Early Iron Age Site Near Rosh Haʿayin, Israel* (ed. I. Finkelstein; Oxford, 1986) 82–84; idem, *Archaeology of the Israelite Settlement*, 275–85.

14. Finkelstein, *The ʿIzbet Sartah Excavations* (Diss., Tel Aviv University, 1983) 110–77; Z. Gal, *The Settlement of the Lower Galilee* (Diss., Tel Aviv University, 1983); A. Zertal, *The Israelite Settlement in the Hills of Manasseh* (Diss., Tel Aviv University, 1986).

15. El Amarna (EA) texts are cited according to J. A. Knudtzon, *Die El-Amarna-Tafeln* (2 vols.; Leipzig, 1907–15); Kumidi (i.e., Kāmid el-Lōz) texts are cited according to D. O. Edzard et al., *Kāmid el-Lōz—Kumidi: Schriftdokumente aus Kāmid el-Lōz* (Saarbrücker Beiträge zur Altertumskunde 7; Bonn, 1970).

"join the enemy."[16] Nothing implies that fugitive brigands are numerous, and the vocabulary neither of flight nor of marginalization attaches to the ḫabiru.

That is, the revisionist vassals are themselves the ḫabiru: there were few if any extra-systemic communities in the hills. But allow Mendenhall's premise about peasant flight: the hills remain empty until ca. 1200. Why did the peasants wait 150 years to flee?

Gottwald suggests that the use of iron made terracing and lime slaking cisterns possible: the hills were uninhabitable until Iron I. But in this very era, Assyrian kings preferred *bronze* pickaxes for hewing chariotry roads through mountains; even in the eighth century Sargon's sappers used "copper" tools.[17] Thus, Mendenhall's LB IIA fugitives had the means to domesticate the uplands.[18] Further, the hills had been settled extensively, with bronze tools, in the Middle Bronze Age. In MB highlands settlements, too, cistern lining was necessary wherever the bedrock was permeable. There is no evidence of a technological breakthrough leading to the opening of the hill country frontier in the twelfth century, and therefore no reason for the peasants to have waited until then to flee.

Mendenhall reacted to Gottwald's epicycle by decrying Gottwald's "cultural-material ideology" requiring "technological innovation to explain change": the villager federation, born of region-wide maelstroms at the start of Iron I, reflects the genius of the original Yahwistic theology—untainted revelation. This federation fell away as local autonomy reasserted itself, along with "the revival of the local cults: the 'Baals.'" This process, and low standards of living, led to the monarchy, its evil soul laid bare by Solomon, whose establishment duplicated those of LB Canaan. Even Jeroboam's secessionists could only "cut the monster in two—they couldn't bring it to an end."[19]

---

16. W. Moran, "Join the ᶜApiru or Become One?" in *"Working with No Data": Semitic and Egyptian Studies Presented to Thomas O. Lambdin* (ed. D. Golomb; Winona Lake, IN, 1987) 209–12; cf. W. Helck, "Die Bedrohung Palästinas durch einwandernde Gruppen am Ende der 18. und am Anfang der 19. Dynastie," *VT* 18 (1968) 473; M. Chaney, "Ancient Palestinian Peasant Movements and the Formation of Premonarchic Israel," in *Palestine in Transition* (ed. D. N. Freedman and D. F. Graf; Sheffield, 1983) 39–90, esp. 72–81.

17. For the Assyrian references, see A. K. Grayson, *Assyrian Rulers of the Third and Second Millennia BC* (Toronto, 1987) 272:40–46; idem, *Assyrian Royal Inscriptions* (Wiesbaden, 1976), 2:7:13; D. D. Luckenbill, *Ancient Records of Assyria and Babylonia* (Chicago, 1926) 1:598; F. Thureau-Dangin, *Une relation de la huitième campagne de Sargon* (Paris, 1912) 3:24; cf. Luckenbill, *The Annals of Sennacherib* (Chicago, 1924) 126:4–5. Cf. also *mupaṣṣidu* in L. W. King, *Cuneiform Texts from Babylonian Tablets in the British Museum*, vol. 15 (London, 1902) no. 35:3.

18. See Gottwald, *Tribes of Yahweh*, 296–97, 655–58; Chaney, "Ancient Palestinian Peasant Movements," 50.

19. Mendenhall, "Ancient Israel's Hyphenated History," in *Palestine in Transition* (ed. D. N. Freedman and D. F. Graf; Sheffield, 1983) 92, 98–99.

These musings conflict with recent attempts on the origins of Israelite kingship. A consensus is emerging that this was introduced under demographic and military-technical pressures.[20] The kings were elective dynasts, whom the lineages held the theoretical power to unseat; the Absalom revolt, thus, marked the watershed in the relationship of the crown to its constituents. That is, it was demographic and agricultural wealth (note the wealth of ᶜIzbet Ṣarṭah stratum II) which laid the ground for kingship. And it was David who in fact centralized power.

But the key point is Mendenhall's homily, his prophetic judgment on the kingship. Yahwism sustained the premonarchic federation. Apostasy created kingship. This schematic judgment abolishes historical method. It typified Mendenhall's approach, and conditioned his analysis. In the end, the case for peasant origins amounts to a surmise about the covenant—the very source of the model is theological. Mendenhall's "model" furnished a lever into the past. But theology was his Archimedean point.

True Israels Are New Israels: Theology in Evidence

Israel's egalitarianism, if any, was domestic. Its ecumenism is a mirage: even connubium (Genesis 34) and cultic assimilation (Josh 9:26) did not always produce integration (Gen 34:25; 2 Sam 21:1-2, 4:2-3). How did a theory so abundantly contraindicated gain credence? How did it arise?

When Mendenhall proposed the theory, several vectors converged on a definition of the Jews in apolitical and non-ethnic terms. A non-ethnic definition could repudiate Nazi racial theory. Non-ethnic Jews had a place in a pluralistic society; and, since their Judaism would be affective, simple disavowal offered immunity against a recurrence of the Holocaust.

The strategy of preemptive deracination—conversion of the Jews by ukase—has a history in recent times. It was first proposed in connection with the Khazars, who, according to a Karaite legend, had adopted Judaism *en masse* in medieval times. In the 1930s, an act was introduced in the Hungarian parliament to distinguish the Khazars from ethnic Jews. Not long after, the Nazi's applied the same logic to the Karaites, who, not being racial Jews, were spared the gas chambers.

In the years before Mendenhall wrote, Moscow chose the same strategy. In 1956, on their own application of the previous year, the Kamchaks were deracinated by the Soviet Ethnographic Institute. This body subsequently ruled that other groups, such as the Tats and the Khazars, were late converts. Deracination exempted these Jews from restrictions attaching

---

20. On population, see my *Emergency of Israel in Canaan*, 98–99, 230; R. Coote and K. Whitelam, "The Emergency of Israel," *Semeia* 37 (1986) 107–47; C. E. Hauer, "From Alt to Anthropology: The Rise of the Israelite State," *JSOT* 36 (1986) 3–15; for the physical data, see Finkelstein, *Archaeology of the Israelite Settlement*.

to ethnic Jews, broadening their educational and occupational possibilities. This was a by-product of de-Stalinization, when Soviet persecution of Jews was exposed in the world press (along with the survival of three hundred Karaites in the Crimea). "Jew" on Soviet internal passports became "Khazar," "Tat," and the like.

Mendenhall deracinated all Israel—all were converts. The corollaries of this scheme, which Mendenhall did not explore in print, were consistent with his subsequent fulminations against Zionist "racism" and Israel.[21] One might reason, for example, that Israel had no right to a "national liberation," like those advocated by "liberation theologians" of the 1960s and 1970s. There being no "Jewish People," there need be no "Jewish state": above all, wrote Mendenhall, "the Kingdom of God could not be identified . . . with any ethnic group." Thus deracinated, Jews have no more legitimate claim to the title "Israel" than does a church: the true Israel is that of the true religion ("the new Israel of God, the New Testament Church").[22]

Such factors may have figured at the theory's subliminal wellspring. Mendenhall had had the complicity of the theological community in the Holocaust on his mind.[23] And his attack on Gottwald's consolidation of his "model" piercingly expressed the emotional primacy of theology for him. Mendenhall compared Gottwald to Alfred Rosenberg, "official ideologist for the Nazi party,"[24] because Gottwald presumed that theology mirrors society, rather than existing in the abstract. Mendenhall's rhetoric set Yahwism, Moses, the(!) prophets, the New Israel, Paul, and ecumenism against paganism, Solomon, Nazism, Marxism, Zionism, and racism.

Mendenhall started from a vision of a pristine revelation, the "Mosaic" covenant: Israel began with an epiphany, a credo, a renunciation of the things of this world. This anti-politicism, Mendenhall reasoned, appealed to peasants rejecting stratified monarchic systems: only the victims of pagan statism could have conceived of a deity who usurped royal prerogatives.

At heart, the thesis is one more tired variation on the worn old myth that monotheism expressed disgust with Egyptian "idols," just as prophecy arose from disgust with a "Baal" infestation in the cult, Christianity from disgust with fossilized Pharisaism, and Protestantism from disgust with decadent Catholicism. Mendenhall's later statement, thus, that "the continuing revolution . . . culminated in the Christian reformation" identifies

---

21. See R. L. Rubinstein, "The Besieged Community in Ancient and Modern Times," *Michigan Quarterly Review* 22 (1983) 447–63, esp. 457–58.

22. Mendenhall, *The Tenth Generation: The Origins of the Biblical Tradition* (Baltimore, 1973) 226.

23. Mendenhall, "Biblical History in Transition," in *The Bible and the Ancient Near East: Essays in Honor of William Foxwell Albright* (ed. G. E. Wright; Garden City, NY, 1965) 33–34, n. 31 (written in 1957).

24. Mendenhall, "Ancient Israel's Hyphenated History," 102.

Jesus and Paul implicitly with Calvin and Luther.[25] That is, Mendenhall's "history" was anti-institutional—as though Quakers, Diggers, and Lutherans did not quickly create institutions of their own. Mendenhall's one historical Eden was found in an Israel about whose political organization we lack all basic data.

The echoes of these theological preoccupations sound throughout Mendenhall's first article as well as his subsequent pronouncements. The proposition that the prophets alone preserved the true Mosaic order marries the old theory of an "amphictyonic ideal" to orthodox Reformation theology. The latter was fixated on prophecy both because "classical" prophets inveigh against empty symbol and because prophecy poses the principle of inspiration against the authority of tradition.

Mendenhall claimed that monarchic religion deteriorated into "mere ritual without the moral and ethical dynamic which was essential to the formative period of the faith."[26] The formulation recalls Wellhausen's Pauline characterization of a "wraith-like" Judaism. It is indistinguishable from Reformationist comment on Catholicism.

What was worse, however, than the antique canards ciphered in the last remark was Mendenhall's misprision of Israelite religion. Mendenhall called this a "faith," a theory discrete from the culture. This was the very heart of the thesis: monarchic religion and Judaism were "mere support for a political system, and finally a system of ritual and a cultural tradition which served as a marker in a hostile world"—ritual systems that mark a culture, thus, are inferior. Conversely, Israel first formed as "specifically a *religious* community," by which is meant, "an ecumenical faith, a catholic religion."[27]

To what community before Pauline Christendom could one aptly apply such labels? Paul seems to have been the first Jew to base salvation on faith, divorced not just from ritual but from works in general. Lacking a reflex in life-style, "faiths" are portable religions: one may adopt them without abandoning one's own culture—as the conflicts between Jews and Egyptians, Greeks, and Romans all illustrate, Israelite religion, and late Judaism, was no such cult. To become an Israelite, one did not make a declaration of faith: one rather became an Israelite. But a Christian could be all things to all men. Mendenhall projected an anti-monarchic, American Protestant reading of Paul's antinomianism back into the premonarchic age. Moses' theology had its first competent exposition in Galatians.

The Peasant's Revolt model of the Israelite settlement was, in sum, a theologian's credal statement. Indeed, Mendenhall's idea of "Biblical History in Transition" had been a vision of the history of Israelite theology in

---

25. Mendenhall, *Tenth Generation*, 196; cf. P. Haupt, "The Burning Bush and the Origins of Judaism," *Proceedings of the American Philological Society* 48 (1909) 354–69.
26. Mendenhall, "Hebrew Conquest of Palestine," 108.
27. Ibid., 118.

which the Mosaic and pre-Mosaic periods were "creative," the premonarchic period "adaptive," and the monarchic era "transitional"—this from a thinker in the *sola scriptura* mold. Here is a later formulation:

> Whether or not the thesis corresponds to the historical facts is a problem which may or may not be decided by the accidents of historical and archaeological discovery, but that this approach to biblical history and thought is useful in understanding ancient man and the biblical religious value system can hardly be called into question.[28]

Political history, then, must be deduced from theology. The two mapped one-to-one, in an "if and only if" Boolean relationship. Allow that Gottwald made Israelites Marxists: Mendenhall had turned the methodological clock back past Vico. If the reality was other than he described, he asserted, we should take refuge in Tertullian: *credo quia absurdum*.

"Models": The New Systematics

The foregoing two sections respectively trench on the validity of Mendenhall's thesis, and situate its initial articulation in a theological context. The reasons for the dissemination of the thesis will have differed according to the circumstances of each individual scholar who has adopted it; none need coincide with Mendenhall's theological agenda. Still, published proponents of the scheme are preponderantly Protestant. Subliminally, the model fulfills emotional needs for a particular constituency.

One should add, as J. M. Sasson has observed, that Mendenhall's position was also a fashionable one in its time. Its popularity cannot be dissociated from that of "liberation" theology and left-wing politics in the seminaries in the last two decades.[29] An inclusive "true Israel" (or original Israel, pristine Israel) that is "anti-establishment" is as sure to evoke knee-jerk leftist response as Nixon-baiting was in the 1970s. The appeal of a "sociological" approach to this Israel was another child of fashion, at a time when sociological gurus multiplied exponentially.

The dynamics of biblical studies also contributed to the success of the hypothesis: the "sociological" approach responds to sheer methodological desperation. Interpreting historical fossils is tricky, and, in the last century, biblical studies has endured crisis upon crisis in the process. Literary criticism led to source criticism, source criticism to form criticism, form criticism to anthropological and comparative-religious research. Today, the welter of competing claims, the cacophony of methods, betrays the cumulation of the decades. The synthetic eschaton promised in the apocalypse of

---

28. Mendenhall, *Tenth Generation*, xi.
29. J. M. Sasson, "On Choosing Models for Recreating Israelite Pre-Monarchic History," *JSOT* 21 (1981) 3–24.

philological positivism has not arrived; expectations of its coming grow dim, and strife and heresy mar the brotherhood in Wellhausen. Theoretical sociology offers an end run around the morass of uncertainty, of scientific diffidence, in which the study of Israelite history has for fifty years been mired: how can one get at the early ("creative") periods, the records concerning which German scholarship had cast into such disrepute; in sociology, Mendenhall pronounced in 1957, one could find solid ground for conceptualizing the deep background, for recovering Abrahamic and Mosaic history.[30]

Mendenhall's clarion has produced, a quarter century later, a flourishing scholarly industry, centered on social-scientific data. Sociologically oriented scholars have been moving into the more accessible later eras, foreswearing crypto-fundamentalist inquiries into the "creative" periods. Still, the origins of this development in the study of premonarchic Israel are never far from the surface. Mendenhall's influence is palpable. These new "sociologists," of course, are not the first to adduce sociological theory to Israelite antiquity—scholars recognized in the nineteenth century that all historical reconstructions involve sociological reconstructions, conscious or by default. In 1954, H. Hahn devoted a whole chapter of his history of biblical criticism to "the Sociological Approach" (chiefly, Alt's) without either prescience or fanfare.[31] What distinguishes the recent discovery of sociology is a penchant for applying to external typologies to supply the place of hard data.[32] That is, the recent "sociology" attempts to ground the history of ideas in a comparative framework. In correlating society and theology, these researchers advert to theory, to schematic—predictive, rather than descriptive—sociological models.

At this juncture, my critique recommences. Mendenhall's model parachuted a Protestant paradise onto Israelite earth: extrinsic models always do violence to local particularities. Scholars are all at pains not to impose modern concepts on ancient data. Yet models honed on cultures from the Andes to Micronesia are equally alien to ancient Israel. Such models can be tested on Israel. But no decent historian believes that they can be used predictively, that societies inevitably react identically to circumstantial similarities. Such a conviction regresses to a determinism, like that of Marx or Spengler, to shed itself of which has been the burden of twentieth-century thought.

30. Mendenhall, "Biblical History in Transition," 32 and nn. 36, 41.
31. H. Hahn, *The Old Testament in Modern Research* (Philadelphia, 1954) 157–84.
32. Cf. Mendenhall, *Tenth Generation*; Gottwald, *Tribes of Yahweh*; idem, "The Participation of Free Agrarians in the Introduction of Monarchy to Ancient Israel" *Semeia* 37 (1986) 77–106 (this issue, edited by Gottwald, is entitled "Social-Scientific Criticism of the Hebrew Bible and Its Social World: The Israelite Monarchy"); F. Frick, *The Formation of the State in Ancient Israel* (Sheffield, 1985); D. Hopkins, *The Highlands of Canaan* (Sheffield, 1985); Coote and Whitelam, "Emergence of Israel"; contrast C. H. J. de Geus, *The Tribes of Israel* (Studia Semitica Neerlandica 18; Assen, 1976); see Hauer, "From Alt to Anthropology."

All historians work from "models," as Mendenhall saw.[33] But one can gauge what are the crucial factors of change and which is the apt model only after identifying the coherence of the local evidence. That is, to understand is to impose a "model." But models enter into dialogue with the data, producing fresh evidence: both must be adapted repeatedly to render the model meaningful and the construction of the evidence felicitous. Models teach questions that one might ask, not answers that one must give.

Extrinsic models cannot do duty for intrinsic reasoning. Alt understood this, and adverted purely to textual and historical-geographic data to sustain positions for which he might have leaned on Weber.[34] The opposite approach leads to poor posture: on the one hand, careful interrogation is waived when the sources' claims are congenial; on the other, sociological configurations, such as the impoverishment of the peasantry, are uncritically reconstructed from partisan text—prophetic polemic about injustice supplies statistical documentation of widespread disenfranchisement. The result is fanciful history; it is also unreflective sociology,[35] devoid of what C. Wright Mills called "the Sociological Imagination." This is the net result when theology dictates history. Yet because of its theological double helix, a poll, say, of the Society of Biblical Literature would probably disclose that most American members see "sociology" as the Great White Hope of Israelite history.

The significance of these issues is gradually being recognized, and the defects are being composed.[36] Meanwhile, "sociology" continues to locate intellectual history in immediate political developments, and to short-circuit problems inherent in the use of polemical sources. The "sociologists" are trying to outrun their own theological shadow:[37] again, students of ancient Israel are almost universally drawn more to the history of theology than to that of ancient Israel. Biblical history is not, as Mendenhall claimed, in transition. It remains biblical, not Syro-Palestinian, Canaanite, or Israelite.

The Peasants' Revolt hypothesis introduced a new sociological sensitivity into the study of Israel. The legacy will survive, although one wonders just how far a sense of sociological realism will penetrate the historical-theological fog. To date, those scholars who appeal to sociology seek to supersede the authority of historical method. They have, in the main, done so, consciously or not, to advance Protestant theological programs.

---

33. Mendenhall, "Hebrew Conquest of Palestine," 100.

34. Cf. Alt, *Kleine Schriften zur Geschichte des Volkes Israel* (Munich, 1953), 2:1-65, 116-34.

35. See N. P. Lemche, "On Sociology and the History of Israel: A Reply to Eckhardt Otto," *Biblische Notizen* 21 (1983) 48-58.

36. See Hauer, "From Alt to Anthropology"; also Gottwald, "Introduction," *Semeia* 37 (1986) 7.

37. Halpern, *Emergence of Israel in Canaan*, 249-61.

Can modern comparativism shed academic light on ancient Israel? We should expect its fruits to sweeten our appreciation not of the Settlement, still less of the pre-literary eras, but of the historical periods of Israel's life in its land. What is wanted is a liberation of Israelite history from modern theology—and from a Protestant-Karaite fixation on origins at the expense of developments—such that the objects of comparativism are the historically accessible phenomena of Israelite antiquity, not the inaccessible, such that the font of authority is the evidence directly pertinent to and first produced by the culture in question, such that the comparative data furnish conceptual frameworks, rather than predications. Israelite history can engage a disciplined historical imagination. It wants one abjuration for it to do so: an abjuration of external doctrine, theological or sociological, in favor of the authority of intrinsic data.

1 CHRONICLES 15-16 AND
THE CHRONICLER'S VIEWS ON THE LEVITES

Paul D. Hanson

Whereas the account of the transfer of the ark to Jerusalem in 2 Samuel 6 makes no mention of the Levites, the Levites and the Levitical musicians and caretakers are described in great detail in 1 Chronicles 15-16. A close analysis of these two chapters, including comparison with references to the Levites in other parts of the Chronicler's history, when projected against the background of a general reconstruction of the temple cult in the early Second Temple period, yields some very interesting clues concerning the Chronicler's views on the Levites.

Analysis of 1 Chronicles 15-16

Chapters 15 and 16 are themselves composite. Within the sections dealing with the Levites, it seems evident that 15:4-10 represents a secondary elaboration of 15:11 (note the parallel phrases in 15:4 and 15:11), and that 15:16-24 was added as an elaboration of 16:4-6, 37:42.[1] I shall proceed by analyzing both the original form of the Chronicles narrative, and the changes introduced into the narrative by the two additions. In the last half of this paper I shall seek to relate my findings to developments within the Jerusalem temple cult during the period spanned by the composition history of the Book of Chronicles.

Author's note: It seems fitting to present to my colleague and friend Shemaryahu Talmon an article addressing a topic to which he has made ground-breaking contributions and which he heard in an earlier oral version on December 8, 1987, at the Annual Meeting of the Society of Biblical Literature in Boston, Massachusetts. All biblical quotations are from the RSV.

1. Installation of musicians and others ministering before the ark finds its logical narrative position after the ark has been situated, i.e., as is the case in 16:4-6. The motivation lying behind the addition of 15:16-23 may have something to do with the concern to portray only properly installed Levites as involved in the transportation of the ark. It may also have included the desire to have the contact of the ancestors of Levitical families with the ark traced all the way back to the pre-Jerusalemite phase of the ark's history.

The Chronicler's Adaptation of 2 Samuel 6

As we first consider what would seem to be the original version of the Chronicles ark narrative, we detect a striking thematic change over against 2 Samuel 6. What had been a popular gathering of the people by King David, with the military (כָּל בָּחוּר) occupying center stage, is transformed by the Chronicler into a sacral procession guided by stringent application of sacerdotal law:

> Then David said, "No one but the Levites may carry the ark of God, for the LORD chose them to carry the ark of the LORD and to minister to him for ever." (1 Chr 15:2)

David's command accords with Mosaic law, as found in Deut 10:8:

> At that time the LORD set apart the tribe of Levi to carry the ark of the covenant of the LORD, to stand before the LORD to minister to him and to bless in his name, to this day.

Indeed, the tragic outcome of the first attempt to transport the ark to its new home in which Uzzah was struck dead by the Lord "because he put forth his hand to the ark" (13:10) is supplied by the Chronicler with an explanation that highlights the grave importance of proper sacral procedure in transporting the ark:

> Because you did not *carry it*(?) the first time, the LORD our God broke forth upon us, because we did not care for it in the way that is ordained. (1 Chr 15:13)

From the very beginning of his arranging for the sanctuary in Jerusalem, David is portrayed as one attending to all details of proper cultic sanctity. And the message is clear: unlike Saul, whose failure as a king could not be disassociated from his total negligence *vis-à-vis* the ark, David makes a clean break from the ways of his predecessor, and thus becomes a worthy founder of the institutions that are central to the concerns of the Chronicler. The first episode thus ends with a summary statement drawing explicit attention to the fact that all had been done according to Mosaic Law as set forth in Exod 25:13–14 and 37:4–5:

> And the Levites carried the ark of God upon their shoulders with the poles, as Moses had commanded according to the word of the LORD. (1 Chr 15:15)

1 Chronicles 15:11 and 4:10

Having described the general manner in which the Chronicler applied the story of the transfer of the ark to Second Temple concerns, I turn to examine the sections specifically discussing the appointment of the Levites to their duties. From the original version of the narrative, we read:

> Then David summoned the priests Zadok and Abiathar, and the Levites Uriel, Asaiah, Joel, Shemaiah, Eliel, and Amminadab, and said to them, "You are the heads of the fathers' houses of the Levites; sanctify yourselves, you and your brethren, so that you may bring up the ark of the LORD, the God of Israel, to the place that I have prepared for it." (1 Chr 15:11-12)

Wilhelm Rudolph argues that the phrase "the priests Zadok and Abiathar" was not in the original text, since the Chronicler was solely interested in the Levites.[2] This proposal is unconvincing for two reasons. (1) Textually, it is baseless, inasmuch as the priests are mentioned alongside the Levites throughout these two chapters, a pattern observed as well throughout 1 and 2 Chronicles.[3] (2) As will be noted in my discussion of the Second Temple setting reflected by the text (pp. 74–77 below), the mention of the priests is in harmony with the social realities of its time.

Though the priests are mentioned first in this instance, focus quickly shifts to the Levites. What is the significance of the six Levites mentioned in 1 Chr 15:11? Here, as well as in the later elaboration given in 1 Chr 15:4–10, they are described as heads of Levitical fathers' houses. And that designation seems to be accurate. In identifying those who transported the ark, the Chronicler names the ancestors claimed by the major Levitical houses of his own day. The fact that the attempt in the secondary elaboration to fit these names into the traditional genealogies is only partly successful corroborates the contention that contemporary realities of the historian's time are being described rather than information simply taken from earlier sources (see pp. 72–74 below).

Moving to the elaboration in 1 Chr 15:4–10 itself, the intention of the writer seems clear, namely to secure the Levitical pedigree of the priestly families mentioned in v. 11 by specifically identifying their patronymics with the earliest descendents of Levi. It is the same objective underlying much of the genealogical reconstruction found in the first eight chapters of 1 Chronicles. Indeed, the interconnections between 1 Chr 15:4–10 and the Levitical genealogy in 1 Chr 6:1–15 and between the elaboration of the temple musicians in 1 Chr 15:16–24 and the genealogy of the temple musicians in 1 Chr 6:16–32 suggest that the hand adding 15:4–10 and 15:16–24 is closely related to or identical with the one responsible for the final shape of the Chronicles genealogies. In the case of 15:4–10, the elaborator had no difficulty fitting Uriel into traditional Levitical genealogical lists, where Uriel is named as a descendent of Kohath (1 Chr 6:9 [English 6:24]). Similarly, Asaiah is listed among the Merarites (1 Chr 6:15 [English 6:30]). The situation was more difficult in the case of Joel, a name found among the Kohathites, but not among the Gershomites. But the

---

2. W. Rudolph, *Chronikbücher* (HAT 21; Tübingen, 1955) 115.
3. Cf. 1 Chr 13:2; 23:2; 28:21; 2 Chr 5:5; 7:6; 8:14–15; 17:7–9; 19:8–11; 29:4; 30:15–16, 21, 25, 27; 31:4, 9; 34:30; 35:1–19.

claim to Gershomite lineage was pressed anyway. The problem was even more difficult, however, in the case of the other three Levitical families, since the traditional genealogy limits the sons of Levi to three. To whom can their descendents trace their ancestry? They must be content with a lineage slightly less ancient. Accordingly, Shemaiah is connected to Elizaphan great grandson of Levi (as a son of Uzziel), Eliel is connected with Hebron son of Kohath, and Amminadab with Uzziel son of Kohath (cf. Exod 6:16–22). If the order in which the six families are named is indicative of relative rank or prestige, it is interesting to note that the group with the most shallow genealogical pedigree comes fourth rather than sixth in the list. How this might relate to relations between priestly families in the early Second Temple period will be discussed below (pp. 74–77).

1 Chronicles 16:4–6, 37–42 and 15:16–24

After the ark had been set inside the tent prepared by David, and the festivities had been completed, the original narrative in Chronicles proceeds to describe the king's appointment of those who would minister before the ark on a permanent basis. Actually, they are assigned to two locations, due to the Chronicler's need to explain how King Solomon could sacrifice at Gibeon (cf. 2 Chr 2:3–6). Thus Asaph and those second to him are appointed to minister before the ark in its new location in Jerusalem (16:4–6), whereas Heman and Jeduthun are left in the high place at Gibeon (16:37–42). Similarly, the priests were divided between the two locations, with Benaiah and Jahaziel serving with Asaph before the ark, and Zadok remaining in Gibeon with Heman and Jeduthun.

The names mentioned as second to the three chiefs can best be understood as representing various Levitical families of the Second Temple period. In a daring move, the Chronicler portrays these families, gathered under the larger division of Asaph, as established by David to minister before the ark. In a twofold manner this move is daring. (1) Though Mosaic law (Deut 10:8) was cited in the previous chapter (1 Chr 15:2) as authorization of the Levites' exclusive responsibility to carry the ark, the era of the ark being carried about was fast ending (only the move to the completed temple reported in 2 Chronicles 5 remained). What would be the fate of these Levites once that responsibility had been completed? The similarity of this dilemma to the one faced by the majority of the Levites in the aftermath of Josiah's reform and centralization of the cult is striking, and, as I shall argue later, that similarity was likely in the mind of the Chronicler. The answer given in 1 Chr 16:4–7 is programmatic: the Levitical families mentioned were established by David in permanent positions as ministers before the ark, where they were "to invoke, to thank, and to praise the LORD, the God of Israel." (2) Also daring is the fact that both in order and in emphasis, the Levites eclipse the priests who are assigned to the ark, inasmuch as Benaiah and Jahaziel are mentioned almost as an afterthought in 1 Chr 16:6.

Once the narrative is resumed after the interlude of the psalm in 1 Chr 16:7–36, we find the Chronicler's description of the arrangement for the high place at Gibeon, where Solomon later would sacrifice to the Lord, and hence where proper priestly officials needed to be installed. It is logical that "Zadok . . . and his brethren the priests" (16:39) would be assigned to this place, since until the completion of the temple it was for the Chronicler the place of sacrifice. The Levites chosen and designated by name to minister at Gibeon were Heman and Jeduthun and those under them. By virtue of this appointment, the two other major Levitical groups were secured in positions at the center of the temple cult, since with the consolidation of the cult in the new temple, the priests and Levites assigned to the two places would be united under one roof, and under that roof the daily morning and evening sacrifices would be offered forever as commanded by Moses (1 Chr 16:40).

As the list of Levites mentioned in the original narrative in 1 Chr 15:11 was elaborated in 15:4–10, so too we find that the list of Levitical musicians found in 1 Chr 16:4–6, 37–42 was elaborated in 15:16–24. Several tendencies can be detected within this secondary passage. (1) The phrase "and the rest of those chosen and expressly named" in 16:41 invited other families (whether of authentic Levitical lineage or not it is impossible to determine) who claimed entitlement to roles within the temple cult to enter their names into the list of Levites appointed by David as musicians and gatekeepers; hence alongside the nine names found in 16:5, four others (five in the LXX) were added. (2) No doubt motivated by the desire to strengthen claims to Levitical pedigree, a patronymic element is added to each of the three groups' names, thereby establishing each within a line of descent leading to the three sons of Levi (Heman to Kohath, Asaph to Gershom, and Ethan to Merari; cf. 1 Chr 6:16–33 [English 6:31–48]). (3) Jeduthun has been replaced by Ethan, as an act of assimilation to what had become the normative genealogy. (4) In place of the order Asaph, Heman, Jeduthun, we find Heman, Asaph, Ethan, perhaps reflecting the growing prestige of the Hemanites at the expense of the Asaphites (it is also noteworthy that Heman belongs to the family of Kohath, thus tracing back to the same son of Levi to which the priestly families are traced in the genealogy that emerged as normative in the early Second Temple period (cf. Exodus 6 and 1 Chronicles 6). (5) In this section Obededom is assigned in v. 21 to the lyre (consistent with the earlier version in 16:5), whereas in vv. 18 and 24 he is designated as a gatekeeper. We apparently are dealing with two layers within 15:16–24 that reflect the instability of the status of this family. Such instability was perhaps typical of many Levitical families during the early Second Temple period, and explains the considerable amount of attention given to genealogical reconstructions during this period (besides 1 Chr 15:4–10, 16–24, cf. 1 Chronicles 6 and 2 Chr 29:12–14).

1 Chronicles 15–16 and the Levites in the Early Second Temple Period

Efforts to relate the description of the Levites in 1 Chronicles 15–16 to a reconstruction of the underlying historical setting cannot avoid the problems involved in dating the Chronicler's history. Without being able to reopen the discussion surrounding attempts to identify two or three distinct levels within the Chronicler's history, I shall suggest in what follows that my analysis of 1 Chronicles 15–16 can be related positively to the idea of multiple levels.

Within what I judge to be the original narrative in these two chapters, King David is portrayed, in harmony with a major theme of the Chronicler's history, as the founder of the temple, its institutions, and priestly orders. Two aspects of this theme as it relates to priestly orders are particularly significant.

First, the conciliatory posture of the Chronicler is evident. The priests and Levites are mentioned together. In both the conveying of the ark and in ministering before it (as well as ministering in Gibeon), priest and Levite process and perform side by side, as they do throughout the Chronicler's history.[4] The fact that the priests are superior to the Levites in rank is not denied, though the lack of emphasis given to this fact is itself significant. In 15:11 Zadok and Abiathar are mentioned before the Levites, but the chief interest rests upon the latter. Similar is the mention of Zadok before Heman and Jeduthun in 16:39–42. Clearly priestly rank is not among the Chronicler's central issues.

This non-emphatic acknowledgment of the superior status of the priests characterizes the whole Chronicler's history. Only where the narrative deals with duties reserved for the priests does the relative superiority of priests over Levites come to expression, as in 1 Chr 23:24–32 ("their duty shall be to assist the sons of Aaron," v. 28) and in 2 Chr 5:2–13, where the Levites carry the ark up to its final abiding place in the temple, but must defer to the priests who actually bring it into the inner sanctuary.

The second aspect of the Chronicler's treatment of sacerdotal orders is much more emphatic and central, and involves an explicit posture of advocacy. The Chronicler is fond of seizing opportunities to extol the virtues of the Levites. Both in war with foreign nations (2 Chr 20:19–23), and in revolt against the wicked Athaliah (2 Chronicles 23), the Levites play a central role in achieving victory. In the temple cleansing/restoration of both Hezekiah and Josiah, the Levites occupy center stage (2 Chr 29:5–36 and 34:8–14). At the culmination of the Josianic restoration, the Chroni-

---

4. See the passages listed in n. 3 above.

cler adds a note in no explicit way required by the narrative: "For the Levites were more upright in heart than the priests in sanctifying themselves" (2 Chr 29:34b). Equally noteworthy is the omission of reference to the Levites in an indictment connected with the fall of Judah to the Babylonians: "All the leading priests and the people likewise were exceedingly unfaithful . . ." (2 Chr 36:14).

The extravagant, enthusiastic attention given to the Levites in the original narrative in 1 Chronicles 15–16 is thus perfectly congruous with the Chronicler's history as a whole. While the *de facto* superior status of the priests is not denied, the most significant action revolves around the Levites. They are the ones the Chronicler seems excited about. What situation is thereby reflected?

Any attempt to answer this question involves speculation. Here is mine. The original Chronicler wrote his history during the period of the temple rebuilding under Zerubbabel and Jeshua. Indeed, as F. M. Cross has suggested, his work was motivated by propagandistic intent.[5] There are certain aspects of the temple-rebuilding program that would have been accepted by all involved in the restoration: a Davidic prince was the natural civil leader for the restoration of the temple and nation. And that central sacrificial priestly duties belonged to the Zadokites was hard to dispute for all but dissident groups. What was anything but clear, however, was the relation to the Levites to the temple-rebuilding program. Evidence of that unclarity is to be found in the literature of the time. I have argued elsewhere that Levites joined with other dissidents in raising fundamental questions about the temple project, questions such as those found in Isa 66:1–5.[6] Judging from the downplaying of eschatological motifs in the Chronicler, we can assume that he would not have been pleased with Haggai's exuberant description of Zerubbabel in "messianic" terms. He would have been even less pleased with the scathing Zadokite reply to Levitical criticism found in Ezek 44:10–31; indeed the contrast between the alleged apostasy of the Levites and the unblemished holiness of the priests seems to be refuted explicitly by 2 Chr 29:34: "For the Levites were more upright in heart than the priests in sanctifying themselves" (cf. also 2 Chr 36:14). As a monumental effort to bring reconciliation into a community threatening to destroy itself through bitter infighting, the Chronicler composed a history that acknowledged the role of Davidic prince and Zadokite priesthood, but above all demonstrated the important role that was to be accorded to the threatened Levitical families in the restored temple cult and community. 1 Chronicles 15–16 serve as clear illustration of the Chronicler's intent.

---

5. F. M. Cross, "A Reconstruction of the Judean Restoration," *JBL* 94 (1975) 4–18 (repr. in *Interpretation* 29 [1975] 187–203), who cites the earlier study of D. N. Freedman, "The Chronicler's Purpose," *CBQ* 23 (1961) 436–42.

6. P. D. Hanson, *The Dawn of Apocalyptic* (2d ed.; Philadelphia, 1979).

Elsewhere in the Chronicler's history, other specific problems relating to the Levites received attention. In spite of legal provision having been made for the physical needs of the Levites (e.g, Num 18:21–32), Neh 13:10 illustrates the precariousness of the Levites' situation down through the fifth century. And it may be that that period was fairly typical of the early Second Temple period in that no help was forthcoming from the temple priests (the high priest Eliashib turned the temple chamber designated as the storeroom for the Levitical tithe into a living quarters for Tobiad!). It is therefore no accident that the Chronicler sets the righteous king Hezekiah alongside David, Jehosephat, and Josiah as a champion of the Levitical cause, as he tells how Hezekiah reestablished the portion committed to the support of the Levites (2 Chr 31:4–19). The lesson seems clear: in the new kingdom, it would be one of the responsibilities of the Davidic prince to assure fair treatment of the Levites.

If the period of temple building serves as a plausible setting for the original version of the Chronicler's history, and more specifically of the original stratum in 1 Chronicles 15 and 16, what setting might be proposed for the elaborations found in 1 Chr 15:4–10 and 15:16–24? I have suggested that these sections reflect a situation of instability among various Levitical families, and the efforts of such families to secure their positions within the temple cult. In contrast to the form of Ezekiel that was handed down to them (including the ruthless condemnation of the Levites in chap. 44), the Chronicler's history was a powerful ally in the struggles of such threatened families to regain a secure position within the temple structures. It is not surprising that they preserved it, adding material where they saw fit.

We can glimpse the situation they were facing with the help of the Book of Malachi and parts of Ezra and Nehemiah.[7] Malachi portrays both a corrupt, unfaithful Zadokite priesthood and a severe Levitical protest.[8] That the Levites were not ingratiated in the eyes of the Zadokites by such a bitter polemic is obvious. A persisting problem may have been depleted numbers. Ezra 2:36–58 suggests that in contrast to a massive return of priests, the number of Levites and temple servants was small, a problem persisting down to the time of Ezra (Ezra 8:15–20). If I am correct in detecting infighting with regard to rank in the rearrangements in the order of listing the Levitical families found in 1 Chronicles 15–16, and in the case of Obededom and Jeiel even disputes with regard to responsibilities (and it would be a strange circumstance indeed if we found a biblical era in which priests were not infighting), then the plight of the Levites was further exacerbated by the factiousness of the individual Levitical families.

---

7. See P. D. Hanson, "Israelite Religion in the Early Postexilic Period," in *Ancient Israelite Religion: Essays in Honor of Frank Moore Cross* (ed. P. D. Miller Jr., P. D. Hanson, and S. D. McBride Jr.; Philadelphia, 1987) 485–508.

8. See P. D. Hanson, "Malachi," in *Harper's Bible Commentary* (ed. J. L. Mays; San Francisco, 1988) 753–56.

That the careful ordering of Levitical families according to lineage and the equally careful assignment of duties such as we find in 1 Chronicles 15–16 and other parts of this history (especially the genealogies at the beginning of the work) ameliorated the situation in which the Levites found themselves in the early Second Temple period seems likely. At any rate, the effort put forth by the original Chronicler and to a lesser extent by the hand or hands that added to it must be viewed as an ingenious and noble attempt at reconciliation within the early Second Temple Jewish community.

THE ISRAELITE LEGAL AND SOCIAL REALITY AS REFLECTED IN CHRONICLES: A CASE STUDY

Sara Japhet

The legal reality assumed or reflected in Chronicles has attracted the attention of Scripture scholars since the early stages of biblical criticism, the focus being exclusively on the various aspects of the cult. At the outset, this study was motivated by the main driving force of biblical scholarship at that time—the investigation of the history of the Pentateuch. The analysis of the legal strata which informed the description of religious institutions in Chronicles was to contribute to the reconstruction of the history of the Pentateuch and of the Israelite cult.[1]

The interest of the present study lies neither in the literature on which the Chronicler draws, nor in the cult, but rather in the actual social and legal reality as reflected in Chronicles.[2] Here the path of research is fraught with difficulties, including the many preliminary questions of a literary and historical nature which attend any study of biblical historiography, Chronicles in particular.[3] I will limit myself to one rather neglected passage, 1 Chr 2:34-41:

> Now Sheshan had no sons, only daughters; but Sheshan had an Egyptian slave, whose name was Jarha. So Sheshan gave his daughter in marriage to Jarha his slave; and she bore him Attai. Attai was the father of Nathan and

---

1. Cf. S. Japhet, "The Historical Reliability of Chronicles—The History of the Problem and Its Place in Biblical Research," *JSOT* 33 (1985) 83–88.
2. Very few studies have actually taken this direction. Cf. J. P. Weinberg, "Die Zociale Gruppe im Weltbild des Chronisten," *ZAW* 98 (1986) 72–95; idem, "Das *bēit ʾābōt* in 6-4. Jh. v.u.Z.," *VT* 23 (1973) 400–414.
3. These relate to composition, date, sources, and reliability. In the present context I will refer briefly to relevant aspects of the discussion, but refrain from dealing with the general issues, for which the reader may consult introductions to the Old Testament and commentaries on Chronicles. Cf. also n. 1.

Nathan of Zabad. Zabad was the father of Ephlal and Ephlal of Obed. Obed was the father of Jehu and Jehu of Azariah. Azariah was the father of Sismai and Sismai of Shallum. Shallum was the father of Jekamiah and Jekamiah of Elishama.

Literary Context

A superficial reading of 1 Chronicles 2 suffices to show that vv. 34–41 constitute an independent unit, loosely tied to the broader context. In spite of the ongoing debate regarding the structure, composition, and sources of chap. 2,[4] the relatedness of vv. 25–33 (referring to Jerahmeel) to vv. 42–50a (referring to Caleb) is not questioned. The two passages are often regarded as a continuous composition by the same author.[5] Verses 34–41, which have been interpolated into the original sequence, form an independent, self-contained unit.

Yet, the cause of this interpolation is also obvious: the appearance of Sheshan, a name found nowhere else in the Bible, denoting in this context both a descendant of Jerahmeel (v. 31) and the protagonist of vv. 34–35.[6] The juxtaposition of these two verses immediately creates a contradiction: the reference to "the sons of Sheshan," of whom one is explicitly named in v. 31, cannot be reconciled with the statement of v. 34, "Sheshan had no sons, only daughters." A common means of settling this contradiction is to interpret v. 31 in the light of v. 34, taking Ahlai to be a female name, with "the sons of" having the general connotation of "descendants,"[7] or presuming that Ahlai died childless during his father's lifetime.[8] However, harmonization is not really necessary, as the difficulty is more apparent than real. Each passage represents different presuppositions and objectives, and thus the same name represents different entities, with different roles. In the

---

4. Cf., among others, H. G. M. Williamson, "Sources and Redaction in the Chronicler's Genealogy of Judah," *JBL* 98 (1979) 351–59; and S. Japhet, *The Books of Chronicles* (OTL; forthcoming).

5. Within the broader context of genealogical lists, these passages display a single genre, uniformity of structure, similarity of subject matter, presuppositions, and phraseology, and are expressly linked by the reference in v. 42: "Caleb the brother of Jerahmeel." Compare the parallel introduction: "the sons of Jerahmeel" (v. 25) and "the sons of Caleb" (v. 42); and the parallel conclusions: "these were the descendants of Jerahmeel" (v. 33) and "these were the descendants of Caleb" (v. 50a). Compare also the structure of the introductory verses, where some identifying comment accompanies the clan's eponym: "Jerahmeel, the first born of Hezron" (v. 25) and "Caleb, the brother of Jerahmeel" (v. 42).

6. Regarding the name, cf. M. Noth, *Die israelitischen Personennamen im Rahmen der gemeinsemitischen Namengebung* (Stuttgart, 1928) 41; H. L. Ginsberg and B. Maisler regard the name as of Hurrite origin; "Semitised Ḫurrians in Syria and Palestine," *Journal of the Palestine Oriental Society* 14 (1934) 263–64.

7. Cf. E. L. Curtis and A. A. Madsen, *A Critical and Exegetical Commentary on the Books of Chronicles* (ICC; Edinburgh, 1910) 94.

8. Cf. Pseudo-Rashi and D. Kimhi on 2:34. Also, S. Yeivin, "Judah," *Encyclopaedia Biblica* (Jerusalem, 1958), 3:491–93 [Hebrew].

genealogy of the Jerahmeelites (vv. 25-33), a conventional ethnic/tribal document portraying relationships and developments within the ethnosocial group in terms of family ramifications,[9] Sheshan and Ahlai represent family units. References to "father" and "son" indicate that an original group has branched, the younger element assuming a new name.[10] Sheshan of vv. 34-35 is an individual who is seen to have belonged to the family unit of the same name. The family tree of this individual in vv. 34-41 may be related to the tribal genealogy, but is not part of it. It is taken from another source and has an altogether different purpose.[11]

Historical and Chronological Context

From a literary point of view, vv. 34-41 form a composite unit; the narrative section of vv. 34-35 combines with the genealogical list of vv. 36-41 to introduce the pedigree of one Elishama the son of Jekamiah, the last name in the line. The story implies that Elishama's legitimate descent from Sheshan was questioned, either because of his recognized Egyptian affiliation or because of the common knowledge that "Sheshan had no sons, only daughters." It is the purpose of the introductory story to account for Elishama's unusual ancestry.

While the text does not reveal any details regarding this Elishama or his time—the name itself is very common in biblical and extra-biblical onomastica—the elaborate genealogy may in fact point to distinction and social prominence.[12] One should note that such pedigrees are not too

9. This genre is well attested in the Bible, mainly in the Pentateuch and the introductory chapters of Chronicles. Cf. J. Liver, "*Jaḥas* [Genealogy]," *Encyclopaedia Biblica* (Jerusalem, 1958), 3:663-71 [Hebrew]; M. D. Johnson, *The Purpose of Biblical Genealogies* (Society for New Testament Studies Monograph Series 8; Cambridge, 1969); R. R. Wilson, *Genealogy and History in the Biblical World* (New Haven, 1977).

10. According to this passage, the patriarchal system of Jerahmeel comprises twenty-four subunits, divided into two branches: a more ancient group, affiliated with Jerahmeel's first wife, comprising eight units (Ram, Bunah, Oren, Ozem, Ahijah, Maaz, Jamin, Eker), and a younger group, the offspring of Jerahmeel and a foreign element ("another wife"), a group which eventually became the stronger element in the tribe (Onam, Jada, Shamai, Nadab, Abishur, Ahban, Molid, Appaim, Seled, Ishi, Sheshan, Ahlai, Jether, Jonathan, Peleth, Zaza); with the extinction of Seled and Jether, these sixteen units were eventually reduced to fourteen. Neither the total number nor the proportions seem to be coincidental.

11. Cf. W. F. Aufrecht, "Genealogy and History in Ancient Israel," *Ascribe to the Lord: Biblical and Other Studies in Memory of Peter C. Craigie* (JSOTSup 67; Sheffield, 1988) 205-35. Several scholars regard vv. 34-41 as a later gloss, assuming that the "contradiction" necessarily indicates different authors (cf. W. Rudolph, *Chronikbücher* [HAT; Tübingen, 1955] 19-20, following earlier commentators). I see no reason, however, why the Chronicler himself could not have realized this double function of the passages. One may better understand the chapter if one posits an intentional interpolation at this point.

12. Early rabbinic literature identified Elishama with the grandfather of "Ishmael the son of Nethaniah," who killed Gedaliah the son of Ahikam (2 Kgs 25:25, Jer 41:1ff.; *y. Hor.* 3:14), an identification followed by some modern scholars. G. Richter identifies him with the scribe

common in the Chronicler's genealogical introduction; identical structure and formulaic language are attested only in the parallel lists of David and the high priests (1 Chr 2:10–17, 6:4–14 [MT 5:30–40]), while different formulations are employed for the list of the Judean kings, the three founding fathers of the Levitical singers, and the Saulides (1 Chr 3:10–16, 6:33–47) [MT 6:18–32], 8:33–40, 9:39–44). Shorter, less strictly formulaic registrations are found occasionally in other tribes. This passage is thus an elaborate attempt to consolidate Elishama's position by connecting him to an established, ancient Judahite family. As for Elishama's period, some hints may be gleaned (with all due caution, of course) from the passage itself and the broader Chronistic context. At this point a preliminary remark is indicated. The material under consideration, with its highly conventional and standardized formulas, requires that one distinguish clearly between conventional and historical elements. While the details of the family tree, the number of listed generations, the names, and even the very point of departure may all express conventional patterns (and may or may not contain historical elements), two aspects of the list represent firm historical fact: the person Elishama living sometime during the history of Israel, and the presuppositions underlying the conventional patterns. The study of these conventional structures may reveal the author's view of the list's time, provenance, and objectives, linked with the person Elishama.

The list registers fifteen generations between Sheshan and his late descendant, Elishama, according to biblical conventions a chronological distance of about three hundred years. The crucial point is, therefore, to establish a chronological focus for Sheshan himself. Here one may turn to the more general Chronistic context, discerning carefully between "objective" historical truth, which is not an issue here, and the Chronicler's historical presuppositions.

According to chap. 2 as a whole, Sheshan represents the tenth generation from Jacob's son Judah[13]—a schematic position fully parallel in the genealogy of David, whose father Jesse is also the tenth generation from Judah.[14] This, then, is the Chronistic historical view, expressed by conventional patterns in these introductory genealogical tables: the passage of ten generations between the twelve sons of Jacob and David's era. Indeed, one of the major objectives of this introduction seems to be to draw a "genealogical portrait" of a complete system of tribal family units of the time of

---

of Jehoiakim (Jer 36:12, 20–21; cf. "Untersuchungen zu den Geschlechtsregistern der Chronik," *ZAW* 34 [1914] 123–24), while others regard him a contemporary of the Chronicler (Curtis and Madsen, *Books of Chronicles*, 95) or even later (Rudolph, *Chronikbücher*, 18).

13. Sheshan's line may be traced as follows: Judah – Perez – Hezron – Jerahmeel – Onam – Shamai – Nadab – Appaim – Ishi – Sheshan (1 Chr 2:3–5, 9, 25–31).

14. David's line may be traced as follows: Judah – Perez – Hezron – Ram – Amminadab – Nahson – Salma – Boaz – Obed – Jesse – David (1 Chr 2:3–5, 9–15). For the method of this structure, cf. Japhet, *Books of Chronicles*, forthcoming.

David, as a necessary introduction to the history of Israel, beginning with David.[15] Forging a link between vv. 34-41 and the preceding passages provides the essential integration of Elishama's family tree. With fifteen generations from David, one is brought to the end of the monarchic period, noting that fifteen ruling monarchs have been enumerated between David and Josiah in the stereotypical list of 1 Chr 3:10-14. One wonders which of the persons whose seals have been recently uncovered might represent "Elishama the son of Jekamiah" of this passage.[16] Was he one of the leaders of "the people of the land," representing the ancient tribe of Jerahmeel, the "governor of the house of Judah" (2 Chr 19:11), the person "at the king's hand, in all matters concerning the people" (Neh 11:24), or any other dignitary of the time? A decision on this matter must await more solid information.

Sociological Context

The etiological story of vv. 34-35 is subservient to the list, providing an explanation for the unexpected continuation of Sheshan's line. It therefore must be based, as even the most skeptical will not deny, on valid social conventions, even if the genealogy itself may be approached with various degrees of suspicion or credence.[17] The very function and value of the family tree for the claimant depend on the fact that it reflects rules and customs recognized by the contemporary reader as valid. Any falsification of sociological assumptions would run counter to the list's *raison d'être* and render it useless. Thus, although the protagonists of the little story cannot be identified, and although Sheshan, his daughter, the Egyptian slave Jarha, and the son Attai may all be fictitious, the set of relationships assumed between them, with their social and juridical basis and function, are all valid. This is the social and legal reality to which I now turn.

---

15. S. Japhet, *The Ideology of the Book of Chronicles and its Place in Biblical Thought* (trans. A. Barber; Frankfurt/Bern, 1989) 278-79, 360-61.

16. Among the bullas published recently by N. Avigad and ascribed by him to the time of Jeremiah, there are several bearing the name Elishama; see *Hebrew Bullae from the Time of Jeremiah* (Jerusalem, 1986) nos. 4, 66, 158-60. Bulla No. 4 actually belongs to "Elishama, the king's servant." No. 75 is the bulla of "Jekamiah the son of Meshulam," while in 1 Chronicles 2 Elishama's father is presented as "Jekamiah the son of Shallum." The interchangeability of Meshulam and Shallum is attested by 1 Chr 9:17 and Neh 12:25; it would not be too far-fetched to identify these names with this text. Bullas 158-60 are the seals of one "Shallum the son of Elishama" who does not really belong to the list but may be related to it.

17. Richter advocates the list's "precision and detail" ("Untersuchungen zu den Geschlechtsregistern," 123), and Curtis and Madsen suggest that "there is nothing in the character of the names given against the genealogy being genuine" (*Books of Chronicles*, 95). A. B. Ehrlich identifies the third and fourth generations—Nathan and Zabad (vs. 36)—with "Zabud the son of Nathan" of Solomon's time (1 Kgs 4:5), identifying Nathan as David's prophet; cf. *Mikrâ ki-Pheschutô* (Berlin, 1899-1901; repr. New York, 1969), 3:276, 431-32.

The Social Problem: Survival Through "Name"

The story's point of departure is established by the introductory statement: "Now Sheshan had no sons, only daughters" (v. 34). The problem which confronts Sheshan is the future existence of his "name," denoting in concrete sociological terms the preservation of his family as a living, functioning reality, with full membership and property rights within the tribe, and thus within the broader framework of the people. Only one other case in the Bible shares this point of departure: the well-known story of the daughters of Zelophehad (Numbers 27, 36; Josh 17:3-6), which unfolds from the very same statement: "Now Zelophehad... had no sons, but daughters" (Num 26:33).[18] It is in this story that the common problem of Zelophehad and Sheshan is clearly expressed: "Why should the name of our father be taken away[19] from his family, because he had no sons?" (Num 27:4). Within the context of Numbers 26-27, the establishment of a "name" determines the allocation of "inheritance" among the Israelite tribes, that is, the social unit's property rights: "To these the land shall be divided for inheritance according to the number of names" (Num 26:53). Property, however, while forming the necessary basis of social existence, does not exhaust its implications. A "name" effected the actual social power of a unit, its privileges, and obligations.[20] One may say that as far as tribal society is concerned, the whole system of social controls and balances was dependent on the preservation of these small units, represented by "names."

It is no wonder, then, that Israelite society invested great effort to secure this balance. In the more specific context under consideration, the best known means is levirate marriage, devised to ensure "that his name may not be blotted out of Israel" (Deut 25:6). However, even were it consistently applied[21] levirate marriage would provide only limited remedy for very specific situations; more common problems are left unattended in biblical traditions and legislature. Generally speaking, the major risk threatening a man's name is his own sterility—a possibility which is never

---

18. Cf. K. D. Sakenfeld, "Zelophehad's Daughters," *Perspectives in Religious Studies* 15 (1988) 37-47; idem, "In the Wilderness Awaiting the Land: The Daughters of Zelophehad and Feminist Interpretation," *Princeton Seminary Bulletin* 9 (1988) 179-96.

19. NJPSV renders Hebrew יגרע as "be lost to his clan." Cf. *Thesaurus of the Language of the Bible* (Jerusalem, 1959) 251: subtract, eliminate.

20. The precise establishment of these "families" and "fathers' houses" is the purpose of the census (cf. Numbers 1, 3, 26), upon which all matters, secular and ritual, are then based. Cf. G. E. Mendenhall, "The Census Lists of Numbers 1 and 26," *JBL* 77 (1958) 52-66. Traces of such a census are to be found also in the genealogical material of Chronicles; cf. J. Liver, "So All Israel Was Enrolled by Genealogies; and These Are Written in the Book of the Kings of Israel," in עז לדוד (David Ben Gurion FS; Jerusalem, 1964) 486-99; Johnson, *Purpose of Biblical Genealogies*, 62-68.

21. This is very doubtful, as already in the Bible its abolition is provided for; cf. Deut 25:5-10, Genesis 38, and Ruth 4.

brought up explicitly in biblical evidence.²² Only temporary or conditional male unproductivity is actually assumed, as when a premature death prevents his procreation.²³ All actual cases of childlessness are ascribed to female barrenness,²⁴ which in a polygamic society does not have conclusive effects on the continuity of the social unit. As male unproductivity is not really recognized, no remedy for it is provided.

This story shares the same anthropological and social assumptions as the Zelophehad pericope. Although neither male nor female are infertile, the family line is not ensured—since all the offspring are daughters. That the biological cause—now commonplace—rests with the male is indeed recognized in this story: Sheshan does not take another wife, but appoints a male replacement as procreator. However, even faced with the risk of utter loss of a family's name, the Bible does not provide any structured remedy for either case. Biblical anthropology did not acknowledge any flaws in the male procreative system.

In contrast to biblical law, the legal systems of other ancient Near Eastern civilizations provided adequate solutions for such situations, conceived under the general roof of "adoption." Best known are the texts from Nuzi which have been amply discussed in connection with the patriarchal narratives,²⁵ but the subject is of much broader scope.²⁶ In these extra-biblical systems one finds not only straightforward adoption, but also the formal procedure for transactions of property, as well as the case most similar to this context: "adoption" for the purpose of marriage, where an "adopted" son marries his "father's" daughter.²⁷

The concept of adoption is not employed in biblical law, and scholars still debate its practical application in ancient Israelite society. Several cases in the biblical narrative, in particular the Jacob-Laban cycle, have

---

22. The adjective "barren" appears frequently in the feminine (Gen 11:30, 25:21, 29:33; Judg 13:2; etc.) but only once in the masculine, as part of a general blessing (Deut 7:14). The cause of unproductivity is explicitly described in Gen 20:18 as "the Lord closed the wombs of the house of Abimelech"; also Gen 16:2, 1 Sam 1:5, Prov 30:16.

23. This is certainly the case with Judah's sons (Gen 38:7-10) and Naomi's two sons (Ruth 1:4)—the two cases where some kind of levirate marriage is indicated. This would probably be the case also in Deut 25:5.

24. As in the famous cases of Sarai, Rebekah, Rachel, Manoah's wife, and Hannah (Gen 11:30, 25:21, 29:31; Judg 13:2; 1 Sam 1:2, 11).

25. Cf., among others, E. A. Speiser, "New Kirkuk Documents Relating to Family Laws," *Annual of the American Schools of Oriental Research* 10 (1928-29) 21-22, 31-33; J. S. Paradise, *Nuzi Inheritance Practices* (Thesis, University of Pennsylvania, 1972) 41-47, 303-8; also, differently, J. Van Seters, "Jacob's Marriage and Ancient Near Eastern Customs: A Re-examination," *HTR* 62 (1969) 377-95.

26. Cf. M. David, "Adoption," *RLA* 1 (1932) 37-39.

27. For these cf. E. Neufeld, *Hebrew Marriage Laws* (London, 1944) 56ff. Neufeld regards the case of Sheshan and Jarha as belonging to this category (p. 58), but the meager evidence does not support this conclusion.

been interpreted as reflecting adoption procedures, while several phrases and metaphors—in particular in the framework of God's relationship with the Davidic king—may indicate that the notion itself was not unknown.[28] However, even where the echoes are strongest, one finds no reference to this institution, and the term itself is absent from the biblical lexicon.[29] The solution applied by Sheshan, unique in biblical literature,[30] is found not in the context of "adoption" but in that of slavery laws and customs.

The Legal Solution: Application of Slavery Laws

Sheshan's actions are presented succinctly: having sired only daughters, he marries one of his daughters to his slave; the son born of this marriage is "his," that is, Sheshan's.

No comprehensive slavery law is extant in the Bible, nor any systematic presentation of definitions, modes of acquisition, rights and obligations of the parties, and the like. Yet, each of the main legal corpora in the Pentateuch contains a version of a manumission law,[31] and there are also several regulations pertaining to slaves in the context of other legal sections.[32] Since this story does not belong to any of these categories, my conclusions must be drawn by inference from the material at hand.

Biblical legislation treated the problem of a slave's children as a particular aspect of manumission; it is referred to in two of the three versions of the law, but omitted in Deut 15:12-18.

Exod 21:3-4 establishes, in casuistic detail, the principle that a slave should leave his master's household in the same condition that he entered it. This principle is illustrated by three different cases: "if he comes in single, he shall go out single" (v. 3a); "if he comes in married, then his wife shall go out with him" (v. 3b); and "if his master gives him a wife and she bears him sons or daughters, the wife and her children shall be her master's, and he shall go out alone" (v. 4). These three possibilities are not exhaustive, nor is there a full balance between the opposing situations;[33] neverthe-

---

28. For a detailed list of all these, cf. J. H. Tigay, "Adoption," *EncJud* 2:298-301.

29. Most interestingly, this is followed in post-biblical Jewish law, where "adoption is not known as a legal institution in Jewish law" (B. Scherschewski, "Adoption," *EncJud* 2:301).

30. The case of Zelophehad's daughters, although having a similar point of departure, has different objectives and implications. Its focal point is the problem of property rights, while the issue of "name" (in this case, of "title") as such, is not really attended to, either in Numbers 27 or in Numbers 36. Cf. Sakenfeld, "Zelophehad's Daughters."

31. Exod 21:2-11, Lev 25:39-54, Deut 15:12-18. For their relationship, cf. S. Japhet, "The Relationship between the Legal Corpora in the Pentateuch in Light of Manumission Laws," in *Studies in the Bible* (ed. S. Japhet; ScrHier 31; Jerusalem, 1986) 63-89.

32. For their listing and analysis, cf. S. Cardellini, *Die biblischen Sklaven-Gesetze im Lichte des keilinschriftlichen Sklavenrechts* (Bonn, 1981) 237ff.

33. A full opposition requires three more clauses: a reference to children—either coming in with their father or born to him during his slavery—in the first instance; a reference to a

less, the structure of the passage permits the clear inference that children born to a slave by a wife given him by his master are his master's, and remain so even if the slave regains his freedom and leaves his master's house.

Although the law is here specifically articulated in the context of manumission, it seems to derive from a more general principle, namely, that whatever a slave acquires during his term of slavery and through his master's intervention is the master's. Although this restricts the slave's control over his family, it also imposes certain limitations on the master's power over the slave's property: not all that a slave owns belongs to his master, but only that which he acquired during his slavery.

Exod 21:2-6 deals exclusively with a "Hebrew slave." Scholarly opinion is greatly divided on the meaning of this term, proposals ranging from the ethnic connotation, viewing "Hebrew" as a synonym of "Israelite," to a distinctly social connotation, deriving "Hebrew" from "Habiru." One finds also a combination view, regarding the origin of the term in the social context, but seeing its application in Exod 21:2 as ethnic.[34] Whatever the meaning of the term, it is clear that the specific law is confined exclusively to one category of slaves—the "Hebrew." It is, however, both possible and justified to infer that the rules concerning a slave's children had broader validity and applicability.[35] Following this reasoning, a general ruling may be formulated: a slave's offspring (or any property) born (or acquired) during his term of slavery (naturally, by a wife given to him by his master) are the master's. This is the background against which Sheshan's actions should be considered, in both the common and divergent aspects of the case.

Exod 21:4 does not give the wife's or her children's identity and status, but a reasonable assumption would be that she was a maid and her children were what the Bible designates as "house born."[36] Other possibilities, however, need not be ruled out; the one illustrated by the case of Sheshan is the marriage of a slave to his master's daughter. The context does not specify whether such a marriage involves a change in the slave's status,[37] but it is clear that the child born of this marriage is a free person,

---

wife only, in the second. It seems that the present structure is motivated by rhetorical considerations, putting the emphasis on the explicit statement of v. 4.

34. Cf. N. P. Lemche, "The 'Hebrew Slave,'" *VT* 25 (1975) 129-44; versus E. Lipiński, "L'esclave Hebreu,'" *VT* 26 (1976) 120-23; cf. recently O. Loretz, *Habiru-Hebräer* (BZAW 160; Berlin, 1984).

35. Cf. Ehrlich, *Mikrâ ki-Pheschutô*, 3:431-32.

36. יליד בית in Gen 17:12-13, 23, 27; Lev 22:11; Jer 2:14.

37. Post-biblical Judaism took it for granted that the slave has been manumitted (and converted). This assumption is best expressed by the popular saying, common in Jerusalem: בתך בגרה שחרר עבדך ותן לה, 'If your daughter has attained puberty, free your slave and give him to her' (*b. Pesaḥ.* 113a). Neufeld assumes that the slave was adopted (*Hebrew Marriage*

who is to carry on the master's name and inherit his property. The story formulates this fact in the simplest way: "And she bore him [i.e., to Sheshan] Attai."

The Legal Context: Exodus 21:2–6 or Leviticus 25:39–54?

One aspect of the story has so far not figured in my discussion—the narrative's emphasis on the ethnic identity of the slave, both in the explicit adjective "Egyptian," and in the proper name "Jarha," immediately recognizable as foreign.[38] These details are not coincidental, nor should they be ascribed to merely literary or theological motives; rather, in view of the passage's extreme economy of detail and its socio/legal orientation, they should be regarded as of necessary legal significance. The slave's non-Israelite origin is an essential condition for Sheshan's plan, an aspect which should qualify more precisely the socio/legal situation.

While Exod 21:2–6 is confined to a "Hebrew slave," Lev 25:39–54 establishes a categorical and systematic differentiation between Israelites and non-Israelites in all relevant situations of slave holding. As the manumission of slaves is presented from the master's point of view, the two masters are differentiated first: an Israelite master (vv. 39–46) and a non-Israelite one (vv. 47–54). Beginning with the Israelite master, a further distinction is made between the two categories of slaves, an Israelite (vv. 39–43) and a non-Israelite (vv. 44–46). In the case of a non-Israelite master, however, the law is cited only for an Israelite slave (vv. 47–54); the fourth possible situation—a non-Israelite slave serving a non-Israelite master—is omitted. In each of these oppositions there is a clear preference for the Israelite vis-à-vis his non-Israelite counterpart, whether slave or master.[39]

Two points of this legislation are significant for the present discussion: the application of ethnic identity as a factor in the context of slavery laws, and the precise legal definitions of the slaves' status. The social class of "slaves" is thus conceived as comprising two subclasses, each with its peculiar definitions and rulings. An Israelite sold to a master—any master—is not a slave but a "hired worker," the laws pertaining to him in any other realm would be those of the free man, the citizen:[40] "He shall be with

---

Laws); while Tigay takes the rabbinical view as self-evident: "Since the slave ... married his master's daughter, he was certainly manumitted and, quite likely, was adopted by his master" ("Adoption," 300).

38. Hebrew ירחע. The name has not yet been attested in the Egyptian onomasticon, but the un-Hebrew combination of consonants עח is very common in Egyptian; cf. M. Broshi, "Jarha," *Encyclopaedia Biblica* (Jerusalem, 1958), 3:863 [Hebrew].

39. Japhet, "Manumission Laws," 76–80.

40. This attitude is followed very consistently by post-biblical exegesis, which equates the Hebrew/Israelite slave with his free brother, interpreting all the different rulings (Exod 21:26–27; 32; etc.) as referring exclusively to the non-Israelite. Cf. *Mek. de Rabbi Ishmael*, Tractate *Neziqin*.

you as a hired servant [שכיר] and as a sojourner" (Lev 25:40); "as a servant hired year by year shall he be with him" (Lev 25:53). When the time comes for the slave to leave his master's house, all his family goes with him, to reclaim their family property: "Then he shall go out from you, he and his children with him" (Lev 25:41). In explicit contrast to the Israelite, a non-Israelite slave is never set free. Here the definition of a slave as his master's property is given in the full sense of the term: "And they may be your property; you may bequeath them to your sons after you, to inherit as a possession forever; you may make slaves of them" (Lev 25:45-46).

Taking Lev 25:39-54 as a frame of reference, we see that the plan conceived by Sheshan could be executed *only* by a slave who was non-Israelite. If he were an Israelite, no matter how distant his liberation would be, his children would be his own and bear his name—as would the children of any free citizen.

I may sum up this aspect of the discussion as follows: If the story is seen in the context of Exod 21:2-6, the identity of the slave would be immaterial, for Sheshan's steps would achieve their desired result no matter who the slave was. According to Exod 21:2-6, *even* a Hebrew slave, with the most favorable manumission regulations, leaves his master's house without his new family. The slave being an "Egyptian" would then be an incidental detail. If, however, we regard this detail as essential, it is only in the context of Leviticus 25 that Sheshan's plan has any meaning. Precisely *because* the slave is non-Israelite can Sheshan perpetuate through him his line and name.

I stated at the beginning of my discussion that Elishama's family tree must be based on *valid social conventions*. Thus, for the purpose of studying these conventions, this passage is an "unprejudiced witness," an unbiased reflection of social and legal reality. To the extent that it reflects the social assumptions of Exod 21:2-6 and Lev 25:39-54, these are to be appreciated as thoroughly valid reflections of a specific, patriarchal system of Israelite society.

Further Sociological and Theological Implications

Might this story, "unbiased" as it is, have further implications? Two points are of particular interest: from a sociological point of view, one wonders at the matter-of-fact record of a marriage between a free woman and a slave. Like many surrounding Near Eastern civilizations, ancient Israelite society accepted as standard procedure that a free man could take a slave girl as a (secondary) wife; this is attested most clearly by the patriarchal narratives[41] and the law of Exod 21:7-11. The opposite, however, is not the case: no

---

41. For example, the famous cases of Abraham taking Hagar, and Jacob taking Bilha and Zilpah as secondary wives. In these cases, however, it is the main wife's initiative, who "gave her to . . . her husband as a wife" (Gen 16:3; 30:3-4, 9).

other instance of a free woman being given in marriage to a slave is attested in the Bible.[42] This is no simple discrimination, and the causes of the phenomenon must be sought in the socioeconomic structure and values of Israelite society, a task which is beyond the scope of the present study. Obviously, however, it should be indicated that in Israel the polygamous system was—as in many other civilizations—unilateral, sanctioning plurality of wives but not of husbands. There was thus an essential difference between a man marrying a slave girl and a free woman being married to a slave. Indeed, post-biblical Judaism did not recognize the possibility suggested by this episode, and assumed as a matter of fact that the slave had been duly manumitted.[43] While this interpretation reflects well the problematics of the situation as well as later attitudes, it cannot be regarded as the plain sense of this text; the very fact that Jarha is a slave makes the procedure suggested here socially valid.

Another aspect of sociological and theological interest is the "mixed marriage"—Jarha is not merely a slave but an "Egyptian slave." Here, again, later rabbinic exegesis took it for granted that the slave had converted and become a proselyte (גר), his description as Egyptian referring only to his origin. This is the standard rabbinic interpretation of all Deuteronomic injunctions, where certain people are prohibited from "entering the assembly of the Lord," applying in different degrees to Ammonites, Moabites, Edomites, and Egyptians (Deut 23:4, 8–9). In fact, in the rabbinic view, which tries to reduce the scope of slavery, the two factors came together: a converted slave would become an "Israelite slave" whose manumission would be in the seventh year.[44] Here, again, the text makes no reference to Jarha's conversion; in fact, if my interpretation of the episode is correct, it is precisely his status as non-Israelite which makes the whole transaction possible. The issue of mixed marriage is stated with no hesitation or religious overtones; the acknowledgment of an Egyptian ancestor seems not to detract in any way from the prestige which, no doubt, Elishama's family tree was construed to enhance.

This attitude is very much at variance with the atmosphere prevalent in Deuteronomistic circles and Ezra/Nehemiah,[45] but on the other hand very much in accord with the story of Ruth, and the Book of Chronicles in

---

42. Among the ancient Near Eastern legal traditions, it is known from the Hittites. Cf. Cardellini, *Die biblischen Sklaven-Gesetze*, 146–48.

43. This is assumed by the popular saying quoted in n. 37. Cf. Kimhi *ad loc.*: "And he gave him his daughter after he manumitted him . . . but this is a homiletic interpretation. . . . From this passage they [the Rabbis] learned that: 'If your daughter has attained puberty, free your slave and give her to him.'" Cf. also Pseudo-Rashi, *ad loc.*

44. Cf. *Mek. de Rabbi Ishmael*, tractate *Neziqin* §§1–2. The explicit statement is instructive: "Just as the Israelite serves six [years] so the proselyte should serve six."

45. Cf. Deut 7:3–4; 1 Kgs 11:1–13; Ezra 9–10; Neh 10:31, 13:23–27.

which it is embedded.[46] While the motives of the latter contexts may be different, they share a positive attitude to the phenomenon of mixed marriage. The moving force behind the untiring struggle against mixed marriage may be seen in the *religious factor*, the struggle for maintaining Israel's religious uniqueness in face of all "incitement" and "defilement." This story of marriage to a non-Israelite, by contrast, is anchored in a real-life context, entirely inspired by *social factors*, which extend their influence even to questions of ethnic identity. It is within this social context, with all its norms, objectives, standards, and procedures, that marriage to a non-Israelite slave is to be understood.

46. Cf. Japhet, "Law and 'the Law' in Ezra–Nehemiah," *Proceedings of the Ninth World Congress for Jewish Studies: Panel Sessions, Bible Studies and Ancient Near East* (Jerusalem, 1988) 99–115; idem, *Ideology of the Book of Chronicles*, 334–51.

THE LAW AS CENTER
OF THE HEBREW BIBLE

Otto Kaiser

The Problem of Unity and Redactional Criticism

During the past few decades there has been a lively discussion within the circles of biblical scholars about whether there is a center of the Hebrew Bible. This discussion is not only an academic one but also derives its force from the problem as to whether it is possible to write a theology of the Hebrew Bible as a whole or only of its individual writings and literary layers.[1] No serious scholar will deny the legitimacy of a diachronic approach. But there remains the question as to whether a synchronic approach is also legitimate. This latter would require that there be a "middle" or a central topic and a material principle of the whole. In both respects the theologian need not speculate since the Bible offers its own answer. Its basic topic is that the Lord is the God of Israel and that Canaan is the land of his people.[2] It is this relation which is interpreted by the Law and the Prophets. Furthermore, one has only to observe the organization of the

---

Author's note: This is a reworked paper of that read in May 1987 at the universities of Oxford and Cambridge and at the Leo Baeck College, London. I want to thank E. W. Nicholson, J. A. Emerton, and J. Magonet for their invitation, and their colleagues and students for their stimulating discussion.

1. See the research reports by H. Graf Reventlow, *Hauptprobleme der alttestamentlichen Theologie im 20. Jahrhundert* (Erträge der Forschung 173; Darmstadt, 1982); idem, *Hauptprobleme der biblischen Theologie im 20. Jahrhundert* (Erträge der Forschung 203; Darmstadt, 1983)—both now translated by John Bowden: *Problems of Old Testament Theology in the Twentieth Century* (Philadelphia, 1985), and *Problems of Biblical Theology in the Twentieth Century* (Philadelphia, 1986); J. H. Hayes and F. C. Prussner, *Old Testament Theology: Its History and Development* (Atlanta, 1985); and O. Merk, "Gesamtbiblische Theologie: Zum Fortgang der Diskussion in den 80er Jahren," *Verkündigung und Forschung* 33 (1988) 19–40.

2. I take this opportunity to affirm my consent with the statements of M. Goshen-Gottstein in this regard in a paper on the Jewish approach to Old Testament theology read at Marburg in 1987.

Bible to detect that it is more than an accidental collection of books; indeed, there is a real central idea governing not only the arrangements of the books but also its later redactions. Such observations lead to the canonical approach which has found its zealous advocate in Brevard S. Childs and, in a more restrained form, Ronald C. Clements.³

Despite the danger that this approach might become a new variety of allegory,⁴ one should concede that it provides an important corrective to biblical exegesis which has been heavily influenced by literary criticism and historical exegesis. When adequately used, this approach is nothing else than the last step of literary and redactional criticism. After we have analyzed a book and isolated its literary layers we still have to ask questions about its redactional process and the intentions which shaped the book as a whole.⁵ It is only natural to proceed a step further and inquire into the structure of the whole Bible. Having done this, one may easily conclude that the Law is its center.

The Covenantal Concept as Preaching to the Exiles

Let me then begin by reflecting about whether the *Bundesformel* or covenantal formula is able to serve as a theological middle of the Bible. There is no need to enter here into the discussion on the age of the whole covenantal concept, or of the covenantal formula,⁶ for we are presently interested only in its scope. The exact text of the formula is "I [the LORD] shall be your God, and you shall be my people."⁷ We have only to look at a few references to become aware that the formula covers the whole historical and eschatological dimension of the Bible. In Gen 17:7-8 it indicates the divine election of Israel by the Lord. According to its formulation it is a covenantal promise: It shall be a ברית עולם that the Lord (cf. v. 1) shall be the God of Abraham and his seed, and that he shall give them the land of Canaan as an אחזת עולם 'everlasting possession'. Moreover, the text determines that the מולה 'the circumcision' shall be the sign for the membership of very male to Israel.⁸

If we pass to the end of the Code of Holiness in Lev 26:12, the promise of a peaceful and blessed life in the land (which shall be the consequence of

---

3. See B. S. Childs, *Introduction to the Old Testament as Scripture* (Philadelphia, 1979); R. E. Clements, *Old Testament Theology: A Fresh Approach* (Atlanta, 1978).
4. Cf. J. Barr, *Holy Scripture: Canon, Authority, Criticism* (Philadelphia, 1983) 103-4.
5. See R. Rendtorff, "Zur Komposition des Buches Jesaja," *VT* 34 (1984) 295-320.
6. See the research report by E. W. Nicholson, *God and His People: Covenant and Theology in the Old Testament* (Oxford, 1986) 3-117.
7. See R. Smend, *Die Bundesformel* (Theologische Studien 68; Zurich, 1963); repr. in his *Die Mitte des Alten Testaments: Gesammelte Studien* (Beiträge zur evangelischen Theologie 99; Munich, 1986), 1:11-39.
8. See E. Kutsch, *Verheissung und Gesetz: Untersuchungen zum sogenannten "Bund" im Alten Testament* (BZAW 131; Berlin, 1973) 108-13.

this relation) is made dependent on the fulfillment of the demand to be obedient to the commandments and to keep the covenant. The same observation may be observed from Deut 26:16–19 as well. But before we focus our attention on the central significance of the Law as the true center of the Bible, let me continue my survey of other references of the covenantal formula, as this may provide a solid foundation for my main argument. I choose two references in the Book of Jeremiah. The first demonstrates the basic agreement with those in Leviticus and Deuteronomy. The second draws attention to its eschatological dimension. Jer 7:21–23 contrasts the practice of whole sacrifices and obedience to the word for the Lord. In this context the covenantal formula has the function of reminding the people that the covenantal blessings are dependent on obedience to the Law, as stated in Leviticus 26 and Deuteronomy 28. The formula is by itself a hint that the word of the Lord in v. 23 has to be understood as the word of the תורה. As obedience to the word of the Lord is the presupposition for a peaceful and blessed life, disobedience is the reason for all kinds of misfortune, eventuating in Israel's exile from the land.[9]

During the Exile it became important to explain Israel's deplorable fate as a consequence of its apostasy from the Lord and his covenantal commandments. It was then also necessary to comfort the people with the divine affirmation that the covenantal relation between him and his people was indissoluble. This comfort would give Israel confidence about its future, whereas the explanation of the Exile would serve to exhort the people to return to the Lord and obey his commandments. This has been the reason that the Deuteronomistic and (afterward) the Priestly schools and their successors reinterpreted the whole prior salvation history from the perspective of the central covenantal concept. The preexilic prophets' message of doom became reinterpreted in line with the covenantal curses of Deuteronomy 28 as can be observed in the case of Jeremiah 7, and the prophets themselves became admonishers to observe the word of the Lord (cf. Jer 7:25–26).[10] The people could recognize that the Exile was a consequence of their failings and their fathers' failings and they could hope for their restoration if they would return to the obedience demanded by the Law. Confronted by their own human, religious, and ethical failing, they could wait for the Lord's salvation as prophesied in Jer 31:31–34: the Lord himself shall make a new covenant with the house of Israel and Judah and implant obedience to his תורה in the heart of his people (cf. Ezek 11:14–21,

---

9. For the deuteronomistic character of Jer 7:21–29, see W. Thiel, *Die deuteronomistische Redaktion von Jeremia 1–25* (Wissenschaftliche Monographien zum Alten und Neuen Testament 41; Neukirchen-Vluyn, 1973) 121–28; and R. P. Carroll, *Jeremiah: A Commentary* (OTL; Philadelphia, 1986) 215–20. W. McKane, *A Critical and Exegetical Commentary on Jeremiah* (ICC; Edinburgh, 1986), 1:177–78, is more restrained.

10. For this concept, see O. Kaiser, *Einleitung in das Alte Testament: Ein Einführung in ihre Ergebnisse und Probleme* (5th ed; Gütersloh, 1984) 171.

36:26-27).[11] Thus what all the preaching of the prophets could not attain, the Lord himself would realize, for his election of his people is valid forever. If one should further ask why the Lord should do this in spite of the people's disobedience, the Book of Ezekiel provides the answer: that by this the Gentiles shall know that he is the Lord, whose name is holy and who sanctifies his name, collecting his dispersed people and leading them back to the land given to their fathers (Ezek 36:22-25). Then the covenantal promise shall become reality; then Israel shall really be his people and the Lord their God (Ezek 36:28).

Let us now consider 2 Samuel 7 in order to remind us of the integrating force of this concept. There the promise of the eternity of the Davidic dynasty is answered by David's appeal for its fulfillment, for then shall the name of the Lord be great forever and one shall say that the Lord Sabaoth is Israel's God (v. 26).[12]

In the time of Exile Israel is confronted in all these ways by the demand to be the people of the Lord, to realize what they finally shall become by the grace of the Lord, who will act for his own honor's sake.

It is not necessary here to round off this picture by adding all the details which biblical exegesis has accumulated. My main purpose has rather been to demonstrate that the covenantal formula is anything but an empty predicate. It is in fact the chief thread through the labyrinth of the Bible. Its many and different voices are not discordant, but like a many-voiced choir produce a mighty hymn to the glory of the Lord, the God of Israel.

The Law as Center of the Hebrew Bible

Let us now look at the organization of the תנ״ך as a whole. To give the Hebrew Bible this name clearly underlines the fundamental importance of the תורה by itself: the תורה opens the collection, it comes first, and it is the "canon" within the canon, or, as has been rightly noticed, in a strict sense the only canonical Scripture.[13] The following books, from Joshua to Kings, are named the נביאים ראשנים, and by this ordered together with the real

---

11. See S. Böhmer, *Heimkehr und neuer Bund: Studien zu Jeremia 30-31* (Göttinger theologische Arbeiten 5; Göttingen, 1976) 74-79, esp. 77: "Die Verheissung in Jer 31,33 kommt von diesen Erfahrungen her: die totale 'Erfolglosigkeit' der deuteronomischen und jeremianischen Verkündigung setzt sie voraus. Das Vertrauen in die messianischen Möglichkeiten ist zerstört. Der Blick richtet sich daher allein auf Jahwe."

12. For the literary layers, see T. Veijola, *Die ewige Dynastie: David und die Entstehung seiner Dynastie nach der deuteronomistischen Darstellung* (Annales Academiae Scientiarum Fennicae, ser. B, 193; Helsinki, 1975) 68-80.

13. See M. C. Doubles in E. Schürer, *The History of the Jewish People in the Age of Jesus Christ (175 B.C.-A.D. 135)* (New English version; ed. G. Vermes, F. Millar, and M. Black; Edinburgh, 1979), 2:316-21.

prophetic books, the נביאים אחרנים. But what was the reason for giving these "historical" books the name "prophets," and what was the presupposed concept of prophecy? The answer seems unquestionably to be that prophets are mentioned throughout the books of Samuel and Kings (beginning with Samuel and concluding with Isaiah). One should also remember in this connection how the Chronicler made his claim to authoritative tradition by naming his sources in Samuel and Kings after various seers and prophets (cf., e.g., 1 Chr 29:29; 2 Chr 32:32, 33:19).[14] But this aspect of inspiration and authority is not the only and, I may suggest, not even the prevailing one. It is merely a formal and not a material principle.

To deal with the last matter, we must inquire into the manner in which the message of prophecy became interpreted in those circles responsible for the organization of the Bible. If we take the Targum as a guide, the answer is that prophecy was interpreted along the lines prepared by the Deuteronomists.[15] The prophets were preaching obedience in the Law, and they admonished the people to follow its path. They announced catastrophe in consequence of their breaking the Law, but also—in the end—the restoration by God. For example, the Targum to Isa 1:2 states:

> Hear, O heavens, which trembled when I gave my law to my people, and give ear, O earth, which was shaken from before my word, for the Lord has spoken. The house of Israel is my people, I called them sons, I cherished them and made them glorious, and they have rebelled against my Memra.[16]

This interpretation of prophecy as preaching obedience to the Law was not an invention of later translators, but had its forerunners in the Bible itself. The Deuteronomistic school interpreted the prophets as preachers of obedience and return to the Lord, and, finally, as preachers of obedience to the Law. This interpretation is characteristic of the prose sections in the Book of Jeremiah, but it is provable as well in the books of Hosea, Amos, Micah, indirectly in the Book of Ezekiel, and in a weakened fashion also in the Book of Isaiah.[17] Another example may be brought from Jer 6:19:

> Hear, O earth; behold, I am bringing evil upon this people,
>   the fruit of their devices,
> because they have not given heed to my words;
>   and as for my law, they have rejected it.[18]

---

14. See J. Blenkinsopp, *A History of Prophecy in Israel* (Philadelphia, 1983) 22–23.

15. On the importance and message of the Targum, see E. Levine, *The Aramaic Version of the Bible: Contents and Context* (BZAW 174; Berlin, 1988).

16. Translation from J. Stenning, *The Targum of Isaiah* (Oxford, 1949) 2.

17. See Kaiser, *Einleitung in das Alte Testament*, 223–24 (for Amos), 227–28 (Hosea), 234 (Isaiah), 237 (Micah), 239 (Zephaniah), 255–56 (Jeremiah), and also 308.

18. Translation from Carroll, *Jeremiah*, 199.

The same idea also occurs in the Deuteronomistic history. The most important reference would seem to be 2 Kings 17. There the end of the Northern Kingdom is judged to be a consequence of the apostasy Israel practiced in spite of warnings by the prophets (v. 13):

> So Yahweh testified against Israel and Judah through every prophet and seer saying, Turn back from your evil ways and keep my commandments and my statutes according to the whole law which I commanded your fathers and which I transmitted to you through my servants the prophets.[19]

This verse is the key to the canonical interpretation of all the prophetical books of the Bible, which should be read as a concrete interpretation of the blessings and threats combined with the proclamation of the Law by Moses. The fulfillment of these blessings and curses in the course of Israel's history, as reported in the Deuteronomistic history,[20] possesses the value of a proof of the validity of all the blessings and curses attached to the Law. Their true addressee is the people of God living in exile and dispersion throughout the world. References like Jer 31:31ff. and Ezek 36:26-27 indicate that there is a hope in redemption transcending all that the people may and can do. But sentences such as Deut 30:19-20 remain fundamental, and ask the people to make their decision in obedience to the Law:

> Today I take heaven and earth as witnesses against you: I presented to you life and death, blessing and curse, that you may choose life and that you may stay alive, you and your seed, loving the LORD, your God, and being obedient to his voice and devoted to him; for this is your life and the length of your days to dwell on the land the LORD has sworn to your fathers . . . to give it to them.

The future of the people depends on their obedience to the Law. But one should not overemphasize this aspect by neglecting the fact that, in the end, it is the Lord who will redeem his obedient people. I shall return to this point later on, when we have answered the open question of how to combine the כתובים 'Scriptures' into this central idea. With regard to the Psalms, biblical redaction has facilitated our task by assigning the first and the second psalms their present position: it is generally acknowledged that they are a preface to the whole prayerbook. The congratulation to the man who has his delight in the Law of the Lord and who is reading it aloud by day and by night and the promise that he shall stand up in the judgment are a clear hint to the praying community and the individual that they can hope for the help of the Lord if they remain obedient to the Law. The Messiah may then come, whose authorization from the Lord the reader can

---

19. Translation from J. Gray, *I and II Kings: A Commentary* (2d ed.; OTL; Philadelphia, 1970) 645.

20. See Kaiser, *Einleitung in das Alte Testament*, 173-74.

find in the second psalm.²¹ It is not difficult to include the Wisdom Books in this overall frame. The correspondence between צדקה and שלום, between justice and full life, is the essence of the Law and the Prophets and not the less of these books. The admonitions of wisdom correspond to the individualization of the blessing and curse of the Law, as we might observe not only in the case of Psalm 1 or Psalm 119, but, for example, also in the court stories of Daniel 3 and 6. There it is stated that the obedient Jew escapes all dangers of persecution caused by his zealous devotion. If we remind ourselves of Psalms 49 and 73, we are prepared to understand also the Book of Job and even the Book of Ecclesiastes in a congruent fashion: the innocent sufferer is a theme in these writings as it is in the Psalms and the Prophets. We need only think of the interpretation of Israel's way through Exile to Restoration as the fate of the obedient and suffering servant in Isa 52:13–53:12.²² That the testimony of Ecclesiastes reflects a man on the borderline of traditional belief, which in the end became tolerable only by a redaction which summarized his reflections in 12:13–14, is well known too:

> The sum of the matter, when all is said and done: Revere God and observe His commandments! For this applies to all mankind: that God will call every creature for account for everything unknown, be it good or bad. (NJPSV)

We could easily enlarge this picture, for example, by recalling that the Song of Songs was early interpreted as a simile for the relation between the Lord and his people, or that the Book of Ruth is a mirror of חֶסֶד, a word which is nearly equivalent to אֱמוּנָה. Let us, however, look at the history of the Chronicler,²³ which includes the account of the foundation of the community of the Second Temple in the Book of Ezra/Nehemiah. One could read this history as a sign that the Lord has not forgotten his people, and that he shall not forget it in the future. In this regard, one should not overlook the fact that Nehemiah 8 gives an aetiology for the synagogue service, with its center in the proclamation and explanation of the Law.²⁴

---

21. See, e.g, G. T. Shepard, *Wisdom as a Hermeneutical Construct: A Study in the Sapientializing of the Old Testament* (BZAW 151; Berlin, 1980) 136–44.
22. For the modification of my interpretation of the Ebed-YHWH-Songs since my *Der königliche Knecht: Eine traditionsgeschichtlich-exegetische Studie über die Ebed-Jahwe-Lieder bei Deuterojesaja* (Forschungen zur Religion und Literatur des Alten und Neuen Testaments 52; Göttingen, 1959; 2d ed. in 1962), see my *Einleitung in das Alte Testament*, 278–80. For the discussion, see H. Haag, *Der Gottesknecht bei Deuterojesaja* (Erträge der Forschung 233; Darmstadt, 1985).
23. For the problems of this history, see P. R. Ackroyd, "Chronicles-Ezra-Nehemiah: The Concept of Unity," in *Lebendige Forschung im Alten Testament* (ed. O. Kaiser; Suppl. to ZAW 100; Berlin, 1988) 189–201.
24. See A. H. J. Gunneweg, *Nehemia* (KAT 19/2; Gütersloh, 1987) 112.

And finally, if we look at the strange position of the Book of Chronicles after that of Ezra and Nehemiah, we become aware that its last sentence (2 Chr 36:23b) is:

> Any one of you of all His people, the LORD his God be with him and let him go up [to Jerusalem]. (NJPSV)

The faithful Jew could read this as an admonition to his pilgrimage to the holy city; but by the same token he could also remember what is written in the Prophets about the eschatological glorification of Jerusalem, including the pilgrimage of the Gentiles to Zion as the new center of the world where all shall learn the ways of the Lord (Isa 2:2–5 || Mic 4:1–5). I use the mention of this expectation as occasion to remark that the prophetical books in their transmitted form are eschatological compositions which lead their readers in different, but ultimately corresponding, ways from Exile to Restoration in the land. One may observe how, in those circles responsible for the transmission of the prophetical heritage, the conviction increased that the Day of the LORD which would precede the final glorification of Zion would include an individual judgment of God's people too. For the pious men of early Hellenistic times the criterion applied could be nothing else than the obedience to the Law. Therefore, the whole prophetical collection took as its postscript what is written in Mal 3:22–24 [English 4:4–6]:[25]

> Remember the law of Moses my servant, the rules and precepts which I bade him deliver to all Israel at Horeb.
> Look, I will send you the prophet Elijah before the great and terrible day of the LORD comes. He will reconcile fathers to sons and sons to fathers, lest I come and put the land under a ban to destroy it. (NEB)

This quotation completes this part of my reflections and reminds us that there is a unity in the Hebrew Bible caused by redactional hints about how to understand its manifold testimonies.

The Structure of the Law and the Structure of Human Existence

Let me turn now to a final matter: a theological and existential analysis of the structure of the Law itself. I may best begin with a short summary of salvation history as told in the Pentateuch. The Lord began his elective

---

25. See W. Rudolph, *Haggai, Sacharja 1–8, Sacharja 9–14, Maleachi* (KAT 13/4; Gütersloh, 1976) 291–93. R. Mason, *The Books of Haggai, Zechariah, and Malachi* (Cambridge Bible Commentary; Cambridge, 1977) 160, is prepared to date this postscript even during the time of persecution under Antiochus IV Epiphanes. However, A. S. van der Woude, *Haggai, Maleachi* (De Prediking van het Oude Testament; Nijkerk, 1982) 157, judges the verses only as the closing remarks of the Book of Malachi; his hints about their terminological connections with the later chronistic literature should be noticed.

activity by his call to Abraham and the fulfillment of his promise to give him a son in his old age. As he protected the life of Abraham and Isaac, he blessed and protected Jacob when he had to flee from his brother's hatred, and brought him and his twelve sons, the fathers of the twelve tribes of Israel, safely back to the land of promise. He used the hatred of Joseph's brothers to save their lives in Egypt, from where he delivered their seed, the people of Israel. God made Israel his people by his covenant at Sinai, and then he led them through the desert and gave them the promised land of Canaan. But before this happened, he demonstrated the earnestness of his will to be the God in whom Israel trusts, and whom they must obey, by letting the grumbling generation die in the wilderness. The only exceptions were Joshua and Kaleb, who had constantly remained faithful when the people had lost their trust in the Lord. At the border of the land of promise Moses admonished the people to love the Lord, to serve him alone, and to keep his commandments. Then he placed them under the covenantal obligation to be obedient to the Law, and asked them to choose between obedience or disobedience, between life or death. This ברית was to be valid for all generations.

It is obvious that Israel's obligation is predicated upon what the Lord has done for them. He has chosen them to be his people and liberated them from the bondage of Egypt. The indicative precedes the imperative. Because Israel is really the people of God, it has to be his people Israel, and there is no chance to escape this destiny. This pattern corresponds in an exciting manner to the schema of salvation designed by the Apostle Paul, as well as by the Protestant reformer Martin Luther. The situation of Israel in Exile, who is the true addressee of salvation history, is one of middle ground: it is caught between its divine election and its eschatological salvation, between the indicative and imperative to be the people of God. And as the Lutheran imperative functions to prevent the security of the Christian, the commandments of the Law likewise function for the Jew. The Jew, as the Christian, may be confident that he or she certainly is a member of the people of God. But there is a difference between certainty and security. Certainty leads to the love of the Lord, and, consequently, to obedience to his demands to respect and to serve him as God alone—to respect not less the spheres of one's neighbor's life in regard to his or her corporal integrity, freedom, personal relations, and possessions as ordered in the Ten Commandments, and even more to love one's neighbor as oneself. If Israel will fulfill these demands, they may expect God's final salvation (cf. Deut 30:1-6). The participation in the promised salvation depends on the obedience to the Law. But even then there is, as we have seen, a final hope that the Lord himself shall give to his people the ability for the demanded obedience. Without his gift of a new heart and a new spirit, Israel may not reach its final destination. To compare it again with the Christian pattern of salvation: humans shall be judged according to their deeds, but rescued by God's grace and mercy. It is the Holy Spirit who has to fill the heart to enable the Christian to love the Lord and one's neighbor.[26]

It has long been acknowledged that the legal collections, the תורה inside of the תורה,[27] do not cover the whole field of Israel's religious and civil life, but have to be valued as paradigmatic: they give examples of what it means to love the Lord and to let him alone be Israel's God.[28] Therefore it is not casuistry, but a steadfast trust in God which gives us the sensitivity for the silent or expressive appeal of our neighbor: to respect our neighbor as comrade on the same path toward death, and toward the Lord as our final hope. I do not want to diminish the differences between Judaism and Christianity, but I thought it helpful, in the interest of a mutual better understanding, to point to a similarity of pattern.

I have said all this using traditional language. Today it is obvious how difficult it was for many to understand such implications during the last centuries, and how many problems this has produced for our religious communities. Let me try then to repeat what just has been said about the structure of the Law by means of a transposition into the human condition.[29] Everybody is challenged at every moment to make a response to a situation. Everybody has received life as a gift and a promise; but whether one evaluates this challenge as a law in its negative sense, or as a chance to act, depends on one's confidence or lack of confidence in the invisible and transcendent ground of one's life. Confronted with negative experiences— one's own failings and those of others—everyone needs the word of promise that confidence shall not fall into the void. Every time someone believes that he or she has to be the master of one's own destiny, that person is tempted to abuse other people for one's own selfish purposes. This must be the result of a desperate isolation. Therefore the individual needs also the

---

26. For the relation between indicative and imperative in the theology of St. Paul, see R. Bultmann, *Theologie des Neuen Testaments* (7th ed.; ed. O. Merk; Tübingen, 1977) 332–35. For the Lutheran concept, see G. Ebeling, *Dogmatik des christlichen Glaubens* (Tübingen, 1979), 3:234–41, where he reflects on the relation between justification and new life.

27. For the history of the term, see H. Gese, "Das Gesetz," in *Zur biblischen Theologie: Alttestamentliche Vorträge* (2d ed.; Beiträge zur evangelischen Theologie 78; Tübingen, 1982) 55–84 (trans. by K. Crim as *Essays on Biblical Theology* [Minneapolis, 1981] 60–92).

28. This judgment is also valid for Deuteronomy, which should not be qualified to function as a civil law code.

29. See O. Kaiser, "Von der Gegenwartsbedeutung des Alten Testaments," in *Der Gott, der mitgeht: Alttestamentliche Predigten* (ed. A. H. J. Gunneweg et al.; Gütersloh, 1972) 9–34 (repr. in *Von der Gegenwartsbedeutung des Alten Testaments: Gesammelte Studien zur Hermeneutik und zur Redaktionsgeschichte* [ed. V. Fritz, K.-F. Pohlmann, and H.-C. Schmitt; Göttingen, 1984] 11–36); and idem, "Vom dunklen Grund der Freiheit," *Neue Zeitschrift für systematische Theologie* (1978) 163–74 (repr. in his *Der Mensch unter dem Schicksal: Studien zur Geschichte, Theologie und Gegenwartsbedeutung der Weisheit* [BZAW 161; Berlin, 1985] 244–55).

other word reminding one that life is being gambled away. The structure of election, temptation, and return to confidence and hope determines in the end the life of us all. If it is our belief that the Lord is the creator of us all, we may find in this structure of our existence the hint for his reality. He by himself is speaking to everybody by his voiceless voice. I finish with a statement to me by Martin Buber during his last visit to Germany: "For we all are too noisy to hear him; it is our task to make this voiceless voice perceptible giving our tongue to him."

EZRA AND MEREMOTH: REMARKS ON THE HISTORY OF THE HIGH PRIESTHOOD

Klaus Koch

Ezra's Transfer of the Gifts to the Temple

The arrival of Ezra and his group in Jerusalem and the delivering of the gifts to the temple is narrated in Ezra 8:32-34 in a short and seemingly unproblematic manner:

> We came to Jerusalem, and there we remained three days. On the fourth day, within the house of our God, the silver and the gold and the vessels were weighed [or: we weighed, LXX] into the hands of Meremoth the priest son of Uriah, and with him was Eleazar the son of Phinehas, and with them were the Levites, Jozabad the son of Jeshua, and Noadiah the son of Binnui. The whole was counted and weighed, and the weight of everything was recorded.

If we put this notice into the context of the Ezra narratives, it contains some curious features.[1] According to Ezra 7:16-17 the Persian king had commissioned Ezra himself to buy sacrifices with the money in Jerusalem and to use the rest of the sum to the best of his judgment. Now, however, it is emphasized that Ezra delivered "the whole" of the gifts to the temple authorities as soon as possible. This notice was either written by an author other than the one responsible for 7:16-17, or the text has a real historical background insofar as things developed in Jerusalem in a different manner

---

Author's note: Shemaryahu Talmon has contributed significant research on the dark centuries of the Second Temple period and the growth of the books of Ezra and Nehemiah, the first documents of that period (e.g., "Ezra and Nehemiah," in *IDBSup* 317-28). So it may be appropriate to present him some considerations on a mostly neglected passage in the Ezra narrative. In this connection I intend to strengthen part of the argumentation of my article "Ezra and the Origins of Judaism," *Journal of Semitic Studies* 19 (1974) 173-97, esp. 190-93. I am thankful to Dwight R. Daniels for improving my English.

1. On the significance of the passage as a concluding event within the "second exodus" according to the Ezra narrative see Koch, "Ezra and the Origins of Judaism," 184-89.

than the one planned in Babylon. That would mean that the hierarchy of the temple maintained its authority even toward the emissary of the Persian government.

But the contradiction between 8:33 and 7:16–17 seems relatively insignificant compared with the strange figures who take the gifts from the hands of Ezra's men. It would be expected that the prominent group of pilgrims and their immense donation should be received by the high priest himself. Such was the case in Num 31:48–54, which may have been a canonical model for this scene. But הכהן הגדול is not only lacking here, he is never mentioned in the whole Ezra narrative! In his stead four representatives are waiting for Ezra, two of them priests and two of them Levites. The latter two are members of the first and second Levitical classes (Neh 10:10, 12:8). Jozabad, however, appears later in the list of men married with foreign women (Ezra 10:23), but accompanies Ezra in Neh 8:7 and is one of the chiefs of the Levites in Neh 11:16. Noadiah is not otherwise mentioned; perhaps he died not long after Ezra's arrival. As a member of the second Levitical class he doubtless enjoyed a prominent position with Jozabad among the *clerus minor*.

But what about Meremoth and Eleazar? Mentioned before the Levites, they probably were both priests. The name Eleazar, as well as his father's name Phinehas, is a typically priestly one. Nevertheless, only Meremoth is called הכהן. Why is the title used only with Meremoth? As far as commentators take regard of this curiosity, they understand Meremoth to be the treasurer.[2] But that would be גזבר in Hebrew (Ezra 1:8) and not כהן.

The Title הכהן

The title given Meremoth is even more surprising if we compare the use of הכהן in the Books of Chronicles, that is, in the nearer linguistic environment of Ezra.[3] There הכהן always means the chief priest of Jerusalem. If other priests are mentioned with him, then the complicated formula הכהן ואחיו הכהנים is used (1 Chr 16:39, 2 Chr 26:17; cf. 1 Chr 24:6). The highest priestly representative is also called (ה)כהן הראש (1 Chr 27:5; 2 Chr 19:11, 26:20, 31:10), once even הכהן הגדול (2 Chr 34:9). But more frequently הכהן is written (2 Chr 22:11; 23:8, 9, 14; 24:2, 20, 25; 34:14, 18). This expression goes back to preexilic times when the highest priest was named "gewöhnlich einfach *hakkohen*."[4] In the Book of Nehemiah, also, הכהן seems always to

---

2. So, e.g., S. Mowinckel, *Studien zu dem Buche Ezra–Nehemia*, vol. 3: *Die Ezrageschichte und das Gesetz Moses* (Oslo, 1965) 32.

3. Even if it may be doubtful whether 1 and 2 Chronicles, Ezra, and Nehemiah all derive from the same author, these writings participate in common ideas and belong to the same circles of postexilic Jerusalem.

4. W. Dommershausen, "כהן," *TWAT* 4:74.

refer to the high priest. The contemporary Eliashib is called הכהן (10:39, 13:4) as often as הכהן הגדול (3:1, 20). At some future time a high priest capable of using the Urim and Thummim is expected as הכהן (7:65). In 13:13, however, an otherwise unknown Shelemiah is introduced as הכהן beside a certain Zadok הספר. Both are appointed by Nehemiah to administrate the tithes. Is Shelemiah only one priest among others? Because of the apparent singularity of the position of "the scribe," it is probably best to think also of "the priest" as a single, outstanding position. Given the uncertain and only fragmentarily known succession of high priests during the fifth century, it is by no means excluded that Shelemiah held this position for a longer or shorter period of time after the deep discord had developed between Nehemiah and (Shelemiah's predecessor) Eliashib (13:7-9).

There may be, however, one more exception, because Ezra too is introduced as "the priest," although in the combination הכהן הספר (Neh 8:9, 12:26; and distributed over two verses in 8:1-2). It seems as if, in the view of the author (or redactor), Ezra united two functions in himself which were otherwise performed by two separate persons (Neh 13:13, 2 Chr 34:15; cf. 1 Chr 18:16, 24:5-6; 2 Chr 24:11). Is Ezra also regarded as a kind of high priest? To answer this decisive question it is necessary to return to the Book of Ezra. With the exception of Meremoth in 8:33, הכהן refers here only to Ezra (10:10, 16-18). Has the author of the Ezra narrative ascribed the highest position of the priestly hierarchy to him? Moreover, has Ezra really claimed this office for himself? It was already mentioned that no other high priest plays a role in the Ezra narratives. Some of the enterprises of Ezra, however, certainly belong to the domain of the high priest. At the great fasting assembly of the people Ezra speaks the collective confession of guilt (Ezra 9) like Aaron in Lev 16:21. He organizes the divorces of unclean marriages throughout the country (Ezra 10). Although he is not the convocator of the קהל in the month of Tishri (Nehemiah 8), he is the leader of the ceremony at the place before the temple. Especially the genealogy of Ezra 7 reveals a high priestly consciousness. Only those ancestors are registered who actually functioned as high priests at the temple in Jerusalem or, prior to that, at the tabernacle, going back to Aaron הכהן הראש. The names of his father, grandfather, and others living during the exilic times are lacking. There is no reason to take the title הכהן concerning Ezra in a manner other than that found elsewhere in the Chronistic literature. It ascribes to him the position of the highest priest in Jerusalem during his stay in the holy city.

There is one objection against such an assumption: the name of (Meremoth and) Ezra is missing in the official list of high priests concerning the early postexilic period in Neh 12:10-11, which contains only members of the family of Jeshua. But this list must be incomplete. It registers only one person, Joiakim, between Jeshua, acting about 520 B.C.E., and Eliashib, officiating 445–433! There have been some attempts to fill the gap. F. M. Cross has looked to Ezra 10:6, which reports a stay of Ezra in the chamber of Jehohanan, the son of Eliashib, at mount Zion.[5] Postulating papponymy in priestly circles, Cross inserts a (first) Eliashib and a Jehohanan after Joiakim in the succession of high priests. The assumption, however, is not easy to verify because of the lack of a priestly position for Jehohanan in Ezra 10 and the frequency of the names Eliashib and Jehohanan.[6] So it seems more preferable to insert—among others—Ezra into the above-mentioned gap.

The Division Hakkoz

But what about Meremoth הכהן? if we take the title seriously, he was chief priest when Ezra arrived but must have been removed afterward. He is no unknown person in the books of Ezra and Nehemiah. He and his family play, however, very different roles. Neh 12:3 numbers a Meremoth among the priests returning under Jeshua and Zerubbabel, whereas among the Levites Jeshua and Binnui (the "fathers" of Jozabad and Noadiah) keep the first position (Ezra 8:33). The Meremoth of Nehemiah 12 must be someone other than the Meremoth of Ezra 8 because of the time difference, but he may have been an ancestor of the family. In Neh 10:6 Meremoth as well as the Levites Jeshua and Binnui sign the document. In this case the reference may be to the priestly and Levitical classes and not to the individual signing. More instructive is the list of the builders of the city wall (Neh 3:4, 21), where Meremoth is doubtless the person of Ezra 8. Although the priestly rank is missing, his genealogy is expanded by one member: Meremoth ben Uriah ben Hakkoz.

This last name is connected with a curious notice in the list of the inhabitants of the province in Ezra 2:61–63 = Neh 7:63–65. This passage relates that Hakkoz, together with two other families, was excluded as unclean by the governor of the province from priestly functions, because there was no registration of his name in the documented genealogies. The order contradicts 1 Chr 24:10, where it is recorded that David appointed Hakkoz as the seventh among the twenty-four priestly divisions. The list of Ezra 2 = Nehemiah 7 is an independent document which was secondarily placed into the present context.[7] According to A. Gunneweg it originated

---

5. F. M. Cross, "A Reconstruction of the Judean Restoration," *JBL* 94 (1975) 4–18, esp. 9–17; cf. Talmon, "Ezra and Nehemiah," 327.

6. P. Ackroyd, "The Jewish Community in Palestine in the Persian Period," in *The Cambridge History of Judaism*, vol. 1: *Introduction; The Persian Period* (ed. W. D. Davies and L. Finkelstein; Cambridge, 1984) 159–60.

7. Talmon, "Ezra and Nehemiah," 322; S. Mowinckel, *Studien zu dem Buche Ezra-Nehemia*, vol. 1: *Die nachchronische Redaktion des Buches: Die Listen* (Oslo, 1964) 108.

in the time of Ezra or shortly thereafter,[8] whereas 1 Chronicles 24 is certainly a younger Chronistic document.[9] So the restrictions laid upon Hakkoz in Ezra 2 = Nehemiah 7 were cancelled in later times, although this priestly division never regained its former status. Therefore, it seems improbable that the name and the role of Meremoth הכהן in Ezra 8:33 goes back to the assumption or invention of the Chronicler or some later redactor. The notice is *unerfindlich* and mirrors a historically reliable event.

Changes in the High Priesthood

The ups and downs in the fate of the family Hakkoz reveal vehement quarrels among the priesthood of the Second Temple about the time of Ezra. The Chronistic redaction has apparently suppressed the corresponding reports. When Ezra arrives, the family of the famous first high priest Jeshua acting at the beginning of the Second Temple period has been dethroned. It is still named first in the lists of priests (Ezra 10:18; cf. 2:36; Neh 12:12), but there is no attempt by Ezra to restore the family to the leading position. In the younger list (1 Chr 24:7), its ancestor Jedaiah has deferred to the division of Jehoiarib and kept only the second rank.

Surprisingly, neither Jeshua nor his successor Joiada receive any title anywhere in the books of Ezra and Nehemiah. Whereas Jeshua/Joshua is nearly always called הכהן הגדול in Haggai (1:1, 12; 2:2; etc.) and Zechariah (3:1, 8), his name appears without any designation in Ezra 2:2, 3:9, 4:3, 5:2; Neh 7:7; 12:1, 7. He is only mentioned "together with his brethren, the priests" in Ezra 3:2, 8 (cf. 2:36; Neh 7:39). Especially astonishing is the list of the house of Jeshua (Neh 12:10–11). Here the names of the members remain without any determination, whereas in the foregoing passage (v. 8), "the Levites," and in the following passage (v. 12), "the priests" are each so designated. Certainly the list in v. 10 originally carried the superscript הכהנים הגדולים, which was probably intentionally suppressed by the redaction. So we have to suppose that the house of Jeshua had kept the high-priestly position through the end of the sixth century but that later on it had been replaced (i.e., by Meremoth and Ezra). After the disappearance of Ezra, it regained the chief position again and retrained it from Eliashib to

---

8. A. H. J. Gunneweg, *Esra* (KAT 19/1; Gütersloh, 1985) 65. J. M. Myers, however, supposes the opposite development; see *Ezra, Nehemiah* (AB 14; Garden City, NY 1965) 72. Taking Ezra 2 as an older source, the family Hakkoz must have proven its priestly status in the meantime according to his opinion. But where should have been a priest using the Urim and Thummim between Jeshua and Ezra? The reversal of the status of Hakkoz seems rather possible during the dark fourth century. Moreover, Ezra 2 is scarcely a list from the time of Jeshua; cf. Koch, "Ezra and the Origins of Judaism," 188–89.

9. Some presume a Maccabean origin for 1 Chronicles 24; cf. W. Rudolph, *Chronikbücher* (HAT 21; Tübingen, 1955) 161–62.

Jaddua (Neh 12:10–11).[10] In the time of 1 Chr 24:7, however, the house of Jehoiarib enjoyed the highest status.

The house of Hakkoz, however, and its member Meremoth, chief priest at the time of Ezra, were more severely degraded and lost not only the high-priestly office, but also all priestly functions. Is it too bold to connect the decline of Meremoth and Hakkoz with the consequences of the inquiries which Ezra had to undertake according to the royal decree in Ezra 7:14? Just arrived, Ezra had to accept the existing authorities. Only after precise examination and after contacting the residing governor could he take measures against conditions of cult and temple that contradicted the law of his God which was in his hand (Ezra 7:14).[11] But then Meremoth not only had to resign, but to disappear with his whole family from the temple service. In later times Hakkoz was reactivated, but only in a subordinate position.

Conclusions

1. In 1 and 2 Chronicles, Ezra, and Nehemiah, the expression הכהן refers to the chief priest of the Jerusalem temple.[12] Hence, not only Ezra himself but Meremoth (Ezra 8) and Shelemiah (Nehemiah 13) must also have occupied this position. This observation accords well with the gap in the list of high priests in Neh 12:10–11, where only one name is mentioned between 520 (Jeshua) and 445 (Eliashib).

2. Before Eliashib, no member of the house of Jeshua receives the title הכהן or הכהן הראש in Ezra and Nehemiah (as opposed to Haggai and Zechariah). Their status as high priests seems to be denied.

3. When Ezra arrived in Jerusalem, he at first acknowledged the status of Meremoth as chief priest. But in the course of Ezra's inquiries Meremoth was removed and his whole division disqualified. Ezra himself acted as high priest.

4. After Ezra's disappearance, the house of Jeshua again regained control of the temple and the priesthood, as indicated by the position of Eliashib in the Book of Nehemiah.

---

10. An exception may have been the above-mentioned function of Shelemiah during Nehemiah's second stay at Jerusalem (Neh 13:13). In Neh 13:28 the title "high priest" belongs to Eliashib, not to the contemporary Jehoiada (cf. the construction in Ezra 7:1–5), who probably gained that position after the departure of Nehemiah (according to Neh 12:10–11).

11. R. Rendtorff, "Esra und 'das Gesetz,'" *ZAW* 96 (1984) 165–84, denies any equivalence between the royal דת of Ezra 7:12–24 and the book of תורה. But his basic assumption of a "rein rechtliche Bedeutung" regarding Aramaic דת and Iranian *data* is erroneous; cf. P. Frei and K. Koch, *Reichsidee und Reichsorganisation im Perserreich* (OBO 55; Freiburg/Göttingen, 1984) 60–65.

12. So Ezra is rightly called ἀρχιερεύς in 1 Esdr 9:39–40, 49 (corresponding to Neh 8:1–2, 9).

DEUTERONOMY 6:24: לְחַיֹּתֵנוּ 'TO MAINTAIN US'

Norbert Lohfink

In Deut 6:21–25, the Israelite father answers his son's question about the meaning of the laws. He develops his answer in syllogistic form. In what could be considered as a first premise, he shows that, juristically speaking, God, by rescuing Israel from Egyptian slavery and bringing her into the promised land, became Israel's owner and master (vv. 21–23). In a second premise, he states that this master in fact has commanded Israel to observe the laws (v. 24). So the conclusion is that Israel, to remain in the state of צדקה, is obliged to observe the law faithfully (v. 25).

In 6:24, there is an additional attempt to indicate the positive implications of God's imposing the law:

לטוב לנו כל הימים
לְחַיֹּתֵנוּ כחיום הזה

I would suggest this paraphrase:

> (Obedience to the laws would imply), to our favor, without time limit, that he will maintain us, as is now the case.

But let us slowly move toward such an unusual translation.

The Piel of חיה in Deuteronomy 6:24

The first words of the text, לטוב לנו, as motivation for the observance of the law, seem to represent a stereotyped deuteronomic phrase (cf. Deut 4:40;

Author's note: For Shemaryahu Talmon, to whom these pages are dedicated, what is discussed here may not be a surprise at all, for the proposed meaning of חיה *Piel* does occur in post-biblical stages of the Hebrew language, for example, in the divine title מחיה חיים (on these points, see n. 19 below). May I be allowed to greet this wise and well-known scholar with the words that the rabbanan in Pumbeditha used to say when they greeted one another (*b. Yoma* 71a): מחיה חיים יתן לך חיים ארוכים וטובים ומתוקנין. I thank Brian MacCuarta for correcting my English style.

5:16, 29, 33; 6:3, 18, 24; 10:13; 12:25, 28; 19:13; 22:7; 30:9b; also 28:11; 30:9a).[1] However, the exact formula לטוב ל occurs only in 6:24 and 10:13.[2]

The only other instance of a טוב phrase, as in 6:24, combined with an expression which contains the verb חיה is Deut 5:30: למען תחיון וטוב לכם. Similar promises of life are to be found elsewhere in Deuteronomy in six further passages. Seventeen similar passages with other wordings may be added.[3] The promise of life certainly is an important motif in Deuteronomy. Only in 5:33 and 6:24, however, are the two expressions combined. Moreover, the order of the expressions is not the same in the two texts. What is more, in 6:24 there is not the usual *Qal* form of the root חיה but the *Piel* form. This is unique in the stereotyped deuteronomic reference to God giving life.

So, contrary to a first impression, one may hesitate to see in Deut 6:24 just one of the many more-or-less-empty phrases of the rhetorical style of Deuteronomy which most commentators suppose.

It seems that the Samaritan tradition had difficulties with the *Piel* of חיה. It added a *waw* and modernized the form to a *Hiphil*: ולהחיי(ו)תנו. The Old Greek harmonized the text to the usual *Qal* forms and, possibly, read a *waw* at the beginning.[4] Jerome did not find the phrase in his *Vorlage*, or, what is more probable, translated the verse very freely. The textual tradition as a whole is best explained if we take the reading of the MT as the original one. It is the *lectio difficilior*, and all other readings can be derived from it. There is also a harmonizing tendency in some modern translations (cf. NAB, TEV, JB). Luther (1546), the Revidierte Lutherbibel, and Junker[5] follow the Vulgate. The complex textual situation and the deviating versions prove that there must be a difficulty in understanding and translating the expression לְחַיֹּתֵנוּ.

---

1. For the meaning of the phrase independent of the observation of the laws, cf. Num 11:18; Deut 15:16, 23:15; 1 Sam 16:16, 23; Jer 22:15; Hos 2:9; Ruth 3:1. For the semantics of טוב cf. especially I. Johag, "טוב: Terminus technicus in Vertrags- und Bündnisformularen des Alten Orients und des Alten Testaments," in *Bausteine biblischer Theologie: Festgabe für G. Johannes Botterweck* (ed. H.-J. Fabry; Bonner biblische Beiträge 50; Bonn, 1977) 3–24.

2. The only other occurrence of the formula is Jer 32:19, which may depend upon Deuteronomy.

3. The six passages are Deut 4:1; 6:24; 8:1; 16:20; 30:16, 19. In addition, the seventeen similar passages with חיים are 30:6, 15, 19, 20; 32:47; and with האריך ימים: 4:26, 40; 5:16, 33; 6:2; 11:9; 17:20; 22:7; 25:15; 30:18; 32:47. The expression האריך ימים precedes the phrase טוב ל in 5:16, and follows it in 4:40, 5:33, 22:7. The occurrence of both a phrase with חיה and a phrase with האריך ימים in 5:33 proves that the two expressions cannot simply be taken as identical.

4. For the *waw*, the main support is in the difficult evidence of the Codex Lugdunensis of the Old Latin, which has *et vivatis*. Could *vivatis* mean that the Old Greek actually read a different Hebrew text?

5. H. Junker, *Deuteronomium* (EB; Würzburg, 1952).

In Deuteronomy, there are only two more instances of חיה *Piel*. They substantiate two well-known meanings of this *Piel*: to restore someone to life (Deut 32:39), and to preserve someone from being killed, to let him live (Deut 20:16). The small number and the variation of meaning show that, in Deuteronomy, there is no stereotyped language when חיה *Piel* is used. Some translations of 6:24 seem to imply the meaning the word has in 20:16: RSV, NEB, JPSV, Gute Nachricht.[6] But in the context of 6:24 that does not make much sense. There is no reason why there should be a danger that God, after having given the promised land to his people, would plan to wipe them out.

A Special Use of the Piel of חיה

Outside Deuteronomy, there are some instances of the *Piel* of חיה which may suggest that there was a juridicial and economic use of this *Piel* which, as far as I can see, has not yet been adequately described. In what follows I want to point to that meaning and to prove that it solves the problems of חיה in Deut 6:24.

Jer 49:11 is the end of the first part of Jeremiah's oracle against Edom, 49:12 being the introduction to the second part, in parallel to 49:7.[7] As a closing verse, its connection to the preceding verses may be a very loose one.[8] The whole verse seems to be a rather impressionistic final touch. We

---

6. Those German translations which use the expression "am Leben erhalten" can be so understood. But this expression is also open to a slightly different meaning.

7. For a discussion of the motives of the verse, cf. D. L. Christensen, *Transformations of the War Oracle in Old Testament Prophecy* (Harvard Dissertations in Religion 3; Missoula, MT, 1975) 232–33.

8. There would be a connection if Symmachus had a Hebrew *Vorlage*. He combines the end of the preceding verse with the beginning of this one: καὶ οὐκ ἔστιν ὃς ἐρεῖ· καταλεῖπε τοὺς ὀρφανούς σου (=LXX 29:11–12). Therefore it is often proposed to read ואין אמר at the end of Jer 49:10. But is this more than good exegesis? There is a tradition of interpretation which has God as speaker of 49:11. At the end of an oracle of doom he himself would raise new hope for Edom; cf. most recently R. P. Carroll, *Jeremiah: A Commentary* (OTL; London, 1986) 803. If that is correct the divine words must be taken as highly ironic, at least in the canonical text, for the text which follows brings an escalation of divine punishment. I rather think that, at the end of an oracle, we just hear a voice from the battlefield. There are dying people to whom the survivors are saying what used to be said in such circumstances. So far, the verse is a confirmation of what had been announced in the oracle beforehand. But what is to be heard, by the same token, does not witness a total end. There will be people who return from the war and take care of the victims' families. Thus far, the original oracle which probably ended here was not concerning total destruction, and, in the definitive text of Jeremiah, the verse has to be taken as transitional to the following part of the oracle, which will be much more radical. As for the discussion of 49:11, the various possibilities of connecting the verse to the preceding and following verses do not affect the proposed interpretation. In the supposition of a divine word to Edom, God would utter formulaic words which survivors use to say on the battlefield to their dying comrades.

listen to a soldier who consoles his dying comrade by assuring him that he himself will take over the responsibility for his family. It must be something which used to be said in such circumstances, a kind of human and economic self-obligation with juridicial consequences:

עזבה יתמיך אני אֲחַיֶּה
ואלמנתיך עלי תבטחו

The *Piel* אֲחַיֶּה certainly means something like 'I shall keep your children alive, I shall rear them'. But in a word to a dying father (which is possibly formulaic), there should be a quite definite juridicial coloring to that meaning. So I translate:

Leave your orphans [without fear]—[for] I shall maintain them;
as for your widows—on me they can rely.

Qoh 7:11-12 contains a statement of traditional wisdom upon which, from 7:13 on, the author will give his comment. In the traditional statement, v. 11 is the thesis, v. 12 gives the foundation. Both thesis and foundation are twofold, the second member in each case being an intensification of the first. The whole is shaped in the form of an hyperbaton: v. 12a gives the foundation for v. 11a, v. 12b for v. 11b. So, 7:12b has to prove that for those who behold the sun, wisdom is even better than an inheritance.[9] The reason given is:

יתרון דעת החכמה תְּחַיֶּה בעליה

In Qoheleth's answer to this traditional opinion, premature death plays a part (cf. 7:15, 17). In view of that, it would be sufficiently founded to translate v. 12b as:

The advantage of intelligence [when compared to rich inheritance] is: wisdom preserves the life of him who possesses it [if a danger of death approaches].

On the other hand, it is quite possible that only Qoheleth himself, in his comment, introduces the idea of premature death while the traditional statement did not yet touch upon it. Under certain economic conditions it may happen that it is more profitable to live, by teaching or commercial activities, from a continuous income than from the yields of landed property, even if such an inherited wealth consists of large estates. It seems to

---

9. For this analysis cf. my *Kohelet* (Neue Echter Bibel 1; Würzburg, 1980) 53.

me that it is rather this line of argument which is developed in Qoh 7:11–12.[10] Thus, I would prefer the following translation:

> The advantage of intelligence [when compared to rich inheritance] is: wisdom [more efficiently] maintains him who possesses it.

It is not to be excluded that the mere wording of the sentence could be understood both ways, and that Qoheleth, by insinuating a meaning which, while possible, nevertheless was not originally intended, in a very sophisticated way played on the different possible meanings of the *Piel* of the root חיה.

This use of חיה *Piel* for taking responsibility for the maintenance of a human being is not far from the well-known use of the same form for breeding cattle (cf. 2 Sam 12:3 and Isa 7:21). In Nathan's parable, the connection is explicit:

> ולרש אין כל כי אם כבשה אחת קטנה אשר קנה
> וַיְחַיֶּהָ
> ותגדל עמו ועם בניו יחדו
> מפתו תאכל
> ומכסו תשתה
> ובחיקו תשכב
> ותהי לו כבת

It is to be expected that there was also a theological transposition of this use of חיה *Piel*. We should look for it in the Psalms. Statistically speaking, חיה *Piel* is overrepresented in the Psalter (twenty instances out of fifty-six), and there, with only one exception, God is always the subject.[11] In my opinion, in two of these theological passages the pregnant meaning of חיה *Piel* as 'to maintain' seems to be present although in both cases other meanings cannot definitively be excluded.

Ps 33:19 says that the eye of the Lord looks on those who fear him,

> להציל ממות נפשם
> וּלְחַיּוֹתָם בָּרָעָב

---

10. To simplify the discussion, up to here I spoke of "traditional" wisdom. To be more exact, the quotation gives the opinion of Qoheleth's contemporary wisdom teachers and friends. Their opinion must not be very old. It even sounded very "modern." But it stemmed from ancient and traditional wisdom principles against which Qoheleth was fighting. Only in this sense was it "traditional."

11. Outside the Psalter, there are only eight instances with God as explicit or implicit subject.

The new translation of the Jewish Publication Society (NJPSV) here rightly has more than simply the idea of God's restoring life to people who are starving to death. The Lord's eye is on them,

> to save them from death,
> to sustain them in famine.

In this instance, there is an old tradition of understanding the text in such a way. Whereas Jerome translated *et vivificet eos in fame*, the Old Latin had *et alat eos in fame*, which corresponds to the Old Greek's διαθρέψαι. If this idea of "providing food" is not accepted here, the only honest alternative is M. Dahood's solution, who supposes a strict parallelism. Thus, רָעָב must correspond to 'death' and therefore must be a name of the God of the underworld: "to preserve their lives from the Hungry One."[12]

The opposition between the mighty king of Ps 33:16–17 and those who fear the Lord of vv. 18–19 reminds one of Ahab and Elijah in 1 Kings 17–18. In the famine which the Lord had sent upon the land, Ahab did not find anything to feed his horses (cf. 1 Kgs 18:5: אולי נמצא חציר וּנְחַיֶּה סוּס וּפֶרֶד) but the Lord maintained Elijah (cf. 1 Kgs 17:2–16).

In the blessing of Ps 41:2b–3a, which is for a משכיל אל דל, there is the following sequence of verbs:

> In the day of trouble the LORD delivers him [מלט *Piel*]
> the LORD protects him [שמר]
> חיה [וִיחַיֵּהוּ *Piel*][13]
> so he is considered happy in the land [אשר *Pual*].

Then, by a change to the second person, something new begins. It seems to me that in the series of these four verbs, חיה *Piel* would come too late if it had the meaning of deliverance from imminent death. The man is first delivered, then he enjoys his God's protection. What else can now be expected than that God takes care for his maintenance in the land so that, finally, people will bless him?

There is a further prayer outside the Psalter in which this meaning for חיה *Piel* seems to be present: Nehemiah's penitential psalm in Neh 9:6–37.

---

12. M. Dahood *Psalms I: 1–50* (AB 16: Garden City, NY, 1966) 203. G. Ravasi, *Il libro dei Salmi* (Bologna, 1986), 1:594, translates "nutrirlo in tempo di fame," but in his commentary gives another interpretation: liberation from early death (p. 607). He then mentions Dahood's solution and shows approval for it.

13. This piece of the chain is missing in the LXX[B]. But this rather is an inner-Greek homoioteleuton than a trace of a shorter Hebrew text—as against C. A. Briggs and E. G. Briggs, *A Critical and Exegetical Commentary on the Book of Psalms* (ICC; Edinburgh, 1906), 1:364.

Before beginning with Abraham's vocation, there is a passage on the creation and conservation of the universe (9:6).[14] There we read:

את עשית את השמים   שמי השמים וכל צבאם
הארץ וכל אשר עליה   הימים וכל אשר בהם
ואתה מְחַיֶּה את כלם   וצבא השמים לך משתחוים

The third line, in chiastic order, returns to the inhabitants of the parts of the universe named in the first and second line.[15] The inhabitants of the heavens are the צבא השמים. They worship their creator. The inhabitants of the earth and the waters, on the other hand, receive something from the Lord. Here too the most fitting sense for the root חיה *Piel* seems to be, 'he maintains them'.

So there is at least a certain probability that חיה *Piel* could be used in the sense of feeding someone, maintaining someone, and that a theological transposition of this usage was possible.

The Idea of "Maintaining" in Deuteronomy 6:24

Returning to Deut 6:24, it is evident that this meaning makes perfect sense in this text. The Lord has brought his People into the promised land. For life in the land, he has given them his laws, and, correspondingly, he will maintain them. This idea will return, in expanded form, later on in Deut 11:10–17 and, certainly, it underlies all the blessings and curses throughout the book. It is not at all alien to the thinking of Deuteronomy. Merely the use of חיה *Piel* is specific to this text.

The choice of this word may be based on two considerations. First, by the common root חיה the expression is linked to one of the stereotypical deuteronomic expressions for blessing. Second, it fits especially well into the juridicial reasoning which dominates the father's answer to his son.[16] The text follows the model of a slave's change of master. Israel was Pharaoh's slave in Egypt; she was set free lawfully by the Lord (using the technical term יצא *Hiphil*). The person who was "brought out" of a "house," by the same token was brought into the house of the liberator (using the technical term בוא *Hiphil*). That means that the liberator is now the new

---

14. Cf. W. Rudolph, *Esra und Nehemia samt 3. Esra* (HAT 20; Tübingen, 1949) 158: "Die ihm nicht nur ihre Existenz, sondern auch ihre Erhaltung verdanken."

15. Most commentators, without any discussion, ignore that and subsume צבא השמים under את כלם. But is it probable that the inhabitants of the earth and the waters do not bow down before God? It is better to assume a chiastic distribution of the statements, and then, on a second level of meaning, the interchange of what is said in the first part of the parallelism with what is said in the second part.

16. For a larger analysis, cf. my *Das Hauptgebot: Eine Untersuchung literarischer Einleitungsfragen zu Dtn 5–11* (Analecta Biblica 20; Rome, 1963) 161–62.

master, the liberated person is the slave. From this point on, the Book of Deuteronomy avoids the use of this terminology. It neither speaks of the land as the Lord's "house" nor does it designate Israel as the Lord's "slave"—the priestly language, later on, will not hesitate to do so (cf. Lev 25:42, 45). But if the words are avoided, the juridicial structure nevertheless is to be supposed. The Lord, therefore, now lawfully has the rights of a master over his slaves: to tell them what he wills. By the same token, he is obliged by law to maintain the new members of his household. For this last-mentioned obligation, חיה *Piel* seems to be the technical term.

We may wonder if, in Deut 6:24, the expression לטוב ל has not a juridicial meaning too, for example, 'in favor, for the benefit of somebody'. The usual expression for such a meaning seems to be simply לטוב (cf. Deut 30:9, Jer 15:11, Ps 119:122, Esth 2:9, 2 Chr 10:7). Only the rhetorical language of Deuteronomy has the fuller expression with a following ל (Deut 6:24, 10:13, imitated by Jer 32:39).

Comparative Evidence

Finally, I want to point to a comparative fact which, to be sure, cannot prove the thesis of this essay but at least may show that this thesis is not at all far fetched in the cultural context of the ancient Near East. In Accadian, the D stem of the word *balāṭu* 'to live' has the meaning 'to maintain someone'.[17] I. M. Diakonoff, in an article on "Agrarian Conditions in Middle Assyria," discusses some varieties of intermediate conditions between freedom and slavery.[18] The first one he treats is what the Middle Assyrian lawbook calls *balluṭu ina lumne* 'reviving in distress' (§39) which, as he himself remarks, would be better translated by the pregnant meaning 'maintaining in distress'. A free citizen who has debts and therefore is in distress transfers his paternal authority over his daughter to another citizen who, in this context, is called the "maintainer," in recompense for cash he needs for paying his debts. The interest of the maintainer is to obtain additional hands for work in his household and eventually to marry the girl to someone and so to receive the "marriage gift." His own obligation is, as the name of the institution says, to "maintain" the girl. It is not just slavery, as she herself remains an Assyrian citizen, but it is very near to it. There is no need to

---

17. Cf. *CAD* B 61–62, s.v. *balāṭu* v., sub nos. 7 and 11; "to provide with food"; *AHW* 1:99 s.v. *balāṭu(m)* II, sub D2c and Dt: "jemanden unterhalten, versorgen." For the biblical use, it may be especially interesting that in *CAD* there are six quotations from the letters of El Amarna (68:28; 74:55; 85:18, 38; 114:56; 215:16). W. L. Moran, *Les Lettres d'El Amarna* (Littératures anciennes du Proche-Orient 13; Paris, 1987), is a little more cautious. He retains for this meaning only three of them.

18. I. M. Diakonoff, "Agrarian Conditions in Middle Assyria," in *Ancient Mesopotamia: Socio-Economic History* (ed. I. M. Diakonoff; Moscow, 1969) 204–34, esp. 224–26, 231–32.

suppose a similar institution in Israel, but a comparable semantic development of the corresponding Hebrew root חיה *Piel* appears at least a little more probable.

Conclusion

Therefore, I propose the meaning 'to maintain someone' for חיה *Piel* in Deut 6:24; Jer 49:11; Ps 33:19, 41:3; Qoh 7:12; Neh 9:6. I point to a similar semantic development of the Accadian root *balaṭu*, and to later Hebrew usage.[19]

---

19. For חיה *Piel* 'to maintain' in post-biblical Hebrew, see A. Even-Shoshan, מלון חדש מנקד ומצוּיר (Jerusalem, 1961), 1:397, who quotes Isa 7:21 and a text from *Exodus Rabbah* for the meaning נתן אפשרות לחיות על ידי מזון וכדומה. For the use of חיה *Piel* in the divine name מחיה חיים, see J. Levy, *Wörterbuch über die Talmudim und Midraschim* (Berlin/Vienna, 1924), 2:44: "der die Lebenden erhält, ernährt."

JERUSALEM AND ZION AFTER THE EXILE: THE EVIDENCE OF FIRST ZECHARIAH

Carol L. Meyers
Eric M. Meyers

The centrality of the Jerusalem and Zion traditions in biblical and post-biblical thought and in the life of ancient Israel and of the Jewish people has long been recognized. It stands to reason that, over such a long span of time, the conceptualization of Jerusalem and Zion underwent development and change while retaining certain critical aspects of meaning. Nonetheless, biblical scholarship on the subject has tended to focus on the preexilic period: on the foundations of the traditions at the time of David's conquest of Jerusalem and Solomon's construction of the temple; on the transfer of traditions about Sinai, as the premier locus of divine revelation, to the capital of the new nation-state; and on the impact of the vicissitudes to which Judah was subjected over the succeeding centuries on the meaning and role of Jerusalem/Zion.

All these levels of research have been productive. Yet they do not deal adequately with the fact of the ongoing vitality of the Jerusalem/Zion idea,[1] despite the termination of the political state in which it originated.[2]

Authors' note: Shemaryahu Talmon is among those who have contributed to our understanding of Zion, as in his "Biblical Concept of Jerusalem," *Journal of Ecumenical Studies* 8 (1971) 300-316. Professor Talmon has been our teacher, colleague, and friend; and we are pleased to offer this contribution in his honor.

1. Discussions of the Jerusalem/Zion tradition tend to focus on its Near Eastern (particularly Canaanite) analogues and precursors and on its form and function in the First Temple period. For example, R. J. Clifford's discussion of "Zion Traditions" in his work on *The Cosmic Mountain in Canaan and the Old Testament* (Harvard Semitic Monographs 4; Cambridge, MA, 1972) omits any reference to First Zechariah. Similarly, J. J. M. Roberts's entry on "Zion Tradition" in *IDBSup*, 985-87, moves from the historic Davidic kingdom to transhistorical apocalyptic without any consideration of early postexilic continuations and transformations.

2. As supposed by many, such as J. J. M. Roberts, "The Davidic Origin of the Zion Traditions," *JBL* 92 (1973) 329-44; and J. D. Levenson, *Sinai and Zion* (Minneapolis, 1985)

And even where the role of the postexilic Jewish community in sustaining and reshaping the Jerusalem/Zion ideals to fit the altered status of a people without political autonomy is examined, the role of the early postexilic prophets in this process has not been given sufficient attention.[3] Haggai and then First Zechariah were instrumental in the process of national and institutional revitalization in the late sixth century. As such, their conceptualizations were critical in continuing the Jerusalem/Zion traditions into the postexilic and, ultimately, post-biblical eras. Consequently, our attention here will focus upon early postexilic prophecy, notably First Zechariah (Zechariah 1–8), who (unlike Haggai) is explicit in his mentions of both Jerusalem and Zion and who is innovative and vivid in his portrayal of the holy center of Judah.

The prophet Zechariah played a critical role in postexilic Judean history. By himself, or with a group of followers, he was probably responsible for the promulgation of a composite work, Haggai–Zechariah 1–8,[4] which was prepared for the occasion of the rededication of the Jerusalem temple in 516 or 515 B.C.E.[5] The temple-restoration project was a landmark event in biblical history, not only because of the continuity and comfort it provided to the postexilic community but also because it was accomplished within, and represented an adaptation to, an entirely new political framework, under Achemenid sovereignty and with prophetic support.[6] Without either a dynastic ruler or full autonomy, the postexilic community was led by a governor and high priest. This dyarchic mode of leadership, supported by both Haggai and First Zechariah, was built upon foundations deep within Israel's past[7] yet pointed in a new direction.

95–101. But see B. C. Ollenburger, *Zion: The City of the Great King* (JSOTSup 41; Sheffield, 1987), for the view that the strength of the Zion symbolism lies apart from royal Davidic interests and ideology.

3. See Levenson, *Sinai and Zion*, 178–84, although he discusses the post–70 C.E. period more fully than the preceding centuries.

4. This is the thesis we present in our recent Anchor Bible commentary: *Haggai, Zechariah 1–8* (AB 25B; Garden City, NY, 1987), esp. pp. l–lxiii of the introduction. Among the many factors contributing to such a conclusion are the literary correspondences between Haggai and Zechariah 7–8 (see chart 5, p. lii), the overlapping dates of the careers of the two prophets (chart 2, pp. xlvi and 4–9), and the temple focus of both books.

5. The rededication of the temple is not mentioned in Haggai or First Zechariah, as it is in Ezra (6:15). For further discussion of chronological matters see ibid., 116–18, 388–89.

6. Ibid., xxxii–xliv, 380. The management of the satrapies through local dynasts loyal to the Persian king and faithful to local concerns was the heart of Achemenid strategy that led to centuries of relative peace in the provinces. Darius the Great's role in establishing such a policy has been treated in a surprisingly original manner by J. M. Cook, *The Persian Empire* (New York, 1983). See also E. M. Meyers, "The Persian Period and the Judean Restoration: From Zerubbabel to Nehemiah," in *Ancient Israelite Religion: Essays in Honor of Frank Moore Cross* (ed. P. D. Miller Jr., P. D. Hanson, and S. D. McBride; Philadelphia, 1987) 509–21.

7. Zechariah's support of the temple-rebuilding project, normally associated with a temple-king typology, may well have been influenced by earlier biblical precedents. The tabernacle was commissioned by Moses, who, although he may have performed the functions

As facilitator of this transition, Zechariah drew upon ancient Jerusalem/Zion traditions. With vivid imagery and through resounding oracles, he proclaimed for all in the Second Commonwealth the idea that this city and its temple transcended normal political considerations while never forsaking their material and territorial dimensions. Furthermore, the prophet infused the historical and mythic aspects of his portrayal of Jerusalem/Zion with the universalistic notions that became prominent in later Judaism. To put it in the prophet's words, the idea of "holy land" (Zech 2:16) was tied to the idea of holy city—"City of Truth... Mountain of Holiness" (Zech 8:3)—for all humankind, "many peoples and mighty nations" (8:22).[8]

The integration of these various aspects of the Jerusalem/Zion tradition characterizes both the specific content and also the general features and overall structure of First Zechariah. We will first examine the texts or sections in which Jerusalem and Zion are explicitly mentioned: (1) the First Vision (1:8–13) with Supplements (1:14–17), (2) the Second and Third Visions (2:1–9) with Expansion (2:10–17), (3) the Prophetic Vision (3:1–10), and (4) the Address to the Bethel Delegation (7:1–17) with Oracles (8:1–23). Then we will consider the way the structure and features of this prophetic book provide and portray the symbolic context that enables the Jerusalem/Zion traditions to remain viable and to function simultaneously at manifold levels of spiritual, historical, temporal, and moral reality.

Jerusalem and Zion in First Zechariah's First Vision: Specific Texts

First Vision (1:8–13) and Oracular Supplements (1:14–17)

The language of Zechariah's First Vision sets the stage for the universal scope that characterizes the prophet's world view. At the same time, it focuses on the historical reality that confronts Zechariah in Darius's second regnal year, in February 519 B.C.E. Jerusalem is mentioned for the first time in First Zechariah in 1:12, where the angelic messenger that plays such a prominent role in Zechariah's visions challenges Yahweh about the condition of "Jerusalem and the cities of Judah, with whom you have been angry these seventy years."

The reference to Jerusalem and to other Judean cities is an explicitly historical designation. The two terms together apparently have a direct

---

of a king, was never called by such a title. Moses supervised the construction of a perfectly legitimate sanctuary. In addition there was a tent shrine (Josh 18:1) or temple (1 Sam 1:9) at Shiloh before the days of the monarchy. The postexilic community therefore knew that a sanctuary could be built without a king and dedicated by priests alone. Moreover, Moses as a civilian leader worked in tandem with his brother Aaron, the high priest.

8. Cf. the ideas of Talmon, "Biblical Concept of Jerusalem," esp. pp. 313ff. All translations of Zechariah used in this article are those of the authors, as they appear in *Haggai, Zechariah 1–8*. Translations of other biblical passages are also those of the authors.

political reference, as a designation for the realm of a Davidic sovereign.[9] They occur frequently elsewhere in the Bible, notably in Jeremiah and Isaiah, although the addition here of "cities" is not typical of the combined, geopolitical reference. In Zechariah, at the opening of the sequence of visions provoked by and centered around the act of restoring the temple, Jerusalem and Judah used together indicate prophetic concern for the status of the traditional Davidic territory, now lying dormant with respect to political autonomy for nearly seventy years, a period representing the maximal span of divine wrath.[10]

The orientation toward *Realpolitik*, indicated by the references to Judah and Jerusalem, and to the desolation during the years since the Babylonian conquest, is set within a global context. The messenger posing the challenge to Yahweh does so because other emissaries have just reported to him, after having "roamed about the earth," that "all the earth indeed rests quietly" (1:10, 11). The use of "earth" (ארץ) in vv. 10 and 11, along with the global imagery of the four horses of 1:8, denotes the universal surveillance of Yahweh. The juxtaposition of the condition of Judah and Jerusalem with the status of the whole world is what provokes the angelic challenge. The integration of Jerusalem, the center, with the world as a whole is present from the outset of Zechariah's visionary sequence.

The challenge in the vision itself (1:8–13) is resolved by an attached series of three oracles (1:14–17) uttered by Yahweh. Jerusalem figures prominently in all three oracular responses; Zion also appears directly in two of them and is implicitly present in the third. In the first oracle (1:14–15), God proclaims the intense and affective nature of the relationship between God and Israel: "I have shown great zeal for Jerusalem and Zion" (1:14). The pairing of Jerusalem and Zion surely reflects traditional Zion theology.[11] Yet, as in 8:3 below, the terms should be viewed as complementary designations rather than as synonymous expressions. Jerusalem is a somewhat broader term, although it frequently assumes the characteristics of its chief component Zion, the mountain of God's temple. The two words together signal the religious and political centrality of the postexilic capital of Judah (Yehud).

The second oracle (1:16) proclaims that Yahweh's house will be rebuilt in Jerusalem. Although it doesn't mention Zion, the location of the house is, of course, Zion. A builder's string ("line," reading קו with LXX and *Qere*) is stretched out to demarcate the walls of the city. The idea of physical limits to Jerusalem, indicated by the line stretched over it, is continued in an entirely positive way in the third oracle (1:17), which anticipates that Yahweh's cities will not be able to contain the products of

---

9. See M. Noth, *The Laws in the Pentateuch and Other Studies* (trans. D. R. Ap-Thomas; London, 1966) 138.

10. See our discussion of the use of "seventy years" in *Haggai, Zechariah 1–8*, 117–18. Cf. Zech 7:3, 5; Jer 25:11–12, 29:10; and n. 5 above.

11. Roberts, "Davidic Origin of the Zion Traditions."

God's bounty once all is restored. Not only will "my cities" (= Judah) flourish, but also Zion and Jerusalem will resume their special, sacred place in the land by dint of Yahweh's choosing them.

The repeated mention of Jerusalem in so concentrated a space as the three oracles of 1:14-17 signifies God's renewed presence in the city of choice. The idea of the selection of Jerusalem occurs elsewhere in Zechariah and also in preexilic prophecy.[12] It denotes the historic role of Jerusalem as site of the temple (1 Kgs 8:44, 48; 2 Chr 6:6, 34, 38) and thus the sacred and special role of Jerusalem as Yahweh's designated earthly city. Jerusalem takes on the attributes of holiness and cosmic centrality of the temple within it, both because of its recurrent usage in these oracles, the central one of which specifies temple restoration, and also because of the way it precedes "Zion" when the two terms are paired. The normal sequence, elsewhere in Zechariah and also in Joel 4:17, Amos 1:2, and Ps 125:1-2, is "Zion . . . Jerusalem." Here Jerusalem takes precedence, thereby drawing the three oracles into a unified presentation and at the same time asserting the special status of the city that is the focus of God's global scrutiny.

Second (2:1-4) and Third (2:5-9) Visions, and Oracular Expansion on the Themes of the First Three Visions (2:10-17)

In contrast to its political and restorative as well as cosmic aspects in the First Vision and its oracles, Jerusalem in the Second Vision is more limited in scope and is in fact confined to the political realm. Yet this specific role of Jerusalem in the world scheme is presented, as for all the visions, against a more universal backdrop.[13] It is all the Judeans (inhabitants of the province of Yehud) and even past Israelites—"Judah, Israel, and Jerusalem"—who are now placed under the political hegemony of Persia. They have been subjected to a past dispersion and are still fearsome of a potential repetition of history (2:4).

The use of these three geographical terms in 2:2 asserts that Assyria, Babylonia, and Persia have all been involved in shaping the destiny of the Jewish people. The Second Vision refers back to the Neo-Babylonian conquest. At the same time it is sensitive to the possibility that, although prospects appeared to be good for cooperation between the restoration community and Persia, there could well be further interference in the land of Judah by the Persian authorities. Persia thus is represented by the "smiths" (2:3),[14] whose actions ultimately will mean autonomy for Jerusalem and the supremacy of Yahweh rather than of Darius in the world.

---

12. Zech 2:16, 3:2. See our discussion below of both those verses; for preexilic prophecy, see Talmon, "Biblical Concept of Jerusalem," 312.

13. The structural and thematic aspects of Zechariah that convey this universal dimension are discussed below.

14. Our reasons for this identification are laid out in *Haggai, Zechariah 1-8*, 135-36. On the power and might of Persia at this time see E. Kuhrt, "The Cyrus Cylinder and Achaemenid Imperial Policy," *JSOT* 25 (1985) 83-97.

Zechariah's Third Vision, "The Man with the Measuring Cord" (2:5–9), is the briefest of all the visions. Because of its placement just prior to the oracular expansion in Zech 2:10–17 and also because of the inclusion of oracular elements within it, it is among the more complex texts of the entire Book of First Zechariah. Although many scholars would like to remove 2:8b–9 from the vision, we regard these verses as essential components of the explication for the measurement of Jerusalem, which is the symbolic action that constitutes the major theme of the visionary scene.

The individual in the scene who has had the visionary experience and who reports it to his audience is the prophet. However, the man with the measuring cord (2:5), who performs the task of marking Jerusalem's perimeter, plays the key role in the vision. That individual is probably the same as the "official" of 2:7, an identification that provides an association between the physical measurement of Jerusalem's boundaries and the more subtle notion of expanded boundaries connoting future, possibly monarchic, hopes. The twofold use of Jerusalem in the Second Vision thus presents the belief that Yahweh is still involved in Jerusalem's ever-unfolding history.

While accepting Judah's modified political role under governor and high priest within the Persian Empire, the prophet still holds open the possibility of a Davidic state ruled by a king. Zechariah expresses this eschatological ideal in an interwoven fabric of visionary and oracular speech. For, wedded to the political aspect of the significance of Jerusalem is the additional notion of Jerusalem as sacred center, the site of Yahweh's earthly dwelling and locus of his universal rule. God will be for Jerusalem "an encircling wall of fire, and as Glory . . . within her" (2:9). This language ("glory" = כבוד) is meant to specify God's relation to the restored temple, God's glorious presence in Jerusalem being an extension of his presence in the temple. All Jerusalem in such a view is a holy temple precinct, and all of it is Yahweh's domain. This concept of the city, which Talmon calls "metropolis" of the world for late-biblical Judaism,[15] is still rooted in the political/territorial and temple as sacred center dimensions.

The first three visions, by participating simultaneously in these several aspects of the meaning of Jerusalem, set the stage for a second, more wide-ranging oracular expansion on themes from all the preceding visions. This material (2:10–17) represents the largest block of oracular material in First Zechariah except for the oracles of part three (chaps. 7–8). The oracular expansion of 2:10–17 recapitulates in reverse order the themes and content of the first three visions.

The expansion commences in 2:10–11 with a bold call to the exiled Judeans to leave their temporary homes in "the land of the north," that is,

---

15. Talmon, "Biblical Concept of Jerusalem," 315.

Babylon, and return to Zion (v. 11). In calling for those in the Diaspora to go back to Zion, the oracle develops one of the central themes of the Third Vision: the focus on Jerusalem itself and on the eventual repopulation of the city and its environs (2:8). The twofold use of the prophetic interjection הוי in v. 10, along with its repetition in v. 11, has the quality of an enthusiastic call to attention.[16] The prophet is clearly committed to the idea of resettling the land of Yehud.

In 2:12-13, the second oracle in this series, Zechariah communicates God's assurance that, despite Persian rule, Judah plays a special role in Yahweh's scheme. Yahweh's special relation to the people means that no power can harm them: "Israel is the apple of his [God's] eye" (2:12).

The final verses (2:14-17) provide a fitting conclusion to the whole oracular expansion while developing several themes central to the First Vision: God's universal dominion and the return of his presence to Jerusalem. The idea of God's return to Jerusalem, here and in the entire visionary sequence, has apparently been evoked by a ceremony of refoundation of the temple, which Zechariah views as the beginning of God's renewed dwelling among his people "on the Holy Land" and in Jerusalem (v. 16), "from his holy abode" (2:17).[17]

The language of these final verses is the language of the older, premonarchic period, and is symbolic of God's association with tabernacle and temple: "I am coming to dwell [שכן] in your midst" (2:14). Verse 15 articulates most clearly the theme of universality but couches it in covenant language to underscore Yahweh's special relationship to Israel: "They will be a people to me." Even the nations (גוים) will come closer to Yahweh and will apparently share in the relationship that had heretofore characterized Israel's relation to God. This is an inclusive eschatological picture, with Judah's destiny part of an international setting. The expression of God's

---

16. And not a prophetic lament, as elsewhere. See G. Gerstenberger, "The Woe-Oracles of the Prophets," *JBL* 81 (1962) 249-63; R. J. Clifford, "The Use of *Hôy* in the Prophets," *CBQ* 28 (1966) 458-64; and W. Jenzen, *Mourning Cry and Woe Oracle* (BZAW 125; Berlin, 1972).

17. We have identified the "premier stone" (האבן הראשה) of Zech 4:7 as the focal point of the ceremony of refoundation; so *Haggai, Zechariah 1-8*, 246-50. Such a ceremony is borrowed from widespread Near Eastern practice. Many of the relevant texts have been collected by R. S. Ellis in *Foundation Deposits in Ancient Mesopotamia* (Yale Near Eastern Researches 2; New Haven, 1968). The date on which the Second Temple was refounded was probably December 18, 520 B.C.E., a date which also receives special attention in Haggai (2:18). Elsewhere in biblical tradition (e.g., 1 Kings 8) it is the dedication of the temple that receives important recognition. In Haggai and Zechariah, however, it is the refounding of the temple that is imbued with cosmic significance. The real beginning of the Second Commonwealth was the day of the refoundation of the Second Temple, five years before its actual rededication.

universality in covenant language in v. 15 not only resumes the central theme of the First Vision but also provides a fitting link to v. 16, where such language combines a universalistic theme with a more particularistic one.[18]

God's place of choice, through which "many nations will be joined to Yahweh on that day" (2:15), is Jerusalem. God has taken (נחל) Judah as "his inheritance on the Holy Land" (2:16). The use of נחל as verb with God as subject is one of two such cases (cf. Exod 34:9) in the Bible. It occurs here along with the sole attestation of the term "Holy Land" (אדמת הקדש) in all of Hebrew Scripture. The particular place through which God manifests universal covenant love is the land which has Jerusalem, the site of the refounded holy temple, as its center.[19]

Prophetic Vision (3:1–10)

The sequence of seven visions that constitute the unique contribution of First Zechariah to the prophetic corpus and to the literature of the human imagination is interrupted, in 3:1–10, by a vision that departs from the structure and form that bring the other seven visions into a unified configuration. Zechariah 3 is a prophetic vision that unfolds in dramatic form. The prophet participates directly in the visionary experience, and this fact, along with formal or structural differences, sets this vision apart.[20] Yet, while differing from the seven visions, it nonetheless participates in the overall scheme of the visions and their meaning. It is paired with the centerpiece of the seven visions, the lampstand vision (Fourth Vision) of Zechariah 4. Chapters 3 and 4 together thus focus directly on the Jerusalem temple, its paraphernalia, and its personnel.

The symbolic and mythic dimensions of this prophetic vision will be treated separately below. Here the specific meaning of the use of "Jerusalem" is under consideration. Jerusalem is mentioned early in the dramatic sequence of the first part of the vision, which deals with the heavenly court and the investiture of the high priest Joshua (3:1–7; vv. 8–10 are a supplementary oracle). Yahweh, one of four dramatis personae with speaking parts in this vision, is the first (and last) to speak out. He chastises one of the central figures of the heavenly court, the Accuser (השטן): "Yahweh said to the Accuser, 'May Yahweh rebuke you, O Accuser; Yahweh who chooses Jerusalem will rebuke you! Is this not a brand plucked from the fire?'" (3:2).

---

18. A universalistic element may also be seen in the expression "Lord of all the earth," which occurs in 4:14 and 6:5.

19. Just as in Haggai (2:18–19) so in Zechariah the day of temple refoundation is associated with plenty and blessing (8:9–13).

20. These differences, and our reasons for numbering the visions as we do, are explained in *Haggai, Zechariah 1–8*, liv–lviii, 213–19.

Jerusalem once again, as in 1:17 and 2:16, is the object of divine favor, indicated by the verb בחר. It would at first seem gratuitous for God's choice of Jerusalem to be signified here. After all, the very setting—the heavenly court examining the high priest—is an overt representation of the special role of temple and city. What can be the function of this reassertion of Jerusalem's prominence in God's plan? Enmeshed in the cosmic symbolism of the divine council is a response to an historic reality, the fear that God's rejection of Jerusalem, as the events of 587 B.C.E. are understood, might be repeated or sustained, that Jerusalem might become like Shiloh (cf. Jer 26:6; Ps 78:59-61, 67-78) and never again serve as the terrestrial home of God's immanence. God has the first word in the scene, but his statement is a response to the indirect and unrecorded concern of the Accuser, and others, about the security of Jerusalem's role as the locus of God's presence.

The second statement in God's opening speech is a rhetorical question, apparently referring to Joshua, whose presence in the court scene is the result of his survival in exile and his return to Jerusalem. Miraculously, a descendant of the last chief priest has managed to become part of the revived temple hierarchy. If that could, and indeed has, happened, it becomes a sign both to the heavenly host and to the audience of the prophet's report that God surely favors Jerusalem, the place of choice.

The selection of Jerusalem here, however, is linked to the priestly rule of Joshua and his "associates ... men of portent" (3:8) rather than to a Davidide.[21] It remains for the Fourth Vision, which is the next section of First Zechariah and the companion piece to this prophetic vision, to work out the role of a royal figure in the renewed Jerusalem and temple. Meanwhile, the historic Joshua partakes of the cosmic meaning of the temple city. Furthermore, the eschatological significance of this moment is also part of the vision, for the supplementary oracle concludes with the language of abundance that denotes an ideal future and anticipates the universalized bounty of the oracles of 8:12 and 8:22-23.

Address to the Delegation from Bethel (7:1-7) and Concluding Oracles (8:1-23)

The only mention of Jerusalem in Zechariah 7 occurs in v. 7, which reflects the language of 2:8. The oracle in the Third Vision, however, depicts a future Jerusalem which, along with its "villages," will be inhabited.

---

21. There is only one indirect reference to a Davidic scion in Haggai, in the final oracle (2:20-23). First Zechariah, however, has several key passages that allude to the future Davidide: 4:6b-10a, the so-called Zerubbabel insert, and 6:9-15, the Crowning. We assert in our commentary, *Haggai, Zechariah 1-8, ad loc.*, that the eschatological tone of all of the so-called Davidic messianic passages is original to Zechariah and represents an accommodation to current political realities.

In 7:7 the Jerusalem that is depicted is the former, preexilic Jerusalem, "along with its cities around it." The subtle difference between the preexilic and postexilic situation must be emphasized. The postexilic setting, indicated by "Jerusalem . . . with its villages [פרזות]" (2:8), refers to the urban-rural continuum of the day. The language of 7:7 denotes a capital city within a larger political entity including many cities, each with secondary settlements, all acknowledging the administrative authority of Jerusalem. The picture in v. 7 is rounded out by the geographical terms "Negev" and "Shephelah," which designate areas less populous than those in which cities dominated the geographic and demographic landscape of preexilic Judah.

All of the remaining mentions of Jerusalem and Zion occur in Zechariah 8, mostly in vv. 1–17, a cluster of seven oracles concerning the restoration of Zion and Judah. The specific role of Jerusalem in world history is the focus of the final oracle of chap. 8, which is the most directly universalistic portrayal of Jerusalem in the postexilic biblical corpus and is surely one of the most eloquent statements in all of Hebrew Scripture.

Because the first oracle (8:2) is strongly reminiscent of the oracular expansion in 1:14–15, the positive connotation of God's zeal is to be emphasized: "I have shown for Zion great zeal." The second oracle (8:3) emphasizes God's abiding presence in Jerusalem, thereby establishing the commitment of Yahweh to the present, restoration community: "I have returned to Zion; I will dwell in the midst of Jerusalem." We have discussed the use of שכן ("dwell") in connection with 2:14 above. Suffice it to say once again that here it similarly is part of temple terminology. Jerusalem as a result becomes the symbol of all that accompanies sacred space, including the authority of the temple's administrative institutions.

Perhaps the most innovative of Zechariah's references to Jerusalem/Zion and to its political/mythic aspects occurs in 8:3b: "Jerusalem will be called the City of Truth, the Mountain of Yahweh of Hosts, the Mountain of Holiness." The unique epithet of Jerusalem, עיר האמת, conveys the importance of the holy city as a place where justice is meted out in society and also serves as an effective link to the oracular unit of 7:9–10, which begins its list of four precepts with the command to carry out "true justice" (משפט אמת). The epithet here perhaps draws on the designation of Isa 1:21 of Jerusalem as "a faithful city full of justice in which righteousness has dwelt." The moral imperatives (7:9–10) to be followed in Jerusalem are reiterated in 7:16–17 and signify that the restoration of God's presence to Jerusalem involves the ideals of justice inherent in Torah and prophecy. The terms "Mountain of Yahweh" and "Mountain of Holiness" complete the oracle. The close connection between sanctuary and mountain, in 4:7 and here, includes mention of Zion (cf. Joel 4:17, Isa 2:2–3). Jerusalem and Zion together, here as in 1:14–17, convey the combined religio-political centrality of the city.

The third oracle (8:4-5) extends the time perspective of Zechariah into the future. Jerusalem is characterized as a city in which little children play and elders are at peace. These images contrast greatly with the destruction and death of the Babylonian conquest and exile. They epitomize a healthy society rejuvenated by God's presence. This beatific view of Jerusalem, with its future orientation, anticipates the three eschatological oracles at the end of Zechariah 8 (vv. 18-23), where the happy state of Jerusalem is extended to all humankind.

In his final oracles the prophet most eloquently addresses the fate of the world and relates it to Jerusalem: "Many peoples and mighty nations will come to seek Yahweh of Hosts in Jerusalem and to entreat the favor of Yahweh" (8:22). There is a progression in the final verses (8:19-23) from Judah to all peoples, the most inclusivistic perspective provided in v. 23 where "ten" and "all tongues" combine with "nations" to symbolize global participation in the acknowledgment of Jerusalem as legitimate terrestrial seat and as locus and symbol of Yahweh's universal rule. The prophet never loses sight of the locative dimension of Yahwism with its epicenter in Jerusalem.

In the final eschatological scheme there is no royal palace or human king; the temple as earthly residence of God is the object of the international gathering in Jerusalem. Despite Jerusalem's central role for *all* humans under Yahweh's rule, Judah will still have a distinctive role in the end of time: "In those days ten men from nations of all tongues will take hold, they will take hold of a Yehudite by the hem, saying, 'Let us go with you, for we have heard that God is with you'" (8:23).[22] This image—of the tiny restoration community symbolized by a single Yehudite (resident of Yehud)—provides the historical and functional contact between the future worldwide membership in Yahweh's domain and the past-present relationship of Yahweh with a tiny portion of the population of the world. The rest of the people in the world will eventually find their way to Yahweh through those who already stand in relationship to God.

From Temple Mount to Holy Land: Symbolic Context of the Jerusalem/Zion Tradition

The way in which Mount Zion, with its temple building, and Jerusalem figure in the prophecies of First Zechariah demonstrates a vitality and versatility that encompasses both historic reality, from past to future, and

---

22. The idiom "to take hold ... by the hem" depicts an act of submission or supplication; see, e.g., 1 Sam 15:27. Hence the picture of ten foreign men taking hold of the hem of a Yehudite conjures up a picture of submission and loyalty. The eschatological prospect is that all nations will come to Jerusalem to accept the one God and that they will accept the primacy of Yahweh by "taking hold of the hem."

suprahistorical sanctity. That Zion and the territories surrounding it—from Jerusalem to Judah and to the entire "holy land"—can function simultaneously in the worlds of politics and vision derives from the mythic context[23] of the ancient Hebraic and Near Eastern conceptualization of the temple's role in the life of a community.

The Jerusalem temple built in the days of David and Solomon exhibits a full measure of the cosmic symbolism that gave the building its sacred role in the newly formed nation-state and also afforded Jerusalem its acclaimed power as capital of an extensive empire.[24] Despite the erosion of the political status of Jerusalem over the ensuing centuries, the temple's sanctity and the concomitant sense of its inviolability remained vital to many Judeans. The radical blow to that conceptualization of Jerusalem and the temple represented by the Babylonian conquest may have interrupted the confidence in Zion's sanctity. Yet the early postexilic community, in agreeing to restore the temple, reactivated the mythic power of the Zion tradition, albeit in a form now distinct in its historical manifestation from the royal Davidic promise.

The biblical prophets of the early postexilic period, both Haggai and First Zechariah, show clear evidence of the continued vitality of the mythic consciousness surrounding the conceptualization of the temple. Because Haggai mentions neither Jerusalem nor Zion but rather concentrates on the temple building itself, our above exegetical comments focused on Zechariah 1–8. Similarly, this discussion of the symbolic context of the temple will center on Zechariah.[25]

Contemporary scholarship has identified and refined a typology of characteristics that constitute the conceptualization of the temple, and by extension its territory, as a place of prime significance within the realm of history and humanity, but also in another realm—of divine existence, cosmic scope, and eternal time.[26] The prophecies of First Zechariah exhibit in striking measure the mythic consciousness that enabled Zion to be reaffirmed by the devastated postexilic community.

---

23. For a useful discussion of what "mythic" means in looking at ancient Israel, see Levenson, *Sinai and Zion*, 102–11.

24. See C. Meyers, "Jachin and Boaz in Religious and Political Perspective," *CBQ* 45 (1983) 167–78, for an analysis of architecture as a mode of communication concerning Jerusalem's imperial role.

25. By choosing not to discuss Haggai here, we do not mean to imply that mythic aspects of temple imagery are absent from Haggai. See our notes and comments to Hag 2:18–19 in *Haggai, Zechariah 1–8, ad loc.*

26. So M. Eliade, *The Sacred and the Profane* (New York, 1961) 36–47; Clifford, *Cosmic Mountain*; M. A. Fishbane, "The Sacred Center: The Symbolic Structure of the Bible," in *Texts and Responses: Studies Presented to Nahum N. Glatzer* (ed. M. A. Fishbane and P. R. Flohr; Leiden, 1975) 6–27; C. Meyers, *The Tabernacle Menorah: A Synthetic Study of a Symbol from the Biblical Cult* (American Schools of Oriental Research Dissertation Series 2; Missoula, MT, 1976) 170–74; Levenson, *Sinai and Zion*, 111–76.

To begin with, the very form of First Zechariah's prophecies signifies the merging of historical and suprahistorical reality. Although traditional oracular presentation is part of its prophecies, the special character of Zechariah 1-8 derives from the visionary mode. That mode, with its focus on Jerusalem and the temple, in itself expresses the prophet's complex perception of present and mythic realities. The visionary mode involves a presentation of the prophet's experience that arises from reality and yet is distinct from the mundane. The vision as a form of prophetic experience is like a dream:[27] supernatural yet built upon the natural. The use of this mode is magnificently appropriate to what it presents, namely, the temple and Zion, which are composed of matter within time and yet have eternal and transcendent dimensions.

Not only does the visionary form suit the conceptualization of Zion that compels the prophet to speak out, but also the very structure of the visionary sequence represents the mythic value of Zion in the prophetic consciousness. The seven visions are arranged in a scheme that can be characterized as a series of superimposed, concentric circles.[28] At the center is the temple itself, represented by the lampstand vision. The two visions closest to the center, visions 3 and 5, widen to a national focus, examining Jerusalem's territory (vision 3; 2:5-9) and self-rule (vision 5; 5:1-4). The next two (visions 2 and 6; 2:1-4 and 5:5-7) have yet a broader scope: they have an international purview in their concern for Judah's (Yehud's) relationship to the imperial powers (Assyria, Babylon, and Persia) that determined Judah's fate in the exilic and postexilic periods. Finally, the visions of the outermost circle (visions 1 and 7; 1:7 and 6:1-8), each with its globe-encircling horses, have a universal dominion in their presentation of Yahweh's worldwide scrutiny and power.

This structure conveys a graphic view of a harmonious world, with Jerusalem and Zion at the center. The temple is not a discrete entity; it is embedded in and empowered by the widening circles of national, international, and universal interests that encompass it. Through all these facets of the temple's simultaneous centrality and broad scope runs the involvement of Yahweh, mediated by prophetic vision, angelic emissaries, and—in the case of the prophetic vision accompanying the central vision—priestly figures.

In addition to the formal and structural characteristics of the visionary sequence of First Zechariah, a plethora of specific details of the individual visions conveys various components of the mythic formulation of Zion. Our Anchor Bible notes and comments contain explications of all of these, and we will here only draw attention to the range of motifs associated with Zion, and Jerusalem, as partaking in spatial and temporal eternity.

---

27. This analogy is developed in *Haggai, Zechariah 1-8*, 126ff.
28. Graphically presented in ibid., chart 8 on p. lvi; see also discussion on pp. liv-lvi.

Perhaps the most prominent feature in the way Near Eastern and other cultures portray their unifying center is that of the sacred or cosmic mountain.[29] Zechariah heralds that aspect in his apostrophic address, "O great mountain" (4:7), to the temple mount in the celebration of refoundation that constitutes the oracular insertion (4:6b–10a) to the central (fourth) vision. The mountain language, present also in the oracles (8:3), is supplemented in this verse by other symbols of the cosmic import of Zion: the premier or foundation stone (4:7; cf. 3:9 and 4:10), and the platform (4:7) that signifies the primal emergence of dry land and thereby assures the temple of its microcosmic status.

Insofar as the sacred tree is linked with holy mountain at the center, the olive trees of the Fourth Vision likewise contribute to the mythic role of Zion. These trees provide a broad range of meaning and symbolism in Israelite and Near Eastern culture in general, where they signify permanence, stability, and fertility.[30] In the context of the vision, they also relate to the specific dyarchic political arrangement of the postexilic community. Furthermore, the trees flank the golden menorah and are connected to it by golden conduits, thus introducing the aspect of light and shining brilliance to the array of mythic symbols concentrated in the central vision.

Another aspect of the mythic presentation of Zion and Jerusalem is found in the visionary mode already discussed. The visions of Zechariah take the appearance and function of angelic beings, already present throughout the Hebrew Bible, to a new stage. Similarly, the idea of the heavenly court or divine council,[31] in which the divine messengers figure prominently, appears in full-blown form in the prophetic vision of Zechariah 3.

Throughout the visionary sequence, the presence of the language of direct speech and of reported speech, and the various features of the heavenly court, together attest to the connection between heaven and earth that is a critical dimension of Zion. The temple partakes of earth and heaven, of God's earthly presence and celestial abode. Zion mediates divine involvement in the affairs of humankind. The visions present the visual dimensions of God's availability to Israel and all the world, and the spoken words of the messengers and courtiers proclaim the divine will to Jerusalem and all nations.

As dramatic and powerful as are these sensory portrayals of Zion in First Zechariah, another dimension of similar import is also presented in vivid form. The court scene of chap. 3, in which the historic figures of Joshua and the prophet enter the heavenly realm of the divine council, is concerned with matters of purity. The temple as God's domain is one of

---

29. See references in n. 26 above.
30. Meyers, *Tabernacle Menorah*, 95–164.
31. See E. T. Mullen, *The Assembly of the Gods: The Divine Council in Canaanite and Early Hebrew Literature* (Harvard Semitic Monographs 24; Chico, CA, 1980).

perfection and holiness, and the human attendants must be similarly pure. The focus is on Joshua and his vestments. Yet these are not simply symbols of ritual purity; they also stand for moral purity, for the absence of iniquity (3:4, 9). Furthermore, by virtue of their religio-political roles, Joshua and his cohorts are to extend such a standard of morality, in accordance with Torah, to all residents of Yehud. Yahweh, through his mediating angel, presents a fourfold charge to Joshua—to "walk in my ways and . . . keep my service . . . render justice in my House and . . . administer my courts" (3:7).[32] The centrality of the vision of Zechariah 3, linked with the lampstand vision of Zechariah 4 in the overall visionary sequence, thus signifies the integral importance of the moral aspect of Zion's role.

Other passages in Zechariah's prophecies echo this message. The Fifth Vision—the Flying Scroll (5:1–4)—presents the authority of Torah throughout the land and under the supervision of Yahweh. The scroll represents a theocratic covenant, the restoration of divine authority in the social sphere, that accompanies the reaffirmation of divine presence in the renewed temple. The purview of the flying scroll with its intended moral imperative seems, in the Fifth Vision, to be limited to Judah. But the ultimate universal scope of Zion as source of and force for social stability and justice is found in the concluding oracles of the prophet where, as noted above, the unique epithet "City of Truth," along with "Mountain of Yahweh of Hosts, the Mountain of Holiness" (8:3; cf. 8:7), is attached to Zion and Jerusalem.

Many of these features of First Zechariah's conceptualization of Jerusalem are present in or adumbrated by preexilic biblical materials. And many are given even fuller expression in post-biblical rabbinic, apocalyptic, and sectarian sources. Surely Zechariah's views of Jerusalem/Zion as preserved in Zechariah 1–8 and as functional aspects of the Second Commonwealth were instrumental in moving those traditions from their place in ancient Israel to their ultimate destiny within Judeo-Christian literature and post-biblical Jewish history.

---

32. This verse represents one of the most comprehensive listings of the functions of the postexilic priest; so *Haggai, Zechariah 1–8*, 76–79, 194–97. Cf. Hag 2:10ff. and E. M. Meyers, "The Use of *tôrâ* in Haggai 2:11 and the Role of the Prophet in the Restoration Community," in *The Word of the Lord Shall Go Forth: Essays in Honor of David Noel Freedman* (ed. C. L. Meyers and M. O'Connor; Winona Lake, IN, 1983) 69–76.

THE PRIESTLY LAWS OF SANCTA CONTAMINATION

Jacob Milgrom

The ancients feared impurity because they imputed to it malignant power of supernatural origin. They conceived it as demonic, aggressively alive, contagious not just to touch, but reaching out through air and solid matter to assail its victims:

> The highest walls, the thickest walls,
> Like a flood they pass.
> From house to house they break through,
> No door can shut them out,
> No bolt can turn them back,
> Through the door like a snake they glide,
> Through the hinge like the wind they blow.[1]

Airborne Impurity: Mesopotamia and Israel

That impurity is dangerous from a distance is a commonplace in Mesopotamian ritual texts like the one cited above. One is contaminated "if he talked to an accursed man," or "[Namburbi] for the evil of a dove or strange bird which... has hovered (literally stood) [over a m]an," or "when a man looketh upon a corpse," or

> The roving Evil Eye
> Hath looked on the neighbourhood and hath vanished far away,
> Hath looked on the vicinity and hath vanished far away,

Author's note: I gratefully acknowledge the assistance of Randy Wohl, graduate student in mathematics at the University of California, Berkeley, in formulating the mathematical equations on p. 146.

1. Translation from R. C. Thompson, *The Devils and Evil Spirits of Babylonia* (2 vols.; London, 1903–1904; repr. New York, 1976), 1:53, lines v:25–35.

Hath looked on the chamber of the land and hath vanished far away,
It hath looked on the wanderer
And like wood cut [for kindling(?)] it hath bent his neck.[2]

B. Landsberger could without hesitation speak of "the circumambient danger" of Mesopotamian impurity.[3]

The airborne quality of impurity was amplified many times over in the presence of the sacred: "an unclean person has come near the sacrifice" (*CAD* E 106); or, "an unclean man or woman must not see (the ritual proceedings)" (*CAD* A/2 8). Moreover, impurity as the embodiment of divine evil was even a threat to the gods themselves, particularly to their sanctuaries. One recalls the images of the protector gods, the *šēdu* and *lamassu*, set before the entrances of Mesopotamian temples and palaces, and, above all, the elaborate purification rituals for both temples and homes to rid them of demons and prevent future incursions.[4] Indeed, to say that impurity attacks from a distance is to admit that it is demonically alive.[5]

Turning to Israel, we find that animate impurity has completely disappeared. Its devitalized traces, however, are still detectable in the rules for the scale-diseased (Lev 14:46–47) and the corpse (Num 19:14–16): everything under the same roof is contaminated except the contents of tightly sealed vessels (Num 19:15). Here we can still discern impurity as a gaseous substance, a volatile force, a miasma exuded by the source of impurity. To be sure, this impurity is no longer of pagan dimensions; it has "clipped wings," being airborne only within an enclosure. Above all, it has lost its malignancy: contaminated objects and persons need merely undergo ritual purification.

In the sacred sphere, however, an entirely different situation exists. The very power which has been stripped from impurity in contact with the common is now revealed in all of its primeval force. This fact can be demonstrated by examining the system of scaled sancta taboos upon which the Priestly legislation is structured. First, however, the nomenclature must

---

2. The four quotations in this paragraph are from, respectively, E. Reiner, "Lipšur Litanies," *JNES* 15 (1956) 137, line 85 (cf. idem, *Šurpu: A Collection of Sumerian and Akkadian Incantations* [AfO Beiheft 11; Graz, 1958] 22, line iii:130); R. Caplice, "Namburbi Texts in the British Museum," *Or* 36 (1967) 35, lines 1–2; Thompson, *Semitic Magic* (London, 1908; repr. New York, 1971) 26; idem, *Devils and Evil Spirits of Babylonia*, 2:113, lines 6–11 (cf. E. Ebeling, "Beschwörungen gegen den Feind und den bösen Blick aus dem Zweistromlande," *Archiv Orientální* 17 [1949] 203–6, lines 5–15).

3. Cited by E. Ritter, "Magical-Expert and Physician," in *Studies in Honor of Benno Landsberger* (ed. H. G. Güterbock and T. Jacobsen; Assyriological Studies 16; Chicago, 1965) 302 n. 13.

4. H. W. F. Saggs, *The Greatness That Was Babylon* (New York, 1962) 315–16.

5. D. P. Wright, *The Disposal of Impurity: Elimination Rites in the Bible and in Hittite and Mesopotamian Literature* (SBLDS 101; Atlanta, 1987) 247–61.

be clarified. I begin by noting two sets of opposites: holy (קדש) and common (חל); pure (טהור) and impure (טמא). The common and the holy are presumed pure, their normal status, unless we are told they have been contaminated. The holy is divided into two classes: sacred (קדש) and most sacred (קדש קדשים). The latter, found exclusively in the sanctuary, are further subdivided by their location, depending on whether they are in the outer courtyard, the sanctuary building, or the inner shrine.[6]

Since the common and the holy are presumed to be pure—their normal and acceptable condition—three of the four categories listed above can interact: the holy, the common, and the impure. They can interact in five different pairs: (1) most sacred and common, (2) sacred and impure, (3) sacred and common, (4) most sacred and impure, and (5) common and impure.

Contact 1 (most sacred–common) yields the following correlations. The common object (but not person) is rendered "holy" on touching all "most sacred" objects—even those in the sanctuary courtyard such as the altar (Exod 29:37) or the sacrifices (Lev 6:11, 20; Ezek 46:20). A common person, that is, a non-priest, will pay with his life if he encroaches upon them (Num 1:51; 3:10, 38; 4:19; 17:5, 28; 18:3, 7).[7] Moreover, if he but gazes upon the sancta while they are being dismantled—even if he does so through inadvertence—the consequences are fatal (Num 4:20, Neh 6:11). Only the priest may handle the most sacred because he is like them: both have been anointed to sacred status (Exodus 28, Leviticus 8). But even he is barred from the adytum except under severe restrictions (Leviticus 16). The Levite is like the layman in all respects (Num 18:3) except that, if he is a Kohatite, he carries the most sacred sancta when the camp is in transit and when they have been covered by the priests (Num 4:5–20). It must be borne in mind that in these examples the sancta are not being contaminated because their contact is with the common, not with the impure. The common is an inert category, devoid of active power. The activity is on the part of the "most sacred" which "sanctifies" the common person (and thing) or can kill him on sight if he is inside the shrine. Thus, the super-holiness with which the most sacred is charged exhibits the same airborne quality that obtains in severe impurity.

Contact 2 (sacred–impure) is illumined by the contrast with contact 1. The prescribed penalty is not death by divine agency (מות) but excision (כרת), for example, "The person who, while impure, eats flesh from the LORD's sacrifice of well-being, that person shall be cut off [ונכרתה] from his kin" (Lev 7:20).

Contact 3 (sacred–common) has no effect whatsoever as long as the common remains uncontaminated. So indeed reads the rule of eating the

---

6. J. Milgrom, *Cult and Conscience* (Leiden, 1976) 35–37.
7. Milgrom, *Studies in Levitical Terminology* (Berkeley, 1970) 16–33.

flesh of the well-being offering (Lev 7:19b, 10:14). However, the illegitimate contact of the sacred and the common (i.e., desecration) is subject to severe penalties: if inadvertent, a fine of twenty percent and a reparation offering (Lev 5:14–26); if deliberate, death at the hands of God (Lev 5:14–26). Even the legitimate contact of the sacred and common is subject to the twenty percent penalty (Leviticus 27).

As for contact 4 (most sacred–impure) the texts are silent, but only because the death penalty is obvious, an *a fortiori* deduction from the capital punishment prescribed for the most sacred–common cases (contact 1). There is also the precedent of Nadab and Abihu whose immediate death was caused by "a strange fire" (Lev 10:1) which, whatever its nature, resulted in the contamination of the sanctuary. Perhaps the most sacred–impure clash results in even greater calamity if we note the frequent reference to the wrath of God punishing not only the offending priest but his community as well (e.g., Lev 4:3, 10:6; Num 18:5).

Having discussed the penalties for bringing sancta into contact with the common and the impure, we can now focus exclusively on sancta–impure contacts (nos. 2 and 4) to study the processes involved, that is, how a sacred object is contaminated and then purified. Contact 5 (impure–common) need not be discussed here since it has been the subject of all the impurity laws in Leviticus 11–15. It is rarely prohibited (e.g., Lev 11:8) and never penalized, unless the prescribed purification is not observed. When this occurs, even minor impurities become major ones, polluting the sanctuary from afar (Lev 5:2–3).[8] However, then, we are dealing with the contact of the sacred and the impure. The pollution of the sanctuary by airborne impurity has already been discussed in connection with its purification by the blood of the purification offering.[9] It remains to discuss the impact of impurity on Israel's other dominant sanctum, the priest.

The Contamination of the Priest: Mesopotamia and Israel

It comes as no surprise to find airborne and deadly impurity in texts dealing with the pagan priest of the ancient Near East. The Babylonian *mašmašu* is contaminated if he even glances at dirty water or a person with "unwashed hands."[10] The *šešgallu*, the main priest of Babylon's Esagila, "shall not view the [New Year's] purification of the temple. If he does view (it), he is no (longer) pure" (*ANET* 333, lines 364–65). The "loosening" of

---

8. Milgrom, "The Graduated Purification Offering (Leviticus 5:1–13)," *JAOS* 103 (1983) 249–54.

9. Milgrom, "Israel's Sanctuary: The Priestly 'Picture of Dorian Gray,'" *RB* 83 (1976) 390–99.

10. For these two forms of contamination, see, respectively, G. Meier, *Die assyrische Beschwörungssammlung Maqlû* (AfO Beiheft 2; Berlin, 1937) 11, lines i:105, 107; and Thompson, *Devils and Evil Spirits of Babylonia*, 2:139–40.

the impurity from the temple walls and its transfer to the scape-ram has, in effect, made it airborne once again and doubly dangerous to the holiest of the priests. The human corpse, in particular, can contaminate from afar but the priest is its special target. Note the alarm sounded in Ur warning of the approach of Dumuzi from the land of the dead:

> O (city of) Ur! At my loud cry
> Lock your house, lock your house, city lock your house!
> O temple of Ur! Lock your house, city lock your house!
> Your *entu*-priestess must not go out of (her house) the Giparu,
> City lock your house![11]

The dead must be kept away from the city and temple, but the chief priestess (*entu*) may not even expose herself to the open air of the street. The susceptibility of the priesthood reaches down to the end of pagan times: the Roman high priest, the Flamen Dialis, sins as did his ancient Babylonian counterpart if he but glances at a corpse (Servius, *On the Aenid* 6:76). So too in Hellenistic Syria: "Those priests who bore the corpse of a Galloi priest of Syria were not allowed to enter the temple for seven days; if any priest looked at a corpse he was impure for that day and could only enter the temple the following day if he was cleansed" (Lucian, *The Syrian God* 2:62).

In these essentials, the priest of Israel is not different from his pagan colleague. His sensitivity to impurity is greater than the layman's, and the high priest, by virtue of his supreme holiness, is the most vulnerable of all. Accordingly, the ordinary priest is permitted to attend the burial of his immediate blood relatives only (Lev 21:1–4); the high priest—not even for his parents (Lev 21:11). In Ezekiel's system, the priest is further set apart from the layman in that his purification from corpse contamination lasts two weeks, climaxed by a *ḥaṭṭāʾt* sacrifice (44:26–27), whereas the layman needs only sprinkling with *ḥaṭṭāʾt* waters on the third and seventh day (Num 19:9). Thus, of the three bearers of corpse contamination, the Nazirite, Ezekiel's priest, and the layman, the two consecrated classes require sacrifices for their purification but not the layman. Finally, the prohibition issued to Israel's high priest that "he may not leave the sanctuary" to follow after the bier is strikingly reminiscent of the Babylonian high priestess who "must not go out of (her house)" (cited at n. 11 above). In this instance, Babylonian and Israelite ritual law coincide exactly.

The susceptibility of the high priest to airborne impurity persists into rabbinic times: "If any of his [the high priest's] near of kin die he may not follow after the bier, . . . but he may go forth with the bearers as far as the

---

11. Translation from T. Jacobsen, "Toward the Image of Tammuz," *History of Religions* 1 (1961) 208 (repr. in idem, *Toward the Image of Tammuz and Other Essays on Mesopotamian History and Culture* [ed. W. L. Moran; HSS 21; Cambridge, MA, 1970] 96).

city gate, *if he and they come not within sight of one another.* So R. Meir. But R. Judah says: 'He may not go forth from the temple, for it is written, "Neither shall he go out of the sanctuary"' [Lev 21:12]" (*m. Sanh.* 2:1, emphasis added). R. Meir and R. Judah do not differ at all. As the Roman and Babylonian parallels teach, R. Meir is correctly citing the reason for the biblical prohibition. Moreover, just as the Flamen Dialis was not allowed to spend a single night outside Rome, so Israel's high priest was never allowed to lodge outside the temple.[12]

The Contamination of Israel's Sanctuary: First Law

The contamination of Israel's sanctuary needs only be summarized here: (1) the accidental sins or impurities of the individual contaminate the outer altar requiring purification blood on its horns (Lev 4:22–35); (2) the accidental sins or impurities of the community invade and contaminate the shrine requiring purification blood on the horns of the inner altar and before the veil (Lev 4:1–21); and (3) the deliberate sins penetrate the veil into the adytum requiring purification blood on and before the ark cover (Lev 16:14–15). Thus, the contamination of the sanctuary varies directly with the intensity of the impurity charge. This law will hold true for all sancta. The sanctuary, however, is set apart from other sancta in that (1) it is capable of different levels or degrees of contamination, and (2) it is automatically contaminated by impurity no matter where it occurs in Israel's camp (P) or land (H). This property is not shared by other sancta. Instead, as already observed, the latter are governed by another correlation, that the closer the impurity source to the sanctum and the greater the holiness charge of the sanctum, the more readily contamination takes place. More precisely the comprehensive law reads: *Sancta contamination varies directly with the charge (holiness) of the sanctuary, the charge of the impurity, and inversely with the distance between them.* If we resort to the vocabulary of electromagnetism (but not to equate the phenomena), we could describe the workings of the law as follows: opposites attract and, in the priestly system, holiness is opposite in charge to the impure. If either the holiness or impurity source is strong enough or the distance between them small enough, impurity will become airborne, spark the gap, and impinge on the sanctum (see the mathematical formulation, p. 146 below).

The Contamination of Israel's Sanctuary: Second Law

The fixed levels of penetration observed for the contamination of the sanctuary yield a second law: *Impurity displaces an equal amount of*

---

12. S. Lieberman, *Hellenism in Jewish Palestine* (New York, 1950) 165 n. 12.

sanctuary holiness. This correlation is adumbrated, outside of P, in the ancient regulation of the holy war camp: "Let him not find anything unseemly among you and turn away from you" (Deut 23:15b; cf. contact 4). Thus, God withdraws from the contaminated camp. In P, this general principle becomes mathematical law. Holiness and impurity are finite quantitative categories; impurity displaces sanctuary holiness in fixed amounts until a saturation point is reached beyond which the sanctuary cannot endure. It might be termed Archimedes' law of holiness displacement. It certifies that holiness can abide with a limited but fixed amount of impurity, and it accounts for the repeated admonitions not to pollute the sanctuary (e.g., Lev 12:4, 15:31, 20:1-4; Num 19:13, 20).

In P's own terms this law can be understood as follows: God will tolerate inadvertent wrongs which contaminate the outside altar (Lev 4:22ff.) and the shrine (Lev 4:1-21) for they can be purged through purification offerings. However, as for the perpetrator of *pešaʿ* 'rebellious acts' (Lev 16:16) "who acts defiantly [and] reviles the LORD" (Num 15:30), personal sacrifice will not avail him. The nation as a whole must expiate for him and others like him at the annual purgation rite of the sanctuary (Leviticus 16), cleansing the contaminated adytum with the purification blood and transferring the released impurities to "the goat for Azazel" (Lev 16:10, 20b-22). Even then, only a limited amount of deliberate sin will be tolerated. There is a point of no return. One day, purgation will no longer avail; the impurities, especially the accumulated *pešaʿ* in the adytum, will go beyond the set limit; God's endurance of his people's impurities will end; he will forsake his abode and abandon it and his people to destruction.[13]

In essence, this priestly theology of sanctuary contamination is structured on the lines of pagan analogues. Indeed, all laws controlling Israel's system operate with equal validity in the polytheistic world, but with one crucial distinction. The pagans, who gave highest priority to protecting their sanctuary from impurity, believed the latter to be personified demonic forces intent on driving out their patron god from his sanctuary, and they sought magical apotropaic rituals, mediated by the priesthood, to enhance the life-force of the deity and shield the sanctuary from invasion. In Israel, however, these universal laws are recast in terms of its monotheism: impurity is not the outcome of demonic force but of the people's sin. The cause of impurity had radically changed. Man has replaced the demon. Rather, the demon is in man. Man has the unique power to obey or resist God. If he chooses to rebel—to use the priestly idiom—he will pollute the sanctuary to the point where God will no longer abide in it. But whether the cause is the demon or the man, the net effect is still the same: God is evicted from his earthly abode.

---

13. Milgrom, "The Function of the חַטָּאת Sacrifice," *Tarbiz* 40 (1970) 1-8 [Hebrew]; idem, "Israel's Sanctuary."

Only a theological structure as just outlined can explain the thought and imagery of Ezekiel, prophet-priest par excellence. The first section of his book (chaps. 1–11) is a vivid description of Jerusalem's forthcoming destruction, dramatized by P's conceptual imagery of God's departure from his temple. Equally characteristic of the Priestly source is Ezekiel's indictment solely stressing the presumptuous, rebellious sin, the *pešaᶜ* and its semantic equivalents, as having contaminated the adytum and forced God's departure (note the similar vocabulary of Ezek 39:24a and Lev 16:16). Six times he explicitly labels the contamination of the temple as the end result of Israel's sin (Ezek 5:11, 8:6, 23:38, 23:39, 24:21, 44:7), and seven times he prophesies its ultimate purification (Ezek 11:16; 37:26, 27, 28; 48:8; 48:10, 21). Indeed, only by recognizing that the priestly laws of sancta contamination inform Ezekiel's thought are we able to explain the ideological framework of his book. God's abandonment of his contaminated temple is complemented by his return to an uncontaminable temple, so assured because Israel will never be less than pure. Ezekiel is his own best witness:

> Son of man, do you see what they are doing, the great abominations that the house of Israel is committing here, to drive me from my sanctuary? (Ezek 8:6)
>
> They shall not contaminate themselves any more with their idols and their detestable things, or with any of their transgressions [*pešaᶜ*]; . . . but I will purify them . . . and I will set my sanctuary in the midst of them for evermore. (Ezek 37:23a, bβ, 26bβ)

Thus, the blueprint of the new temple is not a chance appendix to the book; it is a logical fitting climax to all that has preceded it. First comes the reunification, restoration, and purification of Israel, ending with a promise of a Davidic ruler and a new temple (Ezekiel 36–37). Then follows the purification of the land after the slaughter of Israel's enemies therein (Ezekiel 38–39, esp. 39:12–16). With purging of people and land complete, the new temple can be built (Ezekiel 40–48).

The Contamination of Israel's Sanctuary: Third Law

Having described the process and effect of impurity impinging on the sacred and the common, I am now ready to extrapolate the third and final law. Previously, I have argued that the ablution removes impurity to the extent that it can no longer contaminate the common, but it may contaminate the sacred until evening or, in severer cases of impurity, till sacrificial purification on the following day.[14] On the other hand, prior to

---

14. Milgrom, "The Priestly Impurity System," in *Proceedings of the Ninth World Congress of Jewish Studies*, Division A: *The Period of the Bible* (Jerusalem, 1986) 115–20.

the ablution, both the common and the sacred are subject to contamination, except that the latter process can take place from a distance.

Thus, the pre- and post-ablution periods offer a new criterion for comparing the realms of the sacred and the common, to wit: (*a*) *The sacred is of greater sensitivity to contamination than the common by one degree*, and (*b*) *each purification stage reduces contagion to both the sacred and the common by one degree*. There are three possibilities to contaminate an object: from afar, by direct contact, or at home. Specifically, a severely impure person contaminates a common object by direct contact and a sacred object from afar. After the ablution, he is no longer contagious to the common object but can contaminate a sacred object by direct contact (but not from afar). Finally, after the last stage of purification he is no longer contagious even to sancta. If these two correlations are correct, then a reconstruction of the entire system of ritual impurities contained in the Priestly source is now feasible. Despite the large gaps in the biblical data we would only need to know either the number of ablutions required or the final purification procedure to deduce the missing stages.[15]

Occasionally, lacunas are also filled by the rabbinic evidence, accepted whenever it proves an ancient and uncontested tradition. This also corroborates my general laws, which nearly always predict independently the same results. For example, tannaitic sources (*m. Kelim* 1:4; *m. Neg.* 13:7, 11) and Josephus (*Against Apion* 1:31, *Antiquities* 3:264) affirm that the scale-diseased person has the impurity status of a corpse and analogously contaminates everything under the same roof. This "overhang" principle creates an extra stage in my contamination scale.[16] An additional stage for the scale-diseased person is also predictable, since he alone among the contaminated requires not one but two ablutions for his purification, and my third law states that each ablution reduces contagion by one degree. A third, converging line of evidence stems from the analogy of the "scale-diseased" house which also contaminates by overhang (Lev 14:46–47).

Other correlations with rabbinic tradition can be found, but differences also appear. However, because the biblical assumption of post-ablution sensitivity of sancta also informs the rabbinic system, the differences are in details rather than in principle. Herein, I maintain, lies the greater harvest of my study. The discovery of the biblical laws of sancta contamination will lead to the isolation of the rabbinic laws which veer from their biblical predecessors. These can now be studied for the concrete, historical situations that brought about their change.[17]

---

15. Tentatively, see ibid.
16. Ibid.
17. Milgrom, "Graduated Purification Offering."

The laws of sancta contamination, derived in this paper, are summarized as follows:

1. The contamination of a sanctum varies directly with the intensity of the impurity source, directly with the holiness intensity of the sanctum, and inversely with the distance between them. Also, contamination has a threshold, a fixed value, below which it cannot be activated.
2. The sanctuary is a special case of the general law (1), whereby:
    a. Contamination is a function of the intensity of the impurity source alone, that is, impurities of a severe amount and from any distance (in the camp) will contaminate the sanctuary.
    b. Contamination takes place at three ascending thresholds: the outer altar, the shrine, or the adytum.
    c. Contamination displaces an equal volume of the sanctuary holiness (the Archimedean principle) until a saturation point is reached.
3. Sancta are related to common things in regard to their contamination and purification, as follows:
    a. Sancta are more vulnerable to contamination by one degree.
    b. Each purification stage reduces the communicability of the impurity source to both sancta and common things by one degree.

These laws can also be expressed mathematically,[18] as follows:

Contamination occurs in accordance with the equation of

$$c = f\,[p + (i\text{-}n) + k - 4]$$

where,

- c is the degree of contamination
- f is an increasing, discretely valued function of one discrete variable satisfying $x \leq 0 \Rightarrow f(x) \equiv 0$
- $p \equiv$ contagion factor of the contaminating process (airborne = 1, overhang = 2, direct = 3)
- $i \equiv$ initial impurity of source (0, 1, 2, or 3)
- $n \equiv$ number of relevant purification rituals
- $k \equiv$ holiness constant of sanctum (holy = 1, common = 0)

In the case of the sanctuary there exists a critical level of contamination, C_s, such that

(1) $C \leq C_s$
(2) if $C < C_s$, purification is possible
(3) if ever $C = C_s$, then this condition becomes permanent

---

18. The following symbols are employed: = equals; ≤ less than or equal to; ⇒ implying; ≡ defined as; < less than.

POLYSENSUOUS POLYVALENCY
IN POETIC PARALLELISM

Shalom M. Paul

A fundamental feature of human speech inherent in the basic structure of language is the polyvalency of words.[1] Lexical polyvalency may be subdivided into two different, but at times overlapping, categories: homonymy, two words identical in sound (i.e., homophony, similarly sounding but different in meaning: e.g., bow/bough)[2] or in spelling (i.e., homography, identical spelling but different in meaning: e.g., the noun "can," a metal container, and the verb "can," to be able),[3] and polysemy, one word which bears several meanings.[4] A polysensuous word refers to one thing while alluding to yet another within the same single context; it has both an explicit and implicit meaning. This rhetorical phenomenon, which has been described as "accumulated intension,"[5] has been called by many names:

Author's note: To Professor Shemaryahu Talmon: יערף כמטר לקחך ותזל כטל אמרתך.

1. See, in general, the works of J. Ullman: *Words and Their Use* (London, 1951) 46–56; *Language and Style* (Oxford, 1964) 75–77; *Principles of Semantics* (Oxford, 1967) 117–25 (for additional literature on the topic of polysemy, see pp. 118–19 n. 3); *Semantics: An Introduction to the Science of Meaning* (Oxford, 1970) 156–92; *Meaning and Style* (Oxford, 1973) 54–55. See also W. Empson, *Seven Types of Ambiguity* (New York, 1966).

2. Cf. also, e.g., Molière, *Femmes Savantes*, act 2, scene 6: "Belise: Veux-tu toute ta vie offenser la grammaire? Martine: Qui parle d'offenser grand-mère ni grand-père" (*Oeuvres de Molière* [Paris, 1925], 9:98–99).

3. See the marvelous little poem by E. Merriam, "Nym and Graph," in *It Doesn't Have to Rhyme* (New York, 1965) 54–55, where she creates a contest dialogue between "a sound-alike homophone" and "a spell-alike homograph."

4. In Proust's *Le Côté de Guermantes* (Paris, 1949) 26, the maid Francoise believes that the Guermantes are "une *grande* famille," both because of their illustriousness and their many members: "Car m'ayant que ce seul mot de 'grand' pour les deux choses, il lui semblait qu'elles n'en formaient qu'une seule" (cited by Ullman, *Language and Style*, 237).

5. W. M. Urban, *Language and Reality* (London, 1938) 112–13.

משנה הוראה, מלתא דמשתמעה לתרי אפי, ἀμφιβολία, ἀντανάκλησις, *ambiguitas, dilogia, tawriyya*,[6] *talḥin*,[7] *double entendre*. Since this stylistic device is a fertile source for intentional ambiguity, it has been the subject of severe criticism ever since the time of Aristotle, who wrote in his *"Art" of Rhetoric*: "Words of ambiguous meaning are chiefly useful to enable the sophist to mislead his hearers." However, it also may be the source of a bountiful wellspring for the talented writer who wishes to display his artful and witty literary propensities.[8] Its presence has also been noted in several studies of biblical poetry.[9] Needless to say, the recognition of polysemy

---

6. See E. W. Lane, *An Arabic-English Lexicon* (London, 1893), 8:3052: ندى "signifies the using [of] a word, an expression, or a phrase, which has an obvious meaning, and intending thereby another meaning, to which it applies, but which is contrary to the obvious one." He also compares مِفْرَاض, which is "an oblique, indirect, obscure ambiguous or equivocal, mode of speech" (5:2012).

7. See ibid., 8:3009, under لحن: "An oblique, or ambiguous, mode of speech: ... an inclining of speech to obliqueness, or ambiguity, and equivocal allusion." See also R. Gordis, *A Commentary on the Book of Lamentations* (New York, 1968) 16: "In *talḥin* the author's choice of a particular word instead of its synonym is dictated by his desire to suggest both meanings simultaneously to the reader. The one serves as the primary or dominant meaning, and the other as the secondary concept, thus enriching the thought or emotion of the reader."

8. Here are some other clever examples:

> Where Bentley late tempestuous wont to sport
> In troubled waters, but now sleeps in *Port*
>
> (Pope, *Dunciad*, book 4, lines 201–2)

When Oliver Twist was told by Rumble that he should "bow to the board ... seeing no *board* but the table, [he] fortunately bowed to that" (Dickens, *Oliver Twist* [ed. K. Tillotson; Oxford, 1966] 8).

> Come, thick Night,
> And pall thee in the dunnest smoke of Hell,
> That my keen knife see not the wound it makes,
> Nor Heaven peep through the *blanket* of the dark,
> To cry, "Hold, hold!"
>
> (*Macbeth*, act 1, scene 5, lines 50–54)

> Oh, Nelly Gray! Oh, Nelly Gray!
> Is this your love so warm?
> The love that loves a scarlet coat,
> Should be more *uniform*.

(Thomas Hood, "Faithless Nelly Gray," in *The Works of Thomas Hood* [London, 1862], 1:277)

9. Most of these studies have been published only in modern Hebrew: D. Yellin, in *Tarbiz* 5 (1934) 1–17; idem, *Ketavim Nivḥarim* (Jerusalem, 1939), 2:86–100; A. Weiser, "Mishneh Horaʾah BeSefer Mishle," in *Sefer Niger* (ed. A. Biram et al.; David Neiger FS; Jerusalem, 1959) 140–47; idem, "Mishneh Horaʾah BeSefer Yeshayahu," *Beth Miqra* 20–21 (1964) 25–32; R. Gordis, "Lisegulot Ha-Meliṣah BeKitve HaQodesh," in *Sefer Seidel* (Jerusalem, 1962) 253–66; Y. Kutscher, *Words and Their History* (Jerusalem, 1961) 85–89; R. Weiss, *Mishuṭ BaMiqrah* (Jerusalem, 1976) 186–89 (for additional bibliography on paronomasia, see p. 163 n. 9); M. Paran, "LeMishneh Horaʾah BaMiqrah," *Beer-Sheva* 1 (1973) 150–61.

helps one achieve a fuller and richer understanding and appreciation of the biblical text.[10]

This present article, which is the second part of a study of polysensuous *double entendre*,[11] will concentrate on what has been called Janus parallelism. Named after the Roman deity who is represented with two faces looking in opposite directions, Janus parallelism is a specialized use of the phenomenon of polysemy. Here a single word is found in a pivotal position which parallels what precedes it with one meaning and what follows it with yet another meaning. It literally faces both ways, but in a polysensuous fashion.

An example may be supplied from the Qurʾān, Sūra 55:5-6: "The sun and the moon run their courses, and the نجم and trees bow in adoration." The substantive means both 'stars' (and thus retrospectively continues the list of celestial bodies) and 'sprouts/herbs' (which prospectively joins the "trees" bowing in adoration).[12]

Only recently has this unique "two-faced" stylistic device become a subject of scholarly discussion in biblical circles.

Though the device had been noted by E. König, *Stilistik, Rhetorik, Poetik in Bezug auf die biblische Literatur* (Leipzig, 1900) 10-12, it hardly is mentioned (if at all) in most recent works on biblical poetry. For rare exceptions and then only *en passant*, cf. W. G. E. Watson, "An Example of Multiple Wordplay in Ugaritic," *UF* 12 (1980), 443-44; idem, *Classical Hebrew Poetry* (JSOTSup 26; Sheffield, 1984) 237, 242; R. Alter, *The Art of Biblical Poetry* (New York, 1985) 197-202, who calls it *double entente*. See also E. L. Greenstein, "Two Variations of Grammatical Parallelism in Canaanite Poetry and Their Psycholinguistic Background," *JANES* 6 (1974) 88-89; idem, "How Does Parallelism Mean?" in *A Sense of Text: The Art of Language in the Study of Biblical Literature* (Winona Lake, IN, 1983) 50-51. (I was unable to see the doctoral dissertation of W. Herzberg, *Polysemy in the Hebrew Bible* [New York University, 1979].) There is a wealth of examples primarily in the Hebrew works cited above and in the various commentaries to biblical books, to which the reader is directed. Obviously not all the passages cited will be met with general agreement. The rhetorical device examined here is a literarily sensitive one and is open to multiple opinions. Paran, "LeMishneh Horaʾah BaMiqrah," attempted to clarify the issue by establishing some rules to help determine the validity of this phenomenon. Nevertheless, the ultimate decision must be made by the exegete on each individual verse. For an excellent treatment of this phenomenon in medieval Hebrew and Arabic poetry with many superb examples, see D. Yellin, *Introduction to the Hebrew Poetry of the Spanish Period* (Jerusalem, 1972) 243-51 [Hebrew].

10. For the sake of convenience, most of the English translations of the biblical verses are drawn from NJPS (and occasionally NEB). The references to Rashi, ibn Ezra, Kimchi, Ramban, Meṣudat Zion, Meṣudat David, Minḥat Shai, and the Aramaic translations are all taken from the standard editions of the Rabbinic Bible, *Mikraʾot Gedolot*. For Y. ibn Ganaḥ, see *Sepher Haschoraschim* (Berlin, 1896) [Hebrew]; for D. Y. Abarbanel, see *Commentary to the Latter Prophets* (Jerusalem, 1957) [Hebrew]; for S. D. Luzatto, see *Il Profeta Isaia* (Padua, 1867) [Hebrew].

11. The first part of this study will be published elsewhere.

12. This example is quoted by J. Finkel, "An Interpretation of an Ugaritic Viticultural Poem," in *Joshua Starr Memorial Volume: Studies in History and Philology* (New York, 1953) 35. For the dual meaning of Arabic نجم, see Lane, *Arabic-English Lexicon*, 8:3028.

Canticles 2:12

The blossoms have appeared in the land.
the time of the זמיר has come.
The song of the turtledove is heard in our land.

This first example was proposed by C. H. Gordon.[13] Retrospectively the *hapax legomenon* זמיר evokes the agricultural imagery of the first stich and means 'pruning' (cf. LXX, Aquila, Peshitta, Vulgate, Tg. Ket., Rashbam; for the verb, cf. Lev 25:3–4, Isa 5:6, Gezer Calendar, line 6: זמר). And prospectively, alluding to the song of the turtledove, it refers to 'singing' (cf., e.g., Rashi, ibn Ezra, Kimchi; for the root, cf. 2 Sam 23:1; Isa 24:16, 25:5; Ps 95:2, 119:54; Job 35:10).

Genesis 49:26

The blessings of your father
Surpass the blessings of הורי
To the utmost bounds of the eternal hills.

The second example was the subject of an article by G. Rendsburg.[14] Hebrew הורי (which Rendsburg connects with the following word עד against the Masoretic division) retrospectively is related to the prior stich, paralleling 'father', and means 'parents' (cf. Hos 2:7, Cant 3:4), that is, 'progenitors of old' (cf. Tg. Onq. and Tg. Ps.-J.: אבהתי; Vulgate: *patrium eius*). Then prospectively, paralleling גבעת עולם 'eternal hills', it also means 'eternal mountains' (הרי עד).[15] Compare LXX: ὀρέων μονίμων 'steadfast mountains'; Rashbam: ברכות אביך גברו על ברכות הרים . . . כי הורי לשון כפל של גבעת עולם. For the set pair hills–mountains, see Deut 33:15. Both interpretations were

---

Compare also the following translations of this word in this Sūra: G. Sale, *The Koran* (London, 1877) 513: "vegetables"; R. Bell, *The Quran* (Edinburgh, 1909): "star"; M. M. Pickthall, *The Meaning of the Glorious Koran* (New York, 1954) 549: "the stars"; A. Y. Ali, *The Holy Quran* (New York, 1946) 1472: "herbs," but adds in a note, "*Najm*: may mean stars collectively, or herbs collectively; perhaps both meanings are implied."

13. C. H. Gordon, "Asymmetric Janus Parallelism," *EI* 16 (1982; Harry M. Orlinsky FS) 80*–81*. Cf. also W. Rudolph, *Das Buch Ruth, Das Hohe Lied, Die Klagelieder* (2d. ed.; KAT 17/1–3; Gütersloh, 1962) 133; G. Gerleman, *Ruth, Das Hohelied* (Biblischer Kommentar: Altes Testament 18; Neukirchen-Vluyn, 1965) 124; E. Würthwein, *Die Fünf Megilloth* (2d ed.; HAT 18; Tübingen, 1969) 45; O. Keel, *Das Hohelied* (Zürcher Bibelkommentar Altes Testament 18; Zürich, 1986) 98.

14. G. Rendsburg, "Janus Parallelism in Gen 49:26," *JBL* 99 (1980) 291–93.

15. For the translation "mountains," see also E. A. Speiser, *Genesis* (AB 1; Garden City, NY, 1964) 369.

skillfully interwoven by Tg. Yer.: ברכתא דאבוך יתוספן עלך על ברכתא דבריכו
יתך אהבתך אברהם ויצחק מטולין לטוריא:

May the blessings of your father's be added to the blessings wherewith your <u>fathers</u>, Abraham and Isaac, who are like <u>mountains</u>, blessed you....

To the above may be added the following examples of Janus polysemy.[16]

Isaiah 7:11

The LORD spoke further to Ahaz: "Ask [שאל] for a sign from the LORD your God, העמק שאלה, or up to the sky."[17]

Retrospectively שְׁאָלָה is to be interpreted as a lengthened imperative (cf. Dan 9:19) reinforcing the initial imperative שאל, and means 'ask profoundly, deeply' (cf. Rashi, ibn Ezra, Kimchi, Luzatto [who is aware of the other interpretation found in the versions], Ehrlich).[18] Yet in the context of the end of the verse, "or up to the sky," the word, when interpreted as a substantive (pointing שְׁאֹלָה), prospectively creates an artistic merism: "Ask [anywhere] from *deepest Sheol* up to the highest heaven" (cf. Aquila, Theodotion, Symmachus: εἰς ᾅδην; Vulgate: *in profundum inferni*).[19] For the set pair שמים-שאול, see Amos 9:2 and Job 11:8; for the "depths of Sheol," see Prov 9:18, 25:3.

Isaiah 9:3

> For the yoke [עול] that they bore,
> And מטה of their back,
> The rod [שבט] of their taskmaster,
> You have broken as on the day of Midian.

---

16. Other examples which have been cited, but are totally unconvincing, are E. Zurro, "Disemia de *brḥ* y paralelismo bifronte en Job 9,25," *Bib* 62 (1981) 541–47 (Hebrew ברח simply does not mean 'ser malo'); G. Rendsburg, "Double Polysemy in Genesis 49:6 and Job 3:6," *CBQ* 44 (1982) 48–51; D. T. Tsumura, "Janus Parallelism in Nah 1:8," *JBL* 102 (1983) 109–11 (who misunderstands Hebrew מקומה); D. Grossberg, "Pivotal Polysemy in Jeremiah XXV 10-11a," *VT* 36 (1986) 481–85, where the suggested אור 'tilled land' is totally unfounded.

17. Cf. Yellin, *Ketavim Nivḥarim*, 93–94, who did not, however, catch the Janus construction.

18. A. B. Ehrlich, *Randglossen zur hebräischen Bibel* (7 vols.; Leipzig, 1912), 4:29, vocalizes the word as a substantive, שְׁאֹלָה.

19. Cf. N. H. Tur-Sinai, *Peshuṭo shel Miqra* (6 vols.; Jerusalem, 1967), 3/1:24 [Hebrew]. Many modern commentaries simply translate "Sheol" or the "underworld." The Masoretic pointing שְׁאֹלָה creates an assonance with the following לְמָעְלָה; see G. B. Gray, *Isaiah* (ICC; Edinburgh, 1912) 122, 132.

Prospectively the Hebrew substantive מטה 'staff' parallels the following שבט 'rod'. For this set pair in Isaiah, see Isa 10:5, 24; 14:5 (cf., e.g., Kimchi, Abarbanel). However, the very same מטה can also be interpreted as a verbal participal from the root נטה 'that which bends (the back)', and thus retrospectively would be a direct continuation of the first colon: "For the yoke that they bore which bends their back. . . ."[20] Compare Rashi: . . . עול מטה זה פועל, כמו שפירש רש״י ,;שהיה מטה את שכמו למשא כבד and Ehrlich: ולא שם; ופירוש הדברים האויב שהיה מטה את שכמם לסבול עולו.[21] The imagery is drawn from the work animal that bears a heavy yoke on the back of its shoulders (cf. Gen 49:15; Isa 10:27, 14:25; Ps 81:7).

Isaiah 19:10

And שתתיה shall be crushed,
And all עשי שכר shall be despondent.

The multiple difficulties inherent in this passage are readily apparent upon comparing three different translations:

> Her foundations shall be crushed,
> And all who make dams shall be despondent. (NJPSV)

(NJPSV adds this note: "Meaning of verse uncertain; emendation yields "Her drinkers shall be dejected, / And all her brewers despondent.")

> Egypt's spinners shall be downcast,
> and all her artisans sick at heart. (NEB)

> And the nobles shall be depressed,
> And they that work for hire grieved in soul.[22]

Since the previous verses (8–9) describe the various professional classes in Egypt who will suffer and lament because of the severe drought—"the fishermen" (הדיגים), "all who cast lines in the Nile" (משליכי ביאור חכה), "those who spread nets in the water" (פרשי מכמרת על פני המים), "the flax workers" (עבדי פשתים), "female carders" (שריקות), and "weavers" (ארגים)—it is perfectly logical that here, too, two further professions are added to the

---

20. Paran, "LeMisneh Hora^ᵓah BaMiqrah," 155–56, cites this verse, but did not note the pivotal Janus construction.

21. Ehrlich, *Mikrâ ki-Pheschutô* (3 vols.; Berlin, 1899–1901; repr. New York, 1969), 3:22 [Hebrew]; cf. idem, *Randglossen zur hebräischen Bibel*, 4:37.

22. E. J. Kissane, *The Book of Isaiah* (Dublin, 1960), 1:204; cf. pp. 208–9.

list.[23] Following the MT and vocalization, שָׁתֹתֶיהָ would refer to the 'pillars or foundations' (cf. Ps 11:3) of the society, that is, the nobles or landowners, who, along with עֹשֵׂי שֶׂכֶר 'the hired laborers' (those who work for שכר 'hire', i.e., the working classes) are crushed and despondent (cf. Kimchi).[24] The first substantive, however, has been also interpreted as referring to yet another specific profession, 'weavers' (reading שֹׁתֶיהָ 'her weavers'). This is based on Hebrew and Aramaic שְׁתִי 'warp' (cf. also Akkadian *šutû*; see *AHW* 1293–94); see Lev 13:48–49, 51–53, 56–59 (cf. Tg. Neb.: משתיתא, which renders Hebrew מסכת in Judg 16:13–14; and Arabic: سَدَّى سَتَى 'to set the warp'), and explains LXX: οἱ διαζόμενοι αὐτά, derived from the verb διάζομαι 'to set the warp in the loom'.

Yet another possibility exists if one understands שֹׁתֶיהָ as 'her drinkers' (Vulgate: *inrigua eius*; cf. שתי מים in Ezek 31:14, 16; שתי יין in Joel 1:5; and שתי שכר in Ps 69:13)[25] or 'those who make drinking utensils',[26] which, in turn, would create an apt parallel to עשי שכר, if pointed שֵׁכָר 'strong drink', hence 'her brewers' (cf. LXX: οἱ τὸν ζῦθον ποιοῦθες). Luzatto, after commenting on the verse, cites Tg. Neb.: אתר בית שתי 'the place of drinking,' and adds, ואין הדבר רחוק, ולפי זה יתכן לפרש גם שתתיה העשים מיני שתיה.

It is also of interest to note that Kimchi interprets שתתיה as 'nets', referring to Aramaic שותא, apparently a loan word from Akkadian *šētu*;[27] while ibn Ezra understands the word to mean 'fish ponds'. Both, in turn, connect שכר to the verb סכר (cf. Gen 8:2), meaning 'to dam', thus continuing their exegesis of fish imagery. They also explain the other difficult *hapax legomenon* phrase at the end of this verse, אגמי נפש (usually explained as a byform of עגם נפש; see Job 30:25), in a like manner, by understanding אגם as 'pool, pond' (so, too, Rashi) and נפש, as the 'fish' in the ponds; compare Vulgate: *omnis qui faciebant lacunas ad capiendos pisces*.

In the light of these multifarious interpretations, it may be conjectured that the prophet's choice of שתתיה was deliberate. For retrospectively, in connection with the previous verse, it could refer to another class of weavers (ארגים) and prospectively, in the present verse, it would create a parallel with עשי שכר (pointed שֵׁכָר).

---

23. For this verse, see also Weiser, "Mishneh Horaʾah BeSefer Yeshayahu," 26.
24. Cf. the commentaries of Buhl, Duhm, and Marti; it is also mentioned as a possibility by Luzatto.
25. Cf. Ehrlich, *Randglossen zur hebräischen Bibel*, 4:70.
26. Tur-Sinai, *Peshuṭo shel Miqra*, 3/1:59.
27. See M. Held, "Pits and Pitfalls in Akkadian and Biblical Hebrew," *JANES* 5 (1973; T. H. Gaster FS) 187.

Isaiah 27:12

And on that day the LORD will beat out the grain [i.e., the people like grain] from the שבלת of the Euphrates to the Wadi of Egypt; and you shall be gleaned one by one, O children of Israel.

Hebrew שבלת הנהר, when paired with the followed נחל מצרים 'the Wadi of Egypt', explicitly refers to 'the stream of the Euphrates' (cf. Judg 12:6; Ps 69:3, 16); thus LXX, Vulgate, Saadia, ibn Ganaḥ, Kimchi, Luzatto, Ehrlich.[28] However, in view of the agricultural imagery in this verse, retrospectively in relation to the verb חבט 'to beat out' (employed in the process of threshing a quantity of corn with a stick; cf. Judg 6:16, Isa 28:27, Ruth 2:17), and prospectively with the verb לקט 'to glean', שבלת implicitly refers to 'ears of grain' (cf. Job 24:24). For the combination of the latter verb, לקט, with 'ears of grain' (in the masculine, שבלים), see Ruth 2:2. Compare also the simile for the devastation of the land employed in Isa 17:5: "After being like the standing grain / Harvested by the reaper— / Who reaps ears [שבלים] by the armful— / He shall be like the ears that are gleaned [כמלקט שבלים] / In the Valley of Rephaim."[29]

Isaiah 52:2

Shake off the dust, arise, שְׁבִי Jerusalem!
Loose the bands from your neck,
O captive one [שביה], Fair Zion!

Retrospectively the feminine imperative שְׁבִי refers to personified Jerusalem, who is commanded to "arise" (קומי) and "sit" (שבי) once again on her throne (cf. Tg. Neb., Saadia, Rashi, ibn Ezra; for the opposite order in reference to the dethroning of personified Babylon—from the throne to sitting in the dust—see Isa 47:1). For the complementary pair of verbs, see 1 Sam 28:23: ויקם וישב.

Prospectively, moreover, שבי also implicitly alludes to the female שביה, at the end of the verse, and thus takes on the overtones of her masculine counterpart, 'captive one' (cf. Kimchi; NEB has "captive Jerusalem").[30] Though there are several examples in the Bible of the employment of masculine nouns counterbalanced by their feminine counterparts (e.g., Jer 48:46: שבי/שביה, as in this present verse; Nah 2:13: טרף/טרפה;[31]

---

28. Ehrlich, *Randglossen zur hebräischen Bibel*, 4:97.
29. See also Yellin, *Ketavim Nivḥarim*, 95; F. Delitzsch, *Biblical Commentary on the Prophecies of Isaiah* (Edinburgh, 1890), 1:457–58.
30. Cf. Paran, "LeMishneh Horaʾah BaMiqrah," 155–56. For this verse, see also M. Dahood, "Some Ambiguous Texts in Isaias," *CBQ* 20 (1958) 43–45.
31. For this literary device, see U. Cassuto, *Lešׁ* 15 (1947) 102 [Hebrew]; idem, *The Goddess Anat* (Jerusalem, 1965) 37 [Hebrew].

cf. also Jer 23:19, Ezek 25:15), the pairing of masculine שבי with feminine שביה, both relating to Jerusalem, is anomalous. Yet in this unprecedented fashion, the prophet creates a Janus-like poetic construction. Compare the remark of Luzatto: ואמר "שביה" בת ציון דרך צחות, לשון דומה למלת "שבי" שהזכיר.

Isaiah 57:8

. . . .
כי מאתי גלית
You have gone up [ותעלי] on the couch you made so wide.
. . . .

Though this verse is a classic example of a multiple *crux interpretum*,[32] the predominant erotic context of the various idolatrous practices conducted on the high places makes the meaning of 'stripped' for גָּלִית very plausible—whether the stripping refers to the participants in the cult (e.g., McKenzie,[33] NEB) or the stripping of the couch (e.g., Westermann).[34] For the various nuances of uncovering or stripping, see Rashi, ibn Ezra, Luzatto, Ehrlich.[35] The *Piel* of the root גלה, moreover, is the standard way of expressing immodesty and "uncovering" nakedness (cf. Lev 18:6-19, 20:11-21; Ezek 22:10, 23:18), though only here is it employed without an object.

This, in turn, provides a lead to a further possibility of exegesis. For the verb גלית—vocalized as a *Qal*, גָּלִית, and combined with the initial two words in this verse, כי מאתי 'for from me'—can also be interpreted as meaning 'you have removed yourself from me, you have abandoned me' (cf. NJPS). Thus a clever Janus *entendre* is created: when vocalized as a *Qal*,[36] retrospectively it describes the act of abandoning God; and when vocalized as a *Piel*, it describes yet one more of the licentious activities indulged in by the people, as further amplified by the continuation of this difficult passage.

This phenomenon of polysemy, *mirabile dictu*, extends to the next verb as well, ותעלי. On the one hand, as the continuation of the former stich, it, too, expresses the concept of "departing"; see Rashi: ותעלי מאצלי (so, also, Meṣudat Zion: ענין הסתלקות; and Meṣudat David); Luzatto: ומלת "ותעלי" ענין התרחקות כמו "העלי מסביב קרח" (במדבר טז:כד); Ehrlich: "עלה מן in der Bedeutung 'plötzlich verschwinden" (cf. Gen 17:22). However, when examined in connection with the continuation of this very same

---

32. For a brief comment on the possibility of polysemy here, see Weiser, "Mishneh Horaʾah BeSefer Yeshayahu," 30.
33. J. L. McKenzie, *Second Isaiah*, (AB 20; Garden City, NY, 1968), 156.
34. C. Westermann, *Isaiah 40-66* (OTL; Philadelphia, 1969) 323.
35. Ehrlich, *Mikrâ ki-Pheschutô*, 3:137; idem, *Randglossen zur hebräischen Bibel*, 4:203.
36. Cf. Tur-Sinai, *Peshuṭo shel Miqra*, 3/1:138.

stich, ותעלי (הרחבת) משכבך, the verb also refers to the "going up on the couch / mounting a bed"—an idiom attested in Gen 49:4 and Ps 132:3, and thereby continues the description of the nation's licentious behavior.

Isaiah 57:9

ותשרי the king with oil
. . . .

As the direct continuation of the former verse, just partially examined above, the present verse, too, commences with a difficult clause.[37] The initial verb, וַתָּשֻׁרִי, has been the subject primarily of two different interpretations (irrespective of whether one reads the following word as לַמֶּלֶךְ 'to the king' or לַמֹּלֶךְ 'to Molech'): (a) 'to travel, journey', Hebrew שור (cf., e.g., BDB 1003: "journey"; NJPSV: "approach"; and already Kimchi and Luzatto— both relating the verb to Cant 4:8 and post-biblical שיירה 'caravan'); (b) 'to behold', also derived from Hebrew שור (cf., e.g., Num 23:9, 24:17; Job 24:15), which, in turn, is attested in the substantive, תשורה 'an interview fee/gift'[38] (1 Sam 9:7; cf. Rashi, ibn Ezra, and Kimchi, who also cites Saadia).

It appears that, in the present context, both meanings may have been intended in a "multiple *entendre*."[39] Retrospectively, the verb, when derived from שור (b), may be related to the last verb in the previous verse (v. 8), חזית 'to look'; and prospectively, when derived from שור (a), two additional possibilities exist: (1) since v. 9b states, "You have sent your envoys afar," hence 'to travel'; and/or (2) since "oil" is the direct object of the verb ותשרי למלך בשמן, the reference may very well be to the custom attested in treaty traditions of the sending of oil to the overlord. Compare Hos 12:2: "Now they make a *covenant* with Assyria, / Now *oil* is carried to Egypt."[40] Thus, ותשרי could then be interpreted as a denominative from תשורה, and thus would parallel the next stich: "You have provided many perfumes." Compare the insightful remarks of Ehrlich (who unnecessarily emends the verb to וַתְּשַׁחֲדִי 'you send a gift payment'): "Demgemäss sind aber auch die darauf erwähnten Spezereien bloss als Landesprodukte genannt, mit denen man gleichfalls fremde Könige beschenkte; vgl. Kimchi . . . Danach handelt es sich hier nicht mehr um Götzendienst, sondern um politische Beziehungen zu heidnischen Völkern und Bündnisse mit solchen."[41]

---

37. Cf. Weiser, "Mishneh Horaʾah BeSefer Yeshayahu," 31.

38. See S. M. Paul, "I Samuel 9:7: An Interview Fee," *Bib* 59 (1978) 542–44.

39. For yet another possibility, see P. Wernberg-Møller, "Two Notes," *VT* 8 (1958) 307–8, who, based on LXX ἐπλήθυνας 'to become full of' (from πίμπλημι) and Arabic ثر, interprets the verb to mean 'multiply'. He, in turn, is followed by Westermann, *Isaiah 40–66*, 323.

40. See D. J. McCarthy, "Hosea XII 2: Covenant by Oil," *VT* 14 (1964) 215–21. See also Weiser, "Mishneh Horaʾah BeSefer Yeshayahu," 31.

41. Ehrlich, *Randglossen zur hebräischen Bibel*, 4:204.

Isaiah 57:18

> Then I considered his ways [דרכיו] and will heal him [וארפהו];
> ואנחהו,
> And mete out solace [נחומים] to him . . .

This Janus construction hinges upon the dual meaning of ואנחהו. The verb as presently pointed, וָאַנְחֵהוּ, is the *Hiphil* of the root נחה 'to lead, guide'. Thus, retrospectively, it is attached to the prior דרכיו 'his ways' and refers to guiding and leading the people. Compare, for example, Rashi: אוליכהו בדרך מרפא; Kimchi: ואנחהו בדרך טוב; and Luzatto: להנחותו בדרך הטובה.

However, the verb may also be pointed וַאֲנִחֵהוּ, which is the *Hiphil* of the root נוח, meaning 'to give rest, relief', and thus would be parallel both retrospectively to "will heal him" and prospectively to "mete out solace to him." Compare Rashi, who caught sight of both the above possibilities: אוליכהו בדרך מרפא או ואנחהו לשון הנחה. Ehrlich, on the other hand, suggests yet another possibility: וכבר אמר חכם אחד מחכמי הגוים שדין תיבה זו וַאֲנִחֵהוּ, ופירושו נתתי לו מנוחה; ולי נראה שדינו וְאַנְחֵהוּ, ופירושו הרפיתי ממנו מיסרו. (For this dual *Hiphil* form [הֵנִיחַ, הִנִּיחַ], both derived from the root נוח, but with different meanings, see KB 628.)

This same polysemy is also present in Isa 63:14: "The spirit of the LORD תְּנִיחֶנּוּ [interpreting, along with most commentators, the suffixal ending נו as a ligature for the suffix *mem* [ם],[42] i.e., תְּנִיחֵם] gave them rest"; compare ibn Ezra: והנה תניחנו תחת תניחם, Kimchi, and Luzatto. However, others, for example, Rashi, ibn Ezra, NEB, NJPSV margin, interpret the verb as being derived from the root נחה, תַּנְחֵנּוּ (or תַּנְחֵם) 'guided us [or them]'. Thus Kimchi remarks: ויונתן תרגם [מדברא] . . . תניחנו כמו תנחנו מן נחה את העם. This, in turn, would complement the verbs מוליכם in v. 13 and נהגת, the next verb in v. 14, both referring to God's leading Israel. See also Ehrlich and Tur-Sinai, both who vocalize, תַּנְחֶנּוּ.[43]

Isaiah 60:5

> Then you will תראי and you will glow [ונהרת];
> Your heart will פחד and thrill [רחב].

Yellin discussed the dual meaning of the verb תראי in this verse.[44] It already appears in the previous verse (v. 4), שאי סביב עיניך וראי: 'Raise your eyes and look about', and complements the second verb in this verse, ונהרת: 'You will look in astonishment, you will glow/beam'. However, in the light

---

42. For this phenomenon, see R. Weiss, "On Ligatures in the Hebrew Bible," *JBL* 82 (1963) 188–94, who does not, however, cite this example.

43. Ehrlich, *Mikrâ ki-Pheschutô*, 3:154; Tur-Sinai, *Peshuṭo shel Miqra*, 3/1:147; see, too, McKenzie, *Second Isaiah*, 189. For a discussion of this verse, see J. S. Kselman, "A Note on wᵊnḥhw in Isa 57:18," *CBQ* 43 (1981) 539–42.

44. Yellin, *Ketavim Nivḥarim*, 100.

of other manuscript readings, תִּירְאִי, תִּרְאִי (cf. ibn Ezra, Kimchi, Minḥat Shai), the meaning would be 'you shall be in awe', thus creating an apt parallel to the verb פחד in the next stich.

This phenomenon of a different retrospective and prospective interpretation can also be attached to the verb פחד. When connected with the reading תיראי, it too refers to trembling from fear. But when understood in relation to the following, ורחב לבבך 'your heart shall thrill/be enlarged/expand',[45] it expresses a very positive emotional experience, trembling with joy. For this usage, see also Hos 3:5 and Jer 33:9.[46]

Jeremiah 9:3

> Beware, every man of his friend!
> Trust not even a brother!
> For every brother עקוב יעקב,
> Every friend is base in his dealings/slanders.

The Hebrew expression עָקוֹב יַעֲקֹב means 'to act craftily, to deceive', and thus prospectively parallels the final stich, "to act basely/slander." Yet retrospectively, when read in connection with "Trust not even a brother," it constitutes a skillful pun on the personal name Jacob (יַעֲקֹב)[47] and clearly alludes to his own acts of deceiving his brother. Compare Gen 27:36: הכי קרא שמו יעקב ויעקבני זה פעמים: '[Esau replied], "Did they name him Jacob [יעקב] so that he should cheat/supplant me [ויעקבני] twice?"'[48] See also Hos 12:4. Ehrlich caught this nuance perfectly:

> הקורא המבין יקרא את המקרא הזה וישמע מתוכו קול דברים ככתוב האומר
> [49]כנגד יעקב, "בבטן עקב את אחיו" (הושע יב:ד).

And Bright deftly translated, "For every brother's as crafty as Jacob."[50]

Hosea 2:18-19

> And on that day, declares the LORD,
> You will call me my husband [אישי],
> And no more will you call me בעלי.
> For I will remove the name of the Baalim [בעלים] from their mouth,
> And they shall nevermore be mentioned by name.

---

45. Cf. also the Akkadian interdialectal cognate equivalent: *libbu rapšu*; e.g., *rapaš libbašu* in *Enuma Elish* vi:138; see *AHW* 547 A4f, 957 4c.
46. For this nuance, see Tur-Sinai, *Peshuṭo shel Miqra*, 3/1:143.
47. For the difference in vocalization, see Kimchi.
48. Cf. W. McKane, *Jeremiah*, (ICC; Edinburgh, 1986), 1:200.
49. Ehrlich, *Mikrâ ki-Pheschutô*, 3:193.
50. J. Bright, *Jeremiah* (AB 21; Garden City, NY, 1965) 67, 71–72. See also Weiss, "Ligatures in the Hebrew Bible," 188.

In this well-known example,[51] Hebrew בעלי pivots both ways: retrospectively it parallels אישי and means 'my husband' (cf. Exod 21:3, 22; Deut 24:4, 22:22), and prospectively it creates a polemical diatribe against the mention of the idol Baal.

Amos 1:11

. . . .
Because he pursued his brother with the sword,
And destroyed רחמיו.
His anger seethed ceaselessly,
And his fury raged incessantly.

In an article pertaining to the concatenous literary pattern of the oracles against the nations in Amos 1:3–2:2, I pointed out that the unique expression in v. 11, שִׁחֵת רַחֲמָיו, was to be interpreted as Edom's having 'destroyed the female population' of their enemy.[52] The Hebrew substantive רחם 'womb' > 'young woman' is attested in Judg 5:30 (רחם רחמתים) and most likely in Isa 49:15: התשכח אשה עולה מרחם בן־בטנה גם־אלה תשכחנה: 'Can a woman forget her infant, a young woman the child of her womb? Even these forget . . .' (cf. NEB).[53] It also appears in the Moabite Mesha inscription, רחמת (line 17), and in Ugaritic, where rḥm parallels btlt (cf. rḥm ʿnt ‖ btlt ʿnt; see UT 49:ii:27). This, in turn, provides the contextual literary link between the crimes which Edom and Ammon have in common: both nations are accused of wielding a sword to decimate the female population.

By selecting this rare poetic substantive, Amos created a very clever Janus construction. When related to the prior colon, רחמיו together with אחיו 'his brethren' constitutes a literary merism: the entire population, both male and female, was annihilated. But prospectively, when read in light of the following, it implicitly bears another meaning. For Amos continues his accusation against Edom by condemning their "wrath and fury" (. . . אפו ועברתו) which "seethed and raged" (שמרה . . . ויטר)[54] "incessantly forever"

---

51. Many medieval (e.g., Kimchi) and modern commentators were cognizant of this paronomasia, but did not relate it to a Janus polysemy. Cf. H. W. Wolff, *Hosea* (Hermeneia; Philadelphia, 1974) 49. For a discussion of this verse, see M. A. Friedman, "Israel's Response in Hosea 2:17b: 'You Are My Husband,'" *JBL* 99 (1980) 199–204.

52. S. M. Paul, "Amos 1:3–2:3: A Concatenous Literary Pattern," *JBL* 90 (1971) 397–403.

53. Cf. M. Dahood, "Denominative *riḥḥam*, 'to conceive, enwomb,'" *Bib* 44 (1963) 204; M. I. Gruber, "'Will a Woman Forget Her Infant?' Isa 49:15," *Tarbiz* 51 (1982) 491–92 [Hebrew]; and already R. Gordis, "Studies in the Relationship of Biblical and Rabbinic Hebrew," in *Louis Ginzberg Jubilee Volume on the Occasion of His Seventieth Birthday* (ed. S. Lieberman et al.; New York, 1946) 186.

54. See M. Held, "Rhetorical Questions in Ugaritic and Biblical Hebrew," *EI* 9 (1969; W. F. Albright FS) 73 n. 19.

(נצח . . . לעד). Thus, he is clearly implying that the enemy had subdued all sparks of "his mercy" (רחמיו). Hence, Hebrew רחמיו occupies a pivotal position, primarily meaning 'his young women' and by secondary anticipation 'his mercy'.

For the employment of both these root words in two other passages, see Jer 13:14: לא ארחם מהשחיתם, 'I will show no mercy, but will destroy them'; and, especially, Ps 78:38, which contains no less than three of the key terms found in the verse in Amos (within, of course, an entirely different context):

But he, being <u>merciful</u>, forgave iniquity	כי הוא <u>רחום</u> יכפר עוון
And would not destroy.	ולא <u>ישחית</u>
He restrained his <u>wrath</u> time and again,	והרבה להשיב <u>אפו</u>
And did not give full vent to his <u>fury</u>.	ולא יעיר כל <u>חמתו</u>

(A fourth correspondence may also be cited since חמתו in Psalms is the exact equivalent of עברתו in Amos.)

Nahum 3:6-7

I will throw loathsome things [שקוצים] on you.
I will disfigure you [ונבלתיך],
And will make you like ראי.
All who will see you [ראיך] will recoil from you.

The root ראה, meaning 'excrement, filth', has already been noted in Zeph 3:1 (מוראה) (cf. Lev 11:16).[55] It is common in post-biblical Hebrew, written either ראי or רעי.[56] This interpretation fits very well retrospectively in the present verse, where כְּרֹאִי constitutes the third in a series of actions by which the Lord will humiliate Nineveh: (1) "I will throw loathsome things on you"; (2) ונבלתיך: "I will treat you with contumely" (BDB 614) / "I will count you obscene" (NEB) / "I will disfigure you" (NJPSV); and (3) then last, but not least, "I will treat you like excrement/filth." Cf. Rashi: כזבל; ibn Ezra: "הוי מוראה", "כטנוף וכמוהו"; and Tur-Sinai.[57]

But prospectively the substantive serves yet another exegetical role. For when it is related to the beginning of the next verse (v. 7), "All who see you [רֹאֶיךָ] . . . ," ראי may also be interpreted as, 'I will make a *spectacle/showpiece* of you'. Note that Tg. Neb. incorporated both meanings by translating, ואשויניך <u>מכערא</u> לעיני כל חזך.

---

55. For Zeph 3:1, see Rashi, ibn Ganaḥ, ibn Ezra, Kimchi, Tur-Sinai, *Peshuṭo shel Miqra*, 3/2:531. In *The Book of Job* (Tel Aviv, 1954) 285 [Hebrew], Tur-Sinai suggested that it also appears in Job 33:21.

56. M. Jastrow, *Dictionary of Talmud Babli, Yerushalmi, Midrashic Literature and Targumim* (New York, 1950), 2:1436, 1487.

57. Tur-Sinai, *Peshuṭo shel Miqra*, 3/2:511.

Zephaniah 3:3

> The officials within her are roaring lions;
> Her judges are wolves of the ערב.
> They leave no bone until morning [בקר].

Most versions (Tg. Neb., Vulgate, and Peshitta, with the exception of LXX (τῆς Ἀραβίας 'wolves of Arabia'), interpret ערב in its usual sense, 'evening', that is, 'wolves of the evening', which, prospectively, correlates with the following reference to morning. However, since it is unprecedented (but not impossible) that an animal is referred to in the Bible by a temporal description (the referent is always spatial: קאת מדבר in Ps 102:7; חיתו יער in Ps 50:10, 104:20; בהמות יער in Mic 5:7; חיתו שדה in Isa 56:9, Ps 104:11; with the exception of Hab 1:8, where the same expression as Zeph 3:3 appears), the substantive ערב may also mean 'plain/steppe', that is, 'wolves of the steppes' (cf. Jer 5:6: זאב ערבות).[58] Thus, retrospectively, it creates a description of the wolves, as the prior stich describes the lions. There is, moreover, no need to emend ערב (*contra*, Ehrlich, ערבה/ערבות),[59] since the prophet intentionally resorted to the singular here in order to create this dual impression.

Lamentations 1:1

> Lonely sits the city once great [רבתי] with people.
> She that was רבתי among nations,
> Is become like a widow.
> The princess [שרתי] among states,
> Is become a thrall.

This Janus construction revolves around the second occurrence of רבתי. Retrospectively parallel to the identical word in the first stich, it, too, means 'great, having many [people]' (cf. 1 Sam 2:5: רבת בנים). But, at the same time, the second stich complements the fourth stich: "She that was

---

58. Cf. Yellin, *Ketavim Nivḥarim*, 102–3.
59. Ehrlich, *Randglossen zur hebräischen Bibel*, 5:315. Cf. as well KB 831, which also provides a bibliographical list; and L. Sabottka, *Zephanja* (Biblica et Orientalia 25; Rome, 1972) 104 n. 11, 105 n. 13. For additional discussions of this verse, see K. Elliger, "Das Ende der 'Abendwölfe' Zeph 3,3, Hab 1,8," in *Festschrift Alfred Bertholet zum 80. Geburtstag* (ed. W. Baumgartner et al.; Tübingen, 1950) 158–75; M. Stenzel, "Zum Verständnis von Zeph iii 3b," *VT* 11 (1951) 303–5; B. Jongeling, "Jeux de mots en Sophonie III 1 et 3?" *VT* 21 (1971) 541–47; A. S. van der Woude, "Bemerkungen zu einigen umstrittenen Stellen in Zwölfprophetenbuch," in *Mélanges Bibliques et Orientaux en l'honneur de M. Henri Cazelles* (ed. A. Caquot and M. Delcor; Alter Orient und Altes Testament 212; Neukirchen-Vluyn, 1981) 496; C. Cohen, "The 'Widowed' City," *JANES* 5 (1973; T. H. Gaster FS) 81 n. 57c; and the very clever note and translation of L. Zalcman, "*Di Sera*, Desert, Dessert," *Expository Times* 91 (1980) 311.

רבתי among nations has become . . ." ‖ "The princess [שרתי] among states has become . . . ," and thus רבתי and שרתי constitute a word pair. For the employment of רב and שר as titles of officials of high status, compare רב ביתו (cf. Akkadian *rāb bīti*) in Esth 1:8, שר וגדול in 2 Sam 3:38, and especially the interchangeability of the two, שר הטבחים in Gen 37:36 and רב הטבחים in 2 Kings 25:2.[60] Thus, prospectively the translation would be, 'She that was noble among nations'.

This pair of epithets has been further elucidated by the Ugaritic interdialectal semantic and cognate equivalents *rbt* and *ṯrrt*. Greenfield adduces ample evidence of the employment of these two as epithets of cities (*Udm rbt, Udm ṯrrt; Arṣḫ rbt, Arṣḫ ṯrrt*) and explains *ṯrrt* as a transcription of Akkadian *šarratu* 'queen, noble lady,' an epithet also applied to cities.[61]

Lamentations 1:7–8

> Enemies looked on and gloated [שחקו] over her downfall.
> Jerusalem has greatly sinned,
> Therefore she is become נידה.
> All who admired her despised her [הזילוה],
> For they have seen her nakedness.

The continuation of the end of v. 7 ("Enemies looked on and gloated [שחקו] over her downfall") is related to the next stich: "All who admired her despised her/held her in contempt." Thus the *hapax legomenon* נידה refers elliptically to the 'derisive shaking of the head'; Jerusalem has become an object of scorn. This line of exegesis is followed, for example, by ibn Ezra, Rudolph, Gordis, all referring to the idiom להניד ראש in Jer 18:16 and מנוד ראש in Ps 44:15.[62] Compare Jer 48:27, where שְׂחֹק 'laughingstock' parallels the verb תתנודד 'you shake (your head in mockery)'.

But prospectively, as a unique *plene* spelling of נדה 'unclean, menstruating woman', it relates, as well, to the final stich: "They have seen her

---

60. See A. Berlin, "On the Meaning of *rb*," *JBL* 100 (1981) 90–93, who also translated, "noble among nations."
61. See J. C. Greenfield, "The Epithets *rbt* ‖ *ṯrrt* in the KRT Epic," in *Perspectives on Language and Text: Essays and Poems in Honor of Francis I. Andersen's Sixtieth Birthday* (ed. E. W. Conrad and E. G. Newing; Winona Lake, IN, 1987) 35–37, who compared these city epithets in KRT to Lam 1:1. Cf. also D. R. Hillers, *Lamentations* (AB 7A; Garden City, NY, 1972) 6, to whom Greenfield also refers; and T. M. McDaniel, "Philological Studies in Lamentations," *Bib* 49 (1968) 29–31. See, too, F. M. Cross, "Studies in the Structure of Hebrew Verse: The Prosody of Lamentations 1:1–22," in *The Word of the Lord Shall Go Forth: Essays in Honor of David Noel Freedman in Celebration of His Sixtieth Birthday* (ed. C. L. Meyers and M. O'Connor; Winona Lake, IN, 1983) 136.
62. Rudolph, *Das Buch Ruth, Das Hohe Lied, Die Klagelieder*, 306; Gordis, *Lamentations*, 8, who also raises the possibility of this being an example of *talḥin*.

nakedness."⁶³ For the association of the exposure of nakedness and uncleanness, see, for example, Lev 20:21 and Ezek 22:10.

Job 9:30–31

> If I washed with soap [מי שלג],
> Cleaned my hands in בר,
> You would dip me in שחת,
> Till my clothes would abhor me.

Hebrew בֹר, parallel to מי שלג 'soap, nitre', retrospectively refers to the cleansing vegetable alkali, 'lye' (cf. Isa 1:25 MT), and is identical with בֹּרִית in Jer 2:22 and Mal 3:2. Prospectively, however, when read in connection with the beginning of v. 31, בֹר (or בור, according to Rashi and other manuscript readings recorded in Minḥat Shai) constitutes a synonym of שחת 'pit'; for the parallel pair, see Ps 7:16. The implicit meaning would be, "If I cleaned my hands in one pit, you would dip me in another."⁶⁴

There may very well be an additional *double entendre* in connection with שחת. Paralleling בֹר, it maintains its usual meaning, 'pit'. However, in light of a tradition preserved in LXX ἐη ρυπό 'in mud' and Vulgate *sordibus*, and taking into consideration the Syriac noun שוחתא 'rust' (as noted by Epstein on this verse),⁶⁵ it may also have an additional implicit overtone of 'filth',⁶⁶ thus NEB's translation:

> Thou wilt thrust me into the mud
> and my clothes will make me loathsome.⁶⁷

---

63. See also Hillers, *Lamentations*, 23. Cross, "Prosody of Lamentations 1:1–22," 141, prefers the reading לנוד as found in 4QLam.

64. See Yellin, *Ketavim Nivḥarim*, 104, who did not realize the Janus construction; and M. Greenberg, "Job," in *The Literary Guide to the Bible* (ed. R. Alter and F. Kermode; Cambridge, 1987) 302.

65. Quoted by Yellin, *Ketavim Nivḥarim*, n. 69. Cf. also Akkadian *šuḫtû*; see *AHW* 1262. There is no need, therefore, to emend to בַּשָּׁחָה/בַּסָּחָה/בַּסָּחוֹת, as suggested by some commentators, including Ehrlich, *Randglossen zur hebräischen Bibel*, 5:219.

66. See M. Pope, "The Word שחת in Job 9:31," *JBL* (1964) 269–78; idem, *Job* (AB 15; Garden City, NY, 1979) 72–74. For a poignant criticism of Pope, see Held, "Pits and Pitfalls," 188–90.

67. For another pivotal term, see S. M. Paul, "A Technical Expression from Archery in Zechariah IX 13a," *VT* 39 (1989) 495–97.

THE IMAGE OF POSTEXILIC ISRAEL IN GERMAN BIBLE SCHOLARSHIP FROM WELLHAUSEN TO VON RAD

Rolf Rendtorff

Several years ago Shemaryahu Talmon directed some "critical inquiries" to European Christianity. His point of departure was the different approaches toward the Hebrew Bible that are to be found in Judaism and Christianity. His summary was that in many crucial points "in Christian theological thinking Judaism represents the negative pole, while Christian faith claimed the positive one for itself."[1]

One of the most characteristic fields of this kind of Christian behavior is the depiction of postexilic Judaism in modern German Old Testament scholarship, where we find a certain well-known set of stereotypes. The intention of this paper is, first, to look for the origins of those stereotypes; second, to follow their development through certain significant stages; and, third, to ask how we might deal with these traditions in our present theological situation.

De Wette: From Hebraism to Judaism

It was Wilhelm Martin Leberecht de Wette who in the earliest period of modern biblical scholarship established the distinction between preexilic and postexilic Israel. In 1813 he divided the Old Testament part of his *Biblical Dogmatics* in two parts, which he called Hebraism (*Hebraismus*) and Judaism (*Judentum*).[2] In his view, during the Babylonian Exile the

---

Author's note: This paper was read at the Annual Meeting of the American Academy of Religion, Chicago, November 1988, in the History of Judaism section.

   1. S. Talmon, "Kritische Anfragen der jüdischen Theologie an das europäische Christentum," in *Einladung ins Lehrhaus: Beiträge zum jüdischen Selbstverständnis* (ed. W. Licharz and M. Stöhr; Frankfurt am Main, 1981) 65.
   2. W. M. L. de Wette, *Biblische Dogmatik Alten und Neuen Testaments; oder, Kritische Darstellung der Religionslehre des Hebraismus, des Judenthums und Urchristenthums* (Berlin, 1813; 2d ed. in 1818).

Hebrew nation was changed so deeply by foreign religious influences that it actually became a different nation with a different way of thinking and a different religion (§76). The most characteristic element of this new religion was *devotion to the letter*. The Hebrews understood their disastrous fate as divine punishment for their violation of the law, and therefore now tried to fulfill the law as strictly as possible (§77). But by this devotion to the letter of the Mosaic law, they became estranged from Moses' spirit. This occurred under the influence of the Chaldean or Persian religion (§78). The first sentence of de Wette's chapter on the "doctrine of Judaism" reads: "Judaism is the unsuccessful restoration of Hebraism and a mixture of its positive components with foreign mythological-metaphysical doctrines . . . : a chaos which is longing for a new creation" (§142). Here already almost all stereotypes are present.

A more detailed study of de Wette's conception, however, reveals a remarkable inconsistency. He takes a considerable part of postexilic literature as a continuation of the spirit of Hebraism (cf. §74), and therefore develops his description of Judaism mainly from the postcanonical literature (§149ff.). In the New Testament part of the book, Jesus' teaching is depicted as a "spiritually reborn and developed prophetism" (§211), whereas Pharisaism is the "cutting contrast" to his teaching. Here it becomes obvious that the main interest in the negative characterization of postexilic Judaism is to build up a dark background for the New Testament, and at the same time to save the "better" parts of the Old Testament as a precursor of Jesus and the New Testament.[3]

Wellhausen: The Law Came in Between

Let me now turn to Julius Wellhausen, with whom begins the era of Old Testament scholarship we still live in. In his work the antithesis between preexilic Israel and postexilic Judaism is omnipresent. In 1879 he wrote in a letter that for ten years he had been "exclusively taken up" by the historical study of "Judaism and ancient Israel in its contrast."[4] The results of these studies shaped his later publications.

Wellhausen's basic characterization of the contrast between the two epochs of Israelite and Jewish history is closely related to that given by de Wette. First of all it is the *law* that achieves a predominant role in postexilic Judaism. Wellhausen makes it quite clear upon what he bases his

---

3. The relation of Jesus' teaching to Mosaism is like that of "the full light to a glimmer, the perfect idea to the unperfect picture": he is in harmony with the "original [Mosaic] spirit full of presentiment" (§211).
4. Cf. R. Smend, "Wellhausen und das Judentum," *Zeitschrift für Theologie und Kirche* 79 (1982) 252.

evaluation of the law when he quotes from Paul's Letter to the Romans (5:20): "The Law came in between."[5] Paul's understanding of the law, in its Lutheran (or Augustinian) interpretation, explicitly serves as a criterion for Wellhausen's own assessment of the law.[6]

In Wellhausen's view, like in that of de Wette, the function of the law since the Babylonian Exile had undergone a fundamental change. Two aspects seem to me to be of particular relevance. The first one is the individualization of religion and thereby also of the law. Earlier religion had been "a common possession of the people. "Now, the Jew by birth still had to make himself a Jew by intentional working" because the core of the ideal of justice was "the individual moral."[7] Here the main point is the separation of the law from the nation, which contradicts their connection as given by nature. This aspect later played a crucial role in Martin Noth's concept.

The second point is the relation of law and *cult*. According to Wellhausen, the cult had become part of the law and thereby had changed its very nature: "Religious worship was a natural thing in Hebrew antiquity; it was the blossom of life.... The law... severed this connection"—in particular by the centralization of the cult. "The warm pulse of life no longer throbbed in it to animate it; ... [the cult] had its own meaning all to itself.... The soul was fled; the shell remained....Technique was the main thing, and strict fidelity to rubric." Wellhausen concludes by saying: "The connection of all this with the Judaising tendency to remove God to a distance from man, it may be added, is clear." And: "The cultus, after nature had been killed in it, became the shield of supernaturalistic monotheism."[8]

---

5. Wellhausen uses this verse as the motto to the chapter on "Israel and Judaism" (part 3) in *Prolegomena zur Geschichte Israels* (Berlin, 1883). Quotations are from the English translation by J. S. Black and A. Menzies: *Prolegomena to the History of Ancient Israel* (Edinburgh, 1885; repr. New York, 1957). Wellhausen has taken this quotation from Vatke, as he explicitly indicates (p. 363). The German reads: "Das Gesetz ist zwischenein getreten." Since Luther's translation, "Das Gesetz aber ist neben ein kommen," German translations usually stress the double preposition of the Greek παρεισῆλθεν, which is not expressed in the RSV: "Law came in." Lou Silberman, with reference to Sanday and Headlam, proposes the translation "to sidle in"; see "Wellhausen and Judaism", *Semeia* 25 (1983) 75–82. According to LSJ the word means "come or go in beside."

6. Silberman ("Wellhausen and Judaism," 76) refers to the first edition of the *Prolegomena* where (in a later omitted passage) Wellhausen makes it clear that he "has admittedly pushed Paul beyond what Paul said, that legalism sidled in."

7. J. Wellhausen, "Israelitisch-jüdische Religion," in *Die Kultur der Gegenwart* (ed. P. Hinneberg; Berlin/Leipzig, 1905), 1/4:1–38; repr. in Wellhausen, *Grundrisse zum Alten Testament* (ed. R. Smend; Theologische Bücherei 27; Munich, 1965) 65–109, quotation at 102–3.

8. Quotations in this paragraph from Wellhausen, *Prolegomena to the History of Israel*, 77, 78, 79, 425.

In sum, in Wellhausen's romanticizing view[9] the main aspect of the decline from preexilic Israel to Judaism is the separation of law and cult from the original, natural religion.[10] Yet there is a remarkable inconsistency insofar as individualization on the one hand is highly praised, for example, in the case of Jeremiah, but on the other hand is viewed as an indication of denaturing.[11]

Noth: Only the Law Remained

Compared with Wellhausen's, Martin Noth's view of postexilic Israel shows some similar features, but also some characteristic differences. First of all, Noth felt it to be a problem where to draw the line between "Israel" and "Judaism." In his earlier writings he followed the traditional approach from de Wette through Wellhausen by taking the Babylonian Exile as a dividing line. He made a distinction between "an *earlier* period up to the end of the independent states of Israel and Judah, and so to the factitive end of the Israelite nation, . . . and a *later* period, in which . . . there was no more than a small community in and about Jerusalem, with a widely scattered diaspora."[12] His interest is clearly focused on the political, and in particular on the institutional aspect. "Israel" existed only as long as its institutional form of one or two states existed. But despite this clear distinction, Noth speaks only about the preexilic and postexilic periods, avoiding the term "Judaism" for the latter.

Later he changed his opinion. In his *History of Israel* (1950) he writes that the disappearance of the institution of the Davidic kingdom "did not mean the end of Israel, just as its emergency had not represented the beginning of the history of Israel."[13] Instead he speaks explicitly about "Israel's end" in connection with the Jewish war against the Romans and

---

9. For the influence of romanticism on Wellhausen see also J. Blenkinsopp, *Prophecy and Canon: A Contribution to the Story of Jewish Origins* (Notre Dame, IN, 1977) 17ff.: "Wellhausen and the Origins of Judaism."

10. Smend ("Wellhausen und das Judentum") tries to defend Wellhausen against the accusation of anti-Semitism. In doing so, he responds to my own article ("Die jüdische Bibel und ihre antijüdische Auslegung," in *Auschwitz—Krise der christlichen Theologie* [ed. R. Rendtorff and E. Stegemann; Munich, 1980] 99–116). Yet I want to emphasize that I never claimed Wellhausen to be an anti-Semite. I am fully aware of the fact that there were, and still are, many Christian theologians who in their theological thinking and writing express themselves in a strictly anti-Jewish manner, while in the political and social field fighting anti-Semitic discrimination.

11. For Noth's evaluation of individualism, see n. 16 below.

12. M. Noth, *Die Gesetze im Pentateuch: Ihre Voraussetzungen und ihr Sinn* (Halle, 1940); repr. in Noth, *Gesammelte Studien zum Alten Testament* (2d ed.; Munich, 1960), 1:9–141. Quotations are from the English translation by D. R. Ap-Thomas: *The Laws in the Pentateuch and Other Studies* (Edinburgh, 1966; Philadelphia, 1967) 12.

13. M. Noth, *Geschichte Israels* (Göttingen, 1950). Quotations are from the English translation by P. R. Ackroyd: *The History of Israel* (2d ed.; New York, 1960) 290.

the destruction of the Second Temple in 70 C.E. Now he prefers to use the term "Judaism" for the new phenomenon which arose out of Israel's decline (*Untergang*).[14]

There is nevertheless also in this concept a fundamental difference between preexilic and postexilic Israel. While the former had been constituted in alternating forms of political structures, the latter existed only as a *cultic* community. Noth calls it "the cultic congregation of Jerusalem" (*die Jerusalemer Kultgemeinde*). In this respect he has not changed his view, since already earlier he characterized postexilic Israel in this way. But now he has made his view more explicit so that the consequences are clearer: if Israel in postexilic times existed only as a cultic congregation which gathered around the temple in Jerusalem, then it is evident that after the destruction of the temple this congregation ceased to exist. From that time on there is no Israel any more, but only diaspora.

Moreover, another basic element of Noth's approach shows its effect here. His hypothesis of an ancient Israelite tribal league, the "amphictyony," has the consequence that actually an Israelite *people* had never existed. Even during the period of the monarchy the tribal system worked as a substructure. But how then could Israel continue to exist after the end of an independent political organization?

Here the *law* comes in. According to Noth, originally and essentially the Israelite laws had their *Sitz im Leben* only within the tribal league. This league was built upon the idea of a covenant between YHWH and "Israel," the latter being the name of the league. Only because of the continuing existence of the tribal substructure could the laws serve as a legal basis for monarchically organized Israel as well. But what happened to the laws after the cessation of this structure?

According to Noth, not only the tribal structure, and thereby the political structure in general, had come to an end, but also the covenant between YHWH and Israel was terminated and dissolved, as the prophets had announced. Therefore, in any respect the basis for the validity of the laws was lost. Only the expectation and hope for a "new covenant" according to Jeremiah 31, for a restoration of the previous order of things, enabled the Jerusalem community to survive. One of the means for this survival was the continuous observance of the laws, notwithstanding the fact that they had actually lost their *raison d'être*. This development had fundamental consequences:

> Actually the primary relationship of affairs and regulations became more and more reversed. Whereas it was originally the relationship of God and man depicted as a "covenant" which had constituted the ancient sacral confederacy of the tribes, and whereas it had been the presence of this institution which

---

14. Ibid., 7.

had provided the necessary prerequisite for the validation of the old laws, it was now the acknowledgement and observance of the law by the individuals which constituted the community—for whoever undertook to keep the law joined the community.[15]

There is a slight but very revealing shift of language in the above quotation. In the first part of this long sentence dealing with the original order, Noth speaks of "laws," but in the second part dealing with the individual acceptance and observance, he shifts to "law." And later he writes "the law" (*das Gesetz*) in quotations marks. In Noth's concept of postexilic Israel, this is the decisive turning point. Its consequences he explains again and again: "The reason for this was the transfer of the decisive emphasis from *divine* activity to the behaviour of individual *mortals*—which is a decline from the original basis of the faith."[16] Finally "the law" became an "*absolute entity*," which was

> no longer tied to anything. . . . The law became a power in its own right. . . . It was the law, as the unprecedented primary entity, which fashioned this community, which was nothing but the union of those people who submitted to the law on all points. . . . So when the edifice of the old establishment collapsed, the law which had formed a single pillar in the framework of the whole was the only part which finally remained erect. It then became the centre column and stay of a new edifice erected on the ruins of the old.[17]

One special feature of Noth's conception should at least be mentioned briefly. Noth argues that the terms "law" and "covenant" in postexilic times were separated from each other. I can't discuss this point in the present framework, but want to say only that in my opinion there is no exegetical evidence for this thesis.

In sum, Israel did not exist any longer; only a group of individuals remained whose sole relation to each other was submission to the law. As long as this group gathered around the temple in Jerusalem it deserved the name of "the cultic congregation of Jerusalem"; "but as the centre of worship had been abolished and there was no homeland and therefore no change of united historical action it was in fact something substantially new," namely "Judaism."[18]

---

15. *Laws in the Pentateuch*, 80.
16. Ibid. Immediately before this sentence there is an interesting remark on the function of individualism: "It is customary to speak of the 'individualism' which arose during exilic and post-exilic times in place of an earlier 'collectivism', and often we tend to see an element of progress in this change." The following sentence explains that in Noth's view the opposite is true. For a similar ambivalence in Wellhausen's evaluation of individualism see at n. 11 above.
17. Ibid., 86–87.
18. *History of Israel*, 7. Noth adds that the modern state of Israel "is separated from the Israel of old not only by the long period of almost 2000 years but also by a long history full of vicissitudes and it has come into being in the midst of entirely different historical conditions. It

At first glance, there is an obvious continuity between Wellhausen and Noth in the view of postexilic Israel. For both of them the law is of crucial relevance. But while for Wellhausen the loss of naturalness is the decisive negative point, for Noth it is the loss of the institutional structure of the community. For Wellhausen, Judaism ossifies in legalism; for Noth, Israel ceases to exist and turns into an assembly of individuals who keep the law.

Von Rad: A New Appreciation of the Law

In his *Theology of the Old Testament*, Gerhard von Rad depicts postexilic Israel more or less along the same lines. In particular, with regard to the law he quotes Noth: "The law becomes an absolute entity, unconditionally valid irrespective of time or historical situation." But while he admits that "it is now beginning to become the 'law' in the theological sense of the word," he explicitly denies that there is as yet "any legal casuistry proper."[19] His own depiction of the Priestly Code is full of sympathetic empathy.

Yet for him the crucial point is the problem of *history*. Since in Israel's understanding the law had become absolute and timeless, von Rad sees the consequence that Israel must step out of its history with YHWH, out of salvation history (*Heilsgeschichte*). With such a timeless and ahistoric concept of the Torah as a "law," Judaism finally came into being.

In a certain sense one could say that what the law was for Noth, history was for von Rad. Nevertheless, it was his conception of the law that elicited harsh critique from a dogmatic point of view. One year after the first volume of von Rad's Theology appeared, Gerhard Ebeling published an article on the doctrine of law. In that article he criticized von Rad, not because of his view of the postexilic understanding of law, but on the contrary, because of his opinion that the earlier concept of law, in particular that of Deuteronomy, was less legalistic than the usual Christian interpretation believes. Ebeling comments on von Rad's position: "That of course would lead perforce to the further conclusion that the way to overcome the late Judaistic[!] view of the law is to return to the deuteronomic concept of the Torah"—an idea which from his own dogmatic point of view appears to be simply absurd. In contrast to von Rad's evaluation of Deuteronomy, he argued that the Old Testament in general had not yet realized the very nature of the law, and that Paul was the first to recognize the existence of two lines in the Old Testament, the one coming from

---

would therefore be improper to extend our historical enquiry from the end of the 'Israel' of old to the 'Israel' of the present day."

19. G. von Rad, *Theologie des Alten Testaments* (2 vols.; Munich, 1957–1960). Quotations are from the English translation by D. M. G. Stalker: *Old Testament Theology* (2 vols.; Edinburgh/New York, 1962–1965), 1:91. In the revised fourth German edition (1962), as a consequence of Ebeling's critique (see below), he changed the expression in the second quotation from "theological sense of the word" to "dogmatic sense of the word."

Abraham and the other coming from Moses, the line of promise (ἐπαγ-γελία) and faith (πίστις) as over against the line of law (νόμος) and deeds (ἔργα). Therefore, according to Ebeling, Paul does not argue against the "late Judaistic" understanding of the law but "has in view the Mosaic Law as a whole, and precisely as it is embedded in the totality of the Old Testament revelation of the divine will."[20]

Von Rad took up the challenge. In the revised fourth German edition of the first volume of his *Theology of the Old Testament* (1962), he writes the following: "Our task is clear enough: To understand theologically, as precisely as possible, YHWH's will for Israel, and to take care that this emerging knowledge will not be obscured by a traditional, yet no longer fitting terminology."[21] By this, he veritably denies the applicability of preformulated dogmatic conceptions and terminologies to theological problems of the Old Testament.

From this discussion von Rad drew a remarkable consequence. In the second volume of his *theology of the Old Testament* we find a final chapter on "the law" where he summarizes the whole discussion about the theological understanding of the law. There he writes that it would be a complete misunderstanding of the prophets to believe "that they made the renewal of the broken covenant relationship dependent upon a more meticulous fulfillment of the commandments." And he adds: "It is not easy to give an answer to the question of when it was precisely that Israel began to seek her salvation along the road of the meticulous fulfillment of divine commandments." At least, he is convinced that this did not happen in Old Testament times, and that "there is no basis in the Old Testament for the well-known idea which early Lutheranism exalted to almost canonical status, that Israel was compelled by God's law to an ever greater zeal for the Law."[22]

This debate made it evident how Protestant theologians tried to judge the Old Testament by their own theological criteria, even by those that are explicitly not applicable.[23] Von Rad, though having grown up in the same tradition, intensely and successfully tried to develop a new theological understanding and appreciation of the theological thoughts and intentions of the Hebrew Scriptures from within, avoiding, as far as possible, the

---

20. G. Ebeling, "Erwägungen zur Lehre vom Gesetz", *Zeitschrift für Theologie und Kirche* 55 (1958) 270–306; repr. in Ebeling, *Wort und Glaube* (Tübingen, 1960). Quotations are from the English translation by James W. Leitch: *Word and Faith* (Philadelphia, 1963) 264–66.

21. Von Rad, *Theologie des Alten Testament* (4th ed.; Munich, 1962), 1:214.

22. *Theology of the Old Testament*, 2:404–5.

23. Ebeling writes: "Admittedly, his [i.e., Paul's] own concept of law is then not identical with that of the Old Testament, and cannot be identical with it"; *Word and Faith*, 266. This goes still beyond Wellhausen who himself "has admittedly pushed Paul beyond what Paul said, that legalism sidled in" (cf. n. 6 above).

application of prejudices and theological systems alien to them. When Ebeling attacked him, he clearly decided in favor of an independent theological evaluation of the Hebrew Bible on its own terms.

Thereby he opened the eyes of many readers of his *Theology of the Old Testament*, including myself, to the dangerous and illegitimate dependence of Old Testament theology upon theological values and systems coming from the outside. He insisted, in other contexts as well, that in particular Protestant theology—with its claim to be based on "Scripture"—has to work in the opposite direction, not imposing its own theological ideas on the Scriptures, but taking the Scriptures themselves as a starting point, and first of all developing their intrinsic theological thoughts and insights.

It would go beyond the scope of this paper to discuss the influence of von Rad's approach in the years since. I personally feel it to be significant, but still in a stage of development. I hope that one fruit of this new approach might be better mutual understanding, and even cooperation between Jewish and Christian Bible scholars.

LEGAL TERMINOLOGY IN PSALM 3:8

Nahum M. Sarna

The Problem

Psalm 3 is a petition recited in the first person by an individual who must certainly be the king of Israel or the commander-in-chief of the army. Verses 6–7 show the occasion to be the eve of battle. The army of Israel finds itself outnumbered by far and encircled by the enemy (v. 2). The military situation appears to be desperate; there is demoralization in the camp, and forebodings of disaster are heard on all sides (v. 3). However, the psalmist knows that in the last resort the fortunes of war rest in God's hands (v. 4). His unshakable faith saves him from despondency. He is certain that God will answer his prayer and deliver his people (vv. 5–7). Emboldened, the psalmist exhorts God as follows:

> Rise, O LORD!
> Deliver me, O my God!
> For You slap all my enemies in the face;
>   You break the teeth of the wicked.[1]

Initially, this verse looks beguilingly simple. Nevertheless, it presents problems:

1. The invocation hardly seems to match the reality of the grim situation. Anyone surrounded by an overwhelming mass of enemy troops, and in danger of being annihilated, would surely pray for something far more drastic and decisive than that the foe receive a slap on the cheek and some broken teeth!

---

1. Translations of biblical texts follow the rendering of NJPSV. For the present purposes, it is of no consequence whether or not the verbs הכית and שברת are precatives, as claimed by M. Buttenwieser, *The Psalms Chronologically Treated* (Chicago, 1938; repr. New York, 1969) 396, 400; see also pp. 18–25.

2. Superficially, the breaking of the teeth might be seen as the consequence of the slap on the cheek.² However, in none of the other four biblical occurrences of slapping the cheek is any such connection even hinted at. Is there, then, another explanation for the association of the two?

3. The Hebrew phrase used for breaking the teeth would seem to be quite straightforward, requiring no further elaboration or clarification. Nevertheless, it is unique in the Hebrew Bible, other verbs being used to describe this action: the *Hiphil* of נפל is found in Exod 21:7, and הרס in Ps 58:7. Why, then, did the psalmist employ שבר? The phrase "to smite the cheek" occurs in four biblical contexts. (*a*) In 1 Kgs 22:24 (= 2 Chr 18:23) we read:

> Zedekiah son of Chenaanah stepped up and struck Micaiah on the cheek.

This incident takes place "at the entrance of the gate of Samaria" (v. 10) in the presence of the kings of Judah and Israel and four hundred prophets (v. 6). (*b*) Mic 4:14 discloses:

> They strike the ruler of Israel
> On the cheek with a staff.

This fragment of an oracle dealing with a siege of Jerusalem most likely refers to a real historical circumstance, and describes the action of the Assyrian commander. (*c*) Job 16:10 laments:

> They open wide their mouths at me;
> Reviling me, they strike my cheeks;
> They inflame themselves against me.

Here it is uncertain whether Job complains of an actual assault upon his person or uses metaphoric language. (*d*) Finally, Lam 3:30 recommends:

> Let him offer his cheek to the smiter;
> Let him be surfeited with mockery.

The various contexts make it absolutely clear, beyond the peradventure of a doubt, that to be struck on the cheek was an intolerable insult, a deep humiliation, not a mere slight to be soon forgotten.³ Obviously, the psalm-

---

2. So C. A. Briggs and E. G. Briggs, *A Critical and Exegetical Commentary on the Book of Psalms* (ICC; Edinburgh, 1906), 1:26.

3. So recognized by Rashi and Kimhi, who use the phrase מכת בזיון. E. Dhorme, *Le Livre de Job* (Paris, 1926) 213 (Engl. trans.: *A Commentary on the Book of Job* [trans. H. Knight; London, 1967; repr. Nashville, 1984] 235), points out that "to strike the cheeks, to

ist, in employing that phrase in his invocation has in mind a secondary, figurative sense. He is beseeching God to inflict a humiliating, crushing defeat on the enemy.

Smiting the Cheek in Imprecations and Incantations

This biblical understanding of the serious nature of a slap on the cheek reflects the universal attitude of the peoples of the ancient Near East, whichcan be documented over a wide area for a long period of time. I shall first examine the phenomenon in magical and imprecatory texts, for if a curse against one's enemies includes striking the cheek, then it is a sure index of the severity with which it was viewed.

In the composition generally known today as the "Descent of Ištar into the Netherworld," we read that the goddess Ereškigal, mistress of the abode of the dead, curses Asušunamir, a eunuch. She says to him, "I will curse you with a great curse [*lū-zir-ka iz-ra rabâ*]," which she promptly does, as follows:

> The food of the gutters of the city shall be your food;
> The sewers of the city shall be your drink;
> The shadow of the wall shall be your station;
> The threshold shall be your habitation;
> The besotted and the thirsty shall smite your cheek
> [*šak-ru ù ṣam-mu-ú li-im-ḫaṣ li-it-ki*].[4]

The identical curse is found once again on the lips of the ailing Enkidu in the Gilgameš Epic. Conscious of his impending death, he curses the harlot lass who had been hired to decoy him and teach him the arts of civilized living. Decreeing what he describes as a never-ending fate, he says:

> I will curse you with a great curse. . . .
> The besotted and the thirsty shall smite your cheek.[5]

In the Akkadian *Maqlû* texts, the incantation series composed for priests who specialized in magic, we find among the conventional repertoire of curses that the magician recites,

---

give a slap in the face, is the supreme outrage." Similarly, R. Yaron, *The Laws of Eshnunna* (Jerusalem, 1969) 191 n. 86, notes that it was "the insult *par excellence*."

4. *ANET* 108, rev. 23–28. On the stem *m-ḫ-ṣ*, see M. Held, "*mḫṣ*/*mḫš in Ugaritic and Other Semitic Languages," *JAOS* 79 (1959) 169–76.

5. *ANET* 86, VII:iii:19–22. On the relationship between the Ištar and the Gilgameš passages, see J. H. Tigay, *The Evolution of the Gilgamesh Epic* (Philadelphia, 1982) 128–29, 170–73.

I strike your cheek, I tear out your tongue

a-maḫ-ḫaṣ li-it-ki a-šal-la-pa lisan-ki.[6]

Another instance of this action occurs in the Babylonian text on the New Year ritual, which details ceremonies performed in the Esagila. This includes a ritual in which the *urigallu* priest strips the king of all the insignia of royalty and then humiliates him by slapping his face. After this the monarch enters the innermost sanctuary, and in the presence of the image of the god Bel he makes a "negative confession" for the past year. Among the sins he disavows is smiting on the cheek a subordinate who has the status of *kidinnu*.[7]

Moving from Mesopotamia and Akkadian to North Syria and the Aramaic language, we find at Sfira the treaty between Barga'yah, king of KTK, and Matti'ᶜ'el, a king of Arpad, deriving from ca. 750 B.C.E. This treaty concludes with fearful curses to be heaped upon the violator, one of them being that his wives will be struck on the face.[8]

Smiting the Cheek in Legal Texts

If this strikingly humiliating action has been incorporated into the ancient Near Eastern inventory of curses and magical incantations, then we should expect it to turn up in legal documents that relate to the offense of assault and battery. We are not disappointed; the evidence is at hand.

As early as ca. 1850 B.C.E. the laws of Ešnunna, the Amorite city-state east of the Tigris (now Tell Asmar), treat the slap on the face as an actionable assault, along with biting off the nose and knocking out an eye and a tooth:

A slap in the face—he shall weigh out 10 shekels of silver

me-ḫe-eṣ le-tim 10 šiqil kaspam išaqqal[9]

A court document from the Old Babylonian period (eighteenth century B.C.E.) is a record of a trial for assault and battery of an Amorite infantry man, Bir-ilišu. He was accused of striking the cheek of Apil-ilišu son of Aḫušina. The defendant denied the charge, but balked at making a disclaimer under oath. He was fined three and one-half shekels of silver.[10]

---

6. G. Meier, *Die assyrische Beschwörungssamlung Maqlû* (AfO Beiheft 2; Berlin, 1937) 50, 8:101; cf. T. Abusch, *Babylonian Witchcraft Literature: Case Studies* (BJS 132; Atlanta, 1987) 90, 92.

7. *ANET* 334, line 425.

8. *KAI* 1:42, no. 222:A:41–42; *ANET* 660.

9. *ANET* 163, line 42; Yaron, *Laws of Eshnunna*, 43.

10. *ANET* 545, no. 11.

Hammurabi's laws similarly feature the slap in the face, and treat it very severely in no less than four paragraphs.[11] The penalty for this particular offense varies according to the social standing of the assailant and victim. Paragraphs 202–3 are revealing, particularly in the contrasting penalties:

> If an *awilum* strikes the cheek of an *awilum* who is his superior, he shall be beaten sixty times in the assembly with an oxtail. If a *mar awilum* has struck the cheek of his equal, he shall pay one mineh [i.e., sixty shekels] of silver.[12]

Nearly two thousand years after Hammurabi, striking on the cheek is again featured as an actionable offense, this time in tannaitic sources. *Mishnah Baba Qamma* 8:6 prescribes a penalty of two hundred zuz (= one hundred shekels) for it and double that amount if the aggressor uses the back of his hand.[13] This ruling is expanded in *Tosepta Baba Qamma* 9:31:

> If one struck someone with the back of his hand ... he must pay four hundred zuz, not because it is a painful blow but because it is a humiliating blow.[14]

The Tosepta does not specifically mention the face as the object of the smack but from its citation of Ps 3:8 as a proof text, it is clear that such is understood.

In modern times, Abraham Shapira (1870–1965), head watchman of Petah Tikvah and a keen student of the ways and customs of the Bedouin, once observed the trial of two members of a tribe. One had been accused of stabbing someone with a sword, the other of having smacked someone on the face. The presiding sheikh dealt leniently with the stabber but severely with the other one. In explaining his verdict, he stated: "The striking of the cheek is a graver offense than stabbing with a sword, for the latter enhances the dignity of a man, while striking him on the cheek humiliates him."[15]

The Legal Sitz-im-Leben

From all the foregoing, one may conclude that in choosing his phraseology, the psalmist of Ps 3:8 has carefully drawn on the conventional language of

---

11. *ANET* 175, §§202–5; G. R. Driver and J. C. Miles, *The Babylonian Laws* (Oxford, 1952), 1:409, cf. 412 n. 5.

12. On this penalty, see the remarks of J. J. Finkelstein, "Ammisaduqa's Edict and the Babylonian 'Law Codes,'" *JCS* 15 (1961) 98–99.

13. סטרו נותן לו מאתים זוז לאחר ידו נותן לו ארבע מאות זוז.

14. M. S. Zuckermandel (ed.), *Tosefta, Mischna und Boraitha* (repr. Jerusalem, 1938) 366: הכה באחר ידו ... נותן ארבע מאות זוז ולא מפני שמכה של צער ת'א אלא מפני שמכה של בזיון היא שנא' קומה יי"י ... כי הכית את כל אויבי לחי.

15. Cited in the Israeli daily *Maʿariv*, 10 June 1983.

incantation and imprecation or on legal terminology.[16] We can only decide which after examining the second sentence of the couplet.

As in the preceding clause, we are dealing with a figure of speech, not with the primary meaning. Rashi takes note of this by glossing "teeth" by "might" (גבורתם). David Kimhi further explicates the underlying imagery. He says that the reference is to "those whose intention it is to tear him to pieces." By employing the verb טרף, Kimhi shows his understanding of the enemy being compared to a ravenous, ravaging beast (cf. also Ps 124:6, Zech 9:7), and he cites Job 29:17:

> I broke the jaws of the wrongdoer,
> And I wrested prey from his teeth.

I might also add Ps 58:7:

> O God, smash [הרס] their teeth in their mouth;
> shatter the fangs of lions, O LORD.

To break the teeth is to render impotent, ineffective, powerless to do harm.

All this is clear and uncomplicated, except that, as noted above, Ps 3:8 is the only text in the Hebrew Bible in which the phrase שִׁבֵּר שִׁנַּיִם occurs. Does the uniqueness have any significance? In a recent article, Jo Ann Hacket and John Huehnergard pointed out that the exact Akkadian equivalent of this Hebrew term appears in a thirteenth-century B.C.E. legal document from the vicinity of ancient Emar (modern Meskeneh, about 100 km east-southeast of Aleppo).[17] The document in question is a will, and it contains a penalty clause, as it were, for anyone who would contest its legality. The specific phrase is:

> If they contest, this tablet will break their teeth.
>
> *šumma iraggumū ṭuppu annû šinnātīšunu ušabbar*

This tablet thus establishes a definite legal as well as incantatory context for the phrase. In other words, both clauses of Ps 3:8 under discussion can be documented as legal terminology.

We can go even further than this in elucidating the jurisprudential setting. The laws of Ešnunna (§42) and Hammurabi both exhibit a sequence of legal topics; for example, in the Hammurabi law code, injury through assault to the eye (§§198–99) is discussed first, then injury to the teeth (§§200–201), immediately followed by the cases of the striking of the face

---

16. Abusch, *Babylonian Witchcraft Literature*, 92, 97, 130, and esp. 131–47, draws attention to the interrelation of incantatory and legal language.
17. J. A. Hackett and J. Huehnergard, "On Breaking Teeth," *HTR* 77 (1984) 259–75. I thank Marc Brettler for drawing this article to my attention.

(§§202–5).[18] The likelihood of an Israelite psalmist having been directly influenced by Ešnunna's or Hammurabi's laws is, of course, utterly remote. But it is certainly within the realm of possibility, indeed of probability, that some Israelite legal text, not preserved, featured the same two laws juxtaposed as in these two collections. It is elementary that the legal corpora of the Torah represent only a small part of a much larger body of common law, perhaps orally transmitted, that was current in ancient Israel.

An analogy to the above may be drawn from *lex talionis*. This "eye for an eye" formula is featured three times, once in each of the legal corpora of the Torah (Exod 21:22–25, Lev 24:17–22, Deut 19:18–19, 21). A careful analysis of their surrounding contexts and of the relation of the legal formulation to the specific topic to which each is attached leaves no doubt that the *lex talionis* once circulated quite independently of its present pericopes as a discrete fossilized, general statement of legal policy.[19] Whatever its original intent, the standardized formula came to express an abstract legal concept, the law of equivalence. In the same way, I would suggest that the two clauses of Ps 3:8 go back to some ancient juristic compilation. They then came to be used abstractly and figuratively in literary texts to connote the infliction of humiliation and reduction to impotence. Such a development should occasion no surprise, for the judicial system was not detached from the life of the community; justice was carried on at the city gate, in public, so that legal terminology easily penetrated everyday speech.

Having mentioned the *lex talionis*, it is appropriate to round out this paper with a brief mention of the well-known passage in Matt 5:38–39 (cf. Luke 6:29):

> You have heard that it was said, "An eye for an eye and a tooth for a tooth." But I say unto you, Do not resist one who is evil. But if one strikes you on the right cheek, turn to him the other also.

I shall not relate to the problem that Jesus is here referring to private injury and that he must surely have known that, in his day certainly, the Pharisaic interpretation of the *lex talionis* rejected the literal application and required monetary compensation. Rather, I am struck by the juxtaposition of a blow to the eye, tooth, and cheek in that order as in the laws of Ešnunna and in Hammurabi.[20] Jesus cites all three as examples of "evil," which would make no sense unless "striking the cheek" was taken to be an offense of the utmost severity. Is the sequence pure coincidence or does it, perhaps, reflect some fossilized legal formulation?

---

18. *ANET* 163, 175.
19. See N. M. Sarna, *Exploring Exodus* (New York, 1986) 185–89.
20. See *ANET* 163, 175.

TIME . . . TO BEGIN

Jack M. Sasson

In the literary artistic chronotope, spatial and temporal indicators are fused into one carefully thought-out, concrete whole. Time, as it were, thickens, takes on flesh, becomes artistically visible; likewise, space becomes charged and responsive to the movements of time, plot and history. This intersection of axes and fusion of indicators characterizes the artistic chronotope.

M. M. Bakhtin[1]

As he pondered one more mystery of life, Ben Sira once asked, "Why is one day better [or: more important] than another, when every day in the year has its light from the sun?" He answers, "It was by the Lord's decision that they were distinguished; he appointed the various seasons and festivals; some days he blessed and made holy, and others he assigned to the common run of days" (Sir 33:7-9; NEB, slightly altered). Ben Sira is, of course, commenting on Israel's religious calendar, but most especially he is musing over the Genesis account wherein after extraordinarily creative days God paradoxically chose to sanctify a day when divine omnipotence is not at all exhibited.[2]

Author's note: Shemaryahu Talmon, to whom this paper is affectionately dedicated, may recognize the arguments I advance in this paper for we discussed them when he was a fellow of the National Humanities Center (1987-1988). Moreover, he had read and annotated an earlier draft of the study which became the text of my 1988 Southeast Region Society of Biblical Literature Presidential address, delivered in Macon, GA. I have altered slightly the introductory paragraph of that address, since it alludes to information of local interest only. I am beholden to B. Schmidt for improving my phraseology.

    1. Cited by P. Michalowski, "Mental Maps and Ideology: Reflections on Subartu," *The Origins of Cities in Dry-Farming Syria and Mesopotamia in the Third Millennium B.C.* (ed. H. Weiss; Guilford, CT, 1986) 130. The full text of the quotation is in M. M. Bakhtin, *The Dialogic Imagination: Four Essays by M. M. Bakhtin* (ed. M. Holquist: Austin, 1981) 84.

    2. On the argument that Ben Sira is referring to the Sabbath, see M. Tsevat, *The Meaning of the Book of Job and Other Studies* (New York, 1980) 52.

The Sabbath

In this paper, I reexamine the Genesis verses upon which Ben Sira bases his answer and urge that we turn to Greek "scientific" speculation rather than to Near Eastern mythmaking when looking for comparative material for the first four days of creation. In the process, I try to demonstrate that the Hebrew text did not begin the world's history until that fourth day. What happened during the first three days will soon become clear.[3]

Frequent in Scripture, but absent from the Book of Genesis is the term שבת. The word has so far defied the philologian's grasp. It is peculiar not only in having a double middle radical, but also in doubling the third one as well when a suffix is attached to it. It is certain that שבת cannot mean what the Hebrew implies: a day in which either God's work stops or God stops work. Most likely שבת means 'the day which stops', or 'the day which marks a limit'.[4] Both the etymological distortion and the various scriptural explanations of this institution cast doubt on how much the Hebrews really knew about the origins of שבת.[5] Consequently, when among other early exegetes Theophilus of Antioch sought another solution for the name שבת, he derived it from the number 'seven' שבע.[6] Although this theory too is hardly credible philologically, it is not much worse than a spate of contemporary learned hypotheses which link the word and the institution to alleged Mesopotamian prototypes.[7] At the very least Theophilus's solution recognizes the overpowering control that the number seven and its multiples

---

3. Much has been written on this subject. Good overviews are available in J. Barr's *Biblical Words for Time* (Studies in Biblical Theology 33; London, 1962); J. H. Wilch, *Time and Event* (Leiden, 1969), Introduction.

4. See R. de Vaux, *Ancient Israel: Its Life and Institutions* (New York, 1961) 475–76. Such etymological and etiological difficulties are of course not unknown to Scripture; consider the name משה, for example, which means 'the retriever' when the narrative in Exodus implies 'the retrieved'.

5. About this uniquely Hebraic and obviously ancient institution, Israel's redactors retained various explanations, operating on a widely shared assumption that truth is more potent when observed from multiple perspectives. The Deuteronomist (at 5:14–15) speculated that שבת perpetuated a testimonial to God's involvement in the Exodus. Various hands contributing to Exodus agree on the seventh day as a sign of a covenant between God and his chosen fold or as a day in which human beings may vicariously participate in creation by emulating divine satisfaction at its completion (Exod 20:8–11; enlarged in 31:12–17; cf. 23:12).

6. Actually, Theophilus wanted to show that the Greeks labeled their seventh day from שבת, which he derived from the Hebrew for seven. On the theology of Theophilus and his polemic against Hesiod's cosmology, see P. Nautin, "Genèse 1,1–2, de Justin à Origène," in *In Principio: Interpretations des premiers versets de la Genèse* (ed. P. Vignaux; Paris, 1973) 69–79.

7. The hopelessly muddled debate about the Sabbath's Babylonian origins is, however, finally coming to a sane end, with a clear rejection that Israel had (to use a quaint but commonly used term) "borrowed" the concept and the institution from Mesopotamia. See the conclusions of W. W. Hallo, "New Moons and Sabbaths: A Case-study in the Contrastive Approach," *Hebrew Union College Annual* 48 (1977) 15–18.

have on the Genesis account.[8] This leads us to look at another institution, the week, which binds seven days into a calendar unit.

The Week

No less than the Sabbath, the week, שבוע, also proves to be a curious and arbitrary convention. It is a subdivision which has absolutely no reference to celestial motions. While the moon periodically completes cycles, these differ substantially in length according to how they are calculated. When measured as successive new moons or successive conjunctions with stars, the cycle takes about 29½ days to complete. However, when measured by successive perigees or nodes, the cycle can be two days shorter.[9] Thus, while the month is not an exact fraction of the solar year, the week also is not an exact fraction of the month.

The Month

In fact, because Israel's culture was neither uniform nor homogenous even during the monarchic period, a number of calendars prevailed at one and the same time. The Hebrews as well as their neighbors apportioned the month into thirty or so days. The Hebrews could divide it into three units, each of ten days (עשורה), a reckoning also known to ancient Greece; but they were alone in recognizing the week as a regular and meaningful subdivision for the month. Israel conferred ordinal numbers as names for a series of seven days and repeated the roster when reaching the seventh, which as often as not, was called the Sabbath. There is an attractive theory that the Hebrews arrived at this heptad because they knew seven major celestial bodies: five planets plus the moon and the sun. (In fact, this is how we have names for our own days of the week.) This theory is perfectly plausible but is beyond proof due to the paucity of biblical information. All that we have, however, is a biblical tradition which explains why we have a seven-day sequence. This tradition gathered authority and came to dominate the Hebrew calendar because it justified the existence of the Sabbath day.[10] I refer, of course, to the Priestly creation narrative in Genesis 1:1–2:4a.

---

8. On the number seven as a controlling device in the P account of creation, see U. Cassuto, *A Commentary on the Book of Genesis* (Jersualem, 1961), 1:12–15.

9. Respectively, 27.55 or 27.21 days. The numbers come from the *Random House Dictionary*, s.v. "month".

10. While we can indulge in endless speculation on how Israel invented the Sabbath, for our purpose it is enough to note that at least by the exilic period, the שבת had come to represent God's sovereignty over his people. This is succinctly stated by Second Isaiah, a prophet who rejected the implication that God needed to rest on a given day but wholeheartedly supported the Sabbath as God's gift to humankind (58:13–14): "If you restrain your

Creation in Genesis 1

The commentaries commonly observe that this creation narrative follows a sophisticated and symmetrical design. The pattern of creation for the first three days is said to parallel that of the next three.[11] However, this balanced scheme seems plausible because it reflects our own sense of symmetry. The commentaries themselves record so many doubts about its validity that if we want to unlock the narrative's design we should best turn to the Hebrew's own vocabulary for clues.[12] Once we remove the verbs ברא and עשה as useful criteria because they obviously function *here* as synonyms, the language of creation permits us to divide the narrative into two major phases.[13] The controlling idiom in the first phase is קרא ל 'to assign a name [to something]'. This block lasts three days and I call it the "cosmological phase." The second segment, which I name the "animate phase," covers two days: the fifth and sixth. Because this phase deals with living creatures, נפש is its critical term. However, its controlling language is ברך 'to bless', a word which becomes increasingly significant as God selects Israel and its ancestors.

The fourth day is pivotal and the narrator pays it more attention than all other days with the exception of the sixth. Although this fourth day has no vocabulary which is singular to itself, I nevertheless assign it to the "cosmological phase" because it repeats the vocabulary crucial to the first day. In locating אור, חושך, יום, לילה, and the verb הבדיל in both days, the Hebrew thus invites us to treat as one unit everything bracketed between their occurrences.

---

movement during the Sabbath, and avoid doing whatever pleases you on my Holy Day... then you can seek the LORD's favor. I will place you on top of the world, and will let you savor Jacob's inheritance."

11. The first and fourth days feature the creation of light and the luminaries; the second and fifth days focus on the isolation of waters on either side of the firmament and on the creation of fish and birds to fill the spaces thus obtained; finally, the third and sixth days, which are unique in containing double activities, feature the segregation of the dry land and the creation of earth creatures—beasts and human—to fill the soil.

12. What about the doubling of activities on the third and sixth days, which in fact leaves us not with six but eight units of activities? Why are logically dependent activities (e.g., the creation of water) divided over two separate days? What logic lay behind the creation of plants in the third day, but of sun and moon in the fourth? How is light born at least two full days before there were luminaries? See J. Skinner, *A Critical and Exegetical Commentary on Genesis* (ICC; Edinburgh, 1930) 10–11.

13. This is so despite the fact that in Hebrew the subject of ברא is God, while human beings as well can be subjects for עשה; see A. Caquot, "Brèves remarques exégétiques sur Genèse 1,1–2," in *In Principio: Interpretations des premiers versets de la Genèse* (ed. P. Vignaux; Paris, 1973) 9–21. Notice how the LXX (but not Aquila or Josephus) uses ἐποίησεν 'he made [i.e., עשה]' when translating ברא in 1:1; see A. Paul, "Le Récit de la création," in *Hellenica et Judaica* (ed. A. Caquot; Paris, 1986) 131. On distinguishing among these verbs as well as הבדיל, see S. Talmon, "Biblical Understanding of Creation and Human Commitment," *Christian/Jewish Relations* 20 (1987) 69–89. ברא, however, fosters a pun when the opening words בראשית ברא are made to share the same sequence of three consonants.

The complete account of creation features ten ויאמר statements, the first of which occurs at v. 3. These expressions are allocated over six creative days and are punctuated by seven expressions of satisfaction. They are themselves flanked by a two-verse prologue and an epilogue of about three verses. The epilogue tells us that God ceased to work on the seventh day. Because the number six has little symbolic meaning in Scripture except as precursor for seven; because the Genesis creation account replays words such as day, night, earth, heaven, and God seven times or multiples of seven; and because the Hebrew *may* well be establishing harmony between the length of creation and the number of known planets, this epilogue is structurally neither an addendum nor a later insertion. Instead, it logically resolves previously stated information. Notice also how the crucial ברא אלהים 'God created' frames the whole creation narrative by its presence at its beginning and end: at Gen 1:1, בראשית ברא אלהים את השמים ואת הארץ, and at 2:3, אשר ברא אלהים לעשות.

The vocabulary of the prologue is equally protean. Because Hebrew is concrete when seeking to achieve the abstract, the prologue's vision is couched in a seemingly prosaic vocabulary. However, its syntax and its virtuoso use of paronomasia allow these brief verses to surmount the language's limitation, and invites us to share the narrator's imaginative recreation of the unconceived.

"In the Beginning"?

Most Bible translations offer two radically different renderings for the first two verses. Up until recently we read only, "In the beginning, God created the heaven and the earth." However, a translation based on an exegesis long espoused by medieval Jewish sages has recently won many followers. This translation recognizes that the first word of Genesis, בראשית, must be dependent on the verb following; this forces us to treat the whole phrase as a temporal sentence, "When God began to create. . . ." More importantly, when we analyze בראשית as in construct to the verb following, we are required to treat the whole of v. 2 as a parenthetical statement. Although there are competent philologists who still defend the traditional translation, I personally think that this exegesis is really beyond dispute: first, because it is supported by grammar and syntax;[14] second, because other creation

---

14. All the examples of בראשית are in temporal clauses, and the examples of ראשית in the absolute state (with or without prefixed propositions) are found only when the term is used in ceremonial context; see Skinner, *Genesis*, 12–13. A bibliography on the traditional exegesis of Gen 1:1 can be found in B. W. Anderson, "Introduction: Mythopoeic and Theological Dimensions of the Biblical Creation Faith," in *Creation in the Old Testament* (Philadelphia, 1984) 23–24. For more details on the controversy, see C. Westermann, *Genesis 1–11: A Commentary* (Minneapolis, 1984) 93–98. The Book of Hosea begins with a similar construction (v. 2): תחלת דבר יהוה בהושע ויאמר יהוה אל הושע, which is correctly rendered in NJPSV: "When the LORD first spoke to Hosea, the LORD said to Hosea. . . ."

narratives similarly open with temporal or circumstantial clauses; and third, because the first of God's creative injunctions does not come until v. 3.

Verse 1, then, offers the premise that "when God began to create *the universe*, earth was in a state of תהו ובהו."[15] Despite some learned protest to the contrary, I nevertheless treat "heaven and earth" (שמים and וארץ) as a *merismus*, that is, as one unit of thought formed of two juxtaposed opposites. (We meet with the same rhetorical device in Gen 2:17 when "total knowledge" is given as "the knowledge of good and evil.") Those who inspect the twenty or so occurrences of תהו are doubtlessly right in showing how it invariably connotes 'desiccation' or 'devastation'.[16] Because תהו is linked to בהו, however, the phrase תהו ובהו must be treated neither as another merismus nor even as a hendiadys (as suggested by Speiser and Westermann); rather, it should be understood as a *farrago*, wherein two usually alliterative words combine to give a meaning other than their constituent parts. I would certainly avoid the common rendering 'unformed and void', poetic though it may seem, at least because it would stress the negative, whereas the Hebrew is referring to a definite condition. I would also resist Westermann's 'desert waste' because it conveys much too concrete a vision to the English reader. As it happens, תהו ובהו is manifestly onomatopoeic, and we are lucky to have its equivalent in a nice English onomatopoeic farrago, 'hodgepodge' (originally meaning a 'goulash'). So, the earth was 'hodgepodge'. But there was also חשך על פני תהום.

Darkness upon the Deep

חשך has a crackly sound to it; but there is nothing sinister in this first mention of 'darkness'. As with neighboring cosmogonies, darkness merely emphasizes how indistinct was the primordial. We do something similar when we speak of a "black hole" to suggest a celestial body of impenetrable density. What I find more impressive is the way the Hebrew links this articulation of the unfathomable with another expression for the undifferentiated.

תהום has become an interpretive *bête noire* ever since cuneiform documents introduced the Tiamat of Babylonian myths; so much so that it is now practically impossible to locate a biblical commentary which does not devote many pages to *Enuma Elish* and its influence on the Genesis creation account. I doubt, however, that Israel was much interested in the theologies of other nations, if only because its own theologians did not have ready access to Pritchard's hefty *Ancient Near Eastern Texts Relating*

---

15. Notice how the Hebrew begins with "earth," thus promoting it as the creation's principal objective.
16. Westermann, *Genesis 1–11*, 102-3.

to the Old Testament from which to mount their polemics.[17] Linguistically, *tehom* could be related to Tiamat only indirectly, through a link which is missing from the evidence at hand. *Tehom* as an adversary for God makes fullest sense only in creations where the combat metaphor is dominant. While this particular metaphor appears frequently in Scripture, it is not featured in Genesis where there are metaphors of rearrangement and of craftsmanship.[18] Therefore, we should recognize that here, as elsewhere, *tehom* is a poetic term for bodies of water.[19]

The dictionaries show that על פני is a complex preposition which refers to the movement over and around something rather than just to an arrested condition above a specific surface.[20] In v. 2, darkness envelops *tehom*. However, in the next phrase, ורוח אלהים מרחפת על פני המים, a divine or awesome wind (both adjectives have merits) is to sweep the waters.[21]

The Hebrew writer has so far adopted a lapidary style by which to communicate his information about the primordial. If inclined to do so, we may imagine ourselves in a photographic exhibit where we can only see what the camera can frame. Because chronology and movement cannot be part of the illustration, the portraits we inspect seem frozen beyond time. We therefore react neutrally to the series of sharply focused likenesses the Hebrew has left for us to inspect: images of earth, darkness, air, and water.

"Creatio ex nihilo"?

Already in antiquity, the Hebrew concept of the primordial was identified with Greek notions regarding the four hylic elements—sea, air, earth, and fire, the last manifested primarily as the brightness in the sky.[22] Modern

---

17. That *Enuma Elish* was kept away from nonpriestly hands and that it was recited only in the inner recesses of Mesopotamian temples are also reasons why the text was not likely available to Israel's own priests.

18. These distinctions are nicely developed in L. G. Perdue, "Job's Assault on Creation," *Hebrew Annual Review* 10 (1986) 295–315.

19. See conveniently Caquot, "Brèves remarques exégetiques sur Genèse 1,1–2," 17–18.

20. In the fifth day birds are to flutter over the earth *across* the heavens (v. 20). In the sixth day, earth creatures are to partake of all seed-bearing plants found *all about* the earth (v. 29).

21. Because the darkness and wind clauses share the same preposition as well as pair of words referring to water, I would not be averse to collapsing the two clauses as follows, "Darkness and an awesome (or divine) wind whipped about the watery Deep."

22. For the Greek material, see M. C. Stokes, "Heraclitus of Ephesus," *The Encyclopedia of Philosophy* (ed. P. Edwards; New York, 1967), 3:478–79. Hellenistic Jewry also was alert to this equation, as is obvious from the following Genesis Rabbah anecdote: "A philosopher said to Rabban Gamaliel that God found good materials which He used in the creation of the world, '*Tohu, Bohu*, darkness, water, wind, and the deep,' to which Gamaliel vigorously replied, 'Woe to that man! The term creation is explicitly used of them'" (quoted by L. I. Rabinowitz, "Creation and Cosmogony: Rabbinic View of Creation," *EncJud* 5:1063).

scholars who make a similar suggestion implicitly doubt that the Hebrews had the capacity to imagine a creation from nothing.[23] I want here simply to point out that in Genesis the preexistence of earth, water, air, and darkness in no way deters God from creating many things out of nothing. For example, light is neither a primordial element nor does it evolve from it. It is created *ex nihilo*, and then simply contrasted with darkness. Neither is the רקיע 'firmament' of v. 6 created out of any preexisting element; nor are the מארת 'lightmakers' of v. 14 concocted from anything previously available. In fact, no item which God orders into being by using the jussive יהי within a ויאמר statement can be said to emerge from preexisting materials.[24]

God's first command is that there be light. I do not believe that the Hebrew wants us here to find a polemic against light-centered theologies; nor do I find it necessary to worry about the nature of a sunless or moonless lighting. Rather, the Hebrew is solving a difficulty in the same way that we would when forced to formulate what is beyond our language's capacity to describe: witness how physicists speak of the "Big Bang" when referring to a creative moment, without ever implying that it involves sound, big or small for that matter. In fact, this light has no future and achieves no role until God establishes a contrast between it and darkness. Therefore, we are told, "When God perceived how appropriate 'light' was, he sets it apart from darkness."

What the Hebrew is striving for, however, comes in v. 5. Here occurs the first of three successive appeals to the idiom קרא ל 'assigning a name to something'. We are told that "God named the light 'day,' whereas he named darkness 'night.'" The Hebrew is again struggling with an ambiguous vocabulary; יום is as imprecise in what it denotes as is the English word "day." To solve the limitation of language and to achieve a precise connotation for what is now meant by יום, the Hebrew immediately provides

---

23. The debate commonly posed under the rubric *creatio ex nihilo* is fought almost exclusively around the first twenty words or so of Genesis. The controversy does not properly belong to our field of research because it is fundamentally theological and apologetic, not philological or exegetical. Among these concerns are the following: (1) to harmonize the opening lines in Genesis with those in John ("In the beginning was the Word . . ."); (2) to establish sharp demarcation between Hebrew and pagan concepts of God; and (3) to neutralize scientific speculation on the origins of the universe by placing God beyond nature. Interesting remarks on these matters can be found in A. Momigliano, "Time in Ancient Historiography," in his *Essays in Ancient and Modern Historiography* (Middletown, CT, 1975).

24. Second Isaiah states, "I am the LORD and there is none else, I form light and create darkness, I make weal and create woe—I the LORD do all these things" (45:6–7). Far from reflecting a rejection within Israel of Genesis 1:1–5 and its implication, such a quotation shows a deep understanding of how complex and enriching is the message. See M. Weinfeld, "God the Creator in Gen 1 and the Prophecy of Second Isaiah," *Tarbiz* 37 (1968) 105–32 [Hebrew]. M. Fishbane, *Biblical Interpretation in Ancient Israel* (Oxford, 1985) 321–26, also lists Deut 4:16b–19a, among other passages, which carry on a debate with Gen 1.

contrast with "night," the name now assigned to primordial darkness. The writer pauses in the narrative briefly to tell us parenthetically that "it was evening, it was morning." This sequence faithfully proceeds from what there was (i.e., darkness) to what ensued (i.e., light). The phrase becomes formulaic to the rest of the creation narrative and thus reinforces the deliberate and methodical pace of God's activity; it ought not, therefore, be cited as relevant evidence that Israel began its day on the evening previous.

The writer concludes by assessing this alternation between darkness and daylight as equivalent to "one day." Here we must be particularly careful not to fudge, not to declare this reckoning as equivalent to "first day." Indeed, while for calendar purposes the Hebrew writer does use the cardinal number to modify the word "day," this is invariably followed by the word "month"; for example, ביום אחד לחדש.[25]

Time

By telling us that God is responsible for one day, the writer does not want to declare light as God's first creation; rather, we are being alerted to the invention of time, a medium forged out of darkness, decidedly the least promising element available to the universe. And by choosing one day as the primary scale for the passage of time, the writer acutely observes how the day is the only period in Israel's calendar to depend exclusively on celestial motions. In contrast, the nonsolar year, the lunar month, the week, the (seasonably variable) hour, the minute, and the second are but conventions fixed and accepted by tradition.

Initially, then, "one day" is just a *measure* for time, an alternation between light and day; it is only retrospectively, at the end of another similar stretch of divine creativity, that the formula begins to function as the *unit* of time which is equivalent to our own civil day.

The verses which tell of the invention of one day also make sweeping claims. They maintain that as long as God had not made available to human beings a mechanism for chronology, human beings cannot effectively discuss the relationship among God and primordial substances. From this perspective, theogony or the birth and emergency of God from preexisting matter is a theme which the Hebrew writer could not profitably discuss. It is this reluctance which makes the Hebrews so different from their more mythopoeic neighbors who repeatedly retold how deities emerge either from unformed matter or from each other.[26] Rather than espousing a form

---

25. Additionally, I have great respect for the narrator's paronomastic prowess; "first day," *יום (ה)ראשון, would have so perfectly served to bracket the opening word, בראשית, that if the Hebrew resisted it, something much more challenging was at stake.

26. It is not surprising therefore that when a document such as the Sumerian king list speaks of the descent of kingship as a gift from the gods, its author does not seem particularly

of mythmaking wherein time is elastic and thematic progression is more crucial than historical chronology, the Hebrew adopts a more abstract yet more controllable illusion. Time becomes a cosmological feature of God's own devising and its mysterious flow is not entirely beyond human understanding.

For the ancient Hebrew, then, time is no mirage of the human mind nor is it the riddle which so embarrassed St. Augustine; time is not beyond adequate definition and measurement, as the nearly contemporaneous Pythagoreans would have it. Its rules can be explained theologically—I would say "scientifically"—allowing human beings thereby to chart adequately their own future. It is not surprising therefore that when Israel's sages imagine the other side of beginnings, namely the closing of historical time, they return to this paradigm and initiate apocalyptic unfolding with another "one day" period, namely the "Day of the Lord."

As far as I can tell, in the ancient Near East these positions are unique to Israel.[27] They are not, however, unknown to the nearly contemporaneous Classical Greece of the sixth and fifth centuries. In *Timaeus* §38, Plato crystallizes earlier speculation on time, history, and cosmology:

> For before the heavens came into being there were no days or nights or months or years, but [the father] devised and brought them into being at the same time as the heavens were put together; for they were all parts of time, just as past and future are also forms of it, which we wrongly attribute, without thinking, to the Eternal Being.... So time came into being with the heavens in order that, having come together, they should also be dissolved together if ever they are dissolved; and it was as like as possible to eternity which was its model.[28]

Plato continues, "As a result of this plan and purpose of [G]od for the birth of time, the sun, and moon, and the five planets as they are called came into being to define and preserve the measure of time." The ancient Hebrew writer, however, does not immediately move to the creation of the luminaries, but proceeds instead to define space and mass. Not surprisingly, these two dimensions of nature are commonly linked to time in modern scientific literature.

---

interested in the management of time and its allocation to various city-states. He may simply have had no tradition wherein the emergency of time was an event of singular significance.

27. As two sets of paired deities (Dūri/Dari; Halma/Hallama) time occurs as a component in Mesopotamian cosmogony, but it plays a negligible role there. See W. G. Lambert, "Kosmogonie," *RLA* 6 (1983) 218–22.

28. H. D. P. Lee, *Timaeus and Critia* (New York, 1971) 51–52. In *Biblical Words for Time*, 75–76, Barr refers to Plato's speculations in connection with Genesis 1, adding, "It remains likely that Genesis 1 and other sources would be read as suggesting that time began with ͗ eation" (p. 79).

Space and Mass

During the second day God maps out space within which to set future creations. God generates through divine fiat a רקיע, a hammered item—perhaps a dome—which then splits the primordial waters into two entities. God names the uppermost "heaven." The nethermost is set aside for the next day's task.

The third day, God forms the two physical masses which will be home for human beings. Manipulating a cherished tradition wherein waters are said to retreat at God's order, the narrator establishes a rigid distinction between the seas and the hard land. God gives a second command on that selfsame day, investing this hard land with generative powers. However, by recording this order for the earth to seed itself, the Hebrew writer is not endowing plants with life-giving potential; in fact, this capacity will not be a feature until the "animate phase," when animals and human beings are placed on the earth. Rather, the narrator treats the event as a cancellation of a primordial condition when earth, being תהו ובהו, could not bear any seed or fruit, let alone living beings.[29]

Only at this stage, during the fourth day, does the writer introduce the luminaries, and we can understand why he labors to avoid calling them by name; for the names of the sun, the moon, and the stars can easily suggest the existence of foreign deities. God sets them in space and then surrenders to them control of the diurnal oscillations.[30] Henceforth, human beings need no longer scrutinize the acts of God to realize a pattern for cultic behavior; rather they turn to these astral bodies to compute the yearly festal calendar.

The fifth day is about to dawn. The universe is in harmony: time is charted, space is mapped out, land and sea masses are now ready; the

---

29. Westermann seems to be alone among modern scholars to recognize the importance of time and space as features of the Genesis creation account: see *Genesis 1-11*, 112, 114. However, he hardly develops his views and offers neither an explanation nor an intellectual context for the phenomenon. These insights are made more prominent, albeit still short of adequate discussion, in a more sharply focused restatement of his conclusions, *Genesis: A Practical Commentary* (Grand Rapids, 1987) 8-9. Throughout the ages, "one day" has elicited interpretations which depended on the then current philosophical debates. For Augustine's Plotinian understanding, see A. Solignac, "Exégèse et Metaphysique: Genèse 1,1-3 chez saint Augustin," in *In Principio: Interpretations des premiers versets de la Genèse* (ed. P. Vignaux; Paris 1973) 164-65. On pp. 37-45 of the same volume, C. Touati studies the mystical interpretation of Gersonides: "La lumière de l'intellect, création du Premier Jour; L'exégèse de Genèse 1,1-3 chez Gersonide." A useful collection of Greek primary material on the issue is found in S. Sambursky and S. Pines, *The Concept of Time in Late Neoplatonism* (Jerusalem, 1971).

30. Here, the vision of the narrator is Janus-like, albeit its sequence reverses what we might expect: it skips toward the sixth day in which appears the only creature for whom the luminaries can serve as religious clock, then lurches backward to emulate vocabulary essential to the first day.

luminaries, infinitely more convenient to fathom than is God, are now measures for human existence. As with those dreamers who lived in Qumran, we may be justified, therefore, in believing that it is only on this one day—the fourth—that the history of Israel, indeed our own history, truly begins.[31]

Our response to Ben Sira's query has led us to reassess the import of Genesis's earliest verses. But it has permitted us also to realize better how uncommonly sophisticated and rigorous is the mind of one cosmologist in ancient Israel. I can pay it no better tribute than to apply to it what Thomas Gilby said in appreciation of another fine theologian, Thomas Aquinas:

> [His] style remains an instrument of precision once we appreciate that he was not writing a mathematical treatise or a legal document where single terms can be treated as atoms of discourse or forced into their fixed univocal sense. . . . He was addressing himself as a philosopher to the things first shown us through the senses and not to disembodied essences, and as a theologian to the works of God in history. . . . He had to render things that were at once dark and shimmering, deep and on the surface, single and complex, firm and supple, irreducibly individual yet sharing in the common whole; and he paid them the compliment of attempting to do so without breaking into poetry.[32]

---

31. S. Talmon, "The Calendar Reckoning of the Sect from the Judaean Desert," in *Aspects of the Dead Sea Scrolls* (ed. C. Rabin and Y. Yadin; ScrHier 4; Jerusalem, 1958) 176.

32. Cited by A. Mandelbaum, "Introduction," in *The Divine Comedy of Dante Alighieri: Inferno: A Verse Translation* (New York, 1982) xv.

JACOB IN SHECHEM AND IN BETHEL
(GENESIS 35:1–7)

J. Alberto Soggin

(1) Then God said to Jacob: "Lo, go up to Bethel and settle there; build an altar there to the God who appeared to you when you were running away from your brother Esau." (2) So Jacob said to his household and to all who were with him: "Rid yourselves of the foreign gods which you have among you, purify yourselves and change your clothes, (3) lo, let us go to Bethel and there I shall build an altar to the God who answered me in the time of my distress, and who has been with me during my journey." (4) So they handed over to Jacob all the foreign gods in their possession and the rings from their ears, and he buried them under the terebinth tree near Shechem. (5) Then they left and the surrounding cities were panic-stricken, so that their inhabitants dared not to pursue the sons of Jacob. (6) Then Jacob and all the people with him came to Luz, that is Bethel, in Canaan. (7) There he built an altar and called the place אל בית אל, because it was there that God had revealed himself to him when he was running away from his brother (NEB, slightly modified).

Commentary

Gen 35:1. "To Bethel": the LXX reads εἰς τὸν τόπον βαιθελ, which would be אל מקום בית אל in Hebrew. It could well be an expanded reading,[1] but since מקום often indicates a '(holy) site' it seems rather to be the original. If this longer reading is considered original, it may be supposed that a later scribe intentionally obliterated what would have been a clear indication that Bethel was a "holy site."

---

1. The LXX has a longer text in many cases in this passage; see E. Nielsen, *Shechem* (Copenhagen, 1959) 234.

Gen 35:2. "The foreign gods": the obvious meaning of the text is images or statuettes of foreign gods. It is to them that "the God who appeared to you" (v. 1) is opposed.

Gen 35:4. I have discussed the use of the root טמן with this specialized meaning elsewhere.[2] Normally the root means 'to hide', and this is the only meaning appearing in *HALAT* (pp. 360–61), but F. Zorell suggests both meanings: 'to hide' and 'to bury'.[3] Against this latter rendering see O. Keel, whose arguments have not convinced me.[4] The LXX adds: "And destroyed them until this day," but this is an unnecessary, if not contradictory, detail. If the people rid themselves of the images in whatever way, they need not destroy them. It could be, however, that the LXX simply wanted to stress the unique and final character of what happened, and this was the most adequate way of doing so.

Gen 35:5. According to C. Westermann this verse ought to be added to the end of chap. 36, since it still deals with "the sons of Jacob" and not with Jacob himself.[5] The LXX has sensed the problem just mentioned and renders "they left" with "Israel left," thus avoiding having Jacob's name changed twice (v. 9).

Gen 35:7. אל is lacking in the LXX and in the Vulgate. Could this be a monotheistic correction of the Hebrew text? One should also notice the plural verb with אלהים, translated as singular in the ancient translations.

An Ancient Ritual?

Following the classical study by A. Alt, this text has often been considered to reflect an ancient custom.[6] According to Alt (as is well known), the text has preserved the memory of an ancient ritual of purification,[7] during, or rather before, a pilgrimage from Shechem to Bethel. Alt has rightly stressed the centrality of the burial of the foreign gods and of their personal jewels at the hands of Jacob and his entourage, a burial performed "under the

---

2. J. A. Soggin, "La radice *ṭmn*, 'nascondere,' 'sepellire,' in ebraico," in *Atti del secondo congresso internazionalle di linguistica amito-semitica* (Florence, 1978) 241–45. See also idem, "La 'sepoltura della divinità' nell'iscrizione di Pyrgi (lin. 8–9) e motivi paralleli nell'Antico Testamento," *Rivista degli studi orientali* 45 (1970) 245–52; English trans. in idem, *Old Testament and Oriental Studies* (trans. D. Henderson and C. Rockwell; Biblica et Orientalia 29; Rome, 1975) 112–19.

3. F. Zorell, *Lexicon Hebraicum et Aramaicum Veteris Testamenti* (Rome, 1984) 286.

4. O. Keel, "Das vergraben der 'fremden Götter' in Genesis XXXV 4b," *VT* 23 (1973) 305–6.

5. C. Westermann, *Genesis* (Minneapolis, 1986), 2:551.

6. A. Alt, "Die Wallfahrt von Sichem nach Bethel," in *In piam memoriam Alexander von Bulmerincq* (Riga, 1938) 218–30; repr. in idem, *Kleine Schriften zum Alten Testament* (Munich, 1953), 1:79–88.

7. For such rituals, cf. the details in B. Jacob, *Das erste Buch der Tora: Genesis* (Berlin, 1934).

terebinth tree near Shechem." This or a similar tree is often mentioned in relation to Shechem, and must have been a sacred tree, belonging to the sanctuary.[8] But Alt has also stressed the extraordinary character of such a ritual, performed at a first sanctuary, albeit in preparation for another, a most unusual practice.[9] Whatever we may think of such a *Sitz im Leben* (and I shall soon return to the matter), the present form of the text can be shown to be relatively late. The verb הסרו in such a context is Deuteronomic and Deuteronomistic (cf. Josh 24:14, Judg 10:16, and 1 Sam 7:3).[10] The expression אלהי הנכר also appears more often than not in Deuteronomic and Deuteronomistic texts (cf. Deut 31:16, Josh 24:20, Judg 10:16, 1 Sam 7:3, and Jer 5:19). Furthermore, the *Hithpael* form of טהר is found only in exilic and postexilic texts,[11] while the root טמן with the special meaning 'to bury' instead of the usual one 'to hide', is also late and becomes in medieval Hebrew, especially in Spain, synonymous with קבר.

Thus, there is consistent evidence that the text is Deuteronomic, Deuteronomistic, or in some parts even later. A *direct* connection with an *ancient* cultic ceremony performed before a pilgrimage, as suggested by Alt, becomes highly unlikely, at least as far as this phase of the transmission is concerned. Another matter remains to be clarified. If this text is predominantly Deuteronomic or Deuteronomistic, how could this act be related to and performed in Shechem in preparation for the abhorred sanctuary of Bethel? Why is there not some kind of relationship to the sanctuary of Jerusalem (e.g., with one of the Deuteronomic/Deuteronomistic typical allusions to this holy place before the times of Solomon)? Could it be connected with a ritual that occurred, originally, in the north, to be adopted by Judah after 722/720 B.C.E.? The vindication and claim by Judah after the destruction of the north, and especially after the Exile, to be the true heir also of "Israel" is well known, and could account for the topography of the ceremony.

Parallels

This text is not without parallels. The first and most obvious is Gen 28:10–22 (cf. vv. 1, 3, 7), but this is a very complex narrative, whose stratification has not as yet been definitively worked out. Blum has convincingly shown that a division into the sources J and E cannot be maintained.[12] Gen 35:1–7

---

8. On the localization of this tree, see L. Wächter, "Zur Lokalisierung des sichemitischen Baumheiligtums," *Zeitschrift des Deutschen Palästina-Vereins* 103 (1987) 1–12.

9. On the pilgrimage motif, see Jacob, *Genesis, ad loc.*

10. See L. Perlitt, *Bundestheologie im Alten Testament* (Wissenschaftliche Monographien zum Alten und Neuen Testament 36; Neukirchen-Vluyn, 1969).

11. Westermann, *Genesis, ad loc.*

12. E. Blum, *Die Komposition der Vätergeschichte* (Wissenschaftliche Monographien zum Alten und Neuen Testament 57; Neukirchen-Vluyn, 1984) 7–35.

presupposes, however, that Gen 28:10–22 had been completed in all its phases, so that it can function as a sort of conclusion to it; and this is true even if it must be doubted that it is referring to the fulfillment of the vow mentioned in Gen 28:20–22.[13] In any case Genesis 35 proves to be more recent than Gen 28:10–22. It is therefore impossible to maintain E. Otto's contention that we have in Gen 35:1–7 "an etiology of the sanctuary of Bethel, independent from Gen 28:11–22."[14] In any event, Perlitt has demonstrated conclusively that we are not dealing here with an etiological legend at all.[15] A second, obvious parallel in action and in words is to be found in Josh 24:14–23, also located in Shechem, and in Judg 10:6ff., especially vv. 14–16. Both of these passages are Deuteronomistic, the latter an enhanced and therefore later phase of the redaction of the Book of Judges.

Aim

Can anything be said about the aim of Gen 35:1–7? The answer to this question presupposes another: when could a ritual which contemplated a solemn act of renunciation of foreign gods and the burial of their images become something to be performed with a certain urgency, within a context of a ritual of purification? To this second question there is only one answer, albeit a hypothetical one: such a ceremony could have been performed within the context of what the Hebrew Bible describes as King Josiah's "reformation," but what I would rather see as the elimination of Canaanite polytheism from Judah's faith and ritual, in favor of monotheism. This could hardly happen over a short period of time; it was certainly not a decision taken and carried out within a few years, nor did it restore some mythical, primitive monotheism. It was the concluding phase of a long process, initiated probably with the prophets of the ninth century B.C.E., and continued by those of eighth and seventh centuries. It seems therefore a reasonable assumption that sometime during the second half of the sixth century B.C.E., maybe already in late preexilic times, a ritual was performed in which God's people solemnly pledged to adore YHWH and no other god. This pledge was dated in prehistoric times, and its origins attributed to the ritual performed by Joshua in Shechem, with an important forerunner in Jacob at the same place. That this ritual started as a northern custom could explain its present location.

---

13. To which compare 31:3, 13—with Alt, "Die Wallfahrt von Sichem nach Bethel," 77 n. 1, and against Jacob, *Genesis, ad loc.*

14. E. Otto, *Jakob in Sichem* (Beiträge zur Wissenschaft vom Alten und Neuen Testament 4/10 = 110; Stuttgart, 1979) 72–73.

15. Perlitt, *Bundestheologie im Alten Testament*, 257–58.

WAS SAMUEL A NAZIRITE?

Matitiahu Tsevat

The Tradition

The question under discussion refers to Samuel the literary persona, and not to Samuel the historical person. The tradition is as follows. In the Hebrew text of 1 Sam 1:11 (R *textus receptus*, being the standard consonantal text)[1] Hannah vows that the son to be born in answer to her prayer shall not have his hair cut. In the LXX she adds before the hair vow that he shall not drink wine or (other) intoxicating drink. 4QSam^a of the Judean desert is fragmentary at this point;[2] abstinence from alcohol may have been mentioned in a lacuna. But 4QSam^a 1:22 contains the explicit pronouncement of Hannah, shortly after giving birth to Samuel, that he shall be a lifelong Nazirite.[3] Further, it just may be that προφήτην of Josephus's *Antiquities* 5:347 points to the same word נזיר in his *Vorlage* of v. 22; cf. προφητεύσων, said of Samson the Nazirite in *Antiquities* 5:285, but this is by no means certain. Having introduced Samuel as a prophet (*Antiquities* 5:340) in a context that looks to his prophethood (cf. 1 Sam 3:20), Josephus resumes the word against the narrative background of 1:22–28, thereby foreshadowing Samuel's career.[4] From the time of the LXX or a little before we have the very uncertain testimony of the Hebrew

---

1. M. Goshen-Gottstein eschews the term; see "The Hebrew Bible in the Light of the Qumran Scrolls and the Hebrew University Bible," in *Congress Volume: Jerusalem 1986* (ed. J. A. Emerton; VTSup 40; Leiden, 1988) 49.

2. F. M. Cross, "A New Qumran Biblical Fragment Related to the Original Hebrew Underlying the Septuagint," *BASOR* 132 (1953) 15–26; E. C. Ulrich, *The Qumran Text of Samuel and Josephus* (Harvard Semitic Monographs 19; Missoula, MT, 1978) 39; P. K. McCarter, *I Samuel* (AB 8; Garden City, NY, 1980) 54.

3. Ulrich, *Qumran Text of Samuel and Josephus*, 165; McCarter, *I Samuel*, 56.

4. The opinion of Ulrich that the *Vorlage* of the LXX in v. 11 also had נזיר (*Qumran Text of Samuel and Josephus*, explicitly on p. 39, guardedly on p. 165) is hardly tenable. The verbal adjective δοτόν possibly renders נָתוּן (or נָתִין, נָתִין, although the LXX leaves נָתִין almost always untranslated), but in any case it is noted that the LXX never translates נזיר by δοτός.

(and Syriac) Sirach, בנבואה (ייי) נזיר (46:13; the word ייי is not in the Syriac) which perhaps means 'a Nazirite of the Lord through prophecy' but more likely 'the exalted/consecrated [cf. Gen 49:26, Deut 33:16] of the Lord through prophecy'. The value of this passage as a support of 4QSam^a is diminished by the uncertain meaning of נזיר here, by the absence of נזיר from the LXX, and especially by the position of the phrase within panegyric Sirach 44–50. Conclusions about details of an Old Testament passage—text or content—that are based on its reflection in those chapters are precarious. Finally, the Mishnah records two opinions from the middle of the second century A.D. about Samuel's Naziritism, one positive (R. Nehorai) and one negative (R. Yose [ben Chalafta]; *m. Nazir* 9:5).[5]

The Examination of the Tradition

The law concerning the Nazirite (Num 6:1–21) contains three prohibitions: (1) consumption of wine, grapes, and intoxicating drink in general (vv. 3–4), (2) cutting the hair (v. 5), (3) contact with a human corpse (vv. 6–8). To Samson, whom before his birth a messenger of God ordains to be a Nazirite, the first two apply (Judg 13:4–7; abstinence of the child to begin "from the womb"). Avoidance of "unclean food" (v. 4) somewhat corresponds to avoidance of defilement by contact with a human corpse of Num 6:6–8. Where (as in the Hebrew of 1 Samuel 1) only one prohibition of the three is named and the word Nazirite not used, the assumption of Naziritism is altogether unjustified. For example, the Rechabites abstain from wine, one abstention of three (the others being agriculture and dwelling in houses; Jer 35:6), but they are not called Nazirites then or today. A special hairdo or haircut (of medium length?) is an injunction laid on the priests of Ezekiel's plan for the future temple and service (Ezek 44:20), but again, the word Nazirite is not found there. The Hebrew of 1 Samuel 1 R is identical with Jeremiah 35 and Ezekiel 44 in this respect, whereas 4QSam^a and the LXX are different: 4QSam^a uses the word Nazirite, and the LXX has two injunctions. (The texts of Sirach and Josephus are too uncertain for conclusions.) There are then two traditions of materially different contents. The difference can hardly be blamed on inattentive copying, for such would presuppose the coincidence of two inadvertent omissions in R (abstinence in v. 11 and Nazirite in v. 22) and one in the *Vorlage* of(?) the LXX (Nazirite in v. 22).

Yet the traditions—absence of Naziritism in R on the one hand, and presence in 4QSam^a and the LXX (and in the Hebrew and Syriac Sirach) on the other hand—are not of equal standing. (1) It is a rule of critical

---

5. As is to be expected, the Mishnah stands in the line of tradition of R, not of 4QSam^a and the LXX. Otherwise, R. Yose would not have denied that Samuel was a Nazirite.

philology that traditions grow rather than shrink.[6] When the rule is brought to bear on the issue examined in this article, Naziritism in 1 Samuel is judged to be the result of later growth, present in 4QSam[a] and the LXX, but absent in R. (2) In particular, bestowing "Nazirite" on Samuel is but one more case of the tendency to have various distinguished features and prominent offices converge in Samuel: priest, prophet, judge, kingmaker, and, in Chronicles (the lists of 1 Chr 6:(1), 11–13, 18:23), Levite. (3) Hannah, rejecting Eli's accusation of drunkenness, says that she did not drink alcoholic beverages (1:15–16). If the promise of the abstinence of the child to be born, perhaps in conjunction with the promise not to have his hair cut, would have been an element in the background of R, nothing would have been more natural narratively than the mother countering that not only did she not consume strong drink, but that also the child for whom she had been praying should never drink such if God were to grant her fervent request. The absence of this argument from her defense against the accusation of drunkenness in all texts supports the presumption that abstention from alcohol was not a part of the oldest form of the story. One by one the three reasons speak against the Naziritism of Samuel with various degrees of force; in combination they come as close to proof as one may look for in such circumstances.

The History of Research

The LXX (and Josephus) have always been known to students (and the Hebrew Sirach has been known since 1901), but until the second half of this century Samuel's Naziritism hardly played a role in exegesis. Pisano lists fourteen commentaries on Samuel, not counting translations, from about the middle of the nineteenth to the middle of the twentieth centuries, and their number can be augmented, that do not accept the narrative detail of abstinence in v. 11 LXX as genuine or trustworthy; he mentions two that accept it. On the other hand, from 1953 and later he names three critics, Cross, Ulrich, and McCarter, who side with the LXX in this detail as against two who do not.[7] As to the shift of positions, Pisano points sensibly to v. 22 4QSam[a] where Samuel is called a Nazirite, and 1953, the year of the publication of the Judean desert fragment. The comparatively early age of the attestation, the first century B.C., and its language, Hebrew, can probably be credited with having played an important role in the ascendance of Samuel the Nazirite in recent Old Testament criticism. But whatever the reason, the importance of 4QSam[a] for this detail is exiguous. 4QSam[a] and the LXX mostly stand together over against R (and a similar

---

6. The rule does not apply to splits of traditions and/or breakoffs of substantial parts.
7. S. Pisano, *Additions or Omissions in the Books of Samuel* (OBO 57; Göttingen, 1984) 20 n. 9, 21.

grouping of 4QSam^a and Josephus as opposed to R is noted). The affinity between 4QSam^a and the LXX has been recognized since the discovery of 4QSam^a and has subsequently been substantiated;[8] it is appropriate to say that they belong to one family of textual tradition. Once a text is recognized as a member of a given family, the fact that it attests to a distinctive trait or detail that is already known from another member of the family counts critically for very little; the concept of family warrants the expectation to encounter that trait or detail before it is observed. The measure of expectation is directly proportional to the number of shared traits or details per textual unit. In the present case the number is large. The relevant chapter in Ulrich's *Qumran Text of Samuel and Josephus* (chap. 2: "The Agreement of 4QSam^a with the Greek Version") is the longest of his book (pp. 39–93).[9] In the words of Ulrich: "Part A of this chapter is inordinately long. But that very length is eloquent testimony to the agreement of 4Q[Sam^a] with the Old Greek Version."[10]

As for the question of Samuel's Naziritism, nothing material has changed. The testimony from Qumran about 1 Sam 1:22 is new respecting text and composition; respecting narrative substance it is not. Concerning the latter we are today where we were a hundred years ago. No sufficient reason can be cited for the change of scholarly opinion, however moderate it is, to which Pisano has invited attention. One can only point to similar phenomena in other human affairs and muse: "The pendulum is now swinging in the opposite direction. It is probably futile to look for a rational cause for the present change. How large an amplitude will it reach before the next change?"

Appendix

Shortly after this article had gone to the editor, *ZAW* 100:3 (1988) arrived and brought to my attention (on p. 435) an article by A. Catastini: "4QSam^a: 1. Samuele il 'Nazireo,'" *Henoch* 9 (1987) 161–95. Catastini's thesis that Samuel was a Nazirite rests prominently on his interpretation of

---

8. The 1953 article by Cross is appropriately entitled: "A New Qumran Biblical Fragment Related to the Original Hebrew Underlying the Septuagint." Ulrich provided the substantiation for Cross's thesis in *Qumran Text of Samuel and Josephus* (conveniently surveyed in the table of contents, pp. v–vi). See also n. 9 below.

9. At first glance, it seems that the agreements of 4QSam^a and the LXX are largely canceled out by chap. 4: "The Disagreement of 4QSam^a with the Greek Version" (ibid., 119–49), but this is not the case. I am not concerned here with the matter in its full extent, but only those instances where 4QSam^a goes with R and against the LXX (see pp. 140–46). For an analysis of all possible combination of this disagreement, see Ulrich's conclusion to chap. 4 (pp. 146–49). The shortness of the listing in pp. 140–46 shows that the full length of chap. 2 (55 pages) should be reduced by no more than these 7 pages. Ulrich's conclusion (pp. 146–49) bears this out qualitatively.

10. Ibid., 92.

three passages: 1 Sam 1:23 (pp. 166–69), 1:24–25 (pp. 169–76), and 1:22 (pp. 176–86). The following comment deals with his treatment of vv. 24–25.

Catastini holds, and I agree, that 4QSam^a and the LXX form one tradition over against the tradition of R, and that in this tradition Samuel is a Nazirite. He then asserts that the 4QSam^a–LXX tradition represents a stage in the history of tradition that is older than that of R, as can be seen from the inclusion of bread in the sacrifice of vv. 24–25 (present in 4QSam^a–LXX, absent in R), since bread is an element of a Canaanite (festival) sacrifice. In order to show the Canaanite nature of sacrificial bread in combination with animal sacrifices he has recourse to the Ugaritic text *UT* 3:22 (=*CTA* 35=*KTU* 1:41), where—supposedly—bread is mentioned as part of a sacrifice of a periodic festival. This feature of an ancient (before 1200 B.C.) rite is an indicator of the comparatively old age of the version that mentions it. To be sure, Catastini allows that bread might have been mentioned in an ancestor of R and was later omitted by a scribal error, but he does not seem to believe in such a "mechanical cause." He says that R distances itself (*prende la distanza* and *allontanandosi*) from a manifestation of the Canaanite cult (p. 175). (He does not consider a third possibility besides scribal error and intended doctrinal change, viz., free variation of a text that has not solidified and assumed a final form.)[11] The argument is flawed regarding facts as well as method and reasoning.

The Ugaritic word in question, mostly read *ḥṯ*, may just as well be read *ḥ^c* (cf. *UT* §4:18 that it "is often hard to tell *ṯ* and ^{c} apart"). A. Herdner (*CTA*, p. 119) avers in effect that this is not true of *UT* 3 as the positions of the two signs in relation to their vertical and horizontal axes are different, but she qualifies this by adding (that this is so [only]) *parfois*. Looking at the good photograph in *CTA*, vol. 2, pl. xl, makes me think that this is not a case of *parfois*.

Assuming that the word is really *ḥṯ*, the meaning 'bread' goes back to J. C. de Moor, who, basing himself on Arabic *ḥuṯṯ*, translates it 'unseasoned bread'.[12] But this Arabic word is an adjective meaning "coarse, lumpy, dry, crumbly" and is said of sand, a meal of parched grain, bread, dates, and straw; in its nominalized form it may denote some of the things having the above-mentioned features, bread among them. But its utilization for the elucidation of Ugaritic *ḥṯ* is precarious. Had there been a Ugaritic root *ḥṯ*, otherwise established and meaning 'coarse', etc., then a noun proposed to denote the same or a similar food as Arabic *ḥuṯṯ* would have

---

11. See S. Talmon, "The Textual Study of the Bible—A New Outlook," in *Qumran and the History of the Biblical Text* (ed. F. M. Cross and S. Talmon; Cambridge, MA, 1975) 321–400.

12. J. C. de Moor, *New Year with Canaanites and Israelites* (Kampen, 1972), 2:15; after E. W. Lane, *An Arabic-English Lexicon* (London, 1865), 2:512b. R. Blanchère, *Dictionnaire arabe-français-anglais* (Paris, 1976), 3:2086a, disregarding classical lexicographers, does not list this specific meaning.

had a good chance of admittance to the Ugaritic dictionary. But since ḥṯ 'coarse' is not attested in Ugaritic or in any other North Semitic or East Semitic language, one would have to make two independent assumptions: (1) there was a Ugaritic root ḥṯ 'coarse', and (2) this root produced a word meaning 'unseasoned bread' in Ugaritic as it did in Arabic two thousand years later. The assumptions are independent because coarseness in and of itself has nothing specific to do with bread and vice versa, to say nothing of unseasoned bread. To make this assumed coincidence of circumstances the foundation of a dictionary entry means to open the Ugaritic dictionary to a host of suspect migrants showing passports stamped "Etymology."

The assumption that the Ugaritic word is ḥṯ and that it means unseasoned (or some other kind of) bread invites the challenging question, "Is bread an un-Israelite, unbiblical element of sacrifices?" The following incomplete list of sacrifices, each minimally comprising animals and bread, shows that this is not the case: Exod 29:1ff.; Lev 7:11ff., 8:1ff., 23:17ff.; 1 Sam 10:3(!). And should one nevertheless want to argue that "bread" in 1 Sam 1:24-25 according to 4QSam^a and the LXX indicates affinity of the sacrifice of those passages with that of *UT* 3, one should not overlook that both this text and *UT* 173, its duplicate (except for its last 8 lines), list materials that are not known as ingredients of Old Testament sacrifices, viz., perfumed oils and honey. With or without bread, the sacrifices of 1 Samuel 1 and *UT* 3 are for this reason moderately different.

Concerning Catastini's reasoning and method, it is unconvincing in the extreme that a redactor of 1 Samuel 1 R would eliminate bread offering from his text for doctrinary reasons when bread offerings were all around him in life as in literature and when he lets bread stand in 10:3. For all we know, the sacrifices of the Old Testament and those of Israel's neighbors are tolerably similar, yet prophets and psalms that inveigh against sacrifices do not argue that the nations around Israel also bring sacrifices, and similar ones to boot, and that therefore Israel should not bring them. And if we grant for argument's sake that bread was intentionally eliminated from (an ancestor of) R, and that thereby, in this detail, 4QSam^a and the LXX have preserved the original, does this fact make them representatives of the original text, or other early text forms, of other passages as well? Does the motive of anti-Canaanitism which brought about the elimination of bread also bring about the elimination of Naziritism? Not if we trust Amos 2:11-12.

The limited scope of these comments does not permit me to examine Catastini's interpretation of 1:22 and 1:23, which takes a similar approach. If such similarity is granted, it will not be necessary to also subject the interpretation of those two verses to a similar analysis. The thesis of my article is not likely to be affected by it.

Textual Criticism

THE REDACTION OF THE GREEK ALPHA-TEXT OF ESTHER

Michael V. Fox

Redaction criticism is inevitably a speculative enterprise. To use the final form of a text to reconstruct the process whereby the text reached its final form requires several postulations, each one increasing the uncertainty of the reconstruction. Uncertainty is reduced, though not, of course, eliminated, when we have some external witness to the process, such as a prior version of the text or at least a parallel version that developed from a common ancestor. A further layer of uncertainty is eliminated when we can work with exemplars in the same language.

The Greek books of Esther allow a case study in controlled redaction criticism, for we have two distinct versions of that story, the Alpha-Text (AT) and the Septuagint (LXX), both in Greek. The AT exists, in somewhat variant forms, in four Greek manuscripts: 19 (12th cent.), 93 (13th cent.), 108 (13th cent.), and 319 (11th cent.). The AT is found in R. Hanhart's Göttingen edition at the bottom of the page, and in A. E. Brooke, N. McLean, and H. St. J. Thackeray's Cambridge edition after the Septuagintal Esther.[1] The latter text, together with a new English translation, appears in D. J. A. Clines's recent book.[2]

---

1. The AT has its own chapter-verse numbering system, which is sometimes disordered by attempts to adjust it to the MT's system. In this essay I refer to MT and LXX chapters by Arabic numerals (e.g., 9:6) and to AT chapters by Roman numerals (e.g., viii:44). The proper chapter-verse numeration is used in A. E. Brooke, N. McLean, and H. St. J. Thackeray's edition (*The Old Testament in Greek, 3.1: Esther, Judith, Tobit* [Cambridge, 1940]); R. Hanhart's edition (*Esther* [Göttingen Septuagint 8.3; Göttingen, 1983]) uses the correct verse numbering, but applies the LXX chapter numbers, which are one behind the AT numeration until viii:33 (|| 8:14), since the AT counts Add A as chap. 1. In the AT, all the verses paralleling LXX chaps. 7, 8 (including Add E), 9, 10, and Add F are counted as a single chapter, designated chap. 7 in Hanhart's numeration, chap. viii in Brooke-McLean-Thackeray's edition.

2. D. J. A. Clines, *The Esther Scroll* (JSOTSup 30; Sheffield, 1984) 215-48.

1. The Nature of the AT

The AT is very close to the LXX in some passages, sharply different in others. In the latter, it presents a complete and coherent version of the Esther story distinct from both the LXX and the MT.

The special value of the AT for redaction criticism lies first of all in its initial independence from both the LXX and the MT, and then in its secondary dependence of parts of the LXX. The present study focuses on the second stage.

C. A. Moore showed that the AT is not, as once had been thought, a Lucianic recension of the LXX.[3] Moreover, he suggested, the AT is a translation of a Hebrew (or possibly Aramaic) text quite different from the MT. Clines, following leads from Moore, C. C. Torrey, and H. J. Cook, showed that the Septuagintal Additions and the current ending (in his view, viii:18–21 + 33–38; Add E intervenes between these two blocks) are secondary.[4]

In a forthcoming article in *Textus* I discuss the various attempts to account for the formation of the AT.[5] There I argue on behalf of Moore's and Clines's thesis but define the scope of the two layers somewhat differently:

1. The original AT (proto-AT) included most of AT ii:1–viii:17 (corresponding approximately to MT/LXX 1:1–8:5), but also viii:18–21 + 33–38. This layer comprises the material remaining after the removal of the identifiable Septuagintal material, and it coheres as a narrative unity. It offers an Esther story different from the LXX as well as from the MT, both in wording and in details of the story.

2. A later redactor (designated R-AT) transferred from the LXX the seven Additions (A–F), the ending corresponding approximately to LXX chap. 9 (viii:39–52; this I designate AT-end), several miscellaneous verses, and a block of material after Add D (vi:12–18). The dependency of these sections on the LXX is evident from a comparison of the two versions and is statistically verifiable (see §1.1 below).

---

3. C. A. Moore, *The Greek Text of Esther* (Ph.D. diss., Johns Hopkins University, 1965); idem, "A Greek Witness to a Different Text of Esther," *ZAW* 79 (1967) 351–58. Previous scholars had commonly thought the AT to be a Lucianic recension of the LXX. This notion arose because P. A. de Lagarde (*Librorum Veteris Testamenti Canonicorum Pars Prior Graece* [Göttingen, 1883]) classified three of the AT manuscripts as Lucianic in other books, which B. Jacob ("Das Buch Esther bei den LXX," *ZAW* 10 [1890] 241–98) understood to mean that the version of Esther in those manuscripts was likewise Lucianic; see Hanhart, *Esther*, 92–95.

4. Clines, *Esther Scroll*; C. C. Torrey, "The Older Book of Esther," *HTR* 37 (1944) 1–40; H. J. Cook, "The *A* Text of the Greek Versions of the Book of Esther," *ZAW* 81 (1969) 369–76.

5. M. V. Fox, "The Alpha-Text of the Greek Esther," *Textus* 15 (1991). This forms part of my book, *The Redaction of the Books of Esther* (forthcoming in the Society of Biblical Literature Monograph Series).

This essay compares the AT with the LXX in passages where direct dependency is most evident and statistically provable (the Additions and AT-end), investigating the changes the Septuagintal material received when it was transferred to and imbedded in the original AT.[6] I do not pursue the more usual course of comparing the AT with the LXX to see how both relate to the MT. The MT had no part in the redaction that transformed the proto-AT to the AT in its present form. Nor do I deal with the rest of the AT, which is usually, though in my view wrongly, considered a revision of the LXX.[7]

Studying R-AT's treatment of the LXX provides an "empirical" model for redaction criticism, along the lines of those offered in J. Tigay's anthology, *Empirical Models for Biblical Criticism*.[8] Like those, this study will reveal some of the editorial techniques used in the reworking of a sacred text and show how a redactor can import his own ideology into the new text through small changes, even after that text has achieved some degree of canonicity.

I will first summarize the types of changes R-AT made in the material he borrowed, then consider some of the ideological factors motivating these changes.

1.1. Transfer of LXX Wording

The LXX is the redactor's source, and for the most part he simply draws upon it to supplement the original AT. Of the 281 words in AT-end, 187 (66%) match words in the LXX. The average frequency of Septuagintal

---

6. See ibid. There are a few additional passages that also seem dependent on the LXX; see §1.1 below.

7. See my *Textus* article for a survey of scholarly views of the AT. O. F. Fritzsche, the first scholar to analyze the version, described it as "eine tiefeingreifende Umarbeitung" of the LXX; see *Zusätze zu dem Buche Esther* (Kurzgefasstes exegetisches Handbuch zu dem Apokryphen des Alten Testament 1; Leipzig, 1851) 71. B. Jacob ("Das Buch Esther bei den LXX," 258–62) considered the AT a Lucianic recension based on a very poor text which often led Lucian astray. E. Bickerman ("Notes on the Greek Book of Esther," *Proceedings of the American Academy of Jewish Research* 20 [1951] 101–33), who rejected the attribution of the AT to Lucian, still argued that it descended from the same translation as the LXX. E. Tov ("The 'Lucianic' Text of the Canonical and Apocryphal Sections of Esther: A Rewritten Biblical Book," *Textus* 10 [1982] 10) argued that the AT is a recension of the LXX that underwent revision toward a Hebrew or Aramaic version differing from the MT. J.-C. Haelewyck ("Le Texte dit 'Lucianique' du Livre d'Esther: Son étendue et sa cohérence," *Muséon* 98 [1985] 5–44) presented an intricate theory of intertwined development for the three Greek versions (LXX, AT, and G III—the latter being the *Vorlage* of the Old Latin). He considered the AT, for the most part, a revision of G III, but influenced by the MT, while Add A 11–18 is supposedly the first AT redactor's creation. A later AT redactor borrowed Adds B, C, and E from the LXX. Haelewyck's reconstruction proceeds entirely by a "critique littéraire" (p. 7), which means discovering which combinations of text are more "coherent," and thus, presumably, more original.

8. J. H. Tigay, *Empirical Models for Biblical Criticism* (Philadelphia, 1985).

matches in the redactional sections (Adds A–F and AT-end) is 75%, whereas only 35% of the words in the rest of the AT have Septuagintal matches.[9]

R-AT did not set out to borrow the deuterocanonical Additions from the LXX, for these did not exist apart from the body of the Septuagintal text prior to Jerome, and there is no reason to think the redactor would have recognized them as distinct from the rest of the LXX. Rather, the redactor's procedure, insofar as this can be reconstructed from the end product, was to move sequentially through the two texts, comparing them and transferring material from the LXX to fill gaps he perceived in the receptor text (the proto-AT). For the most part the gaps coincide with the Additions, but they were not all that was lacking in the proto-AT or all that was borrowed. After copying Add D, he continued and transferred 5:3-8 (AT vi:13-18) as well. A few other sentences too were probably transferred from the LXX to fill small lacks in the receptor text (i:1a, i:6-8, v:4b-5, iv:2, iv:9b-11-10a, v:9b, vi:21aβ, vii:1). At the end of the book, the redactor found no parallel to most of LXX 8:15-10:3 or to Add F, and so proceeded to copy most of that material from the LXX, making no distinction between the "canonical" ending (8:15-10:3) and the "deuterocanonical" Addition (F). By this process, R-AT created a new ending from Septuagintal material.

1.2. Substitution of Synonyms

Often the redactor replaces a work with a synonymous word or phrase. In some cases the substituted synonym seems more vivid or specific, for example, ἐπέπεσεν ἐπ' ('fell upon') for ἐνέκειτο ('pressed upon'; viii:42) and πότος κώθων ('drinking and banqueting') for εὐφροσύνη ('merrymaking, festivities'; viii:40). But usually the substitution has little perceptible effect on the meaning, for example, ἐσθῆτα for LXX στολὴν (viii:39) and πένησιν for πτωχοῖς (viii:48; taken from later on, the end of 9:22, which is otherwise lacking in the AT).

One type of synonym substitution is the use of prefix variants in compound verbs: περιπόρφυρον ('purple') for πορφυροῦν ('edged in purple'; viii:39 || 8:15), ἐπανέστη for ἀντέστη (viii:41 || 9:2), ἀπέστειλε for ἐξαποστέλλοντας (viii:48 || 9:22). A detailed examination might reveal the reasons

---

9. By "match" I refer to cases where the words are identical in the two versions, but I also include different grammatical forms of the same lexeme, prefix variants of the same stem, and words of different parts of speech from the same stem. These classes of words were included in the definition of "matches" because they are manifestly in the range of variations the redactor allowed himself in the AT passages indisputably dependent on the LXX. Matches need not appear in the same position in the sentence in each version, but they must fill the same syntactical slot. The radically lower concentrations of Septuagintal matches in the proto-AT sections point to an indirect relationship, namely that both the LXX and the proto-AT derive from the same story, with the MT intermediate between that story and the LXX.

for some of these substitutions, but for the most part the prefix changes seem to have little lexical significance.

Substitution of synonyms is a common phenomenon in manuscript transmission (in Egypt as well as in ancient Israel), but the substitutions in this case are far too frequent to be incidental fluctuations occurring in the course of copying. Still, the phenomenon belongs to the intersection of copying and redaction. It is difficult to say what lies behind this freedom the redactor allows himself, especially when the changes do not clarify or update the text. The redactor is probably deliberately asserting his creative role by making these changes.

1.3. Substitution of Non-synonyms

The replacement of a word by an element (a word or short phrase) that differs in meaning but fills the same slot in the new sentence as in the donor text is what I call substitution of non-synonyms. Synonyms and non-synonyms are not discrete categories—other scholars might distribute some of the items differently—but in principle I consider substitutions as synonymous when they have no noticeable effect on the content.

Some substitutions of non-synonyms are interpretive, as when the redactor substitutes ἐχθρῶν 'enemies' for ἐθνῶν 'nations' (iv:22 || C 21). The redactor is less hostile toward Gentiles in general and prefers to be more specific in defining the Jews' enemies. Mordecai says that he will not bow to anyone but God in πειρασμῷ (v:15) for LXX's ὑπερηφανίᾳ (C 7): it seems no special virtue not to bow "in arrogance"; more heroic is it not to bow even "under trial."

While most prefix variants are synonymous, one case that does produce a shift in meaning is ἡγεῖτο αὐτῶν 'he led them' (viii:52) for διηγεῖτο τὴν ἀγωγὴν 'he led his life' (10:3). This change emphasizes Mordecai's leadership of the Jews.

Variation of numbers is a type of non-synonymous substitution, as when the AT increases the body counts (700 for 500 in viii:44a, and 70,100 for 15,000 in viii:46b).

An interesting example of non-synonymous substitution is in viii:41a, where the redactor has Jews instead of Gentiles: "And many of the Jews circumcised themselves." (I will look at the ideological implications of this change later.)

1.4. Transpositions

Often the redactor changes the order of the words or phrases, usually with no discernible effect on the meaning. The transpositions in AT-end are all minor, for example: τοῖς μακρὰν καὶ τοῖς ἐγγύς for τοῖς ἐγγὺς καὶ τοῖς μακράν (viii:47a). Transpositions are more extensive elsewhere and include both limited metatheses of two words and phrases and long-range displacements of phrases and sentences.

1.5. Additions

The redactor made numerous additions in the material he copied from the LXX. Most are of minor scope, though they sometimes gain greater significance in conjunction with other changes. Some additions are for emphasis and vividness, some for exegetical clarification, some for harmonization, others to add a new concept or nuance. For example, the AT adds "and Mordecai praised [the king]" (viii:51) and also adds "he surrounded [all his people] with honor" (viii:52) in the closing encomium on Mordecai, thereby emphasizing how the successful Jew enhanced the glory of both his king and his people. "Adar" is prefixed to "Nisan" in the date of Mordecai's dream. The redactor is probably influenced by the importance of Adar in the Purim story. To explain how Esther put on τὴν δόξαν αὐτῆς (D 1)—a phrase open to misunderstanding—the redactor adds τὰ ἱμάτια: "She put on the garments of her glory" (vi:1).

1.6. Omissions

Omissions range in scope from scattered words, mostly inconsequential, to the major blocks excised in AT-end. Examples of shorter omissions of repetitions are "and manly virtue" (10:2); "what more would you ask— you shall have it" (9:12; the king's standard promise, but somewhat awkward here); "having a golden chaplet [στέφανον]" (8:15; the LXX already has διάδημα among the appurtenances of Mordecai's glory).

The major omissions occur in the latter part of AT-end, corresponding to MT/LXX 9:14–32. Thirteen whole verses and two half-verses of the seventeen in the LXX are missing (MT's 9:30–31a is not represented in the LXX; while MT 9:32 = LXX 9:31). For the most part the omissions are of repetitions. This section tells of the series of letters sent to confirm the holiday, the people's own confirmation of the holiday and its acceptance by future generations, the distinction between Susan Purim and provincial Purim, and the historical rationale for the holiday.

The repetitiveness of this passage in the MT has been pointed out by many commentators who, however, assume that repetition is a sign of redaction and excise some of the repetitions on those grounds. In this case, however, redaction has *removed* repetition, not produced it. Redundancy in such matters made sense at a stage when the legitimacy of the holiday had still to be argued and when the dates of celebration were likewise a matter of uncertainty. But the status and observance of the holiday do not seem to have been an issue for R-AT (who was at work no earlier than the latter part of the first century C.E.).[10] The redactor is satisfied with condens-

---

10. The dating of the redaction is very uncertain. A *terminus a quo* is indicated by the identification of Adar-Nisan with Dystros-Xandikos (i:1). A retardation in the Macedonian series in the Macedonian-Babylonian month correlations was introduced sometime between 15/16 C.E. and 46/47 C.E. Prior to 15/16 C.E., Adar-Nisan corresponded to Xandikos-Artemisios (see A. E. Samuel, *Greek and Roman Chronology* [Munich, 1972] 142–43).

ing these matters into a few sentences. Also, we can imagine the redactor, as he nears the end of his task, deciding to make do with reporting the gist of material of dubious relevance to his own concerns. Redundant material is excised in viii:40b (9:17a), 44b (9:11), 46 (9:14-19), 48 (9:22a, 23b, 24-25, 26b-32).

An interesting case of restructuring by omission is viii:48b. LXX 9:23 begins καὶ προσεδέξαντο οἱ Ἰουδαῖοι, 'And the Jews accepted [what Mordecai had written]'. By omitting everything after προσεδέξαντο, the redactor makes this word part of the preceding sentence, so that its subject is the poor who προσεδέξαντο 'accepted' Mordecai's gifts. The redactor does not believe that the people had to confirm this holiday, so he puts the word to another use.

Sometimes excisions are entailed by other changes, for example, in viii:41a, after turning the self-circumcision of Gentiles into Jewish repentance, the redactor must omit "because of fear of the Jews." LXX 9:1, reporting the arrival of 13 Adar, is omitted because the redactor has a different understanding of the slaughter of the Jews' enemies (it is not a battle, but a punishment of the foe by royal decree). The omission of 9:26b, the derivation of the holiday's name from Haman's lots, is part of a change in the etymology of the holiday's name (see §2.2.3).

It is clear that the gaps in AT-end (and for that matter the gaps elsewhere in the AT) are no evidence whatsoever for minuses in the original Hebrew, because the redactor is working off of the LXX at every step, with no traceable Hebrew influence, and its omissions are self-consistent.

1.7. Condensation

Sometimes the redactor does not merely omit blocks of words from the LXX, but condenses them. Condensation may take the form of summarization, as in viii:46a, where the seventeen words of 9:14, which state that Esther's request was carried out, are summarized by καὶ συνεχώρησεν 'and he agreed'.

A clever condensation device, one characteristic of this redactor, is the "cut-and-splice" technique, which omits material in such a way as to create new sentences out of the words remaining on either side of the omission, often producing a significantly different sense. Cutting-and-splicing condenses material while giving some representation to omitted sentences, and it can also produce a new idea while deriving its wording from its "source."

A significant use of this technique is at 9:26-27, where the LXX reads, "For this reason these days are called Phrourai, because of the lots," and goes on to explain the etymology of "Phrourai," the historical background of the holiday, and the people's confirmation of it. The AT follows the LXX through the word "lots," then jumps over forty-nine words, takes up the next five, then skips the rest of 9:27 (as well as the next four verses), producing this sentence: "Therefore these days are called Phouraia because of the lots which fell upon these days for a memorial." Only the words "which fell upon" (two words in the Greek) are not borrowed (see § 2.1.1).

One of Shemaryahu Talmon's notable contributions to the basic concepts of Bible study was to show that many of the types of variants arising in textual transmission are continuations of literary techniques used in the formative stages of literary creativity.[11] These are (1) stylistic and textual interchangeability of words, (2) stylistic and textual conflation, and (3) stylistic metathesis and textual inversion. In the redaction under study, there may be conflations of the LXX and the proto-AT in miscellaneous verses, though in the absence of an independent witness to the proto-AT it is impossible to verify this. Types 1 and 3, however, are clearly in evidence. The redactor of this text exemplifies the continuum Talmon described: he is both an author, creating a new form of the Esther story, and a copyist, transferring blocks of material from the LXX to the receptor text. He practices techniques common to authors and copyists, though of necessity less freely than the former and more freely than the latter.

2. The Redactor's Ideas and Attitudes

While most of the changes the redactor introduces in the borrowed Septuagintal material are not substantive, many of them suggest new ideas and an individual ideology. They reveal a redactor reinterpreting the sources and rethinking the meaning of the holiday. In the confines of this paper I will speak of the redactor's interpretation and ideology only insofar as it emerges from AT-end, but this is consistent with the profile one gets from a study of all the redactional units.

2.1. Interpretive Changes

Some changes are interpretive, in the sense that they present an understanding of the Esther story and of the Purim holiday that differs from the Septuagint's.

2.1.1. The etymology of Purim (viii:49) at AT-end differs from the Septuagint's interpretation, though the LXX wording is maintained as much as possible. The AT connects the name Φουραία to lots "that fell upon these days as a memorial" (viii:49), instead of to Haman's lots. This second set of lots, for which the holiday is named, were not mentioned previously. However, in Add E (viii:30) the redactor does have the king say that the Jews have decided to celebrate the 14th and 15th of Adar, and one can understand the lot-casting mentioned in viii:49 with that decision.

---

11. S. Talmon, "The Textual Study of the Bible—A New Outlook," in *Qumran and the History of the Biblical Text* (ed. F. M. Cross and S. Talmon; Cambridge, MA, 1975) 321–400.

2.1.2. The AT construes the names of the slaughtered enemies in viii:44b as belonging to men other than Haman's sons, whereas in the LXX they are his sons. This difference may originate in copyist errors,[12] but it is carried into deliberate reinterpretation. Some manuscripts of the LXX had added a name to the list (by false division of Φαρσανvεσταιν). If this was the case in the redactor's manuscript, he did not have ten names before him. Uncertain about the relation between "ten" and the names, he simply added καὶ and left Haman's sons unnamed. Such an interpretation would have been reinforced by the proto-AT, according to which Esther is allowed both to put Haman's sons to death with their father (viii:19) and to slaughter other enemies (viii:20–21).

2.1.3. The praise of Mordecai in 10:2 is reinterpreted by means of a change in syntax. In the LXX, the king's glory "is written" (γέγραπται) in the chronicles. The AT (viii:51) adds "and Mordecai praised," then changes the voice to active, making Mordecai the subject of "wrote [ἔγραψεν] [sc. the praise recorded in the chronicles]." (The syntax of the verse is subsequently restructured.) The new version emphasizes Mordecai's value to his king.

2.1.4. Although the redactor preserves a two-day celebration for the holiday (viii:47b), he omits the distinction between two days of fighting, as well as the one between Susan Purim and provincial Purim, both of which are of great interest in the MT and taken over by the LXX. In the AT, Esther neither requests a second day of battle nor mentions Susa, but simply asks that the Jews be allowed to proceed with the slaughter (viii:45). Having interpreted Esther's request in 9:13 as a desire for more vengeance, the redactor accomplishes the same effect simply by raising the body count from 15,000 to 70,100.

2.2. Imposition of the Redactor's Ideology

Most of the modifications made in the LXX material transferred to the AT have no noticeable ideological significance. But some redactional changes do work together to convey a modified ideology. Overall there is a tendency to emphasize the positive, giving the celebration and the events behind it an affirmative significance where possible. The redactor does this mainly by reducing Gentile initiative and dissociating Purim from Haman and his would-be pogrom.

---

12. Thus Tov, "'Lucianic' Text of ... Esther." Apparently the name Δελφων was misunderstood as ἀδελφων, then τὸν ... αὐτοῦ was added, producing the AT's καὶ τὸν ἀδελφόν αὐτοῦ. Τὸν ἀδελφὸν is present in some Hexaplaric LXX manuscripts as well.

2.2.1. Circumcision. According to the LXX, many Gentiles circumcised themselves out of fear of the Jews (9:17). The redactor substitutes Jews for Gentiles and eliminates mention of the fear of the Jews (viii:41a). The notion of Jews circumcising themselves may at first seem absurd,[13] but it in fact speaks to a time when Hellenizing Jews avoided circumcision. Using the cut-and-splice technique (omitting LXX 9:1) and a clever word substitution, R-AT reinterprets the effect of the Gentiles' fear of the Jews. In the LXX (9:2) this fear is the reason no one was able to resist (ἀντέστη) Jewish martial power. In the AT (viii:41b), in which 9:2 is joined to the modified viii:41a, this fear becomes the reason that the Gentiles did not oppose or rise up against (ἐπανέστη) the Jews in the matter of Jewish circumcision—nothing else is mentioned in the preceding context to which opposition would be relevant. In this way the redactor substitutes an occasion of Jewish repentance for a fear-inspired conversion of Gentiles, teaching at the same time that the Gentiles did not dare oppose Jewish circumcision.

2.2.2. Jews and Gentiles. The Gentiles are viewed with less hostility by the revised AT than by the proto-AT or the LXX. In the AT, Israel's enemies are more clearly circumscribed. There are malevolent nations in the AT (cf. viii:54b), but these are certain nations, not all of them.

This attitude is in evidence in the changes made in Add A, where the AT, in contrast to the LXX, does not envision all the nations gathering to attack the "nation of the righteous" (i:6; contrast LXX A 6). The Gentiles are themselves endangered by the forces of evil (i:5). There is no simple dichotomy between "every nation" and the "righteous nation, Israel." In the AT's version of Add E, the Gentile king is pictured favorably, even more so than in the LXX. R-AT and the redactor make the king unambiguously a monotheist who calls Israel's God the "sole and true God [τοῦ μόνου θεοῦ καὶ ἀληθινοῦ]" (viii:27).[14]

In line with his reduced hostility toward the Gentiles, the redactor looks forward not to the judgment (LXX κρίσις; F 8) of the Gentiles, but to God's rule (κυριεύσις) over them (viii:56).

2.2.3. The events of Adar. The redactor has a different idea of what happened after Haman's undoing and what ensued in Adar. The AT, in both the original and the redactional sections, is much vaguer than the LXX about the dates of events, not even noting when Haman's plotting took place and when it was undone. R-AT carries over from the proto-AT

---

13. Clines, *Esther Scroll*, 81. On p. 189, Clines apparently grants that this might refer to Hellenizing Jews avoiding circumcision.

14. LXX (E 16) has "the highest and greatest living God [τοῦ ὑψίστου μεγίστου ζῶντος θεοῦ]."

the 13th of Adar as the date projected for the pogrom by Haman's lots (iv:7), but gives no further dates, except to specify 14-15 Adar as the days chosen for celebration (viii:30, 47).

Without going into the chronology implied in the AT as a whole, I note that the lack of specific dating produces a sequence of events without major gaps. The redacted version does not set any fighting on 13-14 Adar. The Jews do slaughter a great many enemies, but this is conceived as punishment by royal license, not as a defensive battle, and the first wave ensues immediately upon Haman's downfall (viii:20-21). There is never an attempt to carry out Haman's plot. Since the AT lacks the motif of irreversible Persian law, the crisis ends with the death of Haman and his allies. The result of this major restructuring, reinforced by changes in Add E,[15] is to distance the holiday from Haman's plot. The holiday is not to be sullied by contiguity with slaughter, nor does it commemorate battles or even the respite from them, nor is its date determined by Haman's lots. To the same end, the redactor, as stated earlier, creates a new set of lots for determining the date of the holiday, rather than contaminating the day's name by association with Haman's murderous, idolatrous lots.

These changes are clearly intentional departures from the LXX. The 14th and 15th of Adar become solely days of happiness and success, a celebration undertaken and defined by the Jews and their God alone.

2.2.4. The confirmation of Purim. The MT (9:20-32) deals at length with the process whereby Purim became a holiday. The institution was a new one, and its authority depended on the validity of the process of institutionalization. The LXX takes over most of this material except for MT 9:30-31aα. R-AT omits almost all of it, an omission, it is reasonable to surmise, motivated first by a loss of interest, since the validity of the holiday was no longer a live issue, and second by a belief that the dates of the festival were divinely ordained (viii:30, 49) and so did not require popular validation. The proto-AT's version of Mordecai's epistle, which the redactor maintains, has Mordecai issuing a command to the Jews to celebrate their deliverance rather than a call for confirmation of the holiday as a permanent institution.

2.3. *The Author's Attitude toward His Texts*

The redactor uses the proto-AT as his basis, working the LXX into it and rarely altering its wording. He is creating a recension of the AT—a supplemented AT not a supplemented LXX. The AT is authoritative and is to be transmitted. It is not enough simply to replicate the LXX.

---

15. Particularly by the replacement of the LXX's reference to the Jews' preparations for self-defense on 13 Adar by a statement that "it has been decided by the Jews throughout the kingdom to celebrate" the 14th and 15th of Adar (viii:30).

On the other hand, the redactor does not regard the proto-AT as sufficient either. It tells the truth but not the whole truth. The redactor looks to the LXX to fill in the gaps in the proto-AT and transfers the missing material with few additions. Hence for the redactor, the LXX too is authoritative, and a book of Esther that fails to report the essential events and discourses as the LXX recounts them is, for this redactor, inadequate. The AT is the result of the interplay between two authoritative versions that have not, however, attained a degree of fixity that precludes adjustments in either.

The redactor has the freedom to add, subtract, substitute, and transpose. But even when making substantive changes, he seeks to maintain the wording of the LXX, insofar as this is utilized. But often it is not utilized. The redactor omits material from the Septuagintal transfers far more often than he adds to them. The relative scarcity of additions within the transferred text suggests a redactor who hesitates to "create" material, to add his own words to an authoritative text, but seeks rather to draw upon an authoritative source.

The way R-AT extracts material from a text he treats as authoritative shows that he sees himself neither as a transmitter of the Septuagintal Esther nor as the creator of a new book of Esther. Rather he seeks to create a recension of the AT without displacing the LXX. Both tell the story of Esther, and the AT only needed some supplementation to do so adequately—with the LXX as the standard of adequacy. The redactor could "omit" material at will because doing so meant simply not using everything available, and one may always extract material from a sacred text or quote part of it. In other words, R-AT treats the LXX as a source, available to be mined as necessary. The AT is to be *haggadah*, reinterpretation by retelling.

3. Recovering Redaction

Knowing as we do just what R-AT did to his base text, in the redactional sections at least,[16] we may ask to what extent this activity would be recoverable if we had only the end product, as is the case when examining the redaction of most of the Hebrew Bible. Could source criticism work on the AT?

Add A could easily be recognized as secondary, for it makes Mordecai appear too soon and reach prominence too soon. In the proto-AT, as in the LXX and the MT, Mordecai is introduced when a substitute for Vashti

---

16. The possibility that R-AT excised short passages from the proto-AT cannot be excluded, though it is unlikely, since the main thrust of the redaction is to supplement the proto-AT, not to correct it. There were almost certainly no major excisions, since the narrative of the proto-AT proceeds without noticeable lacunas.

is sought (iii:5 || 2:5).¹⁷ Moreover, the dream slackens the tension of the story and turns the characters into symbols of cosmic processes—thereby dulling the story's vivid and naturalistic character portrayal. Furthermore, the dream does not completely fit the events it predicts (nor does it do so in the LXX). And if Add A is secondary, Add F is as well.

Adds B and E might not be recognized as secondary. Their peculiar style could be justified as an attempt to imitate the air of a royal edict (as indeed it is). Still, Add E in the AT has little integral connection with the narrative (even less than in the LXX), and the wisdom and monotheistic piety ascribed to the king seem out of character. Also, the king's permission to ignore the first decree comes too late in the AT (viii:20), and his declaration that the Jews have decided to celebrate 14–15 Adar (viii:30) is premature and unrelated to the preceding narrative in the AT.

Add C is not manifestly secondary. Its portrayal of Esther and Mordecai is not sharply incongruous with their portrayal in the proto-AT. This addition is, however, much more concerned with prayer and supplication than most of the AT (especially once Adds A and F are removed), and so might be suspected of being a pious addition for that reason. Furthermore, Esther's interest in the temple (v:22b) and *kašrut* (v:27) have no echo in the rest of the narrative.

Add D is not obviously secondary. To be sure, Esther is far frailer and more obsequious in Add D than elsewhere. But those differences could be explained by the circumstances described in this context, namely her perilous first approach to the king.

AT-end *was* recognized as secondary. Torrey and Clines argued the case on literary grounds.¹⁸ To be sure, they had the MT and the LXX available for comparison, but that did not suffice to seal the argument for the secondary character of AT-end, since it diverges significantly from the MT, while parts of the proto-AT approach the MT closely. Thus the argument had to proceed on literary considerations internal to the AT. Clines's basic argument is that the "literary logic" of the AT falls apart after viii:16. The subsequent narrative is not coordinated with the preceding and evinces a lower level of literary quality. While I do not consider all of Clines's arguments valid, and while I define the scope of AT-end differently, I must grant that as a whole his literary criteria do succeed in isolating AT-end from the proto-AT.

On the other hand, some redactional changes in the receptor text could never, as far as I can tell, be identified without the existence of the

---

17. The AT shows a high degree of correspondence to the LXX in iii:5 (fourteen of nineteen AT words) and might be influenced by it—though the correspondence of name and genealogy need not require direct influence. In any case, it is clear from iii:7 that Mordecai was introduced at this point in the proto-AT as well.

18. Torrey, "Older Book of Esther," 14–15; Clines, *Esther Scroll*, 78–84.

donor text. We could not detect the isolated Septuagintal transfers scattered throughout the AT—and in fact there may be other small redactional transfers that I have not identified. These, however, have little effect on the overall message. More significantly, we could not recognize any of the changes the redactor made *within* the Septuagintal material in the course of transfer. The small transfers are not too important, but the internal changes often have considerable bearing upon the redactor's ideology. The final product would convey the redactor's ideology, but we could estimate only vaguely to what degree this ideology was particularly the redactor's contribution.

Having identified the Additions and AT-end as supplements, we could try to reconstruct the character of the source from which they derived. We might conclude that this source was more religious, setting far more importance on divine control of history, on the hero's spiritual stance, and on the historiosophic import of events. These conclusions would be correct, though in this case we would be misled into thinking that these characteristics were present throughout the donor text, whereas in fact it was the differences between these blocks and the rest of the donor text that made them candidates for transfer.

I conclude that most, though not all, of the redactional blocks in the AT could be identified by criteria traditionally used in literary-historical criticism. This can be done even without reliance on analysis of diction (which, as far as I can tell, would be of little help here, especially given the diverse origins of the redactional sections). Thus redaction criticism could produce correct results, but the arguments for the identification would not be equally decisive for all units. And we could not recognize the smaller transfers or the changes internal to the supplementary blocks. The primary gain from the exercise would be the largely accurate reconstruction of the receptor text at a stage prior to supplementation.

EDITIONS OF THE HEBREW BIBLE—PAST AND FUTURE

Moshe Goshen-Gottstein

Early Editions and the Biblia Rabbinica

Almost five centuries have passed since the master printer Daniel Bomberg published his complete edition of the Hebrew Scriptures, mainly intended for non-Jewish humanists. The very fact that, after editions by Jewish printers were on the market since 1488, a non-Jewish printer dared to invest a large sum of money in what must have seemed a doubtful enterprise may not look like a frightening business venture to modern scholars, but in the beginning of the sixteenth century it did present immense problems—editorial, financial, and especially typographical.

The center for printing editions of classic texts was in those days mainly the city of Venice, where Aldus Manutius had set up his famous press, and a few years later Basle, where printers such as Amorbach or Froben published the works of humanists such as Erasmus, who had come all the way from the Netherlands where the new art of printing was not as yet so advanced. Only men who had a personal interest as humanists, as well as the necessary funds, could expect a readership for the printing of the entire masoretic Bible only a few years after Johannes Reuchlin had published the first grammar of Hebrew (1506) in Pforzheim in the state of Swabia and had thus laid the foundations for Christian Hebraic studies.

Printing a masoretic Bible presented problems which Johann Gutenberg of Mainz never had to face when, a few decades before, he printed the first Bible in a European language in movable type. However, Gutenberg had to deal with letters only, that is, typesetting in one line. But the typesetting of letters is only one aspect of what is needed for a Hebrew Bible. For this, two additional sets of fonts had to enter the picture: vowel and accent markers beneath the base line, as well as on top of the letters. For the moment, we need not deal with the issue of the function of dots and strokes of the accent markers, whether indicating interpunctuation, stress, or musical cantillation. Suffice it to say that letters, vowels, and accents—all three together compose the image of the masoretic text, written or printed.

What concerns us at present is only that the text had to give clear instruction for the liturgical recitation and hence accent (or cantillation) markers were essential. In short, for centuries scribes had toiled to accommodate vowels and accents on top and underneath the letters. Around 1500 master printers had to invent a way of achieving that aim in print. The techniques for such an enterprise had never confronted the heirs of Gutenberg's invention and Hebrew non-masoretic texts did not raise that kind of problem, since such markers were not used as a rule.

The success of the Soncinos—the first printers of Hebrew Bibles—and Bomberg can only be appreciated if one realizes that the greatest printer of those days, Aldus Manutius, failed in his efforts to print a Hebrew Bible and gave the attempt up before he even started printing one page. This puts the achievement of the Soncinos and Bomberg in an even brighter light.

At this point I should also add that some other Jewish printers tried their hand at printing a Hebrew biblical text, generally of the Pentateuch only. As far as we know, the first printing of the entire Hebrew Bible was carried out in 1488, soon after the first Hebrew font had been cut. In any case, since 1494 Jewish printers could habitually publish parts of the Hebrew Bible with all necessary paraphernalia, such as vowels and accent markers, as well as markers of closed and open sections indicated by the Hebrew letters ס and פ.

In retrospect, one wonders in how many places in Italy Jewish printers did set up shop, for example, Soncino, Naples, Bologna, and Pesaro, but also outside Italy, for example, Spain, Portugal, or Constantinople. At present, we are only speaking of so-called incunabula, all printed south of the Alps. Only after 1500 did non-Jewish printers enter the field, so there was no competition for customers between Jewish and non-Jewish printers.

It is generally agreed that the printers who carried out the first printing of the entire Hebrew Bible were of the family of Soncino, who had moved to Italy from Germany and probably printed their Bibles according to Ashkenazi manuscripts in their possession. Since we only know of the master printers, we cannot make any statement whether and how non-Jews fitted into that framework. In any case, Jewish printers employed non-Jewish help, both for type cutting and illustration, as we can learn from a case of a specialist who had learned his art at the press of Aldus and later on worked for Soncino. But as far as we know, Jewish presses never used human figures for illustrations.

The reason why those printings were made by Jews and for Jews only seems to be quite obvious. Although a few scholars of the Florentine academy had already gained in the late fifteenth century some knowledge of Hebrew, only after 1500 was the ideal of the *homo trilinguis* conceived and a market for non-Jewish buyers thus became a reality.

It is against this background that one should view the enterprise of Bomberg, the first non-Jewish printer of a masoretic Bible, who skillfully applied the recently awakened interest in Hebrew of Christian humanists and for the first time arranged printing a Hebrew Bible for the use of non-Jews. However, we have no information how Jewish customers reacted to the first printing by a non-Jew for non-Jews, and whether Jewish laymen ever used it.

As a practicing Catholic, Bomberg needed a non-Jew to arrange that edition. The man responsible for the first effort seemed ideally suited. Felix Pratensis (1517) was a scion of a family of rabbis who had converted about 1506, joined the Augustine order, and then added the knowledge of classical languages to his Hebraic heritage. Thus Felix fitted the ideal picture of a *homo trilinguis* and through this edition opened up a new market for Hebrew Bibles.

Actually, Felix was not the only convert at that time who made use of his Jewish background for printing a Hebrew Bible text. About the same time, the Archbishop of Toledo, Cardinal Ximenes de Cisneros, began his preparation for publishing the Hebrew text of the Bible as part of his Bible polyglot (the *complutensis*, 1514–1517) in Alcala. The dedication of that enormous work to the pope was meant to make his aim clear beyond doubt. The very idea of printing the Hebrew, side by side with the Greek and Latin Bible, teaches us that the humanist ideal of the "three languages" formed the background for that enterprise. However, Ximenes could not find at that time any native Christian to edit the Hebrew part of the polyglot and therefore had to rely on one of the recent Jewish converts (neophytes) to do that job. Thus, Alfonso de Zamora, who served as teacher of Oriental languages at the University of Alcala (Complutium) had to join forces with Pablo Coronel of the University of Salamanca to carry out the special task of editing the Hebrew text for the polyglot.

However, with regard to the Hebrew text, the Spanish edition strikes us as odd: they printed the square letters only, not the full masoretic text. The reason was not that the fully vocalized text could raise questions regarding the correctness of the Latin Vulgate, but whereas the Italian printers had already overcome the typographic problem of setting vowels and accents in type, the Spaniards lagged behind. Since both the Bomberg and Alcala printings were published at the same time, that technical difference in craftsmanship is striking.

Let us now return to the work of Felix Pratensis. As far as we know, Felix was the first humanist in Italy who was able to realize the deficiencies of Jerome's Latin rendering. In any event, he was the first scholar who felt impelled to offer an alternative Latin version of Psalms, and even got the approval of the pope.

The relationship between Felix the editor and Bomberg the financing patron apparently was somewhat complex. Bomberg had fallen under the spell of the humanist ideal and was more than willing to arrange for the printing of a Hebrew Bible. Felix was only too happy to teach Bomberg some Hebrew and to undertake the edition himself. Although Felix must have had a reasonable Hebraic background, by the time he undertook the task he was a member of a church order and was already far removed from whatever masoretic competence he might have possessed. For Bomberg, this was essentially a first attempt at printing Hebrew, just as for Felix.

We have no way to judge why the text of the first Rabbinic Bible came out so poorly. To be sure, true to the spirit of those days, Felix praised the munificence of his patron for having acquired for his edition many good Hebrew manuscripts. He was aware that he could not rely on one single manuscript and was forced to make up his own eclectic text as best he could. Since we can only venture an educated guess regarding the nature and quality of the manuscripts on which Felix based his edition, his description of his toil in preparing a text from those manuscripts must be taken *cum grano salis*. In all probability, they represented a mixture of Sephardi and Ashkenazi manuscripts which were abundant in Jewish communities in Italy, especially because of the influx of refugees from Spain and Germany.

In any event, while the *Biblia Rabbinica* edited by Felix Pratensis was a considerable achievement for its time, its Bible text turned out to be far from satisfactory with regard to the *plene* and defective spellings. Even more so, the vowel markers as far as used were often put in the wrong place. Since Bomberg had entered the printing business, it must have been with a heavy heart that he soon afterward stopped the distribution of his major achievement. An added reason was that while in the beginning Felix was the teacher and *spiritus rector*, in the early 1520s a much more qualified person came to Venice. This was Jacob ben Ḥayim ben Adoniya, who came from Tunis, and when he started working for Bomberg he still was a practicing Jew who possessed both masoretic and kabbalistic competence. But he also converted in the end as one can learn from the bitter remarks of another colleague of his, who also published his books at Bomberg's press, that is, Elias Levita, who was the most important grammarian of his time.

Jacob ben Ḥayim edited for Bomberg a much improved text—the so-termed second Rabbinic Bible, according to similar eclectic principles as did Felix Pratensis. We have no idea whether Bomberg acquired additional and better manuscripts for him or whether the difference in the quality of the text resulted only from ben Ḥayim's superior judgment of the masoretic facts. With a view to the fact that this is the first eclectic text arranged in the early sixteenth century, it seems amazing that, until the twentieth century, this early humanistic edition served as the basis for all later texts. To be sure, some later masoretic scholars discovered minor discrepancies between the text of the second Bomberg Bible and certain evidence in masoretic manuscripts. Those corrections were made first by R. Menahem de Lonzano, some decades after ben Ḥayim's edition and put in the form of a masoretic critical commentary by R. Solomon Yedidya Norzi in the early seventeenth century.

A further point should be clarified before we go on. The subject of this essay is Bible editions. All the large Bomberg editions were termed *Biblia Rabbinica* (in Hebrew: *miqraot gedolot*). The reason for this name is that, while the Bible text is the centerpiece, around the margin several rabbinic commentaries—such as Rashi, Ibn Ezra, and Redak—on the relevant verses of the text are printed similar to the fashion of Christian Bibles which may include not only medieval commentaries, but also some excerpts from the Church Fathers. The question how these rabbinic commentaries were printed and on which basis is not my concern at this moment. The point is that the base-text around which they were printed was reprinted over and over again, notwithstanding the minor corrections that were made in later reprints.

Since we cannot refer to the text of two millenia ago as *masoretic* without committing an anachronistic blunder, we can speak of that early stage only as pre-masoretic, foreshadowing what became the actual facts about one thousand years later. Whereas for purposes of textual criticism proper our main interests are the facts of pre-masoretic evidence, for purposes of dealing with editions of the Hebrew Bible our sole interest is the masoretic text as transmitted for the past thousand years. To be even more exact, we ought to speak of the Tiberian masoretic text (TMT) in order to differentiate clearly between Tiberian and other non-Tiberian forms.

I have already remarked that the special character of printed Bibles is that they contain, since the time around 1500, notations of vowel and accent signs on top or underneath the letters. But for the slight differences regarding the usage of *matres lectionis*, the major differences in masoretic times centered on the minute variations between vowel, accent, and *meteg* markers. Another point was the way of marking sections as open or closed—an issue of considerable halakhic consequence—and keeping count of *plene* and defective spellings. But generally speaking, for the past two millenia, all Hebrew texts were identical.

We can now begin to tackle the issue of Bible editions, which is the main topic of my essay. Given the fact that all printed editions of the Hebrew Bible stem from the same source, what point is there in repeatedly trying to publish "better" or more reliable editions? Why do editions compete with each other claiming on their title pages that this or that edition conforms exactly to the masoretic norm or best represents the *textus receptus*? Are all such claims simple eyewash or ever-improved "public-relations" boasting? In light of what we have already seen, the only justification for such a claim must be the nature of the masoretic foundations on which a certain edition is built.

I have noted above that all present-day editors use as their basis the masoretic text established by Jacob ben Ḥayim in the second edition of the *Biblia Rabbinica*, incorporating corrections from other manuscript sources made in Menahem de Lonzano's *štey yadot* and especially in Solomon Yedidya Norzi's *minḥat šay*. While these two were traditional masoretic scholars whose corrections entered all later editions, Johann Heinrich Michaelis printed his edition in the early eighteenth century, introducing his text as the first achievement of modern textual criticism, using additional masoretic manuscripts to underpin his text.

Buxtorf

Whereas the great Swiss Hebraist Johann Buxtorf had attempted to reedit the edition of Jacob ben Ḥayim in the mid-seventeenth century using his Jewish expert, Braunschweig, to carry out the actual work, Michaelis was the first textual critic (in modern times) who thought that he could carry out his corrections without having masoretic expertise. However, neither Buxtorf nor Michaelis left any lasting mark on later editions and today these are past attempts to be looked at only by historians of the progress (or standstill) of Bible editing.

Perhaps those remarks look somewhat ungracious, since those scholars were not even aware of the complexity of the work they had undertaken, but that extenuating circumstance cannot be granted to the most recent attempt to edit a new edition for the British and Foreign Bible Society by Norman Snaith. Snaith attempted to concoct his edition from various sources, but his result hardly presents an improvement on previous attempts. As my personal impression, I might even suggest that we had gotten used to the edition of the *Biblia Rabbinica* and whatever mistakes still occurred in it. The new edition by the Bible Society was the outcome of a long period of preparation, and the disappointment in the result was rather depressing. In short, if proof was needed and even had Snaith been not just a theologian like many others but an expert on textual criticism, his edition proves that both Jews and non-Jews who attempt to produce a new edition of the Bible should at first acquire an expert proficiency in masoretic matters before they can dare to approach the task of an editor.

Snaith tried to improve on the work of Christian David Ginsburg, whose expertise was superior by far. But his result turned out to be a correction for the worse. Snaith believed that the Spanish manuscript BM Or 2626-28 could be taken as representing the Ben Asher text, although written five hundred years after his time, especially if the Yemenite manuscript BM Or 2375 confirmed the readings. (The unhappy background of Snaith's delusion can be seen in a series of papers published by him in the decade before the publication in 1958.)

While the mishap of Snaith should serve as a general warning to less competent scholars, the main question still has to be answered. Should a new edition of the Hebrew Bible start from the basis of the *Biblia Rabbinica* or be based on an eclectic or diplomatic new effort? To be sure, this question is intricately combined to another issue: the character of the various manuscripts of the Hebrew Bible. At the present stage of textual criticism, that central question cannot be evaded, the more so since almost each expert holds on to his own pet theory and remains firmly convinced that his theory reflects the perfect truth. One almost longs for the simple naïveté of former generations, which did not have to contend with so many conflicting assumptions.

Since practically all Tiberian masoretic manuscripts seem to offer the same text, each manuscript looks on the face of it like all others and the search for a "better" text looks meaningless. But the raw facts do not bear out such a simplistic picture.

I have already stressed that basically all later editions of the Bible ultimately go back to the text arranged by ben Ḥayim and some later corrections based on what seemed to Lonzano or Norzi more reliable manuscripts. Even though it became fashionable for each editor to claim that *his* edition was based on the best masoretic evidence and that what he printed was *the* masoretic text, such boasts were queried, especially once one had to come to terms with the variations between the masoretic text and the versions. But only by 1776 such queries took a more tangible form, when Benjamin Kennicott of Oxford attempted to get funds for a worldwide hunt for the best manuscript on which a Hebrew Bible should be based, and from which the "true" Bible text could be regained.

Kennicott's Collations

By the late eighteenth century, Hebrew biblical manuscripts were dispersed in many European public collections. Thus Kennicott needed the assistance of many co-workers, each of whom could only see that much, so that the final collations published by Kennicott must be used with utmost care.

But the main snag was that Kennicott had given instructions to collate only the consonantal skeleton. Nobody at that time realized that such collation would be a self-defeating enterprise, because the consonantal text had been fixed in the second century C.E. and whatever difference remained could only be found by checking the tiny masoretic details of *plene* orthography, vowels, and accents. Thus, Kennicott had the correct idea that for the Hebrew text to be compared in detail with the ancient versions, the Hebrew text must be studied before everything else. However, since the aim was to search for the "correct" Bible text, collating the consonants only was absolutely meaningless. Thus, the search which had been proclaimed with resounding fanfares finally ended in a whimper of disenchantment and all the sums raised by presubscriptions were spent in vain. Of course, it is only by hindsight that we realize this.

Since Kennicott was the first to publish his collations, it is his name that always comes up in discussions on variations in Hebrew manuscripts. But only a few years later (1784) the Italian scholar Giovanni Bernard de Rossi launched a similar project for which he did not collate the consonants only, but also arranged for collation of vowels (though not of section dividers or accents.) But the *variae lectionis* of de Rossi were as disappointing for scholarship as the collations published by Kennicott a few years earlier.

From our point of looking at the facts today, we can say that all those many manuscripts collated by both Kennicott and de Rossi were of such a late date that it would have been impossible to find in them textual variants which might have made any change to the text established in 1525 at the time of the printing of the second *Biblia Rabbinica*. We know today that basically all Tiberian masoretic manuscripts can offer only one text-form and, if we find any textual differences, they crept in secondarily and cannot compete with the type of variants in the Qumran scrolls.

However, this knowledge was borne out of hindsight, once we could see real textual variations in the Qumran scrolls, which are earlier than the pre-masoretic fixation of the text in the second century C.E. All the entries of textual variations in Hebrew manuscripts found in the Stuttgart *Biblia Hebraica* simply are not worth the printing cost, regardless from which manuscript those quotations are taken.

Since the large collation by Kennicott had ended in a fiasco, hardly any editor who published his edition before the present century dared to move away from the text of the Rabbinic Bible as corrected by Lonzano and Norzi, which had become the "*textus receptus*" of all editions of the Hebrew Bible—claims to the contrary on title pages notwithstanding. Facts are facts and editorial claims may perhaps increase the sales but cannot change the facts.

The last attempt in the nineteenth century (1869) of trying to publish a different edition was the result of the cooperation of a Christian theologian with a Jewish primary-school teacher, who saw in masoretic work a unique challenge. Franz Delitzsch was taken in by Seligman Baer and thus in the end he became responsible for another fiasco. But neither Delitzsch nor Baer ever tried to find out what the real text of Ben Asher had been, simply because such a text was not yet known.

Biblia Hebraica

A new chapter in the history of Bible editions only started in 1906, when Rudolf Kittel conceived the idea to publish a new edition based on the traditional text with apparatuses culled from ancient versions. That hybrid monstrosity—in its various editions—still stands out to this day as the best critical edition of the Hebrew Bible and as a model of what a Bible edition should offer. Although Kittel felt that his *Biblia Hebraica* should become a model edition, he could think of nothing more original than reediting the text of the *Biblia Rabbinica*, which served in those very years as the text of C. D. Ginsburg's edition for the British Bible Society. It seemed that the old habit of using the text established for the first humanist edition still held scholars spellbound. Since ben Ḥayim prepared his edition on the basis of relatively late manuscripts, it looked as if Bible editions could never break out of that deadlock. The text established for the *Biblia Rabbinica* had become the *textus receptus* and scholarship seemed landed with it.

I have repeatedly remarked on the issue that new editions necessarily depend on the character of the manuscripts available to the editor. Ben Ḥayim had at his disposal the typical Ashkenazi and Sephardi manuscripts used by everyone at the time. The deadlock could only be broken once completely different manuscripts had become available. That secret only was unraveled once manuscript evidence of a completely different character became known.

The broadening of manuscript evidence was the result of two different events: the discovery of manuscripts still kept in their original Oriental communities which had never found their way into the libraries of western nations, and the discovery of Bible manuscripts or fragments in the Cairo Geniza. Each of these events had its own specific results. As a result of these discoveries, the entire process of the development of the Tiberian masora appeared in a new light. Much—though not all—of this work is connected to the name of Paul Kahle, who became the dominant figure regarding the Hebrew Bible text during the first decades of this century.

First, let me deal with the issue of the relationship between Ben Asher and the Tiberian masoretic text. For centuries that name had been known from masora lists, as well as from references in halakhic literature. It had long been known that Ben Asher was a masoretic authority of the first rank. But that was only a name. Was this *one* specific person, or more? What achievement made Ben Asher into such an authority that his name popped up in almost every source? Was he one link in a long chain of a "dynasty" of masoretes? Was he of the Karaite persuasion or a Rabbanite? Dealing with such an authority, every detail mattered. Had the text been fixed by a Karaite without anyone objecting, the person behind that name remained hidden in ignorance of the correct facts.

It seemed that almost every scribe claimed that he relied in executing his work on Ben Asher and almost every masora manuscript used his name freely. But if he was just *one* authority on masora, why did no manuscript from other authorities survive and which were the manuscripts prepared by him? From masoretic lists, we know the name of his opponent, Ben Naftali, who disputed many masoretic minutiae. But we did not know of any manuscript which could be reliably traced to either authority. Were these only two heads of rival schools, or did their differences stem from religious positions? Were they possibly responsible for the two types of different Tiberian manuscripts known to us, both using the same type of vowel signs? In any case, the Tiberian vocalization used by us is not the only one that existed as one can see from old manuscripts. It seems that such "non-receptus" type of vocalization still existed in different places in western Europe almost up to the beginning of printing. How do such non-receptus manuscripts fit into the history of the Tiberian masoretic text and is there perhaps some connection to the lost tradition of Ben Naftali?

There are obviously many more questions than answers. But looking at the ancient codexes which survived till our time, one point seems certain: what seems at first sight to be one standardized Tiberian masoretic text very soon turns out to be a large variety of textual types—all of them part of the Tiberian masoretic tradition. To be sure, this variety has nothing to do with what the textual critic looks for, since all those variations only reflect minutiae, which the run-of-the-mill textual critic does not even notice. But those differences which are only of concern for the expert in masoretic studies are there, after all.

Moreover, the decisive advances in the study of old biblical manuscripts took place in the last decades before scholars had learned how to go about judging their character and script. The interest in old manuscripts was not yet matched by adequate knowledge and there were not, as yet, experts in Hebrew paleography who could serve as undisputed authorities. Even more: given this state of affairs, almost every scholar tried to prove his theories and to grind his own axe.

Firkovich

If this was dangerous for any scholarship, the more so in the nascent discipline of Jewish studies when some knowledgeable scholars happened to have also a streak of adventurism. Two figures immediately come to mind. On the one hand was the champion of Karaite revival, Abraham Firkovich (Firkowitz), known by his Hebrew pen name, Even Reshef. Firkovich undoubtedly had a flair for discovering old manuscripts or graveyard inscriptions. He came from the Crimean Karaite center and traveled extensively through all Jewish centers in the Near East, and acquired many manuscripts as presents or tokens of goodwill. Most of those manuscripts finally ended up in the Firkovich collection in St. Petersburg (today Leningrad).

The judgments of Firkovich were influenced by his Karaite persuasion. Inside the czarist empire, strict measures were enforced against Jews. The strategy of the Karaites was rather simple. They claimed that their ancestors had settled in the Crimea long before the Jews had disowned Jesus and therefore they could not be held responsible for his crucifixion. Laws against Jews did not apply to them. The obvious proof was the age-old rift between Jews and Karaites. That old antagonism from Gaonic times was now transferred to the political climate of czarist Russia. Firkovich was held in high esteem by the Karaite community and his statements were never questioned.

This sideline may seem of little importance for my discussion. But Firkovich was not only a connoisseur of Hebrew manuscripts, but had also acquired a skill of imitating old-fashioned letters. Thus, he did not refrain from using his skill from changing the colophons of some ancient manuscripts and putting in the name of Cufut-Kale—the Karaite center—as place of origin of such manuscripts. To be sure, this is a rather short, generous description of the facts as they slowly became public.

Given the general ignorance of his contemporaries with regard to ancient script and the high esteem for a man who had traveled to far-away countries, hardly anyone dared to suspect that he had tampered with the manuscripts he had brought back to Russia. Since those manuscripts were obviously ancient and their discoverer a scholar of renown, nobody would suspect that he himself had rewritten the colophons. The situation arose that the oldest and best masoretic manuscripts became the object of suspicion. In this way, the history of the best ancient Bible manuscripts became a source of further confusion.

There existed at the time only one other specialist on Hebrew manuscripts in Russia: Daniel Chwolson, himself a rather controversial convert to Christianity. Thus, the discussion flared up between two experts—neither one a part of recognized Russian Jewry. The truth seemed to be that Chwolson for some time had his suspicion regarding the authenticity of the findings of Firkovich. But suspicions are not proofs, and Chwolson as a recent convert had to be very careful in debunking the claims put forward in an issue which could jeopardize the claims of the Karaite community and its position *vis-à-vis* orthodox Jewry.

Not all codexes reached Russia directly via the collection of Firkovich. Some came via the collection of the Odessa Society for History and Antiquities. But most, if not all, found their place in the end in the St. Petersburg (= Leningrad) library. But while nineteenth-century scholars such as A. Harkavy or H. L. Strack already realized the value of the manuscripts which had reached St. Petersburg, the scholar who is rightly renowned for having realized which codexes reflected the Ben Asher masora was Paul Kahle, who very fast became *the* authority on the Hebrew Bible text. To be sure, in the twentieth century Ben Asher was already well known, but the problem remained which codex could be taken as the most reliable witness to his text and should therefore serve as the base-text of the new edition of the *Biblia Hebraica* about to be reedited in Stuttgart.

The first editions of this handbook for students had reprinted the text of Jacob ben Ḥayim's *Biblia Rabbinica*. It remains to the merit of Kahle that he convinced Rudolf Kittel to use for the third edition the manuscript known as Leningrad B19A (L), a manuscript singled out long before him as a very good specimen of the Ben Asher masoretic text.

The Leningrad Codex

Kahle was quite aware that there existed another and better manuscript of the Ben Asher text, that is, the codex guarded for centuries by the community of Aleppo in Syria. The truth must be told that Kahle knew only the one page clandestinely published as a photograph by W. Wickes in 1887 and therefore could not form a judgment of the entire Aleppo codex. Thus, L was the only existing codex of the entire Bible which Kahle could study and publish, especially since the Leningrad authorities allowed him to use that manuscript in his home town in Germany. We find in Kahle's writings many vacillations regarding his decision to use L as the basis of his edition, and it stands to reason that since that was the only possible codex he could use and the Aleppo codex (A) was never studied by modern Bible scholars—whether Jews or non-Jews—L became for modern Bible study *the* correct Bible text. Many efforts were expended to prove the reliability of L not only by analyzing its text, but also by studying the treatise concerning the differences (*kitab al-ḫilaf*) composed by Mischael ben Uzziel.

However, already Kahle and his assistant, G. Quell, realized that L was not originally a Ben Asher codex, but as the unusual number of secondhand corrections finally proved, it had been secondarily adapted to the text of Ben Asher at a time when Ben Asher's text was already recognized as the model. The same kind of observation was made by F. Perez Castro in 1955.

It may be a sign of Kahle's preoccupation with the minutiae of vowels and accents that, in basing his edition on L, he did not realize that L was almost the worst codex in regard to orthography that he could choose, as was noted by several experts when A could be compared. With regard to the most important issues of masora, L definitely was an inferior codex—if we study its *plene* and defective orthography and the division of its sections. If we add this to the fact that also its vocalization was a secondary harmonization, we can see that for the past decades, L had held pride of place with little justification.

If we study with care the way which made L into *the* representative of the Ben Asher text, we see it was mainly the notice that it was based on "correct" codexes in accordance with what the master (המלמד) Aaron Ben Asher had fixed. In hindsight, the following picture emerges: Aaron was the last-known member of the dynasty of masoretes, who all were descendants of the "old" Asher. Each generation tried to improve upon the system of graphic notation, but we can today only study the Cairo codex of the prophets by Moshe Ben Asher in comparison with the final stage reached by his son Aaron. Paying attention to the amount of detailed work needed for the execution of *one* part of the Bible, the success of Aaron in supervising the work of the entire Bible is, by itself, enough of an explanation why his codex became the model codex for later practitioners of the masoretic craft and why Maimonides relied on that codex for his halakhic statements how a scroll of the Pentateuch should be laid out.

True enough, A today lacks the explicit colophon that Aaron Ben Asher was the masorete responsible for the work. If there ever was such a colophon, which one would expect, it got detached long ago and the specific relationship between A and Aaron Ben Asher is known only from a note added by a later hand, finally lost in the 1948 pogrom in Aleppo. Thus, the ironic blemish remains to this day, that, although A is *the* oldest Ben Asher codex of the Bible, anyone can argue that the evidence is not complete and, if so inclined, he can deny the status of A altogether.

The Aleppo Codex

But one point is certain: A replaced L as the text for the edition in the Hebrew University Bible, which was the only step possible for modern responsible scholars. While the unfortunate events in Aleppo made some scholars doubt that decision forty years ago, today no scholar can dare to counter our proof.

Some final points are now in order. I have already noted that for a long time the name Ben Asher was taken as a generic term for all texts which could be understood by that term without any additional qualification. Thus all statements in the earlier literature which attempt to look for *a* Ben Asher codex—with an eye on the Cairo codex of Moshe ben Asher—have to be judged today as "shredding paper." Once we know the true facts, earlier tentative trials should be disregarded.

This is not to deny that Aaron stood on the shoulders of his father, or even his great-grandfather. What counts for us are the facts. None of the descendants of that dynasty ever attempted to write down the text of the entire Bible, except its latest scion, that is, Aaron. Since we can judge the degree of difference only with regard to the prophets—for which we have codexes by both father and son—nobody can say to what degree they differed from each other in other parts of the Bible and how different codexes supervised by them show internal developments. At the beginning of the 1990s we need not look any more for reconstructing *a* Ben Asher text. Either we have *the* text, or, if someone claims the opposite, it is up to him to disprove our point.

To be sure, all early codexes show an almost identical text. But it remains the issue of "almost," which is ultimately decisive. Another point to be mentioned at this juncture: for many centuries masoretic lists contrasted the name of Ben Asher with that of Ben Naftali. The trouble is that we may be able to label certain specific readings as being in accordance with Ben Naftali's reading. But apparently once the Ben Asher text had gained general recognition, the text of Ben Naftali was neglected to such a point that after all these centuries we are unable to connect any remaining codex to that masorete. If we had trouble identifying a codex as belonging to Ben Asher, with regard to Ben Naftali this is a "mission impossible." Thus, Ben Naftali is for us a ghost name and anyone is welcome to speculate on how a Ben Naftali codex was written.

Coming back to Ben Asher: until the 1950s, we had only one codex (C) which claimed in its colophon that the masorete responsible for it belonged to the family of Ben Asher and a somewhat larger number of codexes which claimed affinity to the codexes bearing that name. But none could claim that Aaron Ben Asher was the masorete in charge. While Kahle—and after him A. Dotan—was aware of the imperfections of L, both he and Dotan used for their editions what they, in good faith, thought was the nearest to *a* Ben Asher text. If others were misled by their editions, that was their own fault. The trouble seems to be that since the publication of the third edition of the *Biblia Hebraica*, almost every nonspecialist among Bible scholars was under the impression that L was the best existing representative of a Ben Asher text. Since introductions to editions usually remain unread, none of these editors can be blamed for later misunderstandings by nonspecialists.

The halakhic ruling by Maimonides regarding the correct layout of a Tora scroll apparently was caused by lack of binding rules in both Talmuds. To be sure, there existed a noncanonical (*Massekhet soferim*) collection of this kind of halakhic literature, but we do not even know whether that collection already existed at the time of Maimonides. If it did, he did not mention it. In any event, the statement made by Maimonides that in his time such confusion reigned regarding the different ways of writing a Tora scroll and that he felt the need to lay down the ways for laying out a Tora scroll is evidence enough.

In the three or four centuries between Ben Asher and Maimonides the name of Ben Asher had become so prominent that Maimonides decided that the codex arranged by him represented such a model, and he therefore wrote his own Tora scroll in conformity with that of Ben Asher. It also stands to reason that the pronouncement by Maimonides secondarily helped to raise the position of the codex of Ben Asher. But I should stress that Maimonides only spoke about the way the codex was laid out, but did not even mention anything about the masora compiled by Ben Asher. Details of masora were only of secondary interest to him. What counted was the division into sections and the layout of the pentateuchal poems.

Of course, we may assume that if Maimonides relied on the layout of Ben Asher—the main issue for the halakhist—he saw him as the master masorete. But we have to be exact with whose prestige was at stake and how history developed. Also, a further point should be stressed: there was a strict division of labor between scribe and masorete. The scribe calligraphed the text according to the instructions given by the masorete. But the scribe copied the text as he found it in front of him and inevitably some of these readings went counter to the intentions of the masorete. If that happened, the masorete was forced to correct the work of the scribe, and it may be that that kind of give and take is sometimes to be detected in the finished codex. That may—at least partly—account for the many corrections we find in L. The masorete had absolute control over the nonconsonantal part of a codex. But the orthography itself—the *pièce de résistance* of the work—does not necessarily reflect the tradition of the masorete himself.

All these seem to be trivial points, but with regard to the holiness of the Bible text no detail may be thought to be trivial and consequently ignored. Whatever our opinion of the codex as a whole, we should never lose sight of the possibilities of development.

Moreover, Maimonides explicitly refers to the issue of "open" and "closed" sections as a main concern of the masorete, so much so that he decreed we should follow the division employed by Ben Asher. Since we find in A no signs of correction regarding the division into sections, and it seems rather hard to assume that the scribe of A followed specifically in this respect the instructions given by Ben Asher, we must not ignore these divisions as laid down in the *Code* of Maimonides.

As I have stated, the greater part of the Pentateuch of A got lost in the pogrom of Aleppo and we cannot compare the divisions into sections between A and the other early codexes through autopsy. Yet we know for a fact that other masoretes made the divisions into sections differently. But even so, the facts seem to be beyond doubt that A is not only *a* Ben Asher text, but *the* first one which enables us to see for ourselves how his text was arranged.

It is today common knowledge among experts that since I first made that claim thirty years ago, I have an axe to grind in order to uphold my view. Other scholars joined my judgment, but as cruel fact has it, A cannot be said anymore to be the earliest *complete* Bible manuscript in our possession, as L still is.

After the pogrom in Aleppo, it has become the custom to blame the Arab mob for all that is missing from the codex. Since that codex was held in great reverence by the community and earlier on went through rough treatment by pillaging armies, we cannot exclude the possibility that some of the missing parts disappeared earlier. I do not wish to put forward the idea that over the centuries Jews tore out some of the missing parts and even kept them as souvenirs. In the long time of over a thousand years, many fates may interfere with a precious codex and we ought to consider all the possibilities. The trouble seems to be that the codex was treated with such reverence that nobody ever checked its condition.

Hebrew University Bible

Having extolled at length the merits of A as *the* Ben Asher text that justly serves as the basis of the Hebrew University Bible, we can now look at its weaknesses, as the basis for the Everyman's Bible edition of tomorrow. First and foremost: we cannot choose for an edition a Bible text which does not include most of the Pentateuch. As it happens, the Hebrew University Bible starts its edition with the first book of the latter prophets and as far as human foresight goes, A will suffice for most of the lifetimes of the present editors. But on principle, editors cannot follow forever an ostrich policy.

I have already stressed that L would be the worst basis for an edition and to fabricate another eclectic edition from heterogenous sources would be unthinkable in our time. Moreover, although our *textus receptus* was built on the belief that it represented the text as sanctioned by Ben Asher, today we cannot work with that same simplicity. Our *textus receptus* has undergone so many changes in every respect that a proper Ben Asher text would seem so strange to the eye of the run-of-the-mill Jewish user that we must end up on the horns of a multiple dilemma. Whatever text we choose, the choice will be unwelcome for both scholars and common folks. In this respect, our better knowledge will turn out to be a curse in disguise. Let us then see how earlier editors proceeded.

If we disregard for a moment the first attempts by Jews such as the Soncinos, who simply took a manuscript which was in their hands and printed the text, both the Spaniards who prepared the Hebrew text for the Complutensis and Jacob ben Ḥayim proceeded the way of contemporary humanists: both reconstructed a text the best they could. Obviously, Jacob ben Ḥayim was the better connoisseur and Bomberg had better printing facilities. Allowing for minor mishaps in the preparation of the second Rabbinic Bible, that text stood the test of centuries, so much so that both Kittel and Ginsburg took it as the basis of their editions.

It was only in the early eighteenth century that modern scholars started to distrust the Hebrew *textus receptus* just as some distrusted the Greek text of the New Testament. Perhaps the first instance of distrusting the Hebrew *textus receptus* can be detected in the *Biblia Hebraica* which Johann Heinrich Michaelis published in 1720, which was the first edition using textual material from outside the *textus receptus* based on Bomberg's *Biblia Rabbinica*. Michaelis used, not only comparative readings from some ancient version, but also *selectae variantes* of the Hebrew, basing himself not only on text editions of his predecessors in the polyglots and editors such as Stephanus, Buxtorf, Hutter, Jablonski, and Athias, but also on a few specially chosen Hebrew manuscripts which mainly had survived in Erfurt.

It should be noted that both Jews and Christian theologians used one and the same tradition of the *textus receptus*. But when consciousness on the Jewish side grew that only editions especially prepared for synagogue use should be used, then the orthodox wing insisted that for such use they should have their own editions. Again, this was not really a new edition, but another copy of the *textus receptus*.

Delitzsch

The only publication which might deserve the name of an edition was the result of a new type of cooperation, that is, the one published since 1869 under the name of one of the best-known German theologians, Franz Delitzsch, who relied with regard to the masoretic details on the expertise of Seligmann Baer, an erstwhile follower of Wolf Heidenheim, the guiding spirit of the revival of masora consciousness among orthodox German Jews in the nineteenth century.

While Baer had made for himself a name as a masoretic expert and editor of Jewish liturgy, neither he nor Delitzsch ever spent time studying old codexes. In short, while their edition was thought of highly by German theologians it was based on nothing valuable and only created more confusion. Small wonder that both Ginsburg and Kittel based their editions on the original publication by Jacob ben Ḥayim.

That was the state of affairs when Kahle entered the stage in the beginning of the present century. Kahle, who had both first-class eyes for old manuscripts and a first-class nose for smelling out promising young co-workers, was not necessarily more erudite than his contemporaries. But (basing himself on the insights of his predecessors) he was the first one to suggest using an old Ben Asher codex as the basis of his edition, that is, L, and to realize that the son Aaron ben Asher was a greater masoretic expert than his father. To be sure, after one thousand years we can only say that the son must have perfected the achievements of his forefathers and the final model codex made him *the* famous Ben Asher and his codex *the* model which influenced the later experts.

While Kahle reported at length on both L and C, apparently he never used photographs of those codexes side by side. Since he had in his possession photocopies of both, it remains inexplicable why he spent so much space reporting about them but did not publish any notes as to how and where L differed from C. This deficiency has been corrected in some way in the recent volumes on the text of C published under the editorship of F. Perez Castro in Madrid, who at the time received the photographs of C through Kahle.

Although C was prepared by the father Moshe ben Asher, himself a master masorete, we cannot report for sure on the proportion of how many erasures and corrections can be found in that codex in comparison with A. To be sure, the speculation of U. Cassuto that C was the codex referred to by Maimonides was borne out of Cassuto's disillusionment with A, but unfortunately that fact was not realized by later scholars who repeated the initial judgment of Cassuto as one of the possibilities to be reckoned with. Of course, the colophon of C makes it clear that Moshe ben Asher never intended to include more than the prophets. To contemplate proofing the text of an entire codex of the Bible was so much of an innovation that the older father could hardly undertake such a task.

Another point of doubt concerns the question to what extent Kahle checked all the other codexes kept in St. Petersburg—at least those which we are able to study today. But even had he checked all the treasures of that library he would not have found another codex like L, as one can learn from the catalog prepared long before by A. Harkavy and H. L. Strack. Thus, both in the western and the eastern libraries there was only one codex of the entire Bible which could be used to replace the old *textus receptus*, and that was precisely the codex Kahle chose. As it turned out, that was not the ideal choice to make.

Of course, the story concerning A was known at the time Kahle made his choice and already in 1887 W. Wickes had been able to include a photograph of one page of A in his treatise on the accents of the twenty-one so-called prose books of the Bible. One page was sufficient to raise a discussion among scholars but this did not mean that scholars got an exact idea of the value of that codex, even if the Aleppo community would have given the permission for such a study. That story sounded so much more like an oriental fable than a solid basis on which Bible critics could erect their structure.

Ben Asher and Maimonides

Most Bible critics of that time had hardly heard the name of Ben Asher and knew even less about Maimonides. The information that Maimonides had relied in his great halakhic opus on the authority of Ben Asher would have been wasted on them. The position of Ben Asher as masorete was as undisputed among biblicists as that of Maimonides among the halakhists. To be sure, nobody had the slightest idea why Maimonides based his ruling on A, but then most present-day specialists in textual criticism would hardly be able to make a connection between the two specialities and use halakhic expertise side by side with text-critical acumen.

Be this as it may, nobody but Wickes and J. Segall (1909) (apart from Cassuto) had ever seen A before it was mutilated, much less studied it. Kahle was a seasoned entrepreneur who should not have been so naïve as to assume that the elders of the Aleppo community would allow an ex-missionary to handle that codex which was held in great veneration by them. However, both Wickes and Segall were suspect of missionary interests and both were allowed to study that codex. So why would Kahle not be allowed to use A as the basis for the edition he was preparing? What, to us, may seem unrealistic or even preposterous, was not seen that way by Kahle, who had connections as much as Wickes. Having experienced the mutual accusation of the present-day responsible guardians regarding the permission to prepare a facsimile photograph, one can only assume what the conditions were a century ago. Did those worthies from Aleppo expect some money under the table for the permission to use that codex? To think otherwise would be unrealistic. In this light, we ought to see the difficulties which Cassuto encountered on his visit to Aleppo half a century ago.

Altogether, this story explains why, to this day, the student edition of the *Biblia Hebraica* is still based on L and what are the interests which prevented A from taking the place which belonged to it by right.

It is only since Cassuto's family finally managed to find the notes that Cassuto took in 1943 and allowed J. Ofer to use them for publication in 1989 that we have a much better idea of the way codex A had been written and how exact were the halakhic remarks on which Maimonides based his judgement and how Cassuto was misled by the common printings of the *Code* of Maimonides. On a personal level, I may add how gratified I am that the detective work I had to carry out for my 1960 statement regarding A is finally validated from Cassuto's own notes.

Dotan, Koren, and Snaith

To return for a moment to the issue of L versus A: we have seen how Kahle had to base his edition on the text of L which, in 1936 seemed to be the best available text of Ben Asher's Bible. It is not so clear why Aaron Dotan made the same choice in 1973 since photographs of A were already available in 1960. Contrary to Kahle, Dotan was fully aware of the shortcomings of L as a Ben Asher manuscript. But another edition conquered the market that Dotan deserved.

For many years, the publisher of the Koren Bible—who laid no claim to expertise in masoretic issues—had conceived the plan to publish a new "Jewish" edition of the Hebrew Bible. Since he was aware of his lack in masoretic expertise, he sought the help of three scholars, all of whom suffered from the same lack of masoretic expertise, though they were competent in other areas of Jewish studies. Since that publisher's competence was in designing new Hebrew fonts—the only area in which changes of forms were possible—and at that time, no proper technique existed to use machine to add markers of vowels and accents, the publisher apparently decided to deface his "first-time" undertaking by putting in vowel and accent signs by a scissors-and-paste job. Aesthetically, the job turned out quite pleasing and hardly anyone noticed how the master copy—which was later reproduced in reduced form—had come into being.

But while the publisher made persistent claims that this was the first edition set and printed by Jews in their old/new homeland, this was, in fact, a good reproduction of the text printed for a long time by orthodox Jewish printers, especially in the Pentateuch part. Basically, the Koren edition is hardly an edition like that of Dotan, but another rehash of the material prepared by ben Hayim.

So far, my survey has taken us up to 1973 and we have found that in recent years only two printings deserve to be termed "edition," being based on previously unknown material: the *Biblia Hebraica* and Dotan's work, both based for the first time on a new codex, that is, L.

As noted, in 1958 another attempt appeared on the market: the edition published for the British and Foreign Bible Society by Norman Snaith. In contrast to the edition by Kahle, that of Snaith continues the work on the Hebrew Scriptures in the spirit of the old Bible Society. Snaith built his edition in the main on manuscript BM Or 2626-28, a rather fair Spanish example of the text prepared much earlier by Aaron Ben Asher. Snaith seemed convinced that good Ben Asher manuscripts had been preserved in Spain and noted that what he found in that manuscript looked very near to the text used by Norzi and, in a way, that of Ben Asher's original.

Since he felt that his edition gave a text similar to that published by Kahle—each of them following his own source—he took this as an indication that a Ben Asher text could be arranged not only from an early codex such as L, but also from later Sephardi or Yemenite sources. While the way of Snaith's argument does not seem convincing, the result is almost as good as that of Kahle's edition. While I would always prefer to use the prototype manuscript, the edition prepared by Snaith goes a long way to show that the opinion of medieval and post-medieval experts in masoretic learning that Sephardi manuscripts are, on the whole, more trustworthy than Ashkenazi ones remains correct, even if today we have no need for substitutes.

The main disadvantage of Snaith's edition is the fact that its text is eclectic, similar in its character to that of ben Hayim. Having reached the stage of the diplomatic text based on L the choice of Snaith seems to me a regress.

Breuer

Leaving aside the editions based on L, the essential result of this survey of recent editions seems to be the unsuitability of eclectic editions in the area of Bible text similar to the state of the art in other textual areas. Whereas up to recent times the preferred method of editing was that of eclectic texts in most areas of classical studies, the wheel has now turned around, and in spite of the fact that there exist only minor differences, the preferred recent practice for the masoretic Bible is the use of the diplomatic method. This, then, will take us to the most recent attempt in this field. Since 1977 one of the more renowned publishing houses of traditional Hebrew texts—Mosad

Harav Kook—has been publishing its own Bible edition which was prepared by Mordechai Breuer.

Breuer took great pains to publish an edition as near as possible to the text of the Aleppo codex, but the trouble was soon spotted. If one does not print according to one given manuscript, one might end up by concocting one's own text. In other words, while Breuer tried to offer a text as near as possible to A, he could not carry out his intention for all parts of the Bible—but especially not for the main part, that is, the Pentateuch. Breuer was aware of the superiority of A as *the* Ben Asher codex, since he adopted results similar to my own. But since generations of rabbinical scholars had spilled so much ink over that issue, and A was not available for the Pentateuch itself, he was forced to publish the text as "based on the Aleppo codex and manuscripts akin to it" for all three parts of the Bible.

What could have become a new model edition of the entire masoretic text was watered down, thanks to the exactitude sought by the editor. Since any edition of the Bible must perforce start with the Pentateuch and that part was missing from A, Breuer was forced to concoct yet another text and, in spite of his basically sound principles, the user can never be sure where his readings originate from. Whereas Koren's text is not much of an edition in its own right, it reproduces some traditional form and does not concoct a fresh text. Thus, while the edition produced by Breuer conforms much more to the Ben Asher ideal, the discerning user is in the end left bewildered whether a specific reading represents the correct Ben Asher text or whether it is the offshoot from a corrected edition of the *Biblia Rabbinica* and what had become over the centuries some kind of *textus receptus*.

I feel strongly that Breuer was on the correct way to create an edition, based—as far as possible—on the only existing Ben Asher codex, but through his own hyperakribia he spoiled his chance and in the end printed a text of which the user can never be quite sure on what it is based. If we look at Breuer's edition as the outcome of "mission failed," this might perhaps show how not to fail in a future attempt.

A Future Edition

In my view, the best way is to publish a Bible text based on *the* Ben Asher codex and to try to fill the lacunas of A in one of the following ways. Each of these possibilities has its disadvantages, but as long as an editor sticks to one method and states clearly what is done, not much harm can result.

The first possibility is to use as substitutes for the missing parts the best available single source and to state in the introduction which parts have been filled in and from which source. This would insure that we can trace every reading exactly to one specific codex and thus prevent the subjective element which cannot be avoided in an eclectic text edition.

The trouble with this choice is that there exists no *one* alternative codex we can use for filling in the portions missing from A and even the use of two codexes would create great difficulties, since the main issue is precisely the text of the Pentateuch.

The alternative possibility would be to restore A to its original form by using the few pages found since, as well as the notations made from it in various lists. But, again, while this could be arranged with some success for the Pentateuch, this would hardly work for the rest of the Bible.

The third—and, to my mind, almost the worst—possibility would be to fill in the missing parts from more than one of the old codexes written about the same time as A. I feel this is almost the worst solution, since it would lead to the kind of subjective eclecticity which we just tried to avoid.

The fourth—and really worst—possibility would be to use L wherever A is missing. This would save us from the need of subjective choices but give us the guaranteed worst text, even if only used to fill the lacunas of A.

All these ideas are only meant if we intend to publish a new edition of the entire Bible and do not confine our work to what can be used as the basis for the Hebrew University Bible. But I shudder at the thought that sooner or later we are going to be faced by this issue in the framework of a critical edition.

While this paper has attempted to discuss the problem of Bible editions—old and new—I refrain, on purpose, from making absolute recommendations as to how one can avoid all the pitfalls. The more we know of the history of the Bible text, the more imposing the problems we have to face. At present, I am just hinting at some of the possibilities and I hope that Shemaryahu Talmon will be granted many more fruitful years and may perhaps finally see what, at this moment, I can only hint at. One final remark is self-understood: in today's field of Bible studies, the edition of a masoretic Bible text as the basis for a scholarly edition must not be confused with the use of the text in a common edition for laymen. If nothing else results from this survey, my goal has been achieved.

THE THEOLOGICAL SIGNIFICANCE OF THE *HEBRAICA VERITAS* IN JEROME'S THOUGHT

Sarah Kamin ז"ל

Jerome's decision to translate the Hebrew Bible into Latin directly from the Hebrew source[1] raises a basic question: what led Jerome to leave the path on which he had begun his literary work, that is, the revision of the existing Latin translation on the basis of the Greek translation?[2] The answer to this question would appear to be quite obvious. The general dissatisfaction with the existing Latin translation called for a new translation; the original text is Hebrew; therefore, returning to the source in order to write a new translation should not be surprising. Indeed, Jerome himself points to these motivating factors. So, for example, he argues:

> In dealing with the New Testament, whenever among the Latin writers a doubt arises and there occurs a discrepancy between individual copies, we have

---

Author's note: I would like to thank my good friend Nechama Leiter who translated this essay with devotion, completing that which I alone could not have completed.

1. Jerome apparently began this translation in a "corner of his monastery" in Bethlehem about 390 C.E. (for the expression *in angulo monasterii* see Epistle 112; *Patrologia Latina* 22:931). It seems that he began with the translation of Samuel and Kings and, after fifteen years, completed his work with the translation of the Pentateuch.

2. Jerome began his revision of the Latin version, the *Vetus Latina*, on the basis of the Greek with his revision of the Gospels in Rome in 383 C.E. at the request of Pope Damasus. When he became aware of the great number of errors in the Latin version, he continued, on his own initiative, with the revision of Psalms according to the LXX. His discovery of the Hexaplaric column of the LXX in 386 C.E. in Caesarea led Jerome to continue his revision of the Latin translation on the basis of the Hexapla. He also made a second revision of the Book of Psalms. However, the extent of this revision is not clear; according to Jerome (Epistle 134, addressed to Augustine), the manuscript of this revision was stolen. Jerome's familiarity with the Hexapla and the work of Origen convinced him to make a new translation of all the books of the Bible from the original Hebrew text. Furthermore, Jerome accepted the Jewish conception of the canon. See the prefaces to his translations of Samuel and Kings, Daniel, and the books of Solomon.

recourse to the original Greek in which the New Testament was written. So, also, in the Old Testament, if there are discrepancies between the Greek and Latin texts, we go back to the Hebrew.[3]

Nevertheless, as we shall see, Jerome's motivation is not self-evident; it requires clarification.

In deciding to turn to the Hebrew text and write a completely new Latin translation, Jerome turned his back on the *Vetus Latina*, the accepted version that had been traditional in the Latin-speaking churches for hundreds of years. Indeed, letters written to Jerome as well as Jerome's own letters and the prefaces to his translations and commentaries indicate the very strong opposition which his work engendered.[4] So, for example, Augustine warns Jerome that a new Latin translation might cause a schism within the Christian church. Such a translation would not only evoke opposition within those congregations that spoke Greek, but would also evoke opposition within those congregations that spoke Latin since the latter based their liturgy upon the *Vetus Latina*, which was itself based upon the Greek. Augustine asks Jerome to continue the work he had begun, that is, the revision of the Gospels according to the Greek and the revision of the Book of Job according to its Hexaplaric text. Moreover, Augustine stresses the weight of the recognized authority of the LXX translators and discounts the possibility that Jerome might improve upon their work.[5] In a letter written after he had received Jerome's translation of the Hebrew text of Job, Augustine expresses shock; implicit in the translation is the fact that Jerome set himself and the authority of the Hebrew text above the authority of the LXX.[6]

---

3. Epistle 106:2: "Sicut autem in novo Testamento, si quando apud Latinos quaestio exoritur, et est inter exemplaria varietas, recurrimus ad fontem Graeci sermonis, quo novum scriptum est Instrumentum: ita in Veteri Testamento, si quando inter Graecos Latinosque diversitas est, ad Hebraicam confugimus (al. recurrimus) veritatem" (*Patrologia Latina* 22:838).

4. See the preface to the translation of Job (392 C.E.): "I am compelled at every step in my treatment of the books of the Holy Scripture to reply to the abuse of my opponents, who charge my translation with being a censure of the Seventy" (*The Principal Works of St. Jerome* [trans. W. H. Fremantle] in *A Select Library of Nicene and Post-Nicene Fathers of the Christian Church*, 2d ser. [ed. P. Schaff and H. Wace; New York, 1893; repr. Grand Rapids, 1979], 6: 491); *Vulgata* (ed. R. Weber; Stuttgart, 1983) 731: "Cogor per singulos Scripturae divinae libros adversariorum respondere maledictis, qui interpretationem meam reprehensionem Septuaginta interpretum criminantur." Nor is Jerome exaggerating; his complaints about slanderers and his apologies are found in almost everything he wrote. See, e.g., *Apologia contra Rufinum*, 2:24–35, 3:25 (Corpus Christianorum 79:60–72, 97); and Rufinus, *Apologia contra Hieronymum*, 2:35–41 (Corpus Christianorum 20:110–15).

5. See Epistle 28:2 [= Jerome, Epistle 56] written to Jerome in 394 or 395 C.E., Epistle 71 [= Jerome, Epistle 104], and Epistle 82:35 [= Jerome, Epistle 116]. See, too, Augustine's observations regarding Jerome in *The City of God* 18:43.

6. In Epistle 71 [= Jerome, Epistle 104:3–5], Augustine warns of the danger of a schism within the church as a result of Jerome's translation. Augustine demonstrates the danger by a story of an occurrence which took place in Oea (Tripoli) during the reading of Jerome's translation of Jonah. A disturbance broke out in which the contention was so great that the bishop,

Obviously, Augustine was not guided solely, or primarily, by such practical considerations as a possible schism within the church. His primary consideration was theological. Believing the Seventy translators to have been divinely inspired, Augustine considered the authority of the LXX to be derived from divine inspiration (*City of God* 18:42). Augustine's arguments against Jerome's bold undertaking were, therefore, twofold: (1) Jerome's lack of consideration for the ancient traditional liturgy of the church, and (2) Jerome's opposition to the prevailing belief of the Church Fathers in the sanctity of the LXX.

The tendency among modern scholars is to consider Jerome's translation from the Hebrew text as having been motivated by philological, "scientific" factors:[7] the inferior style of the *Vetus Latina*, the sad state of the *Vetus Latina* manuscripts,[8] the fact that this Latin translation was twice removed from the original Hebrew text,[9] and the many differences between the LXX and the Hebrew text. Jerome attributed some of these differences to copyists's errors;[10] he attributed a number to the Latin translators' misunderstanding of the Greek version.[11] However, Jerome attributed some of the differences to the Greek translators themselves, that is, to the considered judgment of the Seventy (see his preface to the translation of Genesis, quoted on p. 247 below). In attributing intent and judgment to the translators, Jerome places them on the level of scholars. Their status is that of wise men working within the limits of human wisdom and understanding, without divine inspiration. Thus, in pointing to the changes which the Greek translators made in respect to the original Hebrew text and claiming that these changes were made on the basis of the translators' judgment,

---

after turning to the Jews for their opinion, discontinued the reading of Jerome's translation. In fact, according to Augustine, the need to turn to the considered opinion of the Jews, the authorities in the Hebrew language, was one of the dangers inherent in Jerome's translation.

7. D. Barthélemy, "La place de la Septante dans l'Eglise," in *Aux grands carrefours de la révélation et de l'exégèse de l'Ancien Testament* (by C. Haruet et al.; Recherches Bibliques 8; Paris, 1967) 17 and 23; idem, "L'Ancien Testament a mûri à Alexandrie," *Theologische Zeitschrift* 21 (1965) 370 (= *Festgabe zum Internationalen Kongress für alttestamentliche Studien in Genf, vom 22. bis 28. August 1965* [Basel, 1965]) (both of these essays are reprinted in Barthelemy's *Études d'histoire du texte de l'Ancien Testament* [OBO 21; Freiburg/Göttingen, 1978], see pp. 115, 121, 139). See, too, P. Benoit, "L'Inspiration des Septante d'après les Pères," in *L'Homme devant Dieu: Mélanges offerts au Père Henri de Lubac* (Paris, 1963), 1:169-87 (repr. in Benoit's *Exégèse et théologie* [Paris, 1968], 3:81-86, 88-89).

8. See Jerome's preface to his revision of the Gospels, "For if we pin our faith to the Latin texts, it is for our opponents to tell us *which*; for there are almost as many forms of texts as there are copies" (trans. Fremantle, p. 488); *Vulgata* (ed. Weber) 1515: "Si enim latinis exemplaribus fides est adhibenda, respondeant quibus; tot sunt paene quot codices."

9. See, too, the preface to the translation of the books of Solomon (Proverbs, Ecclesiastes, and Canticles) from the Hebrew text.

10. See the preface to the translation of Job and the preface to *Hebraicae Quaestiones in Libro Geneseos*. Jerome also refers to his reliance on authoritative manuscripts (*libri authentici*) in the preface to his revision of the Gospels. See, too, Epistle 106:41.

11. See A. Vaccari, *S. Gerolamo*, (Rome, 1921) 98.

Jerome negates the very ground of Augustine's claim (*City of God* 18:43) that the divine Hebrew text and the LXX have one and the same divine source.

Jerome's training in philology was extensive.[12] He studied with Donatus in Rome and his admiration of the classics is well known.[13] Nevertheless, it would appear that philological, "scientific" considerations alone cannot account for Jerome's revolutionary step in undertaking his translation of the Hebrew biblical text. Certainly, it is difficult to assume that purely scientific reasoning would provide sufficient cause for Jerome setting himself against the Christian world, or that on the basis of philological grounds alone, Jerome, noted for his conservatism, would be prepared to endanger the Christian church and run counter to the accepted opinion of the venerated Church Fathers regarding the sanctity of the LXX.

Furthermore, the position of Augustine demonstrates that philological factors in themselves cannot provide sufficient grounds for rejecting the sanctity of the LXX. Although he apparently did not know Hebrew, Augustine was well aware of the differences between the Hebrew text and the Greek of the LXX. However, he explained such differences not only by maintaining the sanctity of the LXX, but by attributing the same degree of sanctity to the Hebrew text and the LXX, for, in his view, both were divinely inspired. All differences between the Hebrew and Greek texts were, therefore, purposeful differences, inspired by divine design. One should recognize them and attempt to grasp their meaning. Thus, according to Augustine, the words of Isaiah in Hebrew and the words of Isaiah in the LXX are both divinely inspired. In other words, the prophet Isaiah and his translator are both prophets. The differences between the Hebrew text and the LXX are significant and the exegete is required to unfold this significance (*City of God* 18:42–43). Obviously, philological considerations similar to those of Jerome did not lead Augustine to reject the sanctity of the LXX! It is apparent, therefore, that we must look beyond philological factors and look for a theological reason which can account for Jerome's rejection of the sanctity of the LXX and acceptance of the authentic Hebrew text, the *Hebraica veritas*, as the decisive text.

Jerome does not write at length regarding theological motivation and we find almost no explicit statements regarding a basic theological motivation for his undertaking a new translation on the basis of the *Hebraica*

---

12. See the preface to the translation of Job: "We have but a poor knowledge of Hebrew, but regarding Latin, we have been in the company of grammarians, rhetoricians, and philosophers almost from our cradle"; *Vulgata* (ed. Weber) 732: "Qui et hebraeum sermonem ex parte didicimus et in latino paene ab ipsis incunabulis inter grammaticos et rethores et philosophos detriti sumus." In the preface to the translation of Isaiah, Jerome tells of his endeavors to learn Hebrew, and in the preface to the translation of Daniel, he tells of his attempt to learn Aramaic.

13. See J. N. D. Kelly, *Jerome* (London, 1975) 10–17, 42.

veritas.[14] My suggestion that such was his motivation rests on but one source in Jerome's writings,[15] or more specifically, on my interpretation of this one source, Jerome's preface to his translation of Genesis.

> And I do not know who was the first author to invent the lies about the seventy cells of Alexandria, in which they were divided, and wrote the same things, since Aristaeus, a champion of . . . Ptolemy, and Josephus, many years later, made no mention of such an incident, but write that they were all gathered together in one apartment and consulted and did not prophesy. For it is one thing to be a prophet, quite another to be a translator. In the one case, the sprit foretells what is to come; in the other, learning and abundance of words translate what is known. . . . Are we condemning the ancients? Absolutely not!. . . . They translated before the coming of Christ, and what they did not know, they expressed in doubtful terms. What we write after His Passion and Resurrection is not so much prophecy as it is history. For things that are heard are narrated in one style, things that are seen in quite another style. What we understand better, we also express better. Therefore, listen, my dear rival, and pay attention, my dear detractor. I am not condemning, I am not reprehending the Septuagint translators, but I am preferring the apostles to all of them with confidence. Christ speaks to me through the lips of those who, I read, have been set above the prophets in spiritual gifts; in this respect, the translators occupy practically the lowest level.[16]

In this preface, Jerome's views concerning the LXX and its translators are stated most explicitly, without apologetic camouflage. Jerome strips the

---

14. Jerome's case for the need for a new translation is embodied in his criticism of the LXX. A repeated argument is that verses vital to the Christian faith, verses on which the apostles relied, are not found in the LXX but are found in the original Hebrew text (for references, see nn. 25, 27). However, this argument does not really justify a new translation of the whole of Scripture. The problem might have been resolved by a revision of the LXX and of the Latin version based on the LXX. In any event, Jerome justifies these omissions, as did his predecessors Origen and Eusebius (see n. 22). It should be added that Jerome cites verses in which the apostles do quote according to the Hebrew and Jerome sees the Hebrew text as the apostles' source. See Epistle 57 and Rufinus, *Apologia contra Hieronymum*, 2:36–38.

15. But see n. 23 below on Epistle 112 and on the preface to the translation of Job.

16. *St. Jerome: Dogmatic and Polemical Works* (trans. J. N. Hritzu; The Fathers of the Church: A New Translation 53; Washington, D.C., 1965) 147–48; *Vulgata* (ed. Weber) 3–4: "Et nescio quis primus auctor septuaginta cellulas Alexandriae mendacio suo extruxerit, quibus divisi eadem scriptitarint, cum Aristheus eiusdem Prolomei ὑπερασπιστής et multo post tempore Iosepphus nihil tale rettulerint, sed in una basilica congregatos contulisse scribant, non prophetasse. Aliud est enim vatem, aliud esse interpretem: ibi spiritus ventura praedicit, hic eruditio et verborum copia ea quae intellegit transfert; . . . . Damnamus veteres? Minime; sed. . . . Illi interpretati sunt ante adventum Christi et quod nesciebant dubiis protulere sententiis, nos post passionem et resurrectionem eius non tam prophetiam quam historiam scribimus; aliter enim audita, aliter visa narrantur: quod melius intellegimus, melius et proferimus. Audi igitur, aemule, obtrectator ausculta: non damno, non reprehendo Septuaginta, sed confidenter cunctis illis Apostolos praefero. Per istorum os mihi Christus sonat, quos ante prophetas inter spiritalia charismata positos lego, in quibus ultimum paene gradum interpretes tenent."

LXX of any trace of the miraculous. He ridicules the tale of seventy translators who, while working alone in separate compartments, thought alike in every detail. Most important, Jerome asserts that a prophet and a translator are decidedly different; he unequivocally distinguishes between them.[17] The reason behind this distinction becomes clear when we consider Jerome's apparently strange observations that the translation of the Seventy was made before the coming of Christ and what the Seventy did not understand, they expressed in vague terms. Based upon these two assertions, Jerome's argument runs as follows: The translators were not prophets but merely wise men. Their translation was made before the advent of Christ. Not being prophets, they could not have known about his coming. Because they did not know of the future advent of Christ, they failed to understand Scripture.

We must add one more link to Jerome's chain of reasoning, for Jerome makes an assumption that is not explicitly stated. According to Jerome, the meaning of the "Old Testament" could become clear only with the coming of Christ since this was the "true" meaning of Scripture. It follows that the Seventy, who did not know of the future coming of Christ, could not have fully understood the word of God in the Scriptures! In light of this explication of Jerome's train of thought, we can appreciate the point of his statement: "What we understand better, we also express better." We can appreciate his claim, when speaking of himself in relation to the Seventy, that though he, too, is no prophet, he translates after the crucifixion and the resurrection. His translation, therefore, is not prophecy, but history.[18]

It is clear that, according to Jerome, the coming of Jesus provided the key to the understanding of Scripture. Whoever lived before Jesus would be faced with scriptural texts that, of necessity, could not be understood. Thus, the Seventy, living before Jesus, met with what they could not understand and, of necessity, had to err in their translation. However, he, Jerome, living as he did after the coming of Jesus, had the key to understanding Scripture.

Jerome judged the Seventy as he might judge any translator, whether a translator of Scripture or a translator of secular literature. All translators were subject to the danger inherent in all translating, the possible misunderstanding of the text to be translated. So, too, as wise as they might be, the Seventy might err. However, the Seventy's misunderstanding of Scripture was not comparable to such misunderstanding as might occur in the translation of any text. Their lack of understanding was inescapable,

---

17. On the source of this claim in Philo, see W. Schwarz, *Principles and Problems of Biblical Translation* (Cambridge, 1955) 25.

18. According to what follows in the preface, Jerome considers "history" to be that which is seen to be real, that which actually occurred.

ineluctable. Because they lived before Jesus and were not prophets, the Seventy necessarily erred in their understanding of the meaning of Scripture. It follows that the Old Latin translation serving the Latin-speaking congregations of the Christian church, based as it was on the LXX, was necessarily based on a misunderstanding of the divine source.

Jerome did not make this assertion explicit in any of his writings. This view was too daring, too dangerous, to be stated clearly. Nevertheless, it appears that this is the very point made in Jerome's preface to Genesis. It is here that we find the theological motivation for a new translation directly from the Hebrew source. Jerome wished to establish a *Christian* translation for the Christian world. For Jerome, the significance of the Hebrew text lay in the fact that it was the original word of God which, he believed, prophesied the coming of Jesus. In contrast to the original Hebrew text, the text of the LXX was a translation of the word of God made by translators who were necessarily precluded from understanding the original text, the word of God.[19] Recognizing that translation is always exegetical,[20] Jerome came to the natural conclusion that only one who understands the text better or more correctly can translate the true meaning of the original text.[21]

---

19. Indeed, Isidore of Seville is said to have praised Jerome's translation as being more exact and more correct because it is the translation of a Christian: "Cuius [i.e., Hieronymi] interpretatio merito ceteris antefertur; nam est et verborum tenacior, et perspicuitate sententiae clarior atque, utpote a Christiano, interpretatio verior"; Isidorus, *Etymologiarum sive Originum Libri XX* (ed. W. M. Lindsay; Oxford, 1911), 6:4–5.

20. Jerome was well aware of the problems involved in translation. As is clear from his preface to the translation of Eusebius's *Chronicon* and from Epistle 57 (which is mostly devoted to the problems of translation in general and to the problems of translating Scripture in particular), Jerome advocated translating according to the sense of the text rather than giving a literal translation which, he believed, would distort the meaning of the original text. In this epistle, Jerome expresses conflicting views regarding Scripture: at one point he suggests that Scripture, too, be translated according to its meaning, but elsewhere in the epistle, he claims that in translating Scripture he turned from his usual manner of translating and attempted to translate word-for-word, since, in Scripture, even the word order held meaning and significance. It is difficult to say that Jerome followed this principle in translating Scripture; his translations, particularly of the last books, are not literal. Nevertheless, the inference to be drawn from Jerome's conflicting assertions is that one who does not understand the significance or the mystery embodied in the word order cannot give a faithful translation. Interestingly, in the preface to his translation of Job, Jerome notes: "At times I have reflected an exact translation, at times, the sense"; "Nunc verba nunc sensus nunc simul utrumque resonabit"; *Vulgata* (ed. Weber) 731.

21. It should be noted that another non-philological motivation for the new Christian translation based on the Hebrew text was the fact that such a translation could be accepted by the Jews and could serve in polemics with them. (Origen made a similar claim to justify the Hexapla in his epistle to Africanus.) See, too, the end of Jerome's preface to the translation of Isaiah: "The Jews will no longer be able to laugh at the mistakes in our holy Scriptures"; *Vulgata* (ed. Weber) 1096: "Ne Iudaei de falsitate scripturarum ecclesiis eius diutius insultarent" (see *Apologia contra Rufinum*, 3:25).

I suggest that it is this motivation, the drive to save the Christians from gross error, that explains why Jerome, a conservative by nature, set out to destroy accepted views. This motivation explains his being able to withstand the criticism and slander of his opponents, great and influential leaders of the Church.[22] Surely, philological or polemical factors alone cannot account for Jerome's stand.

There are two weaknesses in my thesis. (1) It is based on but one source in Jerome's writings.[23] (2) Jerome himself expresses views in contradiction to those I have attributed to him.[24] Because of the revolutionary nature of his views, it is not surprising that Jerome did not repeat them. And, for this very reason, it is not surprising that in other places he tempers his views. Indeed, Jerome expresses conflicting views depending upon his audience. However, Jerome expresses conflicting views concerning the Seventy even within the preface to Genesis itself. He points to verses which he believes to be of decisive importance to the Christian faith which are found in the Hebrew text and are quoted by the apostles in the New Testament, but which are not found in the LXX or in the Old Latin version.[25] Here Jerome does not attribute the omissions to a lack of

---

22. Although Origen and Eusebius both noted that the Seventy hid the mystery that was concealed within Scripture, they maintained that the translators were prophets. Their very "misunderstanding" was, according to Origen and Eusebius, determined by divine providence (see n. 30). Jerome makes similar observations in the preface to his translation of Isaiah.

23. Jerome presents a similar argument in Epistle 112:18, the epistle answering Augustine's Epistle 71. In this letter Jerome criticizes Augustine because he prefers the translation of a Jew, Theodotion, over his, Jerome's, translation though he is Christian: How can he prefer the translation of a Jew who desecrates the name of God over Jerome's translating as a Christian? Moreover, there is a strange remark in this epistle which I find difficult to explain. In justification of his translation, Jerome claims that he wished to translate those testimonies that the Jews deleted or perverted. But who are the Jews to whom he refers? The Seventy? The Three? Indeed, Augustine asks the same question in his Epistle 82 (= Jerome, Epistle 116:34). And in his preface to his translation of Job, Jerome argues: The Three deceived and concealed as unbelieving Jews; nevertheless they are accepted in the church by men of the church. Do I, a Christian of Christian birth, zealous to return what has been lost and to correct what has been corrupted ... deserve disgrace? (Jerome also expresses a different attitude toward the Three; see n. 31.)

24. In the preface to his first translation of Chronicles, Jerome claims, in complete contradiction to his statement here, that the Seventy were divinely inspired when translating! Regarding Jerome's ambivalent attitude toward the Seventy, see Colette Estin, *S. Jerôme traducteur des Psaumes* (Paris, 1977), chap. 2 ("Étude sur une approche de la 'verité hebraïque'"); idem, "Saint Jerôme, de la traduction inspirée à la traduction rélativiste," *RB* 88 (1981) 199–215.

25. The verses cited in the preface to the Pentateuch are Hos 11:1 which is cited according to the MT in Matt 2:15, Isa 11:1 cited in Matt 2:23, Zech 12:10 cited in John 19:37, Prov 18:4 cited in John 7:38, and Isa 64:4 cited in 1 Cor 2:9. In the last two instances the citations in the New Testament are not identical to their Hebrew source. In Epistle 57:7–8, however, Jerome specifically refers to those verses in the New Testament in which the citations differ from their original Hebrew source in order to support his claim that the Seventy, the evangelists, and the apostles translated according to the sense and not according to the literal

understanding on the part of the Seventy. Rather, in decided contrast to the views expressed elsewhere in the preface and referred to above, Jerome attributes these omissions to their understanding of the original text. Thus, according to Jerome, the Seventy understood that those particular verses referred to the Father, the Son, and the Holy Spirit. Nevertheless, the Seventy either left these verses untranslated or changed their meaning in translation in order to conceal them from Ptolemy, because they feared that Ptolemy, a monotheist and Platonist, would think the Jews and their writings were polytheistic.[26]

I can offer no explanation of this contradiction in Jerome's preface to Genesis. On the one hand, the Seventy left verses untranslated or changed their meaning in translation precisely because they did understand these verses; on the other hand, they translated decisive verses "but vaguely" because they did not understand (and could not have understood) because they lived before the coming of Jesus. Nevertheless, despite its inherent contradiction, Jerome's preface leads to two fundamental conclusions: (1) the Seventy based their translation on their considered opinion, not on divine inspiration; (2) their translation is of no particular value to the Christian community since Scriptures relating to the very principles of the Christian faith are not found in the LXX; nor are they found in the Old Latin version based on the LXX.[27]

Perhaps Jerome expressed the view that the deletions in the LXX were introduced intentionally because this view had some basis in Christian tradition. Origen, whose erudition was highly respected by Jerome, had voiced similar views, as did Eusebius.[28] Both Origen and Eusebius noted

---

meaning of the word. On the other hand, in *Hebraicae Quaestiones in Libro Geneseos*, in his commentary on Gen 46:27, noting the discrepancy between the "seventy souls" in the Hebrew text and the "seventy-five souls" in the versions of the Seventy, the *Vetus Latina*, and in the Book of Acts, Jerome apologizes for the fact that the error also appears in the New Testament. Moreover, in Epistle 57:7, Jerome explicitly criticizes the evangelist for incorrectly citing Zech 13:7 in Matt 26:31.

26. Cf. *b. Meg.* 9a. However, the verses cited there as having been changed by the Seventy because of Ptolemy differ from the ones cited by Jerome.

27. Jerome states this explicitly in Epistle 121:2 in the year 407. On the verse "From Egypt I called my son" (Hos 11:1), which the LXX renders καὶ ἐξ Αἰγύπτου μετεκάλεσα τὰ τέκνα αὐτοῦ ("Out of Egypt I have called his children"), Jerome says: Quod utique nisi sequamur Hebraicam Veritatem non pertinere ad Dominum manifestum est" ("If we do not follow the *Hebraica veritas*, it is clear that this does not pertain to the Lord"). In other words, only according to the Hebrew text does the verse speak of Jesus. See, too, Jerome's commentary on Matt 12:20 and Epistle 57:7. In Epistle 121, Jerome exhibits his awareness of the differences between the New Testament and the Hebrew text; nevertheless, he claims that if the evangelists did not translate according to the literal meaning of the words, they did translate according to the sense of the Hebrew text.

28. Barthélemy, "Eusèbe, la Septante et 'les autres,'" in *La Bible et les Pères: Colloque de Strasbourg (ler-3 octobre 1969)* (Paris, 1971) 57-58 (repr. in *Études d'histoire du text de l'Ancien Testament*, 185-86).

that verses of vital significance to the Christian faith were "but vaguely" translated in the LXX.[29] However, since they considered the translation to be divinely inspired, they considered its lack of clarity to be intentional. The time was not ripe for spreading the mysteries of the Christian faith among the Gentiles; the nations were not ready to receive them. The mysteries would be revealed at the proper time, when the revelation would be accepted.[30]

Origen and Eusebius were aware of the fact that the versions of the Three, especially that of Symmachus, contained more instances of translations that were in conformity with the Christian faith than appeared in the LXX. Jerome, following Origen and Eusebius, also preferred these later translations. Of course, one might question how it was possible that the Three, who were Jews, did not accept the fundamental principles of the Christian faith even though they lived after Jesus. However, this question posed no real problem. The translations of the Three were considered to reflect the Hebrew text in which the mysteries were concealed.[31] The conclusion drawn was somewhat paradoxical: though the Seventy understand, they concealed; the Three, who did not understand, faithfully reflected the original, and, therefore, did not misrepresent the Christian faith even though they rejected the tidings that Christians believed were contained in the Hebrew source.[32]

In their theological preference of, for example, the version of Symmachus, Origen and Eusebius opened the way for preference of the Hebrew source over the translation of the Seventy. Jerome's position reflects nothing but a logical deduction stemming from their thinking. They simply did not go as far as Jerome.[33] In any case, the contradiction found in Jerome's

---

29. For a discussion concerning verses that Symmachus translated in closer accord to the Christian faith, see ibid., 52 (repr., p. 180); regarding Ps 9:1, see p. 57 (repr., p. 185).

30. This is in accord with the conception of pedagogic preparation (*praeparatio evangelica*) of divine providence (*oikonomia*; or what Augustine termed the *divina dispensatio*), which, working in history, reveals the mysteries at the proper time according to the ability of the one who receives the revelation. For a broad discussion, see ibid., 63–65 (repr., 191–93); and idem, "Origène et le texte de l'Ancien Testament," in *Épektasis: Mélanges patristiques offerts au Cardinal Jean Daniélou* (ed. J. Fontaine and C. Kannengiesser; Paris, 1972) 258–59 (repr. in *Études d'histoire du texte de l'Ancien Testament*, 214–15).

31. Jerome states that "the later translators did not translate their own works [*non sua*], but translated the works of God"; *Apologia contra Rufinum*, 2:35 (Corpus Christianorum 79:72).

32. For a different evaluation of the Three in the writings of Jerome, see n. 23. So, too, several of the Church Fathers censured them for being Jews who, though they lived after Jesus, did not accept him, as opposed to the Seventy who lived before the coming of Jesus and therefore could not be censured for being Jews.

33. According to N. R. M. de Lange, Origen maintained the view that the LXX was divinely inspired only because he yielded to the accepted view; see "The Letter to Africanus: Origen's Recantation?" *Studia Patristica: Papers Presented to the Seventh International Conference on Patristic Studies Held in Oxford, 1975* (Studia Patristica 16; Texte und Untersuchungen 129; Berlin, 1985) 247.

preface to Genesis still stands. I have attempted to explain it by pointing to Jerome's fidelity to the views of his predecessors.

Some further observations should be made regarding the inconsistencies and lack of clarity in Jerome's writings. As we can see from his prefaces, Jerome originally began translating from the Hebrew source as a private undertaking, initiated at the request of friends.[34] Moreover, Jerome's translations replaced the Old Latin translation very gradually, over a period of several hundred years.[35] Indeed, it is questionable whether Jerome ever wanted his translation to replace the Old Latin version. It is quite possible that Jerome distinguished between the liturgical use of the sacred text and its use in theological and exegetical studies. In fact, there is some evidence of such a distinction in Jerome's Epistle 106: "One should sing what the Seventy translated because of its antiquity, but the *Hebraica veritas* should be studied by scholars for an understanding of the sacred writings."[36] However, whether or not Jerome distinguished between the liturgical and the theological or theoretical use of the text, it is clear that only the Hebrew text could serve to clarify the meaning of the sacred writings and their significance for the Christian faith. It appears to me, therefore, that those views of Jerome in his preface to Genesis on which I have based my hypothesis reflect the principal motivation of his work. Jerome, like Origen before him, refrained from a harsh, open confrontation. However, he could not repress his deep-seated conviction that a new translation of Scripture was necessary for the Christian faith.

In the final analysis, Jerome's translation does not meet the criteria which he himself set. Instead, it reflects the on-going struggle within Jerome's "Christian conscience." The compromises within his translation, his agreement with various LXX renderings despite the fact that they had no basis in the Hebrew text, stem from the fact that Jerome was a believing Christian faithful to the Church. However, his translation from the Hebrew stems from his firm belief in the need for a Christian translation of the *Hebraica veritas*.

---

34. See his prefaces to the translations of the Book of Solomon, Samuel and Kings, and Esther.

35. During the Middle Ages Jerome's translation and the Old Latin version were used together. In fact, Jerome's translation did not receive official sanction until 1546 at the Council of Trent.

36. Estin, "Saint Jérôme," 206. So, too, Epistle 57:11: "One should use the LXX because of its age and because it was written before the coming of Jesus." The very fact cited here as the reason for using the LXX is, according to Jerome, reason for not using it.

INTERCHANGES OF CONSONANTS BETWEEN THE MASORETIC TEXT AND THE *VORLAGE* OF THE SEPTUAGINT

Emanuel Tov

Background

The biblical text consists of many details, each of which is usually called a "reading." When sources differ from each other, these readings are "different" or "variant" readings, or simply "variants." There are thousands of such variants, subdivided into pluses, minuses, transpositions, and differences. Some of the latter are the topic of the present paper. More precisely, since there are so many differences between the biblical manuscripts, one source is taken as the point of departure. In this case the MT is taken as the basis for all comparisons, as it is the central text in Judaism, readily available in good editions. The MT, however, is known in many variations, so that for the purpose of a precise examination a specific text must be chosen. Thus at one time the *Biblia Rabbinica* served as the source for such a comparison, while nowadays we use Codex Leningrad B19ᴬ (L), whose text has been recorded both in the *Biblia Hebraica Stuttgartensia* and the Adi edition by Aaron Dotan.[1] All differences between codex L and the

---

Author's note: This essay is offered as a token of appreciation for a dear friend from whom I have learned more than can be expressed here. Shemaryahu Talmon has contributed much to the topic under investigation. In addition to his numerous articles on the text of the Old Testament and variants in general, the following articles, both entitled "The Ancient Hebrew Alphabet and Biblical Text Criticism," bear directly on the topic under investigation: in *Mélanges Dominique Barthélemy* (ed. P. Casetti, O. Keel, and A. Schenker; OBO 38; Freiburg/Göttingen, 1981) 497–530; and in *Mélanges bibliques et orientaux en l'honneur de M. Mathias Delcor* (ed. A. Caquot, S. Légasse, and Mt. Tardieu; Alter Orient und Altes Testament 215; Neukirchen-Vluyn, 1985) 387–402. This essay is a revised version of my third "Grinfield Lectures on the Septuagint" for 1986–1987, delivered at Oxford University.

1. A. Dotan, תורה נביאים וכתובים (Tel Aviv, 1976).

other sources of the Bible, both in Hebrew and retroversions from one of its many ancient translations, are considered "variants."

One such source differing from the MT is considered here, namely, the LXX. That translation reflects several thousand variants, which should be defined as details whose Hebrew *Vorlage* differed from the MT. Although these details are called variants, their evaluation is problematic. The LXX is written in Greek, but the MT is in Hebrew; any comparison of details between these two texts is therefore difficult, as all details in the LXX have to be retranslated into Hebrew.[2] These reconstructed variants are as important as Hebrew variants, as long as they are based on reliable reconstructions.

The thousands of details in the LXX whose reconstructed parent text differed from the MT are called "reconstructed variants," but the terminology may be confusing.[3] Such terminology may give the wrong impression that every reliably retroverted variant was once found in the Hebrew scroll from which the translation was made. This, however, is not true, and the situation is more complicated. Even if a variant seems to be reliably retroverted from Greek, that reading may never have existed anywhere but in the translator's mind. This applies in particular to retroverted variants which are mistakes, for as a rule one cannot know whether the mistake was made by the translator who misread his *Vorlage*, or by the scribe of the Hebrew source. For example:

Jonah 1:9   (ויאמר אליהם) עברי אנכי (ואת ה׳ אלהי השמים אני ירא)

δοῦλος κυρίου ἐγώ εἰμι

In this verse the MT reads עברי for which the LXX has δοῦλος κυρίου, retroverted into Hebrew as עבד יהוה. In this instance the LXX probably reflects an abbreviation of the tetragrammaton as *yod*, as well as a *dalet-reš* interchange. In my view this retroversion yields an inferior reading, but this issue is not important in the present context. The central point in my argument is that there once *existed* a tangible or abstract reading עֶבֶד, even though we do not know at which level that reading was created. One possibility is that the translator found in front of him a reading עבד י in which the *yod* indicated (or was thought to indicate) an abbreviated tetragrammaton. However, possibly such a reading עבד י׳ never existed in reality, but only in the mind of the translator who mistakenly took the letters עברי as עבד י׳. Likewise, any misreading of ארם (Aram = Syria) as אד(ו)ם (Edom), or vice versa, could have occurred in the scroll from which

---

2. For a discussion of the various problems involved, see my book *The Text-Critical Use of the Septuagint in Biblical Research* (Jerusalem, 1981).

3. Cf. J. Barr, *Comparative Philology and the Text of the Old Testament* (Oxford, 1986; repr. Winona Lake, IN, 1987) 238–39; Tov, *Text-Critical Use of the Septuagint*, 140–41.

the translation was made, but by the same token it could have existed only in the translator's mind.

There are hardly any criteria for distinguishing between retroverted variants that existed in writing and those that existed only in the translator's mind. This point should be stressed, because not all scholars use the ambiguous term "variant" in the same way. Some use the term "variant" or *Vorlage* with the implication that every retroverted reading actually existed in writing. In my view, however, even the most reliable retroversions of variants refer to readings that may not have existed in writing. Unfortunately, due to lack of suitable controls, retroverted variants that existed only in the mind of a translator are also called variants. Accordingly, when referring below to variants reflected in the LXX, I refer to variants which are reliably retroverted, but may not have existed in reality.

Of the differences between the MT and the LXX, I am interested here especially in interchanges on the scribal level of single letters or combinations of two letters, mainly because of their similar shape. This focus thus excludes interchanges of letters or words because of other reasons, such as context, language, exegesis, or theology. Of course, often it is very hard to distinguish between the two. For example, is the interchange between וקטלו and יקטלו in a given context linguistic or did it derive from a scribal mishap? In the present context I do not deal with linguistic interchanges, but since it is often hard to distinguish, I will have to include some of these as well. Clear cases of the interchanges of synonymous pairs (e.g, בני ישראל and בית ישראל) will not be included. But the following instance is not excluded. In Jer 2:18 the LXX reads Γηων, which in Hebrew would point to גחון instead of שחור in the MT's מי לשתות (מצרים לדרך לך מה ועתה) שחור; the LXX has τοῦ πιεῖν ὕδωρ Γηων. Does Γηων imply interchanges of *šin* and *gimmel* and of *reš* and *nun* on the scribal level, or a substitution of two geographic entities? It is hard to decide, but the scribal interchange *šin* / *gimmel* is at least possible, and that of *reš* / *nun* is very likely.

The Question

After these introductory remarks I now turn to the topic of this paper, namely, the actual differences in consonants (letters) between the MT and the reconstructed *Vorlage* of the LXX. When referring to interchanges I mean that one letter is replaced with another one, or even two, presumably because of their external similarity. Added and omitted letters such as שמעו/שמו or שמע/ישמע are excluded.

My study of the interchange of consonants between the MT and the LXX focuses on the following aspects:

1. Which letters interchange on the scribal level?
2. What is the frequency of a given interchange in an individual biblical book?

3. Can we point to certain stages in the development of the Aramaic and/or square scripts reflected by the interchanges in the LXX?
4. Do certain books reflect more interchanges than other books?

Proper Nouns

The most fertile ground for the study of interchangeable letters both in Hebrew sources and between the Hebrew and Greek sources is the realm of proper nouns. For in this area, as a rule, no content considerations are involved, so scribal interchanges rather than content variation must have taken place. The lists of names in Chronicles and its parallel sources provide a fertile field of investigation into the interchange of these consonants.

For example, in the parallel list of David's mighty men in 2 Samuel 23 and 1 Chronicles 11, the following pairs of names refer to the same persons, even though their name and provenance vary slightly in the lists; this variation seemingly makes them different persons.

2 Sam 23:25–26   שמה החרדי . . . חלץ הפלטי
1 Chr 11:27   שמות ההרורי   חלץ הפלוני

The interchanged letters mentioned are known from many other places. שמה and שמות imply an interchange of *he* and *tav*, with an added *waw* as *mater lectionis* in Chronicles. Furthermore, the provenance of this person is חרד according to Samuel, but הרור according to Chronicles. Here we encounter interchanges between *he* and *heth* and between *dalet* and *reš*, again with an added *waw* in Chronicles. Also the provenance of the second person, Heleṣ, differs according to the two sources. In Samuel he is referred to as הפלטי and in Chronicles as הפלוני, reflecting an interchange between *tet* and a *waw–nun* ligature (this ligature is also known elsewhere). Needless to say, in both cases the text mentions individuals who had but one name and place of origin, transmitted in different forms.

2 Sam 23:27   אביעזר הענתתי מבני החשתי
1 Chr 11:28–29   אביעזר הענתותי סבכי החשתי

The second example is more complicated. Was the second "mighty man" named Mevunay as in Samuel or Sibkay as in Chronicles? At the level of pronunciation the difference is considerable, but it is slight at the level of writing, before the time of the Masoretic vocalization. Actually the differences are interchanges of *mem* and *samek* and of *nun* and *kap*, later to be enhanced by the added vocalization.

Similar interchanges are found between the MT and the LXX and they add to our knowledge of what happened in ancient Hebrew manuscripts. The evaluation of the Greek form of these names is, however, not easy since scribes who did not know Hebrew corrupted many a name.[4] Thus there are many cases in which the exact *Vorlage* of the LXX cannot be reconstructed any more, such as:

1 Kgs 4:10　לו שכה וכל ארץ חפר
Λουσαμηνχα καὶ Ρησφαρα

The translator took לו as part of the name. As for the transliteration of the name, he probably read one or more letters between the *kap* and the *he*. A case such as this is not included in the present statistics.

Josh 10:3　פראם
Φιδων

It is clear that the Greek translator read a *dalet* for the *reš* of the MT, but it is not clear whether the end of the word reflects a variant or an inner-Greek variation. The *dalet–reš* interchange is included in my statistics below.

Josh 15:23　וחצור ויתנן
καὶ Ασοριωναιν

The two words have been combined to one, and it is not clear how the first three letters of the second word were read by the translator. This word is excluded from my statistics.

A more advanced knowledge of the possible interchanges of Greek letters eliminates incorrect reconstructions of Hebrew variants. Thus uncial *lambda* and *delta* are known to interchange in Greek manuscripts, a situation which makes the assumption of an interchange *dalet–lamed* unnecessary.

Ezek 27:16　ראמת
Λαμωθ (BQL)
Δαμωθ (C)
Ραμωθ (967)

In order to understand what kind of interchange has occurred here, one has to know what the original text of the LXX was. Taking a clue from the Hebrew text, both Ραμωθ of MS 967 and Δαμωθ of MS C could reflect the original Greek reading, as they could reflect either the MT's ראמת or a variant דאמת, created by an interchange of *dalet* and *reš*. It seems that the solution comes from MSS BQL, since their reading Λαμωθ could only have

---

4. The literature on this topic is rather extensive: see the relevant section (§19) in S. P. Brock, C. T. Fritsch, and S. Jellicoe, *A Classified Bibliography of the Septuagint* (Arbeiten zur Literatur und Geschichte des hellenistischen Judentums 6; Leiden, 1973) 41–42; see also the editions and accompanying volumes of the Göttingen Septuagint.

developed on the inner-Greek level from a reading starting with a *delta* by the frequent *delta-lambda* interchange. Therefore Δαμωθ of codex C is taken as the original Greek reading corrupted to Λαμωθ in mss BQL, while Ραμωθ reflects a correction toward the MT in the Chester Beatty papyrus 967. If this reasoning is correct, the original reading of the LXX Δαμωθ of codex C thus reflects a *dalet-reš* interchange.[5]

However, it often remains difficult to determine whether a particular interchange is inner-Greek or is between the Greek and Hebrew. A particularly difficult case is the possible interchange at the ends of words as either *mem-nun* in Hebrew or *mu-nu* in Greek. Ziegler suggests that the Greek scribes were prone to interchanging these letters without any connection to Hebrew sources,[6] as in Αχικαμ / Αχικαν, Σαλωμ / Σαλων, Συχεμ / Συχεν, Ελυαθαν / Ελυαθαμ. In all these cases indeed some Greek witnesses change a majority reading from *mu* to *nu* or vice versa. However, at the same time a Hebrew *mem-nun* interchange is evidenced in Hebrew sources, so that a number of these cases must be ascribed to Hebrew variations. Further study is needed, but it should be pointed out that recent research has found many unusual forms with *mem-nun* interchanges. From Rabbinic Hebrew forms such as שלון for שלום are known, as well as אדן for אדם and אין for אם. These forms are also known from the Samaritan Pentateuch and inscriptions from the Second Temple period. 1QIsᵃ has מדים for מדין in 9:3 and 60:6, so that the LXX transliteration Μαδιαμ could thus be ascribed to a Hebrew rather than inner-Greek interchange. The same applies to a long series of names such as Γεσεμ for גושן, Εγλωμ for עגלון (Josh 12:12A), and Μαρρων for מרום (Josh 11:7). In his study of the LXX of Isaiah, Seeligmann subscribed to the same opinion before the full evidence was known.[7]

A similar problem obtains with regard to the added *nu* in words ending with a vowel in the MT. One thus notices a frequent transliteration of תימא as Θαιμαν (Jer 25:23 [32:9], Isa 21:14), of שבא as Σαβαν (Gen 25:3), and of אלעשה as Ελεασαν (Jer 29 [36]:3b). Ziegler ascribes to the view that this is an inner-Greek addition of a *nu*.[8] However, the alternative view cannot be discarded easily. תימן next to תימא is known from the MT, and various byforms with a *nun* for nouns ending with vowels are known from Hebrew sources. Thus we know of יהודן and יודן next to יהודה.[9] In all these cases we must thus consider the possibility that the LXX reflected a Hebrew form ending with a *nun*.

---

5. Cf. J. Ziegler, *Beiträge zur Ieremias-Septuaginta* (Mitteilungen des Septuaginta-Unternehmens 6 = Nachrichten der Akademie der Wissenschaften in Göttingen, I: Philologisch-historische Klasse 1958/2; Göttingen, 1958) 61.

6. Ibid., 66–67.

7. I. L. Seeligmann, *The Septuagint of Isaiah: A Discussion of Its Problems* (Leiden, 1948) 65 n. 40.

8. Ibid., 73.

9. See the data in P. Benoit, J. T. Milik, and R. de Vaux, *Les Grottes de Murabbaʿât* (DJD 2; Oxford, 1961) 104.

Common Nouns

Retroversions from the LXX based on transliterated Hebrew words are considered a relatively easy part of the act of retroversion, but even these cases are often problematic, as pointed out above. Much more problematic are the retroversions of common nouns. The subjectivity of this procedure needs hardly to be demonstrated here. One example will suffice.

Jer 2:12 MT   שמו שמים על זאת ושערו חרבו מאד
          reconstruction   הרבה מאד ...
          LXX   ἐξέστη ὁ οὐρανὸς ἐπὶ τούτῳ καὶ
                          ἔφριξεν ἐπὶ πλεῖον σφόδρα

If the reconstruction of the *Vorlage* of חרבו to הרבה is correct, it provides information on interchanges between *het* and *he* and between *waw* and *he*. If the retroversion is incorrect, by implication this information is irrelevant.

The Data

Information of this kind is included in the data to be digested below on interchanges of letters between the MT and the LXX, involving proper and common nouns. All this information is subjective, as it is based on subjective reconstructions as exemplified above, although for proper names reasonable objectivity can be obtained. Nevertheless, it would be worthwhile to take a next step, namely, to record and analyze the data on the interchanged letters.

Table 1 records the data on these interchanges, book by book, giving the total number of interchanged consonants in a given book, counting, for example, עבר for עבד (such as עָבֶד for עֶבֶד), but disregarding an interchange בני ישראל and בית ישראל, since presumably this is not a scribal phenomenon. I also disregard interchanges of person and form in the verb as well as prepositions, since these are too uncertain. Possible interchanges of בשמע and כשמע are thus disregarded, since it is hard to infer from the Greek on such interchanges. The numbers of the interchanges are based on the data of the CATSS (Computer Assisted Tools for Septuagint Studies) database and are necessarily subjective.[10] The major types of interchanges, *dalet-reš*, *yod-waw*, and *mem-nun*, are listed next. The last column provides comparative statistics regarding the total number of assumed interchanges compared with the overall number of words in any given book.

The same data are repeated in table 2, this time arranged according to the relative frequency of the interchanges in the books.

---

10. For details, see E. Tov, *A Computerized Data Base for Septuagint Studies: The Parallel Aligned Text of the Greek and Hebrew Bible* (Computer Assisted Tools for Septuagint Studies 2 = Journal of Northwest Semitic Languages Supplement 1; Stellenbosch, 1986).

TABLE 1. Interchange of Consonants in the Individual Books

Book	Type of Interchange ד/ר	י/ו	מ/נ	Total Number of Interchanges	Number of Words in Book[a]	Percentage
Gen	22	11	27	106	20,613	0.51
Exod	5	2	—	20	16,713	0.12
Lev	2	1	1	22	11,950	0.18
Num	27	7	5	71	16,408	0.43
Deut	3	1	4	35	14,294	0.24
Josh	29	12	51	166	10,051	1.65
Judg–A	6	1	—	21	9,886	0.21
Judg–B	3	1	—	15	9,886	0.15
1 Sam	29	6	2	83	13,264	0.63
2 Sam	32	10	—	100	11,040	0.91
1 Kgs	33	8	5	104	13,140	0.79
2 Kgs	12	12	14	88	12,284	0.72
Isa	38	20	4	98	16,934	0.58
Jer	55	21	5	190	21,836	0.87
Ezek	38	13	16	164	18,730	0.88
Hos	15	10	—	60	2,381	2.52
Joel	2	1	—	4	957	0.42
Amos	7	4	—	19	2,042	0.93
Obad	3	3	—	7	299	2.34
Jonah	—	—	—	—	688	0
Mic	12	3	—	21	1,396	1.50
Nah	2	1	—	12	558	2.15
Hab	2	1	—	6	671	0.89
Zeph	1	1	—	3	767	0.39
Hag	—	—	—	—	600	0
Zech	1	1	—	5	3,128	0.16
Mal	5	—	—	6	876	0.68
Ps	10	14	—	46	19,587	0.23
Job	8	2	—	19	8,351	0.23
Prov	29	16	—	115	6,915	1.66
Ruth	—	—	—	4	1,296	0.31
Song	—	—	—	5	1,250	0.40
Qoh	3	—	—	10	2,987	0.33
Lam	1	2	—	11	1,542	0.71
Esth[b]	—	—	—	—	3,045	0
Dan	6	2	1	21	5,919	0.35
Dan–Θ	2	1	—	7	5,919	0.12
Ezra	4	20	—	26	3,754	0.69
Neh	6	15	3	39	5,312	0.73
1 Chr	41	57	25	178	10,746	1.66
2 Chr	4	5	—	17	13,315	0.13

[a] The data on the number of words for the individual books of the Bible have kindly been provided by P. Cassuto of the CATAB (Centre d'Analyse et de Traitement Automatique de la Bible et des Traditions Écrites) project in Villeurbanne, France.
[b] Without Apocrypha.

TABLE 2. Comparative Analysis of
the Frequency of Interchanges

Book	Total Number of of Interchanges	Number of Words in Book	Percentage
Jonah	—	688	0
Hag	—	600	0
Esth[a]	—	3,045	0
Dan–Θ	7	5,919	0.12
Exod	20	16,713	0.12
2 Chr	17	13,315	0.13
Judg–B	15	9,886	0.15
Zech	5	3,128	0.16
Lev	22	11,950	0.18
Judg–A	21	9,886	0.21
Job	19	8,351	0.23
Ps	46	19,587	0.23
Deut	35	14,294	0.24
Ruth	4	1,296	0.31
Qoh	10	2,987	0.33
Dan	21	5,919	0.35
Zeph	3	767	0.39
Song	5	1,250	0.40
Joel	4	957	0.42
Num	71	16,408	0.43
Gen	106	20,613	0.51
Isa	98	16,934	0.58
1 Sam	83	13,264	0.63
Mal	6	876	0.68
Ezra	26	3,754	0.69
Lam	11	1,542	0.71
2 Kgs	88	12,284	0.72
Neh	39	5,312	0.73
1 Kgs	104	13,140	0.79
Jer	190	21,836	0.87
Ezek	164	18,730	0.88
Hab	6	671	0.89
2 Sam	100	11,040	0.91
Amos	19	2,042	0.93
Mic	21	1,396	1.50
Josh	166	10,051	1.65
1 Chr	178	10,746	1.66
Prov	115	6,915	1.66
Nah	12	558	2.15
Obad	7	299	2.34
Hos	60	2,381	2.52

[a]Without Apocrypha.

Conclusions

1. There is no direct correlation between table 1 and the lists of pluses and minuses occurring in the LXX. That is, the books occurring here with either a small or large number of interchanged consonants do not appear in the other lists with a small or large number of pluses and minuses. This situation is actually not surprising. The frequency of pluses and minuses presumably relates to the *Vorlage* of the LXX and reveals in some cases different stages in the literary growth of the books, while the present study of the interchange of consonants refers to the textual transmission of the Hebrew text and in some cases only to the translators.

2. The statistics in the tables indicate differences in the frequency of interchanges of consonants. The smaller the number of interchanged consonants, the more evidence there is for a stable textual transmission and careful translation. The opposite is true for a large number of interchanges of consonants. Most of the books have up to 0.5 percent interchanges when compared with the number of their words, while a few have between 0.5 and 1.0 percent. Of interest are the books with a greater number of interchanges, as seen from the last seven lines of table 2. Of special interest is the high frequency of interchanged consonants in Hosea, which may indeed point to its textual corruption as has often been claimed in the past. The same applies to the book of 1 Chronicles in contradistinction with that of 2 Chronicles, but here the data may be misleading for 1 Chronicles contains more names than the other books of the Bible and much of the confusion relates to the names. It is hard to evaluate the evidence of the other books (Micah, Nahum, and Obadiah), since the absolute numbers are small, and statistics may be misleading; yet, it should be noted that all belong to the Minor Prophets.

At the other end of the scale we note with interest books which show evidence of little scribal activity, as seen from the first nine lines of table 2. This group contains a few late books: Esther, 2 Chronicles, Daniel–Θ, and Haggai, as well as two books of the Pentateuch.

3. Of equal interest are the *types of interchanges*, that is, which specific interchanges of letters are reflected in the LXX. In this listing no special mention is made of metathesis. I refer only to the interchanges of single letters or pairs of letters. The great majority of interchanges occur in every single book only once or twice and sometimes three times. The only interchanges which occur frequently in most books of the LXX are ד/ר and י/ו. Some of the numbers may be misleading as they include a large number of the same names.

Thus of the 33 interchanges of ד/ר in 1 Kings, 14 refer to the change of הדד to בן הדר (υἱὸς Αδερ), and 6 are of הדד to הדר (Αδερ). In 2 Kings there are 4 similar instances of בן הדד, as well as four cases of סנחריב/Σενναχηριμ and 6 of יהויכין/Ιωακιμ. In 2 Samuel there are 9 instances of

הדדעזר rendered as Αδρααζαρ. In Numbers 14 of the 27 interchanges of ד/ר refer to the interchange of גדשון / גרשון and גדשני / גרשני.

4. As for absolute numbers, one of the interesting questions in the study of interchanges is whether a certain pattern in the *direction* of the interchange can be detected. So far I have found little positive evidence on this issue. That is, with one exception I have not found cases in which there were, for example, more interchanges from *dalet* in the MT to *reš* in the LXX than from *reš* in the MT to *dalet* in the LXX. Usually the numbers are more or less equal, for example, 27 instances of ד/ר between the MT and the LXX of Jeremiah as against 28 cases of ר/ד. The one exception is in Ezra, which contains 17 instances of an interchange י/ו and only 3 of the reverse ו/י, almost all in personal names.

5. In almost all books the only two interchanges occurring with any frequency are ד/ר and י/ו and in many books they occur in a large frequency. In 1–2 Samuel one-third of all interchanges are between ד/ר, and the same applies to 1 Kings and Isaiah. In Micah that number is about one-half of the total instances. In Ezra, of the 26 interchanges, 4 are between ד/ר and 20 are of י/ו. Usually all other interchanges occur with much less frequency.

A second observation is that in almost all books the interchange ד/ר is much more frequent than that of י/ו. Exceptions are Psalms and 1–2 Chronicles with some preponderance of the interchange י/ו over ד/ר, and Ezra and Nehemiah, with much preponderance of י/ו. Thus in Ezra there are 20 instances of י/ו as against 4 of ד/ר.

6. When trying to locate the *period* in the history of the Hebrew alphabet to which these interchanges may attest, I should admit that this type of research is actually still in its infancy. For the *Vorlage* of the LXX of Samuel, Driver thinks of "an early form of the square character," while for the base text of the LXX of 1–2 Chronicles, Allen speaks about the semicursive script of the middle of the second century B.C.E.[11] I. Douglas Miller tried to prove that the interchanges between the MT and the LXX in Hosea attest to the fifth and sixth centuries, but in view of the many uncertainties it remains difficult to make any firm statements.[12] In view of the lack of distinction between *waw* and *yod* in most of the Qumran scrolls, it seems that the books of the LXX which show a preponderance of י/ו interchanges would reflect a relatively late stage of the textual transmission.

---

11. S. R. Driver, *Notes on the Hebrew Text and the Topography of the Books of Samuel* (2d ed.; Oxford, 1913) lxiv; L. C. Allen, *The Greek Chronicles: The Relation of the Septuagint of I and II Chronicles to the Massoretic Text* (VTSup 27; Leiden, 1974), 2:162–65.

12. I. D. Miller, *The Text of Hosea: A Demonstration That Most of the Differences in Meaning between MT, LXX, and PSH Arose in the Late Sixth and Fifth Centuries BC* (Ph.D. diss., Melbourne College of Divinity, 1984).

Indeed the books for which this is the case are the late biblical books: Ezra–Nehemiah, 1–2 Chronicles, and, interestingly enough, also Psalms. On the other hand, all other books display earlier stages in the development of the Hebrew script, as the interchange ד/ר is possible in both the square Aramaic script and the earlier paleo-Hebrew script, and is actually more likely in the paleo-Hebrew script.

THE CANONICAL PROCESS, TEXTUAL CRITICISM, AND LATTER STAGES IN THE COMPOSITION OF THE BIBLE

Eugene Ulrich

In antiquity there were certain scribes engaged in the process of handing on the texts of the Hebrew Scriptures who intentionally went beyond the simple copying of the text. They worked creatively on the traditional sacred text, dared to augment it and enrich it for the community, and thus became contributors to the composition of the Scriptures. Shemaryahu Talmon has described this type of scribe as "a minor partner in the creative literary process."[1]

The present generation of textual critics has made a major contribution to our understanding of the history of the biblical text, and I hope to show how recent textual study of the Hebrew Bible has opened a window on a previously dark stage in the composition of the Bible. James Sanders is correct that study of the areas of text and canon can be mutually illuminating.[2] Textual study has illumined some of the latter stages in the composition of the Bible, stages that (depending upon terminology) we cannot yet call "canon," but stages that have been termed "the canonical process."

In my view, "the canon" as such is a post-biblical topic. The way in which the work that I have been doing over the past years positions me to address the complexus of issues associated with the canon is the way it was

---

Author's note: I wish to thank Professor Shemaryahu Talmon for inviting me to give an earlier version of this paper at a symposium he organized on "The Hebrew Bible—From Literature to Canon," held at the National Humanities Center, Research Triangle Park, NC, April 27-29, 1988.

    1. S. Talmon, "The Textual Study of the Bible—A New Outlook," in *Qumran and the History of the Biblical Text* (ed. F. M. Cross and S. Talmon; Cambridge, MA, 1975) 321-400, esp. 381.

    2. James A. Sanders, *From Sacred Story to Sacred Text* (Philadelphia, 1987).

formed, or more precisely, aspects of the canonical process—tracking the tradents and scribes as they developed and handed on their sacred, traditional literature. There are various aspects in the canonical process: the process by which the individual traditions were collected and composed as present books of the Bible, the process by which books of a similar nature were collected into groupings as sections of the present canon, and the process by which differing parties within Judaism struggled for the supremacy of the section of the canon they believed to be more important (e.g., the Law or the Prophets).

In this paper I wish to explore the stage in the canonical process between the completion (more or less) of one early edition of what we could recognize as a given biblical book and the completion of a later (sometimes the final) version or edition of that book. Thus, just as it is important to consider the earlier stages of growth and collection in *books* such as Genesis or Isaiah or Proverbs, and the stages of growth and collection in *sections* such as the narrative or legal or prophetic or wisdom collections, so too I would like to consider the latter stages of the composition of the biblical text in general, stages common to the majority of the books and extending widely through the materials in the various collections or sections of the Bible.

Specifically, I wish to explore how textual study of the Bible helps one see what the creative scribes (those "minor partners" in the biblical process) were doing, what their contribution was to the Bible as we know it today. As I see it, this exploration will erase even more the line between "higher criticism" and "lower criticism" which has been disappearing for some time.[3] That is, the outmoded distinction between higher criticism and lower criticism has as its premise that the major authors of a book wrote and did their creative work and completed a book, and then accurate or sloppy scribes copied that completed work accurately or sloppily. Higher criticism works on the side of the line marked "composition," and lower criticism operates on the side of the line marked "copying." The data presented below will make the attempt to draw such a line yet more difficult.

Because of the widespread absence of agreement concerning terminology related to canon, I must preface my remarks with some reflections and clarifications. Hopefully these will help advance thinking about canon, but in any case they will at least make clear the sense in which I am using the terms. I then want to focus on one form of the creative activity of the scribes of the Second Temple period, what I will term "multiple literary editions" of biblical texts. Perhaps it would be more factual to say "double literary editions," since we seldom have more than two editions that are extant for any particular example; but I wish to focus attention, not simply

---

3. Cf. E. Ulrich, "Horizons of Old Testament Textual Research at the Thirtieth Anniversary of Qumran Cave 4," *CBQ* 46 (1984) 613–36, esp. 616–18.

on the data which happen to be still extant, but on the general phenomenon which I believe was multiple. An examination of this phenomenon will probably suffice both to show heuristically what other similar creative activities of the scribes were like, and to show that the procedures of these scribes were equivalent to the procedures of those tradents we normally think of as the successive composers of the Scriptures.

Terminology Concerning "Canon"

Recent literature and debates demonstrate a need for a thorough and nuanced definition and description of "canon" and related terms: canonical process, Scripture, canonical text, authoritative text, etc.[4] Brevard Childs states that the "initial difficulty in discussing the issue of the canon arises from the ambiguity of the terminology,"[5] but though he discusses a number of the aspects of the complexity, he does not arrive at a satisfactory definition.[6] Sid Leiman has offered a useful definition of "a canonical book": "A canonical book is a book accepted by Jews as authoritative for religious practice and/or doctrine, and whose authority is binding upon the Jewish people for all generations. Furthermore, such books are to be studied and expounded in private and in public."[7] But there are many complex factors involved. Does Leiman's definition include all the factors that ought to be included? Can we properly speak of canon at periods before the sacred writings were commonly considered and widely agreed by reflexive judgment to be canonical? That is, do not all the characteristics

---

4. A recent somewhat sustained attempt at some definitions and distinctions, with bibliography, can be found in T. A. Hoffman, "Inspiration, Normativeness, Canonicity, and the Unique Sacred Character of the Bible," *CBQ* 44 (1982) 447-69, esp. 454, 463-65. In addition to the general complexity of the issue, the welcome setting of ecumenical searching and dialogue compounds the difficulty of the task but at the same time offers the possibility of more penetrating and accurate results. We are all forced to ask to what extent, and to what advantage or disadvantage, one's presuppositions and views are influenced by denominational histories and approaches, and even within these to distinguish between traditional understandings and attempts at modernization in light of new discoveries and vantage points.

5. B. S. Childs, *Introduction to the Old Testament as Scripture* (Philadelphia, 1979) 49.

6. I tend to agree with Bruce Metzger, *The Canon of the New Testament: Its Origin, Development, and Significance* (Oxford, 1987) 36, "Since [Childs's] use of the word 'canon' has three distinct meanings (as a fixed collection of books, as the final form of a book or group of books, and as a principle of finality and authority), the reader is struck by the seemingly indiscriminate way in which the word 'canonical' is attached to a vast range of words, creating a kind of mystique." Also, Gerald H. Wilson's book, *The Editing of the Hebrew Psalter* (SBLDS 76; Chico, CA, 1985), would have been stronger if he had more thoroughly examined "canonicity" (pp. 88-89) and pushed the questions more penetratingly (p. 64).

7. Sid Z. Leiman, *The Canonization of Hebrew Scripture* (Transactions of the Connecticut Academy of Arts and Sciences 47; Hamden, CT, 1976) 14; cited by Wilson, *Editing of the Hebrew Psalter*, 88.

which constitute canon have to be present before we can legitimately speak of canon? Historical evidence is usually lacking for decisive answers. Is it at all meaningful to speak of an "open canon"? That is a contradiction in terms according to some views. The issue of canon is both a historical and theological issue, and these two perspectives cannot be either totally fused or totally kept separate.[8]

Eichhorn said that "it would have been desirable if one had never even used the term canon"—but nonetheless he did.[9] Furthermore, his division is unfortunate: he divides between "general" and "special" matters—treating text and canon under general and individual books under special matters. This division is unfortunate, because issues of text and canon must be probed also for individual books and sections, and the individual books have certain constitutive characteristics that are best studied as a general phenomenon (e.g., the editorial history of prophetic books).

As far as terminology is concerned, I have not yet been persuaded to agree with anyone more than with Barr, who holds that the canon is a later concept and term, and that it is a technical term requiring precise definition and precise usage.[10] It seems that we must adopt a definition of canon that is either on the broad side or on the strict side. A broad definition will include the notions of traditional, sacred texts considered authoritative, but not necessarily the notions of a reflexive, articulated decision that specific texts and not others belong to a special category and are binding for all believers for all time. A strict definition of canon will also include these latter concepts: conscious decision, unique status, necessarily binding.

I had sanguinely hoped, in the process of constructing this paper, to sort out all these issues and come to a clear decision. But I rather quickly learned that that task was impossible in the time available and that it would require book-length treatment.[11] Among other things in dealing with canon, we have a problem similar to that of "midrash," where the term traditionally referred to "biblical interpretation in the rabbinic milieu," but, because it "has clear analogues with respect to presuppositions, procedures, and functions in literature outside and prior to the rabbinic movement," the term has broadened considerably in the last forty years to include "the study of the origin, evolution, and varieties of biblical interpretation in

---

8. In the original context in which this paper was read (a symposium on the making of the Hebrew Bible), the parallel issue of the canon of the New Testament (and in certain views even the Mishnah and the Talmud) need not raise greater confusion, but perhaps we should not forget that views on canon with respect to the Hebrew Bible ought to remain plausible in the latter contexts as well.

9. Cited by Childs, *Introduction to the Old Testament as Scripture*, 36.

10. J. Barr, *Holy Scripture: Canon, Authority, Criticism* (Philadelphia, 1983) 50.

11. It is unfortunate that, for all the commendable industry which went into Roger Beckwith's *The Old Testament Canon of the New Testament Church* (Grand Rapids, 1985), the project fails on the level of judgment; see also the review by Albert C. Sundberg Jr., "Reexamining the Formation of the Old Testament Canon," *Interpretation* 42 (1988) 78–82.

early Judaism, including the NT."[12] This is not the place to discuss whether the broadening of the definition of midrash is legitimate. But, because I think that the use of strict definitions in general requires us to bring greater sharpness to our thinking and thus greater advances in common knowledge, I continue to hold, tentatively, for the stricter definition of canon.

Canon is a technical term with an established usage in theological discourse. Nonetheless, it is important to begin discussion of its meaning, not within the context of Jewish or Christian religious literature, but within the broader context of Hellenistic culture. Although in Greek it had a concrete original meaning and then metaphorical uses, in Latin and derivative languages and literatures the word has a range of metaphorical uses. Beyer's article in *TDNT* correctly summarizes that in secular use the Greek word had the figurative sense of "norm" or "ideal": in sculpture, the "perfect form of the human frame"; in philosophy, the "basis . . . by which to know what is true and false"; in law, "that which binds us, . . . specific ideals"; and also a "list" or "table."[13]

It is significant that the term does not occur in the LXX in any sense relevant to this discussion,[14] just as it is significant that there is no Hebrew word for canon even long after the biblical period. Gal 6:16 seems to be the only New Testament use that is relevant, and there it is used in the rather general sense of "measure of assessment, norm of one's own action, norm of true Christianity."[15] Until the fourth century the term was used in Christian circles

> generally to emphasise what is for Christianity an inner law and binding norm. . . . After the 4th century the general use was supplemented by the description of certain things in the Church as κανών or κανονικός. . . . Most significant is the fact that from the middle of the 4th century the term canon came to be used for the collection of the sacred writings of the OT, which had been taken over from the Synagogue, and of the NT, which had already taken essential shape from *c.* 200. . . .[16]

Even were we to agree on the meaning of canon in Christian usage, it is not a necessary next step to argue that the same precise usage should hold

---

12. Merrill P. Miller, "Midrash," *IDBSup* 593–97, esp. 596–97.
13. H. W. Beyer, "κανών," *TDNT* 3:596–602.
14. Beyer (ibid., 596) notes that it does occur in Judith for "bedpost"; in Mic 7:4 with no clear meaning; and in 4 Macc 7:21 in a philosophical context.
15. Ibid., 598, 600.
16. Ibid., 600–601. Beyer continues: "The use of κανών in this sense was not influenced by the fact that Alexandrian grammarians had spoken of a canon of writers of model Greek. Nor is the decisive point the equation of κανών and κατάλογος, formal though the use of the term may be. What really counted was the concept of norm inherent in the term, i.e., its material content as the κανών τῆς ἀληθείας in the Christian sense. The Latins thus came to equate *canon* and *biblia*." These conclusions, however, need further scrutiny in the light of the texts and descriptions given by Metzger, *Canon of the New Testament* 312–13 and 210–12.

concerning the canon of the Hebrew Bible. Nonetheless, I think it functionally expedient to appeal to consistency here and to use the term according to its traditional, strict definition as the collection or list of books of the Scriptures.[17]

There are three aspects of the technical use of canon that I think it will be important to note: (1) it represents a reflexive judgment, (2) it denotes a closed list, and (3) it concerns biblical books. Thus, I would argue that there is no canon as such in Judaism prior to the end of the first century C.E. or in Christianity prior to the fourth century, that it is confusing to speak of an "open canon," and that "the canonical text" is an imprecise term, at best an abstraction (not a text one could ever pick up and read). In what follows I do not claim to solve the issues but rather note aspects of the problem in the hope of eliciting finer resolution in the future.

(1) In philosophical terms a reflexive judgment is a judgment that is made in retrospect, self-consciously looking backward and recognizing and explicitly affirming that which has already come to be. It represents the difference between sense experience and judgment, the difference between living and "the examined life." It represents the difference between pre-conceptual knowledge, which animals share, and post-insight ("aha!," "click!") human knowledge, the difference between the habitual conviction that the sunrise will be there in the morning and the scientific knowledge about the physical rotation of the earth on its axis. Thus, for a long while the community handed down sacred writings which increasingly functioned as authoritative books, but it was not until questions were raised and communal or official agreements made that there existed what we properly call a canon. The simple practice of living with the conviction that certain books are binding for one's community is a matter of authoritativeness. The reflexive judgment when a group formally decides that it is a constituent requirement that these books which have been exercising authority are henceforth binding is a judgment concerning canon.

(2) Canon denotes a closed list. Exclusion as well as inclusion is important: as Bruce Metzger says, the process by which the canon was formed "was a task, not only of collecting, but also of sifting and rejecting."[18] He is speaking of the New Testament, of course, but the same process was at work with respect to the Hebrew Bible. The simple judgment that certain books are binding for one's community is again a matter of authoritativeness; the reflexive judgment that these books *but not those books* are binding is a judgment concerning canon. Thus, I would argue

---

17. Note also the dictionary definitions: "The collection or list of books of the Bible accepted by [Jews or] the Christian Church as genuine and inspired" (*OED* 2:74), and "a collection or authoritative list of books accepted as holy scripture" (*Webster's Third New International Dictionary*).

18. Metzger, *Canon of the New Testament*, 7. Note Athanasius's directive (cited by Metzger, p. 212): "Let no one add to these; let nothing be taken away from them."

that it is confusing to speak of an open canon. The fact that there were disagreements on the extent of the canon was not so much a toleration of an open canon but a lack of agreement concerning which particular closed list was to be endorsed.

(3) Canon concerns biblical books, not the specific textual form of the books. One must distinguish two senses of the word "text": a literary opus and the particular wording of that opus. It is the literary opus, and not the particular wording of that opus, with which canon is concerned. Both in Judaism and in Christianity it is books, not the textual form of the books, that are canonical. For the rabbis it was scrolls, that is, books, which made the hands unclean (*m. Yad.* 3:5, 4:6). The Mishnah discusses the permissibility of diverse languages for the biblical scrolls (*m. Meg.* 1:8, 2:1; *m. Yad.* 4:5), the script ("Assyrian" [=square], not "Hebrew" [=Palaeo-Hebrew]), the materials (ink and leather [presumably not papyrus]; *m. Yad.* 4:5), and even the blank spaces which border a scroll (*m. Yad.* 3:4); but to my knowledge there is no discussion of a distinction between textual forms. Similarly for Christian writers:

> Eusebius and Jerome, well aware of such variation in the witnesses, discussed which form of text was to be preferred. It is noteworthy, however, that neither Father suggested that one form was canonical and the other was not. Furthermore, the perception that the canon was basically closed did not lead to a slavish fixing of the text of the canonical books.
>
> Thus, the category of "canonical" appears to have been broad enough to include all variant readings (as well as variant renderings in early versions). . . .
>
> In short, it appears that the question of canonicity pertains to the document *qua* document, and not to one particular form or version of that document.[19]

Thus, "the canonical text" is an imprecise term, an abbreviated expression for "the text of a canonical book" or "the text of the canonical books." It is an ideal, referring to the text of a book or books without focus on any particular form of the text. It is an abstraction, not a text that one can pick up and read.[20] It appears that Childs would agree at least partially:

> However, the point needs to be emphasized that the Masoretic text is not identical with the canonical text, but is only a vehicle for its recovery. There is no extant canonical text. Rather, what we have is a Hebrew text which has been carefully transmitted and meticulously guarded by a school of scribes through an elaborate Masoretic system. . . . The canonical text of first-century

---

19. Ibid., 269–70.
20. The later decisions by diverse believing communities to endorse a specific text form or (perhaps more precisely) a form of the Bible in a specific *language*, were juridical, probably sociopolitical, and possibly polemical, but not critical, decisions; and they are conceptually distinct from the decisions concerning the books as canonical.

Judaism is now contained within a post-canonical tradition. Therefore, even though the expressed purpose of the Masoretes was to preserve the canonical text unchanged, in fact, a variety of factors make clear that changes have occurred and that a distinction between the MT and the canonical text must be maintained.[21]

I would agree with Childs that there is no extant canonical text but disagree with him insofar as he holds that the ideal canonical text is necessarily within the Masoretic textual tradition, especially insofar as he is speaking as a Christian theologian. And I would further suggest that the canonical text is a term usually used improperly and, in light of terminological confusion, should be avoided.[22]

I will conclude this section on the canon with some comments to support my earlier view that the canon as such is a post-biblical topic. According to the criteria which I have outlined above, I think that the canon represents a reflexive judgment, denotes a closed list, and concerns biblical books. Thus I think that Childs is theologically seeking something that historically is not yet there.[23] He appears to focus rather rigidly on

> that official Hebrew text of the Jewish community which had reached a point of stabilization in the first century A.D., thus all but ending its long history of fluidity. From that period on, the one form of the Hebrew text of the Bible became the normative and authoritative expression of Israel's sacred scripture. Stabilization marked the point which separated the text's history into two sharply distinguished periods: a pre-stablization period marked by a wider toleration of divergent text types, and a post-stabilization period characterized by only minor variations of the one official text.[24]

There is, to my knowledge, no evidence prior to the late first century C.E., either in Judaism or in Christianity, to suggest that there was either a *fixed list* of books, or a *fixed text* either of individual books or *a fortiori* of the unified collection of books.[25] Thus, prior to the end of the first century, we do not have a canon in either Judaism or Christianity. We have a canon-in-the-making, but we do not have a canon. We have, well documented by practice, the concept of authoritative sacred books which are to be preserved very faithfully. And we have a "canonical process," that is, the activity by which the books later to become accepted as the canon were produced and treated as sacred and authoritative. But we do not have a canon or a canonical text before the end of the first century. Nor do we

---

21. Childs, *Introduction to the Old Testament as Scripture*, 100.
22. That is, except in those rare instances in which someone is discussing precisely that which the term denotes.
23. This and what follows would hold *a fortiori* with regard to Beckwith's position.
24. Childs, *Introduction to the Old Testament as Scripture*, 100.
25. Even Childs (ibid., 102) agrees concerning the absence of a fixed text: "The period of textual fluidity extended from at least 300 B.C. to A.D. 100."

have such until noticeably later, except possibly within rabbinic Judaism insofar as the Masoretic stream of textual tradition is seen as the only legitimate textual form of the canonical books; but is there evidence to show that diaspora Judaism or even widespread Palestinian Judaism generally accepted, prior to the middle third of the second century, the proto-Masoretic stream that emerged as exclusive?[26]

Do we have a canonical list prior to the end of the first century? Yes and no: Torah—yes; Prophets—mostly; Writings—partly. Can the entries on the list change? If, using the technical definition, one answers "no," then there cannot be a canon until the middle of the second century at the earliest. Those who would choose to use the broader definition could answer "yes," but they would always have to add quickly that that list was not stable and that contemporary believers were not fully conscious of, and were not in agreement on, this aspect of the sacred texts. Is it not better to describe the situation this way: there was a category of sacred, authoritative books to which further entries could be added, and that category contained a number of books which were always included and always required to be included (the five Books of Moses, Isaiah, Psalms, etc.), even though others could also be included (Ezekiel, Song, Esther, Jubilees, etc.). If so, then one would say that there was a canon-in-the-making, but there was not yet a canon.

Some of the contents (e.g., the Torah and, for most, the Prophets) would, of course, have met widescale agreement as a central core. But for other books—first, there would not have been agreement on whether they were meant to be included (such agreement had not been reached well into the second century in Judaism, nor even until later in Christianity). But second and more importantly, the multiplicity of "titles" and the general lack of concern about expressly naming and delimiting the contents forcefully indicate that the many authors who refer to this anthology of literature with such diverse and generic designations were obviously unconcerned about the issue concerning which later Jews and Christians made decisions and still later called canon.[27]

The contents of "the Law" seem clear: the five Books of Moses. But what about the contents of "the Prophets"? Was the Book of Daniel included? Was the Book of Psalms included?[28] Since at that time books were generally separate entities, written on individual scrolls, not sequentially ordered in codexes, it is one step more difficult to answer that

---

26. The Masada and Murabbaᶜat manuscripts positively document a proto-Masoretic text tradition, but the assumption of an official, definitive rejection of other textual forms is an *argumentum e silentio*.

27. *Contra* Beckwith, *Old Testament Canon*, 1, 105–10.

28. See Barr, *Holy Scripture*, 54–55. In this regard, Talmon's oral observation at the symposium is very pointed: at Qumran the only books for which *pešarim* are extant are books of the prophets and the Psalms (considered to be included among the prophets?).

question. But Barr's view has much to recommend it, namely that "instead of the three-stage organization familiar to us, there probably was for a considerable time a two-stage conception, using only the two terms, the Torah and the 'Prophets'. Some books, which to us are in the Writings, may well have been in the Prophets...."[29] Indeed, Daniel is considered among the prophets at Qumran, by Josephus (*Antiquities* 10:249, 266–67), and in the New Testament, whereas the rabbinic tradition that resulted in the present arrangement of the MT presumably did not consider the book among the Prophets (cf. *b. B. Bat.* 14b) but rather among the wise (cf. *b. B. Bat.* 14b, and *b. Yoma* 77a).[30] If the contents of the Prophets was unclear, how can one even entertain the notion that the contents of "the Writings" would have been clear?

Again, I do not claim to have solved the issues but rather to have pointed out what I see as issues to be clarified, how I think they might be further pursued, and pragmatically where I position myself in the terminological haze. I can now turn to an examination of the scribes' contribution to the growth of the text which will become the canon.

Examples of the Editorial Work of the Scribes

Talmon has noted "that a great number, probably an overwhelming majority, of Qumran [and other] variants in biblical scrolls and in Bible quotations resulted from insufficiently controlled copying and/or sometimes represent diverging *Vorlagen*."[31] Indeed, the scribes of scriptural manuscripts often intended simply to produce a new copy of an older *Vorlage*, and from time to time they made mistakes. But let us grant general amnesty to all scribes for their errors and corruptions. Let us concentrate on what they were trying to accomplish beyond simple copying. Let us examine the creative role of these scribes in helping to compose what we now call the Bible. Textual criticism has revealed some of the details of what they were doing, and their role in the composition of the Bible at least partially constitutes the canonical process.

I am not the first, of course, to take up this project. Shemaryahu Talmon devoted most of his long and rich article on "The Textual Study of

---

29. Barr, *Holy Scripture*, 54.
30. For the Qumran reference, see J. M. Allegro, *Qumrân Cave 4 I (4Q158–4Q186)* (DJD 5; Oxford, 1968) 54, 4Q174:ii:3: [כ)אש]ר כתוב בספר דניאל הנביא]. Matt 24:15, the only place where Daniel is mentioned in the New Testament (and secondarily in some manuscripts in the parallel in Mark 13:14), refers to "[the Book of] Daniel the prophet." Note also the speculation in *b. B. Bat.* 14b that the Book of Hosea was perhaps not written on a separate scroll and placed before Jeremiah, Ezekiel, and Isaiah [*sic*] because it is small and could possibly have gotten lost. It is interesting now to speculate further that, since the Book of Daniel is not so much larger than the Book of Hosea, the Book of the Twelve could have been arranged in such a way as to include it.
31. Talmon, "Textual Study of the Bible," 380.

the Bible" to what he terms "biblical stylistics" contrasted with what are normally seen as textual variants. In it he was engaged in demonstrating "that an undetermined percentage of these *variae lectiones* derive from the impact of ongoing literary processes of an intra-biblical nature."[32] One can learn much also from Emanuel Tov's article on biblical harmonization.[33] And many further aspects of this creative activity are illumined by the approach designated "comparative midrash."[34]

Let me briefly recall some of the types of scribal creativity that Talmon analyzed, and then focus on another major type of creative scribal activity. He presented examples of stylistic and textual interchangeability of words, stylistic and textual conflation, and stylistic metathesis and textual inversion. Each of these he considered as "fundamental formative elements which assumedly were operative on the author level as stylistic patterns and in the transmission-stage as their editorial and textual modification."[35]

In this paper I would like to focus on yet another major type of creative scribal activity: namely, multiple literary editions of biblical texts. Now the usual scenario for textual variants is the recognition of plausible variants in other textual witnesses for individual words or phrases in the MT, thus *individual variant readings*, and it is generally this type that Talmon studied, presenting a veritable textbook or chrestomathy of text-critical cases and analyses. But the specific type of textual variant that I wish to explore is that of *variant editions*, multiple literary editions of biblical texts.[36]

32. Ibid. See also Talmon, "DSIa as a Witness to Ancient Exegesis of the Book of Isaiah," *Annual of the Swedish Theological Institute* 1 (1962) 62–72; and idem, "Aspects of the Textual Transmission of the Bible in the Light of Qumran Manuscripts," *Textus* 4 (1964) 95–132. Both of these essays are reprinted in *Qumran and the History of the Biblical Text* (ed. F. M. Cross and S. Talmon; Cambridge, MA, 1975) 116–26, 226–63.

33. E. Tov, "The Nature and Background of Harmonizations in Biblical Manuscripts," *JSOT* 31 (1985) 3–29.

34. R. Bloch, "Écriture et tradition dans le judaisme: Aperçus sur l'origine du midrash," *Cahiers sioniens* 8 (1954) 1–34; idem, "Midrash," in *Approaches to Ancient Judaism: Theory and Practice* (ed. W. S. Green; *BJS 1*; Missoula, MT, 1978) 29–50; "R. Le Déaut, "A propos d'une définition du midrash," *Bib* 50 (1969) 395–413; M. D. Herr, "Midrash," *EncJud* 11:1507–14; Miller, "Midrash"; Sanders, "Torah and Christ," in *From Sacred Story to Sacred Text*, 41–60; idem, "Work to Do," in *Canon and Community: A Guide to Canonical Criticism* (Philadelphia, 1984) 61–68. See also James L. Kugel and Rowan A. Greer, *Early Biblical Interpretation* (Philadelphia, 1986).

35. Talmon, "Textual Study of the Bible," 334.

36. Much of the content in this section appeared as part of an earlier article in which I explored the same data in a different direction: the ramifications of preserved double literary editions for selecting the form of the biblical text which the Bible translator should translate; see "Double Literary Editions of Biblical Narratives and Reflections on Determining the Form to Be Translated," in *Perspectives on the Hebrew Bible: Essays in Honor of Walter J. Harrelson* (ed. James L. Crenshaw; Macon, GA, 1988) 101–16 [=*Perspectives in Religious Studies* 15/4 (Fall 1988) 101–16]. The material is reused here with the kind permission of Mercer University Press.

By multiple literary editions I mean a literary unit—a story, pericope, narrative, poem, book, etc.—appearing in two or more parallel forms (whether by chance extant or no longer extant in the textual witnesses), which one author, major redactor, or major editor completed and which a subsequent redactor or editor intentionally changed to a sufficient extent that the resultant form should be called a revised edition of that text. The subsequent redactor or editor could, of course, be the same person who produced the original edition, as sometimes happens in literature, painting, music, or other art forms, but presumably the subsequent editor would be a different person. In fact there are seldom more than two parallel forms of subsequent editions of biblical passages; but that is chiefly an accident of history, and the process I am intending to describe was a much richer and more frequent process, especially when viewed from a canonical-process perspective, and so I will speak of multiple editions.

Sometimes the scope of the variant editions encompasses only a single story, narrative, chapter, or set of chapters. Sometimes the scope extends to the entire biblical book, as in the case of Jeremiah. At the shorter end of the spectrum, if the scope of the variant tradition is smaller than a single pericope, then "literary edition" is too elevated a term and "textual variant," or "set of textual variants," is more appropriate.[37] At the longer end of the spectrum, one could consider the double edition of the entire Deuteronomistic History.[38]

I would like to reflect on samples of multiple editions found in the various parts of the Hebrew Bible: from the Torah, the Book of Exodus; from the *Nebiʾim Riʾšonim* (or historical books), the Books of Samuel; from the *Nebiʾim ʾAharonim* (or prophetic corpus), the Book of Jeremiah; and from the *Ketubim* (or wisdom corpus), the Book of Daniel. I propose to explore the phenomenon of multiple literary editions of these books and then reflect on what it tells about the process by which the canonical books were produced.

The Book of Exodus

For the Book of Exodus, the MT presents a form of the book that I call "edition I," because we have no texts which preserve an earlier edition

---

37. For individual variants, the selection of a given reading in the MT, a Qumran manuscript, the LXX, or some other version usually does not have ramifications for the selection of variants in subsequent passages. For variant literary editions of extended passages, however, the process of selection must begin with the selection of the *edition* to be used (i.e., the edition as encountered in a certain textual witness, e.g., the MT, the LXX, etc.), and only then should individual variants be considered, and only insofar as they are textual variants within the textual form of that edition.

38. See, e.g., Richard D. Nelson, *The Double Redaction of the Deuteronomistic History* (JSOTSup 18; Sheffield, 1981).

of the book as a whole.³⁹ A subsequent edition has generally been recognized in the Samaritan Pentateuch, an intentionally reedited form based on the form transmitted in the MT. In 1955 Patrick Skehan published some fragments from 4QpaleoExod^m containing Exodus 32.⁴⁰ Initially he described the character of its text as "in the Samaritan Recension," but subsequently he refined his assessment: the scroll had "proved on further study to contain all the expansions of the Samaritan form of Exodus, with one notable exception: it did not contain the addition to the Ten Commandments after Exod 20:17, referring to the unhewn altar on Mt. Gerizim."⁴¹ Thus, this text of Exodus appears to be positioned between the form found in the MT and that found in the Samaritan Pentateuch. Is it a different edition?

If Skehan is correct (and after spending several years on that scroll I will affirm that he is), then it seems that there are two Jewish editions of Exodus, one in the MT and a second in 4QpaleoExod^m. Judith Sanderson, who collaborated with me on the completion of Skehan's edition of this scroll, has published an excellent analysis of its textual character in *An Exodus Scroll from Qumran: 4QpaleoExod^m and the Samaritan Tradition*.⁴² Her analysis demonstrates that the scroll is a descendant of a text of Exodus similar to that of the MT. But one or possibly more scribes took the edition of Exodus as found now in the MT and intentionally developed it. The scroll displays a text-type of Exodus intentionally reedited in conscious distinction from the Masoretic text-type. The Samaritans subsequently used that reedited text-type, perhaps uncritically. That is, I think it probable that the Samaritans used the text-type as in 4QpaleoExod^m without conscious reflection on the different available text-types of Exodus and without a conscious decision to use this text-type as opposed to the different text-type which was also transmitted in Jewish circles and eventually used by the Masoretes. The Samaritans then inserted a single additional expansion, referring to the altar on Mt. Gerizim, and they did this according to the same method by which the expansions characteristic of the edition in 4QpaleoExod^m were made. I would hesitate to say that the

---

39. The Old Greek of Exodus witnesses to an earlier form of the text for at least eight individual readings, but those readings are sporadic and do not constitute an earlier "edition"; cf. Judith E. Sanderson, "The Old Greek of Exodus in the Light of 4QpaleoExod^m," *Textus* 14 (1988) 87–104.

40. P. W. Skehan, "Exodus in the Samaritan Recension from Qumran," *JBL* 74 (1955) 182–87. In the early days the manuscript was designated 4QExod^α and was on occasion confusingly cited as 4QExod^a.

41. Skehan, "Qumran and the Present State of Old Testament Text Studies: The Masoretic Text," *JBL* 78 (1959) 21–25, esp. 22. See also the following note.

42. Judith E. Sanderson, *An Exodus Scroll from Qumran: 4QpaleoExod^m and the Samaritan Tradition* (HSS 30; Atlanta, 1986).

Samaritan text constitutes yet a third edition of Exodus on the basis of this single, though monumental, expansion. But we need not decide the Samaritan issue here.

My point is that there are two Jewish editions of Exodus, that found in the MT and that found in 4QpaleoExod^m. The revised edition of Exodus from Qumran is a text intentionally expanded by *systematic harmonization*.[43] A scribe enriched the traditional edition of Exodus by excerpting and minimally rewording parts of the scriptural text and inserting them virtually word-for-word in a new, related context. Sometimes the text was from nearby places in Exodus, sometimes it was from parallel passages in Deuteronomy. Thus one has in the MT and the LXX an earlier form of the text, but in 4QpaleoExod^m a secondary edition of the text produced in Hebrew by Jewish tradents on the principle of harmonization.[44]

The Books of Samuel

In the Books of Samuel one meets a different type of editorial activity contributing to the composition of the biblical text. Some ancient scribe took a traditional form of the story of David and Goliath and intentionally interwove into it another account of Davidic traditions, thereby creating a significantly different edition of the text in quantity and in content. The David-Goliath story is a clear example of two different editions of a biblical narrative, both attested in textual witnesses which have had longstanding and widespread claim as "the Bible" in different communities.[45] An earlier edition of the text with its own integrity and its own specific viewpoint is still found in the witnesses of the Old Greek, and a second, later, developed edition is now found in the MT.[46] The edition embedded in the MT has intentionally expanded the narrative with identifiably different types of material and different David-traditions.[47]

---

43. Ibid., 196–220; Tov, "Harmonizations in Biblical Manuscripts," esp. 7, 13–14.

44. To complicate matters, the MT and the Old Greek may well exhibit a different type of variant editions for Exodus 35–40, but I shall not explore this here.

45. For the detailed characteristics of the two editions, see D. Barthélemy, D. W. Gooding, J. Lust, and E. Tov, *The Story of David and Goliath: Textual and Literary Criticism: Papers of a Joint Research Venture* (OBO 73; Freiburg/Göttingen, 1986). The detailed characteristics should not distract one here, nor should one's judgment concerning the priority between the two editions (see the following note). It should also be pointed out for clarification that the issue here is not "earlier" or "later" in the origin of the traditions, but "earlier" or "later" in the redaction of the stories as they appear in the LXX and the MT.

46. Here I clearly agree with Tov and Lust and disagree with Barthélemy and Gooding. The correctness of either position, however, should not deflect one from the main point that there do exist double literary editions of the biblical text, because (*a*) all four scholars agree that this is an example of double literary editions, and (*b*) even if this particular example should fail, other examples will swiftly take its place.

47. Lust (*Story of David and Goliath*, 13–14) characterizes the material of the earlier, shorter edition as "heroic epic" material, and the supplemental material as "romantic epic" material.

One can list further examples within Samuel where there is evidence, not just of variant words or phrases within the text, but of variant editions of portions of the book. For example, the story of Hannah in 1 Samuel 1–2, which has long been recognized as rich in the textual variants,[48] is probably not a single edition of the story with haphazard textual variants. A striking number of the Greek variants against the MT are quite probably faithful reflections of a different Hebrew text as exemplified now by the somewhat later and very fragmentary 4QSam^a.[49] My strong suspicion is that a number of the variants coalesce to constitute a pattern indicating that the Hebrew text which lay behind the Old Greek may well have been a variant edition from that which has been transmitted through the Masoretic *textus receptus*.

Stanley Walters has recently proposed "the thesis that M and B [the MT and the LXX Codex Vaticanus] are alternate versions of the story of Samuel's birth. The texts of each, while not in perfect condition, can be given a reasonable and internally consistent reading which shows them to be discrete narratives, each with its own interests and design."[50] One need not agree with all the individual arguments adduced by Walters or with his interpretations of the significance of the individual variants in order to espouse his general conclusion that, as I would rephrase it, in 1 Samuel 1 the MT and the LXX (in basic fidelity to its Hebrew *Vorlage*) may well present two different editions of the text, one intentionally different from the other, each internally consistent.[51]

---

48. See the commentaries of Thenius, Wellhausen, Driver, McCarter, Gordon, and Klein.

49. See F. M. Cross, "A New Qumran Biblical Fragment Related to the Original Hebrew Underlying the Septuagint," *BASOR* 132 (1953) 15–26; and E. Ulrich, *The Qumran Text of Samuel and Josephus* (Harvard Semitic Monographs 19; Missoula, MT, 1978) 39–41, 48–49, 62, 71–72.

50. Stanley D. Walters, "Hannah and Anna: The Greek and Hebrew Texts of 1 Samuel 1," *JBL* 107 (1988) 385–412, esp. 408. Walters goes on to say (p. 409), and in this view I heartily concur, since "M and B are discrete narratives, each with its own *Tendenz*, that any use of either to correct the other must be guided by a very precise and exacting method." See n. 37 above.

51. I will mention only two examples where I disagree. The reading "Her distress was equal to the depression caused by {her} a co-wife [sic]. So she would become depressed on account of..." (LXX B) is listed by Walters ("Hannah and Anna," 389) as if it were a divergent element of the narrative from the reading "Her co-wife used to vex her bitterly in order to..." (MT). I think that methodologically it is more sound to view these readings as parallel: to see the Greek as attempting to offer a translation of a consonantal text close (at the time of translation, but later augmented by a conflation in the transmission process) to the text now reflected in the received Hebrew: וכעסתה צרתה גם כעס בעבור. It is possibly, but not necessarily, correct to assume that the reading of the early Hebrew text has been accurately transmitted in the medieval Codex Leningradensis. Walters also sees the need to posit a variant Hebrew *Vorlage* for the Greek (pp. 394–96). The question is, were the particular variations in the text here made *intentionally* in order to produce variant editions so that it is meaningful to maintain that "in M it is the harassment that goes on and on; in B it is Anna's

In one sense, it does not matter whether the example of 1 Samuel 1–2 is verified as an instance of two intentionally different literary editions of that narrative, since literary and textual critics will probably continue to identify more examples of variant literary editions. Thus, I work on the hypothesis that 1 Samuel 1–2 is preserved in one edition in the MT and in another edition in the LXX, and that one of these two editions was intentionally reedited from the other.[52]

The critical reader of Samuel, comparing the scribes' work in producing multiple editions, will note that the features distinguishing the two intentionally literary editions of 1 Samuel 1–2 are not at all the same as the features distinguishing the two intentionally different literary editions of 1 Samuel 17–18. That is, the ways in which the MT and the LXX differ from each other in the Hannah story are quite different from the ways the MT and LXX differ in the David and Goliath story.[53]

For 1 Samuel 1–2 one finds in the earlier edition (perhaps the MT) a straightforward account with one portrait of Hannah. In the secondary edition (perhaps the LXX) one finds the intentional and consistent *reshaping* of that account, arguably for theological motives, to give a *changed portrait* of Hannah. But for 1 Samuel 17–18, in the earlier edition (this time the LXX) one finds a single version of the story, whereas in the secondary edition (the MT) one finds a *composite* version: the same version as in the LXX, basically unchanged, but now augmented with inserted components of a second version quite different in content, details, and style.[54]

---

passive resistance that goes on and on. And neither feature is found in the other story. In M there is provocation but no response; in B there is depression but no provocation" (p. 392). I would not agree that the Greek translation here is due to an intent to paint the portrait of Hannah in a different character. Second, I do not think that the B addition (from its *Vorlage*?) ἰδοὺ ἐγώ, κύριε can bear the weight of the interpretation as "extreme deference" (p. 392). One needs only to hear the potent quadruple echo of ἰδοὺ ἐγώ in Samuel's call narrative (1 Sam 3:4, 5, 6, 8) and to hear the proud and confident Bathsheba as favored wife address the failing David as κύριε (1 Kgs 1:17) in order to demur with respect to the interpretation that "M portrays Hannah more positively than B, giving to her person—both words and actions— a more substantive importance" (p. 392). It is true that communities hearing the two stories separately would get slightly different impressions of Hannah; the question is whether the difference is due to an editor's intention to paint a different portrait.

52. It is not necessary to assume that the edition in the MT and the one in the Old Greek or its *Vorlage* are directly related. But except for some extraneous variants and for those variants which coalesce to form the variant edition, the texts are close enough to hold a direct relationship as a point of departure for a working hypothesis.

53. For the present I will not digress to the larger issue of the editing of Chronicles from the sources of Samuel–Kings.

54. Even if Barthélemy and Gooding were correct, the point made here still holds: the rationale for the difference between the two literary editions of the Hannah story is different from the rationale for the difference between the two literary editions of the David-Goliath story.

What is found in the revised edition of Exodus from Qumran is different from what is discovered in either of the revised editions in the Samuel narratives. The secondary edition of the text of Exodus was characterized primarily by *harmonization*; in Samuel one finds intentional *reshaping* of stories to give a changed emphasis or *changed portrait* (in the Hannah story), and an intentionally *composite* edition made by supplementing a single tradition with additional contents of sizable proportions from a quite different type of narrative (in the David-Goliath story).

The Book of Jeremiah

The two editions of the Book of Jeremiah have become widely known. 4QJer^b (now probably to be divided as 4QJer^b and 4QJer^d) and the LXX display a form of the story which Emanuel Tov has labelled "edition I," and the MT, 2QJer, 4QJer^a, and 4QJer^c display a subsequent, intentionally expanded edition, "edition II."[55] Tov has outlined very convincingly the characteristics by which edition II goes beyond edition I, including both editorial aspects and exegetical aspects. Under editorial aspects Tov lists the rearrangement of text, the addition of headings to prophecies, the repetition of sections, etc. Under exegetical aspects, he lists the clarification of details in the context, the explicitation of material that was implicit, minor harmonistic additions, and the emphasizing of ideas found in other parts of the book.[56] Thus the two editions of Jeremiah exhibit yet another type of contrast. Here the scope of the secondary edition is the entire book, and the method is basically rearrangement plus expansion—expansion not by relatively infrequent, large-scale harmonization (as in 4QpaleoExod^m) but by routine minor explicitation, clarification, lengthened forms of titles, etc.

The Book of Daniel

Turning to the Book of Daniel, one finds yet a fourth type of intentionally different editions in the biblical text. The text-type of Daniel reflected in the MT is well documented from the early period of its textual

---

55. Tov, "Some Aspects of the Textual and Literary History of the Book of Jeremiah," in *Le livre de Jérémie: Le prophète et son milieu, les oracles et leur transmission* (Bibliotheca ephemeridum theologicarum lovaniensium 54: ed. P.-M. Bogaert; Louvain, 1981) 145–67, esp. 146, correctly maintains that "the scroll resembles the LXX in two major features in which the reconstructed *Vorlage* of that translation differs from MT, viz., the arrangement of the text and its shortness as opposed to the longer text of MT. It should be remembered that the fragment is rather small, but the recognition of these two main characteristics in the fragment is beyond doubt." See also Tov's newer formulations in "The Literary History of the Book of Jeremiah in the Light of Its Textual History," in *Empirical Models for Biblical Criticism* (ed. Jeffrey H. Tigay; Philadelphia, 1985) 213–37; and "The Jeremiah Scrolls from Qumran," *RevQ* 14 (1989) 189–206.

56. Tov, "Textual and Literary History of the Book of Jeremiah," 150–67.

transmission. Qumran provides eight exemplars of the book (as compared with only six of Jeremiah), one of which dates from the end of the second century B.C.E., only about a half century after the book's composition.[57] And all eight, insofar as the fragmentary evidence allows one to judge, are generally in the same textual tradition in which the MT stands. I hasten to qualify that in some of the individual variants the MT is clearly secondary, just as each of the Qumran manuscripts also displays secondary readings *vis-à-vis* the MT. But my point is that, even though there are many minor discrepancies among the various scrolls and between each and the MT, the Qumran manuscripts display the same general *edition* as that in the MT. There are no witnesses to the additions of Suzanna, Bel and the Dragon, the Prayer of the Three Youths, etc., or to the alternate order as found in Papyrus 967.[58]

I will also mention, though it is not my main point here, that for certain individual readings the scrolls provide in Aramaic or Hebrew the *Vorlage* of certain individual Old Greek readings; but again, the general *edition* of each of the scrolls appears to be that of the MT, not that of the Old Greek.

For most of the book, when the MT and the Old Greek are compared, they both witness to the same edition. They do exhibit, however, significant discrepancy in chaps. 4-6, and the Old Greek translator of Daniel has been severely criticized.[59] The forthcoming dissertation of Dean Wenthe, however, on the Old Greek intends to demonstrate that Bludau, Montgomery, and Jeansonne were correct in exonerating the Old Greek translator with regard to the book in general, and in considering chaps. 4-6 of a different order.[60] I agree with Montgomery that "careful study relieves much of the

---

57. The editions of 1QDan^a and 1QDan^b are in D. Barthélemy and J. T. Milik, *Qumrân Cave 1* (DJD 1; Oxford, 1955) 150-52; that of pap6QDan in M. Baillet, J. T. Milik, and R. de Vaux, *Les "Petites Grottes" de Qumrân* (DJD 3; Oxford, 1962) 114-15, pl. 23. See also the recent editions by Ulrich, "Daniel Manuscripts from Qumran, Part 1: A Preliminary Edition of 4QDan^a," *BASOR* 268 (1987) 17-37; and idem, "Daniel Manuscripts from Qumran, Part 2: Preliminary Editions of 4QDan^b and 4QDan^c," *BASOR* 274 (1989) 3-26. 4QDan^d and 4QDan^e, both very small, will be published in a later volume of DJD.

58. I will not even attempt here to bring up the question of the variant editions in the larger Book of Daniel with the "additions," further complicated by the appearance of that longer edition in the presumably Jewish recension, possibly based on a Hebrew-Aramaic *Vorlage*, attributed to Theodotion.

59. See the discussion by J. A. Montgomery, *A Critical and Exegetical Commentary on the Book of Daniel* (ICC; Edinburgh/New York, 1927) 35.

60. D. Wenthe, Ph.D. dissertation on the Old Greek of Daniel 4-6 (University of Notre Dame, forthcoming); August Bludau, *Die alexandrinische Übersetzung des Buches Daniel und ihr Verhältniss zum massorethischen Text* (Biblische Studien 2/2-3; Freiburg im Breisgau, 1897) 31; Montgomery, *Book of Daniel*, 35-37; Sharon Pace, "The Stratigraphy of the Text of Daniel and the Question of Theological *Tendenz* in the Old Greek," *Bulletin of the International Organization for Septuagint and Cognate Studies* 17 (1984) 15-35; and, now more fully, Sharon Pace Jeansonne, *The Old Greek Translation of Daniel 7-12* (Catholic Biblical Quarterly Monograph Series 19; Washington, DC, 1988).

odium that has been cast upon the translation."[61] When the entire book is carefully studied, one finds that for chaps. 1–2, perhaps 3, and 7–12 the Old Greek translation is a faithful translation of a Semitic text close to that in the MT and the scrolls. In chaps. 4 and 6, however, the MT is considerably shorter than the Old Greek, whereas in chap. 5 the Old Greek is noticeably shorter than the MT. The least that can be said is that the same process is not consistently at work in these three chapters. But one can get much more specific. When one analyzes the MT and the Old Greek in parallel for each of the three chapters, the principal factors become clear. (1) I have already mentioned that occasionally the scrolls demonstrate that the MT incorporates secondary readings. (2) Though for chaps. 4–6 the Old Greek is noticeably different from the MT, the nature of the Greek in those chapters is the same as that in the remainder of the book; that is, the Greek of chaps. 1–12 is of one piece. (3) The differences in the quantity of text are not, as often in the MT of Samuel, caused by loss of sizable amounts of material through parablepsis. Rather, in Daniel 4–6 *both* the MT and the Old Greek are apparently secondary, that is, they each expand in different directions beyond an earlier common edition which no longer survives. For example, for each of the three speeches in 5:10–12, 13–16, 17–23 the edition preserved in the MT greatly expands for rhetorical and dramatic effect beyond the edition preserved in the Old Greek. In contrast, the variant editions for chap. 4 are signalled by the differing arrangements of various components and are confirmed by expansions in the Old Greek, such as the expansion (perhaps a Babylonian astrological motif) of the sun and moon dwelling in the great tree (4:8), etc. The conclusion to be drawn, but still to be demonstrated in detail, is that the Old Greek translator translated the entire book faithfully from his Semitic *Vorlage*; he simply had a version of the book which contained a variant edition of the text for those three chapters. Furthermore, the variant editions found in the MT and in the Old Greek for Daniel 4–6 appear to be two different later editions of the story, both secondary, both expanding in different ways beyond a single form which lies behind both but which is no longer extant.

In summary, then, I have shown examples of four different books of the Bible with text forms preserving intentionally variant editions of the biblical text. For the Book of Exodus, the MT and the LXX preserve an earlier form of the text, whereas 4QpaleoExod^m (and subsequently the Samaritan text) preserves a secondary edition of the text produced on the principle of *harmonization*, spanning the majority of the book.

For the Books of Samuel, there is one clear example and another plausible example, offering two different types of intentionally new edition of individual narratives. On the one hand, in 1 Samuel 1–2 the MT may be

---

61. Montgomery, *Book of Daniel*, 36.

the earlier form, and the text translated in the LXX may witness to a secondary edition with an *intentionally altered portrait* for theological motives. On the other, in 1 Samuel 17–18 there are clearly two intentionally different editions, the Greek now displaying the earlier edition and the MT a secondary edition *supplemented by diverse traditions* about David.

For the Book of Jeremiah, the LXX displays an earlier edition of the entire book with one arrangement ("edition I") and the MT an expanded second edition ("edition II"), in substance basically unchanged, but with a *variant arrangement and systematic expansion* by numerous, routine, minor additions.

For the Book of Daniel, the MT and the Old Greek exhibit two different editions of chaps. 4–6, this time *both* apparently being *secondary*, that is, *expanding in different directions* beyond an earlier common edition which no longer survives.

All the editorial work I have been discussing was done at the Hebrew stage.[62] That is, the second of the two different literary editions in each of the four biblical books discussed above was produced at the Hebrew (or, for Daniel, Aramaic) stage, not by a Greek translator. That is important for our consideration of the creative activity of the scribes. But let me add a tangential *obiter dictum*.

With regard to the question of "theological *Tendenz*" or "actualizing exegesis" on the part of the LXX translators, I have yet to examine an allegation of a major interpretative translation by an Old Greek translator and be convinced that the Old Greek translator was responsible for a substantively innovative translation. Most who make such allegations have failed to distinguish the three stages of (*a*) the Hebrew *Vorlage* which is being translated into Greek, (*b*) the results of the transformational process by the original Greek translator, and (*c*) the subsequent transmission history within the Greek manuscript tradition.[63] In most cases the Old Greek translators were attempting to produce a faithful translation of the sacred text, not to produce an interpretation remarkably innovative in content. Nonetheless, it is methodologically important to examine the question for each instance, because it remains a possibility that, since the various Old Greek translators operated on partially differing applications of principles, a certain individual translator may turn out to have exercised substantively creative interpretation in the translation.

The point to bring out in this present discussion is that in a number of instances of multiple literary editions, some of which are still preserved in

---

62. See Ulrich, "Double Literary Editions," 108–10.

63. One clear example of such allegation and its subsequent correction is F. F. Bruce, "The Oldest Greek Version of Daniel," in *Instruction and Interpretation* (by H. A. Brongers, et al.; Oudtestamentische Studiën 20; Leiden, 1977) 22–40, corrected by Pace, "Stratigraphy of the Text of Daniel," 28–32.

the textual witnesses, the creative, secondary editorial work was already done at the Hebrew (or, for Daniel, Aramaic) level within the Jewish community and cannot be discounted as the unimportant or regrettable work of a Greek translator. The parallel editions were current, available forms of the sacred text in the original language, and apparently up to the end of the first century of the common era they were seen as having equally valid claims to being "the biblical text."

Aspects of the Canonical Process

The canonical process is that series of actions, or complex of activity, viewed both individually and as an organic whole, by which the collection of sacred books now recognized as the canonical books was produced, especially with regard to the characteristics by which it became the canon as such. That activity includes, as Sanders says, selectivity and repetition with interpretation—tradition being retold and reshaped faithfully but creatively.[64]

Sanders compares the canonical process to comparative midrash, and I would like to go further and add the very composition of Scripture as another equivalent, and to suggest moreover that the homiletical, liturgical, and spiritual use of Scripture involves a similar process.

A decade ago I suggested that there was a dynamic operative in modern theological reflection which had its roots in the very process by which the Scriptures were composed. Using an analysis of the biblical account of the exodus, I made the claim that the method of composition of the Scriptures is "a *process* and that the process of the development of Scripture is dialectical—Scripture, which began as experience, was produced through a process of tradition(s) being formulated about that experience and being reformulated by interpreters in dialogue with the experience of their communities and with the larger culture."[65] Using the exodus as an example, it seems clear that what (according to the documentary view) the Yahwist, the Elohist, and the Priestly editions were doing was each taking the tradition and *repeating it faithfully* but *reshaping it creatively* in the light of the exigencies of their current cultural situation.

Since the biblical narratives are usually not eyewitness accounts of events but "classic retelling(s)" of the traditions, one must carefully analyze and differentiate the epistemological levels from experience or "raw event" to the final written text: experience, understanding, and judgment, followed

---

64. Sanders, *Canon and Community*, 33.
65. Eugene Ulrich and William G. Thompson, "The Tradition as a Resource in Theological Reflection—Scripture and the Minister," in J. D. Whitehead and E. E. Whitehead, *Method in Ministry: Theological Reflection and Christian Ministry* (New York, 1980) 31–52, esp. 36.

by explicit articulation of the judgment. We usually do not have direct witnesses to "what really happened," but later communities' proclamations of the significance of what had been experienced. Even the very early layers of the biblical text are already selected and interpreted repetitions of Israel's traditions.

Thus, though the events behind the biblical account of "the exodus began in human experience," they were not limited to raw, unreflective experience. It was human experience recognized in faith as shaped by God's presence and purpose. That is, it was interpreted and formulated in traditional religious categories, and it was told and retold, shaped and reshaped, in light of the developing needs and worldviews of the believing communities.[66]

I continue with the modern analogy because it is similar to the attitudes and methods of the creative scribes in antiquity who were at once handing on and composing the scriptural text. "Reading the Bible in the process of theological reflection today is also an event of dynamic interaction between the minister and the text.... The dynamic interaction includes several elements: the text and the reader or hearer, each with a definite worldview and each in a particular concrete situation...."[67] The use of Scripture—whether homiletical or liturgical, whether ancient or contemporary—involves a tripolar dynamic of interaction between the traditional text, the contemporary cultural situation, and the experience of the minister within the community. This tripolar dynamic is a reflection of, and is in faithful continuity with, the process by which the Scriptures were composed.[68]

Returning to the creative biblical scribes, these tradents were actively handing on the tradition, but they were adding to it, enriching it, making it adaptable, up-to-date, relevant, multivalent. One must assume that by and large they knew explicitly what they were doing. Insofar as the scribes were handing on the tradition, they became part of the canonical process: handing on the tradition is a constitutive factor of the canonical process. Sanders refers to this aspect as "repetition."[69] The repetition, in a sense,

66. Ibid., 38–39.
67. Ibid., 40–41.
68. This, by the way, I would see as the theological basis or warrant, if needed, for "conjectural emendation." When Bible translators see ambiguous Hebrew expressions, they must make a decision, an interpretation; they must use their God-given minds to determine as best they can what the meaning is. Translation is an attempt to understand the intention of the "author." The translator must be attentive to the tradition, must understand the culture in which the text originated and has been transmitted, and rely on his or her experience. There clearly are instances where none of the few surviving witnesses preserve the original reading or intended meaning of the author. In such instances the translator must first listen to the three resources just mentioned and then have them vigorously interact and debate with each other. It then becomes the translator's duty to provide the best possible reading, whether by chance attested or not.
69. Sanders, *Canon and Community*, 22.

works like a hammer, pounding home again and again that this material is important. The texts were authoritative texts, and through the traditioning process they were being made more authoritative.[70]

But the scribes were also updating the tradition, contemporizing it, making it relevant. That is, sometimes when the tradition was not adaptable, these scribes *made* it adaptable, thus giving it another of its canonical characteristics, a complementary factor that Sanders terms "resignification."[71] That is, the tradition, important in its original setting, and important in itself beyond its importance for that original concrete situation, is found also to be important to me here and now in my present situation. The tradition proves adaptable, capable of having new significance in this new particular situation. The resignification—insofar as the tradition has proved useful or true—shows that indeed the tradition is *important in itself* (thus genuinely in the category of "tradition") and that it is *important to me* (thus genuinely in the category of "adaptable tradition"). The "authority" of such tradition is not an extraneous characteristic (authority imposed)[72] but is intrinsic (the community recognizes the life-giving power of the tradition).

Conclusion

It remains, then, to sum up how I see textual criticism illuminating the very composition of the canonical Scriptures, that is, illuminating the scribal procedures which in turn constitute an important aspect of the compositional process for the texts of the books which eventually became the canon of Scripture.

The canon as such, as I now see it, is a topic that belongs to the period after the close of the composition of the Scriptures. But aspects of the canonical process can be charted by text-critical research. Textual critics, sparked by the discoveries in the Judean Desert, have been quite active in recent decades. One area of results that I think particularly suggestive is the demonstration that creative scribes produced multiple literary editions of

---

70. This provides another argument, though not a conclusive argument, against calling the material "canonical" at this stage: insofar as the composition is canonical, it should not be changed; it should already be "tradition" and should already be "adaptable" as it is. Also, paradoxically, insofar as the scribes thought they were copying "Scripture," they did not create Scripture; insofar as they thought they were handing on and developing sacred textual traditions, they were creatively producing Scripture.

71. Sanders, *Canon and Community*, 22.

72. One entire avenue that I have not had time to explore here but that deserves exploration is the approach to canonical criticism which sees that part of the present arrangement and certain parts of the content of the text are a direct result of the tradents or scribes vying to establish or enhance the authority of the books or sections they considered more important. Joseph Blenkinsopp has developed this idea in *Prophecy and Canon* (Notre Dame, IN, 1977).

various biblical passages. Though we are grateful for the manuscript remains from the period of 250 B.C.E. to 70 C.E., one must remember that this is but a tiny percentage of the textual activity on biblical literature. Research on the small sampling of surviving evidence shows that this creative scribal activity took different forms—easily recognized in that each of these forms corresponds to well-known procedures by which in even earlier times many parts of the biblical text were produced.

The Book of Exodus displayed harmonization of texts, that is, what one could call "biblical" text added to "biblical" text. The Books of Samuel exhibited both the interweaving of "non-biblical" supplementary traditions into a "biblical" account and possibly the changing or reshaping of a story to present a theologically different portrait. The Book of Jeremiah contained systematic amplification of the entire book of routine minor expansion, although this did not greatly alter the book's overall meaning. One section of the Book of Daniel gave indication that all the extant editions of the book display one or other of two alternative revised editions, both of which are based on an earlier edition no longer preserved.

Many of the procedures that characterize "the canonical process" can be found very early in the composition of the biblical literature and continue to be exercised until well past the latest books accepted into the canon. This is true for the Torah; true for the Former Prophets (it is easier to see if one thinks rather of "the Deuteronomistic History"); true for the Latter Prophets (consider redactional layers of the Book of Amos, the Book of Isaiah, etc.);[73] true for Psalms, Job, Proverbs, Daniel, etc.[74]

The creative scribal work of harmonization and transplanting of text that was observed in Exodus can be seen also in other passages, namely, Isa 2:2-4 || Mic 4:1-4, Obad 1-10 || Jer 49:7-22, etc.[75]

The editorial procedure of weaving into one narrative a quite different version of the same or a similar narrative, observed in 1 Samuel 17-18, is also well known. That is exactly what happened, for example, in the Flood narrative with the versions commonly attributed to the Yahwist and the Priestly editions, and indeed in much of the composition of the Torah and in the far-reaching compositional work of the Deuteronomistic editors.

---

73. See Robert B. Coote, *Amos among the Prophets: Composition and Theology* (Philadelphia, 1981). Note the subtitle of William L. Holladay's book, *Isaiah: Scroll of a Prophetic Heritage* (Grand Rapids, 1978). Note also the description by O. Kaiser, *Isaiah 1-12* (OTL; 2d ed.; trans. J. Bowden; Philadelphia, 1983) 7-8, of the composition by successive layers in the first portion of the Book of Isaiah.

74. This is also true, of course, for the Gospels.

75. Harmonization presupposes that both texts are important in the same or compatible ways, and it presupposes the unity or homogeneity of the two. To put it baldly: sometimes the presupposition behind harmonization is that this text can be juxtaposed to that text because God is the author of both. That presupposition is clearly behind some of the Qumran, New Testament, and rabbinic texts.

And insofar as I am correct concerning 1 Samuel 1–2, one must assume that a number of biblical passages in their present form similarly resulted from a later editor's reshaping of earlier, now lost, narratives for theological motives.

Finally, the general type of creative scribal work which characterizes the revised editions now found in the MT and in the Old Greek of Daniel 4–6 is pervasive and can be seen throughout the Bible. It is, in fact, similar to the secondary edition of Jeremiah on a larger scale. This "later edition" activity represents one of the major ways in which the latter stages of the many texts which come to form the Bible were composed.

Thus, the methods of the late scribes are basically similar to the methods one recognizes in the earlier "authors" and tradents who produced the Scriptures. They were interweaving into traditional materials other material, either their own insightful creations or other available traditions, which they considered important to add for what would now become "the text." These are early and late forms of the same phenomenon, at the early and late stages of the canonical process.[76] What they can teach with a high degree of reliability is that this process was intermittently at work in the development of many parts of the texts of the canonical books where there is no direct evidence to prove it.

---

76. Insofar as this is true, it is another argument for hesitating to speak of "the canonical text" in Childs's sense. The stabilization of the text, which in a developed form is inherited as the Masoretic *textus receptus*, was—not religiously speaking, but textually and historically speaking—an accident of history. I am not aware of any evidence which demonstrates that, for each of the books, the choice of specifically those textual forms which were included in the Masoretic collection was made on any kind of literary, or theological, or other objective criteria. As Childs (*Introduction to the Old Testament as Scripture*, 103) remarks, the MT was not selected because it was "the best, or the most original, Hebrew text."

Qumran
_____

AN ALLEGORICAL AND AUTOBIOGRAPHICAL POEM BY THE *MOREH HAṢ-ṢEDEQ* (1QH 8:4-11)

James H. Charlesworth

The most intriguing passage in the Hodayot is also the most difficult to comprehend. Scholarly exegesis of it, specifically 1QH 8:4-40, has been divided.[1] The purpose of the present essay is to focus upon only a portion of the psalm (1QH 8:4-11), to translate it, to clarify its poetic construction and the meaning of its major symbolic words, to discern if it is an allegory, to present an exegesis of it, and to decide if it is autobiographical. If the psalm is autobiographical, I will then examine if the thought can be traced back to the *môrēh haṣ-ṣédeq*, and, if so, to explore if one can discern his intent and perhaps his history.

Translation of 1QH 8:4-11

In order to focus attention on the Semitic syntax behind the English I present here a literal, yet coherently lucid, translation of 1QH 8:4-11 (asterisks denote the beginning of a line):

Author's note: It is a great pleasure to dedicate this research to Professor Shemaryahu Talmon, a dear friend and cherished colleague, who has contributed significantly to the clarification of both the history of the Qumranians and their founder.

1. Obviously, limitations of space preclude full bibliographical notes and an examination of the entire psalm, 1QH 8:4-40 (which seems to be one long psalm probably written by one author). It is important to stress that we do not know where the psalm ends; it may continue as far as 9:36. J. Carmignac argued that 1QH 8:4-9:36 is one psalm with seven strophies; see his *Les textes de Qumran* (Paris, 1961); and P. Schulz, *Der Autoritätsanspruch des Lehrers der Gerechtigkeit in Qumran* (Meisenheim am Glan, 1974) 27.

4 I [praise you, O Lord, because you]² placed me³
   as⁴ an overflowing fountain in a desert,
   and (as) a spring of water in a land of dryness,⁵

2. Restore the Hodayot formula: [כי אדוני אוד]כה. The first two consonants are visible at the beginning of line 4, and line 3 is *vacat*. See the photograph of column 8 in E. L. Sukenik, אוצר המגילות הגנוזות (*The Treasure of the Hidden Scrolls*) (Jerusalem, 1954), pl. 42. New photographs will be published in J. H. Charlesworth (ed.), *The Dead Sea Scrolls: Hebrew, Aramaic, and Greek Texts with English Translations* (Princeton, in preparation). The restoration of the Hodayot formula was advocated by Sukenik, *Treasure of the Hidden Scrolls*, 42, and by J. Licht, מגילת ההודיות (*The Hodayot Scroll*) (Jerusalem, 1957) 133. Many of the hymns in the Hodayot begin with this formula. All of column 8 was composed by scribe A, who copied everything up to the middle of column 11. For a discussion of the scribes of 1QH see S. Holm-Nielsen, *Hodayot: Psalms from Qumran* (Aarhus, 1960) 9–16.

3. Restore [נ]תתני. A tear and a lacuna obliterate the text at this point. The final four consonants are clear.

4. The most difficult philological decision is confronted here. What does the *beth* before 'an overflowing fountain' mean; and why is it not repeated before 'a spring of water' and before 'the irrigator of the garden'? The easiest translation would be 'by an overflowing fountain', with 'by' placed in parentheses before the second phrase, and the third phrase translated so that the autobiographical meaning is ignored. The allegorical and autobiographical meaning, however, must not be ignored, and the meaning of the psalm must not be blurred. A translation must correspond to its interpretation, and—of course—every translation is an interpretation. Hence, after finishing this essay I returned to the translation and changed my rendering of the opening of this psalm. I now take the problematic *beth* to be an example of the rare so-called *beth essentiae* (see GKC §119i; for the Qumranic extended use of *beth*, see E. Qimron, *The Hebrew of the Dead Sea Scrolls* [HSS 29; Atlanta, 1986] 400.07). It should be translated 'as' or 'in the capacity of' and it denotes identity (see R. J. Williams, *Hebrew Syntax* [Toronto, 1976] 249) or the quality or manner in which a singular subject is shown or shows itself (KB 103). See the probable *beth essentiae* in Deut 26:14 (P. Joüon, *Grammaire de l'hébreu biblique* [Rome, 1923] 404); Exod 6:3, 18:4; Isa 40:10 (=LXX μετὰ ἰσχύος, which is supported by the Peshitta's *bᶜwshn*ᵓ; contrast, however, the scribal emendation in 1QIsaᵃ; see E. Y. Kutscher, *The Language and Linguistic Background of the Isaiah Scroll (1QIsaᵃ)* (STDJ 6; Leiden, 1974) 373); Ps 54:6 ('the Lord is *as* those who uphold my *nepeš*'), 35:2 ('and stand up *as* my help'), and 146:5 ('happy is the one who has the God of Jacob *as* his help'; see M. Dahood, *Psalms III: 101–150* [AB 17a; New York, 1970] 341). The parallelism is in favor of this construction and interpretation. Mystery (*rāz*) is usually linked with a description of the Righteous Teacher; hence 8:11 ('his mystery') refers to him, as does 8:6: he is 'the mysterious water source' beside which are his followers, 'the trees of life'. Long ago A. Dupont-Sommer correctly translated the opening of this psalm (*Les écrits esséniens découverts près de la mer morte* [4th ed.; Paris, 1980] 240):

> Je [te] rends [grâces, ô Adonaï]!
> [Car] tu m'as placé comme une source de fleuves dans un lieu desséché
> et un jaillissement d'eaux dans une terre aride
> et une [ir]rigation de jardin [dans un désert].

It could be objected that '[you] placed me' would demand an object and not *beth essentiae*. The object is clear: the Lord has placed the author 'in a desert as an overflowing fountain, in a land of dryness (as) a spring of water, and (as) the irrigator of the garden.' The object is clear and is almost placarded by this translation; but I prefer to follow the order of the Hebrew in my translation; and not to disturb the flow within the strophes.

5. The implication seems clear: the author is the (source of) water for 'the trees of life'. After completing this article I was led to agree with Dupont-Sommer and Carmignac:

5   and (as) the irrigator[6] * of the garden.[7]
You [have plant]ed[8] a planting of cyprus, and elm,
with cedar together[9] for your glory;
6   (these are) the trees of * life hidden[10]
among all the trees of the water[11]
beside the mysterious water source.
And they caused to sprout the shoot [nṣr][12]
for the eternal planting.
7   Before they shall cause (it) to sprout they strike root,
then send forth their roots to the river [ywbl].
And its trunk[13] shall be open to the living water;
8   and it shall become the eternal fountain.

Dupont-Sommer (*Écrits esséniens*, 240) argued that "le Maître de justice . . . est lui-même la source vivifiante"; Carmignac (*Textes de Qumran*, 236) claimed correctly that "l'ensemble de l'allégorie (surtout line 14) monte que la fontaine représente l'auteur."

6. Read וּמַשְׁקִ֯י (cf. Licht, *Hodayot Scroll*, 133); the *waw* and the curved right vertical stroke of the *mem* can be discerned. There is no need to restore the *mem* (cf. Sukenik, *Treasure of the Hidden Scrolls*, 42). Lit. 'the waterer of' the garden (*Hiphil* part. cstr. sing. of שקי, שקה), or 'cup bearer of' (noun cstr. sing.); the noun obtains the meaning 'irrigation' in rabbinic writings. Sometimes in Qumran, *yod* appears in final position for the single construct state of ל"י verbs. See Qimron, *Hebrew of the Dead Sea Scrolls*, 20. Employing Tiberian vocalization the construct chain would be pointed as follows: וּמַשְׁקֵי גַן. See also the preceeding notes.

7. The images of the Garden of Eden and of Paradise seem to be behind the thought here. The symbolism is more explicit in line 12 with the reference to 'the fiery flame that turns every way' (cf. Gen 3:24).

8. Sukenik (*Treasure of the Hidden Scrolls*) did not restore the words behind the stained leather. Licht (*Hodayot Scroll*) read [רווה אשר נטעת]ה. The final *he* is clear; and the two preceding consonants are barely discernible; read [נט]עָ֯תָ֯ה.

9. Either the author (or possibly another member of the Qumran community) later developed the concept of the *Yaḥad*, 'the community', from such seminal reflections and experiences, or he is alluding to this *terminus technicus* here. See S. Talmon, "The Sectarian יחד—A Biblical Noun," *VT* 3 (1953) 133–40.

10. Lit. 'those who hide themselves' (*Pual*); but the meaning of the hymn seems to be that their hiddenness is not something the trees of life have done. It is their characteristic, possibly due to the predestinarian tone of the major scrolls. See the small monograph on this subject by E. H. Merrill, *Qumran and Predestination: A Theological Study of the Thanksgiving Hymns* (STDJ 8; Leiden, 1975).

11. Note the clear evidence of Qumranic dualism. See the comments on pp. 300–302 about the exegesis of this hymn.

12. As is well known, the term נצר is a highly symbolic term that refers to the coming shoot of David who will bring in the promises of God on this earth. This traditional meaning must not be transported into these verses without careful examination of the precise context of this column.

13. For גיזעו read וגזעו, as in 8:8. The *waw* and *yod* are often indistinguishable in 1QH; the scribe is guilty of metathesis. Sukenik (*Treasure of the Hidden Scrolls*) agreed with my transcription, but as far as I know no one has explained it as I have. Contrast Licht (*Hodayot Scroll*) who read גזעו.

But upon the shoot [nṣr]
every [beast][14] of the forest shall feed.
And its trunk (shall become) a place of trampling
9   for all those who pass over * the way [drk].[15]
And its branches (shall be)[16] for every bird.
And all the tre[es][17] of the water
shall exalt themselves[18] over it,
because they shall become magnified in their planting.
10 But they shall not send forth a root to the river [ywbl].[19]
And he who causes to sprout[20] the hol[y][21] shoot [nṣr]
for the planting of truth is concealed
11 with the result that he is not * esteemed,
and the sealing of his mystery is not perceived.

Poetic Construction

The psalm is composed, under the influence of the Davidic Psalter and Semitic poetry elsewhere, especially in the prophets, according to the rules of *parallelismus membrorum*, which in this psalm is not so loose as elsewhere in the Hodayot. Synonymously parallel, for example, to 'an over-

---

14. Restore חית, with Licht (*Hodayot Scroll*).

15. The term דרך became a *terminus technicus* at Qumran for the community; see my comments on יחד in n. 9. This hymn was probably composed in the middle of the second century B.C.E. By that time possibly, and certainly later, this phrase was understood to mean 'all transgressors of the way'.

16. The meaning seems to be that the branches shall be destroyed or impaired by the birds. Here the translations vary considerably. Cf. Holm-Nielsen, *Hodayot*, " and its foliage (shall be) for all winged birds." Similarly, G. Jeremias, *Der Lehrer der Gerechtigkeit* (Studien zur Umwelt des Neuen Testaments 2; Göttingen, 1963]): "und seine Zweige für alle geflügelten Vögel," Contrast, however, M. Mansoor, *The Thanksgiving Hymns* (STDJ 3; Grand Rapids, 1961): "The road and its branches (shall be trampled) by every winged fowl. . . ." The *parallelismus membrorum* is against Mansoor's translation.

17. Restore [עצ]י. The initial consonant is clear, but the tear and resulting hole have left no trace of other letters. Sukenik (*Treasure of the Hidden Scrolls*) did not restore the form. The restoration was supported by Licht (*Hodayot Scroll*).

18. The form is probably *Hithpael* (to clarify the pejorative sense); the *taw* has probably assimilated to the *reš*, causing a compensatory lengthening of the vowel. Qimron (*Hebrew of the Dead Sea Scrolls*, 311.5) notes only other examples of an assimilated *taw*, but does astutely point out the weakening of *reš* at Qumran (200.14; cf. Kutscher, *Isaiah Scroll*, 531).

19. The implication is that like 'the sons of darkness', according to 1QS 4, the evil trees have no hope or survival.

20. This person is probably to be identified with the one who is the 'irrigator' of the garden; note the causative meaning of the *Hiphil* in both verbal forms.

21. The top right and curved portion of the *qop* is visible to the right of the tear. The *waw* is completely missing. The top left side of a *dalet* or *reš* is visible to the left of the tear; the consonant is probably a *dalet*, because the horizontal stroke is slanted and not somewhat parallel to the line for hanging consonants, as is the case with the *reš*.

flowing fountain in a desert' is 'a spring of water in a land of dryness'. The *Gattung* of this psalm is an individual psalm of thanksgiving ('I [praise you, O Lord, because you] placed me', 8:1) which is mixed with forms from the psalm of lamentation (8:8–10).[22]

The author of this passage is gifted linguistically. For example, he uses different words for 'fountain', 'spring', and 'water source': מקור, מבוע, מעין. He emphasizes the importance of water, especially 'living water' (8:7), which in this psalm, as in the Qumran scrolls generally, in contrast to Biblical Hebrew, means not 'running water', but salvific water that brings eternal life (see 8:7–8).[23] The use of יובל is also indicative of the key concern of the author: his community shall be linked to the 'river' (8:7) but his opponents will not (8:10).

The author's community is the only one which shall send forth the נצר to the eternal source (8:6, 10). All his comments are centered on his community, which is described in agricultural terms[24] as God's eternal planting that God has planted; it is the paradisiac garden (cf. Genesis 1–3).[25] Clearly, the Lord is the one who planted "the planting" (8:5, 6). In contrast, the 'tre[es] of the water' have planted their own 'planting' (8:9). Similar observations led Jeremias to state that the *Stichworten* are "source" and "planting" so that these two provide the *Aufbau* of the *Loblied*.[26]

Allegory

Is this psalm an allegory? The scholarly opinions have varied. Holm-Nielsen warned not to interpret this psalm as if it reflected "the history of the community."

He severely criticizes scholars, like B. Otzen,[27] who interpret this psalm allegorically: "It is a misinterpretation of the text to undertake this sort of allegorisation." He argues that "the lack of clarity in the illustration, with the unmotivated flitting from the illustration of water to that of a plant, from singular to plural, and from the trees of life to the shoot, seems to show that

---

22. See the informed comments by G. Morawe, *Aufbau und Abgrenzung der Loblieder von Qumran: Studien zur gattungsgeschichtlichen Einordnung der Hodayoth* (Berlin, 1961).

23. See my comments on מים חיים in "Les Odes de Salomon et les manuscrits de la mer morte," *RB* 77 (1970) 522–49, esp. 534–38.

24. See S. Talmon's judicious comments about the use of agricultural terms used by the Qumranians to denote "their life-style" in *King, Cult, and Calendar in Ancient Israel* (Jerusalem, 1986) 197.

25. Licht also pointed out that the "description of the trees ... has an allusion to the Garden of Eden"; *Hodayot Scroll*, 133. By the time of the Righteous Teacher the Jewish symbols for the Garden of Eden and Paradise—once separate—had begun to coalesce and present a complex ideological concept.

26. Jeremias, *Der Lehrer der Gerechtigkeit*, 256.

27. B. Otzen, "Takkesalmerne (1QH)," in *Dødehavs teksterne: Skrifter fra den jødiske menighed i Qumran i oversættelse* (ed. E. Nielsen and B. Otzen; Copenhagen, 1959) 99–148.

it is impossible to carry any real allegorical interpretation through. . . ."[28] In contrast, however, Jeremias claimed that it "kann kein Zweifel sein, dass wir eine ausführliche *Allegorie* vor uns haben, deren Auflösung freilich nicht im Text steht, sondern jeweils vom Leser zu vollziehen ist."[29] Licht, Dupont-Sommer, and Carmignac were the first scholars to be convinced that this psalm was an allegory.[30]

Since no meaning can be derived from reading the psalm without some appeal to allegory, it is wise to attempt an interpretation based on a self-critical exploration of the use of allegory by this author, with the recognition that this text demands an interior interpretation: we must attempt to grasp what the psalm would have denoted and connoted to its author and to his earliest followers within the יחד. This task is formidable, because, as Talmon states, in the Qumran scrolls "facts and fancy, historical realism and wishful thinking coalesced indiscriminately."[31]

Exegesis

An interpretation[32] must be guided by the recognition that the psalm was written originally in Hebrew (the language in which it is extant), that the text is marred by lacunas and tears, that the psalm was composed in the second century B.C.E. by one of the leaders of the Qumran community, and that the author was a Jew who knew large portions of the Scriptures by heart, especially Psalms (1:3-4, 80:10, 103:20), Isaiah (11:11; 27:6; 35:7; 40:24; 41:3, 18-19; 44:3; 49:10; 56:9; 58:11; 60:13, 21), Jeremiah (17:8), Ezekiel (17:23 [LXX A]; 31:6, 14), Genesis (3:24), Job (1:10, 5:3, 14:8), and Daniel (4:9). It seems certain that the author of this psalm knew and was influenced by the allegory of the cedar in Ezek 31:14 (as Licht stated long ago):[33]

> All this is in order that no trees by the waters may grow to lofty height or set their tops among the clouds, and that no trees that drink water may reach up to them in height; for they are all given over to death, to the nether world among mortal men, with those who go down to the Pit. [RSV]

---

28. All quotations by Holm-Nielsen in this paragraph are from *Hodayot*, 149. Holm-Nielsen later admitted that some of the Hodayot did reflect personal histories and feelings; some of the compositions thence would be autobiographical; see his "'Ich' in den Hodajoth und die Qumrāngemeinde," in *Qumran-Probleme* (ed. H. Bardtke; Berlin, 1963) 220-21.

29. Jeremias, *Der Lehrer der Gerechtigkeit*, 256.

30. Licht, *Hodayot Scroll*, 131-35. Also, see the notes to the translation. Schulz (*Der Autoritätsanspruch des Lehrers*, 27) also perceived that the psalm was an allegory.

31. Talmon, "The New Covenanters of Qumran," *Scientific American* 225.5 (1971) 77.

32. See the notes to the translation, some of which are necessarily exegetical. Many were added after this essay had been completed and it became clear that the psalm was both allegorical and autobiographical.

33. Licht, *Hodayot Scroll*, 133.

The means to comprehend the psalm, however, is not a detailed study of the origins of the author's symbols and words. One must examine the meaning he intended them to have as he brought them together in the way that he did. He did not produce an exegetical or even a hermeneutical psalm. He did not compose a *pesher*; but using his memory he took up old *tessarae* and created a new mosaic.

What did the author intend to say to whom, and how were they interpreting him? The answers here are readily available only at the preliminary level of research. The author intended to tell the members of his community—the Qumran covenanters—that they were God's elect and that the Lord is to be praised for what he has done and is about to do on their behalf. They were the eschatological community; but he exhorted them, through revelatory poetic phrases that the trees would not bloom immediately (they are planted and waiting for the root to supply sufficient 'living water') and that the greatness of the community was assured and part of the present dimension of the future (the roots are hidden but present).[34] Subsequently, in private and public meetings his followers probably read, recited, and chanted this psalm to celebrate—and reinforce—the belief that they were God's eternal planting, 'the planting of truth'.

Given these broad strokes, what other meanings seem obvious? First, there is a strong dualism: 'the trees of life' and 'the trees of the water'. Second, the thought is eschatological, since the 'trunk' is to 'become the eternal fountain' (8:7-8).

At this point a flood of questions arise. Is not the preceding comment an example of mixed metaphors? The answer seems to be, "Not necessarily," since the 'trunk' when linked to the 'living water' can be said to become the conduit for the water and hence 'the eternal fountain'.

Why did the author use 'trees' to express his dualism here, when elsewhere at Qumran, especially in 1QS 3:13-4:26, we read about a light-darkness paradigm: 'the sons of light' and 'the sons of darkness'? How can there be an antithesis, similar to the one that separates the contraities 'light' and 'darkness', when both 'water' and 'life' are positive and desirable symbolic words in this hymn? Is it not difficult to understand either 'the trees of life' of 'the trees of the water' as pejorative?

If one of these constructs denotes the author's own community, then which is it? The answer is contained in lines 6-7. The 'trees of life' are the ones that are 'hidden among all the trees of the water'. That statement clarifies that 'the trees of the water' denote a large group of which 'the trees of life' are only one element. It is the 'trees of life' that 'caused to sprout the shoot for the eternal planting,' because they 'send forth their roots to the river' and are 'open to the living water.' The little group of 'trees of life'

---

34. See the excellent exegetical comments by Licht, ibid., 133-34.

suffer: they are devoured, trampled upon, and bruised (8:8-9).³⁵ Moreover 'the trees of the water' are proud, exalt themselves (8:9), and magnify themselves (8:9).³⁶ While 'the trees of life' send forth 'their roots to the river' (8:7), 'the trees of the water' do 'not send forth a root to the river' (8:10). Hence, the author's community is represented by the metaphor 'the trees of life.'³⁷

This exegesis raises one serious objection. How can 'the trees of the water' then be a negative term? Is not the water symbolism against such an interpretation? Are not both 'life' and 'water' positive symbols in this psalm, and stressed by the salvific meaning of 'living water' (8:7)? This question leads into issues related to the possibility that the psalm is autobiographical.

Autobiography

It is slowly becoming clear that in some ways this psalm is autobiographical. Note how the author refers to himself, and in terms that are not generic but specific:

1. He has been placed by the Lord as a fountain in a desert.
2. He is the irrigator of the garden, which is a symbolic way of referring to the eschatological community of which he is the founder and to which he is passionately devoted.
3. He is the one, who through the Lord, 'causes to sprout the hol[y] shoot for the planting of truth' (8:10).
4. He is thence the one who is 'concealed' and 'not esteemed' (8:10-11).
5. He possesses a mystery that is 'not perceived' (8:11).

These comments are so specific that it seems probable that in this psalm "eine erkennbare Einzelpersönlichkeit spricht."³⁸ They were most likely composed by some leader who has not been given the honor and recognition that seems appropriate, at least to the author himself. Recognizing that the Qumranians did not write historical works, like 1 Maccabees or Josephus's *Antiquities*,³⁹ let me now ask the following key question: Is it possible that this author is the Moreh haṣ-Ṣedeq?

---

35. Licht (ibid., 133) also drew attention to this dimension of the allegory.

36. Licht (ibid.) also saw the allegorical and autobiographical character of the psalm. He perceived that 'trees of the water' are the wicked.

37. Jeremias wisely concluded that the psalm portrays the following picture: "Auf der einen Seite stehen die feindlichen Wasserbäume—auf der anderen Seite die Lebensbäume, die den heiligen Spross hervorbringen"; *Der Lehrer der Gerechtigkeit*, 260.

38. Ibid., 173.

39. Long ago F. Cross astutely saw that the Qumran scrolls do not contain a "document which can be called properly a historical work. Historiography was not an interest of the sect's authors"; *The Ancient Library of Qumran and Modern Biblical Studies* (rev. ed.; Grand Rapids, 1980) 109.

Among many Qumran specialists today, there is wide agreement about the general features of the Moreh haṣ-Ṣedeq,[40] thanks to the publications of Jeremias, Stegemann, Murphy-O'Connor, and other scholars.[41] I summarize the consensus as follows:

1. While it is not clear that ultimately the Qumranians can be traced back to a group of returnees from Babylon (as Murphy-O'Connor contends), it is certain that the group antedated the leadership of the Righteous Teacher (CD 1:1–12). It is conceivable that the Qumranians were once associated with the Hasidim (1 Maccabees).
2. The Righteous Teacher and the Qumranians were priests. Before being exiled at Qumran they officiated as priests in the temple cult.[42]
3. The Righteous Teacher and his earliest followers were in the lineage of the high priest and they could trace their ancestry back to Zadok (CD 3:19–4:4a). It is not impossible that the Righteous Teacher had served sometime as high priest, perhaps even during the sacerdotal interregnum of 159 to 152 B.C.E. (*Antiquities* 20:10), as Stegemann, Murphy-O'Connor, Knibb, and others have concluded.
4. The Righteous Teacher and his closest followers were expelled from the temple, sometime around the middle of the second century B.C.E., and eventually found refuge at what is now Khirbet Qumran. They lived in tents on the marl terrace or in the caves to the west of the Dead Sea.
5. The Righteous Teacher was persecuted by 'the wicked priest', probably the reigning high priest, and by 'the man of lies', perhaps the leader of a group that splintered away from the Qumranians, conceivably at the time of the exodus from Jerusalem. The Righteous Teacher may have been injured by 'the wicked priest' on the Day of Atonement, according to the Qumran calendar (1QpHab 11:5–8).[43]
6. The Righteous Teacher was the revered authoritarian leader at Qumran. As Talmon perceived, "He is presented as a priestly preceptor invested with the spirit of prophecy." He embodies more than one of the types of religious virtuosi described by M. Weber,[44] and "in his personality *Amtscharisma* coalesces with

---

40. Obviously there is considerable debate over the elements in the consensus; but here I intend to build upon the strong areas of agreement. They are considerable and impressive, and are often lost in scholarly debates.

41. See my discussion in "The Origin and Subsequent History of the Authors of the Dead Sea Scrolls: Four Transitional Phases among the Qumran Essenes," *RevQ* 10 (1980) 213–33. See also M. A. Knibb, *The Qumran Community* (Cambridge, 1987); and P. R. Callaway, *The History of the Qumran Community: An Investigation* (Journal for the Study of the Pseudepigrapha Supplement 3; Sheffield, 1988).

42. Knibb rightly states, in my opinion, that "the emergence of the Essenes is to be associated with the activities of Jews living in Palestine"; *Qumran Community*, 8.

43. Here I wish to acknowledge Talmon as one of the leading experts on the Qumran calendar. His publications on the subject are well known, and can be seen in the list of his publications in this *Festschrift*.

44. See especially M. Weber's "The Pariah Community," in *Ancient Judaism* (trans. H. H. Gerth and D. Martindale; New York, 1952) 336–55; idem, "The Sociology of Charismatic Authority," in *From Max Weber: Essays in Sociology* (trans. H. H. Gerth and C. W. Mills; New York, 1958) 245–52; idem, *The Sociology of Religion* (trans. E. Fischoff; Boston,

persönliche Berufung."[45] Hence, it is misleading to label him simply a charismatic prophet. He was, however, claimed by the Qumranians to be the prophet expected in the end day, or at the יום יהוה, by many Jews (Mal 3:23, 1 Macc 14:41).[46]

7. The Righteous Teacher was primarily an interpreter of Scripture. God had revealed to him "all the mysteries of the words of the prophets" (1QpHab 7:4–5). He was not an innovator, but a teacher who possessed the key to the mysteries of God's word.[47] His interpretation was eschatological. Decades ago Cross wisely contended that the "tradition of Essene exegesis was initiated, no doubt, by the founder of" the Qumran community.[48]

The leader of the Qumranians was not thence "the Teacher of Righteousness," as if he taught the need for righteousness above any other religious virtue. He was "the Righteous Teacher," in contrast to false leaders in Israel who were not to be trusted, and who did not understand the meaning of God's word.

Summary

It should now be obvious that there is significant correlation with the list of five autobiographical elements in the psalm and the list of seven elements of consensus regarding the Righteous Teacher. The psalm was obviously written sometime in the second century B.C.E. by one of the early leaders of the Qumran community. Was the author the Moreh haṣ-Ṣedeq?

Recognizing that historical research, especially when it is based on autobiographical comments in a psalm, can never produce certainty, one undeniable point in favor of the possibility that the author is the Moreh haṣ-Ṣedeq is the authoritative, powerful personality behind the words. We know that the Qumran community was founded by the actions of an allegiance to one charismatic, prophetic figure, the Moreh haṣ-Ṣedeq.

Is there not a key that will help move such a possibility to impressive probability? There are in fact two, and neither has so far been grasped and utilized.

The first key is the problem confronted when facing the exegesis of 'the trees of the water' (8:6). Who are they? Can they really be antithetical to

---

1963). These handy English versions draw attention to more definitive publications in the original German.

45. Both quotations by Talmon are from *King, Cult, and Calendar*, 198

46. K. Schubert wrote, "Für die Qumran-Essener war nun der Lehrer der Gerechtigkeit dieser erwartete letzte Prophet"; see his *Die Qumran-Essener* (Uni-Taschenbücher 224; Munich, 1982) 100.

47. As Talmon states, the Righteous Teacher "seemingly did not innovate any religious concepts and maxims, but rather was an inspired interpreter of the traditional lore"; see *King, Cult, and Calendar*, 199.

48. Cross, *Ancient Library of Qumran*, 113.

the author's own community, 'the trees of life' (8:6)? If antithetical, can they really be pejorative, when 'water' is a central appreciative term both in this psalm and throughout the major scrolls? How is it possible in 'trees of the water' to comprehend both the esteem and contempt held by the author?

The *terminus technicus* 'the trees of the water' may denote one of three possibilities. First, it may refer to the group of 'the man of lies' who separated from the Qumranians. This possibility is to be dismissed, because 'trees of the water' is not the smaller, but the larger group 'among' which 'the trees of life' are 'hidden' (8:6). It is also unlikely that a Qumran leader would have held in esteem such an apostate group. Second, it is possible that 'the trees of the water' are the masses, the Jews generally. This was the position suggested by Jeremias: "Die Wasserbäume . . . sind also das Normale, Gewöhnliche, die Umwelt, die das Aussergewöhnliche verdeckt."[49] This possibility does not explain the tension between esteem and contempt in the psalm, the refusal of the Qumranians to have commerce with others,[50] and the major point that 'the trees of life' are not merely בתוך 'the trees of the water'; they are מחובאים 'among all the trees of the water' (8:6).

The only satisfactory solution is to perceive that 'the trees of the water' are the priests officiating in the temple cult. These are the former associates and colleagues of the Righteous Teacher; hence the esteem and connection with 'water'. They are, however, related to the Hasmonean rulers who caused the expulsion of the Righteous Teacher and his followers from the temple. The Righteous Teacher and his followers, despite their priestly lineage, could no longer gather together without the permission of the illegitimate Hasmonean "high priest." Whether Jonathan or Simon was 'the wicked priest', whether this *terminus technicus* is mere typologic, whether it may refer first to Jonathan and then to Simon, one thing is clear: after Simon was elevated to full control of the temple, the Righteous Teacher and his priestly associates could not longer convene, gather together, or ἐπισυστρέψαι συστροφὴν (1 Macc 14:44). But, perhaps—one must ask— did the Righteous Teacher continue to have some dialogue, or connection, with the ruling priests, not necessarily the Hasmonean high priest, in the temple?

The second key for interpreting the autobiographical meaning of this psalm, mentioned earlier, is the one which clinches the identification, and

49. Jeremias, *Der Lehrer der Gerechtigkeit*, 257.

50. Note the numerous points made by L. Schiffman in the following valid summary: "Over and over we are told that only the sect and its leadership is capable of properly interpreting Jewish law. All other groups and their sins are catalogued so as to explain the necessity for the physical and spiritual separation of the sect from the rest of the people of Israel. We also learn of the role of the *moreh ṣedeq*, the 'correct teacher,' who, along with the Zadokite priests, led the confused initial members to the path of truth"; *Sectarian Law in the Dead Sea Scrolls* (BJS 33; Chico, CA, 1983) 7.

raises to the highest level of historical probability that 1QH 8:4-11 was composed by the Righteous Teacher. The conciliatory tone of the psalm is remarkable. This selfsame tone of a conciliator has recently led J. Strugnell and E. Qimron to argue that *Miqṣat Maʿaśe Hattorah* (4QMMT) is a letter composed around 150 B.C.E. and sent to the officiating priests in the Jerusalem cult, by none other than the Righteous Teacher.[51]

Conclusion

In conclusion, there is impressive cumulative evidence that this allegorical and autobiographical psalm was composed by the Righteous Teacher,[52] who looking around the 'desert' and 'land of dryness' at Qumran (8:4),[53] thanked God for the 'overflowing fountain' and 'spring of water' given to his fellow priests, through him, 'the irrigator' of the eternal garden. His self-understanding and feeling are extremely personal and evocative not only to his followers, who probably knew this psalm by heart, but to many sensitive readers today, removed from him by more than two thousand years. He reminisces about his former colleagues, 'the trees of the water' who did not recognize the revelation bestowed upon him. He and his followers—'the holy ones' and the 'most holy ones'—were sadly 'hidden among all the trees of the water', who regrettably even exalted themselves (8:9) over them. He was 'not esteemed' and 'his mystery'—the mystery given to him by God to be the first to understand 'all the mysteries of the words of the prophets'—was 'not perceived' (8:11). He and his followers are 'the trees of life' because they are alive, and alone possess the source of life.

---

51. According to my notes of a lecture given by E. Qimron at Princeton in 1987, 4Q171 contains palpable evidence that around 150 B.C.E. the leading Qumran priest, probably the Righteous Teacher, sent the following to the leading Jerusalem priest, whom Qimron is convinced is 'the wicked priest': "We have sent you some of the precepts of the Torah that we consider important for your welfare and those of the people." Hence, there must have been some continuing discussions with the earliest Qumranians and their associates in the temple cult. The arguments were centered on the meaning of certain laws (*halakot*), especially those that pertained to the calendar and the temple. I wish to express appreciation to Professors Strugnell and Qimron for permission to refer obliquely to this important text, which should be available soon, and also to acknowledge numerous fruitful and enjoyable conversations with them. The roughly 120 lines of the fragments from Cave 4 have no yet been published; see, for the present, the photograph and preliminary discussion in E. Qimron and J. Strugnell, "An Unpublished Halakhic Letter from Qumran," *Israel Museum Journal* 4 (1985) 9-12.

52. These insights may sway some specialists who have been unduly influenced by the skepticism of G. Vermes and B. Kittel, who see only vague poetic strains in 1QH. See Vermes, "The Essenes and History," *JJS* 32 (1981) 18-31; and Kittel, *The Hymns of Qumran* (SBLDS 50; Chico, CA, 1981) 8-12.

53. P. R. Davies rightly traces 1QH 8:4-11 back to the Righteous Teacher, and concludes that in these lines "he perhaps offers us a view of his place of retreat..."; *Qumran* (Grand Rapids, 1982) 89.

These observations, and this research, transport us back over two millenia to an eyewitness, the one who failed in his struggle to restore the traditional link with David's high priest and to purify the temple cult. The eyewitness report is synchronous with the epochal historical events of the second century B.C.E., and displays the spirit and ethos of the Righteous Teacher. We are even confronted by the intent, personal history, devotion to God, and feeling of the מורה הצדק.

TWO NOTES ON THE APOCRYPHAL PSALMS

Jonas C. Greenfield

After the initial publication of the Apocryphal Psalms found in the Psalms Scroll from Qumran Cave 11 there was a flurry of publication dealing with these psalms.[1] One of the important points made by various scholars was that these psalms were replete with words, terms, and usages which were best known and explained from Late Biblical Hebrew, Ben Sira, Mishnaic Hebrew, and Aramaic.[2] The two notes presented here center about words with which I have had occasion to deal recently. The intent is not to present a new interpretation of these verses, but to focus attention on their proper meaning.

11QPs^a xix:14–16

In the "Plea for Deliverance" (11QPs^a xix) we read:[3]

14–15	רוח אמונה ודעת חונני	אל אתקלה בעויה
15	אל תשלט בי שטן	ורוח טמאה
15–16	מכאוב ויצר רע	אל ירשו בעצמי

This was translated by Sanders as follows:

    14–15   Vouchsafe me a spirit of faith and knowledge,
                and let me not be dishonoured in ruin.
    15   Let not Satan rule over me,
                nor an unclean spirit;

---

1. E.g., J. A. Sanders, *The Psalms Scroll of Qumrân Cave 11 (11QPs^a)* (DJD 4; Oxford, 1965); idem, *The Dead Sea Psalms Scroll* (Ithaca, NY, 1967).
2. Reference to some of these studies will be found in the notes below. Shemaryahu Talmon was among those who noted this important feature of these texts in his study of (Syriac) Psalm I (= 11QPs^a 151) in *Tarbiz* 35 (1965–66) 214–34 [Hebrew].
3. Sanders, *Psalms Scroll*, 76–79.

15–16   Neither let pain nor the evil inclination
        take possession of my bones.

Most of the other published translations do not differ greatly.[4] It was, however, pointed out soon after the initial publication that the verb אתקלה in line 15 was to be vocalized אֶתָּקְלָה, the *Niphal* of the root תקל, with the meaning 'to stumble'.[5] This verb is well known in Mishnaic Hebrew, and is already found in Ben Sira 15:12. Reading the word that follows as בעויה, rather than Sanders's בעווה,[6] this verset must then be translated 'and let me not stumble in transgression'.

The first half of the next line has a parallel in a Qumran fragment of the Aramaic *Testament of Levi* (4QTLevi[a]).[7] It is a line whose first half is preserved in Aramaic, but in its entirety in Greek:

אל תשלט בי כל שטן

And let not any satan have power over me
(to make me stray from your path).[8]

It is clear from this passage and from others in the *Testaments of the Twelve Patriarchs* that Satan, as such, is not meant, but rather a satan or a demon, that is, an evil spirit that can beset a person and lead him astray. In all likelihood the same is true of the passage under discussion here, and the proper translation should be satan rather than Satan. This argues also for interpreting רוח טמאה as רוּחַ טְמֵאָה 'an unclean spirit' rather than רוּחַ טֻמְאָה 'spirit of impurity' with Zech 13:2.[9] It also indicates that יצר רע in the following verset should be translated 'an evil inclination' rather than 'the evil inclination'; this would fit better with מכאוב 'pain' at the beginning of

---

4. E.g., G. Vermes, *The Dead Sea Scrolls in English* (3d ed.; Sheffield, 1987) 212.

5. Fragments of the "Plea for Deliverance" were published by J. van der Ploeg, "Fragments d'un manuscrit de psaumes de Qumran (11QPs[b])," *RB* 74 (1967) 409. For the text under study here only the word אתקלה was fully preserved.

6. Sanders reads עווה but in a note queries: "Read עויה (cf. Dan 4:24)?" Examination of the plate shows that the correct reading is עויה. There is a clear distinction between *waw* and *yod*. This word is an Aramaism. For אתקלה see, among others, the review of Sanders's *Psalms Scroll* by J. A. Goldstein in *JNES* 26 (1967) 307, where the Ben Sira passage is cited.

7. This was first published by J. T. Milik, "Le Testament de Lévi en araméen," *RB* 62 (1955) 400, line 17. The comparison of the two passages was made by D. Flusser, "Qumran and Jewish 'Apotropaic' Prayers," *Israel Exploration Journal* 16 (1966) 197–200 (reprinted in his *Judaism and the Origins of Christianity* [Jerusalem, 1988] 217–20). See also M. Weinfeld, "The Morning Prayers (*Birkhoth Hashachar*) in Qumran and in the Conventional Jewish Liturgy," *RevQ* 13 (1988) 492–93.

8. The translation is that of J. C. Greenfield and M. E. Stone, "The Aramaic and Greek Fragments of a Levi Document," in *The Testaments of the Twelve Patriarchs: A Commentary* (ed. H. W. Hollander and M. de Jonge; Leiden, 1985) 459. The translation of the second part of the line from Greek is in parentheses.

9. As suggested by Goldstein (*JNES* 26 [1967] 306–7) on the basis of that passage.

that verset. The last words of this verse, אל ירשו בעצמי, also deserve further discussion. Sanders had obviously derived ירשו from ירש and translated it as 'take possession'. But the use of ירש for taking possession of the land cannot be extended to the possession of a person by pain or evil. Instead, the root here, as has been noted, is רשה.[10] This root is not found in Biblical Hebrew, but it is found in Ben Sira and Mishnaic Hebrew, as well as in Akkadian, Aramaic, and Phoenician. As I have discussed the semantic development of this root in detail elsewhere, suffice it to say that the basic stem means 'to acquire, have control/power over' and in the causative' to empower, permit, etc.'.[11] Thus, in the much quoted Ben Sira 3:22 we read:

במה שהורשית(ה) התבונן   ואין לך עסק בנסתרות

Consider that which has been permitted to you,
and have no concern with what is hidden.

The causative is also found in the Damascus Document (11:18–20).[12]

The root רשה is used as a virtual synonym of the more common שלט. In legal contexts they are often interchanged, thus in some texts a person is רשאי / רשי, that is, 'is empowered' or 'has control over', and in other texts the term שליט is used. In the divorce document from Wadi Murabbaʿat (P. Mur. xix:17–18) the woman is addressed with רשיא בנפשכי 'having control over yourself', that is, she may in the future be married to whomsoever she wishes.[13] In the standard divorce document (גט) known from Gaonic times, and in use today, the form is expanded to רשאה ושלטאה. This was not really a late innovation for these two terms are found together twice in an as yet unpublished document (P. Yadin 7) from the Babatha archive of Naḥal Ḥever. In this double document (גט מקושר) after his death Babatha's father gives his property, or better, what will remain of it, to his wife and declares (outer text, line 24) that after his death she will be רשיה ושליטה באתרי מתנתא דא או במה די אשבוק מנהון, 'in full control over the places of this gift or what I will leave of them'. In this document a dwelling is provided for Babatha if she becomes a widow, but there is a limitation (lines 39–40): ולא רשיה ולא שליטה תהוא למנעלו לביתא הו בעל, 'she is not empowered to bring a husband into that house'.

---

10. Ibid., 307; and R. Polzin, "Notes on the Dating of the Non-Massoretic Psalms of 11QPsa," *HTR* 60 (1967) 469–70.

11. See J. C. Greenfield, "Studies in the Terminology of the Nabatean Funerary Inscriptions," in *Henoch Yalon Memorial Volume* (ed. E. Y. Kutscher, S. Lieberman, M. Z. Kaddari; Ramat Gan, 1974) 79–82 [Hebrew].

12. See C. Rabin, *The Damascus Documents* (Oxford, 1954) 58–59.

13. Published in P. Benoit, J. T. Milik, and R. de Vaux, *Les Grottes de Murabbaʿât* (DJD 2; Oxford, 1961) 104–9; and *Inscriptions Reveal: Documents from the Time of the Bible, the Mishna and the Talmud* (Jerusalem, 1973) no. 189, p. 200 (English translation, pp. 90–91).

In the various Aramaic dialects there is a preference for the use of one root over the other. Thus שלט is found in all the dialects, but due to diverse semantic development רשה has, at times, in some of the dialects a divergent meaning. The use of רשה in parallelism with שלט is a good example of the breakup of a stereotyped phrase, in this case taken from the legal language of the period.

In the light of this discussion of the use of שלט and רשה, the following translation for these lines is proposed:

> Grant me a spirit of faithfulness and knowledge,
> and let me not stumble in transgression.
> Let not a satan rule over me,
> nor an unclean spirit;
> let pain and evil inclination
> not have control over me.

11QPs^a 155:5–8

In (Syriac) Psalm III (= 11QPs^a 155), lines 5–8 deserve further consideration.[14] Sanders, following the Syriac text, has set the lines in the following order, with English translation:

5 בנה נפשי ואל תמגרה
6 ואל תפרע לפני רשעים
7 גמולי הרע ישיב ממני דין האמת
8 ה' אל תשפטני כחטאתי כי לוא יצדק לפניך כול חי

> Edify my soul and do not cast it down
> And abandon (it) not in the presence of the wicked.
> May the Judge of Truth remove from me the rewards of evil,
> O Lord, judge me not according to my sins;
>   for no man is righteous before thee.

Although at first blush the verb 'edify' to translate בנה seems successful, there is nevertheless a misleading element in the choice of this word.[15] The reader who may have no Hebrew would not know that the archaic meaning of edify (i.e., build) is being used here and would undoubtedly think that the contemporary usage of instruct or improve is meant.[16]

---

14. Sanders, *Psalms Scroll*, 70–72.
15. P. W. Skehan, "A Broken Acrostic and Psalm 9," *CBQ* 27 (1965) 2; and J. Strugnell, "Notes on the Text and Transmission of the Apocryphal Psalms 151, 154 (= Syr. II) and 155 (= Syr. III)," *HTR* 59 (1966) 277.
16. Strugnell ("Apocryphal Psalms," 277) suggested translating בנה as 'build up', while Goldstein (*JNES* 26 [1967] 306) preferred 'restore my soul'. Both J. Magne ("Le Psaume 155," *RevQ* 9 [1977–78] 106) and J. Auffret ("Structure littéraire et interprétation du Psaume 155 de

The verb מגר in the second part of the line shows that a more literal translation such as 'build, raise up' is required. Also, מגר is stronger than 'cast down' as the following examination of its use will show. In Biblical Hebrew it is limited to one passage: השבת מטהרו וכסאו לארץ מגרתה (Ps 89:45). The first verset is difficult and a variety of emendations have been proposed. Since two symbols of authority, the scepter and the throne, are found together in royal inscriptions, literary texts, and imprecations, it is plausible that in this line the original was something like: שברת מטה הדו וכסאו לארץ מגרתה, 'You broke his glorious staff, and hurled his throne to the ground'.[17] In the Targumim מגר serves as the translation of (1) the causative of נפל in Gen 49:17 and Ezek 39:3; (2) שמט 2 Kgs 9:33; (3) הרס in Isa 22:19; (4) the causative of שחח in Isa 25:12; (5) the Pa‘el of צמת in Ps 119:139; and (6) the causative of צמת in Ps 101:5, 8; 143:12. It also functions well as the opposite of בנה. This is the use of מגר in Ezra 6:12, ימגר כל מלך ועם די ישלח ידה להשניה לחבלה, where the punishment ומגר fits the crime חבלה. These two verbs are found together in the petition of the Jews of Elephantine to rebuild their temple. They report that it had been standing even before Cambyses came to Egypt: וכזי כנבוזי על למצרין אגורא זך בנה השכח ואגורי אלהי מצריו כל מגרו ואיש מנדעם באגורא זך לא חבל, 'And when Cambyses entered Egypt he found that temple built, and they destroyed all the temples of the gods of Egypt, but no one damaged anything in that temple'.[18] The Syriac version of this psalm also took the verse quite literally: בנה נפשי ולא תחרביה.

The second line is problematic, for the meaning of ואל תפרע is not evident. Sanders translated it "and do not abandon (it)," following the use of פרע in Ps 88:15 and Prov 4:14–15. The Syriac, following the use of פרע in Aramaic (and Mishnaic Hebrew) as 'uncover, reveal' translated ולא תגלוה as 'and do not uncover it'.[19] An examination of the following lines might prove useful for understanding this line.[20] As was noted by various scholars, there is an imbalance in the size of the lines and also a disruption of the

---

la Grotte 11 de Qumran," *RevQ* 9 [1977–78] 325) offer "restaure mon âme." But "restore" and "restaure" properly translate other verbs in the psalms.

17. See J. C. Greenfield, "Scriptures and Inscription: The Literary and Rhetorical Element in Some Early Phoenician Inscriptions," in *Near Eastern Studies in Honor of William Foxwell Albright* (ed. H. Goedicke; Baltimore, 1971) 254–58.

18. See B. Porten and J. C. Greenfield, *Jews of Elephantine and Arameans of Syene (Fifth Century B.C.E.): Fifty Aramaic Texts with Hebrew and English Translations* (Jerusalem, 1976) 90 (= text 30, lines 13–14 in A. Cowley, *Aramaic Papyri of the Fifth Century B.C.* [Oxford, 1923]). I should note that the root מגר is recorded by native Syriac lexicographers such as Bar Bahlul, but it does not occur in known texts.

19. W. Baars's edition of the Apocryphal Psalms is found in *The Old Testament in Syriac according to the Peshiṭta Version*, vol. 4.6 (Leiden, 1972). The passage under discussion is on p. 9.

20. Strugnell ("Apocryphal Psalms," 277–78) suggested pointing this word as תִּפָּרַע and translating it as 'let it not be laid bare'—but this does not make sense.

acrosticon. The verse division and rearrangement of versets suggested by Skehan is preferable:

5	בנה נפשי ואל תמגרה	[6] ואל תפרע לפני רשעים	
7	גמולי הרע השיב ממני²¹	(כי לא יצדק לפניך כל חי)²²	
8	דין אמת ה'²³	אל תשפטני כחטאתי	

If seen in this light it is clear that the writer asks God to not punish him for his misdeeds. The words גמולי הרע do not mean 'the rewards of evil' but 'retribution for evil deeds'.²⁴ One of the two verbs usually found with גמול in Biblical Hebrew is the causative of שוב, and it usually means 'to punish someone for his evil deeds'. In this verset the direction of the idiom is changed by the use of ממני. The writer asks God as the "judge of truth" not to punish him for his acts.

In the light of vv. 7 and 8, the verb תפרע must be taken as yet another instance of the writer using a verb known to us from Mishnaic Hebrew, in this case פרע with the meaning 'to pay, requite', as noted by some scholars.²⁵ The *Niphal* with the nuance 'to exact payment, punishment' or simply 'to punish' fits the needs of the verse best. וְאַל תִּפָּרַע would then mean 'and do not exact punishment'.

These lines, following Skehan's rearrangement, should be translated in this manner:

> Raise up my soul and do not tear it down,
> and do not exact punishment in the presence of the wicked.
> Turn away from me my recompense for evil,
> for before you no creature is in the right.
> O Lord, judge of truth,
> do not judge me according to my sins.

---

21. As noted by Skehan ("Broken Acrostic and Psalm 9," 3), the Syriac has ʾaphēk, and this must be for השיב. Since throughout the psalm direct address is used, I would agree with Skehan and Goldstein (*JNES* 26 [1967] 306) that this was probably the original reading.

22. In the Qumran text this line, which is also found in Ps 142:2b, is the second verset of line 8. If these lines are left in place when דין האמת is shifted to the beginning of line 8, then the line is clearly too long. It should be noted that the Syriac version agrees with the Qumran text here.

23. That דין האמת followed by the tetragrammaton begins the *dalet* line was seen by B. Uffenheimer ("Psalms 192, 193 from Qumran," *Molad* 22 [1964] 13 [Hebrew]; who refers to an article on this psalm by A. M. Haberman in *Haʾaretz*, 10 July 1964), Skehan ("Broken Acrostic and Psalm 9," 2–3), and Hurwitz ("Observations on the Language of the Third Apocryphal Psalm from Qumran," *RevQ* 5 [1964–66] 227).

24. As seen by Uffenheimer ("Psalms," 12) and Goldstein (*JNES* 26 [1967] 306).

25. Uffenheimer ("Psalms," 13), Goldstein (*JNES* 26 [1967] 306), and Hurwitz ("Third Apocryphal Psalm from Qumran," 228).

A NEGLECTED MEANING OF THE VERB כול AND THE TEXT OF 1QS VI:11–13

Alexander Rofé

The Meaning of כול

One of the meanings assigned to the verb כול by BDB is 'hold in, restrain' for the *Pilpel* stem and 'hold in' for the *Hiphil*. This acceptation deserves a few words of illustration and explanation.

Jer 2:13:

... אתי עזבו
מקור מים חיים
לחצב להם בארות
בארת נשברים
אשר לא יָכִלוּ המים

They have forsaken me, a spring of living water, and hewed them out cisterns, cracked cisterns, which cannot hold the water.

The description of the cisterns as cracked does not call into question their capacity, but their impermeability; the cisterns are cracked, and therefore leak. יָכִלוּ here means 'hold in, retain'.

Jer 6:11:

ואת חמת ה' מלאתי
נלאיתי הכיל
שפך על עולל בחוץ
ועל סוד בחורים יחדיו

But I am filled with the wrath of the LORD, I cannot hold it in. Pour it on the infant in the street and on the gang of youngsters together.

Author's note: It is a pleasure to present this essay to Shemaryahu Talmon, who put the academic community in his debt with his outstanding contributions to the understanding of

The prophet cannot *retain* the wrath of the Lord; against his own will, it spills over onto his fellow citizens, even the most innocent of them, such as infants playing in the street.

Jer 20:9:
ואמרתי לא אזכרנו
ולא אדבר עוד בשמו
והיה בלבי כאש בערת
עצר בעצמתי ונלאיתי כַּלְכֵּל ולא אוכל

I thought: "I will not mention him, no more will I speak in his name." But [his word] was like a raging fire in my heart, shut up in my bones, I could not hold it in, nor could I endure.

The *Pilpel* stem of כול here expresses the same idea as the *Hiphil* in Jer 6:11: Jeremiah cannot *repress* the word of the Lord, although its utterance brings shame and contempt upon him. Not being contained, the word of the Lord bursts forth from the prophet against his will.

In post-biblical Hebrew, as attested by Ben Sira, this meaning of the root כול appears to have been preserved in the reflexive stems *Hitpalpel* and *Hitpolel* as well:

Sir 12:15b MS A: עד עת עמד לא יופיע ואם נמוט לא יתכלכל

LXX: ὥραν μετὰ σοῦ διαμενεῖ
καὶ ἐὰν ἐκκλίνῃς, οὐ μὴ καρτερήσῃ

Neither the Hebrew nor the Greek are intelligible; both, however, appear to preserve elements of the original which may be reconstructed as follows:[1]

עת תעמד עמך יעמד ואם תמוט לא יתכלכל

While you stand, he will stand by you, but if you falter, he will not contain himself.

The subject of this passage is the concealed enemy. He pretends to assist his friend while successful, but as soon as the friend falters, his enemy cannot *contain* or *repress* his rancor.

---

the Dead Sea Scrolls. Some of his important studies were dedicated to semantic or textual aspects of the new discoveries; I shall try to pursue this inquiry along similar lines. I was prompted to take up this study by my students (especially Daniel Matt and Michael Morgan) in an undergraduate seminar on the Manual of Discipline at the University of Pennsylvania in the spring of 1971. Scripture translations have been adapted from the NEB and the NJPSV.

1. The reconstruction is mainly based on the Greek, while using elements of the late Hebrew manuscript. The utmost corruption of the latter is proved by the doublet preserved in 12:15a: ספר בן — יפול להציליך ואם תפול לא ית גלה לך עמך יבוא כאשר; cf. M. H. Segal, סירא השלם (Jerusalem, 1953), *ad loc*. In the first stich I add תעמד assuming that it had dropped out from the LXX's *Vorlage* through haplography.

Sir 43:3 MS B:	בהצהירו ירתיח תבל
	לפני חרבו מי יתכלכל
MS Masada:[2]	בהצהירו יר[ות]יח תבל
	לפני חרבו מי יתֹכֹולל
LXX:	ἐν μεσημβρίᾳ αὐτοῦ ἀνεξηραίνει χώραν
	καὶ ἐναντίον καύματος αὐτοῦ τίς ὑποστήσεται

The basic agreement between the Masada and the Genizah manuscripts proves them to be close to the original, while the Greek offers a free rendering. The rare *Hitpolel* stem of the ancient Masada manuscript, מי יתֹכֹולל, is to be preferred. In context, it seems to mean 'will hold himself'. Who can stand the sun's heat and not run away to shut himself indoors?

Qumran writings offer one more instance of כול *Hitpalpel*, as well as a *Hiphil* form, the latter being most relevant to the conclusions of the present study.

4Q511:1:6–8:[3]	כיא א[ין] משחית בגבוליהם ורוחי רשע
	לו יתהלכו בם כיא הופיע כבוד אלוהי
	דעות באֹמֹתוֹ[4] וכול בני עולה לוא יתֹכלכלו

For there is no destroyer in their boundaries and spirits of evil do not roam therein, because the glory of the God of omniscience has shined in his truth, and all the sons of iniquity will not hold themselves.

The use of כול *Hitpalpel* in this passage is very similar to that of Sir 43:3: both התכולל and התכלכל refer to the conduct of a man who contains himself so as not to flee in the face of danger.

4Q491, frag. 11, i:17:[5]	ומיא יג'דן בֹ[ני]אֹ[6] בפתן]חי פיא] וֹמזל שפתי
	מיא יכיל ומיֹאֹ יועדני וידמה במשפטי

And who will injure me when I open my mouth? And who will restrain the flow of my lips? And who will sue me and destroy (me) in my trial?

---

2. Cf. *The Book of Ben Sira: Text, Concordance, and Analysis of the Vocabulary* (Historical Dictionary of the Hebrew Language; Jerusalem, 1973) [Hebrew], which reading better conforms to the photographs published by Yadin than his own decipherment; cf. Y. Yadin, *The Ben Sira Scroll from Masada* (Jerusalem, 1965), pl. 6, line 19.

3. M. Baillet, *Qumrân Grotte 4 III (4Q482–4Q520)* (DJD 7; Oxford, 1982) 220, pl. lvii.

4. *Aliter* Baillet, who reads באֹמֹרֹיו, but compare the plate: the text allows either completion, yet the analogy with 1QS iv:20, which presents a similar vision of the future, favors my reading.

5. Baillet, ibid., 27, pl. vi.

6. Baillet reads יגדֹוֹנֹאֹ.

The trope "flow of lips" for speech[7] is properly completed by יכיל with the meaning 'contain, restrain'. One is reminded of Jer 2:13 and 6:11 where the *Hiphil* of כול is also used for the holding in of water or of the wrath of the Lord which is eventually poured out like a liquid.

Finally one should mention a rare instance found in rabbinic literature, *Midrash Sipre Bemidbar* 116:

... להזהיר את הכהנים, שתהא העבודה נעשית כתקנה, שכשעבודה נעשית כתקנה, הם כלים את הפורענות מלבוא לעולם[8]

... to warn the priests, that the worship should be done properly, for when the worship is done properly, they restrain disaster from coming to the world.

The basic meaning of כול seems to have been 'measuring', as attested in Arabic, Hebrew, and Aramaic. In the Bible it is present once only, in Isa 40:12: וכל בשלש עפר הארץ, which is reflected in the Qumran writings: יכול עפר הארץ (4Q511:30:5).[9] The petition letter of Meṣad Ḥašabyahu apparently offers three more instances in lines 5, 6(?), and 8 (*KAI* no. 200). The petitioner claims that he reaped (ויקצר), measured (ויכל), and stored (ואסם). Since the measuring of commodities was done by filling vessels, soon a secondary, more common meaning developed for the *Qal* stem: 'filling (vessels)'. This is found in the Gezer Calendar, line 5: ירח קצר וכל, '(the) month of reaping and garnering' (*KAI* no. 182); hence the *Hiphil*, 'comprising within': ארבעים בת יכיל הכיור האחד (1 Kgs 7:26); אלפים בת יכיל (1 Kgs 7:38); מחזיק בתים שלשת אלפים יכיל (2 Chr 4:5). The extended use of כול *Hiphil* for 'containing', without relation to the capacity of a vessel, is evident in 1 Kgs 8:64: קטן מהכיל את העלה, and 2 Chr 7:7: לא יכול להכיל את העלה; it is used in figurative speech in Amos 7:10: לא תוכל הארץ להכיל את כל דבריו.

The meaning 'to hold in, contain, refrain, restrain' appears to be an inner semantic development (as that of Latin *continēre* and English "contain")[10] from the notion of 'comprising' to that of 'continence'. Besides, it is possible that the semantic development of כול was influenced by the similar root כלא and its secondary form כלה.[11] One may note that כלאי האשו‍[ן] למ[ין], the reservoirs of the cistern for water mentioned in the Mesha Stone, line 23 (*KAI* no. 181), correspond to the יָכְלוּ הַמַּיִם ... אֲשֶׁר ... בארת of Jer

---

7. Cf. 4Q511:63–6:ii:4; Baillet, ibid., 247, pl. lxvi.

8. Cf. H. S. Horovitz, *Siphre D'be Rab . . . ad Numeros* (Leipzig, 1917; repr. Jerusalem, 1966) 132–33. My thanks go to M. Kister (Jerusalem) who checked the reading of the Berlin manuscript of *Midrash Sipre*.

9. Baillet, *Qumrân Grotte 4*, 236, pl. lxi.

10. On these two words see the *Oxford Latin Dictionary* (ed. P. G. W. Glare; Oxford, 1982) 430; and *OED* 2:890–91.

11. A. Baumann, "כול kwl," *TWAT* 4:91–95.

2:13. Other semantic developments of the verb כול, such as 'to sustain, support, nourish', frequent indeed in biblical and post-biblical Hebrew, do not concern us here.

The Meaning of 1QS vi:11–13

Keeping in mind the evidence so far gleaned, I now approach a difficult passage found in 1QS vi:11–13. The text, as deciphered by M. Burrows, reads:[12]

(11) . . . ובמושב הרבים אל ידבר איש כול דבר אשר לוא לחפץ[13] הרבים וכיא האיש (12) המבקר על הרבים וכול איש אשר יש אתו דבר לדבר לרבים אשר לוא במעמד האיש השואל את עצת (13) היחד ועמד האיש על רגלוהי[14] ואמר יש אתי דבר לדבר לרבים אם יומרו לו ידבר . . .

The problem arises when we reach the last two words of line 11, as made evident by the following tentative translation:[15]

> And in the session of the members[16] no man shall speak anything not to the wish of the members. And if the man who supervises[17] the members and any man who has a word to speak to the members, while the man who queries the counsel of the community is not standing,[18] then the man shall stand up on his feet and say: "I have something to speak to the members." If they tell him, he shall speak.

According to this punctuation of the passage, the second sentence, opening with וכיא 'and if', begins with a conditional subordinate clause, which would require a verbal predicate, יחפוץ לדבר or the like.[19] The absence of

---

12. M. Burrows, *The Dead Sea Scrolls of St. Mark's Monastery*, vol. 2/2: *Plates and Transcription of the Manual of Discipline* (New Haven, 1951).

13. An obvious, accepted correction; the text has להפץ.

14. Thus in the text; Burrows reads רגליהו.

15. My version combines elements from the translations of Talmon and Marcus; see nn. 17–18 below.

16. Pace J. Carmignac, *Hrbym*: Les 'Nombreux' ou les 'Notables,'" *RevQ* 7 (1971) 575–86. In my opinion, the title denotes their plurality, not their rank.

17. Rightly translated as a verb by S. Talmon, "A Note on DSD VI:11–13," *JJS* 8 (1957) 113–15. In instances where המבקר is not preceded by האיש, the translation by a noun, 'supervisor', is appropriate.

18. For this rendering cf. R. Marcus, "*Mebaqqer* and *Rabbim* in the Manual of Discipline vi.11–13," *JBL* 75 (1956) 298–302.

19. Indeed, J. Licht, *The Rule Scroll* (Jerusalem, 1965) 144 [Hebrew], defined this sentence as elliptical; A. R. C. Leaney, *The Rule of Qumran and Its Meaning* (London, 1966), translates "when *there is* a man who is acting as inspector . . ."; thus he tacitly corrected the text into וכיא יהיה איש מבקר וגו׳. E. F. Sutcliffe, "The General Council of the Qumran

such a predicate has led most translators and interpreters to a different sentence division, that is, to connect וכיא האיש המבקר על הרבים with the preceding sentence, and to begin a new sentence with וכול איש.[20] Indeed, a sentence starting with "any man" does not include a protasis and therefore its predicate would show in line 13: ועמד האיש על רגלוהי. However, following this punctuation, we encounter two other difficulties. One is the opening (ו)כול איש which is rare in 1QS (vii:22; viii:16, 21) and never occurs in the middle of a series of case laws, but rather at its opening. A more serious problem yet is created by connecting וכיא האיש המבקר על הרבים with the preceding sentence which would translate as follows:

And in the session of the members no man shall speak anything not to the wish of the members, וכיא the man who supervises the members.

Various renderings have been suggested for this וכיא: 'except, or, and also, especially, (not) even, indeed',[21] but none of them conforms either to biblical or post-biblical Hebrew diction. Others have suggested correcting וכיא to ופיא,[22] a totally unwarranted conjecture. Thus the passage has so far remained a *crux interpretum*.

In search of a solution, a fresh examination of the text of the scroll is in order. This will result in the surprising find that the reading וכול in line 12 is by no means certain. The reading יכיל is equally plausible.[23] The first letter is a small angular letter with a short right stroke—more akin to *yod* than to *waw*. As for the third letter, its right stroke is a bit longer, yet not as long as that of the *waw* of אתו and השואל in this line (eighth and sixteenth words respectively); in form and size it is similar to the *waw* of לוא in this line (thirteenth word), but no less so to the *yods* of איש (line 9, fourth word) and מישראל (line 13, last word).[24] All in all, taking into account the sound recommendation that "in cases of doubt ... the immediate context of every dubious reading should be examined,"[25] I come up

---

Community," 40 (1959) 971–83, deletes the first אשר in line 12, thus detecting the predicate in יש אתו דבר לדבר וגו'.

20. Cf. Marcus, "*Mebaqqer* and *Rabbim*," with reference to Vermes, Milik, Lambert, Vincent, Reicke; see also P. Wernberg-Møller, *The Manual of Discipline* (STDJ 1; Leiden, 1957).

21. Cf. the scholars mentioned in the preceding note; see also J. Pouilly, *La régle de la communauté de Qumran: Son evolution littéraire* (Cahiers de la Revue Biblique 17; Paris, 1976) 123.

22. W. H. Brownlee, *The Dead Sea Manual of Discipline: Translation and Notes* (BASOR Sup. 10–12; New Haven, 1951), on the authority of H. L. Ginsberg.

23. For what follows, cf. P. Wernberg-Møller, "*Waw* and *Yod* in the 'Rule of the Community' (1QS)," *RevQ* 2 (1960) 223–36.

24. As a general characteristic of this scribe, I note that his *waws* and *yods* are longer toward the end of a word than at its beginning.

25. Wernberg-Møller, "*Waw* and *Yod* in the Rule of the Community (1QS)," 230.

with the following decipherment of the problematic sentence (lines 11–12): וכיא האיש המבקר על הרבים יכיל איש אשר יש אתו דבר לדבר לרבים, rendering the entire passage (lines 11–13) as follows:

> And in the session of the members, no man shall speak anything not to the wish of the members. And if the man who supervises the members *will restrain* a man who has a word to speak to the members, while the man who queries the counsel of the community is not standing, then the man shall stand up on his feet and say: "I have something to speak to the members." If they tell him, he will speak.

Thus, the general purport of the passage seems to me to have been clarified. The regulations for the sessions of the community reserve for the assembly the right of granting the word to each member. The supervisor appears to act in the name of the assembly, as a kind of chairman, and may thus restrain members who wish to speak. His action is not appealable when the session is dedicated to the procedure known as "querying the counsel of the community" (cf. lines 4, 9–10, 15–16, 18–19; viii:25). Since this procedure is considered most important, no one is allowed to interfere with questions or motions. The outward indication that this kind of session is taking place is the officiating of the person known as "the man who queries the counsel of the community"—when on duty he is standing. In other sessions, however, the member restrained by the supervisor is entitled to appeal against his being silenced. The assembly can overrule the supervisor's decision in this case. Hence the assembly must be considered the sovereign body of the community.

THE DEAD SEA SCROLLS AND BIBLICAL STUDIES

James A. Sanders

I should like to address four areas where the influence of the Dead Sea Scrolls has been probably most pronounced: (*a*) they have dramatically altered the history of Early Judaism; (*b*) they have provided a remarkable store of information about the inner thinking of a Jewish denomination in existence when Christianity was born, with which to compare Christianity in its early Jewish-Christian phase; (*c*) they have revolutionized First Testament text criticism; and (*d*) they have helped launch canonical criticism and comparative midrash, as I understand them. For none of these do I intend to give anything like a thorough review of what has been said about them; on the contrary I intend rather to append a few critical observations to a very general, broadly drawn picture of each.[1]

The scene has shifted considerably in the past twenty-five years. Literary critical tools have begun to be used with results that significantly change how one reads the scrolls. Differentiation has set in with theories advanced about the history of formation and composition of the various key documents, especially 1QS and 1QH.[2] By the time Yigael Yadin published the Temple or Torah Scroll (11QT) in the late seventies, the literary critical method was well in place. The method was variously followed and did not issue always in compatible results, but it should be noted that there has not been anything since then like the density of controversy in the earlier period, especially the fifties.

Author's note: It is with distinct pleasure that I dedicate the following to my friend and colleague Shemaryahu Talmon. It is over forty years since the discovery of Qumran Cave 1 and time perhaps for general assessments of the significance for biblical studies of the plethora of scrolls and fragments found in numerous loci along the west bank of the Jordan Rift.

1. What follows is intended to supplement rather than update Sanders, "The Dead Sea Scrolls—A Quarter Century of Study," *BA* 36 (1973) 109–48. A fine update has been done by Michael Wise, "The Dead Sea Scrolls, Part 1: Archaeology and Biblical Manuscripts" and "The Dead Sea Scrolls, Part 2: Nonbiblical Manuscripts," *BA* 49 (1986) 140–54, 228–43. A reassessment of their value especially for history of transmission of the text has been made by G. Vermes, "Biblical Studies and the Dead Sea Scrolls 1947–1987: Retrospects and Prospects," *JSOT* 39 (1987) 113–28. See also Sanders, "The Works of the Qumran Sect," forthcoming in vol. 2 of *The Cambridge History of Judaism*.

2. H. Stegemann, *Die Entstehung der Qumrangemeinde* (Ph.D. diss., Bonn, 1965), was among the first to use thorough-going literary critical methods.

Literary critical differentiation has effected two main areas, the reconstruction of the history of the denomination and their relations to other such groups of the time, and the history of development of theology or beliefs in the group. Whereas in the earlier period after their discovery it was hotly debated whether the group was Essene, or zealot, or an apocalyptic sect, or even Qaraite, complexity has set in, hence more accurate reflection of reality. It is now standard to admit that the denomination associated with the scrolls shifted theological positions as the generations came and went, and that what was seen in the scrolls in the early days may well be there but is now related to aspects of its history. It is also important to remember that some of the scrolls may have been acquisitioned from outside the community.[3]

History of Early Judaism

Even before "economy of explanation" yielded ground to the more realistic historical principle of seeking the complexity of human enterprise (the ambiguity of reality), the scrolls had begun to have a profound effect on the history of Early Judaism.

Nearly everyone grants that the winner in the debate at the turn of the century between Schürer, Boussett, and Gressmann, on the one hand, and George Foot Moore, on the other, was Moore.[4] For Moore, pharisaic-rabbinic Judaism was normative or orthodox, while that which is reflected in much of the pseudepigrapha (*in sensu lato*) was heterodox. This was reflected as well in Hermann Strack and Paul Billerbeck's *Kommentar zum Neuen Testament*. On the other hand, Liebermann's two volumes on the considerable amount of Greek influence in Jewish Palestine, and indeed finally in the Babylonian Talmud, set the stage for what was to become a counterpoint to the Moore synthesis.[5] Moses Hadas, Elias Bickermann, and Morton Smith pioneered the position which has become, in part

---

3. See E. Tov, "The Orthography and Language of the Hebrew Scrolls Found at Qumran and the Origin of These Scrolls," *Textus* 13 (1986) 31–57; and now idem, "Hebrew Biblical Manuscripts from the Judaean Desert: Their Contribution to Textual Criticism," *JJS* 39 (1988) 10–16. Tov and Johann Cook of Stellenbosch are compiling a computerized database which will be invaluable for all future such work; see "A Computerized Data Base for the Qumran Biblical Scrolls with an Appendix on the Samaritan Pentateuch," *Journal of Northwest Semitic Languages* 12 (1984) 133–37. Cook and his students have done encoding on the basis of the Dead Sea Scrolls film collection at the Ancient Biblical Manuscript Center in Claremont.

4. G. F. Moore, *Judaism in the First Centuries of the Christian Era* (3 vols.; Cambridge, MA, 1927–1939), esp. 3:17–22.

5. S. Liebermann, *Greek in Jewish Palestine* (New York, 1942); and idem, *Hellenism in Jewish Palestine* (New York, 1962).

because of the scrolls, the regnant position associated with the work of Jacob Neusner in one direction and Martin Hengel in another.[6]

Traditions in Tannaitic literature from the period of Formative Judaism remain for the most part difficult to date, while we now have a plethora of very datable literature from the pre-Christian period which indicates a complex picture of Early Judaism in which religious pluralism was its hallmark. The significant term is *relecture*. The scrolls emanating directly out of Palestinian soil itself and, according to most of those who now work on them, dating to the Hellenistic-Roman period, have caused a re-reading of all of Jewish literature of the period; and that re-reading has issued in what Michael Stone of Hebrew University has described as the broad pluralism of Early Judaism.[7] As one reads through contribution by contribution of the various scholars who worked on James Charlesworth's two-volume *Pseudepigrapha*,[8] one sees with what firmness the new position has taken hold. A small but significant aspect of the new picture is that we now have among the scrolls the original language forms, among others, of Tobit, Sirach, the Testaments of Levi (Aramaic) and Naphtali (Hebrew), Enoch (Aramaic), and Jubilees (portions from caves 2, 3, 4, and 11).[9] More significant perhaps is the fact that some previously unknown texts from Qumran can now be classified as pseudepigraphic in the same sense.

Not only do we know a great deal more about the Early Judaism of the Hellenistic-Roman period, but we know increasingly more about the Persian period. The same re-reading of other sources that has issued in greater clarity about the second half of Early Judaism is issuing in some clarity now about the earlier period which for so long has resisted probing. Shemaryahu Talmon, whom we honor in this volume, has undertaken a major study of Early Judaism in the Persian period. This is a most felicitous prospect since surely Talmon is the person of the moment who has his hands on the resources necessary to reconstruct this all-essential link in a history which has heretofore largely escaped us.

---

6. M. Hengel, *Judaism and Hellenism: Studies in Their Encounter in Palestine during the Early Hellenistic Period* (2 vols.; trans. J. Bowden; Philadelphia, 1974). The Neusner corpus up to 1984 is indicated in the Neusner issue of *Biblical Theology Bulletin* 14 (1984) 122–25 (incomplete listing but indicative of his work). A recent title pertinent to the point here would be Neusner's *The Mishnah before 70* (BJS 51; Atlanta, 1987).

7. M. Stone, "Judaism at the Time of Christ," *Scientific American* 288 (Jan. 1973) 80–87; idem, *Scriptures, Sects and Visions* (Philadelphia, 1980); Stone and David Satran, *Emerging Judaism: Studies in the Fourth and Third Centuries B.C.E.* (Philadelphia, 1988).

8. J. Charlesworth, *The Old Testament Pseudepigrapha* (2 vols.; Garden City, NY, 1983–1985).

9. See J. Fitzmyer, *The Dead Sea Scrolls: Major Publicaqtions and Tools for Study* (Society of Biblical Literature Sources for Biblical Study 8; Missoula, MT, 1977); J. Sanders, "Palestinian Manuscripts 1947–1972," *JJS* 24 (1973) 74–83; and see n. 1 above.

The history of Judaism from its inception in the sixth century B.C.E. through what Jacob Neusner calls Formative Judaism by the close of the Talmud has gone within a generation from uncertainty to increasing clarity. Combined with the work proceeding in the literatures and history in cognate fields of the same time frame, work in Early and Formative Judaism is providing greater possibilities for responsible theories about the sociopolitical contexts out of which these many texts arose. And while secure dating for much of early rabbinic tradition still eludes us, even there we may hope some day to have firmer theories of dating than heretofore precisely because of what has transpired in these forty years.

Second Testament Study

There are a number of areas of Second Testament study in which the scrolls have been influential. I shall touch on four only.

One of the most foundational impacts the scrolls have had is in study of the languages of Palestine in the first centuries B.C.E. and C.E. Most of the scrolls of whichever provenance are in Hebrew, though a sizeable minority are in Aramaic, such as the Genesis Apocryphon, the Job Targum, the Books of Enoch, Tobit, the Testament of Levi, and others. While finds in Cave 7 may be unrelated to the Qumran library, the Greek fragments from that provenance as well as the Greek materials from the caves related to the period between the two Jewish wars of the late first and early second centuries C.E., in addition to continuing discoveries of hard-media inscriptions, have caused a reassessment of what languages were commonly used in first-century Palestine—just as Liebermann had found in the more erudite and scholarly rabbinic literature. Nor can the use of Greek be limited to the decapolis or Galilean area. Bar Kochba used Greek in the tense situations of sending commands to his lieutenants in the Judean area itself. Sevenster, Emerton, Diez-Macho, Fitzmyer, Lapide, and Maxey have convincingly demonstrated the widespread and common use of Greek throughout Palestine in the late Hasmonean and Herodian periods.[10] Jesus himself was in all likelihood trilingual, and I shouldn't wonder, as Morton Smith has long said, if he could not also read signs in Latin posted for Roman troops.

One of the widely recognized areas in which the scrolls have been helpful in New Testament work is word studies. While this is a disputed

---

10. J. Sevenster, *Do You Know Greek?* (Leiden, 1968); J. Emerton, "The Problem of Vernacular Hebrew in the First Century A.D. and the Language of Jesus," *Journal of Theological Studies* 29 (1973) 1-23; A. Diez-Macho, "La lengua hablada por Jesuscristo," *Oriens Antiquus* 2 (1963) 95-132; J. Fitzmyer, "The Languages of Palestine in the First Century A.D.," *CBQ* 32 (1970) 501-31 (repr. in *A Wandering Aramean: Collected Aramaic Essays* [Society of Biblical Literature Monograph Series 25; Atlanta, 1979]); P. Lapide, "Insights from Qumran into the Languages of Jesus," *RevQ* 8 (1975) 483-501; Z. Maxey, "The Languages of Jesus," an unpublished paper for the Claremont Graduate School.

area and while it is not certain whether the new light cast on certain New Testament Greek words is pertinent in all contexts, there can be little doubt that the scrolls have provided a glossary of theological terms used in Palestine in the first centuries B.C.E. and C.E. Four come to mind without specific searches. One was the focus of Raymond E. Brown's dissertation at Johns Hopkins University which showed that the word μυστήριον in the New Testament was comparable to the word רז in the scrolls; in both it is used in certain contexts to mean an ingroup kind of hermeneutic whereby to read Scripture.[11] Light may also be shed on the enigmatic phrase in 2 Thess 2:7, μυστήριον ... τῆς ἀνομίας, which shows up in the Cave 1 Book of Mysteries (1Q27) as רזי פשע, the mysteries of transgression or of lawlessness. Another was the topic of a study by James Robinson on *Die Hodayot Formel* as it shows up in some New Testament prayers and hymns.[12] Yet another was the recognition that οἱ πολλοί in the New Testament were not necessarily 'crowds'; that is, the term and its morphological variants in the New Testament may mean in some passages the same as הרבים in some Qumran passages where it designates not crowds but rather an ingroup with decision-making power. Many more could be listed; these are but acceptable examples. As in the case of determining the exact contextual meaning of any word in any passage, especially in the onerous task of having to choose only one for translation purposes, care must be taken in this type of cross-reference as well. A New Testament writer may or may not be using a Palestinian adaptation of a Greek word or term; but the fact that we now have a valuable resource of theological vocabulary used in Palestine in the first century cannot be gainsaid.

Beyond word study is the area of theological concept. The fact that some of the Qumran literature seems to verge on dualism on the one hand and determinism on the other may help understand similar difficulties in the New Testament. It has always been a problem in a theocentric, monotheizing religion to understand the use of certain non-monotheizing cultural idioms and mores to address the problem of evil. The New Testament at times seems to embrace Hellenistic-era idioms which in other non-Jewish, non-Christian contexts of the time were patently polytheistic. The fact that the Qumran denominational literature also does not completely avoid such idioms provides a control study in how to understand the use of ancient contemporary polytheistic idioms in a monotheizing context. Once one has addressed that problem, one realizes that all biblical literature reflects the idioms and mores of the several cultural eras out of which it has

---

11. R. Brown, *The Semitic Background of the Term "Mystery" in the New Testament* (Philadelphia, 1968). For other studies on the bearing of the scrolls on Second Testament issues see Fitzmyer, *Dead Sea Scrolls*, 124-30.

12. J. M. Robinson, "Die Hodayot-Formel in Gebet und Hymnus des Frühchristentums," in *Apophoreta: Festschrift für Ernst Haenchen* (ed. W. Eltester and F. H. Kettler; Beihefte zur Zeitschrift für die Neutestamentliche Wissenschaft 30; Berlin, 1964) 194-235.

emerged and through which it has passed. Precisely a canonical perspective evolves from the exercise so that one learns how to understand and exegete literary expressions from the five cultural eras over some twelve to eighteen hundred years from the Bronze Age, the Iron Age, the Persian period, the Hellenistic era, and the Roman period, no one of which is more important or imposing than another. Thus the idioms of the Hellenistic-Roman era no longer stand isolated but can be addressed in a series of control studies about how to understand the monotheizing process without tripping over the idioms of the various cultures in which the monotheizing struggle took place within the biblical paradigm.

Various prominent figures in the New Testament now have counterparts for control study as well, such as Melchizedeq, Enoch, Beliaal/Beelzebub, various angelic as well as denomic figures, and others which populate the literature of Early Judaism.

Perhaps the most important area in which study of the scrolls has influenced New Testament study is that of the function of Scripture and tradition in early Jewish literature. If one focuses one's study of the *Nachleben* of Scripture and tradition in the LXX, the Apocrypha and Pseudepigrapha, and the scrolls, one feels right at home when turning to study the same in the New Testament. It is no more or less apologetic or proof-texting there than elsewhere. On the contrary, one encounters the same range of function as earlier. The differences begin to show up not in the New Testament but in later forms in rabbinic literature, where function of Scripture is at times similar as in the earlier Jewish literature, but with distinct and describable differences. This is one major reason some of us find it difficult to limit the concept of midrash to the literary forms to which the word was later applied in rabbinic literature. Midrash means searching Scripture for the light it can cast on new situations where applied; it clearly does not imply commentary on Scripture in the modern sense of the term.

Scripture and tradition function in early Jewish and Christian literature in five different modes:

citation with formula
citation without formula
allusion
paraphrase
literary shape

The first three modes have been the object of considerable study. In the case of the first two one can proceed immediately to the question of the ancient hermeneutics by which the Scripture or tradition is caused to function in the passage under study. Whether it is an allusion or a citation, the question of the hermeneutics whereby the New Testament author or speaker re-presents the tradition or figure remains the same. How does the newer author or speaker cause the citation, the tradition or the scriptural figure, to function in the new situation, and to what effect? Once one has done so, the work has only begun; but I shall return to this crucial point in a moment.

The fourth and fifth modes, paraphrase and literary shape, require stricter control measures. If one moves through study of the Qumran literature as well as other pre-Christian early Jewish literature focusing on the function of Scripture and tradition there—and one can hardly avoid it—then one sees clearly that paraphrase of Scripture into the "other words" of the newer day is normal and necessary both (*a*) for understanding the old Bronze or Iron Age idiom, or for understanding the early Hellenistic Greek of the LXX in later *koiné* speech; and (*b*) for the adaptation the tradent wishes to make of it. Then if one moves on into similar study of Scripture and tradition in the New Testament, one not only feels quite at home in this regard, but one can apply the same methods of study.

The observation is inescapable (*a*) that later believing communities paraphrased Scripture for clearer understanding of the older mode of speech, and (*b*) that later authors and writers, whether orally or in written form, often wanted to compose what they had to say scripturally. This means not only the literary phenomenon of rewriting Scripture, such as the Chronicler's use of the Genesis-to-Kings literature, or the Genesis Apocryphon and the Temple Scroll, it also means the phenomenon of writing new material in the mode, style, and shape of the older literature which had become or was becoming sacred. After careful study of the products of earlier believing communities, both the highly Hellenized literature and the less so, one recognizes similar literature in the New Testament. And while there are a few literary forms in the New Testament which seem dissimilar, there are many which exhibit what must have been a conscious desire on the part of early Christians, whether previously Jewish or not, to write up scripturally what they believed God had done in Christ and was doing in the early church.

While such study may not solve the problem of the genre gospel, I am convinced that the problems which that genre presents would appear less intractable if Scripture, including the LXX form of it, were understood as a source for gospel writing every bit as important as Mark, Q, and whatever other Christian sectarian source was used in their composition, and if the sociopolitical situation and needs of early Christian communities are factored into consideration of what was written, as much as an individual evangelist's intentions or literary redactional and compositional contribution.

First Testament Text Criticism

The area of study which has perhaps been most affected by the scrolls is First Testament text criticism. There are two major text critical projects in place at the present time which reflect impact of the discovery of the scrolls: the Hebrew University Bible Project (HUBP) and the United Bible Societies' Hebrew Old Testament Text Project (HOTTP). Due to the new situation, caused by work on the scrolls rather than on Codex Aleppensis, both projects had to revise the history of transmission of the Hebrew text. The remarkable thing is that without collusion between them they each reached a simialr revision.[13] This revision has been as remarkable as the revision of the history of Early Judaism, noted earlier.

The UBS project started in 1969 and published its results as *Critique textuelle de l'Ancien Testament*, vol. 1 dealing with the so-called historical books and vol. 2 with Isaiah, Jeremiah, and Lamentations; vol. 3 is nearly ready with at least two to follow.[14]

The basic ground shift took place when it became obvious that the history of transmission of the text had to be rewritten. The first and clearest observation from discovery of the scrolls was that a remarkable difference could be observed between the Qumran biblical scrolls and the supposed *Vorlage* to the LXX, on the one hand, and the biblical scrolls that were found in the later caves at Masada and in the Buqeia, ranging in date between the fall of Jerusalem in 70 C.E. and the defeat of the Second Jewish Revolt in 135. The Qumran scrolls and the LXX (*Vorlage*) are now the oldest biblical literature that we have, ranging in date from the third century B.C.E. (both the LXX of the Pentateuch and the earliest fragments of Samuel from Cave 4). All these, along with the citations of Scripture in the scrolls, Apocrypha, Pseudepigrapha, and the New Testament, indicate that the earliest biblical literature we have exhibits a certain amount of textual fluidity. This was the starting point.

The next observation was that we have no biblical manuscripts from the close of the Bar Kochba Revolt until the Cairo Codex of the Prophets (896 C.E.) and the great Tiberian Masoretic manuscripts in the tenth century C.E. (925 for A and 1009 for L; rumors persist about eighth-century manuscripts, but they await confirmation).

The situation that presented itself, therefore, was that we now have a plethora of texts and versions from the late early Jewish period, a signifi-

---

13. See S. Talmon, "Aspects of the Textual Transmission of the Bible in the Light of Qumran Manuscripts," *Textus* 4 (1964) 94–132; idem, "The Old Testament Text," in *The Cambridge History of the Bible*, vol. 1: *From the Beginnings to Jerome* (ed. P. R. Ackroyd and C. F. Evans; Cambridge, 1970) 159–99; M. Goshen-Gottstein, *The Book of Isaiah: Sample Edition with Introduction* (Jerusalem, 1965) 11–20; idem, "Hebrew Biblical Manuscripts: Their History and Their Place in the HUBP Edition," *Bib* 48 (1967) 243–90; D. Barthélemy, "Text, Hebrew, History of," *IDBSup* 878–84. The first, second, and fourth items are reprinted in *Qumran and the History of the Biblical Text* (ed. F. M. Cross and S. Talmon; Cambridge, MA, 1975) 226–63, 1–41, 42–89.

14. D. Barthélemy (ed.), *Critique textuelle de l'Ancien Testament* (OBO 50/1–2; Freiburg/Göttingen, 1982–1986). An English translation is in preparation by UBS.

cant number from the very beginning of the Formative Jewish period, then nothing but versional evidence (especially the Peshitta and Vulgate) until the ninth/tenth century and the fruit of the work of the tireless Masoretes. When conjoined with the observation that we still have no autographs of any biblical document, and that the debate between Lagarde and Kahle has not been neatly solved, there emerged a four-period history of transmission of the text.

The first period may be called the period of the *Urtext*, that is, the so-called and supposed originals. In contrast to earlier concepts of text criticism, this is simply not the province of text criticism as it is presently conceived. That is the rightful province of historical criticism, of the historian in the workshop who continues to be interested in what someone actually said or wrote in the Iron Age or Persian period. The fact that historical criticism has fallen on relatively hard days underscores perhaps the point that this is beyond the competence of text criticism. It is difficult any longer to say that the task of text criticism is to establish the original text; in fact, we now wonder how much sanguinity there was in targeting such a goal. It is better to say that the task of text criticism is to establish the most responsible critical text available from use of the best methods now in place based on all the readings now available. This was a point discussed in the HOTTP annual meetings in Freudenstadt.

The second period extends from the earliest available fragments in the third century B.C.E. to the fall of Jerusalem in 70 C.E. This we call the period of the accepted texts. It is a period marked not only by (limited) textual fluidity but also perhaps by different families of texts; this latter point is rather warmly debated at the moment. The third period is that of the received text, which extends from the fall of Jerusalem to the close of the pre-Masoretic period. The fourth period is, of course, the Masoretic and post-Masoretic. Again, the salient observation is that the fluidity so characteristic of the Qumran/LXX texts and of the citations in the literature of the Early Jewish period and in the New Testament ceases toward the end of the first century C.E. with the biblical manuscripts from the period between the revolts and the creation of the Greek texts we call Aquila, Theodotion, and Symmachus (all of which exhibit remarkable tendencies, Aquila and Theodotion notably so, not only toward stability of text, and indeed a very proto-Masoretic text, but even literalism, as well).

Following the lead of Moshe Greenberg already in 1955,[15] but especially taking account of evidence in the Dodecapropheton he was assigned to study, D. Barthélemy in 1963 developed a theory of text stabilization. This stabilization began with proto-Theodotionic tendencies in Dodecapropheton (dating to the middle of the first century B.C.E.) and was

---

15. M. Greenberg, "The Stabilization of the Text of the Hebrew Bible, Reviewed in the Light of the Biblical Materials from the Judean Desert," *JAOS* 76 (1956) 157–67.

complete by the last quarter of the first century C.E. With his publication the stage was set for revision of the history of text transmission.[16]

The next most significant event was Moshe Goshen-Gottstein's watershed article that finally dealt the death blow to the earlier modes of "establishing original texts."[17] In that article Goshen-Gottstein showed beyond serious challenge that the famous collations of medieval manuscripts in Kennicott and de Rossi were almost entirely post-Masoretic and could not be depended on to reflect pre-Masoretic readings. The various efforts to find in those collations the reading one wanted based on literary and historical critical study were summarily checked. Such readings as one may find in Kennicott, de Rossi, or even late medieval and Renaissance manuscripts depart from the MT and for the most part do not antedate it. This is not to say that one can totally ignore them; there are some that are more interesting than others and sometimes offer variants worthy of note, such as Kenn. 248 and others.[18]

As the new concepts and method develop it has become increasingly clear that the integrity of the full manuscript context in which a supposed variant reading is found must be respected before an isolated text or versional reading is pillaged for emendation of the MT. Fortunately structural analysis of texts has now developed to the point that it has become a major tool for discovering the integrity of an ancient witness, in order to perceive how the supposed variant fits into the text of the witness as a whole, whether the witness be a text or a version; and it has become a crucial control factor for discerning whether a supposed variant, or a plus or a minus, reflects true variants, or reflects a different concept on the part of the copyist or translator of what the text being copied or translated was actually saying, or indeed should say to his or her community. Clearly most ancient copyists and translators wanted to convey *their* understanding of the *Vorlage* to their communities; they wanted to do their best for their people. And that understanding, due to the later problems they faced in their sociohistorical contexts, was sometimes a resignification of what modern scholarship perceives "the original" should have said due to our supposed advanced knowledge of the earlier biblical period. The perception of the later copyist or translator of what the *Vorlage* meant would clearly have an influence on how they "corrected" what they copied or on how they understood a multivalent term being translated. This is especially the

---

16. D. Barthélemy, *Les Devanciers d'Aquila* (VTSup 10; Leiden, 1963); E. Tov and R. Kraft, *The Greek Minor Prophets Scroll* (DJD 8; Oxford, 1989); see Sanders, "Text and Canon: Concepts and Method," in *From Sacred Story to Sacred Text* (Philadelphia, 1987) 125-51.

17. Goshen-Gottstein, "Hebrew Biblical Manuscripts."

18. See Barthélemy, *Critique textuelle de l'Ancien Testament*, 1:*65-*114, for explication of method.

case in the period before textual stabilization, but occurs thereafter as well. A careful structural analysis of each larger unit or pericope in a manuscript or family of manuscripts, which apparently has "a superior reading" at a crucial point in it, may simply indicate a different conception of what the *Vorlage* meant and not a true variant. This is a major reason the Ancient Biblical Manuscript Center has been established in Claremont: it has become crucial to be able to see supposed variants in their fuller contexts, where manuscripts are available, and not only in prior collations, apparatus, and footnotes—or even in printed cricial editions, which have been of necessity filtered through the biases of competence and interests of their editors.

There are two worthy questions that need addressing at this point in discussion of recent text-critical developments. The one has to do with the importance of philology in discerning earliest readings; and the other concerns the range of readings targeted by the new method in text criticism. They are related questions having to do with the continuing desire to arrive at a so-called original reading.

Not only philology, but numerous other disciplines enter the picture of decision making about which reading of those available should be chosen. Both HUBP and HOTTP agree that outright conjecture is not the province of text criticism, but of literary and historical criticism, and is the prerogative of the historian rightly interested in the *ipsissima verba* of a biblical composition. Such conjectures will continue to be the base of individual scholars' translations, just as dramatic shifts in meanings of Hebrew terms based on philology will continue to be used in similar scholarly translations. It is the position of both text-critical projects that such conjectures—that is outright creations of new readings based on no firm textual evidence whatever, and variant meanings based on comparative philology which in effect amount to conjectures—are not only not the province of text criticism but are improper in translations designed for believing communities. Leaps to other meaning based on undifferentiated use of Arabic, Ugaritic, or other languages cognate and contemporary to Hebrew must be restrained by careful control in comparative philology.[19]

The text critic of the sort I have been describing takes into account all the available data and in interdisciplinary discussion around the worktable reconstructs what an original text might have been in order to be able as well as possible to understand the beautiful ruins left in the text. But when it comes to choosing a reading and its meaning, only those readings which ancient believing communities bequeathed us in the available manuscripts, texts, and versions are the valid options. Having looked at what scholarly

---

19. As suggested in J. Barr, *Comparative Philology and the Text of the Old Testament* (Oxford, 1968); repr. with corrections and additions, Winona Lake, IN, 1987.

expertise of our day can reconstruct, the text critic then looks critically, once more and again, at the available readings and makes a decision based on as sound method as possible, including evaluation in terms of the conceptuality and reality lying back of full textual and versional contexts. What the individual scholar or translator does with all the evidence and expertise is another matter. The text critic observes the limitations of the task with the best possible methods that have been honed and developed in the past twenty-five or so years, largely because of the discovery of the Dead Sea Scrolls.

Canonical Criticism

The current position of text criticism can only be understood in depth if it is seen in the light of recent studies in canon, for text and canon have to be seen in the same light. Stabilization of text and stabilization of canon are interwoven. This is the case in New Testament text criticism as well if the latest views of the date of the Muratorian fragment are observed.[20] But the important point is the question of authority and inspiration.

The historian wants to know as well as possible what happened. And as historians, text critics will continue to reconstruct the history of the formation of the Bible, including all the original moments it is possible to rebuild. But one must ask why. Is it only because we are by training and trade historians, or are we historians perhaps because of an uninvestigated theory of authority and inspiration, namely, that what we want to be in the Bible is what the original contributor said or wrote because of a tacit understanding of what was inspired, or impacted in antiquity by Reality (*die Realität*—a term some theologians use for God).

This whole amorphous area of our work might be illuminated if we were more self-conscious of theory of authority and were to modify it to fit the givens. The tacit, or expressed, understanding of inspiration has been God or Holy Spirit (or Shekinah, or Reality) working with an individual in antiquity, whose words were then more-or-less accurately preserved by disciples, schools, and scribes. The more responsible theory, given the data and facts we actually have, would be that of God or Holy Spirit (or Shekinah, truth, or Reality) working all along the path of formation of

---

20. A. C. Sundberg, "Canon of the New Testament," *IDBSup*, 136–40; for arguments recently advanced for maintaining the earlier date of the Muratorian fragment, see B. Metzger, *The Canon of the New Testament* (Oxford, 1987) 191–201; for the later date (350–400 C.E.), see Lee McDonald, *The Formation of the Christian Biblical Canon* (Nashville, 1988) 135–39. On the principal point see Sanders, "Text and Canon: Old Testament and New," in *Mélanges Dominique Barthélemy* (ed. P. Casetti, O. Keel, and A. Schenker; OBO 38; Freiburg/Göttingen, 1981) 373–94.

these texts.[21] This theory of authority could then include all the so-called spurious or secondary passages (which are in the Bible whether we like it or not), all the discrepancies and anomalies, and that fact that more often than not what we have in the beautiful ruins of many passages is what the Reality of later believing communities bequeathed us.[22] This theory could include the fact that in the canonical paradigm there are numerous cases of resignification of what a passage might originally have meant, not only the doublets and triplets, but also what Samuel Sandmel called Haggadah within Scripture, the numerous cases of the reappearance of an early idea or passage in which they are considerably resignified.[23]

Text and canon go together; they cannot be separated if we are to account responsibly for the data so far accumulated and move forward to more responsible study of these texts as the tradents of the current generation and the next to come. Tradents always engage in the two factors of stability and adaptability if the texts and traditions studied are to make sense; and they must make sense in the tradent's idiom if study of them is responsible. Tradents are always engaged simultaneously in the two tasks of preservation and re-presentation.[24] The basic reason for having a manuscript center where scholars are no longer dependent on others' apparatus and notes, but can do comparative study of as many of the received texts as possible, is so that each generation can obey its own best lights and follow its own developed and responsible methods. William F. Albright was apparently wont to say that the archeologist should leave more of a tell undug then dug, for two reasons: the next generations will probably have better tools with which to work, and sharper questions to put to the data. Another way, a more traditional way of putting that might be to say that the reason for such a collection of enhanced images of ancient and medieval manuscripts of the biblical texts (and nonbiblical for comparative study) is that each generation, and each scholar, may investigate the primary evidence, confident that they are not perpetuating past errors but can see for themselves all the possible readings in the integrity of the full context of the texts and versions in the manuscripts where found.

21. An idea at least already latent in J. Barr, *Old and New in Interpretation* (New York, 1966) 26–27. For an explicit statement of it see Sanders, *Canon and Community* (Philadelphia, 1984) xv–xviii.

22. See S. Talmon, "The Textual Study of the Bible—A New Outlook," in *Qumran and the History of the Biblical Text* (ed. F. M. Cross and S. Talmon; Cambridge, MA, 1975) 321–400; idem, "Heiliges Schrifttum und Kanonische Bücher aus jüdischer Sicht—Überlegungen zur Ausbildung der Grösser 'Die Schrift' im Judentum," in *Die Mitte der Schrift* (ed. M. Klopfenstein et al.; Bern, 1987) 45–89.

23. S. Sandmel, "The Haggadah within Scripture," *JBL* 80 (1961) 110–11.

24. See, e.g., D. Knight, *Rediscovering the Traditions of Ancient Israel* (SBLDS 9; Missoula, MT, 1973) 5–20; and M. Fishbane, *Biblical Interpretation in Ancient Israel* (Oxford, 1985) 1–19.

Humanists need not shy from a traditional concept such as *Shekinah* or Holy Spirit; it is but the acceptance of human humility even while using the most advanced tools of the Enlightenment on the received texts, indeed the recognition that we have much, much more to learn about Reality than we ever "now know." The revealing of that knowledge, the combination of types of knowledge, the coming by it, has an immeasurable dimension which needs to be recognized if responsibility in any generation is to be recognized by the next, and passed on.

Judaism

REFLECTIONS ON TERRITORY IN JUDAISM

W. D. Davies

The doctrine of the Land emerges unmistakably in the foundation document of Judaism—the Tanakh (the Old Testament)—and in its classical sources (the Mishnah, the Midrashim, and the Talmud) and in its religious observances and centuries of its history. There is an undeniable theological tradition that the Land of Israel was promised (more accurately "sworn") by the deity (Yahweh) to Abraham and through him to the people of Israel, and that the Land belonged to Yahweh himself and is his gift to Israel, although Israel can never absolutely claim the Land as its own by right. There is an unseverable, eternal relationship among the people of Israel, the Land, and the God of Israel. This relationship is personalized and conceived in mythological conjugal terms so that Israel is the Bride of

---

Author's note: The grounds for these reflections are provided in my books *The Gospel and the Land: Early Christianity and Jewish Territorial Doctrine* (Berkeley, 1974) and *The Territorial Dimensions of Judaism* (Berkeley, 1982). What I have written will be altogether familiar to the honoree of this volume: we discussed it frequently when he was a Fellow at the National Center for the Humanities here in Durham, North Carolina. One thing our conversations made more clear to me than ever before: if the continuous significance of the Land in the Jewish tradition is obvious, equally obvious is it that the significance, and even centrality, sometimes ascribed to it has fluctuated at various times and places as the vicissitudes of Jewish history have demanded. At times it has been crucial to concentrate on return to the Land and settlement within it; at other times the Land was relegated to a less dominant concern which one might even describe as "a benign neglect." Jewish history compels the questions: what is the permanent or persistent center or heart of Judaism and, in this context, what is the comparative importance of the Land over against and alongside other aspects of Judaism which have been inescapable—ethnicity or peoplehood or Torah? Recent events in Israel have propelled these questions to the forefront in such a way that they may perhaps now be the crucial ones which Judaism has to face. I had hoped to deal precisely with them in this tribute to an old and revered friend, but circumstances hindered. I can only offer this strictly preliminary, inadequate tribute to him as a small token of gratitude, admiration, and affection born of the warmth of his friendship over many years and the intense stimulus and largesse of his work and spirit.

Yahweh and the Land flows "with milk and honey" as bride of Yahweh and spouse of Israel. There is a "chosen" people and a "chosen" land: Israel's vocation is in terms of geography.

There are two main reasons why many have dismissed the doctrine as unworthy of serious consideration. To begin with, in varying degrees we are all now children of the Enlightenment, which searched for the universal in every sphere. To deal with any particularism, not to speak of a geographic-religious particularism, was not congenial to the Enlightenment. It still predisposes us to pass by the necessity of understanding a doctrine such as that of a chosen people in Judaism. And the dismissal of the doctrine of the Land is usually coupled with dismissal of the doctrine of "election," which in the judgment of many has irrationally afflicted the Jewish people.

The other chief reason for the negative response to the doctrine is Christian in origin. It arises from the traditional and contemporary approach of Gentile, even of much Jewish, scholarship to Judaism. Unlike other first-century religions, that religion has persisted as a living faith to the present, so that a contemporaneous urgency has always remained in the discussion of the relationship between it and Christianity. One might have expected that Judaism would have helped to formulate the terms of the discussion between the two faiths. In fact, because of the dominance of Christianity, this discussion has been governed by the concerns that Christians have deemed important. It is doctrines in which Christians have been particularly interested—God, creation, man, sin, and especially time, etc., that is, theological and metaphysical abstractions (despite Christian concentration on the Incarnation)—that have been emphasized in attempts to understand how the gospel emerged from and impinged upon Judaism. The Jewish faith came to be understood largely as a body of ideas which could be examined in Christian categories but was seldom looked at in terms native to itself. Certain consequences followed. Ideas, to be true, must be valid for all persons at all times and places. Any geographic particularistic elements in Judaism could be regarded as insignificant and safely overlooked. Even rabbinic theology, in reaction to Christian theology, from which it borrowed its philosophical tools and methods, concentrated on themes dictated by specifically Christian challenges, and neglected such awkward, particularistic doctrines as that of the Land. Rabbinic thinkers themselves, understanding Judaism in terms of Christianity, asked what significance a particular place, Palestine, could have in their faith; and Christian scholars governed by their own doctrinal interests, naturally neglected Judaism's traditional concentration on the Land.

To overlook the Jewish emphasis on the Land, however, is to overlook one of the most tenaciously held doctrines with which the early church had to come to terms. And certain developments have created a new climate for the approach to it. Historians of religion have discovered similar attitudes toward their particular lands among other peoples. The Jewish doctrine can no longer be dismissed as an oddity of Jewish history. In the light of new knowledge of various cultures, such a dismissal appears simplistic. However much a mark of "primitive" Jewish particularism, the doctrine casts its roots deep into what seems to be human need: Jews are not the only people to have conceived of their "manifest destiny."

Recently the biological roots of the doctrine have been emphasized. R. Ardrey urged that in insisting on their eternal relationship with the Land, Jews were obeying what he called "a territorial imperative" which governs human no less than animal behavior. Ardrey's understanding is not in agreement with what the sources reveal. But his insistence on the importance of territory and its loss for a people can hardly be gainsaid. Aspects of Jewish history confirm him in this. The psychological, linguistic, and political consequences of de-territorialization all demand that the doctrine of the Land in Judaism be more seriously examined. And, apart from all this, any simple dismissal becomes even naïve in the light of one historical fact, that is, the chronologically enduring attachment of Jews to the Land across centuries, and indeed millennia, and the not only heroic and tragic consequences of their separation from it but the immense creativity of that exile. In terms of history it is difficult not to concede that there is here a most extraordinary phenomenon which cries for understanding.

A new openness in the approach to this theme is also emerging in the theological sphere. In Christianity, the Land is relativized and placed under the judgment of Christ: life "in Christ" replaces life "in the Land" as the highest blessing, so that the traditional Jewish territorial doctrine is not upheld. But by insisting that the doctrine has been transcended in the gospel, Christianity has often failed to do justice to the dimensions which it has preserved. To ponder this matter is to be made aware (*a*) that Judaism's insistence that the people of Israel needed a land through which and within which to express its identity, that that people had to have a "space" which it could turn into its own "place," points to a truth about most if not all peoples—a human community needs a geographic sphere of its own within which and through which to express itself; (*b*) that Judaism's insistence that the occupancy of the Land is not absolute but conditioned by obedience to the Torah, that observance and nonobservance of the commandments have geographic, territorial, and cosmic consequences, points to a truth that ecology is dependent upon morality, land and law being mutually dependent, that a people is ultimately responsible for the maintenance of its "place"; and (*c*) that the Jewish people's experience of exile reveals the horrendous price paid by all peoples wherever their territorial roots are cut. The Jewish engagement with the Land is, therefore, a paradigm of most if not all peoples' engagement with their lands.

It is now possible to recognize that without the concreteness of the demand to express community in and through the actualities of space, we are in danger of unrealism. The false romanticism and the individualistic, otherworldly spirituality and false dualism of much in Christian history, although it has other sources in Hellenism and Gnosticism, and in the contemporary revolt against technology, may not be wholly unconnected with the radical break with the doctrine of the Land as much of Judaism understood it. And, in time, this may have been one of the factors that ultimately led to the massive protest against false spirituality in Marxist materialism. The neglect of the positive aspects of the concentration on the Land in Judaism has often been to obscure those biological, cultural, psychological, and historical relations between peoples and their lands that historians of religion and the long wandering of the Jewish people— culminating in the Holocaust and in the creation of the State of Israel—are teaching us. Christian peoples in the West have often been able to ignore these consequences and to escape conceptually into an unrooted universalism. The challenge of Jewish particularism, now so often taken as an affront, could therefore be very salutary.

But do these considerations exhaust the significance of the interpretation of the Land with which Judaism confronts us? There are two other aspects of it to note. The first is its theological dimensions. What I have suggested to be true of all peoples in the light of that interpretation is by it rooted in the divine. At this point the choice is clear. One may assume that Jewish religion, as is the case with all religions, is a *natural* growth of a people's efforts to ensure its own survival and find answers to the problems of existence. If so, the *theological* aspect of the doctrine of the Land can be dismissed. But one may follow another path and claim that without the "materialism" of its territorial doctrine, Judaism could not have made its fundamental contribution to Christianity, nor could it continue to bear its full witness to the world. It is true that the new faith universalized Zion. But the peoples of the world each have their own form of rootedness and love of land; and the Creator blesses and rules in and through these dimensions, even as he limits and judges them all, including Zionism, in terms of his wider purposes.

This reference to the judgment on all nations leads to a second aspect of the territorial doctrine which is fundamental. By some alchemy this earthly doctrine has often been transformed almost to its opposite. The Land has been spiritualized and transcendentalized, that is, made into a symbol of an ideal order either in this world or in the supernatural "world to come." In Judaism and Christianity such a process has persisted from the first century to the present, in the hope for "a land of pure delight, where saints immortal reign" and for "Jerusalem the Golden." It is natural to see in all this a means of divesting the doctrine of the Land of the "crass" materiality which constitutes it a scandal to the spiritual and of circumventing the problem posed by territorial particularity both for Judaism and Christianity. But the process of transcendentalizing and spiritualizing the

Land is more than this. It points to the recognition in both religions that, however desirable, the fulfillment of the terrestrial hope for the Land, or for any land, would not suffice to assuage the more than territorial aspirations of Israel or of any other people. Peoples have been concerned not only with a terrestrial destiny, but with that which will be "when earth and man are gone / and suns and universes cease to be," when all terrestrial concerns have been swallowed up in "that day" when the whole temple of human achievement will be buried in the debris of a universe in ruins. The hope for "the Land," transcendentalized and spiritualized, has enabled many to face "that day," and has given assurance that their destiny lies in an eternal order, which "eye hath not seen nor ear heard." Paradoxically, the Land, as actual geographic reality, has sustained the people of Israel in its historical pilgrimage. In the twentieth century this paradox is particularly significant. A new sensitivity, born of our experience in the space age, to our common perilous existence on what Archibald MacLeish calls "the little, lonely, floating planet, that tiny raft in the enormous empty night" which we call earth, has made us more acutely conscious of the questionableness of overemphasizing territorial divisions however desirable. But simultaneously our awareness of spatial immensities has increased our felt need to have "roots," "a place," "a territory." The need to be rooted, which has engendered among Jews the doctrine of the Land, anchored in the will of the deity, is now more than ever a living need for most peoples and indeed individuals. And, at the same time, the transitoriness and precariousness of human existence in the nuclear age compels the search for "the Land" which defies time and space. The doctrine of the Land as cherished by Judaism and reinterpreted both in that faith and in Christianity, points to the twofold human need for terrestrial roots and for the transcendent. The words of Ps 62:11 can be applied to this doctrine: "One thing God has spoken: two things have I learned." It is certain that the potency of the Land in the imagination of Israel and its influence on human affairs remains. The inevitable conflict between the doctrine and the claims of inhabitants of the Land other than the Jews can only be referred to here, but Shemaryahu Talmon is acutely aware of them.

BIBLICAL EXEGESIS
AND THE FORMATION OF JUDAISM:
SIFRA AND THE PROBLEM OF THE MISHNAH

Jacob Neusner

The author of Sifra composed the one (and the only truly successful) document to accomplish the union of the two Torahs: Scripture (or the written Torah) and the Mishnah (or the oral Torah). This was achieved not merely formally but through the interior structure of thought. It was by means of the critique of practical logic and the rehabilitation of the probative logic of hierarchical classification (*Listenwissenschaft*) in particular that the author of Sifra accomplished this remarkable feat of intellect. That author achieved the (re-)union of the two Torahs into a single cogent statement within the framework of the written Torah by penetrating into the deep composition of logic that underlay the creation of the world in its correct components, rightly classified, and in its right order as portrayed by the Torah.

Specifically, by systematically demolishing the logic that sustains an autonomous Mishnah and by equally and thoroughly demonstrating the dependency, for the identification of the correct classification of things, not upon the traits of things viewed in the abstract, but upon the classification of things by Scripture in particular, the framers of Sifra recast the two parts of the Torah into a single coherent statement through unitary and cogent discourse. At stake, therefore, for Sifra is the dependency of the Mishnah upon Scripture, at least for the encompassing case of the Book of Leviticus.* So in choosing, as to form, the base-text of Scripture, Sifra

---

* That Sifra's authors can have demonstrated the same propositions of topical program and order, logic of cogent discourse, and logic of probative demonstration of propositions, for other parts of the Mishnah that relate to other legal codes in the Mosaic composite is beyond all doubt shown in the two Sifrés. But the program of this document certainly is not particular to the Book of Leviticus, and the polemic and propositions encompass the entirety of the dual Torah, wherever finally written down. That is why I offer the present study as a chapter in the

made its entire statement *in nuce*. Then by composing a document that for very long stretches cannot have been put together without the Mishnah, and at the same time subjecting the generative logical principles of the Mishnah to devastating critique, Sifra took up its mediating position. The destruction of the Mishnah as an autonomous and free-standing statement, based upon its own logic, is followed by the reconstruction of large tracts of the Mishnah as a statement wholly within, and in accord with, the logic and program of the written Torah in Leviticus. I therefore represent as a triumph of intellect the work of Sifra, as we now know it in its recurrent and fixed forms of rhetoric and logic and equally permanent protocol of relationships with other documents, particularly Scripture and Mishnah (with Tosefta). What we have in Sifra is simply one of the great, original, and successful works of the critical mind in the Judaism of the dual Torah as it emerged from late antiquity.

The former, and dominant, approach to uniting the two Torahs, oral and written, into a single cogent statement, involved reading the written Torah into the oral. In form, this was done through inserting into the oral Torah a long sequence of proof texts. That is the solution taken by the authorities who received the Mishnah, the initial and authoritative writing down of the Oral Torah, and subjected it to four hundred years of amplification and paraphrase and internal augmentation. They carried out that solution through the Tosefta (ca. A.D. 300), then through the Talmud of the Land of Israel (ca. A.D. 400), and then, in the most successful, thoroughgoing manner, through the Talmud of Babylonia (ca. A.D. 600). The other solution required reading the oral Torah into the written one, by inserting into the written Torah citations and allusions to the oral one, and, as a matter of fact, also by demonstrating, on both philosophical and theological grounds, the utter subordination and dependency of the oral Torah, the Mishnah, to the written Torah—while at the same time defending and vindicating that same oral Torah.

The Problem of the Mishnah

When, in ca. A.D. 200, the Mishnah reached closure and was received and adopted as law by the state-sanctioned Jewish governments in the Roman Empire, the land of Israel, Iran, and Babylonia, the function and character of the document precipitated a considerable crisis. Politically and theologically presented as the foundation for the everyday administration of the affairs of Jewry, the Mishnah ignored the politics of the sponsoring regimes. Essentially ahistorical, the code hardly identified as authoritative any known

---

problem of how biblical exegesis has framed the history of Judaism, a subject to which my dear friend and long-time teacher, Shemaryahu Talmon, has so richly endowed with his own scholarship.

political institution, let alone the patriarchate in the land of Israel or the exilarchate in Babylonia. True, that political-institutional flaw (from the viewpoint of the sponsoring authorities) scarcely can have proved critical.

But silence of the author of the Mishnah on the theological call for their document presented not a chronic but an acute problem. Since Jews generally accepted the authority of Moses at Sinai, failure to claim for the document a clear and explicit relationship to the Torah of Moses defined that acute issue. Why should people accept as authoritative the rulings of this piece of writing? Omitting reference to a theological, as much as to a political, myth, the Mishnah also failed to signal the relationship between it and Scripture. Since, for all Judaisms, Hebrew Scriptures in general, and the Pentateuch in particular, represented God's will for Israel, silence on that matter provoked considerable response. Let me now spell out in some detail the political, theological, and literary difficulties presented by the Mishnah to any theory that the Mishnah formed part of God's revelation to Moses at Sinai. To make its way into Israelite life, the Mishnah as a constitution and code demanded for itself a theory of beginnings at (or in relation to) Sinai, with Moses, from God. The character of the Mishnah itself hardly won confidence since, on the face of it, the document formed part of or derived from Sinai. It was originally published through oral formulation and oral transmission, that is, in the medium of memorization. But it had been in the medium of writing that, in the view of all of Israel until about A.D. 200, God had been understood to reveal the divine word and will. The Torah was a written book. People who claimed to receive further messages from God usually wrote them down. They had three choices in securing acceptance of their account. All three involved linking the new to the old.

Insofar as a piece of Jewish writing did not find a place in relationship to Scripture, its author laid no claim to present a holy book. The contrast between the Book of Jubilees and the Testaments of the Patriarchs, with their constant and close harping on biblical matters, and the several Books of Maccabees, shows the differences. The former claim to present God's revealed truth, the latter, history. So a book was holy because in style, in authorship, or in (alleged) origin it continued Scripture, finding a place therefore (at least in the author's mind) within the canon, or because it provided an exposition on Scripture's meaning. But the Mishnah made no such claim. It entirely ignored the style of Biblical Hebrew, speaking in a quite different kind of Hebrew altogether. It is silent on its authorship through sixty-two of the sixty-three tractates (the claims of ʾAbot are *post factum*). In any event, nowhere does the Mishnah contain the claim that God had inspired the authors of the document. These are not given biblical names and certainly are not alleged to have been biblical saints. Most of the book's named authorities flourished within the same century as its anonymous arrangers and redactors, not in remote antiquity. Above all, the Mishnah contains scarcely a handful of exegeses of Scripture. These, where they occur, play a trivial and tangential role. So here is the problem of the Mishnah: different from Scripture in language and style, indifferent to the claim of authorship by a biblical hero or divine inspiration, stunningly aloof from allusion to verses of Scripture for nearly the whole of its discourse—yet authoritative for Israel.

The Two Solutions to the Problem of the Mishnah

One response was represented by the claim that the authorities of the Mishnah stood in a chain of tradition that extended back to Sinai; stated explicitly in the Mishnah's first apologetic, tractate ²Abot, that circulated from approximately a generation beyond the promulgation of the Mishnah itself, that view required amplification and concrete demonstration. This approach treated the word *torah* as a common noun, as the word that spoke of a status or classification of sayings. A saying was *torah*, that is, enjoyed the status of *torah* or fell into the classification of *torah*, if it stood in the line of tradition from Sinai.

A second and distinct response took the same view of *torah* as a common noun. This response was to treat the Mishnah as subordinate to, and dependant upon, Scripture. Then *torah* was what fell into the classification of the revelation of *Torah* by God to Moses at Sinai. The way of providing what was needed within that theory was to link statements of the Mishnah to statements ("proof texts") of Scripture. The Tosefta (ca. 300)—a compilation of citations of and comments upon the Mishnah, together with some autonomous materials that may have reached closure in the period in which the work of redaction of the Mishnah was going on, as well as the Talmud of the Land of Israel (ca. 400)—fairly systematically did just that.

The former solution treated Torah with a small *t*, that is to say, as a generic classification, and identified the Mishnah with the Torah revealed to Moses at Sinai by claiming a place for the Mishnah's authorities in the process of tradition and transmission that brought torah—no longer, the Torah, the specific writing comprising the Five Books of Moses—to contemporary Israel, the Jewish people. It was a theological solution, expressed through ideas, attitudes, and implicit claims, but not through sustained rewriting of either Scripture or the Mishnah. The latter solution, by contrast, concerned the specific and concrete statements of the Mishnah and required a literary, not merely a theological, statement, one precise and specific to passages of the Mishnah, one after the other. What was demanded by the claim that the Mishnah depended upon, but therefore enjoyed the standing of, Scripture, was a line-by-line commentary upon the Mishnah in light of Scripture. But this too, I stress, treated *torah* as a common noun.

The third way, which is Sifra's, would set aside the two solutions, the theological and the literary, and explore the much more profound issues of the fundamental and generative structure of right thought, yielding, as a matter of fact, both Scripture and the Mishnah. This approach insisted that *torah* always was a proper noun. There was, and is, only the Torah. But this—the Torah—demanded expansion and vast amplification. When we know the principles of logical structure and especially those of hierarchical classification that animate the Torah, we can undertake part of the task of expansion and amplification, that is, join in the processes of thought that, in the mind of God, yielded the Torah. For when we know how God thought in giving the Torah to Moses at Sinai and so accounting for the classifications and their ordering in the very creation of the world, we can ourselves enter into the Torah and participate in its processes.

Sifra's Solution to the Problem of the Mishnah

The authors of Sifra attempted to set forth the dual Torah as a single, cogent statement, doing so by reading the Mishnah into Scripture not merely for proposition but for expression of proposition. On the surface that decision represented a literary, not merely a theological, judgment. But within the deep structure of thought, it was far more than a mere matter of how to select and organize propositions. Presenting the two Torahs in a single statement constituted an experiment in logic—that logic, in particular, that made cogent thought possible, and that transformed facts into propositions, and propositions into judgments of the more, or the less, consequential. In this respect, Sifra did something no one else in Judaic antiquity even imagined attempting to do, and that is, to state the dual Torah in a single, coherent, cogent piece of writing, a piece of writing in which new thought came to expression in a very particular medium indeed.

While the Mishnah's other apologists wrote the written Torah into the Mishnah, Sifra wrote the oral Torah into Scripture. That is to say, the other of the two approaches to the problem of the Mishnah, the one of Sifra, to begin with claimed to demonstrate that the Mishnah found its correct place within the written Torah itself. Instead of citing verses of Scripture in the context of the Mishnah, Sifra cited passages of the Mishnah in the context of Scripture, Leviticus in particular. Let me concentrate on the other solution, the one that characterized authorities from ʾ*Abot* and the Tosefta through the Babylonian Talmud, which we may call "the appeal to the Torah for a solution to the problem of the Mishnah."

Sifra's position is that the Mishnah is authoritative not because it is *torah* in the generic sense, but because it simply amplifies or depends upon the Torah, in the particular sense of the Five Books of Moses. The earliest exegetical strata of the two talmuds and the legal-exegetical writings produced in the two hundred years after the closure of the Mishnah took the position that the Mishnah is wholly dependent upon Scripture and authoritative, in the status (*but not the classification*) of the Torah, because of that dependency. Whatever is of worth in the Mishnah can be shown to derive directly from Scripture. So the Mishnah was represented as distinct from, and subordinate to, Scripture. This position is expressed in an obvious way. When the talmuds cite a Mishnah pericope, they commonly ask, "What is the source of these words?" And the answer invariably is, "As it is said in Scripture." This constitutes not only a powerful defense for the revealed truth of the Mishnah. It presents, also, a stunning judgment upon the standing (and, as a matter of fact, the classification) of the Mishnah. For when the exegetes find themselves constrained to add proof texts, they admit the need to acknowledge that the Mishnah is not (part of) the Torah but only a secondary expression or amplification of the Torah.

That judgment upon the Mishnah forms part of the polemic of Sifra—but only part of it. Sifra conducts a sustained polemic against the failure of the Mishnah to cite Scripture very much or systematically to link its ideas to Scripture through the medium of formal demonstration by exegesis. Sifra's rhetorical exegesis follows a standard redactional form. Scripture will be cited. Then a statement will be made about its meaning, or a statement of law correlative to that Scripture will be given. That statement sometimes cites the Mishnah, often verbatim. Finally, the author of Sifra invariably states, "Now is that not (merely) logical?" And the point of that statement will be, can this position not be gained through the working of mere logic, based upon facts supplied (to be sure) by Scripture?

The polemical power of Sifra lies in its repetitive demonstration that the stated position, citation of a Mishnah pericope, is not only not the product of logic, but is, and can only be, the product of exegesis of Scripture. That is only part of the matter, as I shall explain, but that component of the larger judgment of Sifra's authors does make the point that the Mishnah is subordinated to Scripture and validated only through Scripture. In that regard, Sifra stands at one with the position of the other successor writings, even though Sifra's writers carried to a much more profound level of thought the critique of the Mishnah. They did so by rethinking the logical foundations of the entire Torah.

The Importance of Classification in the System of the Mishnah

The system of philosophy expressed through concrete and detailed law presented by the Mishnah consists of a coherent logic and topic, a cogent world view, and comprehensive way of living. It is a world view which speaks of transcendent things, a way of life in response to the supernatural meaning of what is done, a heightened and deepened perception of the sanctification of Israel in deed and in deliberation. That paramount concern accounts for the centrality of classification, the appeal of the logic of

Biblical Exegesis and the Formation of Judaism 351

hierarchical classification in the demonstration of comparisons and contrasts, in the formation of the thought of the document. For sanctification in the Mishnah's system means establishing the stability, order, regularity, predictability, and reliability of Israel in the world of nature and supernature in particular at moments and in contexts of danger. And it is through assigning to all things their rightful name, setting of all things in their proper position, that we discover the laws of stability, order, regularity, and predictability. Danger means instability, disorder, irregularity, uncertainty, and betrayal. Each topic of the system as a whole takes up a critical and indispensable moment or context of social being. Through what is said in regard to each of the Mishnah's principal topics, what the system as a whole wishes to declare is fully expressed. Yet if the parts severally and jointly give the message of the whole, the whole cannot exist without all of the parts, so well joined and carefully crafted are they all.

What this means for the requirements of logical demonstration is quite obvious. To show something to be true, one has to demonstrate that, in logic, it conforms to the regularity and order that form the guarantee of truth. Analysis is meant to discover order: the rule that covers diverse (and by nature disorderly) things, the shared trait, the general and prevailing principle of regularity. And to discover the prevailing rule, one has to know how to classify things that seem to be each *sui generis*, how to find the rule that governs diverse things. And that explains the centrality in the system of the Mishnah of the classification of things. At issue between the framers of the Mishnah and the authors of Sifra is the correct sources of classification. The framers of the Mishnah effect their taxonomy through the traits of things. But the authors of Sifra insists that the source of classification is Scripture. We shall now see two expressions of the considerable debate. Here we shall show how Sifra time and again demonstrates that classification without Scripture's data cannot be carried out without Scripture's data, and, it must follow, hierarchical arguments based on extra-scriptural taxa always fail.

In the Mishnah we seek connection between fact and fact, sentence and sentence, by comparing and contrasting two things that are like and not alike. At the logical level the Mishnah falls into the category of familiar philosophical thought. Once we seek regularities, we propose rules. What is like another things falls under its rule, and what is not like the other falls under the opposite rule. Accordingly, as to the species of the genus, so far as they are alike, they share the same rule. So far as they are not alike, each follows a rule contrary to that governing the other. So the work of analysis is what produces connection, and therefore the drawing of conclusions derives from comparison and contrast: the *and*, the *equal*. The proposition then that forms the conclusion concerns the essential likeness of the two offices, except where they are different, but the fundamental assumption is that we can explain both likeness and differences by appeal to a principle of fundamental order and unity. To make these observations concrete, we turn to the case at hand. The important contrast comes at the outset. The high priest and king fall into a single genus, but speciation, based on traits particular to the king, then distinguishes the one from the other. All of this exercise is conducted essentially independently of Scripture; the classifications derive from the system, are viewed as autonomous constructs; traits of things define classifications and dictate what is like and what is unlike.

Sifra's Critique of Designating Classifications without Scriptural Definition: A Preliminary View

Let us now examine one sustained example of how Sifra rejects the principles of the logic of hierarchical classification *as these are worked out by the framers of the Mishnah*. I emphasize that the critique applies to the way in which a shared logic is worked out by the other writing. For it is not the principle that like things follow the same rule (unlike things, the opposite rule) that is at stake. Nor is the principle of hierarchical classification embodied in the argument *a fortiori* at issue. What Sifra disputes is that we can classify things on our own by appeal to the traits or indicative characteristics, that is, utterly without reference to Scripture. The argument is simple. On our own, we cannot classify species into genera. Everything is different from everything else in some way. But Scripture tells us what things are like what other things for what purposes, hence Scripture imposes on things the definitive classifications, and not traits we discern in the things themselves. When we see the nature of the critique, we shall have a clear picture of what is at stake when we examine, in some detail, precisely how the Mishnah's logic does its work. That is why at the outset I present a complete composition in which Sifra tests the modes of classification characteristic of the Mishnah, resting as they do on the traits of things viewed out of the context of Scripture's categories of things.

5. Parashat Vayyiqra Dibura Denedabah, Parashah 3:v:i

1.A. "[If his offering is] a burnt offering [from the herd, he shall offer a male without blemish; he shall offer it at the door of the tent of meeting, that he may be accepted before the Lord; he shall lay his hand upon the head of the burnt offering, and it shall be accepted for him to make atonement for him]" (Lev 1:2):
  B. Why does Scripture refer to a burnt offering in particular?
  C. For one might have taken the view that all of the specified grounds for the invalidation of an offering should apply only to the burnt offering that is brought as a freewill offering.
  D. But how should we know that the same grounds for invalidation apply also to a burnt offering that is brought in fulfillment of an obligation [for instance, the burnt offering that is brought for a leper

who is going through a rite of purification, or the bird brought by a woman who has given birth as part of her purification rite, Leviticus 14 and 12, respectively]?
E. It is a matter of logic.
F. Bringing a burnt offering as a freewill offering and bringing a burnt offering in fulfillment of an obligation [are parallel to one another and fall into the same classification].
G. Just as a burnt offering that is brought as a freewill offering is subject to all of the specified grounds for invalidation, so to a burnt offering brought in fulfillment of an obligation, all the same grounds for invalidation should apply.
H. No, [that reasoning is not compelling. For the two species of the genus, burnt offering, are not wholly identical and can be distinguished, on which basis we may also maintain that the grounds for invalidation that pertain to the one do not necessarily apply to the other. Specifically:] if you have taken that position with respect to the burnt offering brought as a freewill offering, for which there is no equivalent, will you take the same position with regard to the burnt offering brought in fulfillment of an obligation, for which there is an equivalent? [For if one is obligated to bring a burnt offering by reason of obligation and cannot afford a beast, one may bring birds, as at Lev 14:22, but if one is bringing a freewill offering, a less expensive form of the offering may not serve.]
I. Accordingly, since there is the possibility in the case of the burnt offering brought in fulfillment of an obligation, in which case there is an acceptable equivalent [to the more expensive beast, through the less expensive birds], all of the specified grounds for invalidation [which apply, in any case, to the more expensive burnt offering brought as a freewill offering] should not apply at all.
J. That is why in the present passage, Scripture refers simply to "burnt offering," [and without further specification, the meaning is then simple:] all the same are the burnt offering brought in fulfillment of an obligation and a burnt offering brought as a freewill offering in that all of the same grounds for invalidation of the beast that pertain to the one pertain also to the other.
2.A. And how do we know that the same rules of invalidation of a blemished beast apply also in the case of a beast that is designated in substitution of a beast sanctified for an offering [in line with Lev 27:10, so that, if one states that a given, unconsecrated beast is to take the place of a beast that has already been consecrated, the already consecrated beast remains in its holy status, and the beast to which reference is made also becomes consecrated]?
B. The matter of bringing a burnt offering and the matter of bringing a substituted beast fall into the same classification [since both are offerings that in the present instance will be consumed upon the altar,

and, consequently, they fall under the same rule as to invalidating blemishes].
- C. Just as the entire protocol of blemishes applies to the one, so in the case of the beast that is designated as a substitute, the same invalidating blemishes pertain.
- D. No, if you have invoked that rule in the case of the burnt offering, in which case no status of sanctification applies should the beast that is designated as a burnt offering be blemished in some permanent way, will you make the same statement in the case of a beast that is designated as a substitute? For in the case of a substituted beast, the status of sanctification applies even though the beast bears a permanent blemish! [So the two do not fall into the same classification after all, since to begin with one cannot sanctify a permanently blemished beast, which beast can never enter the status of sanctification, but through an act of substitution, a permanently blemished beast can be placed into the status of sanctification.]
- E. Since the status of sanctification applies [to a substituted beast] even though the beast bears a permanent blemish, all of the specified grounds for invalidation as a matter of logic should not apply to it.
- F. That is why in the present passage, Scripture refers simply to "burnt offering," [and without further specification, the meaning is then simple:] all the same are the burnt offering brought in fulfillment of an obligation and a burnt offering brought as a substitute for an animal designated as holy, in that all of the same grounds for invalidation of the beast that pertain to the one pertain also to the other.

3.A. And how do we know [that the protocol of blemishes that applies to the burnt offering brought as a freewill offering applies also to] animals that are subject to the rule of a sacrifice as a peace offering?
- B. It is a matter of logic. The matter of bringing a burnt offering and the matter of bringing animals that are subject to the rule of a sacrifice as a peace offering fall into the same classification [since both are offerings, and consequently under the same rule as to invalidating blemishes].
- C. Just as the entire protocol of blemishes applies to the one, so in the case of animals that are subject to the rule of a sacrifice as a peace offering, the same invalidating blemish pertain.
- D. And it is furthermore a matter of an argument *a fortiori*, as follows:
- E. If to a burnt offering when in the form of a bird, [which is inexpensive,] the protocol of invalidating blemishes applies, to peace offerings, which are not valid when brought in the form of a bird, surely the same protocol of invalidating blemishes should also apply!
- F. No, if you have applied that rule to a burnt offering, in which case females are not valid for the offering as male beasts are, will you say the same of peace offerings? For female beasts as much as male beasts

may be brought for sacrifice in the status of the peace offering. [The two species may be distinguished from one another.]

G. Since it is the case that female beasts as much as male beasts may be brought for sacrifice in the status of the peace offering, the protocol of invalidating blemishes should not apply to a beast designated for use as peace offerings.

H. That is why in the present passage, Scripture refers simply to "burnt offering," [and without further specification, the meaning is then simple:] all the same are the burnt offering brought in fulfillment of an obligation and an animal designated under the rule of peace offerings, in that all of the same grounds for invalidation of the beast that pertain to the one pertain also to the other.

The systematic exercise proves for beasts that serve in three classifications of offerings—burnt offerings, substitutes, and peace offerings—that the same rules of invalidation apply throughout. The comparison of the two kinds of burnt offerings, voluntary and obligatory, shows that they are sufficiently different from one another so that, as a matter of logic, what pertains to the one need not apply to the other. Then come the differences between an animal that is consecrated and one that is designated as a substitute for one that is consecrated. Finally, we distinguish between the applicable rules of the sacrifice: a burnt offering yields no meat for the person in behalf of whom the offering is made, while one sacrificed under the rule of peace offerings does. What is satisfying, therefore, is that we run the changes on three fundamentally dissimilar differences and show that, in each case, the differences between like things are greater than the similarities. I cannot imagine a more perfect exercise in the applied and practical logic of comparison and contrast.

Sifra concurs in the fundamental principle that sanctification consists in calling things by their rightful name, or, in philosophical language, discovering the classification of things and determining the rule that governs diverse things. Where Sifra differs from the view of the Mishnah's concerns—I emphasize—*the origins of taxa*: how do we know what diverse things form a single classification of things? Taxa originate in Scripture. Accordingly, at stake in the critique of the Mishnah is not the principles of logic necessary for understanding the construction and inner structure of creation. All parties among sages concurred that the inner structure set forth by a logic of classification alone could sustain the system of ordering all things in proper place and under the proper rule. The like belongs with the like and conforms to the rule governing the like, the unlike goes over to the opposite and conforms to the opposite rule. When we make lists of the like, we also know the rule governing all the items on those lists, respectively. We know that and one other thing, namely, the opposite rule, governing all items sufficiently like to belong on those lists, but sufficiently unlike to be placed on other lists. That rigorously philosophical logic of analysis (comparison and contrast) served because it was the only logic that could serve a system that proposed to make the statement concerning order and right array. Let me first show how the logic of proving propositions worked, then review Sifra's systematic critique of the way in which the Mishnah's framers applied that logic, specifically, how they proposed to identify classifications.

Sifra's Critique of the Mishnah:
The Taxonomic Attack on Taxonomic Logic

As is now clear, the source of classifications proves to define the decisive point at issue between the authors of Sifra and the framers of the Mishnah. No one denies the principle of hierarchical classification. That is an established fact, a self-evident trait of mind. The argument of Sifra is that, by themselves, things do not possess traits that permit us finally to classify species into a common genus. There always are traits distinctive to a classification. Accordingly, it is the argument of Sifra that, without the revelation of the Torah, we are not able to effect any classification at all, we are left, that is to say, only with species, no genus—only with cases, no rules. I shall now review a series of specific statements of that general position.

The Fundamental Critique:
The Limitations of Monothetic Classification

The thrust of Sifra's attack on the Mishnah's taxonomic logic is readily discerned. Time and again, we can easily demonstrate, things have so many and such diverse and contradictory indicative traits that, comparing one thing to something else, we can always distinguish one species from another. Even though we find something in common, we also can discern some other trait characteristic of one thing but not the other. Consequently, we also can show that the hierarchical logic on which we rely, the argument *a fortiori* or *qol vehomer* will not serve. For if (on the basis of one set of traits which yield a given classification) we place into hierarchical order two or more items (on the basis of a different set of traits), we have either a different classification altogether, or, much more commonly, simply a different hierarchy. So the attack on the way in which the Mishnah has done its work appeals to not merely the limitations of classification solely on the basis of traits of things. The more telling argument addresses what is, to *Listenwissenschaft*, the source of power and compelling proof: hierarchization. That is why, throughout, we must designate the Mishnah's mode of

Listenwissenschaft a logic of hierarchical classification. Things are not merely like or unlike, therefore following one rule or its opposite. Things also are weightier or less weighty, and that a particular point of likeness of difference generates the logical force of *Listenwissenschaft*.

Sifra repeatedly demonstrates that the formation of classifications based on monothetic taxonomy, that is to say, traits that are not only common to both items but that are shared throughout both items (subject to comparison and contrast) simply will not serve. For at every point at which someone alleges uniform or monothetic likeness, Sifra will demonstrate difference. Then how to proceed? Appeal to some shared traits as a basis for classification: this is not like that, and that is not like this, but the indicative traits that both exhibit is such and such, that is to say, polythetic taxonomy. The self-evident problem in accepting differences among things and insisting, nonetheless, on their monomorphic character for purposes of comparison and contrast cannot be set aside. Who says? That is, if I can adduce evidence for a shared classification of things, only a few traits among many characteristic of each thing, then what stops me from treating all things alike?

Polythetic taxonomy opens the way to an unlimited exercise in finding what diverse things have in common and imposing, for that reason, one rule on everything. Then the very working of *Listenwissenschaft* as a tool of analysis, differentiation, comparison, contrast, and the descriptive determination of rules yields the opposite of what is desired. Chaos, not order; a mass of exceptions, not rules; a world of examples, each subject to its own regulation, instead of a world of order and proportion, composition and stability, will result.

How Sifra Affirms Taxonomic Logic

Sifra demonstrates that *Listenwissenschaft* is a self-evidently valid mode of demonstrating the truth of propositions. But *the* source of the correct classification of things is Scripture and only Scripture. Without Scripture's intervention into the taxonomy of the world, we should have no knowledge at all of which things fall into which classifications and therefore are governed by which rules. How then do we appeal to Scripture to designate the operative classifications? Here is a simple example of the alternative mode of classification, one that does not appeal to the traits of things but to the utilization of names by Scripture. What we see is how, by naming things in one way rather than in another, Scripture orders all things, classifying and, in the nature of things, also hierarchizing them. Here is one example among many of how Sifra conceives the right way of logical thought to proceed.

7. Parashat Vayyiqra Dibura Denedabah, Parashah 4:vii:v

1.A. "... and Aaron's sons the priests shall present the blood and throw the blood [against all sides of the altar that is at the door of the tent of meeting]" (Lev 1:5):
  B. Why does Scripture make use of the word "blood" twice [instead of using a pronoun]?
  C. [It is for the following purpose:] How on the basis of Scripture do you know that if blood deriving from one burnt offering was confused with blood deriving from another burnt offering, blood deriving from one burnt offering with blood deriving from a beast that has been substituted therefor, blood deriving from a burnt offering with blood deriving from an unconsecrated beast, the mixture should nonetheless be presented?
  D. It is because Scripture makes use of the word "blood" twice [instead of using a pronoun].
2.A. Is it possible to suppose that, while if blood deriving from beasts in the specified classifications, it is to be presented, for the simple reason that if the several beasts while alive had been confused with one another, they might be offered up,
  B. but how do we know that, even if the blood of a burnt offering were confused with that of a beast killed as a guilt offering, [it is to be offered up].
  C. I shall concede the case of the mixture of the blood of a burnt offering confused with that of a beast killed as a guilt offering, it is to be presented, for both this one and that one fall into the classification of Most Holy Things.
  D. But how do I know that, if the blood of a burnt offering were confused with the blood of a beast slaughtered in the classification of peace offerings or of a thanksgiving offering, [it is to be presented]?
  E. I shall concede the case of the mixture of the blood of a burnt offering confused with that of a beast slaughtered in the classification of peace offerings or of a thanksgiving offering, [it is to be presented,] because the beasts in both classifications produce blood that has to be sprinkled four times.
  F. But how do I know that, if the blood of a burnt offering were confused with the blood of a beast slaughtered in the classification of a firstling or a beast that was counted as tenth or of a beast designated as a passover, [it is to be presented]?
  G. I shall concede the case of the mixture of the blood of a burnt offering confused with that of a beast slaughtered in the classification of firstling or a beast that was counted as tenth or of a beast designated as a passover, [it is to be presented,] because Scripture uses the word "blood" two times.

Biblical Exegesis and the Formation of Judaism 359

H. Then while I may make that concession, might I also suppose that if the blood of a burnt offering was confused with the blood of beasts that had suffered an invalidation, it also may be offered up?
I. Scripture says, "Its blood," [thus excluding such a case].
J. Then I shall concede the case of a mixture of the blood of a valid burnt offering with the blood of beasts that had suffered an invalidation, which blood is not valid to be presented at all.
K. But how do I know that, if such blood were mixed with the blood deriving from beasts set aside as sin offerings to be offered on the inner altar, [it is not to be offered up]?
L. I can concede that the blood of a burnt offering that has been mixed with the blood deriving from beasts set aside as sin offerings to be offered on the inner altar is not to be offered up, for the one is offered on the inner altar, and the other on the outer altar [the burnt offering brought as a freewill offering, under discussion here, is slaughtered at the altar "that is at the door of the tent of meeting," not at the inner altar].
M. But how do I know that, even if the blood of a burnt offering was confused with the blood of sin offerings that are to be slaughtered at the outer altar, it is not to be offered up?
N. Scripture says, "Its blood," [thus excluding such a case].

In place of the rejection of arguments resting on classifying species into a common genus, I now demonstrate how classification really is to be carried on. It is through the imposition upon data of the categories dictated by Scripture: Scripture's use of language. That is the force of this powerful exercise. The first section (1.A–D) sets the stage, simply pointing out that the double use of the word *blood* encompasses a case in which blood in two distinct classifications is somehow confused in the process of the conduct of the cult. In such a case it is quite proper to pour out the mixture of blood deriving from distinct sources, for example, beasts that have served different, but comparable, purposes. Sifra then systematically work out the limits of that rule, showing how comparability works, then pointing to cases in which comparability is set aside. Throughout the exposition, at the crucial point Sifra invokes the formulation of Scripture, subordinating logic or in this instance the process of classification of like species to the dictation of Scripture. I cannot imagine a more successful demonstration of what the framers wish to say.

The reason for Scripture's unique power of classification is the possibility of polythetic classification that only Scripture makes possible. Because of Scripture's provision of taxa, we are able to undertake the science of *Listenwissenschaft*, including hierarchical classification, in the right way. What can we do because we appeal to Scripture, which we cannot do if we do not rely on Scripture? It is to establish the possibility of polythetic classification. We can appeal to shared traits of otherwise distinct taxa and so transform species into a common genus for a given purpose. Only Scripture makes that initiative feasible, so Sifra maintains. What is at stake? It is the possibility of doing precisely what the framers of the Mishnah wish to do. That is to join together masses of diverse data into a single, encompassing statement, to show the rule that inheres in diverse cases. In what follows, we shall see an enormous, coherent, and beautifully articulated exercise in the comparison and contrast of many things of a single genus. The whole holds together, because Scripture makes possible the statement of all things within a single rule. That is, as I have noted, precisely what the framers of the Mishnah proposed to accomplish. Sifra maintains that only by appeal to the Torah is this feat of learning possible. If, then, we wish to understand all things all together and all at once under a single encompassing rule, we had best revert to the Torah, with its account of the rightful names, positions, and order, imputed to all things.

22. Parashat Vayyiqra Dibura Denedabah, Parashah 11:xxii:i

1.A. [With reference to 5:5:] There are those [offerings which require bringing near but do not require waving, waving but not bringing near, waving and bringing near, neither waving nor bringing near; these are offerings which require bringing near but do not require waving: the meal offering of fine flour and the meal offering prepared in the baking pan and the meal offering prepared in the frying pan, and the meal offering of cakes and the meal offering of wafers, and the meal offering of priests, and the meal offering of an anointed priest, and the meal offering of Gentiles, and the meal offering of women, and the meal offering of a sinner. R. Simeon says, "The meal offering of priests and of the anointed priest—bringing near does not apply to them, because the taking of a handful does not apply to them. And whatever is not subject to the taking of a handful is not subject to bringing near."] [Scripture] says, "When you present to the Lord a meal offering that is made in any of these ways, it shall be brought [to the priest who shall take it up to the altar]:"
   B. What requires bringing near is only the handful alone. How do I know that I should encompass under the rule of bringing near the meal offering?
   C. Scripture says explicitly, "Meal offering."
   D. How do I know that I should encompass all meal offerings?
   E. Scripture says, using the accusative particle, "The meal offering."
2.A. I might propose that what requires bringing near is solely the meal offering brought as a freewill offering.
   B. How do I know that the rule encompasses an obligatory meal offering?

Biblical Exegesis and the Formation of Judaism 361

C. It is a matter of logic.
D. Bringing a meal offering as a freewill offering and bringing a meal offering as a matter of obligation form a single classification. Just as a meal offering presented as a freewill offering requires bringing near, so the same rule applies to a meal offering of a sinner [brought as a matter of obligation], which should likewise require bringing near.
E. No, if you have stated that rule governing bringing near in the case of a freewill offering, on which oil and frankincense have to be added, will you say the same of the meal offering of a sinner [Lev 5:11], which does not require oil and frankincense?
F. The meal offering brought by a wife accused of adultery will prove to the contrary, for it does not require oil and frankincense, but it does require bringing near [as is stated explicitly at Num 5:15].
G. No, if you have applied the requirement of bringing near to the meal offering brought by a wife accused of adultery, which also requires waving, will you say the same of the meal offering of a sinner, which does not have to be waved?
H. Lo, you must therefore reason by appeal to a polythetic analogy [in which not all traits pertain to all components of the category, but some traits apply to them all in common]:
I. the meal offering brought as a freewill offering, which requires oil and frankincense, does not in all respects conform to the traits of the meal offering of a wife accused of adultery, which does not require oil and frankincense, and the meal offering of the wife accused of adultery, which requires waving, does not in all respects conform to the traits of a meal offering brought as a freewill offering, which does not require waving.
J. But what they have in common is that they are alike in requiring the taking up of a handful and they are also alike in that they require bringing near.
K. I shall then introduce into the same classification the meal offering of a sinner, which is equivalent to them as to the matter of the taking up of a handful, and also should be equivalent to them as to the requirement of being drawn near.
L. But might one not argue that the trait that all have in common is that all of them may be brought equally by a rich and a poor person and require drawing near, which then excludes from the common classification the meal offering of a sinner, which does not conform to the rule that it may be brought equally by a rich and a poor person, [but may be brought only by a poor person,] and such an offering also should not require being brought near!
M. [The fact that the polythetic classification yields indeterminate results means failure once more, and, accordingly,] Scripture states, "Meal offering,"

N. with this meaning: all the same are the meal offering brought as a freewill offering and the meal offering of a sinner, both this and that require being brought near.

The elegant exercise draws together the various types of meal offerings and shows that they cannot form a classification of either a monothetic or a polythetic character. Consequently, Scripture must be invoked to supply the proof for the classification of the discrete items. The important language is at 2.H-J: these differ from those, and those from these, but what they have in common is.... Then we demonstrate in 2.M, with appeal to Scripture, the sole valid source of polythetic classification. And this is constant throughout Sifra.

While setting forth its critique of the Mishnah's utilization of the logic of comparison and contrast in hierarchical classification, Sifra is careful not to criticize the Mishnah. Its position favors restating the Mishnah within the context of Scripture, not rejecting the conclusions of the Mishnah, let alone its authority. Consequently, when we find a critique of applied reason divorced from Scripture, we rarely uncover an explicit critique of the Mishnah, and when we find a citation of the Mishnah, we rarely uncover linkage to the ubiquitous principle that Scripture forms the source of all classification and hierarchy. When the Mishnah is cited by Sifra, it will be presented as part of the factual substrate of the Torah. When the logic operative throughout the Mishnah is subjected to criticism, the language of the Mishnah will rarely, if ever, be cited in context. The operative language in dealing with the critique of the applied logic of *Listenwissenschaft* as represented by the framers of the Mishnah ordinarily is, "Is it not a matter of logic?" Then the sorts of arguments against taxonomy pursued outside of the framework of Scripture's classifications will follow. When, by contrast, Sifra wishes to introduce a verbatim passage of the Mishnah into the context it has already established, it will ordinarily, though not always, use, *mikan amru*, which, in context, means, "in this connection [sages] have said." It is a simple fact that when the intent is to demolish improper reasoning, the Mishnah's rules in the Mishnah's language rarely, if ever, occur. When Sifra wishes to incorporate paragraphs of the Mishnah into its re-presentation of the Torah, it will do so either without fanfare, as in the passage at hand, or by the neutral joining-language "in this connection [sages] have said."

The Rehabilitation of Hierarchical Classification

Sifra never called into question the self-evident validity of taxonomic logic. Its critique is addressed only to how the Mishnah's framers identify the origins of, and delineate, taxa. But that critique proves fundamental to the case that Sifra proposed to make. For, intending to demonstrate that *the Torah* was a proper noun, and that everything that was valid came to expression in the single, cogent statement of the Torah, Sifra identified the fundamental issue. It is the debate over the way we know things. In insisting, in agreement with the framers of the Mishnah, that there are not only cases but also rules, not only species but also genera, Sifra also made its case in behalf of the case for the Torah as a proper noun. This carries us to the theological foundation for Sifra's sustained critique of applied reason.

In appealing to the principle, for taxonomy, of *sola Scriptura*, I mean to set forth what I conceive really to be at stake. It is the character of the Torah and what it is (in the Torah) that we wish to discern. And the answer to that question requires theological, not merely literary and philosophical, reflection on our part. For I maintain that in their delineation of correct hierarchical logic, Sifra uncovered, within the Torah (hence by definition, written and oral components of the Torah alike) an adumbration of the working of the mind of God. That is because the premise of all discourse is that the Torah was written by God and dictated by God to Moses at Sinai. And that will in the end explain why Sifra for its part has entered into the Torah long passages of not merely clarification but active intrusion, making itself a component of the interlocutorial process. To what end we know: it was to unite the dual Torah. But on what basis?

If Sifra had taken first place in the curriculum of Judaism, its representation of the written Torah and the oral Torah all together and all at once would have opened a different path altogether. For it is one thing to absorb the Torah, oral and written, and it is quite another to join in the processes of thought, the right way of thinking, that sustain the Torah. Sifra proposed to regain access to the modes of thought that guided the formation of the Torah, oral and written alike: comparison and contrast in this way, not in that, identification of categories in one manner, not in another. Since those were the modes of thought that, in Sifra's conception, dictated the structure of intellect upon which the Torah, the united Torah, rested, a simple conclusion is the sole possible one. A related but different issue is the question of the basis on which Sifra represented itself as participant in, and interlocutor of, the Torah, such that it was prepared to re-present, that is to say, simply rewrite (and therefore, itself write) the Torah.

Ancient Near East

RITUAL AND INCANTATION: INTERPRETATION AND TEXTUAL HISTORY OF *MAQLÛ* VII:58–105 AND IX:152–59

Tzvi Abusch

A magical ceremony is formed by the joining together of schematic ritual action and freer lyrical incantation. Not surprising, incantation and ritual are often related. Thus, a particularly interesting and useful way of classifying and analyzing incantations is according to the rituals that underlie or are mentioned in them. One of the simpler kinds of relationships occurs when the incantation itself contains a more or less straightforward description of the ritual actions.[1] When the text of such an incantation is provided with written instructions for the ritual that is to be performed alongside the

Author's Note: My examination of *Maqlû* VII:58–105 and IX:152–59 exemplifies the close connection of interpretation and textual formation, and, thus, it is surely an appropriate offering in honor of Professor Shemaryahu Talmon. From my days as a student of Bible, I recall Talmon's emphasis on the continuity of literary composition and textual transmission and his belief that students of the biblical text should not draw sharp distinctions between lower and higher criticism. I offer this example from the related field of cuneiform literature in support of the claim that interpretation and textual criticism are part of the same enterprise and should not be pursued in isolation from each other.

An early version of this paper was read before the 179th meeting of the American Oriental Society at New York in 1969. The present paper should be read in conjunction with my "The Ritual Tablet and Rubrics of *Maqlû*: Toward the History of the Series," in *A Highway from Egypt to Assyria: Studies in Ancient Near Eastern History and Historiography Presented to Hayim Tadmor* (ed. M. Cogan and I. Eph‹al; Jerusalem, forthcoming). The following sigla are used in this essay for texts in the British Museum: K., Rm., and Sm.; *STT* is used for texts published in *The Sultantepe Tablets*, vol. I (ed. O. R. Gurney and J. J. Finkelstein; London, 1957).

1. Knowing that this kind of a relationship exists can be quite useful. See, e.g., the textual notes on E. Ebeling, *Keilschrifttexte aus Assur religiösen Inhalts* (Leipzig, 1919–1923) no. 71 obv. 9–10 in B. Landsberger, "Zu den Übersetzungen Ebeling's ZDMG. 74, 175ff.," *Zeitschrift der Deutschen Morgenländischen Gesellschaft* 74 (1920) 440; and cf. idem, "The Old Babylonian Charm against *Merḫu*," *JNES* 14 (1955) 21 n. 30.

recitation, these prescriptions should in principle correspond to the ritual activity described in the incantation itself. In practice, however, the expected agreement is not always to be found. Such discrepancies often illumine one or another aspect of religious, social, literary, or textual history.

In this paper, I shall offer an example of such a discrepancy. More precisely, I shall note and explore a discrepancy between an individual incantation in the magical series *Maqlû* and the accompanying ritual instructions in the Ritual Tablet of the series, and offer an explanation for the discordance.[2] I wish, thereby, to reiterate the need to look closely at the connections between incantations and their ritual instructions. Moreover, I hope to provide a clear exegetical basis and confirmation for the judgment given elsewhere[3] that manuscripts of the Ritual Tablet of *Maqlû* preserve readings from, and may themselves even represent, two different recensions of the Ritual Tablet—an earlier shorter recension and a later expanded one—and that the expansion observed therein was motivated in part by the desire to render the instructions more detailed and explicit. The textual instance examined in this paper exemplifies one way in which ritual instructions were revised in the course of transmission. Forming part of the revision, this example sheds light on the history of composition of the text of the Ritual Tablet.

The Incantations and Their Rituals: Internal Analysis

Maqlû VII:58–83 is a straightforward incantation. It is a victim's address to a witch who has bewitched him. The speaker first describes the witch's malevolent activities against him (lines 58–65) and then states that he has performed similar actions against her (lines 66–72).[4] In his statement, he asserts that at the bidding of Ea, god of water and magic, he has drawn a flour representation of the witch before the sun-god Shamash:

yâši ᵈ*Ea mašmaš ilī umaʾʾeranni*
maḫar ᵈ*Šamaš ṣalamki ēṣir* . . .
ina ᵈ*Nisaba elleti bunnannīki umaššil*

---

2. Except where otherwise indicated, the magical series *Maqlû* is referred to according to the text and line numbers given in G. Meier's edition, *Die assyrische Beschwörungssammlung Maqlû* (AfO Beiheft 2; Berlin, 1937); and idem, "Studien zur Beschwörungssammlung *Maqlû*," *AfO* 21 (1966) 70–81. Minor corrections in Meier's edition are normally made without notice. I quote texts in transcription except when it is necessary to indicate the actual signs used.

3. See my "Ritual Tablet and Rubrics of *Maqlû*."

4. Line 68 should read: *lānki aṭṭul lamassaki abni baltaki āmur* (instead of *lānki abni baltaki āmur*). See Ebeling, *Keilschrifttexte aus Assur religiösen Inhalts*, no. 268 obv. 28: *lānki aṭ-ṭul*, and K. 8882: *lamassaki abni*; compare lines 59–60 (in line 59, read *ibnû* instead of *ēpušu*), which contain the parallel statement in the speaker's description of the witch's actions against him.

I am sent by Ea, exorcist of the gods,
Before Shamash I have drawn your representation . . .
With pure flour have I reproduced your likeness. (lines 66–67, 70)

He then states that he has turned back against her the evil magic that she had performed (lines 73–75),[5] and expresses the wishes that her own evil magic seize her (lines 76–80) and that it take leave of his body together with the water with which he washes himself and pour down upon her head:

itti mê ša zumriya u musâti ša qātēya liššaḫiṭma
ana muḫḫiki u lāniki lillikma anāku lubluṭ

May it rinse off with the water of my body and the washing of my hands
And come upon your head and face so that I may live. (lines 81–82)

He concludes with the wish that a substitute stand in for him (line 83).[6]

In short, the bewitched man states that he is washing himself over a flour representation of the witch and that he hopes, thereby, to transfer the witchcraft back to the witch and to rid himself of its evil effects. The content of the incantation and the kinds of correspondences that exist between similar incantations and their ritual instructions[7] lead one to expect that also here the patient will simply perform the ritual action of washing over a flour representation of the witch. But upon examination, the instructions for this incantation as recorded in Meier's edition of the Ritual Tablet of *Maqlû* ("Tablet IX") only partially fulfill these expectations. There, in lines 152–54, we read:[8]

arkišu É[N] *attī-mannu kaššaptu ša ēpušu* [*ṣalmī imannu*]
ṣalam kaššapti ša qēmi ina libbi namsê [*teṣṣer*]
ṣalam ṭīṭi ša kaššapti ina muḫḫi tašakkan qātēšu ana muḫḫi imessi[9]

---

5. Cf. *Maqlû* I:126–30.

6. *Maqlû* VII:83: *ēnītu līnânni māḫirtu limḫuranni*. For this line, cf. Abusch, *Babylonian Witchcraft Literature: Case Studies* (BJS 132; Atlanta, 1987) 33 n. 40.

7. Among many examples, compare (*a*) *Maqlû* VII:119–46 (esp. 136ff.) with IX:163–64; (*b*) H. C. Rawlinson, *The Cuneiform Inscriptions of Western Asia*, vol. 4: *A Selection from the Miscellaneous Inscriptions of Assyria* (2d ed.; ed. T. G. Pinches; London, 1891) no. 17 rev. 8–30 (esp. 18ff.) with rev. 31–34 (as restored by J. Laessøe, *Studies in the Assyrian Ritual and Series bît rimki* [Copenhagen, 1955] 51); and (*c*) Laessøe, *Assyrian Ritual and Series bît rimki*, 37–40: 1–55 and duplicates (esp. p. 39: 37ff.) with p. 40: B rev. 4′–5′ and D: 31′–33′.

8. Meier, *Die assyrische Beschwörungssammlung Maqlû*, 63. Meier's edition of these lines is based on K. 2385+ and K. 3584+. These pieces are now physically joined and include two additional fragments (K. 2385 + 3331 + 3584 + 3645 + 7274 + 7586 + 8033 + 11603).

9. See below, pp. 376–80, for important variants from Sultantepe. Rather than repeating *tamannu* in line 152 after Meier, I have construed ŠID-*nu* as *imannu* (cf. below n. 10). In line 154, I have replaced the first *ana* with *ina* (*ina muḫḫi tašakkan*). The tablet K. 2385+ has *ina*,

Afterward, he recites the incantation *Attī-mannu kaššaptu ša ēpušu ṣalmī*;
You draw a flour representation of the witch in a washbasin;
You place a clay figurine of the witch thereon; he washes his hands over it.

Accordingly, the Ritual Tablet prescribes that the officiating exorcist[10] draw a flour representation of the witch in a wash basin, that he then place a clay figurine of a second witch upon the flour representation of the first witch, and that finally the patient wash his hands over them. What is perplexing is that the incantation mentions nothing that might correspond to the part of the ritual instructions which prescribes the placing of a clay figurine of a second witch. The placing seems incongruous, and the incantation offers no comment whatsoever on the significance of this part of the ritual.[11]

But since the Ritual Tablet continues with a similar set of instructions for the next incantation in the series, VII:84–105,[12] we should examine that ritual in the hope of finding an explanation for the placing of the clay figurines. *Maqlû* IX:155–59 in Meier's edition reads:

ÉN *bāʾirtu ša bāʾirāti*
ṣalam kaššāpi u kaššapti
ša qēmi ina libbi namsê teṣṣ[*er*]

---

as does already K. Tallqvist, *Die assyrische Beschwörungsserie Maqlû* (Acta Societatis Scientiarum Fennicae 20/6; Leipzig, 1895), 2:92. In any case, *ina* is to be preferred; cf. *Maqlû* IX:158 || *STT* no. 83 rev. 71′.

10. In the Ritual Tablet, instructions in second person refer to the officiating exorcist, those in third person refer to the patient; cf. Abusch, "Mesopotamian Anti-Witchcraft Literature: Texts and Studies, Part I: The Nature of *Maqlû*: Its Character, Divisions, and Calendrical Setting," *JNES* 33 (1974) 254–55 n. 11.

11. I need hardly mention that the substitute of *Maqlû* VII:83 is not the verbal correspondence to the clay figurines. The substitute provides a further object to which the evil may be transferred. In witchcraft incantations, the substitution theme is probably secondary and foreign; here, in this incantation, it serves as an additional parallel or equivalent to the witch = flour representation upon whom the water is poured. Cf., e.g., *Maqlû* VII: 136ff. || IX:164.

12. Line 105 is the end of the incantation. According to Meier ("Studien zur Beschwörungssammlung *Maqlû*," 79), "Nach Z. 105 ist in AfO, Beih. 2, S. 50, die Trennungslinie zu tilgen, ebenso das [én] am Anfang von Z. 106." It is true that K. 2950+ does not contain a dividing line after VII:105 or the notation ÉN of the beginning of line 106, but VII:106–11 does not form part of the previous incantation. Note that the Ritual Tablet, IX:160, treats VII:106–11 as a separate incantation. In fact, the Sultantepe recension of the Ritual Tablet places the incantation VII:119–46 between VII:84–105 and VII:106–11. See *STT* 1 no. 83 rev. 72′; IX:163–64b || VII:119–46; IX:160 || VII:106–11; IX:161 || VII:112–18.

ṣalam ṭīṭi ša kaššāpi u kaššapti ina muḫḫi ṣalam qēmi[13] tašakkan qātēšu ana[14] muḫḫi imessi ina ḫuṣāb eʾri ana šalāšīšu ikar[rit]

Incantation. Bāʾirtu ša bāʾirāti;
You draw flour representations of the warlock and witch in a washbasin;
You place clay figurines of the warlock and witch on the flour representations;
He washes his hands over it; he makes three cuts with an ashwood twig.

This second ritual differs only slightly from the immediately preceding one cited above: instead of preparing images only of a witch, the exorcist draws flour images of both a warlock and a witch in a washbasin and places clay figurines of a second warlock and witch upon the flour representations. The patient washes his hands over them and then, in addition, incises them (perhaps only the flour representations) three times with a twig.

Perhaps, we would be able to make sense of the first ritual if we understood the second ritual better: for this purpose, we should address three questions: (1) Does the second ritual (IX:155–59) reveal a more satisfactory correspondence to its incantation (VII:84–105) than does the first ritual (IX:152–54)? (2) What is the meaning of this second ritual? (3) What is the relation between the two rituals?

In the second incantation (VII:84–105), the speaker begins by setting the scene (84–91). He presents a vivid picture of the witch roaming the main thoroughfares in search of the speaker, first, among the young men of the town and, then, among the maidens. He then continues, in lines 92–105, with an address to a second person. The interpretation of the latter section of the incantation, as well as of the whole incantation, depends upon the identities of the speaker and the addressee and upon their respective relations to the sorcerers enumerated in lines 94–100.

Each one of these lines begins with a designation of a kind of sorcerer; with the exception of the different designations, the lines are identical:[15]

kaššāpū	līpušūki	rikiski	aḫeppe
kaššāpātu	līpušāki	rikiski	aḫeppe
kurgarrû	līpušūki	rikiski	aḫeppe
eššebû	līpušūki	rikiski	aḫeppe

13. Ṣalam qēmi in line 158 is absent in STT 1 no. 83. For the significance of the presence of these words in the Nineveh text, but their absence in Sultantepe, see below, pp. 376–80.
14. Ana muḫḫi imessi of STT 1 no. 83 is to be preferred over ina muḫḫi imessi of K. 2385+.
15. But note the expected feminine form līpušāki in line 95.

naršindû	*līpušūki*	*rikiski*	*aḫeppe*
mušlaḫḫū	*līpušūki*	*rikiski*	*aḫeppe*
agugillū	*līpušūki*	*rikiski*	*aḫeppe*

Various translations, and thus implicitly various interpretations, have been offered for these lines; for example:

1. "(Though) the *e*[*ššebû*] bewitch you, I shall break the spell that is on you." (VII:97)[16]
2. "Though the *a*[*gugillu*]-sorcerers have protected you with charms, I will break your bands." (VII:100)[17]
3. "Die Zauberer mögen dich behexen, deinen Knoten zerbreche ich!" (VII:94)[18]

We may immediately disregard the first translation, which is predicated on the assumption that the addressee is the victim, since lines 101–5 treat the addressee as the enemy of the speaker:

amaḫḫaṣ lētki ašallapa lišānki
umallâ ru'āta ēnēki
ušallak aḫīki lillūta
u akkâši ruqbūta ušallakki
u mimma mala tēteppušī utâr ana muḫḫiki[19]

The addressee is the witch. Thus, these lines demonstrate that the aforementioned assumption and the first translation must be wrong.

Accordingly, the only translations which merit serious consideration are those which treat the speaker as the victim and the addressee as the witch. The translations which meet this requirement are the last two: (2) "Though the X have protected you with charms, I will break your bands," and (3) "May the X bewitch you, and I will break your bands." The second translation treats the sorcerers enumerated in this section as allies of the witch. In contrast, the third translation treats these sorcerers as allies of

---

16. *CAD* E 371.
17. *CAD* A/1 159.
18. Meier, *Die assyrische Beschwörungssammlung Maqlû*, 50. Cf. *AHw* 510 ("*kurgarrû*"): "gegen Hexen Maqlû VII 92.96"; *AHw* 258 ("*eššebû*"): "Pl. lúeš-še-bu-ú sollen dich behexen [*Maqlû* VII] Z. 97"; and *AHw* 17 ("*agugillu*"): "*a-gu-gil-lu*meš *līpušū-ki* (mögen dich behexen) Maqlû VII 100." More recently, *CAD* M/2 277: "MUŠ.LAḪ₄.MEŠ *līpušuki rikiski aḫeppi* let the snake charmers put a spell on you (sorceress) so I can break your spell *Maqlu* VII 99"; *CAD* N/1 362: "*nar-šin-du-u*.MEŠ *līpušuki* may the n.-sorcerers bewitch you ... *Maqlu* VII 98."
19. "I strike your cheek, tear out your tongue. . . . And I turn back on your head whatever (evil magic) you have repeatedly performed against me" (lines 101, 105).

the speaker in his confrontation with the witch. I prefer the third translation for several reasons, but notably because line 92 ([ē] uba⁾⁾akimma kurgarrî eššebê) is set up as the opposing counterpart to lines 88–89 (eṭlūt āli ubtana⁾⁾â / itti eṭlūt āli ubtana⁾⁾â⁾inni yâši).[20] Lines 92–93 are then to be translated, if somewhat freely, as "I call forth against you the cult players and the ecstatics[21] (and/so that) I (for my part) will break your bond."[22] Accordingly, these lines indicate that enemies of the addressee (= the witch) are summoned to aid the speaker and harm the witch. This conclusion is confirmed by the fact that the magicians in lines 94–100 are asked to līpušū the witch. When epēšu, meaning 'to practice magic,' governs only a nominal or pronominal personal object, it does not mean 'to protect' or 'to aid magically'. Rather, it means 'to bewitch (harmfully)'. Accordingly, the magical personnel who function as the grammatical subjects of līpušūki must be enemies of the witch.

We can, therefore, only accept that translation which treats the sorcerers enumerated in lines 92–100 as allies of the speaker and enemies of the witch. While it is true that most of the sorcerers mentioned are associated in Mesopotamian witchcraft texts with evil magic, there is evidence that originally witches would sometimes perform useful magical actions on behalf of clients[23] and that, in any case, certain of the sorcerers mentioned in VII:92–100 were known to side with the victim against the witch; for example:[24]

---

20. Note especially the use of bu⁾⁾û in VII:88–89 and 92. The intervening lines, VII:90–91, are possibly a literary addition: these lines interrupt and seem to be intrusive; moreover, they are governed by a different subject than lines 87–89. Their subject is singular, the witch, while the subject of lines 87–89 is a dual or feminine plural, her eyes.

21. Cf. Meier, "Studien zur Beschwörungssammlung Maqlû," 79 on VII:102, where W. von Soden notes: "ú-ba-⁾a-kim-ma 'ich suche für dich (auf)'."

22. Elsewhere I shall discuss the use of riksu in the witchcraft corpus.

23. See my discussion of the popular views of the witch in "The Demonic Image of the Witch in Standard Babylonian Literature: The Reworking of Popular Conceptions by Learned Exorcists," in Religion, Science, and Magic in Concert and in Conflict (ed. J. Neusner et al.; New York, 1989) 32–34. There, I have already mentioned this incantation as an example of a popular layer of witchcraft.

24. H. F. Lutz, Selected Sumerian and Babylonian Texts (Publications of the Babylonian Section, University Museum, University of Pennsylvania, 1/2; Philadelphia, 1919) no. 120 rev. 7–9 (|| Sm. 275 + Rm. 329 || K. 8933). In 1969 I identified Sm. 275 as a duplicate on the basis of F. W. Geers's copy, and surmised that Rm. 329 duplicates Lutz, no. 120 and joins Sm. 275 on the basis of the entry, "One section begins: ÉN an-nu-ú šu-ú an-ni-tu ši-i i-la-as-su-ma [ ]," in C. Bezold, Catalogue of the Cuneiform Tablets in the Kouyunjik Collection (London, 1889–1899) 4:1604, s. Rm. 329. C. B. F. Walker kindly checked and confirmed the suggested join. In 1976 I identified this incantation also on K. 8933 (the lines quoted are not preserved there). This incantation is part of an ušburruda genre of incantations. Note that these were brought together on collection tablets. Elsewhere, I shall treat the genre and cite the compositions, duplicates, and joins. Here I note only that in 1976 Walker confirmed my suggestion that K. 8079 (+) 8112 + 9666 (+) 8933 (+) 10358 (+) 12936 may all belong to the same tablet.

aššu yâši ana lemutti tarteneddênn[i]
mārū ummāni āšipū mušlaḫḫ[ū]
*lipašširūkima a-a-il-ki ú-pa-x x*²⁵

Because you have repeatedly pursued me with evil intent,
May the experts, the exorcists, and the snake charmers
    Disengage you. . . .

Accordingly, VII:84–105 can be understood only if we disregard translations that assume that the addressee is the victim or that the sorcerers enumerated in lines 92–100 are allies of the witch, and instead view the speaker as the victim, the addressee as the witch, and the sorcerers of lines 92–100 as allies of the speaker in his confrontation with the witch. These lines should then be translated:

> I call forth (lit., seek out) against you (O witch) cult players and
>   ecstatics;
> I (for my part) will break your bond.
> May   warlocks   bewitch you, I will break your bond.
> May   witches   bewitch you, I will break your bond.
> May   cult players   bewitch you, I will break your bond.
> May   ecstatics   bewitch you, I will break your bond.
> May   *naršindu*-sorcerers   bewitch you, I will break your bond.
> May   snake charmers   bewitch you, I will break your bond.
> May   *agugillu*-sorcerers   bewitch you, I will break your bond.

Maqlû IX:155–59 (the ritual instructions for VII:84–105) both supports and is rendered understandable by the contention that these sorcerers are enemies of the witch. For the ritual is easily and convincingly interpreted when we assume that the clay figurines placed upon the flour representations symbolize adversaries of the witch and that these adversaries are intended to overpower the witch who is symbolized by the flour representations.

Based on the preceding interpretation of VII:84–105 || IX:155–59, I now summarize this incantation and ritual as follows: the speaker (= the victim) describes the witch's activities, invokes against her a group of

---

25. Lutz, *Selected Sumerian and Babylonian Texts*, no. 120 rev. 9: *li-pa-áš-ši-ru-ki-ma a-a-il-ki ú-pa*-x(=? *ṭar/šar*) x. In this incantation, the second-person referent is the witch. Not uninfluenced by *rikiski aḫeppe* of the *Maqlû* passage, I read *a-a-il-ki* and interpret the signs as a verbal or possibly nominal form derived from *eʾēlu*. For a different interpretation, see E. Reiner, "La Magie babylonienne," in *Le Monde du sorcier* (Sources Orientales 7; Paris, 1966) 87: "Puisque tu m'as poursuivi pour de mauvais desseins, les savants exorcistes et les charmeurs de serpents feront une conjuration contre toi, feront une conjuration contre ton lit." Reiner's translation assumes *lipaššīruki ma-a-a-al-ki*. . . . But the tenth sign in Lutz, *Selected Sumerian and Babylonian Texts*, no. 120 rev. 9 seems to be *-il-* (collated from photograph); Sm. 275+ also has *-il-* at this point (] x i[*l*]).

sorcerers, and concludes his address with the threat that he will cause her own evil to overpower her. On the ritual level, the clay figurines represent allies of the victim, while the flour representations stand for the warlock and witch whose hold must be broken; the placing of the clay figurines upon the flour representations denotes the dominance of the victim's allies over his foes, and the washing represents and achieves transferral of the witchcraft from the patient onto his witch.

I now turn back to the preceding incantation and ritual, VII:58–83 and IX:152–54, and try to resolve the difficulties they present. We have seen that this first ritual does not agree with its incantation, but that the following ritual (IX:152–54), an almost identical ritual to the first (IX:152–54), does agree with its incantation (VII:84–105): in this second ritual, the placing of the clay figurines is not a random action and this second incantation (VII:84–105) and ritual (IX:155–59) even form a meaningful magical complex.[26] In view of the meaningful connection between incantation and ritual in VII:84–105 and IX:155–59, two of my earlier observations—the similarity of the two rituals IX:152–54 and IX:155–59 and the discrepancy posed by the juxtaposition of VII:58–83 and IX:152–54—lead me to surmise (*a*) that the incantation VII:58–83 and its ritual would have once also formed a congruous unit, (*b*) that the accepted text, the recension in the library of Ashurbanipal, is at fault, and (*c*) that the second ritual (IX:155–59) must somehow be implicated or responsible for the introduction of the error into the first ritual. Insofar as there is a correspondence in the second incantation and ritual between the invocation of magical allies in the incantation (VII:92–100) and the ritual placing of clay figurines representing these allies upon the witch, but nothing in the first incantation that corresponds with the problematic ritual placing of the clay figurines in IX:154, I would treat the first half of line 154 (*ṣalam ṭīṭi ša kaššapti ina muḫḫi tašakkan*, 'You place a clay figurine of the witch thereon') as an addition and disregard it in order to regain the original text and proper meaning of the first ritual. Accordingly, the original wording of this ritual would have been:

ṣalam kaššapti ša qēmi ina libbi namsê teṣṣer
qātēšu ana muḫḫi imessi

You draw a flour representation of the witch in a washbasin;
He washes his hands over it.

---

26. Even if my interpretation of VII:84–105 turns out to be wrong and the sorcerers are really the allies of the witch, this would not invalidate the conclusion that placing the clay figurines in IX:158 is a meaningful act or that a close agreement exists between this second incantation and its ritual. The ritual would then represent the transference of evil onto both groups.

The Ritual Instructions: Manuscript Evidence and Textual History

Starting from the recognition that a close correspondence should exist here between incantation and ritual, I have come to the conclusion that the text of the Ritual Tablet is the source of the difficulty posed by VII:58–83 || IX:152–54 and that a better and more original text of the ritual instructions for VII:58–83 would not have contained the first half of IX:154. This conclusion finds confirmation in the following observation: in *STT* 1 no. 83, a Sultantepe copy of the Ritual Tablet of *Maqlû*, which represents a recension that is typologically more primitive than the Neo-Assyrian recension copied at Nineveh, we find virtually the very text which I have just reconstructed by internal analysis. *STT* 1 no. 83 rev. 68'–69' read:

> ... *arkišu* ÉN *attī-mannu kaššaptu ša ēpušu* (*ṣalmī*) *imannu*
> *ṣalam kaššapti ša qēmi ina libbi namsê teṣṣer qātēšu ana muḫḫi imessima*. . . .[27]
>
> ... Afterward, he recites the incantation *Attī-mannu kaššaptu ša ēpušu ṣalmī*;
> You draw a flour representation of the witch in a washbasin; he washes his hands over it. . . .

A number of considerations render it virtually certain that the shorter text (without IX:154a) preserved by *STT* 1 no. 83 is the more original text and is not simply an equal variant or the result of contraction. The preceding detailed internal analysis has shown that the shorter text makes better sense than the longer one: while the shorter version of the instructions fits the incantation, the longer version does not and introduces a discordant note or discrepancy between ritual and incantation. In this instance, coherence and good sense form a reasonable and sound basis for judging the short version to be original and superior. Sense and meaning may serve as a first criterion. This specific decision finds overall support in the observation that, generally, the texts of Mesopotamian prayers, incantations, and rituals tend over time to expand in wording rather than contract.

Actually, the development that I have posited from the shorter text of IX:152–54 (represented here by *STT* 1 no. 83) to the longer text (repre-

---

27. *STT* 1 no. 83 rev. 68'–69' reads:
... EGIR -*šú* ÉN *at-ti man-⌈nu⌉* MÍ.UŠ$_{12}$.ZU *šá* [DÙ-*šú* (*ṣal-mi*) ŠID -*nu*]
[NU MÍ.UŠ$_{12}$].Z[U *šá* ZÌ.D]A *ina* ŠÀ URUDU.*nam-se-e te-eṣ-ṣer* ŠU.II-*šú ana* UGU LUḪ-*ma ana* X [. . .]
The restorations are fairly certain; they remain tentative because of the width of the breaks in lines 69'–70'; further collation is required. The end of line 69' might read: *ana* ⌈É⌉ [GUR-(*ma*)]. It is possible that *imessi* in IX:154 is the last word on the line and in the entry in K. 2385+ (cf. the copy of K. 8033 in Tallqvist, *Die assyrische Beschwörungsserie Maqlû*, 2:92) and that we should retain Meier's restoration LUḪ-[*si*] for the Kuyunjik text, but I cannot be sure of this from my own examination of a photograph of K. 2385+.

sented by K. 2385+) fits with and is confirmed by my observation elsewhere of the existence in *Maqlû* of a marked tendency to add material to the Ritual Tablet in order to render the ritual instructions more detailed and explicit. Manuscripts of the Ritual Tablet are not identical. Leaving aside those additions of individual incantations to the series which reflect the expansion of the ceremony itself, I have noted that some manuscripts have transformed and expanded individual ritual entries that are attested in shorter form in other manuscripts; it is from such differences between manuscripts of the Ritual Tablet that I would infer the existence of the aforementioned type of expansion. The absence of IX:154a in one text, but its presence in another, provides further insight into the growth and development of the Ritual Tablet and help to understand the differences between two recensions of that tablet. The example of the erroneous insertion of IX:154a is particularly important, for it exemplifies the change and establishes unambiguously the direction of the development.

This point requires elaboration, and for this purpose, we must again look closely at IX:152–54 as well as at some of the aforementioned variations. In order to set IX:154a into its larger textual context and use it as part of an overall evaluation, I should first note that the addition or insertion of IX:154a is not the result of an inadvertent or mechanical error. Such an error would probably be due to a mechanical vertical dittography, unconditioned by the context, from IX:158 to IX:154. But, this possibility is highly unlikely for several reasons: (1) if this were a dittography, we would have expected the appearance of the *kaššāpu* and *kaššaptu* in both rituals; instead, only the *kaššaptu* is mentioned in IX:154, whereas both appear in IX:158; (2) several lines intervene between the relevant lines, and a mechanical dittography backward from line 158 to line 154 is unlikely; and (3) the result is not a linguistically unintelligible or garbled passage, but two very similar sequences.

We are thus dealing not with mechanical error but rather with some form of harmonization as evidenced by the fact that the result of the insertion is two nearly identical adjoining sequences. But this harmonization is not motivated simply by the desire to produce two similar adjoining units. Rather, it reflects a redactional attempt to expand the ritual information provided in IX:152–54 by using the following section as a prototype. The editor did not wish to expand the ritual. Rather, he regarded some of the entries before him as too elliptical and not sufficiently informative and detailed,[28] and he intended to render the instructions in IX:152–54 more explicit on the basis of the similar but more detailed instructions in IX:155–59.

---

28. See my "Ritual Tablet and Rubrics of *Maqlû*" for a description of the style of the Ritual Tablet, a characterization of the different kinds of instructions, and an explanation of the elliptical nature of so many of the entries.

As noted, the manuscripts provide a number of instances of variation where the longer text is intended to provide more detailed and explicit ritual information. Here, for the sake of clarity, I repeat some of the simpler examples:[29]

1. IX:163-64

   ÉN *amsi qātēya ubbab zumri⟨ya⟩ mīs qātē*
   Incantation: *amsi qātēya ubbab zumri⟨ya⟩*: hand washing.

   ÉN *amsi qātēya ubbab zumriya ana muḫḫi ṣalam niğsağilê qātēšu imessi*
   Incantation: *amsi qātēya ubbab zumriya*: he washes his hands over a figurine of a substitute.

2. IX:161-62

   ÉN *kiṣrīki kuṣṣurūti* [*mīs qātē* / KI.MIN = *mīs qātē*]
   Incantation: *kiṣrīki kuṣṣurūti*: hand washing

   ÉN *kiṣrīki kuṣṣurūti mīs qātē epru ana libbi namsê tanassuk*
   Incantation: *kiṣrīki kuṣṣurūti*: hand washing; you throw a clump of earth into the washbasin.

3. IX:158

   ṣalam ṭīṭi ša kaššāpi u kaššapti ina muḫḫi tašakkan
   You place clay figurines of the warlock and witch thereon.

   ṣalam ṭīṭi ša kaššāpi u kaššapti ina muḫḫi ṣalam qēmi tašakkan
   You place clay figurines of the warlock and witch upon the representation made of flour.

4. IX:176

   pû ana karpati lā šaḫarrati tanaddima
   You put straw into a nonporous pot.

   pû ana libbi karpati lā šaḫarrati tanaddima
   You put straw inside a nonporous pot.

5. IX:151-52

   ... *tušeṣṣima arkišu*. ...
   ... you take out. Thereafter. ...

   ... *tušeṣṣima tan*[*assuk*] *arkišu*. ...
   ... you take out and throw away. Thereafter. ...

---

29. See my discussion in "Ritual Tablet and Rubrics of *Maqlû*." In the five examples that follow, the Sultantepe version (from *STT* 1 no. 83) is listed first in each case, followed by the Nineveh version (nos. 1-3 are from K. 2385+; nos. 4-5 from K. 2385+ and K. 2691).

There are of course more expansions of this sort. Among other examples, see IX:143ff., where the Nineveh version K. 2385+ has replaced GAR *šamni* 'one tenth of a sila of oil' (IX:143) of the Sultantepe and Babylonian versions with the instruction *šamna kala šērēšu [tapaššaš]* 'you rub all of his flesh with oil' (IX:145).[30] In addition, note what may be related variations between the shorter Babylonian K. 8879+ ... (+) Sm. 139 (+) Sm. 1901 and the longer Nineveh K. 2385+ in IX:183-86, and between *STT* 1 no. 83 || K. 8879+ ... (+) Sm. 139 (+) Sm. 1901 (*teppuš*) and K. 2385+ || K. 2691 (*teppušma*) in IX:179.

Looking back at these examples, we note that, generally speaking, the Neo-Assyrian Nineveh texts preserve the more explicit version of the ritual instructions. The Sultantepe and Babylonian recensions preserve a more primitive text, while the Kuyunjik recension has an expanded version. The differences between *STT* 1 no. 83 and K. 2385+, generally—and the addition of IX:154a found in this Nineveh text, specifically—are part of this process. These variations reflect the tendency to supply additional information. The redactor contributed to the transformation of what may have begun in effect as an *aide de mémoire* into a more definitive set of prescriptions by adding what he deemed to be necessary details in order to make the written instructions more explicit and useful for exorcists. Dissatisfied with short catalog-type entries, the scribes or editors sometimes transformed abbreviated entries without finite verbs into more explicit verbal clauses or even added new clauses.

Maqlû IX:152-54, the example studied in this paper, reflects the addition of such a clause: *ṣalam ṭīṭi ša kaššapti ina muḫḫi tašakkan* (IX:154a). The scribe added IX:154a on the basis of IX:158: *ṣalam ṭīṭi ša kaššāpi u kaššapti ina muḫḫi* (var.: + *ṣalam qēmi*) *tašakkan*. In view of the variation in example 3 between two versions of IX:158, I surmise that the addition was made on the basis of an early version of IX:158 (immediately [?]) prior to the addition there of *ṣalam qēmi*. Both IX:154 and IX:158 were expanded as part of the same editorial tendency.

The expansion of the ritual instructions evidences an attempt by the scribe to provide instructions that reflect and describe the ritual he presumed or knew to have been performed. In expanding the text, the redactor drew upon various sources. He may have drawn upon his own personal knowledge of the actual ritual. He certainly made use of several types of textual sources. He drew on, and extrapolated from, information and statements in the accompanying incantation tablets, in related rituals, and in the Ritual Tablet itself. It is often difficult to specify one source rather than the other because of their interrelation and interdependence. But here are a few likely examples. (1) Incantations: for the addition of *ana muḫḫi*

---

30. Meier's edition of these lines is a fragmentary modern conflation of the two recensions. See my "Demonic Image of the Witch," 57 n. 40.

ṣalam niĝsaĝilê qātēšu imessi in IX:163–64 (example 1 above), the instructions for the incantation VII:119–46, see VII:135–37: *lumnū kišpī . . . itti mê ša zumriya u musâti ša qātēya liššaḫiṭma ana muḫḫi ṣalam niĝsaĝilê lillik*, 'May the evil of witchcraft . . . rinse off together with the water of my body and the washing of my hands and come upon the image of a substitute'; for the addition of *epru ana libbi namsê tanassuk* in IX:161–62 (example 2 above), the instructions for the incantation VII:112–18, see VII:116: *pīki lemnu epru limli/â*, 'May your evil mouth be filled with earth.' Given the verbal correspondences between the incantations and the ritual instructions, these lines in the respective accompanying incantations could well have served as a source—perhaps the principal source—for the expansions. (2) Other rituals: for at least part of the expansion of IX:141–49, compare, for example, the rituals cited by me in "Mesopotamian Anti-Witchcraft Literature."[31] (3) Ritual Tablet: for the addition of *ṣalam qēmi* in IX:158 (example 3 above), see *ṣalam kaššāpi u kaššapti ša qēmi ina libbi namsê teṣṣer* in the immediately preceding two lines (IX:156–57) of the Ritual Tablet.

Far from wishing to introduce innovations or expansions into the actual ritual, the redactor in the examples I have cited here was trying to eliminate the ambiguities and rectify the shortcomings that are inherent in very abbreviated instructions, and to provide more precise guidance for exorcists who might study, supervise, and participate in the actual ritual. The short forms known from the shorter and more original Babylonian and Sultantepe texts have been made over into more explicit longer forms by expert, if occasionally misguided, scribal scholars.

To be sure, these expanded instructions normally fit the accompanying incantations. The passage examined in this paper, IX:152–54, is one more example of the redactor's attempts to provide additional information. Here, too, the redactor of the Kuyunjik recension intended to provide more explicit ritual instructions in lines 152–54 when he modeled this section on the adjoining section, lines 155–59. But, as we have seen, he thereby erred and distorted the meaning of the complex of incantation and ritual.[32] Insofar as the longer text of IX:154 is erroneously conceived and makes less sense than the shorter text to which it is inferior, this passage provides exegetical support for the judgment that the shorter recension of the Ritual Tablet has a more original text than the longer recension and that differences between the recensions are due to expansion rather than contraction. By virtue of the mistaken addition of IX:154a, this redactor confirms the existence of an expansionistic tendency, and even provides conclusive proof for the existence of this type of revision of the ritual instructions for *Maqlû*.

---

31. Abusch, "Mesopotamian Anti-Witchcraft Literature," 256 nn. 8, 10.

32. It should be stressed that the placing of the clay statues on the flour representations is attested for IX:158 in both the Sultantepe and Kuyunjik recensions of the second ritual.

ROYAL ANCESTOR WORSHIP IN THE BIBLICAL WORLD

William W. Hallo

The Levant and Egypt

To cover the dynamics of ancestor worship in the biblical world would take many monographs. So no attempt will here be made to do so in the compass of a single article. Fortunately the interested reader can be referred to recent, exhaustive treatments of some of the areas necessarily omitted here. For example, the evidence of the Bible itself has been thoroughly and imaginatively assembled by H. C. Brichto in his "Kin, Cult, Land and Afterlife—A Biblical Complex."[1] Brichto, after carefully distinguishing between immortality and resurrection, shows that the biblical belief, before Daniel,[2] was confined strictly to immortality, but, where that was concerned, "the veneration of ancestors occupied so central a place in Israelite thought" that even the relative silence of Scripture, especially as to prescriptions for it, cannot be interpreted as evidence to the contrary.[3] But "veneration is not worship"[4] and ancestor *worship* as such was presumably abhorred as a foreign rite.[5]

Author's note: The substance of this paper was presented to the 198th meeting of the American Oriental Society, Chicago, March 21, 1988, in the context of a plenary session on "Dynamics of Ancestor Worship." It benefitted from discussions with Brian Schmidt (University of North Carolina) and with Shemaryahu Talmon while the latter and I were both fellows of the National Humanities Center, Research Triangle Park, North Carolina (1987–1988). It is a pleasure to include it in a volume in Professor Talmon's honor.

1. H. C. Brichto, "Kin, Cult, Land and Afterlife—A Biblical Complex," *Hebrew Union College Annual* 44 (1973) 1–54, esp. 28–29 and 47–48 (n. 75). Among older studies note, e.g., L. André, *Le Culte des morts chez les Hébreux* (1895); and C. Grüneisen, *Der Ahnenkultus und die Urreligion Israels* (Halle, 1990) (cited by F. C. Conybeare, "Ancestor-Worship," in *Encyclopaedia Britannica* [11th ed.], 1:947).
2. Brichto, "Kin, Cult, Land and Afterlife," 53.
3. Ibid., 52.
4. Ibid., 47.
5. Cf. ibid., 28.

Another recent and even more comprehensive study is that of Klaas Spronk entitled *Beatific Afterlife in Ancient Israel and in the Ancient Near East*.[6] Although his book is not devoted to the question of ancestor worship as such, Spronk deals critically with earlier studies on that subject.[7] I note in passing H. Oort, C. Grüneisen, J. C. Matthes, and G. Margoliouth.[8] But he also rejects more recent studies, including Brichto and his distinction between veneration and worship,[9] and concludes that we have hard evidence in the biblical text only for the normal respect paid to the departed,[10] and perhaps some "traces of a royal cult of the dead."[11] He is also unconvinced by Oswald Loretz's attempt to see a survival of a suppressed ancestor cult in the (late) biblical veneration of the patriarchs.[12]

What needs more than passing mention in connection with the biblical evidence is the concept of the *rĕpā'îm*, the spirits of the dead in general[13] but more particularly of the elite—deceased kings,[14] leaders of tribes, chieftains of clans.[15] The notion of Rephaim as an ethnic group, for example, in the "War of the four kings against the five" (Gen 14:5), is a

---

6. K. Spronk, *Beatific Afterlife in Ancient Israel and in the Ancient Near East* (Alter Orient und Altes Testament 219; Kevelaer/Neukirchen-Vluyn, 1986). See the extensive and critical reviews by M. H. Pope in *UF* 19 (1987) 452–63, and by M. S. Smith and E. M. Bloch-Smith, "Death and Afterlife in Ugarit and Israel," *JAOS* 108 (1988) 277–84.

7. Spronk, *Beatific Afterlife*, 28–54 ("Looking for Worship of the Dead") and 247–50 ("Cult of the Dead").

8. H. Oort, "De doodenverering bij de Israëlieten," *Teologisk Tidsskrift* 14 (1881) 350–63; Grüneisen, *Der Ahnenkultus und die Urreligion Israels*; J. C. Matthes, "Rouw en doodenverering in Israel," *Teologisk Tidsskrift* 34 (1900) 97–128; idem, "De doodenverering bij Israel," *Teologisk Tidsskrift* 35 (1901) 320–49; and G. Margoliouth, "Ancestor-Worship and Cult of the Dead (Hebrew)," *Encyclopedia of Religion and Ethics* (ed. J. Hastings; Edinburgh, 1908), 1:444–50.

9. Spronk, *Beatific Afterlife*, 48–51.

10. Ibid., 247–49.

11. Ibid., 250.

12. Ibid., 51–53, citing O. Loretz, "Vom kanaanäischen Totenkult zur jüdischen Patriarchen- und Elternehrung," *Jahrbuch für Anthropologie und Religionsgeschichte* 3 (1978) 149–204; and idem, "Ugaritisch-biblisch *mrzḥ* 'Kultmahl, Kultverein' in Jer. 16,5 und Am. 6,7: Bemerkungen zur Geschichte des Totenkultes in Israel," in *Künder des Wortes: Beiträge zur Theologie der Propheten: Josef Schreiner zum 60. Geburtstag* (ed. L. Ruppert, P. Weimar, and E. Zenger; Würzburg, 1982) 87–93.

13. Cf. Isa 26:14, 19; Prov 2:18, 9:18, 21:16; Job 26:5.

14. Cf. Spronk, *Beatific Afterlife*, 250, for "traces of a royal cult of the dead" in Israel.

15. So, e.g., in Isa 14:9, where the Rephaim are in parallelism with the "kings of nations"; cf. H. L. Ginsberg, "Reflexes of Sargon in Isaiah after 715 B.C.E.," *JAOS* 88 (1968) 51 (= *Essays in Memory of E. A. Speiser* [ed. W. W. Hallo; AOS 53; New Haven, 1968]); J. C. Greenfield, "Scripture and Inscription: The Literary and Rhetorical Element in Some Early Phoenician Inscriptions," in *Near Eastern Studies in Honor of William Foxwell Albright* (ed. H. Goedicke; Baltimore, 1971) 258; Spronk, *Beatific Afterlife*, 213–27; M. Dietrich, O. Loretz, and J. Sanmartín, "Die ugaritischen Totengeister *rpu(m)* und die biblischen Rephaim," *UF* 8 (1976) 47; B. A. Levine and J.-M. de Tarragon, "Dead Kings and Rephaim: The Patrons of the Ugaritic Dynasty," *JAOS* 104 (1984) 649–59.

figment of the popular (biblical) imagination, according to M. Dietrich.[16] For a conceivable etymology of the term, I note Robert Good's suggested understanding: "healed, embalmed, interred."[17] Of the Rephaim more soon.

The Hittite evidence was sifted by Heinrich Otten in his *Hethitische Totenrituale* (1958) and subsequent studies,[18] and a French rendering of the principal texts was provided by L. Christmann-Franck.[19] More recently, A. Archi has discussed the cult of the dead among the Hittites,[20] and the "funerary ritual" has been reviewed by Oliver Gurney in his Schweich Lectures.[21] V. Haas and M. Wäfler have shown that, as in Mesopotamia and Israel, the "care and feeding" of the departed[22] is an obligation on their progeny, on pain of being haunted by their spirits;[23] in particular, this is incumbent on royal progeny.[24] It is worthy of note that the requisite offerings are made, not at the grave, but before the statue or image of the departed.[25] As elsewhere, "the Hittite royal dead were represented in these [funerary] rituals by statues before which the offerings were set."[26]

For the sake of completeness, I mention R. D. Barnett's comparison of the "sirens" on the so-called Urartian cauldrons with the Rephaim, and

---

16. In Dietrich, Loretz, and Sanmartín's terminology, "Schöpfung des Volksglaubens"; see "Die ugaritischen Totengeister *rpu(m)*," 46.

17. R. M. Good, "Supplementary Remarks on the Ugaritic Funerary Text RS 34.126," *BASOR* 239 (1980) 41–42. Cf. previously C. E. L'Heureux, "The Ugaritic and Biblical Rephaim," *HTR* 67 (1974) 269–70.

18. H. Otten, *Hethitische Totenrituale* (Berlin, 1958); idem, "Bestattungssitten und Jenseitsvorstellungen nach den hethitischen Texten," in K. Bittel, *Die hethitischen Grabfunde von Osmankayasi* (Boğazköy-Hattuša 2; Wissenschaftliche Veröffentlichungen der Deutschen Orientgesellschaft 71; Berlin 1958) 81–84; idem, "Eine Lieferungsliste zum Totenritual der hethitischen Könige," *Die Welt des Orients* 2 (1959) 477–79; idem, "Zu den hethitischen Totenritualen," *Orientalische Literaturzeitung* 57 (1962) 229–33.

19. L. Christmann-Franck, "Le rituel des funérailles royales hittites," *Revue hittite et asianique* 29 (1971) 61–111.

20. A. Archi, "Il dio Zawalli: sul culto dei morti pressi gli Ittiti," *Altorientalische Forschungen* 6 (1979) 81–94.

21. O. R. Gurney, *Some Aspects of Hittite Religion* (Schweich Lectures of the British Academy 1976; Oxford, 1977) 59–63.

22. Cf. "The Care and Feeding of the Gods" in A. L. Oppenheim, *Ancient Mesopotamia* (rev. ed.; ed. E. Reiner; Chicago, 1977) 183–98.

23. Oppenheim (ibid., 201) notes that in Akkadian "the protective spirit called *šēdu* . . . is connected with the spirits of the dead," while its Hebrew cognate, which refers to idols, is rendered in the LXX by Greek δαίμων.

24. V. Haas and M. Wäfler, "Bemerkungen zu ᴱ*heštī/ā*-," *UF* 8 (1976) 65–99; 9 (1977) 87–122, esp. 113ff.

25. Ibid., 114.

26. W. T. Pitard, "The Ugaritic Funerary Text RS 34.126," *BASOR* 232 (1978) 67 and n. 10; cf. H. Otten, "Zur Datierung und Bedeutung des Felsheiligtums von Yazılıkaya: Eine Entgegnung," *ZA* 58 (1967) 237; cf. n. 111 below. For the commemorative funerary monuments called *huwaši*, see most recently J.-M. Durand, "Deux 'Slave Documents,'" *NABU— Nouvelles assyriologiques brèves et utilitaires* 1988: 4–6.

his interpretation of "Assurbanipal's feast" on the famous relief from Nineveh as a *marzeaḥ*.[27]

Between the Israelite and the Anatolian spheres lies the newly recovered site of ancient Ebla. This Syrian city is most famous for its third-millennium finds contemporary, as I think, with the Early Dynastic III period in Mesopotamia, including a list of deceased and deified beings and the earliest evidence of the *marzeaḥ*.[28] But it has yielded important results for the early second millennium as well, and among them Paolo Matthiae has identified a whole complex of graves and cult installations which he associates with the worship of deceased royalty. In fact, he has suggested that the objects of this worship belong to a class of beings comparable not only to the biblical Rephaim but also to the Ugaritic *rapiuma* (*rpʾm*).[29]

I must thus mention the Ugaritic evidence as well, if only long enough to cite the explicit offerings to such *rapiuma*—in the guise, not of chariot warriors (or other aristocrats),[30] but of royal ancestors, specifically, it has been suggested, in the form of statues.[31] These offerings are the subject of a number of so-called Rephaim texts in Ugaritic, but the royal connection is particularly evident in one entitled in its superscript a "tablet of sacrifices to the protective spirits [shades]" of the dynasty (*spr.dbḥ.ẓlm*), which has been

---

27. R. D. Barnett, "Assurbanipal's Feast," *EI* 18 (1985; N. Avigad FS) 1*-6* and pl. i; idem, "Sirens and Rephaim," in *Ancient Anatolia: Aspects of Change and Cultural Development: Essays in Honor of Machteld J. Mellink* (ed. J. V. Canby et al.; Madison, 1986) 112-20. Cf. the review by B. R. Foster in *American Journal of Archaeology* 91 (1987) 618. These winged "sirens" are often represented with six fingers, like the Philistine offspring of the Rephaim (2 Sam 21:20) and are, according to Barnett, "meant to represent the Rephaim or divinized ancestors or their equivalents who are invited to a funeral feast" (p. 119). For the *marzeaḥ*, see n. 132 below.

28. A. Archi, "Die ersten zehn Könige von Ebla," *ZA* 76 (1986) 213-17; P. Fronzaroli, "Il culto dei re defunti in *ARET* 3,178," in *Miscellanea Eblaitica* 1 (Quaderni di Semitistica 15; Università di Firenze, 1988) 1-33 and fig. 1. (I owe this and several other references to Brian Schmidt.)

29. P. Matthiae, "Princely Cemetery and Ancestors Cult at Ebla during the Middle Bronze II: A Proposal of Interpretation," *UF* 11 (1979) 563-69. For possible precedents at third-millennium Ebla, see G. Pettinato, "Culto ufficiale ad Ebla durante il regno di Ibbi-sipiš," *Oriens Antiquus* 18 (1979) 115-16. Cf. now also Matthiae, "Cult of the Ancestors and Tutelary God at Ebla," in *Fucus: A Semitic/Afrasian Gathering in Remembrance of Albert Ehrman* (ed. Y. L. Arbeitman; Current Issues in Linguistic Theory 58; Amsterdam, 1988) 103-12.

30. See L'Heureux, "Ugaritic and Biblical Rephaim," 270-72, cited by Dietrich, Loretz, and Sanmartín, "Die ugaritischen Totengeister *rpu(m)*," 49 n. 45. Cf. also W. J. Horowitz, "The Significance of the Rephaim," *Journal of Northwest Semitic Languages* 7 (1979) 37-43.

31. Dietrich and Loretz, "Totenverehrung in Māri (12803) and Ugarit (KTU 1.161)," *UF* 12 (1980) 381, ad KTU 1:161:13-17. Cf. also G. del Olmo Lete, "The 'Divine' Names of the Ugaritic Kings," *UF* 18 (1986) 83-95, who thinks kings were deified and given divine names (cf. pp. 92-93 for this text). Cf. idem, "Un ritual funerario de Ugarit (KTU 1.105)," *Aula Orientalis* 6 (1988) 189-94.

at the center of the discussion since its publication in 1975.[32] I note here especially the studies by Pierre Bordreuil and Dennis Pardee, J. F. Healey, Baruch Levine, Baruch Margalit, Wayne T. Pitard, and Marvin H. Pope.[33] All these scholars have addressed the Ugaritic Rephaim texts, among which the just mentioned tablet of sacrifices has been characterized as a veritable "Ugaritic Feast of all Souls"[34] or as a coronation text for the last king of Ugarit, Ammu-rapi, intended "to secure blessings from the deceased kings" for the occasion.[35]

To Pope, in addition, we owe the interesting interpretation of the royal epithets "man of *rpi*" and "man of *hrnmy*," regularly applied in Ugaritic to King Daniel. Both, according to him, apply to the netherworld. He compares *hrnmy* with the toponyms Hinnom (*hnnm*) near Jerusalem and *hrnm* in Lebanon, and the epithets themselves with the antediluvian personal names *mtwšlḥ* and *mtwš$^{\circ}$l*, both standing for 'man of the netherworld'.[36] Indeed, the name Hammu-rapi (Ammu-rapi), explained in Akkadian sources as *kimta-rapaštum* ('extensive as to family'), reflects the understanding of *rp$^{\circ}$* as deified ancestral spirits guaranteeing fertility to their living descendants.[37]

Not all the ancestral spirits of deceased and deified royalty were subsumed under the concept of Rephaim, however. If Levine and Tarragon are right, we must distinguish between "dead kings and rephaim." The former are the historic kings, the latter the prehistoric ancestors of the dynasty, at Ugarit beginning with Keret. Yaqaru, the first historic king, may represent the transition from the one class to the other.[38] A still more nuanced classification has been proposed by A. Malamat, according to whom the typical ancient Near Eastern (Amorite?) royal genealogies begin

---

32. KTU 1:161 (= RS 34.126), first published by A. Caquot, "Hébreu et Araméen," *Annuaire du Collège de France* 75 (1975) 427–29. Cf. Spronk, *Beatific Afterlife*, 189–93.

33. P. Bordreuil and D. Pardee, "Le rituel funéraire ougaritique RS.34.126," *Syria* 59 (1982) 121–28; J. F. Healey, "Ritual Text KTU 1.161—Translation and Notes," *UF* 10 (1978) 83–88; idem, "*Mlkm/Rp$^{\circ}$um* and the *Kispum*," *UF* 10 (1978) 89–91 (cf. also idem, "The Ugaritic Dead: Some Live Issues," *UF* 18 [1986] 27–32, where kingship and immortality are related [p. 28]); Levine and Tarragon, "Dead Kings and Rephaim"; B. Margalit, "The Geographical Setting of the *Aqht* Story and Its Ramifications," *Ugarit in Retrospect* (ed. G. D. Young; Winona Lake, IN, 1981) 131–58; Pitard, "Ugaritic Funerary text RS 34.126," 65–75; idem, "RS 34.126: Notes on the Text," *Maarav* 4 (1987) 75–86; M. H. Pope, "Notes on the Ugaritic Rephaim Texts," in *Essays on the Ancient Near East in Memory of J. J. Finkelstein* (ed. M. de J. Ellis; Hamden, CT, 1977) 163–82; idem, "The Cult of the Dead at Ugarit," in *Ugarit in Retrospect* (ed. G. D. Young; Winona Lake, IN, 1981) 159–79.

34. T. H. Gaster, "An Ugaritic Feast of All Souls," in *Concepts, Critiques, and Comments: A Festschrift in Honor of David Rose* (New York: privately printed, 1976) 97–106, cited by Pope, "Ugaritic Rephaim Texts," 182 n. 92.

35. So Pitard, "Ugaritic Funerary Text RS 34.126," 67. Cf. Levine and Tarragon, "Dead Kings and Rephaim," 654, and n. 81 below for a comparable Akkadian case.

36. Pope, "Ugaritic Rephaim Texts," 166.

37. Ibid., 167, citing *CAD* K 377, s.v. *kimtu*.

38. Levine and Tarragon, "Dead Kings and Rephaim," 656.

with genealogical stock, determinative lines, and tables of ancestors before passing on to the "historical line."³⁹

Mention may also briefly be made of the Phoenician inscription of King Yaton-baᶜal from Lapethos on Cyprus attesting to semimonthly offerings, on the new moon and the full moon, in the sanctuary of Melqart, not only to that Phoenician deity but also, in one opinion, to the votive statue (*mšpn*) of his father.⁴⁰ Elsewhere, too, in the Northwest Semitic-speaking world, these days of the lunar month were occasions for special offerings, perhaps to deceased royalty.⁴¹ It may even be suggested that, in the Hebrew Bible, the generally negative tones in which the prophets refer to unnamed cultic practices in connection with "new moons and sabbaths" allude to proscribed ancestor worship on new moon and full moon, the presumed original meaning of *šabbat*.⁴²

To round out the Northwest Semitic evidence, I cite the Aramaic inscription of Panamu, king of Yaudi (Yaʔdiy), which enjoins on his successor a rite that, although not designated by name, involves causing the deceased royal spirit to eat and drink with the deity as in the Mesopotamian *kispu* and *pagru* rites.⁴³

The available material from ancient Egypt is particularly massive, given the skew of the evidence. Papyrus survived much better in the dry necropolises of the desert than in the constantly reoccupied and reinundated settlements of the living, whether along the Nile or in the Delta; in addition, the monumental remains on stone and other more durable mediums are more often than not funerary. Hence we know more about the "care and feeding of the dead" in ancient Egypt than about the living. The firm belief in a Ka, very roughly equivalent to our concept of soul, laid the basis for the ancient Egyptians' notion that such a soul, or the Ba and Akh, bird-shaped souls released at death, could survive the death of the physical body, sometimes as ghosts or revenants. But beyond that, the attempt to arrest physical decay led to elaborate measures to assure the afterlife of the king and, in lesser measure, of commoners too and even of animals.⁴⁴ Not

---

39. A. Malamat, "King Lists of the Old Babylonian Period and Biblical Genealogies," *JAOS* 88 (1968) 163–73, esp. 172 (= *Essays in Memory of E. A. Speiser* [ed. W. W. Hallo; AOS 53; New Haven, 1968]).

40. A. Tsukimoto, *Untersuchungen zur Totenpflege (kispum) im alten Mesopotamien* (Alter Orient und Altes Testament 216; Kevelaer/Neukirchen-Vluyn, 1985) 64 and nn. 248–49. Cf. esp. the review by W. G. Lambert in *Or* 56 (1987) 403–4.

41. Tsukimoto, *Untersuchungen zur Totenpflege*, 64 nn. 250–51.

42. For biblical traces of "new moon and sabbath" in the sense of new moon and full moon, see M. Fishbane, *Biblical Interpretation in Ancient Israel* (Oxford, 1984) 149–50.

43. J. C. Greenfield, "Une rite religieux araméen et ses paralleles," *RB* 80 (1973) 46–52; idem, "Aspects of Aramean religion," in *Ancient Israelite Religion: Essays in Honor of Frank Moore Cross* (ed. P. D. Miller Jr., P. D. Hanson, and S. D. McBride; Philadelphia, 1987) 67–78. For *pagru* at Mari, Ugarit, and Alalakh, see n. 129 below.

44. See H. Frankfort, *Ancient Egyptian Religion: An Interpretation* (New York, 1948) 9–10, for mummified animals.

only did the departed pharaoh continue to enjoy divine honors after death, but private individuals too were blessed and fed by their descendants. Essentially, this was done by reciting the inscriptions on their tombs—a form of ancestor worship, or at least veneration, which was economical in a material sense but demanding in the sense that it required the perpetuation of family ties. In return, the departed were expected to honor specific requests from the living as expressed in "Letters to the Dead."[45] The evidence has been assembled by, among others, Hermann Kees in *Totenglauben und Jenseitsvorstellungen der alten Ägypter*.[46]

Mesopotamia: The Early Dynastic Evidence

I do not control the Egyptian material and will thus confine my remaining remarks to the evidence from ancient Mesopotamia as preserved in the cuneiform record. But even here I will not presume to cover the whole topic. Instead, I will confine myself to the cult of *royal* ancestors, taking royal, however, in the broader sense of the ruling *family*—not just the ruling king.[47] My focus on the king (and his family) is not only demanded by the time constraints but by the fact that the evidence for a cult of non-royal ancestors in Mesopotamia is so negligible and elusive as to raise the legitimate question whether it existed at all.[48] If it did, it is immediately distinguished from the cult of the *royal* ancestor by the fact that it rarely goes back more than one or two generations in depth.[49] An apparent

---

45. R. J. Demarée, *The ꜣḫ ỉḳr n Rᶜ-Stelae: On Ancestor Worship in Ancient Egypt* (Egyptologische Uitgaven 3; Leiden, 1983) 213–18. Demarée's work, in spite of its subtitle, is largely confined to a study of some fifty-five funerary steles—forty-seven of them from Deir el-Medîna—characterized by the formula "able spirit [Akh] of the Reᶜ."

46. H. Kees, *Totenglauben und Jenseitsvorstellungen der alten Ägypter* (Berlin, 1956). Cf. also Siegfried Morenz, "Ägyptischer Totenglaube," *Eranos-Jahrbuch* 34 (1965) 399–446 (repr. in his *Religion und Geschichte des alten Ägypten* [Cologne/Vienna, 1975] 73–213).

47. For the cult of the deceased high priestesses of the moon-god, who were daughters of the king that controlled Ur, referred to (along with minor deities) as *dingir-dingir-èš-didli é-ᵈNin-gal* ('deities of the individual sanctuaries, temple of the goddess Ningal'), see P. Weadock, "The *Giparu* at Ur," *Iraq* 37 (1975) 110.

48. For some evidence of private ancestor worship at Nuzi, see briefly A. Skaist, "The Ancestor Cult and Succession in Mesopotamia," in *Death in Mesopotamia: Papers Read at the XXVIᵉ Rencontre Assyriologique Internationale* (ed. B. Alster; Copenhagen, 1980) 123–28. For funerary practices *apart* from ancestor worship, cf. M. T. Barrelet, "Les pratiques funéraires de l'Iraq ancien et l'archéologie," *Akkadica* 16 (1980) 2–27; J.-D. Forest, *Les pratiques funéraires en Mésopotamie du cinquième millénaire au début du troisième: étude de cas* (Éditions Récherche sur les Civilisations, Mémoire No. 19; Paris, 1983).

49. For one generation, see M. Bayliss, "The Cult of Dead Kin in Assyria and Babylonia," *Iraq* 35 (1973) 115–25, with the comments of J. M. Sasson, "Accounting Discrepancies in the Mari NÌ.GUB [NÍG.DU] Texts," in *Zikir Šumim: Assyriological Studies Presented to F. R. Kraus* (ed. G. van Driel; Leiden, 1982) 326 n. 1. For the Ugaritic catalog of filial duties see n. 131 below. The old notion that Sumerian *ibila* derives from *ì-bíl-a* 'fat-burning' as a filial duty in the ancestor cult, still defended by A. Falkenstein, *Die neusumerischen Gerichtsurkunden* (Munich, 1956), 1:111–12, is refuted by F. R. Kraus, "Erbrechtliche Terminologie im

exception is a prayer to the moon-god on behalf of four generations of deceased(?) relatives of an ordinary person, dated to the thirty-third year of Ammi-ditana, that is, just five years before the presumed date of the "Genealogy of the Hammurapi Dynasty."[50] Moreover, I have dealt with so many other aspects of Mesopotamian kingship, from the birth of kings through their death,[51] that a study of their afterlife is a logical extension of my interests.

At the outset I must draw an important distinction between *deceased* royalty and *deified* royalty. Among the Hittites, it is true, such a distinction apparently did not exist. The living king was addressed as "my Sun" (or even "my Sun-god") but he was *not* a god. The deceased king, on the other hand, was; the very idiom for the death of a Hittite king (or queen) was "he [she] became a god" (*šiuniš kikkištat*)—an idiom *not* employed for ordinary mortals.[52] In Mesopotamia, however, deification was a status bestowed on some kings in their lifetime, whether (1) at accession, (2) shortly thereafter, (3) sometime thereafter, (4) occasionally even at birth, and (5) retained or respectively acquired after their death.[53] But such royal deification was the

---

alten Mesopotamien," in *Essays on Oriental Laws of Succession* (by J. Brugman et al.; Studia et Documenta ad Iura Orientis Antiqui Pertinentia 9; Leiden, 1969) 36–38. For evidence of non-royal ancestor worship going back two generations, see Tsukimoto, *Untersuchungen zur Totenpflege*, 159–83: "*kispu(m)* für die Totengeister der Familie," esp. 161–62, where the incantation for the spirits (GIDIM = *eṭimmu*) of the deceased family members includes grandparents (AD.AD-*ia₅* AMA.AMA-*ia₅*) and the whole clan (*kimtia nisutia u salatia*), as many as lie in the earth; cf. n. 121 below. Other texts mention only the spirits of the family in general (GIDIM.MEŠ IM.RI.A); cf. also J. Bottéro, "Les Morts et l'au-delà dans les rituels en accadien contre l'action des 'revenants,'" *ZA* 73 (1983) 172 and (with a different interpretation) 178 n. 87, 180 and n. 96.

50. C. Wilcke, "Ein Gebet an den Mondgott vom 3. IV. des Jahres Ammiditana 33," *ZA* 73 (1983) 49–54; F. R. Kraus, "Ein altbabylonisches Totenopfer," *ZA* 77 (1987) 96–97. For the genealogy of the Hammurapi Dynasty, see n. 81 below.

51. See most recently Hallo, "The Death of Kings: Traditional Historiography in Comparative Perspective," in *A Highway from Egypt to Assyria: Studies in Ancient Near Eastern History and Historiography Presented to Hayim Tadmor* (ed. M. Cogan and I. Ephʿal; Jerusalem, forthcoming).

52. Ibid., n. 39; idem, "Texts, Statues and the Cult of the Divine King," in *Congress Volume: Jerusalem 1986* (ed. J. A. Emerton; VTSup 40; Leiden, 1988) 62 n. 50; for the queen, cf. Christmann-Franck, "Le rituel des funérailles royales hittites," 61. For the Hittite expression, see Otten, *Hethitische Totenrituale*, 119.

53. Examples of no. 1 are Amar-Suen, Šu-Sin, and Ibbi-Sin of the Ur III Dynasty, whose names are invariably preceded by the "divine determinative" in all their monumental inscriptions and in their date formulas; see Hallo, *Early Mesopotamian Royal Titles* (AOS 43; New Haven, 1957) 60–62; N. Schneider, *Die Zeitbestimmung der Wirtschaftsurkunden von Ur III* (Analecta Orientalia 13; Rome, 1936). On no. 2, note that the earliest texts from each of these reigns actually write the accession-year date formula *without* the determinative; see Schneider, *Die Zeitbestimmung der Wirtschaftsurkunden*, 24, 30, 36. An example of no. 3 is Šulgi of the Ur III Dynasty; cf. Hallo, *Early Mesopotamian Royal Titles*, 60–61. An example of no. 4 is Šu-Sin of Ur, who figures as divine in a poem celebrating his birth; cf. *ANET* 496.

ruling ideology *only* in a relatively brief period from ca. 2200–1800 B.C., that is, from midway through the reign of Naram-Sin of Akkad to the accession of Hammurapi of Babylon. In another context, I have assessed the meaning and possible origin of this phase of Mesopotamian ideology, its expression in the cult, and its relationship with a far more enduring cultic expression of Mesopotamian ideology—namely the worship of the "real" gods. Focusing on the role of the statue in the cult, I have suggested a kind of dialectic evolution that may be summarized as follows: initially only the departed royal ancestors were worshiped in the form of cult statues (i.e., in effect, life-size effigies); with the deification of kings, both *living* royalty and "real" deities were represented by and worshiped as cult statues; after the "secularization" of royalty was restored by Hammurapi,[54] cult statues of the deceased royal ancestors continued to be worshiped alongside those of the "living gods."[55] What evidence is there for this dialectic pattern, as far as statues of royal ancestors are concerned?

The Mesopotamians had a well-developed notion of departed spirits. In Sumerian they were known as GIDIM or UDUG, both written with variants of the same sign—variants which the late orthography writes, curiously enough, as "⅓ of a goddess" and "⅔ [or ⅚] of a goddess," respectively.[56] They passed into Akkadian as *eṭimmu* and *utukku* respectively—and it is hard to distinguish between them, though Jean Bottéro's recent study helps.[57] They, and especially the *utukku*, could be good or bad, probably depending on whether they belonged to properly buried persons or not.[58] The evil *utukku*s, that is, presumably, the restless spirits of unburied or improperly buried ancestors, were a particular threat to their living descendants,[59] and elaborate rituals and incantations were evolved to deal with them, beginning in Old Babylonian times, as conveniently shown in Mark Geller's new edition, and greatly elaborated by Neo-Assyrian times, as long known from the edition of R. Campbell

---

An example of no. 5 is Ur-Nammu of Ur, who is deified in some late copies of his royal hymns; cf., e.g., Hallo, "The Coronation of Ur-Nammu," *JCS* 20 (1966) 133–41, esp. 134. Presumably in periods when living kings were deified, departed rulers could also be worshiped, or provided with offerings, in the guise of their statues, even if they had not enjoyed divine status in their own lifetimes; cf. nn. 67, 70, and 71 below for Sargon, Ur-Bau, Gudea.

54. R. Harris, "On the Process of Secularization under Hammurapi," *JCS* 15 (1961) 117–20; idem, "Some Aspects of the Centralization of the Realm under Hammurapi and His Successors," *JAOS* 88 (1968) 727–32.

55. Hallo, "Texts, Statues and the Cult of the Deified King," 54–66, esp. 62–63.

56. Ibid., appendix 2; cf. A. Deimel, *Šumerisches Lexikon* (Rome, 1933), 2:576:1.

57. Bottéro, "Les Morts et l'au-delà," 153–203.

58. Ibid., esp. 169–74.

59. Cf. already "Ur-Nammu's death and burial," line 232 in Wilcke, "Eine Schicksalsentscheidung für den toten Urnammu," in *Actes de la XVIIe Rencontre Assyriologique Internationale* (ed. A. Finet; Ham-sur-Heure, 1970) 90, cited by Bottéro, "Les Morts et l'au-delà," 169.

Thompson.[60] But these essentially apotropaic rituals against the ancestral spirits do not constitute an ancestor cult as such, so for this we must look to other sources.

One clue comes from the juxtaposition of two otherwise unrelated texts, the Sumerian King List and the great list of Babylonian gods known as An=*Anum*. They contain at least one entry in common: Hataniš, the sole and wholly obscure king of the dynasty of Hamazi in the Early Dynastic II section of the king list recurs in the god list as Udug-ekurra, that is, an ancestral spirit of the great temple of Enlil at Nippur. From this fact Thorkild Jacobsen long ago drew the conclusion that the deceased king was represented *by* and worshiped *as* a statue in that temple. If he is right, we may point to a number of comparable ancestral spirits that became deified genii of temples.[61]

I will not concern myself with other and in part better known rulers of the Early Dynastic II period who were deified after their deaths, notably those of Uruk, because these entered the realm of "real gods" and were venerated as such, not as ancestors. I have in mind the likes of Lugalbanda, Dumuzi, and Gilgamesh.

When we move on to the Early Dynastic III period, we actually have contemporaneous evidence for the worship of deceased royal ancestors in statue form though it is, again, somewhat less than explicit. Among the numerous archival texts from pre-Sargonic Lagash, Philip Talon has identified one which records offerings of garments for the deceased ancestors of the dynasty, including Gunidu, the father of Ur-Nanshe its founder;[62] they are summarized as "garments of the spirits" (*túg-gídim-e-ne-kam*) instead of the more common "garments of the 'deceased ancestors'" (*túg-en-en-né-ne*) as identified by Anton Deimel and Yvonne Rosengarten.[63] According to Talon, these offerings were made to the *statues* of the royal personages in question. But such statues could (at least in later times) depict *living* beings according to others, who thus distinguish a cult of the dead, as directed to royalty for the welfare of the society as a whole, from the usual

---

60. M. Geller, *Forerunners to Udug-Hul: Sumerian Exorcistic Incantations* (Freiburger Altorientalische Studien 12; Stuttgart, 1985); R. C. Thompson, *The Devils and Evil Spirits of Mesopotamia* (2 vols.; London, 1903–1904). Cf. more recently G. Castellino, "Rituals and Prayers against 'Appearing Ghosts,'" *Or* 24 (1955) 240–74; and n. 112 below.

61. T. Jacobsen, *The Sumerian King List* (Assyriological Studies 11; Chicago, 1939) 89–90; cf. Hallo, "Texts, Statues and the Cult of the Divine King," appendix 1.

62. P. Talon, "A propos d'une graphie présargonique de ŠL 577 (Gídim)," *RA* 68 (1974) 167–68.

63. A. Deimel, "Die Listen über den Ahnenkult aus der Zeit Lugalandas und Urukaginas," *Or* 2 (1920) 32–51; Y. Rosengarten, *Le Régime des Offrandes* (Paris, 1960), chap. 2: "Les offrandes dédiées aux morts"; cf. idem, *Le Concept Sumérien de Consommation* (Paris, 1960), chap. 7: "Offrandes aux morts."

veneration of the dead intended to absorb their powers while warding off their threats.[64]

J. Bauer has also discussed the ancestor cult in pre-Sargonic Lagash, with special reference to the *ki-a-nag*, the libation place, literally the place for drinking water, that is, the place where offerings to the dead were brought.[65]

Mesopotamia: The Classical Phase

In the Sargonic period, Mesopotamian kingship scaled new heights, and the afterlife of these first "emperors" was correspondingly enhanced and prolonged. The evidence was conveniently assembled by Hans Hirsch in 1960.[66] Beginning with Sargon, the founder of the new dynasty, nearly all of its kings received offerings after their death, which can only mean, according to Hirsch, in the form of their statues. Nor did these offerings cease when the dynasty fell. In the case of Sargon and Naram-Sin, the greatest members of the dynasty, such offerings are attested, not in Old Akkadian texts but in Neo-Sumerian texts of the twenty-first century, in an Old Babylonian text of the eighteenth century from as far away as Mari, and even in Neo-Babylonian texts from sixth-century Sippar, as D. A. Kennedy showed.[67] We can hardly speak, at such dynastic, geographic, or chronologic removes, of ancestor worship in the strict sense, except to the extent that the later dynasties may have regarded themselves as descendants

---

64. Tsukimoto, *Untersuchungen zur Totenpflege*, 21 n. 90.

65. J. Bauer, "Zum Totenkult im altersumerischen Lagasch," in *XVII. Deutscher Orientalistentag 1968 in Würzburg* (Zeitschrift der Deutschen Morgenländischen Gesellschaft Supplement 1; Wiesbaden, 1969) 107–14; idem, *Altsumerische Wirtschaftstexte aus Lagash* (Studia Pohl 9; Rome, 1967) 173–74; cf. A. Falkenstein, *Die Inschriften Gudeas von Lagaš I* (Analecta Orientalia 30; Rome, 1966) 138–39.

66. Hirsch, "Die Inschriften der Könige von Agade," *AfO* 20 (1963) 5, 13, 16, 24, 30, s.v. "Das Nachleben . . . im Kult."

67. In the Old Akkadian texts, Šar-kali-sharri, Bin-kali-sharri, and the unnamed king, queen, princes, and princesses on distribution lists from Sargonic Lagash/Girsu are probably *living* members of the ruling house; cf. F. Thureau-Dangin, "Encore la dynastie d'Agadé," *RA* 9 (1912) 81–83; Hallo, "Gutium," *RLA* 3 (1971) 713; E. Sollberger, *Pre-Sargonic and Sargonic Economic Texts* (Cuneiform Texts from Babylonian Tablets in the British Museum 50; London, 1972), no. 52; B. Foster, "Notes on Sargonic Royal Progress," *JANES* 12 (1980) 29–36. For the Neo-Sumerian texts, see Hirsch, "Die Inschriften der Könige von Agade." For the Old Babylonian text from Mari, see M. Birot, "Fragment de rituel de Mari relatif au *kispum*," in *Death in Mesopotamia: Papers Read at the XXVIe Rencontre Assyriologique Internationale* (ed. B. Alster; Copenhagen, 1980) 139–50 (note that the offerings are specifically made to the *lamassātu* of the kings, here equated with their *ṣalmu* 'image' by Birot [pp. 146–47 and n. 5]); cf. also H. D. Galter, *Kulturkontakte* (Graz, 1986) 17, who translates "Heiligenbilder." For the Neo-Babylonian texts from Sippar, see D. A. Kennedy, "Realia," *RA* 63 (1969) 79–80.

of the Sargonic kings—but it is nonetheless impressive that old antagonisms were forgotten[68] in the millennial perpetuation of what began as a veneration of the departed royal ancestors.[69]

The same description applies to the evidence of the late Sargonic, or Gutian, period late in the twenty-second century. Lagash regained its prominence now under the dynasty of Ur-Bau (if I may so designate it) and its principal figure, Gudea. Both Ur-Bau and Gudea (the latter posthumously deified)[70] continued to receive offerings,[71] again no doubt in the form of their statues, well into the twenty-first century and the dominion of the Ur III Dynasty, in spite of the fact that that dynasty had put a bloody end to their own.[72] In fact, M. Civil has shown that the Ur III Dynasty performed the mouth-washing and mouth-opening ceremonies on the statue of Gudea.[73]

The Ur III Dynasty itself is best documented of all. Now, with royal deification at its height, the statue of the living king was the recipient of worship and offerings[74] along with a host of other royal and divine trappings—the throne, the chariot, the ceremonial boat, and, in the case of Šu-Sin, his own temples. The question is, however, whether these honors continued posthumously. The elaborate burial provided for Šulgi and Amar-Sin suggests as much, as do the lamentations for the first and last members of the dynasty who failed of proper burial in the mausoleum at

---

68. Cf. Wilcke, "Literaturwerke als politische Tendenzschriften," in *La Voix de l'Opposition en Mésopotamie Ancienne* (ed. A. Finet; Brussels, 1975) 37–65.

69. Tsukimoto, *Untersuchungen zur Totenpflege*, 29, sees evidence of a cult of the royal grave in Sargonic times in line 69 of the Exaltation of Inanna, taking *ki-sì-ga* as *é-ki-sì-ga* (*kimāhu* or *qubūru*). For a different interpretation of the line see J. van Dijk, "VAT 8382: Ein zweisprachiges Königsritual," in *Heidelberger Studien zum alten Orient: Adam Falkenstein zum 17. September 1966* (ed. D. O. Edzard; Wiesbaden, 1967) 242 n. 44; Hallo and van Dijk, *The Exaltation of Inanna* (Yale Near Eastern Researches 3; New Haven, 1968) 55, 81–82 *ad loc*. In line 90 of the same composition, Wilcke reads *gidim-(ma)-né hu-mu-(un)-te*, which might imply that Lugal-anne's sacrilege extended to the ancestral cult statues; see "Nin-mešár-ra: Probleme der Interpretation," *Wiener Zeitschrift für die Kunde des Morgenlandes* 68 (1976) 87. Cf. also *MSL* 13:151 E 6–7 with note.

70. Tsukimoto, *Untersuchungen zur Totenpflege*, 62–63.

71. Cf., e.g., Schneider, "Ein deifizierter Patesi zur Zeit des 3. Dynastie von Ur," *Or* 9 (1940) 17–24; and now especially T. Maede, "Two Rulers by the Name Ur-Ningirsu in Pre–Ur III Lagash," *ASJ* 10 (1988) 19–35.

72. Based on the prologue to "Ur-Nammu Laws"—but the reading of the crucial passage is now questioned by S. N. Kramer, "The Ur-Nammu Code: Who Was Its Author?" *Or* 52 (1983) 453–56, esp. 455 n. 12; and P. Steinkeller, "The Date of Gudea and His Dynasty," *JCS* 40 (1988) 47–53, esp. 47 n. 2.

73. M. Civil, "Remarks on 'Sumerian and Bilingual Texts,'" *JNES* 26 (1967) 211.

74. Tsukimoto, *Untersuchungen zur Totenpflege*, 21 n. 90, citing R. Kutscher, "An Offering to the Statue of Šulgi," *Tel Aviv* 2 (1974) 55–59. Cf. J. Klein, *Three Šulgi Hymns* (Ramat Gan, 1981) 31 n. 43.

Ur—wherever that might have been.[75] There are numerous references to offering at the libation place (*ki-a-nag*) of departed kings and queens.[76] More persuasive, if indirect, is the later literary evidence. The genre of royal hymns, first attested by one exemplar for Gudea, flourished under the Ur III kings. But it is known to us only in copies of the successor dynasties at Isin, Larsa, Uruk, and Babylon. These copies are, admittedly, products of the scribal schools, and we cannot be sure that they were actually recited in a cult of the deceased kings. But in the case of Šulgi, the most prominent member of the dynasty, we have testimony from a royal hymn to a statue of the king which received posthumous honors and served as a model of a similar statue of Iddin-Dagan of Isin, together with a comparable royal hymn.[77] And we also have a so-called prophecy by Šulgi which, while preserved on tablets of the seventh century, deals with events, according to R. Borger, its editor, of the thirteenth and twelfth centuries,[78] and was probably composed then if, as I think, it belongs to the genre of Akkadian apocalypses which, characteristically, attempt and notably fail to predict the future after successfully (and ostensibly) "predicting" what has already transpired.[79] (The date of composition can then, theoretically at least, be fixed at the transition from pretended to real prediction.) But whether or not my characterization of the Šulgi prophecy is granted, it is undeniable that it occurs in the guise of a fictional royal autobiography,[80] and in a series with a fictional autobiography of Marduk. In the latter, the god of Babylon reviews the history of his various departures, voluntary or otherwise, from his city—clearly in the guise of his cult statue. It is not too much to suppose, then, that Šulgi too is to be conceived of as speaking in the first person out of the mouth of his statue. That such a statue received offerings as late as the outgoing second millennium is a further deduction, but by no means improbable, given the Sargonic analogies already presented.

---

75. P. R. S. Morey, "Where Did They Bury the Kings of the IIIrd Dynasty of Ur?" *Iraq* 46 (1984) 1–18.

76. See most recently G. Frame, "A New Wife for Šu-Sîn," *Annual Review of the Royal Inscriptions of Mesopotamia Project* 2 (1984) 3–4; previously P. Michalowski, "The Death of Šulgi," *Or* 46 (1977) 220–25. Cf. also n. 138 below.

77. J. Klein, "Šulgi and Išmedagan: Runners in the Service of the Gods (SRT 13)," *Beer Sheva* 2 (1985) 7*–38*; cf. Hallo, "Texts, Statues and the Cult of the Divine King," 61 nn. 43–45.

78. R. Borger, "Gott Marduk und Gott-König Šulgi als Propheten," *Bibliotheca Orientalis* 28 (1971) 3–21.

79. Hallo, "Akkadian Apocalypses," *Israel Exploration Journal* 16 (1966) 231–42; idem, "The Expansion of Cuneiform Literature," *Proceedings of the American Academy of Jewish Research* 46–47 (1980) 307–22, esp. 314.

80. T. Longman III, *Fictional Akkadian Royal Autobiography* (Ph.D. thesis, Yale University, 1983), esp. 345–49; see now idem, *Fictional Akkadian Autobiography: A Generic and Comparative Study* (Winona Lake, IN, 1990) 142–46.

The fall of the Isin Dynasty and the accession of Hammurapi at the beginning of the eighteenth century meant a sharp break in the ideology of kingship. The traditional Sumero-Akkadian ethos was replaced by one more congenial to the new Amorite overlords of Mesopotamia, and nowhere perhaps more conspicuously than in the cult of the royal ancestors. This is dramatically shown by a remarkable document published in 1966 by J. J. Finkelstein under the title of "The Genealogy of the Hammurapi Dynasty."[81] Although it is not explicitly a genealogy, it lists the first nine kings of the dynasty (of whom all but the first are known from other sources as ancestors one of the other), preceded by twenty-two other names of what must have been regarded as the more remote ancestors of the dynasty (the first eleven of them more or less identical with the founders of the Assyrian royal house) all summed up as "the dynasty of the Amorite peoples" and followed by the dynasties of the surrounding countries, and all departed spirits not properly buried.[82] These are invited to eat, drink, and bless the tenth (and presumably living) king of the dynasty. The occasion may be his coronation[83] and almost certainly it involves, though not explicitly naming it, a sacrificial rite for the deceased royal ancestors, known from other Akkadian sources as a *kispu* or, in Sumerian, *ki-sì-ga*.[84] The institution of the *kispu* has been described as a commemorative funerary meal by Bottéro and exhaustively studied by Akio Tsukimoto, and I will not review all his evidence here.[85] Suffice it to say that (1) it almost always has a royal focus or (at least) never explicitly a private one.[86] (2) It is not attested before Old Babylonian times.[87] (3) In Old Babylonian times it is attested as far afield as Mari, where a particularly revealing *kispu* ritual has been elucidated by Maurice Birot[88] and where numerous administrative

---

81. J. J. Finkelstein, "The Genealogy of the Hammurapi Dynasty," *JCS* 20 (1966) 95-118.

82. W. G. Lambert, "Another Look at Hammurabi's Ancestors," *JCS* 22 (1968-69) 1-2; Hallo, "Assyrian Historiography Revisited," *EI* 14 (1978) 1*-7*, esp. 4*-5*.

83. Cf. n. 35 above for a comparable Ugaritic case.

84. For other equivalencies, see n. 69 above.

85. Bottéro, "Les Morts et l'au-delà," 171; Tsukimoto, *Untersuchungen zur Totenpflege*, 65-69; idem, "Aspekte von *kispu(m)* als 'Totenbeigabe,'" in *Death in Mesopotamia: Papers Read at the XXVIe Rencontre Assyriologique Internationale* (ed. B. Alster; Copenhagen, 1980) 129-38.

86. See n. 48 above.

87. According to Tsukimoto, *Untersuchungen zur Totenpflege*, 39-40, the first explicit Akkadian reference occurs in the Old Babylonian letter published by H. F. Lutz, *Early Babylonian Letters from Larsa* (Yale Oriental Series: Babylonian Texts 2; New Haven, 1917), no. 20 (= M. Stol, *Letters from Yale* [Altbabylonische Briefe in Umschrift und Übersetzung 9; Leiden, 1981] 14-15). Cf. also *CAD* K 425-27, s.v. *kispu*.

88. M. Birot, "Fragment de rituel de Mari relatif au *kispum*," 139-50. For important observations on this ritual and a new interpretation see D. Charpin and J.-M. Durand, "'Fils de Sim'al': Les origines tribales des rois de Mari," *RA* 80 (1986) 159-70.

texts attest regular *kispu* offerings to the kings called *šarrāni* chiefly on new and full moon, and to those called *mālikū* on the new moon (once on the full moon).[89] In a newly published Mari(?) text, there is even reference to a *kispum* of the kings on the sixteenth of the month occasioned by a dream vouchsafed to the woman(?) *Dagan-nahmī*.[90] (4) An Old Babylonian text noted by van Dijk provides an interesting catalog of the "necessities for a *kispu* of the steppe"; another provides for butter in the same connection.[91] (5) There is some indirect evidence that *kispu* rituals and offerings took place at the grave, given the lexical equations between Sumerian *é-ki-sì-ga* (literally, *kispu*-house) and Akkadian words for grave.[92] In the same direction points the considerable interest in the precise location of royal burials displayed in texts such as Sumerian litanies for departed kings of Ur and Isin, or the Akkadian Dynastic Chronicle, an interest shared by the biblical books of Kings and Chronicles.[93] In the case of Hittite royalty who (like the Greeks)[94] were cremated, in their case at the start of a fourteen-day ceremony,[95] their worship may have taken place at the "urns buried among the rocks at Osmankaya near the capital" where their ashes were

---

89. P. Talon, "Les offrandes funéraires à Mari," *Annuaire de l'Institut de Philologie et d'Histoire Orientales et Slaves* 22 (1978) 52–75; Tsukimoto, *Untersuchungen zur Totenpflege*, 57–78; Sasson, "Accounting Discrepancies in the Mari NÌ.GUB [NÍG.DU] texts," 326–41. Cf. also the *kispu* offering for the departed spirit of King Jahdun-Lim of Mari (*kispi ana iṭemim ša Yahdun-Lim*) published in J. R. Kupper, *Correspondance de Kibri-Dagan, Gouverneur de Terqa* (Archives Royales de Mari 3; Paris, 1950), no. 40:16–18; cited by Tsukimoto, *Untersuchungen zur Totenpflege*, 59–60; by W. von Soden, "Akkadisch *taʾû* und hebräisch *taʾ* als Raumbezeichnungen," *Die Welt des Orients* 1 (1950) 359; and by F. Ellermeier, *Prophetie in Mari und Israel* (Herzberg, 1968) 32ff.

90. Wilcke, "Dagān-nahmīs Traum," *Die Welt des Orients* 17 (1986) 11–16.

91. Van Dijk, "VAT 8382," 242, citing T. G. Pinches, *Old-Babylonian Business Documents* (Cuneiform Texts from Babylonian Tablets in the British Museum 45; London, 1964), no. 99:29–30: *annû hišihti kisip ṣēri*. The text about butter (IM 10135) has since been published by van Dijk, *Cuneiform Texts: Old Babylonian Contracts and Related Material* (Texts in the Iraq Museum 5; Wiesbaden, 1968) 68.

92. Tsukimoto, *Untersuchungen zur Totenpflege*, 60–61, 70–73, goes to some lengths to deny the existence of a *kispu*-house (*bīt kispi), and especially that posited by Y. al-Khalesi, "The *bīt kispim* in Mesopotamian Architecture: Studies in Form and Function," *Mesopotamia* 12 (1977) 53–81. On words for grave, see n. 69 above. Cf. also *MSL* 13:151 E 6–7 with note. Note further É = *qubūri*, translated as 'graveyard' by J. Huehnergard, "RS 15.86 (PRU 3,51f.)," *UF* 18 (1986) 169–76, citing C. H. Gordon, "Ugaritic *ḥrt/ḥirīta* 'Cemetery,'" *Syria* 33 (1956) 102. But in line 15 of the same text he translates É as 'estate'.

93. See, for all these references, Hallo, "Death of Kings." For possible "offerings for (deceased?) Kassite kings and personnel" late in the reign of Samsu-iluna (ca. 1720 B.C.), see Karel Van Lerberghe, *Old Babylonian Legal and Administrative Texts from Philadelphia* (Orientalia Lovaniensia Analecta 21; Leuven, 1986) no. 20 (reference courtesy J. M. Sasson).

94. Cf. Kees, *Totenglauben und Jenseitsvorstellungen der alten Ägypter*, 19, who notes that it was *not* practiced among Egyptians; Christmann-Franck, "Le rituel des funérailles royales hittites," 61, who cites the cremation of Patroclus and Hector in the *Iliad*.

95. Christmann-Franck, "Le rituel des funérailles royales hittites," 62.

preserved.[96] But Mitanni royalty was emphatically *not* cremated, as once thought.[97] The evidence of royal burial practices in Elam, probably during the interval between ca. 1500 and 1350, has been assembled by Erica Reiner.[98] In Babylonia, the bulk of the evidence points to the statues of the deceased as the typical locus for the ritual and offerings.[99]

Mesopotamia: The Later Evidence

As Tsukimoto indicates, the *kispu* ritual in Mesopotamia continued after the Old Babylonian period into Kassite times, when its connection to the new moon (and full moon) was apparently abandoned[100] in favor of a more general connection with the cultic calendar, including all the lunar festivals (*eššeššu*),[101] the statues of departed kings (*ṣalmū*), and the lustration

---

96. Gurney, *Hittite Religion*, 59. Cf., however, p. 62: "There can be little doubt that the remains of the dead were finally laid to rest in the Stone House"; and "the ritual clearly establishes that the bones of the king were laid to rest in a building called a 'Stone House.'" Was this identical with the É-*hešti*? Cf. nn. 24 and 26 above, and n. 111 below.

97. E. Gaál, "'The King Parrattarna Died and Was Cremated'?" in *Wirtschaft und Gesellschaft im alten Vorderasien* (ed. J. Harmatta and G. Komoróczy; Acta Antiqua Academiae Scientiarum Hungaricae 22; Budapest, 1974) 281–86. Gaál showed that in the Nuzi text published as no. 165 in R. H. Pfeiffer and E. R. Lacheman, *Excavations at Nuzi IV: Miscellaneous Texts*, vol. 1 (HSS 13; Cambridge, MA, 1942), it was the blanket (*zijanātu*) which was burned when the king died, not the king! The same conclusion was reached independently by I. M. Diakonoff and N. Jankowska, "Zum Mythos von den vorderasiatischen Ariern: Die 'Leichenverbrennung' des Königs Parrattarna," *Altorientalische Forschungen* 2 (1975) 131–32. Cf. also G. Wilhelm and B. Hrouda, "Leichenverbrennung," *RLA* 6 (1983) 570–71.

98. E. Reiner, "Inscription from a Royal Elamite Tomb," *AfO* 24 (1973) 87–102; for the bearing of the associated Tepti-ahar brick inscription (pp. 95–97) on Exod 38:8, see now D. Marcus, *Jephtah and His Vow* (Lubbock, TX, 1986) 65 n. 55, *contra* W. G. Plaut, *The Torah: A Modern Commentary* (New York, 1981) 674–75.

99. Bottéro, "Les Morts et l'au-delà," 185: "Les Morts y assistaient (à *kispu*), parfois representés par leurs figurines-substituts," citing E. Ebeling, *Keilschrifttexte aus Assur religiösen Inhalts* (Wissenschaftliche Veröffentlichungen der Deutschen Orientgesellschaft 28; Leipzig, 1915), vol. 1/1, no. 22:3–4 (cf. p. 187). For the ancestral spirits (*eṭimmu*) at Nuzi, see E. R. Lacheman and D. I. Owen, "Texts from Arrapḫa and from Nuzi in the Yale Babylonian Collection," in *Studies on the Civilization and Culture of Nuzi and the Hurrians*, vol. 1: *In Honor of Ernest R. Lacheman* (ed. M. A. Morrison and D. I. Owen; Winona Lake, IN, 1981) 386 line 30; and J. Paradise, "Daughters as 'Sons' at Nuzi," in *Studies on the Civilization and Culture of Nuzi and the Hurrians*, vol. 2: *General Studies and Excavations at Nuzi* 9/1 (ed. D. I. Owen and M. A. Morrison; Winona Lake, IN, 1987) 210–11.

100. Tsukimoto, *Untersuchungen zur Totenpflege*, 86. But note, among others, a late ritual against illnesses provoked by an *eṭimmu* (Ebeling, *Keilschrifttexte aus Assur religiösen Inhalts* [1920], vol. 2/1, no. 184: rev.[!] 33–51) which is specifically scheduled for the fifteenth of the month; see Bottéro, "Les Morts et l'au-delà," 174–75.

101. Tsukimoto, *Untersuchungen zur Totenpflege*, 88, citing A. T. Clay, *Documents from the Temple Archives of Nippur Dated in the Reigns of Cassite Rulers* (Publications of the Babylonian Section 2/2; Philadelphia, 1912), no. 8:8–10.

(*rimku*), possibly of such statues.[102] At Nuzi, there is a hint of *kispu* offerings (here pronounced *kipsu, kipsāti*) as among the duties of an (adoptive) son.[103] Tsukimoto also follows the subject into the first millennium.[104] Although I cannot pursue this topic to the end of Babylonian history in the available space,[105] I note that there was a series called *kispu* in the library of Assurbanipal[106] and that, as late as the Seleucid era, there is ritual provision at Uruk for the evil omen implied "if a statue of the king of this country, or a statue of his father, or a statue of his grandfather falls and breaks, or if its features become indistinct."[107] However, I cannot conclude without a glance at the specifically Assyrian evidence. In the more robust environment of Assyria, an almost monotheistic attachment to the tribal deity Assur, and to the tribal traditions of the original Semitic-speaking settlers of the city and land called by his name, combined to reject many aspects of the evolving Sumero-Babylonian ideology, including most particularly the deification of the king. The king was no more than the steward of god on earth, the governor appointed by Assur. So there was no worship of the living king and, for a long time, no statue of the departed king. What characterized the Assyrian scene, more particularly the open space on the citadel of the city of Assur, was a long row of steles, each bearing the name of a king, a member of the royal family, or a high official. That these steles, in more or less phallic shape,[108] were actual objects of worship, may be doubted[109]—despite their analogies to comparable but uninscribed assemblies of steles at cult places like those of Hazor,[110] or the steles and totems (symbols) which preceded anthropomorphic cult images of the deity among the Hittites.[111]

---

102. Ibid., 88–91.

103. Ibid., 201–27; cf. also n. 48 above.

104. Ibid., 92–124.

105. Barnett, "Assurbanipal's Feast," p. 5* and n. 49, claims that Cyrus set up an image of Assurbanipal in the gate (of Babylon) according to the "Yale portion" of the Cyrus Cylinder (C. E. Keiser and J. B. Nies, *Historical, Religious, and Economic Texts and Antiquities* [Babylonian Inscriptions in the Collection of James B. Nies 2; New Haven, 1920], no. 32), but the reference is only to the older king's inscription (*šiṭir šumi*); cf. P.-R. Berger, "Der Kyros-Zylinder mit dem Zusatzfragment BIN II Nr. 32 und die akkadischen Personennamen im Danielbuch," *ZA* 64 (1975) 202–3.

106. S. Parpola, "Assyrian Library Records," *JNES* 42 (1983) 1–29, esp. 23 (2:2!.13′).

107. *CAD* B 318d, cf. *CAD* Ṣ 81d, *ANET* 340b; S. M. Maul, *"Herzberuhigungsklagen": Die sumerisch-akkadischen Eršahunga-Gebete* (Wiesbaden, 1988) 32.

108. Cf. H. Genge, "Sinn und Bedeutung der Menhire," *IPEK: Jahrbuch für Prähistorische und Ethnographische Kunst* 22 (1969) 105–13 and pl. 77.

109. P. A. Miglus, "Another Look at the 'Stelenreihen' in Assur," *ZA* 74 (1984) 133–40.

110. Greenfield, "Un rite religieux araméen et ses parallèles," *RB* 80 (1973) 48 n. 12; C. F. Graesser, "Standing Stones in Ancient Palestine," *BA* 35 (1972) 34–63; J. V. Canby, "The *Stelenreihen* at Assur, Tell Halaf, and *maṣṣēbôt*," *Iraq* 38 (1976) 113–28.

111. Gurney, *Hittite Religion*, 25–27. Cf. n. 26 above.

Another specifically Assyrian contribution to the cult is made up of the magical prescriptions for dealing with ghosts. These are the subject of a doctoral dissertation completed recently by Jo Ann Scurlock.[112] Among the ninety-seven prescriptions, eighty-two are devoted to "expelling ghosts," without exception of Assyrian provenience.[113] There are also nine necromancy texts of Babylonian provenience and six prescriptions using ghosts as substitutes or for general assistance of which two are of Babylonian provenience.[114] While these prescriptions do not in themselves constitute an ancestor cult, let alone a royal ancestor cult (except perhaps in connection with the ritual for the substitute king), they make frequent reference to the *kispu* ritual,[115] and even suggest possible explanations for some of its characteristic features. Thus the predilection for the full moon and new moon (especially of Ululu, i.e., at the end of Abu) for expelling ghosts may be because then the departed spirits were due to come back to earth to receive their funerary offerings[116] or, more likely, *both* rituals favored the full moon "because, on that day, 'Sin and Šamaš stand together,' making it convenient to address prayers to both gods at once,"[117] and the new moon for comparable reasons. The importance of the solar deity is equally conspicuous in both rituals.[118] The *šegūšu* flour plays a significant part in the former[119] despite the proverbial insistence to the contrary.[120] And it is noteworthy that in both rituals the generation of the grandparents is normally the limit of genealogical depth resorted to.[121]

---

112. J. Scurlock, *Magical Means of Dealing with Ghosts in Ancient Mesopotamia* (Ph.D. thesis, University of Chicago, 1988). I am indebted to Dr. Scurlock for furnishing me with a copy.

113. Prescriptions 1–71 and 77–78 in Scurlock's numbering; the discrepancy in the figures is due to inserts in the sequence numbers.

114. The nine necromancy texts are prescriptions 72–76 and 79–82 (see Scurlock, *Ghosts in Ancient Mesopotamia*, 6 nn. 13–14, on their Babylonian provenience); see previously I. L. Finkel, "Necromancy in Ancient Mesopotamia," *AfO* 29/30 (1983–84) 1–17. The six ghost prescriptions are prescriptions 68, 83–88 (correct p. 112 n. 515 accordingly?); prescriptions 85–86 are from Babylon (cf. Scurlock, *Ghosts in Ancient Mesopotamia*, 6 n. 12).

115. The following prescriptions (with page numbers to Scurlock, *Ghosts in Ancient Mesopotamia* in parentheses) refer to the *kispu* ritual: 63:5, 18 (pp. 35, 271–72); 67:15 (p. 304); 68:14 (pp. 114, 309); 77:10, 16 (pp. 34, 328); 83:5, 10 (p. 346); 85:11 and 86:158 (pp. 118, 353, 356). See prescription 83 for the substitute king.

116. Prescription 58:84 (p. 235); cf. Scurlock, *Ghosts in Ancient Mesopotamia*, 105 and n. 485.

117. Ibid., 31 and n. 131, referring to prescription 59:93 (p. 239).

118. Ibid., 79–81, and n. 131 below.

119. Prescriptions 13:i:13′, 14:i:37′, 16:i:55′, and 22:ii:31′ (pp. 66, 166, 169, 174, 186); 26:iii:30 (p. 197); 57:i:60, 62 (pp. 61–62, 266); 60:i:17, 23 (p. 244).

120. Hallo, "Biblical Abominations and Sumerian Taboos," *JQR* 76 (1985) 21–40, esp. 29.

121. Prescriptions 85:9 and 86:155; cf. Scurlock, *Ghosts in Ancient Mesopotamia*, 353, 356; and n. 53 above.

I conclude the Mesopotamian evidence with the case of Adad-guppi, long-lived mother of the last Chaldean king, Nabonidus. She prides herself in her autobiographical funerary inscription as having offered monthly[122] offerings to the departed kings of the dynasty. They had treated her like a lineal descendant so she returned the favor, the more so as their own descendants failed to do their duty in this regard.[123] For her, as for others before her, "the *kispu* offering was at one and the same time a religious duty and a symbol of legitimacy," to quote Jonas Greenfield.[124]

Summary

Let me sum up. The ancient Mesopotamians had a vivid belief in ancestral spirits, and dealt with them as they did with the more concrete phenomena encountered in their daily life—that is, by means of rituals and incantations. To paraphrase Bottéro, the exorcists appeased them by seeing to their legitimate needs on the one hand, and on the other hand neutralized them by banishing them back to the netherworld.[125] But they did not demonstrably worship them *except* where deceased royalty was concerned— and then the worship took the form of offerings to their statues. That such offerings could continue, in the case of particularly venerated royalty, centuries and even millennia after their dynasty had come to an end provides one more demonstration of the pivotal role played by the king in Mesopotamian ideology. And to the extent that each Babylonian dynasty claimed descent from its predecessors,[126] such offerings are a Mesopotamian expression of the worship of deceased ancestors.

But this Mesopotamian expression is only part of a larger phenomenon, larger in both space and time than the cuneiform evidence. It is here submitted that the cult of the royal ancestors grew in prominence throughout the Asiatic Near East precisely at the turn from the third to the second millennium, and that this growth and expansion of the cult may well reflect a change in ideology. The traditional Sumero-Babylonian ethos, nurtured in the great urban centers of lower Mesopotamia, had emphasized the role of the city, its deity, its temple, and its king both in cult and historiography. The Amorite ethos, at home in the Syrian desert and in upper Mesopotamia

---

122. So Tsukimoto, *Untersuchungen zur Totenpflege*, 122–23. But the meaning of *arhišamma* in iii:12 is probably 'every *new* moon' (*arhu*); note also that in a late lexical text the day of the *kispu* ritual (*ūm kispim*) is equated with the new moon (*bubbulu*); see Tsukimoto, *Untersuchungen zur Totenpflege*, 47 n. 193.

123. Ibid., 120–23.

124. Greenfield, "Un rite religieux araméen," 49: "Le *kispu* est à la fois un devoir religieux et un signe de légitimité."

125. Bottéro, "Les Morts et l'au-delà," 182–83.

126. Cf. Lambert, "The Seed of Kingship," in *Le Palais et la royauté: XIXᵉ Rencontre Assyriologique Internationale* (ed. P. Garelli; Paris, 1974) 427–40, esp. 432–33.

at Mari, Assur, and other ramparts between the desert and the sown, emphasized genealogy and tribal or ancestral relationships.[127] As Greenfield has said of the *kispu* ritual, "One has the impression that this rite evolved during the period of Amorite domination in order to allow for conforming to West Semitic usages."[128] Such usages in my opinion include the cult of the corpse (*pagru*) which is equated with the *kispu* at Mari and which even gives its name to a month at Ugarit and at Alalakh.[129] It also includes the steles of Hazor and their reflexes at Assur and elsewhere,[130] and the complicated institution of the *ilib*, the ancestral deity, which may have been the designation of such steles.[131] There is no space here to go into this involved question, nor that of the funerary repast known as *marzeaḥ*.[132] Suffice it to mention the almost invariable offering of food and drink and the invocation of the name of the dead (*zikir šumi*),[133] and the prominence of the solar deity ("king of the ghosts" and "lord of the dead")[134] in the ritual[135]—all elements well attested in the cuneiform sources of Mesopotamia but documented further west as well. To take only one example from the whole complex of elements associated with the cult of the royal ancestors: the *mlkm*. As is well known, this word occurs in West Semitic

---

127. Hallo, "Dating the Mesopotamian Past," *Bulletin* [*of*] *the Society for Mesopotamian Studies* 6 (1983) 7–18, esp. 9–12; idem, "The Nabonassar Era and Other Epochs in Mesopotamian Chronology and Chronography," in *A Scientific Humanist: Studies in Memory of Abraham Sachs* (ed. E. Leichty and M. de J. Ellis; Philadelphia, 1989) 175–90.

128. Greenfield, "Un rite religieux araméen," 47: "On a l'impression que ce rite [*kispu*] a évolué pendant le temps de la domination amorite pour se conformer à des usages ouest-sémitiques."

129. For Mari, see Dietrich and Loretz, "Totenverehrung in Mari . . . and Ugarit," 381 (they transcribe *pagrû(m)*). For Ugarit, see del Olmo Lete, "'Divine' Names of the Ugaritic Kings," 84 (*ad* KTU 1:106); and Greenfield, "Un rite religieux araméen," 47 n. 12. For Alalakh, see Greenfield, "Un rite religieux araméen," 47 n. 12; and J. H. Ebach, "*PGR* = (Toten-)Opfer?" *UF* 3 (1971) 365–68.

130. See nn. 108–10 above.

131. Cf. for now my brief remarks on the cognate(?) Akkadian divine name Ilibanum; see Hallo, "A Mercantile Agreement from the Reign of Gungunum of Larsa," in *Studies in Honor of Benno Landsberger* (ed. H. G. Güterbock and T. Jacobsen; Assyriological Studies 16; Chicago, 1965) 202 n. 32; and the literature on the "catalog of filial duties" in the Aqhat Epic from Ugarit, for which see most recently Spronk, *Beatific Afterlife*, 146–47; previously Dietrich, Loretz, and Sanmartín, "Ugaritisch *ILIB* und hebräisch ʾ(*W*)*B* 'Totengeist,'" *UF* 6 (1974) 450–51.

132. Cf. most recently Spronk, *Beatific Afterlife*, 196–202 and nn. 12, 27–28 above. For a possible analogy with the *kispu*, cf. n. 82 above. For the *marzeaḥ* at Ebla, cf. Pope, "Cult of the Dead at Ugarit," 179 n. 65.

133. Tsukimoto, *Untersuchungen zur Totenpflege*, 164.

134. "King of the ghosts": MAN GIDIM.GIDIM.E.NE (*šar eṭimmē*) with prescription 17:i:56' (Scurlock, *Ghosts in Ancient Mesopotamia*, 177); previously R. C. Thompson, *Cuneiform Texts from Babylonian Tablets in the British Museum*, vol. 23 (London, 1906), see descriptive index; cf. also *bēl eṭimmē* in *CAD* E 397–401, s.v. *eṭemmu*. "Lord of the dead": EN LÚ.UŠ with prescription 19:ii:8' (Scurlock, *Ghosts in Ancient Mesopotamia*, 180).

with the meaning of 'kings', in Akkadian as 'counselors'. Are we then to take the *mālikū* of the Mari *kispu* rituals as 'counselors, princes, or other high court functionaries' in the Akkadian sense?[136] I prefer to follow Dietrich and Loretz[137] who equate the Mari *mālikū* rather with the 'dead kings' (*mlkm*) of the Ugaritic ritual, and go even further, suggesting that this West Semitic usage penetrated even into the Akkadian of lower Mesopotamia, where the (evil) demons known as *malkū* may be the (restless) spirits of departed kings.[138] Ultimately the investigation of ancestor worship may yet prove to be another major institutional phenomenon which—like law, the calendar, language, writing, and various religious practices— distinguish the Sumero-Babylonian core from the Akkadian-Amorite periphery in the Asiatic Near East—and which separate the Semitic Near East from its Sumerian predecessors and even more profoundly from its Hittite and Egyptian contemporaries.[139]

135. Cf., e.g., Birot, "Fragment de rituel de Mari relatif au *kispum*"; Healey, "The Sun Deity and the Underworld: Mesopotamia and Ugarit," in *Death in Mesopotamia: Papers Read at the XXVIᵉ Rencontre Assyriologique Internationale* (ed. B. Alster; Copenhagen, 1980) 239–42; Bottéro, "Les Morts et l'au-delà," 174, 201–2; cf. the six ghosts prescriptions in n. 114 above.

136. So Healey (see the works by him listed in n. 33 above); cf. previously idem, "*Malku : Mlkm : Anunnaki*," *UF* 7 (1975) 235–38.

137. Dietrich and Loretz, "Neue Studien zu den Ritualtexten aus Ugarit (I): Ein Forschungsbericht," *UF* 13 (1981) 63–100, esp. 69–74.

138. Ibid., 73. Note however already the expression *ki-a-nag ma-al-ku-um lugal-lugal-e-ne* 'libation place of the ghost of kings' in V. E. Crawford, *Sumerian Economic Texts from the First Dynasty of Isin* (Babylonian Inscriptions in the Collection of James B. Nies 9; New Haven, 1954), no. 440:31, a text from twentieth-century Isin; cf. M. van de Mieroop, *Crafts in the Early Isin Period* (Orientalia Lovaniensia Analecta 24; Louvain, 1987) 109–10. In connection with the Mari evidence, Charpin and Durand understand *māliku* simply as prince, more particularly as a non-reigning member of the royal family; "'Fils de Sim³al,'" 169. Cf. also Tsukimoto, *Untersuchungen zur Totenpflege*, 105 n. 386, who suggests that at Nuzi the *eṭimmu* became *ilāni* when they lost their definable character, comparing the Japanese situation where the dead are deified after thirty-three (or fifty-five) years and the kindred cult of the dead ceases.

139. After this manuscript had gone to press, I received, through the courtesy of the author, Abraham Malamat's *Mari and the Israelite Experience* (Schweich Lectures 1984; Oxford, 1989). It includes on pp. 96–107 a thorough survey of "The Royal Ancestor Cult," covering much of the same ground as the foregoing. It could not be considered here.

THE SPELL OF NUDIMMUD

Thorkild Jacobsen

In the Sumerian epic tale known as "Enmerkar and the Lord of Aratta" Enmerkar tells his envoy at the end of his instructions to him to recite "this Spell of Nudimmud" to the lord of Aratta.[1] The text of the spell, which he goes on to quote, has been variously read and interpreted by modern scholars including S. N. Kramer, J. van Dijk, B. Alster, S. Cohen, O. E. Gurney, and myself;[2] but since I have recently come to have serious doubts about my own interpretation without being able to feel comfortable with any of the other ones that have been offered, a renewed examination of the problems involved may be allowable. I shall consider first the text of the spell in its setting in the tale, then its translation and the questions to which it gives rise.

Text

The message of which the Spell of Nudimmud forms a part threatens the lord of Aratta with destruction of his city unless Aratta brings gold and silver to Uruk and does corvé work there for Enmerkar, building temples whose hoped-for splendor is described. I begin quoting in the middle of this description.[3]

---

1. S. N. Kramer, *Enmerkar and the Lord of Aratta* (Philadelphia, 1952). See also Sol Cohen's dissertation, *Enmerkar and the Lord of Aratta* (Ph.D. diss., University of Pennsylvania, 1973).

2. S. N. Kramer, "Man's Golden Age: A Sumerian Parallel to Genesis XI.1," *JAOS* 63 (1943) 191–94; idem, "The 'Babel of Tongues': A Sumerian Version," *JAOS* 88 (1968) 108–11 (= *Essays in Memory of E. A. Speiser* [ed. W. W. Hallo; AOS 53; New Haven, 1968]); J. van Dijk, "La 'confusion des langues': Note sur le lexique et sur la morphologie d'Enmerkar, 147–155," *Or* 39 (1970) 302–10; B. Alster, "An Aspect of 'Enmerkar and the Lord of Aratta,'" *RA* 67 (1973) 101–10; Cohen, *Enmerkar and the Lord of Aratta*; O. E. Gurney, "A Note on the Babel of Tongues," *AfO* 25 (1974–77) 170–71; Thorkild Jacobsen, *The Harps That Once . . .* (New Haven, 1987) 283–90.

3. The text and notes are based on Cohen's edition. I follow Kramer's line count in "Babel of Tongues," which is also followed by Cohen. It has the line numbers after 150 one digit lower than in the original publication. My arrangement of the text, blank lines, and

133	A E F	zag-du$_8$-zag-du$_8$-bé^4 urin$_x$ (ŠEŠ) ḫa-ma-mul-e
134	A E F	agrun-agrun-ba sìr-kù-nam-sub-du$_{12}$-a-ba^5
135	A E F	nam-šub-^{d}Nu-dim-mud-da-ke$_4$^{6} e-ne-ra-dug$_4$-mu-na-ab
136	A E F K	ud-ba- muš-nu-g̃ál-àm^7 g̃ir nu-g̃ál-àm^8
137	A E F K	kir$_4$-nu-g̃ál-àm^9 ur-maḫ nu-g̃ál-àm^{10}
138	A E F K	ur-g̃ir$_x$ (GAR!?)^{11}ur-bar-ra nu-g̃ál-àm^{12}
139	A E F K L	ní-te-g̃e$_x$(GÁ)^{13}-e^{14}su^{15}-zi-zi-i^{16} nu-g̃ál-àm^{17}
140	A E F K L	lu-lu$_8$^{18} gaba-šu^{19}-g̃ar nu-tuk^{20}
141/142	A E F K L	ud-ba kur-Šubur^{21}-ki-Ḫa-ma-zi^{22}ki(142) eme ḫa-mun
142	A E K L	Ki-en-gi kur-gal-^{23}-nam-nun-na^{24}-ka^{25}

---

indentations is intended to bring out the structure of the spell more clearly; it does not reflect similar features in the sources. The sigla for the sources are those of Cohen, listed here with those of Kramer's original publication in parentheses:

A (A)   Ni 9601   Kramer, *Enmerkar and the Lord of Aratta*, pls. 3, 4, 17. Collated. Lines 133–57 and 205–8.

E kkk (C iii) UM 29-16-422 Kramer, *Enmerkar and the Lord of Aratta*, pls. 14, 20.

F ii (E ii)   CBS 10435   E. Chiera, *Sumerian Epics and Myths* (Oriental Institute Publications 15; Chicago, 1934) no. 14.

K   Ash. 1924-574 Kramer, "Babel of Tongues," 110.

L   UM 29-16-442 Unpublished. Variants quoted by E. I. Gordon and the textual apparatus to his *Sumerian Proverbs* (Philadelphia, 1959).

Q   U 16897   C. J. Gadd and S. N. Kramer, *Literary and Religious Texts* (Ur Excavation: Texts 6/1; London, 1963) no. 47.

4. Thus A; E has *-ba*.
5. Thus A; F has *-bi*.
6. Thus A; E has *-kam*.
7. A has -A-A]N after lacuna. E has *ud-ba muš-nu-g̃ál-la-àm*. K and probably F omit *-àm* after *-la*.
8. Thus A; E has *nu-g̃ál-la-àm*; F omits *-àm* after *-la*.
9. A has a lacuna here; E has traces only; F has *kir$_6$ nu-g̃ál-⌈la⌉*.
10. Thus A; E has *nu-g̃ál-la-àm*. K omits *-àm* after *-la*.
11. A has a lacuna here; so has K. E and F have *ur-ge$_7$*; see commentary to the line.
12. Thus A; E has *nu-g̃ál-la-àm*; F and K omit *-àm* after *la*.
13. For the reading g̃e$_x$ of GÁ, see D. O. Edzard, "*Ḫamṭu, marû* und freie Reduplikation beim sumerischen Verbum," *ZA* 66 (1976) 51 n. 203.
14. Thus L; E and K omit *-e*.
15. Thus E, F, and L; K has *su$_x$* (ŠUL).
16. Thus E; K, L, and probably F omit *-i*.
17. Thus A; E has *nu-g̃ál-la-àm*; K omits *-àm* after *-la*.
18. Thus E and L; F adds ^{lu}.
19. K mistakenly has *zu* for *šu*.
20. Thus A and F; L has *nu-tuk-àm*; E has *nu-um-tuk-àm*; K by dithography(?) has *nu-g̃ál-àm*.
21. Thus E and L; K has *zu-bir$_4$*.
22. A has [*ki Ḫa-m*]*a-zi*^{ki}; L has *ki Ḫa-ma-zi*; E has *ki Ḫé-me-zi*; K has NA (mistaken for *ki*) *Ḫa-ma-zi*^{ki}.
23. Thus E and L; K has *-la*.
24. K mistakenly has KI for *-na-*.
25. Thus A and K; E and L have *-kam*.

143	AE	KL	ki-Uri	kur²⁶ me-te-ğál-la²⁷
144	E F K L		kur-Mar-dú	ú-sal-la ná-a²⁸
145	E	KL	an-ki-niğin-na ukù	sağ-sè-ga
146	E	KL	ᵈEn-líl-ra eme-aš-àm²⁹	ḫé-en-na-da-ab-bé³⁰
147	E	K	ud-ba a-ada-en	a-da-nun a-da-lugal-la
148	E	K	ᵈEn-ki a-da-en	a-da-nun a-da-lugal-la
149	E	K	a-da-en-ne³¹	a-da-nun-ne a-da-lugal-la
150	E	K	ᵈEn-ki en-ḫé-ğál-la³²-du₁₁-ga-zi	
151	A	K	en-ğeš-túg-PI s[ağ-k]³³ul kalam-ma-ke₄	
152	A	K	maš-su	dingir-re-e-ne-ke₄
153	A	K	ğeš-túg-PI sá(!?)³⁴-pà-da en	Eriduᵏⁱ-ga-ke₄
154	A	K	ka-ba -eme ì-kúr-kúr³⁵ en-na mi-ni-in-ğar-ra³⁶	

26. K has *u*, presumably from [*ku*]*r* in the broken original.
27. Thus A, E, and K; L has *-àm*.
28. Thus E and K; L has *-àm* for *-a*.
29. Thus E; K has *-a* for *-àm*.
30. Thus L; K has *-dug₄* for *-bé*.
31. Thus E; K and L have *-e* for *-ne*.
32. Thus E; K repeats *en* before *du₄-ga*.
33. This reading seems indicated by the traces in K.
34. K, the only source, has *máš*. For the emendation to *sá*(!?) see the comments on the line.
35. Thus A; K omits one *kúr*. The reading of the signs *ì-kúr* in K has been much discussed. Oliver Gurney kindly sent me the following detailed statement: "My original copy for line 154 was correct and so was Sam Kramer's reading, if not *my* reading of it. The note in AFO XXV was prompted by a query from Hirsch, the editor, who saw that the reading had been doubted and asked me to collate it and write a note in his journal. I proposed the new reading *kúr-kúr* because I thought I could see a difference between this straight ⟶ and the *ì* in the next line, which appeared to curve upwards ⟶, and this is the only change in my revised copy in OECT V (apart from more shading in the ⟶). However, I have looked at this again and come to the conclusion that the apparent curve was an illusion due to accidental damage. The *ì* in 155 is as straight as in 154! I see it thus now: ⟶. So I have no doubt that if *ì-kúr* is the expected form it is correct.

"There is another mistake in this copy which was drawn to my attention by Civil in 1983. In the upper wall of the cavity on the right after the *ì-me* in 155, there is clearly the upper part of an *a* (⟶) and even traces of a final AN after it (⟶). The cavity in fact is not a real break but it is the result of something pressing down the soft tablet, so that the surface is actually partly preserved well below its proper level. That's how I missed these traces in my copy. Fortunately they don't alter the sense (*ì-me-àm*!).

"The signs at the end of 154 look exactly as I drew them in both copies. It *cannot* be *gar-ra*."

36. See the end of n. 35 above. The traces shown fit *gùb* and since the scribe of K occasionally used unorthodox writings (see n. 15 above) he may have used *gùb* for the orthodox *gub* of a variant formulation *en-na mi-ni-in-gub* 'as many as he had implanted there'. Or read ⌈*gál-la*⌉? In L, the only other source, the two last signs are *-ğar-ra*. Åke Sjöberg kindly collated the tablet and confirmed that reading. L omits *-in-* before *ğar*, which might indicate a reading of the form as a passive. It is also possible, though, that the variation is orthographical only.

155	A	K	eme-nam-lú-lu$_8$ aš^{37} ì-me-a
156	A	K	mìn-kam-ma-šè^{38} en-e kin-gi$_4$-a^{39} kur-šè-du-úr^{40}
157	A	K	Aratta^{ki}-aš inim mu-na-ab-daḫ-e

In the later section of the text, which tells of the envoy delivering the message, the text of the corresponding lines is:

208	A	F	Q	zag-du$_8$-zag-du$_8$-ba^{41} urin (ŠEŠ) ḫa-ma-mul-e
206	A	F	Q	agrun-agrun-ba sìr-kù nam-šub du$_{12}$-a-ba^{42}
207	A	F	Q	[nam-šub] ^{d}Nu-dím-mud-ke$_4$ e-ne-ra^{43} dug$_4$-m[u-na-ab]
208	A	F	Q	a-na ma-ab^{44}-bé-en^{45}-na-bi ù-mu-[e-dug$_4$]

The two passages quoted may be translated as follows:

133	May doorposts branch for me at doorjamb after doorjamb,
134	and as in all their chambers holy songs and incantations are intoned
135	recite this spell of Nudimmud to him:
136	In those days, there being no snakes, there being no scorpions,
137	there being no hyenas, there being no lions,
138	there being no lionets or wolves,
139	there being no frighteners or terrifiers,
140	mankind had no opponents.
141	In those days the land Subartu and the Ḫamazi region,
142a	regions of opposite persuasions,
142b	Šumer, the great land of princely office,
143	the Uri region a land appropriately endowed,
144	the land Mardu lying in safe pastures,
145	the whole of heaven and earth, the people in (his) care,
146	were verily then holding forth to Enlil with one voice.
147	In those days: into conflicts between lords, conflicts between princes, and conflicts between kings ...

37. My collation of A (Ni 9601) showed no horizontal wedge above AŠ, such as is indicated in the copy. Gurney informs me that Civil had come to the same conclusion from study of a photograph of that text (letter from Civil to Gurney of 19 Dec. 1983). A and K thus agree.

38. L seems to omit *-ma-šè* (so Cohen).

39. L adds *-ar* after *a* (so Cohen).

40. L has *-ra* for *-úr* (so Cohen).

41. Thus F; Q has *-bé*.

42. E probably has *-bi*.

43. Q has *ǧá-ra* for *e-ne-ra*; possibly by wrong restoration of a damaged [*e-n*]*e-ra* in its original.

44. F omits *-ab-*.

45. Q omits *-en-*.

148	did Enki into conflicts between lords, conflicts between princes, and conflicts between kings—
149	into this conflict between lords, this conflict between princes, and conflicts between kings,
150	did Enki, lord of plenty, keeping promises,
151	wise one, (protective) lock before the country,
152	leader of the gods,
153	the wise and resourceful one, the lord of Eridu
154	alienate the tongues in their mouths as many as he had put there
155	the tongues of man that were (as) one.
156	Next the lord added for the envoy going to the mountains
157	a word to Aratta.

The section telling of the envoy's deliverance of the message reads:

205	May doorposts branch for me at doorjamb after doorjamb,
206	and as in all their chambers holy songs and incantations are intoned
207	recite this spell of Nudimmud to him
208	When you have said what you have to say to me about that.

Commentary

Line 133

For *zag-du*$_8$ see *CAD* S 300. For the translation 'doorjamb after doorjamb' compare IV R. 27:6:b.[46] A translation 'at all its/their doorjambs' is also possible. A more full value, *urin*$_x$ for *urì* (ŠEŠ), is indicated by the Akkadian loanword rendering it, *urinnu*. Besides its well-documented meaning 'to radiate rays of light, to shine', the verb *mulu* could apparently also denote 'to radiate branches (from a tree trunk), to branch out'. One may note here the meaning *papallu* 'twig, shoot' of *mulu* in its use as a noun[47] and passages in which, as a verb, it refers to the shade given by the branching crown of a tree, for example: ᵍⁱˢ*mes-úr-gur-ra pa-mul-dagal-la-me-en an-dùl ki-en-gi-ra gissu-du*$_{10}$*-ga me-en*, 'I am a mesu tree of thick base and broad branching crown, I am the umbrella of Šumer of sweet shade';[48] "Enmerkar and the Lord of Aratta," 341–43: *pa-bi Kul-ab*ᵏⁱ*-a an-dùl-eš ì* [var. om.] *-ak pa-mul-mul-la-bi èš É-an-na-ke*$_4$ [var. *-ka*] *kù*

---

46. H. C. Rawlinson and G. Smith, *The Cuneiform Inscriptions of Western Asia*, vol. 4: *A Selection from the Miscellaneous Inscriptions of Assyria* (London, 1875) no. 27:5:6–7.

47. A. Deimel, *Šumerisches Lexikon* (Rome, 1930) 112:16.

48. H. de Genouillac, *Textes religieux sumériens du Louvre*, vol. 1 (Musée du Louvre—Départment des Antiquités Orientales: Textes Cunéiformes 15; Paris, 1930) no. 9:v:50–51.

ᵈInanna-ke₄ ní im-ši-ib-te-en-te, 'Its crown shades Kullab, under its spreading crown at the close Eanna does holy Inanna cool off'; Lugalbanda ii:42–43: ĝiš-bi ĝiš-bi ĝiš [var. om.] ᵍⁱˢtaškarin-na-kam [var. -ka] mušen-e pa-mul-mul-la-bi an-dùl-šè ba-ab-ak, "Its [i.e., Anzu's nests] wood being juniper and woods of the boxwoods, the bird had made their branching boughs into a shelter for her [i.e., its young]'. The verb is also typically used of reed-bundle uprights, urin, and refers apparently to the branching of the reed tops at the end. Note, besides the passage here considered, the great Enlil hymn lines 45–46: kissa ([KI]-URÌ-RÚ)-a urinₓ(ŠEŠ)-mul-la-ba [di]-ir-ga-me-ul-e šu im-ta-du₇-du₇, 'Amid the branching reed uprights of the brick mantle (top edge) the offering table arrangements and ancient sacred offices were carried out to perfection'; Gudea Statue C ii:22–23, E iii:3, F ii:14: ka-al-ka urinₓ(ŠEŠ) [E: ᵍⁱˢŠEŠ] ba-mul, 'Over the brick pit he made reed uprights branch'; Gudea Cylinder A xiii:21–23: ka-al-nam-nun-na mu-ni-ĝar-ra-ni ᵈAnzu(d) šu-riₓ-lugal-la-na-kam urin(ŠEŠ)-šè bí-mul, 'And over the brick pit which he had put in princely domain, he had, as emblem of his master, thunderbirds as uprights spread (their wings)'. The terminology is based on reed architecture and may be more easily visualized if one looks at the sketch by Andrae.[49] Here also belongs probably the epithet mul or mul-mul 'branching out' given to Nidaba who is often pictured on seals with reeds or grain sprouting from her body.[50] Note also: (1) ᵈNida[ba . . .] (2) munus-zi [. . .] (3) munus-sa₆-ga [. . .] (4) munus-mul-mul-la [. . .], 'Nidaba able woman . . . pleasant woman branching out';[51] [munus]-zi-mul an-da šà-kú[š]-ù ᵈNidaba zà-mí, 'Praise be the able branching-out woman, counselor of An, Nidaba'.[52] Lastly one may note the use of mulu with si 'horn' as in si-mul = aia-lum 'stag',[53] where si-mul 'branching horns' may refer to the stag's antlers and their branches. It can also be used, though, of smooth horns branching out from the forehead of a bull as in the great Enlil hymn lines 70–71 where Kiur's brickwork is likened to an aurochs: sig₄-bi kù-ruš-a-uru₄-na₄-za-gìn-na-ka am-gim Ki-en-gi-ra si-mul ba-ni-ib-íl, 'Its brickwork—ruddy gold on a foundation laid on lapis lazuli—is tossing like an aurochs widely splayed horns in Šumer'. The nuance of 'branching out, splaying' may underlie the use of si-mul that is rendered in Akkadian by gêšu 'to split'.

Line 134

My original translation of du₁₂-a-ba as an imperative failed to take into account that an imperative transitive active 'intone!' should have the

---

49. W. Andrae, *Das Gotteshaus und die Urformen des Bauens im alten Orient* (Berlin, 1930) fig. 75.
50. Cf. H. Frankfort, *Cylinder Seals* (London, 1939) 116–17.
51. V. Scheil, "La déese Nisaba," *Orientalistische Literaturzeitung* 7 (1904) 254.
52. J. van Dijk, *Sumerische Götterlieder* (Heidelberg, 1960), 2:145:46 (= E. Chiera, *Sumerian Texts of Varied Contents* [Oriental Institute Publications 16; Chicago, 1934] no. 37).
53. Deimel, *Šumerisches Lexikon*, 112:101.

The Spell of Nudimmud 409

form du_{12}-*ba-ab* and not du_{12}-*a-ba*.[54] This latter form must therefore be analyzed as a *nomen actionis* in -*a* followed by -*ba* < *b(i)-a*, a construction discussed by Poebel as having the force of a verbal conjunction meaning 'after, when' (when pluperfect), and denoting literally 'upon (the occurrence) of this'.[55]

Line 135

ᵈ*Nu-dím-mud-da-ke₄* contains the genitive element followed by an element -*e* which can hardly be other than the demonstrative suffix -*e* 'this' since Nudimmud cannot be a transitive active subject nor a dative object here. The 'this' refers to the particular spell of Nudimmud that Enmerkar is about to recite to the messenger. See also commentary on line 149.

Line 138

The text has *ur-gir*ₓ(ŠÈ) 'domestic dog', which can hardly be right since the context clearly demands the name of a wild animal dangerous to man. It seems therefore likely that at an early point in the tradition a scribe mistook a dictated *ur-ğir*ₓ(ĞAR) = *girru* 'lionet' for the similar sounding *ur-gir*ₓ(ŠÈ) *kalbu* 'domestic dog'. For the value *ğir*ₓ of ĞAR, compare (besides the loanword *girru* for *ur*-ĞAR) *egirru* for *enim*-ĞAR.

Line 141

All the manuscripts begin line 142 with *eme-ḫa-mun*. This leaves Subartu and Ḫamazi without descriptive epithets, which all the other countries have, and very awkwardly makes Šumer and "the great country" appositions to *eme* in *eme-ḫa-mun*. It seems therefore likely that the original text had *eme-ḫa-mun* as an epithet for Subartu and Ḫamazi at the end of line 141, and then line 142 began with *Ki-en-gi* in the expected symmetrical pattern.[56] The translation 'of opposite persuasion' is free. Unlike my 1987 translation 'bilingual',[57] I would now prefer to return to my earlier rendering 'mutually opposed tongues'. Unfortunately most of the occurrences of the phrase are without context, entries from lexical texts, or from broken passages. The clearest example is from the hymn to Utu: *eme-ḫa-mun aš-gim si mu-ni-íb-sá-e:li-šá nu mit-ḫur-ti ki-ma iš-tin šu-me tuš-te-šir*, 'Mutually opposed statements you straighten out as were they one [Akkadian "one line"]'.[58] The same passage, less well preserved, occurs also

---

54. Jacobsen, *The Harps That Once* . . . , 288.
55. A. Poebel, *Historical Texts* (Publications of the Babylonian Section 4/1; Philadelphia, 1914) 38–39.
56. For *eme-ḫa-mun*, see A. Sjöberg and E. Bergmann, *The Collection of the Sumerian Temple Hymns* (Texts from Cuneiform Sources 3; Locust Valley, NY, 1969) 83–84.
57. Jacobsen, *The Harps That Once* . . . , 289.
58. Rawlinson and Smith, *Cuneiform Inscriptions of Western Asia*, 4:19:2:9/10.

in the hymn to Utu as judge in the Third Tablet of *Bit-rimki* lines 79/80.[59] The reference is to the judge's task of sorting out conflicting testimony to arrive at the truth. Since *lišānu* is often used of statements in court one may compare the great Nanše Hymn,[60] which describes Ḫendursaga rendering judgment: *inim-inim-ma-bi si um-mi-in-sá di-bi igi ù-[bi-bar] nam-tag-bi ugu-ama-dumu-ka-ke i-im-ĝá-ĝá-dè*, 'When he has straightened out the testimony about it and looked into that case he is ready to impose the penalty for it on the mother of the child'. *Eme-ḫa-mun si-sá-e* occurs in broken context said about Ningublaga and about Rim-Sîn(?).[61] In the hymn to Ningublaga's temple the god is called *maš-maš eme-ḫa-mun-dungu an-na bí-ĝen*, 'a *mašmašu* priest who makes the mutually opposed tongues of the clouds in heaven agree', that is, makes the clouds, each of which has a different proposal of where to go, all move together.[62] Lastly there is the entry in *Antagal* B. 60: *eme-ḫa-mun silim-sá*$^{si-lim-sa}$ *muš-tar-ri-ḫu*, 'boaster'. Here, since *silim-sá* by itself means 'boaster' the full Sumerian phrase presumably means more specifically 'mutually opposed tongues boaster', that is, a person engaged in logomachia with an opponent. In conclusion, it may be of interest to note that Landsberger orally suggested to me that *ḫa-mun* basically meant 'salted fish' and referred to a fish split in two equal halves and salted to be dried.

Line 142b

Since *kur* is used as an epithet for Šumer it seems clear that it can mean neither 'mountain' nor 'foreign country' here, but stands rather for 'independent country'. The same usage is found in "Enki and the World Order," line 190. The term *me-nam-nun-na* may be translated as 'the office of princeliness', that is, 'the official duties of a prince'. The translation 'prince' for *nun* is traditional and unobjectionable if one takes it as a title of nobility only and disregards its use for a son of a sovereign. As a title of nobility *nun* occurs in *a-nun.ak.ene*, which designates the divine nobility as 'seed of princes'. The term continued in secular use until the Isin-Larsa period. Lipit-Eštar is designated as *nun* in the hymn SK 199.[63] As indicated by its use to characterize Šumer in this line of the text, the realm of a *nun* could be an independent principality. This is supported by lines 147–49,

---

59. H. C. Rawlinson and T. G. Pinches, *The Cuneiform Inscriptions of Western Asia*, vol. 5: *A Selection from the Miscellaneous Inscriptions of Assyria and Babylonia* (London, 1884) nos. 50–51.

60. W. Heimpel, "The Nanshe Hymn," *JCS* 33 (1981) 94:208–10.

61. On Ningublaga, see E. Ebeling, "Sammlungen von Beschwörungsformeln teils in sumerisch-akkadischer, teils in sumerischer oder akkadischer Sprache," *Archiv Orientální* 21 (1953) 373:ii:19–20); on Rim-Sîn, see Gadd and Kramer, *Literary and Religious Texts*, no. 90 obv. 19.

62. Sjöberg and Bergmann, *Collection of the Sumerian Temple Hymns*, 26:153.

63. W. Römer, *Sumerische "Königshymnen" der Isin-Zeit* (Leiden, 1965) 10ff.

which refer to wars between princes (*nun*). It could apparently be held concurrently with that of king (*lugal*) as shown by the Lipit-Eštar hymn,[64] where princeliness is called "the keystone and ornament of kingship [*ḫé-du-gil-sa nam-lugal-la*]"; and by the vase of Lugalzagesi ii:21–25, which locates the office of princeliness (*me-nam-nun*) in Uruk, where it presumably was held by him. Note also that the "lord" (*en*) of Uruk, Enmerkar, sees his scepter, that is, his authority, as having its base in the office of princeliness: *ĝidru-ĝá úr-bi me-nam-nun-na-ka*, 'The base of my scepter is in the office of princeliness' ("Enmerkar and the Lord of Aratta," line 340, cf. 383). In many cases, it is true, the office of princeship appears to be an appointive one, granted by An or Enlil, but the same is true also of kingship which very clearly implies independence; it reflects a shift from popular to divine election of the sovereign.[65] Thus Lipit-Eštar was appointed to the office of king by An[66] and to the office of princeliness by Enki with Enlil and Suen providing the appurtenances, Inanna providing a suitable queen for him: ĝiš*gu-za-maḫ-nam-nun-na ḫé-du₈ gil-sa nam-lugal-la* ᵈ*En-lil-le zi-dè-eš ma-ra-an-sum suḫuš-bi ḫu-mu-ra-ab-*SÈ ᵈ*Sú-en aga saĝ-za mi-ni-in-ga-na múš nam-ba-an-túm-mu* ᵈ*En-ki-ke₄ me-nam-nun-na-ka še-er-ka-an ḫu-mu-ni-in-dug₄* ᵈ*Inanna nin-nam-nun-na-da za-e-da ḫu-mu-ém-dè-gub*, 'The august throne of princely office, the keystone and ornament of kingship, Enlil rightfully gave you, may he ... its foundation for you, may Suen not let the crown he fixed upon your head end functioning, Enki has verily decked you out in princely office and Inanna has made a princely queen stand beside you'.[67] Similarly Enki, the god most consistently given the title of prince, was appointed to that office by An: *aia-zu An lugal en numun-i-i kalam-ki-ĝar-ĝar-ra me-an-ki saĝ-kesda-bi-šè ma-ra-an-sum nun-bi-šè mu-un-íl-e*, 'Your father An, king and enu of the settled countryside who makes the seed sprout up, gave you the offices of heaven and earth to take care of, raised you to prince (in charge) of them'.[68] The offices are specified in the following lines as clearing the rivers, providing rains, and having grain, pasture, and garden plants grow abundantly. Nusku, too, was appointed to the office of prince, in his case by Enlil. A hymn to him says *É-kur èš-maḫ me-nam-nun-na šu-zu-šè im-mi-si*, 'Ekur, the august close and the princely office he [i.e., Enlil] filled into your hand'. Passages dealing with human princes (*nun*) mostly seem to stress responsibility for the building of temples. Gudea's dream telling him to build the temple Eninnu came to him because

---

64. Ibid., 14:43.
65. T. Jacobsen, "Early Political Development in Mesopotamia," *ZA* 52 (1957) 116; repr. in idem, *Toward the Image of Tammuz and Other Essays on Mesopotamian History and Culture* (ed. W. L. Moran; HSS 21; Cambridge, MA, 1970) 145.
66. Römer, *Sumerische "Königshymnen" der Isin-Zeit*, 12:i:25–28, cf. line 42.
67. Ibid., 14:43–47.
68. C. J. Gadd, *Cuneiform Texts from Babylonian Tablets in the British Museum*, vol. 36 (London, 1921) no. 31:6–7.

he was a prince: *siba-me nam-nun-né sag̃ ma-ab-sum-sum*, 'I being the shepherd, the princeliness has given it to me' (Gudea Cylinder A i:26); and later, when he has identified through omina the correct brick-pit, he puts it in princely domain: *g̃á-ù-šub-ba-šè máš ba-ši-ná ka-al-bi-šè igi-zi ba-ši-bar siba-mu-pà-da-Nanše-ke₄ nam-nun-na ì-g̃ar*, 'Toward the brick-mold shed he had an (omen-)kid lie down and the brick was revealed by the omen. Approvingly he looked upon its brick pit, and the shepherd, Nanše's nominee, put it in the princely domain' (Gudea Cylinder A xiii:16–19). Šulgi was similarly concerned: *uru-g̃u₁₀ ᵈUtu-gim ba-ta-è-en šà-ba ki bí-lá é temen-ní-íl-lá ki-ús-sa gug-a nam-nun-né mu-ni-íb-si-nam*, 'Over my city I rose like the sungod, in its midst I sank an area and a house founded on a stepwise rising terrace on carnelian I filled in there by princeliness' (Šulgi C).[69] And Samsuiluna was told: *ki-kù-ki-sikil-la [šu]-mú-mú-da-zu-dè me-nam-nun-na šu gal-bi hé-ni-du*, 'When you pray in a holy place, a pure place, the office of princeliness is verily performed to great perfection'.[70] Interesting also is the statement about *du₆-úr*, the seat on which Enlil makes decisions in Ur. It is *nun-ki-èš-kù-zu nam-tar-re me-nun-me-sikil-la ki-ús-sa*, 'given essential character by a prince with expert knowledge of plots for a close, founded amid princely rites and pure rites'.[71] Since the temple and the divine presence which it implied were of central importance for the welfare of a Sumerian community, the ruler's ability to obtain permission from the gods to build their temples and to guide the work right was an essential part of his office and it is understandable that Enmerkar in the passage quoted earlier ("Enmerkar and the Lord of Aratta," line 340, cf. 383) can see his authority as rooted in that function.[72]

Lines 145–46

Sag̃-sì is rendered as *pa-qa-du* 'entrust, put in the charge (of someone)'.[73] As here used I take it to be a *nomen agentis* in *-a* with passive force which describes the people as Enlil's charges. The verb /e/ is imperfective and renders process. I translate it therefore as 'were holding forth' rather than as 'spoke'. The *dug₄* of the later version is likely to be secondary. The infix *-da-* in *hé-en-na-da-ab-bé* would seem to be used in its temporal

---

69. E. Chiera, *Sumerian Religious Texts* (Upland, PA, 1924) 14:25–27.

70. F. Thureau-Dangin, *Tablettes d'Uruk à l'usage des prêtres du Temple d'Anu au temps des Séleucides* (Musée du Louvre—Départment des Antiquités Orientales: Textes Cunéiformes 6; Paris, 1922) no. 43:46–47.

71. S. N. Kramer, *Sumerian Literary Texts from Nippur* (Annual of the American School of Oriental Research 23; New Haven, 1944) i:79:8.

72. Further passages for *nun*, *nam-nun*, and *me-nam-nun-na* may be found in van Dijk, *Sumerische Götterlieder*, 2:120–21; and Sjöberg and Bergmann, *Collection of the Sumerian Temple Hymns*, 52–53.

73. Deimel, *Šumerisches Lexikon*, 115:131d.

meaning to indicate contemporarity 'with that, at that (time)' as in *nu-da-a-di-ni* 'not until then, not yet'.[74] The overall sense appears to be that the people were driving Enlil to exasperation by their concerted demands. It may be noted that *sağ-sè* also can denote *ṭupālu* 'disrespect, reproach';[75] the possibility of a reading 'the people were then griping to Enlil with one voice', that is, were dissatisfied with his management, cannot be excluded.

Lines 147–49

Proto-izi II 451–52 (*MSL* 13:53) lists *a-da-en* (451) and *a-da-en-lugal* (452) with *a-da-mìn* (449–50) 'contest' and after *šà-íb-ba* 'angry heart', *libiš-tuku* 'to rage', and *libiš-bal* 'wrath' (445–48), a context that strongly advocates a meaning 'conflict' for *a-da* with the contestants defined by the following *mìn* 'two', *en* 'lords', *nun* 'princes', *lugal* 'kings'. The precise syntactic structure is not clear. In line 149 the *-ne* or *-e* following *en* and *nun* is the demonstrative pronominal suffix 'this'[76] and refers apparently to the contest between Enmerkar and the lord of Aratta which the story is about. The *-a* after *lugal* at the end of the lines is the mark of inessive 'into'. (I owe the reference and translation to Aaron Schaffer.)

Line 151

The accepted reading, suggested by Hallo is *ig*[*i-ğá*]*l* 'the intelligent one'.[77] It seems to me that the remnants of signs showed in Gurney's copy are more consonant with *s*[*ağ-ku*]*l*, especially those before the break.[78] They do not fit *ig*[*i*]. The metaphor 'lock' stands for 'protector'. Enki protects Sumer from the invasion as a bolt on a door protects the inhabitants of the house from attack from outside.

Line 153

The phrase *máš pà-da* is common to describe the selection of a human high priestess (*en*) by omens. As an epithet for Enki, a major god, it is inconceivable. I assume, therefore, that the original text has *sá pà-da* 'resourceful', literally 'finding (good) advice', a title for Enki known from elsewhere.[79] In a slightly damaged original a copyist could easily have "restored" the traces of *sá* as part of a partly obliterated *máš* influenced by the common phrase *máš*(*-e*) *pà-da*.

---

74. Cf. also A. Poebel, Review of *Historical Fragments* by L. Legrain, *Orientalistische Literaturzeitung* 27 (1924) 262 n. 1.

75. Deimel, *Šumerisches Lexikon*, 115:131a.

76. See A. Poebel, *Grundzüge der sumerischen Grammatik* (Rostock, 1923) 223–28.

77. W. W. Hallo, as quoted in Kramer, "Babel of Tongues," 111 n. 12.

78. O. E. Gurney, in Kramer, "Babel of Tongues," 110.

79. See A. Falkenstein, "Sumerische religiöse Texte, 1: Drei 'Hymnen' auf Urninurta von Isin," *ZA* 49 (1949) 139, who transliterates *di* 'judgment' rather than *sá* 'counsel'.

Line 154

In the verbal form the infix -*ni*- resumes the inessive -*a* of *ka-ba* 'in their mouths', and -*n*- represents the ergative third-person singular and resumes the -*e* that ends the epithets for Enki in lines 151, 152, and 153. The final -*a* is the mark of clause: 'as he had put therein'. The reference is to Enki as *Nu-dím-mud*, creator of man. *Enna* 'as far as, until, as many as', may be construed as a noun.[80] In the meaning 'as many as' it occurs in *túg-mu mu-da-an-sìg en$_x$-na an-mu$_4$-mu$_4$-:ṣú-ba-tim iš-šaḫ-ṭa-an-ni-ma a-di al-tab-šú*, 'My clothes were torn off me as many as I had put on'.[81]

A different interpretation of line 154 was proposed by Kramer.[82] He considered *en-na* here to be identical with the *en-na* that corresponds to Akkadian *šapsu* 'defiant, disobedient', and rendered it 'contention': "Changed the speech in their mouths, [set up] contention into it." This translation, with minor modifications was followed by Cohen who rendered the line as "changed the speech in their mouth, having there placed contention." The difficulty with this, however, is that *en-na* in all its occurrences denotes persons, 'defiant ones', and never the abstract concept 'contention'. Also, the relative -*a* at the end of the line does not fit. Kramer ignored it, Cohen apparently tries to account for it by using an English participial construction, quite different from what the Sumerian has.

Interpretation

In attempting to interpret the spell and understand its meaning it seems logical to begin with its protagonist from whom it is named, Nudimmud.

Kramer, in his original treatment of the spell, suggested that "it is not unreasonable to deduce that Enki was displeased with this universal sway of Enlil and that he took action to disrupt it, action which led perhaps to the dispersion of mankind and the diffusion of languages."[83] This interpretation rested essentially on line 146, which Kramer restored and translated as "to Enlil in one tongue gave praise." In his later treatment, after the fragment from Sultan Tepe had become available, he maintained his interpretation in all essentials: "Our new piece, therefore, puts it beyond all doubt that the Sumerians believed that there was a time when all mankind spoke one and the same language, and that it was Enki, the Sumerian god of wisdom, who confounded their speech. The reason for this fateful deed

---

80. A. Poebel, "Eine sumerische Inschrift Samsuilunas über die Erbauung der Festung Dur-Samsuiluna," *AfO* 9 (1933/34) 263 with n. 35.

81. F. Thureau-Dangin, "Une Lamentation sur la Dévastation du Temple d'Ištar," *RA* 33 (1936) 104 rev. 31.

82. Kramer, "Babel of Tongues," 111 with nn. 12, 16.

83. Kramer, "Man's Golden Age," 194.

is not stated in the text; it may well have been inspired by Enki's jealousy of Enlil and the universal sway over mankind that he enjoyed."[84]

A serious difficulty with following Kramer in this interpretation is the absence of any convincing evidence that Enki was ever jealous of Enlil.[85] The only times he acted to oppose Enlil, as in the story of the Flood and the similar Akkadian story of Atraḫasīs, it was to save mankind, his own creation.

Looking afresh, then, at Enki and his action in the spell, one can hardly fail to see that the poet presents him very much in his traditional role of friend to mankind. In the title of the spell he figures as Nudimmud, that is as "the creator of man," a title that implies fatherly concern, and as performer of the crucial action in the story the poet presents him as "lord of plenty, keeping promises, wise one, (protective) lock before the country, leader of the gods, the wise and resourceful one."

If that is so, however, if Enki is to be seen in his familiar role of friend and savior of man, then primeval human conditions as they are described

---

84. Kramer, "Babel of Tongues," 111.

85. Kramer in support of assuming such jealousy refers to a highly speculative passage in his contribution to the proceedings of the 9th Rencontre Assyriologique Internationale ("Sumero-Akkadian Interconnections: Religious Ideas," in *Aspects du Contact Suméro-Akkadien* [Geneva, 1960] 276) (= *Genava* 8 [1960]), in which he suggests that the Semitic god Ea was adopted by the Sumerians and given the Sumerian name Enki: "As pointed out in an earlier study it seems rather strange that the epithet *en-ki* 'Lord of the Earth' should be given to a deity who is primarily the god in charge of waters rather than of the earth. The title 'Lord of the Earth' seems to point to an effort on the part of the Sumerian theologians to make him a rival of Enlil who 'had carried off the earth' after heaven had been separated from it, and would therefore presumably be the real 'Lord of the Earth'. However, the title *en*, traditionally translated 'lord', never denotes 'owner' in Sumerian but rather 'productive manager'; as Enki's name refers to the role of water in fertilizing the earth and making it produce, it implies no challenge to anybody. Nor do I think the Sumerians lacked a god for something as vital for them as water and had to borrow one. In "Babel of Tongues" (111 n. 13), Kramer also refers to de Genouillac, *Textes religieux sumériens du Louvre*, no. 9:7, where ^{d}*En-ki* ^{d}*En-ki* seem to parallel *dingir-gal-gal-e-ne* 'the great gods' and ^{d}*A-nun-na-ke$_4$-ne* 'the divine aristocracy', literally 'the sons of princes', in some not fully clear way. Kramer assumes that ^{d}*En-ki* ^{d}*En-ki*, literally 'the Enkis', refers to the god of waters and wisdom whose full name was *Enki(k)*, but there never were more than one of him. The plural form thus shows that reference is to the gods called *En-ki*, who figured as ancestors of Enlil. They are mentioned as ^{d}*En-ki-ne* in H. F. Lutz, *Selected Sumerian and Babylonian Texts* (Publications of the Babylonian Section 1/2; Philadelphia, 1919) no. 107 rev. 7: *En-ki-ne* ^{d}*Nin-ki-ne* 'the Enkis and Ninkis'. There is thus no reason to assume a body of Enki gods identical with the Igigi who defeated the Anunnaki, the An gods; nor is it at all clear how such a victory could have shown that Enki was jealous of Enlil. For the term Igigi see my essay "*Inuma Ilu awīlum*," in *Essays on the Ancient Near East in Memory of Jacob Joel Finkelstein* (ed. M. de J. Ellis; New Haven, 1977) 117, where I give reasons for translating it 'the Seven'. I would now see this as referring, at least originally, to 'the seven lawmaking gods'; on these see Jacobsen, "Early Political Development in Mesopotamia," 101 n. 13 (repr. p. 372 n. 13); idem, "Primitive Democracy in Ancient Mesopotamia," *JNES* 2 (1943) 168 n. 50 (repr. in *Toward the Image of Tammuz*, 404 n. 50).

in the text, man having no opponent, cannot have seemed as ideal to him—and to the poet—as they appear at first glance; rather there must have been in them a clear and present danger.

As to what that danger would have been, one may turn for a parallel to the similar situation in the story of the Flood where the noise of a proliferating mankind keeps Enlil sleepless and makes him bring on the Flood to obtain quiet.[86] In Nudimmud's spell, too, we may have a situation that could exasperate Enlil and lead to catastrophe. One will notice here that Enki's preventive measure is conflict between rulers, and that the conflict of Enmerkar and the Lord of Aratta is included as "this conflict of lords." That present conflict had as its purpose the acquisition of rare building materials and corvé labor for Uruk, things which before Enki's action could only have been obtained by an appeal to the gods since neither war nor trade existed. It may therefore be proposed that the fact that man had no enemies, and so would multiply beyond bounds, would be likely to lead to an overwhelming clamor of identical demands on Enlil, certain to exasperate him and thus threatening that he might decide to wipe out mankind. Enki's action forestalled this by providing a way for the human rulers to obtain what they needed by conquest, and the wars they waged to that end would in addition serve to keep mankind's numbers down.

The interpretation here proposed, besides preserving the traditional, well-established image of Enki as friend and savior of man, has the added advantage of providing an acceptable answer to the otherwise troubling questions of what was the purpose of reciting this tale to the lord of Aratta at all. Why is the tale called a spell, *nam-šub*, a term that implies that it would have magic powers to some specific purpose? And why is the envoy to recite it only after the enforced building activity has come to an end?

Seen as a spell, the tale hallows Enmerkar's aggression by making it the carrying out of a necessary task imposed by Enki. By reciting it at the end of the work the divine justification it invokes would presumably counteract any evils that resentment by the builders might have caused to the structures and any continuing resentment on the part of the lord of Aratta. Enmerkar's action had divine sanction. It was Enki's will.

---

86. As more remote parallels one might mention the biblical story of the tower of Babel in which the power of a united mankind is felt as a threat by God, a threat countered by the confusion of languages and the dispersal of mankind throughout the earth. Also worthy of comparison, perhaps, are the Greek myths about Prometheus who created mankind and repeatedly gained advantages for them against Zeus's wishes. He was less successful, however, than Ea in avoiding ultimate vengeance on himself and on man. None of these, however, has the theme of preventive action by a wise, but less powerful, deity in substituting a lesser evil for a threatening catastrophic one.

INDEX OF REFERENCES

Hebrew Bible

Genesis
1   51, 186–94
1–2   48, 50
1–3   299
1:1   47, 186 n. 13,
    187, 187 n. 14,
    188
1:1–2   184 n. 6,
    189 n. 19
1:1–3   193 n. 29
1:1–5   190 n. 24
1:1–2:4   185
1:2   187, 189
1:3   187, 188
1:5   190
1:6   190
1:14   190
1:20   189 n. 20
1:27   47
1:28   47
1:29   189 n. 20
2:1   51
2:3   187
2:5   51
2:17   188
2:21–22   47
2:23   47–51
2:24   47
3:24   297 n. 7, 300
8:2   153
10:14   58
10:25–30   58
11:1   403 n. 2
11:14ff.   59

Genesis (cont'd.)
11:30   85 n. 22,
    85 n. 24
11:31   58
12:1–3   58
14:5   382
14:15   21 n. 11
15:16   58
16:2   85 n. 22
16:3   89 n. 41
16:14   4
17:1   94
17:7–8   94
17:12–13   87 n. 36
17:22   155
17:23   87 n. 36
17:27   87 n. 36
18   22
19   17, 21 n. 10,
    28 n. 27, 29
19:1   23
19:2   23
19:4   23, 30,
    31 n. 34
19:5   23, 27
19:8   44 n. 20
19:11   28
19:15   22 n. 13, 23
19:15–22   23
19:16   41 n. 17
19:23   22 n. 13, 23,
    23 n. 16
19:23–24   31 n. 36
19:27   23, 23 n. 15

Genesis (cont'd.)
19:30–38   xvii,
    27 n. 24
19:33   23, 23 n. 15, 27
19:35   27
20:18   85 n. 22
24   4
24:12–27   4
24:42–48   4
24:65   xxiii
25:3   260
25:11   4
25:21   85 n. 22,
    85 n. 24
26:15–25   4
26:16   4
26:19   4
26:23   4
27:36   158
28:1   197
28:3   197
28:7   197
28:10–22   197, 198
28:11–22   198
28:20–22   198
29:23   27 n. 24
29:31   85 n. 24
29:33   85 n. 22
30:3–4   89 n. 41
30:9   89 n. 41
30:15–16   27 n. 24
31:3   198 n. 13
31:13   198 n. 13
34   61

Genesis (cont'd.)
34:25   61
35:1   195
35:1–7   195–98
35:2   196
35:4   196
35:5   196
35:7   196
35:9   196
37:36   162
38   84 n. 21
38:7–10   85 n. 23
38:14   xxiii
38:19   xxiii
39:11–12   27 n. 24
46:27   251 n. 25
49:4   156
49:6   151 n. 16
49:15   152
49:17   313
49:26   150–51, 200

Exodus
2:15–21   4
3:6   56
6   73
6:3   296 n. 4
6:16–22   72
14:28–29   7
15:1   7
15:1–18   7
15:13–14   58
15:19   7
18:4   296 n. 4
18:13   21 n. 12
20:8–11   184 n. 5
20:17   279
21:2   87
21:2–6   87, 88–89
21:2–11   86 n. 31
21:3   86, 159
21:3–4   86
21:4   86, 87, 87 n. 33
21:7   176
21:7–11   89
21:22   159
21:22–25   181
21:26–27   88 n. 40

Exodus (cont'd.)
22:1   22 n. 13
22:2   22 n. 13
23:12   184 n. 5
25:13–14   70
28   139
29:1ff.   204
29:37   139
31:12–17   184 n. 5
32   88 n. 40, 279
34:9   128
35–40   280 n. 44
37:4–5   70
38:8   396 n. 98

Leviticus
1:2   352
1:5   358
4:1–21   142, 143
4:3   140
4:22–35   142
4:22ff.   143
5:1–13   140 n. 8
5:2–3   140
5:5   360
5:11   361
5:14–26   140
6:11   139
6:20   139
7:11ff.   204
7:19   140
7:20   139
8   139
8:1ff.   204
10:1   140
10:6   140
10:14   140
11–15   140
11:8   140
11:16   160
12   353
12:4   143
13:48–49   153
13:51–53   153
13:56–59   153
14   353
14:22   353
14:46–47   138, 145

Leviticus (cont'd.)
15:16–18   27 n. 24
15:31   143
16   139, 143
16:10   143
16:14–15   142
16:16   143, 144
16:20–22   143
16:21   107
18:6   28 n. 26
18:6–18   28 n. 26
18:6–19   155
20:1–4   143
20:10–21   28 n. 26
20:11–21   155
20:21   163
21:1–4   141
21:11   141
21:12   142
22:11   87 n. 36
23:17ff.   204
24:17–22   181
25   89
25:3–4   150
25:39–43   88
25:39–46   88
25:39–54   86 n. 31, 88–89
25:40   89
25:41   89
25:42   118
25:44–46   88
25:45   118
25:45–46   89
25:47–54   88
25:53   89
26   95
26:12   94
27   140
27:10   353

Numbers
1   84 n. 20
1:51   139
3   84 n. 20
3:10   139
3:38   139
4:5–20   139

Index of References

Numbers (cont'd.)
4:19   139
4:20   139
5:15   361
6:1–21   200
6:3–4   200
6:5   200
6:6–8   200
11:18   112 n. 1
15:30   143
17:5   139
17:28   139
18:3   139
18:5   140
18:7   139
18:21–32   76
19:9   141
19:13   143
19:14–16   138
19:15   138
19:20   143
20:5–11   7
21:4   6
21:6   7
21:10   6
21:11   6
21:14   6
21:15   6
21:16   6
21:17–18   6
21:18   xxi, 7, 13
21:19   6
22–24   56
23:9   156
24:6   xxiii
24:17   xxi, 10 n. 11, 156
26   84 n. 20
26–27   84
26:33   84
26:53   84
27   84, 86 n. 30
27:4   84
31:48–54   106
36   84, 86 n. 30

Deuteronomy
2:2–23   58

Deuteronomy (cont'd.)
4:1   112 n. 3
4:16–19   190 n. 24
4:26   112 n. 3
4:40   111, 112 n. 3
5:14–15   184 n. 5
5:16   112, 112 n. 3
5:29   112
5:30   112
5:53   112 n. 3
6:2   112 n. 3
6:3   112
6:10–13   5
6:18   112
6:21–23   111
6:21–25   111
6:24   111–19
6:25   111
7:3–4   90 n. 45
7:14   85 n. 22
8:1   112 n. 3
10:8   70, 72
10:13   112, 118
11:9   112 n. 3
11:10–17   117
12:25   112
12:28   112
15:12–18   86, 86 n. 31
15:16   112 n. 1
16:20   112 n. 3
17:20   112 n. 3
19:13   112
19:18–19   181
19:21   181
20:16   113
22:7   112, 112 n. 3
22:22   159
23   28 n. 29
23:1–3   28 n. 29
23:4   90
23:4–7   28 n. 29
23:8–9   90
23:11–12   27 n. 24
23:15   112 n. 1, 143
24:4   159
25:5   85 n. 23
25:5–10   84 n. 21
25:6   84

Deuteronomy (cont'd.)
25:15   112 n. 3
26   56
26:14   296 n. 4
26:16–19   95
28   95
28:11   112
30:1–6   101
30:6   112 n. 3, 112
30:9   118
30:15   112 n. 3
30:16   112 n. 3
30:18   112 n. 3
30:19   112 n. 3
30:19–20   98
30:20   112 n. 3
31:16   197
32:33   xxi
32:39   113
32:47   112 n. 3
33:15   150
33:16   200
34:9   14

Joshua
2   17
2:1   25, 26, 27, 29 n. 32
2:2   25, 26
2:5   25, 26
2:7   25
2:8   25, 26, 27
6:3   28 n. 27
6:11   26 n. 22
7:6   21 n. 12
7:9   31 n. 34
8:3   21 n. 11
9   58
9:26   61
10:3   259
11:7   260
12   58
12:12   260
12:17–18   56
12:24   56
15:23   259
17:3–6   84
18:1   123 n. 7

Joshua (cont'd.)
24 56, 57
24:3 57
24:14 197
24:14-23 198
24:20 197

Judges
1:27-36 58
5 38 n. 11, 58
5:30 159
6:16 154
6:27 22 n. 13
7:9 21 n. 11
8:23 33, 34
8:25-30 33
8:33 35 n. 8, 37
8:33-35 35
8:34 34 n. 3
8:35 35
9 33-40
9:1 35, 35 n. 6, 38, 38 n. 12
9:1-6 35
9:2 34, 34 n. 3, 34 n. 4, 35, 35 n. 6, 35 n. 7, 40
9:3 35 n. 7, 38, 38 n. 12
9:4 35 n. 8
9:5 35 n. 6, 38, 38 n. 12
9:6 35 n. 7, 36 n. 9, 37
9:7 35 n. 7
9:7-24 35
9:15 36, 37
9:16 35, 35 n. 6, 37
9:17 38 n. 12
9:17-18 37
9:18 34, 38 n. 10, 38 n. 12
9:19 35, 35 n. 6, 37
9:20 36, 38
9:21 38 n. 12
9:22 36 n. 9
9:22-24 36 n. 9

Judges (cont'd.)
9:23 34 n. 2, 35 n. 7, 36, 37
9:23-24 36, 37
9:24 35 n. 6, 35 n. 7, 36, 38 n. 12
9:25 35 n. 7, 36 n. 9, 37, 39
9:25-41 36
9:26 35 n. 7, 36 n. 9
9:27 35 n. 8
9:28 37, 38 n. 12
9:31 38 n. 12
9:32 21 n. 11
9:34 21 n. 11, 39
9:36 39 n. 13
9:39 35 n. 7
9:39-49 37
9:41 36 n. 9, 38 n. 12
9:42 36 n. 9
9:42-57 36
9:43 39
9:44 39
9:46 35 n. 7, 35 n. 8
9:47 35 n. 7
9:47-49 38
9:48 40
9:49 38, 38 n. 12
9:49-51 38
9:51 35 n. 7, 38, 38 n. 12, 39
9:53 38 n. 12, 39
9:54 37, 38 n. 12, 40
9:56 38 n. 12
9:56-57 36
9:57 35 n. 6, 35 n. 7, 36
10:6ff. 198
10:14-16 198
10:16 197
11:1-3 39
11:37-40 39
12 25 n. 18
12:4 56
12:6 154
13:2 85 n. 22, 85 n. 24
13:4 200

Judges (cont'd.)
13:4-7 200
16:1-3 27, 30 n. 33
16:2-3 22 n. 13, 27 n. 24
16:13-14 153
17-21 43
17:6 43
18:1 43
19 21, 21 n. 10, 40-45
19-21 17, 24, 38 n. 11
19:1 43, 44
19:1-2 41
19:1-30 42
19:3 42, 44 n. 21
19:3-4 41
19:3-9 44
19:4 44 n. 21
19:5 41
19:5-7 41
19:8 23, 24, 41 n. 17
19:8-10 41
19:8-14 23 n. 16
19:9 23, 24
19:10 42, 44
19:11 23, 24, 41, 42
19:11-12 41
19:11-13 44
19:11-14 41, 44
19:12 42, 44
19:14 24, 42, 44
19:15 24, 24 n. 17
19:15-16 42
19:15-21 41, 44
19:16 24
19:21 44
19:22 27, 30, 31 n. 34, 41 n. 16, 42, 44
19:22-26 41
19:23 44
19:23-24 44
19:24 44 n. 20
19:25 24, 27, 42
19:25-26 23 n. 16, 45 n. 22

Index of References

Judges (cont'd.)
19:25–27   42
19:26   24, 42, 44 n. 21
19:27   24, 42
19:27–28   41
19:29–30   41
19:30   42, 43, 43 n. 18
20–21   42, 43
20:5   30
20:19   23 n. 15, 24
20:23   21 n. 12, 24, 25
20:26   21 n. 12, 24, 25
20:43   31 n. 34
21   48
21:2   22 n. 12, 24, 25
21:14   48
21:19ff.   48
21:23   48
21:25   43

1 Samuel
1   200, 204, 281
1–2   281, 282, 285, 291
1:2   85 n. 24
1:5   85 n. 22
1:9   123 n. 7
1:11   85 n. 24, 199, 199 n. 4, 200, 201
1:15–16   201
1:22   199, 200, 202, 203, 204
1:22–28   199
1:23   203, 204
1:24–25   203, 204
2:5   161
3:4   282 n. 51
3:5   282 n. 51
3:6   282 n. 51
3:8   282 n. 51
3:20   199
7:3   197
9:7   156, 156 n. 38
10:3   204
11:5–10   21 n. 11
11:21   40
14:36   21 n. 11

1 Samuel (cont'd.)
15:27   131 n. 22
16:16   112 n. 1
16:23   112 n. 1
17–18   282, 286, 290
19:11–12   21 n. 11
22:22   30 n. 33
26:7   21 n. 11
28:23   154
30:17   22 n. 12
31:12   21 n. 11

2 Samuel
1:12   22 n. 12
2:29   21 n. 11
3:38   162
4:2–3   61
4:7   21 n. 11
6   69, 70
7   96
7:26   96
11:2–4   27 n. 24
12:3   115
12:12   31 n. 36
17:14   37
17:16   21 n. 11
21   58
21:1–2   61
21:20   384 n. 27
23   258
23:1   150
23:25–26   258
23:27   258

1 Kings
1:17   282 n. 51
4:5   83 n. 17
4:10   259
6:32   xxiii
7:26   318
7:38   318
8   127 n. 17
8:44   125
8:48   125
8:64   318
11:1–13   90 n. 45
17–18   116
17:2–16   116

1 Kings (cont'd.)
18:5   116
22:24   176

2 Kings
3:25   30 n. 33
6   28 n. 27
6:14   21 n. 11
6:15   30 n. 33
6:18   28 n. 27
8:21   21 n. 11, 30 n. 33
9:33   313
13:20–21   xvii
17   98
17:13   98
19:35   21 n. 11
25:2   162
25:4   21 n. 11
25:25   81 n. 12

Isaiah
1:2   97
1:21   130
1:25   163
2:2–3   130
2:2–4   290
2:2–5   100
3:23   xxiii
5:6   150
7:11   151
7:21   115, 119 n. 19
9:3   151–52
10:5   152
10:24   152
10:27   152
11:1   250 n. 25
11:2   10
11:11   300
12:3   5
12:13–14   99
14:5   152
14:9   382 n. 15
14:25   152
17:5   154
19:8–9   152
19:10   152–53
21:14   260

Isaiah (cont'd.)
22:19   313
24:16   150
25:5   150
25:12   313
26:14   382 n. 13
26:19   382 n. 13
27:6   300
27:12   154
28:27   154
35:7   300
40:10   296 n. 4
40:12   318
40:24   300
41:3   300
41:18–19   300
44:3   300
45:6–7   190 n. 24
47:1   154
49:7   xix
49:10   300
49:15   159, 159 n. 53
49:23   xix
52:2   154–55
52:13–53:12   99
56:9   161, 300
57:8   155, 156
57:9   156
57:18   157
58:11   300
58:13–14   185 n. 10
60:4   157
60:5   157–58
60:13   300
60:14   xix
60:21   300
63:13   157
63:14   157
64:4   250 n. 25
66:1–5   75

Jeremiah
2:12   261
2:13   6, 11, 16
2:13   315, 318, 319
2:14   87 n. 36
2:18   257
2:22   163

Jeremiah (cont'd.)
5:6   161
5:19   197
6:11   315, 316, 318
6:19   97
7   95
7:21–23   95
7:21–29   95 n. 9
7:23   95
7:25–26   95
9:3   158
12:5   xviii
13:14   160
14:1–8   6
15:11   118
16:5   382 n. 12
17:8   300
17:13   6
18:16   162
20:9   316
22:15   112 n. 1
23:19   155
25:11–12   124 n. 10
25:23   260
26:6   129
29:3   260
29:10   124 n. 10
29:11–12   113 n. 8
31   169
31:31–34   95
31:31ff.   98
32:9   260
32:19   112 n. 2
32:39   118
33:9   158
35   200
35:6   200
36:3   260
36:12   82 n. 12
36:20–21   82 n. 12
39:4   21 n. 11
41:1ff.   81 n. 12
48:27   162
48:46   154
49:7   113
49:7–22   290
49:10   113 n. 8

Jeremiah (cont'd.)
49:11   113, 113 n. 8, 119
49:12   113

Ezekiel
1–11   144
5:11   144
8:6   144
11:14–21   95
11:16   144
16:49   28 n. 25
16:58   28 n. 25
17:23   300
22:10   155, 163
23:18   155
23:38   144
23:39   144
24:21   144
25:15   155
27:16   259
31:6   300
31:14   153, 300
31:16   153
36–37   144
36:22–25   96
36:26–27   96, 98
36:28   96
37:23   144
37:26   144
37:27   144
37:28   144
38–39   144
39:3   313
39:12–16   144
39:24   144
40–48   144
44   76, 200
44:7   144
44:10–31   75
44:20   200
44:26–27   141
46:20   139
48:8   144
48:10   144
48:21   144

Hosea
1:2   47, 48, 187 n. 14

Hosea (cont'd.)
2:7   150
2:9   112 n. 1
2:17   159 n. 51
2:18–19   158–59
3:1   47, 48
3:5   158
8:10   xxiii
11:1   250 n. 25,
          251 n. 27
12:2   156, 156 n. 40
12:4   158
13:15   4

Joel
1:5   153
4:17   125, 130
4:18   5

Amos
1:2   125
1:3–2:2   159,
            159 n. 52
1:11   159–60
2:8   xxiii
2:11–12   204
6:7   382 n. 12
7:10   318
9:2   151
9:7   58

Obadiah
1–10   290

Jonah
1   49 n. 4
1–2   49
1:1–2   49
1:9   256
3–4   49
3:1–2   49
4:11   49

Micah
4:1–4   290
4:1–5   100
4:14   176

Micah (cont'd.)
5:7   161
7:4   271 n. 14

Nahum
1:8   151 n. 16
2:13   154
3:6–7   160

Habakkuk
1:4   31 n. 34
1:8   161, 161 n. 59

Zephaniah
3:1   160, 160 n. 55
3:3   161, 161 n. 59

Haggai
1:1   109
1:7ff.   50
1:12   109
2:2   109
2:10ff.   135 n. 32
2:11   135 n. 32
2:18   127 n. 17
2:18–19   128 n. 19,
             132 n. 25
2:20–23   50, 129 n. 21

Zechariah
1–8   121–35
1:7   133
1:8–13   123–25
1:10   124
1:11   124
1:12   123
1:14–15   130
1:14–17   123–25, 130
1:16   124
1:17   124, 129
2:1–4   125–28, 133
2:1–9   123
2:2   125
2:3   125
2:4   125
2:5   126
2:5–9   125–28, 133
2:7   126

Zechariah (cont'd.)
2:8   127, 129, 130
2:8–9   126
2:9   126
2:10   127
2:10–11   126
2:10–17   123, 125–28
2:11   127
2:12–13   127
2:14   130
2:14–17   127
2:15   128
2:16   123, 125 n. 12,
         127, 128, 129
2:17   127
3   128, 134, 135
3:1   109
3:1–7   128
3:1–10   123, 128–29
3:2   125 n. 12, 128
3:4   135
3:7   135
3:8   109, 129
3:8–10   128
3:9   134, 135
4   128, 135
4:6–10   129 n. 21, 134
4:7   127 n. 17, 130,
        134, 134
4:10   134
4:14   128 n. 18
5:1–4   133, 135
5:5–7   133
6:1–8   133
6:5   128 n. 18
6:9–15   129 n. 21
7   129
7–8   126
7:1–7   129–31
7:1–17   123
7:3   124 n. 10
7:5   124 n. 10
7:7   129, 130
7:9–10   130
7:16–17   130
8   130
8:1–17   130
8:1–23   123, 129–31

Zechariah (cont'd.)
8:2   130
8:3   123, 124, 130, 130, 134, 135
8:4-5   131
8:7   135
8:9-13 128 n. 19
8:12   129
8:18-23 131
8:19-23 131
8:22   123, 131
8:22-23 129
8:23   131
9:7   180
9:13   163 n. 67
12:10   250 n. 25
13:2   310
13:7   251 n. 25
14:8   5

Malachi
3:2   163
3:22-24 100
3:23   304

Psalms
1   99
1:3-4   300
3   175
3:2   175
3:3   175
3:4   175
3:5-7   175
3:6-7   175
3:8   175-81
7:16   163
9   312 n. 15
9:1   252 n. 29
11:3   153
22   31 n. 34
22:13   31 n. 34
23   xvi
33:16-17 116
33:18-19 116
33:19   115, 119
35:2   296 n. 4
35:10   16
36:8-10 5

Psalms (cont'd.)
36:10   16
36:11   5
37   xxii
40:6   48 n. 1
41:2-3 116
41:3   119
44:15   162
49   99
50:10   161
54:6   296 n. 4
58:7   176, 180
62:11   343
69:3   154
69:13   153
69:16   154
73   99
78:38   160
78:59-61 129
78:67-78 129
80:10   300
81:7   152
88:11   382 n. 13
88:15   313
89:45   313
95:2   150
101:5   313
101:8   313
102:7   161
103:20 300
104   xv
104:11 161
104:20 161
105:22 xxiii
106:47-48 xxii
109:3   30 n. 33
114:8   14
119   99
119:54 150
119:122 118
119:139 313
124:6   180
125:1-2 125
132:3   156
142:2   314 n. 22
143:12 313
146:5   296 n. 4

Job
1:10   300
3:3   27 n. 24
3:6   27 n. 24, 151 n. 16
5:3   300
9:25   151 n. 16
9:30-31 163
9:31   163 n. 66
11:8   151
14:8   300
16:10   176
24:15   156
24:24   154
26:5   382 n. 13
28:9   15
28:11   15
29:17   180
30:25   153
33:21   160 n. 55
35:10   150

Proverbs
1:3   48 n. 1
1:6   51
2:18   382 n. 13
4:14-15 313
9:18   151, 382 n. 13
10:11   5
13:14   5
18:4   5, 250 n. 25
21:16   382 n. 13
25:3   151
30   50
30:1   50
30:1-4 50
30:4   50
30:16   85 n. 22
31:1   50

Ruth
1:4   85 n. 23
2:2   154
2:17   154
3   27 n. 24
3:1   112 n. 1
3:1-14 27 n. 24
4   84 n. 21

Canticles
2:12   50, 51, 150
3:4   150
4:8   156
4:15   4
5:7   xxiii

Qoheleth
7:11   114
7:11–12   114, 115
7:12   114, 119
7:13   114
7:15   114
7:17   114

Lamentations
1:1   161–62, 162 n. 61
1:1–22   162 n. 61, 163 n. 63
1:7–8   162–63
3:30   176

Esther
1:1–8:5   208
1:8   162
2:5   219
2:9   118
3:13   49
8:10–13   49
8:15   210, 212
8:15–10:3   210
9   208
9:1   213, 216
9:2   210, 216
9:6–12   49
9:11   213
9:12   49, 212
9:13   215
9:14   213
9:14–19   213
9:14–32   212
9:16   49
9:17   213, 216
9:20–32   217
9:22   210, 213
9:23   213
9:24–25   213
9:26   213

Esther (cont'd.)
9:26–27   213
9:26–32   213
9:27   213
9:30–31   212, 217
9:31   212
9:32   212
10:2   212, 215
10:3   211

Esther-Alpha Text
i:1   210, 212 n. 10
i:5   216
i:6   216
i:6–8   210
i:11–18   209 n. 7
ii:1–viii:17   208
iii:5   219, 219 n. 17
iii:7   219 n. 17
iv:2   210
iv:7   217
iv:9–11   210
iv:22   211
v:4–5   210
v:9   210
v:15   211
v:22   219
v:27   219
vi:1   212
vi:12–18   208
vi:13–18   210
vi:21   210
vii:1   210
viii:16   219
viii:18–21   208
viii:19   215
viii:20   219
viii:20–21   215, 217
viii:27   216
viii:30   214, 217, 217, 217 n. 15, 219
viii:33–38   208
viii:39   210
viii:39–52   208
viii:40   210, 213
viii:41   210, 213, 216
viii:42   210
viii:44   211, 213, 215

Esther-AT (cont'd.)
viii:45   215
viii:46   211, 213, 213
viii:47   211, 215, 217
viii:48   210, 213, 213
viii:49   214, 217
viii:51   212, 215
viii:52   211, 212
viii:54   216
viii:56   216

Daniel
1–2   285
3   99, 285
4   285
4–6   284, 284 n. 60, 285, 286, 291
4:8   285
4:9   300
4:24   310 n. 6
5   285
5:10–12   285
5:13–16   285
5:17–23   285
6   99
7–12   285
9:19   151

Ezra
1:8   106
2   108, 109, 109 n. 8
2:2   109
2:36   109
2:36–58   76
2:61–63   108
3:2   109
3:8   109
3:9   109
4:3   109
5:2   109
6:12   313
6:15   122 n. 5
7   107
7:1–5   110 n. 10
7:12–24   110 n. 11
7:14   110
7:16–17   105, 106
8   108, 110

Ezra (cont'd.)
8:15-20   76
8:32-34   105
8:33   106, 107, 108, 109
9   107
9-10   90 n. 45
10   107, 108
10:6   108
10:10   107
10:16-18   107
10:18   109
10:23   106

Nehemiah
3:1   107
3:4   108
3:20   107
3:21   108
6:11   139
7   108, 109
7:7   109
7:39   109
7:63-65   108
7:65   107
8   99, 107
8:1-2   107, 110 n. 12
8:7   106, 107
8:9   110 n. 12
9:6   117, 119
9:6-37   116
10:6   108
10:10   106
10:31   90 n. 45
10:39   107
11:16   106
11:24   83
12   108
12:1   109
12:3   108
12:7   109
12:8   106, 109
12:10   109
12:10-11   107, 109, 110, 110 n. 10
12:12   109
12:25   83 n. 16

Nehemiah (cont'd.)
12:26   107
13   110
13:4   107
13:7-9   107
13:10   76
13:13   107, 110 n. 10
13:23-27   90 n. 45
13:28   110 n. 10

1 Chronicles
2   83 n. 16
2:3-5   82 n. 13, 82 n. 14
2:9   82 n. 13
2:9-15   82 n. 14
2:10-17   82
2:25   80 n. 5
2:25-31   82 n. 13
2:25-33   80, 81
2:31   80
2:33   80 n. 5
2:34   80, 80 n. 8, 84
2:34-35   80, 81, 83
2:34-41   79-90
2:36   83 n. 17
2:36-41   81
2:42   80 n. 5
2:42-50   80
2:50   80 n. 5
3:10-14   83
3:10-16   82
4:10   70-72
6   73, 74
6:1   201
6:1-15   71
6:4-14   82
6:9   71
6:11-13   201
6:15   71
6:16-32   71
6:16-33   73
6:21   73
6:33-47   82
8:33-40   82
9:17   83 n. 16
9:39-44   82
11   258

1 Chronicles (cont'd.)
11:27   258
11:28-29   258
13:2   71 n. 3
13:10   70
15-16   69-77
15:2   70, 72
15:4   69
15:4-10   69, 71, 73, 74, 76
15:11   69, 70-72, 73, 74
15:11-12   71
15:13   70
15:15   70
15:16-23   69 n. 1
15:16-24   69, 71, 72-74, 76
16:4-6   69, 69 n. 1, 72-74
16:4-7   72
16:5   73
16:6   73
16:7-36   73
16:18   73
16:24   73
16:37-42   72-74
16:39   73, 106
16:39-42   74
16:40   73
16:41   73
18:16   107
18:23   201
23:3   71 n. 3
23:24-32   74
23:28   74
24   109, 109 n. 9
24:5-6   107
24:6   106, 109
24:7   110
24:10   108
27:5   106
28:21   71 n. 3
29:29   97
37:42   69

2 Chronicles
2:3-6   72

Index of References

2 Chronicles (cont'd.)
4:5   318
5   72
5:2–13   74
5:5   71 n. 3
6:6   125
6:34   125
6:38   125
7:6   71 n. 3
7:7   318
8:14–15   71 n. 3
10:7   118
17:7–9   71 n. 3
18:23   176
19:8–11   71 n. 3
19:11   83, 106
20:19–23   74
21:9   21 n. 11, 30 n. 33

2 Chronicles (cont'd.)
22:11   106
23   74
23:8   106
23:9   106
23:14   106
24:2   106
24:11   107
24:20   106
24:25   106
26:17   106
26:20   106
29:4   71 n. 3
29:5–36   74
29:12–14   74
29:34   75
30:15–16   71 n. 3
30:21   71 n. 3
30:25   71 n. 3

2 Chronicles (cont'd.)
30:27   71 n. 3
31:4   71 n. 3
31:4–19   76
31:9   71 n. 3
31:10   106
32:4   4
32:32   97
33:19   97
34:8–14   74
34:9   106
34:14   106
34:15   107
34:18   106
34:30   71 n. 3
35:1–19   71 n. 3
36:14   75
36:23   100

Apocrypha and Pseudepigrapha

1 Esdras
3–4   xviii
9:39–40   110 n. 12
9:49   110 n. 12

2 Esdras (4 Ezra)
14:38–41   10, 12
14:47   10

Sirach
3:22   311
12:15   316, 316 n. 1

Sirach (cont'd.)
15:12   310
24:31   13
24:35   13
33:7–9   183
43:3   317
44–50   200
46:13   200

1 Maccabees
14:41   304
14:44   305

4 Maccabees
7:21   271 n. 14

2 Baruch (Syriac)
59:7   10

1 Enoch (Ethiopic)
48:1   9
48:1–2   10

Odes of Solomon
11:6–7   11
30:1–7   11

New Testament

Matthew
2:15   250 n. 25
2:23   250 n. 25
5:38–39   181
12:20   251 n. 27
24:15   276 n. 30
26:31   251 n. 25

Mark
13:14   276 n. 30

Luke
5:29   181

John
1:1   190 n. 23
4:14   11, 12
7:37–38   10, 11
7:38   250 n. 25
19:37   250 n. 25

Romans
5:20   167

1 Corinthians
2:9   250 n. 25

Galatians
6:16   271

2 Thessalonians
2:7   327

Qumran / Dead Sea Scrolls

1Q27 327
1QDan^{a-b} 284 n. 57

1QH *(Thanksgiving Scroll)*
  2:18 9
  5:10–11 9
  6:18–19 12
  8:1 299
  8:4 306
  8:4–8 9
  8:4–11 295–307
  8:4–40 295, 295 n. 1
  8:4–9:36 295 n. 1
  8:5 299
  8:6 296 n. 4, 299, 304, 305
  8:7 299, 302
  8:7–8 299, 301
  8:8 297 n. 13
  8:8–9 302
  8:8–10 299
  8:9 299, 302, 306
  8:10 299, 302
  8:10–11 302
  8:11 296 n. 4, 302, 306
  9:36 295 n. 1
  11:18 13

1QIs^a 9:3 260
1QIs^a 60:6 260
1QpHab 7:4–5 304
1QpHab 11:5–8 303

1QS *(Manual of Discipline)*
  3:13–4:26 301
  3:17–19 8
  4 298 n. 19
  4:20 317 n. 4
  6:4 321
  6:9–10 321
  6:11–13 315–21
  6:15–16 321
  6:18–19 321
  7:22 320
  8:16 320
  8:21 320
  8:25 321

1QS *(Manual of Discipline) (cont'd.)*
  9:10–11 xx
  11 12
  11:4–8 8 n. 7
  11:5–7 8
  11:6–8 10

2QJer 283
4Q171 306 n. 51
4Q174 ii:3 276 n. 30
4Q491, frag. 11:i:17 317
4Q511 1:6–8 317
4Q511 30:5 318
4Q511 63-4:ii:4 318 n. 7
4QDan^{a-e} 284 n. 57
4QJer^{a-e} 283
4QMMT 306
4QpaleoExod^m 279–80, 283, 285
4QSam^a 1:22 199, 201
4QTLevi^a 310
11QPs^a 19:14–16 309–12
11QPs^a 151 309 n. 2
11QPs^a 155:5–8 312–14
11QPs^b 310 n. 5

CD *(Damascus Document)*
  1:1–12 303
  3:13–17 8
  3:19–4:4 303
  5:1–4 xxi
  5:8–12 xxi
  6:3–10 7, 13
  6:3–11 xxi
  7:8–13 xxi
  7:19–21 xxi
  8:9–12 xxi
  9:2–8 xxi
  11:18–20 311
  19:10–13 xxi

P. Mur. xix:17–18 311
P. Yadin 7 311
P. Yadin 7:24 311
P. Yadin 7:39–40 311
pap6QDan 284 n. 57
Papyrus 967 284

Mishnaic and Other Rabbinic Writings

ʾAbot de Rabbi Nathan
  A/1:14   14
  A/6   15 n. 32
  B/37   13 n. 27

Babylonian Talmud
  Baba Batra 14b   276, 276 n. 30
  Baba Batra 72b   13
  Megilla 9a   251 n. 26
  Pesaḥim 113a   87 n. 37
  Taʿanit 7a   13
  Yoma 71a   111
  Yoma 77a   276

Jerusalem Talmud
  Horayot 3:14   81 n. 12

Mekilta de Rabbi Ishmael
  Neziqin 1–2   90 n. 44

Midrash Sipre Bemidbar 116   318

Mishnah
  ʾAbot 2:11   14
  ʾAbot 6:1   14
  Baba Qamma 8:6   179
  Kelim 1:4   145
  Megilla 1:8   273
  Megilla 2:1   273
  Nazir 9:5   200
  Negaʿim 13:7   145
  Negaʿim 13:11   145
  Sanhedrin 2:1   142

Mishnah (cont'd.)
  Yadayim 3:4   273
  Yadayim 3:5   273
  Yadayim 4:5   273
  Yadayim 4:6   273

Rabbah
  Gen 1:8   8 n. 7
  Gen 18:22   13 n. 26
  Gen 64:8   13
  Gen 70:8   14
  Exod 30:3   14
  Lev 20:4   13 n. 26

Sefer ha-Bahir 5   15 n. 33
Sifra 3:v:i   352
Sifra 4:vii:v   358
Sifra 11:xxii:i   360

Tanḥuma
  Ḥuqqat 48   13 n. 25
  Mišpaṭim 8   14 n. 29

Targum
  Num 20:2   13 n. 26
  Num 21:17   13 n. 26
  Isa 12:3   13
  Isa 44:3   14

Testament of Judah 24:1–4   10 n. 11

Tosepta
  Baba Qamma 9:31   179

Other Ancient Near Eastern Texts

AASOR 23 i:79:8   412 n. 71
AbB 9 14–15   394 n. 87
ʿAnat ii:19–20   48 n. 2
ʿAnat iv:14   50 n. 5
Antagal B. 60   410
ARET 3 178   384 n. 28
ARM 3 40:16–18   395 n. 89
Ash. 1924-574   404 n. 3
Bezold, Cat. 4:1604   373 n. 24
BIN 2 32   397 n. 105

BIN 9 440:31   401 n. 138
Bit-rimki, Third Tablet   410
BM Or 2375   226
BM Or 2626-28   226
CBS 10435   404 n. 3
CT 36 31:6–7   411 n. 68
CT 45 99:29–30   395 n. 91
CTA 4 iv:25–26   xix
CTA 35   203

El Amarna texts (EA)
  68:28   118 n. 17
  71:20–22   59
  71:28–31   59
  74:55   118 n. 17
  76:17–20   59
  85:18   118 n. 17
  85:38   118 n. 17
  114:56   118 n. 17
  195   59
  215:16   118 n. 17

Enki and the World Order   410
Enlil Hymn   408
Enmerkar and the Lord of Aratta
  407, 411, 412
Enuma Elish   158 n. 45
Ešnunna   180
Gezer Calendar   150
Gilgameš Epic   177
Gudea Cylinder A   408, 412
Gudea Statue   408
Hammurabi, Law Code of   179, 180, 181
Hebrew Bullas   83 n. 16
HSS 13 165   396 n. 97
IM 10135   395 n. 91

Josephus, *Against Apion*
  1:31   145
Josephus, *Antiquities*
  3:264   145
  3:276   30 n. 32
  5:7–8   29 n. 32
  5:139   25
  5:143–46   29 n. 31
  5:285   199
  5:340   199
  5:347   199
  10:249   276
  10:266–67   276
  20:10   303

K. 2385   369 n. 8, 369 n. 9, 371 n. 14, 376 n. 27, 377, 378 n. 29, 379
K. 2691   378 n. 29, 379
K. 2950   370 n. 12
K. 3331   369 n. 8
K. 3584   369 n. 8
K. 3645   369 n. 8
K. 7274   369 n. 8
K. 7586   369 n. 8
K. 8033   369 n. 8, 376 n. 27
K. 8079   373 n. 24
K. 8112   373 n. 24
K. 8879   379
K. 8882   368 n. 4
K. 8933   373 n. 24
K. 9666   373 n. 24
K. 10358   373 n. 24
K. 11603   369 n. 8
K. 12936   373 n. 24

KAI
  181   318
  182   318
  200   318
  222:A:41–42   178 n. 8

KAR
  22:3–4   396 n. 99
  71 obv. 9–10   367 n. 1
  184 rev. 33–51   396 n. 100
  268 obv. 28   368 n. 4

KTU 1
  41   203
  105   384 n. 31
  106   400 n. 129
  161   384 n. 31, 385 n. 32, 385 n. 33

Kumidi 1   59
Kumidi 2   59
Laessøe, *Bît Rimki*   369 n. 7
Lugalbanda ii:42–43   408
Lugalzagesi ii:21–25   411
Maqlû vii:58–105   367–80
Maqlû ix:152–59   367–80
MSL 13:53   413
MSL 13:151 E 6–7   392 n. 69, 395 n. 92
Ni 9601   404 n. 3, 406 n. 37
Nudimmud, Spell of   403–16
OIP 16 37   408 n. 52
OLA 21 20   395 n. 93
OLA 24 109–10   401 n. 138

PBS
   1/2 107 rev. 7   415 n. 85
   1/2 120 rev. 7–9   373 n. 24
   1/2 120 rev. 9   374 n. 25
   2/2 8:8–10   396 n. 101
   4/1 38–39   409 n. 55

Proto-izi II 451–52   413
PRU 3:51f.   395 n. 92
Qurʾān 55:5–6   149
4 R 17 rev. 8–30   369 n. 7
4 R 17 rev. 31–34   369 n. 7
4 R 19:2:9/10   409 n. 58
4 R 27:6:b   407
5 R 50–51   410 n. 59
Rm. 329   373 n. 24
RS 15:86   395 n. 92
RS 34:126   383 n. 17, 383 n. 26, 385 n. 32, 385 n. 33, 385 n. 35
SCCNH 1 386:30   396 n. 99
SK 199   410
Sm. 139   379
Sm. 275   373 n. 24, 374 n. 25
Sm. 1901   379
Spell of Nudimmud   403–16

STT 1 83   370 n. 9, 370 n. 12, 371 n. 13, 371 n. 14, 376, 376 n. 27, 378 n. 29, 379
Tallqvist, *Maqlû* 2:92   370 n. 9, 376 n. 27
TCL 6 43:46–47   412 n. 70
TCL 15 9:v:50–51   407 n. 48
TCL 15 9:7   415 n. 85
TCS 3 26:153   410 n. 62
TCS 3 52–53   412 n. 72
TCS 3 83–84   409 n. 56
TIM 5 68   395 n. 91
U 16897   404 n. 3
UM 29-16-422   404 n. 3
UM 29-16-442   404 n. 3

UT
   3   203, 204
   3:22   203
   4:18   203
   49:ii:27   159
   173   204

VAT 8382   392 n. 69, 395 n. 91
YOS 2 20   394 n. 87

המקרא ועסקנו ביחס הגלוי של הפרשנים המסורתיים לשאלת המחוייבות הזאת, כפי שהוא מתבטא בהצהרות עקרוניות ובאזכורם המפורש של הטעמים בפירושים, בין שהם נסמכים על הטעמים ובין שהם מתנגדים להם. ההתייחסות הסמוייה של הפרשנות לטעמי המקרא – היינו: זו שאינה מאזכרת אותם במפורש – הן כשהיא מתאימה להם ומוארת על-ידי העיון בהם, והן – ובמיוחד – כשהיא מנוגדת להם, מצריכה עיון נפרד. שכן היחס הסתום אינו נלמד מן היחס המפורש, שסקרנו לעיל, ואיי״ה נפרש את הסתום במקום אחר.

10. מפרשי המקרא, שהיו מודעים לסמכות המיוחסת לטעמים על-ידי לומדי המקרא, השתדלו ל"גייס" לתמיכה בפירושיהם, או לדחיית פירושי אחרים, כפי שראינו לעיל. אזכורם של הטעמים בהקשרים כאלה, כמו גם הצהרות עקרוניות על מחוייבותו של הפרשן לטעמים, תופעות מובנות הן. כן ברור הוא, שברוב המקרים שבהם פירושו כלשהו עולה בקנה אחד עם פיסוק הטעמים, אין הפרשן מלווה את פירושו בהצהרות או באזכורים כאלה, שכן אין הוא זקוק אז לראיה תומכת בפירושו, בהעדר פירושים אלטרנטיביים. עם זאת, לא מעטים הם המקרים, שבהם חולק הפרשן על פיסוק הטעמים, אלא שהוא עושה זאת בשתיקה, על-ידי הצעת פירושו-שלו, ללא אזכור פיסוק הטעמים ודחייתו. יציאה מפורשת נגד הטעמים עלולה לפעול כבומרנג נגד הפרשן, ובכל זאת ישנם מקרים נדירים, שבהם העז פרשן מסורתי לערער במפורש על סמכות הטעמים ומחוייבותו הפרשן להם. כך הוא בדוגמות הבאות, שהזכירן שד"ל בהקדמתו:[26]

10.1 רד"ק בפירושו להו' יב, יב –

אִם־גִּלְעָ֥ד אָ֛וֶן אַךְ־שָׁ֖וְא הָי֑וּ בַּגִּלְגָּל֙ שְׁוָרִ֣ים זִבֵּ֔חוּ...

– מפרש את 'אך-שוא היו' תחילה לפי הטעמים: 'נוכל להדביקו למעלה... ויהי העניין כפול במלות שונות', היינו: אם גלעד היו אך אָוֶן ושוא. בהמשך מציע רד"ק לקשור את הצירוף עם התיבה 'בגלגל' שאחריו, בניגוד לטעמים, היינו: 'אך שוא היו בגלגל, ...', והוא מוסיף: 'ואף-על-פי שהזקף במלת "היו", אין כל טעמי הפירושים הולכים אחרי טעמי הניקוד'. הרי כאן הצהרה גלויה האומרת, כי לעיתים יש להעדיף את הפיסוק הנדרש לפירוש (= 'טעמי הפירושים'), על פני הפיסוק של הטעמים (= 'טעמי הניקוד' = הטעמים המצויינים בסימנים שבכתב).

10.2 גם ר' חזקיה ב"ר מנוח בפירושו (המכונה 'חזקוני')[27] יוצא בגלוי נגד הטעמים שבכמה כתובים. אין הוא נרתע מהסגת האתנחתא אחורה או מהעתקתה קדימה בפסוק. הסגה אחורה תמצא בפירושו לבר' מז, ו: 'ארץ מצרים לפניך הִ֔יא במיטב הארץ הוֹשֵׁ֣ב אֶת־אָבִ֣יךָ וְאֶת־אַחֶ֗יךָ יֵשְׁב֙וּ בְּאֶ֣רֶץ גֹּ֔שֶׁן וְאִם־יָדַ֗עְתָּ וְיֶשׁ־בָּם֙ אַנְשֵׁי־חַ֔יִל וְשַׂמְתָּ֛ם שָׂרֵ֥י מִקְנֶ֖ה עַל־אֲשֶׁר־לִֽי׃'. עמדתה המנותקת לכאורה של הסינטגמה 'ישבו בארץ גשן' בהביאה אותו לפרש: 'במיטב הארץ הושב את-אביך (בהצבת האתנחתא כאן!) – כי הוא זקן ואינו מבקש רק מנוחה ואויר טוב, אבל אחיך בחורים ישבו בארץ גשן, ארץ מקום מרעה'. והוא מוסיף ומצהיר: 'יואל תשיבני מן האתנחתא לומר שהיא מפסקת, שהרי דוגמתו מצינו: "זְבוּלֻ֗ן עַ֣ם חֵרֵ֥ף נַפְשׁ֖וֹ לָמ֑וּת וְנַפְתָּלִ֕י עַ֖ל מְרוֹמֵ֥י שָׂדֶֽה" (שופ' ה, יח)'.[28] העתקת האתנחתא קדימה תמצא בפירושו לבר' מט, כז: 'בִּנְיָמִין֙ זְאֵ֣ב יִטְרָ֔ף בַּבֹּ֖קֶר יֹ֣אכַל עַ֑ד וְלָעֶ֖רֶב יְחַלֵּ֥ק שָׁלָֽל׃'. חזקוני העדיף לפרש את תיבת 'עד' כמלת יחס (ולא כשם-עצם, כפי שפירשוה אחרים) וקשר אותה לתיבה 'ולערב': 'יטרוף רוב בהמות כל כך, שבכל בקר תהא אכילתו מספקתו עד לערב, שיחלק בו משלל טרפו לגוריו... וי"י ד"ולערב" יתרה היא, וכמה רבות'. ואף כאן הוא מוסיף: 'ואין להשיב מן האתנחתא שב-"עַד"...'.

11. במאמר זה ביררנו את הרקע שהוליד את תחושת המחוייבות של פרשני המקרא לטעמי

---

[26] שד"ל (לעיל, הערה 15), עמ' יד-טו.
[27] חזקוני, פירושי התורה לרבינו חזקיה ב"ר מנוח, מהדורת ח"ד שעוועל^2 (ירושלים, תשמ"ב).
[28] שופ' ה, יח נתפרש בניגוד לטעמים – אך בשתיקה, ללא אזכורם – גם על-ידי רש"י (ורד"ק). אפשר שהחזקוני נתלה ברש"י כבאילן גדול, להצדקת אי-התחשבותו במיקום האתנחתא, ולכן הביא ראיה מפסוק זה.

לפסוק במקרא, ותמצא שדרשת חז"ל מוזכרת בפירוש רק לאחר הפשט, וללא ציון תמיכת הטעמים. פירוש הפשט המוצע על-ידי רש"י (על אתר) — "כל שם גדולה קרויה "משיחה", כמו: "לך נתתים למשחה" (במ' יח, ח)' — מואר יותר בפירושו לצירוף "עד־משיח נגיד" בדנ' ט, כה: "עד בא כרש... שאמר הקב"ה עליו שהוא ישוב ויבנה עירו, וקראו משיחו ונגידו, שנא': "כה אמר ה' למשיחו לכורש..."'. נמצאת למד, שכשהביא רש"י את פירושו לצירוף, היינו: כשתפקד כפרשן המקרא ולא כפרשן התלמוד, הציג את 'למשיחו לכורש' כצירוף של תמורה. וכיוון שראייה זו אינה עולה בקנה אחד עם פיסוק הטעמים, בצדק לא הסתייע בהם.

9. רשב"ם

אף רשב"ם מסתמך לעתים על הטעמים בפירושו. כך במקרים דלהלן:

9.1 בפירושו לבר' יח, כא הלך רשב"ם בעקבות סבו, רש"י, בהסתמכו על הטעמים. על טעותו של רש"י בהביאו ראיה מן הטעמים לפירושו כתבנו עמדנו בסעיף 8.7 לעיל, והדברים חלים גם על דברי רשב"ם בפירושו לכתוב: 'יעשו כָּלָ֑ה — פָּ֣סֵק יש בינתיים, להפריד הדבר. כלומר: אם כן עשו, אעשה אותם כלה.'

9.2 דחיית פירושו של פסוק בטענה שאין הוא הולם את פיסוק הטעמים מלמדת על הכרת הפרשן בערך הסמכותי המיוחס לטעמים על-ידי קוראיו הפוטנציאליים. כך תמצא בפירוש רשב"ם לבר' מט, ט —

גּ֤וּר אַרְיֵ֙ה יְהוּדָ֔ה מִטֶּ֖רֶף בְּנִ֣י עָלִ֑יתָ...

— התנגדות לפירוש המדרשי המתעלם מן הטעמים והמבוטא בתמציתיות בב"ר צח, ז — 'מטרפו של יוסף עלית ונתעלית' — ובדומה בפסוודו־יונתן על אתר, וכנראה גם ברש"י (למרות שמסדר הדיבורים־המתחילים ברש"י התאמים כאן לפיסוק הטעמים).[25] לפי מדרש זה צריך היה פיסוק הטעמים להיות

מִטֶּ֖רֶף בְּנִ֣י עָלִ֑יתָ

ועל כן קובע רשב"ם: 'והמפרשו במכירת יוסף לא ידע בשיטה של פסוק ולא בחילוק טעמים כלל'. מפירושו הפשטני של רשב"ם, המתאים כמובן לטעמים, עולה שיבנ'י אינה משמשת כסומך, אלא כמלת פנייה, המכוונת לנושאו של הפועל 'עלית', ועל-כן חיברוה הטעמים לפועל.

9.3 בפירושו לוי' יט, יד — וְלִפְנֵ֣י עִוֵּ֔ר לֹ֥א תִתֵּ֖ן מִכְשֹׁ֑ל — מסתמך רשב"ם על הטעמים לא באשר לפיסוק המקרא, אלא לקביעת משקלה של התיבה חֵרֵ֔שׁ על-פי הטעמתה: '...וטעמו ברי"ש, כי משקל דגש הוא, כמו עִוֵּ֔ר, גֶּ֣בֶן'. יש עניין מיוחד בהערתו זו של הרשב"ם, המלמדת כי היא מכוונת לקוראים שאין לפניהם טקסט מנוקד, או שבמסורת הקריאה שלהם לא הבחינו בהגייה בין צירה/סגול. נטרול שתי תנועות אלה מקנה לטעם כאן מעמד פונמטי, המונע בלבול בין חֵרֵ֔שׁ (כאן) / חֶ֫רֶשׁ (יהו' ב, א).

למשיחו לכורש | אשר־החזקתי בימינו...'. רש"י יצא מהטעמים הקיימים בפסוקנו והצביע על זרות אחת. הזרויות הנוספות שבפסוק טעונות בירור לעצמן, ומשתקפת מהן התרוצצות בלתי מוכרעת בין פירוש המתאים יותר לפשט, ולפיו 'למשיחו לכורש' = צירוף של תמורה, לבין פירוש המתאים לדרש ואכמ"ל.

25 ואפשר בכל זאת להעמיד את פירוש רש"י (ואולי גם את פסוודו־יונתן) על-פי הטעמים כך: 'מטרף [יוסף], [אתה] בני (= יהודה), עלית'.

בטעמים, באמרו:

> וטעם המקרא מוכיח שהם ('אחרי' ו'דרך') שני דברים, שננקדו (=פוסקו) בשני
> טעמים (מפסיקים): 'אחרי' — נקוד בפשטא, ו'דרך' נקוד במשפל (=יתיב). ואם
> היה 'אחרי דרך' דבור אחד, היה נקוד 'אחרי' במשרת, בשופר הפוך (=מהפך)...

רש"י רואה בטעם המפריד שבמלה 'אחרי' עילה לניתוקה התחבירי מן ההמשך. זאת ועוד: לדידו, בידודה של 'אחרי' במחצית השנייה של תחום שלטון המלך (הזקף), גורם לה להימשך כביכול, מצד העניין, אל המחצית הראשונה שלו, המופסקת על־ידי המשנה (רביע). אולם כבר שד"ל[23] דחה את המשמעות שמייחס רש"י לטעם המפריד שב'אחרי', וקבע כי רש"י נכשל בהבנת כוחם של טעמי המקרא הזה, כי משפטי הטעמים לא היו ידועים יפה בימיו. שד"ל השווה את הטעמים שבצירוף 'אחרי דרך מבוא השמש' לטעמים שבצירוף 'ימי שבע שבתת השנים' (וי' כה, ח), וטען בצדק, כי אמנם 'מילת "אחרי"... אינה סמוכה למילת "דרך" לבדה, אבל היא סמוכה לשלוש תיבות: "דרך מבוא השמש"'. על דברי שד"ל יש להוסיף, כי הסינטגמה המורכבת 'אחרי דרך מבוא השמש' מצויינת על־ידי הטעמים לפי המרכיבים המיידיים הבונים אותה, היינו: {אחרי [דרך (מבוא השמש)]}. וכיון שזוהי שיטתם הרגילה של בעלי הטעמים, אין לייחס למלה 'אחרי' כשהיא בטעם מפסיק תפקיד תחבירי או סמנטי שונה מזה המיוחד לה כשהיא בטעם מחבר. והשווה: 'וַתָּקָם חַנָּה אַחֲרֵי אָכְלָה בְשִׁלֹה וְאַחֲרֵי שָׁתֹה...' (שמ"א א, ט):

המרכיבים המיידיים של הצירוף 'אַחֲרֵי (אָכְלָה בְשִׁלֹה)' מחייבים כאן הצבת טעם מפסיק ב'אחרי', מה שאין כן בהמשך — 'וְאַחֲרֵי שָׁתֹה'. אמור מעתה: ארבע התיבות 'אחרי דרך מבוא השמש' מחוברות על־ידי הטעמים ליחידה אחת. הטעמים לא ביקשו לבודד את תיבת 'אחרי' ביחידה, אלא ציינו את היותה האחרונה בסדר הצטרפות המרכיבים של הסינטגמה. ספק הוא, אם הישענותו של רש"י על הטעמים בשלוש הדוגמאות האחרונות מלמדת על אהבתו להם, אך אם כך הוא, הרי האהבה קלקלה כאן את השורה.

8.9 יש להיזהר מלתלות ברש"י הישענות על הטעמים במקום שרש"י לא התכוון לגייס את הטעמים לתמיכה בדעתו שלו, אלא להצביע על הזיקה שבין הטעמים לבין פירוש מדרשי לפסוק. כך למשל נדרש הפסוק 'כֹּה־אָמַר ה' לִמְשִׁיחוֹ לְכוֹרֶשׁ אֲשֶׁר־הֶחֱזַקְתִּי בִימִינוֹ...' (יש' מה, א) בבלי מגילה יב ע"א:

> ...וכי כורש משיח היה? אלא אמר לו הקב"ה למשיח: קובל אני לך על כורש
> (ולכורש' = 'על כורש'). אני אמרתי: 'הוא יבנה ביתי ויקבץ גליותי' (פרפרזה, לפי:
> 'הוא יבנה עירי וגלותי יְשַׁלֵּחַ' — שם, יג); והוא אמר: 'מי בכם מכל עמו... ויעל'.

רש"י בפירושו לתלמוד (שם, ד"ה יקובל אני לך) מציין:

> וניקוד טעם מקרא זה מוכיח על דרש זה, שאין לך טעם זרקא במקרא שאין סגול
> בא אחריו. וכאן ננקד 'למשיחו' בזרקא ו'לכורש' ננקד במאריך (=מונח),
> להפרישו ולנתקו מעם 'למשיחו'.

רש"י תפקד כאן כפרשן התלמוד ולא כפרשן המקרא. הוא הצביע על סיוע הטעמים לא לפירוש הפסוק כשלעצמו, אלא לדרשה התלמודית הנתלית בו.[24] תדע שכן הוא, אם תלך אצל פירושו

---

[23] שד"ל (לעיל, הערה 15) בפירושו על אתר, עמ' 525.
[24] למעשה, הדרשה התלמודית היתה מסתייעת במערכת טעמים פחות מוזרה לפסוקנו, כך: 'כֹּה־אָמַר ה'

פירש מה יהיה ב"אותו וכל אשר לו", ולמטה פירש]'. כדי לאשש את הפירוש המאולץ הזה נתלה רש"י בטעמים — מתוך הנחה שהסמכות שמאחוריהם אכן מספקת הוכחה לנכונות הפירוש — ומשלב בדבריו את הטיעון: 'והזקף שהוא על "באש" מוכיח שהוא נפרד מ"אתו", שכן מצינו מקראות שהטעם מחלקן'. כפי שהראינו בהצגת חלוקת הטעמים, אין הם חורגים מהפשט ואין ללמוד מההפרדה בין 'באש' לבין 'אתו...' את מה שמבקש רש"י לתלות בהפרדה זו.

8.7 הסתמכותו של רש"י על הטעמים בפירושו לבר' יח, כא —

...הַכְּצַעֲקָתָהּ הַבָּאָה אֵלַי עָשׂוּ ׀ כָּלָה...

— בטעות יסודה. לפי פירושו: 'הבאה אלי עשו — ואם עומדים במרדם כלה אני עושה בהם' — משפט תנאי כאן, שהרישא שלו היא 'הכצעקתה... עשו', והסיפא שלו היא 'כלה [אני עושה בהם]'. חלוקת הטעמים, כפי שציינו, אינה כזאת, ותמוהים הם דברי רש"י בהמשך 'ולפיכך יש הפסק נקודת פס(י)ק בין "עשו" ל"כלה", כדי להפריד תיבה מחברתה'. אמנם מונה + פסק יש כאן, אך נתחלף לו לרש"י צירוף זה במונח לגרמיה שאין כאן, וצדק שד"ל[20] בקבעו: 'ומה שהביא רש"י ראיה מן הטעם שבין "עשו" ל"כלה", ... וכל שכן שאין זה מונח לגרמיה, אינו ראיה, ... ואינו אלא פסק, שאין לו שום כוח בענין נתוח המאמרים'. שד"ל הטיב לראות גם את המשמעות התחבירית והסמנטית של 'כלה': 'עשו כלה, הכוונה עשו בהחלט, ובא הפסק ליתן ריוח בין שתי המילות, שלא יובן ש"כלה" הוא היה המושא, ... אבל יובן שהוא תואר הפועל, כמו "כלה גרש יגרש אתכם מזה" (שמ' יא, א)'. נמצא, שהפועל 'עשו' מקבל שני משלימים תיאוריים: כָּלָה, המצטרף אליו ראשונה, וּכְצַעֲקָתָהּ הַבָּאָה אֵלַי, המצטרף אל הצירוף הראשון. הפסק בצירוף הראשון בא לרופף במידת-מה את הקשר[21] שבין הפועל לבין משלים שהוא בלתי-מוצרך, ורש"י טעה בהערכת תפקידו כאן.

8.8 גם בפירושו לדב' יא, ל —

הֲלֹא-הֵ֗מָּה בְּעֵ֤בֶר הַיַּרְדֵּן֙ אַחֲרֵי֙ דֶּ֤רֶךְ מְב֣וֹא הַשֶּׁ֔מֶשׁ...

— תולה רש"י בטעמים מה שלא נתכוונו לומר. מפירוש רש"י ל'אחרי' — 'אחר העברת הירדן הרבה והלאה למרחוק' — ומאזכור הכלל 'וזהו לשון "אחרי": כל מקום שנאמר "אחרי" מופלג הוא'[22] אנו למדים כי לשיטתו מלה זו, המציינת מרחק, אינה מתייחסת ל'דרך מבוא השמש', אלא עומדת מבודדת כביכול, כמעין afterthought ל'בעבר הירדן'. כך עולה גם מהמשך דבריו, בד"ה 'דרך מבוא השמש': 'להלן מן הירדן לצד מערבי'. רש"י קורא אפוא את הפסוק כך: 'הלא-המה בעבר הירדן (אך לא בסמוך לירדן, אלא) אחרי (=להלן מן הירדן), 'הרבה והלאה למרחוק' מן ה'עברי' [=הגדה] שלו דרך (=לצד) מבוא השמש (='מערבי')'. את הסברו זה תומך רש"י

---

20 שד"ל (לעיל, הערה 15), בפירושו על אתר, עמ' 78-79.
21 ראה ברויאר 1 (לעיל, הערה 15), עמ' 83; ברויאר 2 (לעיל, הערה 15), עמ' 133.
22 הכלל השלם, המצביע על דיפרנציאציה סמנטית בין 'אחר' לבין 'אחרי', מופיע ברש"י בפירושו לבר' טו, א: 'כל מקום שנאמר "אחר" — סמוך; "אחרי" — מופלג'. וראה גם רש"י לבר' לט, ז; משי כח, כג. מקורו של הכלל בב"ר מד, ה, שם נחלקים ר' יודן ור' הונא, תרויהון בשם ר' יוסי בן זמרא. רש"י נוקט לעניין זה בשיטת ר' הונא, ואילו שיטת ר' יודן — הפוכה. תן דעתך לכך, שבכל המקומות הנזכרים עוסק הכלל בשדה הסמנטי של הזמן, ואילו בדב' יא, ל הוא מיושם על-ידי רש"י לשדה הסמנטי של המקום. עוד נזכיר, כי פסוקנו מתפרש על-ידי רש"י באותו אופן גם בפירושו לבבלי סוטה לג ע"ב, ד"ה 'הלא המה בעבר הירדן', ושם לאחר שביאר '... שההרים האלה במערב הירדן ואילך הרבה להלן מן הירדן לצד מערבי הוסיף במפורש: יולא סמוך לירדן'.

הניקוד (=פיסוק הטעמים) למדני להבדילם זו מזו, ולהעמיד תיבת 'ופניהם' בפני עצמה. וכן פירושו: ופניהם. לפניהם; וכנפיהם היו פרודות למעלה מפניהם... ודוגמת לשון מקרא זו יש עוד בפרשה זו (פס' יח): ' וְגֻבֵּיהֶן וְגֹבַהּ לָהֶם וְיִרְאָה לָהֶם —
תיבת 'וגביהן' עומדת בעצמה.

פיסוקם של בעלי הטעמים לשני הפסוקים — יח' א, יא ו-יח — היה לרש"י לעיניים, והובילו לפרש את 'ופניהם' ואת 'וגביהן' כמבודדות מן ההמשך. אפשר שרש"י הבין מן הטעמים, שיש לראות בתיבות אלה משפטים חסרי נשוא, היינו: 'ופניהם [להם]'; 'וגביהן [להן]'. ואף שבהציגו תיבות אלה כמשפטים כיוון לעיקר דעתם של בעלי הטעמים, לא ירד לסוף דעתם, כפי שאנו מעדיפים לראותה, ולא הצביע על ייחודו של המבנה התחבירי שבפרדיקציות אלה, שבהן משמש הכינוי החבור כנשואו של שם-העצם הנושאי שאליו הוא דבוק. אמור מעתה: 'ופניהם' = ופנים להם; 'וגביהן' = 'וגַבִּים (=וגַבּוֹת) להן', כדרך שפירשנו לעיל (בסעיף 3) את תפישתם התחבירית של בעלי ההכרע שנדחה בפיסוקו של הכתוב בשמ' כה, לד (=לז, כ), שבודדו את 'כפתריה ופרחיה', בהבינם את הצירוף כשתי פרדיקציות, היינו: 'כפתורים לה ופרחים לה'.[17]

8.6 הסתמכות על הטעמים מחייבת הכרה מלאה של שיטת הפיסוק המתמצית בהם, שכן הכרה חלקית של השיטה עלולה להביא למסקנות מוטעות. נראה שהערכתו של רש"י, שהישענות על טעמי המקרא מחזקת את פירושו, גרמה לו לגייס אותם כהוכחה לפירושו גם כשהסתמך עליהם שלא כדין, מבלי לחוש בכך. כך למשל ברורה היא חלוקת הטעמים — התואמת את פשט הכתוב — ביהו' ז, טו:

וְהָיָה הַנִּלְכָּד בַּחֵרֶם יִשָּׂרֵף בָּאֵשׁ אֹתוֹ וְאֶת־כָּל־אֲשֶׁר־לוֹ...

הקיסרותו של האתנחתא נחצית אחרי חלק הייחוד — 'הנלכד בחרם'; ובמחצית השנייה מופרד החלק הנשואי — 'ישרף באש' — מן החלק-הנושאי-הכולל — 'אתו ואת־כל־אשר־לו',[18] (הנחלק אף הוא לשני חלקיו). רש"י בפירושו על אתר חש מחויבות לפרשנות חז"ל (במ"ר כג, ו; תנחומא מסעי ה), שלפיה נידון עכן בסקילה (כדין מחלל שבת, על שגנב בשבת),[19] פרשנות שהותאמה למסופר ביהו' ז, כד-כה: 'ויקח יהושע את־עכן... ואת־בניו ואת־בנתיו ואת־שורו ואת־חמרו ואת־צאנו ואת־אהלו ואת־כל־אשר־לו... וירגמו אתו כל־ישראל אבן (רש"י: 'שחלל את השבת') וישרפו אתם (רש"י: 'האהל והמטלטלין') באש ויסקלו אתם (רש"י: 'השור והבהמה') באבנים'. הצורך לגשר בין ציווי ה', להמית בשריפה את הנלכד בחרם (פס' טו), לבין מה שבוצע בפועל — סקילת עכן (פס' כה) — הביא את רש"י להידחק בפירושו לפס' טו, ולהוציאו מפשוטו, כך: "'ישרף באש' — האהל והמטלטלין; 'אותו ואת כל אשר לו' — כדין המפורש למטה (בפס' כה: 'וירגמו אתו... אבן... ויסקלו אתם באבנים'): אותו והבהמה בסקילה'. את הפסוק ופתרונו, כמוצע על־ידי רש"י בהמשך, יש להבין כך: 'יהיה הנלכד בחרם [זה דינו]: ישרף באש [הראוי לישרף, היינו: האהל והמטלטלין שלו; ואילו] אתו ואת־כל־אשר־לו [יסקלו (וזה מקרא קצר... לא

---

17 ראה הערה 4 לעיל.

18 'אתו ואת־כל־אשר־לו' = 'הוא וכל אשר לו', ומציינו בלשון המקרא, שנושאו של פועל סביל עשוי לבוא אחרי 'את', כגון: ' וַיֻּגַּד לְרִבְקָה אֶת־דִּבְרֵי עֵשָׂו בְּנָהּ הַגָּדֹל ' (בר' כז, מב). תן דעתך לכך, שאף כאן הפרידו הטעמים בין החלק הנשואי לחלק הנושאי.

19 לפי המדרש (בבמ"ר ובתנחומא שצוינו בגוף) עכן נידון גם לשריפה, על שמעל בחרם. אך בבבלי סנהדרין מד ע"א נשללת האפשרות שנענש הן בסקילה והן בשריפה, ונקבע שהראוי לשריפה — לשריפה (רש"י, שם: 'כסף זהב ובגדים') — לשריפה; הראוי לסקילה (רש"י, שם: 'הוא, שורו ובהמותיו') — לסקילה. רש"י בפירושו ליהו' ז, טו, כה אימץ את מה שאינו שנוי במחלוקת, היינו: סקילה.

פרשנות המקרא המסורתית והמחוייבות לטעמי המקרא

הינם שווי מין ומספר, כגון: אָחִ֥י יְפַ֖ת הַגָּד֑וֹל (ברי י, כא).[16]

8.2 רשיי אכן נועץ בטעמי המקרא ולומד מהם פירושי פסוקים. כך מציין הוא בפירושו ליר׳ ג, ח —

וָאֵרֶ֗א כִּ֤י עַל־כָּל־אֹדוֹת֙ אֲשֶׁ֤ר נִֽאֲפָה֙ מְשֻׁבָ֣ה יִשְׂרָאֵ֔ל שִׁלַּחְתִּ֕יהָ וָאֶתֵּ֛ן אֶת־סֵ֥פֶר כְּרִיתֻתֶ֖יהָ אֵלֶ֑יהָ...

— כי: ׳נקודות טעמי מקרא זה מלמדין על פירושו׳. "ישראל" נקוד זקף, מובדל מ"שלחתיה"; "שלחתיה" נקוד זקף גדול לעצמו. מפירושו בהמשך משתמע, שטעמי המקרא הבינו את המבנה התחבירי של הפסוק כך, שישלחתיה ואתן את־ספר כריתותיה אליה׳ הוא פסוק־תוכן מושאי של ׳וארא׳, היינו: ראיתי (לנכון) לשלחה..., ובין השניים חוצץ פסוק סיבה לפועל ׳וארא׳ — ׳כי... נאפה משבה ישראל׳.

8.3 גם בפירושו למל״א י, כח —

וּמוֹצָ֧א הַסּוּסִ֛ים אֲשֶׁ֥ר לִשְׁלֹמֹ֖ה מִמִּצְרָ֑יִם וּמִקְוֵ֕ה סֹחֲרֵ֣י הַמֶּ֔לֶךְ יִקְח֥וּ מִקְוֵ֖ה בִּמְחִֽיר׃

— נסמך רשיי על הטעמים: יולכן נקוד על ׳ומקוה׳ טעם זקף גדול, ללמוד שהתיבה עומדת בעצמה ואינה דבוקה לאחריה׳. הטעמים באו ללמד, כי יש לראות בצלע השנייה של הפסוק משפט יחוד, שבו התיבה ׳מקוה׳ משמשת כחלק ייחוד, למרות שהיא מופיעה גם בגוף המשפט, ושלא כמקובל אין כינוי מוסב ממיר אותה שם.

8.4 רשיי נזקק לתמיכת הטעמים גם בפירושו לשמ׳ טו, יז:

תְּבִאֵ֗מוֹ וְתִטָּעֵ֙מוֹ֙ בְּהַ֣ר נַחֲלָֽתְךָ֔ מָכ֧וֹן לְשִׁבְתְּךָ֛ פָּעַ֖לְתָּ יְהוָ֑ה מִקְּדָ֕שׁ אֲדֹנָ֖י כּוֹנְנ֥וּ יָדֶֽיךָ׃

בפרשי: ׳מקדש ה׳׳ — הטעם עליו זקף גדול, להפרידו מתיבת ״השם" שלאחריו. המקדש אשר כוננו ידיך, ה׳...׳. לצורך פירוש זה היה יכול רשיי להסתמך על נקוד ׳מקדשי בקמץ, השולל אפשרית של ׳מקדש ה׳׳. סמיכות כזאת סובלת גם מן הזהות שבין ׳ה׳׳ לבין הכינוי שב׳ידיך׳, וכן במצב זה מתבקשת הלשון ׳מקדשך׳ כוננו ידיך. בכל זאת העדיף רשיי להסתמך על הטעמים, שכן העיון בהם מבליט את הסטטוס של התיבה ׳ה׳׳, המשמשת כאן, כמו בצלע המקבילה — ׳מכון לשבתך פעלת, ה׳׳ — במעמד של פנייה. אך שלא כבצלע המקבילה, חוצצת הפנייה כאן בין הזוקק ׳מקדשי לבין פסוק הזיקה האסינדטי שמלווהו — [אשר] כוננו ידיך׳. ועל כן ראה רשיי להצמיד את פסוק הזיקה לזוקק, כפי שהוא בצלע המקבילה, ופירש: ׳המקדש אשר כוננו ידיך, ה׳ ...׳. נמצא שהטעמים לימדו את רשיי גם על התקבולות ׳מקדשי || [אשר] ׳מכון לשבתך׳; ו׳[אשר] כוננו ידיך׳ || [אשר] פעלת׳. והרי כאן לימוד יתר על מה שמלמדים הקמץ שבתיבה ׳מקדשי וזהות ׳ה׳׳ עם הכינוי שב׳ידיך׳.

8.5 הצהרה על תלות מוחלטת של הפירוש בטעמים מצוייה אצל רשיי בפירושו ליחי א, יא -
וּפְנֵיהֶ֥ם וְכַנְפֵיהֶ֖ם פְּרֻד֣וֹת מִלְמָ֑עְלָה...

אלמלא שראיתי טעם זקף גדול נקוד על ׳ופניהם׳ לא הייתי יודע לפרש. אבל

---

[16] הקביעה (בבבלי סנה׳ סט ע״ב) שיפת גדול שבאחים׳ תואמת את טעמי המקרא, ואפשר שכיוון שכבר הוכרע כך בתלמוד, לא נזקק רשיי בפירושו לתורה להסתמך על הטעמים לעניין זה, אף שציין את הבעייתיות התחבירית שבכתוב: ׳איני יודע (היינו: אין לדעת מן הכתוב עצמו) אם יפת הגדול, אם שֵׁם׳, ובפירושו תמך על־פי תיאורכים מקראיים בקביעת חז״ל.

ויאמר ה׳ אלהים הן האדם היה כְּאַחַד מִמֶּנּוּ לָדַעַת טוֹב וָרָע... (בר׳ ג, כב).

ראב״ע דוחה בנימוק מורפולוגי את האפשרות להפסיק במלה 'כְּאַחַד' ולהפרידה מהמלה 'מִמֶּנּוּ' — פיסוק העולה מתרגום אונקלוס, למשל — בציינו כי 'כאשר יהיה אֶחָד בפתח קטן (= סגול), יהיה בטעם (= מוטעם), ועניינו מוכרת (= בסטטוס נפרד), ואם יהיה בפתח גדול (= אַחָד, כבפסוקנו), יהיה סמוך (= בסטטוס נסמך)... על כן לא יתכן מדקדוק הלשון להיות פירושו "כמו אֶחָד", ומה טעם (= מובן) יהיה לו'. ראב״ע אינו מסתפק בנימוק המורפולוגי, ושולל אפשרות חלוקה המנוגדת לטעמים בטענה: 'יהיה בעל הטעמים ראוי לדבק "מִמֶּנּוּ" עם "לָדַעַת" (אילו היה סבור כמו אונקלוס, למשל)... ופי׳ "מִמֶּנּוּ" לשון רבים, ... וזה דבור השם עם המלאכים'.[14] מהדוגמאות שהובאו נמצאנו למדים, כי ראב״ע נצרך להצהרת מחוייבותו 'לשמור דרך הטעמים' כטענה מכרעת המגוייסת נגד פירושים של אחרים, העומדים בסתירה לטעמי המקרא.

7. הצהרות עקרוניות על מחייבות הפרשן לטעמי המקרא לא מצאנו אצל מפרשים אחרים. עם זאת, אזכורים מפורשים של הטעמים מצויים אצל כמה מהם — בעיקר אצל רש״י ורשב״ם — במקומות אחדים, וחלקם צויינו כבר במחקרים קודמים,[15] המזמינים עיון. נעיין כאן בכמה אזכורים כאלה, ונבדוק את תרומת הטעמים באותם פסוקים להבנת המבנה התחבירי של הכתוב. כן ננסה לבחון, אם אזכורים אלה מציינים הכרה מצידו של הפרשן בנחיצות תרומת הטעמים לפירוש הפסוק, עד כדי הישענות על תרומה זו, או שהוא רואה בהם תוספת סיוע לפירושו, המבוסס על שיקולים משיקולים שונים.

8. **רש״י**

8.1 רש״י בפירושו לדב׳ כט, כ — ...הַכְּתוּבָה בְּסֵפֶר הַתּוֹרָה הַזֶּה:

— מציג להשוואה את דב׳ כח, סא — ...אֲשֶׁר לֹא כָתוּב בְּסֵפֶר הַתּוֹרָה הַזֹּאת...

— ומצביע על התאמת הלוואי על־פי מינו לסומך או לנסמך: "הַזֹּאת" לשון נקבה מוסב אל "הַתּוֹרָה"; "הַזֶּה" לשון זכר מוסב אל "הַסֵּפֶר", **ועל ידי פסוק הטעמים הן נחלקין לשתי לשונות**'. אזכור הטעמים כאן אינו מצביע על מחוייבות להם. הוא בא כתוספת לטיעון הדקדוקי, ונראה שכוונתו מתודית. יש בו מעין הזמנה להיוועץ בטעמי המקרא, שכן אלה מסמנים את המרכיבים המיידיים (= immediate constituents) של יחידות תחביריות מורכבות, ועשויים על כן להצביע על זיקת הלוואי לסומך או לנסמך, אף במקרים שבהם שני מרכיבי הסמיכות

הפותחים את המניין בתיבת 'יה' השנייה (וכך רס״ג, כנראה). וראה על כך בתוספות לבבלי ר״ה, יז ע״ב, ד״ה 'שלש עשרה מדות'.

14 בדומה לראב״ע פירוש גם רד״ק את הפסוק.

15 לעניין זה, וכן דוגמאות לזיקה שבין הפרשנות לבין הטעמים, ראה במחקרים החשובים דלהלן: מ׳ ברויאר, פיסוק טעמים שבמקרא (ירושלים, תשי״ח) [להלן: ברויאר 1], בעיקר עמודים 135-158; הנ״ל, טעמי המקרא בכ״א ספרים ובספרי אמ״ת (ירושלים, תשמ״ב) [להלן: ברויאר 2], בעיקר עמודים 368-377; שמואל דוד לוצאטו, פירוש שד״ל על חמשה חומשי תורה[2] (תל־אביב, תשכ״ו), בהקדמה עמודים יד-טו; W. Wickes, *Two Treatises on the Accentuation of the Old Testament:* (reprinted New York, 1970) טעמי כ״א ספרים (2), טעמי אמ״ת (1); ע״צ מלמד, "טעמי המקרא בדברי פרשני המקרא", מחקרי המרכז לחקר הפולקלור א (ירושלים, תש״ל) קצ״ה-קצ״ט; ח׳ ילון, פרקי לשון (ירושלים, תשל״א) 331; ייבין (לעיל, הערה 2), עמ׳ 162-167.

פרשנות המקרא המסורתית והמחוייבות לטעמי המקרא   157*

בעניין זה, עד שכרכו את הטעמים (כמו גם את הניקוד) עם מתן תורה מסיני. ומי שלא ראה אותם כמסורים אז בסימניהם בכתב, הרי לפחות פירש את נתינתם בסיני כמסירה שבעל־פה. כך מצינו במחזור ויטרי, בפירושו למסכת אבות, בדיון על השתלשלות מסירת התורה:

> שטעמי לנגינות הם שנאמרו למשה, מי תולש ומי זוקף, ומי יושב ומי עומד, ומי העולה ומי היורד ומי המונח. אבל סימני הנגינות סופרים הוא שתקנום... ומפני שהטעמים והנגינות משתבחין הוא שתקנום. ולפיכך לא ניתן ספר תורה לינקד, שאע״פ שניתנו פסוקי הטעמים ונגינות הקרייה מסיני במסורת, דכת׳ ׳יושם שכל׳ (נחמי ח, ח), על פה נאמרו, ולא בסימני נקידה בספר...[9]

6. קשירת הטעמים למסורת המשתלשלת מסיני, ואמונה שהבנת הטקסט תלויה בהם — כפי שעולה מן הקשרים האסוציאטיביים שמְסַפקים הצירופים שנתפרשו כמכוונים לטעמים: ׳שׂוֹם שכל׳, ׳וְיָבִינוּ בַמִּקְרָא׳, ׳לְלַמֵּד דַּעַת אֶת־הָעָם׳ — מזמינה מלכתחילה מחוייבות מצד פרשנות המקרא המסורתית לטעמי המקרא. ביטוי ברור למחוייבות כזאת אתה מוצא בהצהרותיו של ראב״ע, המובאות בשניים מספריו. ב״מאזני לשון הקודש״ הוא שולל פירושים המנוגדים לטעמים. וזה לשונו: ׳אזהירך שתלך אחרי בעלי הטעמים, וכל פירוש שאינו על פי הטעמים לא תאבה לו ולא תשמע אליו׳;[10] וב״ספר צחות״ מתייחס הוא במפורש לחכמת ״המפסיק״ בהסתמך על התוצר של עבודתו, שהוא ללא כל דופי. וזה לשונו: ׳איך טעה המפסיק, ואף כי הוא עזרא הסופר! והכלל, כי המפסיק לא היה אחריו חכם כמוהו, כי הנה ראינו בכל המקרא לא הפסיק כי אם במקום ראוי׳.[11]

את מחוייבותו לטעמים מבטא ראב״ע במפורש גם בכמה מקומות בפירושו. כך משל:

לוּלֵי ה׳ צְבָאוֹת הוֹתִיר לָנוּ שָׂרִיד כִּמְעָט כִּסְדֹם הָיִינוּ לַעֲמֹרָה דָּמִינוּ

(יש׳ א, ט) — ׳... ו״כמעט״ דבק עם ״שריד״, בעבור טעם המפסיק, כי **עיקר גדול הוא לשמור דרך הטעמים**׳. אזכורו של ׳עיקר גדול׳ זה חשוב לראב״ע, משום שחז״ל התעלמו ממנו בהתייחסם לפסוקנו,[12] וכן עשר תרגום יונתן ורש״י (והסכים עמהם שד״ל). כיוצא בזה, בהסתמכו על חלוקת הטעמים בשמ׳ לד, ו —

וַיַּעֲבֹר ה׳ עַל־פָּנָיו וַיִּקְרָא ה׳ ׀ ה׳ אֵל רַחוּם וְחַנּוּן...

— דוחה ראב״ע את פירוש רס״ג: ׳אמר הגאון כי ״השם״ הראשון דבק עם ״ויקרא״ (היינו: ׳... ויקרא [= נשוא] ה׳ [= נושא]׳, ורק אחר כך מתחיל הדיבור הישיר המהווה פסוק־תוכן מושאי: ׳ה׳ אל רחום וחנון...׳). ואילו היה כן, **למה לא דָּבַק בעל הטעמים**? והנכון: כי ״השם״ שתי פעמים, כמו ״אברהם אברהם״...׳.[13] טענה דומה באה בדבריו על הפסוק:

---

[9] מחזור ויטרי, לרבינו שמחה מתלמידי רש״י ז״ל, מהדורת שמעון הלוי איש הורוויץ (ירושלים, תשכ״ג) סימן תכד, עמ׳ 462.

[10] אברהם אבן עזרא, מאזני לשון הקדש (אופיבאך, תקנ״א) דף ד עמ׳ ב.

[11] אברהם אבן עזרא, ספר צחות, מהדורת ג״ה ליפמאן (פיורדא, תקפ״ז, מחודש על־ידי י׳מקור, ירושלים, תש״ל) דף עג עמ׳ ב.

[12] בבבלי ברכי ט ע״א; ס ע״א.

[13] הציטוט הוא מפירושו הארוך, ודברים דומים באים בפירושו הקצר. נעיר כי גם לשיטת ראב״ע הנושא של ׳ויקרא׳ הוא ה׳, אלא שראב״ע רואה בפסוק שני נשואים — ׳ויעבר׳... ׳ויקרא׳ — לאותו נושא — ׳ה׳׳. כך יש להבין מדבריו: יואל תתמה בעבור שהשם קורא השם׳! אין ענייננו כאן בסוגיית דרך מנייננו של שלוש עשרה מידות, שיש המונים את שתי התיבות ׳ה׳ ה׳׳ כשתי מידות (וכך ראב״ע!), ויש

מן הדיון על הפסוק 'וישלח֣ אֶֽת־נַעֲרֵי֙ בְּנֵ֣י יִשְׂרָאֵ֔ל וַיַּֽעֲל֖וּ עֹלֹ֑ת וַֽיִּזְבְּח֞וּ זְבָחִ֧ים שְׁלָמִ֛ים לַה' פָּרִֽים׃' (שמ' כד, ה), בבבלי חג' ו ע"ב:

בעי רב חסדא: האי קרא היכי כתיב: 'וישלח את נערי בני ישראל ויעלו עלות' — כבשים, 'ויזבחו זבחים שלמים לה' פרים', או דלמא אידי ואידי פרים הוו? למאי נפקא מינה? — מר זוטרא אמר: **לפיסוק טעמים.**

ההתלבטות של רב חסדא, אם 'פרים' קשורה בפסוק רק לזבחי השלמים או גם לעולות, שאלה פרשנית היא, ובהעדר מסורת פיסוקית נותרת היא ללא הכרע. אך מסיום הפסקה — 'למאי נפקא מינה?' — ומתשובת מר זוטרא — 'לפיסוק טעמים' — אנו למדים על מעגל קסמים שפרשנות וטעמים סובבים עליו. שכן חז"ל הוטרדו לא רק מהעדר ההכרעה הפרשנית לפסוק, אלא אף מחוסר היכולת להכתיב על-פי פירוש הפסוק את פיסוק הטעמים שלו, שנתעלם מהם, ושהוא בגדר מטרה לעצמה.[7] עם זאת, במקרים כגון זה האחרון, אפשר גם שלא נתעלמה מחז"ל ההכרעה הפיסוקית של המקרא, אלא למרות שזו הגיעה לידיהם במסורת ברורה, התעלמו ממנה חז"ל ביודעין, והעדיפו לפסק ולפרש את המקרא בדרך אחרת. מכל מקום, פרשני ימי-הביניים, שלפניהם עמדה כבר בבירור מסורת הפיסוק של הטעמים, יש מהם שהורו היתר לעצמם לסטות ממנה. כך עולה מפירושו הקצר של ראב"ע על אתר: 'ומלת "פרים" על העולות ועל השלמים',[8] ובדומה מפירושו של רמב"ן על אתר: 'וטעם "לה' פרים"... והנה העלו העולות וזבחו השלמים כולם פרים'. אפשר שפרשנים אלה לא נתרעו מסטייה עצמאית ממסורת הפיסוק של הטעמים, אך אפשר גם שסטייה כזאת לא קשתה עליהם, משום שסברו, שחז"ל סללו לפניהם את הדרך להתעלם ממסורת הטעמים, או אף להתנגד לה.

5. לאור האמור לעיל ברור הוא, כי למרות שאין התלמוד מכיר עדיין סימנים גרפיים של טעמים, מודע הוא לקיומו של התפקיד המוסיקאלי-פיסוקי-פרשני שלהם, היינו: של המסורת שבעל-פה, שמאוחר יותר פותחה ובוטאה בשיטה גראפית. זאת ועוד: חז"ל ייחסו את הטעמים לתקופת עזרא. כך עולה מן הדרשות על הכתוב: 'ויקראו בספר בתורת האלהים מפרש ושום שכל ויבינו במקרא' (נחמ' ח, ח): '"ושום שכל" — אלו הטעמים' (ירו' מג' ד, א); '"ושום שכל" — אלו הפסוקין'; '"ויבינו במקרא" — אלו פסקי טעמים' (בבלי מג' ג ע"א; נדר' לז ע"ב). כיוצא בזה דרשו את האמור על קהלת שילַמַּד-דעת את-העם' (קה' יב, ט): 'דאגמריה בסימני טעמים' (בבלי עירובין כא ע"ב). ייחוסם של הטעמים לזמן קדום — לתקופת עזרא, וביתר הפלגה (המיוחסת אולי גם את סימני הטעמים) לקהלת (שלשיטת חז"ל הוא שלמה) — משקף את חשיבותם הרבה בעיני חז"ל. בדרך זו עולה דרגת הטעמים, שמלכתחילה אינם מהווים מרכיב של הטקסט, ומתקרבת אל הטקסט בזמן, כדי להתקרב אליו גם בסמכות. ואמנם בימי-הביניים היו שהפליגו

---

[7] רש"י בפירושו על אתר, ד"ה 'לפיסוקי טעמים', מודע כמובן לטעמים שנקבעו לפסוק, אך משים עצמו בערוס של חז"ל ומציין את שתי האפשרויות לפסק את הפסוק בהתאם לשני הפירושים האפשריים: 'לפסוקי טעמים — בנגינות. אם תאמר שני מינין — צריך אתה לפסוק הטעם של "ויעלו עלת" באתנחתא, כמו שאנו קורין אותו, או בזקף קטן, טעם שמפסיק הדבור ממה שאחריו. ואם מין אחד היה — צריך לקרותו באחד משאר טעמים שאין מפסיקין, כגון פשטא או רביעי.

[8] דבריו בפירושו הארוך על אתר — יזהכיר עם השלמים "פרים", כי האוכלים רבים היו' — ניתן להתאימם לפירושו הקצר, ולומר כי כוונתם להסביר מדוע נסמכה "פרים" דוקא לשלמים ולא לעולות, למרות שהיא מכוונת גם להם. אך אפשר לפרשם גם לפי פיסוק הטעמים, היינו: העולות לעצמן, והשלמים — לעצמם, וכיוון שהשלמים רבו אוכליהם פירט הכתוב את סוגם, מה שלא עשה בעולות.

3. העובדה שחז"ל ציינו שחמש מקראות בתורה אין להן הכרע' (בבלי יומא נב ע"א-ע"ב) מלמדת, שבדרך כלל ידעו את 'הכרעות' הפסוקים ממסורת שבעל-פה, ורק במקרים נדירים נתעלמה מהם ה'הכרעה'. מקרים אלה מצביעים על מסורות "מתרוצצות" באשר לפיסוק מקראות מסוימים, עד שהוכרעה התרוצצות זו וגברה אחת מן המסורות על רעותה. כך הוא המצב לגבי ארבעה מחמשת המקראות שנמנו שם (ברי' ד, ז; מט, ו-ז; שמי' יז, ט; כה, לד [= לז, כ]). בדרך כלל ניתן להבין את הסברה העניינית והלשונית שמאחורי המסורת הפיסוקית שנדחתה,[3] אך בשמי' כד, לד היא משקפת תפישה המייחסת למבנה תחבירי מקראי תפקיד שלא הוכר. כנגד המסורת הפיסוקית שגברה — ׳ובמנרה ארבעה גבעים מְשֻׁקָּדִים כפתריה ופרחיה:׳ — עומדת המסורת הפיסוקית שנדחתה — ׳ובמנרה ארבעה גבעים מְשֻׁקָּדִים כפתריה ופרחיה׳. זו מותירה את ׳כפתריה ופרחיה׳ תלויים על בלימה, כביכול. במקום אחר[4] הראינו, כי הכרע זה מתפרנס מתפישה תחבירית, שלפיה ׳כפתריה ופרחיה׳ = ׳כפתורים לה ופרחים לה׳, היינו: שתי פרדיקציות כאן ולא שתי סינטגמות.[5] הא למדת, שגם מסורות הפיסוק שנדחו לבסוף, הגיון להן ולימוד הן צריכות לא רק בשלב שלפני ההכרעה, כפי שראו חז"ל להתייחס אליהן, אלא אף בדיעבד, לאחר ההכרעה. מקרא חמישי ברשימה החז"לית, שאין לו הכרע, הוא: ׳הנך שֹׁכב עם־אֲבֹתֶיךָ וקם העם הזה וזנה...׳ (דבי' לא, טז). בניגוד לארבעת הפסוקים האחרים שברשימה, אין להניח כאן שהמסורת הפיסוקית שנדחתה נתכוונה להציע פשט חילופי לפסוק,[6] אלא זו נולדה מתוך "צורך" תיאולוגי, להציע פיסוק דרשני לפסוק — ׳הנך שֹׁכב עם־אֲבֹתֶיךָ וקם׳ — שישתול בתורה רמיזה לתחיית המתים. משהגיעו אל חז"ל שתי מסורות הפיסוק למקרא זה, נהגו בו כבמקראות האחרים, שכן חז"ל לא נטלו לעצמם את זכות ההכרעה בין המסורות.

4. בצד חמשת המקראות שאין להן הכרע' מצויים בספרות חז"ל עוד פסוקים שנתלבטו בפיסוקם. סבורים אנו, שההבדל בין המקרים שאין להן הכרע' לבין האחרים הוא בכך, שהראשונים הגיעו אל חז"ל כשהם מלווים במסורות פיסוק קדומות מתחרות, ואילו האחרונים — נתעלמה מחז"ל מסורת הפיסוק שלהם, היינו, זו לא הגיעה לידיהם בבירור. כך עולה, למשל,

---

3 מקרה פשוט הוא הפסוק בשמי' יז, ט. כאן שייכה המסורת שנדחתה את ׳מחר׳ לסוף הקיסורת הראשונה של הפסוק. בברי' מט צירפה המסורת שנדחתה את המלה הראשונה של פסוק ז לסוף פסוק ו, וקראה ׳...וברצונם עקרו שור ארור׳. קריאה זו מלמדת על אפשרות של העצמה של ׳ארור׳ במקרא והעמדתו כסומך בסמיכות ׳שור ארור׳, היינו: ׳שור של ארור׳ (׳שור של שכם, שהוא מארור כנען׳ — לשון רש"י ביומא נב ע"ב). מסורת הפיסוק שנדחתה לברי' ד, ז גרסה: יהלא אם-תיטיב [מוטב]; [אולם] שאת (= ׳יזכר לך העוון] ואם לא תיטיב׳. קריאה זו הניחה אפשרות שסיפא של תנאי תישמט, ותעשה את התנאי לתנאי ריטורי. היינו ׳אם תיטיב׳ = ׳מוטב שתיטיב׳. כמו כן מניחה קריאה זו, שחיבורם של שני תנאים יצמיד את ו"ו החיבור לרישא של התנאי השני, גם כשהוא בנוי בסדר ׳סיפא-רישא׳.

4 ראה ש' קוגוט, "שימושים חליפיים בכינויים פרודים וחבורים להבעת קניין בעברית המקראית", ספר היובל לכבוד פרופ' מ' גושן-גוטשטיין (בדפוס).

5 להלן בסעיף 8.5 נדון במקרים שטעמי המקרא ראו במבנה הנדון מבע פרדיקטיבי, והיו בכך עניינים לפרשן.

6 ראה דברי ראב"ע על אתר, המצביע על חוסר המשמעות של ׳העם הזה וזנה׳. מדרשות חז"ל לכמה פסוקים עולה שיטה של קריאה כפולה של מלה או מלים בפסוק — מעין הפלולוגיה. כך למשל נדרשות המלים ׳בנשך ובמרבית׳ (וי׳ כה, לז) בבלי ב"מ סא ע"א, וכן ׳יתננה ואכלה או מכור׳ (דבי' יד, כא) בבלי פסחים כא ע"ב. אך גם קריאה כפולה של ׳וקם׳ בפסוקנו, עם שתסייע לתחביר המשפט ׳[וקם] העם הזה וזנה׳, לא תהיה בגדר פשט הפסוק.

משורש 'שוב' / 'שָׁבֻ'נוּ — משורש 'שבי'[1] כן מובחנות צורות קָטַלְתִּי, קָטַלְתָּ, מהצורות המקבילות הצמודות לוי"ו ההיפוך — וְקָטַלְתִּי, וְקָטַלְתָּ. עניין זה עשוי היה להזמין ניגודים נושאי משמעות כאלה: וְקָטַלְתִּי, וְקָטַלְתָּ (וי"ו החיבור, עבר רגיל) / וְקָטַלְתִּי, וְקָטַלְתָּ (וי"ו ההיפוך, עבר מהופך). אולם ניגודים כאלה אינם מזדמנים בדרך-כלל במקרא, כיוון שהיצמדותן של צורות העבר הרגיל — קָטַלְתִּי, קָטַלְתָּ — אל וי"ו החיבור מתבקשת בעיקר, כשפעלים אלה מצטרפים אל פועל אחר שקדם להם. אולם בלשון המקרא הצטרפותם של שני פעלים המכוונים לזמן עבר נעשית ברגיל במבנה 'יָאקְטֹל וְאָקְטֹל' (וכיוצא בזה: 'יַתְקְטֹל וַתִּקְטֹל') או גם במבנה 'קָטַלְתִּי וְאָקְטֹל' (וכיוצא בזה: 'קָטַלְתָּ וַתִּקְטֹל'), אך לא במבנה 'קָטַלְתִּי וְקָטַלְתָּ'. על כן, בבר' יז, כ למשל, מנועה כנראה הטעמה אחרת מזו שבכתוב: 'הִנֵּה | בֵּרַכְתִּי אֹתוֹ וְהִפְרֵיתִי אֹתוֹ וְהִרְבֵּיתִי אֹתוֹ', ועל כרחך 'וְהִפְרֵיתִי' וכן 'וְהִרְבֵּיתִי' צורות עבר מהופך הן, והטעמה מלעילית של תיבות אלו ופירושן כצורות עבר רגיל ('וְהִפְרֵיתִי', 'וְהִרְבֵּיתִי') נדחית אפוא, לא רק בשל ההקשר שבהמשך — 'שנים עשר נשיאים יוליד'. נמצא, שמגבלות תחביריות מכתיבות מלכתחילה את ההטעמה המלרעית — וְקָטַלְתִּי, וְקָטַלְתָּ — ואת תפישת הצורות כעבר מהופך. ובכל זאת, אפשר שצורות וְקָטַלְתִּי, וְקָטַלְתָּ, תזדמנה במבנה תחבירי אחר, בהקשר שיתבע מן הפרשן הכרעה לטובת ההטעמה המלעילית. כך למשל בדב' יא, י: 'כִּי הָאָרֶץ אֲשֶׁר אַתָּה בָא-שָׁמָּה לְרִשְׁתָּהּ לֹא כְאֶרֶץ מִצְרַיִם הִוא אֲשֶׁר יְצָאתֶם מִשָּׁם אֲשֶׁר תִּזְרַע אֶת-זַרְעֲךָ וְהִשְׁקִיתָ בְרַגְלְךָ כְּגַן הַיָּרָק'. בעלי הטעמים פירשו יפה פה את 'וְהִשְׁקִיתָ' על-ידי הטעמתה המלעילית, כצורת עבר רגיל הצמודה לוי"ו החיבור, ומסתמא הבינו את 'אֲשֶׁר תִּזְרַע אֶת-זַרְעֲךָ' בהוראת 'אֲשֶׁר הָיִיתָ זוֹרֵעַ' (כפי שעולה גם מהתפסיר של רס"ג על אתר), וההמשך — 'וְהִשְׁקִיתָ בְרַגְלְךָ' — אף הוא מכוון לעבר. 'וְהִשְׁקִיתָ' בפסוק זה עומדת אפוא בניגוד להופעתה הרגילה כצורת עבר מהופך בהטעמה מלרעית, כמו בפסוקים שלהלן: 'וְהוֹצֵאתָ לָהֶם מַיִם מִן-הַסֶּלַע וְהִשְׁקִיתָ אֶת-הָעֵדָה' (במ' כ, ח); 'וְהִשְׁקִיתָ אוֹתָם יָיִן' (יר' לה, ב).

2. הפרשנות המסורתית למקרא, הן זו המפוזרת בספרות חז"ל, והן זו השיטתית של פרשני ימי-הביניים, ראוי לה שתיבדק בזיקה לפרשנות ה"אילמת" העולה מטעמי המקרא. כיוון הזיקה שבין פרשנות ימי-הביניים לבין טעמי המקרא הינו ברור, שכן טעמי המקרא עמדו לנגד עיני פרשנים אלה, ופירושיהם פעמים שספגו את פירוש הטעמים ופעמים שהתעלמו ממנו. לא כזה הוא המצב באשר לזיקה שבין פרשנותם של חז"ל לפסוקי מקרא לבין טעמי המקרא. כאן אפשר מלכתחילה לצפות להשתקפות של פרשנות הטעמים, בפרשנות הטעמים, וכששני אלו אינם עולים בקנה אחד, ניתן לכאורה לדבר על התעלמות הטעמים מפרשנות חז"ל לאותם כתובים, או על כך שבעלי הטעמים לא הכירו פרשנות מסוימת זאת. אולם, למרות שהסימנים הגראפיים של הטעמים הותקנו בזמן סמוך להתקנת סימני הניקוד (ולענייננו אין חשיבות לשאלה הבלתי מוכרעת איזו ממערכות הסימנים קדמה לרעותה), היינו לאחר חתימת התלמוד הבבלי,[2] קדמה להתקנת הסימנים מסורת מוסיקאלית-פיסוקית שנמסרה בעל-פה. על כן מוטב לדבר על קיומה או על אי-קיומה של זיקה בין פרשנות חז"ל לפרשנות הטעמים, מבלי להכריע בשאלת כיוון הזיקה. שכן אפשר שלא הטעמים מתבססים על פרשנות חז"ל או מתעלמים ממנה, אלא פרשנות חז"ל פעמים שהיא משמשת פה למסורת מוסיקאלית-פיסוקית שהולידה מאוחר יותר את סימני הטעמים, ופעמים שהיא מתעלמת ממסורת זו, או מתנגדת לה.

---

1 תן דעתך: 'וְאֶת-נְשֵׁיהֶם שָׁבוּ וַיָּבֹזּוּ' (בר' לד, כט) מתפרש על-פי הטעמים משורש 'שבי'. אך בהטעמה מלעילית היה הצירוף 'שָׁבוּ וַיָּבֹזּוּ' מתפרש על-פי שורש 'שוב', היינו חזרו ובזזו. מאידך גיסא, הפסוק 'וַיִּקַּח יוֹחָנָן בֶּן-קָרֵחַ וְכָל-שָׂרֵי הַחֲיָלִים אֵת כָּל-שְׁאֵרִית יְהוּדָה אֲשֶׁר-שָׁבוּ מִכָּל-הַגּוֹיִם...' (יר' מג, ה) מתפרש על-פי הטעמים משורש 'שוב', אך בהטעמה מלרעית — שָׁבוּ — היה מתפרש על-פי שורש 'שבי', ובעל "מצודת דוד" ראה להדגיש 'אשר שבו — אשר חזרו...'.

2 ראה: י' ייבין, מבוא למסורה הטברנית (ירושלים, תשל"ב) 114-115.

התייחסותה המפורשת של פרשנות המקרא המסורתית לשאלת המחוייבות לטעמי המקרא, והרקע למחוייבות זו

שמחה קוגוט

1. טעמי המקרא, המלווים את הטקסט המקראי, ממלאים בו-זמנית שלושה תפקידים. (א) תפקיד מוסיקלי: הם משמשים מעין מערכת תווים להשמעת הטקסט בלחן מקובל, כשהוא נקרא במסגרת ריטואלית; (ב) תפקיד פוניטי: הם מציינים את ההברה המוטעמת במלה, בהיותם צמודים אליה בדרך כלל (להוציא מספר טעמים פרפוזיטיביים ופוסט-פוזיטיביים); (ג) תפקיד פיסוקי-תחבירי: חלק מן הטעמים מתפקדים גם כסימני פיסוק, במערכת "הייראַרכית" של קיסרים, מלכים, משנים ושלישים, המחלקת את הפסוק בשיטה בִּינָארית (= דו חלקית), חלוקה לפנים מחלוקה, ומצביעה בדרך זו על קשרים תחביריים פנימיים בתוך הפסוק.

1.1 השלכותיו של התפקיד השלישי על פרשנות הטקסט ברורות מאליהן. שכן כל פיסוק וכל חלוקה תחבירית מצביעים על דרך הבנה מסויימת של הכתוב, ואגב כך הם עשויים לכוון לפירוש מסויים ולדחות פירוש אחר.

1.2 גם התפקיד המוסיקלי תורם למעשה לפיסוק, בצד היותו אמצעי שינון מנמוטכני. שכן הלחן מונע קריאה מונוטונית של הטקסט וגוזר עליו פיסוק ענייני בהתאם להפסקותיו שלו. התפקיד הפיסוקי, ולא המנמוטכני, הוא העומד מאחורי הקביעה הנחרצת המובאת בתלמוד בשם רבי יוחנן: "כל הקורא בלא נעימה ושונה בלא זמרה עליו הכתוב אומר "וגם אני נתתי להם חקים לא טובים" (יחז' כ, כה)' (בבלי מג' לב, ע"א). שכן לא העדר שינון הופך את חוקי האל ל'חקים לא טובים', אלא פיסוק מוטעה, המשבש את כוונתם.

1.3 גם לתפקיד הפוניטי של הטעמים ישנה זיקה לפרשנות הטקסט. ציון ההברה המוטעמת במילה, עם שמלכתחילה עניין לו בדיוק ההגייה בקריאת הטקסט, הרי במקרים שהטעם הוא פונימטי, מכריע ציון זה בין שני פירושים אפשריים. כך למשל מבחין הטעם בשורשי ע"י/ע"ו בין צורת עבר נסתרת (בָּאָה) לבינוני יחידה (בָּאָה), וראה פירוש רש"י לבר' כט, ט. במקרים מסויימים מבחין הטעם בין צורת עבר נסתרת של שורשים עלולים שונים, כגון: 'שָׁבוּ —

מפרשינו, כי נרמז כאן קושי (ראב"ע 'מי יוכל למצוא ...'; רלב"ג 'קשה'; מ"ד 'הוא דבר יקר ומילתא דלא שכיחא'), ואילו Kn: A man who has found. את שאלת הַכֶחָש הַשֶּׁבַע 'מִי ה' (משלי ל, ט) מבאר ראב"ע: 'כענין לא ידעתי את ה", ואילו רש"י: 'כלומר, אין אלהים'. 'מי אשר יבחר (קרי: יחבר) אל כל החיים' (קה' ט, ד) מבואר אצל מפרשינו כמשפט חיווי: 'כל מי שהוא מחובר וגו" (ראב"ע), 'בעודו בחיים וגו" (רש"י), ואילו V רואה כאן שלילה: nemo est qui semper vivat. 'כי מי יודע מה טוב לאדם ... מי יגיד לאדם' (קה' ו, יב) נתפש אצל היירונימוס כביטוי לאי-ידיעה כללית (cum ignoret ... quis ei poterit indicare), אך רש"י מעיר: 'צריך הוא שיהא מי יגיד לו'.

8.3 ולסיום שני מקראות, שהתפישה הפילולוגית לגבי תפקיד המלה 'מי' השפעה מכרעת לה על הפרשנות התיאולוגית.
'מי מדד בשעלו מים ושמים בזרת תכן' (יש' מ, יב); פסוק זה ואילך מתפרש בימינו בדרך כלל בתור שאלה מליצית, לגלגנית, הבאה להראות לאדם, כי אין שכלו האמפירי מסוגל להשיג את סוד הבריאה. אך ייתכן, כי בקטע נרמזת תפישה קוסמוגונית של ממש. בכל אופן, כך גורסים הקדמונים: עם שהבינו, כי הדברים נאמרים כלשון בני־אדם (רד"ק 'והוא על דבר משל, כי אין לו יד ואגרוף'; והיירונימוס (humanae consuetudinis verbis utitur), הריהם רואים בפסוקים אלה שבח לאל הבורא. רש"י: 'כל זה היה בו כח לעשותי'; רד"ק: 'מי שברא העולם מאין יכול לעשות זה'; היירונימוס: per quae Dei maiestas et Creatoris potentia demonstratur (IV,487).

8.4 דומה לכך מש' ל, ד, שיש בו קושיא נוספת, הריהי במילים 'מה שמו ומה שם בנו'. שוב החדשים רואים כאן שאילה של לגלוג, אך לא כן המפרשים שלנו. ראב"ע אומר: 'איני יכול לדעתו', ורש"י רואה במעשים 'עלה שמים, הקים אפסי ארץ' נפלאות, ואם יאמר האומר 'כבר היה דוגמתו, אמור מה שם בנו ... ונדע מיהו'. הרלב"ג הסיק מן הקטע מסקנות פילוסופיות לגבי הבריאה, ואין צריך לומר, כי 'שמו' ו'שם בנו' נתפרשו כדברים של ממש במדרש ובמסורת הנוצרית.

9.0 לשון האדם, העמימות והמידע משמשים בה בערבוביה. כלל זה חל גם על משפטי השאלה, שספק שאילה הם, ספק אמצעי סגנוני להבעת דעה; פירצה הקוראה לפרשנות.

6.1 את שאלתו המליצית של איוב 'ומה אתבונן על בתולה' (איוב לא, א) הופכים G (οὐ καὶ ὥς) ו-V (ut ne); תירגום זה מהדק את הקשר עם הרישא: 'כרתי ברית לעיני, כדי שלא...' למשפט חיווי שלילי; כן הרס"ג: 'פמא ...'.[26]

6.2 המגמה לפרש שאלה בתור שלילה, חזקה במיוחד ב-V: 'מי יוכל לתקן' (קה' ז, יג) - nemo possit corrigere; 'במה ישכבי' (שמ' כב, כו); 'למה יבאו (דה"ב לב, ד) - ne veniant; 'למה לי חיים' (בר' כז, מו) - nolo vivere; ועוד. לעומת זאת מוצאים אנו הפיכת שאלה מליצית שלילית למשאלה אצל הרס"ג: 'למה לא מרחם אמות' (איוב ג, יא) - 'ליתני מת פי בטן אמי'.[27]

7.1 השאלה האימפליקטיבית כוללת פרט ומציגה אותו כעובדה, אף שאינו כזאת. כך השאלות במ' כא, ה ו-יהו' ז, ז מנסות להציג את הכחדתם של בני ישראל ברעב ובחרב כמטרת העלתם ממצרים והכנסתם ארצה ולא רק כתוצאה אפשרית מכך. רעי איוב מציגים כעובדה, כי איוב חושב כבהמה, כששואלים הם כאילו רק לסיבת מחשבתו זו: 'מדוע נחשבנו כבהמה' (איוב יח, ג). גוזמה ריטורית מעין זו נובעת מן הרצון העז להביא לידי שינוי פני הדברים; לפיכך מצויה היא גם בדברי תפילה ותחנונים.

7.2 'למה אלהים זנחת לנצח' (תה' עד, א). המתרגמים אמנם מעתיקים את השאלה כצורתה, אולם מ"ד מבאר את הפסוק תוך הדגשה, כי אין מוסר הוא מצב כהוויתו אלא רק הרגשה: '... זה זמן רב עד שנראה כאלו כן יהיה לעולם'. בכל אופן על-פי פסוק זה יש להבין דומיו (שם, י, יג, ב; עט, ה; פט, מז ועוד), אלא שבהם מילת השאלה שברישא, המבקשת לדעת את אורך הזמן, סותרת את ההמשך, הקובע אותו, היינו 'ל(א)נצח'. סתירה זו מסירים המתרגמים על-ידי כך, שמחלקים את הפסוק לשתי שאלות,[28] וכן עושה מ"ד (תה' יג, ב); 'עד מתי אהיה נד ומטלטל, וכי תשכחני נצחי').

8.1 שאלה, הפותחת במלה 'מדוע' מבקשת לדעת, לשם מה נעשתה פעולה ומה תועלת בה, אלא שמילת השאלה צמודה לעתים לפעולה, שמן הבחינה ההגיונית אין השאלה חלה עליה. 'מדוע קויתי לעשות ענבים ויעש באושים' (יש' ה, ד); התמיההּ היא, כמובן, למה עשה הכרם באושים, ולא, מדוע קיוה בעליו לפירות טובים. המתרגמים החדשים מתקנים בהתאם, למשל KJ: Wherefore, when I looked... brought it forth. 'מדוע באתי ואין איש' (יש' נ, ב), BR: Weshalb war kein Mann, als ich kam. גם רד"ק מבאר: 'ולמה היה זה, כי באתי ואין איש עונה לי'.

8.2 כבר הערנו לגבי המלה 'מי', כי אפשר לפרשה כפתיחה לשאלה של ממש או כשלילה. ואף ככינוי סתמי משמע 'כל איש אשר...'.[29] כן לגבי 'אשת חיל מי ימצא' (מש' לא, י) מעירים

המשמעות הריטורית של המלית 'מי' (יודע') (קה' ג, כא) ומעיר: Pronomen enim QUIS in Scripturis sanctis non pro impossibili, sed pro difficili semper accipitur (III, 417).

[26] י' קאפח, איוב עם תרגום ופירוש הגאון רבנו סעדיה (ירושלים, תשל"ג) קנד.
[27] שם, עמ' מב.
[28] למשל, KJ (תה' יג, ב): How long ... O Lord? forever?.
[29] ארליך (לעיל, הערה 21), עמ' 347 מעיר לגבי המלה 'מי' ביח' לא, יח: 'כל החכמים עושים הדברים האלה שאלה ... ובאמת "מי" זה כמו אשר.

ופרשנים מן הפשט (פרט ל-KJ).[20]

G מנסח משפט חיווי (וכן הייתנימוס בפירושו filius dilectus mihi), ת״י מגביל את שלילת מעמדו המיוחד של ישראל לתקופה מסויימת (׳הכבר חביב קדמי ישראל...׳), L מכניס מלית שלילה לתוך השאלה ומחייב תשובה חיובית (...Ist nicht Ephraim), BR מרכך את השלילה (Ist ... ein so teurer Sohn).

ואילו המפרשים מבארים את השלילה בכך, כי אין העם דומה לבן יקיר, ׳שלא חטא ... לעולמ׳ (רד״ק) יעושה (לה׳) כל רצוני׳ (רש״י).

4.3 גם השאלה ׳הזבחים ומנחה הגשתם לי במדבר׳ (עמ׳ ה, כה) מבקשת תשובה שלילית, כפי שהעיר ראב״ע: ׳ה״א הזבחים ה״א התימה והנה הטעם שלא הגישו׳, וכן מתרגמים את השאלה כצורתה. בכל זאת עולה קושי עקב הסתירה למסופר בחומש, כדברי ארליך: ׳מי שעינים לו לראות... הלא יראה שהנביא השואל שאלה זו לא היה יודע שעשה משה במדבר׳.[21] הייתנימוס מנצל סתירה זו לפולמוס: בני ישראל במדבר לא הקריבו לה׳ אלא לאלילים או שלא הקריבו מרצונם אלא מתוך פחד.[22] קדמונינו מצאו תירוצים אחרים: לא בני ישראל נטטו להקריב אלא רק שבט לוי, או שלא ציווה ליחידים אלא לציבור וכיו״ב.[23]

5.0 התגובה החיובית, אשר לה מצפה השואל, בפותחו שאלה במלית ׳הלא׳ — גוני משמעות רבים לה לפי הנסיבות: היענות נדיבה לבקשתו (שמ״א כו, ד), הודאה בעובדה ידועה לכול (שם יב, יז) וכיו״ב.[24] גם בכתובים אלה לא מעטים הקשיים הפרשניים (תה׳ נו, ט,יד; ס, יב; קח, יב; איוב ד, ו), אלא שבהקשר הנושא שלנו נביא רק מקרים אחדים, שבהם הבנתה המדוייקת של השאלה תלויה בתפישתנו את סימניה הצורניים.

5.1 ׳הלא ידעת אם לא שמעת אלהי עולם ה״ (יש׳ מ, כח). הייתנימוס בתרגומו מפריד בין הצורנים הדבקים ׳הֲ/לא׳ בהעבירו את השלילה לתוך הפועל: numque nescis (במקום nonne cognovisti), ובין מפרשינו יש רואים במלית ׳אם׳ לא את מקבילתה הרגילה של ה״א השאלה אלא מלת תנאי, כאילו אמר: הרי ׳מדרך השכל׳ (רד״ק) יכולת להבין, גם אם ׳שמעת ׳ממלמד ומורה׳ (רד״ק, מ״ד).

6.0 מן המפורסמות הקשר בין שאלה לשלילה, המוצאת ביטויו בתיפקודן של אותן מליות בשני המשמעים (אין — מאין, מה — ערבית ׳מא׳ וכו׳); מקורו בשאלה הריטורית:[25] ׳מי מתפקד גם במשמע ׳אף אחד לא...׳, ׳מה׳ במשמע ׳לא כלום׳ וכן הלאה. על כך יש להוסיף, כי בכלל עשויים רגשות עזים למצוא את ביטויים בניסוח אינטרוגטיבי: ׳מי יתן׳ תחת ׳הלוואי, ׳איך׳ תחת ׳הוי׳, ׳מדוע׳ תחת ׳חבל׳ ודומיהם. מתוך תחום רחב זה דוגמאות ספורות, אשר בהן לשון והגות מעורבות בהשפעתן על הפרשנות.

---

20 KJ: Is Ephraim my dear son?.
21 א׳ ארליך, מקרא כפשוטו ג (ברלין, תרס״א) 411.
22 Quae in deserto obtulit Israel, non deo obtulisse, sed Moloch regi suo ... non voluntate, sed poenarum fecerunt metu (VI, 305).
23 ראב״ע: ׳קדמונינו ז״ל אמרו כי הלויים הקריבו, ואם היא קבלה קבלנו, כי על דרך הפשט — לא הקריבו׳.
24 ספק אם קיים קשר — ומהו — עם הצורן האוגריתי ׳הל׳ (= הנה); אך אכמ״ל.
25 C. Brockelmann, *Grundriss der vergleichenden Grammatik der semitischen Sprachen* (2 vols.; Berlin, 1908-1913) 2:111-115. הייתנימוס מנסה לעמוד על

3.3 בשאלתו 'מי יודע ... העלה היא למעלה' (קה' ג, כא) מביע החכם את ספקו בדבר הישארות הנפש, או אף שולל אמונה זו (על הצירוף 'מי יודע' ראה להלן), אולם לפרשנות המסורתית, כיהודית כנוצרית, קשה לקבל, כי שלמה המלך הביא עצמו לידי הרהור, אשר videtur esse blasphemum (היירונימוס). הפרשן הנוצרי תרץ את הקושי על-פי אמונתו, לאמור שהמאמר יפה עד בוא משיחם,[16] ואילו הנקדנים הסירו את השאלה בנקדם ה"א היידוע (הָעֹלָה ... הַיֹּרֶדֶת, ולא: הַ... הַ...; השווה ראב"ע). וכן קובע רש"י: 'רוח בני אדם היא העולה למעלה ועומדת בדין ... צריך שלא להתנהג כבהמה'. בין התרגומים הידועים רק KJ הולך בעקבות פרשנות זו: Who knoweth the spirit of man that goeth upward.[17]

4.0 הכלל הוא לגבי השאלה המליצית, כי מניסוחה החיובי מסתברת תשובה שלילית, ולהיפך, ניסוחה השלילי מחייב תשובה חיובית. ליתר דיוק: אם עובדה ידועה לשואל ולנשאל זה מכבר, אפשר להדגישה דוקא על-ידי שאלה, הטוענת את ההיפך, ואשר מאלצת את הנשאל לסתור את הטענה ולאשר את העובדה מחדש. כלל זה, הכרוך בפסיכולוגיה של הלשון, מוצא, כידוע, ביטוי גם בשפות אחרות.[18] אולם מצויים במקרא מקרים, שלכאורה מופר בהם הכלל הזה.

4.1 'הנגלה נגליתי אל בית אביך' (שמ"א ב, כז). על-פי הכלל דלעיל מתבקשת תשובה שלילית, ואילו המסורת ההיסטורית מחייבת תשובה חיובית, וכן רד"ק יהה"א לאמת הדבר כפשוטו; ואפשר להניח, כי אלהים בוחן, כביכול, את עלי הכהן, כלשון רש"י: 'היֹדעתם ...'. אך מותר לראות בכתוב שאלה ריטורית (הרד"ק מביא את דעת אביו), אם כוללים בה את הסיפא לאמור: הנגליתי ובחרתי אותך, כדי שתבעט? כך עשה BR: habe ich mich darum offenbart etc.

התרגומים בוחרים בדרכים שונות: G משמיט את צורן השאלה בכלל והופך את המשפט להיגד חיובי (כן L), ואילו V מנסח שאלה מליצית אך מכניס לתוכה מלת שלילה: numquid non aperte revelatus sum, ואזי התשובה המצופה, כמובן: 'אכן נגלית ...'.[19]

4.2 גם על השאלה, הנשאלת בשם ה' מפי הנביא 'הבן יקיר לי אפרים' (יר' לא, כ) התשובה המצופה שלילית, ואכן זו הכוונה, והראייה בהמשך: (כיוון שאין הוא בני יקירי, תמוה כי) 'זכור אזכרנו עוד', כאילו היה — אף שאינו כזה — ילד שעשועים. אולם רעיון זה נראה סותר את המסורת בפסוקים כגון 'אמר ה' בני בכרי ישראל' (שמ' ד, כב) ודומיו, ולפיכך סטו מתרגמים

חיווי בפי בית יעקב, אך מן הסתם גרסו 'האומרי' (G: ὁ λέγων).

16 .... ad adventum Christi (bestiae et homines) ad inferos pariter ducerentur (III,416) — למן ימי גייגר מקובלת הסברה, כי הניקוד פרי מגמה תיאולוגית; נימוקיו של גורדיס (R. Gordis, *Koheleth* [New York, 1968] 238) נגד סברה זו אינם משכנעים.

17 G: εἰ ... εἰ; V: si .. si; BR: ob ... ob.

18 H. Müller-Solger, "Zum Problem der Frage in der Textauslegung," *Zeitschrift für Literaturwissenschaft und Linguistik* 17 (1975).

19 מ"צ סגל, ספרי שמואל (ירושלים, 1968) כז, מעיר: 'שאלה מליצית המשמשת להדגיש את אמתות האמור ולהסיר את כל הספקות מלב השומע המוכרח להשיב על השאלה בהסכם לדעת השואל, אך אינו מביא שום ראייה, שאכן קיימת שאלה ריטורית בנוסח חיובי, המכריחה להשיב בחיוב. הפסוקים, אשר סגל מביא, הם בחינת מעשה לסתור: שמ"א כג, יט — מלת השאלה שלילית דוקא 'הלא'; שמ"ב ז, ה — מחייב שלילה, השווה דה"א יז, ד.

1.4 '...גם בעיני יפלא נאם ה'' (זכ' ח, ו); לפי הפשט הרי בעיני ה' נפלאה גאולת ישראל באותה מידה כפי שנפלאה היא בעיני הגאולים. וכן דעתו של רש"י: 'גם בעיני יפלא, איך שבתי מן החרון הגדול', וגם ראב"ע אומר: 'גם בעיני עשיתי פלא גדול... לא עשיתי כמוהו', אולם מביא הוא דעה אחרת, הגורסת, כי יה"א התימה חסר, כאילו כתוב "הגם בעיני יפלא"'. וכך המתרגמים כגון V: numquid in oculis meis difficile erit.[10] אין להתעלם מן השוני שבין הפרשנויות, הכרוכות בשתי התפישות: האחת מבליטה את גודל הנס, עד כי אפילו הקב"ה מתפעל כביכול ממנו, ואילו השניה מהללת את עליונותו של האל מעל בשר ודם.

1.5 אחרי שהזכיר הנביא את חטאי ישראל אומר הוא: 'לא תשיגם בגבעה מלחמה' (הו' י, ט). אף כי הבטחה זו נראית תמוהה, מוסרים אותה התרגומים העתיקים כצורתה, וכן מפרש רש"י. אף רד"ק רואה כאן חיווי, אולם כוזב: 'יואלה חושבים בלבם שלא תשיגם מלחמה'. ממש כך היירונימוס בפירושו sicut ipsi putant, אבל מביא הוא גם דעה אחרת: nonne oportet eum a proelio comprehendi (VI, 114s.), היינו שאלה. כך נוהגים התרגומים החדשים.[11]

2.1 בלשון חז"ל מתפקדת המילית 'אוכי' כפתיחה לשאלה ריטורית, כשתשובתה המצופה שלילית. ייתכן, כי ניתן לגלות את ראשיתו של שימוש זה בטקסטים מקראיים;[12] בכל אופן, היו שפירשו כתובים מתוך הנחה זו. שמ"א כד, כ אפשר להבינו כפסוק מקוטע, שמשמעו 'כאשר ימצא איש את אויבו ושלחו בדרך טוב "האל ישלם לו טובה" (רד"ק), וכן ה' ישלמך וגו' או 'אם ימצא ... האמנם ... (ו'ו התמיהה) ישלח וגו'' (will he send him away).[13] אולם מ"ד: יר"ל, וכי נעשה מעולם כזאת שימצא וגו', וברוח דומה V: quis enim cum etc.

3.1 אפילו מצויה תווית הה"א בראש משפט, לא ברור בכל המקרים, אם היא צורן הידוע או צורן השאלה; ואין צריך להזכיר, כי הניקוד אינו מהימן בנידון, באשר הוא עצמו מהווה פירוש. כך חלוקות הדעות לגבי הפסוק 'האיש אחד יחטא ועל כל העדה תקצף' (במ' טז, כב): KJ, V, G רואים כאן שאלה,[14] הנקדנים והמפרשים שלנו וכן BR, L חיווי (נוסח השומרוני: 'האיש האחד'). ההבדל דק, אך נראה, כי בשאלה כרוך רמז של הרהור כללי אחר דרכי ה'.

3.2 המחלוקת בקשר לפסוק 'האמור בית יעקב הקצר רוח ה'' (מי' ב, ז) נוגעת לענין, מי השואל 'הקצר' וגו'. אם הה"א הידוע יש במלה 'האמור' הרי שהפנייה היא של הנביא אל העם 'שמע, אתה הקרוא בית יעקב' (ראב"ע) – 'הקצר וגו'' (כן רד"ק), ואילו אם ה"א של 'האמור' תימה, הרי שהעם משמיע את השאלה שבסיפא (גם דעה זו אצל ראב"ע: 'הדבר זה שיהיה אמור – בלשון תימה'), כדברי רש"י 'הזאת יאמרו בית יעקב כששומעים וכו''. מחלוקת דומה בקרב המתרגמים.[15]

---

10 KJ: Should it also be marvellous in mine eyes. מ"צ סגל (תנ"ך, מהדורה ספרותית, [תל-אביב, תשי"א]) מוסיף סימן שאלה.
11 Kn: ... was it not; BR: Soll sie nicht... BHS מציעה לגרוס: 'הלא (תשיגם)'.
12 השווה שמ"ב ט, א; איוב ו, כב; מל"ב יח, כב; לד לעומת ישי' לו, יט וכו'. לגבי לשון חז"ל ראה בבלי ר"ה ט, ע"א, שבת ד, ע"א ועוד הרבה.
13 S. R. Driver, Notes on the Hebrew Text of the Books of Samuel (Oxford, 1913) 195 בדומה לתרגומים החדשים.
14 V: ... num uno peccante; KJ: shall one man sin; אבל G:... εἰ.
15 השווה, למשל, KJ: O (thou that art) named ... the house of Jacob, is the spirit etc. לעומת BR:...Wird noch immer gesprochen. גם התרגומים הקלאסיים מוסרים משפט

בבחינת שאלה ריטורית על גוניה; α/א   שקול כנגד חיווי מודגש; β/א   בוחן את הנשאל; γ/א
מפגין את השכלתו של השואל לעומת בורותו של הנשאל; γ/ב   משתף את הנשאל בהרהורי
השואל; γ/ג   מדגיש את חוסר הידע הכללי.

0.3   מסתבר, איפוא, כי מלאכתו של העוסק במקרא אינה פשוטה: קודם כל עליו לקבוע, אם
מבע מסויים הוא שאלה מבחינת הסימנטיקה (וחסרים הסממנים שבדיבור כגון עקומת
הצליל!), ולאחר מכן, אם אכן שאלה לעיניו, עליו לגלות, מה טיבה מבחינת הפרגמטיקה.
במקרים רבים ההכרע קשה, ואין תימה, כי לגבי כתובים רבים חלוקות דעות הפרשנים.[5] להלן
נביא דוגמאות מספר מתוך המבחר הרחב.

1.1   עקב השימוש הפקולטטיבי בצורני שאלה אפשר לפרש כתובים מסויימים לכאן ולכאן.
'גדול עוני מנשוא' (בר' ד, יג) מתפרש על פי רוב כחיווי, בין אם רואים בדברי קין וידוי, כי אכן
חטאו גדול מכדי שייסלח לו,[6] או תלונה על חומרת העונש, שאין כוח לשאתו,[7] אולם רש״י רואה
כאן שאלה מופנית אל אלהים: האמנם לא תוכל לסלוח לי על עווני?[8]

1.2   'זה חסדך את רעך' (שמ״ב טז, יז) נמסר כחיווי, מן הסתם אירוני, על-ידי המתרגמים
הקלאסיים (G, V), ואילו החדשים (KJ, L) רואים כאן שאלה, כפי שכבר מנסח זאת מ״ד: 'וכי
זהו החסד...?'. דברי איזבל 'אתה עתה תעשה מלוכה וגו'' (מל״א כא, ז) הם הצהרה בדבר
סמכותו הריבונית של המלך (V: grandis auctoritatis es) אשר למן הרגע ההוא יוצא מן הכוח
אל הפועל (BR: ... Du-jetzt sollst du), או שאלה של לעג (רד״ק: 'לשון תמיהה', רלב״ג: ר״ל
האם...'), שמטרתה לדרבן את המלך לפעול בתקיפות.

1.3   'ולא אחד עשה' (מלי ב,טו); צירוף זה קשה בהקשרו ורבו פירושיו, עד שאי־אפשר לסקור
אותם. ענייננו להראות, כי התפישה בדבר סוג המשפט משפיעה על הפרשנות. לפי ראב״ע הוא
חיווי: 'ולא אחד מכם עשה כדת', לפי V שאלה: nonne unus fecit, דהיינו: האם לא האל האחד
ברא איש ואשתו? גם לפי רד״ק יש פה שאלה, אלא שבאה מפי סוררים ומורים: 'וכי 'אברהם
אבינו ע״ה שהיה אחד לא עשה כן כמו שאנחנו עושים? שהניח אשתו ובעל הגר שפחתו...'.[9]

---

[5] הקיצורים לציון המפרשים מקובלים (מ״ד = מצודת דוד), ואלה התרגומים:
G = Septuaginta (מהדורת Rahlfs)
V = Vulgata (מהדורת Weber)
L = Luther (מהדורת 1545)
BR = Buber-Rosenzweig (1976-79)
KJ = King James Version
Kn = Knox Version
ההערות הפרשניות של היירונימוס מובאות על־פי מהדורת Vallarsi (כרך, עמודה).

[6] רמב״ן '... והנכון בפשט שהוא ודוי, אמר, אמת כי עוני גדול מלסלוח וצדיק אתה ה״. V: maior
est iniquitas mea quam ut veniam merear. ובדומה כבר G, וכן L, BR.

[7] ראב״ע: '... והטעם כי זה העונש גדול לא אוכל לסבלו'; KJ: My punishment is greater than
I can bear.

[8] רש״י: 'בתמיה. אתה טוען עליונים ותחתונים ועוני אי אפשר לטעון?'

[9] גם לותר, המתרגם את הפסוק כמשפט חיווי, אימץ את הפירוש הזה, שלפיו 'האחד' הוא אברהם,
והוא מעיר בהערת שוליים: Abraham ... nam ein ander Weib nicht aus furwitz, wie jr
thut, sondern das er Gotte Kinder zeugete. BR מעתיק שאלה, אלא שהמלה 'אחד'
הופכת למושא: Und hat er nicht in Eins sie gemacht.

התאמה בין ההיבט הצורני של הפסוק ובין כוונת המבע קיימת רק במקרים א/α, ב/β, ג/γ ואילו בשאר המקרים על השומע לחשוף את משמעו של המבע מבעד התבנית הלשונית, שלתוכה יצק הדובר את כוונתו. הווה אומר לגבי עניננו: אפילו נעדר מן הפסוק הסימון החיצוני, המציין על פי רוב את אופיו האינטרוגטיבי של המבע, חובה עלינו לבדוק שמא שמא הוא מבטא שאלה תמיהה.

0.2 סיבוך נוסף בכך, כי מהותה של שאילה אינה חד־משמעית, כפי שנרמז כבר בהוסיפנו את המלה 'תמיהה' על קודמתה. כמובן, השימוש הבולט בשאילה הוא בפניית השואל אל הנשאל לצורך בקשת מידע (ואף פה יש להבחין בין תת־סוגים, כגון שאלת הכרע, שאלת הכרע מדומה, שאלת השלמה וכיוצא באלה), אולם לעתים אין השאילה מבקשת מידע אלא מביעה את רחשי לבו של השואל: השאלה מליצית, ריטורית, ובה עסקינן.[3]

אולם גם פה המונח וההגדרה הפשטניים עשויים להטעות, כאילו בכל המקרים האלה לפנינו שאלה מדומה, אשר תשובתה ידועה לכול.[4] קשת הנסיבות, שבהן משמשת השאלה הריטורית, רחבה למדיי:
אין נכללות בסוג הזה רק מליצות של נואם או הבעות רחשי לב הדובר; יש גם שאלות הבאות לעורר את מחשבתו של השומע או לבחון את ידיעותיו ועוד. ההכרעה, אם שאלה "ריטורית" היא, דהיינו מדומה, תלויה במידת הידיעות לגבי הנושא הן אצל השואל והן — על פי הערכתו — אצל הנשאל.

השואל	הנשאל		
	ידיעה α	חוסר ודאות β	אי ידיעה γ
א. ידיעה	שאלה רטורית	שאלה רטורית	שאלה רטורית
ב. חוסר ודאות		שאלה רטורית	שאלה רטורית
ג. אי־ידיעה		שאלה רטורית	שאלה רטורית

יוצא כי רק כאשר השואל אינו יודע דבר לגבי הנושא (ג) או אינו בטוח בידיעתו (ב), אך מניח זו אצל הנשאל כוודאית (α) או כאפשרית (β), כוונתו להשיג אינפורמציה; שאר השאלות הן

---

3 (1972) T. E. Pratt, *The Meaning of the Interrogative in the O.T.* (עם ביבליוגרפיה). מ׳ דובשני, "סוגי השאלות בתנ״ך", ספר יוסף ברסלבי (ירושלים, תש״ל) 160־170, מביא דוגמאות לא מעטות, אך מיונן פגום מבחינת הסדר וההגיון. כך למשל, דרים ירי יב, א; תהי ח, ה בכפיפה אחת של שאלות שאין עליהן בכלל תשובה׳, אף כי השאלה הראשונה מביעה מחאה (שלא בדין דין רשעים צלחה), והשניה ענווה (אין אנוש ראוי כי תזכרנו), ועוד כהנה וכהנה. C. Brockelmann, *Hebräische Syntax* (Neukirchen, 1956), index, "Frage, rhetorische"
4 אולריך (לעיל, הערה 1), עמ׳ 45: "Scheinfrage ohne Erwartung einer Antwort"

השאלה המליצית במקרא ופרשנותה

בנימין קדר

0.1 סיווג המשפטים לשלושה סוגים, והם החיווי (declarative), הציווי (imperative), והשאלה (interrogative) מגלה טפח ומכסה טפחיים, קודם כל משום שלא ברור, אם המיון ייעשה על-פי בחנים צורניים-מורפוסינטקטיים או סימנטיים-סיטואטיביים.[1] הרי התבוננות, אף החטופה ביותר, במבעים ממשיים מלמדת אותנו, כי כל אחד משלושת הסוגים, אם נמיינם על-פי צורתם, עשוי לשמש להבעת דעה או פקודה או שאלה; ידגים זאת הלוח:

צורת המבע	משמע המבע		
	היגד α	פקודה β	שאלה γ
חיווי א	מראיך נאוה[2]	לא הודעתני (=הודע נא)	ולא הודעת את עבדיך (=מדוע לא)
ציווי ב	ראה עניי (הנני עני)	הודיעני נא	הגידה נא שמך (מה שמך)
שאלה ג	מה נאוו... רגלי מבשר (נאוו רגלי)	למה זה תשאל לשמי (אל תשאל)	מה שמך

---

1 R. H. Robins, *General Linguistics* (London, 1971) 271ff.; T. Lewandowski, *Linguistisches Wörterbuch* (Heidelberg, 1985) 3.85. הוספת סוג רביעי (exclamation, Ausrufesatz), המצויה לרוב [Cambridge, *Theoretical Linguistics* ,Lyons .J) 123 [Kiel, 1972] *Linguistische Grundbegriffe* ,Ulrich .W ;178 [1971 אינה מצודקת, לא מצד הצורה ולא מצד התוכן התקשורתי.

2 מראי מקום: שה"ש ב, יד; שמ' לג, יב; מל"א א, כז; תה' כה, יח; שמ' לג, יג; בר' לב, ל; יש' מב, ז; בר' לב, כז, ל.

יקבצנו,[19] ועוד מעט יסור מעליו משאם, סבלם,[20] של המלך והשרים. יָחֵלוּ* עניינו לפי פירוש זה "יתירו את קשרי המשא", "יסירו את המשא מעליהם".

אבל לא פירושו של כתוב זה שבהושע הוא במרכז דברינו על שימושו של 'חלל' במקרא. מה שאנו מבקשים להצביע עליו הוא שהסימימה הבסיסית שלו 'התרת הקשר' כמעט שאינה מצויה כלל במקרא (ואפשר שאינה מצויה כל עיקר, שהרי הכתוב בהושע מוקשה הוא ביותר, ואין פירושנו אלא בבחינת הצעה), אבל נגזרותיה הסימנטיות נפוצות. וכן הוא לגבי הסימימה המופשטת של 'אסר', בהוראת "ביקש למנוע עשייתה של פעולה". ואילו בלשון חכמים נתגבשה האנטונימיה בין 'התיר' לבין 'אסר', במשמעותן המופשטת, גיבוש סופי (יחבש' הוא המשמש ברגיל במשמעותו המוחשית של 'אסר' המקראי; והשווה לשימוש לשימוש צורותיהן של שני השורשים: 'אין חבוש מתיר את עצמו מבית האסורים' — ברכות ה ע"ב), והיא מקבילה במלואה לאנטונימיה שבין 'שרא' לבין 'אסר' בארמית.

ולא זו בלבד, אלא שאף הקוינה של היוונית של הברית החדשה עניין הוא לכאן. אנו מוצאים בה התפתחות מקבילה: מן המשמעות המוחשית של האסירה, הקשירה והנחלה, אל המשמעות המופשטת של האיסור.[21]

אשר לסימימה העיקרית השנייה של 'חלל', המציינת את התחלת הפעולה, ניתן להניח שהיא קשורה קשר מיטונימי לסימימה של 'התרת הקשר'. בערבית נפוצות נגזרותיה של סימימה זאת, והן מציינות את החניה במקום (לסאן אלעראב: حَلَّ بالمكان – نزول القوم بمحلة وهو نقيض الارتحال "חניית אנשי השבט במקום מסוים, ומשמעות זאת מנוגדת למשמעות הנדידה"), את המושגים של "שכונה", "מקום", את מושג הדבר המותר בכללו (حَلَال בניגוד לـ حَرَام) את האשה (حَلِيلَة – "המותרת לבעלה") ואת הבעל (حَلِيل – "המותר לאשתו"), ועוד. ייתכן שהקשר בין הסימימה של ההתחלה מסתבר, כאמור, כהתפתחות מיטונימית: התרת קשר המשא שעל גב הגמל, היא ראשיתו של מעשה החנייה במדבר. קווי התפתחותו של 'חלל' הערבית מקבילים לקווי ההתפתחות של 'שרא' הארמי, וגם בו שתי סימימות עיקריות אלה של ההתרה, המוחשית והמופשטת — ומכאן המגורים והשהייה — ושל ההתחלה. עניין לציין שאף šurru(m) האכדי מציין את התחלת הפעולה.

---

19 לעניין הזיקה שבין משמעות הקיבוץ והאיסוף לבין הוראת ההצלה והישועה ראה: יהושעתי את הצלעה והנדחה אקבצי (צפ' ג, יט).

20 לעניין הסרת הסבל כמטאפורה של שחרור וגאולה ראה: 'ביום ההוא יסור סבלו מעל שכמך ועלו מעל צוארך' (ישי י, כז; וכן שם יד, כה); 'הסירותי מסבל שכמו' (תה' פא, ז).

21 ראה דרט (לעיל, הערה 17).

דברי", כבלשון חכמים ובלשוננו היום. כפועל מצויה משמעות זאת ככל הנראה בכתוב אחד, ובו לבדו, והוא בסיפור מעשה יוסף בתהלים קה. ראשיתו של הסיפור במעשה זה בפסוק יז, שלח לפניהם איש לעבד נמכר יוסף', והמשכו בפסוקים כ-כב: (כ) 'שלח מלך ויתירהו מֹשֵל עמים ויפתחהו; (כא) שָֹמוֹ אדון לביתו ומשל בכל קנינו; (כב) לֶאְסֹר שׂריו בנפשו וזקניו יְחַכֵּם'. סביר לומר, שאין הצרף 'לאסר שריו' מכוון לכבילתם של שרי פרעה בכבלים, אלא לסמכותו של יוסף להטיל איסורים על שרי פרעה; אף ההקבלה בין 'לאסר שריו' לבין 'וזקניו יחכם'[15] מלמדת על כך.[16]

אף מצויה כאן מעין הוראת־משנה אנטונימית העולה מן הניגוד שבין הצרף שלפנינו, לבין האמור בפסוקים יח, כ: 'ענו בכבל רגליו ברזל באה נפשו ... שלח מלך ויתירהו משל עמים ויפתחהו'. ומלת 'נפשו' משמשת חוליה המחברת את הכבילה בכבלים (פסוק יח) לבין האיסור הנאמר במאמר פה (פסוק כ).[17] אין צריך לומר שהסימימה של האיסור מצויה בשמות העצם המקראיים 'אָסַר' ו'אָסָר'; אבל בתחום הפועל סימימה זאת היא יחידאית במקרא בכתוב שלפנינו. כידוע היא שכיחה בעברית שלאחרי המקרא.

הסימימה המנוגדת של ה'היתר', במשמעו המוחשי, כלומר "התרת קשר", אינה באה במקרא בשורש 'חָלַל' (כלומר השורש המקביל לערבית حَلَّ, להבדיל מן 'חִלֵּל' = ערבית خَلّ, "נָקַב, פָּרַץ"), אולי להוציא כתוב מוקשה בספר הושע, שבו אפשר שהיא מצויה. אנו עומדים על סימימה זאת מתוך ההשוואה לערבית, שבה משמעו הבסיסי של حَلَّ הוא 'התרת קשר'. נפוצות בעברית הנגזרות המשמעותיות של סימימת יהתרת האיסורי: בתחום הפועל - יַחֲלֵּל' (יח' כה, ג), 'מְחַלְּלַי' ('שמי הגדול המחלל בגוים' – יח' לו, כא) ועוד, ובתחום השם – 'חלי' שהוא ניגודו של 'קדשי', יָחָלָי' (יח', כא, ל: 'ואתה חלל רשע נשיא ישראל' – 'נשיא ישראל שכבודו חֻלַּל'; 'אשה זנה וחללה' – וי' כא, ז, וראה גם שם יד). אף הסימימה העיקרית השנייה שבשורש זה, והיא המציינת את התחלה הפעולה קשורה, ככל הנראה, לסימימה של התרת הקשר, ולעניין זה נחזור בקצרה בהמשכם של הדברים.

אותו כתוב בהושע, שבו אפשר שמצויה סימימה זאת של התרת הקשר הריהו: 'גם כי יתנו בגוים עתה אקבצם וַיָּחֵלוּ מעט ממשא מלך שרים' (ח, י). ניתן לפרש פסוק מוקשה זה – ואיני מזכיר דבר זה אלא בקיצור[18] – ככתוב שיש בו נימת נחומים בתוך נבואה קשה, האומר שאף־על־פי שהעם חטא, התנה אהבים עם הגוים ('גם כי יתנו בגויםי'), לא תבוא עליו כליה גמורה; ה'

---

15 ואפשר ש'יחכם' משמעה 'ימשל', כמשמעות הפועל בערבית.

16 'ובנפשו' 'הוא עצמו' (בְּנַפְשֹׁה), והשווה: 'נשבע ה' צבאות בנפשו' (יר' נא, יד, עמ' ו, ח). ואף 'כי בנפשו דבר אדניהו (מל"א ב, כג) עניין הוא לכאן, שהרי אדניהו עצמו פונה אל בת־שבע בבקשה ששלמה יתן לו את אבישג לאשה (פסוק יז), ואילו בת־שבע, בדבריה אל שלמה אומרת: 'יִתַּן את אבישג השונמית לאדניהו אחיך לאשה', ואינה מפרשת שזאת היא בקשת אדניהו. ולאחר מכן דוד אומר בשבועתו (פסוקים כג-כד) – אדוניהו יומת, כי הוא עצמו אמר את הדברים האלה, ביקש בקשה זאת. והשווה בכתובות חרסי ערד: 'ידבר אתכם המלך בנפשכם' = אתכם בעצמכם (חרס 24, שו' 18; אהרני לא פירש את תיבת 'נפשכם').

17 לשימושו של 'אסרי' בכתוב הנידון בתהלים ראה J. Duncan and M. Derrett, "Binding and Loosing (Matt 16:19; 18:18; John 29-23)," *JBL* 102 (1983) 112-117 (ולעניין זה, שם, עמ' 115).

18 לפירוטם של דברים ראה: ש' מורג, "חקר לשון המקרא: אטימולוגיה וסימנטיקה", דברי הקונגרס העולמי השמיני למדעי היהדות, ישיבות מרכזיות – מקרא ולשון עברית (ירושלים, תשמ"ג) 56-57.

את ההוראה של הגינוי, כלומר "אמירת דברי הסתייגות או תוכחה לגבי מעשים שיש בהם סטייה מדרך הישר".

בערבית היקף תחומו הסימנטי של הסימה של הסטייה המוסרית הוא רחב יותר. נגזרותיו הצורניות של גֹנַי משמשות בשני שדות סימנטיים: שדה הפשיעה ושדה הבשלת הפרי. בראשון משמשות צורות כגון جنى "פֶּשַׁע", ובשדה השני צרפים כגון أجنت الأرضُ "האדמה נתנה יבול שופע".

נדירות הן ההיקרויות שבהן מצויה בנגזרותיו הצורניות של שורש זה הסימה של הסטייה המוחשית, הפיסית, מן הקו הישר. לסאן אלערב אינו מביא אלא דוגמה אחת לכך: وفي حديث ابي بكر رضي الله عنه أنه رأى أبا ذر رضى الله عنه فدعاه فجنى عليه فسارّه (על אבו בכר, ירצהו האל, (מסופר) שהוא ראה את אבו ד'ר, ירצהו האל, וקרא אותו אליו **וכפף עצמו כלפיו** ודיבר עמו בסוד". הילסאן' מסביר: جنى عليه – أكبّ عليه, כלומר "התכופף", והוא מוסיף, שבמקורו השורש הוא جَنَأ, שמשמעו "נטה ופנה אל..." (مال عليه وعطف); לאחר שאיבד ההגה הסופי בו, ההמזה, את עיצוריותו, נעשה جَنَأ לְ- جَنى.[12]

מאחר ששורש זה جَنَأ, בא' סופית, אינו משמש בשדה הסימנטי של הסטייה המוסרית והפשיעה, נמצאים אנו למדים, שהמעבר מן הסימה של הסטייה והנטייה, הקיימת במשמעות של התכופפות, כלומר בנגזרותיו של השורש جَنَأ, חלה בערבית לאחר שֶ- جَنَأ נעשה جَنى. ולאחר שינוי צורני זה, קרה למעשה בידול בערבית. שימושו של جَنى בהוראת ההתכופפות הוא נדיר, ובה משמש בעיקר جَنَأ. במשמע הסטייה המוסרית והפשיעה משמש جَنى (לבד משימושו האחר, שהזכרנוהו לעיל, בשדה הבשלת הפרי). בארמית, לעומת זאת, אין לנו עדויות על שימושו של 'גנא', בא' סופית עיצורית — שהרי שורשי ל"א הפכו בה, רובם ככולם, לשורשי ל"י, ובה חלה ההתפתחות הסימנטית הנזכרת: הסימה ההיסטורית של הסטיה והנטיה נתפתחה במישור המוחשי למשמעות של שכיבה ותנוחה ובמישור המופשט לציונה של סטייה מוסרית (לעניין אחרון זה השווה את ההתפתחות הסימנטית של השורשים 'שטי'/'סטי', שני',[13] ואת 'משבה' במשמע "מחלה", "סטייה" מן ' שוב מן ...' — "סטה", "סר מן הדרך הנכונה").[14] השדה הקשרי הנידון שבין העברית, הארמית והערבית הריהו איפוא:

בעברית: 'נטי' — ובו הסימה של הסטיה והשכיבה; 'גני' — ובו הסימה של הסטייה המוסרית.

בארמית: 'גני' — ובו הסימות של הסטייה המוסרית והשכיבה.

בערבית: 'גני' — ובו הסימה של הפשיעה; הסימה של הנטייה מצויה ב'גני' שהוא מעיקרו 'גנא'.

וראוי להוסיף ששימושו של 'גנה' בעברית אינו נמצא אלא בלשון חכמים, ובעיקר בשכבתה האמוראית — לשון חכמים ב', לפי המינוח שקבעו מורנו המנוח יחזקאל קוטשר — ואפשר שאילה הוא מן הארמית.

נעבור עתה אל ענייני איסור והיתר. השורש 'אסר' נגזרותיו הסימנטיות ברובן אינן משמשות במקרא במשמע של "קביעה המבקשת למנוע עשייתה של הפעולה", רוצה לומר "אסר לעשות

---

12 ראה גם C. Brockelmann, *Lexicon Syriacum*, בערך 'גנא'.

13 ראה: ש' מורג, "על 'מלות מפתח' ומלות עדות בלשונו של ירמיהו", ספר אהרן רוזן, בעריכת ע' אורן ובי"צ פישלר (ירושלים, תשל"ה) 72, הע' 21; וכן תרביץ נג (תשמ"ד) 507.

14 ראה "על 'מלות מפתח' ...", 69-71, ותרביץ שם, 506.

כעצי התמר"⁷, וכן בכתוב 'כי נטה אל־על ידו ואל שדי יתגבר' (איוב טו, כה) — "הרים ידו בעזות כלפי שמיא". השדה הרביעי, הירידה, גילויו לפנינו בעיקר בסימה שביסוד גזרון של תוארי־הפועל 'מַטָּה', 'לְמַטָּה', ודיינו אם נתבונן בניגוד בין 'לְמַטָּה' לבין 'לְמַעְלָה'. ואפשר הוא השדה, גם בעת שנושאיו של 'נטה' הם 'יום' ('נטות היום' — שופ' יט, ח) וצלי ('יִנָּטוּ צללי ערב' — יר' ו, ד).

מבחינת היחסים ההיסטוריים שבין השדות, מסתבר שהסימה הראשונית, הבסיסית, של השורש עניינה היה המתיחה והפרישה, ולא **כיוון הפעולה** הוא החשוב כאן, אלא **מהות** הפעולה. המתיחה והפרישה יכולות להיעשות בכל כיוון שהוא, כלפי מעלה או כלפי מטה, במאוזן (השווה: 'והיה מֻטּות כנפיו מלא רחב ארצך' — יש' ח, ח) או במאונך, או תוך סטייה מן הקו המאונך או המאוזן. מכאן גם ההסבר לעובדה, כי מעיקרו של דבר לא היה ניגוד בין השדה השלישי — ההרמה והזקיפה — לבין השדה הרביעי — ההורדה.

סימה ראשונית זאת, המתיחה, היא הסימה העיקרית של נגזרות השורש הערבי המקביל نطا "מתח, פרש"⁸.

מלבד בארבעת השדות הסמנטיים הנזכרים משמש 'נטה', כפועל, אם כי פעם אחת בלבד, גם בשדה אחר — השדה הסמנטי של תנוחות הגוף: 'ויעל בגדים חבלים יַטּוּ אצל כל מזבח' (עמ' ב, ח); 'יַטּוּ' = "ישכבו". ברורה הזיקה שבין דברי עמוס לכתובי התורה: 'אם חבל תחבל שלמת רעך עד בא השמש תשיבנו לו כי הוא כסותה לבדה שמלתו לערו בַּמֶּה ישכב' (שמ' כב, כה-כו). סימה זאת של השכיבה תולדה היא של סימת הנטיה, נטיית הגוף, שהרי בשכיבה, המסומכת בכרים, נטוי הוא הגוף. ומכאן גם תיבת 'מִטָּה'. שימוש זה של 'יִטֶּה' / יַטָּה' — "ישכב" נוהג בלשון חכמים⁹.

דברים שאמרנו על משמעות זאת של יַטּוּ' בעמוס פתיחה הם לנו לדון בשדה ההקשרי הכולל מכאן משמעים של נטיה, סטיה מן הקו הישר, באופן הפיסי, המוחשי, ובאופן המוסרי, המופשט. לשדה הקשרי זה שייך 'גני' הארמי, אשר לנגזרותיו משמעות של שכיבה מכאן ומשמעות שיש בה סימה של התנהגות שלילית מכאן.

בסורית מציינות נגזרותיו הצורוניות של 'גני' את השכיבה וההישענות בבניין פְּעַל¹⁰ ואת הגינוי בבניין פַּעֵל, וכן הוא במנדעית.¹¹ הסימה של הסטייה הפיסית שהולידה את הוראת השכיבה, בהקבלה להתפתחות שחלה בעברית ב'נטה', פעלה איפוא גם בשדה ההתנהגות המוסרית והולידה

---

7 לעניין 'נחלים' = "עצי התמר" (וכן אפשר שהיא המשמעות של 'נחלי' בצרף 'אבי הנחל' [שה"ש ו, יא] אף המתרגם היווני של בן סירא פירש כך את 'נחלי' בצרף 'כערבי נחלי' [נ, יז])' ראה במאמר הנזכר, עמ' 14-15. תיבת 'נחלים' מקבילה בפסוק ל'גנות', 'אהלים', 'ארזים' — וכולם מעולם הצומח הם. עובדה הראויה לציון היא שאף בשירה הערבית מצינו שימוש של צורה הנגזרת מן השורש נטי לגבי עצי תמר זקופים: הצרף: نطاة الرِّقَال הוא ממש המקבילה של 'נחלים נטויי'.
8 לידה מצויות סימות אחרות, תנייניות, כגון ההתחרות (تاطى). בשימוש הקלאסי העתיק נמצא גם שימושו של השורש כשנושאו הוא יד: اليد المنطية خير من اليد السفلى "היד המורמת עדיפה על היד המוטה כלפי מטה" (לסאן אלערב עמ' 4465 טור א'; מקור מן החדית').
9 ראה: י' קוטשר, מלים ותולדותיהן (ירושלים, תשכ"א) 35.
10 קיימת גם משמעות תניינית של "שכיבה בהחבא", "היעלמות נסתרת".
11 ראה: E. S. Drower and R. Macuch, *A Mandaic Dictionary* (Oxford, 1963) בערכו. בבניין פַּעֵל נוהגת במנדעית גם המשמעות של שכיבה במובנה המיני. שורש אחר לחלוטין הוא 'גנא' בהוראת "השמיע קול רועם" (מצוין אצל מאצוך כ'גנא' III, אשר מבחינה היסטורית אינו אלא 'גנח', השווה בארמית בבלית 'גנח גוהאי' — ברכות נט, ע"א).

וההישנות. מבחינה סינכרונית אין סימה זאת מתגלה בעברית, אבל נראה לנו שבעיון דיאכרוני ניתן לחשוף אותה כיסוד המשמעותי, שממנו נתפתח שימוש השורש בשניים מן השדות, שדה מלאכת האומן במתכת ושדה הלבוש. עניינו של הכתוב יַעֲרֹךְ על הכרובים ועל התמרות את הזהב׳ הוא עשיית שכבת-ציפוי נוספת מעל הציפוי הקיים; אם כך הדבר, הרי שלפנינו סימה המציינת חזרה על פעולה. ככל הנראה, אף בתיבה יְרִדִיד׳, שהיא בלשון המקרא הגזרת השמנית היחידה מן השורש, מופיעה אותה סימה עצמה. ניתן להניח, שמעיקרו של דבר ציינה סימה ירדיד׳ חפץ של לבוש, אפשר יצָעיף׳, שהיה עשוי שתי פיסות-בד שהיו מקבילות או מקופלות זו לעומת זו. (בהמשך דברינו נעמוד על הזיקה שבין ההכפלה לבין הקיפול בארמית, והרי גם בעברית אותו שורש לפנינו יכפל׳ — יקפל׳). גם התיבה יצָעיף׳ נגזרת משורש, שסימת ההכפלה מצויה בו, יצַעֲף׳,[4] שמקבילו הערבי (ضعف) הוא בעל נגזרות רבות בשדה ההכפלה, וכבר צוין הדבר במילונים (מילונם של BDB מתרגם את המלה יצעיף׳ - a doubled or folded thing).

אם סברתנו לגבי יְרִדִיד׳ נכונה, נמצאנו רואים שהסימה הבסיסית של ההכפלה, משותפת לפועל שבכתוב יַעֲרֹךְ על הכרובים ועל התמרות את הזהב׳ ולשם העצם יְרִדִיד׳.

בשורש יצעף׳ אין הסימה הנזכרת מתגלה אלא בתיבה יצָעיף׳. בערבית, שבה נגזרותיה הסמנטיות רבות, היא מהווה כעין קו אנטונימי לסימה אחרת, המצויה בו בשורש, סימת החלושה: ضعيف ״חלש״, והקרובים לו. אם הדבר היה כך אף בעברית המקראית אין אנו יודעים, שכן הנגזרת היחידה העברית מיצעף׳ היא יצעיף׳. בארמית אתה מוצא צאצאים גזרוניים לא מעטים לשורש השמי יצעף׳: השורשים יעיף׳, יעפף׳ בארמית הבבלית (יעיף׳, ״כפול״, עיּף ״הכפיל׳, יְמַעֲפֵי׳ ״מוכפל״) יעוף׳ בסורית (עַף ״הכפיל״, ״קיפל״), יאפף׳ במנדעית — (״הכפיל״, ״קיפל״, ״עטף״). שורשים אלה הם בני שילושים ובני ריבעים של צַעף. חל כאן תהליך המוכר גם משורשים אחרים: מקבילתה הארמית של צ היא, כידוע ע׳. יצָעף׳ העברי מקבילתו הארמית הריהי, אפוא, *יעעף׳. ניתן לשחזר את השלבים הבאים: מתוך הבדלות הופך *יעעף׳ ליאעף׳, ושורש אחרון זה נתפס כאפעל של יעוף׳ (או יעפף׳).

נשוב עתה לעיון קצר בשימושו של יְרִדִּד׳ בכתובים יהרודד עמי תחתי וילך עמים׳. ככל הנראה, ביסוד משמעותו של הצרף נתונה הסימה של הריקוע והירידוד, המצויה, כידוע, בעברית שלאחר המקרא, אבל לא בלשון המקרא, ולפנינו מיטאפורה: יָהֲרֹד עַמִּי׳ — ״הרוקע, העושה אותו כאסקופה הנרמסת והנדרסת״.[5] ואם כך הדבר, מצרפת סימה זאת, מבחינה היסטורית, את שדה השליטה וההכנעה לשדה מלאכת האומן (במתכת).

נהירים הדברים, שסימות דחויות, כסימה של ההכפלה בשורש יצעף׳, שלא שרדה בעברית אלא בתיבה יצעיף׳, מצויות אף בפעלים שכיחים, ודוגמה לכך הפועל ינטה׳. ארבעה הם השדות הסימנטיים העיקריים, שצורותיו של ינטה׳ משמשות בהם:[6] (א) המתיחה והפרישה; (ב) הפנייה והסטייה; (ג) ההרמה, ההקמה, הזקיפה; (ד) ההורדה. הקרויותיהן של צורות הפועל בשני השדות הראשונים שכיחות, ואין צורך להדגימן. בשדה השלישי, ההרמה והזקיפה, נוהג הפועל בצרף נטיוות (הכתיב: נטוות) גרון׳ (יש׳ ג, טז), בכתוב יכְנָחָלִים נָטָיוּ׳ (במ׳ כד, ו) ״הם זקופים

---

[4] בסימן צ אני מסמן את ההגה העברי המקביל ל-ض הערבית.

[5] ראה מילון בן-יהודה, עמ׳ 6440: ירדד עמים׳ = ״דרך עליהם ועשאם כשטיחים תחת רגליו״.

[6] ראה: ש׳ מורג, ״רובדי קדמות — עיונים לשוניים במשלי בלעם״, תרביץ נ (תשמ״א) 15, הערה 54.

כך, למשל, בלקסמות הנגזרות מן השורש 'גאה' יכלול השדה ההקשרי רק סימיות משדה הגאווה ומשדה הגידול והצמיחה, והם הדברים באשר לשורש 'יהר'-'יחר' (ואנו מצמידים כאן לשון משנה ללשון מקרא) שממנו נגזרות ה'ייהיר' וה'יוהרה' מכאן וה'יחור' ('יחור של תאנה' – כלאיים א, ח; 'יחור של זית' – ירושלמי יבמות ו, ד) – "ענף או קטע מענף הנשתל בקרקע או המשמש להרכבה", מכאן. לעומת זאת, כולל השדה ההקשרי של 'עברי' סימיות מארבעה שדות סימנטיים. ההשוואה בין שדות הקשריים בשפות שמיות שונות עשויה ללמד על תולדותיהם של קווי-משמע.

נעיין בקווי-המשמע של שורשים אחרים ונפתח ב'רדד'.

את היקרויות נגזרותיו של שורש זה בלשון המקרא ניתן לשייך לשלושה שדות סימנטיים:

(א) שדה השליטה וההכנעה, ובו הכתובים: 'חסדי ומצודתי משגבי ומפלטי לי מגני ובו חסיתי הרודֵד עמי תחתי' (תה' קמד, ב),[2] 'יֵלֶד לפניו גוים ומתני מלכים אֲפַתֵּחַ' (יש' מה, א).[3]

(ב) שדה מלאכת האומן (וביתר צמצום: שדה המלאכה במתכת): 'ירַדֵּד על הכרובים ועל התמרות את הזהב' (מל"א ו, לב). ענייננו של הפועל כאן, ככל הנראה, יציקת שכבת זהב נוספת מעל ציפוי הזהב שהיה עשוי על הכרובים והתימורות. ראשיתו של הכתוב היא: 'ושתי דלתות עצי שמן וקלע עליהם מקלעות כרובים ותמרת ופטורי צצים וצִפָּה זהב'. כידוע, בשדה סימנטי זה נוהג השורש בלשון חכמים, כגון: 'מרדדין טסין לעבודת המשכן' (תוס' שבת יא, ב).

(ג) שדה הלבוש, ובו סימנטימה אחת בלבד והיא 'רדידי' (יש' ג, כא; שה"ש ה, ז).

השדות הסימנטיים העיקריים שהשורש זה משמש בהם בערבית הם:

(א) שדה ההחזרה, התשובה והתגובה, כמו, למשל, رَدَّ عَلَيْهِ السَّلَامَ "החזיר לו שלום", رَدَّ هُجُومًا "הדף התקפה" (השווה: 'משיבי מלחמה שערה' – יש' כח, ו), رَدَّ لَهُ الشَيْءَ "החזיר לו את הדבר".

(ב) שדה ההישנות, החזרה, הכפלה, כגון رَدَّ قَوْلَهُ "חזר על דבריו".

(ג) שדה השינוי, כגון رَدَّ الأَبْيَضَ أَسْوَدَ "הפך את הלבן לשחור", رَدَّ الأَهْلِيَّةَ "טיהור שם", "ריהביליטציה".

(ד) שדה ההגנה, رَدَّ "הודף, מגן" (رِدَّء "עוזרו ומגנו").

(ה) שדה הסילוק וההסרה رَدَّهُ عَنْ وَجْهِهِ "הסירו מעל פניו"; أَمَرَ اللَّهُ لَا مَرَدَّ لَهُ "אין לדחות, להשיב אחור, את צו ה' ".

בעיון ראשון נראה שבין העברית המקראית לבין הערבית הקלאסית מתגלה קרבה רק ביחס שבין שדה השליטה וההכנעה בראשונה לבין שדה ההגנה באחרונה. וראוי, כמובן, לציין שההשוואה בין שתי הלשונות אינה עשויה להיות שלמה בגלל מגבלות היקרויות של השורש בקורפוס המקראי.

אם נבקש לברר מבחינה היסטורית כיצד נתגבשו השדות, כמות שהם מבחינה סינכרונית, נוכל לעמוד על סימימה, שבלשון המקרא היא נדירה, ואילו בערבית היא שכיחה, והיא תופסת מקום חשוב בנגזרותיו של השורש. כוונתנו לסימימה המציינת את **החזרה על פעולה, את ההכפלה**

---

2 השבעים והוולגטה גורסים, כנוסח המסורה: עַמִּי; לעומת זאת, עקילס, הירונימוס, הפשיטתא והתרגום הארמי גורסים 'עמים' (והשווה תה' יח, מח: 'האל הנותן נקמות לי וידבר עמים תחתי').

3 הצורה 'יְלַד' צורת מקור היא, וראה ספרי דקדוק ללשון המקרא.

הערות אחדות למבנה שדות סימנטיים והקשריים בעברית ובערבית

שלמה מורג

במושג 'שדה הקשרי' אנו מכוונים לכלול של שדות סימנטיים שביניהם נוצר הקשר (אסוציאציה), משום שיחידות־משמע (סימנטימות) מסוימות מופיעות בשדות אחדים שבתוך הכלול. כל שדה עומד לעצמו בתוך כלול זה, ואין בהכרח קשר תוכני בין מהותו של שדה א' לבין זאת של שדה ב' או ג'. הקשר בין השדות נוצר מתוך שיתוף המוצא של סימנטימות המופיעות באחדים מהם; כלומר — באחדים מן השדות נמצאות יחידות־משמע הנגזרות מאותו שורש.

לשם הדגמה: בעברית אנו מוצאים הקשר בין שדה **הגידול והצמיחה** לבין שדות **התנועה, הכעס והגאווה**; סימנטימות מן השורש 'עבר' מצויות בכל ארבעת השדות הללו.[1]
אין צורך לפרט את הנגזרות הסימנטיות משורש זה המשמשות בשדה התנועה, אבל לצורך ההבהרה, נזכיר שהסימנטימה 'עבורי' 'תבואה' ('עבור הארץ' — רק בספר יהו': ה, יא, יב) בשדה הגידול היא משמשת, כמוה כ'תבואה', ששורשה משמש אף הוא בשדות התנועה והגידול כאחד. הפועל 'עִבַּר' ('שורו עִבַּר' — איוב כא, י) עניינו גרימת תחילתו של הגידול והצמיחה, וכיוצאים בו.

מציאותן של נגזרות סימנטיות מן 'עבר' בשדה הכעס ידועות שהרי ממנו נגזרה מילת 'עֶבְרָה'. סימנטימה זאת עצמה משמשת אף בשדה הגאווה: שמענו גאון מואב גֵּא מאד גאותו וגאונו וְעֶבְרָתוֹ לא כן בדיו' (יש' טז, ו). ברי, שעֶבְרָה' כאן אין עניינה "כעס" אלא "גאווה".

אין צריך לומר שהשדה ההקשרי שונה במהותו מן השדה הסימנטי. ניתן לראות בשדה ההקשרי צרוף של סימימות (קווי־ייחוד סימנטיים, סַמָּנים סימנטיים, סוגלים, semantic markers, semantic features), המקובצות מן האלומה של מגבש הסימימות שבתוך הלקסמה, הערך המילוני. כך, למשל, השדה ההקשרי שהדגמנו אותו (גידול־ תנועה־ כעס־ גאווה), מהווה צירוף של סימימות מן הלקסמה 'עבר'.

מבחינה דיאכרונית השדה ההקשרי הוא תולדה של מעתקים סימנטיים, ובעיקר של מטונימיה ומטאפורה. אף ברור ומחוור, ששדה הקשרי יכול להיות רחב לגבי לקסמות מסוימות ומוגבל לגבי אחרות.

---

[1] ראה ש' מורג, "עיונים ביחסי משמעויות", ארץ־ישראל (ספר ח"א גינזברג) יד (תשל"ח) 138.

מזמור לז סוטה איפוא מהצמד השגור והמקובל 'צדק-ישר'. מכל פרקי ספר תהלים רק בו מוצאים אנו את ה'צדיק' כשהוא משמש בסמיכות ענינית לשרש 'חכם', ובכך מתגלה הוא כאן כבעל זיקה הדוקה ביותר לספרות החכמה המקראית. זיקה זו בולטת במיוחד לאור הקירבה המפליגה בניסוחם המילולי של תה' לז, ל ומש' י, לא (השווה לעיל, עמ' 119); אולם, כאמור, אין היא מצטמצמת רק בכך. כפי שראינו, באה כאן לידי ביטוי תפיסה כוללת, המזהה את ה'צדיק' עם ה'חכם' (ואת ה'רשע' עם ה'כסיל'); ותפיסה זו אופיינית, במקרא, באופן **מובהק** לספרות החכמה. מכאן שרשאים אנו לראות בהופעתה החריגה של 'צדיק' + 'חכמה' בתה' לז סממן סגנוני המצביע על ההשפעה החכמתית שמחבר מזמורנו היה נתון לה.

ג

תה' לז הוא מזמור בעל צביון חכמתי מובהק; ועל כך יש, למעשה, אחידות דעים כוללת בין החוקרים השונים אשר עסקו בניתוחו של המזמור.[17] לא בכדי אף התבטא אחד מהם כי 'תה' לז מצדיק את הדיבור על מזמורים חכמתיים בספרות המקראית'.[18] מכל מקום, העובדה אותה מבקשים אנו להטעים כאן היא, שהצביונים החכמתי של הפרק מוצא את ביטויו — בדרך הטבע — גם באוצר-המלים המשוקע בו. מלבד ה'צדיק' = 'חכם' (פס' ל), בו עסקנו לעיל, ניתן להזכיר בהקשר זה את האידיום 'סור מרע' (פס' כז)[19] ואת הצירוף 'צדיק' + 'חונן' (פס' כא);[20] ולמעשה לא יהא זה מוגזם לומר כי הפרק כולו מלא וגדוש בביטויים מרובים אשר השימוש בהם אופייני בצורה מובהקת לספרות החכמה — ובמיוחד לספר משלי.[21]

עובדה זו, שתה' לז משופע ברישומי לשון חכמתיים הפזורים בו מראשיתו ועד סופו, ללמד יצאה כי לפנינו מזמור אשר נתחבר (או נתנסח) בבית-המדרש של החכמים (או בקרב אנשים אשר היו חשופים להשפעתם); ומכאן שאכן רשאים אנו לראותו כ"מזמור חכמתי".

ובחכמתי ובנעם לבי'], ובכתבת פנמו הארמית [KAI 215, 11: 'בחכמתה ובצדקה']). ברור אפוא, כי אף הצמד המקראי 'צדיק' || 'חכם' (ולא רק 'צדיק' || 'ישר') משתלשל ממסורת ספרותית קדומה, המתועדת **במקורות החוץ-מקראיים** (והשווה ויינפלד, שם, עמ' 36-37, הערה 13) — כשבאותה מסורת לא היה הצמד הנדון בעל קונוטציה חכמתית דווקא. מכל מקום, כפי שהתברר לנו לעיל, הרי במסגרת שימוש הלשון של **הספרות המקראית** בודאי מהוה 'צדיק' || 'חכם' סימן היכר חכמתי מובהק (אבישר מצטט בספרו פסוקים רבים מן החמר המקראי המתיחס ל'צדיק' || 'ישרי' [שם עמ' 51-53] ול'צדיק' || 'חכם' [שם, עמ' 50-51]. אולם אין הוא ער לכך, שבניגוד ל'צדיק' || 'ישרי', אשר שימושו שגור בספרות המקראית כולה — ובכלל זה, כמובן, **גם** בספרות החכמה— הרי תפוצתו של 'צדיק' || 'חכם' מתרכזת במקרא בבירור **רק** בטקסטים בעלי זיקה הדוקה לספירה של החכמים).

17 השווה, למשל, L. G. Perdue, "Didactic Poems and Wisdom Psalms," in: *Wisdom and Cult* (Missoula, 1977) 334 n. 74.

18 S. Holm-Nielsen, "The Importance of Late Jewish Psalmody for the Understanding of Old Testament Psalmodic Tradition," *ST* 14 (1960) 45.

19 השווה: הורביץ, (לעיל, הערה 2), עמ' 47-49.

20 השווה: א' הורביץ, "ראשיתם המקראית של מונחים תלמודיים — לתולדות צמיחתו של מושג ה'צדיקי' ", בתוך: מ' בר-אשר (עורך), מחקרים בלשון, כרך ב-ג [ספר א' בנדויד] (ירושלים, תשמ"ז), 155-160.

21 פרטים מלאים יבאו בחיבור הנזכר לעיל, חלק א.

ל'צדקי' הוא בדרך־כלל 'ישרי' (ולא 'חכמי').[13] דרך משל:

דב' לב, ד:	אֵל אמונה ואין עול **צדיק וישר** הוא
יש' יא, ד:	ושפט **בצדק** דלים והוכיח **במישור** לענוי ארץ
לג, טו:	הלך **צדקות** ודבר **מישרים**
משלי כא, יח:	כפר **לצדיק** רשע ותחת **ישרים** בוגד;

והרבה בתהלים; השווה:

תה' ט, ט:	והוא ישפט תבל **בצדק** ידין לאמים **במישרים**
לב, יא:	שמחו בה' וגילו **צדיקים** והרנינו כל **ישרי** לב
לג, א:	רננו **צדיקים** בה' **לישרים** נאוה תהלה
נח, ב:	...**צדק** תדברון **מישרים** תשפטו
סד, יא:	ישמח **צדיק** בה' ... ויתהללו כל **ישרי** לב
צז, יא:	אור זרע **לצדיק** **ולישרי** לב שמחה
צח, ט:	... ישפט תבל **בצדק** ועמים **במישרים**
קיט, קלז:	**צדיק** אתה ה' **וישר** משפטיך
קמ, יד:	אך **צדיקים** יודו לשמך ישבו **ישרים** את פניך.

בדומה לכך מצאנו את 'צדקי' || 'ישרי' גם במקורות החיצוניים; השווה:[14]

ספרות אוגרית:	את׳ת **צדקה** ... מתרחצת **ישרה**
	(אשת צדקו ... רעית ישרו)
כתבת יחמלך:	כמלכ **צדק** ומלך **ישר** לפנ אל גבל קדשמ [הא]
	(כי מלך צדיק ומלך ישר לפני אלי גבל הקדשים הוא)
פילון מגבל:	Μισωρ καὶ Ζυδυκ (= מישור וצדק).[15]

'שפע הצירופים בין השרשים "ישר" ו־"צדק" ... סימן מובהק הוא, שקרבתם הסגנונית נעוצה במסורת עתיקת יומין.[16]

דב' א, יג:	יהבו לכם אנשים **חכמים ונבנים** וידעים לשבטיכם	ואשימם בראשיכם' לעומת
שמ' יח, כא:	'ואתה תחזה... אנשי חיל יראי אלהים אנשי אמת שנאי בצע ושמת עליהם ...'.

---

13 השווה: ש"א ליונשטם, "הערות לתולדות המליצה המקראית", ספר סגל (כתבי החברה לחקר המקרא בישראל, ספר י"ז [ירושלים, תשכ"ה] 180). וראה גם י' אבישור, כתובות פיניקיות והמקרא, כרך א (ירושלים, תשל"ט) 51-53 (במאמרו: "שקיעים מספרות פיניקיה במשלי ג'", שנתון א [תשל"ו] 20, מציין אבישור — בצדק — כי הצמד ישר/צדק מצוי **לרוב** במקרא בצורות ובדרכי צימוד שונות'. [ההדגשה שלי — א.ה.]); ואם כן תמוה מדוע מונה הוא צמד זה בין הראיות המצביעות על קיומה של יתלות טקסטואלית והשפעה ספרותית', שם, עמ' 24, בין הספרות הפיניקית לבין משלי ג דווקא.

14 ליונשטם, שם, עמ' 181-182; אבישור, שם.

15 ובדומה לכך הצמד האוגריתי 'צדק-משר', המופיע ברשימת אלים מאוגרית; ראה אבישור, שם, עמ' 53, הערה 47. ליונשטם מזכיר בהקשר זה (שם, עמ' 182) גם את kittum u mīšarum האכדי — ביטוי שנדון לאחרונה בפרוטרוט אצל מ' ויינפלד, משפט וצדקה בישראל ובעמים (ירושלים, תשמ"ה).

16 ליונשטם, שם, עמ' 181. אמנם מצאנו בכתובות השמיות הצפון־מערביות פעמיים גם את התקבולת 'צדקי || 'חכמי (השווה אבישור, שם, עמ' 50-51: בכתבת אזתוד הכנענית KAI 26, IA 12-13: 'בצדקי

צדיק = חכם בתה' לז ושאלת רקעו החכמתי של המזמור

קה'	ז, טז:	גול יגול אבי **צדיק** (והשי' גם	יולד **חכם** וישמח בו
	יא, ט:	בפה חנף ישחת רעהו	וב**דעת צדיקים** יחלצו?[9]
	ז, טז:	אל תהי **צדיק** הרבה	ואל **תתחכם** יותר
	ט, א:	...אשר ה**צדיקים והחכמים** ועבדיהם ביד האלהים	
ב. קה'	ז, יז:	אל **תרשע** הרבה (ואולי[10] גם	ואל תהי **סכל** למה תמות...
	כה:	...לדעת ולתור ובקש חכמה...	ולדעת **רשע כסל** והסכלות הוללות)
ג. בן־סירא	טו, ט-י:	לא נאתה תהלה בפי **רשע**...	בפה **חכם** תאמר תהלה
ד. מש'	י, כא:	שפתי **צדיק** ירעו רבים	ו**אוילים** בחסר לב ימותו.

מחוץ למשלי וקהלת אין אנו מוצאים במקרא את השרשים 'צדק' ו'חכם' כשהם משמשים בכפיפה אחת אלא בשני הפסוקים הבאים:

תה' לז, ל:	פי **צדיק** יהגה **חכמה**	ולשונו תדבר משפט
(על־דרך משלי י, לא:	פי **צדיק** ינוב **חכמה**	ולשון תהפכות תכרת[11])
דב' טז, יט:	...כי השחד יעור עיני	**חכמים** ויסלף דברי **צדקים**
(כנגד שמ' כג, ח:	...כי השחד יעור	פקחים ויסלף דברי **צדיקים**).

דוגמא אחרונה זו מאלפת במיוחד לעניננו, משום שמשתקפים ממנה שני שלבים עוקבים בתולדות ניסוחה של האימרה; ואת התקבולת 'צדיקי' || 'חכמי' מוצאים אנו דוקא בגלגולה המאוחר שבספר דברים, אשר רעיונותיו וביטוייו מושפעים, כידוע, במקרים רבים, מספרות החכמה.[12] מכל מקום, שימוש זה של 'חכמ' || 'צדיקי' הוא בהחלט מיוחד ובלתי שגרתי; שכן ע"פ המקובל בלשון המקרא — בכתובים המצויים מחוץ למעגלה של ספרות החכמה — השרש הנלוה

---

9 אמנם כאן צמד המלים שמדובר בהן הוא 'צדיקי' — 'דעתי' ולא 'צדיקי' — 'חכמהי'.

10 אם אכן יש להבין פסוק זה: 'and I saw that wickedness is foolishness'; השווה R. Gordis, *Koheleth--The Man and His World* (3d ed.; New York, 1968) 178 והשווה גם עמ' 281-282.

11 על היחס שבין תה' לז, ל לבין משלי י, לא השווה, מ' פארן, הפתגמים הכפולים וחקר התפתחות הפתגם', עבודת גמר לתואר השני, הוגשה בחוג למקרא באוניברסיטה העברית בירושלים (ירושלים, תשל"ה) 72. ע"פ פארן נשתמרה צורתו המקורית של משל זה — כ'פתגם ניגודי' — במשלי; ואילו ניסוחו בתהלים — כ'חרוז נרדף' — מציג התפתחות תנינית. אולם דוק כי לעניננו אין נפקא מינה מי הושפע ממי ומי נטל ממי. העובדה המכרעת לגבי דידנו היא כי מדובר כאן ב**שימוש לשוני**, אשר היקרויותיו במקרא אופייניות באפן מובהק לטקסטים חכמיים; ותקפותו של נתון זה איננה מותנית בנקיטת עמדה בשאלת **התלות הסגנונית** שבין תה' לז, ל ומשלי י, לא.

12 השווה M. Weinfeld, *Deuteronomy and the Deuteronomic School* (Oxford, 1972) 245. שתי דוגמאות מאלפות נוספות מסוג זה המובאות ע"י ויינפלד (שם, עמ' 181, הערה 3; 244 - 245) הן:

דב' לד, ט:	יהושע ...	מלא רוח **חכמה** כי סמך משה את ידיו עליוי	לעומת
במ' כז, יח:	...קח לך את	יהושע ... אשר רוח	בו וסמכת את ידך עליוי

המצביע על אופיו — או רקעו — החכמתי של המזמור.

ב

תה' לז, ל: פי צדיק יהגה חכמה ולשונו תדבר משפט.

צמד המונחים 'צדיק' ו'רשע' נזכר לעתים תכופות בספרות המקראית. אף כי בהקשרים שונים מוצאים אנו אותם בגיווני משמעות מסוימים,[3] הרי אין בכך כדי לטשטש את ההוראה הבסיסית המונחת ביסודו של כל אחד משני השמות הללו. עיקר משמעותה של המילה 'צדיק' הוא 'ישר', 'צודק', 'תמים' — בין שמדובר באדם (בר' יח, כג: '...האף תספה צדיק עם רשע'), באל (יש' מה, כא: 'אֵל צדיק ומושיע') ואפילו בשם עצם מופשט (דב' ד, ח: 'משפטים צדיקם') — וההיפוכה ב'רשע', שהוא 'רע' ו'חוטא'. אופיים וגורלם של הצדיק והרשע נידונים בפרוטרוט בעיקר בספרות החכמה.[4] במסגרת זו מרבים הכתובים לתאר את מעלותיו של הצדיק, המביאות לו אשר והצלחה, כנגד מגרעותיו של הרשע, המובילות אותו לכשלון וחרפה. הניגוד בין 'צדיק' ל'רשע' הוא מוטיב החוזר פעמים אין ספור במיוחד בספר משלי.[5]

ספרות החכמה מרבה לעסוק גם בצמד מונחים אחר — 'חכם' ו'כסיל'.[6] בדומה ל'צדיק', כך גם ה'חכם' זוכה לדברי שבח והלל; ואילו היפוכו מגולם בדמות ה'כסיל', אשר תכונותיו והתנהגותו מתוארים בביקורתיות ובלגלוג. כינוייו של ה'כסיל' שונים ומגוונים — 'אויל', 'בער', 'סכל' — והם מופיעים, במקרים רבים, כתקבלת ניגודית ל'חכם'.

קוי הדמיון המתגלים בין העימותים 'צדיק' — 'רשע' מחד ו'חכם' — 'כסיל' מאידך, והעובדה ששני הצמדים המנוגדים הללו מופיעים עשרות פעמים בספרות החכמה המקראית, הביאו בדרך הטבע להתקרבות ניכרת — ואף לחפיפה מסוימת — בין ה'צדיק' ל'חכם', המסמלים את האדם האידאלי, ובין ה'רשע' ל'כסיל', המציגים את הטיפוס השלילי שבחברה.[7] אין זה מפתיע, אפוא, שבטקסטים חכמתיים לא מעטים מוצאים אנו "ערבוב" בין שני הצמדים האמורים, כאשר ה'צדיק' נתפס כ'חכם', ואילו ה'רשע' מתואר כ'כסיל'.[8] במיוחד מרובים הכתובים החכמתיים שבהם 'צדיק' = 'חכם' (משלי; קהלת), אך מצאנו גם את השרש 'רשע' כשהוא מתייחס ל'סכל' (קהלת), וכמו"כ תקבלת ניגודית בין 'רשע' — 'חכם' (בן־סירא) ובין 'אויל' — 'צדיק' (משלי). השווה:

א. מש'	ט, ט:	תן ל**חכם** ויחכם עוד	הודע ל**צדיק** ויוסף לקח
	י, לא:	פי **צדיק** ינוב **חכמה**	ולשון תהפכות תכרת
	יא, ל:	פרי **צדיק** עץ חיים	ולקח נפשות **חכם**

3 כגון, בהקשר המשפטי שבו ה'צדיק' = 'זכאי (בדין)' וה'רשע' = 'חייב (בדין)', השווה דב' כה, א: '...ונגשו אל המשפט ... והצדיקו את הצדיק והרשיעו את הרשע'.

4 ראה, למשל, י' קויפמן, תולדות האמונה הישראלית, כרך ב, ספר שני (ירושלים, תל־אביב, תשט"ז) 576.

5 השווה R. B. Y. Scott, "Wise and Foolish, Righteous and Wicked," VTSup 23 (Leiden, 1972) 153-154, 160.

6 שם.

7 ראה, למשל, את ניסוח הדומה של שני הפסוקים הבאים:

| מש' טו, | יד: | **לב נבון** יבקש דעת | ופני (קרי: **ופי**) **כסילים** ירעה אולת |
| | כח: | **לב צדיק** יהגה לענות | **ופי רשעים** יביע רעות |

8 השווה, למשל, 133 (Philadelphia, 1966) H. Ringgren, *Israelite Religion* (סקוט שם, עמ' 153, לא עמד על מלוא היקפה של התופעה. הוא סבור שמדובר כאן בשתים-שלש דוגמאות בלבד; אך מספרן גדול בהרבה — ראה להלן).

צדיק = חכם בתה' לז ושאלת רקעו החכמתי של המזמור

אבי הורביץ

א

המונח "מזמורים חכמתיים" רווח מאד בספרות המדעית של חקר המקרא, והוא נזכר תכופות במאמרים ובמונוגרפיות, בפירושים ובמבואות. כפי שניתן ללמוד משני רכיביו של המונח, מתייחס הוא ליצירות שיריות המשתייכות, מבחינת סיווגן המקובל, לספרות המזמורית; אלא שעם זאת ניכרים בהן גם סממנים מסוימים האופייניים לספרות החכמה.

תיאור פשטני זה של המזמורים החכמתיים רחוק, כמובן, מאד מלהוות הגדרה מדויקת וחד-משמעית של הטקסטים המשתייכים לקבוצה הנידונה. לכל היותר ניתן לראות בו איפיון כוללני והצגה של מכנה משותף מינימלי, אשר מעצם טיבו עשוי הוא לחבוק דעות מנוגדות והשקפות סותרות. אולם פגם זה איננו נובע מליקויי הגדרה וניסוח, אלא משקף בנאמנות את מצב-המחקר. עיון בפרסומים העוסקים בסוגיית המזמורים החכמתיים מצביע על כך כי בקושי רב ניתן יהיה לגלות שני מלומדים המסכימים ביניהם על הרכבה המדויק של הרשימה הכוללת את הטקסטים האמורים.[1]

שאלת זיהויים של "המזמורים החכמתיים", כפי שהיא נראית מנקודת מבטו של חקר-הלשון, תידון בפרוטרוט במקום אחר במסגרת חיבור מיוחד אשר יוקדש כולו לנושא זה.[2] כאן מבקשים אנו להתרכז בניתוח של שימוש לשוני מסוים, המופיע בתה' לז והמהווה במקרא — מחוץ למזמור — סימן היכר מובהק לפרזיולוגיה של משלי וקהלת. המסקנה אותה ננסה לאשש במסגרת דיוננו היא כפולה. ראשית, כי לפנינו אמנם דרך ביטוי שהיא מסגולות סגנונה המובהק של ספרות החכמה. ושנית, כי הופעתו של הביטוי הנידון בתה' לז עשויה לשמש כאינדיקטור

---

1 השווה: R. E. Murphy, "A Consideration of the Classification 'Wisdom Psalms'," VTSup 9 (Leiden, 1963) 156 (repr. *Studies in Ancient Israelite Wisdom* [ed. J. L. Crenshaw; New York, 1976]); R. B. Y. Scott, *The Way of Wisdom* (New York, 1971) 193.

2 להצגתה של הבדיקה המוצעת ולדיון בבעיות המיתודולוגיות הכרוכות בה ראה לפי שעה: Avi Hurvitz, "Wisdom Vocabulary in the Hebrew Psalter: a Contribution to the Study of 'Wisdom Psalms'," *VT* 38 (1988) 41-51.

שער הלשון

בקצרה על העיקריות שבהן.

סאנדרס סבור, שהנטייה לתלות את ספר תהילים כולו בדוד המלך, שלדעתו היא ניכרת בברית החדשה ובדברי חז״ל, מגיעה במגילה זו של קומראן לכלל מימוש מלא. והנה לנגד עיני חז״ל ודאי היה כל הכתוב בספר תהילים ואילו מחברי הברית החדשה נסמכו על התרגום היווני למקרא. אבל הנטייה לתלות את ספר תהילים כולו בדוד המלך אין לה שמץ של סימן לא בנוסח המסורה ולא בנוסח השבעים שלפנינו, שיותר ממחצית מזמורי תהילים אינם מיוחסים בהם לדוד, או שהם מיוחסים במפורש לדמויות אחרות. מה שהביא סאנדרס משמם של חז״ל, שידוד כתב ספר תהילים, יש להשלים במקום שהחסיר: ׳על ידי עשרה זקנים׳, מאדם הראשון עד בני קורח (בבלי ב״ב יד, ע״ב). היגד מדרשי כגון זה שידוד נתן להם (לישראל) ספר תהילים׳ (מדרש שוחר טוב, א) לא יוכיח כאן כלום, משום שהמדרש יכול להשתמש בלשון של הכללה ואילו אנו לא לצורת הדיבור של המדרש אנו שואלים, אלא לזהות המחברים שלפי ההנחה עמדו מאחורי כל אחד מן המזמורים שבמגילה זו, כפי שהשיגום אנשי קומראן. ועוד, בפיסקה הפרוזאית $11QPs^a$ DavComp אומרים על דוד שחיבר ארבעת אלפים וחמישים ׳תהילים׳ ושירים, וסאנדרס מניח ששמונה היצירות הבלתי־מקראיות שבמגילה זו מכוונות להיות כלולות באותם ארבעת אלפים וחמישים. אבל הנאמר בפיסקה זו לא יצא מגדר הודעה, או ׳סיפור׳, שלא נתפרש בו היכן חבויים כל אותם אלפי שירים של דוד ואם עדיין הם בנמצא. ממש כך לא נתפרש בכתוב במל״א ה, יב-יג היכן הם אותם שלושת אלפים משל וחמישה ואלף שירים על חיות וצמחים שחיבר שלמה — וודאי שאין הכוונה באלה למשלים הדידאקטיים המיוחסים לשלמה ומונחים לפנינו בספר משלי, שהללו אינם מדברים לא בחיות ולא בצמחים.

עוד סבור סאנדרס, שהטורים האחרונים שבמגילה זו ׳קובעים בבהירות מוחלטת (!) שספר תהילים של קומראן בכללו יוחס לדוד׳,[14] וכל כך משום שבטורים הללו מובאות יצירות המיוחסות לדוד במפורש והן כאילו מלמדות לא על עצמן בלבד אלא על המגילה כולה. והריהו מתעלם מן העובדה, שבטורים הללו מופיע גם מזמור קלד, שלא יוחס לדוד לא בנוסח המסורה ולא בנוסח השבעים.[15] ולא עוד אלא שאין ליצירות המובאות בטורים הללו שום משמעות לגבי החלקים האחרים של המגילה. מזמור קנא גופו, המיוחס לדוד והחותם מגילה זו וגם את ספר תהילים לפי נוסח השבעים, לא היה בכוחו ליטול כלום מן העובדה, שבנוסח השבעים מיוחסים מזמורי תהילים למחברים רבים ושונים לא פחות, ובמקצת אף יותר, מבנוסח המסורה.[16] די אם נוסיף, שבין השאר מחזיקה מגילה זו את השיר בשבח החכמה, החותם את ספר בן סירא ואין טעם שלא לשייך אותו לבן סירא עצמו. ואפילו נניח שלא בן סירא חיברו, הרי כל מהותו מעידה עליו שהוא נובלת מאוחרת של ספרות החכמה ולא יכול להקדים בהרבה את זמנו של בן סירא. סאנדרס הנדחק לומר, שבקומראן נחשב שיר זה ליצירה של דוד, נמצא כמעיד על עצמו, שמשהו פגום בהנחותיו. יתר על כן, הוא עצמו אנוס להודות, שבעצם מתאים השיר לספר בן סירא יותר משהוא מתאים לסדר מזמורי תהילים של דוד׳ (a Davidic psalter). אף־על־פי כן הוא מתעקש לטעון,[17] שבקומראן יוחס השיר לדוד. והרי גם זה אינו סימן יפה לו ולהנחותיו.

---

14 סאנדרס (לעיל, הערה 7), עמ׳ 76, 92.

15 במגילה זו חסרה השורה שהכילה את פתיחת המזמור הזה, אבל לפי רוחב הטור אין שם מקום לשנות מן הנוסח המקובל.

16 תמה אני על גושן־גוטשטיין (לעיל, הערה 10), עמ׳ 27-28, מה ראה להסכים עם סברה זו של סאנדרס, שכל היצירות שבמגילה זו כאילו נתייחסו לדוד.

17 ראה סאנדרס (לעיל, הערה 7), עמ׳ 83, 85.

ג

לאחר שנתפס המהדיר להנחה, שהמגילה 11QPs^a מתכוונת לייצג את ספר תהילים או את שני ה"ספרים" האחרונים שבתהילים, באחד משלבי גידולו של הספר, היה עליו לטעון עוד שתי טענות, שגם הן לא תעמודנה במבחן הביקורת. הטענה האחת היא ששמונה היצירות הבלתי־מקראיות שבמגילה זו, שהזכרנו למעלה, נחשבו לאנשי קומראן כחלק מן האסופה המקראית לכל דבר. שהרי מי שקובע, כפי שהמהדיר קובע, שאנשי קומראן הביטו על מגילה זו בתום לב׳, bona fide, כעל ספר תהילים התקני, אינו יכול שלא לטעון, שאין בעיניין זה הבדל בין אותן שמונה יצירות לבין המזמורים המקראיים, שבתוכם הן משובצות.[11] על טענה זו אפשר, למשל, להקשות, שאם באותו שלב כבר היו שמונה היצירות הנזכרות שוות למזמורי תהילים במעלת הקדושה, אין להבין למה אחרי כן נדחו מתוך ספר תהילים. לאמיתו של דבר, הטענה שבאותו שלב נתפסו שמונה היצירות כמזמורי תהילים לכל דבר, אינה אלא שימוש בהנחה שהיא עצמה טעונה הוכחה. שהרי הנחה זו היא העומדת למבחן, אם באמת נתכוונה המגילה לייצג את ספר תהילים בהתגלמותו המקראית, או שהיא לקט של מזמורים מקראיים שגם כמה יצירות בלתי־מקראיות הוכללו בו.

ולא עוד אלא שבאמת אף שמונה היצירות הבלתי־מקראיות עצמן אינן כולן ממעלה אחת. ארבע מהן, היינו (1)-(4), הגיעו לידיהם של סופרי קומראן מן המוכן ומקומן הוא על גבול האסופה המקראית, אלא שידיהם של סופרי קומראן חלו ביצירות אלו ורידדו את לשונן.[12] ארבע האחרות, היינו (5)-(8), נתחברו כנראה על־ידי סופרי קומראן עצמם, כיצירות אישיות שלהם, או של מישהו מסוים מהם, ומבחינה זו הן מקבילות לתפילות השיריות שבמגילת ההודיות, שגם הן יצירות קומראניות. ואף שהלשון של רובן, להוציא את הפריט הפרוזאי (8), מתאמצת להידמות ללשון השירה במקרא, לא הצליחו המחברים, ושמא לא הצליח המחבר המסוים, להעלים את אופייה החיצוני והתכניני של לשון זו. אלא שיסודן הבלתי־מקראי של כל שמונה היצירות הללו לא הפקיע אותן מכל מידה של קדושה. גם לתפילות השיריות שבמגילת ההודיות ודאי ייחסו אנשי קומראן מידה של קדושה. פחיתותן של שמונה היצירות לעומת כתבי הקודש, וכן הדירוג במעלת הקדושה שנתקיים כנראה בתוכן, לא יכלו למנוע את האפשרות שתהיינה כולן נכללות עם מזמורים מקראיים במגילה אחת. אל נשכח שגם בסידור התפילות המאוחר מעולם לא נמנעו מלכרוך מזמורים מקראיים עם ברכות ופיוטים, חדשים גם ישנים, בכריכה אחת.

ד

הטענה האחרת שביקש סאנדרס להציג, כדי להמחיש שהמגילה 11QPs^a מחזיקה את ספר תהילים באחד משלבי גידולו, היא שכל היצירות שבמגילה זו, המקראיות והבלתי־מקראיות גם יחד, יוחסו על־ידי בעלי המגילה לדוד המלך.[13] כדי לאשש טענה זו, המוזרה אף יותר מקודמתה, ניסה סאנדרס להביא כל מיני ראיות, אבל הבחינה תראה בקלות שאין בהן ממש. אתעכב בזה

---

11 סאנדרס (לעיל, הערה 9), עמ׳ 84-86.

12 על קדמותם של מזמור קנא ושל הפריטים (2)-(4) לימי קומראן ראה במאמרי (לעיל, הערה 2), עמ׳ 320-321, 326. קדמותו של מזמור קנה, הוא פריט (3) לעיל, לימי קומראן יכולה להיות נלמדת גם מן העובדה, שבמגילה 11QPs^a האקרוסטיכון האלפביתי של מזמור זה כבר פגום ומקוטע — בניגוד לשיר התהילה לציון, הוא פריט (6), למשל, שהאקרוסטיכון שלו שלם כולו. השיר בשבח החכמה, החותם את ספר בן סירא, היינו פריט (4), כמוהו כספר בן סירא כולו, ודאי קדם לתקופת החשמונאים. והשווה לעיל, הערה 2.

13 ראה סאנדרס (לעיל, הערה 7), עמ׳ 58, 63-76, 92 ועוד; וכן במאמרו (לעיל, הערה 9), עמ׳ 84-88.

מחתימת ספר בן סירא; (5) שועה לישועה, 11QPs^a Plea; (6) שיר תהילה לציון, 11QPs^a Zion; (7) שיר תהילה לה', 11QPs^a Creat.; (8) פיסקה פרוזאית, שסימנה 11QPs^a DavComp ואין בה שום יומרה של יצירה ואף אפשר שהיא מקולמוסו של הסופר־המעתיק שהיה המלקט של מגילה זו.[8]

המהדיר של מגילה זו, ג"א סאנדרס, הניח שהיא מחזיקה את ספר תהילים ה"קאנוני" וכך גם כינה את התגלית: *The Psalms Scroll*, במשמעות של 'מגילת (ספר) תהילים' ולא 'מגילה של מזמורים'. ההנחה הפכה לו למלכודת, כיוון שניטל עליו למצוא את הקשר בין מגילה זו לבין ספר תהילים שלפנינו. וכך נדחק אל הטענה, שהנמסר במגילה זו הוא אחת הצורות בתהליך הארוך והמורכב של הקאנוניזציה של ספר תהילים, קודם שקיבל את צורתו האחרונה בהחלטה של חכמים ביבנה. אלא שהואיל ומגילה זו מצומצמת בהיקפה לעומת ספר תהילים שלפנינו, הריהו קובע, שזה אחד השלבים בתהליך הגיבוש של שני ה"ספרים" האחרונים שבתהילים, הם הפרקים צ-קו, קז-קנ, שהברכה הרביעית (תה' קו, מז-מח) מפרידה ביניהם.[9] כאילו שבאמת יש משהו שעשוי להסביר את המעבר מן הקבוצה של כארבעים פרקים שבמגילה של קומראן אל רצף ששים ואחד הפרקים שבאותו חלק של ספר תהילים — אפילו נניח, לשם הוויכוח, שבאמת קיבל ספר תהילים את צורתו בדרך של גידול איטי ומודרג. וכאילו שבאמת ניתן לדמות, שקודם שנתבררה צורתו של ספר תהילים ואלו מזמורים שייכים לו וכשעדיין הם מתרוצצים בלא סדר מוסכם, כבר יכולים אנשי קומראן להזדרז ולחבר עליהם פשרים. בנקודה זו הריני מוכן איפוא להסכים עם המשיגים על המהדיר ולומר עמם, שאין המגילה של קומראן מתכוונת לייצג את ספר תהילים ולא איזה חלק ממנו. אין זה אלא לקט ליטורגי, המחזיק מזמורים **מתוך** ספר תהילים וגם כמה יצירות שמקומן על גבול המקרא או מחוץ למקרא.[10]

---

8 לכל שמונה היצירות הללו נתלוו תרגום וביאור בחלק השני של הפרסום של סאנדרס (שם, עמ' 53-93). ה'שועה לישועה', 11QPs^a Plea, מופיעה במגילה נוספת, שהיא מאותה המערה (11QPs^b) ושרדה בשישה קטעים. שתי המגילות דומות בכך שהמזמורים קמא, קלג, קמד באים בהן באותו הסדר וגם צירופי הפסוקים ממזמור קיח היו כנראה שווים בשתיהן. ראה: J. van der Ploeg, *RB* 74 (1967) 408-412; J. A. Sanders, *McCormick Quarterly* 21 (1968) 286-288. אפשר איפוא, ששתי המגילות החזיקו ילקוטים דומים, או שני עותקים של לקט אחד. ואפשר שעקבות של שיר התהילה לציון, 11QPs^a Zion, ניתנים לאבחנה גם במגילה 11QPs^f, שהוכללו בה עוד שני הימנונים בלתי־מקראיים (סאנדרס, שם, עמ' 297-298).

9 ראה: J. A. Sanders, "Variorum in the Psalms Scroll (11QPs^a)," *HTR* 59 (1966) 88-94 ושם (עמ' 88, 90) הוא מדבר במפורש על הגיבוש הנפרד של חמשת ספרי תהילים ותופס את המגילה 11QPs^a כעדות למצבם הרופס של שני הספרים האחרונים שבתהילים באותה השעה. והשווה גם סאנדרס (לעיל, הערה 8), עמ' 291-297. סיקור מפורט של השקפת סאנדרס וגם של השקפות הנחלקות עליו בעניין זה, נמצא בספרו של וילסון: R. G. Wilson, *The Editing of the Hebrew Psalter* (Chico, CA, 1985) 63-81.

10 כך היא עמדתם של גושן־גוטשטיין, סקיהן וטלמון, כל אחד בדרכו ובנימוקיו. ראה M. H. Goshen-Gottstein, "The Psalms Scroll (11QPs^a)," *Textus* 5 (1966) 22-33; P. W. Skehan, "Qumran and the OT Criticism," *Qumran: sa piété, sa théologie et son milieu* (ed. M. Delcor; Louvain, 1978) 163-182; ש' טלמון, "מזמורים חיצוניים בלשון העברית מקומראן", *תרביץ* לה (תשכ"ו) 215-216; הנ"ל, שם לז (תשכ"ח) 100-101. סקירה לבדו מדגיש את התלות של 11QPs^a בספר תהילים הקאנוני, שנתגבש לפני קומראן ובאותה הצורה נתקיים עד היום. טענותיו של וילסון (לעיל, הערה 9), עמ' 81-92, הנוטה לצדד בעמדתו של סאנדרס, נראות לי רופפות מאוד.

העדפה של המעתיק להסתפק במגילה הנמצאת בידיו, בלא להוסיף לה יריעות. ואי-אילו מגילות ודאי היו ליקוטי מזמורים בלבד, בלא שום כוונה להקיף את ספר תהילים הקאנוני, כפי שנראה מיד.

ב

מראית-עין של מפנה בהערכת מגילות תהילים של קומראן אירעה עם פרסום המגילה הגדולה 11QPs^a ואגב כך עלו כמה טענות חדשות-ישנות ביחס לגיבושו של ספר תהילים. כמה שאלות ניצבות בפני המבקש להסביר את חיבורו של ספר תהילים ורובן מותנות זו בזו ומסובכות את הבעיה. שאלת יסוד היא אם קיבל הספר את צורתו בשלבים, תוך גידול מודרג מן הילקוטים הראשונים שנשתקעו בו עד להרחבותיו המאוחרות — או שנתחבר במעשה חד-פעמי של איסוף ילקוטי מזמורים, קדומים ומאוחרים יחסית, למסגרת אחת. שאלה אחרת היא אם יש קשר בין ארבע הברכות המשובצות בספר תהילים (תה' מא, יד; עב, יח-יט; פט, נג; קו, מז-מח) לבין שלבי הגידול המשוערים של הספר — או שהושמו הברכות במקומותיהן לאחר מעשה, לאחר שכבר הגיע הספר למלוא היקפו. ושוב שאלה אחרת היא אם מבחינה זו יש להבדיל בן שלוש הברכות הראשונות, שבהיותן קבועות בנקודות-תפר בין ילקוטי מזמורים אולי שימשו חתימות לילקוטים שלפניהן, לבין הברכה הרביעית, שהואיל והיא תקועה באמצעה של קבוצת מזמורים רצופים אולי שימשה לצורך ליטורגי בלבד — או שדינן של כל ארבע הברכות אחד הוא. הדיון בשאלות אלו ובאחרות כיוצא באלו, מוטב שיהא שמור לעת אחרת.

כאן נגביל את עצמנו לשאלה, אם יש בכתב-היד 11QPs^a כדי לבטל את ההכרה, שברקע כתבי קומראן כבר היה ספר תהילים מגובש במלואו. ובמילים אחרות, אם יש בכתב-יד זה כדי להראות, שחיבורו של הספר היה בגדר תהליך, שנמשך עד לסוף ימי בית-שני ובזמנה של קהילת קומראן עדיין היה בעיצומו.

המגילה 11QPs^a מחזיקה כארבעים מזמורים מבין הפרקים צג-קנ שבספר תהילים, אבל בניגוד למגילות שהזכרנו למעלה, בזו אין דילוגים בלבד, או העברה של פרק זה או אחר ממקומו. בהשוואה לספר תהילים נקבעו המזמורים במגילה זו בערבוביה גמורה, בלא שום סימן לשיטה כלשהי ותוך קפיצות חוזרות ונשנות לפנים ולאחור. וזה סדר פרקי תהילים במגילה זו: (קא-קג, קיט, קיח [פסוקים כה-כט], קד, קמז, קה [עד פסוק יב]), קה (מפסוק כה ואילך), קמו, קמח, קכא-קלב, קיט, קלה-קלו, קיח (פסוקים טו-טז, ח-ט, כט?) ; קמה, קלט, קלז-קלח, צג, קמא, קלג, קמד, קמב-קמג, קמט-קן, קם, קלד.^{7} נוסף לערבוביה של הפרקים הללו שובצו במגילה זו שמונה יצירות קטנות, שלרובן אין שייכות לספר תהילים הקאנוני, לא בנוסח המסורה ולא בנוסח השבעים, וכמה מהן ודאי אף נתחברו על-ידי סופרי קומראן עצמם. גם שמונה יצירות אלו אינן מרוכזות יחד, אלא תקועות לסירוגין בין המזמורים המקראיים שבמגילה זו. כולן משובצות בחלקה האחרון של המגילה, בין מזמור קמה לסופה של המגילה, ואין לגלות שום כוונה בסדר הופעתן. לפיכך נציין אותן בזה שלא כסדרן במגילה. ואלו הן: (1) מזמור קנא, שנודע בנוסח יווני מתרגום השבעים ומכל שמונה יצירות אלו הוא לבדו קשור שם לספר תהילים; (2-3) מזמורים קנד-קנה, שנודעו בתרגום סורי; (4) השיר האלפאביתי בשבח החכמה, שסימנו Sirach 11QPs^a ונודע

---

7 שמונה הפרקים הראשונים, שסגרנו אותם בסוגריים, מופיעים על חמישה קטעים, A עד E, שנקרעו מתחילתה של המגילה. הפרסום הראשון הקיף את עיקר המגילה מן הקטעים A עד D. קטע E נוסף בפרסומו של ידין. ראה: J. A. Sanders, *The Psalms Scroll of Qumran Cave 11* (DJD 4; Oxford, 1965) 3-49; Y. Yadin, "Another Fragment of the Psalms Scroll from Qumran Cave 11," *Textus* 5 (1966) 1-10. השוליים התחתונים של המגילה נתבלו לאורכה, אבל לרוב אין הרווח שבשולי המגילה נראה מספיק כדי להכניס בו פרק נוסף.

ונוסח השבעים בצירופי פרקים זה לזה, יש ביניהם שוויון של ממש בסדר החומר עצמו. משמע שגיבושו של הספר קדם לפחות לתרגומו היווני — אבל זה אינו מאוחר לאמצע המאה ה-ב׳ לפנה״ס.[3] ושוב אין להימלט מן ההכרה, שברקע תקופת קומראן כבר נתקיים ספר תהילים כשהוא שלם כולו.

החריגים מן הכלל שהזכרנו, שבקטעי קומראן באים פרקי תהילים לרוב באותו סדר שנודע מנוסחי המסורה והשבעים, אינם מרובים ואף שלפעמים יש בהם כדי להתמיה, אין הם מספיקים כדי לבטל את ההסכמה הבסיסית שבין הנוסחים. תכופות ניטל עלינו לעמוד בפני פערים גדולים בין הפרקים, כגון הפערים בכתב־יד $1QPs^a$ בין הפרקים צו-קיט, בכתב־יד $4QPs^a$ בין הפרקים ו-כא, בכתב־יד $4QPs^f$ בין הפרקים כב-קז, בכתב־יד $4QPs^k$ בין הפרקים ל-קלה. אין צורך לומר, שבכל מקרה כזה, שחסר בו חלק ניכר מגוף המגילה, אין ללמוד כלום ממה שאין עינינו רואות. אבל בשתי המגילות $4QPs^a$, $4QPs^q$, ברור שפרק לב נעדר בהן ממקומו בין הפרקים לא-לג ואילו במגילה $4QPs^b$ נשמט כל גוש הפרקים קד-קיא.[4] באי־אילו מגילות נשתבש הסדר הנכון של הפרקים. כך, למשל, בכתב־יד $4QPs^a$ הוקדם פרק עא ממקומו ושובץ מיד לאחר פרק לח.[5] בכתב־יד $4QPs^d$, שאינו אלא שתי קבוצות קטעים זעירים, הושם פרק קמז לפני פרק קד. ובכל זאת אין בחריגים כאלה כדי לבטל את ההסכמה הבסיסית בסדר המזמורים בין מגילות קומראן לבין הנוסחים שבידינו. אל נשכח, שכתוצאה של homoioteleuton (״סיום דומה״, שלמעשה יכול להיות גם ״פתיחה דומה״) נשמטו מזמורים גם מכתבי־יד של ימי הביניים וכך אירע לפעמים אפילו במאוחרים שבהם.[6] על אחת כמה וכמה שבתקופת בית שני יכלו להימצא כתבי־יד פגומים. אף אין לבטל את האפשרות, שאי־אילו מגילות לא נתכוונו להכיל את ספר תהילים כולו, אלא מהדורות מקוצרות של הספר, בדילוגים על כמה חלקים. והסיבה לכך אף יכלה להיות פשוטה בתכלית, כגון מחירם הגבוה של העורות, או

---

3. הניסוח שלמעלה הוא במילים שלי. דוגמאות לעוללות של שירה מזמורית מן התקופה ההלניסטית הן: מזמור קנא, שנוסחו היווני נודע מתרגום השבעים ונוסח עברי מורחב שלו נמצא במגילה $11QPs^a$ (ועל זה ראה במאמרי: ״שני הנוסחים של מזמור תהלים קנא״, תרביץ נד [תשמ״ה] 319-329); המזמורים קנד-קנה, שנודעו בתרגום סורי ונוסח עברי שלהם נמצא גם כן במגילה $11QPs^a$; המזמורים קנב-קנג, שנודעו גם כן בתרגום סורי מעברית, אבל נוסחם העברי לא נשתמר; מזמור התודה המובא בסוף ספר בן סירא (נא, א-ח, לפי מ״צ סגל) ומזמור ההלל, שהוא חיקוי לתהילים קלו והובא בהמשך אותו הפרק (נא, כא-לה), אבל הושמט מן התרגום היווני וגם מן התרגום הסורי.

3 במאה ב׳ לפנה״ס כבר הופיעו התרגומים היווניים לדברי הימים ולאסתר ואין לתאר שהתרגום היווני לתהילים היה מאוחר מאלה. מדברי נכדו של בן סירא, בהקדמתו לתרגום היווני לספרו של סבא, משתמע בבירור, שהמקרא כבר מתורגם לפניו כולו ליוונית ונחלק לתורה, נביאים וספרים אחרים׳. ואין לתאר את הקבוצה השלישית בלא ספר תהילים בתוכה.

4 להשמטה זו השווה: P. W. Skehan, "The Qumran Manuscripts and Textual Criticism," VTSup 4 (Leiden, 1957) 153-154. סקיהן מציין, שבהתחשב בטורים הצרים וברווחים הניכרים שביניהם, קשה להניח שהכילה המגילה $4QPs^b$ את ספר תהילים כולו. על השמטת פרק לב מכתב־היד $4QPs^a$ השווה שם, עמ׳ 154 (ושם מציין סקיהן, שכתב־היד השני שפרק לב הושמט ממנו ׳אינו ממערה 4 בקומראן; אבל לפי סאנדרס זהו $4QPs^q$).

5 אין במגילה זו פער בין הפרקים לח-עא, אלא פרק עא בא מיד לאחר לח. סקיהן מסביר את הגלישה לפרק עא על־ידי הדמיון בין החתימות של הפרקים לח ו-ע, שמשום כך גלש המעתיק מפרק לח לפרק עא.

6 דוגמה לכך הוא מקרהו של כתב־יד 9399 במוזיאון הבריטי, שהועתק באמצע מאה י״ג לסה״נ ובגלל הפתיחות הדומות של המזמורים נז, נח, דלג בו המעתיק על פרק נז. ואין להניח שדוגמה זו יחידה במינה.

המגילה 11QPs^a ובעית חיבורו
של ספר תהילים

מנחם הרן

א

משעה שהתחילו להתגלות מגילות תהילים בקומראן, גברה ונתחזקה הכרתם של החוקרים, שכל המגילות הללו תלויות בספר תהילים שלפנינו. כארבעים כתבי-יד של תהילים נתגלו במערות של קומראן ובחלקים אחרים של מדבר יהודה, כולם מקוטעים וברובם הגדול אף נשתיירו בפירורים בלבד.[1] וכל כמה שמרובה בשרידים הללו החסר, אי-אפשר שלא לראות שאם מחזיק כתב-היד כמה פרקים, הריהם סדורים לרוב לפי הסדר העולה מנוסח המסורה וגם מתרגום השבעים. משמע שברקע כתבי-היד הללו כבר קיימת הסכמה בסיסית ביחס לסדר הפנימי של ספר תהילים. לכך מצטרפים כמה שיקולים נוספים, שגם הם מצביעים על הקדמות היחסית של גיבוש ספר תהילים, שבתקופת קומראן, שהתחילה במחצית השנייה של המאה ה-ב' לפנה"ס, כבר היה מוגמר: (א) העובדה שבקומראן כבר מופיעים פשרים לספר תהילים מוכחת בבירור, שחיבורו של ספר זה שייך לתקופה קודמת ולאנשי קומראן נחשב כחלק בלתי-מעורער מכתבי הקודש. (ב) יצירה עצמית של שירה לירית-דתית לא פסקה בתקופת קומראן ודוגמאות שלה מופיעות במגילת ההודיות, אלא שזו כבר מושפעת מספר תהילים וגם מחלקים אחרים של המקרא. משמע שהשירה המזמורית המקופלת בספר תהילים עצמו מייצגת סוג קדום יותר, ששקע ובטל בעיקרו עם תום התקופה הפרסית — אף שחיוניותה היתירה של שירה זו גרמה שתהא השפעתה מוקרנת גם בזמן מאוחר יותר ועוללות שלה צצו בפרק הראשון של התקופה ההלניסטית.[2] ולכך יש להוסיף עוד, (ג) שלמרות השינויים הקלים הקיימים בין נוסח המסורה

---

1 ראה את הרשימה הקטלוגית של סאנדרס: "J. A. Sanders, "Pre-Masoretic Psalter Texts, CBQ 27 (1965) 114-123. סאנדרס מונה שרידים של שלושים ושבע מגילות (שהגדולה שבהן היא 11QPs^a), מהן שלוש שהן קטעים זעירים ביותר (ולפיכך צוינו תחת המספר 21a ולא נכנסו למניין), ארבעה פשרים, קטע אחד מנחל חבר, שניים ממצדה. ממערה 4 של קומראן בלבד זוהו שרידי שש עשרה מגילות ועליהן יש להוסיף את שלושת הקטעים הזעירים.

2 השווה: J. P. Hyatt, *JBL* 76 (1957) 5; M. Burrows, *More Light on the Dead Sea Scrolls* (New York, 1958) 169-171; F. M. Cross, *The Ancient Library of Qumran* (Garden City, NY, 1961) 165-166; idem, *HTR* 57 (1964) 286, 295-

הדבר, הרי במגילת ברד"מ מצורפים לפנינו שני סוגי הלכות שהיו נוהגים גם בעולמם של חכמים: הלכות השנויות בשיטתה של המשנה — כלומר בניסוח כללי ומופשט — והלכות השנויות בשיטתם של מדרשי ההלכה — כלומר הלכות הסמוכות על כתובים.[51] כאשר משווים את דרך פירוש ההלכות בברד"מ, אל דרך מדרש הנבואה בשיטת הפשר, עולה הבדל חריף: לעומת מדרש פשט של ההלכה, חפשית היא שיטת הפשר, נועזת ומעניקה לכתובים פירושים רחוק מן הפשט. והנה, שתי גישות יסוד כאלה אל פירוש הכתובים מוכרות לנו גם הן מעולמם של חז"ל: לעומת מדרש ההלכה עפ"י עקרונות לוגיים בא מדרש אגדה, הדורש דברי נבואה וחכמה בדרך חפשית ונועזת, המתירה, לעתים קרובות, את הקשרים ההדוקים בין הפשט לבין פירושו.[52] נראה לומר, איפוא, שבברד"מ מיוצגים "מדרש ההלכה" ו"מדרש האגדה" של אנשי העדה. ואכן, בספרית קומראן מתגלים חיבורי הלכה בעלי גישות פרשניות שונות וסוגים ספרותיים מגוונים. בצד חיבורי הלכה בסגנון המשנה,[53] יש פסקאות הדומות למדרשי ההלכה, ואילו מגילת המקדש כתובה כחיקוי לתורה. לצדם יש חיבורים רבים ההולכים בשיטת הפשר. יש להניח שאנשי עדת קומראן לא המציאו שיטות פרשנות אלה, והם יורשים וניזונים ממסורת קיימת ומגובשת. אם כן, משקפים כתביהם שלב קדום של שתי גישות-יסוד פרשניות שנהגו ביהדות בימי בית שני, ואשר אנשי העדה התאימום לצרכיהם ולרעיונותיהם.[54]

והאינטרפרטציה המשפטיים... אך המדרש שבא לאחר שכבר היתה ההלכה קיימת, וכל עיקרו רק בקיומה של ההלכה ובשילובה בפסוק - מדרש זה נאחז בפסוק, באותיותיו ובתגיו...' (שם, עמ' 260-261). על קובצי מדרשי ההלכה של החכמים שהגיעו לידינו ראה שם, כרך ב, 857-856.

51 על ההבדל בין מדרש הלכה למשנה השווה אלון, שם, כרך ב, 859-856.

52 וכך מגדיר ש' ליברמן את שתי הדרכים העיקריות שנהגו אצל החכמים בפירוש המקראות: 'החכמים השתמשו במספר מועט לערך של מידות במדרש חלק החוקים שבתורה. מידות אלו היו פרי חירה, הבחנה וגיבוש מתוך ריבוי של דרכים בביאור הכתובים. אבל באגדה ובאסמכתות להלכה נזקקו החכמים לאמצעים המקובלים בעולם הספרות בזמן ההוא'. ראה: ש' ליברמן, יוונית ויוונות בארץ-ישראל (ירושלים, תשכ"ג) 209.

53 ראה, למשל, את המגילה 4Q512, הכוללת הלכות טהרה, ראה בייה (לעיל, הערה 42), עמ' 286-262.

54 למסקנה דומה לגבי הצורה הספרותית של הצעת ההלכה הקדומה הגיע גולדברג (לעיל, הערה 49), עמ' 106. אך מסקנתו שתורתה של מגילת המקדש אינה נלמדת מכתובים ובכך היא דומה למשנה (שם, עמ' 99), היא מוזרה, בלשון המעטה, לגבי מגילה המתאמצת לערוך את כל תורותיה כתורות שניתנו למשה מפי הקב"ה. נראה לי שהמגילה אכן "לומדת" את תורותיה מן הכתובים, אך בשיטה שונה משיטת המשנה או משיטת מדרשי ההלכה של חז"ל.

אף על פי שגם זהו ציטוט ממאמר אלהי ממש.⁴⁵ מכאן שאין נפקא מינה בין שתי נוסחות אלו, והן חילופיות. הציטטה עצמה קצרה וכוללת רק שתי מלים, ומהן הסיק בעל ההלכה את האיסור להקריב כל קרבן אחר בשבת זולת עולת השבת. הוא לא היה יכול ללמוד מפסוק זה את עצם הציווי להקריב קרבן בשבת, שכן ציווי זה נקבע במפורש בבמ' כח, ט-י. מכאן, שלמד ממנו את ההגבלה לעולת השבת בלבד.⁴⁶ נראה שהסיק הגבלה זו מדיוק לשון 'מלבד', שהוא מפרשה במובן מסייג, היינו, שהפרט המצויין על ידה הוא מחוץ לכלל שהוזכר קודם.⁴⁷ לשון אחר, בשבתות **אין** מקריבים את הקרבנות שנמנו בראשית המשפט. פירוש כזה אינו עולה בקנה אחד עם הלכת הפרושים, שגרסו קרבנות חגים וראשי חודשים בשבתות. שלא כבעל ברד"מ, בססו כנראה הפרושים את הלכתם על הבנת התיבה 'בלבד' כשגרתה בלשון המקרא, היינו, שהפרט המצויין על ידה **נוסף** על כל הקרבנות שנמנו קודם. אם-כן, בעל הלכת ברד"מ חלוק על הלכת הפרושים בפירוש תיבת 'בלבד'. ברי שפירוש זה מהווה חלק משיטה יותר רחבה. לדעת באומגרטן אולי משתקפת כאן המחלוקת על הלוח. שכן, לעומת הלוח הירחי-שמשי שנהגו הפרושים היה נהוג בעדת קומראן לוח שמש בן 364 יום, לפחות לגבי חגים ומועדים. לפי לוח זה לא חלו חגים ומועדים בשבתות ועל-כן לא נצרכו אנשי העדה לקרבנות מלבד עולת השבת.⁴⁸

הציטטות שנדונו כאן שונות מן הציטטות שבקבוצה הקודמת הן בצורתן והן באופיין. שתי הדוגמות לקוחות מקובץ הלכות שבת המצוי בברד"מ IX, והן נוגעות לפרטים בשמירת השבת. שמירת השבת עצמה היתה, כמובן, מקובלת על כלל ישראל, והמחלוקות בין הכתות היו בפרטי הלכות. ואכן, זו התמונה העולה גם מהלכות ברד"מ. שתי ההלכות שבעל הלכת ברד"מ סמך על ציטטות מפורשות נוגעות לסוגיות שהיו שנויות במחלוקת, אולי גם משום שהיו מחלוקות פרשניות מוגדרות. נראה שמשום כך נזקק בעל ההלכה בברד"מ לציטטות בדרך של נימוק המסביר ומחזק את הכלל ההלכי שנוסח במשפט העיקרי. יתכן שצדוק שיפמן הרואה בקובץ הלכות השבת מקור לעצמו, הערוך באופן מכוון כך שהכללים עם הציטטות יעמדו בראשו ובחתימתו של הקובץ.⁴⁹

מה שעולה מכלל הדוגמות שדנתי בהן כאן, היא שיטת מדרש הכתובים הקרובה מאד לשיטת מדרשי ההלכה של חז"ל.⁵⁰ היא סמוכה על פרשנות החותרת לגלות את פשט דברי התורה. אם כך

---

45 נוסחת הפתיחה 'כי כן כתוב' מציגה ציטוט מחוק התורה גם בסרך היחד V, 15: '...כיא ירחק ממנו בכל דבר כיא כן כתוב מכול דבר שקר תרחק' (שמ' כג, ז). ובדרך אגב ייאמר שגם כאן מחיל המחבר את האמירה הכוללת של התורה לכלל הנוהג בעדתו בתנך עדתו בלבד (ראה לעיל בדיון על ברד"מ IX, 2-8).

46 לדעת שיפמן יש כאן מדרש הלכה ממש, שכן ההלכה נקבעה מתוך תפיסת הניגוד שבין שני מקראות בתורה (ויי' כג, לח/ במ' כח, י) והתרתו על ידי פירוש אחד מן הפסוקים כבא להשמיע דיוק נוסף או שונה לעומת הראשון. השווה שיפמן (לעיל, הערה 39), עמ' 128.

47 כפי שעולה משימושו של בעל ברד"מ במקום אחר (V, 5-6): 'ויעלו מעשי דויד מלבד דם אוריה ויעזבם לו אלי'. ראה הערת רבין (לעיל, הערה 22) שם. השווה א' בן-יהודה, מילון הלשון העברית ה (ירושלים) 2604.

48 השווה: באומגרטן (לעיל, הערה 42), עמ' 127-128.

49 השווה שיפמן (לעיל, הערה 39), עמ' 85-86. לעומתו סובר א' גולדנברג ש'אין כאן אלא סגנון של ציון להתחלה של רשימה ולסיום של רשימה'. ראה מאמרו: "המדרש הקדום והמדרש המאוחר", תרביץ נ (תשמ"א) 99, הערה 16.

50 על אופיו של מדרש הכתובים בהלכה ראה: מ' אלון, המשפט העברי³ א (ירושלים, תשמ"ח; 260-246. אלון מסכם שם את הדעה שנתקבלה בקרב החוקרים על קיום שני מיני מדרש הלכה: מדרש יוצר ומדרש מקיים. מדרש יוצר 'מגמתו לבאר וליישב את האמור בתורה או ליצור הלכות חדשות מתוך דרישת התורה'; המדרש המקיים 'מגמתו אינה ביאור ולא יצירת הלכות, אלא קיום ושילוב של הלכה קיימת, ידועה, בתוך התורה... המדרש המבאר והיוצר שומר על כלליו ותחומי של ההגיון

הלכה זו מנוסחת כאיסור שולל במשפט הראשי עם ציטטה בחלק השני, במשפט הטפל הסיבתי. הציטטה מוצגת בנוסחה 'כי הוא אשר אמר', ומביאה את הטעם לקביעה שבמשפט הראשון. הרחבת איסור מלאכה — 'תוספת מלאכה' במושגי החכמים — לחלק האחרון של יום ששי, נלמדת איפוא מלשון הכתוב בספר דברים. נראה שכחז"ל לומד גם בעל הלכת ברד"מ את תוספת מלאכה מלשון 'שמור', שבה מנוסח הציווי על השבת שבספר דברים (וכן ו" יט, ג: 'ואת שבתתי תשמרו'), כנגד השימוש בתיבת 'זכור' במקרא המקביל (שמות כ, ח: 'זכור את יום השבת לקדשו').[39] על-פי כמה עדויות קדום היה איסור מלאכה ביום ששי מבעוד יום (ספרא, אמור י"ד ה - ו; יומא פ"א ע"ב; ראש השנה ט ע"א; סוכה פ"ה מ"ה ותוס' סוכה פ"ד הי"א והי"ב; יוספוס, קדמוניות טז, ו, ב; מלחמות ד ט, יב),[40] ורק לאחר מכן הקלו החכמים והתירו מלאכה עד סמוך לשקיעה ('ירו' שביעית פ"א ה"א, לג ע"א).[41] אפשר איפוא, שבעל ההלכה בברד"מ משקף את החומרה הקדומה בעניין תוספת שבת, אך הוא מסיק אותה ממקרא מפורש, אולי משום שביקש לקבוע שתוספת השבת ביום ששי מדאורייתא היא,[42] מתוך פולמוס נגד מגמות מקלות בקרב החכמים. ושמא נשתמר הד מחלוקת קדומה זו במחלוקת בית שמאי לבית הלל בעניין תוספת שבת.[43]

XI, 17-18 (= ו"כג, לח)

אל יעל איש למזבח בשבת כי אם עולת השבת כי כן כתוב 'מלבד שבתותיכם'.[44]

לפנינו קביעת איסור להעלות בשבת עולות אחרות מלבד עולת השבת. גם כאן מוצג תחילה הניסוח הכללי והמופשט במשפט הראשי, והציטטה מופיעה במשפט סיבה טפל. אף כאן נפתח המשפט הטפל במלת הטעם 'כי', אלא שהנוסחה כולה היא 'כי כן כתוב', ולא 'כי הוא אשר אמר',

---

בר-אילן א (תשכ"ג) 116. וזה יותר מתקבל על הדעת מאשר פירוש מוצע שהכוונה לשערי השמים הנזכרים בספר חנוך החבשי ע"ב, ג.

39 השווה מכילתא יתרו, בחודש, פרשה ז' (מהדורת הורוביץ-רבין עמ' 229): 'זכור ושמור. זכור מלפניו ושמור מלאחריו. מכאן אמרו: מוסיפין מחול על הקדש'; מדרש תנאים, עמ' 21: 'זכור, עד שלא יכנס, להוסיף עליו מן החול בתחלתו; שמור, משיכנס, להוסיף עליו מן החול ביציאתו'. ראה גינצברג, (לעיל, הערה 22), עמ' 57-56; L. H. Schiffman, *The Halakhah at Qumran* (Leiden, 1975) 84-85.

40 השווה גילת, שם, עמ' 117-118.

41 גילת, שם.

42 כדעת ספרא אמור, שם. הלכה זו מעידה שאנשי העדה חישבו את היום כחז"ל מערב היום הקודם עד ערבו של היום שלאחריו, דבר המתאשר גם מן התפילות לערב ולבוקר שבמגילה 4Q503. שם מנויות ברכות ערב ובוקר בסדר זה על-פי ימי החודש. ראה למשל 4Q503 col. III, l. 6: 'בחמשה לחודש בע[ר]ב יברכו וענו [וא]מרו'; השווה: M. Baillet, *Qumran Grotte 4 (4Q482-4Q520)* (DJD 7; Oxford, 1982) 106; J. M. Baumgarten, "The Beginning of the Day in the Calendar of Jubilees," *Studies in Qumran Law* (SJLA 24; Leiden, 1977) 12.

43 השווה: תוס' שבת פ"א ה"ד, י"כ; שבת פ"א ה"ה, ד' ע"א, בבלי שבת י"ח ע"ב וכן מדה"ג לשמ' כ, ח. השווה: ש' ליברמן, תוספתא כפשוטה ג סדר מועד (ניו-יורק, תשכ"ב) 17-18 וכן: י"ד גילת, משנתו של ר' אליעזר בן הורקנוס (תל-אביב, תשכ"ח) 102-106.

44 גורס 'שבתותיכם' לעומת 'שבתת ה'' בנוסח המסורה, המקויים ע"י כל התרגומים. אולי רצה בעל ברד"מ למנוע הזכרת השם המפורש; אך שים לב לשאר שמות העצם הנזכרים בפסוק: 'מתנותיכם, נדריכם, נדבותיכם'. ראה גינצבורג (לעיל, הערה 22), עמ' 197 והערתו ב - (1912) 56 *MGWJ* 444. נראה שהפסוק הזה מצוטט גם במגילת הלכה אחרת מקומראן, 4Q513 Col. I, ll. 3-4: [ביום שבת ל[ ] מלבד שבתות[. השווה: בייה (לעיל, הערה 42), עמ' 290.

להסמיכן למה שנאמר קודם לכן על שבועת האסר. זוהי שבועה מובהקת השייכת למערכת חייה של עדת מדבר יהודה, והעובדה שהיא המוצעת כדוגמה הראשונה לחובה לקיים נדר או התחייבות כלפי שמים, אפילו תחת איום מוות,[34] שוב חוזרת ומעידה שבכללה עוסקת מגילת ברד"מ בהלכותיה של העדה. שתי ההלכות שהוצעו עד כאן עניינן בכללים הנוהגים בקרב אנשי הכת. כל אחת מהן הוצגה כנובעת מחוק מקראי, על-פי שיטת הפרשנות המיוחדת של העדה. שיטה זו, כפי שהיא באה לידי ביטוי בדוגמות שלפנינו, היא שיטה מצמצמת המפרשת את לשון הציווי הכללית של התורה על אנשי העדה ותנאי חייהם. עתה מתברר שהמבנה המיוחד והאפייני להלכות כאלה עם הציטטה בראש והצגתה בנוסחת 'ואשר אמר', משרת את האופי והתפקיד של הלכות אלה כפירושים מיוחדים של כללי התנהגות לקבוצה מסויימת.

מבחינת מבנה ומטרה מצויה ציטטה נוספת מסוג זה: 'אשר אמר לא תושיעך ידך לך, איש אשר ישביע על פני השדה אשר לא לפנים השפטים או מאמרם, הושיע ידו לוי' (ברד"מ IX, 10-8). גם כאן מקדימה הציטטה את ההלכה הכללית, וגם כאן היא מוצגת בנוסחה 'אשר אמר'. כקודמותיה מפרשת גם הלכה זו כלל הנהוג בקרב אנשי העדה. אך שלא כדוגמות האחרות אין הציטטה כאן לקוחה מן התורה אלא ממקור שאינו ידוע לנו.[35] טבע הלכות אלה וצורתן האופיינית מרמזים שאולי הן לקוחות ממקבצי הלכות כתתיים שהיו לעדה, בדומה לקבצים שאנו מכירים ממגילות המערה הרביעית מקומראן.[36] ראוי לציין שנוסחה דומה לנוסחה הפותחת את הציטטות שנדונו עד כאן, 'ואשר אמר', מופיעה גם בציטטות נבואה המתפרשות בדרך הפשר.[37] אפשר שהנוסחה מציגה מאמר אלהי, בין אם אמירת חוק ובין אם נבואה. אך אפשר ששיתוף הנוסחה נובע גם משיתוף פרשני, היינו, גם הציטטות שלעיל וגם הפשרים מפרשים מאמרים אלוהיים על עניני העדה, בין אם צווי חוק להתנהגות ובין אם מאמרי נבואה על מאורעות לעתיד.

לעומת הציטטות שהוצעו למעלה, מצויות בהלכות שבת שתי ציטטות הבנויות באופן שונה. תחילה בא משפט ראשי ובו מנוסח הכלל בלשון כללית, ובמשפט טפל סיבתי התלוי בו באה הציטטה. וכבר מבנה זה יש בו נימה פולמוסית, שכן הוא רואה צורך להוסיף טעם להלכה הכללית, והטעם לקוח ממקור הסמכות עצמו, מציווי אלוהי.

IX, 17-18 (= דב' ה, יב)

אל יעש איש ביום הששי מלאכה מן העת אשר יהיה גלגל השמש רחוק מן השער מלואו[38]
כי הוא אשר אמר 'שמור את יום השבת לקדשו'.

הקבוע המשמש במגילות לעניין זה, 'להקים אסר על נפשו', מבוסס על לשונות של במ' ל, אך כצורתו
הוא מיוחד לעדת קומראן. ראה: Y. Thorion, "The Use of Prepositions in 1Q Serek,"
RQ 10 (1979-1980) 426.

34 כך רבין (לעיל, הערה 3), עמ' 76.

35 אבל ראה שופ' ז, ב: 'פן יתפאר עלי ישראל לאמר ידי הושיעה לי'; שמ"א כה, כו: '...אשר מנעך ה' מבוא בדמים והושע ידך לך'. מעניין שהצירוף 'הושיע יד ל...' אינו מופיע בתורה, ואין שום פסוק שמשתמש בו בניסוח חוק, דוגמת הציטטה בברד"מ. לכן אפשר שצודק רבין, שם, עמ' 45 בהשערתו שהציטטה לקוחה מתוך חיבור כיתתי של העדה.

36 השווה רבין, שם, עמ' 45; והערת שיפמן (לעיל, הערה 22), עמ' 39.

37 השווה VI, 13-14, 'וכל אשר הובאו בברית לבלתי בוא אל המקדש להאיר מזבחו חנם...אשר אמר אל מי בכם יסגור דלתו ולא תאירו מזבחי חנם' (=מל' א, י); VIII, 8-10: 'ויבחרו איש בשרירות לבו ולא נזרו מעם ויפרעו ביד רמה ללכת בדרך רשעים אשר אמר אל עליהם חמת תנינים יינם וראש פתנים אכזרי' (=דב' לב, לג). השווה גם הנוסחה הקרובה 'ואשר אמר משה' המופיעה ב-VIII, 14; XIX, 26. כל המקרים הללו מופיעים בקטעי פולמוס העדה נגד מתנגדיה.

38 גילת מפרש: מן העת אשר גלגל השמש יהיה רחוק משער ירושלים, או השער המערבי במקום מושבם של אנשי הכת. השווה: י"ד גילת, "לקדמותם של איסורי שבת אחדים", בר-אילן ספר השנה של אונ'

לאחר שפירש את הציווי ואת תחולתו על אנשי העדה, הוא מוסיף וקובע את תחולתו בזמן: 'אם החריש לו מיום ליום', כלומר, אם שתק במשך יום שלם,[27] לא מילא את חובתו ולא השמיע את התוכחה בפני עדים, הריהו חוטא, שכן חל עליו הכתוב 'ולא תשא עליו חטא'. קביעת פרק הזמן לתוכחה מנוסחת כאמירה סתמית, בלי נוסחת פתיחה לציטטה, ועל כן אין היא נכנסת לגדר של ציטטה מפורשת. אך למעשה משתמש בעל ההלכה בלשון במ' ל, טו, הקובעת את פרק הזמן הדרוש לבעל להשמיע התנגדות לנדר או אסר של אשתו. כאן יש שימוש בציטטה בלתי מפורשת כדי ללמוד את גדר הזמן מעניין נדרים לעניין ההתראה.[28] מהצעת הדברים יוצא ששתי הציטטות המפורשות מתוך וי"ט מובאות כבסיס ההלכה, ועל-כן בעלת משמעות היא העובדה ששתיהן מוצגות בנוסחה 'ואשר **אמר** (האל)'. היותן דבר האל הוא מקור חיובן וסמכותן. אך כשבא בעל ההלכה לדייק בדברי התורה על ידי ציטטה מדברי נבואה, הציגה בנוסחה אחרת, ו'אין **כתוב** כי אם'.

איסור נקמה ונטירה על-פי פירושו כאן נזכר כתקנה מפורשת בסרך תקנות העדה הן בספר ברד"מ עצמו (VII , 2), והן בתקנון סרך-היחד (VII,8)[29] מרכזיותו של איסור זה וקיומו בחיי העדה עולה גם מהיפוכו, היינו, מכך שאויבי העדה הואשמו בכך שהם נוקמים ונוטרים (ברד"מ VIII, 5; XIX, 18).

כללו של דבר, איסור התורה על נקימה ונטירה מצוטט כאן כדי לפרש את חלותו על חברי עדת קומראן וכדי לפרש את כללי הנהגתו.

XVI, 6-9 (=דב' כג, מב)

ואשר אמר: 'מוצא שפתיך תשמור' להקים,[30] כל שבועת אסר אשר יקום[31] איש על נפשו ל[עש]ות דבר מן התורה עד מחיר מות אל יפדהו; כל אשר [יקי]ם איש על נפשו לסור מ[ן התו]רה עד מחיר מות אל יקימהו.

בהלכה זו משולבת הציטטה כדרך שנעשתה בהלכת נקימה ונטירה (XI 2). כאן פותחת הציטטה מספר דברים קובץ הלכות בענייני נדרים, אסרים ונדבות. פרטי העניינים מבוססים על חוקי פרשת שבועות ונדרים שבבמדבר ל, אך את החובה הכללית לקיים שבועה או נדר קובעת ציטטה מפורשת מן הפרשה המקבילה בספר דברים כג, כד. סדר כגון זה מצוי גם בקובץ מקביל במגילת המקדש נ"ג, 11 - נ"ד, 7.[32] אף שם מקובצים חוקים בענייני שבועות ונדרים הלקוחים מצווי התורה בבמדבר פרק ל; אך הקובץ פותח בפסוקים המקבילים בדב' כג, כב-כד, כדי להציע תחילה את החיוב הכללי לקיים נדר או שבועה. בסדר עניינים כזה מוצגת לשון ספר דברים כחוק הכללי המתפרט בשורה של אסרים ונדרים שנתפרשו בתורה בפרשת מטות. אך בהצעת הדברים בברד"מ, פותחת את רשימת פרטי האסרים שבועתם המיוחדת של אנשי עדת קומראן, היא שבועת האסר שנשבעו המצטרפים לעדה ובה התחייבו לשמור את תורת משה בפירושה המיוחד של העדה.[33] ואכן, נראה שבעל ברד"מ סדר כאן הלכות שבועות כיון שביקש

יט, יז; ראה רמב"ן למקום).

27 במשמע יום ולילה או מזריחה לשקיעה. השווה שיפמן, שם, עמ' 91.

28 השווה דמיון הלשונות בין הציווי על התוכחה (וי' יט, יז: 'ולא תשא עליו חטא') לציווי על הנדר (במ' ל, טז: 'ונשא את עונה').

29 השווה י' ליכט, מגילת הסרכים (ירושלים, תשכ"ה) 162- 163.

30 השווה המשך לשון הפסוק שם: 'ועשית (כאשר נדרת...)'.

31 אולי יש לקרוא 'יקים' (גם בש' 4? וזה שיעור תרגומו של רבין בשני המקומות), כפי שהשלים רבין בשורה 9. והשווה גם שורה 5. תיבת [יקי]ם נזכרת גם בהמשך, וקימרון קורא כאן ל[ק]ום.

32 השווה הערותיו של י' ידין, מגילת המקדש ב (ירושלים, תשל"ז) 168-169.

33 ראה ברד"מ IX, 12 ובקביעה מפורשת בסרך היחד ה, 7-8. השווה גם הודיות יד, 17-18. מטבע הלשון

נוקם הוא ונוטר; ואין כתוב כי אם 'נוקם הוא'[20] לצריו ונוטר הוא לאויביו' (נח' א, ב); אם
החריש לו מיום ליום ובחרון אפו דבר בן, בדבר מות ענה בו; יען אשר לא הקים את מצות
אל אשר אמר לו 'הוכח תוכיח את רעיך'[21] ולא תשא עליו חטא' (ויי' יט, יז).

ההלכה שלפנינו עשויה שני חלקים הנובעים זה מזה ומשלימים זה את זה, וכל חלק נתמך
על-ידי ציטוט: א. תחילה מצוטט איסור התורה לנקום ולנטור. המחבר מוסיף ומפרש מהן
נקימה ונטירה. לדידו נקם ונוטר הוא מי מאנשי העדה המאשים את חברו מן העדה בלא
שהוכיחו, כלומר בלא שהזהירו קודם לכן בפני עדים. מניסוח זה יוצא שבעל ההלכה פירש את
לשון הכתוב 'בני עמך' על אנשי העדה בלבד, שכן הוא מחיל את האיסור רק על 'איש מבאי
הברית' המאשים את רעהו. ובודאי פירש באופן כזה גם את צו התורה הסמוך 'הוכח תוכיח את
רעיך'.[22] בעל ההלכה השלים את צו האיסור על נקימה ונטירה בציטוטה מדברי הנביא נחום,
המוצגת בנוסחת הפתיחה המצמצמת 'ואין כתוב כי אם', ובה נאמר שהקב"ה נוקם ונוטר לצריו
ולאויביו.[23] על פיה יש ללמוד ממדות האל, שנקמה ונטירה אמורים בעל עצמו או רק בצר ואויב
אך לא ברע. ואם 'רעי' הוא חבר העדה, 'צר ואויב' נראה להיות כל מי שהוא ממתנגדי העדה. כאן
נראה יפה הבדל בין תפקוד ציטטה מחוק התורה לבין תפקוד ציטוטה מדברי נבואה. את ההלכה
עצמה לא גזר המחבר מדברי הנבואה,[24] אך סמך עליהם כדי לדייק ולהגדיר את חלות חוק
התורה. ב. החלק השני חולץ פרט אחד מן האיסור — התוכחה — ומרחיב ומפרש את חיוב
התוכחה ואת טיבה. על יסוד סמיכות ענייני תוכחה לנקימה בלשון החוק המקראי (ויי' יט, יז-יח),
הסיק בעל הקטע שהם חלים זה על זה, כלומר, שהאיסור לנקום וליטור פירושו איסור על אדם
להאשים את רעהו בעבירה כלשהי בלא שהוכיחו קודם לכן. נראה שעל יסוד כפל הלשון 'הוכח
תוכיח' הסיק שהתוכחה חייבת להעשות בפומבי, כלומר בפני עדים.[25] כלומר שאינו מוכיח באופן
כזה הוא 'נוקם ונוטר' וחוטא בעצמו.[26]

---

20 בנוסח המסורה 'נוקם ה''. ושימוש בתיבת 'הוא' כנגד שם הויה רגיל במקורותינו. ראה גינזברג
   (להלן, הערה 22), עמ' 40 ורבין, שם למקום.
21 בנוסח המסורה 'עמיתך'; אבל ראה 'רעך' בפסוק שלאחריו (וי' יט, יח).
22 גם במגילות אחרות של עדת קומראן נתפרשה לשון 'רעהו' על חבר העדה בלבד; השווה לשון
   תקנות העדה בסרך היחד V-VIII; לקטע כולו השוה: H. L. Ginsberg, *An Unknown Jewish
   Sect* (New York, 1976) 40-44, ודיונו של: L. Schiffman, *Sectarian Law in the
   Dead Sea Scrolls* (BJS 33; Chico, 1983) 89-94.
23 באגרת אל הרומיים יב, יט, אוסר פאולוס על הנקמה על יסוד הכתוב בדב' לב, לה: 'אל תתנקמו,
   יקירי, אלא תנו מקום לחרון־אף (האל), כי כתוב: "לי נקם ושלם, אמר ה'"'. גינזברג, שם, עמ' 41
   ושיפמן שם, עמ' 90, שואלים מדוע משתמש בעל ברד"מ באסמכתא מן הנבואה ואינו נסמך על דברי
   התורה בעניין הנקמה, כפי שעשה פאולוס. גינזברג, שם, עמ' 40-41 מסביר זאת בכך שדברי הנביא
   כוללים עניין נוסף שאינו נזכר בשירת האזינו: לא זו בלבד שהנקמה שמורה לאל אלא שהוא מפעיל
   אותה רק לגבי אויביו, ודבריו נראים. שיפמן מתרץ זאת בכך שעדת מדבר יהודה נהגה, שלא
   כחכמים, ללמוד הלכה מדברי נבואה. אבל הבדלי נוסחת הפתיחה והקשר הדברים מעידים שאין
   כאן אסמכתא מקראית לצורך פירוש הלכה אלא פירוש חלות ההלכה. גם מבחינת הפסוק מספר דברים
   עצמו, אין הכרח להניח שבעל הלכת ברד"מ פירש את דברי משה כפאולוס; אפשר שפירשם לעניין
   אחר, למשל, על הדין לעתי"ל (כמסורת התרגום הארמי הארצישראלי [כ"י ניאופיטי ותרגום
   הקטעים] שפירשה את הפסוק לדין שיעשה הקב"ה ברשעים לעתי"ל). ושמא (כפי שכבר הציע גינזברג,
   שם, עמ' 41), בדומה לתרגום השבעים (ודומה לו גם נוסח השומרוני) גרס בדב' לב, לה 'ביום נקם
   אשלם' במקום נוסח המסורה 'לי נקם ושלם'.
24 כפי שסובר שיפמן, שם, עמ' 90. ראה הערה קודמת.
25 אפשר שכך הבין גם הירונימוס בשעה שתרגם בוולגטה, eum argue publice; השווה שיפמן, שם,
   עמ' 90.
26 ובדרך זו תרגם גם אונקלוס את לשון הפסוק 'ולא תשא עליו חטא': 'ולא תקבל על דיליה חובה' (וי'

אך עד עתה לא נעשה נסיון לדון בהן באופן שיטתי במסגרת אחת ולראותן כמשקפות שיטה פרשנית. סקירה שיטתית של כל הציטטות המפורשות בספר ברד"מ על שני חלקיו מעלה שהן נחלקות לשתי קבוצות שונות באופיין, במטרותיהן ובניסוחן:

I. ציטטות מחוקי התורה — המכוונות לפרש חוק מן התורה. בברד"מ יש שני סוגי ציטטות מחוקי התורה: הקבוצה האחת כוללת ציטטות מפורשות של חוקי תורה על מנת לסמוך אותן להלכה. הקבוצה האחרת כוללת ציטטות מחוקי התורה המובאות כדי לבחון לאורן התנהגות של אישיות או קבוצת אנשים בעבר או בהווה.[16] כל הציטטות מן הסוג הראשון מופיעות בחלק ההלכי, הערוך כסדר את הכללים וההנהגות לחברי עדת קומראן, ואילו הציטטות מן הסוג השני מופיעות בחלק הראשון, הדרשתי, בקטעי פולמוס עם מתנגדי העדה. ההבדל זה בסגנון ובהקשר משקפים יפה את השוני בין שני הסוגים ובשימוש שנעשה בם.

II. ציטטות מן הנבואה ומשירות התורה — והן ציטטות המתפרשות בסגנון הפשרים כרמזים למאורעות ואישים מן ההיסטוריה. העובדה ששירות התורה מתפרשות על דרך הפשר מעידה על שהן נחשבו לדברי נבואה.[17]

במסגרת מצומצמת זו אסתפק בניתוח ציטטות מן התורה השייכות לקטיגוריה הראשונה, כלומר ציטטות הלקוחות מחוקי התורה, ואף מהן אעסוק רק בסוג הראשון של ציטטות שעניינן פירוש הלכות. יש עניין מיוחד בציטטות כאלה בברד"מ גם משום שהן יוצאות-דופן בהלכת ברד"מ עצמה, וגם משום שהן שונות מהלכתה של מגילת המקדש, או הלכת ספר היובלים; שכן, אף-על-פי שיש להלכה במגילת המקדש ובספר היובלים זיקת תוכן להלכת ברד"מ, שלא כברד"מ הן מוצגות כחיקוקי פסוידואפיגרפי לתורה עצמה.

ציטטות מחוקי התורה בברד"מ

הציטטות מחוקי התורה הנדונות כאן לקוחות כולן מן החלק ההלכי של ברד"מ, ולכולן תפקיד אחד, להוות סמך מן הכתוב להלכה שהוצמדה אליה. אך גם בהלכת ברד"מ נדירות הן ציטטות כאלה, שכן רוב ההלכות שנויות בלשון כללים מופשטים, כדרך ניסוח המשנה, בלי כל סמך מן הכתוב. משום כך עולה השאלה מה ראה בעל ההלכה בברד"מ לשנות ממנהגו ולסמוך הלכות מסוימות על ציטטות מפורשות? אפשר שרמז לתשובה יעלה לנו מן הדיון עצמו. מיון ראשון מראה שציטטות-אסמכתא להלכות מוצגות בברד"מ בשני דגמים פורמליים: בדגם אחד מוצגת הציטטה בנוסחת הפתיחה 'אשר אמר', והיא הפותחת, ואילו הכלל ההלכי מובא אחריה ומנוסח כפירוש לה. בדגם השני בא הכלל ההלכי הכללי במשפט הראשי הפותח, ואילו הציטטה המקראית באה אחריו במשפט טפל סיבתי. בדגם זה מוצגת הציטטה בנוסחה הפתיחה שבראשה מלת הטעם 'כי'. בחינה מקרוב מעלה שהשוני בדגמים משקף שוני גם בטיב ההלכות ובמטרתן.

IX, 2-8 (= וי' יט, יז-יח; נח' א, ב)

ואשר[18] אמר 'לא תקום ולא תטור את בני עמך' (וי' יט, יח) וכל איש מביאי[19] הברית אשר יביא על רעהו דבר אשר לא בהוכח לפני עדים והביאו בחרון אפו או ספר לזקניו להבזותו,

---

16 השווה למשל, ברד"מ V, 4-1, המצטט את דב' יז, טו בקשר לדוד המלך, או V, 8-12 המצטט את וי' יח, יג בפולמוס נגד המטמאים את המקדש.

17 השווה: IV, 4-3; VII, 21-19; VIII, 12-9. העובדה ששירות התורה נחשבו כנבואה, להבדיל מחוקי התורה, מעידה שבימי המחבר עדיין לא נתפסה התורה כמקשה אחת. כאן גם חוזר ומתאשר הכלל ששיטת הפירוש של הפשר נוהגת אצל אנשי עדת מדבר יהודה רק ביחס למה שנחשב על-ידם כדבר נבואה.

18 אף שיש 'ו' מקשרת אין ההלכה שייכת לכלל שלפניו, העוסק בחרם אדם.

19 צ"ל 'מבאי'. השווה II, 2. ראה רבין (לעיל, הערה 3), עמ' 45. במהדורה חדשה של נוסח הגניזה שהכין א' קימרון (ושתצא לאור בהדרתו של מ' ברושי) הוא מעיר: יש לקרוא: מבואי = מְבָאֵי.

כמו רבות ממגילות מדבר יהודה כך גם מגילה זו עושה שימוש מיוחד במינו במקרא, אך הוא
עדיין לא נחקר ותואר באופן שיטתי. בדיקת השימוש הזה ובדיקת דרכה של המגילה בשילוב
החמרים המקראיים אל המרקם הסגנוני והרעיוני שלה עשויים ללמדנו הרבה לא רק על המקרא
ופירושו, אלא גם על טיב דעותיה ומקורותיה של מגילת ברד"מ עצמה, ועל מקומה בספרות בית
שני בכלל.[10] מבחינה זו יש עניין מיוחד בברד"מ דווקא, שכן חיבור זה תוחם לו מקום משלו
בכלל המגילות. מצד אחד יש בו חלק של דרשה, השוזר הרצאת מעשים עם פירוש מקראות,
ומצד שני יש בו חלק של הלכות ותקנות, המשולב בציטטות מקראיות. כך, עניינים המוכרים
לנו כנפרדים בחיבורי מגילות שונות נמצאים משולבים בברד"מ. יתר על כן, מבחינת צורתו
הספרותית אין החיבור הזה בנוי על פי דגם מקראי, אלא הוא מציג את ענייניו בסגנון מיוחד לו.
לכן נוח הוא להפרדה בין היסודות המקראיים ליסודות אחדים המשמשים בו. ריבוי פנים זה
מרמז לעושר השמור לעיון בדרך השימוש במקרא בברד"מ, וממנו יהא נשכר לא רק חקר ברד"מ,
אלא גם מחקר ספרות התקופה כולה.

אכן, מגילת ברד"מ גדושה ומשופעת ביסודות מקראיים בשימושים שונים ומגוונים ועיון
מדוקדק בהם ימלא דפים הרבה. מקוצר היריעה בחרתי לדון רק בצד אחד ממכלול זה. הבחירה
נעשתה על יסוד הגדרה של תיפקוד יסודות מקראיים בספרות בתר־מקראית, שהצעתי במקום
אחר.[11] על־פי הגדרה זו משמשים יסודות מקראיים בספרות בית שני בשני מיני תיפקוד:

א. תיפקוד פרשני, המאופיין על ידי שימוש מפורש בחמרים מקראיים והמציג את החלק
המקראי ואת החלק הפרשני בתבניות פורמליות נבדלות. לכאן שייכים מדרש חז"ל הפרשני,
הפשרים מקומראן, פירושי פילון האלכסנדרוני, וציטטות מפורשות המשולבות לצורות ספרותיות
אחרות (למשל ציטטות בספרי האפוקריפה[12] ובספרי הבשורה שבברית החדשה[13] וכן ציטטות
כגון אלו שנדונות במאמר זה).

ב. תיפקוד יוצר, המאופיין על־ידי שימוש משתמע, והמשתמש בחמרים מקראיים בלי לזהותם
במפורש ככאלה. בשימוש כזה משולבים יסודות המקרא אל כלל חמרי הבניין הבונים את
החיבור החדש. קטיגוריה זו רחבה ומגוונת מאד, והיא כוללת ציטטות שאינם מוצגים במפורש,
רמזים מסוגים שונים, מבנים ומוטיבים.

ספר ברד"מ כולל דוגמות לרוב משתי הקבוצות, אך כאן אעסוק רק בסוג אחד של שימושים
מפורשים, כלומר בציטטות מפורשות.[14] בעבר נדונו ציטטות שונות בברד"מ כמקרים בודדים;[15]

---

10 מבחינה זו יש לברד"מ מעמד מיוחד בין מגילות מדבר יהודה על שום זיקתה הגלויה לחיבורים
    פסוידואפיגרפיים יהודיים כגון ספר היובלים, ספר חנוך וצוואת לוי.
11 ראה מ"ש ב־380-382 (1988 ,Assen ;Mulder .J .M .ed) *Mikra*. פיצמאייר (לעיל, הערה 1),
    מיין את הציטטות שמצא לארבע קבוצות: א. ציטטות מילוליות ב. ציטטות המפורשות ברוח זמנו
    של המחבר. ג. ציטטות המותאמות לצרכי המחבר. ד. ציטטות אסכטולוגיות. למעשה מהווה
    הקבוצה הראשונה את ציטטות חוקי התורה הנדונות כאן על ידי, והקבוצה השניה מהווה את
    ציטטות הפשר. בחינה מקרוב מעלה שהציטטות הכלולות בקבוצות השלישית או הרביעית, נתונות
    למיון בראשונה או בשניה. ייחודן של ציטטות ברד"מ מטשטש בדיונו של פיצמאייר הן משום שכלל
    עוד חיבורים מקומראן, והן משום השוואתו הכוללנית מדי עם ציטטות הברית החדשה.
12 דנתי ברובן במאמרי לעיל (הערה 11).
13 ראה סקירתו של: ",D. Moody Smith, "The Use of the Old Testament in the New
    The Use of the Old Testament in the New and Other Essays: Studies in Honor of
    W. F. Stinespring (ed. J. M. Elfrid; Durham, 1972) 3-65.
14 במקום אחר אני מקוה להשלים את החסר. קיים סוג נוסף של שימוש מפורש שאינו בגדר ציטטה,
    כגון איזכור שמות ומאורעות (ראה המיון במאמרי [לעיל, הערה 11], עמ' 391-400), ואף הוא מצוי
    בברד"מ (השווה למשל, הזכרת נח והאבות בברד"מ III, 4-1 או את הזכרת משה ואהרן ב־V, 17-18).
15 ראה, למשל, ברוק (לעיל, הערה 1), עמ' 302-309 על ברד"מ V II 8, 13-, ושם ספרות קודמת.

החיבור המכונה "ברית דמשק" נודע משני כתבי יד בגניזת קהיר[3] ומקטעים של כתבי יד שנתגלו במערות קומראן.[4] החיבור הועתק באופן רצוף בכתבי היד מן הגניזה, אך הוא עשוי משני חלקים השונים בתוכנם ובסגנונם. בכ"י A תופס החלק האחד את הדפים 1-8, והוא כתוב בסגנון דרשת תוכחה המספרת את תולדותיה של עדה בעלת דעות מיוחדות במינן. החלק השני משתרע על דפים 9-16 והוא מאגד אוסף הלכות וכן תקנון (= סרך) הקובע את סדרי חייה של עדה מסויימת, כנראה העדה המתוארת בחלק הראשון.[5] מכ"י B שרדו רק שני דפים 19-20, מן החלק הדרשתי. אפשר שבנוסח המקורי והמלא היו שני החלקים הללו משולבים במבנה כולל אחד, אבל דבר זה לא יתברר כל צרכו עד שלא יתפרסמו קטעי קומראן.[6] ואכן, עיקר מאמציהם של החוקרים כוונו עד עתה להגדרת העדה המתוארת בחיבור, אופייה, דעותיה ומקומה בהיסטוריה של ימי בית שני,[7] אף כי עדיין טעונים בירור וליבון מקומו של חיבור זה בכלל מגילות מדבר יהודה ומהות זיקתו אל חיבורים כגון סרך היחד ומגילת המקדש.[8] לעומת זאת, בחיתוליה היא החקירה על אפיו הספרותי, סגנונו ופרשנותו של החיבור.[9] אבל אף-על-פי שעדיין אין בידי החוקרים קטעי החיבור מקומראן, אין אנו פטורים מליתן את הדעת על שאלות אלו.

---

3 מהדורה ראשונה: S. Schechter, *Documents of Jewish Sectaries* I (Cambridge, 1910). הפקסימיליות בשלמותן פורסמו רק כארבעים שנה לאחר מכן ע"י: S. Zeitlin, *The Zadokite Fragments* (JQRMS 1; Philadelphia, 1952). מהדורה מתוקנת: C. Rabin, *The Zadokite Documents* (2d ed.; Oxford, 1958). כל הציטטות במאמר זה הן על-פי מהדורתו של רבין; דפים 19-20 מצוטטים עפ"י הנוסח הנפרד של כל אחד מהם (ולא עפ"י נוסחתו המשולבת של רבין).

4 קטעים מן המערות החמישית (5Q12) והששית (6Q15) פורסמו ע"י: M. Baillet, J. T. Millik and R. de Vaux, *Les 'Petites Grottes' de Qumrân* (DJD 3; Oxford, 1962) 128-131, 181; M. Baillet, "Fragment du Documents de Damas: Qumran, Grotte 6," *RB* 63 (1956) 513-552. על קטעי ברד"מ מן המערה הרביעית שעדיין לא פורסמו ראה: J. T. Milik, "Fragment d'une source," *RB* 73 (1966) 105 וכן ב- 410-416 *RB* 67 (1960). שם נתנה רשימת שינויי נוסח בקטעים אלה לעומת נוסח הגניזה. עפ"י מה שפרסם מיליק ניסה פיצמאייר לשחזר את מבנה ברד"מ על-פי נוסח מגילות קומראן. ראה את ההקדמה שכתב להדפסה מחודשת של ההוצאה הראשונה של שכטר :J. A. Fitzmyer, "Prolegomenon," in: S. Schechter, *Documents of Jewish Sectaries* (New York, 1970) 9-34.

5 הקרבה בסגנון ובתוכן בין מגילת ברד"מ למגילות כיתתיות אחרות, ובייחוד לסרך היחד, מצביע על כך שנוצרו בחוג קרוב או זהה. אף-על-פי-כן יש הבדלים בפרטים בין מבנה העדה העולה מברד"מ לבין זה שמשתקף בסרך-היחד ובעית היחס בין שני החיבורים עדיין מחכה לפתרונה. ראה סקירתי "Qumran Sectarian Literature," *Jewish Writings of the Second Temple Period* (ed. M. E. Stone; Assen, 1984) 502-503.

6 לפי שעה ראה את נסיון השחזור של פיצמאייר (לעיל, הערה 4).

7 ראה, למשל: P. R. Davies, *The Damascus Covenant* (JSOTSup 25; Sheffield, 1982), והספרות הנסקרת בהקדמתו (עמ' 3-47).

8 עד עתה עבר מחקר ברד"מ שלושה שלבים: מגילוי החיבור בגניזת קהיר עד לגילויי מגילות קומראן; מגילויי המגילות עד לפרסום מגילת המקדש; מפרסום מגילת המקדש עד עתה. ראה סקירתו של דייויס שם.

9 המחקר הספרותי המקיף ביותר שנעשה עד עתה על ברד"מ הוא של: J. Murphy-O'Connor שכתב סדרת מאמרים על הנושא ב- *HTR* 64 (1971) 210-232; 78 *RB* 77 (1970) 201-229; 544-564, 200-216 (1972) *RB* 79; 379-386 (1971). עבודתו של דייויס לעיל מבוססת במידה רבה על קביעותיו של מרפי-אוקונור ואולם יש פרכות רבות בניתוח הספרותי ובמסקנות ההיסטוריות שהסיקו השניים ממנו.

בין מקרא למגילות: ציטטות מן התורה במגילת ברית דמשק

דבורה דימנט

זכה שמריהו טלמון להיות ממניחי היסוד למחקר המגילות הגנוזות ומחדי העין שהאירו אותן. את יתדותיו במחקר זה תמך בעיון מדוקדק במקרא, ועליהן בנה את בניין מחקרו רב ההשראה במגילות, בתרגומים ובספרים אחרים הנשענים על המקרא ויונקים ממנו. מקווה אני שעיון זה שאני מניחה לפניו על מקרא ועל מגילות ראוי יהיה לבעל היובל ולדרכו במחקר.

העיון הקצר המובא כאן מוקדש לדרכי השימוש בציטטות מקראיות במגילת ברית־דמשק (=ברד״מ). מצויים בידינו כמה מחקרים על השימוש במקרא במגילות מדבר יהודה בכלל, וגם סקירות על ציטטות של ממש,[1] אך אין הם יוצאים מגדר של איסוף החומר ותיאורו, ואף זאת באופן ראשוני בלבד. מבחינה זו לא נשתנתה גורלה של מגילת ברד״מ, אף על פי שזכתה להתוודע אל החוקרים כארבעים שנה קודם לגילוי המגילות.[2]

---

1   ראה את רשימותיהם של: J. Carmignac, "Les citations de l'Ancien Testament dans la 'Guerre des Fils de Lumière contre les fils de Ténèbres'," *RB* 63 (1956) 234-260, 375-390; J. A. Fitzmyer, "The Use of Explicit Old Testament Quotations in Qumran Literature and in the New Testament," *Essays on the Semitic Background of the New Testament* (London, 1971) 3-58 ושם ספרות קודמת. על פירוש המקרא ראה למשל: W. H. Brownlee, "Biblical Interpretation among the Sectaries of the Dead Sea Scrolls," *BA* 14 (1951) 54-76 וספרו של: F. F. Bruce, *Biblical Exegesis in the Qumran Texts* (London, 1959), העוסק בעיקר בפשרים. כן הוא דין ספרו של: G. J. Brooke, *Exegesis at Qumran* (JSOTSup 29; Sheffield, 1985). מטבע הדברים הוקדשה עיקר תשומת לב המחקר לפרשנות הנבואה בפשרים. ראה את סיכומה של M. P. Horgan, *Pesharim* (CBQMS 8; Washington, 1979); ולאחרונה ב' ניצן, מגילת פשר חבקוק (ירושלים, תשמ״ו) 29-79.

2   ברוס, שם, עמ' 32-40 מקדיש פרק קצר לברד״מ, בעיקר לציטטות פשרים. כך גם ברוק, שם, עמ' 205-209, 302-309, העוסק בשתי ציטטות פשר בברד״מ. סקירה קצרה על הציטטות המפורשות בברד״מ, בסרך היחד, במגילת מלחמת בני אור וב־4QFlor כלולה במאמרו הנ״ל של פיצמאייר; סקירה מפורטת, אך חסרת מסגרת שיטתית, על השימוש במקרא בחלק הדרשני של ברד״מ מצויה בעבודת הדוקטור של: O. J. R. Schwarz, *Der erste Teil der Damaskusschrift und das Alte Testament* (Lichtland, 1966).

לאורך כל הספרות של בני הכת ומשולב בה. על טכניקת השילוב של כתובי הנבואה במחשבה הכת כתבתי לעיל אגב הדגמה בכתובים נבחרים.

כמו אצל חז"ל ובעלי הברית החדשה אף בקומראן התפיסה היא, שהנבואה אינה קיימת עוד,[16] על כן הם פונים לעניין בשתי פנים, מחד הם ממנים עצמם כתחליף חי לנבואה המתה, ומאידך הם מצפים להתחדשות הנבואה.

כמו לגבי כלל ישראל כך גם בתפיסה האסכטולוגית של הכת מצוי גם המרכיב של ציפיה להופעה מחודשת של הנביאים. דבר זה בא לידי ביטוי באמרות כגון "עד בוא נביא ומשיחי אהרון וישראל" (הסרכים IX, 11-10).[17] מכאן, שבהשקפת הכת ראו לצרף לצד המשיח(ים) גם את הנביא. והשווה ללשון בחשמונאים א' ד, מו ייניחו את האבנים על הר הבית במקום מיוחד עד בוא נביא להורות עליהו'.[18] וכן תנחומא בהעלותך וא"ו: 'כשיעור הקב"ה ברחמיו ויבנה ביתו והיכלו הוא מחזיר (ולפני כן נזכרה גניזת הארון והמנורה **ורוח הקודש** והכרובים) למקום ומשמחן את ירושלים' (נוסח שונה במקצת בא בתנחומא באבער בהעלותך י"א). והשווה תנחומא באבער בהעלותך כ"ח: 'אמר הקב"ה בעולם הזה יחידים נתנבאו, אבל לעולם הבא כל ישראל יהיו נביאים, שנאמר והיה אחרי כן אשפוך את רוחי על כל בשר ונבאו בניכם ובנותיכם' וגי'. באותה מידה ניתן לראות ב-Testimonia ציפיה להופעת נביא. המדובר בטקסט המצטט, בין השאר, (שם, שורות 5 ואילך) את חוק הנביא שבדברים יח:[19] 'נבי אקים להאמה מקרב אחיהמה כמוהי'.[20] כן בא שם שימוש בדברים ה ו-לג ובמדבר כד. אין ספק, ששיבוץ עניין זה במסגרת האחרית מלמד, שלפי שיטתם יזכו אז בני הכת לחידוש הנבואה. אלא שבהווה, בחיי הכת, יש תחליף לנבואה, המכוון הוא ליצירות הפרשניות שנוסדו בכת על בסיסם של הנביאים הקלאסיים שבמקרא.

---

16 על ישו כתחליף לנבואה ואף עולה עליה, ראה י' ידין, "מגילות ים המלח והאיגרת אל העברים", מחקרים במגילות הגנוזות (ירושלים, תשכ"א) 194-193, 206-205 כמקביל לרעיון שבפשר חבקוק, וראה גם: M. Burrows, "Prophecy and Prophet at Qumran," *Israel's Prophetic Heritage: J. Muilenburg Jubilee Volume* (London, 1982) 223-232. לפי בץ, שם, עמ' 68-61, מורה הצדק ראה את עצמו כנביא. לפי פלוסר יש בנצרות מקום מיוחד לתפיסת ישו כנביא ושהתגלמותו מבטלת את הכתרים המקובלים: נבואה, מלוכה וכהונה באשר הוא נביא האמת, ראה: יהדות ומקורות הנצרות (ת"א, תשל"ט) 408-407 וכן הערה 8 (ושם ספרות) על מתי יב, מא-מב, ועיין אצל בורוס שם, תכופות. לעניין זה ראה עתה גם את המאמר: F. E. Greenspahn, "Why Prophecy Ceased," *JBL* 108 (1989) 37-49.

17 עיין בפירושו של ליכט למקום, וכן י' ליוור, "המשיח מבית דוד במגילות מדבר יהודה", עיונים במגילות מדבר יהודה (ירושלים, תשי"ז) 74 וכן בהערה 67, שם. לפי ליוור תפקיד הנביא לקבוע את זהות המשיח מאהרון, ובכלל זה לבשר על בוא אחרית הימים, וכן ידין, עמ' 206. כתוב מקביל לנ"ל הוא ברית דמשק VI, 11-10 'עד עמד יורה הצדק באחרית הימים', שניתן לפרשו כמביע את הרעיון, שאנשי הכת ציפו להופעתו מחדש של 'מורה (=יורה) הצדק'. בנוסח מקביל לאמור 'עד בוא נביא ומשיחי אהרון וישראל' שבסרכים.

18 לנושאים אלו עיין אצל א' סגינין, "נבואה ואפוקלפטיקה ביהדות של ימי בית שני", פרקים בתולדות ירושלים בימי בית שני, ספר זכרון לאברהם שליט (ירושלים, תשמ"א) 458-453.

19 ראה .4Q175 ll. 5 ff., לנוסח אחר ראה 4Q158, 6, ll. 6-10. נושא הנבואה היה, איפוא, במוקד התעניינותה של הכת.

20 מאידך הופעתו של חוק הנביא במגילת המקדש אין לייחס לה אלמנט אידיאולוגי, באשר הדברים מובאים במסגרת הבאות מרובות ורצופות מספר דברים, מקום שבמקרה 'מכסה' גם את דברים יח - חוק הנביא.

מקום מרכזי לנושא 'פי ה'' תופס הכתוב בספר ירמיה העוסק במינויו מחדש לתפקיד לאחר שניסה לברוח ממנו: 'אם תשוב ואשיבך **לפני תעמוד** ואם תוציא יקר מזולל **כפי תהיה**' (יר' טו, יט). היינו, ירמיהו יהיה ראוי לחזור ולהיחשב 'פי ה'' אם יעמוד בתנאים הנזכרים. למעשה זה השימוש "הגבוה" ביותר מבין שימושי 'פי ה'', באשר בעוד שהלשונות הקודמים עניינים בסמכותיות של האישים בכך שדבריהם באו להם מפי האל, הרי כאן הוגדר הנביא כפי האל ממש.

במגילות בא, כאמור, צירוף זה בהקשרים שונים וראוי להפנות לאחד הכתובים המרכזיים בנדון: הודיות I,20 'יועל פיכ[ה ודברכה נה]יה כול ומבלעדיך לא יעשה'. כתוב זה מקיף יותר מאלה שהבאנו מן המקרא, באשר בו נאמר באורח כללי ועקרוני, שהכל נהיה על פי האל ועל פי קביעתו והחלטתו.

עוד על תפקיד מנהיגי הכת

בפתיחת מגילת ברית דמשק מובאת סקירה של קורות עם ישראל מנקודת מבטה של הכת: 'הסתיר (האל) את פניו מישראל וממקדשו ויתנם לחרבי' (4-3,I). בהמשך נזכרו מעמדו המיוחד של מורה הצדק 'ויקם להם מורה צדק להדריכם בדרך לבו ויודע לדורות אחרונים את אשר עשה בדור אחרון בעדת בוגדים הם סרי דרך היא העת אשר היה כתוב עליה..........' (שם, 11-13). מעמדו של מורה הצדק הוגדר כמי שהאל 'הקימו' (לתפקידו) (השווה לעמ' ב, יא 'יואקים מבניכם לנביאים'), התפקיד מוגדר בלשון 'להדריכם בדרך לבו ויודע לדורות אחרונים את אשר עשה בדור אחרון' (12-11,I). יצוין, שלא כבשני הטקסטים מפשר חבקוק (דפים II -VII) לא נאמר כאן, שהוא נתמנה לפרש את רזי הנבואות, אבל נאמר, שהוא נצטווה להודיע לבריות את אשר יקרה 'בדור אחרון' (12,I; השווה פשר חבקוק II, 7), דבר שיש בו ממסמני העיסוק בנבואות העתיד של הנביאים. דבר זה אינו רחוק מן האמור בפשר חבקוק.

בסיום הקטע של התיאור ההיסטורי (15-14,II) הוא פונה אל העדה ואומר: 'ועתה בנים שמעו לי ואגלה עיניכם לראות ולהבין במעשי אל' וגו'. הרי זה לערך תפקידו המוגדר של מורה הצדק כפי שעולה לעיל בעקבות I, 11. נמצא, שתפקידו של בעל המגילה קרוב לתפקיד מורה הצדק בהארת עיני העם בדבר משמעות הנבואה לגבי חייהם בהווה. מקטע אחר במגילה זו, 33-32,XX, אף למדנו, שבהאזינם לקול מורה הצדק דבקים הם בחוקי הצדק, ומכאן עולה, שלהטפת המורה יש אופי של מצוות, והשווה לעיל בסעיף 3 על הקשר בין מצוות התורה ודברי הנביאים.

סיכום: השקפת הכת על הנבואה

כפי שהעלינו במאמר עשו אנשי כת מדבר יהודה שימוש רב בספרות הנבואה המקראית. בכתביהם הם מזכירים את אמרות הנביאים ואת המובא בספרי הנביאים. אף ראינו, שהמגילות משופעות במובאות מפורשות מדברי נביאים. הפנייה לגוש זה מתוך כלל הספרות המקראית באה משום הרוח של דברי הנביאים הפונה לעתיד ושאינה מתייחסת בהכרח לתקופה קונקרטית. מחברי קומראן ראו את הנביאים כאישים שבאו אחר משה, היינו, אחר התורה, כממשיכיה וכמפרשיה. עם זאת פירשו בכת את האמור בנבואה כמכוון אל דור שלהם ואל קורותיהם הספציפיים. מימושה של תפיסה זו הוא במערכת פירושים, שבהם הצביעו על זיקתה של ספרות הנבואה לחייהם העכשוויים. פירושים אלה חלקם מסודר וערוך לדבר, אבל רובו הוא מפוזר

---

15 אף בץ (לעיל, הערה 12), עמ' 75-76 הקביל מקום זה לפשר חבקוק II ו- VII.

לשון מקביל לאמור על הכהן, שהאל נתן בלבו בינה לפשור את כול דברי עבדיו הנביאים. נמצא, ששני אלה הם דמויות המפתח בכת לגבי התפקיד והיחס לכתבי הנביאים.[12] אף בדף זה (VII) נמסרה אימרה נוספת בנדון ובה נאמר 'אשר יארוך הקץ האחרון ויתר על כול אשר דברו הנביאים כיא רזי אל להפליא' (VII, 7-8). היינו, שהתגשמות דברי הנביאים תארך מעבר לזמן שהנביאים ציפו, 'כי רזי אל להפליא' - ואין לשער את המועד להתרחשויות, באשר הם בגדר רזי אל הפלאיים.[13]

גם בטקסטים נוספים עולה תמונה קרובה. כך ב- 4Q171 1-2, I, l. 19 'ולוא שמ[עו] למליץ דעתי'. והדין הוא עם בראונלי, שימליץ דעתי' הוא תואר למורה הצדק.[14] עוד בא רעיון זה בניסוח כללי ועקרוני בברית דמשק VII, 17-18 'ספרי הנביאים אשר בזה ישראל את דבריהם'. וכן נאמר בפשר חבקוק II, 2-3 'כי לא [האמינו בדברי] מורה הצדקה מפיא אל ועל הבוג[דים] וגו'. ואין לשונות הללו רחוקים מאלה האמורים על הכהן. על זאת יש להוסיף, שטענות כאלה כנגד העם באות במקרא פעמים הרבה על אי ציות לנביאים. נמצא, שמנהיגי הכת משתמשים ממשיכיהם של הנביאים המקראיים גם בייחס לנושא הזה.

צירוף לשון אחר החוזר לאותה תמונה על הבינה שניתנה בידי יחידי סגולה בא גם בהודיות XIV, 8 '[אודכה] אדוני הנותן בלב עבדכה בינה'. מן הסתם מכוון מתן הבינה למערכת מסועפת של כשרים, השייכים לפינות השונות של החיים, ואין מניעה, שאף הכושר לפירוש הנבואות עתיקות-היומין כלול בזה. נמצאת למד, שתפילה שגרתית בקומראן, כגון זו שבהודיות יכולה לכלול תודה לאל על הענקת החסד הגדול למנהיג המכונה כאן 'עבדכה'. אף תן דעתך להמשך הכתוב בו נאמר (שורות 12-13): 'ואני ידעתי **ומבינתך** כי ברצונכה בא[ר]וח קודשך וכן תגישנו **לבינתך**'. נמצא, הקטע ממוקד בין שני מרכזים - בינת האל מחד והבינה האלהית שהוענקה לו מהאל עצמו מאידך. אף נאמר 'וכן תגישנו לבינתך' המקשר בין שני 'סוגיי' הבינה.

ללשון 'מפי אלי' שמצאנו לעיל והמביע את הסמכות האלוהית של דברי השווה הודיות XII, 9 'מפי אלי'. אף נכתב כזאת בטקסט 4Q163, 8-10, l. 8 'ואשר [כתו]ב בספר זכריה מפ[י] אלי'. אם ההשלמה נכונה, מה שיוחס לפנים לנביאים שדבריהם הם 'מפי אלי', עתה זכה מורה הצדק לכך: 'כי לא [האמינו בדברי] מורה הצדקה מפיא אל ועל הבוג[דים]' וגו' (פשר חבקוק II, 2-3). שווה גם הודיות XI, 34. עניין הלשון 'מפי אלי' הוא משמעותי, לדעתי, לעניין בדיקת הייחס לנבואה ולנביאים בספרות הכת.

יש לציין, שאחד השימושים של הלשון 'מפי אלי' במקרא הוא לתיאור מקור סמכותם האלהית של הנביאים. כך דה"ב לו, יב 'לא נכנע מלפני ירמיהו הנביא מפי ה", יר' ט, 'ואשר דבר פי ה' אליו'. ואף כשרוצים להגדיר את מעמדם המזוייף של נביאי השקר משתמשים הכתובים בלשון זה 'חזון לבם ידברו לא מפי ה" (יר' כג, טז). אף במגילות השתמשו בלשונות כאלה לציון נביאי שקר: 'מפי נביאי כזב מפותי תעות' (הודיות IV, 16), שהוא ציון לכך שאין דבריהם 'מפי אלי'.

---

8), עמ' 57-58. השווה, למשל, שוחר טוב צ, ד, שפרט למשה ולישעיהו לא ידעו הנביאים עצמם את תוכן נבואותיהם ומשמעותן, השווה אגרת פטרוס א' א, י-יב, שהנביאים לא ידעו כלל את תוכן דבריהם. לפי קוה"ר א, ח הנביאים ראו רק מקצת מן העתיד 'כמבין סדקו של פתח', השווה גם פילון *Quis Rerum*, 265-266 וראה גם בראונלי, שם, עמ' 28-30.

12 הרבה הצביעו על תפקיד מורה הצדק כמקביל לתפקיד דניאל אשר 'פשרי' הוא את דברי ירמיהו ויחזקאל, השווה דנ' ט, ב. חיא גינזברג סבר למצוא פירוש לשירי עבד ה' בספר דניאל, וראה אנציקלופדיה מקראית ב (ירושלים, תשי"ד) 950; וראה גם בראונלי, שם, עמ' 28-30; O. Betz, *Offenbarung und Schriftforschung in der Qumransekt* (Tübingen, 1960) 61-68.

13 עיין בפירוט אצל ב' ניצן (לעיל, הערה 1), עמ' 173-174.

14 השווה בראונלי, עמ' 111, ועיין גם עמ' 55, שם.

יהיה לי לבן׳ וגו׳, העוסק במקורו בהבטחת השושלת הנערצת של בית דוד, על המנהיגות באחרית הימים (4QFlor 1-2, I, ll. 10-11).
מכל אלה עולה, שכמעט כל כתובי הספרות הנבואית שנדרשו במגילות נתפרשו על הכת ועל קורותיה ותקוותיה.

5. תפקיד הכת ביחס לנבואה המקראית

בפרק הקודם עמדנו על תפיסת הכת את ספרות הנבואה כמבשרת הקורות האקטואליים והאידיאולוגיים של הכת. עתה נפנה לצד שונה של הנושא, והוא עניין ראיית מנהיגי הכת את תפקידם שלהם ביחס לנבואה הקדומה. שני טקסטים בסיסיים קיימים בנדון: פשר חבקוק II ו-VII.

במקור הראשון (II,6-10) נאמר: ׳אשר לוא יאמינוא בשומעם את כול הבא[ות על] הדור האחרון מפי הכוהן אשר נתן אל ב[לבו בינ]ה לפשור [את] כול דברי עבדיו הנביאים [אשר ב]ידם ספר אל את כול הבאות על עמו וע[ל עדתו]׳.
המקור השני בא בדף VII שורות 1-8: ׳וידבר אל אל חבקוק לכתוב את הבאות על הדור האחרון ואת גמר הקץ לא הודיעו ואשר אמר למען ירוץ הקורא בו פשרו על מורה הצדק אשר הודיעו אל את כל רזי דברי עבדיו הנבאים כיא עוד חזון למועד יפיח לקץ ולוא יכזב פשרו אשר יארוך הקץ האחרון ויתר על כול אשר דברו הנביאים כיא רזי אל להפלה׳.
מכאן יוצא, שלפי השקפת הכת דברי הנביאים מבשרים את דבר האל לעת מסויימת, אלא שמשמעם המדוייק ובעיקר זמן תחולתם לא נזכרו ושמא לא נודעו אף לנביאים עצמם. לפי דף II לכהן יש כושר לומר ׳את כול הבא[ות על] הדור האחרון׳ בזכות האל ׳אשר נתן אל ב[לבו בינ]ה לפשור [את] כול דברי עבדיו הנביאים׳.
באידיאולוגיה זו יש, איפוא, חלוקה ברורה בין שני כוחות:

1. הנביאים (המקראיים) שבהם הפקיד האל את סיפור הקורות לבוא.
2. הכהן (בכת) אשר לו נתן האל בינה לפשור את דברי הנביאים.

נמצא, ששני הכוחות הללו פועלים מכוח המנדט והיכולת, שהאל העניק להם:

הכהן - ׳אשר נתן אל ב[לבו׳
הנביאים - ׳אשר ב]ידם ספר אל את כול הבאות׳

מכאן עולה, שדברי הנביאים אינם יכולים להיות ברורים ביחס לזמן ולנתונים נוספים של התקיימותם, ובלא פעולת הכהן, לו ניתנה ההבנה לפשור את דברי הנביאים, לא היו אלו מובנים לבני הדור האקטואלי.[10] וכל כך משום שלנביאים לא נאמרה תמונת העתיד בשלמותה ורק באמצעות מורה הצדק יודיע האל את רזי דברי עבדיו הנביאים (פשר חבקוק VII,4-5).[11] הרי זה

---

10 בכך אני מפרש אחרת מאשר פיצמאייר: J. A. Fitzmyer, "The Use of Explicit O.T. Quotations in Qumran Literature and in the N.T.," *Essays on the Semitic Background of the N.T.* (London, 1971) 22-23. לדעתו, הדברים נאמרו לחבקוק בדורו ובהם משמעות על ׳הדור האחרון׳, אולם דברים אלה הועברו אל ימי הכת בזכות אישיותו הכריזמטית של מורה הצדק. לעניין מתן משמעות אקטואלית לטקסט עתיק מפנה פיצמאייר לאל הרומיים טו, ד, וראה גם אל הקורונתיים א׳ י, יא, אל הרומיים ד, כג-כד על ערך נוסף לכתוב לבד מעניין זמנו המקורי גם לקורא האקטואלי. ועיין עוד לקמן. וראה אליגר: K. Elliger, *Studien zur Habakuk Kommentar vom Toten Meer* (Tübingen, 1953) 171, 190-191, על המורה והכהן כפרשני הספרות הנבואית שבמקרא.

11 במקורות יש תפיסות שונות בדבר היקף הידע של הנביאים וראה על כך אצל בראונלי (לעיל, הערה

הנביאים'. וכבר העירותי לעיל על מעמדו של הלשון 'פשרו' בספרות הפשרים. הדבר קשור בסמכות, שנטלו בעלי הפשרים להודיע על המשמעות של ההתגשמות **האקטואלית** של דברי הנביאים (ועיין לקמן).

עוד מוצאים כאן נסיונות של פירוש כתוב נבואי אחד ('מה נאוו על הרים רגלי מבשר' וגו') על ידי זיהויו לכתוב אחר ('יהוא הכתוב אשר אמר עליו נחם א[בילי ציון]'). זו היא טכניקה של פירוש אקטואלי של דברי נביא בדברים אחרים משלו. בהמשך בא פשר נוסף על ידי השוואתם וזיהויים לדברי דניאל: יוהמבשר (=שבדברי ישעיהו) הו[אה מ[שיח הרו[ח] אשר אמר דני[אל[9] עליו עד משיח נגיד שבועים שבעה]'. כלומר, שני כתובים מחברים שונים הופגשו במאמץ פרשני לקבוע את תחולתם בהתאם לאידיאולוגיה ולסמכות הפרשנית של המחבר. הלשון '[דברי] הנביאי[ם' מצביע על אחד היסודות העיקריים ללימודו של אנשי הכת. ועיין לעיל על השוואת צירוף לשון זה ללשון 'ספרי הנביאים' שבברית דמשק.

מבנה הפירוש של הטקסט הנדון כך הוא: ההרים שבכתוב נתפסו ככלל דברי הנביאים והמשך הפסוק ('הנה על הרים) רגלי מבשר' נתפרש על כתוב מסויים. יש להעיר, ששימוש הכתובים בקטעים שהזכרנו שונה ממה שמצאנו במגילות הפשרים הגדולות, באשר שם יש שיטה קבועה להבאה: פסוק ופשרו, פסוק ופשרו, ואילו כאן משום דרך בחירת הכתובים, שאינה כפויה על המחבר, הוא בוחר את כתוביו לפי הקו שהוא קבע. ועוד: פעמים כתוב מסויים משמש למחבר חלק ממערכת הפירוש לכתוב אחר.

לאור מכלול הכתובים של גוש הנביאים, שסופרי קומראן עשו בהם שימוש בכתביהם, יש להעיר הערות נוספות על אלו שהעירונו לעיל: הרוב הגדול של כתובים מספרות הנבואה בא במגילות לצורך הדגמה של סיוע קדום לציפיות בני הכת לעניינים השונים של זמנם שלהם. כך נתפרשו כתובים מקראיים על הדור האחרון ועל הקורות בו וזאת מתוך הודעה, שהאל הודיע לישראל מראש באמצעות הנביאים את משמע הקורות.

כתובים שונים מן הנבואה נתפרשו על מעבר אנשי הכת לדמשק (ברית דמשק VII, 13) וגם הכתוב 'במדבר פנו דרך ה'' פורש על קורות הכת (הסרכים VIII, 14 ואילך). 'דורש התורה' ממנהיגי הכת נתפרש ככלי שהאל העמידו לתפקידו, ולכן הוא מושא הפירוש של הכתוב 'מוציא כלי למעשיהו' (ברית דמשק VI, 8-7). טוהר מוצאם והתאמתם המלאה לתפקידם של מנהיגי הכת נלמדו מתוך הפירוש לכתוב 'יהכהנים והלויים בני צדוק' שביחי מד, טו (ברית דמשק III, IV-21, 1) והם מקיימי הכתוב במל' א, י (=ברית דמשק VI, 13-12) והם הם 'מסגירי הדלת'. לפי שיטת הכת המקדש מחולל עתה מפשעי בני ישראל ומה להם להוסיף חטא ולבקר במקדש כזה, על כן הם נמנעים מלבוא אליו ולקיים בו את ההליכים הפולחניים. את עונשי האל הנזכרים בכתובי הנבואה הם מפרשים על אויביהם, כך לגבי הכתוב ביחז' בחזקת [היד ויסרני מלכת בדרך] העם הזה והמה אשר כתוב עליהמה בספר יחזקאל הנביא אשר לו[א יטמאו עוד] [בג[ל[ו]ליהמה' (4QFlor 1-2, I, ll. 15-17). ועליהם יבוא בליעל משולח (ברית דמשק IV, 13-12) והם מסיגי הגבול ועברת ה'' תשפוך עליהמ' (VIII, 3). נפש האל נקעה מהם והוא יענישם בהחרבת מוסדות השלטון ('אין מלך ואין שרי הוי ג, ד - ברית דמשק VIII, 39 = XX, 16).

הגורל הרע מכוון, כאמור, לרשעים, ואילו העתיד הטוב מכוון לכת ולאנשיה. האויב יסולק - כפירוש הכתתי לכתוב שמספר ישעיה - 'ונפל אשור בחרב לא איש' (ישי' לא, ח - מגילת המלחמה XI, 11). ועליהם יחילו את בוא יום הישועה בידי מלכיצדק, שבו יבוא הזמן לנחם לאבילי ציון (מדרש מלכיצדק טור II, שורות 20-17). הכת פירשה על עצמה את בוא המשיח באחרית יהוקימותי את זרעכה אחריכה והכינותי את כסא ממלכתו [לעו[לם' וכן פירשו את הכתוב יהוא

---

9 על השלמה זו השווה קובלסקי (לעיל, הערה 1), עמי 21.

נמצא, שההתייחסות לפסוק הנבואי, דברי ישעיהו, מלופפת משני צדדיה: תחילה - בדברי צפייה לעתיד משל המחבר 'ובכל השנים האלה יהיה...כאשר דברי וגו'. אחרי הציטטה בא הסבר נוסף הפותח ב'פשרו', שהוא כאמור, פתיחה שגרתית בפשרים לפירוש האקטואלי של דברי נבואה. המיוחד כאן הוא, שחלק מן הפשר הוא ציטוט נוסף והפעם של מקור חיצוני, דברי לוי בן יעקב.

גם ב־VI, 7 בא נוסח של השוואה פרשנית ואקטואלית 'והמחוקק (על פי במ' כא, יח) הוא דורש התורה' לזה מוסיף המחבר את הסימוכין הנבואי שהוא בסיס הפירוש: 'אשר אמר ישעיה מוציא כלי למעשיהו' (VI, 7-8). תפקיד משפט הזיהוי הוא לקשר את המציאות עם נבואת הנביא. דין הצירוף 'הוא....אשר אמר ישעיה' כדין הלשון הקודם 'כאשר דבר אל כיד ישעיה הנביא'. ויש לציין, שבשני הכתובים בא הביאור (או חלק ממנו) **לפני** הפסוק, בניגוד לספרות הפשרים בה בא הפירוש בדרך כלל **אחר** הכתוב המצוטט.

נוסחה מפורטת יותר באה שם VII, 10 ואילך: 'יבבוא הדבר אשר כתוב בדברי ישעיה בן אמוץ הנביא אשר אמר יבוא עליך ועל עמך ועל בית אביך ימים אשר [לא] באו מיום סור אפרים מעל יהודה בהפרד שני בתי ישראל שר אפרים מעל יהודה וכל הנסוגים הוסגרו לחרב והמחזיקים נמלטו לארץ צפון'.

תן דעתך למבנה הקטע: מתוארת בו מציאות, שהמחבר רואה כהתגשמות דברי האלהים. זהו פשר הצירוף 'כבוא הדבר'. יש לשים לב לניסוח הכפול של פעולת הנביא, מחד ההפנייה היא **לכתוב** בספרו ('יאשר כתוב בדברי ישעיה בן אמוץ הנביא') ומאידך לנאמר על ידיו ('ישעיה בן אמוץ הנביא אשר **אמר**') וגו'. מכאן עולה, שפעולתו הוגדרה כאמירה. היינו, שבתודעת בעל ברית דמשק יש שתי תמונות על מפעלי הנביאים, מחד הוא רואה אותם כאישים נואמים ומדברים, ומאידך הוא מכיר כבר את דבריהם בכללותם בספר, על כן הוא מזכיר את הכתוב בהם. ועיין על כך לעיל בסעיף 1 - נביאים וספריהם.

שיטה זו של ביאור אקטואלי לדברי הנביאים באה גם בפלורילגיום 4QFlor 1-2, I, l. 16 'והמה אשר כתוב עליהמה בספר יחזקאל הנביא אשר לו[א יטמא עוד] [בג]ל[ו]ליהמה המה בני צדוק' וגו'. יושם אל לב, ששיטת הזיהוי הכפול מופעלת גם כאן. ראשית בזיהוי 'והמה אשר כתוב' וגו', ושנית - 'המה בני צדוק' וגו'. בכך ממסגר המחבר את הכתוב הנבואי בין שתי אמרות משלו המהוות פירוש מיידי ואקטואלי לכתוב. בטקסט שלפני כן (15-16) נאמר 'אשר כתוב בספר ישעיה הנביא לאחרית [ה]ימים ויה יכחזקת [היד ויסרני מלכת בדרך] העם הזה'. הכתוב מספר ישעיה הובא להצדקת הפירוש הפותח 'פשר הדב[ר על] סרי מדרך [ ]העם' וגו', שהוא פירוש לפסוק מתהילים א 'ומדרש מאשרי [ה]איש אשר לוא הלך'. נמצא, שלפנינו שיטה של פשר אקטואלי, המדבר על התחולה הכתתית של דברי המקרא ובעיקר של קטעי הנבואה שבו. שיטת הפירוש ערוכה לפי עקרונות של שרשור, עירוב והשתלשלות של כתובים מקראיים בקטעי פירוש אקטואלי.

ודוגמא אחרונה בפרק זה: במדרש מלכיצדק טור II, 15-20 אנו מוצאים שוב את לשונות הזיהוי הפרשנים הללו. '....הזואת הואה יום ה[ישועה א]שר אמר [אל עליו ביד ישע]יה הנביא אשר אמר [מה] נאוו על הרים רגלי מבש[ר מ]שמיע שלום מב[שר טוב משמיע ישוע]ה אומר לציון [מלך] אלהיך פשרו ההר[י]ם [דברי] הנביאי[ם] המה א[שר] נב[או] לכול [אבילי ציון] והמבשר הו[אה מ]שיח הרו[ח] אשר אמר דנ]יאל עליו עד משיח נגיד שבועים שבעה ומבשר [טוב משמי[ע ישועה] הואה הכ[תו]ב אשר [אמר] לנח[ם] א[בילי ציון]' וגו'.

בטקסט יש צירוף של דרכי ביטוי חשובות לנדון: ראשית יש כאן הודעה, שהמציאות היא על פי בשורת ישעיהו (השני). עוד בא כאן כמו בברית דמשק הלשון 'פשרו' - 'פשרו ההרים דברי

לדיון באספקטים דומים ראה בראונלי: W. H. Brownlee, *The Midrash Pesher of Habakkuk* (Ann Arbor, MI, 1979) 28-30.

מסויימים בשמותיהם המפורשים בצירוף לכתובים מנבואתיהם.

4. תפקיד הנביאים המקראיים ומעמדם במחשבת הכת

עתה נעמוד על טקסטים אחדים שמהם ניתן לראות את תפיסת אנשי הכת בנדון מעמד הנביאים. מתוך האמור במגילת המלחמה XI, 7-8 ניתן לראות בבירור את צורת הערכת הדמויות הנבואיות, שכן אמור שם, 'וביד משיחיכה חוזי תעודות הגדתה לנו ק[צי] מלחמות ידיכה להלחם באויבינו להפיל גדודי בליעל....ביד אביוני פדותכה'. כינויי הנביאים 'חוזי תעודות' והציון 'הגדתה' זורעים אור בהיר על התפקיד, שהאל הטיל על הנביאים: האל 'מגיד' באמצעותם את העתיד לקרות ועל כן הקורות בעתיד — 'התעודות' — ייאמרו בידם. גם בהודיות II, 14-15 נזכר רמז לתפקידם, 'לכול חוזי נכוחות'. אף עולה מזה, שתחילת דבריהם של נביאי המקרא היא על הימים הנוכחיים, קורותיהם האקטואליים של בני הכת.

בשורת כתובים במגילות ניתן ללמוד על תפקיד הנביאים לפי תפיסת הכת:

כבר בכתובים שנדונו בפרק הראשון ניתן לראות פן מסויים של תפקיד הנביאים וכתביהם בחיי הכת. נחזור ונביא קצת מן הכתובים של סעיף 1 - נביאים וספריהם - כדוגמה להוכיח את דברינו, ועליהם יתוספו כתובים אחרים, שיש בהם אותו כיוון.

בברית דמשק VII, 10-11 נאמר: 'כבוא הדבר אשר כתוב בדברי ישעיה בן אמוץ הנביא אשר אמר'. הרי שהמחבר רואה במציאות שבהווה את התגשמותם של דברי ישעיהו, 'כבוא הדבר אשר כתוב' וגו'. וכן נזכרה התייחסות לספר נבואה בלשון 'אשר כ]תוב עליהם בספר ירמ[יה]' ב-4Q182 1, l. 4.

צד חשוב של עניין זה הוא יחס מנהיגי הכת לכתובים מספרות הנבואה המקראית. בשורת טקסטים מן המגילות עולה, שהיוצרים בקומראן נוקטים פירוש של פשר לגבי כתובי הנביאים. מגמת הפשר היא להצביע על כך, שהכתובים מספרי הנביאים משמשים מקור לראייה לגבי ימי הכת וחייה. אביא עתה מספר כתובים שעולה מהם תפיסה מעין זו.

נפתח בברית דמשק IV, 12-15 שם נאמר, 'ובכל השנים האלה יהיה בליעל משולח בישראל כאשר דבר אל ביד ישעיה הנביא בן אמוץ לאמור פחד ופחת ופח עליך יושב הארץ פשרו שלושת מצודות בליעל אשר אמר עליהם לוי בן יעקב' וגו'.[7]

טכניקת הציטוט כך היא: בתחילה מובא כתוב ובצידו הלשון 'פשרו' כשיטת הפשרים המלאים, אך בברית דמשק זו הופעה חד פעמית של המונח. ניתוח האמור בשני טקסטים מתוך פשר חבקוק (II, 9-8; VII, 1-8) (על טקסטים אלה ראה דיון בהמשך) מלמד, שבכת ראו את מנהיגיה (=הכהן ומורה הצדק) כפרשנים הלגיטימיים של ספרות הנבואה: 'אשר הודיעו אל את כול רזי דברי עבדיו הנביאים' (VII, 4), 'נתן אל ב[לבו בינ]ה לפשור [את] כול דברי עבדיו הנביאים' (II, 9-8). נמצא, שהשימוש בלשון 'פשרו' חוזר לאותה נקודת מוצא, היינו, כוונת הלשון 'פשרו (על)' לקשור בין האמרה הנבואית לבין פירושה האקטואלי. מכאן שהכהן, למשל, רואה את עצמו כמי שהאל נתן לו בינה לפשור את כל דברי עבדיו הנביאים.

נחזור עתה לכתוב מברית דמשק. בעל החיבור טוען, שהקורות עתה ('יהיה בליעל משולח בישראל') הם 'כאשר דבר....ישעיה'. היינו, שהמחבר נוטל סמכות כפרשנה של נבואת ישעיהו. 'כאשר דברי' הוא לשון הזיהוי הטכני. המחבר אינו מסתפק בזיהויי פרשני זה, אלא הוא נעזר במאורעות כדי לאתר בעזרתם את משמעות דבר ה' הקדום, שנתבטא בהטפות הנביאים.[8]

---

7 כאן דוגמה נדירה לציטוט מקור חיצוני כדרך שהם מתייחסים בדרך כלל לפסוקי מקרא וכדומה.

8 על עקרונות הפשר ראה: B. E. Thiering, *Redating the Teacher of Righteousness* (Sydney, 1979) 10-12, 50, 194, etc. כגון על שיטת האטומיזציה; על פירוש קבוע למניח הבא בכתובים; ועוד. הזמנים בפשר מתפרשים, לדעתו, כך: החטאים - בעבר, העונשים - בעתיד.

תפיסת הנבואה המקראית בכתבי קומראן

גם ב- 2 ,4Q280, שמיליק כינה אותו וטקסטים נוספים מן המערה הרביעית 'סרך הטהרות', ניתן ללמוד על השוואת מעמדם של התורה והנבואה.[6] במסגרת הקללה כנגד מלכי רשע נאמר:

שורה   1   אר[ור אתה מלכי רשע בכול מח]שבות... [
        5 ....   וארורים עוש[י מחשבות רשעכה
        6 ....   לזום על ברית אל [ולמאוס את התורה ואת]
        7   [דבר]י כול חוזי אמ[תו וכ]ול המואס לבוא[‏

נזכרו כאן שני מקורות הסמכות העתיקים — התורה והנביאים ('חוזי אמ[תו) — שהרשעים חטאו כנגדם.
יש לשים לב שלפני טענה זו וגם אחריה תוארה בטקסט בגידת הרשעים בברית אל (שורות 6-7). ושמא 'ברית אל' הוא לשון כינוי למפעלם המשותף של התורה והנביאים.
אף ב- II ,4Q286 10 נאמרים דברים קרובים:

שורה 11   [וארורים כ]ול עוש[י מחשבות רשע]תמה ומקימי מזמתכה [בלבבמה לזום
        12   [על ברית א]ל ול[מאוס את דברי חוזי אמ]תו ולהמיר את משפ[טי] התורה

מהעמדת שני הטקסטים 4Q280 ו- 4Q286 זה בצד זה ניתן לאשר את ההשלמות בשניהם. בשני המקורות מדובר בהשוואת מעמד הנביאים למעמד התורה. יתרה מזאת - בקטע האחרון (4Q286) אף קדמה כנראה הזכרת הנביאים לתורה.
עוד בא הצירוף של התורה והנביאים בסמיכות במגילת הסרכים VIII, 15-16: '[אשר] צוה ביד מושה לעשות ככול הנגלה עת בעת וכאשר גלו הנביאים ברוח קודשו'. גם כאן מצויייה התייחסות לדרישת התורה כפי שנגלה 'עת בעתי' וכפי שגילו הנביאים, ונראה, שנרמז כאן לתפקיד הנביאים לבאר את תורת משה. אולם ברור, שעל פי פשט הדברים נראה, שהנביאים נזכרים בצד התורה כשני המקורות שבהם מתגלים דברי האל ומצוותיו. והשווה גם הסרכים I, 2-3 'לדרוש אל [   ] לעשות הטוב והישר לפניו כאשר צוה ביד מושה וביד כול עבדיו הנביאים'. ממקור זה עולה, שהוראות האל החשובות המחבר רואם כפי שרשומות בתורה ובספרות הנביאים, ונראה, שלפי השקפתו קדושת שתי החטיבות זהה, או לפחות קרובה ביותר.
יצויין, שאף מקורות שמחוץ למגילות ים המלח מקיימים שיטה זו, כך בברית החדשה ועוד. השווה, למשל, לוקס טז, כט-לא על ציות למשה ולנביאים, מפעלות כו, כב על השוואת הטפתו של פאולוס למפעלם של 'הנביאים וגם משה'.
צירוף מעניין ביותר של התורה והנביאים בא במגילת ברית דמשק VII, 14-20. בשיטה של כתובים המפרשים זה את זה נתבאר חלק ממרכיבי עמ' ה, כו-כז כמכוון לספרי התורה ('ספרי התורה הם סוכת המלך') והוא פירושם ללשון 'סכות מלככם' שבעמוס (בשינוי הנוסח). ההנמקה לביאור מובאת בהמשך הטקסט על פי כתוב אחר מספר עמוס (ט, יא) 'כאשר אמר והקימותי את סוכת דוד הנפלתי'. אחר כך בואר חלק אחר של הכתוב - עמ' ה, כו-כז - על ספרי הנביאים, 'וכיון הצלמים הם ספרי הנביאים אשר בזה ישראל את דבריהם'.
נמצא, שספרי התורה וספרי הנביאים נזכרו זה בצד זה כבסיס לתפיסת המחבר, התורה נזכרת בקוטב החיובי לגבי העתיד הטוב, והיא הושוותה לסוכה, שהאל עתיד להקים באחרית, ואילו ספרי הנביאים מוצבים בקוטב של העבר וההווה על שנזנחו ברשעת בני העם.
צירוף דברים קרוב לזה בא אולי במגילת מלכיצדק 17 .II 11QMelch, 1 'פשרו ההר[י]ם [דברי] הנביאי[ם] המה א[שר] נב[או] לכול [אבילי ציון]'. אם אמנם ההשלמה נכונה אזי כוונתה כאן יצירתם הכוללת של הנביאים 'דברי הנביאים', בעוד שלפני כן נזכרו בטקסט נביאים

---

6   J. T. Milik, "Milki-Ṣedek et Milki-resaʿ dans les anciens écrits juifs et chrétiens," *JJS* 23 (1972) 127-129; קובלסקי (לעיל, הערה 1), עמי 37-48.

אשר כתב מושה ועבדיכה
הנביאים אש[ר ש]לחתה ל[קר]תנו הרעה באחרית.

אף שהקטע קטן ועל אף שהההקשר אינו ברור ניתן להסיק ממנו על המעמד השווה של משה
והנביאים כמו בכתובים אחרים במגילות. יצוין, שהייחוס למשה כיוצר הוא על מעשי כתיבה,
והוא תיאור קבוע המיוחס לו במקורות שונים. גם ההתייחסות לנביאים בנוסח 'אשר שלחתה'
הוא מן המקובלים, השווה יר' ז, כה 'ואשלח אליכם את כל עבדי הנביאים', השווה עוד שם כג,
כא; דה"ב כד, יט, ועוד.

בגלל קיטוע הטקסט אין אפשרות להכריע מה נאמר בייחס לכתיבת משה, ומה הוא תפקיד
שליחת הנביאים אל העם. אף אפשר, שהלשון 'שלחתה' מכוון גם למשה.
מכל מקום המובא בהמשך מתייחס לתוכן אזהרת הנביאים, והוא קשור להודעה על הרעה,
שתבוא על העם באחרית.

בקטע מפשר הושע נאמר:

.....וישכחו את אל המ[ ]
מצוותיי השליכו אחרי גום אשר שלח אליהם [בפי]
עבדיו הנביאים ולמתעיהם שמעו ויכבדום.[5]

נוסף על 'עבדיו הנביאים' שהאל 'שלח אליהם' (ראה גם במקור הקודם) נזכרו כאן 'מצוותיי' של
האל שציווה לעם, ושהרשעים השליכו אחרי גוום. נראה לי, שהלשון 'מצוותיי' מכוון לתורה.
נמצא, גם כאן יש הצירוף של התורה (ספר המצוות) והנביאים. ואף אפשר, שניתן ללמוד מן
הטקסט עניין נוסף. הרי נאמר כאן:

אשר שלח אליהם [בפי]
עבדיו הנביאים...

כלומר, אף לפי מקור זה אחד מתפקידי הנביאים הוא לבשר ולהודיע את מצוות האל, הרי
שנתקרבו עוד יותר תפקידי הנביאים והתורה.
בפשר נאמר, שדחיית המצוות (=התורה) והנביאים לוותה בציות וכבוד למתעים, והוא רעיון
מקביל לאמור בברית דמשק V, VI-21,1: 'כי דברו (מסיגי הגבול) סרה על מצות אל ביד משה וגם
במשיחי הקודש'. כלומר, שמפעלם של משיחי הקודש נזכר כאובייקט להתקוממותיהם של מסיגי
הגבול, ועל פי ההקשר מסתבר, שמכוון בכינוי זה לנביאים. נראה, שהצירוף 'מצות ביד
(משה)' חל גם על ההמשך 'במשיחי הקודש', ואפשר שעולה מכך, שהאל מסר את מצוותיו גם
ביד הנביאים.

יש לציין, שפעולתם של מתנגדי הכוחות הללו מוגדרת כנבואה, 'וינבאו שקר להשיב את ישראל
מאחר אל' (שם, VI, 1-2). כלומר, המתעים הם נביאי השקר, שפעלו נגד משה ונגד נביאי האמת
המייצגים את הדת הנכונה. יש לציין עניין נוסף העולה בהשוואת הטקסטים הנדונים: בפשר
הושע הדיבור מכוון כנגד ישראל המותעים, ואילו בברית דמשק הפנייה היא כנגד 'מסיגי הגבול'
המתעים את ישראל.

טיעון דומה על דבקות בשליחי כזב, נביאי שקר, וזניחת השליחים האמיתיים, נביאי ה', עולה
ממגילת ההודיות IV, 15-18 'ומכשול עוון שמו לנגד פניים ויבואו לדורשכה מפי נביאי כזב
מפותי תעות. והם[ב]ל[וע]ג שפה ולשון אחרת ידברו לעמך להולל.....כי לא [ידעו אמרת]כה ולא
האזינו לדברכי'; כך הוא באשר לדבקות ברע. ואשר לזניחת השליחים הלגיטימיים נאמר: 'כי
אמרו לחזון דעת לא נכון ולדרך לבכה לא היאה'.

---

5 4Q166 II, ll. 3-5.

המכוון הוא ללא ספק לספר נבואי. כך, למשל, נאמר במגילת הסרכים VIII, 14-15 'כאשר כתוב במדבר פנו דרך....היאה מדרש התורה.........וכאשר גלו הנביאים ברוח קודשי, וברור, שמכוון לציטוט דברים מספר יש' מ, ג '(קול קורא) במדבר פנו דרך' וגו', אף שכאמור אין שם הנביא נזכר כאן במפורש.

2. פריסת החומר הנבואי במגילות

ניתן לעמוד על מידת השימוש בנבואה המקראית בספרות קומראן על ידי דיווח סטטיסטי של היקף השימוש בספרות זו על פי שלש מגילות, שבחרתי לצורך העניין.
בדיקת שלש מגילות גדולות בקומראן עשויה לשפוך אור על היקף השימוש המפורש של כתובים נבואיים בהן:[3] מגילת מלחמת בני אור בבני חושך, מגילת הסרכים ומגילת ברית דמשק.
במגילת מלחמת בני אור בבני חושך מופיעה רק מובאה **מפורשת** אחת מן המקרא: בדף XI, 11 מצוטט יש' לא, ח 'ונפל אשור בחרב לא איש וחרב לא אדם תאכלנו'.
במגילת הסרכים מופיעות שתי מובאות **מפורשות** מספרי הנבואה. כך בדף V, 17-18 מצוטט יש' ב, כב 'כאשר כתוב חדלו לכם מן האדם אשר נשמה באפו כיא במה נחשב הואה'. VIII, 14-15 מצטט את יש' מ, ג 'כאשר כתוב במדבר פנו דרך......ישרו בערבה מסלה לאלוהינו'. בברית דמשק מצויות שלש-עשרה מובאות **מפורשות** מספרי הנבואה. הכתובים שנזכרו במובאות אלו הם מן הספרים הבאים: ישעיה, יחזקאל, הושע, עמוס, מיכה, מלאכי. מבין אלה הספרים ישעיה והושע הם החיבורים, שהירבו לצטט מהם במגילה זו (שבע מובאות מכלל הנ"ל).

הכתובים שמן הנבואה הובאו לשם הדגמה של שנים-שלשה נושאים. בעיקרו של דבר במגילה זו נדונו כתובי הנבואה לשם הנושאים הבאים: תיאור חטאם של ישראל, העונש שייענשו בו על חטאים אלה, שאלות הגמול וכיו"ב.
מבדיקה פשוטה זו נסתבר, שהמשופעת ביותר במובאות מפורשות מן הנבואה היא מגילת ברית דמשק. הדבר בולט במיוחד משום שמדובר במגילות בגודלן דומה לערך. על כן נראה, שהשוני ה"כמותי" הוא פרי נטיית המחברים השונים של המגילות הללו, בכפוף, כמובן, לצרכים הנובעים מתוכני המגילות ומרעיונותיהן העיקריים, ובזה נבדלות המגילות זו מזו. מגילת הסרכים שבאו בה שתי מובאות בלבד היא יצירה משפטית תקנונית, ומובן שאין לזה קשר כלשהו עם הנבואה, שתוכנה ורוחה שונות מן האווירה המשפטית הנ"ל.

3. מעמד ספרי הנביאים בהשוואה לתורה במחשבת הכת

עתה נעסוק בשורת טקסטים בסיסיים מספרות הכת, שניתן ללמוד מהם את תפיסת מעמד הנבואה בייחס לחלקים אחרים של המקרא, ובעיקר לתורה.
בפרק זה נעמיד על תפיסת הכת את מעמד הנביאים. מסתבר, שלגבי נושאים שונים ראו מנהיגי הכת את הנבואה בנוסף להיותה ממשיכתה של התורה גם שוות ערך לה מבחינת קדושתה וכיו"ב. על כלל הצדדים הללו של הנושא אני עומד בפרק הנוכחי.
בטקסט ממגילה שנתפרסמה לאחרונה (4Q504 1-2, III, ll. 12-13) נאמר:[4]

---

3 בציטוט מפורש כוונתי לכתוב מקראי המובא במפורש ובמוצהר בתור שכזה. זאת להבדיל משימוש ברמזי לשון המעידים על בקיאותם של סופרי הכת בחומר המקרא. על לשונות הציטוט המפורש עיין אצל: 505-514 (1969-1971) 7 *RQ* ,F. L. Horton.

4 M. Baillet, *Qumran Grotte 4:III (4Q 482-4Q 520)* (DJD 7; Oxford, 1982) 141-142.

במגילת הסרכים IX, 11 'עד בוא נביא ומשיחי אהרון וישראל'. ושמא שייך לכך אף עניין חוק הנביא החוזר אצלם בהקשרים שונים.

מבנה המאמר יהיה כדלקמן:

1. נביאים וספריהם
2. פריסת החומר הנבואי במגילות
3. מעמד ספרי הנביאים בהשוואה לתורה במחשבת הכת
4. תפקיד הנביאים המקראיים ומעמדם במחשבת הכת
5. תפקיד הכת ביחס לנבואה המקראית

1. נביאים וספריהם

א. איזכור נביאים

סופרי קומראן משתמשים בדבריהם בכתובים מתוך גוש ספרי הנבואה שבמקרא, והוא סימן לחשיבות שהם ייחסו לנביאים. במיוחד ראוי לציין את הכתובים, שבהם יש התייחסות ישירה לנביאים מסוימים. כך, למשל, נזכר ישעיהו שלש פעמים בברית דמשק: IV, 13-14 'כאשר דבר אל ביד ישעיה הנביא בן אמוץ'; VI, 7-8 'אשר אמר ישעיה'; VII, 10 'כבוא הדבר אשר כתוב בדברי ישעיהו בן אמוץ הנביא אשר אמר'. וכן נאמר במדרש מלכיצדק II, 15-16 'א[שר אמר [אל עליו ביד ישע]יה הנביא אשר אמר [מה] נאוו על הרים רגלי מבש[ר' וכו'.

יחזקאל הנביא נזכר בכתוב בברית דמשק III, 20-21 'כאשר הקים אל להם ביד יחזקאל הנביא לאמר'; וכן בא הצירוף 'ביד זכריה הנביא' (ברית דמשק XIX, 7). ניסוח מיוחד של הזכרת נביאים בא בברית דמשק VIII, 20-21 'הוא הדבר אשר אמר ירמיה לברוך בן נרייה ואלישע לגיחזי נערו'. ועוד הזכרות כיוצא באלה.

ב. איזכור ספרי הנביאים

בטקסטים אחרים במגילות ההתייחסות היא ל**ספרי** הנביאים. הדברים מסתברים מתוך כך שהנביא לא נזכר באורח אישי אלא ההתייחסות היא ל**כתוב** בספרו. כך, דרך משל, כתוב ב- 4QFlor 1-2, I, l. 15 'אשר כתוב בספר ישעיה הנביא'; שם, שורה 16 'אשר כתוב עליהמה בספר יחזקאל הנביא' וכן נזכר ספרו של יחזקאל הנביא ב-3-1 .l ,7 ,4Q177 'אש[ר כתוב בספר יחזקאל הנ(ביא]' וכן 4Q182 1,l. 4 'אשר כ]תוב עליהם בספר ירמ[יה]'; והשווה שם, 4Q163 1. 4 וכן 4Q177 5-6, l. 5. ספר זכריה נזכר בטקסט קטע -8 4Q163 l. 8 'כת]וב בספר זכריה מפ [ ] '.

צירוף מיוחד במינו הוא 4QFlor 1-3, II, l. 3 'אש]ר כתוב בספר דניאל הנביא' והוא צירוף נדיר, באשר סברו שכינויו של דניאל כנביא הוא עניין מאוחר יחסית, שהרי עד כאן הכרנו את כינויו כנביא רק בכתבים נוצריים וכדומה, והנה הופעתו בטקסט הנוכחי מלמדת, שראשית השימוש בכינוי זה בייחס לדניאל מוקדמת יותר ממה שחשבו.[2]

עוד צריך להוסיף, שבקטעי מגילות מצויות כמה וכמה הזכרות של נוסחים קרובים לכתוב בקבוצת הטקסטים הנ"ל. כך 'כאשר כתוב בספר [ ] או בדומה, עיין 4Q177 5-6, l. 11 אבל שם הספר חסר בקטע. לפי המקבילות בטקסטים האחרים נראה לסבור, ש**בחלק** מן הקטעים

---

[2] על דניאל כנביא בקטע זה ראה: 338 (1972) J. A. Fitzmyer, CBQ 34 המצביע על כיוון כזה של הערכת דמותו כנביא על פי שיבוץ ספר דניאל בגוש נביאים בשבעים ובוולגטה. על דניאל כנביא בברית החדשה ראה מתי כד, טו, ועיין א"א אורבך, "מתי פסקה הנבואה", תרביץ יז (תש"ו) 6 וכן בהערה 42, שם.

תפיסת הנבואה המקראית בכתבי קומראן

גרשון בריןבמאמר זה אדון בגישת כת קומראן לספרות הנבואה המקראית. היות והנושא הוא מורכב ומפורט אעסוק רק בקווים אחדים מתוכו. אני סבור, שצירוף קווים אלו עשוי ללמדנו על נושא חשוב זה, גם אם לא נדון בכל חלקיו.[1]

מכלל ספרות המקרא מצאה הכת למתאים להיתלות בנבואה לצורך ענייניה. זאת משום שעל פי טיבה זו ספרות, שזיקתה להווה מעומעמת ועיקרה חזון לעתיד. הכת פנתה לספרות זו והסבה אותה מבחינה פרשנית באופן כזה, שיתבאר שכבר הנבואה שבמקרא התייחסה לכת ולקורותיה, ואמנם זו שיטת הלימוד של חלקי המקרא המשתייכים לספרות הנבואה.

עוד צריך להביא בחשבון, שהכת יצאה מנקודת מוצא שבתקופתה אין נביאים. לקביעה זו השלכות אחדות לגבי הכת ועניניה: 1. בהעדר נביאים עלתה יוקרתה של הספרות הנבואית של העבר, זו שנכללה במקרא. נתון זה הגביר את השאיפה ללמוד ולחקור את הכתוב בה, ובפרט לפתח את דרכי הקישור בין ספרות הנבואה המקראית לבין 'הדור האחרון', דורם של בני הכת. עיקר הקישור מתבטא בפיתוח הכלי הספרותי של הפשרים, שבעזרתו הצביעו הוגי הדעות הכתתיים על האפליקציה הכתתית של דברי הנביאים הקדומים. 2. בהיארארכיה של מנהיגי האומה העמידו בכת את מנהיגי ההווה שבכת בתפקיד קונקרטי בייחס לנביאים המקראיים, אם בייחס לסמכויות האלהיות לגבי הפירוש האקטואלי של דברי הנביאים ואם בתפקידי המשך לנביאים הקדומים. 3. היתה בכת ציפיה מעומעמת לגבי חזרת מוסד הנבואה. רמז לכך בא

---

[1] כל הטקסטים מ- 4Q158 ועד 4Q186 מצוטטים על פי J. M. Allegro, *Qumran Cave 4:I* (DJD 5; Oxford, 1968). הטקסט 4QFlor מכוון ל- *Florilegium* מובא על פי 4Q174 שבכרך זה של DJD. ברית דמשק מצוטטת על פי C. Rabin, *The Zadokite Documents* (Oxford, 1954); מגילת ההודיות על פי י' ליכט, מגילת ההודיות (ירושלים, תשי״ז); מגילת הסרכים על פי י' ליכט, מגילת הסרכים (ירושלים, תשכ״ה); מגילת המלחמה על פי י' ידין, מגילת מלחמת בני אור בבני חושך (ירושלים, תשט״ו); פשר חבקוק מצוטט על פי ב' ניצן, מגילת פשר חבקוק (ירושלים, תשמ״ו); מדרש מלכיצדק מובא על פי P. J. Kobelski, *Melchizedek and Melchirešaʿ* (CBQMS 10; Washington, D.C., 1981) 5-10. בהשלמות לקטעים החסרים בתעודות המצוטטות בחיבורי גרסתי לפעמים לפי הצעה שונה מזו שבמקורות הנ״ל.

שער קומראן

צבא ומדיניות: פרשיות עגומות בקורות ממלכת הצפון97*

שהעוינות כלפי עמרי כרוכה היתה בהרס העיר החשובה הזאת, ובהתעוררות של תגובה שלילית פעילה באוכלוסיית סביבתה.

היחסים הלא־תקינים בין עמרי לבין אזור מנשה מסתברים אף מן העובדה שעמרי בנה בירה חדשה — שומרון — וזנח את תרצה.[16]

הצלחת עמרי היא ראיה לחשיבות הצבא בהכרעות לתפיסת השלטון. אולם מעשיו שתוארו בקצרה (מל״א טז, כה-כח) היו פרי לשיתוף פעולה רב היקף ואוהד מצד בעלי העוצמה הפוליטית והכלכלית שהתקבצו בבירה החדשה. הקשרים הבינלאומיים־הכלכליים עם צור ועם יהודה שהחלו בימי מלכות עמרי שרתו בראש ובראשונה את מגמותיו של הרובד העליון והבטיחו את גיבושו לשליט. ואין זה מקרה כלל ועיקר שימי עמרי וימי יורשו, נתאפיינו בפיתוח, בשגשוג וביציבות, שמהם נהנו בעיקר בני השדרות העליונות. המאבקים בין הקצונה הבכירה לבין השלטון פסקו עד הפיכת יהוא (מל״ב ט-י). מכל מקום, התוצאות העגומות של ההתרחשויות מאז מלכות נדב מחד גיסא והתבססות שושלת בית עמרי מאידך גיסא מראות כי שלטון יציב לא הושג בכל מקרה רק על־ידי המעורבות של הכוח הצבאי.

---

16 M. Lurje, *Studien zur Geschichte der wirtschaftlichen und sozialen Verhältnisse im israelitisch-jüdischen Reiche* (BZAW 45; Giessen, 1927) 57ff. סבור כי המאבק היה בין קפיטליסטים וסוחרים מחד (לצד תבני) ובעלי מקרקעין אמידים מאידך (לצד עמרי).

פיקד.⁹ כנמסר, הקדים זמרי בימים ספורים את עמרי 'שר הצבא על ישראל', שנהנה מתמיכת חילות אחרים, לרבות אלה שחנו בגבתון (מל"א טז, טו-טז). קשה להניח אם שהה עמרי במקום כמפקד המצור שעדיין לא הוכרע או שמא חזר בעל הכתובים על הסיטואציה מראשית ימי בעשא. מהות המניעים שהדריכו את התמלכותו בראש צבאותיו אינם מחוורים. אפשר שכוונתו הראשונית היתה ליטול את השלטון מיד אלה. אבל אין זה מן הנמנע כי אלה חשש מפני האפשרות הזאת והקיף עצמו ביחידות רכב עליהן פיקד "נאמנו" זמרי. מכל מקום, הזדרז עמרי להתמלך עת הגיעה אליו השמועה על מות המלך ועלית זמרי על הכס בתרצה.¹⁰

התאבדותו של זמרי ותפיסת תרצה בידי עמרי לא הביאו לרגיעה. על עמרי קם גורם אופוזיציוני בהנהגת תבני בן גינת. מאלף הוא כי הכתובים לא מזכירים התנגשויות בין עמרי לתבני. אבל הדגישו חלוקת העם לשני חצאים, חלוקה סכימטית, ללא ספק, שבאה ללמד על התנגדות נרחבת לעמרי.¹¹ סביר הוא שפעולות אלימות נרמזות בעצם החלוקה הזאת ובהתגברות 'חצי העם' שנהו אחר עמרי על המחצית האחרת (מל"א טז, כא-כב).¹² יתר על כן, מרווח הזמן של ארבע שנים שבין המלכת עמרי בגבתון (מל"א טז, טו) לבין התמלכותו על ישראל (שם, כג) מורה על מאבק אלים בין שני האישים.

תבני לפי הנמסר, לא נשא תואר צבאי ובכתובים אודותיו לא נזכרה המעורבות של יחידה צבאית כלשהי. אבל אין ללמד מכך בהכרח שצבא לא עמד לימינו. האיזכור של 'עם' משמעו בהקשר הנידון 'צבא'. המונח 'עם' משמש במל"א טז, טז לציון גייסות. ואמורים הדברים גם בעוד כתובים במקרא (שופ' ט, לה-לו; שמ"א יא, יא; שמ"ב יב, כח-כט; יח, טו-טז; דה"א יט; כא, ה ועוד). באור השתלשלות הארועים והנסיבות בזמן ההוא, בו הומלכו מפקדים ביד חייליהם וחתרו לכיבוש השלטון, מתקבל על הדעת שגם תבני היה שר במערכת הצבאית. כמה נימוקים תומכים בכך. במקום ראשון, התקופה הממושכת ביחס, בה עמדו זה מול זה "חצאי העם" מורה שלרשות תבני עמד כוח צבאי ניכר. שהרי אחרת ההכרעה לטובת עמרי, שצבאות סרו למרותו, היתה מושגת במהירות. במקום שני, תבני התמלך אחר ההתאבדות של זמרי ותפיסת תרצה ביד עמרי. לכאן תואמת האפשרות שהגורם אשר העלה את זמרי ונסוג מפני עמרי אחר התנגדות שגרמה להריסת הבירה¹³ – הוא 'מחצית הרכב' – המליך שר צבא אחר תחת מפקדו שהתאבד.¹⁴ זאת ועוד, המאבק בין תבני לבין עמרי מחייב לא רק מציאותו של צבא שסר למרות תבני, אלא גם עורף טריטוריאלי נרחב. רווחה הדעה שמוצאו של תבני בגינת.¹⁵ אם כך היה הדבר, הרי שנשען גם על יסודות מנשיים. תרצה החרבה, מצויה היתה בנחלתו המסורתית של מנשה וסביר

---

9 על הזיקה בין אנשי הרכב של זמרי לעילית הכנענית של המרין (שאין לה על מה לסמוך) ראה גריי (לעיל, הערה 3), עמ' 327.

10 עיין פארקר (לעיל, הערה 4), עמ' 319 המבחין בסטטוס נרכש אצל זמרי ועמרי.

11 H. J. Hayes and J. M. Miller, *Israelite and Judaean History* (London, 1977) 398-399.

12 N. K. Gottwald, *The Hebrew Bible* (Philadelphia, 1985) 374-375 חתר להניח כי תבני ממלכה מוגבלת בעוד עמרי נתמך על-ידי הצבא המקצועי. לדעתו אפשר שעמרי היה ממוצא כנעני ושאף משום כך למלוכה ריכוזית. והשווה: A. Alt, "Das Stadtstaat Samaria," *Kleine Schriften* (Munich, 1959) 3:258-302.

13 R. de Vaux, "The Excavations at Tell el Farʿah and the Site of Ancient Tirzah," *PEQ* 88 (1956) 125-140; cf. *Encyclopedia of Archaeological Excavations in the Holy Land* (Jerusalem, 1976) 2:401-406.

14 פארקר (לעיל, הערה 3), עמ' 319: תבני לחם במייצגי השררה (זמרי, עמרי).

15 S. Yeivin, "The Divided Kingdom," *WHJP* 4/1 (Jerusalem, 1979) 333 n. 51.

מפקדיהן התגלו כמכשיר פוליטי יעיל להגשמת יעדי הקצונה הבכירה, אמצעי יעיל יותר מהשענות על שדרות האוכלוסיה לבדן.

השאיפות לתפיסת כס המלוכה בקרב בכירי הצבא קבלו תנופה והגשמתן זורזה בגלל הכשלונות של ירבעם ועושי דברו במלחמה. כיבוש הטריטוריות ביד אביה (דה"ב יג, ד ואילך)[6] היה מכה ניצחת ליוקרתם והוא הדין בהעדר ההכרעה במצור על גבתון. התיצבותו של מחנה גבתון נגד נדב מצביעה על מרי בקרב דרגי הפיקוד בשדה הקרב, וזקיפת המחדלים גם לחובת המלך שהתמלך לא מכבר משום שלא שינה את הקו שנקבע ביד אביו (ואפשר שלא היה בידו סיפק לעשות כן). אלה היו ככל הנראה, מניעיו של בעשא (אשר פיקד על החונים ליד גבתון, אף שתיאורו הצבאי לא נזכר מפורשות בכתובים) להכתיב את המלכים על־ידי סילוקו של נדב. בעיני הצבא שהוצב למצור היה בעשא אלטרנטיבה שעשויה היתה להביא למפנה בשלטון ובמלחמה כאחד (מל"א טו, כה-לב).[7]

עלייתו של בעשא לשלטון לא נתקלה בהתנגדות ומכאן יש להסיק כי בחצר המלוכה ובקרב המקורבים למוקד ההכרעות המדיניות היתה הזדהות עם מטרותיו. אכן, מלכותו סימנה מפנה בתפיסה המדינית והצבאית. ביטויו — מלחמת תנופה רבת עצמה ביהודה ששמה קץ להתנגשויות המתמשכות ולמפלות. נראה שמגמתו של בעשא היתה להכריע בהכרעה צבאית מהירה את היעד שלא התגשם מאז הפילוג — ניתוק מוחלט מיהודה ובתנאים רצויים לממלכת ישראל. ההישגים המהירים נועדו גם להעלות את המוראל הלאומי ולאחד את האוכלוסיה תחת שלטונה של אישיות חזקה ובחסות הצבא. ההתקדמות לעבר ירושלים וההשתלטות על אזורי הגבול, שירתו היטב את מגמות העצמאות השלמה שלא הוגשמו במלואן ביד ירבעם ויורשו (מל"א טו, טז-יז, לב; דה"ב טז, א). אם אכן יש רקע ריאלי לביקורת שהושמה בפי יהוא בן חנני (מל"א טו, א-ז) הרי שההקבלה בין ירבעם לבין בעשא מעידה על כוונת האחרון ללכת בעקבות היעדים שהציב הראשון.

האקטיביזם של בעשא, שנתקל, כאמור, בביקורת, תאם את הלכי הרוח בקרב הצבא והחוגים שעמדו לימינו בהמלכתו בתרצה. הראיה לכך — לפי הנמסר שלט בעשא כשלוש עשרה שנה ללא הפרעה (מל"א טו, כח, לג; טז, ח). וקשה לשער מה יכלו להיות הישגיו אלמלי הפלישה של ארם דמשק לישראל (מל"א טו, יח-כח; דה"ב טז, ב-ה). אז אבדו לישראל טריטוריות בחלקה הצפוני וככל הנראה גם האחיזה הישראלית במואב.[8]

מות בעשא (בקרב?) לא הותיר מקום לשלטון יציב ביד בנו אלה. התקדים שנקבע ביד בעשא, הכשלון הצבאי ועצם התמלכותו של שליט חדש עודדו שוב שרים בכירים והעמיקו את הכרתם ושאיפותיהם למלא תפקיד מרכזי בממלכה בגיבוי יחידותיהם. בעת ובעונה אחת קמו שני מפקדים כדי ליטול את ההנהגה בידיהם. האחד, זמרי, "עבד" אלה, ממקורבי המלך בתרצה ביצע הפיכת חצר מהירה (מל"א טז, ח-יד) בתמיכת יחידות 'מחצית הרכב' המוצבות בבירה עליהן

---

6 על העדר אמינות היסטורית בכתובים על כבושי אביה: R. W. Klein, "Abijah's Campaign against the North (II Chr. 13): What Were the Chronicler's Sources?" *ZAW* 95 (1983) 210-217. לאמינות המידע בדה"ב יג, יט: J. M. Myers, *2 Chronicles* (AB; Garden City, NY, 1965) 81; H. G. M. Williamson, *1 and 2 Chronicles* (London, 1982) 291-295.

7 ראה פארקר (לעיל, הערה 4), עמ' 318-319 לזהותו של בעשא כבעל סמכות מסורתית אשר מילא תפקידו של מנהיג עממי על רקע ההתנגשויות בין ערכי האוכלוסיה לבין המניפולציות של הכוח של ירבעם, בדומה לאלה של שלמה (!) לדעתו התאים בעשא את חלוקת העבודה של השיטה המונארכית לערכים המסורתיים וכך כונן את הלגיטימיות של הקשר שיזם.

8 ב' מזר, "מישע", אנציקלופדיה מקראית ד (ירושלים, תש"ל) 921-922.

חלקם, אם לא רובם ככולם, היו רמי מעלה ומילאו תפקידים חשובים בחילות שלמה. לאחר מכן פעלו השרים הללו בצבא הצפון.

העילית הצבאית בממלכת הצפון מודעת היתה לכוחה ולתרומתה לשלטון ובמיוחד נוכח נסיבות כינונה של המסגרת הפוליטית החדשה. המודעות הזאת, כך נראים הדברים, הדריכה את הקצונה הבכירה בפעילותה ובמעורבותה הפוליטית והקנתה תוקף רב לשאיפותיה; נאמנותה לשלטון והזדהותה עם יעדי הפילוג היו מותנות בהיענות מלכותית לציפיותיה וכרוכות בעידוד, קידום ובתמלוגים הולמים.

החיוניות של השררה למערכת הצבאית והפוליטית לא נזכרה במישרין בכתובים הנוגעים בדבר; היא מתחייבת מן ההתרחשויות בימי מלכותו של ירבעם בן נבט.

הלכי הרוח בקרב הסגל הבכיר במרוצת שלטונו של המלך הזה ניכרים בארועים שנרמזו בהקשר למות בנו, נדב. מלכותו הקצרה היתה, כמו סיטואציות דומות ומוכרות של ימי חלופין בין אב ליורשו, שעת בין־ערביים פוליטית — פרק זמן מתאים לפעולתם של גורמים לא מרוצים, לרבות אנשי צבא שנשאו עיניהם לתמורה בשלטון ולתפיסת כס המלוכה.

מעשי הקצונה שתוארו במל״א ט״ו-ט״ז עשויים להתפרש באופנים שונים: על רקע הרכבה הפלורליסטי של ממלכת ישראל והמבנה החברתי המסורתי שלה אפשר שהם משקפים יריבות בין־שבטית שבה ייצגו קציני צבא את האינטרסים של חלקי האוכלוסיה השונים; ואין זה מן הנמנע שהיו גורמים בקרב האוכלוסיה, כגון יסודות המקור של הקצינים או של חיילי היחידות שהשליכו את יהבם על שרי הצבא בקוותם לקדם את השאיפות שלהם. יצויין כי המקורות המקראיים הנוגעים בדבר אינם מותירים מקום ורמז על יריבות מעין זאת. אפשרות אחרת להסבר: התנגשויות בין המלוכה לבין האוכלוסיה על רקע הניגוד בין מגמות השלטון לבין מצבם של הנתינים ועמדותיהם. אף לאפשרות הזאת אין יסוד בכתובים. שאלה נכבדת היא באיזו מדה יכלה האוכלוסיה להפעיל כוח כדי להכריע בעימות. קשה גם לשער אם התגבש השלטון בממלכת הצפון במרוצת שמונה עשר השנים בקירוב לקיומו עד כדי כך שנדחה על־ידי נתיניו.

יתר על כן, בחר ירבעם בן נבט כזכור, להשען על קבוצות מוגדרות ומצומצמות ולא על ה״עם״. סימני העדפה ״שבטית־רגיונלית״ לא ניכרו בימיו ולא בימי המולכים אחריו בממלכת ישראל. אף מכאן ניתן להסיק שלא היה רקע ״שבטי״ לסכסוכים שפקדו את המדינה. אבל נעלה מכל ספק היא הסתייעותם של הקצונה ביחידות שסרו למרותם והתיצבו לימינה. דומה איפוא, שרחוקות היו פעילותיהם של שרי הצבא המעורבים ממה שקרוי ״מהפכה״ (עממית, חברתית או אחרת).[4] לפיכך נראה שהודרכו בידי מניעים, שאיפות וציפיות של בני חוגם[5] ולא היה בינם לבין מאווים ״שבטיים״ ולא כלום — הם אספקלריה לעמדות פוליטיות ואחרות של השדרות העליונות, שהפיקוד הבכיר נמנה עם רכיביהן. נסיונות ההשתלטות על מוקד ההכרעות המדיניות מלמדים על מגמה להעמיד בראש השלטון אנשים מתאימים תחת השליטים שלא השביעו את רצון הרובד העליון, תומכי קצינים בכירים שונים.

כך או כך, המאורעות אחרי מות ירבעם אינם מותירים מקום לספק שיחידות הצבא שנהו אחר

---

4 ראה דיון המסתייע בתפיסות על מהפכה במדעי החברה: S. B. Parker, "Revolutions in Northern Israel," SBLSP 3 (Missoula, MT, 1976) 311-319. השלמת התאור של הארועים בדיון הזה היא בהתאם לסממני ההתנגשויות במהפכות ומרידות ובעיקר — המתיחות והעדר האיזון שבין חלוקת העבודה בשיטה המלכותית לבין הערכים המסורתיים.

5 באור האמור קשה להסביר את החלופין התכופים על כס המלוכה שניזומו בידי הקצונה על־ידי הדגשת אופיה המיוחד של המלוכה הצפונית ברוח תפיסתו של: A. Alt, "Das Königtum in den Reichen Israel und Juda," VT 1 (1951) 2-22. והוא הדין בהסבר הארועים על רקע המורשת האמפיקטיונית הקדומה: J. Bright, A History of Israel (2d ed.; London, 1979) 234-235.

צבא ומדיניות: פרשיות עגומות בקורות ממלכת הצפון

חנוך רביב ז"ל

התיאורים המתומצתים במל"א יב, כה-לג, שלחקרם תרם שמריהו טלמון תרומה נכבדה,[1] מותירים מקום לקביעה כי שלטונו של ירבעם בן נבט נשען על קבוצות בעלות מעמד רם, השפעה ויוקרה. עם אלה נימנו כהונה מיוחסת, וחוגים אקטיביסטיים מקרב יוזמי הפילוג ומיישמיו.[2] ויש לשער כי השליט הראשון של ממלכת הצפון נזקק גם לגיבוי הצבא ומפקדיו.

אכן, צבא נאמן ומסור היה הכרח לקיומו וליצובו של שלטון המצוי בתהליך התגבשות על רקע מערכת פוליטית מתהווה והנתון ללחצים של קבוצות כוח שונות. יתר על כן, הוטלה על הצבא ההגנה על גבולות המסגרת המדינית החדשה במלחמה המתמשכת במלכי יהודה (מל"א יד, ל; טו, ו-ז והשווה דה"ב יג, ב ואילך).

מקורו של סגל הפיקוד בצבא ממלכת הצפון היה, כמסתבר, במערכת הצבאית של הממלכה המאוחדת. דוד שילב מבני האוכלוסיה בטריטוריות הצפוניות בגדודי, במוסד הגיבורים שלו (דה"א יא, מא-מו; יב). הוא ושלמה יורשו קידמו יסודות צפוניים מקורבים בצבאם, כשם שעשו בתחום האדמיניסטרציה הבכירה והזוטרה (דה"ב כז; מל"א ד). נראה איפוא, כי לא חסר לירבעם בן נבט כוח אדם מיומן לאייש בו את כל דרגות הפיקוד, אלה ששירתו את הממלכה המאוחדת והצטרפו לאחר מכן לצבאות הממלכה הישראלית. אם אכן אמינה היא התוספת בתרגום השבעים למל"א יב, כד, הרי שקצינים על יחידותיהם נטלו חלק במרידה של ירבעם בשלמה.[3]

ניכר כי עוד בראשית דרכה של ממלכת ישראל התגבשה עילית צבאית של שרים בכירים אשר

---

1   S. Talmon, "Divergencies in Calendar-Reckoning in Ephraim and Judah," *VT* 8 (1958) 48-74.

2   ראה: ח' רביב, "דרך ירבעם בממלכתו", שנתון למקרא ולחקר המזרח הקדום (בדפוס). השווה: B. Halpern, "Sectionalism and the Schism," *JBL* 93 (1974) 519-532; idem, "Levitic Participation in the Reform Cult of Jeroboam I," *JBL* 95 (1976) 31-42.

3   ראה: D. W. Gooding, "The Septuagint's Rival Versions of Jeroboam's Rise to Power," *VT* 17 (1967) 173-189. אבל השווה: J. A. Montgomery, *A Critical and Exegetical Commentary on the Books of Kings* (Edinburgh, 1951) 251f.; J. Gray, *I and II Kings* (2d ed.; London, 1970) 310ff.

לעומת זאת בולט היעדרן של נוסחאות אלו בסיפורי אליהו (להבדיל מהלשונות 'נפל', 'כרע', מל"א יח, לט; מל"ב א, יג). אפשר שעם התבססות נימוסי המלכות נעלם הצורך לפאר אותם בדרך הסיפור, ואף ייתכן שהמספר הדתי חש צורך להימנע מרמזים לטיקסיות זו. בסופו של דבר, אשת ירבעם מוצגת כמי שהולכת בגפה אל הנביא, וזה גוער בה בלא גינוני טקס כלל. האם מקרה הוא, שבסיפורי אליהו ואלישע אין זכר להשתחוויה לפני המלך, אלא רק לפני הנביא (מל"ב ב, טו; ד, לז; והקבל א, יג)?

ומצד שני, גם בתיאור טיקסי הפולחן ובשירת המזמורים ויתרו על הנוסחאות המורכבות. ניתן לשער שגם תופעה זו קשורה לשינוי ביחס לגינוני המלכות. הרי אפשר שהמשורר הדתי ביקש ליצור הבדל בין נימוסי החצר ובין עולמם של טיקסי הדת. אך אין זה הגורם היחיד להיעלמותן של נוסחאות אלו. הרי גם המספר החצרוני שיצר (או ערך) את ספר דברי שלמה נמנע מלהשתמש בהן. דומה שמדובר בתופעה כללית יותר. כבר הראו, שבמשך הזמן חלה הידלדלות כללית באוצר הנוסחאות המסורתיות. הגוף הסיפרותי האחרון שבו נוסחאות אלו ממלאות תפקיד של ממש, הוא מכלול הסיפורים על ראשית הממלכה, החל בסיפורי שמואל וכלה בסיפור המלכת שלמה (פולק, תדירות). נוסחאות אלו עדיין מהדהדות בסיפורי אליהו ואלישע (והקבל עמ' ז, יד; הו' א, ג, ו, ח), כדי להיעלם כמעט לחלוטין מהאופק בספרות מאוחרת יותר. דומה שחל שינוי בטעמם הסיפרותי של הבריות: סר חינם של הצירופים השגורים ורוחב הלשון. ושמא תופעה זו קשורה בהתפשטות ידיעת הקריאה והכתיבה. תהליך זה השפיע גם על הלשונות הקשורות בהשתחוויה. רק בעל ספר דברי הימים השיב עטרה ליושנה, מתוך מגמה מובהקת לפאר את מלכות ישראל ואת הפולחן שבבית המקדש בימי הבית הראשון.

ועוד, בתוך המסורת הישראלית ניכרים סימנים להתפתחויות מיוחדות. בתופעות יחידות במינן אנו נתקלים, כאשר אנו נוגעים במוסד המלוכה, ובפרשיות העוסקות במוסד זה. הרי בסיפורי האבות (וכן בסיפורי משה) משמשות בעיקר הנוסחאות של 'השתחוה' עם 'קדד', עם 'קום', או עם המשלים 'ארצה'. בסיפורי דוד, לעומת זאת, הנוסחאות השכיחות הן 'ויפל ... וישתחו', 'וישתחו אפים ארצה'.

בסיפורים אלו בא הצירוף 'ויפל וישתחו' בששה כתובים, כנגד היעדר בולט בסיפורי אברהם, יעקב ויוסף (לשם השוואה: בפרשיות אלו באה הנוסחה 'ויקד וישתחו' שלוש פעמים, כנגד ארבע פעמים בסיפורי דוד). הנוסחה 'וישתחו אפים ארצה' באה פעמיים בסיפור יוסף (בסיפורי אברהם הקבל 'ויקם וישתחו אפים ארצה', בר' יט, א) כנגד ארבע פעמים בסיפורי דוד. מסתבר אפוא, שבעניין זה סיפורי דוד מצטיינים בגוון מיוחד. ותן דעתך שבסיפורי שמואל ושאול (שמ"א א-ט) אין זכר לנוסחאות אלו, למרות ריבוי לשון 'השתחוה'. מניין נובעת תופעה זו? האם מדובר בקנייניו של מספר אחד ויחיד או של חוג מספרים מוגדר? דומני שלא. הרי הנוסחה 'וישתחו אפים ארצה' מזדמנת גם בסיפור יוסף, ויש להניח שכבר היתה קיימת בסיפורת הישראלית הקדומה (הקבל בר' יט, א). אך לאור השימוש בנוסחה זו בסיפורי יוסף ודוד מסתבר שיש לה זיקה מיוחדת למוסד המלוכה ולגינוני הטקס החצרניים. דבר זה ניכר יפה בצירוף השני, הוא 'ויפל... וישתחו'. צירוף זה קרוב לנוסחה האוגריתית הבאה בראש במכתבים אל המלך ואל בני בית המלוכה לציון השתחוויה ('לרגלי... אני נופלי'). מכאן ההנחה שמא יש בצירוף המקראי משום נסיון ליצור נוסחה קבועה לציון מחוות הסגידה לפני המלך, בהתאם למנהג החצרני הכנעני הידוע. מגמה מעין זו היתה משתלבת יפה בין הסימנים לשאיפה לאמץ ולפתח את נימוסי החצר כפי שהיו מוכרים בין בתי המלוכה הכנעניים. עדות למגמה זו בימי דוד אתה מוצא במה שנאמר על תמר 'כי כן תלבשנה בנות המלך' (שמ"ב יג, יח), ובהערה על האנשים שאבשלום ואדוניהו הריצו לפניהם, ועל המרכבה שעשו לעצמם (טו, א; מל"א א, ה). על הרגישויות הרבה לדרכי אדנות אלו מעידה, כידוע, פרשת משפט המלך, אשר מתריסה כנגד מרכבת המלך והרצים לפניה כאחד (שמ"א ח, יא). מכאן ההנחה, שבתקופה זו גילו מספרים מסוימים, ובעיקר אנשי החצר המעודדים אותם (לעולם יש יחסי גומלין בין גורמים אלו),[33] עניין בנוסחאות המפארות את ההשתחוויה לפני המלך. מסתבר, שנוסחאות אלו נוצרו על ידי הרחבתם של צירופים מסורתיים. בנוסחה 'ויפל על פניו ארצה וישתחו' ניתן לראות הרחבה של הצרף 'ויפל על פניו'/ 'ויפל ארצה' (ראה לעיל). אך בעוד שבדרך כלל צירוף זה אינו מכוון למלך, הרי שהגירסה המורחבת, כמוה כמו הנוסחה הכנענית, אופיינית לטיקסיות החצרנית. את הצירוף המורכב 'וישתחו אפים ארצה' העדיפו אנשי החצר על פני הנוסחה הפשוטה 'וישתחו ארצה'.

תקופה מסוימת המשיכו לטפח את המסורת הנוסחאית. אך במשך הזמן נטשו אותה המספרים. בספר דברי שלמה' (מל"א ג-יא), שלא נוצר לפני התקופה האשורית (יעיד הצירוף 'עבר הנהר', שם ה, ד), אין להן זכר, למרות שבסיפור המלכת שלמה הנוסחאות הקשורות בהשתחוויה הן נפוצות ביותר. כן נעדרות נוסחאות אלו לחלוטין מתיאור קורותיהן של ממלכות יהודה וישראל, על אף שבוודאי היה להן מקום. הד למסורת זו תמצא רק בסיפורי אלישע (מל"ב ב, טו; ד, לז;

S. E. Loewenstamm, אוגרית ובסיפורת המקראית מזה ובין הרחבותיה בשירה המקראית עמד: "The Address 'Listen' in the Ugaritic Epic and the Bible," *The Bible World: Essays in Honor of C. H. Gordon* (New York, 1980) 123-31. על פיתוח הנוסחה 'יישא עיניו וירא' בשירה המקראית עיין הנ"ל: *Comparative Studies in the Bible and Ancient Oriental Literatures* (Neukirchen-Vluyn, 1980) 289-91 n. 16.

33 על הכנענים (חורים) בחצר דוד ראה: ב' מזר, "סופר המלך דוד ובעיית הפקידות הגבוהה בממלכת ישראל", כנען וישראל (ירושלים, תשל"ד) 208-221.

וישתחו'). זאת אומרת, כאן לשון השירה אמנם השפיעה על סגנון הפרוזה, אך השפעה זו מוגבלת לתקופת הבית השני דווקא; לנוסחה 'ויכרע וישתחו' אין זכר בסיפורת הקדומה.

לאמיתו של דבר נמצא רק צירוף אחד המשותף לשירה המקראית ולסיפורת, והוא 'בוא והשתחוה', כגון: 'אבוא ביתך, אשתחוה אל היכל קדשך' (תהי' ה, ח; וכן: צו, ח-ט = דהי"א טז, כט; פט, ט; צה, ו; קלב, ז; ישי' כז, יג; סו, כג; יר' ז, ב = כו, ב; יחי' מו, ט; תשע דוגמאות בשירה ובחזון).

בסיפורת אתה מוצא אחת עשרה דוגמאות, כגון: 'ויבא בית ה' וישתחו' (שמ"ב יב, כ; וכן: בר' לז, י; מב, ו; שמ"א ב, לו; שמ"ב יד, לג; מל"א א, כג, נג;[31] מל"ב ב, טו; ד, לז; ה, יח; דהי"ב כד, יז). נמצא, בין כל הצירופים עם לשון ההשתחוויה זה הצרף הנפוץ ביותר. מבחינה סגנונית הדבר מובן מאליו. הרי לשון 'בוא' היא ההקדמה הנפוצה ביותר לכל פעולה. בסיפורת המקראית תמצא לכך יותר ממאתיים דוגמאות, כגון 'ויבא וישב באלוני ממרא' (ברי' יג, יח), 'ויבאו אל יעקב אביהם ארצה כנען ויגידו לו' (מב, כט). גם מבחינה ענייני ריבוי הדוגמאות לצמד זה נראה סביר. שכן, במקרים רבים אין מחווה זו אלא ברכה לאחר הכניסה לפני מלך או נכבד, כגון יוסף (מב, ו). וכן נוהג גם מי שמתייצב לפני האל, כמו דוד (שמ"ב יב, כ). ולא ייפלא שבכתבי אוגרית ניתן למצוא זכר לשורת פעולות דומה. לפני שהשאלה אשרה השתחוותה לפניו אלו, נכנסה אל היכלו: 'ותבא קרש מלך אב שנמ', ומיד: 'לפעני אל תהבר ותקל, תשתחוי ותכבדה' (=יהיא באה אל בית המלך [או: בית מלכות] האב הנשגב [ ]; או: אבי השנים], לפני אל וכרעה ונפלה, השתחוותה וכיבדה אותי', הרדנר 4, VI: 23-26; וכיוצא בזה הרדנר 2, III: 5-6). בסיפור דוד מסורת זו היתה לנקודת מוצא למשחק מעודן: 'ויבא עד הראש אשר ישתחוה שם' (שמ"ב טו, לב). על יוסף ואחיו נאמר: 'ויבא יוסף הביתה ויביאו לו את המנחה אשר בידם הביתה וישתחוו לו ארצה' (ברי' מג, כו). והנה, רק בפרשת השונמית (מל"ב ד, לז) ובסיפור יוסף משמש צמד זה בצד המשלימים הנוסחאיים: 'הבוא נבוא אני ואמך... להשתחות לך ארצה' (בר' לז, י); 'ויבאו אחי יוסף וישתחוו לו אפים ארצה' (מב, ו), מאחר שכתובים אלו מהווים מעגל של מבט של פנים והתגשמותו, אין תמה בדמיון בניסוח). אלו הן דוגמאות לעיצוב סגנוני מיוחד באמצעות הנוסחאות השגורות. ריבויין של נוסחאות אלו וההתאמה שבין הזוג הקבוע שבספרות המקראית ובין הצירוף האוגריתי, מהווים סימן נוסף לאחדות המורשת השמית-מערבית הקדומה.

ואולם, אחדותה של מסורת זו היא לעולם אחדות מתוך שוני וגיוון, מתוך ריחוק בצד קירבה. הקירבה באה לידי ביטוי בעצם השימוש בלשון 'השתחווה', וכן בצירופים של פועל זה עם הלשונות 'בוא' ו'קל'/'נפל'. השוני, לעומת זאת, ניכר בזה, שבכתבי אוגרית אין אח ורע לנוסחה 'ויקד וישתחו', ואף לא ללווי הפעלים נפל והשתחוה ו'השתחוה' עם המשלימים 'אפים', 'פנים', ו'ארץ'. תופעות אלו מעידות, שהמספר הישראלי לא שאב ממסורת אוגרית, אלא מענף אחר של שירת העלילה השמית-המערבית הקדומה.

כן ניכר הדבר, שיש זיקה ישירה בין מורשת שירת העלילה ובין הסיפורת הקדומה, כפי שזאת באה לידי ביטוי בסיפורי האבות, ובמידה פחותה בסיפורי שמואל, שאול ודוד. הרי אותן נוסחאות המצויות בחטיבות אלו תדיר, מקומן לא יכירם בשירה המקראית (או רק בשירה המאוחרת, בהשפעת סיפורי הפרוזה). לא מספרות המזמורים והנבואה שאב המספר את נוסחאותיו, אלא משירת העלילה.[32]

---

31 בתה"ש למל"א ב, יג הקבל: 'ויבא... אל בת-שבע אם שלמה וישתחו לה'.
32 על הפער בין הצירוף הפרוזאי 'יישא קולו ויקרא' ובין גירסאותיו הפיוטיות עמד קאסוטו (לעיל, הערה 1), עמ' 28 (בשירה אין זכר לצרף 'יישא קולו ויבד'). על היחס בין הקריאה 'שמעי' שבכתבי

בסיפורת המקראית - שכן הם הקרובים ביותר לשירת העלילה, על כן יש להניח שגירסה פשוטה זו, קדומה היא.

נוסחה המשותפת לסיפורי האבות ולחטיבות על דוד ושאול היא הצירוף 'ויקם וישתחו', שבה הפועל 'קום' משמשת הקדמה לפעולה העיקרית, בדומה לצירוף השכיח 'ויקם וילך'.[27] יש שהכתוב מציין במשלים את מי ההשתחוויה באה לכבד, כגון: 'ויקם המלך לקראתה וישתחו לה' (מל"א ב, יט; [תה"ש: 'וישק לה']; וכן בר' כג, ז; שמ"א כה, מא). ויש שהדבר עולה מההקשר בלבד: 'ויקם לקראתם וישתחו אפים ארץ' (בר' יט, א; וכן שמ' לג, י; סך הכל חמש דוגמאות). מחווה זו משמשת בדרך כלל לשם ברכה: מי שמבחין באורח קם ממושבו ומשתחווה לו. וכן אתה מוצא בכתבי אוגרית: 'לפננה ידד ויקם, לפענה יכרע ויקלי' (=לפניו...? וקם, כרע ונפל'; הרדנר II,10: 18-17), באכדית הקבל izzizū iknušū (כלומר 'קמו וכרעו'; עלילת הבריאה ה, 88). האם מקרה הוא, שבמקרא מחווה זו אינה מכוונת למלך?

צירופים אלו, אין להם מקבילות בשירה המקראית, אלא בחזיונותיהם של נביאי גלות בבל שצורפו לספר ישעיה בלבד. לצירוף 'ויקם וישתחוו' ניתן להקביל את ההיגד 'מלכים יראו וקמו, שרים וישתחוו לך' (יש' מט, ז); בהתאמה לאופיו הפיוטי של כתוב זה נפרטה הנוסחה הרצופה לשתי צלעות. על החופשיות שבה נהוג המשורר נוהג בנוסחאות, מעיד גם היפוך הסדר שבהיגד 'אפים ארצה ישתחוו לך ועפר רגליך ילחכו' (מט, כג). הד נוסף תמצא בהכרזה: 'והלכו אליך שחוח בני מעניך, והשתחוו על כפות רגליך כל מנאציך' (ס, יד). באזכור 'כפות' 'רגלי ישראל שומע אתה את בת קולו של הצירוף הקדום, כמו בסיפור השונמית ('ותפל על רגליו ותשתחו', מל"ב ד, לז; וכיוצא בזה 'ותפל על רגליו', שמ"א כה, כד). נמצא, בעניין הנוסחאות הקשורות בלשון 'השתחוו' לא הסיפורת תלויה במסורת השירה הקדומה, אלא להפך, לשון החזון של ימי גלות בבל תלויה במסורת הפרוזה הקדומה. ואל ייפלא הדבר בעיניך, שכן בחזיונות אלו מצינו רמזים למסורת אברהם (יש' מא ח; נא, ב; וכן סג, טז) וליייעוד דוד (יש' נה, ג-ד); סימן מובהק לתלות הנביא בסיפורי דוד תמצא בלשון נגיד ומצוה לאמים', הקבל שמ"א ט, טז; כה, ל; מל"א א, לה).

יחד עם זאת, גם השירה המקראית שומרת זכר לצירופים שכדוגמתם תמצא בכתבי אוגרית: מלבד הזוג 'השתחווה/כבד' שעליו הצבענו לעיל, אתה מוצא גם את הצמד 'השתחוה/כרע', כגון: 'אכלו וישתחוו כל דשני ארץ, לפניו יכרעו כל יורדי עפר' (תה' כב, ל;[28] וכן: צה, ו). בכתבי אוגרית מצינו לשון דומה: 'יכרע ויקלי' (= 'יכרע ונפל'; הרדנר II,10: 18-17).[29] הצמד הפיוטי נקלט בסיפורת המקראית המאוחרת, כגון: 'וכל עבדי המלך... כרעים ומשתחוים להמן' (אסי ג, ב), 'ומרדכי לא יכרע ולא ישתחוה' (שם, שם; וכן שם, פס' ה; דה"ב ז, ג [תה"ש 'ויפלו...ישתחוו'];[30] כט, כט). צירוף דומה משתקף בתה"ש לדה"א כט, כ: 'ויכרעו על ברכיהם וישתחוו' (נחמ': 'ויקדו

---

27 כגון בר' יג, יז; כב, ג; רשימה מלאה תמצא אצל: פולק, תדירות 451.

28 בדבר 'אכלי'/'השתחוה' הקבל 'ייאכל העם וישתחוו לאלהיהן' (במ' כה, ב).

29 בעניין הצמד 'יכרע/נפלי' הקבל שופ' ה, כז; יש' י, ד; תה' כ, ט, תמיד בעניין תבוסה ומוות. בסיפורת לשון 'יכרעי' אינה נפוצה, והופעותיה מוגבלות כמעט לחלוטין לעניין השתחוויה, על פי רוב בצירוף המשלים 'על ברכים' (שופ' ז, ה, ו; מל"א ח, נד; יט, יח; מל"ב א, יג; עז' ט, ה; וכן דה"ב כט, כ לפי תה"ש). כן ראה תיאור מות יורם (מל"ב ט, כד); בדבר הכריעה כתנוחת היולדת (שמ"א ד, יט; איוב לט, ב-ג) ראה גרובר (לעיל, הערה 17), עמ' 324-325, הערה 2.

30 בכתוב זה תמצא בצד המשלים 'אפים ארצה' הרחבה נוספת בלשון המאוחרת 'על הרצפה' ועיין: A. Hurvitz, *A Linguistic Study of the Relationship between the Priestly Source and the Book of Ezekiel: A New Approach to an Old Problem* (CahRB 20; Paris, 1982) 135-37.

(מל"א א, לא). באחד הכתובים המאוחרים באות ההרחבות בצלע השנייה של הנוסחה: ויקדו וישתחוו לה' אפים ארצה' (נחמ' ח, ו; אך בספר עזרא החיצון [ט, מט] הדבר בא על תיקונו: ויפלו ארצה וישתחוו).

נמצא, נוסחה זו מזדמנת ארבע פעמים בסיפורי שאול ודוד, שלוש פעמים בסיפורי משה, פעמיים בסיפורי עבד אברהם, ופעם אחת בסיפור יוסף ובפרשת בלעם (סה"כ אחת עשרה דוגמאות). בספרות ימי הבית השני היא מזדמנת שלוש פעמים, לרבות חריג אחד (נחמ' ח, ו). יוצא דופן נוסף תמצא, כאמור, בפסוקית 'ויקד יהושפט אפים ארצה' בלא 'וישתחוו' (דה"ב כ, יח).

תופעה בולטת היא ההעדפה לשימוש בנוסחה זו בלא משלימים 'אפים', 'פנים' ו'ארץ'. וזה נבדל צירוף זה מהנוסחה 'ויפל... וישתחוו', אשר באה לעולם בליווי משלימים. מסתבר שדי בלשון 'יקד' בלבד כדי להגדיר את אופי הפעולה; אך לשון 'נפל' זקוקה לעולם למגדיר נוסף, כבצירוף 'ויפל על פניו'. כן יש לתת את הדעת על ההבדל בתפקיד ובתפרוסת שבין הנוסחה 'ויקד וישתחוו' ובין 'ויפל וישתחוו'. הנוסחה האחרונה משמשת בעיקר למעמד לפני המלך או משנהו (בר' מג, כח; שמ"א כ, מא; שמ"א א, ב; ט, ו; יד, ד, כב), או לפני בני אדם הראויים לכבוד מיוחד (שמ"א כה, כג; מל"ב ד, לז; רות ב, י). יהושע משתחווה לפני המלאך (יהו' ה, יד), ומחוותו של איוב באה בעיקר להביע אבל וזעזוע. נמצא, נוסחה זו אינה משמשת להשתחוויה לפני האל. הצירוף 'ויקד וישתחוו', לעומת זאת, משמש בעיקר לשם עבודת שמיים (בר' כד, כו, מח; שמ' ד, לא; יב,כז; לד, ח; וביימי הבית השני: נחמ' ח, ו; דה"ב כט, ל). לשון זו נאה לכיבוד המלאך (במ' כב, לא), או הנביא העולה משאול בתור רוח רפאים (שמ"א כח, יד), ואף למעמד לפני המלך (שמ"א כד, ח; מל"א א טז, לא); למלך ואל כאחד מכוונת מחווה זו בסיפור המלכת שלמה (דה"א כט, כ). על השאלה מה פשר תופעות אלו, לא נוכל להשיב בטרם נדון במספר נוסחאות נוספות.

הרי מלבד זאת אתה מוצא לשון 'השתחוויה' בצירוף משלימים, אך ללא פועל מקדים. שני המשלימים 'אפים' ו'ארץ' עשויים לבוא זה בצד זה: 'ויבאו אחי יוסף וישתחוו לו אפים ארצה' (בר' מב, ו; וכן: מג, כו לפי תה"ש; 'ויבא אל המלך וישתחוו לו על אפיו ארצה' (שמ"ב יד, לג; תה"ש: 'וישתחוו לו ויפל על אפיו ארצה', מתוך חריגה מסדר המלים הנוסחאי; והקבל יח, כח; בר' מח, יב); 'ויצא ארונה וישתחוו למלך אפיו ארצה' (שמ"ב כד, כ; לפי דה"א כא, כא: 'וישתחוו לדוד אפים ארצה'; וכיוצא בו מל"א, כג; סך הכל שבע דוגמאות). בסיפור לוט תמצא את הצירוף המורכב 'ויקם לקראתם וישתחוו אפים ארצה' (בר' יט, א). ודוק, שהנוסחה 'וישתחוו אפים ארצה' אינה ראויה למעמד לפני האל. היא משמשת אך ורק לכריעה למלך (שמ"ב יד, לג; יח, כח; כד, כ; מל"א א, כג), למשנה למלך (בר' מב, ו), ולאב הזקן (מח, יב); בסיפור לוט היא מכוונת לעוברי אורח-מלאכים. ותן דעתך להבדל בין נוסחה זו ובין הצירוף 'ויפל על פני ארצה וישתחוו'. הרי בצירוף האחרון משמש בדרך כלל המשלים 'על פנים' (פרט לשמ"א כ, מא), כנגד לשון 'אפים' שבנוסחה 'וישתחוו אפים ארצה' ובצירוף 'ויקד אפים ארצה וישתחוו'.

כן אתה מוצא את המשלים 'ארצה' בלבד, כגון: 'וירץ לקראתם וישתחוו ארצה' (בר' יח, ב; וכיוצא בו לג, ג). על פי רוב בא משלים לציין למי ההשתחוויה מכוונת, בין שמדובר במעמד לפני האל (כד, נב), ולאמיתו של דבר גם יח, ב), ובין שמדובר באדם הראוי לכבוד זה: 'ובא אני ואמך ואחיך להשתחות לך ארצה' (לז, י; וכן מג, כו [לפי תה"ש: 'אפים ארצה']; מל"א ב, טו; וכיוצא בו לג, ג; סך הכל שש דוגמאות). תפרוסת זו דומה אפוא לזו של הנוסחה 'ויקד וישתחוו'. צד שווה נוסף בין צירופים אלו, הוא פשטותם. כבר ראינו שבדרך כלל הנוסחה 'ויקד וישתחוו' מכילה פועל ופועל מקדים בלבד, בלא משלימים. והנה, הצרף 'וישתחוו ארצה' מכיל רק פועל ומשלים. ודווקא צורות פשטות אלו, הן הנפוצות ביותר בסיפורי האבות ובסיפור יוסף. ולא זו בלבד, אלא עוד שדווקא הצרף 'וישתחוו ארצה' אינו מזדמן בסיפורי דוד ושאול. מכיוון שלאור תפרוסת הנוסחאות הכללית במקרא מסתבר שסיפורי האבות מהווים את הרובד הקדום ביותר

הקבלה לצירוף הנוסחאי נפל על פנים: 'ויפל על פניו וישתחו' (שמ"ב ט, ו). ובשני המשלימים גם יחד: 'ויתפל על פניה ארצה ותשתחו' (שמ"ב יד, ד; וכן כב); 'ויפל יהושע אל פניו ארצה וישתחו' (יהו' ה, יד; בתה"ש משתקפת הנוסחה הקצרה: 'ויהושע נפל על פניו ארצה' בלבד); 'ויפל לאפיו ארצה וישתחו שלש פעמים' (שמ"א כ, מא; בתה"ש ליתא 'ארצה'). ויש שהציון 'ארצה' מצטרף אל לשון 'השתחוויה', באופן שנוצרת תקבולת: 'ויתפל לאפי דוד על פניה ותשתחו ארצה' (שמ"א כה, כג; וכן רות ב, י). וכן אתה מוצא את המשלים 'רגלי': 'ויתפל על רגליו ותשתחו ארצה' (מל"ב ד, לז). הד מאוחר של נוסחה זו בא בסיפור יהושפט: 'וכל יהודה וישבי ירושלים נפלו לפני ה' להשתחות לה'' (דה"ב כ, יח). דבר זה שהמקור החבור מחליף את הפועל הנטוי, הוא כנראה סימן לסגנון המאוחר של בעל דברי הימים. מרבית הדוגמאות לצירוף זה באות מספר שמואל (ששה מקרים); הן מורות על כריעה לפני המלך (שמ"ב ט, ו; יד, ד, כב) או לפני המלך בכוח (שמ"א כ, מא; כה, כג; שמ"ב א, ב). אין לנו אף דוגמה אחת בסיפורי אברהם ויעקב.

לעומת זאת, בסיפורי האבות אתה מוצא תדיר גירסה אחרת של צירוף זה, גירסה שבה הפועל 'ויקדי' ירש את מקומו של לשון 'ויפלי'. פועל זה, אינו בא כלל ברשות עצמו, פרט לכתוב המאוחר על השתחוויתו של יהושפט, 'ויקד יהושפט אפים ארצה' (דה"ב כ, יח), בסמוך לצירוף החריג 'ויפל...להשתחות' שכבר הזכרנו. הפעל 'יקד' מצוי באכדית (quddudu, qadādu), אך הוראתו שנויה במחלוקת. במקרים מסוימים (בעיקר בבניין קל, G) דומה שאין משמעו אלא 'לכופף', כגון 'ardu ša iqdudu kišāssu', הוא 'עובד (האל) שהרכין ראשי'.[24] פירוש דומה אפשר לתת לצירוף 'liqdud 'appašu, כלומר 'שישפיל פניו',[25] אך בעלי המילון האשורי מעדיפים את הפירוש 'לקוד קידה' (בייחוד בבניין D, פיעל), וטעמם עמם.[26] בין כך ובין כך, מבחינה סמנטית שני המשמעים קרובים זה לזה. מסתבר אפוא, שבלשון המקרא שרש זה אינו אלא שריד של הלשון האפית הקדומה.

במקרא משמש הפועל 'יקד' הקדמה ללשון 'השתחוויה', ומסתבר שהוא מציין פעולה הקודמת למחווה העיקרית. יש ששני הפעלים באים זה בצד זה בלא הרחבה: 'ויקדו וישתחוו' (ברי' מג, כח [כתי' 'וישתחו']; וכן שמ' ד, לא; יב, כז; דה"ב כט, ל). כן אתה מוצא 'ויקד האיש וישתחו לה'' (ברי' כד, כו, וכן פסי' מח), ואף: 'ותקד בת־שבע ותשתחו למלך' (מל"א א, טז), 'ויקדו וישתחוו לה' ולמלך' (דה"ש כט, כ; תה"ש: 'ויכרעו על ברכיהם וישתחוו', וראה להלן). ויש שהמשלים 'ארצה' בא בתור הרחבה לאחר לשון 'יקד' (ולא לאחר 'השתחוויה' כבנוסחה 'ויפל... וישתחו') : 'ויקד ארצה וישתחוו' (שמ' לד, ח). המשלים 'אפים', לעומת זאת, בא לאחר לשון 'השתחוויה': 'ויקד וישתחו לאפיו' (במ' כב, לא). בנסף לכך באה פה ושם ההרחבה בשני משלימים, כגון: 'ויקד דוד אפים ארצה וישתחו' (שמ"א כד, ח, וכן כח, יד; הקבל 'ויפל על פניו ארצה וישתחו'). ויש שבעקבות לשון 'השתחוויה' תבוא הרחבה נוספת: 'ותקד בת־שבע אפים ארץ ותשתחו למלך'

---

24 ראה: CAD K 447, מתוך השוואה לצירוף kišāda kanāšu; וכן: גרובר, (לעיל, הערה 17), עמ' 126-128.

25 והקבל qaddā lētāšu quddudū panūšu (מובא אצל CAD Q 45), כלומר: 'לחייו נפלו, פניו נפולים'.

26 וראה: E. Ebeling, *Tod und Leben nach den Vorstellungen der Babylonier, I: Texte* (Berlin, 1931) 71-72, text 18, col. 2, line 13: appašu liqdud, ina erṣete lippalsiḫ (= 'יעל אפיו יקוד, על הארץ ישכב', כסימן לאבל ותענית). והנה, בזכות הפירוש 'יקידה' מעיד כתוב מקביל באותו טכסט: appašu tušaqdassu ana Sin (שי 3 שם). לדעת אבלינג פירוש הכתוב הוא 'תגרום לו להרכין את פניו לסין', אך מכיוון שמדובר בטקסי תענית יותר סביר לפרש תורה לו להשתחוות לפני סין', ועיין: CAD N 271.

ולכניעה תמצא בשמ"א ה, ד: 'והנה דגון נפל לפניו ארצה'). בכתובים הקרובים לדיני הכהנים הנוסחה תיפל על פניו' שכיחה למדיי (בר' יז, ג, יז; וי' ט, כד; במ' יד, ה; טז, ד, כב; יז, י, כ, ו; יח' א, כח; ג, כג, ט, ח; יא, יג; מג, ג; מד, ד; וראה גם דנ' ח, יז). שלא כמו הנוסחה האוגריתית, שהיא מכוונת למלך ולבני ביתו, הנוסחה המקראית אינה נפוצה בתיאורי המעמד לפני המלך (אך ראה 'יפל לפני', שמ"א יט, יט; בר' מד, יד; נ, יח).

במכתבים בלשון אוגרית, כמו גם במכתבי אל-עמארנה הכתובים בבלית, זכתה נוסחה זו למספר הרחבות שיש להן מקבילות בכמה כתובים מקראיים. מכתב אל אם המלך פותח בלשון 'לפעני אדתני מרחקתם קלני' (='לפני גבירתנו שנינו נופלים ממרחק', הרדנר 51, 5-7). לכך מקבילה ההוראה האלהית למשה: 'והשתחויתם מרחק' (שמ' כד, א). זכר לנימוס-נוסחה כנעני נוסף תמצא במעמד יעקב לפני עשו: 'וישתחו ארצה שבע פעמים עד גשתו אליו' (בר' לג, ג). הכריעה 'שבע פעמים' מקבילה לנוסחה בראש מכתב נוסף: 'לפעני אדתי שבעד ושבעאד מרחקתם קלת' (='שבע ושבע פעמים אני נופל ממרחק לרגלי גבירתי', הרדנר 52, 6-11).[22] וכיוצא בו בפרשת דוד ויונתן: 'ויפל לאפיו ארצה וישתחו שלש פעמים' (שמ"א כ, מא). ריבוי ההשתחוויות אינו נהוג במקרא. בכתובים שלפנינו יש להן הצדקה בגלל ייחודן: יעקב חייב לפייס את עשו; דוד מביע נאמנות ליורש העצר, שעה שהוא בורח מפני המלך עצמו. בסיפור משה הציווי להשתחוות מרחוק מובן לאור העובדה, שרק כאן מורשים בני תמותה לעלות אל מעון האל ולהשתחוות לפני האדון בכבודו ובעצמו. בזכות מעמדם המיוחד של כתובים אלו, כך מסתבר, נשתמר בהם זכר לנימוס הכנעני ולנוסחה המשקפת אותו. במקרא היו המחוות הכנעניות הקדומות למוטיב ספרותי. תופעה זו מגבירה את הקשר בין הספרות הישראלית ובין מורשת הספרות הקדומה.

כעת נחזור לשירה ולנוסחה הפיוטית שבכתבי אוגרית. כצפוי, החרוז האוגריתי זכה למקבילה בשירה המקראית. הצלע השנייה שבנוסחה זו, 'תשתחוי ותכבדה' (=השתחווה וכיבדה אותו'), יש לה בת קול במשאלת המשורר: 'יבואו וישתחוו לפניך ויכבדו לשמך' (תה' פו, ט); 'יהבו לה' כבוד שמו, השתחוו לה' בהדרת קדש' (תה' כט, ב; צלע ב ליתא בתה' צו, ט). צירוף זה נשנה וחוזר בבקשת שאול מעם שמואל: 'עתה כבדני נא נגד זקני עמי ונגד ישראל ושוב עמי והשתחויתי לה'' (שמ"א טו, ל). בבקשה שההשתחוויה תשמש הוקרה למלך, ולא כבוד לאל, אתה שומע נימה אירונית. ושמא תמצא בזוג זה את מקורו של צמד נוסף הקרוב לו מבחינת הצליל: 'יעבד'/'השתחווה', כגון בברכת יצחק: 'יעבדוך עמים וישתחוו (כת': וישתחו') לך לאמים' (בר' כז, כט); 'וישתחוו לו כל מלכים, כל גוים יעבדוהו' (תה' עב, יא).[23]

ואולם, מקבילה הרבה יותר משכנעת לנוסחה האוגריתית תמצא בפרוזה המקראית. לצרף יותקל, תשתחוי' (כלומר 'ינפלה והשתחוותה') מתאים הצירוף 'יפל ... וישתחו' (עשר דוגמאות). ובחלק הארמי של דניאל 'נפל וסגד'). אך המספר הישראלי מוסיף משלימים, אם תיאור מקום (כגון 'ארצה'), ואם ציון לחלק הגוף הנוגע באדמה ('פנים'). לרוב באה ההרחבה לאחר הפועל הראשון. בלשון 'ארצה' בלבד: 'ויפל ארצה וישתחו' (שמ"ב א, ב; איוב א, כ); בלשון 'על פניו', מתוך

---

22 עיין: S. E. Loewenstamm, "Prostration from Afar in Ugaritic, Akkadian, and Hebrew," *BASOR* 188 (1967) 41-43. וכן: *UT* 2008, 4-5; 2063, 5-8.

23 ומכאן חדר זוג זה לספרות החוק, לעריכת המשנה-תורתית ולפרוזה של ספר ירמיה, בייחוד בכתובים שעניינים באיסור עבודה זרה: שמ' כ, ה; כג, כד (אך בלא ההרחבה: לד, יד; וכן מי' ה, יב; תה' פא, י); דב' ח, יט, טז, יא; יז, ג; כט, כה; ד, יט; ה, ט; ל, יז; ומכאן: יהו' כג, ז; טז, שופ' ב, יב, יז, יט; מל"א ט, ו, ט (=דה"ב ז, יט, כב); טז, לא; כב, נד; מל"ב יז, יז, לה; כא, ג, כא; וכן גם יר' א, טז, י; טז, יא; כב, ט; כה, ו; דה"ב לג, ג. ובתקבולת עם לשון 'קטר': יר' א ,טז; דה"ב כה, יד; לב, יב (בניגוד למקבילה בספר מלכים).

הגיעה לספרות הישראלית מהאגרון הספרותי השמי-המערבי הקדום. הרי מקבילה מובהקת לה בשירת העלילה האוגריתית, כגון בשורה 'לפעני אל תהבר ותקל, תשתחוי ותכבדה' (= 'לרגלי אלו כרעה ונפלה, השתחוותה וכיבדה אותי'; הרדנר 4 VI: 25-26).[19] ועוד, בעברית אין למלה זו גיזרון סביר,[20] ואילו בלשון אוגרית ניתן לייחס אותה לשרש 'חוי' בבניין השתפעל, ויהי משמעה 'להתקפל כמו נחש' ('חויתא' בארמית).[21] באוגריתית לשון מזדמנת רק בשירה; במכתבים הנוסחה הנפוצה לעניין השתחוויה נוקטת לשון 'קלי' בלבד, (='נפלי'), כגון 'לפעני אמי קלת' (='לרגלי אמי אני נופל'; הרדנר 50, 5-6). במקרא מקביל לכך הצירוף הקבוע יופל על פניו המוצג גם בסגנון הקלאסי (דה"א כא, טז; מל"א יח, ז; יהו' ז, ו, י). בסיפור שמשון אתה מוצא את הצירוף המורחב 'יופלו על פניהם ארצה' (שופ' יג, כ); לשון דומה משתקפת בנוסח היווני של ספר יהושע: καὶ Ἰησοῦς ἔπεσεν ἐπὶ πρόσωπον ἐπὶ γῆν (יהו' ה, יד: 'ויהושע נפל על פניו ארצה'). על אביגיל נאמר 'ותפל על רגליו' לשם תחינה (שמ"א כה, כד), מתוך הקבלה ללשון 'לפעני' (='לרגלי') שבנוסחה האוגריתית. ברובד זה של הסיפורת המקראית אתה מוצא גם את הצירוף 'נפל לפני' (בר' מד, יד; נ, יח; שמ"ב יט, יט; והקבל אס' ח, ג; סימן לתבוסה בדו-קרב

אחת בסיפור יוסף); שמ' יא, ח; יח, ז; כד, א (שלוש פעמים בסיפורי משה); שופ' ז, טו; שמ"א א, ג, יט, כח; כה, כג, ל, לא (שש פעמים בסיפורי שמואל ושאול); שמ"ב ט, יח; טז, ד; יח, כא (שלוש פעמים בסיפורי דוד); מל"א ה, ח, (שלוש פעמים בסיפורי אלישע); מל"ב יח, כב (='יש' לו, ז); יט, לז (='יש' לז, לח); נחמ' ט, ו; דה"ב כט, כח (פעם אחת בספר דברי הימים). על הגוסס נאמר 'וישתחו על המטה' (בר' מז, לא; מל"א א, מז), ושמא גם זאת נוסחה. ובשירה: יש' מה, יד; ובתקבולת עם 'סגד' מד, טו, יז; מו, ו; יח' ח, טז; מיכה ה, יב; צפ' א, ה; ב, יא; זכ' יד, טז, יז; תה' מה, יב; סו, ד; פא, י; צז, ז; קז, יט; ובתקבולת עם 'רום': צט, ה, ט; עם 'יהודה': קל"ח, ב (וכן בר' מט, ח) עם לשון 'עבד': עב, יא (וכן בר' כז, כט, כט).

19 בשם המחברת הרדנר אציין את: Andrée Herdner, *Corpus des tablettes cunéiformes alphabétiques, découvertes à Ras Shamra-Ugarit de 1929 à 1939* (Paris, 1963) וכן: הרדנר IV ,17: 51-50, ועוד שש פעמים. כן מצינו בתקבולת: 'אל תפל ואל תשתחוי' (הרדנר 2, I: 51), ועיין, Y. Avishur, *Stylistic Studies of Word-Pairs in Biblical and Ancient Semitic Literatures* (Neukirchen-Vluyn, 1984) 388.

20 בניגוד לדעתם של אמרטון (J. A. Emerton, "The Etymology of hištaḥawah," *OTS* 20 [1977] 41-55), וקרויצר (S. Kreuzer, "Zur Bedeutung und Etymologie von hištaḥawah / yšṯḥwy," *VT* 35 [1985] 39-60).

21 עיין: W. F. Albright, "The North-Canaanite Epic of 'Al 'eyan Ba'al and Mot," *JPOS* 12 (1932) 197 n. 14. לגבי בניין השתפעל באוגריתית הקבל הלשון 'ישתקלי' מהשורש 'יקילי', כלומר 'יהזדרז'; ועיין: S. E. Loewenstamm, "YŠTQL," *UF* 16 (1984) 357. ויצוין שגם זה לשון פיוטי מובהק, ואין זה מהנמנע שמוצאו לא מהאוגריתית אלא משפה שמית-מערבית אחרת, קדומה יותר.) אחרת: J. C. Greenfield, "The Root ŠQL in Akkadian Ugaritic and Aramaic," *UF* 11 (1977) 325-327; והמשמע 'להתקפל כמו נחש' תואם היטב את תנועתו של המתפלש בעפר לפני שליט או אל (הקבל למשל את סגידת יהוא לפני מלך אשור, *ANEP* 351). גרובר (לעיל, הערה 17), עמ' 92-91 הביע את הדעה שלשון ההשתחוויה מכוונת לקידה בחלק העליון של הגוף (מהבטן ומעלה) אם כשלעצמה ואם כהקדמה להתפלשות על הארץ; סדר הלשונות בנוסחה האוגריתית (תחילה 'יתקל', לאחר מכן 'ישתחוי') נובעת לדעתו מזה שהמלה הארוכה ביותר, היא 'ישתחוי', תבוא בסוף, בהתאם לחוקי הסגנון. ואולם, במקרה זה לא נוכל להסביר איך זה שלפני המלך גם מבצעים קידה ('וישתחו') וגם מתפלשים בעפר ('ויפל'), בעוד שלפני האל ניתן להסתפק בקידה בלבד ('והשתחויה לשיטתו). נמצא, לשון השתחוויה מורה על התפלשות בעפר דווקא.

וישתחו: קבוצת נוסחאות בשירה ובסיפורת שבמקרא

דיון זה, מטרתו להרחיב את היריעה ולהראות מה תורם העיון בקבוצת נוסחאות הקשורות בהשתחוויה, קבוצה שקאסוטו לא נתן עליה את הדעת. לעניין זה נודע ערך מיוחד, מכיון שהוא כרוך בבעיות של סגנון, של מבנה חברתי ושל מנהגי פולחן כאחד. לעונג ולכבוד הוא לי להגיש שורות אלו לפרופ׳ שמריהו טלמון, שתמיד שם לב למכלול החברתי־ספרותי־דתי ואשר היה בין הבודדים שהגיבו על השערתו של קאסוטו, ואף השכיל להצביע על מקצת מחולשותיה.[16]
באוצר הנוסחאות המסורתיות תופסים הצירופים הקשורים בלשון 'השתחוויה' מקום מיוחד. מחוות ההשתחוויה, פנים רבות לה. לעולם יש בה משום ביטוי להכרה בגדולה ובאדנות, בין שהיא מביעה ברכה (בר' יח, ב), תודה (מל"ב ד, לז), או תחינה (שמ"א כה, כג), כניעה וקבלת מרות (מל"א א, נג) או הישמעות לפקודה (שמ"ב יח, כא).[17] ההשתחוויה עשויה להוקיר אל, מלאך, רוח רפאים, מלך, נביא ואדם נכבד כגון אב (בר' מח, יב) או נדיב (רות ב, י). בסופו של דבר ניווכח לדעת שתפקידיה החברתיים והדתיים של מחווה זו השפיעו הן על עיצוב נוסחאות אלו והן על תדירותן. ואולם, תחילה יש לדון בצד הסגנוני.
לשון 'השתחווה' שכיחה בסיפורת (91 דוגמאות) ובשירה (40 מקרים) כאחד.[18] אין ספק, שהיא

---

16 S. Talmon, "Did There Exist a Biblical National Epic?," *Proceedings of the Seventh World Congress of Jewish Studies: Studies in the Bible and the Ancient Near East* (Jerusalem, 1981) 50-57. בהתנגדותו למגמה למצוא שרידים של שירת העלילה במקרא תומך גם: C. Conroy, "Hebrew Epic-Historical Notes and Critical Reflections," *Bib* 61 (1980) 28-30. קונרוי מגלה את דעתו שיש פער גדול בין שירת העלילה הטיפוסית, היא השירה ההומירית, ובין שירת העלילה של המזרח הקדום. טענה זו אמנם נכונה, אבל אין בה משום ראייה שהשירה המספרת של שומר, בבל ואוגרית אינה שירת עלילה. חייבים להבחין בין אפיון ספרותי ובין קביעת סוג ספרותי. טענתו של טלמון, ששירת העלילה הקדומה נדחתה בישראל בכוונה תחילה אומצה והורחבה על־ידי D. Damrosch, *The Narrative Covenant: Transformations of Genre in the Growth of Biblical Literature* (San Fransisco, 1987) 36-47. אך מצד שני מקבל דאמרוש את טענות קאסוטו וקרוס שהסיפורת המקראית צמחה מתוך השירה האפית (שם, עמ' 1-16).

17 על ריבוי תפקידיה של מחווה זו עמד גרובר: M. Gruber, *Aspects of Non-verbal Communication in the Ancient Near East* (Studia Pohl 12; Rome, 1980) 94-124. בהשתחוויית איוב לנוכח הפורענות ראה דוגמה להתפלשות בעפר באבל ותענית (איוב א, כ); אסמכתה לכך מצא מצד אחד בשימוש בלשון ארצה׳ יפול בלבד כסימן לבהלה ואבל (יהו׳ ז, י; יח׳ ט, ח; יא, יג) ומצד שני בפועל האכדי napalsuḫu (ויפול ארצה, להשתופף על הארץ׳) אשר משמש גם כסימן לאבל (גרובר, 469-464). כנגד זאת יש לומר, שהקבלות אלו אינן מוכיחות דבר מכיון שלשונות אלו משמשות במשמעים שונים ומשונים, לאו דווקא 'כריעה'. אין להן אותה קונוטציה קבועה של הכרה באדנות שיש ללשון 'השתחוויה'. היות שהמספר מעדיף את הצירוף ׳יפול ארצה וישתחו׳ על לשון ׳יפול ארצה׳ גרידא, הוא מעמיד את צערו של איוב בסימן של כניעה לגדולת האל (וראה פס' כא שם). לדעת גרובר (104-102) לשון 'השתחווה לה׳ ' מכוון לעבודת שמיים בכלל, ולאו דווקא להשתחוויה. ואולם, איך יתבארו כתובים המזכירים השתחוויה לבשר ודם, מתוך הצרכה בלמ"ד השימוש דווקא, (שמ"א יח, כא; וכיוצא בו: בר' לז, ז; שמ"א ב, ל)? לשון זו מציינת השתחוויה דווקא.

18 כאן יצוינו רק הדוגמאות ללשון זו בלא הרחבה נוסחאית: בר' כב, ה; כג, יב (פעמיים בסיפורי אברהם); לג, ו, ז, (שלוש פעמים בסיפור יעקב, תמיד לאחר לשון ׳נגש׳); לז, ז (לאחר ׳תסבינה׳; פעם

לדיון זה היא תגליתו של קאסוטו, אשר הראה שסיפורי המקרא, וסיפורי האבות בפרט, מכילים כמה צירופים כבולים, שכדוגמתם תמצא גם בשירת העלילה האוגריתית,[7] כגון הנוסחאות 'וישא עיניו וירא',[8] 'וישא קולו ויקרא/ויבך',[9] 'ויען ויאמר',[10] 'ויקח ... ויצא ללכת/וילד',[11] 'וישם פניו',[12] ו'ויחבש חמורי'.[13] ועל אף שלא כל דוגמאותיו משכנעות,[14] ולמרות המספר המצומצם של הדוגמאות, יש בדבריו משום בסיס לטענה שהמספר הישראלי הקדום שאב ממסורת שירת העלילה השמית-מערבית הקדומה. השערה זו מתחזקת במידה ניכרת לאור בדיקה סטטיסטית ממוחשבת מקיפה, הכוללת נוסחאות נוספות רבות. בדיקה זו מוכיחה באופן חד-משמעי, שבכמות הנוסחאות יש הבדל מובהק בין סיפורי האבות והפרשיות על שמואל, שאול ודוד (שמ"א א—מל"א ב) מזה ובין מרבית הסיפורים בשאר המקרא מזה.[15]

---

5 ראה סיפור סרמוגי לפי: R. C. Steiner and C. F. Nims, "Assurbanipal and Shamash-shum-ukin: A Tale of Two Brothers in Aramaic in Demotic Script," *RB* 92 (1985) 74, col 19, lines 9-10; 'סלקו שכי על שר בבל, שכי ענון יאמרן' (=עלו הצופים אל חומת בבל, ענו הצופים ואמרו'; וחוזר חלילה' טור XXI, ש' 1; שם, עמ' 77). בכתוב זה משתקפת יצירה מתקופת אשורבניפל. טופס הצופים, יש לו מקבילות בשמ"ב יח, כד-כז; מל"א ט, יש"י כא, ו-י ובשירת העלילה האוגריתית (הרדנר I,2 :19- 21) ואכמ"ל.

6 פ' פולק, "פרקי יואב: דמותו של יואב בסיפורי דוד", ספר יצחק אריה זליגמן א (י' זקוביץ-א' רופא עורכים, ירושלים, תשמ"ג) 212-228. יש לכך מקבילות בשירת הומירוס (איליאדה ד 456-462; 480-492; 501-504; ה 34-74; יא 91-98; 425-420, כב 321-366). ושמא מוצאו של מוטיב זה בשירת העלילה של האריסטוקראטיה ההודו-אירופית בארץ ישראל בתקופת הברונזה ואכמ"ל.

7 קאסוטו (לעיל, הערה 1), עמ' 24-28.

8 'וישא עיניו וירא': קאסוטו שם, עמ' 24-25; פ' פולק, "הנוסחאות האפיות בסיפורי המקרא ושורשי הסיפורת העברית הקדומה", תעודה ז (בדפוס; להלן: פולק, שרשים); וכן: F. H. Polak, "Epic Formulas in Biblical Narrative: Frequency and Distribution," *Les Actes du second colloque international: "Bible et Informatique: méthodes, outils, résultats"* (Geneve, 1989) 447. (להלן: פולק, תדירות).

9 'וישא קולו ויקרא'/'וישא קולו ויבך'; קאסוטו, שם, עמ' 28; פולק, תדירות, שם.

10 קאסוטו שם; 80 דוגמאות בסיפורת (פולק, תדירות, שם).

11 קאסוטו, שם עמ' 26-27; י' אבישור, "נוסחאות ספרותיות לתיאור מסע במקרא ובספרות אוגרית", בית מקרא ל (תשמ"ה) 133-141; פולק, תדירות, 449.

12 קאסוטו, שם; מרבית דוגמאותיו של קאסוטו אינן לעניין, אך יש משקל רב לדוגמה בסיפור יעקב (בר' לא, כא בעקבות 'ויקם') ועיין פולק, שרשים, הערה 14; וכן: S. Layton, "Biblical Hebrew 'To Set the Face' in the Light of Akkadian and Ugaritic," *UF* 17 (1986) 169-81.

13 מ"ד קאסוטו, האלה ענת (ירושלים, תשי"א) 33, וספק אם זאת אכן נוסחה שכן אי אפשר להביע את העניין בדרך אחרת (ועיין פולק, שרשים, הערה 14).

14 צירופים נוסחאיים נדירים: 'וישא רגליו וילך'; 'ויתן קולו בבכי'; צירופים שמוצאם בטיקסי המשפט: 'ויצק שמן על ראשי' (כגון בר' כח, יח), 'ויצל ויתן' (בר' לא, ט); ועיין: ,J. C. Greenfield "Aramaic *hnṣl* and Some Biblical Passages," *Meqor Hajjim, Festschrift G. Molin* (Graz, 1983) 115-19; 'ויקח ויתן' ראה: פ' פולק, "'לקח' ונתן': הערות נוספות על הנוסחה וגלגוליה במקרא", שנתון ז-ח (תשמ"ג-תשמ"ד) 179-186; הנ"ל, "'ויקח יהושע את כל הארץ (...) ויתנה יהושע לנחלה לישראל' (יהו' יא, כג)", שנתון ט (תשמ"ח) 234-235; ושמא גם 'אשר ילדה' (כגון בר' כא, ט).

15 פולק תדירות. הביסוס הפילולוגי ניתן אצל פולק, שרשים.

וישתחו: קבוצת נוסחאות בשירה ובסיפורת שבמקרא

פרנק פולק

ייחודה של הסיפורת המקראית אינו שנוי במחלוקת. קוצר היריעה היחסי, אפילו בפרשיות המצטיינות בסגנון רחב יותר, הביא לריכוז הסממנים הספרותיים ותחבולות המספר בתחומים צרים ביותר, ומכיון שכך הוגברה עוצמתם לאין ערוך. רושם שונה לחלוטין יוצרת השירה האפית של המזרח הקדום, החל בספרות השומרית וכלה בכתבי אוגרית: כאן שולטים רוחב הלשון, ההתקדמות האיטית, ההדרגתיות, וההחזרה. ואמנם תמצא עוצמה ופאתוס, אבל אלה מתפרסים על כר נרחב ומידלדלים לא מעט. למרות זאת כבר הבחינו כמה חוקרים, שסגנון זה נתן את אותותיו גם בסיפורת המקראית. ריבוי החזרות שבו, הוא סממן אפי מובהק.[1] קרוס טוען שחלק מהמוטיבים המרכזיים של הסיפור המקראי מהווים המשך לשירת העלילה, כגון מוטיב האל כגבור מלחמה.[2] כיום מסתבר שמורשת העיצוב האפי משתקפת גם בטפסים מסורתיים אחרים,[3] כגון טופס הסעודה,[4] התצפית מעל החומה,[5] וחיסול הלוחם היריב.[6] התרומה העיקרית

---

1 ראה: מ״ד קאסוטו, ספרות מקראית וספרות כנענית (ירושלים, תשל״ב) 31-34; V. Hurwitz, "The Priestly Account of Building the Tabernacle," *JAOS* 105 (1985) 21-30.

2 F. M. Cross, *Canaanite Myth and Hebrew Epic-Essays in the History of the Religion of Israel* (Cambridge, 1973) 112 n. 3, 124, 193; idem, "Biblical Archeology Today: The Biblical Aspect," *Biblical Archeology Today* (ed. A. Biran et al.; Jerusalem, 1985) 11.

3 על מעמד הדפוס המוצק (הטופס) לשם היצג מוטיב מסוים בספרות שבעל-פה ראה: A. B. Lord, *The Singer of Tales* (Cambridge, 1960) 60-98.

4 ראה לעת עתה פ׳ פולק, הרובד העיקרי בפרקים א׳-ט״ו של ספר שמואל א׳, חיבור לשם קבלת תואר דוקטור לפילוסופיה (ירושלים, תשמ״ד) 200, 211 הערה 61, 222 הערות 133-136; וכן: J. A. Ferrara and S. B. Parker, "Seating Arrangement at Divine Banquets," *UF* 4 (1972) 37-39; י׳ אבישור, ״סיפור ביקור המלאכים אצל אברהם (ברי י״ח, א-טז) ומקבילו האוגריתי (2 אקהת V: 4-31)״, בית מקרא לב (תשמ״ז) 168-177.

מידת "קל וחומר"", אך נראה לי שנושא זה מתקשר במישרים לקודם לו. שהרי אפשר להניח כי המלים 'בארץ שלום אתה בוטח' עדיין מכוונות לזירת הריצה. הכוונה שזו טריטוריה שלווה ונוחה למירוץ לעומת ההמשך 'גאון הירדן'. שטח זה הנו סבוך ונפתל ודומה לג'ונגל ובו חיות טרף (השווה יר' מט, ט; נ, מד), שטח שאיננו כשר כלל לריצה.[7] הזיקה בין שני חלקי הפסוק מתעצמת והולכת על סמך הבנה נכונה של הפועל 'בטח' בניב 'בארץ שלום אתה בוטח'. בניגוד לפירוש המקובל לפיו השורש 'בטח' מכוון לשלווה וביטחון נודעת לו במקרא הוראה שונה במספר מקראות, וככל הנראה, גם בכתוב שלנו. ההוראה היא במקביל ללשון הערבית: ליפול ארצה, להשתטח על הבטן/הפנים, כלומר להשתרע על הארץ במלוא הגוף. משמעות זו, הוצעה כבר על-ידי אלפאסי בימי הביניים ונתקבלה על דעת כמה פרשנים מודרניים.[8] למעשה היא מצויה כבר בתרגום הארמי לירמיה.[9] אם נקבל איפוא את המובן הבלתי שיגרתי של 'בטח' הרי אף חציו השני של פסוקנו מעלה תמונה של מירוץ וכישלונו עקב קריסת האיש הרץ. במילים אחרות לא זה בלבד שהנביא איננו יכול לשאר הרצים, אף בזירה נוחה לריצה ('ארץ שלום') הנו מתמוטט ואיננו משיג את היעד הנכסף.

בסיכום, אחד הלקחים שניתן להעלות מן הדיון הנ"ל שאף בישראל, כמו במצרים וביוון,[10] ולו במידה צנועה יותר, היתה שוררת רוח של תחרויות ספורטיביות לפחות לגבי הריצה.

---

7 וראה דברי רש"י למקום: 'בארץ שלום ... שם הלאוך', היינו הדברים חוזרים אל הקטע הקודם וקשורים זה בזה.

8 ראה דוד בן אברהם אלפאסי, כתאב גאמע אלאלפאט (מלון מקראי עברי-ערבי), מהדורת S. L. Skoss, *Kitāb Jāmiʿ Al-Alfāẓ* (New Haven, 1936) 1:2/5 וראה גם רש"י על משי' יד, טז, המזכיר שם את הכתוב שלנו. בין החדשים עמד על הוראה זו בין השאר: S. L. Skoss, *Jewish Studies in Memory of G. A. Kohut* (1935) 549-53.

9 התרגום הארמי מוסיף למלה 'את מתבטחי' (אולי כבר בהוראה שאנו דנים בה) במפורש את התיבה 'ונפילי'.

10 השווה: W. Decker, "Das sogenannte Agonale und der alt-ägyptische Sport," *Festschrift Elmar Edel* (Bamberg, 1974) 90ff.

מירוצים, ביחוד ארוכי-טווח, נזכרים בעולם העתיק לעתים קרובות בספרות היוונים ולכך יש
להוסיף גם מירוצי סוסים, וכן התאורים הפלאסטיים על גבי כדים.[2] לעומת זה ביחס למזרח
הקדום חומר מסוג זה נדיר ביותר ועל אחת כמה וכמה כאשר מדובר בתחרויות של רצים. אולם
באחרונה נתגלו בשטח זה במצרים פרטים מאלפים. ב-1981 נתפרסמה מצבה מצרית של פרעה
תהרקה מן השושלת הכ״ה במצרים (השושלת הנובית-הכושית) שהיא בחזקת מקור יחיד במינו
לעניינו. המצבה, שתאריכה הוא שנת 685 לפני הספירה, כלומר כשבעים-שמונים שנה לפני
ירמיהו הנביא, מכונה בצדק הן בכתובת גופה והן בידי החוקרים החדשים בכינוי האופייני
״אסטילת המירוץ של תהרקה״.[3] האסטילה הוצבה, כמצבותיהם של פרעונים אחרים בנתיב
המדבר ליד האתר דהשור, נתיב שהוליך מבירת מצרים נוף לנווה המדבר פאיום. עיקר תכנה נוגע
לנו ומתאר חיילים של צבא פרעה המתאמנים מדי יום בריצות בנתיב הנזכר הלוך וחזור, מרחק
של מאה קילומטרים בשני הכיוונים.[4] צוין משך הזמן שהרצים נזקקו לו כדי לגמוע מרחק זה,
והוא בן תשע שעות, היינו אחד עשר קילומטרים לשעה בממוצע. האסטילה באה להנציח את
מירוץ החיילים שפרעה פיקח עליו אישית, ואף נטל בו חלק לאורך כברת דרך מסוימת, והרצים
המצטיינים זכו לגמול.

כאן דוגמה יחידה במינה של מירוץ ארוך-טווח במתכונת שכמותה בוודאי לא עמדה לעיני מחבר
ספר ירמיה. לעומת מירוצי רגלים אין לנו ידיעות ברורות על תחרות של ריצת רגלים נגד סוסים
או פרשים ושמא הכוונה בירמיה אפילו למרכבות (אותן מסמלת המלה ׳סוסים׳). אכן תבליטים
מצריים על גבי קירות מקדשים או קירות קברים מתארים לעתים חיילים שרצים לפני מרכבת
המלך או אחריה. אולי הם משמשים כליווי למרכבה או כמגינים עליה, אך מכל מקום עליהם
לשמור על קצב דהרת הסוסים.[5]

לעתים הכוונה היא לשיטת לחימה של המצרים שלפיה אחד מאנשי צוות הרכב יורד ממנו
בהמולת הקרב ומתקדם רגלית בצד הסוסים נגד האויב.[6] עם זה מן הסתם אפשר לשער שמירוצי
רגלים עם סוסים היו קיימים אצל זה או אחר וכי לא מן הנמנע שדברי ספר ירמיה
מושתתים על יסוד ריאלי.

בחצי השני של הפסוק בספר ירמיה אנו עוברים לכאורה לנושא אחר, אף הוא במתכונת של

---

2 על הספורט בעולם העתיק ראה את הסקירות: I. Weiler, *Der Sport bei den Völkern der alten Welt* (2d ed.; Darmstadt, 1988) 146ff.; J. Jüthner, *Die athletische Leibesübungen der Griechen* (2 vols.; Wien, 1968) 2:15-156 (Wettlauf).

3 הטכסט המצרי פורסם על-ידי: A. M. Moussa, "A Stela of Taharqa from the Desert Road at Dahshur," *Mitteilungen des Deutschen Instituts für Ägyptische Altertumskunde in Kairo* 37 (1981) 331-37; H. Altenmüller and A. M. Moussa, "Die Inschriften auf der Taharkastele von der Dahschurstrasse," *Die sumerischen und akkadischen Königsinschriften* 9 (1981) 57-84 של לניתוח ההיבט הספורטיבי התעודה השווה: -68 (München, 1987) *W. Decker, Sport und Spiel im alten Ägypten*; מחקרו של הנ״ל: 74; "Die Lauf-Stele des Königs Taharqa," *Kölner Beiträge zur Sportwissenschaft* 13 (1984) 7-37.

4 פרטים טכניים על המירוץ ראה במאמרו של דקר (לעיל, הערה 3), עמ׳ 71 ואילך, וכן הערכים בלקסיקון המצרי פרי עטו של אותו המחבר: 6 *LÄ* "Wettkampf,"; 1161ff. (1984) 5 *LÄ* ,"Sport" 1238ff. (1986).

5 השווה: Decker, "Die Lauf-Stele des Königs Taharqa," 20 ושם תמונה מס׳ 6, מקבר מאהו שבאל-עמרנה.

6 השווה: A. R. Schulman, "The Egyptian Chariotry: A Reexamination," *Journal of the American Research Center in Egypt* 2 (1963) 89-90.

'כי את רגלים רצתה וילאוך' (יר' יב, ה)

אברהם מלמט

בכלל עשרת המקרים הנמנים בספרות חז"ל ביחס למידת "קל וחומר" (למשל בר"ר צב, ז) מצויה הפיסקה התמוהה כלשהו מספר ירמיה יב, ה: 'כי את רגלים רצתה וילאוך ואיך תתחרה את הסוסים? ובארץ שלום אתה בוטח ואיך תעשה בגאון הירדן',[1] כתוב זה, שאולי היה מעין משל רווח, בא בשמץ של הפתעה כתשובת ה' לתלונות הנביא וכדי להדגים את חוסר האונים והמציאות הקודרת שבהם נתון ירמיהו. לדברי ה' אין הנביא מסוגל להתמודד עם מכשולים קלי ערך קל וחומר עם נסויים כבדים ונצורים. לא נעמוד ברשימה קצרה זו על ההיבט התיאולוגי של דברי ה' ונברר אך ורק את הרקע הריאלי המשתקף בדברים אלה.
בראש הפסוק נרמזת תחרות בין רצים, או אצנים בלשון ימינו, שבה הללו גוברים בקלות על כושרו של הנביא ומתישים ומוגיעים אותו ('וילאוך'). ניתן להציע פירוש שונה במקצת, שעד כמה שידוע לי לא נשקל עד כה, שלפיו 'הרַגלים' הם אף כאן אנשי צבא הנלחמים רגלית, כשם שמעינו תיבה זו גם במקומות אחרים במקרא (למשל, שמ' יב, טז). במקרה זה המירוץ נועד לאימון או להסתערות של חיילים, פירוש ההולם יפה הן את הזכרת ה'סוסים' בהמשך הפסוק, והן את התעודה המצרית שנביא להלן. אמנם אין ההבדל בין שני הפירושים, המקובל והמוצע כאן, בעל משמעות לגבי הנושא שלנו. על-פי שני הפירושים אמורים הדברים במירוץ של רגלים נגד רגלים או בתחרות של רגלים עם סוסים.
רצים נזכרים לעתים נדירות במקרא. שתי דוגמאות מרשימות למירוץ ארוך-טווח (אך לא לתחרות) הן: האיש הנמלט משדה המערכה באבן העזר — אפק, בה ניגפו בני ישראל מפני פלשתים, רץ לשילה (מרחק קרוב לשלושים קילומטרים) כדי לבשר את תבוסת ישראל לעלי (שמ"א ד, יב). ריצה זו מעלה על דעתנו את ריצת מרתון "המקורית" ביוון העתיקה, רק שהבשורות בפי הרצים היו הפוכות בתכנן. שלוש ריצות ארוכות טווח נוספות נזכרות במקרא: שני הרצים (הכושי ואחימעץ) המבשרים לדויד את תבוסת אבשלום (שמ"ב יח, יט-כו), וגיחזי, המתיימר לשמש שליחו של אלישע, ורודף אחרי מרכבתו של השר נעמן ומצליח להשיג את הרכב (מל"ב ה, כ-כב), היינו, מעין התמודדות בין רץ למרכבה, כמו במשלו של ירמיהו. הדוגמה האחרת היא ריצת אליהו הנביא לפני מרכבת המלך אחאב מראש הכרמל ועד לעיר יזרעאל שבעמק (מרחק של עשרים וחמישה קילומטרים בקירוב) (מל"א יח, מו).

---

1 ראה פירושים על ספר ירמיה למקום וביחוד הפירוש האחרון והמפורט ביותר: W. McKane, *Jeremiah* (ICC; Edinburgh, 1986) 1:263-66.

לשאלת לשון המקור של סיפור שלושת הנערים 75*

ניגש אל מלאכת התרגום.⁵⁹ העיבוד המונח לפנינו בעזה״ח אינו מעיד אפוא על תולדות הקורפוס היווני אלא על תולדות ספרי דה״י, עזרא ונחמיה.

---

59 אם מסתברת טענה זו, ממילא גם הלבוש היווני של הספר כולו, סיפור הנערים כחלקים האחרים, תפור באותה יד. ואכן, הסיפור והחלקים המקבילים לדה״י, עז׳ ונחמ׳ טבועים באותו חותם. דיברנו לעיל על התפלגות דומה של שימושים לשוניים בסיפור הנערים וביתר עזה״ח. להלן כמה דוגמאות לשיתוף בסגנון: הנוסח πάντα ἄλλα τὰ καὶ הן בא ב-ו, ד (עז׳ ה, ג) והן בסיפור, ד, ה; χρυσώματα משמשים הן ב-ג, ה והן ב-ח, נו (עז׳ ח, כז); והליווי בדרכים מתואר ב-ח, נא (עז׳ ח, כב) על ידי ἡ προπομπή, ובסיפור, ד, מז: ἵνα προπέμψωσιν αὐτόν; האיזור נקרא פה ופה: κοίλη Συρία καὶ Φοινίκη, בסיפור — ד, מח, ובשאר הספר פעמים הרבה; המקדש הוא בשניהם τὸ ἱερόν, בסיפור — ד, נא, סג, בשאר הספר פעמים הרבה. וכולן התבטאויות יוצאות דופן בקורפוס של תרגום השבעים.

יסודות היקום. אך אילו נתן דעתו לכך שמינה של **קשוט, קושטא** הארמית הוא זכר,[55] לא היה נזקק לכך. ודווקא משום שמינה של **אמת** ושל ἀλήθεια נקבה הוא, ואילו של **קושט** — זכר, יוצא המרצע מן השק ומורה על מקורו הארמי של הסיפור. פסוק לו סובב סביב האמת ועל כן מסתבר שאף סופו כן: μετ' αὐτοῦ ἄδικον οὐδέν ἐστιν καὶ, היינו: 'ולא איתי עמה כל עולה',[56] אין עמה, עם האמת, כל 'עולה'. הכינוי (עמיה) לא חזר במקור אל האל אלא אל **קשוט**; היה על המתרגם לשנות לנקבה בהתאם ליוונית, וטעה ולא שינה, ונמצא הכינוי חוזר אל האל. ובפסוק מ, εὐλογητὸς ὁ θεὸς τῆς ἀληθείας, אפשר היה לפניו: 'מְבָרַךְ/בְּרִיךְ אלה קשטא', כלומר 'מבורכת/ברוכת אלוה (היא) האמת', והמתרגם הבין 'ברוך (הוא) אלהי האמת'.[57]

* * *

אם הצלחנו להביא די ראיות — ובהחלט יש חשיבות לעדות המצטברת — כדי לקרב אל הדעת שהסיפור מתורגם משפה שמית, ככל הנראה מארמית, עדיין איננו יודעים על פי זה בידי מי הגיע להקשרו הנוכחי בתוך ספר עזרא. קטע הביניים המקשר בין סיפור הנערים לבין הספר שהוא נתון בו, ה, א-ו או ד-ו, אפשר נכתב ארמית ואפשר עברית, אך קשה להניח שנכתב יוונית, ולו רק משום שהוא, יותר מכל קטע אחר בסיפור, כתוב בדפוס לא יווני.[58] לפיכך, מעשה שילוב הסיפור בספר והשינויים שהוכנסו בספר כדי להכשירו לקליטת הסיפור היו כבר לעיני המתרגם כאשר

---

55 כך בכל הדיאלקטים הארמיים 'קשוט, קושטא' — מינה זכר; ואף בסורית, אשר הושפעה מן הדיסימילאציה של הנחציים: קושטא>קושתא והת"יו יכלה להיתפש כמציינת נקבה — אומר עליה בר עלי במפורש: 'ידכרנאית ולא נקבאית': R. Payne Smith, *Thesaurus Syriacus* (Oxford, 1901) 2:3773.

56 עולה היא המלה המנוגדת לאמת הן בס' חנוך הארמי, ראה 4QEn^{c}1 V, 3, מיליק (לעיל, הערה 37), עמ' 189, והן בסורית (פיין סמית, שם).

57 ושמא היה כתוב במקור: 'בריך/מברך יהוה קושטא', דהיינו: ברוכה/מבורכת תהיה האמת, והמתרגם פירש את הפועל **יהוה** כשם האל. והשווה: 'יהוה בריך דין קושטא' בחנוך הארמי 4QEn^{d}1 XI,2 (מיליק, שם, עמ' 218).

58 לציין את המעט: 1. שלושה משפטים ראשיים רצופים פותחים ב-καί, עדות שדי בה כדי להטיל ספק חמור באפשרות שלפנינו כתיבה יוונית חפשית. 2. הדפוסים הפותחים את שני הקטעים המרכיבים את הפסוקים הללו: פסוק א - μετὰ δὲ ταῦτα..., פסוק ד καὶ ταῦτα τὰ ὀνόματα... 3. האפיון של קבוצות העולים: κατὰ πατριὰς αὐτῶν εἰς τὰς φυλὰς ἐπὶ τὴν μεριδαρχίαν αὐτῶν (פסוק ד). 4. דרך ציון החודש בפסוק: τοῦ μηνὸς Νισὰν τοῦ πρώτου ἔτους. ולבסוף, 5. נראה הדבר שביסוד הטקסט היווני המוקשה בפסוק ה עומד שיבוש שנגרם במעבר ממקור לתרגום: Ἰησοῦς ὁ τοῦ Ἰωσεδέκ· οἱ ἱερεῖς υἱοὶ Φινεὲς υἱοὶ Ἀαρών... τοῦ Σαραίου καὶ Ἰωακεὶμ ὁ τοῦ Ζοροβαβὲλ τοῦ Σαλαθιήλ. הפתיחה ב- οἱ ἱερεῖς... מבקשת יותר מכאן אחד ויויקים הלוא היה בנו של ישוע בן יהוצדק ולעומת זאת לא ידוע מי בשם זה שהיה בנו של זרובבל. אין זאת אלא שיבנו' או 'ברה' שהגדיר את יויקים כבנו של ישוע הובן ללא הכינוי והפך יויקים לבנו של זרובבל. לפני המתרגם היה אפוא: 'הכהנים בני פנחס בן אהרן ישוע בן יוצדק בן שריה בן **ויויקים בנו (ו)זרובבל** בן שאלתיאל...' (השמטת וי"ו ווי"ו לפני האות זי"ן אולי מסתברת על רקע דמיון מה בין האותיות, השווה יבוזים ב-ד"ה ב, טז לעומת יבוסים בעזה"ח א, מט), או כיוצא בזה בארמית: '...ויויקים ברה ו)זרובבל...'.

כבוד ל-οἰκογενεῖς. אך הוראת המלה היוונית היא 'עבדים ילידי הבית', ואין היא תואמת את ההקשר. נראה שאין זה אלא תרגום של 'בני ביתא'. בארמית הממלכתית והבינציימית **בר ביתא** הוא פקיד גבוה בחצר המלכות,[50] ואילו בעברית **בן בית** הוא עבד שנולד בבית האדון.[51] המתרגם מצא לפניו את הצירוף הזה ותרגמו על פי הוראת מרכיביו, אף שאין זה הולם את הקשר הדברים.[52]

ד, יד הריהו מקום מפורסם בכל דיון מסוג זה: οὐ μέγας ὁ βασιλεὺς καὶ πολλοὶ οἱ ἄνθρωποι ὁ οἶνος ἰσχύει. משמעו הרגיל של πολλοί אינו תואם את העניין, שהרי צפויה שימת דגש על הכוח, הגודל, לא על הריבוי. רודולף (עמ' ix) לשיטתו חיפש ומצא שהמלה היוונית נושאת גם גון-משמע של 'חזקים', אך ספק אם מחבר יווני היה נדחק לבחור דווקא במלה זו, שלפניה הכל מעלה על הדעת משמעות של 'רבים'. אין זאת כי אם תרגום טעות לפנינו. טורי (עמ' 24) טען שהמתרגם טעה לתרגם את **רברבין** במשמע 'רבים', כלומר ראה במלה הארמית את בת דמותה העברית. לעומת זאת אם נניח שהיה לפניו טקסט ארמי: 'שגיאין בני אנשא' — הכל יתבאר מאליו, שהרי **שגיאין** עניינה בארמית 'רבים' הן בכמות[53] הן בגודל,[54] והמתרגם בחר במשמע הראשון במקום שהיה ראוי לו לבחור בשני.

תרגום טעות המסתבר על רקע שימוש הלשון הארמי הרבה יותר מאשר על רקע העברית חוזר על עצמו בפרק ד, בפסוקים מט ואילך: שוב ושוב מתקבל הרושם מן הטקסט היווני שהמלך כותב אל היהודים, אל העולים, אל הכוהנים, הלויים והשומרים. משום ש-**על** עניינו גם 'אודות' וגם 'אל', טעה המתרגם להבין שהמכתב של המלך הופנה אל היהודים וכו', אלא שהופנה אל פחוות עבר הנהר, כפתוב בפסוק מח, ועניינו נסב על היהודים. דו-המשמעות של **על** היא לחם חוקה של הארמית הממלכתית, אך יש להודות שאינה נעדרת מן העברית, וראה עז' ד, ו, ז.

ד, לז: εὐλογητὸς ὁ θεὸς τῆς ἀληθείας. ד, מ: καὶ οὐκ ἔστιν μετ' αὐτοῦ ἄδικον οὐδέν. רבים ציינו את הקושי שבהופעת האל כנושא לעצמו בדברים על האמת, ד, לה, לו, מ. אם מבינים את פסוק לה, ὁ μέγας ὃς ταῦτα ποιεῖ καὶ οὐχί, כהמשך הדברים על השמש ולא כהגדרת האל, שאינו נזכר מפורשות, הנה הופעת האל כנושא בפסוקים ו-מ יכולה להתפרש כתולדה של מסירת המקור הארמי. טורי (עמ' 55-56) הציע פתרון בכיוון זה אך הטיל על כתפי המתרגם שינוי מגמתי: לתת לאל מקום של כבוד בסיפור שעניינו עליונות

---

[50] אפשר שהרשימה מונה את הפקידים הגבוהים על פי סולם החשיבות ובראש הרשימה מוצבים ה-οἰκογενεῖς. **בר ביתא'** היה תוארו של ארשם, מבכירי הממשל הפרסי, והשוה את האמור במגילת בראשית יט, כד: 'תלתא גברין מן רברבי מצרין מן בני ביתא די פרעו צען', באייר (לעיל, הערה 41), עמ' 173. קשה לקבל את גישת רונדגרן המייחס ליוונית את משמע הארמית על סמך שימושה של המלה במקומנו, ראה: F. Rundgren, "Zur Bedeutung von οἰκογενής in 1 Esra 3,1," Eranos 55 (1957) 145-52.

[51] בברי' טו, ג הוא שם נרדף ל-בן משק הבית הנזכר בפסוק הקודם, אך ראה במיוחד קוהלת ב, ז: 'קניתי עבדים ושפחות ובני בית היה לי'. צימרמן (לעיל, הערה 1), עמ' 199, לא דק בעניין זה.

[52] עם זאת אין להתעלם מכך שהצורה הצפויה ביסוד המונה המתאים היטב להקשר, οἰκονόμος, ד, מו, מט, אף היא **בר-בית**. ייתכן שבא לידי תרגום שונה משום שבכתובים הללו ההקשר אינו סובל מכל וכל את המשמעות שמביא עמו οἰκογενής ואילו ב-ג, א יכול היה לטעות ולחשוב שמדובר בעבדי חצר המלכות.

[53] השוה 'ישניו שגיאן', עז' ה, יא.

[54] השוה 'צלם חד שגיא', דני' ב, לא, 'מתגן רברבן שגיאן' שם, מז; וכשימוש הזה (**שגיאין** בהוראת 'גדולים') אף בתרגומים הארמיים מארץ ישראל, כגון לברי' ד, יג.

σύσκφ   בא לומר שנתיני המלך מעלים לו את המסים על תוצרתם, ונמצא מסגיר את מקורו הארמי בשלושה אופנים. בלשון המקרא **מס** עניינו 'מס עובד', 'אנגריה'; הוא משמש ברגיל בלשון יחיד,[44] ומעלה המס הוא השליט המקבל את האנשים לעבודות הכפייה. התרגומים מלמדים על דרכה השונה של הארמית: **מס** אינה מוגבלת, ככל הנראה, למס עובד,[45] וכל מקום המלה באה תמיד בריבוי: **מסין**, ומעלה המס אינו המקבל אלא המוסר.[46] הכתוב שלנו מדבר על מסי התוצרת החקלאית (ולא על אנגריה) אשר האזרחים נאלצים להעלות למלך, והוא משקף אפוא בצורה ובתוכן מבע מעין **מ(נ)סקין מסין**.

נזכיר בקיצור עוד צירופים אחדים כגון זה.

- ד, ה: πάντα τὰ ἄλλα, יכול משקף צירוף ארמי כלאחרן כלאי, שסימוכין לו במכתבם של יהודי יב אל בגוהי (קאולי 30: 11-12).[47] הצירוף חוזר ב-ו, ד (עז׳ ה, ג), ללא מקביל ישיר בנה״מ.

- ד, י, לא: εἰς τοῦτο σκπ. שמא עמד לעיני המתרגם הצירוף **לקבל דנה**, או בצורתו השכיחה יותר **כל קבל דנה**. הוראתו המילולית היא 'לנוכח זה', אך משמעו למעשה יבו בזמן, 'אז', והוא ההולם את ההקשר.[48]

- ד, כב: ἄγνωναι ξαμᾶς ἰσθ. טורי (עמוד 53) הציע שהמתרגם בחר במבנה תחבירי זה היות שצירו של המשפט שעמד לנגד עיניו סב על **אָרִיךְ** הארמי (עז׳ ד, יד: ׳לא אריך לנא למחזא׳) ואין כיו״ב בעברית המקרא.

ובסיומה של פרשה זו ייזכר מקומו של הפועל בסוף המשפט, אחד מסימני ההיכר של הארמית הממלכתית, אשר בא לה בירושה מן האכדית.[49] נראים הדברים, שמקומות אחדים בסיפור הנערים מעידים על נוהג לשון ארמי זה: ג, ו; ד, מב, מג, מד, מו, נ.

2. עניני תוכן.

לעתים, תמיהות בתוכן הסיפור מתבררות על רקע אי הבנה של מקור ארמי.

ג, א: οἰκογενεῖς. בפתיחת הסיפור נזכרים מוזמני המלך למשתה שערך ובין אלה יש מקום של

---

44 בצירוף 'שרי מסים' בשמ' א, יא נגרר הריבוי אחרי הנסמך, כדרך 'לחות אבנים' השכיח בתורה; ומעניינו שבתרגומים לא נתבארה צורת הסומך היחידאית הזאת כפשוטה. לשון המגילות ממשיכה את לשון המקרא ואילו לשון התנאים, אולי בעקבות הארמית, פנתה אף היא ללשון רבים (על פי עדות הקונקורדאנציה של המילון ההיסטורי של הלשון העברית).

45 כעדות התרגומים האיי״מ לברי׳ מט, טו.

46 בדב׳ כ, יא נאמר על תושבי העיר הנכנעת: ׳יהיו לך למס׳. משפט זה נמסר בתרגומים היהודיים: ׳יהון לך למסקי מסין׳ (כך באונקלוס וכיו״ב בתרגומים הארץ-ישראליים). ׳מס׳ מומר אפוא ב**מסים**׳ ומעלי המסים הם המשלמים אותו. ובעל תרגום-יונתן לנביאים נאלץ לשנות את האמור במ״א ה, כז: ׳ויעל המלך שלמה מס מכל ישראל׳, כך: ׳יומני מלכא שלמה מסקי מסין׳, ר״ל המיר את ה׳מס׳ ב׳מסיני׳ ומעלה המס שוב אינו שלמה אלא מי שמסקפו.

47 זו לשון המכתב: יואחרן (זי תמה) הוה כלא באשה שרפו׳ – (וכל דבר) אחר, אשר שם היה, כולו שרפו באש, עיין למשל, ז׳ בן-חיים, ׳יב״, אנציקלופדיה מקראית ג (ירושלים, תשי״ח) 433-434. אך נראה יותר ש׳אחרן כלא׳ עניינו יכל השאר׳, ושיעור הדברים: וכל השאר, אשר היה שם – שרפו באש.

48 על הצעת טורי ראה לעיל הערה 31.

49 S. Segert, *Altaramäische Grammatik* (Leipzig, 1975) 422. תן דעתך שקו לשוני זה, הזר ללשונות השמיות, נעלם מן הדיאלקטים התופסים את מקומה של הארמית הממלכתית.

עזה"ח אכן מצטיין בהמרת מבני הסמיכות שמצא לפניו במבנים אחרים, 'יווניים' יותר, אך המבנה היווני שיצא מתחת ידיו בפעם הזאת אינו עושה חסד עם לשון המטרה, אם ננקוט לשון המעטה, ובו שהוא חוזר למקור שהכתיב את הצורה היוונית.[35]

ד, לו: σείεται καὶ τρέμει. מן הסתם זהו תצלומו של אחד הביטויים הארמיים: 'זאעין ודחלין', ראה דני ה, יט; ו, כז,[36] או: 'ירעדין ודחלין', ס' חנוך הארמי 4QEn^d 2 II,30.[37] בארמית זהו אפוא ביטוי שגור ואילו בעברית לא מצאנו שכמותו.[38]

ד, לט: ἀπὸ πάντων τῶν ἀδίκων ποιεῖ τὰ δίκαια. בלשון המקרא עושים משפט או שפטים במישרה (לא ממישהו).[39] טורי (עמ' 25) השכיל להצביע על מלת היחס המוצרכת הזרה ליוונית אשר נספחה לכאן בהסח דעתו של המתרגם היווני, והפנה אל: 'ידינה להוא מתעבד מנּה' (עז' ז, כו). טקסטים שנתגלו מאוחר יותר מספקים אישור נוסף לכך. בס' חנוך הארמי 4QEn^{e}1 XXII,3: 'דינא רבא די מנהון יתעבד', ובמכתבי בר-כוכבא: 'מזכון פרענותא תתעבד';[40] ודוגמות ההולמות עוד יותר את לשון הכתוב היווני, בבניין קל עם מן מוצרכת, ב-4QEn^{g}1 IV,16: 'למעבד דין קשוט מן כול רשיעין', ובמגילת בראשית כ, יד: 'יעבד לי דין מנה' (וכיו"ב בתרגום אונקלוס לדב' לג, ז).

ד, מב: σοφώτερος ὑπερέθετο. שימוש כזה של 'ימצא' כפועל עזר מודאלי ('להתגלות כנכון') המשמש כאגוד במשפט אינו נוהג בעברית המקרא,[41] אך הוא מצוי בארמית המקרא, ראה דני ה, כז: 'השתכחת חסיר'.

מטבעות הלשון שהבאנו מזדקרים לעין מבעד למעטה התרגום ומהווים ראיה מובהקת לקשר הבלתי אמצעי עם הארמית. אין הם אלא קצה הקרחון, אך באחרים רב הנסתר על הנגלה. כך דרך משל בצירוף הבא: ד, ו: ἀναφέρουσιν τοὺς φόρους. המונח המתאים לציין 'מסי' בארמית הממלכתית הוא מ(נ)דה (עז' ד, יג, כ; ו, ח; ז, כד), ובעקבותיה 'מדה' בעברית (נחמי ה, ד). האם הוא שהיה לעיני המתרגם ובחר למוסרו בלשון רבים: φόροι? אפשר שכן, אם משווים את מנהגו של מתרגם עזרא ונחמיה. אך, בעל התרגום המונח לפנינו בעזה"ח בוחר למסור את מ(נ)דה באופן עקבי ב-φορολογία.[42] קשה להניח אפוא ש- מ(נ)דה היא שעמדה ביסודה של φόρος, בפרט שהפועל ἀναφέρειν אינו בא אף באחד מן המקומות הללו.[43] הפעלים המלווים הם δοῦναι ו-ἐπιβάλλειν בהתאמה עם המקור הארמי הנוקט לשון נת"ן/יה"ב ו-רמ"י, ואילו ἀναφέρειν הוא האקויוולנט של 'להעלות' (80x) ודומיו. ἀναφέρουσιν τοὺς

---

[35] טורי, (לעיל, הערה 1), עמ' 53 הערה e, מגדיר את הצירוף הזה כברבריזם. על התקצרות הביטוי במעבר מן המקור לתרגום ראה לעיל, הערה 25.

[36] ובהיפוך הסדר: 'דאלין וזאעין', מג' בראשית 0, ג, K. Beyer, *Die aramäischen Texte vom Toten Meer* (Göttingen, 1984) 176.

[37] J. T. Milik, *The Books of Enoch* (Oxford, 1976) 223, והשווה אף 4QEn^{c}4,1 (מיליק, עמ' 204).

[38] הביטוי העברי הקרוב ביותר שמצאנו הוא: 'פחדו ורגזו', ירי' לג, ט.

[39] כגון: 'ובכל אלהי מצרים אעשה שפטים' שמ' יב, יב, וכיו"ב במד' לג, ד, תהי' קיט, פד; קמט, יט.

[40] י' קוטשר, מחקרים בעברית ובארמית (ירושלים, תשל"ז) לח. בעמ' מ הוא מציע לעניין זה: 'העובדה כי הפועל מתקשר במלת-היחס "מן", מתפרשת בשורש זה בהוראה "לגבות תשלום", השוה אף "להיפרע מן" בלשון חז"ל.

[41] במקראית המאוחרת, אסי' ו, ב, דני' יב, א, יש כבר שימוש דומה, אך עדיין בולט הקשר שבין החיפוש למציאה. בלשון התנאים לעומת זאת כבר נשתגר שימוש זה.

[42] ראה ב, יח; ו, כז; ח, כב (עז' ד, יג; ו, ח; ז, כד בהתאם) והשווה ב, כג (עז' ד, כ).

[43] דומה שהיינו מצפים ברגיל ל-φέρειν (או לפועל אחר, כמו ἀπάγειν) לעניין העלאת מסים, ואילו ἀναφέρειν בא לענות על פועל גורם במקור שלפניו.

בנגהא...'. וכסיוע לזו הראשונה, שמא היה לפניו מעין: *ישנת המלך נהיתה עליו*, במשמע — נפלה עליו שינה,[30] והבין, אולי, על דרך דנ' ב, א: *יתתפעם רוחו ושנתו נהיתה עליו*, במשמע — היתה ממנו והלאה. למרות שלהסבר האחרון אין בסיס מוצק בשימוש הלשון, הוא מתאים יותר לרוח הסיפור, באשר אין הסיפור נבנה ממוטיב נדודי השינה, ולהפך. גם מבחינת אוצר המלים והביטויים יקשה להסביר את הצירוף ἐγένετο ἄϋπνος καὶ מבלי להניח שהכותב הלך שבי אחרי המקור שלפניו.[31]

מתברר אפוא — גם מבלי להתחייב לגבי דמותו המדויקת של המקור — שמרכיבים מסוימים בתוכן סיפור הנערים, בלשונו ובעיצובו החיצוני, מלמדים שאכן בצורתו הנוכחית הינו תרגום. נפנה עתה להתבונן מקרוב בשפת המקור בנסיון לגלות אם עברית היתה או ארמית. ממילא נזכיר את הראיות החשובות שהעלה טורי בחכתו, אך נדייקן ונבססן ונשלים אחריו בחומר משלנו.[32]

ג

מהי אפוא לשונו של המקור שעמד לנגד המתרגם, ארמית או עברית? האם ניתן לגלות מבני-לשון המשתקפים מבעד לטקסט היווני ואשר מצויים רק באחת מן הלשונות הללו? שמא יכול הקשר להצביע לעבר לשון המקור? אין זו משימה קלה, ולו רק מפני שקשה ללמוד על מצב הטקסט והלשון מכלי שני. נוסף על כך, תמונת הלשונות הללו מבוססת על מקורות מוגבלים, וחוסר תיעוד באחת מהן יכול להיות אקראי. ולבסוף, קירבת הלשון הגדולה שבין העברית לארמית מכבידה על הכרעה חותכת בין שתי הלשונות, שהרי חלק נכבד מן האוכלוסיה בארץ-ישראל באותה התקופה היה דו-לשוני (עברית וארמית) ומבני לשון האופייניים ללשון אחת יכלו בנקל להפוך נחלת הלשון האחרת. אף על פי כן, במקרים אחדים דומה שהטקסט היווני שלפנינו מוסבר היטב על יסוד מקור ארמי, ואילו נוסח עברי לא יסכון לכך. מאידך, קשה למצוא עדויות אקסקלוסיביות למקור עברי, במלים אחרות, זרויות בלשון או בהקשר שאין ניתן להסבירן גם על דרך הארמית.

1. ענייני לשון

דפוסי-לשון אחדים משקפים את הארמית הממלכתית והביניימית, אך אין להם אח בעברית. ראשית תיזכר אותה מלת קישור שהעמיד עליה טורי (23-24) והכל מחרים־מחזיקים אחריו: שכיחותה הגבוהה של המלה τότε בסיפור הנערים — ג, ד,ח; ד, לג, מא (2x),מב,מג,מז, כמו גם בשאר עזה"ח (7 פעמים) — אינה אופיינית ליוונית ואין לה הסבר מתקבל על הדעת אלא במלת הקישור השכיחה בארמית הממלכתית **(ב)אדין**.[33]

ד, יח: καλλει τῷ εἴδει καὶ τῷ. דרך הבעה זו זרה ליוונית ויש לשער שהיא בבואה של לשון המקור. כנגד העברית הנוקטת סמיכות שם-התואר במקרים כאלה, כגון: *יפת תואר ויפת מראה'* (בר' כט, יז), גורסים התרגומים הארמיים: *יאיא בריוא ושפירא בחזווה*,[34] ודרך זו היא המשתקפת ביוונית. אמנם גם היוונית, כארמית, מתרחקת מסמיכות, והמתרגם של

---

30 השווה שמ"א א, יח: *יפניה לא היו לה עוד', ר"ל ופניה לא נפלו. בלשון התנאים מצוי הביטוי **יש שינה לפני*** בהוראת *להירדם*, כגון: מכילתא דר"י, שירה, ה (הורוביץ־רבין, עמ' 134).

31 הדפוס התרגומי בולט עוד יותר בדנ' ב, א הנזכר: τότε αὐτοῦ ἀπ' αὐτοῦ ἐγένετο ὕπνος καὶ.

32 ודוק: טורי לא טרח להוציא את העברית מפני הארמית. כך, למשל, יכול להציע (עמ' 25) עם דנה' כמקור ל-ἐκ τούτου σπᾷ (ד, י, לא), על סמך עם זה', המזדמן דוקא בעברית, נחמ' ה, יג.

33 מקבילתה העברית *אז' אין שימושה כמלת קישור מרובה והוא הדין ביורשתה המאוחרת: בכן (עברית ובארמית).

34 כך בשרידי התרגום (כ"י E), P. Kahle, *Masoreten des Westens* (Stuttgart, 1930) 2:34 וכיו"ב בשאר התרגומים הארמיים.

ישוער ביוונית והוא חב את קיומו לצירוף העברי 'נש״א/משא פנים' או בן דמותו הארמי 'נס״ב/מסב אפין'.[25] גם הרישא, καὶ οὐκ ἔστιν παρ' αὐτῇ καὶ οὐκ ἔστιν μετ' αὐτοῦ... נושאים חותם שמי. כל הכתוב כולו מוצא לו מקביל קרוב בדה״ב ט, ז: 'כי אין עם ה' אלהינו עולה ומשא פנים ומקח שחד'.

כך גם ד, לח, מ: εἰς αἰῶνα τοῦ αἰῶνος...τῶν πάντων αἰώνων...., משקפים ככל הנראה את הביטויים השגורים 'לעולם ועד', 'כל עולמים'.[26]

אף צירוף כמו ג, א: ἐποίησεν δοχὴν, ספק אם היה מי נוקט בו אלמלא השתייך על משפחת המתרגמים המוסרת 'עשה משתה' (אסתר), 'עבד לחם' (דניאל) ב-ποιεῖν δοχὴν.

3. עניינים שבתוכן.

ולבסוף, זרויות בתוכן, אפשר פירות בוסר של תרגומי־טעות, שאין כמותם כדי להסגיר את קיומו של מעשה־התרגום.

שיבוש מסתתר, ככל הנראה, מאחורי הכתוב ב-ד, ד: ἐὰν δὲ ἐξαποστείλῃ αὐτοὺς πρὸς τοὺς πολεμίους βαδίζουσιν καὶ κατεργάζονται τὰ **ὄρη** καὶ τὰ τείχη καὶ τοὺς πύργους. מדוע עם צאתם בפקודת המלך נגד אויביו הם כובשים דוקא **הרים** בצד חומות ומגדלים? שמא במקור נסמכו החומות והמגדלים לערים, לא להרים. השיבוש חל או על גבי טקסט עברי: הרים־ערים,[27] או ארמי: טיריא,[28] או קוריא־טוריא, אך לא ביוונית.[29]

סתירה בולטת יש בין ג, ג: καὶ ἐκοιμήθη καὶ ἔξυπνος ἐγένετο, ובין ההמשך, במיוחד ג, יג: καὶ ὅτε ἐξηγέρθη καὶ. בזה אמר שהמלך היה ער ובזה אמר שהקיץ משנתו. הכיצד? ייתכן שיש כאן צירוף של מסורות שונות, פתרון מרחיק לכת לכשעצמו, וייתכן שהמתח בסיפור נולד במעבר ממקור לתרגום: אפשר שבמקום הראשון נאמר שהמלך נרדם והבין בו המתרגם את ההפך, ואפשר שבמקום השני נאמר שהמלך קם והבין שהמלך ניעור משנתו. כסיוע לאפשרות האחרונה השווה דנ' ו, יט-כ: '...ושנתה נדת עלוהי. באדין מלכא בשפרפרא **יקום**

---

25 השווה דב' י, יז: 'לא ישא פנים ולא יקח שחד'. חיות הביטוי בארמית עולה מן השימוש העצמאי בתרגומים הארמיים: אונקלוס המיר את המבנה בדב', שם, ב־'דלית קדמוהי מסב אפין...'; ניאופיטי תירגם אף את דב' א, יז: 'לא תכירו פנים במשפט' ב־**ענס״ב אפין**; ובפשיטתא שגור: **נסב באפא**. מכל מקום, הדגש צריך להיות על λαμβάνειν πρόσωπα, החסר כל נשמה ביוונית. הערת רודולף במבוא לפירושו (לעיל, הערה 1) עמוד ix שביטוי שמי צריך לפועל גם לפני διάφορα - שחדי, אינה מבטלת את הקביעה הקודמת, אם כי יש טעם בדבריו. הרי אפשר לומר שחסרון פועל או שם פעולה לפני 'שחדי' מוכיחה שלפנינו יווני המשתמש בביטויים העבריים בצורה חפשית. אלא שגם בצורתה המקוצרת זוהי דרך התבטאות כשרה בעברית, או בארמית, מה שאין כן ביוונית. עוד יש לציין שמצאנו קיצור דומה בחלקים המתורגמים: 'יקש את ערפו ויאמץ את לבבו' (דה״ב לו, יג) נמסר בעזה״ח א, מו ללא מקביל לפועל השני: σκληρύνας αὐτοῦ τὸν τράχηλον καὶ τὴν καρδίαν. מעניין שגם καλὴν τῷ εἴδει καὶ τῷ κάλλει הוא בחינת תרגום מצמצם של ביטוי המחזיק אלמנט חוזר. ראה להלן עמ' 64.

26 היחוד הכפול, בקשר גנטיבי, כמו זה בפסוק לח, בא מול 'לעולם ועד' בתרגום המילולי של תהלים, אך גם בתה״ש לדנ' יב, ג (ראה גם שושנה סד). 'כל עלמים' בא בתה״י קמה, יג, ובספרות ארמית, מגילת בראשית ב, ז: 'מלך כל עלמים' (ורווח בטוביה). ביוונית בלתי־תלויה היו מוסיפים את πᾶς אצל לשון יחיד.

27 כהצעת א' כהנא, הספרים החיצוניים א (ירושלים, תרפ״ט). והשווה דה״ב יד, ו: 'ויאמר ליהודה נבנה את הערים האלה ונסב חומה ומגדלים דלתים ובריחים'.

28 כהצעת צימרמן (לעיל, הערה 1), עמ' 192.

29 וליוסיפון יש כפל: 'ואם יצום להפוך **ערים** יהפכו ואם לחצוב **הרים** יחצבו ואם להרוס חומות ירוסו'.

καθήσῃ καὶ ἐχόμενός μου καθήσῃ (ד, מב). אין ספק שב-ד, מב מתגשם מה שהובטח ב-ג, ז, ונקל לראות זאת על פי ההמשך המשותף. אלא שבתהליך התרגום נפל דבר: מטבע ההבטחה המלכותית היה זהה כאן וכאן במקור, אך המתרגם מסר בראשונה בצורה אחת, ובאחרונה בצורה אחרת.

ופרט סגנוני אחד המרמז על מוצאו של הכתוב בשפה אחרת. ד, ז-ט מונה שבעה צמדי פעלים. בששה מהם מורכב הצמד מפועל אחד בשתי צורות, ורק אחד מתבלט כצמד של שני פעלים שונים: **πατάξαι** ... ἀποκτεῖναι ἀποκτέννουσιν... ἀφεῖναι ἀφίουσιν ... **τύπτουσιν** ... ἐρημῶσαι ἐρημοῦσιν ... οἰκοδομῆσαι οἰκοδομοῦσιν ... ἐκκόψαι ἐκκόπτουσιν ... φυτεῦσαι φυτεύουσιν. ונראה הדבר שהחריג הוא מוצר של תרגום, לא של מקור.[22]

2. דגמי לשון

היזקקות לפראזיולוגיה מקראית אינה בהכרח תווית-זיהוי לתרגום, אך מן הראוי להדגיש שלשון הסיפור משופעת בה, דרך משל:

• ד, נד, τὴν ἱερατικὴν στολὴν ἐν τίνι λατρεύουσιν ἐν αὐτῇ, השוה יח׳ מב, יד: ׳בגדיהם אשר ישרתו בהן׳.

• ד, ס, εὐλογητὸς εἶ ὃς ἔδωκας μοι σοφίαν καὶ σοὶ ὁμολογῶ δέσποτα τῶν πατέρων, מוצא לו מקביל קרוב בדנ׳ ב, כג: ׳לך אלה אבהתי מהודא ומשבח אנה די חכמתא וגבורתא יהבת לי׳,[23] כמו גם בדה״א כט, י-יב.

• ד, סג, τὸ ἱερὸν οὗ ὠνομάσθη τὸ ὄνομα αὐτοῦ ἐπ᾽ αὐτῷ, השוה יר׳ ז, י: ׳בבית הזה אשר נקרא שמי עליו׳ ועוד.

ובמיוחד כדאי לשים לב אל מקומות כגון: ג, ו: καὶ πορφύραν περιβαλέσθαι καὶ ἐν χρυσώμασιν πίνειν καὶ ἐπὶ χρυσῷ καθεύδειν καὶ ἅρμα χρυσοχάλινον καὶ κίδαριν βυσσίνην καὶ μανιάκην περὶ τὸν τράχηλον, כתוב שיש לו הד, בעניין ובמינוח, בדנ׳ ה, ז: ׳ארגונא ילבש והמניכא די דהבא על צוארה...׳ (וכמוהו בפסוקים טז, כט),[24] והשווה עוד אס׳ א, ו-ז; ח, טו. או, הרשימה ב-ג, יד: καὶ σατράπας καὶ στρατηγοὺς καὶ τοπάρχας καὶ ὑπάτους הזהה לתה״ש לדנ׳ ג, ב: ׳לאחשדרפניא סגניא ופחותא אדרגזריא׳. הללו, נוסף על כך שהם מראים על הקירבה ללשון המקרא, הם גם תולים במקור דפוסים שהיה בהם כדי להקנות ליוונית ממד של אותנטיות, של לשון-החצר, והנה מסתבר שהם יכולים להיות באותה מידה תרגום.

מעבר לקירבה הכללית בדפוס הלשון מזדקרים לעין כמה וכמה צירופי-לשון יווניים, והם ראויים לתואר **תרגומי-שאילה**. ראשון ביניהם ד, לט: καὶ οὐκ ἔστιν παρ᾽ αὐτῇ λαμβάνειν πρόσωπα οὐδὲ διάφορα λαμβάνειν πρόσωπα. צירוף כגון לא

---

22 ראה עוד רשימת הפעלים החוזרת בגיוון חלקי ביוונית ב-ד, כג-כד. יש עוד אי אלה דברים הקרובים אל הלב אך קשה להוכיחם, כמו אפשרות של משחק צלילים עול-הבל בדברים על האמת, ד לו-לז, או השתקפותו של הצירוף ׳בגדי כבוד׳, בן-סירא ו, כט (ביוונית, בעברית: בגדי כתם), לא; נ, יא, וראה תה״ש ליש׳ נב, א, או בארמית ׳לבושין דיקר׳ (ומעניין שאותו הציב אונקלוס למול ׳כתנות עור׳ בבר׳ ד, כא), על פני שתי צלעות ב-ד, יז, למרות שכוונות הצלע השנייה יכולה להיות כפשוטה, והשווה אס׳ א, כ.

23 וראה גם ד, מ על יד דנ׳ ב לז; ז, יד,כז.

24 אפשר אתה בא לידי טעות בציון קירבת היתר לדניאל מפני המלים האחיות ׳המניכאי׳ - ὁ μανιακής (זו כמו βύσσινος שאולות ליוונית).

לשאלת לשון המקור של סיפור שלושת הנערים   67*

בשטח ההפקר שבין יוונית מתורגמת למקורית.[20]
יחס אחר שבדק מרטין הוא השימוש ב-καί לעומת השימוש ב-δέ. הוא מצא שביוונית
התרגומים יש לפחות שני καί על כל δέ בעוד ביוונית מקורית יהיו פחות מאשר δέ
באופן משמעותי. במדגמים ממשיים נעה העקומה בתה״ש בין 6 καί על כל δέ (פרקים מתה״ש
לבראשית ולחלקים הארמיים בדניאל) ועד 343 καί על כל δέ (תיאודוטיון לחלקים העבריים
של דניאל). לעומת זאת, ביוונית המקורית יש 0.06 καί על כל δέ (פוליביוס) ועד 0.39 καί על
כל δέ (פפירוסים). מבט חטוף בעזה״ח מגלה מיד שהספר כולו, הסיפור כחלקים המקבילים
לנה״מ, מוצא את מקומו בבטחה בצד של תה״ש, באשר יש בו באופן ברור שימוש יותר
אינטנסיבי ב-καί מאשר ב-δέ. בחלקים המתורגמים היחס הוא 7:1 ובסיפור אף יותר מזה —
8.5:1. כמו הקווים שהצטיירו עד כה גם על פי זה עומד הסיפור, כמו עזה״ח כולו, קרוב יותר
ליוונית הבלתי תלויה מרוב ספרי תה״ש, אך עדיין ניכר בו היטב שהוא שייך למשפחת הספרים
המתורגמים.

ב

בפרק הקודם ביקשנו להראות שלשון המקור הטביעה חותמה על לשון הסיפור ושפתו היא
יוונית תרגומית. ננסה עתה להתחקות אחר רישומים מיוחדים שמעשה התרגום השאיר אחריו
בסיפור היווני, מצד עיצוב החומר, הלשון והתוכן.

1. עניינים שבצורה.

נזכיר תחילה כתוב שצורתו כמו מוכיחה בפועל את קיומו של מעשה־תרגום. הכוונה ל־ג, ד: οἱ
σωματοφύλακες οἱ φυλάσσοντες τὸ σῶμα τοῦ βασιλέως. יהי מקורו של
הטקסט הזה אשר יהי, מה הסבר טוב לו מתרגום כפול? מה טעם לפירוש המונח במרכיביו
הישירים, אם לא התלות במקור הבנוי מרכיבים נפרדים? דומה הדבר לכתוב ב־ז, ב:
ἐπεστάτουν τῶν ἱερῶν ἔργων...ἱεροστάταις. אף שאין לו אקויוולנט ברור
במקבילו בעז׳ ו, יג, מסתבר שאינו אלא תרגום כפול.[21]
מן הסתם, הופעתם של נוסחים שונים במקום שצפויה חזרה על אותו נוסח, יכולה לשמש ראיה
להעברה משפה לשפה. בין זכויות היתר לנער שיימצא חכם מונים הנערים: καὶ δεύτερος
καθιεῖται Δαρείου (ג, ז). אך, בבוא עת המלך לפרוע את השטר הזה, אומר הוא:

20 טבלת השכיחות של מלות היחס השונות לעומת ἐν:

	תרגום השבעים		עזרא החיצוני	יוונית במקור
	תרגום	סיפור		
διά	0.1	0.3		0.19-3.0	0.01-0.18
εἰς	0.51	0.1		0.79-11.0	0.01-0.49
κατά	0.3	0.23		0.26-2.1	0.01-0.19
περί	0.05	0.41		0.28-1.2	0.01-0.27
πρός	0.15	0.47		0.19-0.26	0.01-0.024
ὑπό	0.06	0.11		0.13-0.51	0.01-0.07

בחלקים המתורגמים בעזה״ח: ὑπό, περί, διά נמצאות בגבול תה״ש, πρός, εἰς בשטח
הביניים, κατά בגבול הלשון המקורית. בסיפור: περί, διά בגבול הלשון המקורית,
πρός, ὑπό בשטח הביניים, εἰς בגבול תה״ש.

21 אפשר זהו תרגום כפול של ׳בנין׳, הבא בפסוק הזה ללא מקביל בעזה״ח, ונתפש כ׳מניין׳, מלשון
מיני, על דרך דנ׳ ה, מט: ימני על עבידתא׳, ג, יב: ׳די מנית יתהון על עבידת...׳. והשווה טיפוס
התרגומים הכפולים החוזר על אלמנט אחד, ברי לט, כא-כג: ׳שר בית הסהר׳ - ἀρχιδεσμοφύλαξ
τοῦ δεσμωτηρίου.

ראשית, אמנם הפער בין לשון הסיפור ללשון היוונית הבלתי־תלויה קטן נוכח המרכיב החשוב של לשון הפאפירוסים בני הזמן — אך עדיין אי אפשר להגדיר את לשון הסיפור בפשטות כקוינֶה, עדיין מפרידה ביניהן כברת דרך רצופה דפוסים שמיים. ויש להדגיש נקודה נוספת העולה מפן אחר של חקר עזה״ח, דהיינו חקר טכניקת התרגום בחלקים שמקורם בידנו. בדיקת דרכו של המתרגם מגלה, שאין הוא מעביר את התוכן עם הכלי, אלא מרבה להמיר את כלי הביטוי המועדפים בעברית ובארמית בכלי ביטוי שהם בני בית ביוונית. אם מתרגם כזה אחראי ליוונית של סיפור הנערים, הרי אין לצפות לפער עמוק בינה ובין הלשון בת הזמן שאינה תרגום. על רקע זה עולה ערכה של הרצועה שעדיין מבחינה בין לשון הסיפור ללשון בת הזמן שאינה תרגום, ויש בה הוכחה נאמנה עוד יותר למעשה התרגום של הסיפור.

הוא הדין ביחס שבין פעלים במשפטים עיקריים ומשועבדים. המתרגם מחליף 35 פעמים מבנים פאראטאקטיים במבנים היפוטאקטיים, ואפשר להוסיף על כך מספר לא קטן של מקומות שהפסוקית המשועבדת דוחה פנייה מבנים תחביריים אחרים. היחס של 2:1 בין פעלים במשפטים משועבדים לראשיים מקבל לאור זה משקל יתר כראיה לטיבה התרגומי של לשון הסיפור.

ובאותו עניין במגזר אחר. בלוחות של סולאמו המציבים את תמונת השימוש במילות־יחס־למחצה, כהגדרתה, ודרכי תרגומן, מוצא לו עזה״ח, ומדובר בספר כולו ללא הפרדה בין הסיפור לחלקים המתורגמים, מקום של כבוד כספר שקשה למצוא בו שימוש טועה, בלתי יווני, במלות היחס. ובכלל, הוא עומד בתחתית הסולם של הספרים החיצוניים, בין אלה שממעטים ביותר במלות יחס פיזיוגנומיות.[16] אין בכך די לקרבו אל הספרים הלא־מתורגמים,[17] אך הוא קונה לו מעמד מיוחד בין תרגומים אחרים ובעליו מתאפיין כמי שעלה בידו להשתחרר משפת המקור ולשמור על חיוניותה של שפת המטרה.[18]

החזות היוונית האותנטית באופן יחסי של סיפור הנערים אינה אפוא חריגה במסגרת עזה״ח וכמו החלקים המתורגמים אפשר גם הסיפור חייב את טיב לשונו למתרגם.

לאור הדברים הללו כדאי לשים לב אל היחסים הפנימיים בין הסיפור ובין החלקים המתורגמים בנוגע לתופעות מסויימות. נשתמש כאן בשניים מן הקריטריונים שהעמיד מרטין.[19] הוא בדק את שכיחות הופעתה של מלת היחס ἐν לעומת מלות יחס אחרות, והגיע למסקנה שבחומר יווני מקורי רווחות מילות יחס אחרות הרבה יותר בעוד בתרגומים ἐν עולה עליהן ללא שיעור. בדיקת היחס הזה בעזה״ח, בסיפור ובחלקים המתורגמים מזה, מגלה שהספר כולו עומד איתן

רב לשימוש במבנים מורכבים של פעלים ראשיים ומשועבדים.

16 R. Sollamo, *Renderings of Hebrew Semiprepositions in the Septuagint* (Helsinki, 1979) 290ff.

17 בעזה״ח מלת יחס אחת כזאת על כל 16 פסוקים, בעוד במק״ב־ד היחס הוא 90:1, 277:1, 284:0 בהתאם.

18 אף על פי כן, מדי פעם מתעוררת תמיהה על הבחירה במלות היחס, כמו הצרכת חָפֵּץ ל־νικᾶν ב־ ג, יב: ὑπὲρ δὲ πάντα νικᾷ ἡ ἀλήθεια; או εἰς־לπλεῖν ב־ד, כג: εἰς τὴν θάλασσαν πλεῖν (ביוונית שטים אל מקום מסויים, אך שטים בים, או מוטב: πλεῖν τὴν θάλασσαν, ללא מלת יחס. עם זאת, קשה להצביע לבטח על דמות המקור; צימרמן (לעיל, הערה 1), עמ' 200, הציע שהמתרגם מצא לפניו 'פרש לימא', אך לא מתועד שימוש ארמי כזה, בעברית ראה ירו' מעשר קטן ראש פרק ג פא ע״ג: 'יאסור לפרש לים הגדול').

19 R. A. Martin, *Syntactical Evidence of Semitic Sources in Greek Documents* (SBLSCS 3; Missoula, MT, 1974) 5ff.

לשאלת לשון המקור של סיפור שלושת הנערים 65*

הצרכת πρὸς לפעלי אמירה, אם כי אינה נדירה בקוינה:[7] ג, ד: εἶπαν ἕτερος πρὸς τὸν ἕτερον. ואף הקדמת הכינוי:[8] ד, טז: ἐξέθρεψαν αὐτοὺς τοὺς φυτεύοντας. ἄρχειν, כפועל־עזר במשמע 'להתחיל', אין השימוש בו חזון נפרץ ביוונית,[9] והנה הוא חוזר ופותח את דברי הנערים: ג, טז: ἤρξατο ὁ πρῶτος...καὶ ἔφη וכיוצא בו: ד, א, יג, לג. גם המלית ἵνα, שאפשר משקפת את **די** הארמית,[10] שבה ומופיעה, ועצם החזרה על המלית בפסוקים סמוכים יכולה להעיד על היגררות אחר מקור לא־יווני:

ד, מו: ...δέομαι οὖν ἵνα ποιήσῃς.
ד, מז: ...καὶ ἔγραψεν...ἵνα προπέμψωσιν.
ד, נ: ...καὶ ἵνα οἱ Ιδουμαῖοι ἀφιῶσιν.

נזכיר כאן עוד את השימוש ב־ποιεῖν, שאפשר משקף פועל גורם בעברית או בארמית: ג, כ: καὶ ἐποίησεν αὐτοὺς συναναβῆναι;[11] ה, ג: Ποιεῖ πλουσίας... ποιεῖ λαλεῖν. הנתונים שלהלן אף הם יצאו ללמד על דפוס שמי, אך בצורה מבוקרת יותר.

ראיה נכבדה לקיומו של מקור שמי לסיפור הנערים עולה מפרט משני כמו מקומה של המלית πᾶς, ובמשניותו חשיבותו: מארבעת הדפוסים שהמלה יכולה לבוא בהם ניכרת בסיפור הנערים העדפה ברורה לדפוסים המקראיים. הצורות המקובלות ביוונית הבלתי תלויה, ὁ πᾶς X או ὁ X πᾶς, ביחיד וברבים, מיוצגות בסיפור במדה מזערית, שלוש פעמים, לעומת הצורות πᾶς X ו־πᾶς ὁ X, בעיקר ברבים, כשלושים פעם. נטייה דומה יש בחלקים מן הברית־החדשה,[12] והיא מנוגדת למגמה בפאפירוסים מן המאה ה־ג' לפנה"ס, ועוד יותר מן המאות הבאות שלפנה"ס, המראים העדפה בולטת להרכבים היווניים הקלאסיים.[13] אין ההרכבים המועדפים בסיפור הנערים בלתי אפשריים ביוונית, והם מופיעים עשרות פעמים בפאפירוסים, אך אילו נכתב הסיפור מלכתחילה יוונית, היינו מצפים ליחס אחר בין ההיקרויות של המבנים מן הסוגים השונים.

על אותה המגמה מצביע לוח ההיקרויות של פעלים ראשיים לעומת משועבדים.[14]

בדגמים מן הברית־החדשה נמצאו	על כל פועל ראשי כ־0.4 פעלים משועבדים.
בדגמים מן הפאפירוסים נמצאו	על כל פועל ראשי כ־0.7 פעלים משועבדים.
ומן היוונית הקלאסית	על כל פועל ראשי כ־1.4 פעלים משועבדים.
בסיפור הנערים מצאנו	על כל פועל ראשי כ־0.5 פעלים משועבדים, משמע, בנטיה

הפוכה מן השפה הקלאסית, יש בסיפור יותר פעלים ראשיים ממשועבדים, בערך פי שניים; וכי אין בכך ללמד על מקור המעדיף משפטים פאראטאקטיים?[15]

משקלם של היחסים בין דרכי ההתבטאות ביצירות השונות עולה לאור שיקולים נוספים.

---

7 ראה: N. Turner, in J. H. Moulton, *A Grammar of New Testament Greek* (4 vols.; Edinburgh, 1976) 4:54.

8 M. Black, *An Aramaic Approach to the Gospels and Acts* (3d ed.; Oxford, 1967) 96ff.

9 טרנר, שם, עמ' 20, 46.

10 C. F. Burney, *The Aramaic Origin of the Fourth Gospel* (Oxford, 1922) 69ff.

11 ראה: E. Tov, "The Representation of the Causative Aspects of the Hiph'il in the LXX," *Bib* 63 (1982) 417-24.

12 טרנר, שם, 95.

13 על פי: E. Mayser, *Grammatik der griechischen Papyri aus der Ptolemaerzeit* (Berlin & Leipzig, 1934) 2:2:102.

14 טרנר, שם, עמ' 51.

15 הממצא מן הפאפירוסים במקרה זה הוא פחות מכריע מפני אופיים הסיפרותי שאינו משאיר מקום

תוך שימת דגש על טיבה של היוונית ההלניסטית ובחינת הזיקה בין העברית והארמית.
השאלה הכפולה העומדת על הפרק היא אפוא: האם נכתב הסיפור במקורו יוונית, ואם לאו —
האם נכתב ארמית או עברית? ביסוד הבעיה עומד הקושי לדלות מן החומר ראיות שליליות,
דהיינו ראיות לכך ש**אי אפשר** שמבעים מסוימים היו כתובים בשפה מסוימת. לכאורה אין קושי
להכריע בין השפה היוונית ובין שפה שמית; אלא שאפשר לנפץ את רוב הטענות ל'ברבריזמים'
ביוונית, כאשר חיפוש מדוקדק יכול להעלות מן האפלה גון־משמעות של מלה או מבנה תחבירי
שיאשש את המבע הצורם כשימוש לשוני יווני לגיטימי. ואף אם לא נמצאה מקבילה בנבכי
הטקסטים היווניים, תמיד אפשר לתרץ את הזרויות בטיבה של היוונית שבפי המחבר וברקע
התרבותי שלו.[5] מן הכיוון השני אין טעם רב לבלוש אחר הרכבים שאי אפשר שהיו כתובים
בשפה שמית. שהרי כאן יש מענה לכל בעיה בדמות המתרגם. דרך משל, אם מושג יווני par
excellence כמו φιλανθρωπία, שקשה להעלות דמות מקור לו בארמית או בעברית, יכול
היה להיחשב טענה בין טענות לכך שתוספת E לאסתר נכתבה במקורה יוונית, הנה באה הופעתו
של אותו המונח בעזה״ח, בחלקים המתורגמים, לא בסיפור הנערים, ואין זה משנה אם אין לו
שם אקוויוולנט ברור, ומקעקעת את יסוד הטענה. הוא הדין גם בניסיון להכריע בין עברית
לארמית; שתי השפות היו אחיזות זו בזו זמן רב, ואין לדעת מתי או בפי מי נדדו צורות ודגמים
מן הלשון האחת אל רעותה. ועם זאת, דומה שהערכה מדייקת יותר של טיב היוונית של סיפור
שלושת הנערים יש בה כדי להכתירה כיוונית תרגומית, והתבוננות בטיב הלשון המשתקפת ממנה
תטה את הכף לצד הארמית.

א

לא פעם אפיינו את שפת סיפור הנערים כיוונית חופשית וקולחת. מן הראוי להתחקות אחר טיב
היוונית שהסיפור כתוב בה באמצעות בחונים מדויקים במידת האפשר ולראות מה עומד מאחורי
החזות החיצונית הזאת. האם שפת הסיפור קרובה יותר ליוונית מקורית או ליוונית תרגומית?
ככלל, אם מציבים את שפת הסיפור בסולם השוואה של דגמי לשון ביוונית החופשית וביוונית
השייכת למעגל הסובב את תה״ש, מגלים שאין היא משתחררת בקלות מחוג היוונית התרגומית.
כדי להעמיד הערכות אלה על בסיס של נתונים, נשתמש בקני־המידה שהציבו חוקרי הלשון של
הברית־החדשה, בחיפושיהם אחר מקורה.
נזכיר תחילה כמה דגמים המכבידים על רהיטות לשון הסיפור; הללו, גם אם אין בהם כדי
להטביע בו חותם מובהק של תרגום, תימה הוא מדוע חברו יחד לדור בכפיפה זו.[6]
כך שני הדפוסים: ד, נח: λέγων...εὐλόγησεν, ד, מא: εἶπαν...εὐλόγησεν καὶ ἐφώνησεν .... או

בעיקרו עברי, חלק שאבד מפרוטו־נה״מ ועמד במקורו בין עז׳ א לעז׳ ב. אך מה הצדקה הגיונית לכך
שאגרות המלכים האחרים מצוטטות ארמית ואילו אגרות כורש (כך על פי תיקונו של טורי, שהרי
עזה״ח מדבר על דריוש) מצוטטות דווקא עברית? גם מצד העניין אין זה מתקבל על הדעת שהחלק
הזה אכן גישר אי פעם בין עז׳ א ו־ב.

5 אלה בדיוק שתי הפנים של שיטת רודולף, שם: ראשית, זוהי יוונית יהודית. שנית, לכל קושיה על
דמות הטקסט היווני יש בהכרח תשובה אחרת מאשר בדמות מקורו.

6 ראה דברי הביקורת של מובינקל כנגד רודולף: "Es wäre jedoch merkwürdig, wenn es dem
behaupteten griechischen Verfasser gelungen wäre, fast sämmtliche Anomalien
des gesprochenen Judengriechisch in seine Erzählung zu unterbringen" (S.
Mowinckel, *Studien zu dem Buche Ezra-Nehemia* [Oslo, 1964] 1:11).

לשאלת לשון המקור של סיפור
שלושת הנערים (עזה"ח ג-ד)

ציפורה טלשיר ודוד טלשיר

זה זמן רב קופא על שמריו המחקר על שפת המקור של סיפור הנערים, עזרא החיצוני (להלן: עזה"ח) ג, א - ה, ו. דעות החוקרים אינן יוצאות, בדרך כלל, מגדר התרשמות כללית, ונר לרגלי כולם דברי טורי.[1] טורי סבור היה שגוף הסיפור נכתב במקורו ארמית ותר אחר אחר דפוסים ארמיים הניבטים מבעד למסך לשון התרגום. ראייתיו מהוות בסיס בכל דיון בטיב המקור של סיפור הנערים. גם מי שנושא שפת המקור של הסיפור משמשת נקודת מוצא למחקרו אינו מחפש ראיות חדשות ומסתפק בהזכרת ההוכחה העיקרית שהביא טורי מן השימוש התכוף, הזר ליוונית, במלה τότε, כדי לומר בה שאכן ביסודו של הסיפור עמד מקור שמי.[2] מאידך, הבא לטעון שהסיפור נכתב יוונית במקורו ומתרץ את טיב לשונו באופיה של היוונית היהודית, ובתוך כך מעלים עין ממלת המפתח הזאת, נמצאת שתיקתו תמוהה למדי.[3] משום מרכזיותה של τότε, האמורה לשקף את מלת הקישור הארמית **אדין**, נוטה הכף ממילא לצד הטענה שאותו מקור שמי משוער ארמי היה ולא עברי.[4] מטרתו של עיון זה היא לבדוק מחדש את שאלת לשון המקור של סיפור הנערים,

---

1 בדרך הטבע, הטוענים שהסיפור יווני במקורו הסתפקו בהתרשמות כללית, כביכול לא עליהם הראיה. כך למשל: O. F. Fritzsche, *Exegetisches Handbuch zu den Apokryphen* (Leipzig, 1851) 1; H. Guthe, "Das dritte Buch Esra," *Die Apokryphen und Pseudepigraphen des AT* (2 vols.; ed. E. Kautzsch; Tübingen, 1900) 1:1. מן הצד השני עמד יאן, שהציע לסיפור שחזור מלא לעברית; שחזור זה מתמיה מבחינה מתודית באותה מידה כהצעות השחזור שלו **לעברית** של טקסטים אחרים מעזה"ח שיש להם מקביל **עברי וארמי** בנה"מ. G. Jahn, *Die Bücher Esra und Nehemja* (Leiden, 1909) 177-188. הראיות של טורי, C. C. Torrey, *Ezra Studies* (Chicago, 1910), נרשמו בשלושה מקומות, עמ' 23-25, 56-50, 125-131. מי שהלכו בעקבותיו ציטטו את עיקרי דבריו, כך: P. E. Bayer, *Das dritte Buch Esdras* (Freiburg, 1911) 123ff.; B. Walde, *Die Esrasbücher der Septuaginta* (Freiburg, 1913) 119-20, ועוד רבים. צימרמן ניסה להמשיך את דרכו של טורי ולדלות ראיות חדשות, אך אף שהעלה רעיונות מעניינים רוב הצעותיו מרחיקות-לכת, F. Zimmermann, "The Story of the Three Guardsmen," *JQR* 54 (1963-64) 179-200.

2 כך רודולף, W. Rudolph, *Esra und Nehemia* (HAT; Tübingen, 1949) viii-ix; K. F. Pohlmann, *Studien zum dritten Esra* (Göttingen, 1970) 49.

4 טורי סבור היה שרוב הסיפור אכן היה ארמי, להוציא את חלקו האחרון, מ-ד, מז ואילך, שהיה

רביעי, ח, מח, וסוטה יג, ע"ב, וכבר הצביע ליונשטט על כך שסיפור מות משה שבתורה אינו אלא פולמוס עם המסורת שלא מת משה — כמוהו כאליהו — כדי שלא יהפכוהו, חלילה, לאל.[31] אם הסיפור שבתורה גימד אפוא את המסורת על הסתלקות משה מעולמנו הרי שסיפור מות אלישע התאכזר עמו כפל כפליים!

לסיכום עיוננו בסיפור הן בבידודו והן על רקע הקשריו המתרחבים נוכל אולי להשיב על השאלות שהיצבנו בפתח דברינו; בראש ובראשונה נתברר לנו כי הסיפור לא נועד להיקרא ברצינות גמורה: המכשולים שפיזר המספר לאורכן של שלושים ואחת מלות הסיפור, מכשולים הנובעים בראש ובראשונה מקוצר היריעה, מן האליפטיות, מבטיחים מעין קומדיה של טעויות ותמיהות: כיצד הלך הנקבר בקבר אלישע קודם ששב לחיים? ואולי כלל לא מת והקברנים אצו לקבור אדם חי? (וממל"א יג למדנו שאין עצמותיו של איש אלוהים מחיות אלא רק ממלטות מן הביזיון ...), ויתרה מזאת, סיפור על נביא מת המחייה נביא אחרים ואינו מסוגל להועיל לעצמו, ממילא מעלה חיוך על שפתינו. ואם יאמר האומר שמגע החייאה את הנביא והוא הקם לתחייה הרי גם בכך יש מן הגיחוך שחיי הנביא ינתנו לו בדרך המקרה ועל־ידי מי שלא חננו ה' בכישורים של בעל־נס.

הסיפור החסכן אכן מציג את אלישע באור נלעג בעיקר לאורם של שאר סיפורי אלישע — מותו שאינו מעורר צער, קבורה בלתי מכובדת במקום בלתי נודע, נס שאין לה' חלק בו ועדים אין לו, נס שאיש אינו צריך לו ואיש אינו מודה עליו, ובלשונו של אברבנאל: 'כי הנה הנביאים יפעלו הנסים והנפלאות בהדבקותם בו יתברך, כי אז יגזרו אומר ויקם להם, ואחרי שבמותם נפסק אותו דבקות איך יהיה אפשר שבזולת דבקות יעשו עצמותם היבשות נס תחיית המתים כזה? הלא ראית שכאשר אליהו ואלישע בחייהם הוצרכו להחיות את המת הרבו בתפילותיהם ועשו מעשים רשומים בהשתטחם עליהם כמו שנזכר בסיפוריהם, ואיך מזולת כל זה יעשו עצמותיו אותו הנס עצמו? כל שכן שיהיה הנס לבלתי תכלית, כי מה היה המונע שישכבו עצמות הנביא עם עצמות איש אחר?...'

וכאן אנו מגיעים לשאלת סמכותו של המספר: דומה כי בסיפורנו אין המספר מבקש לזכות במוניטין של מספר כל יודע ואין הוא מתאמץ לשכנע את קוראיו להאמין בסיפורו בכל מחיר: סתימות הפרטים, אלמוניות הדמויות, הסתלקות העדים הפוטנציאליים מן הזירה ואי־ידיעת מקום ההתרחשות אינם תורמים ליצירת אמון ואמינות, מה גם שבסיפורי ניסים אחרים במחזור סיפורי אלישע נמצאים אמצעי בקרה שתכליתם לשכנע את הקורא באמיתות הנס.[32]

השאלה השלישית והקשה ביותר לתשובה היא אם ראוי סיפורנו לשבח, אם הוא ראוי שנראה בו "סיפור טוב". ניתן להתחמק, כמובן, מתשובה ולציין שהערכה שכזאת היא ממילא סובייקטיבית ואין לה במה לתמוך יתדותיה. אך דומה שדווקא סיפור שלא נועד אולי לגדולות מלכתחילה השיג דווקא בעירפולו, בעליבותו, וברב־משמעויותו את התכלית לשמה נוצר: הקלת ראש בקבר הנביא ובניסים המתרחשים אצלו, לבל יגיע הקורא לידי הערצה וסגידה לקבר אלישע. ואם השיג הסיפור את מטרתו זו ממילא ראוי ראוי הוא לשבח.

---

31. ראה ש"א ליונשטט, "מות משה", תרביץ כד (תשי"ח) 16-31.
32. על תופעה זו בסיפורי הנסים ראה מאמרי: "מנגנוני בקרה בסיפורי ניסים במקרא", שנתון ז-ח (תשמ"ו) 61-75.

מבית־אל מבקש בסיפור זה מבניו כי במותו יקברוהו בקברו של איש האלוהים מיהודה, שהוא גרם למיתתו: 'ויהי אחרי קברו אתו ויאמר אל בניו לאמר במותי וקברתם אתי בקבר אשר איש האלוהים קבור בו, אצל עצמתיו הניחו את עצמתי. כי היה יהיה הדבר אשר קרא בדבר ה' על המזבח אשר בבית אל ...' (פס' לא-לב). טעם בקשתו של הנביא מתבאר עם התגשמות נבואתו של איש האלוהים (כינויו המובהק של אלישע): לשאלת יאשיהו, למראה הציון על קברו של איש האלוהים מיהודה, משיבים לו אנשי העיר: 'הקבר איש האלהים אשר בא מיהודה ויקרא את הדברים האלה אשר עשית על המזבח בית אל' (מל״ב כג, יז). ובעקבות השמועה מצווה המלך: '...הניחו לו איש אל ינע עצמתיו וימלטו עצמתיו את עצמות הנביא אשר בא משמרון' (שם פס' יח). בעקבות כתוב זה הושלמה על דרך ההרמוניזציה גם בקשת הנביא מבית־אל במל״א יג, בנוסח תרגום השבעים: Παρὰ τὰ ὀστᾶ αὐτοῦ θέτε με ἵνα σωθῶσι τὰ ὀστᾶ μου τοῖς ὀστοῖς αὐτῶν μετὰ τῶν ὀστῶν 'אצל עצמתיו הניחו אתי למען תימלטנה עצמותי עם עצמותיו'. המעשה בעצמותיו של נביא, הממלטות עצמותיו של אחר ומצילות אותן מגורל מביש הוא לדעתי רציונליזציה של מעשה נס על עצמות נביא שיש בכוחן להחיות גוף המובא לקבורה אצלו.[28]

הסיפור במל״א יג הוא אפוא שלב נוסף בסילוק הרכיב הניסי; אם בסיפורנו שבמל״ב יג בכל זאת נתרחש נס כולשהו, אם גם נלעג או אף בלתי מעורר אמון, הרי הנס נעלם כליל במל״א יג. אם נרחיק מבטנו אל מעבר לגבולות ספר מלכים, נתבונן במסורת על הסתלקותו של נביא אחר, אדון הנביאים משה (דב' לד). בסיפור מותו של משה כמה קווי דמיון לסיפורנו: מקום קבורתו המדוייק של משה אינו ידוע: 'ויקבר אתו בגי בארץ מואב מול בית פעור ולא ידע איש את קברתו עד היום הזה' (דב' לד, ו). בעוד שכאן המספר מעיד על כך במפורש הרי שבסיפורנו הוא נמנע מציין את מקום הקבורה כאילו מתוך חסכנותו במילים. עם זאת, דומה כי המטרה אחת, וכדברי ארליך:[29] 'ונדמה לי שנמנעו סופרי כתבי־הקודש מלהזכיר קברות הנביאים כדי שלא יהיו מקדשים עצמותם וקבריהם, ומן הטעם הזה לא ידע איש את קבורת משה ...', ודוק: ההשוואה לסיפור מותו של משה מבהירה את טעם אזכרתם של גדודי מואב. דומה כי הן משה, הן אליהו והן אלישע נסתלקו על־פי המסורת מן העולם באותו המקום ממש.[30]

קירבה נוספת בין סיפור אלישע לסיפור משה היא בציון הקוברים אותם על דרך הסתמי: באלישע — 'ויקברהו', ובמשה — 'ויקבר אותו בגי' (פס' ו). אלא שבסיפור משה ניתן להבין שה' הוא הקוברו משום שהוא הנזכר בסיום הכתוב הקודם: 'וימת שם משה עבד ה' בארץ מואב על פי ה'' (פס' ה).

בניגוד לאלישע שמת בחוליו (כפי שלימדנו ההקשר המיידי) משה מת בבריאות טובה וגמורה רק משום שה' מצא לנכון לאוספו: 'ומשה בן מאה ועשרים שנה במתו לא כהתה עינו ולא נס לחה' (פס' ז). והפרש נוסף בין הסיפורים — שלא כקבורת אלישע שאינה מותירה כל רושם, הרי קבורת משה מלווה באבל גדול: 'ויבכו בני ישראל את משה ... שלשים יום' (פס' ח). סיפור מות משה כסיפור הסתלקות אליהו מעמידים אפוא בצל את מעשה מות אלישע הנושא אופי עלוב ביותר.

ועוד, בסיפור אלישע מצינו כי אחד הפרושים יאפשר לנו להבין כי הקם מן המתים הוא אלישע עצמו. והנה, גם אודות משה נשתמרו מסורות שלא מת וזכה לחיי אלמוות, ראה: קדמוניות ס'

---

28 ועוד על תופעה זו ראה מאמרי: ״רציונליזציה של מוטיבים ניסיים בסיפורת המקראית״, דברי הקונגרס העולמי התשיעי למדעי היהדות (חטיבה א' תקופת המקרא; ירושלים, תשמ״ו) 27-34.

29 א״ב ארליך, מקרא כפשוטו ב (ברלין, תר״ס) 362.

30 למסורות בדבר קבורת אלישע במקומות אחרים (שומרון, הר־הכרמל) ראה א' יערי, מסעות ארץ ישראל (רמת־גן, 1976) 639; מ' איש־שלום, מסעי נוצרים לארץ־ישראל (תל־אביב, 1979) 219; ז' וילנאי, מצבות קדש בארץ ישראל א (ירושלים, תשמ״ה) 354-356.

שנים ברוחך אלי' (ב, ט), היינו שהחייה אלישע שני מתים ואליהו אחד,[23] בן האלמנה מצרפת (מל"א יז, כד): 'דאמר רבי חמא בר חנינא גדולים צדיקים במיתתן יותר מבחייהן שנאמר "ויהי הם קברים איש והנה ראו [את] הגדוד וישליכו את האיש בקבר אלישע וילך ויגע האיש בעצמות אלישע ויחי ויקם על רגליו". אמר ליה רב פפא לאביי ודלמא לקיומי ביה ברכתא דאליהו דכתיב ביה "ויהי נא פי שנים ברוחך אלי'" אמר ליה אי הכי היינו דתניא על רגליו עמד ולביתו לא הלך אלא במה איקיים כדאמר ר' יוחנן שריפא צרעת נעמן שהיא שקולה כמת שנאמר "אל נא תהי כמת"' (חולין ז, ע"ב; ראה גם סנה' מז, ע"א).[24]

החכמים פוסלים, אפוא, את הפירוש המוצע ומעדיפים לראות בנס ריפוי נעמן את ההחייאה השנייה. חז"ל חשו בנלעגותו של סיפורנו, בשוני המובהק שבינו ובין שאר סיפורי הניסים ולפיכך לא ראו בנס זה משום השבת המת לחיים בני קיימא אלא דרך להרחיקו מקבר אלישע.[25] ואכן, בכל סיפורי הניסים האחרים של אלישע ייזכר שם שמיים בין אם יאמר במפורש שהיה לו חלק בנס כגון בסיפור החייאת בן השונמית שם פונה הנביא בתפילה לה': 'ויתפלל אל ה'' (ד, כג), ובין על־ידי כינויו של אלישע בתואר 'איש אלוהים' (כגון בסיפור ריפוי הנזיר [ד, לח-מא] או הצפת הגרזן [ו, א-ז]). כמו כן אין עוד סיפורי ניסים בהם אין עדים לנס, ויתרה מזאת: בכל שאר סיפורי הניסים מתעוררת המחייבת בעייה את התערבותו של הנביא על דרך עשיית נס. בסיפורנו, לעומת זאת, אין כל בעייה, מותו של האיש אינו מעורר צערו של אדם, ואין מי שיבקש על חייו. ההחייאה אינה אלא "תאונה"![26]

סיפור הפתיחה למחזור אלישע, הלוא הוא סיפור הסתלקותו של אליהו, כורך את דמות הרב עם דמות התלמיד ומציע לנו להרחיב את מעגל הקשר ולכלול בו את מחזור סיפורי אליהו. גם אליהו כאלישע מקים נער מן המתים (מל"א יז, יז-כד) ובסיפור זה כבסיפור השונמית מתעוררת בעייה המחייבת את התערבות הנביא: אם הילד מביעה את טרוניתה (פס' יח) והנביא מתפלל לה' (פס' כ, כא) זוכה ונענה: 'וישמע ה' בקול אליהו ותשב נפש הילד על קרבו ויחי' (פס' כב, וראה לשון 'ויחי' גם בסיפורנו). אמנם גם במעשה אליהו יש מגע גופני בין הנביא לבין המת, אך זה שולי 'ויתמדד על הילד שלש פעמים' (פס' כא) והנס נעשה מכוח התרצותו של ה' לנביא. גם כאן מודה אם הנער לנביא (פס' כד) ונמצא שגם סיפור ההחייאה של אליהו נאצל לאין שיעור מסיפורנו שלנו.[27]

רש"י בפירושו לגמרא סנה' מז, ע"א יודע לספר כי הנקבר האלמוני בקבר אלישע הוא: 'נביא השקר היה, הוא הנביא אשר השיב את עדו לאכול ולשתות בבית־אל וענשו על־ידי והמיתו הארי, וכשמת לאחר ימים קברוהו אצל אלישע ולא הוכשר אצל המקום שיקבר אצלו והחייהו'.
הקישור הנועז שיוצר רש"י בין סיפורנו לבין הסיפור במל"א יג אינו משולל יסוד: הנביא הזקן

---

23 פירוש זה אינו פשט. ב'פי־שנים' הכוונה לשני חלקים כחלק הבכור (ראה דב' כא, טו-יז; וכן זכ' יג, ח). בן־סירא מח, יב כבר מבאר 'פי שנים' במשמעות כפליים אך קובע זאת לגבי כלל ניסיו של אלישע ולאו דווקא לגבי ניסי ההחייאה. ראה רופא, שם, עמ' 46, הערה 15.
24 ועוד לעניין הקשר בין מוות וצרעת ראה ספרי גבה מעל גבה (לעיל, הערה 1), עמ' 43.
25 דווקא רד"ק מקבל פירוש זה: 'מרז"ל כי חיה והוליד בנים והטעם שחייב לקיים ברכת אליהו שניתן לו פי שניים ברוחו, ואליהו החייה מת אחד והוא החייה שניים. אחד בן חייו בן השונמית ואחד במותו זה האיש ...'.
26 אף בסיפורי ההחייאה שבברית החדשה כגון החייאת בן האלמנה על־ידי ישוע (לוקס ז, יא-יז), החייאת לעזר (יוחנן יא) והחייאת הנער על־ידי פטרוס (מפעלות השליחים ט, לו-מא) אין המת קם לתחייה אלא לאחר הפנייה לבעל הנס הפותר את הבעייה בנוכחות קהל. זאת ועוד, בסיפורים אלה יהא תמיד מי שיעודה על הנס.
27 סיפור ההחייאה של אליהו יונק מזה של אלישע, וראה הראיות בספרו של רופא (לעיל, הערה 20), עמ' 113-114.

ב: 'וארם יצאו גדודים' והן בפרק ו, כג: 'ולא יספו עוד גדודי ארם לבוא בארץ ישראל', וראה באמת הציטוט המשובש בתוספתא סוטה ספי"ב: "כל זמן שהיה אלישע קיים לא היו גדודי ארם מתגרין בישי. משמת מהו אומר "וגדודי ארם באו לארץ..."'. לפני שננסה לתת טעם לבחירת המואבים נעיר כי סמיכות הפרשיות בין סיפורנו לבין הקשרו המיידי יוצרת מצב נלעג. בחייו מכונה אלישע 'אבי אבי רכב ישראל ופרשיו', היינו מגינו הצבאי של ישראל, והנה אך נסתלק וכבר מעיזים אויבי ישראל פניהם ועושים בארץ כבתוך שלהם.

בואם של גדודי מואב דווקא עשוי להיות מוסבר על רקע הכישלון הצרוב במערכה עם מואב (פרק ג). בסיפור זה ניבא אלישע את נצחון ישראל ויהודה (פס' יח), אך בסיומו של הסיפור משתבש מהלך העניינים: 'וירא מלך מואב כי חזק ממנו המלחמה ... ויקח את בנו הבכור אשר ימלך תחתיו ויעלהו עלה על החמה ויהי קצף גדול על ישראל ויסעו מעליו וישבו לארץ' (פס' כו-כז). כשלונם של ישראל – כשלונו של אלישע – מותיר כוח צבאי ביד המואבים והם ממשיכים לעשות בו שימוש גם לאחר מותו של אלישע. סיפור קבורת אלישע אינו מחמיא לנביא גם מבחינה זו שהוא מנציח אפוא את זכר כשלונו.

הופעת גדודי מואב אכן מזכירה מבחינה מסוימת את הופעת גדודי ארם. האחרונים לא הופיעו כאילו אלא כדי לשבות נערה קטנה מארץ ישראל (ה, ב), ואילו כל הופעתם של גדודי מואב לא הייתה לכאורה אלא למען עורר את יראתם של הקברנים המשליכים את האיש בקבר אלישע. בעוד שבמלחמות ארם הופיעו תחילה גדודי הגדודים, ומשלא עלה בידם לגרום נזק של ממש הופיע הצבא הארמי כולו (פרק ז), הרי שסדר הדברים מהופך במה שנוגע לאויב המואבי: תחילה נלחם ישראל במואב (פרק ג) ואחר כך משלחים המואבים את גדודיהם בישראל.

דומה שהטעם העיקרי להיות הגדודים מואבים דווקא, יתברר לנו אם ניתן דעתנו על מקום עלייתו של אליהו בסערה השמימה, בעבר הירדן מול יריחו. גדודי מואב נמצאים אפוא בטריטוריה הקרובה למואב, ומבקש המספר לרמוז לנו כי מקום הסתלקותו של אליהו ומקום קבורתו של אלישע חד הם. וראה עוד בהמשך.

את סיפורנו ראוי להשוות עם סיפור החייאה אחר של אלישע, סיפור החייאתו של בן השונמית (ד, ח-לז). גם סיפור השונמית אינו מחמיא לאלישע יתר על המידה.[22] אלישע מנסה להתחמק מחובתו כלפי השונמית ובנה ומשלח תחילה את גיחזי ומשענתו – משענת הנביא – בידו (פס' כט-לא). כשלון נסיון ההחייאה על-ידי שליח ומשענתו מחזק בנו, על כל פנים, את ההכרה כי הנער אכן מת, מה שאין כן בסיפור האיש המושלך אל קבר אלישע, שאינו מעיד בוודאות על מות האיש. בשני הסיפורים קם אדם לתחייה בעקבות מגע עם גוף הנביא: בסיפור השונמית: 'ויעל וישכב על הילד וישם פיו על פיו ועיניו על עיניו וכפיו על כפיו ויגהר עליו ויחם בשר הילד'. וישב וילך בבית אחת הנה ואחת הנה ויעל ויגהר עליו ויזורר הנער עד שבע פעמים ויפקח הנער את עיניו' (פס' לד-לה), ובסיפורנו קם המת לתחייה בעקבות מגע עם גוף הנביא המת, עם עצמותיו. כח החיות שהיה בו באלישע בעודנו חי הוסיף לפכות בו גם אחרי מותו. אך רב ההבדל בין שני הסיפורים: בסיפור השונמית יש תיעוד מלא על הנס – יש לנס עדים ויש מי שמכיר תודה לנביא: 'ותבא [=השונמית] ותפל על רגליו ותשתחו ארצה ותשא את בנה ותצא' (פס' לז), ויתרה מזאת: גיחזי הוא שהיה עד לנס מעיד עליו בפני המלך (ח, ה) ובו ברגע מופיעים האשה ובנה, וכדברי גיחזי: '... אדני המלך זאת האשה וזה בנה אשר החיה אלישע'.

את שני סיפורי ההחייאה הללו כורכים חז"ל בהצביעם על האפשרות שהחייאת המת האלמוני המצטרפת להחייאת בן השונמית יש בה כדי למלא אחר בקשת אלישע מאליהו: 'ויהי נא פי

---

[22] ראה רופא (לעיל, הערה 20), עמ' 32-33.

אמיתותו מלבד המספר שאף הוא מקצר מאד בדבריו ומותיר בסיפורו פרטים סתומים לרוב. הדברים כה קצרים וכה רב-משמעיים עד שאתה יכול להניח שהנקבר לא היה מת, ולפיכך לא קם לתחייה. אפשרות אחרת, מגוחכת לא פחות, היא שאלישע הוא שקם לתחייה מכח נגיעתו של המת האחר...

נעבור עתה לבחינת סיפורנו על רקע הקשרו המיידי, מה שלפניו ומה שאחריו. מעשה קבורת אלישע ניצב אחרי המעשה בנבואתו האחרונה למלך יואש, נבואה שעניינה מלחמת ישראל בארם (יג, יד-יט), ובעקבות סיפורנו אכן מתגשמת נבואת אלישע, ותן דעתך לזיקה בין דברי הנביא: '...ועתה שלש פעמים תכה את ארם' (פס׳ יט) לבין התגשמות הנבואה: '... שלש פעמים הכהו יואש וישב את ערי ישראלי' (פס׳ כה).[18]

סיפור הנבואה האחרונה נפתח במילים: 'ואלישע חלה את חליו אשר ימות בו' (פס׳ יד) ומכאן קשר ברור לסיפורנו שימות אלישע' (פס׳ כ). עתה מתבארת אף סיבת מותו-חוליו (ועוד לעניין זה להלן).[19] בסיפור הנבואה האחרונה מכנה המלך הנרגש את הנביא: 'אבי אבי רכב ישראל ופרשיו' (פס׳ יד) אותו כינוי בו מכנה אלישע את אליהו רבו בסיפור הסתלקותו של אליהו ומעבר הרוח מאליהו לאלישע, סיפור שהוא בבחינת פתיחה למחזור סיפורי אלישע (מל״ב ב, יב).[20] זיקה זו בין הסיפור שסיפורנו נסמך אליו לבין סיפור הסתלקותו של אליהו מעבירה אותנו לבחינת סיפורנו על רקע מחזור סיפורי אלישע כולו, ונפתחת בזיקה למל״ב ב: בניגוד להעלמותו המרשימה של אליהו העולה בסערה השמיימה בעודנו במלוא אונו וכוחו, העלמות שאין עימה מיתה, הרי שהסתלקותו של אלישע מותירה רושם עלוב משהו: אלישע חולה ואינו יכול לרפא לעצמו, וכך מגיע עד שערי מוות. האיש אשר ריפא למי יריחו (ב, כא) והסיר מוות מן הנזיד המורעל (ד, לח-מא), מת ככל האדם. בניגוד לקהל הגדול, קהל בני הנביאים המבשרים את הסתלקות אליהו ואף צופים בה (ב, ג, ה, ז) הרי שמות אלישע מעוצב בקול דממה דקה, ללא קהל ובעליבות רבה. אמת, נושא האלמוות מופיע גם בסיפור הסתלקות אלישע, אך בין אם נפרש כי המושלך על קבר הנביא קם לתחייה ובין אם נעדיף את הפירוש כי אלישע הוא הקם בעקבות המגע עם הגוף המושלך אל קברו, השוואת שני הסיפורים אינה מחמיאה לאלישע, אם לנקוט לשון המעטה.

לפי הפירוש על-פיו אין אלישע קם לתחייה הרי הניגוד בינו ובין אדוניו חריף כפליים. בעוד שאליהו עלה בסערה השמיימה הרי שאלישע מת ונקבר, וגם אם יש בכוחו לחלץ אחרים מן המיתה הרי לא יוכל להקים את עצמו מן המתים.

מעניין כי שני סיפורי ההסתלקות משלבים רכיב של השלכה במעשה האלמוות. במל״ב ב מעלים בני הנביאים את ההשערה המוטעית כי רוח ה׳ נשא את אליהו וישלכהו באחד ההרים או באחת הגאיות' (פס׳ טז), ולבסוף מתברר כי לא הושלך אלא בשמים מקומו. בסיפורנו, לעומת זאת, מושלך אדם מת על קבר הנביא וגם אם אלישע הוא הקם לתחייה הרי לא מכוחו שלו הוא קם, ואין קימתו מעוררת רושם.

התבוננות בגוף מחזור סיפורי אלישע, במה שבין שני סיפורי ההסתלקות שבמסגרת, עשויה להבהיר כמה סתומות בסיפורנו. כבר תמהנו לעיל מה ראה המספר לציין דוקא את דבר בואם של גדודי מואב בארץ[21] ולא, דרך משל, את בואם של גדודי ארם הנזכרים במחזור הן בפרק ה,

---

[18] מעניין כי הנוסח הלוקיאני של תה״ש מעביר את שני הפסוקים הקודמים למעשה הנבואה האחרונה, הפסוקים המספרים במות יואש וקבורתו (פס׳ יב-יג) לאחר פס׳ כא כדי שלא ידובר במות יואש קודם שיכה את ערי ישראל.

[19] קשר אסוציאטיבי-לשוני בין שני הסיפורים: 'וישליכו את האיש' (פס׳ כא); 'ולא השליכם מעל פניו' (פס׳ כג).

[20] ראה א׳ רופא, סיפורי הנביאים (ירושלים, תשמ״ג) 45.

[21] נסיון עקר לבאור מדיני-היסטורי של בואם של גדודי מואב, ראה בפירושו של גריי (לעיל, הערה 6), עמ׳ 544.

ויקם על רגליו", האם חי המת ההוא בקרבת עצמות אדוננו אלישע כפי שנראה מפשטו של המקרא או לא?[12]

האם מיעוט מילותיו של הסיפור, הנמנע מלדבר הן בכבוד אלישע וקבורתו והן בשבח הנס, מעיד על כוונה מכוונת למעט מכבוד הנביא ומעשהו? האם האפשרויות השונות שנפתחו לנו במלאכת הפירוש, אפשרויות היוצרות סיטואציות הומוריסטיות, ואולי אף נלעגות, מעידות אף הן באותו הכיוון? מחד גיסא ימצא מי שיאמר שבא הסיפור לדבר בשבח אלישע, בכוחו להחיות מתים אחרי מותו שלו, וכדברי יוסף בן מתיתיהו המסיים ומסכם את תולדות חייו של אלישע במילים: "ובזה סיפרנו את מעשי אלישע הנביא, את הדברים שחזה ואמר בהיותו בחיים ואיזה כוח אלוהי היה בו אחרי מותו" (שם).

מאידך גיסא יש אפשרות לראות בסיפור מעשה הלועג לנביא — סיפור על-פיו חייה, אמנם, אלישע אדם לאחר מותו, אך מה טיבו של נס זה המסייע לאחרים ואינו יכול לסייע לעצמו? העובדה שאין המספר מרבה בדברי שיכנוע לאמיתות סיפורו — והרי, כפי שאמרנו, אין מי שיעיד על הנס — מבהירה שהמספר משאיר כאילו לשיפוטו של הקורא את ההחלטה אם יאמין למעשה, אם לאו.[13]

אם כוונה של לעג לנביא יש כאן הרי מזכיר הדבר את טיפוס המהתלה האיסופית על חוזים העוסקים בגורלות ומנבאים לאחרים, שעה שהם עצמם נכשלים כשלון צורב. במשל ה"חוזה בכוכבים",[14] מסופר על חוזה אשר "בהיות כל רוחו נתון לשמים לא נזהר ונפל לתוך באר", ולקחו: 'את העניינים שבשמים אתה מתאמץ לראות ואת מה שבארץ אינך רואה'.

ובמשל נוסף, "המגיד עתידות",[15] מעוצב כשלונו של מגיד עתידות שפרנסתו על ניחוש לאחרים, ובעודו עוסק במלאכתו אין הוא חש כי ביתו נפרץ וגנגב רכושו: 'אתה מתפאר לדעת מראש את עסקיהם של אחרים ואת שעלול לבוא עליך לא ניחשת'.[16]

במקרא מצוי טיפוס סיפורי זה במעשה בלעם ואתונו (במ' כב, כב-לה): החוזה המפורסם אינו רואה ואינו יודע מה שנהיר לאתונו הרואה את מלאך ה' הניצב בדרך לפניה ומונע ממנה לילד; האתון היא המטיפה מוסר לנביא![17]

ולא רק לעג לנביא יש בסיפורנו אלא אף מניעה ברורה להפוך את מקום קבורתו (אשר לא נודע) למקום עלייה לרגל; סיפור כה נלעג אין בו כדי לעורר רגש של הערצה לאיש ולמקום בו ארע לכאורה הנס.

לסיכום העיון בסיפור בבידודו נציין אפוא כי בין כך ובין כך אין אנו מתרשמים שהסיפור מחמיא לאלישע ולכוח ההחיאה שיש בו לאחר מותו. הסיפור מספר מעשה בנס כאילו בעל כורחו — מעשה נס ללא קהל, ללא השתאות, ללא שבח לנביא ולאלוהיו, נס שאין מעיד על

---

12 על-פי שטיינזלץ (לעיל, הערה 9), עמ' 114.
13 סיפור "החיאה" שהוא בבחינת מהתלה על סיפורי ניסים מביא דרויאנוב בספר הבדיחה והחדוד, א (תל-אביב, תשי"ט) רכ"ט: 'בחבורה של חסידים סיפרו מופתים של רבייס. נענה אחד מן החבורה ואמר: באזנינו שמענו ובעינינו לא ראינו. מוטב שאספר לכם כה מה שראיתי בעיני ממש ... ביום קיץ אחד של אשתקד היה המעשה. בעצם היום יצא אחד מאנ"ש מביתו, בריא ושלם כאחד האדם, ופתאם מעד ונפל לארץ. רצנו והודענו לרבי יחיא. מיד הפסיק משנתו, יצא אל הנופל, הניח ידו על ראשו ולחש לו: מה לך? — קום! — ותיכף קם! נתלהבה החבורה. — לא, לא קם. כבר פרחה נשמתו. רגנה החבורה. מה מופת הוא זה? החזיר המספר: מופת? ... איני יודע ... אבל זה ראיתי בעיני ממש'.
14 ראה ש' שפאן, משלי איסופוס (ירושלים, 1961) משל רצ"א (עמ' 140-141).
15 שפאן, שם, משל שי"ד (עמ' 146).
16 מוטיווים דומים ראה שם במשלים: ההולכים בדרך והעורב (משל רע"ג, עמ' 132); המכשפה (משל ש"ו, עמ' 148).
17 ראה א' רופא, ספר בלעם (ירושלים, תשמ"ם) ובמיוחד 49-52.

לא הלך אלא שחיה לשעה ומת ונקבר במקום אחר שנאמר 'אל תאסוף עם חטאים נפשי...' (שו"ט למזמור כו), כלומר 'שלא היתה עמידתו אלא לשעה לפרוש מאותו צדיק בלבד' (קה"ר פ"ח, י ראה גם סנה' מז, ע"א).

האיש נוגע אפוא בעצמות אלישע, ותוצאות המגע: 'ויחי'. מלת 'ויחי' עשויה לבטא קימה מן המתים (כגון מל"א יז, כב; יח' לז, ג, ט, י) ובחזון העצמות היבשות שביחזקאל אף משתקף רצף ארועים כזה שבסיפורנו: 'ותבוא בהם הרוח ויחיו ויעמדו על רגליהם' (פס' י). עם זאת יש ומלה זו מבטאת אך התחזקות או ריפוי מן החולי (שופ' טו, יט — בעקבות צמא; מל"ב כ, ז; ישי' לח, ט).

ומהו הפירוש הראוי למילת 'ויחי' בסיפורנו? לכאורה ברור שקם המושלך מן המתים בעקבות המגע בעצמות אלישע. אך אם נדייק ונזכור שלא העיד המספר על הנקבר כי מת תחילה — בניגוד לעדותו המפורשת על אלישע: 'וימת אלישע' — אפשר לנו לפרש כאילו בטעות בקשו לקברו, ומשהשליכוהו נזדעזע, נתעורר וקם על רגליו. ושמא דווקא פירוש זה יעלה בקנה אחד עם מלת 'וילך' במקומה וכצורתה בנה"מ, היינו שיכול היה לילך האיש שלא מת? פירוש זה יקנה מיד הומוריסטי לסיפור שהרי אין בו לא נס ולא בן נס!

אם בכל זאת נבאר כי אל קבר אלישע קם לתחייה הרי שכוח החיות שהיה בעצמות אלישע הוא שחייהו. ראוי לזכור כי מילת 'עצמות' עשוייה להתייחס לעצמות ממש (כגון יח' לז, א ואילך; מל"ב כג, יד וכן רבים) אך גם לגוף השלם (כדוגמת תה' לב, ג; נא, י; משי' טז, כד; איוב ז, טו). פירושה האחרון של התיבה 'עצמות' מאיר באור שונה את מהלך העניינים: הנקבר השני נגע בעצמות אלישע ואלישע הוא שקם על רגליו ושב לחיים. ואם יבקש הקורא לדייק ולומר שהפועל הקודם לפועל 'ויחי', 'ויגע' מדבר באיש ולפיכך הוא קם ולא אחר, ניתן להשיב לו מחילופי הנושאים הקיימים בסיפור, בין סוף פס' כ וראש פס' כא: 'וגדודי מואב יבאו ... ויהי הם קברים' (והרי יוסף בן מתיתיהו טעה, כזכור, במשמע החילופים הללו!). על קימת אלישע עצמו לתחייה הבין את הסיפור בן-סירא: 'כל דבר לא נפלא ממנו ומתחתיו נברא בשרו. בחייו עשה נפלאות ובמותו תמהי מעשה' (מח, טז-יז).[11] גם כאן מאפשרת אפוא האליפטיות של הסיפור הקצר פירוש הומוריסטי — איש אלמוני הוא שעשה נס עם הנביא; אלישע שמת בראש הסיפור: 'וימת אלישע', קם לתחייה בסיומו: 'ויחי ויקם על רגליו'.

אם בכל זאת נדבק בפירוש היותר פשוט היינו שהאלמוני הוא הקם לתחייה נשאלת השאלה מה עושה המת כשהוא שב לחיים? הסיפור אינו משיב על השאלה, אינו מגלה בה עניין. גם אם נעביר את מילת 'וילך' לסוף הסיפור הרי זו תציין אך את פינוי הבמה ולא את שיבת האיש לביתו. מצטיירת פה אפוא סיטואציה הומוריסטית נוספת: קברניו של המת נעלמו, האויב היה כלא היה והמת-החי שבוודאי לא ידע את נפשו ולא הבין מה שארע לו ואיך הגיע למקום שהגיע — עומד נבוך על עומדו. לפנינו אפוא מעשה בנס שאין לו עדים, שרק המספר מכוחה של סמכות שהוא נוטל לעצמו יכול להעיד עליו. אין בסיפור זה יד וחלק לה', אין הקם לתחייה מודה על הנס שנעשה עמו ואינו מעיד עליו קבל עם ועדה. מקום התרחשותו של הנס (שאינו ידוע) אינו הופך למקום של עלייה לרגל, ובקצרה: אין המעשה מותיר אחריו כל רושם ואין המספר מתאמץ לחזק את תוקף המעשה ואמיתותו. כך אפוא עשוי להתעורר פיקפוק באמיתות הנס, כגון בשאלה עליה משיב ר' אברהם בן הרמב"ם: 'ילמדנו רבנו מה פירוש הכתוב "ויגע האיש בעצמות אלישע ויחי

---

[11] היוני משקף נוסחה שונה: ימתחתיו נבא בשרי' (καὶ ἐν κοιμήσει ἐπροφήτευσεν τὸ σῶμα αὐτοῦ) אך זהו תקון הנובע מהבנה שונה של הסיפור — שגופו של אלישע החיה את האחר, ולפיכך נבא = עשה מעשה נביא, חולל נס. רבים פרשני בן-סירא המעדיפים את הנוסח היוני משום שאינם ערים לאפשרות האחרת הגלומה בסיפור שבמלכים, וראה לאחרונה: P. W. Skehan and A. A. Di Lella, *The Wisdom of Ben Sira* (AB; New York, 1979) 532.

כהנחת רד"ק כי 'אפשר שתהא האל"ף תמורת ה"א הנקבה והוא כמו "בה שנה"', כלומר באותה שנה עצמה שמת אלישע, והיא גם דרך הבנתם של הפשיטתא והוולגטה: in ipso anno ('בה בשנה').[6]

הסיפור הקצר נמנע גם מלציין מיהו שקבר את 'האיש'. צורת הסתמי 'ויהי הם קברים' עלולה לגרור אחריה אי-הבנה, ואכן יוסף בן מתיתיהו נפל בפח וקבע כי מואבים הם שקברוהו: 'אותה שעה (בעת קבורתו של אלישע) קרה גם הדבר ששודדים השליכו איש אחד אל תוך קברו של אלישע...' (שם). אף זהותו של האיש, של המת, אינה חשובה בעיני מספרנו, עובדה שהפריעה לבעלי המדרש המבקשים לקרוע את מסכת האלמוניות מפניהן של דמויות שוליות במקרא. כך דרך משל, מצינו בפדר"א ל"ג שהיה המת הקם לתחייה בן שלום בן תקוע שנמצא ראוי מכח צדקתו שישוב ויחיה אחרי מותו.

לשון 'והנה' – לשון מובהקת של ציון הפתעה[7] – רומזת לפליאת הקברנים נוכח הגדוד המואבי, ליראתם כי רבה: 'וישליכו את האיש' – 'מרוב חופזם מפחד הגדוד השליכוהו בקבר אלישע' (רד"ק). השלכת המת יש בה משום ביזיונו (ראה דרך משל שמ"ב יח, יז; יר' יד, טז) אף שלא נתכוונו לבזותו ולא השליכוהו אלא מתוקף הנסיבות. המת הושלך לקבר אלישע, 'במערת אלישע שנקבר בה ולא היה להם אלא לפתוח פי המערה ולהשליכו בתוכה' (רד"ק).

קברניו של המת נסו על נפשם, הגדוד הלך לדרכו מבלי לשית ליבו לקברנים ולמנוסתם ולא נותר על הבמה אלא המת-החי לבדו.

ומה אנו שומעים אודותיו? 'וילך ויגע האיש בעצמות אלישע...'. הנוסח קשה שהרי לא שמענו על המתים שהם הולכים. רד"ק מבאר: 'ונתגלגל האיש עד שנגע בעצמות אלישע, וזהו "וילך ויגע"' ואכן אפשר שהל"ך משמש בציוויים כלשון זירוז (כדוגמת בר' יט, לב; שמ"א כו, יט; מל"א טו, יט), וראה השימוש בפועל זה לעיצוב פעולה המביעה צמיחה או התעצמות (כגון שמ"ב ג, א; יונה א, ב; אסי' ט, ד).

תיקון נוסח המבטל כליל את הקושי: 'וילכו' (בעקבות הנוסח הלוקיאני של תה"ש), היינו הקברנים הם שהלכו, נטשו את המת לגורלו בפחדם מן המואבים.[8] השיבוש המשוער ארע עקב השמטת הוי"ו ממילת 'וילכו' בהשפעת הווי"ו שבראש המילה הבאה 'ויגע' (הפלוגרפיה).

אפשרות אחרת לתיקון הנוסח – ועלינו לזכור כי תיקונים אלה משפיעים על דרך הבנתו של הסיפור – היא להעביר את מלת 'וילך' לסוף הכתוב: 'ויחי ויקם על רגליו וילך', היינו שהלך האיש למקום שהלך ממקום הקבורה, וכפי שמצינו בשו"ת ר' אברהם בן הרמב"ם סימן ע"ט:[9] '...חי וקם והלך'; ההנחה היא שמלת 'וילך' נשמטה בהעתקת הסיפור ממקומה, מי שחש בהשמטה העתיקה בשוליים או בין השיטין, ובהעתקה נוספת מעשה ידיו של מי שלא ידע עוד מהו המקום הראוי לה, הגיעה המלה למקום שהגיעה.[10] אם אכן הלך המת משדה הקבורה הרי שהגיע למקום יישוב ונוכחות הנוכחים בנס שאירע לו. אלא מאי? כיוון שלא שומעים אנו על תגובה כולשהי שעורר מעשה הנס, מדגישים חכמים שלא הלך האיש לאחר שקם והרי הם מקיימים את לשון הסיפור כצורתו על סיומו בקימת האיש על רגליו: 'ויחי ויקם על רגליו' תנא על רגליו עמד לביתו

---

[6] ראה: J. Gray, *Kings* (OTL; London, 1964) 543.

[7] למלת 'והנה' כלשון הפתעה ראה לדוגמא בר' כט, כה, לז, כט; לח, כז; מא, ז; מב, לה; שמ' ב, ו; ג, ב; ד, ו-ז).

[8] ראה למשל: A. B. Ehrlich, *Randglossen zur hebräischen Bibel* (7 vols.; Leipzig, 1914) 7:309.

[9] על-פי ע' שטיינזלץ, פירוש המקרא בספרות השאלות והתשובות מהמאה השמינית ועד השש-עשרה (ירושלים, 1978) 114.

[10] השמטת קטע והעתקתו במקום שאינו ראוי לו היא תופעה שכיחה בתולדות הנוסח. ראה דוגמות סיפוריות לתופעה בספרי חיי שמשון (לעיל הערה 1), עמי 259 והעי 122.

נציב, אפוא, את השאלות המתעוררות אגב קריאה ונבקש להן תשובות הן בסיפור גופו והן — תוך הרחבה הדרגתית ומבוקרת של מעגל הקשריו — בסביבתו הספרותית הקרובה והרחוקה.[4] דווקא קוצר הסיפור יש בו כדי לעורר קושיות מפני שהפרוץ בו על העומד והשמא רב על הברי. תשובות לקושיות הללו עשויות לגלות לנו את מסרו-מסריו של הסיפור.

וימת אלישע
ויקברהו
וגדודי מואב יבאו בארץ בא שנה
ויהי הם קברים איש
והנה ראו את הגדוד
וישליכו את האיש בקבר אלישע
וילך ויגע האיש בעצמות אלישע
ויחי ויקם על רגליו

תחילה נרכז מבטנו בסיפור בבידודו; נציב את השאלות העולות למקרא ונוכח על אילו מהן יכולים אנו להשיב, אילו אינן רלבנטיות ואינן ראויות לתשובה ולאילו אין פתרון עד שלא נרחיב את יריעת ההקשר. הקורא את הסיפור בבידודו — קורא שאינו מצויד בידע מוקדם על אלישע ומעלליו — לא ידע מיהו אותו אלישע שבו פותח הסיפור, דמות יחידה הנזכרת בשמה — ואף לא ידע על מה תפארתה של דמות זו ומהו טיב מעשיה עליהם בא להוסיף סיפור ההחיאה. אי ידיעה זו עלולה לגרור אחריה בלבול גדול בהמשך הקריאה.

הסיפור בבידודו אינו מגלה לנו מהי סיבת מותו של אלישע: זקנתו גרמה? חולי שחלה בו? ואולי המיתו ה׳ על חטאיו? דומה שאין שאלה זו ראויה להישאל מפני שהמספר בחר שלא להציע לה תשובה, מפני שאינה רלבנטית למסר שנושא הסיפור. שאלות אחרות שאינן ראויות להישאל הן זהות המטפלים בקבורת אלישע ומקום קבורתו.

דווקא משום שאין הסיפור נותן דעתו לעניינים אלו יתמה התמה האם לא נמצא אלישע ראוי כי ידובר בקבורתו ביתר פירוט? האם אין מקום לספר, דרך משל, בצער שעוררה הסתלקותו? יוסף בן מתיתיהו שחש בקושי אכן מרחיב בנקודה זו: ׳... הוא זכה גם לקבורה נהדרת כראוי לאיש אהוב אלוהים במידה כזו׳ (קדמוניות ס׳ תשיעי, ח, ו).

המימד ה״היסטורי״ חודר לסיפור באיזכורם של ׳גדודי מואב׳. מדוע דווקא בהם ידבר הכתוב? היש בפרט זה משום רמז למקום קבורתו של אלישע? ושוב, קריאת הסיפור ללא הקשרו-הקשריו מותירה אותנו ללא מענה.

הביטוי המציין את מועד בואם של הארמים ׳בא שנה׳ אינו נהיר ודומה שאין מנוס מתיקון הנוסח. נוסח התרגום הארמי ׳בּמיעל שתא׳ — וכהסברו של רש״י ׳בתשובת השנה׳ (השווה שמ״ב יא, א; מל״א כ, כב, כו) מניח את הקריאה ׳כבא השנה׳, היינו לקראת סוף השנה, לעת צאת המלכים׳ (שמ״ב יא, א), היינו באביב, עם חלוף הגשמים, כאשר מזג האויר יפה ליציאה למלחמה.[5] ומוסיף רש״י טעם נוסף ליציאת הגדודים בתקופה זו של השנה: ׳בעוד הארץ מלאה דשאים ויש מאכל לבהמתם דרך חילות לצאת׳. דרך אחרת להתמודד עם הצירוף הקשה היא

---

4 לשיטת פרשנות הסיפור המקראי — בהקשרים ההולכים ומתרחבים, ראה מאמרי: ״יעלה קרח עלה קרחי — מעגלי פרשנות בסיפור המקראי״, מחקרי ירושלים בספרות עברית ח, (ירושלים, תשמ״ה) 7-23; ״הגם דוד בנביאים״ (בדפוס).

5 ראה לדוגמה: C. F. Burney, *Notes on the Hebrew Text of the Book of Kings* (Oxford, 1903) 317.

'וימת אלישע...ויחי ויקם על רגליו' (מל"ב יג,כ-כא): סיפור קצרצר במעגלי פרשנות

יאיר זקוביץ

ספר התנ"ך מעורר בקוראיו יראת כבוד וכובד ראש, תחושה שעליהם להלך בשביליו על קצות האצבעות ובהנמכת קול, וזאת מפני שאינו ספר ככל הספרים אלא "ספר הספרים", כתבי-הקודש של עם ישראל. אנו, האמונים על "קריאה צמודה" של הטקסט המקראי, על תשומת לב מלאה לפרטי הפרטים של עיצוב היצירה הספרותית, על ביקוש בלתי נלאה אחר משמעה של כל מלה בהקשרה,[1] ודאי שלא נטיף לקלות ראש בגישה לתנ"ך, ונהפוך הוא. עם זאת, ראוי לבחון, מידי פעם, את הנחת היסוד כאילו כל סיפור וסיפור במקרא נכתב מתוך רצינות מקפיאה, ללא חיוך וללא קריצת עין.[2] שאלה נוספת שעלינו לשוב ולשאול את עצמנו היא, האם המספר המקראי אכן מבקש לעצמו, בכל מקרה ומקרה, סמכות בלתי מוגבלת,[3] האם הוא מצפה מאתנו, קוראיו, להאמין אמונה עוורת בכל מלה שלו?

ואם אנו מוסיפים שאלה על שאלה מדוע לא נעז ונתמודד גם עם המשפט הקדום הקובע כי כל סיפור מקראי הוא בבחינת יצירה ספרותית נפלאה, גאונית; אכן, המקרא משופע בפניני ספרות בוהקות באור יקרות ואין הוא צריך להמלצותינו או למחמאותינו, אך האם יעלה על הדעת שאיכות כל סיפוריו ללא יוצא מן הכלל אחת היא?

את תקפותם של "ההרהורי הכפירה" שהעלינו נבחן לאורו של סיפור קצרצר בן שלושים ואחת מלים, מעשה שארע בקבר אלישע, סיפור שלמרות קוצר יריעתו הריהו משופע בדמויות לרוב: אלישע המת, קברניו, גדודי מואב, האיש המושלך לקבר אלישע וקברניו-משליכיו, ובמלים אחרות: שני מתים בודדים (שאחד מהם יקום לתחיה) ושלוש דמויות קולקטיביות: שתי קבוצות של קברנים וגדוד-גדודים מואביים.

---

1 לשיטת הקריאה הצמודה ראה: M. Weiss, *The Bible From Within* (Jerusalem, 1984). דוגמאות ליישומה לתחום הסיפור המקראי ראה בספרי: חיי שמשון (ירושלים, תשמ"ב); גבוה מעל גבוה (תל-אביב, 1985).

2 למימד ההומור בסיפור המקראי ראה לדוגמה מאמרי: "Humor and Theology, or The Successful Failure of the Israeli Intelligence - A Literary Folkloristic Approach to Jos 2" (in press).

3 לשאלת סמכותו של המספר המקראי עיין: ש' בר-אפרת, העיצוב האמנותי של הסיפור במקרא (1979) 48-53.

נימוקים אלה מצטרפים יחד לכלל הוכחה שאין ליחס את הסיפור למקור J כפי שטוענים אנשי הביקורת ההיסטורית והספרותית, לפחות לא על-פי תיארוכו המקובל עליהם,[52] אלא לעורך מתקופת בית שני, בין אם נכנהו "כהני" (P) או בכינוי הסתמי (R). הטענות הסגנוניות שהעלו המפרשים על-מנת לזהות סיפור זה כסיפור יהוויסטי אינן מכריעות. שהרי צמד הביטויים שעליהם הם מסתמכים, 'בכירה—צעירה', 'לחיות זרע', אין בהם כשלעצמם ליחד מקור זה; מה גם שהשם 'יהוה' שהוא המאפיין העיקרי של מקור זה, נעדר בכלל באגדה זו ואילו השם המופיע בחוליה שלפניה, הינו דווקא הכינוי הכללי 'אלהים' (בר' יט, כט).

אם אמנם דלה העורך המאוחר של התורה אגדה אתנולוגית ממקור מואבי-עמוני שנתגלגלה במסורת בעל-פה, השערה שעד כה אי אפשר להוכחה, הרי הוא שהפכה מבלי שחולל בה שינוי פנימי שהוא, מאגדה אטיולוגית-אתנולוגית המספרת על לידת שני העמים מואב ובני-עמון לסיפור אטיולוגי-גניאלוגי שתפקידו להכשיר מראש את היבדלותם של בני-ישראל מהם למרות מוצאם המשותף. על-פיו, קירבת המוצא בין לוט ואברהם נתקיימה בקושי דור אחד בלבד. מעשה התעברותן של בנות לוט מאביהן אמנם קשר יחד את מואב ועמון לאב אחד, אך גם הפריד ביניהם ובין בני אברהם, יצחק ויעקב לדורות. ואולי על-פי השיטה הגניאלוגית ה"טלסקופית" של ההיסטוריוגרפיה הישראלית נמשך דור אחד של קירבה זו ביניהם קרוב לאלף שנה?[53] פתחנו בניסיון לזהות את כוונת הסיפור המקורי על-פי הביקורת הספרותית-הסוגנית וסיימנו בניסיון לזהות את מגמת העורך על-פי ביקורת העריכה. זאת, מתוך הכרה שהמגמתיות איננה בסיפור כשלעצמו, אלא בשילובו ובייישומו בסיפורת על אבות ישראל. מגמתיות זו הינה פרי העריכה ולא פרי הדמיון היוצר. עם-זאת, לא ניתן להוכיח אם נתקיים אי-פעם סיפור עצמאי כזה, מתי נוצר ועל-ידי מי. ואם בגרעינו נולד תמים והירואי, מתי וכיצד נתחוללה בו מטמורפוזה שהכשירה אותו לשמש חוליה בהיסטוריוגרפיה המקראית המורכבת.

---

52 את השקפתי בעניין תיארוכו של J, ובעיקר בעניין אופיו כרובד עריכתי של הסיפורים על האבות הבעתי בספרי מיעקב לישראל (ירושלים, תשמ״ו).

53 את התואר "טלסקופית" שאלתי ממאמרו של א' מלמט: "ראשיתו של עם ישראל — לחקר קדם-ההיסטוריה הישראלית", קתדרה לתולדות ארץ ישראל ויישובה יח (שבט, תשמ״א) 1-21.

אתנולוגיה, אטיולוגיה, גניאלוגיה והיסטוריוגרפיה בסיפור על לוט ובנותיו

באשדוד שבנבואת זכריה (ט, ו)[45] ונדרוש אותו בעקבות קזל כזהה עם הממזר שבדב׳ כג, ג,[46] הרי שנוצר "משולש" הזהה לזה שמופיע בנחמ׳ יג, כג המצוטט לעיל. אין זה מקרה שברשימת עמי הארצות שבני ישראל, כולל הכהנים והלויים, לא נבדלו מתועבותיהם שבעז׳ ט, א נמנים 'העמוני והמואבי׳ ובסדר זה כמו בדב׳ כג, ד.[47]

זהו כנראה אף מאחזו ההיסטורי של העורך ה"כהני" ששילב את מעשה בנות לוט באביהן באטיולוגיה הגנטית השלילית של מואב ובני-עמון. למרות שאין כל רמז לסיפור הולדתם של מואב ועמון באיסור של דב׳ כג, ד-ז ואף לא בנחמ׳ יג, א-ב, שבשניהם אין מופיע אפילו הכינוי "בני-לוט", ניתן לשער זאת בעקיפין על-פי הנימוקים המסתברים שהעלינו. אל נימוקים אלה מתוספות העדויות שמן השתיקה, שעל-פיהן אין סיפור לידתם של מואב ועמון נרמז כלל בנבואות על עמים אלה: לא בנבואות המושלים העתיקה על מואב (במ׳ כא כז-ל), לא בנבואות בלעם על הגויים שמהן נעדרים בני עמון (במ׳ כד, טז-כד),[48] ואף לא בנבואה הקלאסית הישראלית.[49] פרט למוטיב השכרות אין שם דבר שיעורר רושם שהנביאים מודעים לסיפור אטיולוגי-גנטי זה.[50] אפילו צפניה המדמה בנבואתו את גורל הצמד "מואב ובני-עמון" אל גורל הצמד "סדום ועמורה" (ב, ט) אינו מודע לסיפור זה.[51]

---

45 מ׳ זר-כבוד, חגי, זכריה ומלאכי (ירושלים, 1968) מפרט הפירושים השונים שניתנו ל'ממזר׳ שבזכ׳ ט, ו ומגיע לפירוש סינטטי שהכוונה כאן 'לאיזה מעמד נמוך שהתגורר בארץ הפלשתים, מעין הצוענים, בניגוד לגאון פלשתים׳.

46 H. Cazelles, "La Mission d'Esdras," *VT* 4 (1954) 121f.

47 במנין העמים מופיע גם המצרי׳ ובסדר זה עצמו כבדב׳ כג, ד-ח כשלאחריו בא 'והאמורי׳. ואמנם מקצת כתבי-יד ותה"ש גורסים 'והאדומי׳ תמורת 'והאמורי׳. על הזיקה שבין חלק מן העמים הנזכרים כאן ובין דב׳ כג עמד מ׳ זר-כבוד בפירושו לעזרא ונחמיה (ירושלים, 1980) נח, הערה 7, אך מבלי שהסיק מכך את המסקנות הנוגעות לדב׳ כג. יש לציין שהסדר בני-עמון ומואב מופיע רק בהיסטוריוגרפיה המאוחרת (עז"נ ודה"י בנוסף לדב׳ כג, ד) בעוד שהסדר המופיע בהיסטוריוגרפיה הקדומה וכן בנבואה (פרט לירי׳ ט, כה), הוא הפוך.

48 לעובדה שאין בני עמון נזכר כלל בשירות הקדומות, שמקורן אינו ישראלי (המושלים, בלעם) ואף לא בשירת הים (שמ׳ טו) יש כמובן משמעות לעניננו. ועיין: ב׳ עודד, "עמון", אנציקלופדיה מקראית ו, 269.

49 על מואב: עמ׳ ב, א-ג; יש׳ טו-טז; יר׳ מח; יח׳ כה, ח-יא; צפ׳ ב, ח-י. וראה גם: שמ׳ טו, טו. על בני-עמון: עמ׳ א, יג-טו; יר׳ מט, א-ו; יח׳ כא, כה, א-ז; צפ׳ ב, ח-ז מופיעים מואב ובני עמון כצמד, ואף שם לא כבינוי בני לוט. קשה, איפוא, להניח שמנבואות לעג כה שנונות וחריפות יעדר המוטיב של לידת בני לוט מערייות, אילו אמנם הסיפור היה ידוע.

50 השכרות מופיעה כמוטיב רק בנבואת ירמיהו על מואב (יר׳ מח, לו), היין כמקור שמחה וגאוה של מואב מופיע גם אצל ירמיהו (מח) וגם אצל ישעיהו (טו-טז). באף מקום אין רמז לסיפור לוט במערה. אין היין מופיע כלל בנבואות על בני-עמון.

51 הנבואה כשלעצמה בעלת נימה פוליטית פולמוסית מובהקת. את המילה 'יבזום׳ יש לקרוא 'יבזום׳, ראה פירושיהם של: J. M. P. Smith, *Zephaniah* (ICC; 4th ed.; Edinburgh, 1959); J. D. W. Watts, *Genesis* (CBC; Cambridge, 1975) 169ff., 227. 'גאונם׳ מתפרש לא כגאווה על מוצאם הטהור, כפי שנתפרש האטימולוגיה שבסיפור לידת מואב ובני-עמון (בר׳ יט, לז-לח) על-ידי גונקל ותלמידיו, אלא על חרפם עם ה׳. דימוי גורלם לסדום ועמורה אינו מיוחד רק להם, אלא מופיע בנבואה הקלאסית אף ביחס לעמים אחרים: בבל (יש׳ יג, יט); אדום (יר׳ מט, יח); כשדים (יר׳ נ, מ) ואפילו ישראל (יש׳ א, ט; עמ׳ ד, יא). הרקע ההיסטורי של הנבואה בצפניה על-פי ח"א גינזברג הוא קודם לכיבושי יאשיהו, ראה: H. L. Ginsberg "Judah and Transjordan: Status from 734 to 582 B.C.E," *Alexander Marx Jubilee Volume* (New York, 1950) 354.

אין ביכולתנו לברר במסגרת מאמר זה מהו מוצאם הטבעי של צווי-טאבו אלה, ומהם הצרכים החברתיים המיוחדים שהולידו אותם. על-פי ניסוחם בספר דברים משקפים הם כבר חוויות היסטוריות מצטברות ותודעה לאומית מאוחרת. אולם, אפילו נשער מוצא קדום של איסורים אלה,⁴⁰ הרי הניסיון להסתמך עליהם על-מנת לישמם בפועל קשור עם המאבק ההיסטורי על התבדלותו הלאומית-פולחנית של "זרע הקודש" שבתקופת עזרא ונחמיה (עז' ט, ב). על-כך מעידה בראש ובראשונה העובדה שרק על עזרא ונחמיה מסופר במקרא שנחלצו להפעיל איסורים אלה במאבק פנימי אקטואלי, בעוד שבתיאור תולדות ישראל מאז התנחלותו ועד החורבן לא מצאנו התבדלות מסוג זה ביחס לקשרים עם מואבים ועמונים.⁴¹ ההיפך, עדויות שונות מצביעות על השתלבותם של עמונים ומואבים בקהל ישראל.⁴² רק בהיסטוריוגרפיה המקראית המאוחרת נותרו עקבות המאפשרים לנו לעמוד על השינוי הקיצוני ביחס כלפי העמונים והמואבים וממילא על המאחז ההיסטורי של מגמת התבדלות מהם. נחמיה מצטט את האיסור שבדב' כג, ד עם הנמקותיו המופיעות בדב' כג, ה-ו (נחמ' יג, א ואילך) על-מנת להצדיק את צעדיו בסילוק טוביה העמוני מלשכת בית ה' בירושלים (שם, ד-ט).⁴³ בהמשכו של הפרק מתאונן נחמיה: 'גם בימים ההם ראיתי את היהודים השיבו נשים אשדודיות עמוניות ומואביות' (נחמ' יג, כג), וזאת כביכול, אחר ההתחייבות של שרי הכהנים והלויים ושל ישראל בברית לגרש את הנשים הנוכריות (עז' י). מחבר דברי-הימים מדגים יחס זה בתיאור תולדות מלכי יהודה בימי בית ראשון כשהוא משייך את הקושרים שהיכו את יואש מלך יהודה בדמי זכריה בן יהוידע הכהן (בדה״י: בני יהוידע) לאימהות עמונית ומואבית: 'ואלה המתקשרים עליו זבד בן שמעת העמונית ויהוזבד בן שמרית המואבית' (דה״ב כד, כו). די להשוות את גירסתו עם גירסת מל״ב יב, כב על אירוע זה: 'המכים את יואש יוזבד בן שמעת ויהוזבד בן שמר עבדיו', כדי לעמוד על המגמה האנטי עמונית-מואבית המאוחרת.⁴⁴ אם נצרף לעמוני ולמואבי שבמדרש דברי-הימים את ה'ממזר'

---

40 ראה: ש' ליונשטם, "עריות" אנציקלופדיה מקראית ו, 389. על-פי K. Galling, "Das Gemeindegesetz in Deuteronomium 23," *Festschrift für A. Bertholet* (Tübingen, 1950) 176-91, מהווים פסוקים ב, ג, ד, ח קבוצת חוקים אפודיקטיים עתיקים של קהל ה' עוד מתקופת המקדש האמפיקטיוני בגלגל. הוא מבסס בין השאר את מסקנותיו על-כך שהביטוי 'יבקהל ה'' הינו קדם-דויטרונומיסטי ומופיע כבר במי' ב, ה.

41 במל״א יא, א ואילך אמנם משתקפת מגמה כזאת, אולם על צביונם הדויטרונומיסטי המאוחר של פסוקים אלה, ראה: J. A. Montgomery, *The Books of Kings* (ICC; Edinburgh, 1951) 231; J. Gray, *I & II Kings* (OTL; Philadelphia, 1963) 251. רק באיכה א, י משתקפת מגמה זאת לראשונה: 'ידו פרש צר על כל מחמדיה כי ראתה גוים באו מקדשה אשר צויתה לא יבאו בקהל לך', רש״י מפרש: 'אלו עמון ומואב'. אם אמנם לכך נתכוון המקונן, הרי שאין זה קודם לחורבן המקדש. אך ראה גם: T. J. Meek, *Lamentations* (IB; Nashville, 1984) 6:11. הקושר מגמה זאת עם ימי יח' מד, ט ואינו מזכיר בהקשר זה כלל את דב' כג, ד.

42 ברשימת גיבורי דוד מופיעים, לצד עמים שונים: צלק העמוני (שמ״ב כג, לז; דה״א יא, לט) ויתמה המואבי (דה״א יא, מו). יתר על כן, אחד מעבדי המלך יואש שהתקשר עליו ושמוצאו מואבי על-פי דה״ב כד, כו, נושא שם תיאופורי ישראלי 'יהוזבד'. וראה על כך: ש' יפת, אמונות ודעות בספר דברי הימים (ירושלים, 1977) 298.

43 ב' אופנהיימר, חזונות זכריה (ירושלים, 1961) 27, סובר שטוביה היה בן תערובת ישראלי-עמוני.

44 L. Curtis and A. A. Madsen, *The Books of Chronicles* (ICC; Edinburgh, 1952) 139; J. M. Myers, *II Chronicles* (AB; Garden City, NY, 1965) 439. מאירס מייחס גירסת דברי הימים ל"מדרש ספר מלכים" (ראה שם, פסוק כז) שהמניעים הדתיים שלו שקופים יותר מאלו של הדויטרונומיסט. וראה עוד: ש' יפת (לעיל, הערה 42), עמ' 298. יהודה קיל, ספר דברי הימים (ירושלים, תשמ״ו) תשסה.

של העורך ה"כהני" של ספר בראשית להסביר את מערכת היחסים הבינלאומיים באמצעות הגניאלוגי.[33] על-פי מגמה זו לוקח לו עשו בן יצחק את מחלת בת ישמעאל בן אברהם לאשה, ולא מבנות לוט, לאחר שראה 'כי רעות בנות כנען בעיני יצחק אביו' (בר' כח, ח-ט).
בנסיוננו להסביר את מגמת העורך שהביא סיפור זה במקומו, יצאנו מן ההנחה שקיימת זיקה סמויה בין סיפור לוט ובנותיו ובין האיסור על בואם של עמוני ומואבי בקהל ה' (דב' כג, ד). הנחה שמצאנוה כבר אצל פרשנים קדומים וחדשים. אף שחלוקות הדעות בקרב החוקרים ביחס לשחזור קבוצת החוקים הראשונית שבה מופיע איסור זה,[34] הרי אין ביניהם מחלוקת על כך שקיים קשר ישיר בין האיסור בפסוק ד ובין האיסורים הקודמים בפרק זה (כג, א-ג). ולעומת זאת הקשר שלו עם הפסוקים שאחריו (ה-ו) הינו משני. פסוקים ה-ו באו לנמק איסור זה בטעמים היסטוריים-מוסריים. מאידך, מן הקשר שבין פסוק ד לקודמיו הם מקישים שהוא קשור בלידתם של שני עמים אלה מעריות, אף שהטעם לא פורש כלל.[35] היקש זה מתבסס על פסוק א שבו יש איסור מפורש לגלות 'כנף האב' (אף שהאיסור מנוסח בגוף זכר) ועל פסוק ג שבו מופיע איסור זהה בלשונו לזה שבפסוק ד, ביחס לממזר.[36] את משמעותו של "ממזר", מונח המופיע במקרא פעמיים בלבד,[37] גוזרים הם בעקבות חז"ל מן האיסורים המופיעים כאן כמי שנולד מאיסור עריות (במילים אחרות, הוכחה שבמעגל).[38] לפסוק ב 'לא יבא פצוע דכא וכרות שפכה בקהל ה'' לא הוסבה כמעט תשומת לב; אף כי הוא החסר כל צביון אתני, משקף לא פחות מן האחרים את העקרונות של קבוצת איסורים אלה: מום גופני שיש בו משום טומאה פולחנית, והפוסל את הנגוע בו מלבוא בקהל ה'. משמע, המשותף לצווי טאבו אלה הינו הבטחת הטוהר הפולחני של קהל ה',[39] טוהר שאינו מתבסס רק על המוצא המשותף, אלא על סייגים אחרים הבאים להבטיחו.

---

33 ראה: ליוור (לעיל, הערה 20), עמ' 663-671, וראה: R. R. Wilson, "The OT Genealogies in Recent Research," *JBL* 94 (1975) 169-89; T. L. Thompson, *The Historicity of the Patriarchal Narrative* (Berlin, 1974) 380ff.

34 S. R. Driver, *Deuteronomy* (ICC; 3d. Ed.; Edinburgh, 1901) 260-62; G. von Rad, *Deuteronomium Studien* (Göttingen, 1947) 13f.; C. M. Carmichael, *The Laws of Deuteronomy* (Ithaca, NY, 1974) 173.

35 G. von Rad, *Das fünfte Buch Mose* (ATD; Göttingen, 1964) 104f.; A. Phillips, *Deuteronomy* (Cambridge, 1973) 154; P. C. Craigie, *The Book of Deuteronomy* (Grand Rapids, MI, 1976) 296 ff.

36 C. M. Carmichael, *Law and Narrative in the Bible* (Ithaca, NY, 1985) 229ff. טוען שהאיסור על קבלת ממזר בקהל ה' צמח מהמקרה המיוחד של בנות לוט שכוונתן היתה טובה, אבל דרכן במימוש כוונתן לא היתה מקובלת על הדויטרונומיסט. M. Fishbane, *Biblical Inter-pretation in Ancient Israel* (Oxford, 1985) 119 n. 406, טוען שהביטוי 'ערות אביך' שבוי' יח, ז, שאינו תואם את ההמשך, נוסף לאחר הסיפור על בנות לוט שבבר' יט, לא-לח וראה גם מה שכתב בהמשך (עמ' 120) על העריכה הטקסטואלית של דב' כג, א-ט.

37 דב' כג, ג וזכ' ט, ו כשכל אחד מהם מופיע בהקשר שונה וספק אם בהוראה שווה. וראה: א' בן-יהודה, מלון הלשון העברית הישנה והחדשה, כרך ששי (ירושלים-ת"א, 1948); 3066-3067; וכן: BDB, 561; KB, 533.

38 ראה המחלוקת בין התנאים ביחס להגדרת ממזר במשנה יב' ד, יג: 'איזהו ממזר כל שאר בשר שהוא בלא יבוא'; וראה פירושו של ד"צ הופמן לפסוק זה בספר דברים (תל-אביב, תשכ"א) עמי תמה; ארליך, מקרא כפשוטו לספר דברים, (1969) 351.

39 שד"ל (לעיל, הערה 1), עמ' 54, מפרש את דב' כג, ד, בעקבות חז"ל כמוסב על גברים בלבד: 'אין הנשים בכלל, כי לשון ביאה בקהל לא יפול על הזכרים אשר בבואם עם אחר יעשו בקרבו משפחה חדשה, מה שאין כן הנשים, כי משפחת אם אינה קרויה משפחה...'.

העורך, שמצא לנכון לשלב סיפור זה במקום זה, כלומר: אחרי ההבטחות לאברהם בברית על לידת בנו (פרקים טו-יח) ולפני הסיפורים על לידת יצחק בנו ויורשו היחיד והנבחר (פרקים כא-כב). באמצעות סיפור לוט ובנותיו מופקעים צאצאי לוט בדיעבד מקשרי נישואין עם צאצאי אברהם ונותרת משפחת נחור אחיו בלבד.[27] ואמנם לקראת נישואיו של יצחק, לאחר שזכה לרשת את כל ההבטחות האלוהיות שניתנו לאביו שעמד בניסיון העקידה, מופיעה רשימת צאצאי משפחתו של נחור (בר' כב, כ-כד) ובה כלולה רבקה, אשתו היעודה של יצחק (שם, כג). היעדרה של כל רשימת יוחסין של צאצאי לוט ממגילות היוחסין שבספר בראשית והמקרא כולו, מסתברת מן המגמה לנתק את שושלת לוט משושלת אברהם, האגדה האתנולוגית על לידת מואב ובני-עמון מלוט היא הנותנת נימוקו גנטי, אם כי סמוי, להינתקות זו.[28]

באמצעות הנוסחה האטיולוגית החותמת את סיפור המערה (בר' יט, לז[ב], לח[ב]) נכנסים בני לוט למישור ההיסטורי והגיאו-פוליטי עם מורשת כפולה: כיורשים הלגיטימיים של נחלת לוט (בר' יג, י-יא),[29] והאחרת כצאצאי לידת עריות. ככאלה פסולים הם לחיתון עם שושלת אברהם יצחק ויעקב. במזל של כפילות זו מוסברים היחסים שביניהם לבין בני-ישראל במשנה-תורה. מצד אחד, הפרדה גיאוגרפית המבוססת על ההכרה שגבולות מואב ובני עמון הוצבו ושעל בני ישראל לכבדם (דב' ב, ט ואילך). מן הצד האחר, הפרדה פולחנית-לאומית, האוסרת על בואם של עמוני ומואבי בקהל ה' עד עולם (דב' כג, ד).[30] ואולי, לחילופין, סכנת הניתוק מנחלת ה' הארוגה לישראלי הבא להסתפח אליהם (שמ"א כו, יט).[31] הראשון, שקוף יותר והטעה רבים מן הקדמונים והחדשים לראות בו את הכוונה הראשונית והעיקרית של סיפור לוט.[32] האחרון, סמוי ומסתבר בעקיפין ממקומו של הסיפור. דווקא הוא, יותר מן הראשון, תואם את המגמה המטרימה

---

itself obscure the reasons for a prohibition"; R. Wagen, "Taboo," *The Encyclopedia of Religion* 14:234.

27 T. J. Prewitt, "Kinship Structures and the Genesis Genealogies," *JNES* 40(1981) 87-98. הבחין בזאת, אך מבלי שהסיק את המסקנות המתבקשות לעניינו. ראה במיוחד, עמ' 94 הערה 16.

28 שלא כוסטרמן (לעיל, הערה 1), עמ' 379, שראה בשילוב זה רק את הזיקה הגניאלוגית הגלויה כדוגמת זו של הגר וישמעאל.

29 ראה למשל: סימפסון (לעיל, הערה 1), עמ' 631, וכל התולים מוצאה של אגדה זו באיזור הגיאוגרפי של דרום עבר-הירדן המזרחי. על הרקע ההיסטורי-גיאוגרפי ועל העדויות הארכיאולוגיות לצמיחתן של ממלכות מואב ועמון במאה הי"ג לפנה"ס, ראה: N. Glueck, *The Other Side of the Jordan,* (New Haven, 1945); A. H. van Zyl, *The Moabites* (Leiden, 1960); M. Ottosson, *Gilead* (Lund, 1969); J. Sawyer and D. J. A. Clines, eds., *Midian, Moab and Edom* (Sheffield, 1983).

30 חז"ל מבחינים ביסוד בין מואבית למואבי, ואת האיסור בדב' כג, ד מייחסים הם למואבי ולא למואבית. ראה משנה יב' ח, ג 'עמוני ומואבי אסורים, ואיסורן איסור עולם אבל נקבותיהן מותרות מיד ...' ובכל זאת מוצאים אנו במשנה יד' ד, ד מחלוקת בין רבן גמליאל ורבי יהושע אם מותר ליהודה גר עמוני לבוא בקהל, והתירוהו.

31 על המשמעות הפולחנית של 'ספח' (שמ"א ב, לו; ישי יד, א) ראה: P. K. McCarter, *1 Samuel* (AB; Garden City, NY, 1980) 408. על הקשר שבין דוד וביתו ובין מואב ניתן ללמוד משמ"א כב, א-ד, ואולי לשם נתכוון בדבריו אל שאול? על ייחוסו של דוד לרות המואביה, ראה: רות ד, יז-כב.

32 אפילו ון-סתרס הדוחה את שיטת גונקל ותלמידיו לבודד אגדה זו ממסכת הסיפורים הכללית על אברהם, מסכים שהמגמה הראשונית של האטיולוגיה היא לקשר את מוצאם של עמי עבר-הירדן הללו עם לוט. J. Van Seters, *Abraham in History and Tradition* (New Haven, 1975) 221.

אתנולוגיה, אטיולוגיה, גניאלוגיה והיסטוריוגרפיה בסיפור על לוט ובנותיו

הינה הבנת המפתח לפענוח משמעותו האטיולוגית וההיסטוריוסופית, כפי שנתפרשה על־ידי המחבר הישראלי. לקשר זה נקדיש את הבחנותינו הנוגעות גם לסיפור מלגוו וגם לאינטרפרטציות שנתלו בו מלברו.

בסיפור עצמו אין כוונה לגנות את בנות לוט על המעשה שעשו, וספק אם יש כוונה כזו לגבי לוט אביהן.[21] בנסיבות המתוארות בסיפור, אפילו נפרידו ונבודדו לחלוטין מסיפור סדום ועמורה כדרך שהציעו גונקל ותלמידיו, עשו בנות לוט את ההכרחי להמשך קיומו של המין האנושי. פעמיים חוזרת ההנמקה יונחיה מאבינו זרע׳ (פס׳ לב, לד).[22] אלא, שעל־מנת לממש מטרה חיובית זו כשלעצמה, נהגו שלא ׳כדרך כל הארץ׳. מודעות לסטייתן מן הנורמות המקובלות השקו את אביהן יין. בכך קיבלו על עצמן את האחריות עבור החטא והסירוה מעל אביהן.[23] במושגים שאולים ניתן להגדיר את מעשה בנות לוט כ״מצוה הבאה בעבירה״. הסתירה הפנימית הזו, של מצוה הבאה בעבירה הינה מהותית בסיפור זה, וכל שיפוט מוסרי הנוטה לדון מעשה זה כולו לזכות, או כולו לחובה, מתעלם מן המשמעות האמיתית של הסיפור שהיא דווקא דו־ערכיות המוסרית שלו.[24] כל ניסיון לפרש דו־ערכיות זו כתולדה של שתי השקפות שונות על המעשה: האחת מואבית־עמונית הרואה בו מעשה הירואי שיש להתפאר בו, והאחרת, ישראלית, הרואה בו חטא של עריות שיש לגנותו — אין לו אחיזה בסיפור עצמו.[25] אם קיימים בסיפור שני רבדים הם הינם במימד הזמן, כפי שהבהרנו לעיל, אבל לא במימד המוסרי.

כיצד מתקשרת, איפוא, פרשנותנו על דו־ערכיותו של הסיפור עם מסקנתנו שסיפור זה הובא על־מנת לרמוז מדוע לא נוצרו קשרי נישואין בין בני אברהם ובני לוט? הקשר ביניהם הינו תיפקודי ויישומי, והוא משקף את מגמתו של מי שערך את הסיפורים על האבות במסגרת גניאלוגית. הבדלתו של זרע אברהם מזרע לוט על־ידי הימנעות מקשרי חיתון ביניהם אכן קשורה ללידתם של בני לוט מעריות, אך פסילתם לנישואין לא באה בשל חטאם המוסרי של הוריהם, וודאי שלא בשל חטאם הם. התייחסותו של עורך זה הינה לתוצאת המעשה ולא לסיבותיו. הנולדים מ״נישואי־בוסר״ אלו נושאים עמם פגם גנטי מלידה, מעין טומאה מרחם, המונע מזרע אברהם, יצחק ויעקב מלהתחתן בהם. אין בסיפור עצמו לא נימוק מוסרי ואף לא נימוק דתי לכך בדומה למנהגים אחרים של ״טאבו״, שהם כביכול מובנים מאליהם גם כאשר סיבותיהם נעלמות.[26] אולם הקשרו התפקודי במסגרת הסיפורים על אברהם משקף את מגמת

---

[21] כבר חז״ל נחלקו ביניהם ביחס להערכת התנהגותם של לוט (ראה בר״ר נא, י). המצדדים בזכותו מסתמכים בעיקר על מידת הכנסת האורחים שגילה בסיפור על הפיכת סדום (בר׳ יט, א-ח) ועל העובדה שהיה שיכור בעת ששכב עם בנותיו. ראה למשל רד״ק (לעיל, הערה 1), עמ׳ נא. אך ראה הסתייגותו של ליונשטם בעניין זה, (לעיל, הערה 4), עמ׳ 448. לביקורת סרקסטית זוכה לוט בפירושו של: B. Vawter, *On Genesis* (New York, 1977) 242.

[22] כך אצל גונקל ורוב המפרשים ההולכים בעקבותיו. אך ראה גם: בנו יעקב (לעיל, הערה 1), עמ׳ 464; טליה רודין־אוברסקי, מאלוני ממרא עד סדום (ירושלים, תשמ״ב) 137.

[23] קאסוטו בהתייחסו לסיפור שכרונו של נוח וגילוי ערוותו (ט, כ-כט) מצביע על הזיקה שבין הסיפור ובין חב׳ ב, טו: ׳הוי משקה רעהו מספח חמתך ואף שכר למען הביט על מעוריהם׳. לדעתו מכוונת תוכחת הנביא כלפי בבל שעל־פי לוח העמים (בר׳ י, י) היתה ראשית מלכותו של נמרוד בן כוש בן חם שגילה ערוות אביו. ראה פירושו על ספר בראשית (ירושלים, תשל״ד) 103-104.

[24] קיליאן אכן מציע להשתחרר מן החשיבה המוסרית בפירוש הסיפור, אך הוא עצמו אינו מקפיד על כך, ראה: קיליאן (לעיל, הערה 1), עמ׳ 137 ואילך.

[25] לונג עמד על כך שהניתוח של הסיפור מראה שהפורמולה האטימולוגית־אטיולוגית מתייחסת לסיפור כולו, ראה: B. Long, *The Problem of Etiological Narrative in the Old Testament* (BZAW 108; Berlin, 1968) 51.

[26] "Taboo is not so much a system of regulations as it is a scheme of negative differentiation, in which the fact of prohibition and the prohibited act or object

והעקרוניות שלפנינו אגדה אתנולוגית מואבית בלבוש ישראלי נותרה בעינה. דומה שהגורסים כך
אף לא טרחו לשאול את עצמם: מה הניע את המחבר הישראלי להעתיק אגדה זו שלפי השקפתם
כולה שבח לצאצאי לוט על מוצאם ולהציבה במקום שהציבה? היחיד מבין הפרשנים החדשים
שהציג שאלה זו בפירושו היה ספייזר.[17] מתוך הכרה שהסיפור הזה אינו מכוון לגנות את
המואבים והעמונים על מוצאם, אלא משקף מציאות שקדמה ליחסי האיבה ההיסטוריים שבין
הישראלים ובין שכניהם אלה, הסיק ספייזר ששכנים אלה היו חשובים מדי מכדי להתעלם
מהם.[18] תשובתו אמנם מסבירה את עצם הימצאותו של הסיפור במקרא, אך לא את חשיבותו
ותפקידו בהקשר המיוחד ששובץ בו. מהו, איפוא, התפקיד שנועד לסיפור לידתם של בני-לוט,
מואב ובני-עמון, בתולדות אבי ישראל?

התשובה המוצעת להלן היא שהסיפור שובץ במקומו על-מנת להקדים ולהסביר מדוע לא
נתקיימו יחסי-נישואין בין בני אברהם ובין בני לוט, ומדוע טרח אברהם לקחת ליצחק בנו אשה
ממרחקים, מבני נחור אחיו (בר' כד). לכאורה, ניתן להסביר זאת בכך שללוט נולדו מזיווגין אלו
בנים בלבד, אולם בדיעבד מסתבר שאף יעקב נכד אברהם מצטווה לשאת אשה רק ממשפחת
נחור (בר' כח, א-ב) בעוד שהאפשרות לקחת אשה ממשפחת לוט בן אחי אברהם אינה נזכרת
כלל. מתעורר, איפוא, חשד שיש קשר סמוי בין הסיפור על לידת מואב ועמון ובין האיסור שבדב'
כג, ד: 'לא יבא עמוני ומואבי בקהל ה' גם דור עשירי לא יבא להם בקהל ה' עד עולם', שהרי
על-פי הסיפור לידתם של המואבים והעמונים היתה מראש 'שלא כדרך כל הארץ'. איסור כזה
אינו מופיע בשורת האיסורים שבספר דברים ביחס לישמעאל ואילו ביחס לאדומים הוא מופיע
בצורה הרבה יותר מתונה: 'לא תתעב אדומי כי אחיך הוא ... דור שלישי יבוא להם בקהל ה''
(שם, ח-ט).[19] זהו כנראה גם הטעם מדוע לא מופיעה בספר בראשית, ואף לא במקום אחר
במקרא, רשימת תולדות בני לוט, כדרך שמוצאים אנו רשימות כאלה בקשר לנחור (בר' כב, כ-
כד), לישמעאל (שם, כה יב-יח) ולעשר-אדום (שם, לו).[20]

מבין כל הפרשנים שעיינתי בהם רק אבן-עזרא רמז בכיוון זה, אף שכוונתו היתה שונה משלנו.
בפירושו לבר' יט, לז נאמר: 'וטעם עד היום שלא התערב עמם גוי זר, או זה הדבר ידוע עד היום'.
אם לכך נתכוונו כל אלה מבית-מדרשו של גונקל ואחרים שטענו למשמעות ישראלית מאוחרת
שנשתלתה על אגדה מואבית-עמונית קדומה, הרי שלא הסיקו מזאת את המסקנות הנכונות לגבי
המחבר. והרי הבנת הקשר שבין הסיפור המקורי כשלעצמו ובין ההקשר הרחב שבו הוא משולב

מן המסורת הפרה-ליטררית: ראשיתה, המוטיב של צמיחת חיים חדשים מן החורבן, דרך האגדה
האטיולוגית השבטית של זוג השבטים השכנים מואב ועמון ועד לשילובה בתולדות האבות.

17 ספייזר (לעיל, הערה 1), עמ' 145.

18 ספייזר, שם, עמ' 146, הסברו של נות דומה, ראה: M. Noth, *A History of Pentateuchal Traditions* (New York, 1972) 192.

19 השימוש בביטוי 'לא תתעב', בא כנראה להגדיר את ההבדל המשמעותי שביניהם לבין העמוני
והמואבי שביחס אליהם מופיע הביטוי 'כתעבותיהם', בעז' ט, א.

20 הסבר על העדרה של רשימת יוחסין של בני לוט לא מצאתי אצל: י' ליוור, "יחסי", אנציקלופדיה
מקראית ג, 663-671. אף לא במחקרים העוסקים ביחס שבין הגניאלוגיה להיסטוריה במקרא, כמו
לאחרונה של: R. R. Wilson, *Genealogy and History in the Biblical World* (New Haven, 1971); J. Van Seters, "The Primeval Histories of Greece and Israel Compared," *ZAW* 100 (1988) 1-22. האחרון מזכיר את העובדה שאין המשך לשושלת לוט
ומשווה זאת עם מקבילה מן הגניאלוגיות המופיעות ב"קטלוג של נשים" של הסיוד, ששם נגמרת
רשימת השושלת של חותוס בן הלן בציון שני בניו אלאיוס ואיון שהפכו שמות שני עמים. בעוד
שרשימות השושלת של שני בניו האחרים של הלן, דורוס ואיילוס מתרחבות ביותר, אולם, מהו
הגורם להבדל זה, לא פירש.

אתנולוגיה, אטיולוגיה, גניאלוגיה והיסטוריוגרפיה בסיפור על לוט ובנותיו   45*

פירוש כוונת הסיפור תלויה, איפוא, בפירוש מגמת המחבר, וזו משתקפת מן הדו־מימדיות של הזמן המגולם בו. המימד האירועי־הממשי של המעשה עצמו, והמימד ההיסטורי־פרספקטיבי שבניסוח האטיולוגי החותם אותו 'הוא אבי מואב (בני עמון) עד היום' (שם לז׳, לח׳).[11] הדו־מימדיות ניכרת לא רק בזמן אלא גם בנולדים. אלה הופכים בנוסחת הקדם האטיולוגית־אטימולוגית ('הוא... עד היום') מבנים לעמים היסטוריים. כך מתחוללת בסוף הסיפור תמורה מן האפיזודה הבודדת והכמעט־מיתית אל תחום ההיסטוריה הבינלאומית.

גונקל היה הראשון שניסה לתת לכך הסבר ספרותי־שיטתי שונה מזה של הביקורת ההיסטורית־ספרותית של המאה הי״ט, שזיהתה באגדה זו רק רובד אחד של זמן, את זה של המחבר. הוא הבחין בין האגדה הבודדת, על־פי טיבה וחומריה ובין המשמעות ההיסטורית המאוחרת שנתלוותה אליה מאוחר יותר.[12] את האגדה הגדיר על־פי השיטה הגנטית־ספרותית שפיתח כ״אגדה אתנולוגית״. על־פי טיבה הינה מיתית־פואטית, מה שניכר ממרכיביה, ומן הדמיון המוטיבי שבינה לבין המיתוס היוני על מירה (סמירנה) שהשקתה את אביה יין, הרתה ממנו וילדה לו.[13] במקורה היתה מואבית־עמונית ויצגה את גאות עמים אלה על מוצאם, כפי שניתן ללמוד ממתן השמות על־ידי האימהות: מאב ובן־עמי. המשמעות ההיסטורית המאוחרת משתקפת במגמה הישראלית להציג צאצאי עמים אלה בקלונם, מה שמוצא ביטוי קיצוני באיסור על בוא־ם בקהל ה' בדב' כג, ד. כמו כן בנבואות הלעג לעמים אלו (ישי׳ טז, ז ואילך; ירי׳ מח, יא ואילך). דע־עקא, גונקל לא הוכיח כלל את קיומם של שני רבדים אלה בסיפור עצמו, ולא השכיל להראות היכן מסתיימת האגדה המקורית ומה נוסף אליה בסיפור על־מנת לסגלה להשקפתו של המחבר הישראלי. גם את ההשערה על מוצאה המואבי־עמוני של האגדה שנתגלגלה לאוזני המחבר הישראלי מן הסתם באמצעות המסורת שבעל־פה, לא השכיל לבסס על הכתוב עצמו, לא מבחינת המוטיב, ולא מבחינת הסגנון והלשון. בכתובות המואביות והעמוניות שנמצאו עד כה אין כל רמז לאגדת־מוצא כזו ואף לא נמצא מאחז היסטורי שיסביר מי משני העמים ומתי היה מעוניין להדגיש את מוצאם המשותף.

קוצר ידו של גונקל בניתוח הסיפור לרבדיו לא מנע שורה ארוכה של פרשנים ללכת בעקבותיו.[14] אף לא הניעם להשלים את החסר בכל הנוגע לשיחזורה של האגדה המקורית המואבית־עמונית ולעורטלה מלבושי המגמתי של המחבר הישראלי שעשה בה שימוש לרעה. רובם ככולם אף זיהו מחבר זה כיהוויסט, והגדירוהו על־פי הגירסות השונות של מקור זה.[15] במרוצת הזמן, נוספו כמה הבחנות בפרטים והוארו כמה עניינים, במיוחד על־ידי תלמידו וסטרמן.[16] אולם ההנחה העיקרית

---

11 זהו הסיום המאפיין את האגדות האטיולוגיות על־פי גונקל. בהיותו מנמק תופעה הווית באגדת־קדומים. כאן לראשונה מופיע בספר בראשית, ובצורה זו רק עוד בברי׳ לה, כ, בדרך כלל מופיעה הצורה 'עד היום הזה' וראה: בר׳ כו, לג; לב, לג; דב׳ לד, ו ועוד.

12 גונקל, (לעיל, הערה 1), עמ׳ 217-218.

13 האגדה מובאת בלקסיקון של: W. H. Roscher, *Ausführliches Lexicon der griechischen und römischen Mythologie* (Leipzig, 1884-86) 1:1, 69ff.

14 ראה (לעיל, הערה 1): פרוקש, עמ׳ 129; סקינר, מצדד בפירושו של גונקל בהסתייגות מה, עמ׳ 314; פון־ראד, עמ׳ 218-220; סימפסון, עמ׳ 631 ואילך; קיליאן, עמ׳ 136-141; לוק, עמ׳ 83-95; וסטרמן, עמ׳ 379 ואילך. ראוי לציין שאף בנו יעקב, עמ׳ 464, מקבל את דעתו של גונקל על מגמתו החיובית של הסיפור על בנות לוט מבלי שישכים לרבדים השונים שגילה בו גונקל וכמובן לא לייחוסו ל־J. במגמה החיובית של הסיפור מכיר אף ספייזר, עמ׳ 145, אולם מתקשה להכריע אם הוא ממוצא ישראלי, או ממוצא עמוני־מואבי, כפי שטוען גונקל.

15 גונקל, סימפסון, פרוקש, פון־ראד, ספייזר, קיליאן וסטרמן — כולם מייחסים סיפור זה למקור J וזאת בהסתמך על ביטויים המאפיינים לדעתם את J, כמו: 'הבכירה', 'הצעירה', 'לחיות זרע'.

16 וסטרמן (לעיל, הערה 1), עמ׳ 379-385 מבחין בשלוש שכבות שמהן התהווה הסיפור בתהליך ממושך

שנחלקו בינייהם בנוגע לכוונתן של בנות לוט בהתעברותן מאביהן, בהסתמכם על כתובים אחרים במקרא המספרים על יחסי־מין בין בני ישראל ובנות מואב. בבר״ר נא, י מצאנו:[5] ״הה״ד ״אני ידעתי נאם יי עברתו לא כן״ (ירי מח, ל). ר׳ חננא בר פפא אמר מתחילת עיבורו של מואב לא היה לשם זנות אלא לשם שמים, ״בדיו לא כן עשו״ (שם, שם) אלא לשם זנות ״וישב ישראל בשטים ויחל העם לזנות אל בנות מואב״ (במי כה, א). ר׳ סימון אמר מתחילת עיבורו של מואב לא היה לשם שמים אלא לשום זנות, ״בדיו לא כן עשו״, אלא לשם שמים ״בדיו לא כן עשו״, ״ותרד הגרן כאשר צותה חמותה״ (רות ג, ו)׳. הגישה המשותפת לשניהם היא שאין כוונת האם סימן לבנות, אלא ההיפוך: מהתנהגות הבנות ניתן ללמוד על הכוונה המקורית של האם.[6] שלא כמותם סובר ר׳ לוי, הטוען: ׳אם תחילת עיבורו לשם זנות אף סופו לשם זנות ״בדיו לא כן עשו״, ״וישב ישראל בשטים״, אם תחילת עיבורו לשם שמים אף סופו לשם שמים ״בדיו לא כן עשו״, ״ותרד הגרן״׳. הוא גוזר גזירה שווה מן הכוונה אל התולדה כשהוא דורש את הביטוי ׳בדיו לא כן עשו׳ כלשון תמיהה.[7]

בהערכת המעשה של בנות לוט מתמקדת גם המחלוקת בין הפרשנים החדשים, אלא שהם מבקשים לגלות בו יותר את כוונתו של המספר, מאשר את כוונת גיבוריו. גישתם דומה לזו של ר׳ לוי שאין לחפש הנגדה בין כוונת האימהות ובין התנהגותן של הבנות. אף הם, כקדמונים, מנסים להקיש מן הניסיון ההיסטורי של יחסי ישראל עם העממים בני לוט על טיב המעשה, אולם מבלי שייחסו ניסיון זה רק לקשרי מין עם בנות מואב. על־פי סברתם משקף המעשה על לוט ובנותיו את יחסו של המספר הישראלי לשני עממים אלה: מואב ועמון. כך נוטים פרשנים מן המאה הי״ט למצוא בסיפור זה מגמה להשפיל את שכני ישראל אלה ולבוז להם על מוצאם המגונה. זאת בהסתמך על דב׳ כג, ד האוסר בואם של בני עמים אלה בקהל ה׳. הם תולים מגמה זו באיבה שצמחה בישראל כלפי שני עמים אלה, במהלך היחסים ההיסטוריים הבינלאומיים שביניהם ובין ישראל.[8] אחרים, שביקשו לפרש את מעשה בנות לוט לזכות — כמעשה הירואי שנועד לקיים את המשך הזרע נוכח סכנת הכליון של המין האנושי — הסתמכו על מקורות מקראיים המגלים יחס של כבוד כלפי עמים אלה, כמו: דב׳ ב, ט, יג, שבו מוזהרים בני ישראל לכבד את גבול של בני־לוט.[9] וכבר קדם להם רד״ק בפירושו על התורה שכתב: ׳וכל הספור הזה נכתב כדי להודיע תולדות עמון ומואב כי מבני לוט היו שתי האומות האלה והאל נתן להם ארץ נחלה לאהבת אברהם אביו שהיה לוט בין אחיו ומרבית ביתו, ומנע את ישראל שלא יצורו אותם ולא יתגרו בם מלחמה, כי לא נתן מארצם עד מדרך כף רגל כי לבני לוט נתן אותם ירושה...׳.[10]

״לוט״, אנציקלופדיה מקראית ד (ירושלים, תש״ל) 447-448.

5 בר״ר, עם מראה מקומות וחילופי נוסחאות ופירוש מנחת יהודה מאת יהודה טהעאדאר, מחברת ז (ברלין, תרע״ג) 540.

6 זאת בהסתמך על יר׳ מח, ל: ׳אני ידעתי נאם ה׳ עברתו ולא כן בדיו לא כן עשו׳ שאותו הם דורשים: ׳עברתו׳ במשמעות עיבורו, ו׳בדיו׳ במשמעות צאצאיו. ושיעור הדברים עיבורו של מואב לא היה כמו שעשו בדיו (צאצאיו). גירסה שונה של הפסוק מופיעה בישי טז, ו עליו מסתמך המדרש המובא במדרש הגדול שיצא לאור על־ידי מרדכי מרגליות (הוצאת הרב קוק, ירושלים, תשכ״ז) עמי שכו. גירסת יר׳ מח, ל מורכבת, ובחסרונו משבית סדר הדברים ולא כן בדיו, זה חבור הדברים כתוב בישי טז, ו ודין האתנא בבדיי.

7 המשכו של המדרש שצויין לעיל בהערה 5 והפירוש בעקבות מנחת יהודה, שם עמי 540.

8 ראה ביחוד דילמן (לעיל, הערה 1), עמי 113, המסתמך על קנובל, הופפלד, שרדר, קייזר וולהאוזן. דרייבר (להלן, הערה 34), עמי 203, מצטט אותו אבל בהסתייגות כשהוא עצמו נוטה להערכה מאוזנת יותר ביחס לכוונת הסיפור.

9 ראה דליטש (לעיל הערה 1), עמי 65; הולצינגר (לעיל, הערה 1), עמי 157-158.

10 פירוש רד״ק (לעיל, הערה 1), עמי נא. וראה גם ד״צ הופמן (לעיל, הערה 1), עמי שיג.

אתנולוגיה, אטיולוגיה, גניאלוגיה והיסטוריוגרפיה בסיפור על לוט ובנותיו
(בר׳ יט, ל-לח)[1]

זאב ויסמן

עיון מוקדם בפירושים השונים לסיפור זה מגלה עד כמה נתקשו המפרשים השונים לרדת לסוף כוונתו.[2] אמנם הסיפור עצמו ברור בתוכנו ובלשונו, לא נמצאו בו לא סתירות ולא כפילויות, אף לא שברים ותוספות שיעידו על חוסר שלמות ועל אי-אחידות,[3] ובכל-זאת זכה לפרשנויות שונות ומנוגדות. את אשר לא השכילו הפרשנים לגלות מגוו ניסו לפרש מלברו, כשהם נאחזים בהתייחסויות השונות במקרא אל בני-לוט: מואב ועמון.[4] ראשיתה של מחלוקת זו אצל חז״ל,

---

1 המאמר נכתב בעת שהותי כעמית מחקר אורח בסמינר התיאולוגי של פרינסטון, אביב 1988. תודתי והוקרתי נתונה למארחי.

2 פירושים לבראשית: מקראות גדולות; פירושי רד״ק על התורה, ספר בראשית (פרעסבורג תר״ב לפ״ק) (ירושלים, תשכ״ה); א׳ ארליך, מקרא כפשוטו, א (ברלין, תרנ״ט; דפוס צילום: ניו-יורק, 1969); שד״ל, חמישה חומשי תורה, (פאדובה, התרל״א; תל-אביב תשל״ב); ד׳ הופמן, ספר בראשית ב, (בני-ברק, תשל״א); F. Delitzsch, *New Commentary on Genesis* (2 vols.; New York, 1889); A. Dillmann, *Genesis* (2 vols.; Edinburgh, 1897); H. Holzinger, *Genesis* (Freiburg, 1898); H. Gunkel, *Genesis* (Göttingen, 1969); J. Skinner, *Genesis* (ICC; Edinburgh, 1912); O. Procksch, *Die Genesis* (Leipzig, 1913); B. Jacob, *Das erste Buch der Tora, Genesis* (New York, 1934); C. A. Simpson, "The Book of Genesis" (*IB*; Nashville, 1952); G. von Rad, *Genesis* (OTL; Philadelphia, 1961); E. A. Speiser, *Genesis* (AB; Garden City, NY, 1964); R. Kilian, *Die vorpriesterlichen Abrahams-Überlieferungen* (BBB 24; Bonn, 1966); K. Luke, *Studies on the Book of Genesis* (Always, India, 1975); C. Westermann, *Genesis* (BKAT 2; Neukirchen-Vluyn, 1981).

3 פרט לפסוק ל׳ שהוא כשלעצמו איחוי בין סיפור זה ובין הסיפור על צוער, מחד-גיסא, והסיפור על הפיכת סדום, מאידך-גיסא. כפי שמעידה החזרה ׳וישבי – ׳הוא ושתי בנותיו׳ – שבשני חלקי הפסוק, וראה הפירושים הביקורתיים דלעיל, וביחוד: וסטרמן, עמ׳ 381.

4 הכינויי ׳בני לוטי׳ מופיע רק בדב׳ ב, ט, יט ובתה׳ פג, ט. הוא כשלעצמו אינו מעיד שלוט נחשב כאפונים של מואב ועמון. מאידך, יש משמעות לשימוש בכינויי זה להבנת הזיקה שבין סיפור זה ובין התייחסויות אחרות במקרא בענין היחסים בין ישראל ובין מואב ובני-עמון. ועיין: ש׳ ליונשטם,

בצלע הראשונה של הפסוק האחרון מעצב בעל המזמור את הרגשתו המגובשת, הסופית, את טיב יחסו של ה׳ אליו, בצלע השנייה ממחיש הוא את יחסו שלו אל ה׳ ׳לארך ימים׳. תיאור זמן זה מביע מה שאינו מובע בקודמו, ׳כל ימי חיי׳, היינו את אריכות הזמן שלפי הרגשת בעל המזמור יתקיים יחסו זה של ה׳.

המשפט הפותח את פס׳ ו הוא דינאמי מאוד, המסיים סטאטי. הפסוק כולו עומד אפוא ביחס כיאסטי כלפי פס׳ ב המתחיל בהמחשת יחסו של ה׳ אל בעל המזמור. שם המשפט הראשון סטאטי: ׳בנאות דשא ירביצני׳, בעוד שמשנהו דינאמי: ׳על מי מנחות ינהלני׳. תחושה של סיום, של סגירת המסגרת עולה גם מתוך איזכורו של שם הוויה. זה מופיע בראש המזמור: ׳ה׳ רעי׳, ובסיומו: ׳ושבתי בבית ה׳.׳[78] איזכורו הראשון של ה׳ מציין את יחסו אל בעל המזמור, איזכורו השני את יחסו של בעל המזמור אליו.

---

78 השווה ויסבליט (לעיל, הערה 38), עמ׳ 230; G. H. Carlson, "Shepherd and Host: A Literary Look at Psalm 23," *The Bible Today* 78 (1975) 401.

כפי שמתברר מן ההקשר, המכוון ב'טוב וחסד' הוא יחסו של ה'. בגלל ההדרגה המתבטאת ב'חסדי' לעומת 'טובי', אולי ניתן להניח כי משמעותה של וי"ו החיבור שלפני המלה: אף, אפילו.[69] מכל מקום בדבר הוא בעל המזמור על מצבו במשפט זה, הוא אינו אומר: 'אך טוב וחסד' מנת חלקי או כדומה, אלא 'ירדפוני'. הכוונה בבחירת נשוא זה דווקא תתברר אם ניתן את הדעת על כך, שבהזכרת 'גיא צלמות' (פס' ד) ו'צררי' (פס' ה) משתקף שמבחינה אובייקטיבית בעל המזמור נרדף. מהתייחסויותיו בעקיפין אל מצבו זה בתחילה הוא מעיד על עצמו שגם בהיותו נרדף הוא אינו ירא רע (פס' ד), אחר כך הוא מוסר שבנוכחות רודפיו ה' עורך שולחן לו (פס' ה) ולבסוף הוא מגיע לידי ההכרה שעל־אף צורריו רודפיו: 'טוב וחסד', טובו וחסדו של ה', הם בעקבותי, הם אינם מרפים ממנו כל ימי חייו.

פס' ו[3]: 'ושבתי בבית ה' לארץ ימים' — במחלוקות הפרשנים על המשפט חלוקות הדעות גם על מהימנות הגירסה של הנשוא כנתינתה שלפיה הוא הפועל הגזור מן השורש שו"ב. פירושי המשפט כמדבר על שיבה אל 'בית ה'' גוררים דרשות, מדרשות שונות.[70] ואולם, לאור העובדה שיש מזמורים שבהם מדובר בשהייה בבית ה', ביניהם גם בלשון 'ישבי',[71] ועוד יותר לאור העובדה ששני הפעלים 'שב', 'ישבי' לא־פעם מתחלפים גם בנוסח המסורה,[72] מתקבלת דעת חוקרים לא־מעטים שגם בנוסח האותנטי של משפטנו שימש כנשוא הפועל 'ישבי'.[73] מן השיחזורים המוצעים נראה כסביר ביותר 'ושבתי',[74] היינו 'ישבי' במקור נטוי של בניין קל עם כינוי המדבר. ובכן, הצד היצורי המסור של הפועל מהימן, ואשר לניקודו — השי"ן פתוחה במקום חרוקה. תופעה שיש כי גם בעלי המסורה עמדו עליה.[75] לפי משפטנו, בעל המזמור, הנרדף על־ידי טובו וחסדו של ה', מצהיר שישבתו היא 'בבית ה''.

המכוון בביטוי 'בבית ה'' גם הוא שנוי במחלוקת. הרוב המכריע של פרשני מזמורנו[76] סבורים כי פשוטו כמשמעו, היינו בית המקדש. ואולם כפי שנקבע,[77] לפי פירוש זה אין שום קשר קוהרנטי בין צלע זו של פסוקנו ובין קודמתה. יתרה מזו. משפטו האחרון של המזמור אינו משתלב כלל וכלל במזמורנו, לא בתוכנו ולא בסגנונו. מעניינו וממסכת אריגתו של המזמור מתבקשת המסקנה שכשם שבתמונות דומות המומחש אינו קשור למקדש או לפולחן, כך בדבריו של בעל המזמור 'וישבתי בבית ה'' מתבטא שהוא שרוי באופן קבוע עם ה'.

---

69 כגון שמ"ב א, כג; קה' ה, ו.
70 ראה הפירושים המחזיקים בנוסח המסורה בסקירתו של מק-דניאל (לעיל, הערה 1), עמ' 3-38.
71 תה' כז, ג; פד, ה. השווה גם צא, א. בלשון 'שכן': תה' טו, א; סה, ה. ה'גור': תה' טו, א; סא, ה. דאהוד ופרידמן (לעיל, הערה 23), עמ' 162 מניחים ש'ישבתי' משורש שו"י שהוא צורת משנה של יש"ב.
72 על חילופי שני הפעלים בנוסח המסורה ראה הולדיי (לעיל, הערה 26), עמ' 158-160; מק-דניאל (לעיל, הערה 1), עמ' 192-193. הולדיי הביא גם את הכתובים שבהם הפועל בנוסח המסורה מוחלף בתרגומים העתיקים.
73 נשוא זה כבר משתקף בתרגומים העתיקים או כתרגום של 'וישבתי' (ע' ס' ו') או של 'וֹשַׁבְתִּי' (היארונימוס, פ' ת').
74 מן החוקרים בעשרות השנים האחרונות השוללים את מהימנות הגירסה שבנוסח המסורה, כך סבורים, למשל A. Szörényi, *Psalmen und Kult in Alten Testament* (Budapest, 1961) 529; גינונסן (לעיל, הערה 28), עמ' 262; מיטמן (לעיל, הערה 23), עמ' 14, הע' 11.
75 למשל, יחז' לה, ט, כתוב: 'תישבנה', קרי: 'תשובנה'.
76 מן החוקרים בדורנו, כגון סֶרֶנְיִי (לעיל, הערה 74), עמ' 529; בֶּיֶרְלִין (לעיל, הערה 39), עמ' 111; גינונסון (לעיל, הערה 28), עמ' 262; R. von Ungern-Sternberg, "Das 'Wohnen im Hause Gottes': Eine terminologische Psalmenstudie," *KD* 17 (1970) 216; מק-דניאל (לעיל, הערה 1), עמ' 159-205; מילר (לעיל, הערה 22), עמ' 117.
77 ראה, למשל O. Eissfeldt, "Bleiben im Hause J...s," *Kleine Schriften* (Tübingen, 1973) 5:115.

המקרא כסמל של דבר טוב בגיוונים שונים.[58] הסיכה בשמן, שבה מדובר כאן, היא נוהג רווח שממנו היו נמנעים בימי אבל,[59] הואיל ופעולה זו נחשבה כסימן לשמחה.[60] לציון הפעולות של משיחה בשמן לצרכים שונים משמשים במקרא הפעלים 'משח, סך' וגם 'יצק' כמה פעמים, 'דשן' משמש כאן בלבד. מסתבר שהשימוש היחידאי הזה ודווקא בשורש שעיקר הוראתו קרובה לשורש שמ"ן, הוא בעל משמעות. בצירוף 'דשנת בשמן' מובעת סיכה בכמות גדולה של שמן, ובשמושו בדרך השאלה משמעות הביטוי: גרימת שמחה רבה מאוד, אם אמנם לא בלתי רגילה. במשפט הנדון לא רק השימוש בפועל 'דשן' הוא יחריגי, אלא גם שימושו של הפועל בצורת פעל ('דשנת') בעוד צורת הפועל שלפניו ('תערך') — בעצם כל הפעלים — היא ביפעל. האם גם "חריגה" זו היא מחושבת ולא רק פורמאלית גרידה? בין המתייחסים אל צורת הפועל יש הסבורים ש'דשנת' מציין פעולה בעבר ושהפעולה של 'דשנת' בשמן ראשי קדמה ל'תערך' לפני שלחן' וגו'.[61] אך הסבר זה מוטל בספק בעצם בשל העובדה שדרכה של צורת פעל לציין פעולה בהווה ואף בעתיד,[62] ולא רק בעבר. ואולי (!) אפשר גם לטעון נגד המסקנה ההיא המוסקת מצורת 'דשנת' בשני הפסוקים המזכירים אכילה או שתייה עם סיכה בשמן (עמ' ו; דנ' י, ד), מוזכרת הסיכה אחרונה. כהסבר לשוני בצורת הפעלים שבשתי צלעות פסוקנו, נראית הסברה[63] שכאן, כמו בכתובים לא-מעטים בוא פועל בצורת פָּעַל אחרי פועל ביפעל, משמש הפועל בפעל כביאור של המעוצב בפועל שביפעל. אם כן את שני המשפטים הראשונים של הפסוק יש לפרש: אתה עורך שולחן ... בִּדַשֶׁנְךָ בשמן את ראשי.[64]

'כוסי רויה'. — המלה 'רויה' המופיעה עוד פעם במקרא (תה' סו, יב) מציינת את מצבו של הרווה, שפע, שׂבע. כנראה משמשת היא כאן כנשוא המשפט.[65] וכן באמור בעל המזמור: 'כוסי רויה', מכריז הוא שכוסו היא גדושה — ככל הנראה ביין. נמצא שבפסוק הנדון מביע בעל המזמור שמול צורריו ה' מגלה את דאגתו לו, הוא מכין לו מזון ולא זו בלבד אלא אף מענג אותו במידה יתרה, ולא רק בתענוג חיצוני, בסיכת ראשו בשמן, כי אם גם בתענוג פנימי בנתינת יין ישמח לבב אנוש' (תה' קד, טו). אמור מעתה: גם הפעם משתקפת התעמקות הדרגתית בהכרת יחסי דאגנותו של ה'.

פס' ו': 'אַךְ טוֹב וָחֶסֶד יִרְדְּפוּנִי כָּל יְמֵי חַיָּי' — מלת החיבור 'אך' כאן לשון הדגשה יתרה, או הדגשת ודאות: אכן, אמנם כן, באמת, או הדגשת הגבלה: רק, בלבד.[66] 'טובו' משמש כמו בפעמים לא-מעטות[67] כשם עצם בהתכוונו לטוב הקורה את האדם ואילו 'חסד' מציין 'נאמנות, הזדהות,[68]

---

58 ראה, למשל, קה' ז, א. ראה עוד א' שטרן, "שמן", אנציקלופדיה מקראית ח (ירושלים, תשמ"ב) 124-125.

59 ראה שמ"ב יב, כ; יד, ב; יש' סא, ג; דנ' י, ג. ראה עוד י' ליוור, "משיחה", אנציקלופדיה מקראית ה (ירושלים, תשכ"ח) 527.

60 תה' מה, ח; צב, יא; קלח, ב; קה' ט, ח.

61 כפי שסבורים גונקל; G. Schwarz, "'...einen Tisch angesichts meiner Feinde'?" *VT* 20 (1970) 120; ראה גם: L. Koehler, "Psalm 23," *ZAW* 68 (1956) 232.

62 ראה ג"ק (לעיל, הערה 6), §106g-o.

63 §13 D. Michel, *Tempora und Satzstellung in den Psalmen* (Bonn, 1960); מיטמן (לעיל, הערה 23), עמ' 12.

64 מיכל (לעיל, הערה 63), §13, 22.

65 ג"ק (לעיל, הערה 6), §141c.

66 ראה: "אך" *HALAT*.

67 כגון דב' ו, כד; י, יג; ל, ט; יש' נב, ז; יר' ו, טז; לב, מ; טו; ח, טו, לט; זכ' ט, יז; תה' ד, ז; כה, יג; לג, ה; יא, יג ועוד.

68 ראה: "חסד" *HALAT*.

צורכי האכילה. — יש שהמלה 'לפני' משמשת במובן: לרשותו של, בשביל,[51] זהו שימושה גם הפעם. כוונת 'לפני' אפוא: בשבילי. בפנייתו זו אל ה' אומר בעל המזמור אליו, שהוא, ה', מכין לו אוכל 'נגד צררי'. — 'צורר': גורם צרה, מציק, אויב.[52] אין לדעת מי הם צוררי בעל המזמור, ניתן רק להניח שהם המכוונים בדבר בעל המזמור על הליכתו 'בגיא צלמות' ועל שבטו של ה' (פס' ד). — משמעות 'נגד', לפי ההקשר: נוכח, לעיני.[53]

בציון נוכחות הצוררים בתיאור מעשה ה' להעיד על בעל המזמור מתבטאת שמחה לאיד[54] רק לפי הרואה בו מהירהורי לבו. המסתכל במזמור הוא מוצא שמשתקפת בו התפתחות לעומת הנאמר בפס' ד. בעוד שלפי פס' ד הרגיש הוא שאף בהימצאותו בצרה, ה' עמו, עתה לפי פסוקנו, ידוע לו שבהיות צוררים נוכחים, ה' עורך שולחן לו. נמצא שמכוח עיצוב הרגשתו את יחסו של ה' אליו מתגבשת בו הכרה, כי בצר לו לא זו בלבד שה' עמו אלא שהוא גם דואג לו, ביתר דיוק, להזנתו.

בהשתקפותו זו של השינוי בהרגשתו, בהכרתו של בעל המזמור, כמובן, אין הקשר הספרותי הדרוש בין פס' ד לפס' ה. כמו כן אין לראות קשר זה בתפיסתו של המתואר בפס' ה, של עריכת שולחן בשביל בעל המזמור לעיני צורריו, כהמחשתו של המוכרז בסוף פס' ד, של העידוד שביסורים מידי ה', ובתמיכתו. טיב הקשר שבין שני פסוקים אלה יחשף לאור התהליך שאינו נדיר בעיצובה של מיטאפורה, היינו שמלה בת משמעויות שונות פושטת משמעות ולובשת משמעות בתוך תוכה של המיטאפורה; המשמעות המכוסה תתגלה והגלויה תתכסה בהמשך המיטאפורה.[55] לפי תופעה זו מתבררת שכשם שמנושאי המשפט בפס' ד[ב] מתבקשת המסקנה כי נשואו, הפועל 'ינחם', מציין עידוד, כך מתגלית מן האמור בפס' ה[א], 'תערך לפני שלחן נגד צררי', הוראתו המכוסה של הפועל ההוא, המובן של 'עודד' מפנה את מקומו למובן: דיבר, נתן תנחומים. שכן בצד דברי תנחומים נהוג להכרות את האבל, להגיש לו אוכל.[56] אל נוהג זה, שגרם לטראנספורמציה של המכוון ב'ינחמני', התכוון בעל המזמור בפנותו אל ה' במשפט: 'תערך לפני שלחני. בהנחה זו סמך חזק למדי לסברה שמשפט זה בפס' ה הוא המשכו האורגאני של סוף המשפט שבפס' ד[ב].

ברם הואיל והמשפט מסתיים במילים 'נגד צררי', כלום מתקבל על הדעת שהכוונה היא כי את סעודת ההבראה מכין ה' לעיני הצוררים? הרי מעשה זה מביא לידיעתם שבעל המזמור הוא אבל. פי הרבה יותר סביר להניח כפשוטו של המשפט, כי בהכרזת 'נגד צררי' בסוף המשפט גם כן משתקפת טראנספורמציה שחלה במהלך התהוותו. התיאור של סעודת ההבראה על-ידי ה' עבר מבלי משים לתיאור שבו ה' דואג למחייתו של בעל המזמור בנוכחות צורריו.

פס' ה: 'דשנת בשמן ראשי כוסי רויה' — הפועל 'דשן' שהוראתו: שמן, נעשה שמן, משמש כאן משימושיו בבניין פיעל במשמעות: עשה שמן, השמין.[57] — 'בשמן', היינו בדבר המשמש במליצת

---

51 כגון בר' יג, ט; כד נא; לד, י; יר' מ, ד; דה"ב יד, ו ועוד.
52 ראה: "צרר" II, *HALAT*.
53 לשימושו זה של 'נגד' ראה, למשל, בר' לא, לב, לז; מז, טו; שמ' לד, י; שמ"א יב, ג; טז, ו; יש' מט, טז; נט, יב; סא, יא; יואל, א, טז ועוד.
54 כפי שסבורים, בין היתר, למשל, גונקל, וייזר, גלנדר (לעיל, הערה 14), עמ' 463. ראה גם שטרק (לעיל, הערה 10) שם.
55 ראה וייס (לעיל, הערה 49), עמ' 48-49.
56 ראה שמ"ג ג, לה; יר' סז, ז; יח' כג, יז, כב.
57 יש המייחסים לפועל כאן וכן במש' טו, ל (ובבן-סירא כו, יז) את המשמעות: רענן. ראה: "דשן" *HALAT*.

שמכים בו,⁴² משמש כאן כמיטאפורה שהמכוון בה, לפי ההקשר, כמו שהשם נדרש על-ידי חז״ל⁴³ ונתפס על-ידי פרשנים אחדים מן הראשונים⁴⁴ והאחרונים:⁴⁵ הבאת יסורים. — השם 'משענתי' מציין חפץ שניתן להישען עליו. כאן, שמכונה בו, כמו עוד בשני פסוקים (שמ' כא, יט; זכ' ה, ו), מקל להישען עליו, בשמשו כמיטאפורה בקשר לה', ממחיש הוא את תמיכתו, סעדו של ה'.⁴⁶ כינוי הגוף 'המה' בא להדגשת שני הנושאים, 'שבטך ומשענתך', ליתר דיוק, הוא מדגיש את המובע במפורש בריבוי של נשוא המשפט, ינחמוני, היינו שהוא מוסב על שני הנושאים. מעובדה זו גם מתבקשת המסקנה שמשימושיו של הפועל 'נחם' המכוון כאן הוא ההולם באופן שווה את שני הנושאים. אם, כפי שמתברר כמשמעו של הנושאים אף לאחד אינו מתאים כנשוא הפועל בשום הוראה, יש לברירה לאור פשוטם של שני הנושאים. כך מסתבר שאין הפועל מציין כאן, כמו בשימושו השכיח גם בעברית המקראית, אמירת תנחומים, שכן פעולה זו ניתן לייחס רק ל'משענתך', היינו לתמיכתו, לסעדו של ה'. 'ינחם' כנשוא גם ל'שבטך', ליסורים מידי ה', מתיישב בפיו של מאמין, דוגמת בעל מזמורנו, בשמש הפועל משימושיו הידועים בלשון עידוד.⁴⁷ ובכן באמור בעל המזמור: 'שבטך ומשענתך המה ינחמוני, הוא מכריז: הן היסורים שה' מביא עליו, והן תמיכתו, סעדו, מעודדים אותו.

ההכרזה על 'שבטך', היינו שהמומחש בו אינו מדכא, מייאש אותו, אלא להיפך, מתמצתת את הנאמר בפס' ד^א: 'גם כי אלך' וגו'. ואילו ההכרזה על 'משענתך' היא תמצית הדברים שבפס' ב-ג. שני חלקי ההכרזה מסכמים אפוא את המוכרז בשני פסוקים אלה. מבחינת העניין מהווה משפטנו מכוח סדר המילים 'שבטך ומשענתך' הקבלה כיאסטית למשפטי הפסוקים ההם, לנבואות דשא' וגו' ול'גם כי אלך' וגו', כדרכם של כתובים שמטרתם להתייחס זה לזה.⁴⁸ נמצא שבפס' ב-ד מומחש המוכרז בפסוק א^ב.

בסכם פסוק ד^ב את המובע לפניו האם גם מסיים הוא את חטיבת הפסוקים א^ב-ד, כדעת הרוב המכריע של חוקרי מזמורנו שלפיה בפסוק ה נפתח חלק חדש? ברם, כפי שכבר הועד לעיל, דעה רווחת זו, שגרמה לפירושים ולמסקנות רבים, די שונים, לפעמים משונים, אינה אלא התעלמות מן הכלל הרמנויטי, 'שיש להבין את צורות ובעלות משמעות בחוקיותן העצמית, בהתאם לחוקיות המבנה המיוחדת להן, ... אם כך אין למדוד אותן בהתאם לכושרן לתכלית חיצונית זו או זו, העשויה להיראות כקרובה ביותר בעיני הפרשן'.⁴⁹ מכלל זה מתחייב שלהבהרת היחס בין פס' ה לפס' ד, בעצם לפסוקים א^ב - ד, כהלכה, יש להקדים את בירור הכתוב בפס' ה בהתחשב באופיה של לשון המזמור, שהיא לשון שירה.

פס' ה^א: **'תערך לפני שלחן נגד צררי'**⁵⁰ — הביטוי 'ערך שלחן' מורה על סידורו של שולחן בכל

---

42 "שבט" KB,.
43 שוח״ט למזמורנו [ה], [ו]; יל״ש לפסוקנו.
44 רש״י, רד״ק.
45 ארליך. לפי אהרוני (לעיל, הערה 3), עמ' 28, 'שבטי מסמן את המשפט האלוהי. השווה J. L. Kugel, *The Idea of Biblical Poetry. Parallelism and Its History* (New Haven, 1981) 129 n. 50.
46 קוגל, שם.
47 ראה בין היתר, "נחם" *HALAT*,. לפי הדעה הרווחת בין חוקרי מזמורנו הנוסח האותנטי: יְנַחֲנִי (ראה *BHK*).
48 ראה וייס (לעיל, הערה 16), עמ' 94-95, 113.
49 E. Betti, *Die Hermeneutik als allgemeine Methodik der Geisteswissenschaften* (Tübingen, 1963) 14-15. ראה גם מ' וייס, מקראות ככוונתם (ירושלים, תשמ״ח) 34.
50 מלבד בפסוקנו: יש' כא, ה; סה, יא; יח' כג, מא; תה' עח, יט; משי ט, ב.

פס׳ ד׳: ׳גם כי אלך בגיא צלמות לא אירא רע כי אתה עמדי׳ — לפי הדעה הרווחת, בצירוף ׳גם כי׳ משמש המרכיב ׳כי׳ בהוראה: אם.[34] ׳גם כי׳ אפוא: אפילו, אף-על-פי ש-.[35] באמור בעל המזמור: ׳גם כי אלך ... לא אירא רע׳ כוונתו היא: אפילו אני הולך ... אינני ירא. והמתבטא כאן הוא הודאתו של אדם ההולך או יש שהוא הולך ׳בגיא צלמות׳. — המלה ׳גיא׳ היא כינוי למושג הגיאוגראפי המכונה גם בשם ׳עמק׳.[36] — ׳צלמות׳. כעין מוסכם הוא במחקר, כי המלה היא שם גזור מן השורש צל״ם, לשון קדרות, על משקל ׳מרדות׳, ׳עבדות׳ או ׳חכמות׳, ׳הוללות׳, הגייתו הנכונה אפוא ׳צלמות׳ או ׳צלמות׳, והוראתו: חושך.[37] במיטאפורה ׳גיא צלמות׳ מומחש מצב רע, קשה, שבו בעל המזמור (עדיין) מצוי[38] או אולי היה מצוי.[39] ועם זאת מצהיר הוא: ׳לא אירא רע׳, שאינו ירא מפני אסון. — ׳כי אתה עמדי׳. במקום הדיבור על ה׳ שהיה עד עכשיו בגוף שלישי, יש כאן פנייה ישירה אל ה׳. שינוי זה בוודאי בעל משמעות, ביחוד כיוון שהוא חל כשבעל המזמור מציין את הסיבה להרגשת הבטחון המוחלט על אף הימצאותו במצב שהוא מבחינה אובייקטיבית רע. בשוותו לנגדו את הליכתו ׳בגיא צלמות׳, רואה הוא שה׳ עמו, לכן אינו מדבר עוד עליו אלא אליו.[40] המתבטא בשינוי שבמשפט זה הוא בעצם השלמתו של המעוצב במשפט שבפס׳ ד[aא] ׳גם כי אלך בגי צלמות׳, גם מכוח השינוי שבו, מן העובדה שלא נאמר שם ׳יוליכני׳ בדומה לפרטי התיאור הקודמים שבהם הנושא הדקדוקי הוא ה׳ והמושא בעל המזמור, אלא נאמר ׳אלך׳, היינו הפעם נעשית הפעולה על-ידי בעל המזמור עצמו, הוא פועל לבד, בעצמאות.[41] נמצא שבמשפט בפס׳ ד[א], השונה גם במבנהו התחבירי מיתר משפטי המזמור בהיותו הוא בלבד משפט מורכב, ניתן ביטוי הן להכרתו של בעל המזמור כי להליכתו ׳בגיא צלמות׳ הוא הגורם ולא ה׳, והן לבטחונו שאפילו הוא נמצא בנסיבות הקשות ביותר ה׳ אינו נסתר מאחוריהן אלא ה׳ נוכח עמו בהן.

פס׳ ד[ב]: ׳שבטך ומשענתך המה ינחמני׳ — השם ׳שבט׳ שבהוראתו היסודית מציין מקל

---

23), עמ׳ 8; מילר (לעיל, הערה 22), עמ׳ 115.

34 ראה J. Muilenburg, "The Linguistic and Rhetorical Usages of the Particle כי in the Old Testament," *HUCA* 32 (1961) 115.

35 ׳גם׳ *HALAT*.

36 י״א אהרוני-ש״א ליונשטם, ״מושגים גיאוגרפיים במקרא״, אנציקלופדיה מקראית ד (ירושלים, תשכ״ג) 747-748.

37 ׳צלמות׳, *HALAT*, מקדמונינו כך סבורים מנחם בן סרוק, מחברת מנחם, ערך ׳צלם׳; דונש בן לברט, ספר תשובות דונש בן לברט... לספר מחברת מנחם (מהדורת ד׳ פיליפאווסקי), עמ׳ 89 ובעיקבותיו רש״י לפסוקנו.

38 בעשרות השנים האחרונות כך סבורים, למשל, א״ל שטראוס, ״פרקי תהלים״, בדרכי הספרות (ירושלים, תשי״ט) 69, ש׳ ויסבליט, ״על מזמור כ״ג בתהלים״, בית מקרא יז (תשל״ב) 230; גלנדר (לעיל, הערה 14), עמ׳ 463; שטרוף, (לעיל, הערה 10), עמ׳ 91; פולק (לעיל, הערה 10), עמ׳ 233; מק-דניאל (לעיל, הערה 1), עמ׳ 120, 289.

39 ההליכה ׳בגיא צלמות׳ מאורע של העבר, כגון, לפי ויזר; W. Beyerlin, *Die Rettung der Bedrängten in den Feindpsalmen der Einzelnen auf institutionelle Zusammenhänge untersucht* (Göttingen, 1970) 112 ; דובאש (לעיל, הערה 27), עמ׳ 146-147; C. Westermann, "Anthropologische und theologisch Aspekte des Gebets in den Psalmen," *Zur neueren Psalmenforschung* (ed. P. H. A. Neumann; Darmstadt, 1976) 463.

40 על משמעותו זו של המעבר הזה כאן עומדים, למשל: P. Volz, "Zur Auslegung von Psalm 23 und 121," *NKZ* 36 (1925) 577; שטראוס (לעיל, הערה 8), עמ׳ 69; פולק (לעיל, הערה 10), עמ׳ 233, 236.

41 השווה פולק (לעיל, הערה 10), עמ׳ 233.

המזמור מציין בפועל 'ינחני' (או בנרדף לו), כפי שהיה מתבקש מנשוא המשפט בטור המקביל 'ינהלני',[24] אלא הוא אומר 'ירביצני', שבו מעוצב גם מצב סטאטי של מנוחה, כשם שגם מ'מי מנחות' השתייה היא במנוחה ללא הפרעה, בלי פחד.

פס' ג[א]: **'נפשי ישובב'** — שימושי המלה 'נפש' במקרא הם רבים. כהוראתה המקורית לרוב מניחים את ההוראה היסודית: לוע, גרון כאיבר של נשימה ואכילה שממנה נתפתחו יתר ההוראות המופשטות. עיקר הוראתה הוא 'חיות אינדיבידואלית או מה שמצוי בחי כאשר הוא חי',[25] כמושא לפועל הגזור מן השורש שו"ב בבניין הפעיל, היינו הצירוף 'ישיב נפש', המציין: הציל חיים (תה' לה, יז; איוב לב, ל) או החיה, החזיר את כוח החיים (תה' יט, ח; מש' כה, יג; רות ד, טו; ועוד),[26] נפוץ למדי, ואילו 'נפש' כמושא לבניין פולל, 'שובב', הוא יחידאי. בדרך כלל מייחסים גם לצירוף זה את המשמעות: החזיר, חידש את רוח החיים, את החיות.[27]

המשפט 'נפשי ישובב' מהווה מעבר. מחד גיסא יש בו מעין כלל הבא בעיקבות הפרטים שבפס' ב,[28] היינו מילוי נפשו-גרונו של השה הרעב והצמא, מאידך גיסא, מלשונו של המשפט מסתברת ההנחה שהנושא הדקדוקי אינו עוד רק הרועה והמושא אינו עוד רק השה; אם אמנם לא, כמו בהמשך, גם מבחינה דקדוקית רק על ה' ועל בעל המזמור מדבר הכתוב.[29]

פס' ג[א]: **'ינחני במעגלי צדק למען שמו'** — 'ינחה' דוגמת הפעלים שיש שהוא משמש במקביל להם, 'ינהל' (שמ' טו, יג; תה' לא, ד), 'ינהג' (יש' סג, יג; תה' עח, נג), הוא לשון הדרכה. — 'מעגלי' הוא ערוץ עגלה, מסלול.[30] מהקשריו מתחייבת המסקנה, שפשוטו לא כמשמעו בכל הקרויותיו[31] חוץ מבאחת (תה' סה, יב) אלא השימוש הוא בהשאלה במובן: אופן התנהגות, מידה. 'במעגלי צדק' אפוא: בדרכי צדק, במידות צדק. ואולם הצירוף 'מעגלי צדק' מתיישב כחלק אורגאני מן המזמור רק אם 'צדק' אינו מתפרש כמונח יורידי, המציין את אופן הנהגתו של ה' שהוא במידת הדין, בשפיטת אמת, אלא כמו בכתובים הרבה, ובייחוד במזמורי תהילים,[32] כציוני כולל לטובו, לחסדו ולישועתו של ה'. בדרכים אלה מנחה אפוא ה' את בעל מזמורנו וכך הוא עושה 'למען שמו'. בגלל שמו, היינו מיהותו, בהיותו דואג לבני-אדם.[33]

---

24 'ינחני' מקביל ל'ינהלי' בשמ' טו, יג, ונרדף לו בתה' לא, ד.

25 יש"ל ליכט, "נפש", אנציקלופדיה מקראית ה (ירושלים, תשכ"ח) 903. ראה עוד: H. Seebass, "נֶפֶשׁ næpæš," TWAT 5:531-44.

26 W. L. Holladay, *The Root Sûbh in the Old Testament* (Leiden, 1958) 96-97.

27 כגון, וז-זיל (לעיל, הערה 10), עמ' 69; דאהוד; F. U. Dobiāš, "Der 23 Psalm," *Communio Viatorum* 15 (1972) 145; קראוס; מיטמן (לעיל, הערה 23), עמ' 5; מילר (לעיל, הערה 22), עמ' 114; סבאס (לעיל, הערה 25), עמ' 544; ועוד.

28 וז-זיל (לעיל, הערה 10), עמ' 69; A. R. Johnson, "Psalm 23 and the Household of Faith," *Proclamation and Presence - Old Testament Essays in Honor of G. H. Davies* (ed. J. I. Durham and J. I. Porter; London, 1970) 258; קראוס; מיטמן (לעיל, הערה 23), עמ' 5; מילר (לעיל, הערה 22), עמ' 114.

29 כך סבורים ויזר; G. J. Thierry, "Notes on Hebrew Grammar and Etymology – Psalm XXIII," *OTS* 9 (1951) 13; idem, "Remarks on Various Passages of the Psalms," *OTS* 13 (1963) 92-93; N. H. Ridderbos, *Die Psalmen–Stilistische Verfahren und Aufbau mit besonderer Berücksichtigung von Ps 1-41* (BZAW 117; Berlin, 1972) 193.

30 "מעגל" II, *HALAT*.

31 יש' כו, ז; נט, ח; תה' יז, ה; קמ, ו; מש' ב, ט, טו, יח; ד, יא, כו; ה, ו, כא.

32 כגון תה' לו, ז; פט, יז; צט, ב; קמה, ז ועוד. ראה ש' ליכט "צדק, צדקה, צדיק", אנציקלופדיה מקראית ו (ירושלים, תשל"ב) 683.

33 כוונה דומה מיוחסת ל'למען שמו' כאן כגון ע"י חיות, מן האחרונים, למשל, ע"י מיטמן (לעיל, הערה

ואולם להבהרתו ולהדגשתו של המוכרז בשני משפטי הפסוק, בהיותו כללי, מופשט, נזקק בעל המזמור לפרטו, להמחישו, היינו לומר במפורש מה הם מעשי ה' עמו הגורמים לראות בו את רועהו שלו ולהרגיש שאין חסר לו ולא כלום. בזה מדובר בהמשך.

פס' ב[א]: **'בנאות דשא ירביצני'** — 'נאות' ריבוי נסמך של 'נוה',[17] כינוי למקום מרעה.[18] 'דשא' מציין ירק, כאן עשב רענן.[19] ובכן לא בשדי עשב נשדף אלא 'בנאות דשא' — 'ירביצני', היינו: ישכיבני, ביתר דיוק, משכיב אותי, כפי שיוצא, כאמור לעיל, משימוש הפעלים בצורת יפעל במזמורנו לפי המכוון בו.

מלבד הדאגה שגילויה קביעת מקום ההרבצה 'בנאות דשא', ממחישה את ההכרזה שבפס' א[ב] גם העובדה הנמסרת במשפט שבפס' ב[ב]: **'על מי מנחות ינהלני'**. — 'מנחות': ריבוי זה של 'מנוחה', המופיע במקרא עוד פעם (יש' לד, יח), הוא אחד משימושי הריבוי הבא לתת עוצמת יתר למשמעותו של השם.[20] 'מנחות': מנוחה מוחלטת. אשר להוראת המלה 'מנוחה' — במקרא משמשת היא בשתי כוונות, בפסיכולוגית ובלוקאלית.[21] במשפטנו, לפי דעה אחת,[22] מורה המלה על שקט והמכוון בסמיכות 'מי מנוחות' הוא למים שקטים. לדעה אחרת[23] המשמעות של 'מנוחה' כאן: מקום שקט. 'מי מנוחות' אפוא מים שעליהם אפשר לנוח בנחת. ואולם מן ההקבלה המדויקת של שני משפטי פס' ב, שמבחינה תחבירית בנויים באופן שווה לגמרי ומבחינה תוכנית מתאימים מאוד זה לזה, ניתן להסיק במידה ניכרת של סבירות את המסקנה כי הסמיכות 'מי מנוחות' משמשת באותו התפקיד כמו 'בנאות דשא', היינו כסמיכות התואר. הווי אומר, 'מי מנוחות': מים ההולכים לאט, לא זרמים העלולים לסכן את השה. — הפועל 'ינהל', המביע את ההולכה אל 'מי מנוחות', בציינו את כיוון הפעולה מצריך (דוגמת פעלי תנועה בכלל) את מילות היחס 'אל' (שמ' טו, יג), 'ל-' (יש' נא, יח) וכמו כאן 'יעל' (גם יש' מט, י).

בארץ-ישראל על איזורי הריה ומדבריה הנרחבים, על עונות הקיץ החמות היבשות ועל עונות הבצורת הלא-נדירות בחורף, אין מקומות מרעה ומים מצויים תמיד ובכל מקום. משום כך ההכרחי האלמנטארי למחיית הצאן לפעמים לא-במעטות אינו נמצא אלא אחרי חיפוש ארוך, מייגע וסבל רב. לפיכך כשבעל המזמור ממחיש שבגלל יחסו של ה' אליו מצבו הוא שלם לחלוטין ומזהה את עצמו עם שה כיון שמרגיש בה' את רועהו, אינו מכריז 'יש לי הכל', אלא 'לא אחסר', לא חסר לי כלל וכלל אף פעם מה שלא רק רגיל אלא אף טבעי, מה שלעיתים קרובות חסר לצאן. יתרה מזו. לא זו בלבד שבמרעה ובמים אין לי מחסור, אלא שאפילו 'נאות דשא' ו'מי מנוחות' בתמידות 'לא אחסר'. ולא זו אף זו. את הימצאותו 'בנאות דשא' מתוך חסדו של ה' עמו אין בעל

---

[17] 'נאות' > 'נְוֹת' (צפ' ו, ב). ראה: H. Bauer and P. Leander, *Historische Grammatik der hebräischen Sprache* (Hildesheim, 1922) §21g.

[18] ראה: H. Ringgren, "נָוֶה nāwœh," *TWAT* 5:293-97.

[19] ראה: H. Ringgren, "דֶּשֶׁא dœše," *TWAT* 2:329-31. לשימושה זה של המלה ראה יש' סו, יד.

[20] ג"ק (לעיל, הערה 6), §124e.

[21] ראה: K. D. Preuss, "נוּחַ nûaḥ, מְנוּחָה menûḥāh," *TWAT* 5:304-6.

[22] תפיסה זו את הסמיכות 'מי מנוחות', המשתקפת בכל התרגומים העתיקים והנמצאת בפירושו של המאירי, במצודת דוד ובביאור, מקובלת מן החוקרים בדור האחרון, למשל, על-ידי ון-זיל (לעיל, הערה 10), עמ' 69; דאהוד; קראוס; י' בזק, "תהלים כ"ג (ה' רועי) — כמזמור צורני-גיאומטרי", בית מקרא כו (תשמ"א) 372; P. D. Miller, *Interpreting the Psalms* (Philadelphia, 1986) 114; פרויס (לעיל, הערה 21), עמ' 305.

[23] בדור האחרון כך מפרשים את המלה, כגון: A. L. Merill, "Psalm XXIII and the Jerusalem Tradition," *VT* 15 (1965) 358; פרידמן (לעיל, הערה 2), עמ' 148; S. Mittmann, "Aufbau und Einheit des Danklieds Psalm 23," *ZTK* 77 (1980) 6 ועוד.

יעקב: "האלהים הרעה אתי" (בר' מח, טו). ובכן, הכרזתו של בעל המזמור: "ה' רעי" היא עיצוב אמונתו שטיפולו של ה' בו אינו באחד מתוך כלל ישראל אלא הוא פרטי, אישי לחלוטין.[10] — על-פי מקומו והמובע בו ניתן לראות במשפט כעין מוטו למזמור.

פס' א[ב]: **'לא אחסר'** — משמע הפועל 'חסר' כאן: לא היה לו.[11] בהיותו (כרוב המכריע של הפעלים במזמור זה)[12] בצורת יפעל, המבטאת בין היתר פעולות, אירועים או מצבים מתמשכים[13] פירושו של המשפט הוא: איניני חסר דבר. בקשר למשפטנו נקבע: "אינו דומה האומר ״לא אחסר" לאומר "יש לי הכל". כהבדל שבין שתי אמירות אלה צוין שבאמירה השלילית יש "טעם המעטה".[14] ואכן לא הרי האמירה בלשון שלילה כהרי זו בלשון חיוב. ואף נראית כנכונה ראיית המעטה באמירה השלילית מול האמירה החיובית. ברם, התבוננות בכתובים שהקשרם כמו כאן מעלה, כי שימושו של הנשוא "לא חסר" אינו המעטה של שלמות המצב, אלא התאמת המשפט להקשר, שכך מתחייב מצד העניין.[15] מן העיון בפס' ב יעלה שאת המתואר בו הולם דווקא הנוסח השלילי של ההכרזה "לא אחסר".

המוכרז במשפט ערטילאי, קצר ביותר, בן שתי מילים, 'לא אחסר', הוא התוצאה הישירה למה שמכריז המשפט הקודם של אותו מספר מילים: 'ה' רעי'. עם זאת אין מלת איחוי ביניהם, מלה שתציין את קישרם ההגיוני. הם שני משפטים עצמאיים. צורה זו של הכתוב היא חלק אינטגראלי ממהות המזמור. מתבטאת בה ברוח ומשתקפת תפיסת שתי העובדות: 'ה' רעי', 'לא אחסר', כשוות מכל הבחינות, כאמיתות המוכרזות שאינן זקוקות לציון הקשר ביניהן, בהיותו מובן מאליו. אין אפוא צורך לנמק את ההכרזה 'לא אחסר', ואין לציין את תוצאת ההכרזה: 'ה' רעי'.[16]

---

10 כבר עמדו על כך, בין היתר:2d) W. Staerk, *Lyrik (Psalmen, Hoheslied und Verwandtes)* ed.; Göttingen, 1920) 211; A. H. van Zyl, "Psalm 23," *Studies on the Psalms – Papers read at 6th Meeting of Die O.T. Werkgemeenskap in Suid-Afrika* (1963) 69; גונקל, קראוס. כמו כן פי' פולק, " 'ה' רעי לא אחסר' (תה' כג 1) — על פרשנות ואמנות השירה במקרא", תעודה ב — עיונים במקרא, ספר זכרון לי״מ גרינץ (תל-אביב, תשמ״ב) 235, הוא מעיר, כמו לפני: W. Schottroff, "Psalm 23: Zur Methode sozial-geschichtlicher Bibelauslegung," *Traditionen der Befreiung: Sozialgeschichliche Bibelauslegungen* (ed. W. Schottroff, W. Stegemann; Munich/Gelzhaus, 1980) 1:88-89 ששמות פרטיים תיאופוריים היו גם במיסופוטאמיה המעידים על תפיסת יחס אינדיבידואלי של אלוהות. שוטרוף מביא כדוגמא, בין השאר את השם:šamaš-re'ûa[d] (יְשַׁמֵשׁ רועיי) המזכיר את המשפט הנדון.

11 'חסר' בבניין קל בשמש, כמו במשפטנו, כפועל עומד זוהי הוראתו בנחמ' ט, כא. לפי אחדים (כגון גונקל, דאהוד) גם במשי' יג, כה. לרוב שימושיו הוא במובן: פחת, התמעט (כגון בר' ח, ג, ה; יח, כח; ועוד), לא היה (כגון דב' טו, ח; מל״א יז, יד; טז; יש' נא, יד; ועוד).

12 חוץ מ'דשנתי' (פס' ה [ב]), ו'שבתי' (פס' ו [ב]).

13 ג״ק (לעיל, הערה 6), §107f.

14 ש' גלנדר, "על מצב הדובר במזמור כ״ג", בית מקרא כג (תשל״ח) 462. לדעתו, בהכרזה 'לא אחסר' יכביכול — מציין הדובר "איניני מתאונן".

15 בכתובים כגון: זה ארבעים שנה ה' אלהיך עמך לא חסרת דבר' (דב' ב, ז); 'ארץ אשר לא במסכנת תאכל בה לחם לא תחסר כל בה' (שם ח, ט), בוודאי אין "טעם של המעטה", ובלשון יהיה לך הכל לא היה מובע המכוון בהם, כשם שהכוונה בדברי יעקב: 'יש לי כל' (בר' לג, יא) לא היתה מתבטאת במשפט 'לא אחסר'. (ולא רק מפני שלא היתה ההקבלה בעלת משמעות לדברי עשו 'יש לי רב' [שם, ט]).

16 ראה עוד וייס (לעיל, הערה 5), עמ' 47-49.

'סגנונו המיוחד שתפיסה אמוציונאלית אימפרסיוניסטית גררתו'.[3] אמנם כן הוא. ברם הקביעה המדוייקת של הסיבה לניגודים הגדולים שעדיין קיימים בדעות החוקרים היא, מלבד הסתמכות על עקרונות מקובלים בחקר המקרא, התנכרות לאופן עיצובו של המזמור, לטיבה של הלשון השירית, היינו התעלמות מן הדרך הלגיטימית היחידה להבנתה הנכונה.[4] שגיאה מיתודית היא אפוא הסיבה לפירושים השונים למזמורנו ולמסקנות המוסקות ממנו. הואיל וכך, מוצעת כאן לשיקול תפיסת המעוצב במזמור כג לפי השיטה הפרשנית האדקואטית, שיטת ״האינטרפרטאציה הכוליית״,[5] בשימושה הנכון. הצעה זו מוגשת (גם במקום רפי ז״ל שלנו) בהוקרה, בהכרת טובה, ברגשי ידידות ובברכה שלמה לחברי הפרופ׳ שמריהו טלמון יצ״ו עמו״ש, שתרם רבות גם לעיצוב דרכי הניתוח הספרותי־הרעיוני של המקרא.

פס׳ א[a-b]: *ה׳ רעי* — משפט זה נבדל מן המשפטים הבאים אחריו על־ידי עצם היותו משפט שמני ולא פעלי כמוהם. בהתאם לסדר המילים במשפט שמני,[6] *ה׳* הנושא, *רעי* הנשוא. פירוש המשפט אפוא: ה׳ הוא רועי. בהמחישו בעל המזמור את הרגשתו שיחסו של ה׳ אליו הוא כיחס הרועה לצאנו, משתמש הוא במיטאפורה הנפוצה במקרא גם בקשר לה׳[7] וגם בקשר למנהיג, למלך.[8] המיטאפורה של ה׳ כרועה ממחישה בדרך כלל יחס קולקטיבי, לעם כולו[9] — שהרי הרועה מטפל בעדר ולא בשה בודד. פסוקנו הוא יוצא מן הכלל, וכמוהו הכתוב שבו מובאים דברי

---

3   אהרוני (לעיל, הערה 2), עמ׳ 26, 33. בדומה סבור וייזר: ׳הקושי בפירוש המזמור הוא העושר המזרחי של תמונות לשונו ומחשבתו, המקשה לפעמים לקבוע בדיוק את הגבול בין משל לנמשל, כיוון ששניהם בהבעתו השירית־אליגורית של המזמור תכופות מתמזגים׳. שונה ואופייני הוא הסברו של מק־דניאל (לעיל, הערה 1), עמ׳ 1, 38, ועוד, לניגודים בפרשנות מזמורנו. לדעתו ׳בנוגע לתמונות הלשון לא שמו לב הפרשנים לספרות המזרח הקדמון וגם לא התחקו אחר תמונות לשון אלה בכל ספרי המקרא על מנת לקבוע את גבולות השימוש בהן׳. הווי אומר, לדעתו, על המכוון בפרטי המזמור ניתן לעמוד לא על־פי הקשרם במזמור אלא על־פי שימושים ביצירות אחרות במקרא ואף בספרות שמחוצה לו.

4   מצבו של מזמור כג בפרשנות ה״מדעית״ ראיה חותכת לכשלונן של השיטות ה״ביקורתיות״ המקובלות בחקר המזמורים גם לפי: A. Cooper, "Structure, Midrash and Meaning: The Case of Psalm 23," דברי הקונגרס העולמי התשיעי למדעי היהדות, חטיבה א, (ירושלים תשמ״ז) החלק הלועזי, 107-114. בעקבות נ״ה טור־סיני וד״נ פרידמן מציע הוא לאמץ שיטה חדשה הקרויה ניאו־מדרשית, שעיקרה מציאת אחיזה למזמור באחד מסיפורי המקרא. לדעתו, מזמורנו ׳מדרש על חייו של יעקב — לאמיתו של דבר קרובה המיוסדת על בר׳ מח, טו׳ (׳והאלהים הרעה אתי מעודי עד היום הזה׳). עם זאת מודה קופר שהצעת פרידמן לראות את המזמור כמדרש על יציאת מצרים (כפי שנדרש גם במדרש) ובעצם גם פירושו של רד״ק שלפיו מתייחס המזמור לפרק מחיי דוד (כפי שנתפרש גם על־ידי לנדבלום [לעיל, בהערה 2] ולפניו על־ידי דליטש שקופר אינו מזכירם) אפשריים אף הם. נמצא שקופר מצדד עם הדוגלים בריבוי קריאות אפשרויות של היצירה הספרותית.

5   ראה מ׳ וייס, המקרא כדמותו[3] (ירושלים, תשמ״ז) 27-73. (לדעות מנוגדות אין בחיבור התייחסות אלא לאלה שהן לכאורה סבירות או במקרים שאין להם הכרע.)

6   W. Gesenius and E. Kautzsch, *Hebräische Grammatik* (27th ed.; Leipzig, 1902) §141 l; C. Brockelmann, *Hebräische Syntax* (Neukirchen, 1956) §27a.

7   בר׳ מח, טו; מט, כד; ישי׳ מ, יא; הו׳ ד, טז; מי׳ ז, יד. השווה גם הערה 9. רועה כמיטאפורה לאלוהות שכיחה גם במיסופוטאמיה ובמצרים (ראה מק־דניאל [לעיל, הערה 1], עמ׳ 52-60).

8   ראה מק־דניאל (לעיל, הערה 1), עמ׳ 46-52. לשימוש זה במזרח הקדום שם, 41-46.

9   השווה את כינויי המיטאפורה לישראל: ׳צאן׳ (ישי׳ סג, יא; יר׳ כג, א-ד; יחז׳ לד, ו ואילך; מי׳ ז, יד; זכ׳ ט, טז; תה׳ עד, א; עז, כא; נב, ועוד), ׳עדר׳ (יר׳ יג, יז; תה׳ עח, נב).

בעל מזמור כג על יחסו של ה׳ אליו:
לחקר האמונות והדעות במזמורי תהילים

מאיר וייס

מן המפורסמות הוא שממאה וחמישים מזמורי תהילים רק מעטים נדונו ונחקרו כה תכופות ובאופן כה אינטנסיבי כמו מזמור כג.[1] האתגר שמעמיד המזמור בפני החוקרים נעוץ בנסיון להבין את חיבור החלקים או את פירוש המזמור כיחידה אחת, כשלמות. שכן, התמונה בפס׳ א-ד מופסקת לפתע בפס׳ ה על-ידי פעולות המתאימות רק בקושי רב למתואר בפסוקים שלפניו.[2] קושי זה גורם להעדר תמימות דעים בדבר מספרן ופירושן של תמונות הלשון במזמור. כמו כן שנויות במחלוקת הנסיבות המשתקפות במזמור. יש הרואים בו הצהרה נשגבה על שלווה בלתי מופרעת, בעוד שאחרים מוצאים כי רקעו הוא צרה צרורה. כסיבת המבוכה השוררת בחקר מזמורנו נקבע

---

1 בכל מקום שבו מצויין שם המחבר בלבד ההפניה היא אל פירושו לספר תהילים. É. Beaucamp בפירושו לספר תהילים (115) [Paris, 1976] *Le Psautier, Ps 1-72* רושם יותר משלושים חיבורים על מזמור כג שנתפרסמו בשנים 1934-1972. מספר הספרים והמאמרים על המזמור מן השנים 1973-1986 המוזכרים ב- *Elenchus Bibliographicus Biblicus* עולה על ארבעים וחמישה, ביניהם הדיסרטאציות: F. L. McDaniel, *The Relation between the Shepherd and Banquet Motif of Psalm 23* (Dallas, 1983); C. O'Connor, *Psalm 23: A Closer Look* (Louvain, 1983).

2 D. N. Freedman, "The Twenty-Third Psalm," *Michigan Oriental Studies in Honor of George Cameron* (eds. L. L. Orlin et al.; Ann Arbor, 1976) 139 ואילך. ראה גם: R. Ahroni, "The Unity of Psalm 23," *HAR* 6 (1982) 21-22 ועוד. הפתרונות לבעיות המזמור הנמצאות והמומצאות ראה בסקירתו של מק-דניאל (לעיל, הערה 1), עמ׳ 3-38. פירושו של מק-דניאל, שם, 121-219 ופירושי החיבורים שהופיעו אחרי הדיסרטאציה שלו בעצם אינם נבדלים אלא בגיוונים בלתי משמעותיים מן הנסקרים על-ידו. למשל, לפי: J. R. Lundblom, "Psalm 23: Song of Passage," *Int* 40 (1986) 5-16 מזמור כג הוא "שיר מסע". המכוון בו מסעו של דוד מירושלים למדבר וחזרה לירושלים. לפי: M. S. Smith, "Setting and Rhetoric in Psalm 23," *JSOT* 41 (1988) 61-66, מזמורנו הוא "מסע רוחני". בחלק הראשון מתואר מה היה האדם רואה בדרך לבית המקדש, בחלק השני שיא החוייה, השהייה במקדש. (ראה גם את תפיסת המזמור על-ידי קופר להלן, הערה 4.)

לעומת זאת אנו צריכים להיות מודעים להצגה ספרותית של העובדות. יש להבחין בין הסיפור על הרפורמה Erzählung (מל״ב כב, ג-כג, ג; כא-כט) לבין רישום העובדות כפי שזה מופיע בכרוניקה שבמל״ב כג, ד-כ).[18] הסיפור מעוניין להציג את יאשיהו כמלך ששמר תורת משה ב״כל לבבו ובכל נפשו ובכל מאדו״ ושלא היה כמוהו במלכים, דבר שהופך אותו משוחד מבחינת הערכת האישיות והמפעלים הקשורים בה. לעומת זאת יש להתייחס במלא הרצינות לעובדות המוניות בכרוניקה שבה הדברים מתוארים באופן אובייקטיבי וללא דברי הערכה.

חשיפת הרבדים בפרקי המקרא חשובה איפוא ביותר בטרם ניגשים לניתוח ספרותי-אסתיטי. למעשה תלויות הגישה הספרותית-אסתיטית והגישה הביקורתית-ספרותית זו בזו. כדי להגיע לשיקול ביקורתי מבוסס יש להעריך את החומר מבחינתו הספרותית-אסתיטית ולהיפך כדי לנתח סוגיה מבחינה ספרותית-אסתיטית יש להשתמש בשיקולים ביקורתיים-פילולוגיים הנחוצים לצורך מיון וסיווג החומר שלפנינו. אי-אפשר לגשת בקנה מידה אחיד לכל הספרות המקראית. יש בה חומר שאינו ניתן למדידה בכלים אסתיטיים כגון כרוניקות ודיווחים וגם אם לתוכם מסתננים ניסוחים בעלי אופי ספרותי הרי יש להודות שאי-אפשר לשים אותם על מישור אחד עם סיפורת ושירה. כדי לבודד מקורות יבשים אלה משים בהם בעיקר מסירת עובדות ולא תיאור ספרותי יש להפעיל שיטות ביקורתיות-פילולוגיות. והוא הדין לאותם קטעי הערכה דוגמאטיים שלמרות היותם מנוסחים ניסוחים סטריאוטיפיים אי-אפשר לראות אותם כספרות במובנה הרגיל.

הגישה הספרותית חיונית לחקר המקרא אך בתנאי שהיא מלווה בשיטה פילולוגית היסטורית-ביקורתית.

---

18 ראה מאמרי: "Josiah," *EncJud* 10:288-93.

שמבקש מנושא כליו להמיתו כדי להימלט מחרפה — אצל אבימלך שנפל ביד אשה, השווה שופ׳ ד, ט, ואצל שאול שנפל בידי ערלים — זהה בשני המקרים אלא שדרך הביצוע שונה. במקרה אבימלך אמנם נדקר המנהיג בידי נערו, במקרה שאול — המלך ונערו מתאבדים כאחד. כידוע יש בידינו גירסה שונה על מות שאול בשמ״ב א לפיה ביקש שאול להיהרג בידי עמלקי שנקלע למקום הקרב, וחוקרים רבים סבורים שגירסה זו אינה מהימנה שכן מעוניינת לייחס הריגת שאול בידי עמלק ששאול נכשל בהחרמתו (שמ״א טו). לא נדון כאן בבעיה זו[14] אך נציין שמבחינה ספרותית התקדים בקשר לאבימלך מאלף ושמא עשוי לסייע בהעדפת הגירסה הראשונה בקשר למות שאול. אך כיצד בכל זאת נסביר את השינויים בנסיבות המוות: אצל אבימלך נערו אמנם דוקר אותו ואצל שאול המלך ונערו, כל אחד נופל על חרבו. והנה מצאנו סיפור חיצוני שעשוי להפיץ אור נוסף על המעשה. באנאלים של אשורבניפל קוראים אנו כי נבו־בל־שומאתי, נכדו של מרודך בלאדן, כאשר שמע על בוא שליחי אשורבניפל לעילם שאיתה קשר קשר נגד אשור, פחד מאד וביקש למות: ״אל נערו, נושא כליו, אמר: דקרני ... ודקרו עצמם (uptatteḫu aḫameš) בחרבות שבמחניהם״.[15] האם סיפור זה מחזק את מהימנות הגירסה שבשמ״ב לא? לאו דווקא, נראה לי כי גם המסופר על נבו־בל־שומאתי אינו בהכרח בבחינת עובדה היסטורית כי אם קונבנציה שהיתה מקובלת בתיאורי מות מלכים בשעת מפלה. על כל פנים עיון בספרות ולאו דווקא מקראית עשוי להאיר יותר את הפרובלמטיקה הספרותית, לאור העובדה שבסיפור מות שאול נאמר כי שאול ונושא כליו כל אחד מהם נפל על חרבו יש לשאול שמא גם באנאלים האשוריים יש לפרש לא כמקובל בתרגום האנאלים כי דקרו זה את זה כי אם דקרו את עצמם כאחד דהיינו כל אחד את עצמו, והביטוי האשורי uptatteḫu aḫameš אמנם עשוי להתפרש כך,[16] ואם כן למדנו משהו מסיפור שאול על הספרות האשורית.

אני אמנם מקבל את ההנחה של השיטה הכוליית כי קודם כל יש ללמוד על היצירה מתוך עצמה אך יש מקרים שבהם נבין את היצירה עצמה טוב יותר אם נשים לב למוטיבים דומים ביצירות קרובות, וכל זאת מתוך שיקולים ספרותיים. למרות כל זאת אי־אפשר לשלול אפריורי את התרחשות המאורע עצמו, וזאת במיוחד כאשר מדובר באירועים פומביים. אני רוצה להתייחס — אגב כך — לסוגייה שלאחרונה נזקקו לה רבות דהיינו הרפורמות הדתיות בישראל. הרחקת פולחן זר על־ידי מלכים צדיקים הפך להיות מעין סטריאוטיף בהיסטוריוגרפיה הישראלית (מל״א טו, יא-יג; כב, מג; מל״ב ג, ב; יא, יח; יד, ג-ד; טו, ג-ד) ולפיכך נמצאו לאחרונה שמפקפקים במהימנות הרפורמה בכלל ונוטים לראות ברפורמות נושא ספרותי שנוצר מתוך רצון להתאים מלכים מסוימיים לנורמות שנתפתחו בגולה.[17] אולם לא נוכל לקבל זאת בשום פנים ואופן. אין זה הגיוני שמישהו ייחס באופן פיקטיבי מעשה היסטורי לאומי למלך, כגון יאשיהו, בשעה שיש אנשים שזוכרים עדיין מלך זה ומעלליו.

רוב החוקרים מסכימים כי ספר מלכים הועלה על גבי הכתב — בין אם נערך בבת אחת או שעבר שתי עריכות — בשנים 550-620, כלומר לא יותר משבעים ושתיים שנה לאחר התאריך שלו מיוחסת הרפורמה של יאשיהו. השאלה היא איפוא האם אפשר לבדות עובדות פומביות כאלה ולהציגן בפני אנשים שחיו בתקופה ההיא או בפני דור שהמאורעות שלפני החורבן עדיין טריים וזכורים היטב.

---

14 ראה לאחרונה דיון של י׳ אמית, ״שלש וריאציות על מות שאול״, בית מקרא ק (תשמ״ה) 92-102.
15 M. Streck, *Assurbanipal* 60, VII:31ff.
16 ראה: *CAD* s.v. aḫameš 2b: *jointly*.
17 ראה בייחוד: M. D. Hoffman, *Reform und Reformen* (ATANT 66; Zürich, 1980) ועיין מה שכתבתי בשנתון ט (תשמ״ה) 236-238.

נכון שכדי להבחין ברבדים ומקורות יש להשקיע עמל רב. כדי לנתח פרשה מקראית צריך להצטייד בכלים פילולוגיים, היסטוריים, בלשניים ואנתרופולוגיים, מלאכה שהיא לא קלה; לפיכך יש מעדיפים ליהנות מקריאת היצירה כמות שהיא ולוותר על ניתוח ופירוק החומר. אולם יש לזכור כי אז מזניחים את החקירה, וכפי שראינו עשויים להגיע למסקנות מסולפות בקביעות לגבי אופי היצירה. הניתוח האסתטי חיוני אך הוא צריך לבוא לצד ניתוחים פילולוגיים־היסטוריים.

לאחרונה למדו ההיסטוריונים כי בחקירה ההיסטורית יש להתחשב במודלים ודגמים ובכך רואה אני התקרבות מצידם לתנועה הדוגלת במקרא כספרות. מסתבר כי אפילו סוגיות שנראו היסטוריות טהורות כגון התנחלות השבטים בארץ־ישראל כפופות לדגמים ספרותיים. תוך כדי עיסוק בסוגיה זו גיליתי[11] כי דגמים זהים לאלו שבתיאור ההתנחלות בספר יהושע מצויים גם בתיאורי הקולוניזציה היוונית. גם שם מצאנו כי המייסד או יוזם ההתנחלות ὀιχιστής זקוק לדבר נבואה לפני ההתנחלות ולשם כך הוא משתף פעולה עם כהן־נביא (השווה משה ויהושע מצד אחד ואלעזר הכהן ויהושע מצד שני). בהתנחלות שבעיון בדומה להתנחלות בישראל מחלקים את האדמה ומפילים עליה גורל לפני האלהות — בישראל במקדש שילה, וביוון במקדש דלפוי; כמו בישראל כך גם ביוון מקימים מצבות ומזבחות לאחר שהגיעו למקום ההתנחלות (השווה גלגל והר עיבל). לכאורה לפנינו דגם ספרותי המשמש בסיס לתיאור ההתנחלות אך מאות תעודות מיוון מעידות כי יש לפרטי הדגם הזה עגינה היסטורית וכי הזיקה לדלפוי בתחום הקולוניזאציה היתה בבחינת עובדה. באופן דומה יש לראות גם בישראל את הזיקה לשילה כעובדה אוטנטית ובפרט כשחפירות הוכיחו כי בשילה היה קיים מרכז סקראלי מקדמת דנה.[12] עם זאת אין ספק שבתיאורי הספרות הכהנית הישראלית, שבהם הכל נראה באספקלריה של עדת ישראל השלמה והמאוחדת, הדברים חורגים מהיסטוריה ריאלית והופכים לספרות בעלת אופי אידיאליסטי וסכימאטי. עדיין ניכרים כאן שרטוטים בודדים של התרחשויות היסטוריות ריאליות אך בתיאור כמות שהוא שלטת הכללה בעלת מגמה אידיאליסטית. כאשר אנו מתקדמים לעבר יחזקאל שינק מהספרות הכהנית ובודקים כיצד הוא מתאר את חלוקת הארץ לנחלות שבטי ישראל, הרי התשתית הריאלית נעלמת לגמרי והתיאור הוא אוטופי גמור. במרכז הארץ הנחלקת עומדת ירושלים ולא שילה וכל השבטים ממוקמים בעבר הירדן המערבי כולל ראובן וגד שישבו בעבר הירדן המזרחי (יחז' מח). כאן התיאור הוא ספרותי טהור.

הכרת הספרות על כל רבדיה המגוונים תסייע לנו איפוא בהבנת הדגם הבסיסי שמאחורי יחידה זו או אחרת ואת התפתחויותיו של הדגם.

בדרך זו של חשיפת דגמים נגלה כי גם אירועים שנראים ריאליים וקונקרטיים אינם למעשה אלא דפוס ספרותי שניתן למצאו לא רק במקרא כי אם גם מחוצה לו. נקח לדוגמא את המסופר על מות אבימלך ושאול. לאחר שאישה השליכה פלח רכב על ראש אבימלך ורוצצה את גלגלתו (שופ' ט, כג) קורא אבימלך **לנער נושא כליו** ואומר לו: **שלוף חרבך** ומותתני פן יאמרו לי אשה הרגתהו'. ואז מסופר: 'וידקרהו נערו וימת' (פס' נד). אותו דפוס בסגנון חופף אנו מוצאים בקשר לשאול: **'ויאמר שאול לנשא כליו שלף חרבך ודקרני** בה פן יבאו הערלים האלה ודקרני והתעללו בי ולא אבה נשא כליו כי ירא מאד ויקח שאול את החרב ויפל עליה. וירא נשא כליו כי מת שאול ויפל גם הוא על חרבו וימת עמו' (שמ"א לא, ד).[13] המוטיב בקשר למלך ומנהיג

---

11 ראה מאמרי: "מסורת ההתנחלות של שבטי ישראל בכנען — הדגם ואופיו", קתדרה לתולדות א"י ויישובה מד (תשמ"ז) 3־20.

12 כנ"ל.

13 וראה להקבלה זו: צ' טלשיר, "על זיקה בין סיפורים בהיסטוריוגרפיה המקראית הקדומה", שנתון ה־ו (תשמ"א - תשמ"ב) 71.

ובכך נעמוד על דרך יצירתו ומשמעה.

אולם אפילו בתחום הסיפורת ההיסטורית עצמה, ניתן ללמוד הרבה על-ידי הבחנות רבדים. יש להבחין בין תיאור מציאות היסטורית פוליטית שכל קורא יודע עליה, ואי-אפשר להציג בפניו שקר לבין שיחות אינטימיות ודיאלוגים שהסופר ממציא לשם התיאור. כמו-כן יש להבחין בין תיאור פוליטי-היסטורי המנוסח כרוניקה עובדתית שיש לנו מקבילה לה במקורות חוץ כגון התיאור על תשלום המס לסנחרב במל"ב יח, יד-טז[8] לבין התיאור הסמוך לו שמביא את הסיפור על מפלת צבא סנחרב שיש בו הרבה גלוריפיקציה ורצון להציג את הדברים כנס גדול. לחוקרי הסיפורת יש כאן אתגר דווקא בשל השוני באופי המקורות שלפנינו. אין לשים על מישור אחד כרוניקה עובדתית שיש לה אסמכתא חיצונית לבין סיפור פלא הבא לתאר את התערבותו הישירה של האל במפלת הצבא האשורי באמצעות מלאך ה' המכה במחנה אשור 185 אלף (מל"ב יט, לה).

עד עתה טענתי שהבחנת רבדים תעמיק את ההבנה הסיפרותית. ברצוני גם להראות שההתעלמות מרבדים ומקורות עשוייה להוליכנו למסקנות מוטעות בתחום הניתוח האסתטי של הסיפורת. כך למשל קובע שטרנברג כי הסיפור המקראי יש בו אידיאולוגיה אך אין הוא סיפור דידאקטי שכן איננו מעריך את גיבוריו לטוב או לרע כי אם נותן לקורא להתרשם מהתיאור ולהעריך בעצמו את הגיבורים. איפיון זה כשלעצמו נכון ללא ספק. כך למשל בסיפורי ירושת העצר של דוד אנו תמהים כל הזמן מה יחסו של המספר לדוד: האם שופט אותו לחיוב או לשלילה? גם כשהוא אומר על דוד בקשר ליחסו לאדניה בן חגית: 'ולא עצבו אביו מימיו לאמר מדוע ככה עשית' (מל"א א, ו) אנו שואלים האם הוא רואה בכך טוב לבו של המלך או חולשת אופי ועל הקורא להחליט. אותו דבר מופיע בתה"ש לגבי אמנון בשמ"ב יג, כא, שם נאמר: 'ולא עצב את אמנון בנו כי אהבו כי בנו הוא',[9] ואף שם אותה דילמה. זה כמובן נובע להערכת דמותו של דוד בכלל, האם ניתן להסיק כי התנהגותו המאופקת של דוד ביחס לילדיו גרמה לטרגדיה בחצרו.

והוא הדין ביחס לעמדת המספר לגבי שלמה במל"א א-ב. האם שלמה מוצג כאכזרי ושופך דמים בפרקים אלה או שמא אין הוא אלא ממלא בקפדנות צוואת אביו?

שטרנברג טוען בצדק שהנויטראליות של המספר יש בה קוים אסתטיים מופלאים ואף מגמה חינוכית, אך אינו מודע לעובדה שלצד הסיפור הנויטראלי יש מסגרת דידאקטית-דוגמאטית שהיא ההיפך מהנויטראליות. בעוד שבסיפור עצמו על שלמה לא נאמר דבר על אופיו הרי במסגרת של הסיפור, שאנו מכנים אותה דטרונומיסטית, יש הערכה ברורה ואף קיצונית של אישיותו: 'ויעש שלמה הרע בעיני ה' ולא מלא אחרי ה' כדוד אביו' (מל"א יא, ו).

משפטים חורצים כאלה מצויים במסגרות של ספר שופטים וספר מלכים ואין לשים אותם בשום פנים ואופן על מישור אחד עם הסיפורים עצמם. פער פעור בין המספר על אחאב שהיה מעומד במרכבה נכח ארם לבין בעל המסגרת המעניין למסור כי הכלבים לקקו את דמו (מל"א כב לה, לח).[10] המסגרות האלה שקובעות באופן נחרץ מי עשה הרע בעיני ה' ומי עשה הישר בעיני ה' המלוות את הסיפורים עומדות בניגוד גמור לקביעה הכוללת של שטרנברג שהיצירה הסיפורית המקראית היא א-דידאקטית. לא זו בלבד שבשכבות מסויימות יש דידאקטיקה אלא אף אינדוקטרינציה ברורה. על כל פנים אין זה נכון לומר שהסיפור המקראי בכלל אין בו אינדוקטרינציה ודידאקטיקה.

---

[8] ראה לאחרונה ח' תדמור, "בחינות היסטוריוגרפיות והיסטוריות", ציון נ (תשמ"ג) 65-80.

[9] הקטע הושמט מנוסח המסורה בשל הומויוארכטון (קפיצת עין של הסופר מיו"ו שבתחלת הקטע שהושמט ליו"ו שבתחלת פס' כב), ראה לאחרונה פירושו של מק-קרטר לשמואל בסידרת AB, 1984.

[10] ראה בספרי: *Deuteronomy and the Deuteronomic School* (Oxford, 1972) 20ff.

אולם עם כל היתרונות של השיטה הספרותית יש לשאול אם הגיע הזמן לנטוש את השיטות הקונבנציונליות המבוססות על מציאת רבדים והתחקות אחרי שלבי ההתפתחות ההיסטורית של היצירה. האם, כפי שטוענים אחדים, ניתוח היצירה לרבדים תפריע לראיית כוליותה? או שמא יש לקיים את השיטות השונות זו לצד זו? עניין אחד הוא לראות את דרך התפתחות היצירה ואת המסר ההיסטורי שלה ועניין נפרד הוא להתחקות על היצירה השלמה ומשמעה הספרותי-אסתטי. ברצוננו להראות שהניתוח הביקורתי-ההיסטורי, לא זו בלבד שאינו מפריע כי אם להיפך הכרחי להבנת ההיבטים האסתטיים של היצירה המקראית.

השימוש במימצאי הביקורת הספרותית ההיסטורית יסלק הרבה מכשולים העומדים בדרכה של השיטה הספרותית-האסתטית. כך למשל קביעתו של שטרנברג בספרו *The Poetics of Biblical Narrative*[5] שהיצירה המקראית היא כולה היסטוריוגרפיה שכן מתיימרת למסור היסטוריה, אינה מדוייקת שכן מעמידה על מישור אחד את כל היצירה המקראית מבלי להתחשב ברבדים הספרותיים השונים שבה. כבר העירה אדל ברלין בביקורתה על ספרו של שטרנברג[6] שאין למדוד בקנה מידה אחיד את סיפורי הבריאה עם סיפורי האבות וקורות המלוכה, סיפור קין והבל אינו שייך לאותו ז׳אנר שאליו שייך הסיפור על מלחמת המלכים בבר׳ יד ושניהם שונים תכלית השינוי מסיפור מסע סנחרב ליהודה. ואכן אם מעיינים אנו בספרות המזרח הקדום שם הטכסטים עדיין לא גובשו לכדי תיאור היסטורי רצוף מהבריאה עד החורבן, כפי שנעשה בספרות המקרא, הרי אנו מגלים כי יצירות השייכות לז׳אנרים ספרותיים שונים בוללו בישראל במתכוון, וכי היו קיימים במזרח הקדום כסוגי יצירה שונים הנפרדים זה מזה; אנו מוצאים שם סיפורי בראשית לחוד, ורשימות אבות העולם לחוד, אנאלים מלכותיים המתארים מסעות מלחמה של המלכים לחוד וכרוניקות המסכמות בגוף שלישי תקופות של מאות בשנים לחוד, תיאורי בניין מקדשים לחוד ומזמורי נצחון לחוד. כל אחד מהווה ז׳אנר בפני עצמו. כנגד זאת בספרות המקרא צורפו באופן די מלאכותי ז׳אנרים אלה כדי ליצור היסטוריה רצופה ובשל כך נוצרו לא מעט חיספוסים ואי-הבנות. כך למשל בספר שמות המתיימר להציג לפנינו את תקופת יציאת מצרים צורפו זה לזה סיפור, שירת נצחון (פרק טו), חוק ומשפט, ותיאורי בנין המשכן. וכיוצא בזה ספר מלכים המתאר את תולדות המלוכה צירף ביחד סיפורי חצר (מל״א א-ב)[7] עם רשימות אדמיניסטרטיביות, (מל״א ד) תיאורי בנין המקדש (מל״א ו-ז), אנאלים מלכותיים, סיפורים נבואיים וכרוניקות סינכרוניסטיות. הללו האחרונות מהוות באשור ז׳אנר בפני עצמו.

יש לשאול כמובן מה משמעו של סידור החומר המונח לפנינו אך אסור להתעלם מן השוני במרכיבים העשוי להסביר לנו את הקשיים בהבנת מבנה היצירה השלמה. אדרבה הכרה בשוני זה יגלה לנו את כשרונו של הסופר שהתגבר על פערים ויישב סתירות כדי להשיג אחדות. בדרך זו נעמוד על גדולת הספור המקראי שהגיע מ-Aufzählung = מסירת עובדות, כפי שזה היה נהוג במיסופוטאמיה, ל-Erzählung = סיפור המעשה. בניגוד לחומר של המזרח הקדום שהוא אטומיסטי ופרגמנטארי הרי הסופר המקראי המונע בכח אידיאולוגיה היסטורית יצר היסטוריוגרפיה רצופה מחונכת. כך למשל סיפורי התגלות הם ז׳אנר שונה מקובצי חוקים, אך על-ידי צירוף שני הז׳אנרים נולד הסיפור על מעמד הר סיני שעשה את עם ישראל לעם סגולה. צודק שטרנברג שבשביל הסופר הישראלי תיאור בריאת העולם הוא היסטוריה באותה מידה שכיבוש הארץ הוא היסטוריה. אך דווקא חוקרי ספרות צריכים להיות ערים להבדלים שבז׳אנר, כדי להבחין בתופעות ספרותיות שונות. המעניין הוא לראות כיצד צירף הסופר הישראלי ז׳אנרים

---

5 M. Sternberg, *The Poetics of Biblical Narrative* (Bloomington, 1985).

6 *Prooftexts* 6 (1986) 273-84.

7 כפי שכבר ראה: L. Rost, *Die Überlieferung von der Thronfolge Davids* (BWANT 42; Stuttgart, 1926). שייכים שני פרקים אלה להמשך סיפורי ירושת העצר של דוד הכוללים שמ״ב ט-כ.

המקרא בראי הספרות

משה ויינפלד

בשל הדעה הקדומה שהתנ״ך בא ללמד ולא לענג ולהנות היתה קיימת רתיעה מלקרא את התנ״ך כספרות ולהיזונות ממנה הנאה אסתיטית. אנו נזכרים אגב כך במאמר חז״ל בקשר לכתוב: זמירות היו לי חוקיך בבית מגורי׳ (תהי קיט, נד): ״מפני מה נענש דוד מפני שקרא לדברי תורה ״זמירות״׳ (סוטה לה ע״א). במקרא עצמו מוצגת ההשקפה שכדי להעריך נכונה את דברי הנביא יש לדעת שדברי הנביא לא באו לענג אלא לאלף. על יחזקאל נאמר: ׳והנך להם כשיר עגבים יפה קול ומיטיב נגן ושמעו את דבריך ועשים אינם אתם׳ (לג, לב). עם זאת, דוקא מכתוב זה אנו למדים שעצם השמעת הדברים בשיר וניגון הקלה על הקליטה ולפיכך היתה הכרחית.

ואכן מסתבר לנו בשנים האחרונות כי הממד הספרותי הוא חלק מהמסר של הטקסט. כך למשל מעמד הר סיני, שהפך ערך מרכזי באמונת ישראל, יונק למעשה את כל תוקפו מהתיאור הספרותי המלהיב של עם העומד מלא חרדה מול ההר הבוער באש (ראה בייחוד דברים ד). הספרות עיצבה איפוא את המסר הדתי והחויה הדתית. ואמנם שיקולי אסתטיקה במבנה, צורה וכיאסמוס, מלה מנחה וכמות הופעתה ביחידה וכיוצא בזה, כל אלה עוזרים לנו להבין את מירקם הפרשה ואף מגמתה. השיטה הכוליית שפותחה על-ידי מאיר וייס[1] מלמדת כי כדי להבין את היצירה ולאו דוקא את דרך התהוותה, חשוב לראות את היצירה כמות שהיא לפנינו ולהבינה מבפנים. כמו כן למדנו כי לא רק בסיפור יש לשים לב למירקם הספרותי-אסטיטי, גם בחוקה קיימים אותם כללים. ההבחנה הספרותית בין חוק מנוסח בצורה אפודיקטית לבין חוק מנוסח בצורה קאזואיסטית היא שמאפשרת לנו להבין את מוצא החוקים ותיפקודם בחברה.[2] יתרה מזו בשנים האחרונות למדים אנו כי ניסוח החוקים ובמיוחד החוקים הכהניים מושתת על דגמים ומבנים ספרותיים כמעט פיוטיים ועל כך עמד מי פארן ז״ל בחיבורו.[3] אף רשימות יוחסין יבשות נמסרו לנו בצורה ספרותית.[4]

---

1 ראה לאחרונה ספריו: המקרא כדמותו (מהדורה שלישית מתוקנת ומורחבת [ירושלים, תשמ״ז]); מקראות בכוונתם, לקט מאמרים (ירושלים, תשמ״ח).

2 הראשון שהבחין בין הצורות הללו היה א׳ אלט במאמרו: "Die Ursprünge des Israelitischen Rechts," (1934) *Kleine Schriften* (Munich, 1959) 1:278-323, וראה לאחרונה על דגמי ניסוח בחוק הישראלי והמיסופוטאמי אצל ש׳ פאול, לשוננו לד (תש״ל) 257-266.

3 דרכי הסגנון הכוהני בתורה — דגמים, שימושי לשון, מבנים (ירושלים, תשמ״ט).

4 לדוגמה יפה הנוגעת לדה״א ז, כ-כח ראה לאחרונה: L. Mazor, "The Origin and Evolution of the Curse upon the Rebuilder of Jericho," *Textus* 14 (1988) 1-26.

ורשעים עוד אינם׳.[35] לכאורה, אין בהסברים אלה כדי לבטל את הצרימה המבנית של מעבר חד מדי מתיאורי הבריאה, מן ההפתעה ה"טרייה" של המסקנה בדבר חוסר הודאות במחזוריות היקום, אל הבעת שמחה אישית של המשורר. ואולם טענתי היא, שכיוון שלאורך כל המזמור הוכנה הקרקע למעבר חד זה — אין הוא חד מדי. בעשותו את המפנה המפתיע לנורמה האסטטית השלטת במזמור, לצד הקטלוג, נתן המחבר הכשר (במשמע ׳"כשר" ומשמע "כשירות" כאחת) ספרותי למעבר החד גם בסוף המזמור, וכך היה ההגד בתחום החברי-מוסרי לחלק בלתי נפרד מן המזמור גם מבחינה רעיונית ואסטטית.

---

35 ׳עובדת הרום האינסופי והמכריע של ה׳ ויחד עמה קרבת האלהים אשר כל אחד ואחד יוכל למצוא אותה ... היא הערובה, שבסופו של דבר ישמעו בני האדם לכמיהה אל ה׳ הטבועה בליבם, ועי״כ יתמו מעיקרם מן הארץ כל קלות הדעת ואי הציות לתורה ה׳ ...׳ (ר׳ שמשון רפאל הירש, ספר תהילים, [ירושלים, תשכ״ב] 141) וכן: The poet longs for time when God's joy in his creature and the creature's joy in his Maker will unite in perfect harmony... (וייזר, [לעיל, הערה 5], עמ׳ 670).

(דור הולך ודור בא... וזרח השמש ובא השמש ...סובב סבב הולך הרוח ועל סביבתיו שב הרוח׳
וכדו׳, א, ד-ט), מצטרף כאן לשבחי האל, כחלק בלתי נפרד מתיאור התכליתיות בעולם. אמנם
בניגוד למוטיב התכליתיות, הנישא באופן ברור על-גבי י׳ל׳ התכלית, אין כאן דברים מפורשים על
המחזוריות הנצחית, הבלתי נמנעת, כביכול, בעולם, אך יש במזמור מספיק נתונים התורמים
לבניין ההשערה, שכוונתו לשבח לא רק את תכליתיות היקום אלא גם את המחזוריות שבו.
השערה זו נבנית מתיאורי זרימת המים בפסוקים ו-י; מאיזכור השמש והירח, היום והלילה
בפסוקים יט-כ; מתיאור "חילופי התפקידים" המחזוריים בין האדם לבעלי-החיים בפסוקים כא-
כג. וכך מגיע הקורא לפסוק כד כשהוא מצוייד בהכרה ברורה לגבי המסר הכפול של המזמור:
העולם תכליתי ומחזורי, וזהו שבחו של הבורא. ה-anticlimax בפסוקים כה-כז, העשוי, כאמור,
להיראות "סרח עודף" (וגם בכך הוא ממלא תפקיד פואטי, שהרי כדי להעניין לפסוק כד מעמד של
שיא יש הכרח ליצור אחריו ירידה כלשהיא!) אין בו דבר שיכול לערער את מסקנת הקורא.
ואולם בפסוקים כח-ל חוזרת בפעם השלישית אותה תופעה מבנית — המפנה המפתיע, המעבר
הבלתי צפוי, ושוב נשברת, הפעם רק בחלקה, השערתו ה"וודאית" הקודמת של הקורא. שהרי
הכתוב קובע כאן במפורש, שאין בעולם מחזוריות בלתי נמנעת: ׳תתן להם ילקטון תפתח ידך
ישבעון טוב תסתיר פניך יבהלון תסף רוח יגועון ואל עפרם ישובון. תשלח רוחך יבראון ותחדש
פני האדמה׳. נמצא הקורא מופתע שוב, אולי אף מאוכזב, מכשלונו החוזר ונשנה לגלות את
ה"צופן" של היצירה במלואו: אכן, הבריאה תכליתית, אך אין היא מחזורית כמו שטעה לחשוב.
למקרא המנון אחנתון, שאחד הלקחים העיקריים העולים ממנו הוא כי יש מחזוריות קבועה
ובלתי ניתנת להפרעה בעולם, יובן ההבט הפולמוסי של המסר ההפוך של מזמור קד. אף דרך
הבעתו של מסר זה במזמור — כהפתעה, כתיקון של אי-הבנה, יש בו מן התשובה הסמויה לטענת
ההמנון המצרי.

(ד) אין זו הפעם האחרונה שעושה המחבר שימוש בתכסיס המפנה המפתיע. הפיסקה לב-לה
חורגת מכמה וכמה בחינות מכל שקדם לה: רק כאן חוזר המזמור (לאחר ׳ברכי נפשי׳ שבפתיחה)
לגוף מדבר (פסוק לג); בעוד שלאורך המזמור כולו ממלא האדם תפקיד משני ושולי הרי בפסוקים
אלה הוא העיקר; מוטיב הצדיק והרשע אינו נרמז כלל לאורך המזמור, ונראה לפיכך שלא במקומו
בסופו. ואולם אין בזאת כדי להצדיק את הסברה, שפסוקים אלה אינם מעיקרו של המזמור
המקורי.[34] כבר ציינתי שהקריאה ׳ברכי נפשי׳ והמעבר החד מתיאור הוד הבריאה הם רמז
מטרים, היוצר ציפיות לנימה אישית גם בהמשך המזמור. ציפיה זו מתממשת רק בפסוק לג.
הנימה האישית יוצרת זימון נאה ומקובל בספרות המזמורים לאיזכור מוטיב הצדיק והרשע, וגם
את הבאתו **כסיכום** להמנון אפשר להבין: ההרמוניה המלאה בקיום, עליה עמד המחבר תוך כדי
תיאוריו, הביאתו למסקנה שלא יתכן שיהיה קיום ממושך לרשעים, שהם הגורם היחיד הפוגם
בהרמוניה זו, ומכאן בקשתו (או מסקנתו ההגיונית, לדעת אחרים) ׳יתמו חטאים מן הארץ

---

[34] גונקל, שם, עמ׳ 447, סבור, שבפסוק כג בא המזמור המקורי לסיומו, ופסוק כד פתח מזמור חדש.
ראיה הוא מוצא בריבוי פעלים בבינוני בשבח האל בפסוקים א-כג, שאינו אופייני לחלק השני של
המזמור. לדעתו שני המזמורים נכתבו בידי אותו מחבר, ולאחר מכן צרפם עורך זה לזה. לאחרונה
טען ריינדל שהפסוקים לא-לה נוספו למזמור המקורי בעת שספר תהילים כולו עבר עריכה חכמתית.
ראה: J. Reindel, "Weisheitliche Bearbeitung von Psalmen," VTSup 32 (Leiden,
56-351 (1981. דבריו על מזמור קד תמצא בעמ׳ 350-348. אינני מתכוון להתדיין ישירות עם
טענות אלו, וראה פולמוסו של וייס עם גונקל (לעיל, הערה 24) עמ׳ 55], בתקווה שהניתוח הספרותי
של המזמור יתרום להפרכתו.

המזמור. עתה הוא מצפה לתחושת נחת הרוח המלווה את האישור המוחלט של השערתו. ואולם כבר לפסוק ח מתגנב מוטיב התכליתיות בבריאה: זרימת המים 'אל מקום זה יסדת להם' מונעת שיטפונות בעולם; הנחלים הזורמים משקים את חיות השדה ואת העצים, שבין עפאיהם שוכנות הצפרים. הופעתו הראשונה של מוטיב התכליתיות אינה בולטת, ואי אפשר לאבחן אותה אלא במבט לאחור, משהוצג רצף של מספר פרטים; אך אם אין בה עדיין כדי להעלות השערה חדשה בעניין המסר של המזמור, הרי יש בה כדי לעכב בעד אותה תחושת נחת רוח לה מצפה עתה הקורא. נראה שרק בהגיעו לפסוקים יא-יב הוא יכול לתקן לעצמו את השערתו הקודמת, לפיה עיקר המזמור הוא השבח את יפי הבריאה, ולהעלות בהיסוס השערה חדשה לגבי הצופן של המזמור:[29] עיקרו הוא השבח על **תכליתיות** הבריאה. חיזוקים להשערה חדשה זו אפשר למצוא בפסוקים יד-כג: מילית המפתח בהם היא 'ל' התכלית,[30] והשימוש החוזר ונשנה בה תורם לביסוס התחושה, כי הפעם לא טעה. אישור מוחלט לכך בודאי מוצא הקורא בפסוק כד, המשבח לא את יפי הבריאה אלא את חכמת הבורא.[31] גם המבנה המשולש של הפסוק, החורג ממבנה מרבית הפסוקים במזמור, (מה שהביא כמה חוקרים לפקפק במקוריותו. ראה לקמן, הערה 34) מאשר, שזהו שיא המזמור. עתה, משמגיע לשיא נראה לקורא שיותר אין למזמור מה לחדש: אכן, הוא טעה בשלב ראשון בהבנת המסר, אך עתה אין לו עוד מקום לטעות: חכמת האל בבריאה היא שבחו העיקרי. מה שנראה במבט ראשון יפה בלבד — הלך והתברר גם כתכליתי, מחוכם ומחושב.[32]

(ג) מיקומו של פסוק השיא (כד) הרבה לפני סופו של המזמור, בצורה שקוטעת את רשימת ברואי האל (שהרי רשימה זו נמשכת גם בפסוקים כה-כו),[33] ממלא תפקיד מבני כפול: (1) ביצרו רושם של התפרצות פתאומית, הוא מציג את המשורר כמי שלא היה יכול לעצור בעצמו מלהביע, שלא במקומה, כביכול, את התובנה שהבריקה בו לגבי המסר האמיתי של הבריאה; והרי במצב זה ממש מצוי הקורא. (2) קוטע את דגם הקטלוג, קודם שייגע יותר מדי את הקורא בשל ארכו ובשל השימוש התכוף ב-'ל' התכלית בפסוקים יד-כג.

ואולם הגעה לשיא היצירה בשלב מוקדם מדי, אחד-עשר פסוקים לפני סיומה, יוצרת בעיה מבנית חדשה: יש סכנה שיתרת המזמור תהיה מעין סרח עודף שמיותר אולי לקראו, שהרי כבר אנו מעבר לשיא המזמור, וכבר עמדנו על המסר שבו. אני סבור, שגם בעיה זו באה על פתרונה תוך שימוש מתוחכם באותה טכניקה מבנית של המפנה המפתיע, הפעם בלא שיצטרך הקורא להחליף את השערתו, כי תכליתיות הבריאה היא הצופן להבנת המזמור.

תוך כדי פיתוח מוטיב התכליתיות בבריאה, ובד בבד עם התחדדות ההכרה אצל הקורא בחשיבותה, מתגבשת תחושה, שהמזמור מלמדנו גם על קיומה של **מחזוריות אימננטית** ביקום. הרושם הוא, כי מוטיב זה, שבספר קוהלת נעשה בו שימוש אמנותי ליצירת אוירה מלנכולית

---

29 על הטכניקה של בנית השערות והפרכתן ועל יישומה בפרוזה עמד פרי. ראה: מ' פרי, "הדינאמיקה של הטקסט הספרותי", הספרות כח (1979) 6-46.
30 לבהמה; לעבודת; להוציא; להצהיל; לעלים; לשפנים; למועדים; לטרף; לפעלו; ולעבדתו.
31 ראה על כך דבריו של וייס, שם, עמ' 55-57.
32 על זיהוי היפה עם התכליתי בטבע ומכאן גם תביעה פואטית לתכליתיות באמנות ראה ע"י קאנט, ביקורת כח השיפוט (ירושלים, תשכ"ט) 20-28, 124.
33 בריגס (לעיל, הערה 5), עמ' 339 טען שפסוק כד אינו במקום נאות, הוא מורכב **מכמה** גלוסות שהעתקו ממקומן הראשוני (עמ' 336). בכלל, לדעתו המזמור כולו מלא בגלוסות (כ-15, ראה עמ' 329), שאת חלקן הוא אף יודע לתארך! גונקל (לעיל, הערה 5), עמ' 451 הציע לפרק את פסוק כד לשניים בצורה הבאה: 'מה רבו מעשיך ה' רבה הארץ קנינך + פסוק כה + כלם בחכמה עשית'. וראה דבריו גם בהערה הבאה.

תנה הודך על השמים', ומיד בעקבותיה אכן מתאר המשורר מהו שמאדיר את שם האל ומבטא את הודו. מזמור קג פותח בהמרצה כפולה (פסוקים א; ב) 'ברכי נפשי את ה' זהה לזו שבמזמורנו, ומיד בהמשך באה הנמקה הולמת לקריאה זו 'אל תשכחי כל גמוליו. הסולח לכל עונכי...' וגו'. נוצר איפוא הרושם שבמזמורנו יש מעין קצר בין היסודות A ו-B, על מנת להגיע בפשטות יתרה ליסוד C. אולם למקרא המזמור כולו מתברר, **שהמפנה המפתיע** הוא תכסיס ספרותי דומיננטי ביצירה, שקבע לא במעט את מבנה, ובהופעתו מיד בהתחלה יש משום רמז מטרים לכך. הוכחתה של טענה זו תידחה להמשך הדיון, באשר היא מחייבת ניתוח עניינים נוספים, אך כבר בשלב זה ראוי להתייחס למשפט הסיום, הזהה, כאמור, למשפט הפתיחה.[28] לעומת המעבר התמוה בפסוק א הרי הופעת קריאת 'ברכי נפשי' בסוף המזמור נראית מובנת וטבעית ביותר, משום שפסוקים לג-לה מכשירים עבורה היטב את הקרקע. פסוקים אלה שונים מאלה שבפתיחת המזמור (למעט הקריאה 'ברכי נפשי את ה') משתי בחינות: הם מנוסחים בגוף ראשון, ומדברים על תחושות השמחה והבטחון של המשורר (אשירה, אזמרה, שיחי, אשמח). לפיכך קריאת 'ברכי נפשי' בעקבותיהם היא טבעית, כמעט מתבקשת. בשיבוצה אחרי המלים 'יתמו חטאים מן הארץ ורשעים עוד אינם' ממלאת קריאה זו תפקיד נוסף: היא "מגלה" לקורא, שבעל המזמור הוא ההפך מן ה'חטאים' וה'רשעים', משמע הוא צדיק, אשר על כן הוא קורא לנפשו לברך את האל, מכחיד הרשעים. נמצא שסיום המזמור מתקשר באופן מעגלי לפתיחתו לא רק בעצם החזרה ה"טכנית", לכאורה, על 'ברכי נפשי', אלא גם מבחינה עניינית: אי אתה יכול להבין את פתיחת המזמור אלא אם כן הגעת לסופו.

(ב) עצם הקריאה '...גדלת מאד הוד והדר לבשתי', והתפקיד שהיא ממלאת — לנמק (בצורה בלתי צפויה, כאמור) את קריאת הפתיחה 'ברכי נפשי' — קובעים את התרשמותו הראשונה של הקורא: זהו מזמור שעיקרו ביטוי ל**רגשות** המחבר. התרשמות זו מתחזקת למקרא פסוקי ההמשך, המתארים דברים מפעימים ביפים ובהדרם, כהוכחה לאמירה 'הוד והדר לבשתי': השמים המוארים, העבים וצורותיהם הציוריות מעוררות הדמיון, מלאכים אפופי אש לוהטת, זרימה אדירה של שטפונות מים, נופי הרים וגבעות. ככל שמתמשכים התיאורים הללו כן מתגבשת בקרב הקורא ההכרה, שהוא עומד על הרעיון היסודי של המזמור: הוכחת טענת 'הוד והדר לבשת'. הכרה מעין זו (היכולה לאפיין גם את המאזין ליצירה מוסיקאלית, בהיות המוסיקה כמו הספרות אמנות המתרחשת במימד הזמן) עשויה להיות מורכבת משלושה שלבים. בשלב הראשון **מגשש** הקורא תוך נסיון למצוא את ה"מפתח" להבנת היצירה, ובסופו, משנדמה לו כי אכן הגיע אליו, הוא חש ריגוש אינטלקטואלי של מי שהגיע לתובנה; בשלב השני, עם המשך הקריאה, משתברר לו שהנחתו מקבלת **אישור** וחיזוק, מתחלף הריגוש לנחת רוח שלווה; ואולם אם שלב זה מתמשך יתר על המידה עלולה תחושת הנחת להתחלף בשעמום, במסקנה שאין טעם להמשיך לקרוא, משום שכבר הכל גלוי וידוע וצפוי. נמצא שבסיסה של היצירה על קטלוג פלאי הטבע, שהוגדר לעיל כ"הגד" בפני עצמו, ולא רק כאמצעי טכני, יוצר בעיה מבנית: כיצד להתמיד בדגם הקטלוגי בלא שיגיע הקורא מוקדם מדי לשלב בו יחוש שאין לו עוד חפץ בקריאת היצירה. האם פתר המשורר בעיה זו? דומה כי בעובדה שאנו קוראים במזמור עד סופו בלא להגיע לשלב השעמום יש משום תשובה חיובית חד משמעית לשאלה זו, ולא נותר אלא לבדוק כיצד עשה זאת המחבר.

את הפתרון ניתן להגדיר כהעתקה מודרגת של הדגשים בתיאור הבריאה מן המרגש אל התכליתי. תיאורי האור, השמים, המים, העבים, זרימת המים, המתמשכים עד פסוק ט יוצרים בבירור את תחושת ההוד וההדר, ובהדרגה מגשימים אצל הקורא את ההשערה, כי יפי הבריאה הוא המסר של

---

[28] למעט המלה 'הללויה', שהיא ככל הנראה חותמת עריכה, המופיעה בספר תהלים ב-12 מזמורים נוספים (קה; קו; קיג; קטז-קיז; קלה; קמו-קנ).

נכונה; אין היא אלא ראיה למעמדו האסטרטגי של סיפור **פתיחה**, ולכך השכנוע שיש לסגנון "יבש", ו"סכמטי", כסגנון ברי א, כשמשתמשים בו בדרך ובהקשר הולמים. נמצא שאילו בחר לשבח את האל על-ידי תיאור סדר הבריאה, היה על מחבר המזמור להכריע איזו מסורת בריאה יציג במזמורו. אכן, אפשר לומר, כי מן הסתם יציג את המסורת המקובלת עליו, ואולם זהו פתרון גרוע מבחינת תכלית יצירתו: אם רצונו למקד את דבריו בשבח האל הבורא, מוטב לו שלא ירמוז לסיפור בריאה שיש עליו חולקים, משום שבכך הוא עלול להכניס למזמור יסוד מעורר מחלוקת, שיסיטו את תשומת הלב מן העיקר, ויפגום בתכלית המזמור. ואף זאת: מי לנו ערב, שהייתה למשוררנו העדפה של מסורת בריאה זו או אחרת? נמצא שהשאלה כיצד לספר על הבריאה, באיזה סדר למנות את פרטיה, היא בעית רקע שהמחבר לא יכול היה להתעלם ממנה, כאשר פתרונה עשוי לקבוע במידה מכרעת את מבנה המזמור כולו.[25] מבעיה זו פטורים היו בעלי ההמנונים הקצרים יותר, לא רק משום שקיצורם איפשר להם לאזכר רק פרטים מעטים מן הבריאה, אלא גם משום שהיותה הבריאה רק אחד המוטיבים בהם מחלישה את חריפות הבעיה.

ב

לאחר שנפרשו כמה מנתוני הרקע העשויים לתרום להבנת המזמור, אבקש לעיין בו במגמה לחשוף את הבעיות המזדמנות, שהפתרונות להן קבעו במידה רבה את עיצובה של היצירה.
(א) המזמור פותח ומסיים במשפט קצר זהה 'ברכי נפשי את ה". ויוצא בכך חובת הדגם לפתוח בהכרזה ולסיים במסקנה (יסודות A; D) בדרך קלה ופשוטה, הנקוטה גם בהמנונים אחרים.[26] בנמקו את קריאת הפתיחה במלים הספורות 'ה' אלהי גדלת מאד, הוד והדר לבשת' (יסוד B) יצר לעצמו המשורר מרחב להקדיש את המזמור כולו למוטב העיקרי בהמנונים — פירוט שבחי האל (יסוד C). ואולם הפתיחה 'ברכי נפשי' חורגת מעט מן המוסכמה בפתחה בברכה ולא בהלל לאל, וכך למקרא הפסוקים הראשונים המפרטים את שבח האל נוצר הרושם, כי גיוון זה של הדגם השגור בא על חשבון ההגיון הפנימי של הכתוב: הקשר בין ההמרצה העצמית לברך את האל, לבין הנמקתה המתייחסת **ליופי** הבריאה, נראה מאולץ: כהקדמה לתיאור הוד והדר הבריאה היינו מצפים לקריאת התפעלות ולא להמרצה לברך.[27] השוואה עם מזמורים ח ו-קג תבהיר זאת. מזמור ח פותח בקריאת התפעלות 'ה' אדוננו מה אדיר שמך בכל הארץ אשר

---

25 השאלה האם מחבר מזמורנו הכיר את סיפור הבריאה ברי' א נוגעת לענייננו, ותשובה חיובית הייתה גורמת דיון במהות ה"דיאלוג" בין המזמור לבין אותו סיפור. דא עקא, שהתשובה כרוכה בתיארוך מדויק של מזמורנו ושל ברי' א, המחייב דיון בפני עצמו, שאין זה מקומו, וקשה להמנע בו מטענות מעגליות, כעולה מדבריהם של חוקרים שנקטו עמדה בעניין. ראה גונקל (לעיל, הערה 5), עמי 453; בריגס (לעיל, הערה 5), עמי 330-331 (היודע להצביע על כתובים מקראיים נוספים שעמדו לנגד עיני מחבר מזמור קד). לעומתם קבע קראוס (לעיל, הערה 3), עמי 709 שמחבר מזמורנו לא הכיר כלל את הסיפור בברי א.
26 השווה ח; קג; קמה; וכן קו; קיג; קמו-קנז, הפותחים ומסיימים ב'הללויה'. ראה גם מזמורים קיח; קלה; קלו, שגם אם אינם המנונים לפי המיון שהצגנו לעיל, הרי יש בהם הרבה מיסודות ההמנוניים.
27 מיטשל כפה על משפט הפתיחה את היסוד A השיגרתי בטענו, ש'ברכי' הבא במזמורי תהילים בבנין פיעל ציווי כשנושאו האדם, פרושו 'הלל'. דעה זו אינה מקובלת עלי מה גם שמיטשל עצמו מודה, שהפועל אינו מתנהג כפעלי הלל רגילים. ראה: C. W. Mitchell, *The Meaning of BRK 'to bless' in the Old Testament* (Atlanta, 1987) 82, 138-46. הנכון הוא, ככל הנראה, שהשימוש בפעל 'יברך' בהמנונינו ניתן לו בדיעבד, בהשפעת ההקשר המיוחד, גוון אפשרי של 'הלל', ואין בכך כדי לסתור את טענתנו. בריגס (לעיל, הערה 5), עמי 329 סבור, שהנוסחה 'ברכי נפשי את ה" היא גלוסה ליטורגית, ואף קביעה זו מוטלת בספק.

('הארץ בחשכה כמו מתי'), נתונה לשלטון חיות טרף, 'כי נח יוצרם באפקי, ואילו במזמורנו יש תפקיד חיובי גם לילה',[21] שאין בו כל אנרכיה, וגם בחשכה חיות הטרף שואגות **לבקש** מאל אכלם' (כא). כללו של דבר: אתון הוא חלק ממערכת היקום, ואילו ה' הוא מחוצה לה, אינו כפוף לה. אמירה זו עולה מממזמור קד כשהוא לעצמו, אך מי שרואה לנגד עיניו גם את ההמנון המצרי יכול לעמוד גם על היסוד הפולמוסי שבה.[22]

(ג) הרצוי להטיל על דגם הקטלוג סדר אברים משמעותי מעורר את הבעיה, על-פי איזה עקרון יוזכרו פרטי הבריאה: לפי סדר (עולה או יורד?) חשיבותם (מאיזו בחינה?) ואולי מן הקרוב לאדם (קרקע, עצים וכו') אל המרוחק ממנו (שמים, גרמי השמים)? אחת האפשרויות המתבקשות היא, כמובן, עריכה "כרונולוגית" — לפי סדר בריאתם. והנה מתברר, שבעל מזמור קד לא בחר בשיטה זו. דבר זה עולה הן מן הלשונות בהן נקט והן מן ההגיון הפנימי שבתאוריו. אין המזמור נוקט בשום מקום לשון המרמזת על סדר זמנים כלשהו, כגון 'בראשית', 'ראשון', 'שני', 'יוסף ו...', 'ואחר..', 'לשונות המביעים בריאה, יצירה, פזורים אמנם לאורך המזמור ('יעשה' — ד; יט; כד; 'יסד' — ה; ח; 'יצר' — כו; 'ברא' — ל), ועולה מהם בברור שכל היקום נברא על-ידי ה', אך לגבי מרבית הברואים (כגון השמים, החיות, האדם) אין שימוש בפעלים אלה (אלא: 'מקרה',[23] 'ינוסון', 'יעלו', 'המשלח', 'ישקו' ואף אין אמירה שהם **נבראו**. בדרך זו מתחוור לקורא, שהברואים אינם נמנים על-פי סדר בריאתם ה"כרונולוגי". כזאת עולה גם מסדר הפרטים הנזכרים: המזמור פותח ב"עטה אור ...', אך רק בפסוק יט מדובר במפורש על יצירת הירח והשמש; המים לסוגיהם נזכרים לכל אורך המזמור (ג; ו-י; כה); כך גם בעלי החיים (יא-יב; יד; יז-יח; כ-כא; כה-כא).

מתברר, אם כן, שהמחבר בחר ליצור רושם שאין הוא מונה את הברואים על-פי סדר בריאתם, ונראה לי הדבר תוצאה של ריבוי מסורות בריאה בישראל. על השאלה כיצד נברא העולם נותן המקרא יותר מתשובה אחת. סיפורי הבריאה בבר' א-ב, ג; ב, ד-כה, שאינם עולים בקנה אחד, לצד איזכורים אחרים בספרות המקרא הקשורים בבריאת העולם, כגון יש' נא, ט-י; איוב לח, מלמדים ללא ספק על ריבוי מסורות בריאה בישראל.[24] התמונה המתקבלת כיום אצל הקורא במקרא לפי תומו, כאילו בבר' א מובאת המסורת ה"רשמית" (שלא לומר ה"נכונה") ואילו כל שאר הכתובים הם מעין ואריאציות ספרותיות, המיוסדות על המסורת העיקרית, בוודאי אינה

---

21 מ' וויינפלד סבר, שהכתוב ביש' מה', ז: 'יוצר אור ובורא חושך עושה שלום ובורא רע' מרמז לפולמוס עם בר' א, כאילו החושך שייך לתחום הכאוס, הדימוני, השלילי בעולם. ראה: "האל הבורא בבראשית א ובנבואות ישעיהו השני", תרביץ לז (תשכ"ח) 120-123. אם אמנם סברה זו נכונה הרי ניתן למצוא במזמורנו גם פולמוס עם אמונות ודעות בישראל, בלא קשר להמנון המצרי דווקא.

22 מקוצר היריעה, ומשום שאין לי הרבה לחדש בעניין ההבדלים הרעיוניים שבין מזמור קד לבין ההמנון המצרי, אינני מרחיב בנושא זה, עליו עמדו רבים. ראה בפירושיהם של בוטנוויזר (לעיל, הערה 5), עמ' 158-161; קראוס (לעיל, הערה 3), עמ' 712-713; גונקל (לעיל, הערה 5), עמ' 453. דיון בתפיסה של דת אחנתון וההמנון בכלל זה בהשוואה למקרא ראה: V. A. Tobin, "Amarna and Biblical Religion," *Pharaonic Egypt* (ed. S. Groll; Jerusalem, 1985) 231-77 בעמודים 234-237 מובא גם תרגום אנגלי חדש של ההמנון.

23 על פסוק ג, ראה לאחרונה דיונו הסמנטי של א' רובינשטיין, "המקרה במים עליותיו", שי לחיים רוזן, החברה האירופאית לבלשנות, (תל-אביב, 1987) 8.

24 עם זאת אפשר שאיזכור השמים, האור, המים והתהום בראשית המזמור משקף הסכמה בין מסורות הבריאה העיקריות שרווחו בישראל, שאלו היו הנבראים הראשונים. ואכמ"ל. השוואת סדר הבריאה במזמורנו לבר' א תמצא אצל מ' וייס, המקרא כדמותו (ירושלים, תשכ"ב) 56. בעמודים 50-59 מובא ניתוח ספרותי מעניין, הממוקד בפסוק כו, אך כדרכו של וייס חובק הדיון נושאים הנוגעים לפרק כולו, והרבה למדתי ממנו. וראה לקמן הערה 31.

מבנהו של מזמור קד; שההמנון המצרי, שכולו שיר שבח לאל הבורא אתון, מלא תפקיד דיאלקטי בחיבורו של מזמור קד: נשאבו ממנו חומרים רבים, ודווקא משום כך ניכר ניסיון להשתחרר ממנו, לבנות את מזמורנו בדרך שונה, עצמאית. ברור, מכל מקום, שהמחבר לא התעלם מן ההמנון המצרי, הן משום שהייתה בכך התחמקות מעימות רעיוני עם תפיסתו הדתית, והן משום שראה אתגר **אמנותי** בהתמודדות עמו. ניתן איפוא לראות את מזמור קד כמעין דיאלוג (ואף פולמוס) סמוי עם ההמנון המצרי, במישור האמנותי והרעיוני כאחת. מצב זה עורר בעיה פואטית, וכפי שנראה בהמשך אכן התמודד עמה המשורר, ובהצלחה: המזמור חייב לעמוד כיצירה עצמאית, בלתי תלויה בהמנון אחנתון, אך בלי לוותר על הדיאלוג עמו. והרי זו בעיה פואטית מרכזית בכל תחומי האמנות.[19]

השלד הקטלוגי של ההמנון המצרי העמיד את מחברנו בפני בעיות מן הסוג שציינו לעיל ביחס למזמור קד: כיצד לכתוב המנון, שיר הלל, על תשתית של ז'אנר כה יבש כקטלוג. מתברר שבהתמודדותו עם בעיה זו נקט המחבר המצרי רק **באחת** השיטות אותן יישם מחבר מזמור קד, והיא החריגה מן הסגנון האובייקטיבי היבש (כגון: תופע בהדר; כל הארץ מלאת הדרך; מצרים בחג; דגי היאור יפזזו אל פניך; מה נפלאו דרכיך, ועוד). המאפיין השני של הקטלוג, אדישות לסדר האברים, שבעיני מחבר מזמור קד נראה כבלתי הולם את יצירתו, נשמר ביצירה המצרית.[20]

גם במישור הרעיוני עומד מזמורנו בפני עצמו, חרף הפולמוס הסמוי שהוא מנהל עם ההמנון המצרי. דוגמא מובהקת לכך היא איזכור שם האל הבורא. שם ה' נזכר במזמור קד שבע פעמים (א, טז; כד; לא; לג; לד; לה). בפיזור מעניין ובעל משמעות במזמור כשהוא נידון בפני עצמו: הופעתו מיד בפתיחת המזמור מבטלת כל "מתח", כביכול, באשר לזהות הבורא שגדולתה מתוארת בהמשך; הופעתו במלים האחרונות של המזמור מעמידתהו אף היא במקום איסטרטגי ביותר; על מעמדו המיוחד של פסוק כד במערך המזמור כולו נעמוד בהמשך, אך בשלב זה ראוי לציין, שהוא נותן "תאוצה" לאיזכור צפוף יותר ויותר של שם ה', עד להופעתו הרצופה בכל אחד משלושת הפסוקים האחרונים של המזמור. פרישה זו של שם ה' יש לה איפה הגיון פנימי במבנה המזמור כשהוא לעצמו; אך מי שמכיר את ההמנון המצרי אינו יכול להתעלם מן הרושם שיש כאן גם פולמוס סמוי. ההמנון המצרי מזכיר רבות את שם אתון (תשע פעמים), פסוק כד עצמו, בנוסף על תפקידו האימננטי במזמור, נראה כמתפלמס עם מקבילתו המצרית: לעומת 'מה רבו מעשיך ... האל היחיד', אין אחר מבלעדיו' פונה מזמורנו לאל (בלשון נוכח!) 'מה רבו מעשיך ה'', וכביכול "מתרגם" בכך את המונח "האל היחיד" למקבילתו המובנת מאליה. במקום '[מה רבו מעשיך] **נסתרו** מפניו' נמצא בפסוק כד 'כלם בחכמה עשית' – ובכך מודיענו המחבר, שהוא הצליח לעמוד על אחד היסודות החשובים ביותר בבריאה, וכפי שנראה לקמן אף בנה את המזמור כולו בדרך שתדגיש זאת.

נימה נוספת של פולמוס סמוי יש לראות בתאור הארץ החשכה: בהמנון המצרי משולה היא למת

---

19 כדוגמאות, שלש מתוך אין ספור, אפשר להזכיר את יצירתו של אדוארד מאנה 'הסעודה על הדשא' (1863), שזיקתה ליצירותיהם של מרקאנטוניו רימונדי (משפטו של פאריס, 1520) וג'יורג'יונה (קונצרט פסטוראלי, 1510) היוותה אמירה פולמוסית אסטטית וחברתית, שפתחה שרשרת תגובות אמנותיות; את פתיחת הסימפוניה החמישית של גוסטב מאהלר, שהיא "דיאלוג" מובהק עם הפתיחה לסימפוניה החמישית של בטהובן; את יוליסס של ג'יוייס ביחס לאודיסאה של הומרוס. בדוגמא אחרונה זו דן, לצד עשרות דוגמאות אחרות, ג'נט, אשר העלה את ענין ההתייחסות הסמויה של טקסט ספרותי אחד לקודמו לדרגת עקרון יסוד בקריאת כל טקסט שהוא. ראה: G. Genette, *Palimpsestes, La littérature au second degré* (Paris, 1982).

20 משום כך גם ניתן להחליף את סדר הבתים בהמנון המצרי בלא שייפגם מבנהו כלל ועיקר, ואף משמעותו לא תשתנה מאומה. גם החזרה על פרטים רבים בהמנון (כך גם במזמור קד ובקטלוגים מצריים של ממש) קשורה בתכונה זו של שיר השבח לאתון.

תהילים קד: עיון ספרותי

הרי השוואה של כתובים נבחרים משני ההמנונים, על מנת להזכיר לקורא מעט מן המשותף ביניהם. המובאות הן לפי סדר המזמור המצרי. בסוגריים מראי המקום ממזמור קד:

'תופע בהדר באפק השמים' השווה: '...הוד והדר לבשת... נוטה שמים.' (א-ב)

'תשקע באפק מערב הארץ בחשכה' השווה: 'שמש ידע מבואו. תשת חשך ויהי לילה' (יט-כ)

'יכל ארי יצא ממאורתו, כל הרמש ישכו. חשך ...' השווה: 'תשת חשך ויהי לילה ...הכפירים שואגים לטרף' (יט-כ)

'הצפרים תעופינה מקניהון' השווה: 'אשר שם צפרים יקננו' (יז)

'האניות יהלכון צפונה ודרומה ... דגי היאור יפזזו אל פניך' השווה: 'שם אניות יהלכון לויתן זה יצרת לשחק בו' (כו)

'מה רבו מעשיך, נסתרו מפני, האל היחיד' השווה: 'מה רבו מעשיך ה'' (כד)

'נתת היאור ...וישטוף הריהם ... לרוות שדותם בכפריהם' השווה: 'המשלח מעינים בנחלים בין הרים יהלכון ...משקה הרים מעליותיו מפרי מעשיך תשבע הארץ' (י-יג)

'זרחת ויחיו, תשקע ומתי' השווה: 'תסתיר פניך יבהלון תסף רוחם יגועון ואל עפרם ישובון תשלח רוחך יבראון' (כט-ל)

דומה כי די בכתובים אלה להסיר ספק בקיומה של זיקה בין מזמורנו לבין ההמנון לאתון.[17] מודעות למבנה השלד הקטלוגי אף של המנון אתון[18] מאירה ביתר בהירות את מהות הזיקה בין שתי היצירות. אני סבור, שהשלד הקטלוגי של ההמנון המצרי היה אחד הגורמים אשר קבעו את

לערך, משמע הרבה לפני כתוב מקראי כלשהו), אשר שינה את שמו לאחנתון, בהכריזו על אתון כאל יחיד. הוא נמצא בכמה נוסחים, והשלם שבכולם פורסם על ידי דיוויס: *The* ,N. de G. Davies *Rock Tombs of El Amarna* (London, 1908) 6, pl. 27. הציטוטים מתוך ההמנון הם לפי תרגומו של מ' גרינץ, סיפורים מזמורים ומשלים מספרות מצרים העתיקה (ירושלים, תשל"ה) 136-141.

17 מדוגמאות אלה גם עולה, שהזיקה להמנון המצרי אינה מוגבלת לפסוקים יט-כד, כפי שהציג זאת קראוס (לעיל, הערה 3), עמ' 712-713, בעקבות גונקל (לעיל, הערה 5), עמ' 453. נאגל מוצא מקבילות להמנון המצרי גם בפסוקים הבאים: כא; כג; יד; כה-כו; כז; י-יא. ראה: "G. Nagel, "A propos des rapports du Psaume 104 avec les textes égyptiens," *Festschrift A. Bertholet* (ed. W. Baumgartner, O. Eissfeldt, K. Ellinger, and L. Rost; Tübingen, 1950) 403-395. בנוסף למזמור אתון השלם משווה נאגל למזמור קד גם כמה קטעים מן ההמנון הקצר לאתון, וממספר קטעי המנונים מצריים נוספים. לדעתו הכיר המחבר הישראלי את ההמנונים המצריים בתרגום כנעני. לדעה זו שותפים קראוס, שם; M. Dahood, *Psalms* (AB; Garden City, NY, 1970) 33 ואחרים. זאת בניגוד לברסטד אשר טען להשפעה ישירה מן המצרית. ראה: J. Breasted, *The Dawn of Conscience* (New York, 1933) 336-70. לענייננו וויכוח זה אינו מעלה ואינו מוריד.

18 ראה קראוס (לעיל, הערה 3), עמ' 709. הרי הפרטים המהווים את השלד הקטלוגי של המנון אחנתון: אופק, שמש, ארץ, הארץ העליונה, הארץ התחתונה, אשת מלך, אדמה, ארצות, זהרורים, חשך, מת, חדש משכב, ראש, עין, ארי, רמש, רגליים, גוף, מלבושים, זרועות, צאן, דשא, עצים, צפרים, חיות בר, אניות, דגי היאור, זוב (?) בנשים, זרע בגברים, בטן, אם, מינקת, רוח, אפרוח, ביצה, אנשים, בקר, יאור, ים, כפרים, מדבר, חרף, חרף (42 פרטים). פוקס "M. Fox, "Egyptian Onomastica and Biblical Wisdom," *VT* 36 [1986] 302-10) הזהיר מפני היגררות אחר השוואות שטחיות בין קטלוגים מצריים לבין כתובים מקראיים. הצדק עמו, וטענתו שהמנון אחנתון מושפע מקטלוגים מצריים אינה עומדת בסתירה לכך, כמובן. היא אינה סותרת אף את גישתו המחמירה של טלמון בעניין השוואת יצירות מתרבויות שונות. ראה: "S. Talmon, "The 'Comparative Method' in Biblical Interpretation," VTSup 29 (Leiden, 1978) 320-56.

במזרח הקדמון (ראה לקמן) ובישראל בכלל, ואין זו המסגרת המתאימה להאריך בדוגמאות לכך. די להזכיר שוב את מזמור קלו, המבוסס על דגם זה, כדי לציין, שעצם השימוש בקטלוג במזמורנו אינו יוצא דופן. ואולם חרף היותו כלי מתאים למשוררנו מבחינה אחת, הרי מגבלותיו האסטטיות של הקטלוג גלויות לעין. זהו ז'אנר טכני, יבש, חסר "הוד והדר", ומבחינה זו הוא מנוגד לתכלית ההמנון – להפעים. אני סבור שאתגר זה, הצורך לגשר על הפער בין היתרונות (התיאורטיים) לבין המגבלות (בתחום החוויתי) של דגם הקטלוג, הוא אחד הגורמים החשובים שתרמו לעיצוב המזמור כמות שהוא.

כיצד התמודד המשורר עם קושי זה? בניסוח עקרוני ניתן לומר, שהוא דחה שניים משלשת המאפיינים המובהקים של ז'אנר הקטלוג ואימץ רק את המאפיין הבולט ביותר – ריבוי פרטים בעלי מכנה משותף. שני המאפיינים שנדחו הם (1) הסגנון האובייקטיבי; (2) חוסר החשיבות של סדר אברי הקטלוג.

(1) הוויתור על הסגנון האובייקטיבי, הבולט לעין כבר במלות הפתיחה של המזמור, מתבטא בשלשה אופנים: הערות "הסבר" של המשורר, כגון 'בל תמוט עולם ועד' (ה); 'בל ישבון לכסות ארץ' (ט);[14] שימוש במלים שהקשרם במזמור מקנה להן עצמה רגשית כגון 'ינוסון', 'יחפזון' (ד) 'ישמח לבב אנוש' (טו); הרכבה סלקטיבית של הקטלוג מפרטים יפים או מרשימים בלבד: אור, אש, המים הזורמים, ציפורים וצמחיה עשירה, ולא, למשל, שרצים, רמשים, שטחי מדבר, ארץ מלחה.

(2) אדישותו של הקטלוג לסדרם של אבריו, לדווקנות של רצף מסוים,[15] אינה תכונה מקרית אלא מהותית לדגם הקטלוג: היעדר ההיררכיה, היכולת להחליף באופן חפשי את מקומם של אברי הקטלוג וסעיפיו, מדגישה את החשיבות הסגולית שיש לפרטים עצמם, והרי זה עיקרו של הז'אנר. לפיכך, וויתור על סממן זה עלול לטשטש את עצם האופי הקטלוגי של היצירה. המשימה הספרותית העומדת בפני מי שבא לכתוב "קטלוג מדומה", תוך מתן חשיבות לסדר הפרטים שהוא מזכיר נראית כפרדוכס: ליצור רצף בעל סדר משמעותי, אשר יוסיף עניין לדגם היבש, אך בלא שיטשטש עד לבלי הכר האופי הקטלוגי של היצירה. הפתרון העקרוני שנמצא לבעיה זו במזמורנו הוא רישום הפרטים באופן שמשמעותיות הרצף תתברר רק לאחר שתבנית הקטלוג כבר הוטבעה בתודעת הקורא. דרך יישומו בפועל של עקרון זה תידון בחלק ב של המאמר.

(ב) מיד עם פרסומו של המזמור המצרי לאתון, השמש, הוכרו קווי דמיון בינו ובין תה' קד.[16]

---

14 הערות מעין אלה החוצצות בין פרטי הקטלוג מאיטות את הקצב המהיר הנוצר על-ידי תכיפות הפרטים בקטלוג. ואולם שימוש מרובה בפעלי עשיה ותנועה (נוטה; מקרה; מהלך; ינוסון; יחפזון; יעלו; ירדו; יעברון; משלח וכיו"ב) מאיץ את הקצב. פון ראד (לפי קראוס [לעיל, הערה 3], עמ' 715) ראה בתכונה זו של המזמור ביטוי לראיה הישראלית את היקום כהתרחשות ולא כהוויה. בלא לקבוע עמדה לגבי השקפה זו אבקש להאיר הבט פואטי של היסוד הדינאמי במזמור: לסינג, בספרו לאוקון (1766) תבע מן השירה דינמיות והתרחשות, בהיותן תכונות מהותיות של הספרות, בניגוד לתיאורים סטטיים, המהותיים לאמנות הציור. דומה שבמזמורנו יש הענות אינטואיטיבית לפואטיקה של לסינג, שעל אף הדוגמטיות היתרה יש בה כדי להאיר כמה מאפיינים של הספרות בהשוואה לאמניות אחרות. ראה: G. E. Lessing, *Laocoon* (New York, 1962). עיין במיוחד בעמ' 77-84.

15 הנה, דרך משל, קטע מן הקטלוג המצרי הידוע בכינויו הקטלוג של אמנף, בסעיף 'בניינים, חלקים וסוגי קרקע': 'מבצר, כפר, בית, חדר, חדר-מגורים, חדר צדדי, חלק תחתון, חלק קדמי, אולם רחב, גומחא, סטיו עמודים, חדר עליון, גג, מעלה מדרגות, קבר, מקום מסתור, אסם...' לפי: A. H. Gardiner, *Ancient Egyptian Onomastica* (Oxford, 1947) 2*.

16 המזמור נתגלה באל-עמארנה בקברו של איה, משרי המלך. הוא חובר בימי אמנחתף הרביעי (1380-1362

תהילים קד: עיון ספרותי

שלפחות חלק מהם שימשו אף בפולחן,[8] ועל כן היו מוכרים יפה. בנסיבות אלו ניתן להניח, שאמן אמיתי שבא לכתוב המנון, נתן בכך ביטוי לתחושתו, שכיוצר יש לו מה לחדש בסוג זה, אף שדשו בו רבים. ואכן, בחינת מזמור קד מראה, כי אם גם יש בו חידוד של אי אילו מסרים תיאולוגיים, הרי חידושו הממשי הוא בתחום האמנותי, והוא המקנה עוצמה גם למסר התיאולוגי שבמזמור.

על רקע שבחי הבריאה האחרים בשירה המקראית ובמיוחד בספרות המזמורים ניתן להצביע על ייחודו הבולט ביותר של מזמור קד: הבריאה מתוארת כאן **באריכות** יתרה, ברצף של 22 פסוקים, ב-כג, ולאחר קיטוע קצר (פסוק כד) גם בפסוקים כה-כו. זאת בהשוואה למזמור קלז, בו מתמשך תיאור הבריאה לאורך 5 חצאי פסוקים בלבד (ה-ט); חציו השני של כל פסוק הוא הנוסחא החוזרת 'כי לעולם חסדו'). הצגה מובהקת עוד יותר של ייחודו של מזמור קד יש בנתונים הבאים: המזמור מציין לא פחות מ-36 ברואים[9] לעומת 6 במזמור קלו;[10] 14 במזמור סה,[11] ו-15 במזמור קמז,[12] שהם המנונים הקרובים ביותר למזמור קד מבחינה זו.

במקרים אחדים מתבקש הקיצור היחסי בשבח הבורא מעצם ההקשר והז'אנר, כגון באמירות כבוד הבאות כלוואי לשם האל (כדוגמת 'כה אמר האל ה' בורא השמים ונטיהם רקע הארץ וצאצאיה...', יש' מב, ה), או כשהרחבה יתרה עלולה להסיט את הדובר מעניינו הראשי (כגון בויר' י, יב-יג). לא כן בהמנונים. כאן מבטא אולי הקיצור את הצורך לומר, שאם **השמים** מספרים כבוד אל ומעשה ידיו מגיד **הרקיע** (תה' יט, א), כלומר, אם היקום **עצמו** מעיד על גדולת בוראו — מוטב לא להרבות במילי שבח; די להפנות את הקורא להביט סביבו ('כי אראה שמיך מעשה אצבעותיך...' תה' ח, ד)! מכל מקום מתברר, שעל רקע המסורת הספרותית של אמירות קצרות בשבח הבורא ברר לו מחבר מזמור קד דרך ספרותית חדשה: **להאריך** במקום לקצר; להרבות בפרטי הבריאה במקום להסתפק בדוגמאות מעטות. מן המזמור גם עולה, שפרטנות יתרה זו הולמת יפה את מטרתו ('מה **רבו** מעשיך ה'', פסוק כד), ויש עימה הגד ברור: אין צורך להרבות במילות שבח לבורא; די **למנות** את **מעשיו** אחד לאחד! משמעותו של פתרון זה היא, שככל שירבה באיזכור פרטי הבריאה, כך ייטיב המזמור לשבח את האל. המימוש הז'אנרי היעיל ביותר של עקרון זה הוא צורת הקטלוג: רשימת פרטים, שהמכנה המשותף שלהם ברור ומובן בין מאליו בין בזכות משפט פתיחה המציין אותו.[13] הקטלוג היה ז'אנר ידוע ומוכר

---

8 לאחרונה מקובל להניח שמזמור קד חובר כליטורגיה, אף שהדעות חלוקות באשר לנסיבות הפולחניות המדויקות בהן נעשה בו שימוש. ראה קראוס (לעיל, הערה 3), עמ' 709; וייזר (לעיל, הערה 5), עמ' 670 וכן עמודים 35-52, 60; S.Mowinckel, *Psalmenstudien* (Amsterdam, 1966) 6:32-33 וכן הנ"ל: *The Psalms in Israel's Worship* (Oxford, 1962) 84-89, 144. דעות אלה אינן מבוססות על ניתוח המזמור לגופו אלא על הנחות מוקדמות בעניין התכלית הפולחנית של מזמורי תהילים בכללותם.

9 אור, שמים, מים, עבים, רוח, מלאכים, ארץ, תהום, הרים, רעמים, בקעות, מעיינים, נחלים, חיתו שדה, פראים, עוף השמים, עפאים, חציר, בהמה, אדם, ארזים, חסידה, ברושים, יעלים, סלעים, שפנים, ירח, שמש, לילה, חית יער, כפירים, ערב, ים, רמשים, לויתן. כן נרמזים כרמים דגן וזיתים (פסוק טו- יין, לחם, שמן).

10 שמים, ארץ, מים, שמש, ירח, כוכבים.

11 ארץ, ים, הרים, בקר, ערב, פלג, דגן, רביבים, נאות מדבר, גבעות, כרים, צאן, עמקים, בר.

12 כוכבים, שמים, עבים, מטר, הרים, חציר, בהמה, בני עורב, סוס, איש, ארץ, שלג, כפור, קרח, מים.

13 ההגדרה הז'אנרית התיאורטית של הקטלוג עשויה להסתבך ביותר, ואין זו המסגרת הנאותה להרחיב בעניני. דיון על כך ראה: ב' ערפלי, מבנה ומשמעות בשירת יהודה עמיחי, חיבור לקבלת תואר דוקטור, הוגש לסנט אוניברסיטת תל־אביב (1977) 5-38. תמציתו של דיון זה תמצא אצל הנ"ל, הפרחים והאגרטל (תל־אביב, תשמ"ז) 34-42.

מסקנה, שזיקתה העניינית לחלק הראשון יוצרת מסגרת למזמור כולו.[4] ואולם למעיין בהמנונים מתברר, שמוסכמותיו הספרותיות של סוג זה אינן כה כובלות כאלו שבתחינת היחיד, שהיא מוגבלת למדי בשל המוטיב העיקרי שלה — המאמין הנתון במצוקה, בעוד שמסגרת ההמנון מאפשרת למשורר מרחב תמרון רב יותר: יש לפניו מבחר מגוון של מוטיבים (כגון: האל בורא העולם; אדון ההיסטוריה; חסדי האל לאדם; חסדיו לישראל), מתוכם הוא יכול לברור אחד או יותר בהרכב זה או אחר, בלא שייפגע הדגם היסודי של ההמנון. זאת ועוד: דגם ההמנון אינו מחייב מעבר חד מאוירה אחת לשנייה (כגון מיאוש לתקוה בתחינת היחיד), שהוא קושי אמנותי, אשר חומרתו מכתיבה מראש את הבעיה המבנית העיקרית אותה יהא על המשורר לפתור. ניתן אולי לדמות את הבא לכתוב תחינת יחיד למי שטרם צאתו לדרך הוא משקיף עליה עד סופה, מאתר בה את המכשול העיקרי, וקובע כיצד יתגבר עליו. לעומתו כותב ההמנון הוא כמי שראוה לפניו מספר דרכים, אף רואה את המכשולים הראשונים בכל אחת מהן, אך גם לאחר שהחליט באיזו דרך ילך עדיין אינו יודע אילו מכשולים נוספים צפויים לו, ואין לו אלא לסמוך על תושיתו, שיידע להתגבר עליהם לכשיאלץ לעשות כן. ה'מכשולים' הללו הם משני טיפוסים: בעיות רקע ובעיות מזדמנות.

א

על בעיות הרקע אני מציע למנות את הנתונים הבאים: (א) שכיחותם של הגדים וחיבורים קצרים בשבח האל הבורא בספרות המקראית בכלל, בספרות המזמורית בפרט ובהמנונים במיוחד. (ב) המנון אחנתון לשמש. (ג) קיומן של מסורות בריאה שונות וסותרות בישראל.

(א) המצופה והמובן מאליו הם אויבי האמנות, האורבים במיוחד לפיתחו של אמן הבא לעסוק בנושא שיגרתי. בבואו לכתוב המנון לאל הבורא עמד המחבר בפני מציאות תרבותית של ריבוי אמירות שבח והלל בנושא זה.[5] ושל שאר אין צורך לתארך במדויק את חיבורים של מזמור קד[5] ושל שאר הכתובים שנזכיר להלן כדי לקבוע, שבעת חיבורו של מזמורנו היו נפוצים בתחומים השונים של היצירה הספרותית בישראל אמירות וחיבורים קצרים בשבח האל הבורא ויפי היקום. נמצאם בספרות הנבואה (כגון יש' מ, יב-טו; כב, כו; מא, ד; מב, ה; מה, ז, יב, יח; מח, יג; נא, ט-י; יר' ה, כב; י, יב-יג [= נא, טו-טז]; לב, יז; עמ' ד, יג; ה, ח; ט, ו; יונה א, ט; זכ' יב, א), בספרות החכמה (כגון: משלי ג, יט-כ; ח, כב-לב[6], וכמובן בספרות המזמורית (כגון: תה' ח; יט; כד א-ב; לג, ה-ז; סה; עד, יג-יז; פט, יא-יג; צ, ב; צה, א-ד; צו, ה, יא-יב; קלה, ה-ז; קלו, א-ט; קמז; קמח). נראה

---

4 לפי קוך, שם. הוא מסמן את ארבעת החלקים באותיות A, B, C, D ולהלן אשתמש בסימון זה.
5 מיותר להביא כאן מידע מלא על דעותיהם של כל החוקרים בעניין שולי זה ואסתפק בדוגמאות ספרות בלבד. בריגס קבע את זמן המזמור לתקופה היוונית; בוטנוויזר, וויזר, קראוס קובעים אותו לתקופת הבית הראשון, ואני שותף לדעה זו. גונקל נוקט לשון שלילית 'תיארוך המזמור לתקופה הבתר גלותית אינו מובן מאליו'. ראה: C. A. Briggs, *The Book of Psalms* (ICC; 2 vols.; Edinburgh, 1906) 2:331; M. Buttenwieser, *The Psalms Chronologically Treated* (Chicago, 1938) 161-67; קראוס (לעיל, הערה 3), כרך 2 עמ' 781; A. Weiser, *The Psalms* (OTL; London, 1962) 91-95; H. Gunkel, *Die Psalmen* (5th ed.; Göttingen,1968) 454.
6 שבחי האל הבורא עולים גם מאיוב ט, ד-י; כו, ז-יד; לו-לז; לח-לט. אף כאן אני שותף לדעה השלטת כי ספר איוב כולו נתחבר לאחר החורבן, ושוב, תיארוך זה או אחר של הספר אינו חיוני לטיעוני הכללי במאמר.
7 בספרות ההיסטוריוגרפית מעצם טיבה יש לכתובים מסוג זה מקום שולי: שמ"א ב, ח; מל"ב יט, טו, דה"א טז, כו; דה"ב ב, יא; נחמ' ט, ו.

תהילים קד: עיון ספרותי

יאיר הופמן

במאמר קודם שעסק בתחינות היחיד ביקשתי להראות שאחד המפתחות להבנה ולשיפוט אסטטי של מזמורים היא מודעות למאבק המחברים במוסכמת (קונבנציות) הספרותיות שסוג ספרותי זה מטיל עליהם.[1] טענתי, שעקב הכרתם את אילוצי הז׳אנר ידעו בעלי המזמורים מראש, מהי הבעיה המבנית העיקרית שעליהם לפתור על מנת שייושם המוסכמה — לסיים את התחינה בהבעת תקוה — לא ייראה מאולץ מבחינה אמנותית. במאמר זה אבקש להראות שבמקרה של מזמור קד המצב שונה במקצת. אמנם גם כאן עשויה הבנת מערכת האילוצים עימה התמודד המשורר לתרום לשיפוט האסטטי של יצירתו; ואולם במזמור קד הדגם המסורתי מהווה אילוץ משני בלבד, ובעייתו העיקרית של המשורר אינה התמודדות עם מוסכמה ז׳אנרית נוקשה. למעשה לא בעיה אסטטית מרכזית אחת עומדה בפני מחבר המזמור, אלא שורה של בעיות, שדרך פיתרונן היא אשר קבעה את האופי האמנותי של מזמור קד.[2]

בעקבות מיונו הסוגי של המזמורים על-ידי גונקל מקובל לשייך את מזמור קד לטיפוס ההמנונים,[3] וככל סוג איבחנו גם כאן דגם יסודי, ובו ארבעה מרכיבים: הזמנה להלל את ה׳; משפט מעבר קצר, המציג את נושא ההלל; החלק העיקרי, שהוא הפיתוח וההרחבה של הנושא;

---

1 י׳ הופמן, ״המעבר מיאוש לתקוה במזמורי תחינת היחיד״, תרביץ נה (תשמ״ו) 161-172.

2 אני נדרש שוב לניסוחה של האזרחי, שהובא גם במאמר הנזכר לעיל: ׳הניסיון לנסח את היצירה האמנותית במונחים של בעיות ופתרונן עשוי להיות הדרך המקרבת אותנו ככל האפשר אל עיקרה של המעלה האסטטית׳. ראה פ׳ האזרחי, הפעילות המתבוננת, עיונים באסטטיקה (ירושלים, תשכ״ה) 104. השיפוט האסטטי ינסה על כן לגלות מתוך היצירה המוגמרת מה היו הבעיות האמנותיות אותן היא באה לפתור, כשהשאלה באיזו מידה היה האמן מודע לכל הבעיות הללו היא משנית, אולי אף בלתי רלוונטית. עוד על האמנות במונחים של בעיות ופתרונותיהן ראה: E. Kris and A. Kaplan, "Aesthetic Ambiguity," *Psychoanalytic Explorations in Art* (ed. E. Kris; New York, 1964) 243-64.

3 ראה: H. Gunkel, *Einleitung in die Psalmen* (Göttingen, 1933). בעמ׳ 66 הוא מונה את מזמור קד על קבוצה של ׳המנוני יחיד׳. בעמ׳ 32 מובאת רשימת ההמנונים כולם. עוד על מיון המזמורים ראה: H. J. Kraus, *Psalmen* (BKAT 15; Neukirchen, 1961) 1:xli. וכן: K. Koch, *The Growth of the Biblical Tradition* (London, 1969) 159-70.

them and wrote them"—where did he find God's speeches, and who collected them from God's mouth and wrote them? If you say, "The friends and Job wrote God's speeches," what a wonder it is that there are six interlocutors yet there is no difference in style among them, the style of each being like that of his fellow! Yet the style of each prophet differs from his fellow's (although they say all flows from a single Will—the Holy Spirit), and the speech of each is as distinct from his fellow's as white is from red; as, for example, the case of the twelve minor prophets. . . . Indeed, it is but natural that as people's temperaments differ so do their deeds and manner of speaking. Hence, if Job and his friends were truly as the plain sense of the text presents them and not an allegory, individual differences of speech should have appeared among them besides the differences of opinion that appear among them. . . . Thus anyone familiar with books and the science of language must acknowledge that Job is stylistically uniform from beginning to end, and that a single author composed and invented it. No distinctive styles occur in it; only in opinion and substance are there distinctions. . . .

Beside these evidences is (this final one): What is told at the end of the Book of Job of the doubling of his possessions is ground enough for understanding that it is an allegory.

2. One might object: How can Job be an allegory when Ezekiel mentions him with Noah and Daniel, who do not serve as allegories (Ezekiel 14)? From this it appears that the prophet believed in Job's historicity. . . . We make three responses. (a) Even though the prophet was convinced that Job existed and was no allegory, that does not oblige us to reject the view that he serves as an allegory. For no one knowledgeable about the secrets of prophecy can believe that God said to that prophet in prophetic vision that "Job existed and was created." Hence, if the prophet said that Job existed it proves nothing. (b) We might further suppose that the prophet who mentioned Job did not believe he existed, yet referred to him as though he did in order to hide the truth of the matter from the masses, lest they disparage him, thinking he was only an allegory. (c) Prophets customarily speak in parables—indeed most of what they say is parabolic—hence, they do not hesitate to refer to something that has no reality. . . .

From the content of God's two responses to Job, strange and lengthy as they are, every intelligent person will take it as proven that the entire Book of Job is an allegory. . . .

3. I think it worthwhile to consider the name *Job*, whose reference, according to its derivation, is to איבה—antagonism and hatred—since he was antagonized and banished far from God. First, he was delivered to Satan, though blameless . . . and over and above that he was loathed by society as an enemy (איב) who committed terrible crimes. . . . Moreover, with all his misfortunes his friends added to his vexation by arguing with him and contradicting him. Even if his misfortunes were on account of sins and crimes . . . they should have greeted him with consolation and commiserated with him. Indeed, his friends came with the intention of doing so, but they did just the opposite! . . . They condemned him as though he were a confirmed villain, though he was, as the text says, blameless and upright, fearing God and shunning evil. Surely anyone who is intelligent and knows how to read a book will realize how stupid that person is who fails to perceive that such matters—written and arranged in no logical (natural) order when taken at their plain meaning, and which do not follow ordinary common sense—must serve as an allegory.

Even a fool must realize that God cannot be seduced by Satan or any other creature . . . ; how much less that Satan injure an innocent person. That alone should be enough to quash a fool's inclination to believe that Job ever existed or was created in any shape or form. . . .

If the class (of fools) is not persuaded by these evidences that Job is an allegory, we adduce more. . . . Suppose Job and his friends really existed—how was the series of responses composed? If you say, "These men met together and each spoke his piece and wrote it down in his own idiom; afterward Elihu appeared and spoke his piece and wrote it; afterward God came and spoke his piece"—the question arises: Who compiled all their utterances into one book after they finished speaking? To this you have no answer. If you say, "Our teacher Moses [the putative author of Job] found their speeches written but disjoined and he collected

המפליגה והמפליאה, והמסוכנה. שהרי ישראל שווארץ היה צריך לגאלו מתהום הנשייה באמצע המאה שעברה.[26]

Appendix: Zeraḥya of Barcelona's Commentary to Job (Rome, 1291)

1. What you must know first is that this entire book serves as an allegory (משל). Its primary intention, indeed, was to make known religious and non-religious motives and various beliefs by which men at large of different stripes are distinguished. . . .

As you know, the sages also held this opinion of the book, as they put it: "Job never existed and never was created but serves as a parable [למשל היה]" (*Baba Batra* 15a). But besides, every intelligent person ought to mark the initial words of the book: "There was a man in the land of Uẓ named Job." Nothing is said of his father nor of the time of his story. All this was to advise us that these events were invented, like parables in which names of people and animals, names of places and many other things are invented in order to instruct people respecting social conduct and the like. The word *Uẓ*, as Maimonides pointed out (*Guide* 3:22), is very likely to be understood as alluding to עצה 'counsel', that is, to the application of sound counsel and understanding to its interpretation. For undoubtedly the author might have chosen among the places of the world one commonly mentioned in books, but he intended by the choice of this name, because of the allusion to counsel, to indicate also that this book was composed and arranged with the intention and purpose of alluding to secrets and counsels of wisdom of which every wise person ought to be aware.

---

26 לפי רביצקי (לעיל, הערה 3), עמ' 85-80, נמצאים פירושים לר' זרחיה רק לאיוב (3 כ"י) ולמשלי (2 כ"י). ישראל שווארץ גאלם מגניזה. הסכנה בתפיסת איוב כמשל תוארה יפה בהקדמת ר' יוסף אבן כספי (ספרד, מחצית ראשונה של המאה ה-י"ד) לפירושו לאיוב, בתוך י' לאסט, מהדיר, עשרה כלי כסף, חלק א, (פרסבורג, תרס"ג) (ד"צ: ירושלים, תש"ל) 138-137:

ואני מפליא, איך ראוי לקדמונים ולאחרונים ז"ל לפקפק בזה, כי מה הבדל בין אומרים: איש היה בארץ עוץ וכו' ובין אומרים: ויהי איש אחד מן הרמתים צופים ושמו אלקנה וכו' וכל הספור ההוא, מעלי ומשמואל וזולתם; וכן: ויהי בימי שפוט השופטים; וכן: ויהי בימי אחשורוש; וכן כתוב בתורה: אלה תולדות נח וכו' ויולד נח שלשה בנים וגו', וכל דבר המבול ומעשה התיבה. ואם נאמר בספור איוב ורעיו שחכם כתב זה למשל, להניח בלב הרואים (= הקוראים) דעות ואמונות, כן יוכל לומר באלו כולם. ואם כן, אין לנו לא תורה ולא מקרא וכתובים. ואם קצת קדמונינו ז"ל לא ידעו לו זמן ומקום, מה לנו לזה? ועוד: אחר שענין איוב, כמו שאמר הרמ[ב"ם], נמצא תמיד, כמו שידעט אנחנו גם כן, כי כמה איוב איכא בשוקא, בכל שנה ושנה, אם יש להם מספר בנים ובנות ומקנה רב כמו איוב זה, או פחות או יתר, וכן שאר עניני הספור, למה לא יתכן אצלנו כי בארץ עוץ היה זה הענין באיוב זה ... וחלילה לנו בדבר (=להוציא מקראות מפשוטם למשל) בכל המקרא, רק מה שבא בנבואות שההכרח יביאנו לפרשו במראה הנבואה, לפי שהיותו בהקיץ הוא נמנע.

שזה הספר הוא מחובר למשל. ואם תרצה לאמר שאיוב וחבריו היו[22] על כל פנים, יבוא השואל וישאל אותך איך חוברו סדרי אלו המענים? ואם תאמר שהאנשים ההם התקבצו יחד וכל אחד מהם דבר דבריו וכתב במליצתו, ושאליהו בא אחר מיכן ודבר דבריו וכתבם, והשם בא אחר מכן ודבר דבריו, יענה השואל וישאל עוד: ומי חבר דבריהם בספר אחד אחר שגמרו מלדבר דבריהם? אין לך בזה תשובה. ואם תאמר כי משה רבינו מצא דבריהם כתובים מפוזרים ומפורדים וחברם וכתבם, דברי האל אנא מצאם ומי חברם מפי השם וכתבם?

אם תאמר: החברים ואיוב כתבו דברי השם, ישיב השואל עוד ויאמר: וזה דבר[23] מופלא שיהיה ששה מדברים ולא יהיה הפרש במליצתם וכל אחד מהם ידבר דברי חברו כדברי חברו במליצה? והלא אנו רואים דברי הנביאים מרצון אחד והוא רוח הקודש (אין) מליצת אחד כמליצת חברו ודבריהם נכרים זה מזה ונבדלים כהבדל הלבן מן האדום והארוך מן הקצר, שהרי בתרי עשר נראה כי כל נביא מהם מדבר במליצה מבדלת מאוד ממליצת חברו, וזה באמת דבר טבעי באדם כי בהשתנות המזגים והטבעים באנשים ישתנו גם כן מעשיהם ודבריהם. על כן היה ענין איוב וחבריו כפשוטו וכמשמעו ולא היו למשל, היה נראה מדבריהם הפרש המבואר אשר בין זה לזה במליצה ובדיבור לבד כי בענין כבר נראה הפרשם ודעתם הנבדל זה מזה, כמו שאנו רואים שדברי הנביאים נבדלים במליצתם ואחד אינו מדבר כדמות חברו. אם כן כל יודע ספר ודקדוק הלשון יכיר ויודע כי איוב מראשו ועד סופו מליצה אחת היא ועל אופן אחד הולך, ומליץ אחד חברו וחדשו ואין בדבריו ומליצתו הפרש. וההפרש הוא בענינים ובדיעות לבד. ודע זה והבינהו.

ומלבד אלו הראיות, כי לפי מה שספר בסוף ספר איוב מהכפלת הקנינים שנכפלו[24] לו היה מספיק להבין בו כי הכל יהיה משל. אך זה החולי התפשט מאוד במוחת אנשי דורנו להאמין שיהיו דברי הנביאים כלם כפשוטם ושאין בהם משל כל שכן שהוא קשה עליהם להאמין כי ספר איוב כלו יהיה משל, ודי בזה רמז ורא(י)ה שזה הספר משל.[25]

אנו רואים במחבר זה קני־מידה ספרותיים, ספרותיים־היסטוריים ותיאולוגיים משמשים בערבוביה:

הטענה התיאולוגית העיקרית היא משערורית פיתוי השטן את הקב"ה.

הטענה הספרותית־היסטורית היא מקשי־שיחזור תהליך התהוות הספר (קשה לספר את שלבי התהוותו אם הוא רישום מציאותי של נאומי המדברים).

הטענה הספרותית־ריטורית מתפרקת לכמה צדדים:

סגנון הבדייה — חסרת פרטים מזהים;

עלילה בלתי הגיונית (משתמע מכך כי הספור אינו עיקר);

שמות סמליים;

סיום "חלקי" ו"מעוגל" מדי;

אחדות־הסגנון מפריך את תפיסת הכתוב כרישום מהימן של ששה מדברים (ההיקש מן הנביאים הקטנים).

מתוחכם במיוחד הוא ביטול עדותו של יחזקאל, בנימוקים הלקוחים מתורת הנבואה, מסגנון הנבואה ומהנחת ההתחשבות עם דעות המוניות.

קני־מידה אלה נושאים כוחם יפה לערער את הממשות ההיסטורית של הרבה סיפורי המקרא. אין אנו יודעים אם זרחיה החיל אותם על ספרים אחרים, אך ברור למדי כי לא היה המשך לשיטתו

---

22 בנדפס: 'יהיו'.
23 בנדפס: 'דברי'.
24 בנדפס: 'שנקפלו'.
25 המובאה הזאת היא מתקות אנוש (לעיל, הערה 2). תיקוני הגירסה הם מִסְבָרתי.

הממשלים שמחברים שמות אנשים ושמות שאר בעלי חיים ושמות מדינות ועניינים אחרים רבים להודיע בכל זה עניינים מועילים[17] לבני האדם בהנהגתם קצתם עם קצתם והדומה לזה. וגם מלת 'עוץ' כמו שזכר בן הרב[18] ז"ל הוא דבר קרוב מאד להבין מזה השם שהוא לרמוז בו בעניין העצה לומר להנהיג עצה ותבונה בעניינו. כי בלא ספק הרבה מדיניות היה יכול המחבר לזכור ממדיניות העולם שהם נמצאות ונזכרות בספרים, אבל המחבר הזה שחבר ספר איוב בלא ספק כיון לזכור זה השם הרמוז אליו עניין העצה להורות גם כן שזה הספר חובר וסודר בהסכמה ועצה חכמה לרמוז בו סודות ועצות הנבונות והראויות לכל חכם לדעת אותם ולהתעורר על עניינם ...

ואם יבוא המקשה ויאמר: למה היה עניין איוב משל? והלא זכרו הנביא עם נח דניאל שלא היה למשל, כי נראה מזה שהנביא היה מאמין שאיוב היה בלא ספק ולא היה משל! יש לנו על זה שלוש תשובות: האחת היא שאף על פי שהנביא היה בדעתו והסכמתו שאיוב היה ולא היה משל, אין אנו מוכרחים בעבור זה להרחיק דעת מי שאומר שהוא למשל, כי אין מי שיודע סודות הנבואה שיאמין שהבורא אמר לנביא ההוא במראה הנבואה שאיוב היה ונברא. אם כן אין ראיה אם הנביא אמר שאיוב היה. ועוד נוכל לאמר כי הנביא שזכר איוב אף על פי שלא היה מאמין שאיוב היה, זכר אותו כאלו היה כדי להסתיר עניינו מן ההמון ושלא יחשבוהו למשל כדי שלא יקלו בו. והתשובה השלישית היא שהנביאים רגילים לדבר במשלים ורוב דבריהם הם משל על כן אינם חוששים לזכור בתוך דבריהם דבר אחד שאין לו מציאות. על כן אין להקשות או לתפוש על הכוונה האמיתית הזאת הנאמרת בספר איוב מדברי הנביא ההוא ...

וממה שנראה לי גם כן שצריך לבקש לו עניין ולהשתכל עליו הוא שם זה האיש איוב שעניינו לפי שרשו איבה ושנאה על שהיה נאוב[19] ונרחק מאד מן הבורא יתברך. תחלה שנמסר ביד השטן חנם ולא על פשע כמו שהעיד בו הכתוב באמרו: ותסיתני בו לבלעו חנם. ולא עוד אלא שאפילו מן הבריות היה שנוא ונתאב כאויב שפשע והפליג בעול כמו שתראה כל מה שנגזר עליו מאיבוד הממון על-ידי הכשדים ואיבוד הבנים כשנפל הבית עליהם. ועוד שעם הצרות שחלו עליו חבריו הפליגו להוסיף לו בכעסו ובצרתו כשהיו חולקים עליו וסותרים דבריו, כי מן הראוי היה על חבריו שאפילו חלו עליו הצרות ההם מפשע שעשה או מחטאים שגרמו עליו האיבוד הגדול ההוא היה להם לקבלו ולנחמו ולנוד לו על כל מה שקרה לו. אבל חבריו באו לו על דעת לעשות כן ועשו ההפך כמו שיורה על זה מה שהפסוק אומר כי אף-על-פי שישבו חבריו אתו לארץ שבעת ימי אבלות לא השיגו לדבר לו דברי נחמות ולא לנוד לו ועל בניו ועל בנותיו ולא דברו לו דבר מרוב צערו וכאבו עד שהתחיל איוב לדבר להם מתחילה קודם שחבריו ידברו לו שום דבר. ועם כל זה חבריו לא חמלו עליו אבל הרשיעו וחייבוהו כאחד מן הרשעים הגמורים והוא לפי שהכתוב מעיד עליו איש תם וישר וירא אלהים וסר מרע. אבל כל משכיל ומבין ספר יוכל לדעת אל כמה עולה סכלות מי שלא יבחין בשכלו כי כגון אלו העניינים הכתובים[20] והמסודרים בלא שום סדר טבעי לפי פשוטיהם ושאינם הולכים כסדר הנהוג באנשי העולם כולם הם למשל.

כי איך יעלה אפילו בלב הסכל שהבורא יתברך שמו יהיה נפתה לשטן או לשום נברא מנבראיו ואפילו אם היה מלאך כל שכן שהיה שטן מזיק לבריות בלא פשע ובלא עון, כי זה לבדו היה מספיק להוציא כל סכל וכל פתי מהיותו מאמין שאיוב היה כלל בשום זמן או נברא בשום פנים, כמו שיחשבו אנשים שמחים מלא מזוהמא שאינם נפסקת מהם לעולם ואין ראוי שתפסק מהם כיון שעלה בהמותם וסכלותם לזה הגדר כלו שיאמינו שאיוב היה או נברא בשום פנים בעולם. ואם לא יספיק לזה הכת[21] מה שזכרנו מראיות על שאיוב היה משל נוסיף עוד להביא ראיה על

---

17 בנדפס: 'מועלים'.
18 רמב"ם, מורה, חלק ג, פרק כב.
19 נפעל משורש אוב/איב.
20 בנדפס: 'והכתובים'.
21 בנדפס: 'יהכת''.

פרשת איוב המופלאה והנפלאה ... הוא משל לבאור השקפות בני אדם בהשגחה. וכבר ידעת מאמר א' מהם (מחז"ל) בפירוש: איוב לא היה ולא נברא אלא משל היה; ואשר חשב שהוא היה ונברא ושהוא מעשה שהיה לא ידע לו לא זמן ולא מקום,[14] אלא אחד החכמים אמר שהיה בימי האבות, ואחד אמר שהיה בימי משה, ואחד אמר שהיה בימי דוד, ואחד אמר שהוא היה מעולי בבל. וזה ממה שמחזק דברי מי שאמר שהוא לא היה ולא נברא. כללו של דבר: בין היה בן לא היה הרי כיוצא במאורעו, המצוי תמיד, נבוכו כל החוקרים מבני אדם ... ולפי שתי ההשקפות, לומר אם היה או לא היה, אותם הדברים שהקדימם אותם, כלומר דבר השטן ודברי ה' לשטן, ומסירתו בידו, כל זה משל בלי ספק אצל כל בעלי שכל ... משל שתלויים בו נפלאות ודברים שהם כבשונו של עולם ... (תרגום י' קאפח, עמ' שכא-שכב)

כאן מצאנו לראשונה נימוקים לסברה שאיוב משל הוא: אין לו זמן ואין לו מקום (שהרי עוץ הוא 'שם אדם — את עוץ בכורו', בר' כב, כא — לפי רמב"ם, שם בהמשך), ותמונת אסיפת בני האלהים היא סמלית ליכל בעלי שכלי' — היינו לכל מפרש פירוש שכלתני למקרא.

מה שרמב"ם השאיר במעין צריך עיון, והוא: מעמדו גופו של ספר איוב ושל איוב עצמו ההיה אם לא. פירש תלמידו ר' זרחיה בן יצחק בן שאלתיאל חן מברצלונה, בפירושו לאיוב. קצה נפשו של ר' זרחיה בקריאה מילולית פשטית של המקרא, והוא אינו חושך שבט לשונו מגבם של הקוראים כך. אותנו מעניינת מערכת הטיעונים המצדדים באופיו המשלי של ספר איוב. עד כמה שידוע לי, אין כדוגמתם לתעוזה, ולרגישות ספרותית.

לפי ר' זרחיה, אלה הם הסימנים שספר איוב הוא "מחובר" או "מחודש" כלומר חיבור בדיוני:

א. היעדר קוי זיהוי לגיבור הראשי.
ב. האופי הסמלי של השמות 'עוץ' ו'איוב'.
ג. אי-הסבירות של הסיפור.
ד. הקושי התיאולוגי: התפתות האל לשטן.
ה. אי-היכולת לתאר התהוות הספר בהנחה שדבריו כפשוטם.
ו. אחדות המליצה אצל ששה מדברים.
ז. הכפלת קנייניו של איוב באחריתו.

כנגד הראיה מיח' יד מציע זרחיה שלוש פירכות:

1. גם אם הנביא האמין שאיוב היה, אין זה מחייב אותנו להאמין כן, כי אין זה מסוג הדברים הנמסרים לנביאים במראה נבואה.
2. גם אם הנביא ידע כי איוב משל היה, לא היה מפרסם את הדבר כדי שלא להוזיל את ערך הספר בעיני ההמון.
3. הנביאים מרבים להשתמש במשלים.

ואלה דבריו:

מה שאתה צריך לדעת תחלה הוא כי זה הספר כלו הוא למשל, וכוונתו הראשונה אמנם היתה להודיע בו כוונות תוריות ובלתי תוריות ואמונות מתחלפות אשר אנשי העולם בכללם למיניהם נבדלים בהם, כמו שאנו עומדים לבאר זה אחר זאת ההסכמה במלות אשר הונחו בתחלת זה הספר לזכור מה שראוי לזכור.

כבר ידעת כי חז"ל הלכו כן גם בזה הספר אחר זאת ההסכמה באמרם 'איוב לא היה ולא נברא אלא למשל היה'[15] ומלבד זה יש לכל שכל להשתכל במלות אשר הונחו בתחלת זה הספר והוא שהתחיל 'איש היה' ולא זכר בן[16] 'מי היה זה האיש וגם זמן לא זכר לענין זה האיש. וכל זה אמנם היה להורות לנו ולהודיענו כי דברים אלו היו דברים מחוברים כאחת ממשלי

---

14 רמב"ם ור' זרחיה בעקבותיו מתעלמים מ'ארץ עוץ' שבאיכה ד'. אין בידי להסביר זאת.
15 גירסה מעורבת (משל היה + אלא למשל); ראה מאמרו של ליברמן (לעיל, הערה 6), עמ' קה.
16 בנדפס (ראה הערה 2): 'יבו'.

איוב היה או לא היה: סוגיה בפרשנות ימי הביניים

אלא[10] הוא היה וייסורין לא היו.[10] ולמה נכתבו עליו[11]? אלא לומר[12]
אלו(לי) באו עליו היה יכול לעמוד בהם (קרבן העדה: שצדיק גדול היה, שאלו באו עליו כל
הייסורין הכתובים בקרא לא היה בועט)

ירו׳ סוטה סוף פ״ה, בתרגום הארמית לעברית ובתוספות מפירוש קרבן
העדה לר׳ דוד פרענקיל.

כאן כבר מצטמצמת הבדיוניות: איוב הוא אמנם דמות היסטורית, מימי אברהם אבינו, אלא
שהקורות המסופרות עליו בספר הן בדייה, שנמסרה לדמות בת־אופי כזה שראוי להדביק אליה
מעשה כזה. יש כאן פשרה מתוחכמת למדי בין העמדות האפשריות.

נימה פולמוסית מובהקת בוקעת מקטע במדרש הגדול ויקרא, פר׳ מצורע (מהד׳ שטיינזלץ, עמ׳
תט):

תניא: בית מנוגע לא היה ולא נהיה. א״ר נתן (דור חמישי לתנאים, אמצע המאה ה-ב׳): אני
פניתי את אבניו.
עיר הנדחת לא היתה ולא נהייתה. ר׳ נתן אומר: אני עמדתי על תלה.
בן סורר ומורה לא היה ולא נהיה. אמר ר׳ נתן: אני ישבתי בבית דינו ועמדתי על קברו.
נשר הגדול (של יחז׳ יז) לא היה ולא נהיה. א״ר נתן אני ראיתי את גוזליו.
איוב לא היה ולא נהיה. א״ר נתן אני ראיתי את בני בניו.

לא נחו מוסרי המסורת עד שעקרו את שיני הסברה המבדה מכל וכל על־ידי "תיקון" זעיר בגרסת
התלמוד בבבא בתרא. וכך אנו קוראים בדרשות ר׳ יהושע אבן שועיב (ספרד, תחילת המאה ה-
י״ד):

ור׳ האי ז״ל כתב בתשובה כי דעתו שהיה ונברא, **ולא חלק אדם על זה מעולם**. ומה שאמר
בגמרא: לא היה ולא נברא בעולם אלא להיות משל לבני אדם: ממנו יראו וכן יעשו ... וכתב הוא
ז״ל כי **בגמרא שלהם הגירסא כך: ולא היה ולא נברא אלא למשל**, ואין גורסין משל
היה אלא ודאי היה ונברא ...[13]

גרסה זו המתועדת בספרות המאוחרת כנראה יסודה בחוגי בעלי הקבלה (לדעת ר״ש ליברמן),
ואין צריך לומר שהיא מוכחשת מהמשך הסוגיה, הבא להפריך את האומר שאיוב לא היה כלל
בעולם.

טענה חזקה לממשות איוב היא איזכורו ביח׳ יד:

בן אדם! ארץ כי תחטא לי למעל מעל
ונטיתי ידי עליה ושברתי לה מטה לחם ...
והיו שלשת האנשים האלה בתוכה: נח דנאל ואיוב
המה בצדקתם ינצלו נפשם נאם ה׳ אלהים וכו׳.

בתחילת פירושו לספר איוב, ראב״ע אוחז בראיה זו: ׳ולא יתכן שלא היה בעולם בעבור שאמר
יחזקאל ונח ודניאל ואיוב. ואם אמר טוען: אולי איוב אחר היה שהזכיר הנביא? יאמר לו: אם כן
אמור כן בדניאל ונח?!׳

אנו שמים לב, שאין במסורות אלו אף נימוק אחד מפורש לתפיסה כי אין איוב אלא משל —
וכאלו בקשו להפחית עד כמה שאפשר את משקלה של "כפירה" כזו. אולם דווקא תפיסה זו היתה
נוחה לפילוסופים שביקשו מפלט מקשיים תיאולוגיים במקרא על־ידי קריאה אליגורית. כך
רמב״ם (נפטר 1204) במורה נבוכים, חלק ג׳, פרק כ״ב מעדיף את הדעה "הַמְבַדָּה" ביחס לאיוב:

---

10 בר״ר: ׳לא היה ביסורים שנכתבו לוי.
11 בר״ר: ׳לוי.
12 חסר בבר״ר.
13 מובא ממאמרו של ש׳ ליברמן, "מסורת קבלה בדברי הגאונים?", ספר היובל לבנימין מנשה לוין,
בעריכת י״ל הכוהן פישמן (ירושלים, ת״ש) קה-קח; המובאה בעמ׳ קו.

ארמי שאבד)[4] נכדו של עשו (בר' לו, ד,יג; ולפי התוספתא שם של יובב היא בצרה — פירוש מדרשי על בר' לו, לג: 'וימלך תחתיו יובב בן זרח מבצרה'). וברוח זה שיבצוהו כמה מחז"ל בימי האבות, ואת כתיבת ספרו ייחסו למשה רבינו (בבא בתרא טו ע"א).[5]

אבל לצד גישה זו המאשרת את ממשותו ההיסטורית של איוב היתה הגישה המחזיקה אותו כבדוי, המיוחסת לאמורא ארצישראלי אלמוני בדור שלישי (המאה ה-ד'), והפותחת את הדיון בסגנון הספר:

יתיב ההוא מרבנן קמיה דרבי שמואל בר נחמני ויתיב וקאמר:
איוב לא היה ולא נברא אלא משל היה [אינו דמות בת ממשות היסטורית אלא בדויה]
אמר לו: עליך אמר קרא: איש היה בארץ עוץ איוב שמו
אלא מעתה: ולרש אין כל כי אם כבשה אחת קטנה אשר קנה ויחיה [רש"י משלים: **ותהי** לו כבת (שמ"ב יב, ג)] מי הוה אלא משל בעלמא? הכא נמי משל בעלמא.
אם כן שמו ושם עירו למה? (בבא בתרא טו ע"א).

ההיסמכות התמימה על ה'יהיה' המקראי מתערערת על-ידי שיתוף הסגנון ה'הויתי' במשל כבשת הרש (שמ"ב יב, א-ג) שגוזמתו מעידה על בדיונותו (יותהי לו כבת/ גוזמת שיא — לאחר 'מפתו תאכל ומכוסו תשתה ובחיקו תשכב'; מעניין שהמספר המקראי מניח כי אין בו גוזמה המסגירה לדוד את בדיונותו). ואולם ערעור זה מופרך, במקרה שלנו, על-ידי ציוני הזיהוי הנוספים לגבור — 'שמו ושם עירו' (בניגוד למשל כבשת הרש: 'שני אנשים [אלמונים] היו בעיר אחת' [אלמונית], הרי כאן 'איש היה בארץ עוץ איוב שמו'). לפירכה זו אין תשובה; ואנו נשארים בבוחן הזיהוי כמאשר את ממשות האיש.[6]

מסורת מקבילה אולם מורכבת יותר באה בבר"ר נז, ב, ובירושלמי סוטה סוף פרק ה. תחילה מובאת מסירתו של ר' שמעון בן לקיש (דור שני לאמוראי א"י, סוף המאה ה-ג') בשם בר קפרא כי איוב בימי אברהם אבינו היה; ולאחר מכן:

ר' שמעון בן לקיש אמר: איוב לא היה[7] ולא עתיד להיות[7] (קרבן העדה: שלא נכתב על שם העתיד)
מוחלפת שיטתו של ר' שמעון בן לקיש; שם אמר ר' שמעון בן לקיש בשם[8] בר קפרא בימי אברהם אבינו[9] היה וכאן היה אומר ככה? (קרבן העדה: שלא היה מעולם אלא משל הוא)

---

4   ראה: Pinkus Frankl, "Die Zusätze in der LXX zu Hiob," *MGWJ* 21 (1872) 306-315.

5   אברהם אבן עזרא דוחה את זיהוי יובב עם איוב מאת "היצחקי המהביל" (פירושו לבר' לו, לג), ולועג לו: 'שמא בחלום ראה זה כי אין לו על מה ישען לא על דברי הנביאים ולא על מה שהעתיקו חכמינו' (פירושו לאיוב א, א). עם זאת הוא אוחז בדעה קרובה: 'איוב היה מבני בניו של עשו והענין מוכיח: בארץ עוץ, כמו שישי ושמחי בת אדום יושבת בארץ עוץ' (איכה ד, כא). אהרן בן אליה הקראי (מאה הי"ד, מניקומדיה) בספרו עץ החיים, מהדורת פרנץ דליטש, (לייפציג, 1841), עמ' 137 מביא סברה שמישראל היה, ויוב (בן יששכר, בר' מו, יג) הוא איוב'.

6   מהרש"א, בחידושי אגדות לבבא בתרא טו ע"א תמה על שלא טען הטוען מלשון הויה שבראשית הסיפור: שני אנשים היו בעיר אחת ... לעשיר היה ... ומשיב: מן הוויות אלה אין להקשות וכי אין זאת אלא משל בעלמא? שהרי אפשר שנקט הכתוב למשל בדבר שהיה ונברא; כלומר הוויתם של שני האנשים, והויית הרכוש הרב לעשיר אינן בהכרח בדייה. אבל: יותהי לו כבת/ ודאי אינו אלא משל שלא היה ולא נברא. אפשרות ביניים כזאת — שממשלים משל בדמות מציאותית — עולה במובאה הבאה מן הירושלמי.

7   בר"ר, מהדורת תיאודור-אלבק: 'ולא נברא'.

8   בר"ר: 'משם'.

9   בבר"ר חסר.

איוב היה או לא היה:
סוגיה בפרשנות ימי הביניים[1]

משה גרינברג

הרצאותיו של שמריהו טלמון על "מלאכת הסיפור במקרא" (מפעל השכפול, האוניברסיטה העברית, תשט״ז)[2] היו מן הנסיונות הראשונים בשפה העברית לסקור בשיטתיות את ההבט הספרותי של המקרא; מאז לא פסקה התעניינותו בנושא, ורבים מפרסומיו נוגעים בו. אקוה איפוא כי ימצא חפץ בהעלאת זכרה של מערכת טענות מסוף המאה הי״ג לאופיו הבדיוני של ספר איוב, טענות המפליאות בנועזותן.

מדובר בדברי הקדמה של ר׳ זרחיה בן יצחק בן שאלתיאל ברצלוני לפירושו לספר איוב, בהם הוא מבקש לאשש את הדעה, שהובעה כבר בתלמוד, כי איוב הוא משל ולא ממשות היסטורית; וזאת כדי להצדיק את הפירוש האליגורי-פילוסופי אשר בעיניו מתחייב מהערכת ספר איוב כספר רציני.[3] קרה כאן מה שקורה לפעמים בתולדות היצירה ההגותית: המתכוון לתכלית מסויימת יוצר אמצעים שחשיבותם קיימת בלי קשר לתכלית שלה נועדו. ברוך שפינוזה שאף לערער את הסמכות האזרחית של הכנסיה, ואגב כך פיתח שיטה פילולוגית-היסטורית בפרשנות המקרא החשובה בפני עצמה בלי קשר לנסיבות שבהן קמה. במדה צנועה מזו, כדי להצדיק אלגוריזציה של ספר איוב המציא זרחיה ברצלוני קווים לביקורת ספרותית, אשר בגלל אופיים הבוטה, ובגלל הסכנה הטמונה בהם לקריאה תמימה של המקרא, נשתקעו לא זכו להיות התחלה להתפתחות החוש הביקורתי.

עדות קדומה לשיבוצו איוב לתוך ההיסטוריה המקראית היא מסורת עתיקה כי יואב הוא יובב (צוואת איוב א, א; ב, א) בן זרח (תוספת בתרגום השבעים לסוף הספר, כנראה על סמך תרגום

---

1 לעזר רב בהכנת רשימה זו היה לי ילקוט הקדמות לפירושי המקרא, ערך אוריאל סימון, המחלקה לתנ״ך, אוניברסיטת בר-אילן (רמת-גן, תשל״ג).
2 חיבור זה, שהוא סיכום ההרצאות בידי תלמידים, זכה לכמה מהדורות בשם "דרכי הסיפור במקרא".
3 פירוש ר׳ זרחיה על ספר איוב ראה אור במהדורת ישראל שווארץ, בספר תקות אנוש (ברלין, 1868); דברי המבוא הנוגעים לעניינינו הם בעמ׳ 169-173. ר׳ זרחיה השלים את פירושו ברומה בשנת 1291. לתולדות ר׳ זרחיה וכתביו ראה: אביעזר רביצקי, משנתו של ר׳ זרחיה בן יצחק בן שאלתיאל חן וההגות המיימונית-תיבונית במאה הי״ג, חיבור לשם קבלת תואר דוקטור לפילוסופיה, האוניברסיטה העברית בירושלים (תשל״ח) 66-94.

שער המקרא

רשימת קצורים

רשימת קיצורים נוספת בעמ׳ xiii-xiv. הקיצורים העבריים ע״פ "תרביץ."

ANEP	J. B. Pritchard (ed.), *Ancient Near East in Pictures*
ATANT	Abhandlungen zur Theologie des Alten und Neuen Testaments
ATD	Das Alte Testament Deutsch
BBB	Bonner biblische Beiträge
BHK	R. Kittel (ed.), *Biblia Hebraica*
BKAT	Biblischer Kommentar: Altes Testament
BWANT	Beiträge zur Wissenschaft vom Alten und Neuen Testament
CahRB	Cahiers de la Revue biblique
CBC	Cambridge Bible Commentary
CBQMS	Catholic Biblical Quarterly Monograph Series
HALAT	W. Baumgartner et al., *Hebräisches und aramäisches Lexikon zum Alten Testament*
HAR	Hebrew Annual Review
HUCA	Hebrew Union College Annual
IB	G. A. Buttrick (ed.), *Interpreter's Bible*
Int	Interpretation
JPOS	Journal of the Palestine Oriental Society
JQR	Jewish Quarterly Review
JQRMS	Jewish Quarterly Review Monograph Series
KD	*Kerygma und Dogma*
LÄ	W. Helck and E. Otto (eds.), *Lexikon der Ägyptologie*
MGWJ	*Monatsschrift für Geschichte und Wissenschaft des Judentums*
NKZ	Neue kirchliche Zeitschrift
OTS	Oudtestamentische Studiën
PEQ	Palestine Exploration Quarterly
RQ	*Revue de Qumran*
SBLSCS	Society of Biblical Literature, Septuagint and Cognate Studies
SBLSP	Society of Biblical Literature, Seminar Papers
SJLA	Studies in Judaism in Late Antiquity
ST	*Studia Theologica*
WHJP	World History of the Jewish People
ZTK	*Zeitschrift für Theologie und Kirche*

המדברי--במחקר זה באים לידי ביטוי גישה ספרותית מובהקת והבנה של גישות חברתיות קדומות.

כל מאמריו של שמריהו טלמון משקפים דמיון יוצר וגישה סינתטית המתפתחת כל הזמן. כל אלה היו להשראה לרבים מבין תלמידיו. אכן, הוא העמיד תלמידים הרבה, לא רק באוניברסטאות בישראל, אלא גם בחוץ־לארץ, שם לימד כמרצה אורח במוסדות מחקר מכובדים, החל מאוניברסיטאות לידס, ברנדייס והרווארד, בראשית שנות השישים, ושוב בשנות השבעים, וכלה באוניברסיטאות של היידלברג, לוצרן, ברקלי, ג'ונס הופקינס וונדרבילט בעשור הקודם. בשיעורים שלימד בחוץ־לארץ, בהרצאות הרבות ברחבי העולם, הציג טלמון את חקר המקרא במיטבו לאנשים רבים. השפעתו ניכרת גם מעבר לעולם האקדמי, כפי שיעיד כל מי ששמע על מפעלו החינוכי במחנות העולים בקפריסין וראה אותו בפעולה ביצירת קשרים תרבותיים ורוחניים עם המועצה הבינלאומית של הכנסיות ועם הוַטיקן. תלמידים רבים שלמדו באוניברסיטאות, בסמינרים ובמוסדות תיאולוגיים באירופה, אפריקה וביבשת אמריקה, והשתתפו בסדנאות בהדרכתו של שמריהו טלמון, הגיעו לאחר מכן לירושלים להמשך הלימודים באוניברסיטה העברית. מאמצים "אֶקוּמֶנִיים" אלה מצאו אוזן קשבת בדרגים הגבוהים ביותר בוַטיקן ובמקומות אחרים.

מאמציו לטובת המכון ללימודים יהודיים בהיידלברג (גרמניה) מציגים מימד נוסף של עבודתו, בתחום החינוך והניהול. מיומנויות ותכונות אלה גם באו לידי ביטוי קודם כל במסגרת עבודתו כראש המכון האוניברסיטאי של חיפה, וכדיקן הפקולטה למדעי הרוח באוניברסיטה העברית, וכן בפעילותו למען הדיאלוג היהודי־נוצרי.

חברינו למקצוע, שהגיבו במהירות ובהתלהבות להזמנתנו להשתתף בקובץ זה, מכירים בתרומותיו הרבות של שמריהו למקצוע. ההיקף והאיכות של המחקרים הכלולים בספר — בעברית ובאנגלית — משקפים נאמנה את רוחב אפקיו ותחומי ההתעניינות המגוונים של שמריהו.

חובה נעימה היא לנו להודות לאשתו פנינה טלמון ולבנות משפחת טלמון, אפרת לבני, תמר אלעד, נגה לוין ותמר מורג, על התעניינותן הפעילה בספר. כמו כן אנחנו מודים מאוד לד"ר ווסטון פילדס מעורב בכל שלבי ה"מבצע" והציע את עזרתו ומיומנותו בהתלהבות. אנו מודים גם לגב' דליה עמארה וכן לגב' דורית יוסף שעזרו בעריכת המאמרים העבריים. כמו כן אנו מודים לחברת אייזנבראון, במיוחד לדויד איקן ולמנהל מר ג'יימס אייזנבראון על סיועם ומיומנותם בהכנת החלק האנגלי של הספר וכן לחברת 'ידעי' (הגב' רונית שמגר-הנדלמן) על הכנת החלק העברי.

לבסוף, מלים אחדות על שם הספר, "שערי טלמון". השם טלמון בא במקרא כשמה של משפחת שוערים בין שבי ציון (עז' ב, מב; נחמ' ז, מה; יא, יט; יב, כב; דה"א ט, יז), ולכך רומז שם הקובץ, "שערי טלמון". למלת 'שערי' משמעות נוספת בעברית הבתר-מקראית, דהיינו 'פרק בתוך ספר', ואכן ספר זה מתחלק שערים שערים.

שמריהו, בשם כל הכותבים בקובץ זה ובשם רבים אחרים, אנו מודים לך על תרומתך למדע ועל היותך מופת לאחרים.

עמנואל טוב ומיכאל פישביין   ירושלים תשנ"ו

הקדמה

אנו מתכבדים להגיש את הספר הזה כשי לחבר יקר ולעמית, שמריהו טלמון, החוגג עתה יובל שנים של חיים וחקירה בישראל. עם עלייתו ארצה מגרמניה בשנת 1939 החל שמריהו את לימודי המקרא באוניברסיטה העברית בירושלים. עם תום לימודיו, לימד במוסדות שונים באנגליה ובישראל, וכעבור זמן־מה חזר לאוניברסיטה העברית, שם שימש כפרופסור למקרא בקתידרה על־שם י"ל מאגנס.

במשך שנים רבות הלהיב שמריהו טלמון את תלמידיו בשיעורים מרתקים, ובאותו זמן אף תרם רבות למדע המקרא באמצעות מחקריו הרבים.

צחד ממוקדי התעניינותו המדעית של שמריהו טלמון הוא נוסח המקרא, נושא עליו כתב את עבודת הדוקטור. מחקר זה על 'כפלי גירסה' בנוסח המקרא קבע סטנדרד גבוה לחקירתו, וחידש רבות בתחום זה. במרוצת השנים הוא שיכלל והשלים כיוון חקירה זה במחקרים מגוונים אודות היבטים שונים של תולדות הנוסח והתפתחות אסופת כתבי הקודש, בין היתר בעבודה מסורה כאחד העורכים של מפעל המקרא של האוניברסיטה העברית במשך שנים רבות, וכעורך בטאונו "טקסטוס"; ולבסוף, יישם שיטות השאולות מביקורת הנוסח לחקירת תולדות התרבות והספרות של עם ישראל. ייחודו של טלמון ביכולתו לשלב במחקריו הפוריים תחומי התעניינות שונים, ויכולת זו, המשתקפת גם בהוראתו, הרשימה את כל תלמידיו, לרבות אותנו.

גישתו הסוציולוגית לתולדות הנוסח כמו גם עומק חקירתו בעדי־הנוסח העתיקים הניבו תרומות חשובות להבנת סוגיות רבות של נוסח המקרא, בייחוד בתחום מגילות מדבר יהודה. מחקריו על ההיבטים הפרשניים של מגילת ישעיה הגדולה, שנכתבו לפני שנים הרבה, מאלפים עד עצם היום הזה. סקירותיו השונות על תולדות נוסח המקרא מוזכרות תכופות בספרות המחקר. עניינו של טלמון במגילות קומראן וגישתו הסוציולוגית שולבו באופן פורה במחקריו על תולדות אנשי קומראן וזהותם. אחד ממאמריו החשובים בתחום זה עוסק ברקע החברתי של המונח 'יחד' ובמשמעותו. בו בזמן עסק טלמון בהיבטים אחרים של חקירה סוציולוגית של העולם העתיק ושל מוסדותיו החברתיים -- מחקריו על מוסד המלוכה ועם הארץ' בישראל הקדומה, כמו גם חקירתו המתמשכת של ספרי עזרא ונחמיה — פתחו אופקים חדשים והביאו את עמיתיו לידי קריאה בספרות המחקר הסוציולוגית. מאמרו הפרוגרמטי של טלמון על השיטה המשווה שווה אף הוא לכיוון זה ותרם באופן ניכר לתחום מחקר חשוב בחקירת התרבויות והספרויות העתיקות.

חקירתו של טלמון משלבת בצורה חדשנית את ביקורת הנוסח עם הניתוח הספרותי והעיון בחיבור ספרי המקרא. התעניינותו בחזרות טקסטואליות, שבעזרתה גילה גירסאות 'נרדפות' ו'כפולות' בעדי־הנוסח העתיקים של המקרא, הניבה מחקרים על הבו־זמניות של אפיזודות בסיפור המקראי כמו גם על תפקיד ה'חזרה המקשרת' בתהליך החיבור שמאחורי ספרי המקרא. התעניינותו בהישנות מוטיבים הניבה מאמרים חשובים נוספים, כגון: מחקרו המופתי על 'מוטיב

vii*

שער קומראן

*101 גרשון ברין • אוניברסיטת תל אביב
תפיסת הנבואה המקראית בכתבי קומראן

*113 דבורה דימנט • אוניברסיטת חיפה
בין מקרא למגילות: ציטטות מן התורה במגילת ברית דמשק

*123 מנחם הרן • האוניברסיטה העברית בירושלים
המגילה 11QPs^a ובעית חיבורו של ספר תהילים

שער הלשון

*131 אבי הורביץ • האוניברסיטה העברית בירושלים
צדיק = חכם בתה' לז ושאלת רקעו החכמתי של המזמור

*137 שלמה מורג • האוניברסיטה העברית בירושלים
הערות אחדות למבנה שדות סימנטיים והקשריים בעברית ובערבית

*145 בנימין קדר • אוניברסיטת חיפה
השאלה המליצית במקרא ופרשנותה

*153 שמחה קוגוט • האוניברסיטה העברית בירושלים
התייחסותה המפורשת של פרשנות המקרא המסורתית לשאלת המחוייבות לטעמי המקרא, והרקע למחוייבות זו

תוכן העניינים

vii*   הקדמה
ix*   רשימת קיצורים

שער המקרא

3*   משה גרינברג • האוניברסיטה העברית בירושלים
איוב היה או לא היה: סוגיה בפרשנות ימי הביניים

13*   יאיר הופמן • אוניברסיטת תל אביב
תהילים קד: עיון ספרותי

25*   משה ויינפלד • האוניברסיטה העברית בירושלים
המקרא בראי הספרות

31*   מאיר וייס • האוניברסיטה העברית בירושלים
בעל מזמור כג על יחסו של ה׳ אליו: לחקר האמונות והדעות במזמורי תהילים

43*   זאב ויסמן • אוניברסיטת חיפה
אתנולוגיה, אטיולוגיה, גניאלוגיה והיסטוריוגרפיה בסיפור על לוט ובנותיו (בר׳ יט, ל-לח)

53*   יאיר זקוביץ • האוניברסיטה העברית בירושלים
יומת אלישע...ויחי ויקם על רגליו׳ (מל״ב יג,כ-כא): סיפור קצרצר במעגלי פרשנות

63*   ציפורה טלשיר ודוד טלשיר • האוניברסיטה העברית בירושלים
לשאלת לשון המקור של סיפור שלושת הנערים (עזה״ח ג-ד)

77*   אברהם מלמט • האוניברסיטה העברית בירושלים
׳כי את רגלים רצתה וילאוך׳ (יר׳ יב, ה)

81*   פרנק פולק • אוניברסיטת תל אביב
וישתחו: קבוצת נוסחאות בשירה ובסיפורת שבמקרא

93*   חנוך רביב ז״ל • האוניברסיטה העברית בירושלים
צבא ומדיניות: פרשיות עגומות בקורות ממלכת הצפון

הוכן לדפוס על־ידי דעץ ירושלים
Hebrew section typeset by *Daatz*, Jerusalem

© 1992 by Eisenbrauns.
All rights reserved.
Printed in the United States of America.

שערי טלמון

מחקרים במקרא, קומראן והמזרח הקדמון מוגשים
לשמריהו טלמון

בעריכת
עמנואל טוב ומיכאל פישביין
מזכיר המערכת: וסטון פילדס

Eisenbrauns
Winona Lake, Indiana
1992

שערי טלמון